TO:
Joy, Scott, and Kevin
Mary, Kristen, and Matt

3rd Edition

PRODUCTION AND OPERATIONS MANAGEMENT

Concepts, Models, and Behavior

Everett E. Adam, Jr.
Ronald J. Ebert

Prentice-Hall, Englewood Cliffs, NJ 07632

Library of Congress Cataloging-in-Publication Data

Adam, Everett E.
Production and operations management.

Includes index.
1. Production management. I. Ebert, Ronald J.
II. Title.
TS155.A29514 1986 658.5 85-20493
ISBN 0-13-724857-1

Editorial/production supervision: Susan Fisher
Cover/interior design: Jayne Conte
Cover photo: Paul Silverman
Manufacturing buyer: Ed O'Dougherty

Printed in the United States of America

10 9 8 7 6 5 4 3 2

ISBN 0-13-724857-1 01

Prentice-Hall International (UK) Limited, *London*
Prentice-Hall of Australia Pty. Limited, *Sydney*
Prentice-Hall Canada Inc., *Toronto*
Prentice Hall Hispanoamericana, S.A., *Mexico*
Prentice-Hall of India Private Limited, *New Delhi*
Prentice-Hall of Japan, Inc., *Tokyo*
Prentice-Hall of Southeast Asia Pte. Ltd., *Singapore*
Editora Prentice-Hall do Brasil, Ltda., *Rio de Janeiro*

Contents

16 Material Requirements Planning 639

17 Managing for Quality 673

PART SIX

DYNAMICS OF OPERATIONS MANAGEMENT

18 The Conversion Process in Change 740

19 Useful Technical Approaches to Change 773

Preface

This third edition was developed with an increased awareness of the vital role that production and operations management continues to play in national and world economies. Although the operations function exists in virtually every organization, it is often misunderstood by practitioners and sometimes elusive to students of business and management. Part of the problem lies in the changing nature of the field of study—the historical evolution from shop management to production management to systems analysis and management science and, more recently, to management of operations in goods- and services-producing organizations. By the mid-1980s it is apparent that new technologies, competition from emerging industrialized nations outside Europe and North America, and the productivity and quality demands from owners and consumers are again reshaping production and operations management. In response to these pressures, the production/operations function in many industries has become a key instrument for competitive success, with emphasis on the management of operations within the context of each organization's unique needs. This shift toward a managerial focus has resulted in two gaps, one in education, the other in practice.

In the educational setting, students are often left with the feeling that operations is distinctly different and separate from management. In some instances, analysis and quantitative techniques have been emphasized at the expense of a basic unifying framework for the overall role of operations management in organizations. We continue our efforts to fill this void with the unifying theme of this book: planning, organizing, and controlling—the classic process school of management. Our third edition applies this integrating approach in each chapter, showing how resource conversion into goods and services involves both modeling and behavioral techniques. This edition also relies on operations strategy as a guide for topical integration.

For students and teachers alike, our integrative framework has served admirably in lending coherence to the numerous revisions which now appear in the third edition. These modifications include: a presentation of the major competitive challenges to operations (new Chapter 2); a renewed interest in strategic planning (revised Chapter 4); recognition of the increased role of operations capacity (revised Chapter 6); a comprehensive review of contemporary North American manufacturing planning and control systems (revised Chapters 11 and 12); separate and thorough treatment of information systems in operations (new Chapter 9) and material requirements planning (MRP) (expanded Chapter 16); a reorientation toward managing for quality (major expansion of Chapter 17); and the treatment of worldwide manufacturing techniques, especially those of the Japanese (Chapters 2, 11, 12, 15, 17, and 20). General chapters on management, organizing, and control from previous editions were deleted. Collectively, these changes have re-shaped the book to provide the reader with a contemporary treatment of production and operations management.

In the eyes of many practitioners there is a gap between what they must deal with operationally and what they studied in production/operations books. This is particularly true for those who were introduced to production/operations management as a quantitative/systems analysis discipline. In the first place, practitioners' problems are not all as readily solved by quantitative models as some introductory treatments imply. Second, the systems approach to operations, for some reason, has tended to underemphasize the role of human behavior as an integral part of productive systems. Therefore we continue to emphasize a balance between the quantitative aspects and important behavioral applications. When problems are behavioral (quality motivation, for example), we introduce such contemporary techniques as behavior modification, quality circles, and attitude change procedures to deal with them; when they are quantitative (inventory control, for example) we stress appropriate techniques of quantitative analysis.

Throughout the book, we discuss the basic production/operations management issues and concepts in a way that can be understood by those with minimal mathematical skills. Readers can use the chapter supplements to build upon these fundamentals if they wish. Each supplement emphasizes technique and methodology as it relates to a fundamental topic in the chapter, but it does so at a more rigorous quantitative level. Thus, computer simulation, linear programming, the mathematics of forecasting, some optimization techniques, and other related materials included in the supplements can be an integral part of the course at the option of the user. The book stands alone, however, without the supplements.

As service industries continue to increase in importance, the role of production/operations management in the service sector takes on added significance. Historically, much production management technology was developed and refined in manufacturing organizations; to what extent is it transferrable to service organizations? When technologies can be transferred, we have demonstrated the possibility. Our view is that "operations" is a broad term encompassing manufacturing, agriculture, and services—

not a term that simply replaces traditional production or is applicable only to services.

The major purpose of this book is to introduce the basics of production/operations management in an understandable way. Part I introduces the student to operations management in what we hope is an exciting manner. Each chapter in Parts II through V begins with an operations executive's comment about the chapter, and within the chapter a major production/operations activity is discussed and analyzed in isolation so the reader may have an unclouded perspective of the basic activity under consideration. As the chapter progresses, however, we show how this activity interrelates with the others. In short, Chapters 4 through 17 present the core production/operations management activities. In Part VI, the emphasis shifts to synthesizing—integrating the production/operations management process into a realistic and meaningful whole. Overall, the reader proceeds from the parts to the whole, first learning the concepts and terminology of each subfunction and then seeing how they relate to one another and work together. We believe these fundamentals can be grasped by students with minimal knowledge of statistics, quantitative methods, management, and organizational behavior.

Our intent, as it was in the previous editions, is to provide a student-oriented presentation at an introductory level. The material is presented in a simple, straightforward fashion. To assist student understanding, we provide end-of-chapter materials designed to reinforce the essentials of each chapter. Solved problems at the end of each chapter have been added, while many review questions and problems have been revised. Although some questions and problems are intended to challenge understanding slightly beyond the level of the chapter itself, most directly reinforce the basics. At the end of each chapter the reader will find a glossary and usually a case; these reemphasize the terminology and basic concepts in the chapter. We offer another major feature, the study guide, designed to help students develop a better understanding of operations management through independent study. Some instructors use the study guide as an integral part of the course to improve learning and teaching efficiency. We think you will find it a valuable supplement to this edition.

Distinguishing features of this book, then, are *an integrating framework*, featuring management process, resource conversion, and concepts, models, and behavior; *behavioral applications* within production/operations; inclusion of the service sector via an *operations orientation;* and *a student emphasis* featuring an introductory treatment, continuity among chapters, and learning enhancement within chapters with specially prepared executive comments, numerous examples, chapter summaries, cases, glossaries, review and discussion questions, problems, and the student study guide featuring an independent study approach.

We wish to thank our many peers nationally who, after thoughtful use of the first two editions, provided constructive suggestions for this revision. We appreciate the time and effort expended by the operations managers and executives who prepared the chapter introductions for this edition. They have made a nice voluntary contribution; we hope students will enjoy and benefit from their comments. We are also indebted to those who reviewed this revision: Professors Robert Brown, Boston College; John Castellano, Suffolk University, Boston; Richard Discenza, Northern Arizona University; David M. Dougherty, The University of Texas at El Paso; Douglas A. Elvers, The University of North Carolina at Chapel Hill; Keith Fay, Arizona State University; Barbara M. Fossum, The University of Texas at Austin; Chan K. Hahn, Bowling Green State University; David Lopez, University of Washington; Raymond Lutz, The University of Texas at Dallas; J. R. Minifie, Texas Tech University; W. Kent Moore, Valdosta State College; Walt Newsom, Mississippi State University; David W. Pentico, Virginia Commonwealth University; and Vincent G. Reuter, Arizona State University. Our gratitude is again extended to the following people, whose comments and reviews of the earlier editions were invaluable: Professors Richard Discenza, Northern Arizona University; David M. Dougherty, The University of Texas at El Paso; Douglas A. Elvers, The University of North Carolina at Chapel Hill; Larry Ritzman, The Ohio State University; and Albert R. Wood, University of Western Ontario. We also wish to acknowledge the resource support of the University of Missouri-Columbia.

Everett E. Adam, Jr.
Ronald J. Ebert

Editorial Review Board

1 Operations Management

While all managers are involved in planning, organizing, and controlling, operations managers have the direct responsibility for "getting the job done." They must provide the leadership that is needed to produce the product or service demanded by the customer.

In the aerospace industry, our operations organizations grew out of the manufacturing departments of the past, whose responsibilities were generally fabrication and assembly. They were succeeded by the production organizations of the immediate post-World War II period, where functions like manufacturing planning, tooling, plant engineering, and production control were added. Today's operations divisions are additionally responsible for purchasing, material control, quality assurance, and in some cases, engineering and program management.

This evolution has produced broadly capable operations teams, responsible for the quality of the product, as seen by the customer; for the organization's productivity, which determines the product's competitive cost; and for responsiveness to the customer's needs.

With quality and productivity more competitively significant than ever before, operations management has added behavioral and modeling approaches to its historical use of the classical/scientific schools of management techniques.

All of these many elements come into play in the fascinating field of operations management.

William T. Gross
Executive Vice President
Douglas Aircraft Company
Long Beach, California

Mr. Gross's comments exemplify the widely shared experience of managers in many organizations and industries. Operations management is a significant part of all our lives; it is multi-faceted, involving diverse activities and skills; and it is an interesting, action-oriented area. Looking beyond Mr. Gross's comments, however, across thousands of organizations nationwide, some serious concerns persist about the well-being of operations management and its role in our nation's economic future.

At the onset of the 1980s, while Japan's productivity continued its healthy surges, the leaders of business and government world-wide were alarmed at the productivity stagnation in the United States. What had happened to the giant of commerce and industry? What led to its lethargy? What have we learned in the ensuing years? What can be done to restore its stately posture? Answers to these questions reside in the ways we manage our organizations and their operations.

While her productivity waned, U.S. society was at the same time unrelenting in its concern over other related issues—maintaining adequate energy sources, preserving the environment, and meeting the demand for its goods and services at home and abroad. These factors continue to impose complex demands on our organizations. Today management faces unparalleled challenges from a more educated, affluent, demanding, and concerned society than ever before, as well as from keener international competition. Never before have management challenges and the costs of failure been greater—and never before have the techniques and knowledge to meet these challenges been more available to operating managers.

The complexities of our contemporary world have heightened our dependence on organizations and the people who manage them; yet often we fail to understand and appreciate the process of management. Moreover, as we've learned from our recent costly experiences, we have seriously neglected the operations of our organizations; we have taken for granted our preeminence as capable producers. No longer can we afford to do so. We need to reexamine the processes by which goods and services are created and to revitalize the ways that we manage the human and material resources for doing so. This book aims to meet these needs. It presents the concepts, terminology, problems, and the opportunities that comprise operations management.

We begin this first chapter by describing what is meant by the "operations function" in organizations. Then, by tracing its history, we observe how operations management has evolved from simple beginnings to achieve its current stature as a major element of competitive strategy in contemporary organizations.

THE OPERATIONS FUNCTION OF ORGANIZATIONS

The operations function (system) is that part of the organization that exists primarily to generate and produce the organization's products. In some organizations the product is a physical good (refrigerators, breakfast cereal), while in others it is a service (insurance, health care for the elderly). What do such diverse organizations as manufacturing companies, financial institutions, and health care facilities all have within their operations system? The basic elements they share in common are shown in Figure 1.1. They have a *conversion process,* some resource *inputs* into that process, the *products* resulting from the conversion of the inputs, and *information feedback* about the activities in the operations system. Once they are produced, the goods and services are converted into cash (sold) to acquire more resources to keep the conversion process alive.

Try to recall examples of real organizations as you think about the conversion process shown in Figure 1.1. Perhaps you have worked in a department store, on a farm, for a construction company, or in an automobile assembly plant. What were the inputs? A department store's inputs include the land upon which the building is located; your labor as a stock clerk; capital in the form of the building, equipment, and merchandise; and the management skills of the store managers (see Figure 1.2).

On a farm the operations system is the transformation that occurs when the farmer's inputs (land, equipment, labor, and so on) are converted into such outputs as corn, wheat, or milk. The exact form of the conversion process varies from industry to industry, but it is an economic phenomenon that exists in every industry. Economists refer to this transformation of resources into goods and services as the "production function." For all operations systems the general goal is to create some kind of *"value-added,"* so that the outputs are worth more to consumers than just the sum of the individual inputs. To the consumer, the resulting products offer utility due to the form, the time, or the place of their availability from the conversion process.

FIGURE 1.1
The operations system

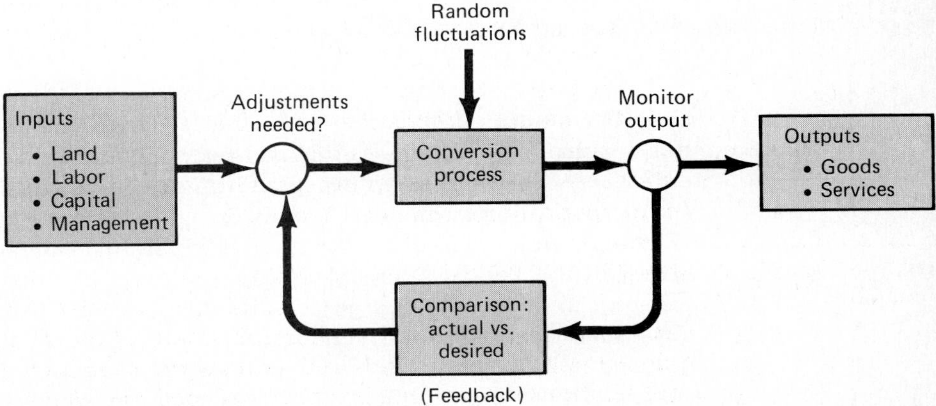

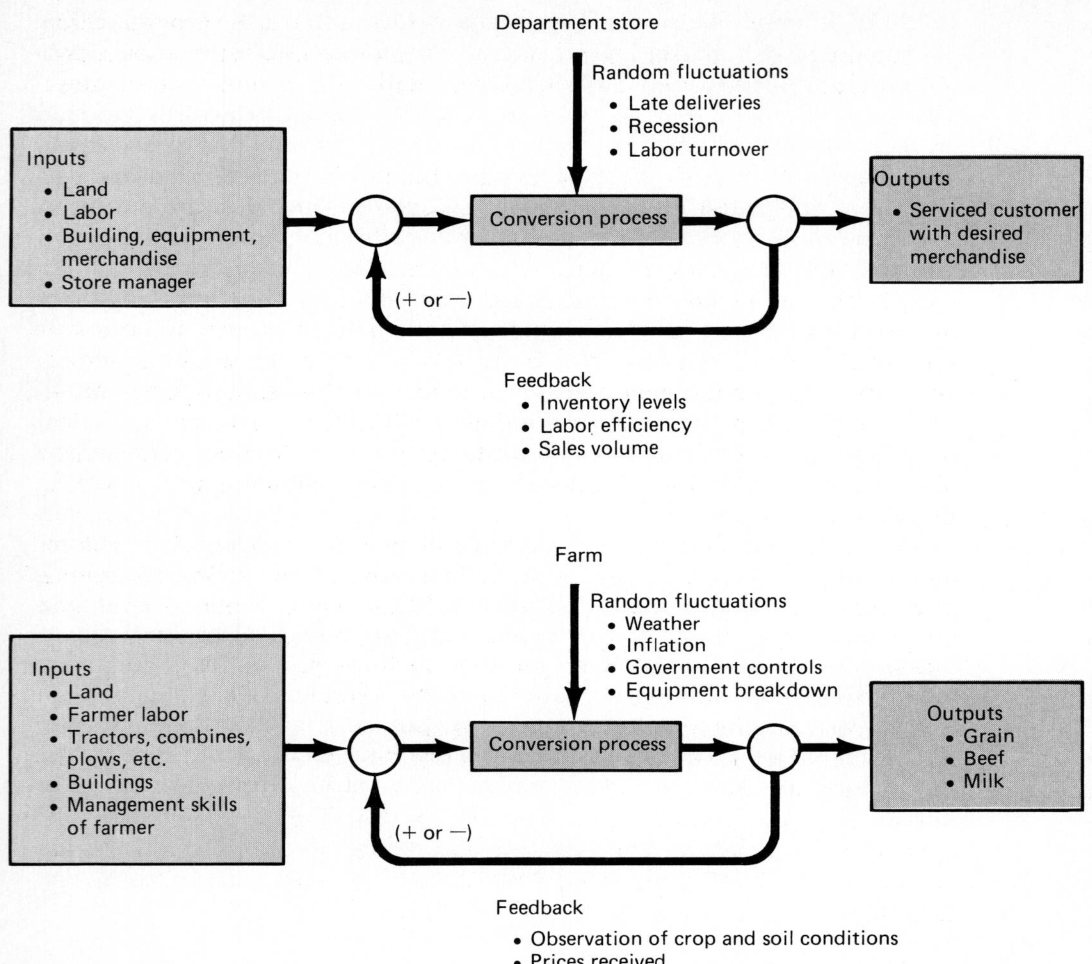

FIGURE 1.2
The operations systems for a department store and a farm

The random fluctuations indicated in Figure 1.1 consist of unplanned or uncontrollable influences that cause actual output to differ from planned output. A Chrysler assembly plant might be plagued with production equipment failures, material shortages, or wildcat strikes by United Auto Workers union members. Random fluctuations can arise from external sources (fire, floods, or lightning, for example) or from internal problems inherent in the conversion process. Inherent variabilities of equipment, material imperfections, and human errors all affect output quality. In fact, random variations are the rule rather than the exception in production processes; error-free performance is virtually nonexistent.

The function of the feedback loop in Figure 1.1 is to provide information linkages. Without some feedback of information, management cannot control operations because they don't know the results of their decisions.

Technologies of Conversion The transformation of inputs into outputs varies considerably with the technology employed. By *technology,* we mean the types of transformation activities taking place, including the level of scientific sophistication in plant, equipment, skills, and product (or service) in the conversion process. A soft-drink bottling operation, for example, features a highly mechanized, capital-intensive conversion process. A scientific research laboratory utilizes highly trained, professional scientists and specialized equipment. Other industries use low-skilled labor intensively in their conversion processes. The level of technological sophistication in any firm affects the services it can offer to customers, its operating efficiency, and the types of costs and problems it encounters in operating its system.

An additional variation among technologies is the extent that customers are present or involved in the conversion process. In service operations, managers sometimes find it useful to distinguish between *output* and *throughput* types of customer involvement. Outputs are the generated services; throughputs are the items going through the process. In a pediatrics clinic the output is the medical service to the child who, by going through the conversion process, is also the throughput. At a fast-food restaurant, in contrast, the customer does not go through the conversion process. The outputs are hamburgers and french fries in a hurry (both goods and services), while the throughputs are the food items as they are prepared and converted. The customer is neither a throughput nor an output. Both the clinic and the restaurant provide services, even though the outputs and throughputs differ considerably.

HISTORICAL EVOLUTION OF PRODUCTION AND OPERATIONS MANAGEMENT

For over two centuries operations management has been recognized as an important factor in our economic well-being.

Progressing through a series of names—*manufacturing management, production management,* and *operations management*—all of which describe the same general discipline, the order of the terms reflects the evolution of modern operations management. The traditional view of manufacturing management began in the eighteenth century with Adam Smith's recognition that the subdivision and specialization of labor can result in economic benefits. He recommended breaking jobs down into subtasks and reassigning workers to specialized tasks in which they would become highly skilled and efficient. In the early twentieth century, Frederick W.

Taylor implemented Smith's theories and crusaded for scientific management throughout the vast manufacturing complex of his day. From then until about 1930, the traditional view prevailed, and many techniques we still use today were developed. Among these were the recognition of differential skills, the development of the scientific approach to studying work, motion and time studies, and scheduling techniques. A brief sketch of these and other contributions to manufacturing management is highlighted in Table 1.1.

Production management became the more widely accepted term from the 1930s through the 1950s. As Frederick Taylor's work became more widely known and other contributors to management adopted the scientific approach, techniques were developed that focused on economic efficiency at the core of manufacturing organizations. Work measurement, wage incentive programs, and other techniques traditionally associated with industrial engineering were applied to management situations. People in their

TABLE 1.1
Historical summary of operations management

Date (approximate)	Contribution	Contributor
1776	Specialization of labor in manufacturing	Adam Smith
1799	Interchangeable parts, cost accounting	Eli Whitney and others
1832	Division of labor by skill; assignment of jobs by skill; basics of time study	Charles Babbage
1900	Scientific management; time study and work study developed; dividing planning and doing of work	Frederick W. Taylor
1900	Motion study of jobs	Frank B. Gilbreth
1901	Scheduling techniques for employees, machines, jobs in manufacturing	Henry L. Gantt
1915	Economic lot sizes for inventory control	F. W. Harris
1927	Human relations; the Hawthorne studies	Elton Mayo
1931	Statistical inference applied to product quality; quality control charts	Walter A. Shewhart
1935	Statistical sampling applied to quality control; inspection sampling plans	H. F. Dodge and H. G. Romig
1940	Operations research applications in World War II	P. M. S. Blacket and others
1946	Digital computer	John Mauchly, J. P. Eckert
1947	Linear programming	George B. Dantzig, William Orchard-Hays, and others
1950	Mathematical programming, nonlinear and stochastic processes	A. Charnes, W. W. Cooper, H. Raiffa, and others
1951	Commercial digital computer; large scale computations available	Sperry Univac
1960	Organizational behavior; continued study of people at work	L. Cummings, L. Porter, and others
1970	Integrating operations into overall strategy and policy	W. Skinner

physical environments were "put under a microscope" and studied in great detail. Jobs were carefully analyzed and reorganized to eliminate wasteful efforts and achieve greater efficiency. At this same time, however, management began modifying its views, having discovered that workers have multiple needs, not just economic needs. Psychologists, sociologists, and other social scientists began to study people and human behavior in the work environment. In addition, economists, mathematicians, and computer scientists contributed newer, more sophisticated, analytical approaches.

With the advent of the 1970s, two distinct changes in our views were emerging. The most obvious of these was the new name, *operations management,* that was a reflection of shifts in the service and manufacturing sectors of the economy. As the service sector became more prominent than manufacturing, the change from production to operations emphasized the broadening of our field to service organizations as well as to those that produced physical goods. The second, more subtle change, was the beginning of an emphasis on synthesis, rather than just analysis, in our management practices. Spearheaded most notably by Wickham Skinner, American industry was awakened to its negligence of the operations function as a vital weapon in the organization's overall competitive strategy. Previously preoccupied with an intensive analytical orientation and an emphasis on marketing and finance, we had failed to ensure that our operations activities were integrated coherently into the highest levels of strategy and policy to provide focused, rather than diverse and fragmented, directions for our organizations. Today, as a consequence, the operations function is experiencing a renewed role as a vital strategic element for meeting consumers' needs throughout the world.[1]

A SYSTEMS VIEW OF OPERATIONS: DEFINING THE SUBSYSTEM

In our discussion, up to this point, we have identified operations as a system of the organization.

Organizations Viewed as Systems

What is a system? Often used loosely, the term can mean different things to different people. In a very general sense, a *system* is a collection of objects united by some form of regular interaction and interdependence. Systems can vary from large physical collections of subcomponents, such as nationwide communications networks, to more minute abstract examples—someone's "system" for processing paperwork in an office, for example. In some professional fields, such as process engineering and biology, *system* has a much more precise definition. Regardless of the precision of the term, however, models are often developed to represent a system or some aspect

[1]See C. G. Andrew and G. A. Johnson, "The Crucial Importance of Production and Operations Management," *Academy of Management Review* 7, no. 1 (1982), pp. 143–47.

of it. These models, which show functional relationships, are used to facilitate communication among people who are mutually interested in whatever system is under consideration.

The systems concept, as applied to organizations, can help develop our understanding of operations. Consider this simple systems model.

EXAMPLE

A business organization can be defined as an identifiable entity created to accomplish specific purposes. It exists within, and is part of, a larger environment. The organization itself consists of numerous subcomponents (subsystems), all of which interact in pursuing the organizational goals.

Several important systems concepts underlie this definition. The organization:

- Has identifiable goals that may be expressed in terms of profit, service, or other accomplishments,
- Has boundaries that limit the nature and types of activities it performs,
- Is part of a larger environment (another system),
- Is made up of subcomponents that are interrelated in many complex ways,
- Engages in efforts and actions to ensure that its goals are being satisfactorily attained.

An organization's goals identify its fundamental reasons for existence; they tell what it is trying to accomplish. A business firm's goals often describe both the general nature of its products (goods and/or services) and what it wishes to accomplish for its customers, employees, and owners. A firm's statement of goals is important because it directs and guides day-to-day activities and alerts management when the firm is headed off course.

The boundaries of an organization are largely determined by society's acceptance of its goals. The business firm cannot exist without the consent and support of the larger environment. Figure 1.3 shows several environmental elements affecting the firm's success. If consumers don't buy the product, if other businesses won't supply needed materials, if governmental regulations are too rigid, the business firm will cease to exist.

A systems model of the organization itself identifies the subsystems, or subcomponents, that make up the firm. Some of these are illustrated in Figure 1.4. The production/operations subsystem is one of many interdependent subsystems in most organizations. As Figure 1.4 shows, a business firm might well have accounting, personnel, engineering, finance, marketing, purchasing, and physical distribution functions in addition to production/operations. These functions are not independent but are interrelated to one another in many vital ways. (The arrows indicate interdependence.) You can see that marketing interacts with purchasing and finance; what

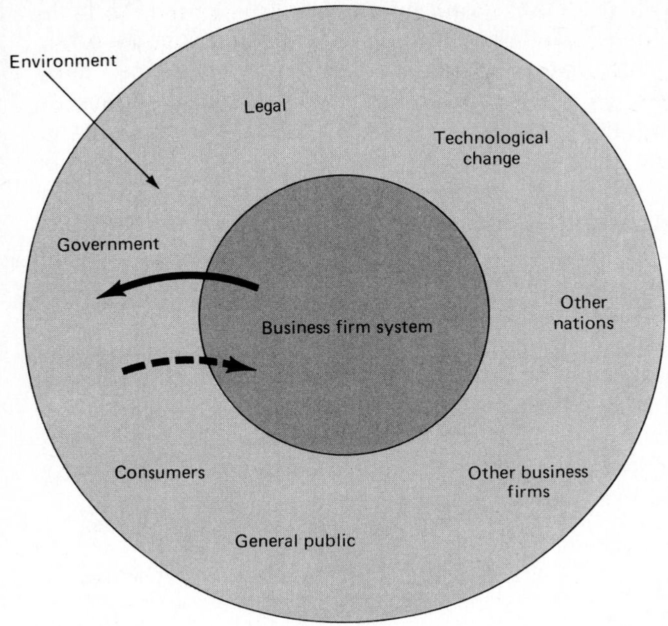

FIGURE 1.3
The business firm and the environment

FIGURE 1.4
The business firm: A systems view

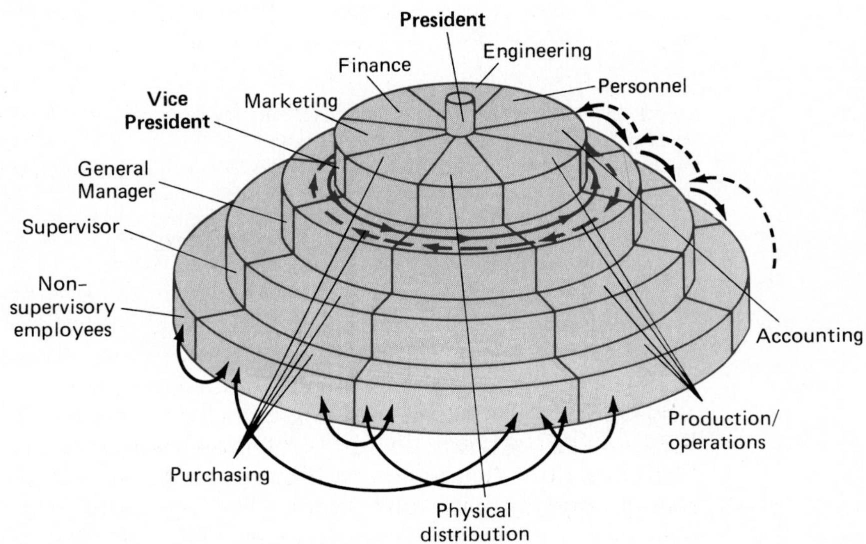

you cannot see so clearly is that marketing interacts with all other subsystems as well. Decisions made in the production/operations subsystem often affect the behavior and performance of other subsystems. Likewise, decisions in the other subsystems affect production/operations as well as one another. Finally, you should understand that the boundaries separating the various subsystems are not clear and distinct. Where do the responsibilities of production/operations end and those of physical distribution begin? The answers to such questions are often unclear and sometimes never resolved.

System Control The final major concept in the systems model of organizations is control. Control in the business firm involves measurement of outputs, evaluation or comparison of actual accomplishments with desired accomplishments, and adjustments of inputs. The results of this comparison are fed back to management, as was shown in Figure 1.1. The "feedback loop" enables management to decide whether or not adjustments in organizational activities are needed; it is an essential element in exercising timely control over the firm's behavior.

EXAMPLE

There are many different kinds of control in technologically advanced societies. Consider the technological control feature in a high-quality automobile that features year-round constant interior temperature. Say that desired temperature is 72°F. If the temperature in the early morning is actually 58°F, when the car is started actual temperature is monitored, a comparison to desired temperature made, and the adjustment made by the heater. In the evening, the temperature in the car might be 84°F. The monitoring, comparison, and adjustment takes place again, this time by cooling.

A similar kind of control exists in organizations. Some executives use a simple system to make sure future organization activities take place in accordance with the organization's plans. Required activities are noted on a calendar date when they are supposed to be performed. At the beginning of each day, the executive checks the calendar to see what activities are planned for the day. He or she seeks information to compare actual progress to date with planned progress. If adjustments are needed, they can be made immediately. Even if no adjustments are necessary, the control process is functioning, since the executive knows that performance is taking place according to the organization's plans.

As you can see, by adopting a systems viewpoint we gain a perspective on what purposes the operations subsystem serves in the overall organization and how it relates to other activities. There are some other management perspectives, however, in addition to the systems viewpoint, that aid us in understanding operations management as we see next.

MANAGING THE OPERATIONS SUBSYSTEM

We have described the operations subsystem; the real problem, however, is not to identify it but to operate it effectively. The conversion process must be managed by someone, and that someone is the operations manager.

The operations manager's job is to manage the process of converting inputs into desired outputs. In doing so the practicing manager uses various approaches from the classical, behavioral, and modeling views of management. As discussed below, and as summarized in Table 1.2, our percep-

TABLE 1.2
Operations management elements from various schools of management thought

School	Some important assumptions	Primary focus	General contributions to management
Classical			
Scientific management	People motivated by economics alone Managerial rationality Organization a closed system (certainty)	Economic efficiency Physical aspects of work environment Scientific analysis of work tasks Applications of techniques to work tasks	Demonstration of benefits from specialization of labor, division of labor, job analysis, separation of planning and doing
Process orientation		Management processes	Identification of principles and functions of management
Behavioral			
Human relations	People complex; possess multiple needs	Behavior of individual in work environment	Awareness of individuals
Behavioral science	Human beings social creatures	Interpersonal and social aspects of work environment	Identification of behavioral variables that relate to organizational behavior
Social systems	Organization an open system	Interactive relationships of organization with its environment	Development of theories relating organizational behavior to human characteristics and organizational variables
Modeling			
Decision making	Decision making processes are the primary managerial behaviors	Information acquisition, utilization, and choice processes	Development of guides for improving decision making
Systems theory	Organization an open system Organization a complex of interrelated subcomponents	Identification of organization boundaries, interrelationships among subsystems, and relationships between organization and larger environment	Development of approaches for predicting and explaining system behavior
Mathematical modeling	Main elements of organizations can be abstracted, interrelated, and expressed mathematically	Quantification of decision problems and systems Optimization of small set of situations	Development of explicit rules for management decisions Development of methods for analyzing organization systems or subsystems

tions of management responsibilities and concepts have evolved through the years, and we have gained insights from a variety of sources with different orientations.

Classical

Classical management has contributed the scientific management and process theories to the operations manager's knowledge.

Scientific Management The basis of scientific management is a focus on economic efficiency at the production core of the organization. Of central importance is the belief that rationality on the part of management will obtain economic efficiency. This school of management thought emphasizes the closed-system logic of engineering, technology, and economics. (A closed system is one that is self-contained, relies little on support from its environment, and operates essentially in a world of certainty.) People at work were considered to be motivated by money alone. Economic efficiency was the single measure of organization performance. Further, it was assumed that by buying the talents of an expert who specialized in engineering technology, management could purchase the rationality it needed. In short, the scientific management school of thought considers the organization to be a closed system unaffected by outside disturbances or influences.

Economic *efficiency*, a vital measure of performance according to classical thought, is a term that many organizations have retained today. Consequently, it is an important concept to understand. Efficiency refers to the ratio of outputs to inputs. Organization efficiency typically is a ratio of product or service outputs to land, capital, or labor inputs.

$$\text{Efficiency (\%)} = \frac{\text{Output}}{\text{Input}} \times 100\% \quad (1.1)$$

EXAMPLE

Management is concerned with labor efficiency, especially when labor is costly. To determine how efficient labor is in a given situation, management sets an *individual standard,* a goal reflecting an average worker's normal amount of output per unit of time under normal working conditions. Say that the standard in a cafeteria is the preparation of 200 salads in one hour. If labor input produces 150 salads per hour, how efficient is the salad operation?

$$\text{Labor efficiency} = \frac{\text{Labor output}}{\text{Labor input}} \times 100\% = \frac{150 \text{ salads}}{200 \text{ salads}} \times 100\% = 75\%$$

Compared to standard, this operation is 75 percent efficient in the preparation of salads.

Perhaps the most significant contribution to scientific management was Frederick Taylor's concept of separating *planning* from *doing* in production because the two tasks require distinctly different skills. He believed that some workers (managers, in modern terminology) should schedule work, purchase materials, analyze jobs, and perform other nonproduction tasks. Others (operative, or production, workers) should perform the manual tasks necessary to transform materials into finished goods. Before Taylor, all industrial tasks were performed by the same person—much like a small family farm is operated by a farmer today.

As our economy becomes more service-oriented, we see managers' increasing reliance on proven scientific management techniques to help them reach their goals. Efforts to gain economic efficiency through labor cost analysis and control are employed not only by goods-producing firms, but also in government, hospitals, and other service organizations. Although we cannot accept scientific management as an all-inclusive definition, we certainly can recognize its influence in many operations today.

Process The *process* school of management thought, also referred to as the administrative or functional approach to management, was developed in the early 1900s by Luther Gulick, Lyndall Urwick, Oliver Sheldon, and Henri Fayol, among others. These pioneers viewed management as a continuous process involving the functions of planning, organizing, and controlling by a manager, who influences others through the functions he or she performs. As elaborated by Fayol, these functions are as follows:

1. *Planning* includes all those activities that result in developing a course of action. These activities guide future decision making.
2. *Organizing* involves all activities that result in some structure of tasks and authority.
3. *Controlling* activities are those that assure that the performance in the organization takes place in accordance with planned performance.

This approach to management, with the process emphasis, will be the one most frequently referred to in this book. As part of the ongoing process of management, operations managers perform functions that involve planning, organizing, and controlling. The process approach is very helpful in structuring our thinking about management since it both examines separate activities in detail and allows for their interdependence (see Figure 1.5). These functions overlap and are not necessarily performed in any fixed order.

Behavioral

Human Relations The behavioral school began in 1927 with a human relations movement that emerged quite unexpectedly from some research studies at the Hawthorne Works of the Western Electric Company near Chicago. The research was originally intended to examine the effects of changes in the physical work environment on production output—a typical

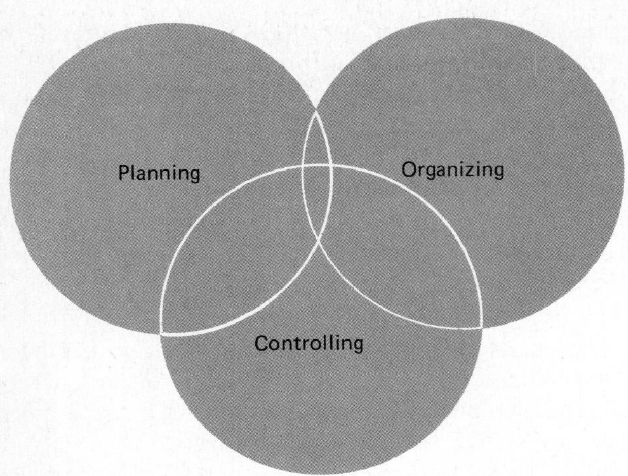

FIGURE 1.5
The management process

scientific management study. Some social scientists on the research team, however, observed that changes in output were often due to factors other than just physical changes in the work area. Specifically, workers seemed to respond favorably to the individual care, attention, and interest that the experimenters had shown toward their work. Productivity increased. The main outgrowth of this research was a new attitude that seriously questioned scientific management's man-as-machine concept.

Behavioral Science and Social Systems The answer to the human relations question has been provided by *behavioral science* and *social systems* theories: people in their work environment, as elsewhere, are extremely complex. Theories concerning such behavioral processes as leadership, motivation, communication, and attitude change have been supported with a great deal of experimental evidence from both laboratories and actual organizations. Applied psychologists have developed *behavioral science* theories of the individual; social psychologists, sociologists, and cultural anthropologists have developed *social systems* theories of people in groups at work. Role relationships, group structure, formal and informal power, and cultural differences have all been found to affect performance. In light of these developments, modern managers have modified their views.

Our study of operations management would certainly be superficial if we chose to ignore the contributions from the behavioral sciences. People in their working environments exhibit behavioral dimensions that are not readily explained either in the closed system of the classical approach or by the logical analysis of the modeling approach to management. Certainly operations managers must take into account individual and group behavior of subordinates, peers, superiors, and other groups in their managerial activities. As managers plan, organize, and control their operations, they must take into account the behavioral implications of their activities. Thus,

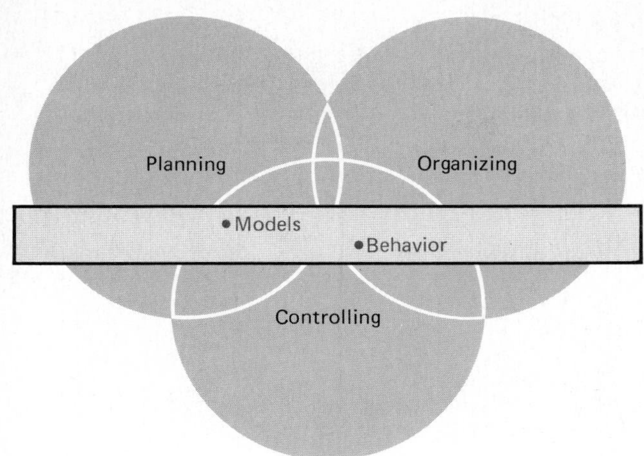

FIGURE 1.6
Management variables in operations

the *process and behavioral approaches necessarily interact,* as depicted in Figure 1.6. Models also have been added to Figure 1.6; let's now see why.

Modeling

The modeling school of management is concerned with decision making, systems theory, and mathematical modeling of systems and decision-making processes.

Decision Making The decision-making orientation considers making decisions to be the central purpose of management. Simply stated, the view of this approach is that management *is* decision making. Managers subscribing to this approach make use of studies dealing with human information needs, information processing, assessing risk, and generating decision alternatives to help them make final choices.

Systems Theory Advocates of systems theory stress the importance of studying organizations from a "total systems" point of view. They consider the organization to be a system of highly interrelated and interdependent parts. When management makes a change in one subsystem, far-reaching effects can be felt in other parts of the total system. A policy change in marketing, for example, can affect finance, production, and personnel subsystems. According to this school, identifying subsystem relationships, predicting effects of changes in the system, and properly implementing system change are all part of managing the total organization.

Mathematical Modeling With its foundations in operations research and management science, mathematical modeling focuses on creating mathematical representations of management problems and organizations. For a particular problem, the variables are expressed mathematically, and the model is then used to demonstrate different outcomes that would result from various possible managerial choices. The modeling approach can also be used to examine organization decisions from a systems viewpoint. After relationships among subsystems have been represented mathematically, management can use a model to determine the consequences possible management decisions would have on various subsystems throughout the organization. Often mathematical modeling is used simply to clarify relationships and provide information that might be useful for management decisions.

EXAMPLE

The breakeven volume of output is that volume at which the total revenue received equals the total cost of production. Let fixed cost be *a*, a unit variable cost *b*, and unit revenue *c*. At what volume of output *x* (expressed in units of product) will the organization break even? Using the linear mathematical breakeven model, equation 1.2, we can find the output level *x* at which total revenue equals total cost.

$$\text{Total revenue} = \text{Total cost} \qquad \textbf{(1.2)}$$
$$cx = a + bx$$

If a city license bureau has fixed operating costs of \$500,000 per year, incurs variable costs of \$1 for each customer it services, and receives \$2 in revenue from each customer, how many customers must it service to cover all its costs of operation? The breakeven volume is determined as follows:

$$cx = a + bx$$
$$\$2x = \$500{,}000 + \$1x$$
$$x = 500{,}000$$

Breakeven volume is 500,000 customers.

This is one simple example of a general approach to management that works very effectively in management situations lending themselves to logical analysis. Breakeven analysis, inventory control, and some resource allocation situations are easily converted into mathematical terms. As we have noticed with all the other schools of thought, however, modeling theories alone cannot supply a total approach to management. Modeling theories have a limited concept of human beings; when mathematical relationships are stressed, managerial activities may be neglected, and these activities cannot always be modeled.

Many of the planning, organizing, and controlling activities of *the managerial process can be modeled*. But although these models of decision making, functional problems, and systems are related to the behavioral dimensions of subordinates and supervisors, integration of the modeling and behavioral approaches to management is difficult; the two schools have adopted very different scientific methodologies. The kinds of measurements used in the empirical, experimental approach of the behavioral school differ somewhat from those used in the mathematical, computerized approach of the modeling school. Nevertheless, in private and public organizations managers draw from the modeling school for those activities that can be modeled, taking into account any behavioral consequences. As indicated in Figure 1.6, we will consider how modeling relates to the behavioral and process dimensions of operations management.

A FRAMEWORK FOR MANAGING OPERATIONS

In this book, we draw from these various approaches a framework for our study of operations management.

Planning The operations manager selects the objectives for the operations subsystem of the organization and the policies, programs, and procedures for achieving the objectives. This stage includes clarification of the role and focus of operations in the organization's overall strategy. It also involves efforts directed toward product planning, facilities design, and the use of the conversion process.

Organizing The operations manager establishes an intentional structure of roles and information flows within the operations subsystem. He or she determines and enumerates the activities required to achieve the operations subsystem's goals and assigns authority and responsibility for carrying them out.

Controlling To ensure that the plans for the operations subsystem are accomplished, the operations manager must also exercise control. Outputs must be measured to see if they conform to what has been planned. If they do, adjustments aren't needed. If the information feedback indicates substantial differences between planned and actual outputs, then inputs or parts of the conversion process must be adjusted. Suppose automobile production one week averaged fifty one cars per working hour, but planned output was fifty nine cars. Investigation reveals that on four occasions some gear box subassemblies were not sent to the main assembly line. These shortages resulted in reduced output levels for the week. Adjustments must be made through the feedback loop to alleviate the shortage. Perhaps inputs have to be readjusted and more direct labor and materials devoted to gear box subassemblies. Actual solutions to such problems might not be so simple, but feedback and control measures can often help identify the sources of problems and suggest ways to solve them.

Behavior In executing planning, organizing, and controlling functions, operations managers are clearly concerned with how their actions affect human behavior. They also want to know how the behavior of subordinates can affect management's planning, organizing, and control actions. In operations we are interested in the behavior of subordinates and managers, especially their decision-making behavior.

Models As operations managers plan, organize, and control the transformation process, they encounter many problems and must make many decisions. They can frequently simplify these difficulties by using models. Types of models and examples of their uses will be illustrated in some detail as we cover the functional problems of operations management.

Problems of the Operations Manager

Operating managers are concerned with many different problem areas: cost control in brokerage houses, quality of services in hospitals, rates of production output in furniture factories. Although operations managers occupy positions at several levels of their organizations, and although they work in different kinds of organizations, they all share some kinds of problems. The results of a study, The Manufacturing Futures Project, conducted at Boston University, reveal the kinds of activities 160 executives are concerned with in U.S. and Canadian firms. The respondents, managers or directors of operations, plant managers, divisional general managers, vice presidents, and others with related duties showed that many of their firms' most prominent activities for improving operations had to do with planning, organizing, and controlling the operations system and its conversion process (Table 1.3). You can see that some of their activities are primarily identified with each of the three functions of management. Production planing, defining manufacturing strategy, and product redesign, for example, are *planning* oriented. Changing the organization, labor/management relations, and developing integrated information systems are examples of *organizing* activities. Inventory control, maintenance improvement, and lead-time reduction exemplify *control* oriented activities.[2] Since we are dealing with a system that has highly interrelated components, however, these problem areas are interrelated, and none is related strictly to planning *or* organizing *or* controlling. It will become clear as we progress in our study of operations management that all these problem areas are encountered to some extent as the operations manager plans, organizes, and controls the operations subsystem and manages the conversion process.

[2]For related studies see Robert R. Britney and E. F. Peter Newson, *The Canadian Production/Operations Management Environment: An Audit* (School of Business Administration Research Monograph, London, Ontario: University of Western Ontario, April 1975); see also Robert R. Britney, "Continuing Education in Production/Operations Management," in *Proceedings of the 34th Annual Meeting of the Academy of Management*, 1974; see also Stephen E. Berry, Hugh J. Watson, and William T. Greenwood, "A Survey as to the Content of the Introductory POM Course," *Academy of Management Journal* 21, no. 4 (December 1978), pp. 699–714.

TABLE 1.3
Activities emphasized by organizations to improve operations

%*	Activity	%	Activity
90.6	Production planning, scheduling/inventory control systems	46.3	Automating jobs
76.9	Supervisor training	44.4	Developing new processes for new products
66.3	Capacity expansion	43.1	Vendor relations, procurement procedures
63.1	Worker safety programs	42.5	Focusing factories
58.8	Defining a manufacturing strategy	41.3	Narrowing product line; standardizing
57.5	Motivating direct labor employees	39.4	Making existing systems work better
55.0	Value analysis-product redesign	35.0	Giving workers a broader range of tasks to perform
54.4	Improved maintenance practices	33.1	CAD (Computer Aided Design)
53.1	Changing the manufacturing organization	31.9	Giving workers more responsibility for planning and organizing work
51.3	Changing labor/management relationships	29.4	CAM (Computer Aided Manufacture)
50.0	Developing integrated information systems	26.9	Plant relocation
48.1	Lead time reduction	25.0	Group technology
47.5	Quality circles	21.3	Office automation
46.9	Developing new processes for old products	20.6	Zero defects programs
		20.0	Reducing size of manufacturing units

*Percentage of respondents whose business unit has placed an emphasis on this activity in the last five years with the objective of improving operations.
Source: *The Manufacturing Futures Project: Summary of Survey Responses* (Boston University School of Management, 1982), pp. 20–21.

THE STRATEGIC ROLE OF OPERATIONS

As one studies and practices operations management, it is easy to become preoccupied with the detailed economic and engineering aspects of the conversion process and lose sight of its fundamental purpose for existence. This, in fact, has occurred in many U.S. companies, and the results have been costly from an overall organizational viewpoint. Economy and efficiency of conversion operations are secondary goals, not primary goals, of the overall organization. Primary overall goals are related to market opportunities. Indeed, an overemphasis on operations efficiency and economy can detract from primary goal accomplishment. We must therefore consider the broader strategic role of operations in the organization.

A Stragetic Perspective

In Figure 1.7 we see the basic downward flow of strategy influence leading to conversion operations and results. The general thrust of the process is guided by competitive and market conditions in the industry, which pro-

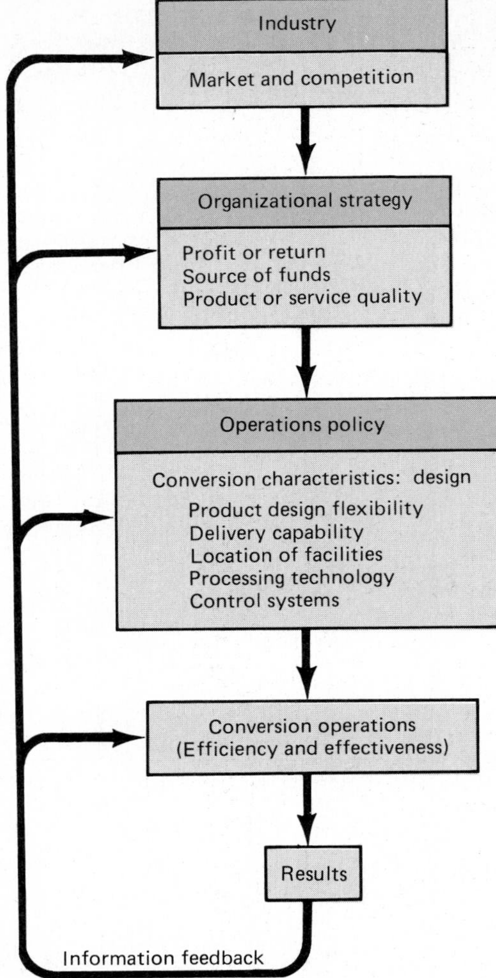

FIGURE 1.7
Operations as a strategic element in accomplishing organizational goals

vide the basis for determining the organization's strategy. Where is the industry now, and where will it be in the future? What are the existing and potential markets? What market gaps exist, and what competencies do we have for filling them? A careful analysis of market segments and the ability of our competitors and ourselves to meet the needs of these segments will determine the most effective direction for focusing an organization's future efforts.

After assessing the potential within an industry an overall organizational strategy must be developed, including some basic choices of the primary basis for competing. In doing so, priorities are established among the following four characteristics:[3]

- Dependability (reliable, timely delivery of orders to customers)
- Flexibility (responding rapidly with new products or changes in output volume)
- Quality (product performance)
- Cost efficiency (low product price)

In recent years, we've learned that most organizations can't be best on all these dimensions and, by trying to do so, they end up doing nothing well. Furthermore, when a competency exists in one of these areas, an attempt to switch to a different one can lead to a downfall in *effectiveness* (meeting the primary objectives). An example is the firm with a product quality management system geared to one orientation at the time that emerging market opportunities require another. Say that current products for existing markets warrant low to medium reliability. They need little or no product-life testing and only periodic performance checks of large volumes of output. When a new market opportunity emerges, the firm might attempt to economize by using its existing quality management system. If the market success of the new product depends on greater product precision, reliability, and a more intensive quality control effort than currently exists, an entirely different quality control technology may be necessary. Left as is, the quality management system overlaid on a new product can lead to a marketing disaster. If the company wishes to capitalize on the new market opportunity, it must be willing and able to implement the necessary quality control technology, even if it involves extensive, costly changes.

These basic strategic choices, then, set the tone for the shape and content of the operations function and what it accomplishes. A conversion process designed for one type of focus is often ill-suited for success in another, alternative, focus.

Operations Objectives

The overall objective of the operations subsystem is to provide conversion capabilities for meeting the organization's basic goals and strategy. The organization's chosen strategic focus can then be translated into operations subgoals, which specify:

1. product (service) characteristics,
2. process characteristics,

[3]Further discussion of these characteristics is given in S. C. Wheelwright, "Reflecting Corporate Strategy in Manufacturing Decisions," *Business Horizons* 21, no. 1 (1978), pp. 57–66; see also W. Skinner, *Manufacturing in the Corporate Strategy*, (New York: John Wiley & Sons, 1978).

3. customer service,
   a. producing quantities to meet expected demand
   b. meeting the required delivery date for goods or services
4. product (service) quality,
5. efficiency,
   a. effective employee relations and labor cost control
   b. material cost control
   c. cost control in facility utilization
6. adaptability for future survival.

The priorities among these operations objectives and their relative emphases should be direct reflections of the overall organization's mission.

Operations Alternatives and Tradeoffs

The operations objectives can be attained through the decisions that are made in the various operations areas shown in Table 1.4. Each decision area involves important tradeoffs. As you can see, the decisions consider not only physical facilities and equipment but the mix of human skills and types of organizational arrangements as well. All these decision areas in combination determine the operations function's basic overall orientation, its ability to perform effectively and to respond to opportunity, and the extent to which it is constrained from undertaking new endeavors. After outlining the decisions and alternatives, how does one proceed to make choices among them?

Depending upon the preferred focus, our choices in the decision areas should be mutually supportive and consistent for attaining the desired operations objectives. This is achieved through operations *policies* that guide our choices in the diverse operations decision areas toward the preferred focus. Suppose our strategy is to pursue several specialized segments of the electronics instrumentation market by featuring a small volume of high-priced, custom-engineered products of high reliability. This choice has important implications for each of the conversion characteristics and decision areas in Table 1.4. We might establish a policy of buying basic product subcomponents rather than making them in several small plants located near specific market segments. This decision could involve relatively low investment in buildings but high investment in general-purpose equipment and research. Production planning and control policies could be oriented toward low inventory levels, with emphasis on high product reliability and on-time deliveries. A specialized professional work force under relatively loose supervision could be appropriate. Within each facility, the "design-as-you-go approach" to product engineering could be employed for meeting customers' specialized product needs. The highly technical nature of the product could dictate the need for a relatively large engineering and product development staff.

These decisions are important because once they're implemented they may be difficult to change. As a result, firms may get themselves locked into situations that are detrimental to pursuing new market opportunities,

TABLE 1.4
Some important tradeoff decisions in manufacturing—or "You Can't Have It Both Ways"*

Decision area	Decision	Alternatives
Plant and equipment	Span of process	Make or buy
	Plant size	One big plant or several smaller ones
	Plant location	Locate near markets or near materials
	Investment decisions	Invest mainly in buildings or equipment or inventories or research
	Choice of equipment	General purpose or special purpose equipment
	Kind of tooling	Temporary minimum tooling or "production tooling"
Production planning and control	Frequency of inventory-taking	Few or many breaks in production for buffer stocks
	Inventory size	High inventory or a lower inventory
	Degree of inventory control	Control in great detail or in lesser detail
	What to control	Controls designed to minimize machine downtime or labor cost or time in process, or to maximize output of particular products or material usage
	Quality control	High reliability and quality or low cost
	Use of standard	Formal or informal or none at all
Labor and staffing	Job specialization	Highly specialized or not highly specialized
	Supervision	Technically trained first-line supervisors or nontechnically trained supervisors
Product design/engineering	Size of product line	Many customer specials or few specials or none at all
	Design stability	Frozen design or many engineering change orders
	Technological risk	Use of new processes unproved by competitors or follow-the-leader policy
	Engineering	Complete packaged design or design-as-you-go approach
	Use of manufacturing engineering	Few of many manufacturing engineers

*Adapted from Wickham Skinner, "Manufacturing—Missing Link in Corporate Strategy," *Harvard Business Review* 47, no. 3 (May–June 1969), p. 141. Copyright 1969 by the President and Fellows of Harvard College.

and they are placed at a competitive disadvantage for long periods of time. This often happens with such basic operations design decisions as how many facilities to build and where to locate them. Should we build one large facility to benefit from economies of scale in operations? Or should we build several smaller specialized facilities to provide better delivery service to various market segments? Each decision has advantages, but each also has long-run implications for the types of future market opportunities it can accommodate. If, for example, a firm decides on four small facilities, each specializing in a particular family of products, the capital requirements of this decision may strain the company financially. Should market demand increase for one of the products, the firm may be unable both to compete with larger firms in the industry and to acquire funds for expansion.

TABLE 1.5
Distinctive characteristics of service organizations*

Characteristics	Some implications for operations management
1. Customer is a participant in the service process.	1. a. Customer is an input/resource. b. Customer has immediate interactions with operations.
2. Production and consumption occur simultaneously.	2. a. Services are not inventoried. b. Capacity to provide service must be available when demanded.
3. Service capacity is time perishable.	3. a. Service capacity and demand must be synchronized. b. Forecasting demand, smoothing demand, and adjusting capacity have important implications for operations.
4. Site selection is dictated by customer location.	4. a. Multiple sites may be needed, each with a small scale of operations. b. Vehicle routing may be affected by site selection.
5. Operations are labor intensive.	5. a. New technologies are difficult to implement while maintaining a personalized atmosphere. b. Employee characteristics influence the value of the service package.
6. Services are intangible.	6. a. Unit of output is difficult to define and measure. b. Quality control systems are difficult to establish.

*Modified from R. S. Sullivan, "The Service Sector: Challenges and Imperatives for Research in Operations Management," *Journal of Operations Management* 2, no. 4(August 1982), p. 212.

In concluding this overview of operations strategy it should be noted that although many of our examples have been manufacturing oriented, strategy in service operations is equally important. Because service organizations possess different characteristics than manufacturers, however, their strategies display somewhat different emphases. These distinctive characteristics, displayed in Table 1.5, are prime considerations in developing service strategies and operations for diverse organizations such as hospitals, hotels, transportation systems, and entertainment companies.

TRENDS IN OPERATIONS MANAGEMENT

What new demands are being made of operations managers today? How will their jobs change in the future? Answers to such questions are speculative, but we can find some clues by observing recent trends in overall economic activities.

Shifts in Economic Activity

Are people doing the same kinds of work today that they have done in the past? The question is important because operations management will usually be found where economic activity is occurring. Table 1.6 provides us

TABLE 1.6
Distribution of employed workers by major sectors of the economy, 1900–1982*

Year	Agriculture and other extractive industries	Industry	Services	Total
1900	38%	34%	28%	100%
1910	34	37	29	100
1920	30	39	31	100
1930	27	35	38	100
1940	25	34	41	100
1950	15	40	45	100
1960	11	39	50	100
1970	5	34	61	100
1980	4	28	68	100
1982	4	26	70	100

*U.S., Bureau of the Census: Victor Fuchs, *The Service Economy* (New York: Columbia University Press, 1968), p. 207, with permission of the NBER; *Statistical Abstract of the United States 1972,* pp. 227–30; U.S., Department of Labor, Bureau of Labor Statistics, 1975, 1979, 1984.

with some answers. We can see that there has been an employment shift from agriculture and other extractive (mining and contract construction) industries to the service sector, agriculture decreasing from 38 percent of the employed workers in 1900 to 4 percent in 1982, and service workers increasing from 28 percent in 1900 to 70 percent in 1982. The percentage of workers employed in industry has dwindled steadily. Will this trend continue? We suspect not. It is quite possible that the percentage of workers in the service sector will gradually continue to grow, but this growth, most likely, will be relatively slow. The most recent data suggest it will come from workers shifting from industry to the service sector, while the percentage of agricultural workers will remain around 4 percent.

One point is clear. The largest sector of the United States economy today is in services. In 1929 of the 47.6 million people employed in the United States, 18.1 million were employed in services. In 1982, 102 million people were employed, 71.4 million in services. The fastest growing service sector has been government services, with repair services a close second. In number of actual workers, the total labor force has increased some 54 million workers—52 million of whom work in the service sector.[4] Personal consumption expenditures, along with employment, have also shifted toward services. In 1983, fifty percent of consumer expenditures were for services and fifty percent for durable and nondurable goods.

[4]U.S. Department of Labor, Bureau of Labor Statistics, 1972, 1975, 1979, and 1984.

More economic activity in the service sector suggests that many of you may find yourselves employed in service industries in the future.[5] In this book we will take the position that operations management concepts, skills, and techniques are transferable *across* the industry/service sectors and *within* industries and services. Our examples and explanations will therefore apply to both kinds of operations, even if only one is mentioned.[6] Modern management continues to transfer manufacturing concepts, techniques, and skills to the service sector. With an understanding of operations management, managers of service operations have been successful in bringing about needed improvements in quality, effectiveness, and efficiency in their organizations.

PRODUCTION AND OPERATIONS MANAGEMENT CAREERS

In 1984 there were 110 million workers in the United States labor force. Some 7 million of these, we estimate, filled supervisory positions in finance, operations, and marketing. The characteristically high labor intensity in operations means there is a disproportionately high share of managerial jobs in this area. In production and operations, many future managers can find careers.

Entry Positions in Production/Operations Management

If your career objectives are to advance to a top management position, operations is a reasonable avenue to travel. One *Fortune* survey of the 500 largest U.S. individual companies found that chief executive officers had a production/operations career emphasis 18.6 percent of the time.[7] Besides the top position in the organization, there is generally a vice president or similar officer responsible for production/operations. This raises the question of how one might gain such a position. What entry positions allow people to gain experience for promotion within operations?

Two entry tracks are evident—a line and a staff approach. Typical line positions include first-line supervisors, management trainees, and foremen. Staff positions include computer analysts, project analysts, inventory and material planning and control, production planning, logistics, and quality control. Our recent experiences indicate ample opportunities in all these areas, especially first-line supervision, computer-related positions, and in materials management positions. In any of these jobs you will likely obtain *product or service knowledge* about the firm for which you work—a necessity for most top management positions.

---

[5]For a discussion of the growth of service versus manufacturing job opportunities see "Are Unemployment Forecasts Too Gloomy?," *Businessweek* (April 23, 1984), pp. 74–79.

[6]The development of operations problem solutions and their transfer to service sector organizations is discussed in V. A. Mabert, "Service Operations Management: Research and Application," *Journal of Operations Management* 2, no. 4 (August 1982), pp. 203–209.

[7]Charles G. Burch, "A Group Profile of the *Fortune* 500 Chief Executives," *Fortune* (May 1976), pp. 173–77, 308–12.

EXAMPLE

In a recent semester two different industry guests visited an undergraduate production/operations management class. In response to student questions on careers, one guest, the personnel manager at a new Quaker Oats Company manufacturing facility, stressed an interest in management, production/operations management, and industrial engineering students for entry first-line foreman positions. As she explained them, the jobs were in a clean, modern facility with good opportunity for line or staff advancement. The second guest, the operations vice president at First National Bank of Kansas City, stressed an interest in operations management majors for entry positions in operations analysis, a staff function directly supporting bank operations. After six months to two years, operations analysts typically move to line supervisory positions. In both cases, promotion was available within operations and to other functions (marketing, finance, etc.) as well.

Career Choice in Production/Operations Management

Because of their importance in our lives, careers deserve reasoned thought and direction. To guide these efforts, personal career management procedures are available from several sources.[8] We suggest that in making career choices in production/operations you consider (1) opportunity for advancement, professional development, and visibility in the organization; (2) expected job satisfaction; (3) monetary rewards; (4) quality of life (climate, entertainment, etc.); (5) work group characteristics; and (6) individual needs and desires (location, health considerations, etc.). P/OM career decisions are amenable to change. Although you might have to learn new technology in a major job change, P/OM skills are generally transferable across services and manufacturing and within each sector. Professional organizations and journals occasionally summarize career opportunities in their operations management areas, thus providing a good source of information.

CONTEMPORARY OPERATIONS MANAGEMENT TOPICS

Modern operations management is a complex proposition. To deal with it, we have divided this book into six major parts. In each part, we relate specific operations management considerations to the contemporary issue under discussion. By organizing our coverage around the management subfunctions of planning, organizing, and controlling, we strive for an integrative perspective (see Figure 1.8). By relating each problem area to a common theme, we hope to suggest a continuity of thought that will help

[8] See, for example, Douglas T. Hall, *Careers in Organizations* (Santa Monica, California: Goodyear Publishing Co., 1976), especially Chapter 2, "Career Choice"; see also M. London and S. A. Stumpf, *Managing Careers* (Reading, MA: Addison-Wesley, 1982).

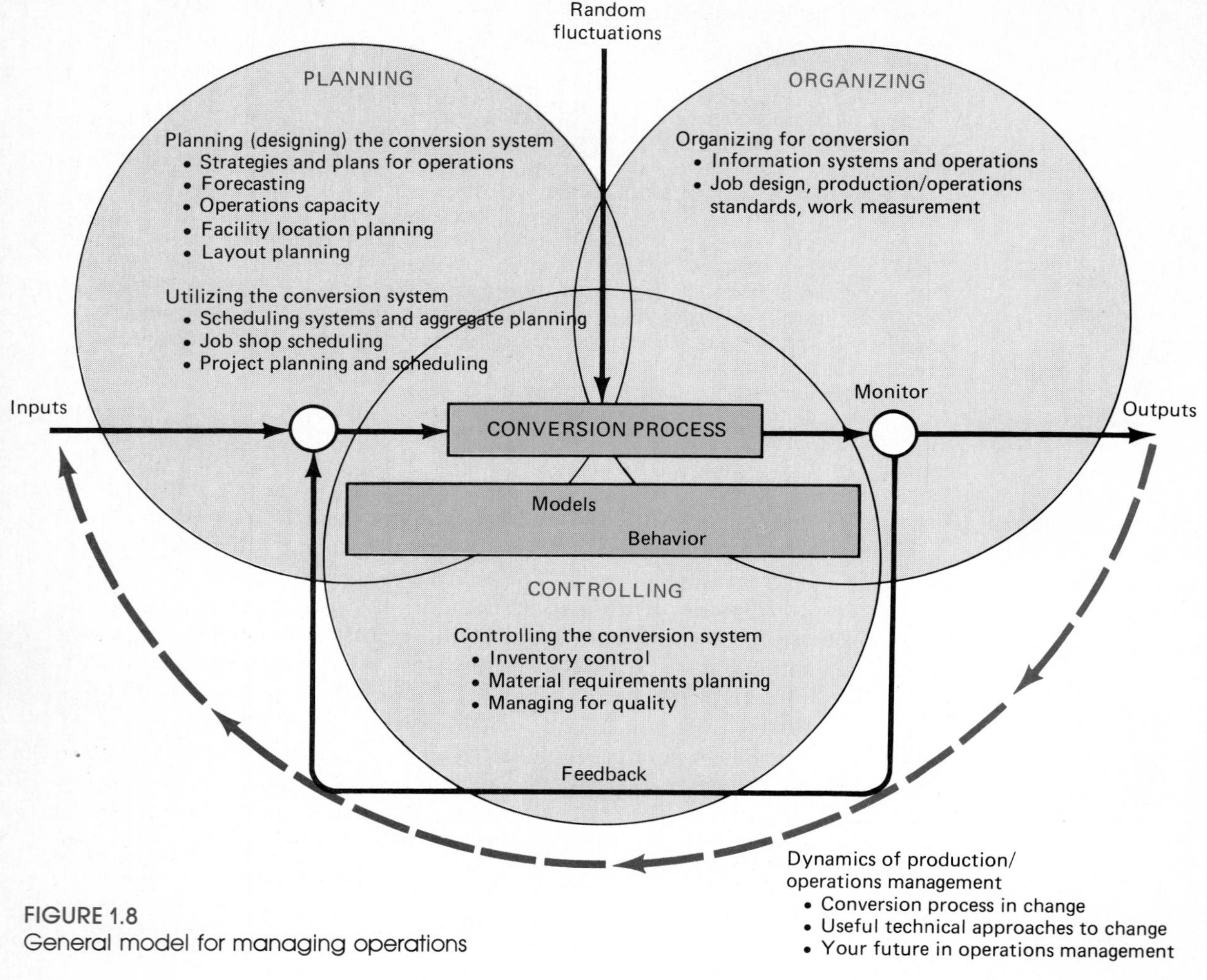

FIGURE 1.8
General model for managing operations

you grasp the fundamentals of operations management. Within this framework, we have found it useful to approach the planning subfunction somewhat differently than is usually the case. We divide this subfunction into two major parts: planning the conversion system and utilizing the conversion system. Planning the conversion system revolves around its design; utilization of the system focuses on operating it once it's in existence. Although this distinction may be somewhat artificial, it allows us to integrate problem areas in a more logical fashion than otherwise.

One major topic, for example, is controlling the conversion system (Part V). In this section we deal with inventory control, materials management, and quality management—all necessary activities of operating managers. As we discuss each of these separately, we develop relevant concepts and terminology, identify problems, and present problem-solving techniques. When problems are behavioral (quality motivation, for example), we introduce contemporary techniques like quality circles and attitude change procedures to deal with them. When problems are process-oriented (quality control, for example), we show why models and such methods as sampling theory and control procedures are appropriate.

Before considering specific solutions to operations problems, however, we must first explore the major problems, issues, and challenges that are facing operations managers. These include questions on productivity, technology, and competition, all of which create the challenges for effective performance today. It is this set of questions that we consider next.

SUMMARY

This chapter has highlighted the role of the operations function in organizations and the importance of managing it effectively. Operations was defined in terms of the mission it serves for the organization, the technology it employs, and the human and managerial processes it involves. Using this approach, we were able to see the breadth of issues the operations manager faces, as well as the kinds of problems and decisions that arise in operations management.

To understand and solve operations problems we adopted a framework that draws upon the concepts from three schools of management thought—classical, behavioral, and modeling. Systems concepts can be useful for understanding organizations and the role of the operations function within them, and pictorial models of these systems show the basic nature of the operations subsystem and its interaction with the environment. Operations management makes use of these systems, models, and various techniques in directing the conversion process, which converts inputs into desired outputs. Operations managers must become involved in planning, organizing, and controlling operations. As they make decisions and decide among alternatives, they must consider the organization's goals and overall strategy.

Historical shifts in economic activity and predicted changes in the growth of major industries indicate the increasing importance of the service sector. These changes present some new challenges to operations management, and transferring our knowledge of production management into the service sector setting is chief among them.

CASE

Kare-Full Katering, Inc.

Harrison T. Wenk III is a forty-three-year-old married man with two children, ages ten and fourteen. Harrison, who has a masters degree in education, teaches junior high school music in a small town in Ohio. Harrison's father passed away two months ago, leaving his only child with an unusual business opportunity. According to his father's will, Harrison has twelve months to become active in the family food-catering business, Kare-Full Katering, Inc., or it will be sold to two key employees for a reasonable and fair price. If Harrison becomes involved, the two employees have the option to purchase a significant, but less than majority, interest in the firm.

Harrison's only involvement with this business, which his grandfather established, was as an hourly employee during high school and college summers. He is confident that he could learn and perhaps enjoy the marketing side of the business, and that he could retain the long-time head of accounting-finance. But he would never really enjoy day-to-day operations. In fact, he doesn't understand what operations management really involves.

In 1984 Kare-Full Katering, Inc., had $3.75 million in sales in central Ohio. Net profit after taxes was $105,000, the eleventh consecutive year of profitable operations and the seventeenth in the last twenty years. There are 210 employees in this labor-intense business. Institutional contracts account for over 70 percent of sales and include partial food services of three colleges, six captive commercial establishments (primarily manufacturing plants and banks), two long-term care facilities, and five grade schools. Some customer locations employ a permanent operations manager; others are served from the main kitchens of Kare-Full Katering. Harrison believes that if he becomes active in the business, one of the two key employees, the vice president of operations, will leave the firm.

Harrison has decided to complete the final two months of this school year and then spend this summer around Kare-Full Katering—as well as institutions with their own food services—to assess whether he wants to become involved in the business. He is particularly interested in finding out as much as possible about operations. Harrison believes he owes it to his wife and children to fairly evaluate this opportunity.

Case Questions

1. Prepare a worksheet of operations activities that Harrison should inquire about this summer.
2. To manage the firm, how much does Harrison need to know about operations? Why?
3. What problems do you expect Harrison to encounter this summer—both at Kare-Full and at other institutions?
4. If you were Harrison, what would you do? Why?

CASE

Operations Management in a Veterinary Clinic

See if you can identify the inputs, outputs, and conversion processes that exist in a veterinary clinic consisting of three veterinarians, a clerical staff, and two animal control assistants. Identify the primary operations management activities (use Table 1.3 as a guide) that exist in this setting. Lay them out in a framework similar to the one in Figure 1.1. You should consider how the addition of an operations manager to the clinic staff would affect the cost and effectiveness of medical services. Normally in a situation like this, the operations manager would be one of the veterinarians. Could you explain to them why they should hire you to manage operations of the clinic?

REVIEW AND DISCUSSION QUESTIONS

1. Organizations may be viewed as systems. The systems view is important to operations managers since (a) the production/operations system is a part of the firm or organization and (b) within the production/operations function there are subsystems. Explain.
2. Using Figure 1.1, explain the conversion process in a fast food outlet (McDonald's, for example) and a public swimming pool.
3. (a) What are operations subgoals?
   (b) What is the overall objective of the operations subsystem?
   (c) How do they relate to each other?
4. Explain how control works in the operations subsystem. A schematic model (a diagram) might be helpful in organizing your discussion.
5. How does production/operations policy interrelate with accounting and financial policy and marketing policy? What does this interrelationship accomplish?
6. Organization goal accomplishment requires that a strategic element of operations is the consideration of the firm's industry, strategy, operations policy, and conversion process. How do these elements relate to one another? How do they relate to organization goal accomplishment?
7. Relate the conversion diagram in Figure 1.1 to the first fifteen activity areas listed by operations managers in Table 1.3.
8. Compare and contrast the three broad categories of management thought: classical, behavioral, and modeling schools.
9. Describe classical management's scientific management theory.
10. A problem with modern assembly line techniques seems to be that workers are apathetic. How could scientific management be used as a basis for solving this problem? How could a human relations philosophy help solve it?
11. Why is there a need for a behavioral school of management thought? Preferably from your own experience or observation, provide a supervisor-subordinate situation that supports your answer.
12. Relate the general model for managing operations (Figure 1.8) to each school of management thought.
13. How do inflation, energy shortages, and a shorter work week each present new challenges to production/operations managers?
14. Energy conservation is an individual, firm, and national concern. If you were a manager of a large department store employing 200 and spending over $10,000 a month on utilities, which approach to (or school of) management might assist you best in reducing energy costs? Why?
15. As an industrialized nation becomes more affluent, people have more leisure time and demand more services than they used to. Many workers enter the labor force later and leave it earlier. How do these changes affect the role of the traditional production/operations manager?

PROBLEMS

1. The manager of a cola bottling plant came to work early on Friday, having been out of town on business throughout the week. Before others arrived, he checked the daily labor efficiency report for the bottling plant. Daily efficiency was 102 percent Monday, 94 percent Tuesday, and 87 percent Wednesday. Going to the assistant manager's desk, he found that actual hours worked on Thursday were 96, cases

bottled Thursday were 1,025. The equivalent labor output, the standard, is 12.5 cases per hour. What, if any, questions should the manager ask when employees arrive Friday?

2. An insurance claims office's group labor standard is 150 claims processed per day. So far this week, 160, 125, 140, and 100 claims have been processed daily. The claims backlog is building. Prepare a graph of daily efficiency. What does the graph indicate?

GLOSSARY

Behavioral science Theories of human behavior and how it is affected by such processes as leadership, motivation, communication, interpersonal relationships, and attitude change.

Classical school of management Focuses on efficiency at the production core and on the separation of planning and doing work; emphasizes management principles and functions.

Controlling All those activities assuring that performance in the organization takes place in accordance with planned performance.

Conversion process Changing labor, capital, land, and management inputs into outputs of goods and services.

Efficiency Some measure (ratio) of outputs to inputs.

Feedback Information in the control process that allows management to decide whether or not adjustments in organizational activities are needed.

Human relations Concept that people are complex and have multiple needs and that the subordinate-supervisor relationship directly affects productivity.

Mathematical modeling The creation of mathematical representations of management problems and organizations in order to determine outcomes of proposed courses of action.

Operations management Management of the conversion process, which converts land, labor, capital, and management inputs into desired outputs of goods and services.

Operations subsystem That part of the organization that exists primarily for generating or producing the organization's physical goods or services.

Organizing All activities that result in some structure of tasks and authority.

Planning All those activities that result in developing a course of action and guide future decision making.

Process management One theory of the classical school; it views management as a continuous process involving the functions of planning, organizing, and controlling so as to influence the actions of others.

Random fluctuations Unplanned or uncontrollable environmental influences (strikes, floods, etc.) that cause planned and actual output to differ.

Scientific management One of several classical theories of management; it emphasizes economic efficiency at the production core through management rationality; assumes the economic motivation of workers and urges the separation of planning and doing work.

Social system One set of behavioral theories examining group relationships and their effect upon productivity.

Specialization of labor Concept of breaking jobs down into specialized subtasks and reassigning work according to the task involved.

System A collection of objects united by some form of regular interaction and interdependence.

System theory Identifies organization boundaries, interrelationships among subsystems, and relationships between the organization and the larger environment.

SELECTED READINGS

Andrew, C. G. and Johnson, G. A. "The Crucial Importance of Production and Operations Management." *Academy of Management Review* 7, no. 1 (January 1982), pp. 143–47.

Barnard, Chester I. *The Functions of the Executive*. Cambridge: Harvard University Press, 1938.

Berry, Stephen E., Hugh J. Watson, and William T. Greenwood. "A Survey as to the Content of the Introductory POM Course." *Academy of Management Journal* 21, no. 4 (December 1978), pp. 699–714.

Britney, Robert R. and E. F. Peter Newson. *The Canadian Production/Operations Management Environment: An Audit*. School of Business Administration Research Monograph. London, Ontario: University of Western Ontario, April 1975.

Fayol, Henri. *General and Industrial Management*. Translated by Constance Storrs. London: Pitman Pub. Corp., 1949.

George, Claude S., Jr. *The History of Management Thought*. 2nd ed. Englewood Cliffs, N.J.: Prentice-Hall, Inc., 1972.

Mabert, V. A. "Service Operations Management." *Journal of Operations Management* 2, no. 4 (August 1982), pp. 203–209.

Roethlisberger, Fritz and William J. Dickson. *Management and the Worker*. Cambridge, Mass.: Harvard University Press, 1939.

Simon, Herbert A. *The New Science of Management Decision*. New York: Harper & Row, 1960.

Skinner, Wickham. "Manufacturing—Missing Link in Corporate Strategy." *Harvard Business Review* 47, no. 3 (May–June 1969).

Skinner, Wickham. *Manufacturing in the Corporate Strategy*. New York: John Wiley & Sons, 1978.

Smith, Adam. *The Wealth of Nations*. New York: Random House, Inc., 1937.

Sullivan, R. S. "The Service Sector: Challenges and Imperatives for Research in Operations." *Journal of Operations Management* 2, no. 4 (August 1982), pp. 211–14.

Thompson, James D. *Organizations in Action*. New York: McGraw-Hill Book Co., 1967.

Wheelwright, S. C. "Reflecting Corporate Strategy in Manufacturing Decisions." *Business Horizons* 21, no. 1 (1978), pp. 57–66.

2 Meeting the Competitive Challenge in Operations

At Westinghouse, we are putting top priority emphasis on productivity and quality improvement, not only because it is necessary for the well-being of our Corporation, but because we believe it is vital for the economic survival of our nation and for our national security.

About three and one-half years ago, we started this Corporate-wide top-priority emphasis on productivity improvement for two basic reasons. First was our need to further improve our Corporate performance, and the second was our concern over increasing international competition. We didn't want this to be a one-shot effort, but rather we wanted productivity improvement to become a way-of-life throughout the Corporation.

In early 1979 we formed a Corporate Committee on Productivity, and I was assigned to chair it. Initially, our Committee spent many months studying the situation—first in the United States; then in Europe; and then in the Pacific Basin—particularly in Japan. Significantly, we didn't anticipate, at the outset, that most of our studies would find the Japanese to be so formidable. In my case, I've been visting Japan for almost 20 years. But—for the first 17 years, as a teacher—and only the past three years, as a student. This "role change" makes an immense difference.

Significantly also, we didn't realize, at the outset, that quality is as important to productivity—as are people and technology.[1]

Thomas J. Murrin, President, Public Systems Company
Westinghouse Electric Company, Pittsburgh, Pennsylvania,

---

[1]Thomas J. Murrin, "Productivity and Quality Improvement," Remarks to Defense Logistics Agency, Bottom Line Conference (Washington, D.C., May 13, 1982).

Consistent with the thrust of Mr. Murrin's comments, this chapter will pursue three aspects of the competitive challenge that faces production/operations managers today—*productivity, technology and mechanization,* and *international business.* These topics will form a background for addressing problem areas that will be critical to operations management in the years ahead. The balance of this book is directed toward providing an approach to operations management that will meet the challenges introduced here.

PRODUCTIVITY

Efficiency, productivity, performance—these are terms we tend to use interchangeably in discussing behavior and achievement. Efficiency and productivity refer to a ratio of outputs divided by inputs, but performance is a broader term incorporating efficiency and productivity in overall achievement. In this section we want to define productivity more precisely and examine its various levels in the economy. Then we will discuss measurement, productivity trends, quality and productivity relationships, and some production improvement efforts underway in selected firms. Our intent is to provide some order in the jungle of terminology surrounding the term *productivity.*

Productivity Defined

Productivity can be expressed on a total factor basis or on a partial factor basis. *Total* factor productivity is the ratio of outputs over all inputs:

$$\text{Productivity} = \frac{\text{Outputs}}{\text{Labor} + \text{Capital} + \text{Materials} + \text{Energy}} \qquad \textbf{(2.1)}$$

Outputs relative to one, two, or three of the inputs (labor, capital, materials, or energy) are *partial* measures of productivity. For example, capital productivity is also measured by an output-to-input ratio; one measure is the dollar value of outputs divided by the number of dollars of capital investment during a year. Output per labor hour, often called labor efficiency, is perhaps the most common partial measure of productivity.

EXAMPLE

A small restaurant has averaged 224 customers served during a day over the past year. Hours are 6:00 A.M. to 2:00 P.M., and three employees comprise the total staff. Average labor productivity could be expressed as

$$\text{Labor Productivity} = \frac{\text{Output}}{\text{Labor Input}}$$

$$= \frac{224 \text{ Customers Served}}{3 \text{ employees} \times 8 \text{ hours/employee}}$$
$$= 8.133 \text{ customers served/hour}$$

On Tuesday of this week, 264 customers were served by a full staff. On Wednesday, 232 customers were served, with two employees working full days and one working but two hours. We can find labor productivity for each day as

$$\text{Labor Productivity (Tuesday)} = \frac{264}{3 \times 8} = 11.0 \text{ customers served/hour}$$

$$\text{Labor Productivity} = \frac{232}{(2 \times 8) + 2} = 12.889 \text{ customers served/hour}$$

For each day, labor productivity was well above this historical average, a level of labor performance that should please the owner (unless it caused customers to wait excessively for service).

Levels of Productivity

Productivity can be viewed at two extremes. We can look at the level of an entire nation or at the level of an individual employee. In between these two extremes are industry, organization (firm), division (business unit), and workgroup levels. Figure 2.1 illustrates total factor productivity—as well as the partial factors, capital and labor—for the United States business economy over a ten-year span. We can see that although it has been relatively stable, productivity declined in the late 1970s before a recent increase. This

FIGURE 2.1
Productivity trends in the U.S. business economy by quarter: 1973–1983 II

Source: *Productivity Perspectives* (American Productivity Center, December 1983), p. 3.

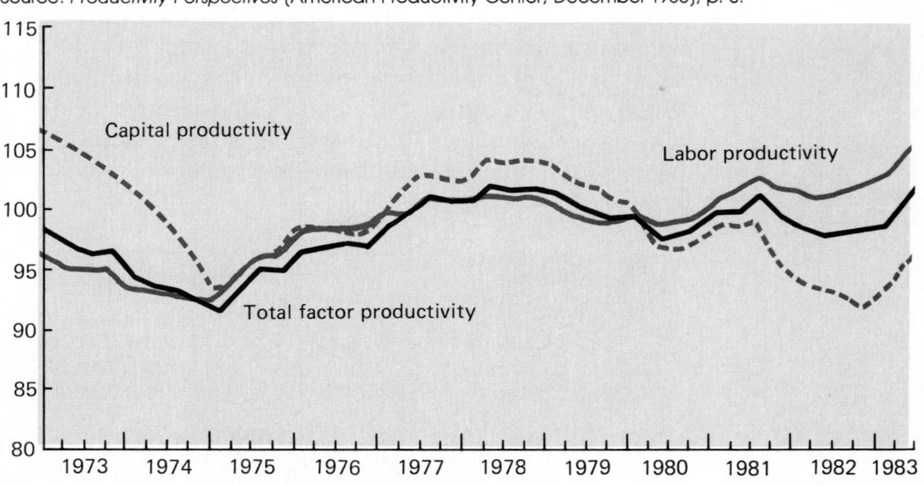

level of analysis, on a national basis, identifies overall trends and guides government policy analysis. However, it leaves us, as individual operations managers, a little uncertain about what we can do to improve a given trend. The information we can gain from lower-level measurements may help us to overcome this uncertainty.

Productivity Measurement

Productivity measurement varies with the level of analysis, in terms of the factors selected for inclusion in the productivity ratio, and how these factors are measured. To illustrate, consider the *industry*-level productivity changes within the U.S. business economy. As Figure 2.2 illustrates, farming has experienced *total factor* productivity gains, while mining has declined. Table 2.1 provides a different industry sector measure, showing the *labor* productivity of selected manufacturing sectors. Labor productivity in tobacco and in petroleum far exceeds the national average ($8.62/labor hour), while levels of productivity in apparel and leather manufacturing are substantially less than the national average.

Similarly, in individual firms, the productivity question involves measurements from standard accounting statements, *the income statement* and *balance sheet*.[2] The data, adjusted for price changes, is a measurement ap-

FIGURE 2.2
Total factor productivity (average annual growth rates)
Source: *Productivity Perspectives* (American Productivity Center, December 1983), p. 9.

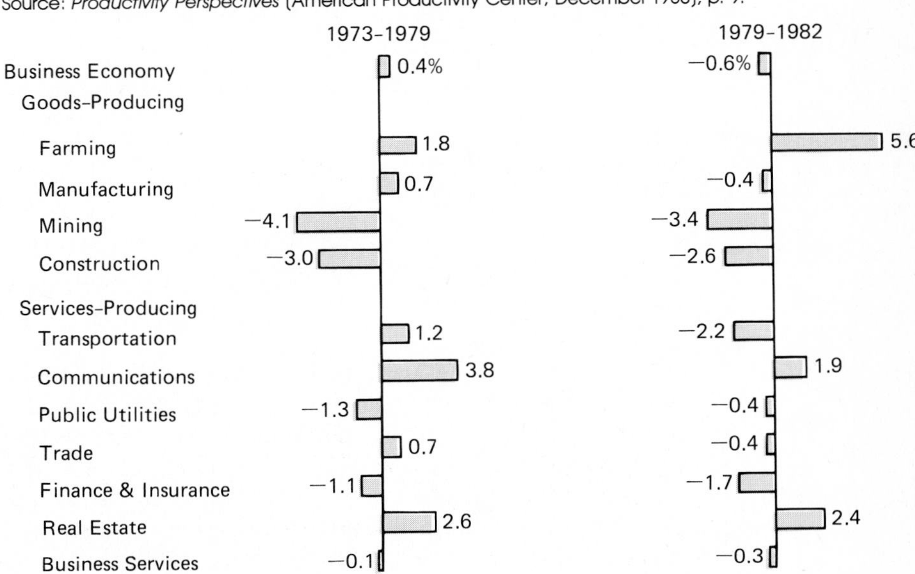

[2]See Gary N. Brayton, "Simplified Method of Measuring Productivity Identifies Opportunities for Increasing It," *Industrial Engineering* (February 1983), pp. 49–56.

TABLE 2.1
Manufacturing labor productivity level, 1982

	Output/hour (1972$)	% of Mfg. hours
Tobacco	$30.40	0%
Petroleum	15.05	1
Chemicals	12.10	6
Food	10.47	9
Transportation equipment	9.76	9
Electrical machinery	9.39	11
Instruments	9.03	4
Nonelectric machinery	8.96	12
Paper	8.81	4
Total manufacturing	$8.62	100%
Primary metals	7.83	5
Rubber	7.80	4
Stone, clay & glass	7.66	3
Fabricated metals	7.44	8
Misc. manufacturing	6.89	2
Lumber	6.87	3
Textiles	6.84	4
Printing & publishing	6.57	7
Furniture	5.53	2
Apparel	5.41	5
Leather	5.30	1

Source: *Productivity Perspectives* (American Productivity Center, December 1983), p. 9.

proach that is used by the consulting firm Touche Ross & Company; it is based on the American Productivity Center productivity measurement procedure.

Practical Guides for Measurement Often we are interested in the measurement question within a business unit, for subunits such as departments, and for individuals. The industrial engineering profession has developed methods for individual work measurement that are used in these areas, as discussed in Chapter 10.

We suggest some simple guidelines for establishing productivity measures for workgroups and individuals. First, be sure top management truly wants to measure productivity and is committed to doing so. Developing and using the measurement activity can be very expensive.

Second, involve employees at all levels in developing measures. Although management is responsible for making the final selection of measures, as well as balancing data collection costs against usefulness, employees at lower levels can also develop measures effectively.[3]

Third, select a variety of productivity measures and performance indicators that will best meet the performance improvement needs of the specific organization. For formal productivity ratios, the numerator of the productivity ratio (equation 2.1) could be expressed as quantity, quality (such as number of good items), sales dollars, number of on-time deliveries, or many other output dimensions. Similarly, there are many variations for the denominator. Rather than choosing one universal measure, a meaningful performance measurement system will incorporate several useful indicators—such as outputs, costs, and schedule achievement—as well as some productivity measures.

Finally, utilize existing data (financial, operations, quality, and computerized management information) wherever it is available. It is counterproductive to generate new data unnecessarily. We are reminded of our conversation with a bank employee in a check reconciliation activity who told us that the time she spent in measuring and reporting her activity equaled or exceeded the time she spent on the activity itself. In this instance, the best productivity gain—and improvement is the ultimate objective of a measurement program—might be to eliminate or drastically reduce the employee's measurement activity.

Productivity Trends

In Figures 2.1 and 2.2, we saw a rather stagnant U.S. productivity picture for the past decade. From 1960 to 1983, labor productivity growth never exceeded 4 percent in any one year. What about the contribution of capital? This is important to operations managers, as the tradeoff between investment and labor is always under scrutiny. As Figure 2.3 illustrates, capital productivity growth rates for the business economy have been negative for both the 1973–1979 period (−0.4 percent) and the 1979–1982 period (−2.8 percent), with substantial declines (−5.6 percent) in the finance and insurance industries.

What does this mean? It means that capital has not contributed positively, overall, to annual productivity growth during the last few years in the U.S. economy. The prudent operations manager should be aware of this and should seek investments that clearly enhance productivity in his or her operations (farming, mining, real estate, or whatever).

Are these trends true reflections of productivity? Or instead, are they caused by price changes? How do prices and productivity interact? Accounting standards boards, stockholders, and many corporate managers are quite interested in the answers to these questions. They believe that profitability growth in the latter part of the 1970s resulted from rising prices (inflation)—not from better-run (more productive) operations. Figure 2.4 il-

[3]For a widely used application of measurement involving employees, see the procedures developed in Everett E. Adam, Jr., James C. Hershauer, and William A. Ruch, *Productivity and Quality: Measurement as a Basis for Improvement* (Englewood Cliffs, N.J.: Prentice-Hall, 1981).

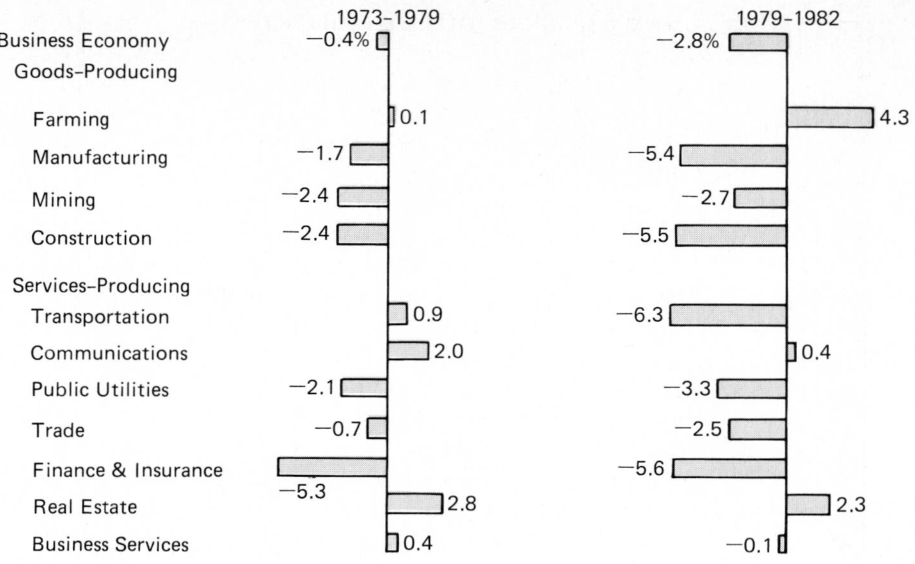

FIGURE 2.3
Capital productivity average annual growth rates

Source: *Productivity Perspectives* (American Productivity Center, December 1983), p. 5.

lustrates that their observation may well be true for some industries. Those industries that appear above the dotted line are gaining through price increases, while those below the dotted line are growing as a result of higher output gains.

Now that we have some productivity background at the national and industry levels, let's look at what some individual firms are doing to improve their competitive position in quality and productivity.

Quality and Productivity

One reason that the competitive position of firms can falter is that the quality of goods and services produced does not meet the customer's expectations. When quality—the appropriateness of design specifications to function and use as well as the degree to which outputs conform to the design specifications—is poor, demand for products and services can diminish quickly. But what does this have to do with productivity?

There is a clear relationship between quality and productivity. Generally, when quality increases, so will productivity. Why? Because waste is eliminated. The amount of resource inputs (the denominator of equation 2.1) required to produce good outputs (the numerator) is reduced. Productivity increases.

If this is so simple, why haven't all U.S. firms figured this out? Many have. Even if one accepts this view, however, achieving high-quality performance is not all that simple. There are also other views of the quality-productivity relationship.

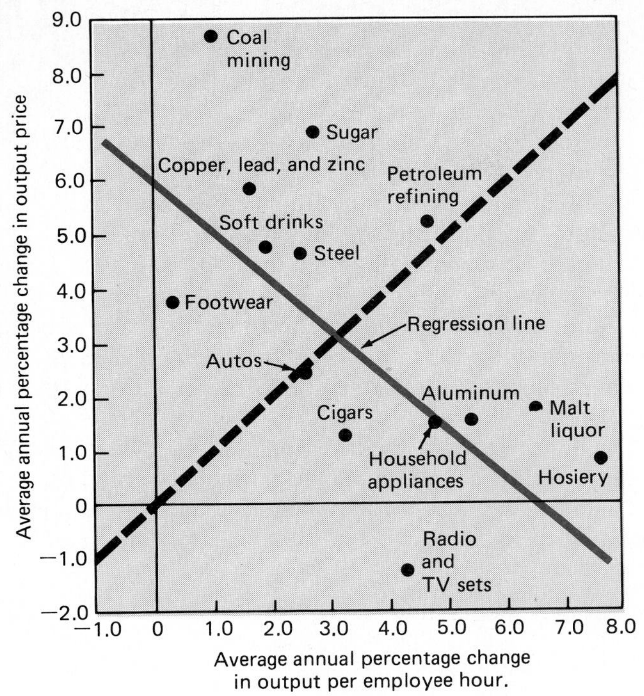

FIGURE 2.4
Prices and labor productivity: average rates of change, selected industries

Source: *The Economic Review* (The Federal Reserve Bank of Kansas City, November, 1979), p. 17. Dotted line added by authors.

One such view is that quality and productivity move in opposite directions. Think about such processes as typing or data entry at a computer keyboard. As your speed increases, what tends to happen? You tend to make more errors, especially when you go "very fast." Logically, it follows that if you type slowly and carefully, you will make fewer errors. There is a tradeoff between speed and accuracy. As quality increases, speed (and productivity) decrease.

How can these two contrasting positions concerning quality-productivity relationships be resolved? We believe the answer is in the concept of *capability*. We suggest that as long as there is unused capability in the individual (such as the typist) or the productive system (such as a manufacturing facility), then increases in speed (and productivity) can be achieved without declines in quality. Or, alternatively, quality can be improved without changing speed. If one focuses on quality, holding speed constant, then quality should increase, waste should be eliminated, and productivity should increase. This can happen as long as the individual, or group of individuals, is willing to exert effort and has the capability to achieve the quality-productivity levels desired. It is the operations manager's task to provide the facilities, tools, and desire (motivation) to do so. This is a very difficult task. Some managers and firms are discovering ways to maintain high quality and increase productivity at the same time. Let's observe some of their techniques.

Deming and Juran Two management consultants, Dr. W. E. Deming and Dr. J. M. Juran, have worked with the Japanese during the past several decades to enhance product quality through statistical methods. Dr. Deming,[4] perhaps the most widely recognized American in Japanese manufacturing circles, has emphasized statistical analysis as the basis for process control and improvement (achieving increased quality and productivity). Successful applications of Deming's approach in the United States have taken place at the Nashua Corporation and Ford Motor Company.

Dr. Juran's approach is more managerial, but it has the same basic intent: to achieve productivity gains through emphasis on quality. He specifies goals for management and lays the blame for poor quality and low levels of productivity on management rather than on the workers. Dr. Juran has consulted with American firms such as Caterpillar Tractor and Texas Instruments.

Both Juran and Deming emphasize data collection and analysis as a basis for informed operative employee and managerial decision making. Starting with Chapter 3, analysis as a basis for decision making will be used throughout this book, including Chapter 17, "Managing for Quality."

EXAMPLE

Ford Motor Company has embraced the advertising slogan "Quality is Job #1." For quality assurance executives, this has indeed been the primary focus within Ford in the 1980s. Ford has utilized management consultants such as Dr. Deming to stimulate the commitment required among its employees. Top executives have diligently stressed quality, and quality education has become a major activity at all levels within Ford. Suppliers have also become a part of the quality emphasis. Ford provides conferences, schools, and manuals to teach suppliers what is expected of them and how to achieve these expectations. Ford's approach was first to improve quality, and then to capitalize on this improvement in its marketing campaign. Company advertisements promote Ford products as the best-made American products. Ford's approach appears to be working, as indicated by the results of data independently collected on customer complaints about new cars and trucks in 1983–1984.

A Quality-Productivity Strategy Improving quality is one important way to maintain a competitive position in today's markets. Quality can be promoted to customers and employees. Consumers want quality products and

[4]See, for example, W. Edwards Deming, "On Some Statistical Aids Toward Economic Production," *Interfaces* 5, no. 4 (August 1975), pp. 1–15; W. Edwards Deming, *Quality, Productivity, and Competitive Position,* MIT Industrial Liaison Program Report (Cambridge, Mass.: MIT, 1983); Joseph M. Juran, *Quality Control Handbook,* 3rd Ed. (N.Y.: McGraw Hill, 1974); and Joseph M. Juran, *Quality Planning and Analysis,* 2nd Ed. (N.Y.: McGraw-Hill, 1980).

services, and employees at all levels in the organization like to be associated with a winner. Most people associate high quality with a winning competitive position. Although employees may balk when they are encouraged to work more productively (because they feel they are being told to work faster), very few, if any, will argue with quality as a goal.

From an economic perspective, when quality is emphasized and subsequently improved, waste is decreased or eliminated. Hours are not wasted reworking products. Material is not thrown away. Operations costs are reduced. At the same time, the customer receives products and services that are "fit" for use. As a result, product prices can be lowered to share this productivity gain with customers, thereby increasing the firm's market share. Or, alternatively, the higher-quality product (as compared with competitors' product offerings) can command a premium price and a more secure market niche. To employees, these results mean increased job security because of a sound competitive position. Stockholders can benefit through higher overall profits and improved asset utilization. In short, high quality can make everyone a winner—a message some firms and managers seem to understand better than others.

Understanding and accepting this quality-productivity strategy is a first step toward its achievement. We encourage you to think seriously about this line of reasoning as you read the balance of this chapter and book.

Quality and Productivity Improvement Efforts

Let's look at a few examples of firms that are seeking productivity and quality gains in order to improve their competitive positions. As we saw in the comments that began this chapter, Westinghouse Electric Company, as a worldwide competitor in a variety of consumer, industrial, defense, and aerospace sectors, has a vital interest in quality and productivity improvement. Members of Westinghouse management were profoundly impressed with Japanese manufacturing technology. They were particularly affected by the devotion to quality among their Japanese counterparts. Since then, Westinghouse has undertaken initiatives to adopt quality circles, new technology, and a quality improvement emphasis by concurrently designing both the product and manufacturing process. What has Westinghouse achieved? Setting a goal in constant dollars of 6 percent a year in value added (by Westinghouse) per employee, the Westinghouse Public Systems Company achieved a 7-percent-a-year gain over three years (1979–82). The Public Systems Company is now seeking a 10 percent improvement per year.

In addition to individual company examples, improvement efforts are being organized into productivity centers and institutes, with more than 300 known centers worldwide.[5] These centers typically have any of four thrusts—training and education, information distribution and promotion,

[5]Robert R. Britney, *1982 International Directory of Productivity Centers* (The University of Western Ontario, 1982).

sociotechnical approaches, and industrial engineering and managerial economic emphasis[6]—reflecting the interests of the firms (consumers of center services) they are serving. Forty percent of the centers were estimated to emphasize training and education, with 20 percent primarily emphasizing each of the other three activities. Relative budgets in various parts of the world were aggregated by the authors, with 23.3 percent of worldwide center expenditures in North America, 32.0 percent in Europe, 21.6 percent in South America, 9.9 percent in Asia, and 11.9 percent throughout the remainder of the world.

One such facility is the American Productivity Center (APC) located in Houston, Texas. This not-for-profit center aids North American businesses in productivity improvement. Based on his observations, C. Jackson Grayson, chairman and founder, has some suggestions for chief executive officer (CEOs) regarding possible pitfalls. Since productivity improvement efforts typically involve operations, and because major expenditures and activities occur in this area, we should be aware of this expert's advice. Dr. Grayson suggests:

> First, the chief executive must be involved. Productivity gains must be made a major management goal with high priority.
>
> Second, a long-term strategy needs to be developed. The strategy should include opportunities for improvement, goals, productivity measures, rewards for achievement, employer involvement, communication, and effective organization.
>
> Third, productivity should be part of the company's regular business plan and budget.
>
> Finally, the greatest potential for improvement may lie in doing things differently. This will involve business risks. Changes will be necessary in organization, management style, and employee relations.[7]

We had the opportunity to participate in an APC-sponsored event, which is summarized in the example below.

EXAMPLE

The American Productivity Center coordinated private sector initiatives for a White House Conference on Productivity authorized by Congress and held in Washington, D.C. during September, 1983. The final reports represent the thinking of 175 senior-level leaders from business, labor, academia, and govern-

[6]R. R. Britney, D. Johnston, J. M. Legentil, and J. Walsh, "Planning for Productivity Gains within the Firm," Working Paper #82–38 (London, Canada: School of Business Administration, The University of Western Ontario, October 1982).

[7]C. Jackson Grayson, "What Every CEO Should Know About Productivity," *Chief Executive Magazine* 15 (1981).

ment who were brought together "electronically" by the American Productivity Center from April to August, 1983. These leaders met "on-line" for this four-month period, using computer terminals, telephone-satellite communication links, and a computer conference system called the Electronic Information Exchange System (EIES).

They exchanged information and ideas. They discussed, debated, and finally hammered out their recommendations in seven areas involving productivity, quality, and quality of work life:

1. Cooperation in the Workplace
2. Health Care
3. Information Workers
4. Quality
5. Reward Systems
6. Technology
7. Training

As C. Jackson Grayson summarized, "I sat at the crossroads of this conference, and the electronic traffic scrolling by my screen was an incredible window on the American state of thinking about productivity, quality, and quality of work life.

"Never has there been such an extended dialogue in such a frank and open manner by practical leaders on these subjects. It was a unique and historic conference. These were no isolated academics engaged in theoretical debates, no public officials posed for political posturing, no special interests pleading their causes. They were a sincere, open cross-section of American leaders, speaking their minds (often from their own homes late at night and on weekends) from a variety of perspectives and talking freely about their views, fears, and hopes.

"There was deep concern.

"A participant, not known to be given to purple prose, expressed his concern one Sunday evening.

"There is some feeling that this problem we face is temporary. That it will go away with the recovery, or that we merely have to find the right combination of magic incantations or techniques.

"I am convinced it is far more serious. It will be of much longer duration than we presently think, and the American public will have to give up its dreams of the automatic promised land forever.

"There is no question in my mind that the forces loose in the world today will inexorably force us to face the problem of producing competitively or sinking from the scene as did Greece and Rome.

"There were also hope and encouraging examples of changes underway. Successful programs. Case studies. Anecdotes. Changed attitudes. Excitement again in plants and offices that were dying."[8]

The above comments indicate that the changes in our thinking apply not just to factories and blue-collar workers, but to service industries and offices as well. What promise is there for productivity and quality improvement in services, particularly in white-collar services? Our concluding ex-

[8]C. Jackson Grayson, "Summary Comments," *White House Conference on Productivity Private Sector Final Report* (American Productivity Center, September 1, 1983).

ample provides some insight into TRW's quest for improved white-collar productivity.[9]

EXAMPLE

TRW is a multinational, highly diversified corporation with over $5 billion in sales, $3 billion in assets, and 100,000 employees operating in 27 different countries. Products range from car parts to satellite systems. TRW is the second largest computer software producer in the nation, behind only IBM. While 40 percent of TRW's workers are now involved in manufacturing, that number will fall to 5 percent by the year 2000, according to Henry P. Conn, TRW's former vice-president for productivity.

TRW has one fundamental objective. "TRW seeks to achieve superior performance as an economic unit, with special emphasis on high-quality products and services." This translates into seven goals summarized to reflect financial performance: high quality at competitive prices, market strength, diversification, management and technological innovation, maximum productivity, and effective use of outside-the-company resources (consultants, training, etc.).

Ruch and Werther illustrate by example how TRW organizes to achieve their objectives. A focus is on people. Managers are doing what they should be doing—planning, guiding, communicating, and supporting employees at all levels. Employees are working with a new sense of involvement.

For example, TRW has improved efficiency in computer software-writer jobs. Writers spend less time talking on the telephone, filing, attending meetings, or staring out windows. Instead, they spend as much time as possible actually writing the lines of code that guide missiles or track satellites. They now have individual rather than grouped terminals, computerized mail, and teleconferencing—all with the intent of working more at line activities that add value to the service the company is producing and selling.

It is clear that TRW is improving productivity, in part by adopting new techniques. Many other organizations have also discovered that new technologies have the potential to affect productivity positively, as we see next.

TECHNOLOGY AND MECHANIZATION

In Chapter 1 we referred to the "conversion process" as the central element of the production and operations function. The work of operations management revolves around conversion, where resource inputs are converted or

[9]See "Faced with a Changing Work Force, TRW Pushes to Raise White Collar Productivity," *Wall Street Journal*, August 22, 1983; William A. Ruch, "The Measurement of White-Collar Productivity," *National Productivity Review* (Autumn 1982), pp. 416–426; and William A. Ruch and William B. Werther, Jr., "Productivity Strategies at TRW," *National Productivity Review* (Spring 1983), pp. 109–126.

transformed into useful products and services. This conversion process is present in most organizations, but it is distinctly different for a bank, an aerospace firm, or a public utility. The basic technologies of operations differ among industries as well as within various organizations in any one industry. Accuracy in clerical tasks, judgment in evaluating a customer's ability to return loaned money, and extremely safe care of customer funds are all labor skills necessary in a bank. In contrast, the public utility requires engineering skills to design facilities, maintenance abilities for various mechanical and electrical applications, and operating skills for larger pieces of equipment used in operations. *The blending of labor, land, capital, and management—and the scientific expertise needed for this task—are at the very heart of technology* in operations.

In some instances, machinery is substituted for hand labor. *Mechanization is the process of bringing about the use of equipment and machinery* in production and operations. In a bank, for example, some jobs—such as checking account reconciliation and statement preparation—are mechanized. Other tasks, such as the interview in which information is initially gathered by a loan officer to start the loan qualification process, are not mechanized.

Organizations today face decisions regarding which variations in technology to employ and what degree of mechanization is best. Many of the challenges for improved productivity and quality are answered by managers and owners as they adopt more sophisticated technologies and increased mechanization. However, the costs associated with an inappropriate strategy for technology and mechanization are great. On the one hand, competitors who effectively substitute capital and equipment for labor in order to gain lower production and operating costs may increase market share very quickly. For example, highly mechanized companies in Japan and Korea caused a loss in market share for the U.S. steel industry. On the other hand, action to increase mechanization, when it is unnecessary or inappropriate, may be quite costly. A firm may be saddled with high fixed costs relative to other companies in the industry. Management may be unable to reduce variable costs of manufacturing sufficiently to recover the costs of mechanization.

What degree of technological change, mechanization, and automation is strategically best? The judgments required by any one organization to respond correctly to this question are often critical to the long-term survival of the business. It takes experience and wisdom to make such a decision; these qualities cannot be learned in a book. However, we can introduce you to some of the mechanization alternatives being faced by businesses today. Through our discussion of these choices—such as computers, robotics, and computer-aided design—you may gain some insights into the complexity of these decisions and the cost/benefit tradeoffs that are involved.

Technology, Mechanization, and the Work Force

In no small part, the technological competitive challenge stems from the Japanese experience since World War II. With help from the United States following World War II, the Japanese have become very adept at using central planning to enhance technological advances. These advances have been focused on several major industries, including steel, automotive, major appliances, and consumer electronics. The high quality of Japanese products, coupled with relatively low prices, have resulted in some excellent values. As a result, Japanese industry has received a great deal of attention from the U.S. consumer, the press, and competitors. This consumer awareness is repeating itself in Europe and other countries throughout the world as the results of mechanization are realized.

While the Japanese have had their successes, not everyone is willing to accept the Japanese experience as an appropriate across-the-board model of industrial policy, high technology, and mechanization for the United States to follow blindly.[10] Instead, we can learn from our own experiences in technology as well as from the more recent Japanese successes. The Japanese concepts of lifetime employment and centralized allocation of capital, for example, may actually inhibit creative high-technology developments in Japan. Indeed, a 1980 survey of 200 top Japanese managers involved in technical innovation at major companies found that 73 percent were convinced that their nation lagged behind the United States in revolutionary new technologies. U.S. innovation and entrepreneurial capability provide one of the competitive edges over industries in Japan, Europe, and other economic communities. There has been a great deal of debate surrounding our national industrial policy; we are refreshed by the following view.

> "It's incredible that some Americans are going to heavy state planning while I'm being asked to go to Europe to help them disband theirs," remarks Boston venture capitalist Peter Brooke, who has also been summoned to Japan to spark entrepreneurial growth. "We shouldn't follow their mistakes. We're the ones with the answers."[11]

The Work Force What impact have rapidly changing technology and increased mechanization had on the work force? Professor Eli Ginzberg traced the changes in the work force from the Industrial Revolution, which occurred two centuries ago, to the present. He found that two-thirds of the labor force has had their human muscle removed from the tasks of production.[12] Agriculture is an excellent example. In 1820 more than 70 percent

---

[10] William J. Abernathy and John E. Corcoran, "Relearning from the Old Masters: Lessons of the American System of Manufacturing" *Journal of Operations Management* 3, no. 4 (August 1983), pp. 155–167.

[11] Joel Kotkin, "On Top of Technology," special to the *Washington Post*, published in the *Columbia* (Mo.) *Daily Tribune*, Sunday, May 6, 1984, p. 67.

[12] Eli Ginzberg, "The Mechanization of Work," *Scientific American* 247, no. 3 (September 1982), pp. 67–75.

of the labor force worked on farms. By 1900 fewer than 40 percent worked in agriculture, and today farming employs less than 5 percent of the labor force. Today service employment is approaching 70 percent of the work force. The balance of the present work force, some 25–30 percent, is involved in manufacturing. Even in manufacturing there are many service jobs. In highly mechanized manufacturing, typically one-third of the workers have nonproduction jobs.[13] In some high-technology aerospace manufacturing environments, as many as 90 percent are employed in nontouch labor (nonproduction) jobs. Mechanization is a primary, but not the sole, determinant of this change in the work force, according to Ginzberg. He lists other contributing factors: later entry into the work force due to a desire for more education, and a much higher percentage of women (43 percent) in the overall work force.

Just as agriculture has changed over the past 200 years, Ginzberg believes that another major shift is underway in the structure of industrialized nations. He feels that the rapid availability and use of the digital computer will have a dramatic impact on employment patterns for the overall work force. We can already see the impact of the computer throughout the economy, wherever people are working—and many are working in operations. Therefore, throughout this book our intent is to focus on the computer, particularly in its applications to production and operations.

Although we often think of mechanization only in the workplace, its impact is actually much more widespread. Examine for a moment the impact of mechanization on tools we use in the home—refrigerators, washing machines, dryers, vacuum sweepers, and microwave ovens, to mention a few. Along with changing social and family norms, the simple application of mechanization to the home has contributed significantly to freeing women from traditional household roles. As a result, women are a major labor resource input in organizations, occupying positions in engineering, management, and other technical areas. People in virtually every sector of the economy are affected by technology and mechanization. We will examine how technology and mechanization have emerged in the manufacturing sector and we will illustrate ways in which these changes may directly affect your career.

Manufacturing, Technology, and Mechanization

Manufacturing specialists refer to both current and anticipated changes in technology and mechanization as the "factory of the future." The driving force behind this factory will be a series of digital computers. Some refer to this concept as *flexible manufacturing systems* (FMS), systems where workstations, automated material handling and transport, and computer control are integrated. Still others refer to this futuristic manufacturing concept as *computer-integrated manufacturing*, a concept we shall discuss in

[13]Thomas G. Gunn, "The Mechanization of Design and Manufacturing," *Scientific American* 247, no. 3 (September 1982), p. 116.

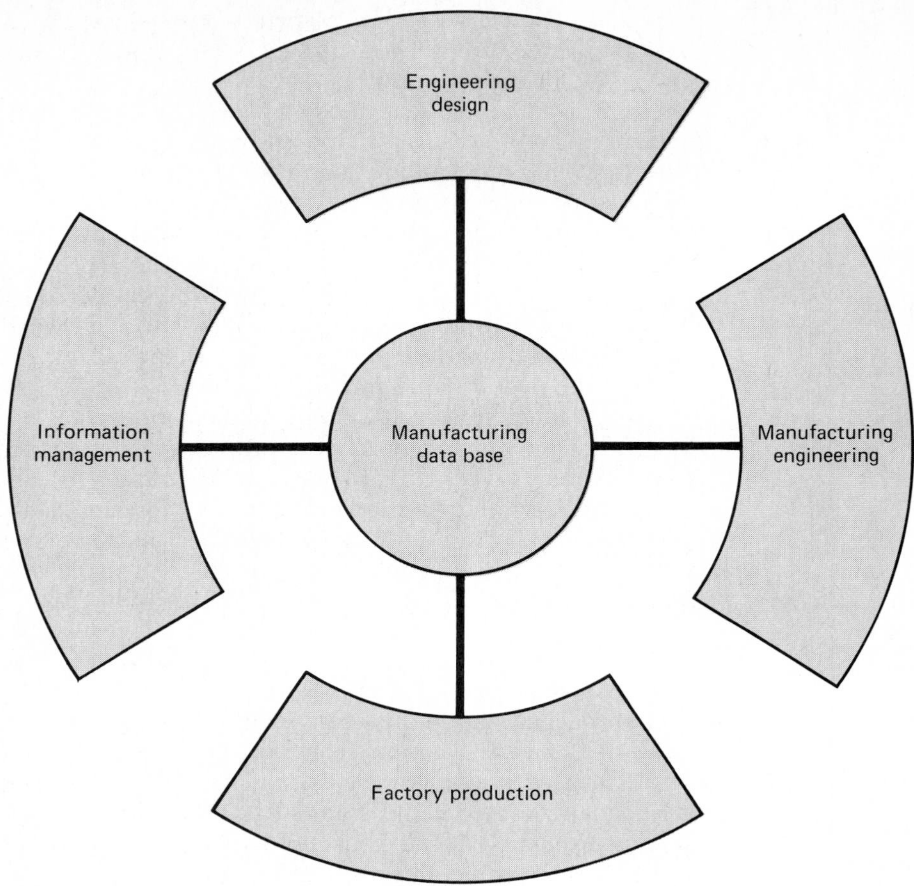

FIGURE 2.5
Computer-integrated manufacturing

this section.[14] Computer-integrated manufacturing centers around a manufacturing data base consisting of four primary manufacturing functions: engineering design, manufacturing engineering, factory production, and information management, as shown in Figure 2.5. The manufacturing data base stores all product–related and process–related information required to produce that part or product. The data base contains information about the machines and tools required, the materials necessary to make the product

[14]Basic reference material utilized in this section includes Thomas G. Gunn, "Computer Integrated Manufacturing," *Proceedings of the 1982 Academic-Practitioners Liaison Operations Management Workshop* (Michigan State University, July 1982) pp. 1–22; Thomas G. Gunn, "The Mechanization of Design and Manufacturing," *Scientific American* 247, no. 3 (September 1982), pp. 114–131; and promotional materials provided by McAuto, a subsidiary of McDonnell Douglas Corporation, St. Louis, Mo.

and all intermediate parts, the sequence of manufacturing steps, and various information items such as quantities demanded, due dates, and vendors for purchased parts.

EXAMPLE

One of the more complex assemblies currently manufactured is that of large airplanes such as the Boeing 727 and 747 and the Douglas DC10 and MD80. In observing the assembly and test flight procedures of one of these large commercial passenger planes, we were told that over 200,000 parts must be assembled to produce a complete airplane. Data is centrally stored in a manufacturing data base. It may be retrieved—and sometimes reentered in the data base in a different form—by members of engineering design, manufacturing engineering, factory production, and information management. The production and support staffs are very large—typically 15,000 or more employees—to design and manufacture one airplane model. Several airplanes a month may be produced, with an approximate sales value of $20 million each. The technological and mechanization challenges associated with such production are great. At present, no nation in the world approaches the sophistication, reliability, and performance of U.S. commercial and military aerospace manufacturers.

Design engineering captures the consumer's intended use and specifies the functional and aesthetic properties of the product; *manufacturing engineering* converts these specifications into the language and drawings necessary to produce the parts. This engineering interface is a source of many problems in businesses. The creative designs must often be compromised so that parts and products are not cost-prohibitive to an affordable end product. *Factory production* is the actual "touch" manufacturing, where direct labor, materials, and machines are blended to produce the product. *Information management* involves support activities associated with planning, controlling, and documenting all engineering and manufacturing activities. We will devote Chapter 9 to a discussion of information systems. As a result, this important aspect of computer-integrated manufacturing will not be stressed in the balance of this chapter.

In Figure 2.6 the subfunctions for each of these four major computer-integrated manufacturing functions are presented. We will briefly introduce you to the shaded subfunctions—computer-aided design (CAD), computer-aided manufacturing (CAM), group technology, and robotics/robots—to illustrate the essentials of the technology and mechanization issues now at the forefront of strategic planning in manufacturing.

Computer-Aided Design (CAD) Computer-aided design involves software programs that allow the designer to carry out extremely rapid geometric transformations. The designer is no longer limited to the top, side, and

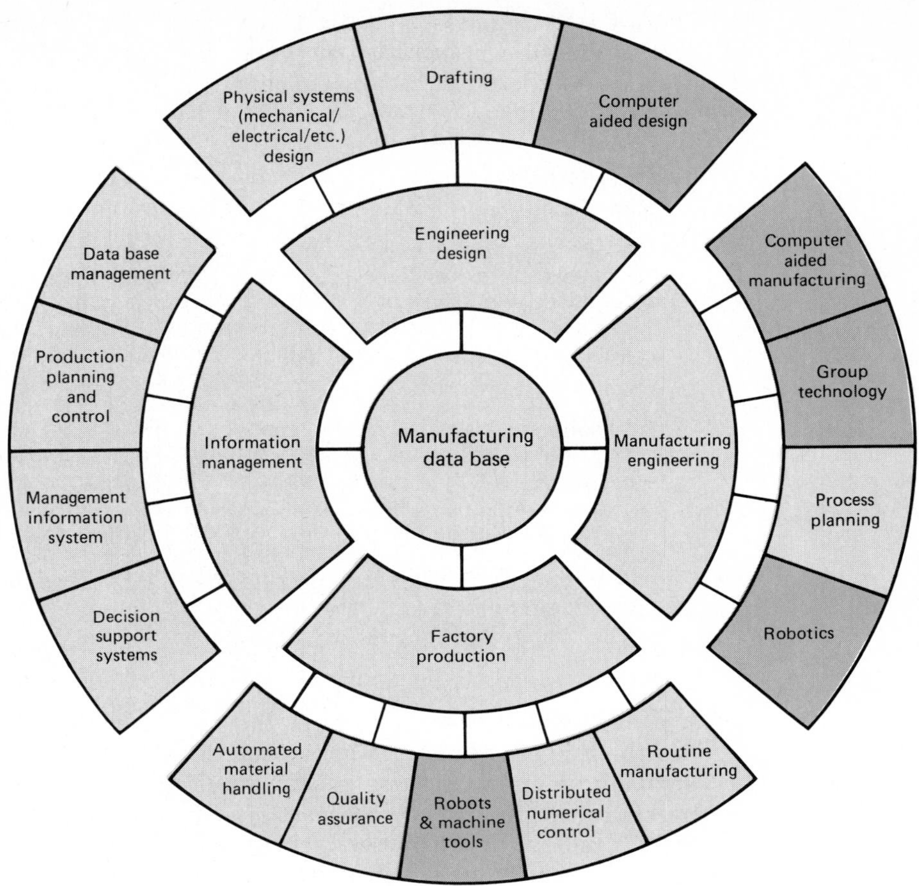

FIGURE 2.6
Computer-integrated manufacturing subfunctions

front views characteristic of traditional drawings. The designer can get rotation of the part about any axis on the screen, "zoom" in for details, take a distant perspective, and display part cross-sections. This eliminates the need for many laborious mock-ups, models, and prototypes.

This type of design work is done on a cathode-ray tube terminal, also referred to as a CRT. The final design is stored electronically in the computer, and a paper copy can be printed at any time. A sophisticated computer program drives and coordinates all these activities and is the heart of any CAD or CAM application. Two important features of CAD are timeliness and accuracy. As soon as the design is completed, it is available to manufacturing—even in remote locations, since the transfer is electronic. Also, accuracy is maintained. When the original design is changed, only the new design is electronically stored. This minimizes the potential for errors associated with planning based on outdated drawings.

What does CAD accomplish? Generally drafting productivity improves by a factor of three or more, and there are several additional overall benefits to manufacturers. At General Motors, for example, the design time for a new automobile has been reduced from 24 to 14 months. A manufacturer of molds for plastic parts was able to increase output from 30 mold cavities per year to 140, solely because of the increased efficiency afforded by a computerized design system.[15] Similar savings in time, along with increased productivity, are common in other manufacturing applications.

Merrill Lynch conducts a survey to trace the market growth of the CAD/CAM industry. The industry grew at a 55 percent compounded rate from 1978 to 1982, with expected sales of $1.15 billion in 1982.[16] Implying a 35 percent annual growth until 1986 would result in a $3.8 billion industry by 1986. New applications in architectural and engineering firms, coupled with the traditional electronic, mechanical, and mapping applications could expand this total further. To illustrate, we recently saw an advertisement for a CAD architectural package offered for $124,000. As you can see, the costs of such packages are not small by any means.

Computer-Aided Manufacturing (CAM) Computer-aided manufacturing is a system that controls the actual machine on the shop floor. A computer program guides the production of a "tape" containing the instructions for numerical control (NC) machines. The machine then automatically cuts, bores, mills, and performs other operations as automatically instructed. Tolerances can be held very tight, up to one ten-thousandth of an inch, for many cutting operations.

For large parts using rare metals, this degree of accuracy is a great improvement over the human level of judgment, wisdom, and dexterity of the master machinist who traditionally performed this job. One major aerospace manufacturer, however, advises that too much CAM can be costly. A wrong computer program, without visual inspection and some flexibility on the part of the machine operator, may result in many erroneous parts being produced—even though they are produced quite efficiently. These comments suggest that human involvement is not being eliminated by the CAD/CAM technology but, rather, that it is being deployed in new ways.

The objective in computer-integrated manufacturing is to take the "/" out of CAD/CAM. Conceptually, it is desirable to have the final engineering design determine the machine settings on the factory floor. McAuto's UNIGRAPHICS is a system that attempts to do just that.

---

[15]Gunn, *Scientific American,* p. 121.

[16]Thomas P. Kurlak, "Computer-Aided Design and Manufacturing Industry: Review and Outlook" (Merrill Lynch Pierce Fenner and Smith, Inc., Securities Research Division, September 14, 1982), pp. 1–17.

EXAMPLE

One user, the Business Forms Division of Harris Corporation, in Dayton, Ohio, uses CAD/CAM to facilitate the production of quality presses.[17] The first five-terminal network was installed in 1976 and paid for itself through increased productivity in just 2.6 years. A second five-terminal network was installed in 1978 with a payback in 1.9 years. Mike Kuntz, manager of the CAD/CAM group at Harris, reflects on the CAD/CAM installations: "In engineering work, our overall productivity increase due to UNIGRAPHICS is 3.5 to 1, although some applications show as much as 24-to-1 savings," Kuntz says.

Group Technology (GT) Group technology is a way of organizing and using data for parts with similarities; it is a tool for standardization. Characteristics of parts, such as their length, diameter, type of material, and density are recorded for each item in the manufacturing system. The computer can then sort for all similar parts—for example, all titanium screws less than 1½ inches long and of ½ inch maximum diameter. A designer—in engineering or manufacturing—might well find a useful titanium screw and avoid the cost of designing a new one. He or she would specify an existing part number to do the desired job. By identifying design attributes and grouping families of items, the computer can aid in tasks too large for the most experienced designer to accomplish manually or mentally.

European and Japanese manufacturers are ahead of the United States in group technology applications, some dating to post-World War II in Europe. Currently, GT is used most often in engineering design. It is used less frequently as a basis for rearranging the manufacturing process into cells for producing like families of parts. This so-called *cellular manufacturing* could be aided by GT classifications, but this would be more helpful for setting up new facilities than for rearranging existing ones.[18]

EXAMPLE

At Otis Engineering, an engineering and manufacturing company with over $5 billion in sales in 1978, a different story emerges.[19] Group technology was applied in an environment with over 200,000 drawings to search; historically,

[17]"Harris Uses McAuto UNIGRAPHICS for Quality Presses," A McAuto Client Profile (St. Louis, Mo.: McAuto, A Division of McDonnell Douglas Corporation, 1984).

[18]See a user survey Nancy Lea Hyer, "Management's Guide to Group Technology," *Operations Management Review* 2, no. 2, (Winter 1984), pp. 36–42.

[19]Bob Alton, "Group Technology," *Proceedings of the 1982 Academic-Practitioners Liaison Operations Management Workshop* (Michigan State University, July, 1982), pp. 38–42.

Otis employees had found that it was usually faster to design a new part than to search for a similar part already in existence. In addition to engineering design savings, substantial operations savings occurred as well. After only ten months of operation, approximately 580 hours of setup time was saved, averaging 12 minutes per part produced. A 55 percent capacity savings was experienced in some work centers. The program was expanded, resulting in approximately 8,500 machine hours saved, a 45 percent capacity savings, and a nine-month payback for training and coding. The scheduling department experienced similar positive results. Parts that workers had previously produced in 80 days now cleared manufacturing in only 38 days.

How did Otis Engineering achieve all of this? Parts were not only grouped (classed) by GT and manufactured in existing layouts, but also by families of parts where efficiency could be realized in setups, run-times, and in-process inventory.

Robotics and Robots A robot is a mechanical machine capable of moving materials and performing routine, repetitive tasks. It is programmable, which means that a sequence of moves can be preset to be repeated time after time, then reset again to perform another set of moves. Robots replace humans for some very heavy, dirty, dangerous, or unpleasant tasks where the job is very routine (monotonous) in nature. The art of selecting robots for various applications—and knowing when *not* to use them—is called robotics.

Among the more common applications of robots in the United States are loading and unloading machine tools, painting, and spotwelding—especially in the automotive and appliance industries. The Japanese accept a much broader definition of robots than North Americans and Europeans. In Japan very simple manual manipulators and fixed sequence devices are called robots. Outside Japan robots are mechanical devices that are programmable; the most sophisticated even have some vision, touch feedback, and limited decision-making capability. By each country's respective definition of a robot, Japan has about 80,000 and the United States between 5,000 and 7,000 robots.[20] Using the U.S. definition of a robot would reduce the Japanese number to the 20,000 to 30,000 range.

The primary advantage of robots over human workers is that their performance never varies. Quality levels are maintained without distraction or fatigue. Reliability is often greater—the robot shows for work each day and is just as consistent Monday morning and Friday evening as every other hour of the week.

[20]Thomas S. Gunn, *Scientific American*, p. 127 and Thomas S. Gunn, *Proceedings 1982 Academic-Practitioners Liaison Operations Management Workshop*, p. 13.

Economically, a robot in the United States costs from $50,000 to $100,000 installed. The following example shows how a robot can be economically justified for the tasks that it can perform.[21]

EXAMPLE

A robot, installed, will cost $76,500 for an unpleasant job involving stacking full cans of paint in a paint factory. The robot can be used 20 hours per day, on the average, seven days a week. The robot should last five to ten years under such usage with but a few major repairs. An employee is paid $10.00 per hour, and $7.00 per hour in fringe benefits, including Social Security payments by the company. To recover only the initial investment, the robot need work

$$\begin{aligned} \text{Hours to Work} &= \frac{\$76{,}500}{\$17.00/\text{hour}} \\ &= 4{,}500 \text{ hours} \end{aligned}$$

The plant operates only two shifts, 16 total hours per day, for five days per week and 50 weeks per year. The total hours a robot would be used per year would be

$$\begin{aligned} \text{Hours plant open per year} &= 16 \text{ hr/day} \times 5 \text{ days/wk} \times 50 \text{ wk/yr} \\ &= 4{,}000 \text{ hours/year} \end{aligned}$$

In a little over a year, the robot would recover its initial outlay. The payback period would be

$$\begin{aligned} \text{Payback (years)} &= \frac{4{,}500 \text{ hrs}}{4{,}000 \text{ hrs/year}} \\ &= 1.125 \text{ years.} \end{aligned}$$

The rapid recovery of the initial investment is indeed very attractive.

Although the operating costs for the robot were ignored in the simplified example, we see that a robot can offer attractive financial returns to the firm. In terms of operating costs, suppose they averaged to 20 percent of the robot's installed cost, spread over its lifetime. Then, the 4,500 hours would become 5,400 hours and the payback would change to 1.35 years. In addition, the primary benefit of robots, improved performance quality, will

[21]In 1983 the average price of spot welding robots was $78,000. In 1965 the average hourly cost of an auto-worker was $5 per hour, as was the hourly cost of a robot. By 1980 costs were $16 and $5 per hour respectively. From Emilia Askari, "The Robots of '1984'," *Miami Herald*, March 19, 1984, p. 9. Also see Kenneth M. Jenkins and Alan R. Raedels, "The Robot Revolution: Strategic Considerations for Managers," *Operations Management Review* 7, no. 2 (Winter 1983), pp. 41–44.

be achieved if the robotics engineer has properly selected a good application. Of course, management must also be involved in selecting a site, educating employees on the benefits of robots, gaining line management support, managing the engineering support staff, and keeping the union (if any) informed on the progress of the installations.[22]

How many robots will we need by 1990 or the year 2000? In 1979 less than ten U.S. companies turned out $28 million worth of robots. By early 1984, American industry was buying $169 million a year worth of robots from more than 60 manufacturers. Giants such as General Motors, the Westinghouse Corporation, IBM, and General Electric incorporated robots into their operations.[23] During the 1979 to 1984 period, the robotics industry came to life. The sophistication of microprocessors—the chips that power the computers that run the arms that pass for robots—increased and their prices fell. Robotics technologies thus became cost feasible.

Robots and Displaced Employees There is, of course, an interaction between mechanization and the work force, as we discussed in a previous section. Emilia Askari estimates that by 1990 United States job displacement due to robots will be between 17,400 to 28,200 employees in welding and 18,400 to 47,600 employees in assembly. What will these workers do? Individually, this is a serious problem because they are typically lower-skilled persons. Retraining, reassignment, and changing occupations are all better alternatives than unemployment. New jobs might be created from economic growth, resulting in some relief.

In the robotics industry alone, between 32,000 and 64,100 new jobs are expected—but these will not necessarily be appropriate for individuals replaced by the robot. In fact, that is quite unlikely; workers will need technological skill to plan, design, and produce robots. It is clear that mechanization provides opportunities as well as problems and challenges.

Trends in Mechanization and Automation

A survey of users, vendors, and "experts" in factory automation uncovered some interesting news. The study cited in the following example included a sample of 57 firms thought to be sophisticated automation users; 38 CAD/CAM, robotics, and numerical control suppliers; and 64 individuals believed to be experts. Each of the participants responded to a questionnaire. Their responses are summarized into three dominant trends that appeared in the data.

[22]For insight into managing installations, see Fred K. Foulkes and Jeffrey L. Hirsch, "People Make Robots Work," *Harvard Business Review* (January–February 1984).

[23]Emilia Askari, "The Robots of '1984'," *Miami Herald*, March 19, 1984, pp. 1, 7–11.

EXAMPLE

"*Leading-edge users of computer-aided manufacturing processes believe in learning by doing.* Most have proceeded in an incremental fashion to develop an internal base of experience with factory automation technologies. They tend to have supportive management and a sense of where they are heading. Their current measurement capabilities, however, restrict the basis for making adoption decisions as well as the subsequent evaluation of impacts from recent technological innovations. These users usually rely heavily on outside suppliers for critical technical assistance and consider reliability factors to be more important than price in selecting a vendor. They generally feel they cannot afford to postpone decisions until improved technologies become available. Current leading-edge users will strongly affect the future direction of these technologies.

"Suppliers claim that *most manufacturers are not sophisticated customers.* They would like potential users to be more aware of their needs for improved manufacturing processes and to be more interested in the long-term strategic benefits of computer-aided manufacturing technologies already on the market. A classic dilemma seems to have arisen: decisions to adopt expensive factory automation technologies are often made by managers who lack the background to assess technological options, while staff familiar with the new technologies are less able to appreciate associated strategic dimensions. A likely outcome is a decision that is either shortsighted or misguided. Suppliers with limited direct experience in new applications of their technologies and little in-depth knowledge of the business situations of their customers cannot be expected to help users avoid such errors.

"*The most difficult problems* in achieving computer-integrated manufacturing *are managerial rather than technical.* Manufacturers contemplating factory automation face different issues depending on whether they adopt a retrofit strategy or whether they attempt to make a fresh start as new facilities are brought on stream. In either case, they often have inadequate internal technical resources, strong barriers to communication across traditional functions lines, and a reward structure that does not encourage risk-taking in the interest of long-term strategic gains. Manufacturing organizations that do not deal directly with these kinds of managerial problems are not likely to succeed in factory automation, even if appropriate technological options exist."[24]

As the above example illustrates, the adoption of these manufacturing technologies has a major effect on each company's strategy and focus.

Mechanization, Technology, and Services

Are there examples of mechanization in service industries and service functions? Certainly. Most of us have benefited from the power lawnmower—and a few of us remember "push" mowers as well; we welcomed the change. Another example is an automatic material-handling system,

[24]Stephen R. Rosenthal, "A Survey of Factory Automation in the U.S.," *Operations Management Review* 2, no. 2 (Winter 1984), pp. 3–13.

common in industry. These systems "pick" items by programmed, manless vehicles.

The universal product code and electronic scanners in retail trade, especially in grocery stores, are a good example of service mechanization. Financial transactions also are mechanized to a high degree. Have you used the automatic teller at a financial institution—the "ugly teller"? Authorities are suggesting we will be paying bills by computer, using our television screen and telephone even more than is done today, in but a few years. Communications advances are all around us—many resulting from increased satellite technology.

We see, then, that mechanization and technology issues are as relevant to services as they are to manufacturing. In fact, service mechanization is probably easier for most of us to relate to because of our personal experiences. An interesting aspect of service automation is the consumer's reaction to the substitution of "unfriendly machines" for "friendly people," regardless of the economics. We will address this issue in several places in this book. What are your feelings as to how much you are willing to pay extra for personal, human service?

INTERNATIONAL PRODUCTION/OPERATIONS MANAGEMENT

The world is shrinking, and worldwide economic competition is intensifying. Transportation and communication improvements make nations seem closer together. As one nation becomes aware of the products and services that are available in the world at large, demand for those items and services tends to increase. And how is that demand met? In some cases it is not met, especially among poor nations. In other cases, products and services are produced by a given country for internal consumption. In still other situations, goods are imported and the services of other countries are consumed at their origin (since most services cannot be stored). Yet another alternative is for the producing nation to transfer its conversion know-how to the consuming nation. This approach is currently being used by companies that provide services; it is also increasingly prevalent among firms that manufacture products (through licensing arrangements). As a result, there is heightened interest in the *international dimension of production and operations*. Although our interest is managerial, that is, an interest in operations management similarities and differences among nations, we really cannot understand the management issues without some understanding of the economics involved. Therefore, we will focus briefly on broad economic differences among nations, especially productivity comparisons that build upon our previous discussions of U.S. productivity. Then, we will explore major manufacturing management differences among the industrial communities of Europe, Japan, and North America. Next, we will take a closer look at Japanese business, especially the production management successes the Japanese have experienced in the 1970s and 1980s. Finally, we'll focus on the key international issues that the United States faces for the next ten years.

The International Productivity Challenge in Production and Operations

How does the productivity growth of the United States compare with that of other industrialized countries? Between 1973 and 1982 the average annual increase in manufacturing productivity was 1.4 percent in Canada, 1.5 percent in the United States, 2.5 percent in the United Kingdom, 4.6 percent in France, and 6.2 percent in Japan, as shown in Figure 2.7. Japan is at the forefront and the United States and Canada bring up the rear.

Rate of growth is important over the long term, but what are the relative bases of each nation? That is, now that we see who is running the fastest (Japan), who is at the head of the pack? As Figure 2.8 illustrates, the United States is first, with most other industrial nations ahead of Japan in terms of gross domestic product (GDP, an output measure) per employee. Two columns are shown in Figure 2.8. One is from the Bureau of Labor Statistics (BLS) and the unit of measure is per employee; the other column is from another source (Maddison) and the unit of measure is per hour worked.

Figure 2.7 indicates that the United States experienced a period of low

FIGURE 2.7
International manufacturing productivity

Source: *Productivity Perspectives* (American Productivity Center, December 1983), p. 14.

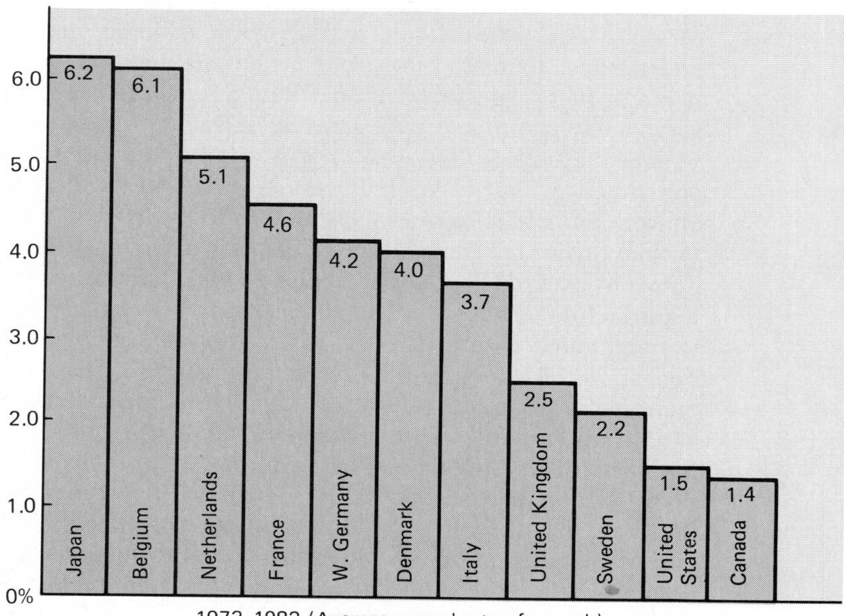

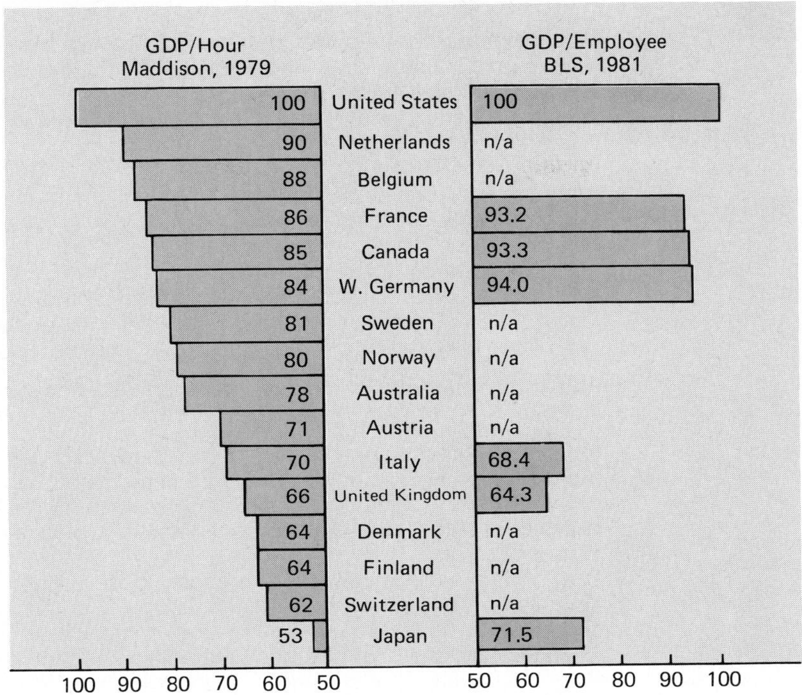

FIGURE 2.8
International productivity levels

Source: *Productivity Perspectives* (American Productivity Center, December 1983), p. 13.

productivity growth—a decline in growth more severe than in many other parts of the world. Yet as Figure 2.8 illustrates, we are still the world productivity leader. In total, we do have a productivity problem in the United States. The following example shows one leader's opinion as to what the Japanese were doing better than Americans as early as 1980.

EXAMPLE

The American Productivity Center located in Houston, Texas, has been established by private industry to consider what can be done to increase productivity. The center's director, C. Jackson Grayson, shared the following report with the news media. It was prepared by a Detroit auto executive who had spent quite a bit of time in Japan. What is that country doing better than America? Here are the executive's conclusions:

- The Japanese automakers are outperforming us in all areas of quality, cost control, planning, employee relations and management.

- Their accomplishments are the result of a totally dedicated work force (from top to bottom) rather than any unique skills, automation, manufacturing techniques, or innovative processes.
- Their total system and resultant productivity have evolved from an endless effort to eliminate waste in *any* form—be it excess manpower, inventory, lost time, repair, or whatever.
- Although they are highly automated in their machining, engine assembly, body shop and frame manufacturing operations, their robots, shuttles, conveyors, transfer machines, etc., are all either American-made or are produced by Japanese firms under U.S. manufacturers license. The N/C tape controlled equipment, their side frame systems, body truck methods of gaging, etc., are practically "photo copies" of U.S. systems—but they are beating us at our own game.

Here is his breakdown of how the Japanese compare with American auto workers:

- Quality: Extremely high product quality levels are achieved at all manufacturers, primarily because all parts fit as specified. About 96 percent of all vehicles go directly to the haul-away lots without any repair. Engine reject rate is only 0.01 percent. Water leaks average 0 percent on passenger cars.
- Cost control and productivity: An overall observation is they are 20 percent better. They provide no relief manpower or standby labor pool for absentee coverage. You see no one in the aisles or canteen areas. Absenteeism runs 3 to 4 percent, including vacation and sick time.
- Inventory control: Their system (called *kan-ban*) typifies the Japanese approach to the no waste ethic and is really the key to their productivity, efficiency, quality and cost control capability. The system operates on the basis of having no more than two hours' worth of stock of any part on hand at the line. The system also operates on the basis of complete trust with the vendors regarding quality and quantity of their shipments. There is no receiving inspection and no count verification with material delivered directly to the point of use.
- Work force and employee attitudes: The major advantage the Japanese manufacturers have is a stable and completely dedicated work force, which is totally committed to the success of the business and to customer satisfaction through quality.

The stability of the work force comes about not only as a result of the fact that employees are hired for life (retirement age is 56–60), but just as important is the fact that everyone is paid the same wage. Therefore, there is no movement of people within the work force. Employees who quit will not be hired by any other manufacturer.*

**Houston Chronicle,* Monday, November 17, 1980, Section 2, p. 13.

Dr. Jackson, and many others in the United States, are attempting to increase nationwide awareness about productivity. The National Association of Broadcasters, for example, has initiated a six-year (1983 to 89) productivity awareness campaign in the media. The television portion of this campaign features Howard K. Smith, a well-known news analyst. Participating in the development of this campaign, as well as the 1983 White House Conference on Productivity, we found insights into the competitive nature of North American executives when they become aroused by the international productivity challenge.

Major Manufacturing Differences Among Japan, Europe, and North America

Further insights into differences among nations are revealed in a major study by Professors Jeffrey Miller (Boston University, U.S.A.), Jinchiro Nakane (Science Institute, Japan), and Thomas Vollman (INSEAD/CEDEP, France), who conduct an annual survey of future directions in manufacturing. Their survey report for 1983 contrasted the opinions of 209 U.S., 151 European, and 260 Japanese executives.[25] In 1982, these high-level executives had average sales of $350 million in their business unit; the parent company of their business unit had average sales of $3.0 billion.

Strategies Overall, it is interesting that strategies vary little among these groups. From eight choices, the rank order of the top four business unit strategies is the same. The strategic objectives, listed in decreasing order of importance, are as follows:

1. developing new products for existing markets,
2. increasing market share in existing markets,
3. developing new products for new markets, and
4. developing new markets for existing products.[26]

Competitive Priorities Although the strategic objectives are the same for these major industrial centers, methods for achieving the objectives differ, as shown by the varying competitive priorities listed in Table 2.2. In this figure, priorities are presented in decreasing order of importance. The North American executives reflect an emphasis on quality, performance, and service. The Japanese are more concerned with price, speed, and new products. European executives are in between; they list quality, performance, and price as being most important.

Concerns and Recent Efforts to Improve Table 2.3 reflects the concerns of each respective industrial group, while Table 2.4 provides the most recent efforts to improve. Each column lists factors in decreasing importance, from most to least important for the factors frequently cited.

From the information presented in Table 2.3, we note that the importance placed on high quality is uniform across all three groups. While industrial groups in North America and Europe are also quite concerned

[25]Jeffrey Miller, Jinchiro Nakane, and Thomas Vollman, "The 1983 Global Manufacturing Futures Survey," Manufacturing Roundtable Research Report Series (Boston University School of Management, Boston University, 1983). The authors express their gratitude for a willingness on the part of these scholars to share their study.

[26]Ibid., p. 5.

TABLE 2.2
Competitive priorities

North America	Japan	Europe
Consistent quality	Low price	Consistent quality
High-performance products	Rapid design changes	On-time delivery
On-time deliveries	Consistent quality	High-performance products
Fast deliveries	High-performance products	Low price
After-sale service	On-time deliveries	Rapid design changes
Low price	Rapid volume changes	Fast deliveries
Rapid design changes	After-sale service	Rapid volume changes
Rapid volume changes	Fast deliveries	After-sale service
SUMMARY: Performance/service	SUMMARY: Price/speed—new products	SUMMARY: Quality/price

Source: Jeffrey Miller, Jinchiro Nakane, and Thomas Vollman, "The 1983 Global Manufacturing Futures Survey," Manufacturing Roundtable Research Report Series (School of Management, Boston University, 1983).

about costs, the Japanese are very interested in qualified supervision and new product schedules.

What are the groups doing about these concerns? Again we see similarities between North America and Europe; both of these groups attach great importance to new production/inventory control systems and super-

TABLE 2.3
Current concerns

North America	Japan	Europe
Producing to high-quality standards	Producing to high-quality standards	High/rising overhead costs
High/rising overhead costs	Yield problems/rejects	Producing to high-quality standards
Excess capacity	Available qualified supervisors	Low indirect labor productivity
Introduction of new products on schedule	Introduction of new products on schedule	High/rising material costs
Low indirect productivity	Falling behind in process technology	Introduction of new products on schedule
High/rising inventories	High/rising material costs	Poor sales forecasts
High/rising material costs	Inability to deliver on time	Low direct labor productivity
Poor sales forecasts	High/rising overhead costs	Excess manufacturing capacity
Low direct labor productivity	Low direct labor productivity	High/rising inventories
Yield problems/rejects	Aging workforce	Impact of government regulations
	Availability of qualified workers	

Source: Miller et al.

TABLE 2.4
Recent efforts to improve effectiveness

North America	Japan	Europe
Production/inventory control systems	Quality circles	Production/inventory control
Supervisor training	Automating jobs	Automating jobs
Reducing size of work force	New processes/old products	Supervisor training
Integrating manufacturing MIS	Reducing size of work force	Manufacturing reorganization
Worker safety	Worker safety	Making existing systems work better
Quality circles	Reconditioning physical plants	New processes/old products
Direct labor motivation	Direct labor motivation	Direct labor motivation
Developing new processes for old products	Giving workers a broader range of tasks	Changing labor/management relationship
Improved maintenance	Value analysis/product redesign	Integrating manufacturing information systems
Making existing systems work better	Manufacturing reorganization	Worker safety

Source: Miller et al.

visor training (Table 2.4). By contrast, the Japanese are involved in quality circles (operative employee participation and training); they are less concerned with supervisor training and introducing technology and mechanization.

Understanding the Japanese Challenge for Production and Operations

As in previous sections, it is helpful if we begin by comparing productivity between Japan and the United States. We recall that Japan has experienced a higher growth rate in productivity (6.2 percent) than the United States (1.5 percent) over the last decade (Figure 2.7). Yet Japan's overall productivity, as measured by gross domestic production per employee, was but 71.5 percent of the United States' in 1981 (Figure 2.8). Japan is catching up with the United States, but it still needs to make a lot of progress.

Japanese Labor Productivity in Selected Industries On an industry sector basis of comparison, the United States generally outperforms Japan. We are not surprised at the Japanese lead in primary metals and electrical machinery as shown in Figure 2.9, since they are known as excellent manufacturers. However, we are quite surprised about the lead they enjoy in finance and insurance, since the United States has such a good record in most services. Examine the level of business services productivity in Figure 2.9. Japan is but 47 percent as productive as the United States. Yet in finance and insurance—both very comparable to business services—Japan is 147 percent as productive as the United States. Perhaps Japan's centralized banking system accounts for some of the difference, as the United States has over 14,000 banks. Regardless, we don't want to lose sight of the fact

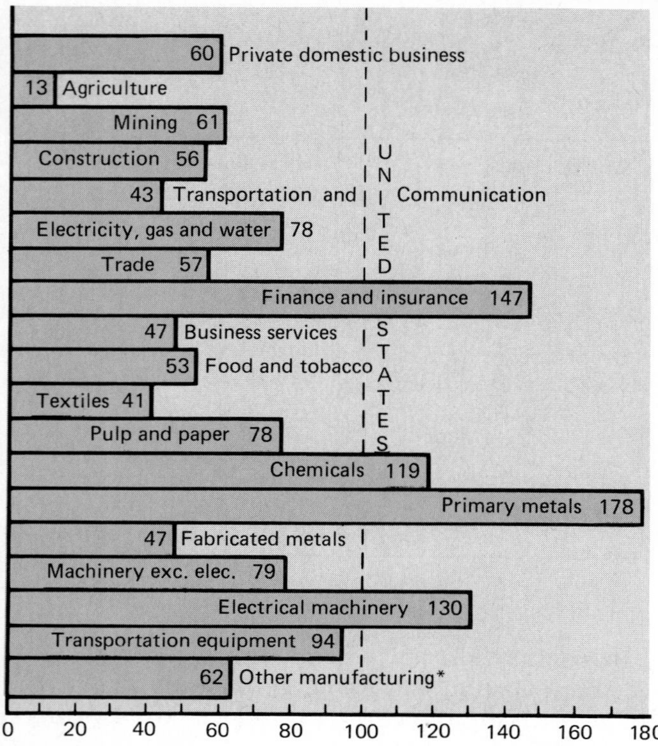

FIGURE 2.9
Japanese levels of labor productivity relative to the United States

Source: *Productivity Perspectives* (American Productivity Center, December 1983), p. 15.

that the United States is more productive than Japan for most of the categories in Figure 2.9.

Economic and Cultural Factors Contributing to Success In a comparative analysis of Japan and the United States, several factors emerge as critical to the Japanese productivity revival.[27] Some experts see the following factors as contributing to the Japanese successes:

- A rate of personal savings averaging four times the U.S. level, which makes possible the financing of gross fixed capital formation at an average ratio exceeding 30 percent of gross national product—roughly *double* the U.S. rate.
- Impetus for continuing technological improvement, an accelerated "learning curve" for both management and worker cadres, and a high average level of plant capacity utilization—all factors which can be seen as by-products of rapid output growth.

[27]Elliot S. Grossman and George E. Sadler, "Executive Summary," *Comparative Productivity Dynamics: Japan and the United States* (Houston, TX: American Productivity Center, November 1982), pp. 1–4.

- A vigorous growth stimulating program, focused on increasing exports, carried out by the Japanese government following the Occupation.
- Careful attention to improving research, development, and the rapid dissemination and use of new technology.
- The close cooperation that exists among labor, management, academic, and government. Central to this is a belief that productivity improvement should be the responsibility of both labor and management—that workers have an obligation to improve quality and efficiency, and that the company must be committed to offering lifelong employment and retraining as necessary to sustain such improvements.
- A cultural dedication to achieving consensus around a superordinate goal and to adapting to change as necessary to concentrate on "what works."

In discussions of Japanese productivity, we have repeatedly seen these, as well as several other, items cited. These authors, however, have presented the economic analysis to support their summary, which removes a good bit of the speculation surrounding Japanese successes.

Japanese Management North American managers are keenly interested in Japanese management style and in discovering what the Japanese do differently. What is it that leads to success in Japan? Is it culture, environment, management skills, or beliefs about people? Management scholars and consultants are probing these issues and offering suggestions.

A popular view was presented in the early 1980s by William Ouchi; his analysis focused on characteristics of *organizations* as the basis for comparison.[28] Ouchi listed such distinguishing features of Japanese organizations as lifetime employment, slow evaluation and promotion, nonspecialized career paths, implicit control mechanisms, collective decision making, collective responsibility, and holistic concern for employees. In contrast, qualities inherent in American organizations include short-term employment, rapid evaluation and promotion, specialized career paths, explicit control mechanisms, individual decision making, individual responsibility, and a more segmented concern for workers.[29] Ouchi offers a new American approach, called Theory Z. He believes that some features of Japanese organizations could be successfully replicated in American organizations. Theory Z would be a synthesis; it would include the best aspects of both approaches.

Richard Pascale and Anthony Athos, taking a different approach than Ouchi's, have developed a model that analyzes Japanese and American firms based on seven variables: the "hard S's"—structure, strategy, and systems—and the "soft S's"—skills, staff, subordinate goals, and style. With-

[28]See William C. Ouchi, *Theory Z: How American Business Can Meet the Japanese Challenge* (Reading, Mass.: Addison-Wesley, 1981).

[29]This comparison is drawn from J. Bernard Keys and Thomas R. Miller, "The Japanese Management Theory Jungle," *Academy of Management Review* 9, no. 2 (April 1984), pp. 342–353.

out elaborating on these definitions (or concepts) and the rationale behind them, it is difficult to evaluate the validity of their argument that American firms are best at the "hard S's" and Japanese firms are best at the "soft S's."[30] The "soft S's" involve people. Pascale and Athos, both business school professors, give the Japanese high scores for their behavioral interactions with, and treatment of, employees. Many of the authors' arguments stem from comparisons of the Japanese firm, Matsushita Corporation, and the American firm, ITT. Those interested in comparative management between Japan and the United States will want to read this book. It is highly relevant to the study of management within operations.

Although there are many more studies that define and explain management characteristics, we feel it is essential to mention the work of Cole, who clearly identifies the setting in which Japanese firms are successful in dealing with people at work.[31] For example, he has excellent insights into why quality circles work well in Japan. Professor Cole has been studying and writing about the Japanese worker for over a decade, and he provides useful observations about Japanese behavior and culture. Cole's work provides something of a transition for us as we now turn to a discussion of successful Japanese management techniques we think are quite important to manufacturing.

Japanese Manufacturing Management In this brief section we will present an overview of some Japanese manufacturing techniques that are having an impact throughout the world. We will identify where in this book these topics will be developed and we will suggest some timely reference sources for further reading.

American manufacturers have been keenly aware of the manufacturing processes and methods of the Japanese, especially their approaches to *quality* (quality circles and the use of statistical quality control), inventory management, and automation in process and repetitive manufacturing. In Chapter 17 we will take a closer look at the quality picture in Japan. Earlier in this chapter we referred to Juran and Deming's contributions to statistical quality control in Japan; we also discussed Cole's contribution to our understanding of quality circles.

In Chapters 14 to 16 *inventory* concepts, techniques, and applications will be developed. This will include a discussion of Japanese approaches to limiting inventory. Robert W. Hall and the American Production and Inventory Control Society have collaborated on an excellent book that explains Japanese inventory methods.[32] The first two chapters of Professor

---

[30] Richard T. Pascale and Anthony G. Athos, *The Art of Japanese Management* (Warner Books, 1981).

[31] R. E. Cole, *Work, Mobility, and Participation: A Comparative Study of American and Japanese Industry* (Berkeley, CA: University of California Press, 1979).

[32] Robert W. Hall, *Zero Inventories* (Homewood, Ill.: Dow Jones Irwin, 1983). For a shorter synopsis see Robert W. Hall, "Driving the Productivity Machine: Production Planning and Control in Japan," A Research Report by the American Production and Inventory Control Society (Falls Church, Virginia, 1981).

Hall's book are particularly insightful as he describes the Japanese desire for zero inventory and provides many excellent detailed case histories in Japanese manufacturing.

We will touch on Japanese *manufacturing processes* in our discussion of planning and utilizing the conversion system, especially in the areas of facility layout (Chapter 8) and production scheduling (Chapters 11 and 12). Schonberger provides useful insights into these subjects as well as into Japanese inventory systems. A helpful study of these Japanese manufacturing techniques and their applicability to American firms is presented by Vollman, Berry, and Whybark. From a broader policy perspective, Krajewski and others believe that the key strategy is to reshape the production environment; they feel that American firms already have the tools to do so.[33]

MEETING THE INTERNATIONAL CHALLENGES IN PRODUCTION AND OPERATIONS MANAGEMENT

Any projections of the critical international issues that will face operations managers into the 1990s are speculative indeed. Clearly, however, as you begin your career in operations, you will encounter issues and problems at the grass-roots level within the organization. And, as you progress through your career, you will become more involved with deciding the overall strategies your firm must pursue in its operations. With this broader perspective in mind, the following operations issues are important to assure success in international competition.

1. Other nations are increasing their levels of productivity at a faster rate than the United States. This progress must be monitored both in terms of nations and individual firms. Which countries are moving fastest to catch the leader, the United States?
2. Industry-by-industry productivity analyses within a national economy will allow the operations executive to focus broadly on his or her competition.
3. Firm-by-firm comparisons and case situations in other nations can be helpful. What are our strongest foreign competitors doing? How? Why?
4. Quality might well be the strategic variable to make our firm competitive internationally.
5. If developing nations have labor advantages, what should our operations strategy be toward replacing high-cost United States workers with (1) mechanization or (2) direct ownership of overseas (foreign) feeder plants in developing countries with low labor costs? What are the economic tradeoffs among mech-

[33]Richard J. Schonberger, "The Transfer of Japanese Manufacturing Management Approaches to U.S. Industry," *The Academy of Management Review* 7, no. 3 (July 1982), pp. 479–487; and idem., *Japanese Manufacturing Techniques*, (New York: Free Press, 1982); Thomas E. Vollman, William L. Berry, and D. Clay Whybark, *Manufacturing Planning and Control Systems* (Homewood, Ill.: Irwin, 1984); Lee J. Krajewski, Barry E. King, Larry P. Ritzman, and Danny S. Wong, "A Viable U.S. Manufacturing Strategy: Reshaping the Production Environment," *Operations Management Review* 2, No. 3 (Spring 1984), pp. 4–10.

anization, world-wide labor costs, transportation, and other cost factors in our operations?

6. What can we learn from the Pacific Basin countries,[34] especially Japan, concerning successes in management style and manufacturing practices?

These and other issues specific to a firm or industry seem critical to successful global operations. We hope that you share our excitement about this challenge.

MEETING THE COMPETITIVE CHALLENGE IN OPERATIONS AND PRODUCTION MANAGEMENT

Our attention has been focused on three major issues: productivity, mechanization, and international competition. The challenges are before us. It should be exhilarating to manage in operations for the remainder of this century. Businesses, government agencies, academics, and students are taking production and operations management seriously. The function is becoming increasingly significant in our society.

In the remainder of this book, we will try to equip you with a knowledge of the concepts, models, and behavioral approaches you will need in order to meet the challenges ahead. In Chapter 3 we will examine modeling and analysis, and we will show how these approaches meet the needs of the contemporary manager.

SUMMARY

Consumers, owners, citizens, and employees are increasingly aware of the competitive environment in which they live. Within individual organizations, operations challenges are substantial. In this chapter we focused on *productivity, technology and mechanization,* and *international business,* as each affects operations management.

We discovered that recent U.S. productivity levels have not increased as rapidly as during the post-World War II period. The quality-productivity connection was discussed as a strategic issue for the firm. In presenting the challenges in technology and mechanization, the focus was upon the work force and manufacturing applications. "Factory of the Future" components, CAD/CAM, group technology, and robotics were introduced. Our presentation of the international challenge in operations built upon previous productivity discussions; we also examined the accomplishments of Europe and Japan as compared to the United States.

In summary, the competitive challenges presented in this chapter abound in

[34]We have not touched on activities in China, both the Peoples Republic of China and Taiwan, which are emerging competitors with Korea and other nations. See, for example, Leon S. Lasdon, "Operations Research in China," *Interfaces* 10, no. 1 (February 1980), pp. 23–27, and Paul Gray and Burton V. Dean, "The Chinese–U.S. Symposium on Systems Analysis," *Interfaces* 12, no. 1 (February 1982), pp. 44–49.

many organizations. The balance of the book will focus on meeting these challenges through a better understanding of operations concepts, models, and behavioral applications.

CASE

Melanie Elizabeth's Dilemma

An established transformer manufacturer supplies high-voltage transformers to utilities throughout the world. Located in southern Indiana, sales the last three years have averaged 60 percent in North America, 20 percent to South America, and 20 percent to the Pacific Basin. The table below shows some selected company data for this manufacturing plant, which does all manufacturing for this division.

Chris, the plant manager, and his brother Nat, director of engineering, are at odds about purchasing several state-of-the-art robots for welding a continuous seam on the transformers. Transformers manufactured by this company are designed to hang on telephone poles near residences or commercial buildings. Since they are used outdoors, they must be totally airtight. This welding operation is critical to an airtight, high-quality transformer. Chris insists that the robots are not cost justified; he also fears they will cause problems with the direct labor employees now doing the welding. Chris is concerned that the use of robots may jeopardize upcoming labor negotiations and that it will force manufacturing to use equipment they don't know how to operate. Nat argues that the use of robots will reduce manufacturing expenses and improve the overall quality of the welding department. Another potential advantage is that the engineering group will develop robotics skills for future use.

Chris and Melanie Elizabeth work for the same group vice-president. Melanie Elizabeth works with the vice-president at corporate headquarters in Chicago. As the vice-president's staff assistant, Melanie Elizabeth has been asked to gather facts concerning the Indiana plant's intended robotics application. She is to make a recommendation to Chris, Nat, and the group vice-president at a meeting at the plant in three weeks. Melanie Elizabeth is also aware of the possibility that the entire plant will be moved to the Philippine Islands in the next two years. Average labor rates and fringe benefits in the Philippines are expected to be $4.75/hour. The decision to move will be based in part upon upcoming union negotiation results and union leader/member willingness to participate in the change. Melanie Elizabeth's assignment is to get all the economics and judgmental issues on the table, not to make a final choice for the company.

Case Questions

1. In the role of Melanie Elizabeth:
   (a) prepare the best case to support Chris's position
   (b) prepare the best case to support Nat's position
2. With three weeks remaining, what would you like to gather in terms of additional information? Why?
3. If you were Melanie Elizabeth and were asked for a recommendation without additional information, what would you suggest? Why?

Indiana plant data

Last Year (1985) Sales	$13,750,000
Cost of Goods Sold (1985)	$11,500,000
Labor	$ 4,750,000
Material	$ 6,000,000
Overhead	$ 750,000
Invested Capital (1985)	$ 3,500,000
Number of Employees	1,150
Direct Labor	750
Direct Labor, Welding	121
Non-Direct Labor	400
Average Direct Labor Wages and Fringes	$18.75/hour
Welding Labor Productivity (current month)	93.7%
Welding Material Usage Variance (positive usage is more than standard; current month)	+16%
Cost One Robot, Installed	$103,000
Robot Characteristics	
Direct Workers Replaced (two shifts)	3
Total Cost Operation Annually	$ 10,300
Estimated Useful Life	5 years
Plant Operations	2 shifts, 50 weeks/yr.

DISCUSSION QUESTIONS

1. Explain total factor productivity. What is partial factor productivity? What partial factor productivity measure is likely to be used in production/operations management most frequently?
2. Discuss the practical guides for establishing productivity measures for work groups and individuals.
3. Explain the relationship between quality and productivity. Discuss the apparent alternative positions that (A) both move in the same direction or (B) each moves in opposing directions. Which do you accept? Why?
4. If a firm were to accept quality as the strategic variable for improvement of operations, what might the firm expect as results? How would the firm go about improving its competitive position in that manner?
5. Discuss TRW's white-collar productivity improvement effort.
6. Explain the relationships between technology, mechanization, and the workforce by (A) defining each and (B) explaining how technology and mechanization are affecting the workforce.
7. Explain computer-integrated manufacturing. Figures 2.5 and 2.6 should be useful in your discussion.
8. Robots, CAD, CAM, numerical control, manufacturing data base, group technology—these all are terms used in manufacturing, but difficult to grasp. After studying each, prepare a short essay that explains these terms in nontechnical language a high school senior could be expected to understand.
9. What do you think are the significant facts about robots and robotics?
10. Contrast the major manufacturing differences among Japan, Europe, and North America based on the executive survey conducted by Miller, Nakane, and Vollman.

11. Discuss the economic and cultural factors that apparently have led to Japanese successes in productivity.
12. Review the Japanese approach to management. What do you believe are the key features that contribute to their successful management style? Why?
13. Near the end of this chapter, the authors speculate on several operations issues important to success in international competition. Select any one of these aspects and explain why you think it is important.
14. Briefly explain how *productivity, technology and mechanization,* and *international business* interrelate as they collectively become a formidable challenge to production and operations managers during the remainder of this century.

PROBLEMS

Reinforcing Fundamentals

1. A robot, installed, is estimated to cost $68,000. This robotics application is directed at replacing one employee per shift on a routine, repetitive task that the employee and robot can do equally well. The plant works three shifts a day, five days a week, 47 weeks a year. Total labor wages and fringes average $9.25/hour in this facility. Absenteeism has averaged 11 percent the last year in this job. Every hour the equipment is idle from absenteeism, the company loses a $5 contribution to profit, which cannot be recovered. The robot is expected to be "down," not available, 1 percent of the time and is expected to have a three-year useful life. Should the company make the investment, based on this economic analysis?
2. Consider the impact of the robot installation on the three employees in the problem above. If you could get absenteeism reduced to one percent by showing this analysis to employees, could they keep their jobs? If not, what alternatives typically exist for retaining the employees?
3. In question one above, what wage rate would be necessary for the employees to be economically equivalent to the robot, if all other factors remained constant? Would employees be likely to accept this rate? Why?
4. An insurance company has a group standard in the claims department to process 1,250 claims per day when fully staffed with 52 employees. Consider the following data and compute labor productivity for each of the last four weeks. What does this mean?

Week (5 days)	Average employees	Claims processed
35	50	6250
36	51	6200
37	51	5850
38	51	5950

5. In the insurance company example above, if the group productivity standard is maintained, the contribution to profit for each claim processed is eleven dollars. To achieve this contribution, $13.75 per hour in total labor and fringe benefits is expended, as well as total computer equipment and labor support of $12,000 per employee per year. In the most recent month, computer costs averaged $1,200 per employee in the claims department.
   (A) Compute total standard costs per month for claims.

(B) Determine the total factor productivity (labor and computer) in claims last month.

(C) What was the net contribution to profit, after productivity gains (or losses), for the month?

GLOSSARY

Computer-Aided Design (CAD) Computer software programs allowing the designer to carry out geometric transformations rapidly.

Computer-Aided Manufacturing (CAM) Computer software programs that control the actual machine on the shop floor.

Computer-integrated manufacturing Digital computers utilizing a manufacturing data base that encompasses engineering design, manufacturing engineering, factory production, and information management.

Group technology A way of organizing and using data for parts with similarities; it is a tool for standardization.

Mechanization The process of bringing about the use of equipment and machinery in production and operations.

Productivity The ratio of outputs over inputs; total factor productivity is outputs over the total of labor, capital, materials, and energy.

Quality The appropriateness of design specifications to function and use, as well as the degree to which outputs (products or services) conform to the design specifications.

Robot A programmable mechanical machine capable of moving materials and performing routine, repetitive tasks.

Robotics The art of selecting robots for various applications.

Technology The scientific expertise in blending labor, land, capital, and management into useful outputs.

SELECTED READINGS

Adam, Everett E., Jr., James C. Hershauer, and William A. Ruch. *Productivity and Quality: Measurement as a Basis for Improvement.* New York: Prentice-Hall, 1981.

American Productivity Center, *Productivity Perspectives,* December, 1983.

Cole, R. E. *Work, Mobility, and Participation: A Comparative Study of American and Japanese Industry,* Berkeley, Ca.: University of California Press, 1979.

Deming, W. E. *Quality, Productivity, and Competitive Position.* MIT Industrial Liaison Program Report, Cambridge, Mass.: MIT, 1983.

Ginzberg, Eli. "The Mechanization of Work," *Scientific American* 247, no. 3 (September 1982), pp. 67–75.

Gunn, Thomas G. "The Mechanization of Design and Manufacturing," *Scientific American* 247, no. 3 (September 1982), p. 116.

Gunn, Thomas G. "Computer-Integrated Manufacturing," *Proceedings of the 1982 Academic-Practitioners Liaison Operations Management Workshop.* Michigan State University, July 1982, pp. 1–22.

Hall, Robert W. *Zero Inventories.* Homewood, IL: Dow Jones Irwin, 1983.

Hyer, Nancy Lea. "Management's Guide to Group Technology," *Operations Management Review* 2, no. 2 (Winter 1984), pp. 36–42.

Juran, J. M. *Quality Planning and Analysis.* 2nd Ed. New York: McGraw-Hill, 1980.

Keys, Bernard J. and Thomas R. Miller. "The Japanese Management Theory Jungle," *Academy of Management Review* 9, no. 2 (April 1984), pp. 342–353.

Miller, Jeffrey, Jinchiro Nakane, and Thomas Vollman. "The 1983 Global Manufacturing Futures Survey," Manufacturing Roundtable Research Report Series, Boston University School of Management, Boston University, 1983.

Schonberger, Richard J. *Japanese Manufacturing Techniques.* New York: Free Press, 1982.

3 Operations Analysis

At American Airlines, the Operations Research Group is deeply involved in many of the important decisions facing senior management. The group utilizes the tools addressed in this chapter, and other tools, to assist operating departments.

- Schedule the airline
- Schedule flight crews
- Manage over $400 million of inventory
- Determine how many seats to sell and how much to charge
- Determine flight times
- Estimate schedule dependability
- Determine hiring, training, and vacation schedules for flight crews
- Develop flight plans
- Develop airport staffing plans
- Forecast passenger demand for new markets
- Design communications networks

In addition, many Operations Research projects support nonrecurring management decision making. Examples of these kinds of projects include:

- Fleet planning decisions
- Airport expansion decisions
- Location studies for crew bases, maintenance bases, and reservations offices

In short, the tools you are going to learn about are used extensively in the airline industry, and at American the results flow directly to the bottom line.

Thomas M. Cook, Director of Operations Research
American Airlines, Inc.
Dallas, Texas

Mr. Cook has identified a great variety of problem areas, including some that recur daily and others of a less frequent, long-run variety. Operations analysis offers some basic concepts and tools that can be used to deal with diverse problems in a formal, systematic way that yields better performance.

One of the distinguishing features of contemporary operations management is its use of systematic formal analysis. Formally analyzing problems allows managers to plan, organize, and control the conversion process in a systematic way; it gives them information and guidance for the decisions they have to make. As they analyze problems or alternatives, managers often make use of modeling techniques. In this chapter, we introduce the analytic orientation that typifies much of production/operations management (P/OM). As you read it, you will see that analysis and modeling are closely related (see Figure 3.1).

DECISION MAKING

As we discussed in Chapter 1, decision making is a key activity that sets managers apart from other employees of the organization. Faced with difficult and complex problems, managers must often take decisive action under severe time constraints. To help them, a variety of decision-making and analysis aids have been developed over the past sixty years. This abundance of decision-making aids distinguishes P/OM from many of the other subsystems of the organization. It is difficult to find another area of management in which more effort has been devoted to finding formal methods of analysis, and it is equally difficult to find areas where these developments are more widely employed. How does analysis help a manager make decisions? The answer becomes clearer when we examine the process of decision making.

The Decision-Making Process

Decisions usually involve several identifiable stages. First is the recognition that a problem, an obstacle to achieving a goal, exists. Second, attempts are made to identify alternatives, evaluate them, select one alternative, and implement the decision. Although it has a role to play throughout the process, formal analysis is used most extensively in the evaluation and choice stages. Some additional, "in between" steps are also involved in the decision-making process: identifying criteria, identifying relevant variables, and experimenting. To evaluate alternatives, managers must choose a criterion to distinguish between "good" and "bad" choices, and they must know how all the alternatives would affect the organization. The parts of the organization that would be affected are called the *relevant variables*. Next, managers use some experimentation to estimate the impact each alternative would have if it were adopted. This experimentation may range from very informal to highly formal. Figure 3.2 shows the stages managers go through in making a decision.

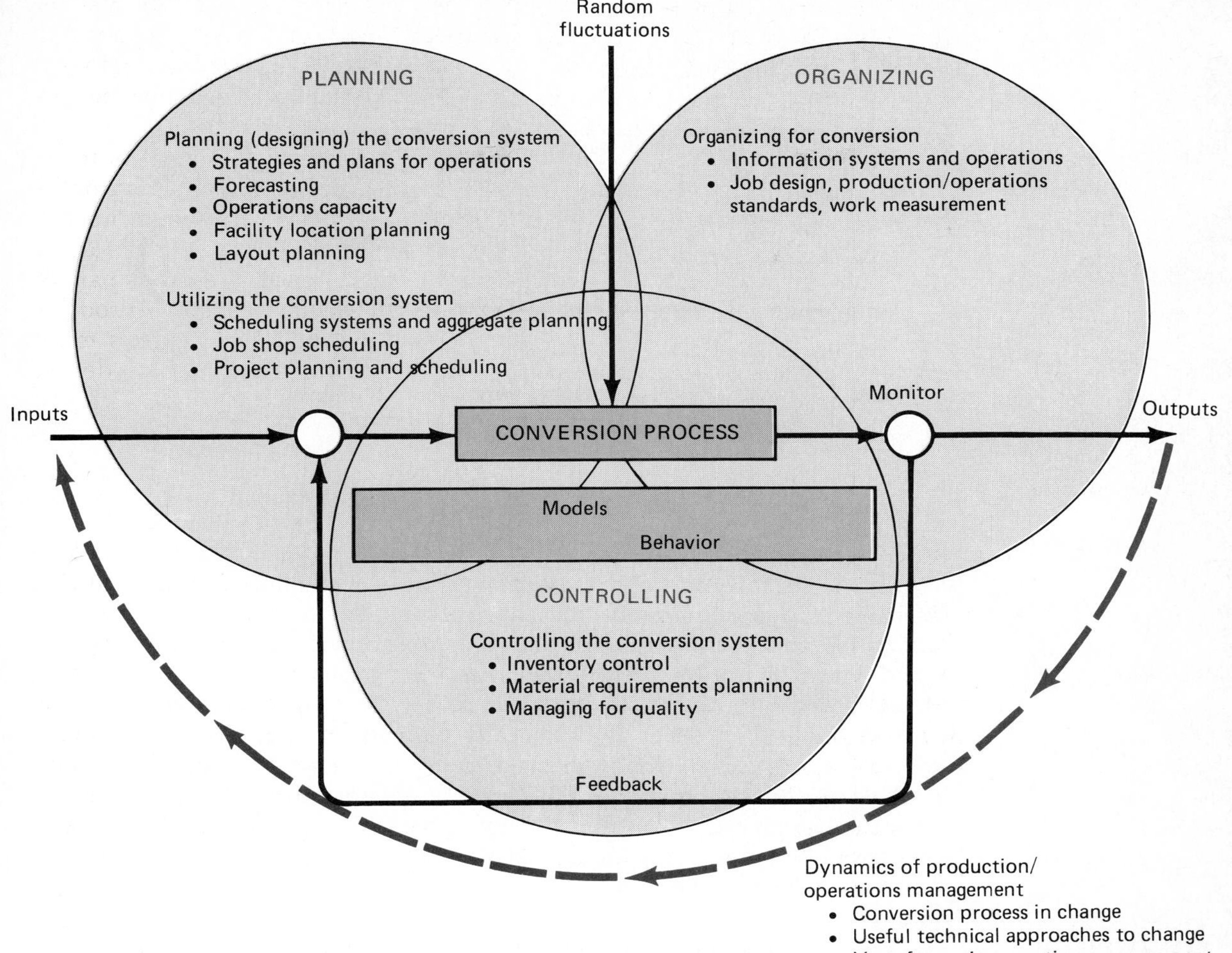

FIGURE 3.1
Framework for production/operations management

Management Science Approach to Decision Making

Management science (operations research) is a contemporary term encompassing both a philosophy and an approach to analyzing and solving organizational problems. Philosophically it assumes that explainable causes underlie organization problems and that systematic study of these problems can suggest how they may be resolved. The management science approach relies heavily on the scientific method of problem solving and on the use of quantitative models. *A model is a representation of something real; it shows relationships among variables and can be used to predict or explain.* Coupling the scientific method with quantitative models provides a

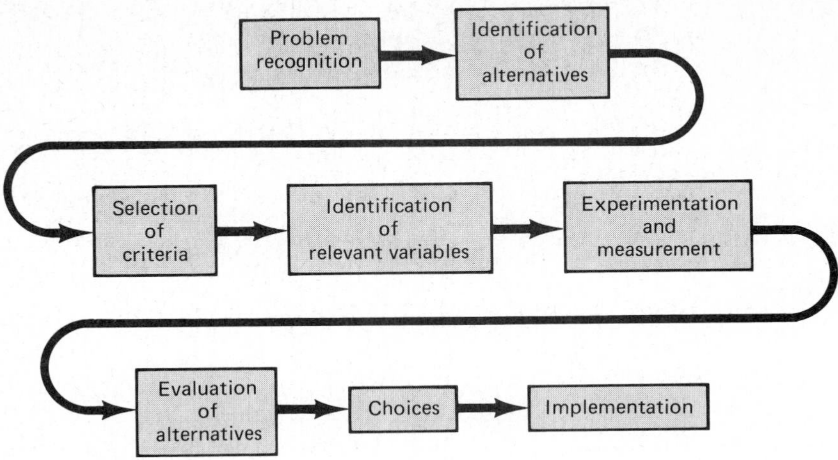

FIGURE 3.2
The decision-making process

powerful basis for analysis. Analysts can build a model of the operating system or of one or more system subcomponents. Then they can experiment to see how the model performs under various conditions. The idea is to find ways of improving the real operating system without tampering with it directly. Actually changing the real system to observe whether or not performance improves is potentially dangerous. Real changes in productive systems can be costly to make, and once made they can have unexpected costly consequences, which may be irreversible. Predicting system responses to various changes before those changes are actually made is the purpose of the management scientist.

With a model, the effects of experimental changes can be measured and observed more rapidly, more conclusively, and in some respects at less risk than would be possible by manipulating the real system. The difficulty is that sometimes the model may not accurately reflect the real system. If it doesn't, changes that looked good in the model may turn out to be disappointing when they're actually implemented. Did the analyst build into the model all the relevant aspects of the real system? It's a good idea to find out with a validity check.[1] Either or both of these steps can help make sure the model is accurate:

1. People responsible for the system being modeled should approve the model's operation.
2. The model and the system being modeled should be operated simultaneously for some time to make sure they're equivalent in performance.

[1]Using an invalid model is a major cause of failure cited in J. S. Annino and E. C. Russell, "The Seven Most Frequent Causes of Simulation Failure—And How to Avoid Them," *Interfaces* 11, no. 3 (June 1981), pp. 59–63.

Management science can help operations managers solve many of the problems they confront. But which problems should be tackled by management science and which by another approach is a decision that has to be based on experience and judgment.

THE ROLE OF MODELS IN ANALYSIS

In spite of their utility, we must recognize models for what they are—artificial representations of things that are real. As such, they fall short of fully duplicating their real world counterpart.

> **EXAMPLE**
>
> Descriptions of the conversion process in this book are one kind of model, a *written* model. These descriptions are not, of course, the conversion process itself. The conversion process is the ongoing, real-life activities that are occurring right now in most organizations; our descriptions merely explain that process.

This incompleteness of models should not be interpreted as a strictly negative feature. In fact, it can be desirable, because it clears away extraneous elements and concentrates on the heart of the problem. Real decision problems are complicated enough without trying to reconstruct all their complexities into a model. Instead, what we want, and what the modeling process gives us, is a simplified version of the situation, a representation in which all the minor considerations have been stripped away so the major factors are clearly visible.

Types of Models in Production and Operations Management

In production and operations management, we use several types of models of varying levels of sophistication.

Verbal Models Verbal or written models are descriptive. *They express in words the relationships among variables.* Suppose a passing motorist asks you to give directions to the nearest gas station. Rather than actually driving along the roads to show the way, you *abstract* the situation by describing road signs, traffic lights, perhaps landmarks. If you tell him the way, you are giving a verbal model. If you write the directions in words (not pictures), you are giving a descriptive model.

Schematic Models *Schematic models show a pictorial relationship among variables.* If you gave the passing motorist a map showing the way to the nearest gas station, you would be giving a schematic model. Charts and diagrams are also schematic; they are very useful for showing relationships among variables, as long as all the legends, symbols, and scales are explained.

Iconic Models *Iconic models are scaled physical replicas of objects or processes.* Architectural models of new buildings and highway engineering replicas of a proposed overpass system are iconic models. In chemical engineering, scaled operating physical replicas of new chemical processing facilities are often constructed. These are operated before actual construction to assess whether the hypothesized relationships among chemicals, temperature, and other variables really hold.

Mathematical Models *Mathematical models show functional relationships among variables by using mathematical symbols and equations.* In any equation, x, y, and similar symbols are abstractions (they represent real variables) used to represent precise functional relationships among the variables.

Choosing the Right Model

What is the most appropriate form of model? The answer depends on the purpose of the analysis and the nature of the problem. The selection of a model and the level of detail are guided by one overriding consideration: what kind of information do I need to make a decision?

Consider an office layout problem. Two different models may be appropriate. First, we may use a mathematical model to measure how much work volume flows among all the different work centers in the office. This would give us a general idea of where to relocate work centers to eliminate unnecessary work flows. Then we might use a schematic model to specify exact positioning of equipment in work centers. The schematic model could be as simple as a rough sketch or very detailed, including replicas of equipment, walls, and even wiring. From the entire modeling effort, we could recommend an efficient layout design.[2]

Mathematical Models in P/OM

Optimization Operations managers often use formal models to help analyze problems and suggest solutions. To assist, they often find it helpful to use an *algorithm,* a prescribed set of steps (a procedure) that attains a goal. In *optimization* models, for example, we want to find the *best* solution (the goal), and an *optimization algorithm* identifies the steps for doing so. In operations management we strive for optimization algorithms as aids in problem solving.

[2]See J. S. Dyer and R. N. Lund, "Tinker Toys and Christmas Trees: Opening a New Merchandising Package for AMOCO Oil Company," *Interfaces* 12, no. 6 (December 1982), pp. 38–52. The authors explain how mathematical, iconic, and schematic models were combined to aid decision making at Standard Oil (Indiana).

Heuristics In other cases, a *heuristic* approach is used. A heuristic is a way (a strategy) of using rules of thumb or defined decision procedures to attack a problem. In general, when we use heuristics we do not expect to attain the best possible solution to a problem; instead, we hope for a *satisfactory* solution *quickly*. Formally developed heuristic procedures are called *heuristic algorithms*. They are useful for problems for which optimization algorithms have not yet been developed. Among their uses is the assembly line balancing problem (discussed in Chapter 8).

Modeling Benefits

The extensive use of models, especially schematic and mathematical models, is sometimes questioned by students and practitioners of P/OM. The application of well-defined models often requires assumptions that are sometimes questionable, costs and other data that are difficult to obtain, and forecasts of future events that are not easily obtained. Even so, using a particular model is frequently justified. The knowledge gained from working with models and attempting to apply them can yield valuable insights into the decision problem. The use of explicitly defined models:

1. forces managers to recognize a problem area and decide what types of decisions are required. Simply recognizing the decision points can be a major step forward in many situations,
2. makes managers recognize the factors involved in the problem and determine what variables can be controlled to affect performance of the system,
3. forces managers to recognize *relevant* costs and gain some knowledge of their magnitudes, and
4. enables managers to identify the relationships of costs to the decision variables, recognize important tradeoffs among costs, and gain knowledge of the overall interaction of variables and costs.

Breakeven Analysis

Sometimes a simple formal analysis can clarify one of the most fundamental sets of relationships encountered in operations management. *Breakeven analysis is a graphical or algebraic representation of the relationships among volume, cost, and revenues in an organization.* Breakeven analysis is very useful for helping the manager conceptualize these relationships.

As the volume of output from a productive facility increases, costs and revenues also increase. Costs can generally be divided into two categories, fixed and variable. Fixed costs are those incurred regardless of output volume. They include heating, lighting, and administrative expenses that are the same whether one or one thousand units of output are produced. Variable costs are those that fluctuate directly with volume of output; higher output results in higher total variable costs. Typically, they are the costs of direct labor and material. In Figure 3.3, total revenues and total costs are shown as linear functions of output volume. Both total costs and total revenues increase with higher levels of output. Costs exceed revenues over the initial range of volume up to point V_{BE}. Point V_{BE} is *the breakeven point—that level of operating volume at which total cost equals total revenues from operations.* Thereafter, revenues exceed costs of operation.

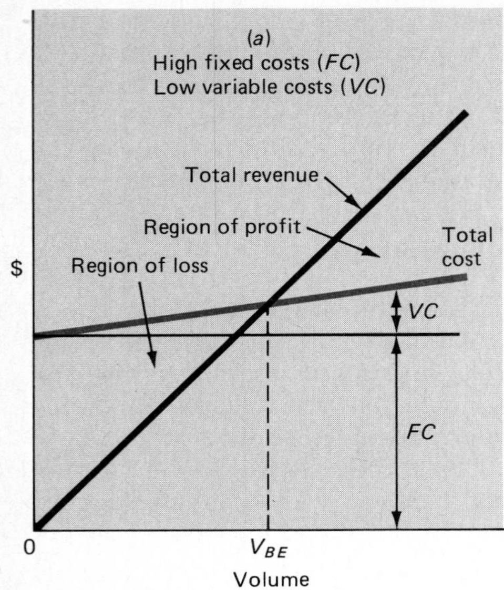

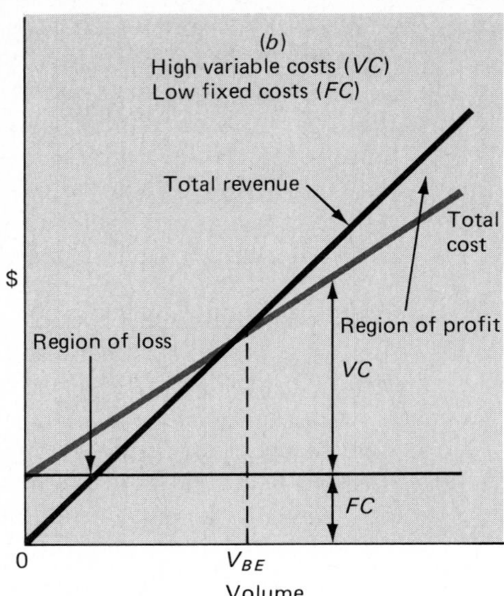

FIGURE 3.3
Cost structures and breakeven charts for two contrasting conversion processes

Breakeven analysis is useful for identifying the level of operations (output) that must be reached in order to recover all the costs of operation from revenues. The breakeven point depends on the selling price of the product and the operating cost structure. Operating costs vary from company to company depending on the type of conversion technology, administrative structure, and operating policies they employ. Some conversion processes require large capital outlays and high overhead expenses but low unit variable costs. They require a large volume of output to reach breakeven, but once they have attained it profitability increases rapidly. Other conversion processes have low fixed costs and high unit variable costs. Figure 3.3 shows both kinds of cost structures.

Breakeven with Discontinuous Revenues and Costs Revenues and/or costs may be curvilinear rather than linear functions (with constant slope) over some ranges of output volume, and the functions may not be continuous with increasing volume. Indeed, a major purpose of breakeven analysis is to reveal how the organization's costs and revenues change with volume of output. The analysis can then be used to help make decisions about the organization's output goals.

Consider the situation in Figure 3.4. The organization has two facilities, *A* and *B*, which may be operated during the coming year. Facility *A*, working a single shift, has a breakeven volume of BE_1 units. Thereafter, profitability increases up to the output V_A. If greater profit is desired, facil-

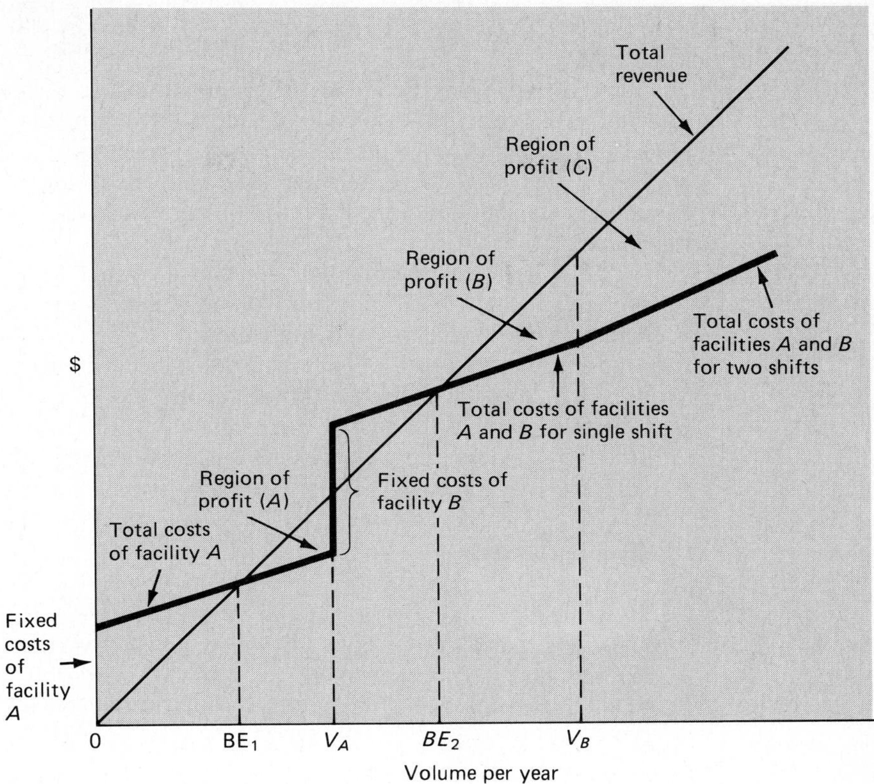

FIGURE 3.4
Breakeven chart for operating one facility, two facilities, and two facilities on double shifts

ity B must be opened and additional fixed costs incurred. The overall operation (facilities A and B) will not be profitable until a volume of BE_2 units is achieved. Output volumes above BE_2 result in higher profit rates until volume V_B is reached. To achieve outputs above V_B, second shift operations are necessary, and variable costs increase accordingly. Beyond V_B, profits continue to increase, but at a slower rate.

Information from the breakeven chart (a schematic model) can now be used for aiding managerial decisions. Once the desired level of profitability for the year has been stated, we can show the volume of output necessary for achieving it. We can also identify how many facilities and shifts will be needed, and we can estimate operating costs and working capital requirements. It is also possible to present the analysis as a mathematical model using equations to represent the relationships among output volume, cost, and sales revenues.

SELECTING DECISION CRITERIA

The decision-making process ultimately involves choosing one of several alternatives. What constitutes a "good" alternative or a "bad" one? The answer to this question is often not clear. Alternative *A* may be good in one sense but not so good in another. The same may be true for alternative *B*. Somehow we must decide; we must have *criteria* that will help us compare alternatives.

The criteria managers use are those system characteristics deemed most crucial for meeting system objectives. A formal analysis not only identifies these characteristics but attempts to measure the performances of each alternative for each objective. The criteria measurements then become formal indicators by which alternatives are evaluated. One of the primary reasons for formal analysis in decision making is to determine the criteria values of each decision alternative. Were the criteria values of alternatives already known, formal analysis would be unnecessary.

EXAMPLE

The manager of banking operations at Downtown National Bank has been allocated a budgetary increase of $10,000 for the purpose of streamlining bank operations. Her job is to improve service to customers with minimum additional resource expenditures during the coming year. As part of this program the manager is considering two decision alternatives: *A*, employ an additional teller during peak business hours, or *B*, change existing business hours from 9 to 4 o'clock to 9 to 5 o'clock daily. A formal analysis of both alternatives was made using two criteria, average customer waiting time, and annual added cost of operations. The analysis revealed the following:

Alternative	Reduction in average customer waiting time (minutes)	Additional operating cost per year
A	2.73	$10,000
B	.68	10,000

Since the alternatives are equally attractive in terms of the cost criterion, the manager chooses alternative *A* because it reduces customer waiting time more than alternative *B* does.

Notice that many additional factors could also have been considered. These two alternatives, for example, may differ in terms of the number of new customers they would attract. The operations manager has necessarily discarded some criteria and selected only those that she believes to be realistic and reasonable. On the basis of the alternatives' effectiveness according to established criteria, the manager was able to make a decision.

Conflicting Criteria

Identifying the criteria and measuring the criteria values for each alternative do not always resolve the decision problem. Often a very difficult phase of decision making remains. This occurs when the chosen criteria values conflict, usually when there are multiple criteria. Suppose the analysis in our banking example had shown the following:

Alternative	Reduction in average customer waiting time (minutes)	Additional operating cost per year
A	2.73	$10,000
B	.68	2,000

Alternative *A* is most attractive in terms of reducing average customer waiting time. *B*, however, is far less costly. The operations manager is concerned with both cost and service. Now which alternative is better? There is no simple answer; the manager will have to use her experience and judgment. She may attempt to combine the two criteria into a single measure of desirability, the cost per minute of reduced waiting time.

Alternative	Cost per minute of reduced waiting time
A	$\frac{\$10{,}000}{2.73 \text{ minutes}} = \$3{,}663$
B	$\frac{\$\ 2{,}000}{.68 \text{ minutes}} = \$2{,}941$

Alternative *B* is more efficient in terms of offering greater reductions in waiting time for each dollar expended. In addition, $8,000 is still available to spend on other service improvement opportunities that may exist. If additional improvement opportunities don't exist, alternative *A* may become more attractive than *B*.

The perplexing problem of conflicting criteria becomes even more challenging as our economy continues to shift from manufacturing toward service industries. Many of the criteria that were appropriate for manufacturing analysis are not suited to analysis of labor-intense service industries.[3] Still, service industries managers can use formal analysis to identify relevant criteria and measure the criteria values of each alternative before they make decisions.

---

[3]Recognizing the measurement problem that exists in the service sector, the National Science Foundation has developed a program for research into productivity measurement in service industries. See, for example, *Proceedings of the Grantees Conference on Research on Productivity Measurement Systems for Administrative Services*, ed. William A. Ruch, National Science Foundation Program 75–14 (Washington, D.C., November 1977).

CLASSIFYING DECISION PROBLEMS

Since many different kinds of decision problems are encountered by the operations analyst, it's a good idea to have a convenient starting point, or frame of reference, for initiating the analysis effort. Classifying problems into different types makes it easier to select models and criteria to use in the analysis. We'll consider two ways of classifying problems: by the degree of uncertainty of outcomes and by the degree of interdependence among decisions.

Uncertainty of Outcomes

When we know for sure what the outcome for each decision alternative will be, we are dealing with a problem under conditions of *certainty*. When a decision alternative can result in more than one possible outcome and we know the relative chances (probabilities) of each outcome's occurrence, we are facing a decision problem under conditions of *risk*. Finally, when an alternative has more than one possible outcome and we do not know their relative chances of occurrence, we face a decision problem under *uncertainty*.

These three categories possess both common features and some important differences. These characteristics are shared by all three:

1. there are two or more alternatives,
2. possible outcomes for each alternative are identified, and
3. a decision criterion is identified as a basis for evaluating the alternatives.

The three differ in:

1. the extent to which the ultimate outcome of the decision is known,
2. the extent to which the chances of each outcome's occurrence (state of nature) is known, and
3. the computational procedure used for evaluation.

Some examples may clarify the problems of certainty, risk, and uncertainty.

EXAMPLE: CERTAINTY

A chain of supermarkets is going to open a new store at one of four possible locations. Management wishes to select the location that will maximize profitability over the next ten years. An extensive analysis was performed to determine the costs, revenues, and profits for each alternative. The results are shown below.

Location	Ten-year profit ($ millions)
1	.70
2	.95
3	.60
4	.84

Management has a high degree of confidence in these figures. The decision criterion (profit) has been explicitly identified and accurately calculated for each alternative. Management's strategy is to select the alternative with the highest criterion value, in this case location 2.

EXAMPLE: RISK

An extensive analysis of the supermarket chain's problem reveals that the profit associated with each alternative is not known for sure. Management is convinced that the ten-year profitability of each location alternative will depend upon future regional population growth. Therefore, the ultimate outcome is not totally within the control of management; it also depends on external considerations. Three possible levels of population growth have been identified: low, medium, and high. The profitability ($ million) associated with each alternative under each possible level of population growth has been established below.

	Rate of Population Growth		
Location	Low (5% or less)	Medium (above 5% but below 10%)	High (10% or more)
1	$.3	$.8	$ .9
2	.2	.6	1.1
3	.4	.5	.6
4	.6	.7	.8
Probability (p)	.2	.3	.5

At the bottom of the table, the analyst has recorded the probability of occurrence for each possible rate of population growth. Decision strategy in this situation is more difficult than it is under conditions of certainty.

EXAMPLE: UNCERTAINTY

If the supermarket chain's management knows that profitability depends on future population growth, but it doesn't know the probabilities of low, medium, or high growth, it is faced with a decision problem under uncertainty. Obviously, strategy is much harder to come by in this case.

Under conditions of certainty, the best location alternative is easily identified. Location 2 clearly yields the highest profit. Under conditions of risk, however, the choice is not so easy. We do not know which location will be best because the rate of future population growth is unknown. In analyzing this situation, we have to arrange the data differently than we did under certainty conditions. Look at the table in the risk example. (A table arranged like this is called a *matrix.*) The levels of profit for low, medium, and high population growth are listed separately for each location. Which alternative is best? If population growth turns out to be low, location 4 is best ($.6 million). If growth is medium, location 1 is best ($.8 million), and if it is high, location 2 is best ($1.1 million). In the analyst's language, the three rates of population growth are called *states of nature.*

To help guide our decision, we use a procedure that adjusts the profits for each alternative to account for the chances of obtaining those profits. This results in a criterion called *expected value,* an averaging technique in which each possible outcome is weighted by its chances of occurring. The expected value procedure follows these steps:

1. Select one alternative for evaluation.
2. List all possible outcomes for this alternative.
3. Multiply each of these outcomes by its chance of occurrence.
4. Add the products from step 3 to obtain the expected value for that alternative.
5. Repeat steps 1 to 4 for each of the remaining alternatives.
6. Select the alternative with the highest expected value (for profits) or lowest expected value (for costs).

This procedure has been applied to our example in Table 3.1. The expected value criterion is highest for alternative 2. Although profits for location 2 vary from lower than the others ($.2 million) to higher ($1.1 million), it is the best choice because it yields the highest expected profit of all ($.77 million). If management faced this situation many times and always chose alternative 2, its average profit would be higher than for any other alternative. The expected value criterion is helpful in many decisions faced by the operations manager, and we will use it frequently.[4]

Decision problems under uncertainty can also be structured in matrix form. Since the probabilities are not known, however, rational strategies for decision making are not well-defined or straightforward. Three approaches from among several that analysts use in these circumstances are discussed here. The first, *maximax,* is an optimistic approach; the analyst considers only the best outcome for each alternative. In Table 3.1, the outcomes considered would be $.9 million for alternative 1, $1.1 million for alternative 2, $.6 million for alternative 3, and $.8 million for alternative 4. Among

[4]You may have noticed something important about location 3. For every population rate (state of nature), location 4 has a better outcome than location 3. When one alternative is equal to or better than another for every possible state of nature, analysts say that it *dominates* that alternative; in this case, 4 dominates 3. Therefore 3 could be eliminated immediately.

TABLE 3.1
Calculation of expected value ($ Million)

Alternative	Outcomes × chances			Summation	Expected value (profit)
1	$.3 × .2 = .06	$.8 × .3 = .24	$ .9 × .5 = .45	.06 + .24 + .45	= $.75
2	.2 × .2 = .04	.6 × .3 = .18	1.1 × .5 = .55	.04 + .18 + .55	= .77
3	.4 × .2 = .08	.5 × .3 = .15	.6 × .5 = .30	.08 + .15 + .30	= .53
4	.6 × .2 = .12	.7 × .3 = .21	.8 × .5 = .40	.12 + .21 + .40	= .73

these, alternative 2 yields the maximum profit, and that is the one that would be chosen.

The second approach under uncertainty is *maximin*, a pessimistic approach. With this approach, the analyst considers only the worst possible outcome for each alternative and chooses the "best of the worst" (maximum among the minimums). In Table 3.1, the figures would be $.3 million for alternative 1, $.2 million for alternative 2, $.4 million for alternative 3, and $.6 million for alternative 4. The best of these is 4.

The third approach, the *principle of insufficient reason*, assumes that since we know absolutely nothing about the probabilities of any state of nature, we should treat each with equal probability and choose on the expected value basis. Using this approach, we would choose alternative 4.

Interdependence Among Decisions

Another way of classifying decision problems is in relation to the number of decision stages that must be considered. At one extreme are single-stage, or static, problems; at the other are multistage, or sequential, problems. Although real problems don't always fall into either of these two pure types, we usually treat them as such for purposes of analysis. Both types are encountered in operations management.

Static problems are essentially "one-time-only" decisions. Inventory, "make vs. buy," product mix, and location of new facility decisions are often treated as static problems. Our supermarket chain example was treated this way.

With static problems, the analyst focuses on the immediate consequences of the decision without much formal concern about how these consequences affect other future decisions. To simplify the situation, the decision is treated as if it were independent of other decisions.

Multistage treatments, on the other hand, explicitly consider how several sequential decisions are related to one another. The outcome of the first decision affects the attractiveness of the choices at the next decision stage, and so on down the line at each decision point. With multistage problems, the concern is not how to get the best outcome of any single stage but how to make a *series* of choices that will finally result in the best overall set of outcomes from beginning to end. Sequential decision problems are commonly encountered by the operations manager in project management, capacity planning, and aggregate scheduling.

Decision Trees: Analysis of a Two-Stage Problem

One method for dealing with sequential problems is decision tree analysis, used to systematically structure and analyze problems.[5] Not only the results are useful; the process of structuring a problem into a decision tree framework is itself very helpful. The manager must identify decision alternatives, identify chance events that can influence the outcomes, and explicitly assess the chances that various outcomes will occur. The process of clarifying these aspects of the problem can lead to more enlightened decisions, even if the analysis is not carried to completion. Typically, the expected value criterion is used to identify the best course of action.

Decision trees are most beneficial when applied to sequential, multistage problems involving time-phased decisions. Decision tree analysis consists of these steps:

1. Tree diagramming
   (a) Identify all decisions (and their alternatives) to be made and the order (sequence) in which they must be made.
   (b) Identify the chance events that can occur after each decision.
   (c) Develop a tree diagram showing the sequence of decisions and chance events.
2. Estimation
   (a) Obtain a probability estimate of the chances of occurrence for each chance event outcome.
   (b) Obtain estimates of the financial (criterion) consequences of all possible outcomes and actions.
3. Evaluation and selection
   (a) Calculate the expected value of all possible actions.
   (b) Select the action offering the most attractive expected value.

These steps can be illustrated by a problem example.

EXAMPLE

The city transit system in Smalltown has been operating its bus system at a $400,000 deficit annually. The city council has decided to raise bus fares to help offset the operating deficit. The director of City Transit believes the fare increase will decrease ridership unless transit system services are expanded. The director suggests that expanded services be offered simultaneously with

---

[5]An example of extensive use of decision trees yielding substantial economic benefits is presented in T. J. Madden, M. S. Hyrnick, and J. A. Hodde, "Decision Analysis Used to Evaluate Air Quality Control Equipment for Ohio Edison Company," *Interfaces* 13, no. 1 (February 1983), pp. 66–75.

the fare increase to offset negative community reaction. He believes this action will result in one of three levels of ridership: increased, sustained, or reduced.

An influential council member suggests an alternative plan. He would increase the fare now but delay the expanded service decision for two years. If this is done, the director is sure, ridership will not increase during the next two years; it will either decrease or be sustained at current levels. If service is expanded two years after the fare increase, ridership may be increased, sustained, or reduced. If service is not expanded in two years, however, the most optimistic estimates are that ridership will either be sustained or reduced, not increased. The director has decided to use a decision tree analysis to evaluate this problem for an eight-year time horizon (the desired length of the planning period).

Tree Diagramming Figure 3.5 shows the initial tree diagram developed by the director. The sequence of decisions and chance events flows from left to right. Labels have been added to each branch of the tree. At the left side of the diagram, we see the first decision (represented by a square) and its two alternatives, each represented by a branch emanating from the square. If service is expanded now (alternative *B*), the decision will be followed by a chance event (circle), which can lead to any of three outcomes: annual ridership during each of the next eight years will either increase, remain unchanged, or decrease. The annual operating deficit (ultimate outcome) depends on the outcome of the chance event. If service is not expanded now (alternative *A*), annual ridership during the next two years is expected to be either reduced or sustained at the current level. After two years, a second decision must be made. Service will either be expanded or not be expanded (alternatives *C* and *D*). If service is not expanded (*D*), ridership during the next six years will either be sustained or reduced. If service is expanded (*C*), it is also possible that ridership might increase above the current level.

Estimation The next stage of the decision tree analysis involves estimating the outcomes and probabilities of chance events. Probability estimates are needed *wherever a chance event appears* in the diagram. Notice that probabilities for the chance event *f* (Figure 3.6) sum to 1.0. This is because one and only one of these three outcomes must occur. The one-time cost of expanding service is $300 thousands if done now (branch *B*) and $450 thousands if done two years from now (branch *C*).

For the chance node following decision alternative *B*, the director believes that by expanding services now, the chances for increased ridership are .2, for sustained ridership .5, and for reduced ridership .3 for each of the next eight years. With alternative *A*, the chances for sustained ridership are .3 and for reduced ridership .7 in years one and two. Similarly, probabilities have been estimated for each possible outcome for the chance events that follow alternatives *C* and *D*. These various probability estimates

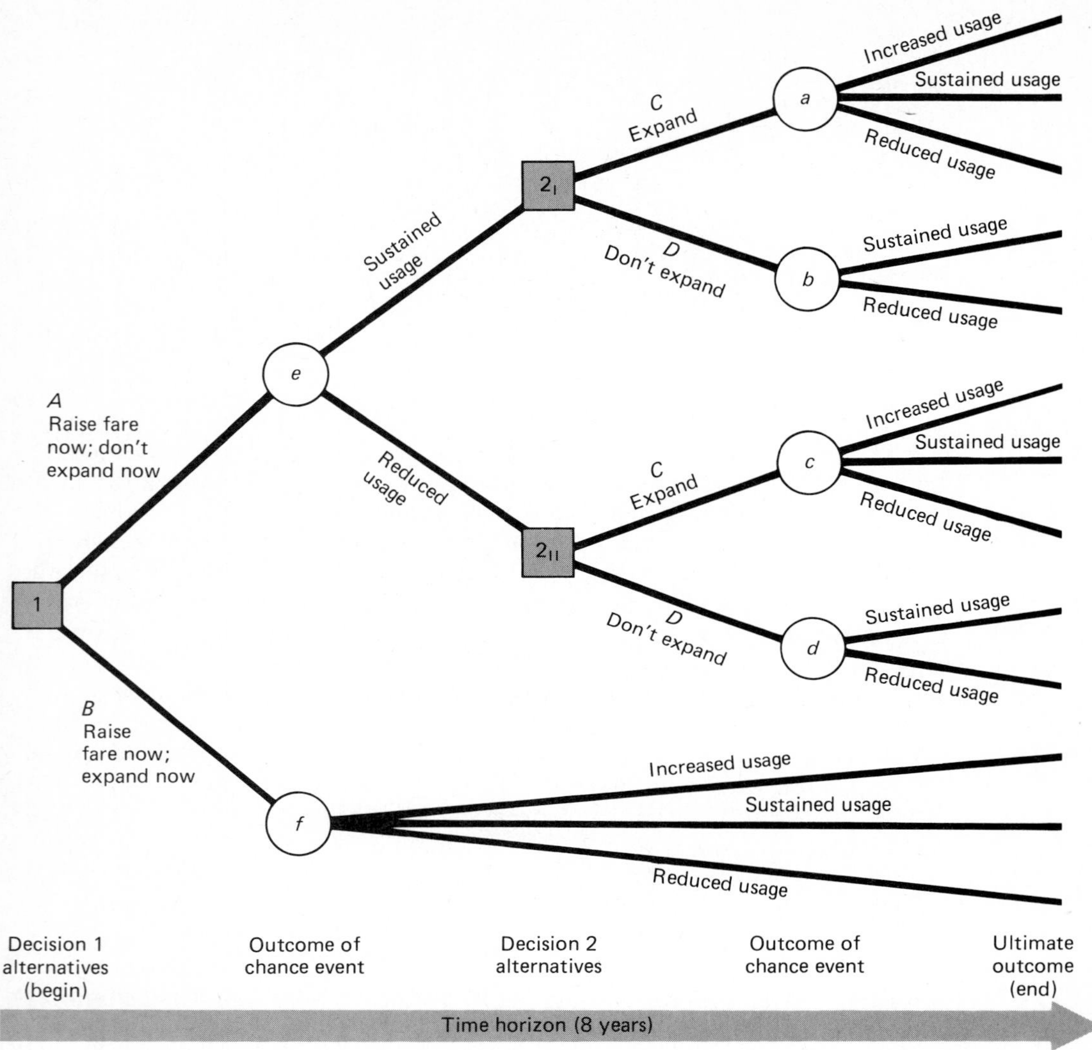

FIGURE 3.5
Decision tree diagram for a city transit system

for all chance events are shown in Figure 3.6, as are the cost consequences of all outcomes and actions.

Evaluation and Selection The final phase of the analysis is to calculate expected values of all possible actions. For our example, we will calculate the expected cost of each chance event node and decision square in the diagram. That will allow us to identify the set of actions that will lead to

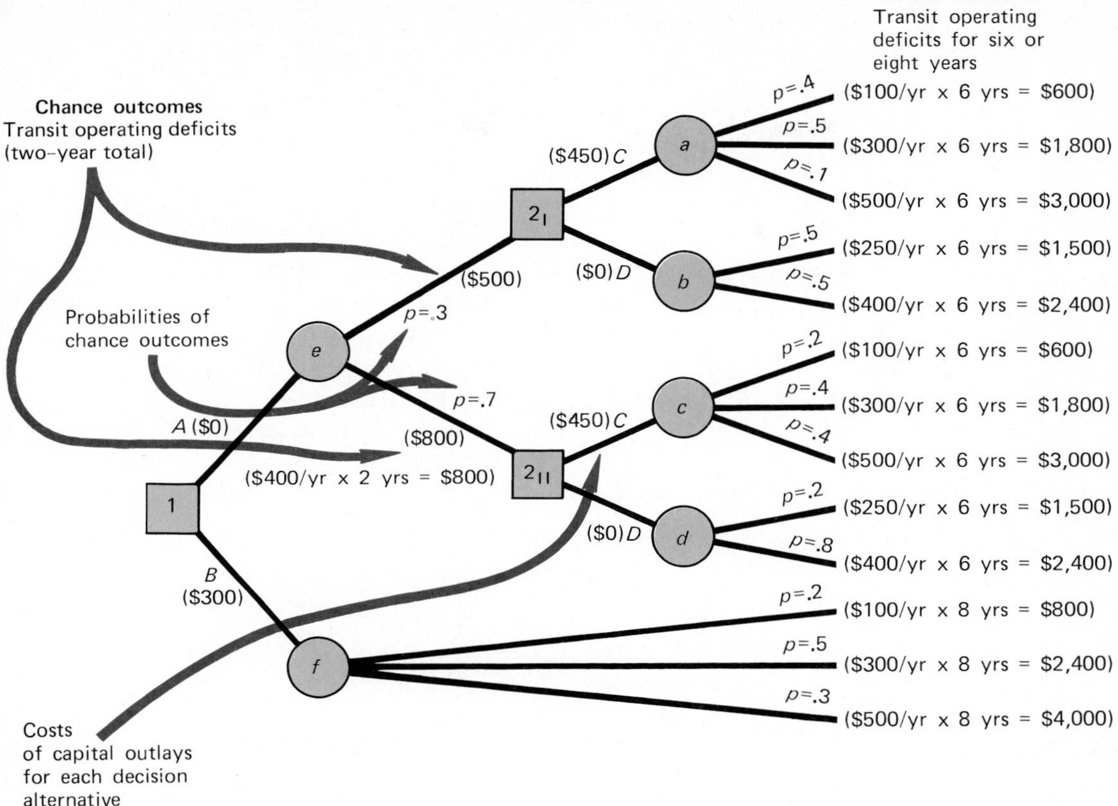

FIGURE 3.6
Tree diagram with probabilities, outcomes, and costs (cost figures in $ thousands)

minimum expected cost for the eight-year decision horizon. We begin by calculating expected cost of nodes at the right side of the diagram, at the last stage of the problem, and then work backwards.

Look at Figure 3.6 again. Suppose the city had taken a course of action that resulted in its being located at node *a*. This would be the case if service was not expanded initially, ridership was sustained in years one and two, and service was expanded after two years. What will happen to ridership in years three through eight? We don't know for sure: this is a chance event. We can, however, calculate the *expected cost* of the outcomes that follow node *a*:

$$\begin{aligned} EC_a &= (.4)(\$600) + (.5)(\$1{,}800) + (.1)(\$3{,}000) \\ &= 240 + 900 + 300 \\ &= \$1{,}440 \end{aligned}$$

This tells us that if we ever do reach node *a*, the expected cost of all possible outcomes thereafter is \$1,440. We can similarly calculate the expected costs associated with nodes *b*, *c*, and *d* and record these costs for each node on Figure 3.7.

$$EC_b = (.5)(\$1{,}500) + (.5)(\$2{,}400) = \$1{,}950$$
$$EC_c = (.2)(\$600) + (.4)(\$1{,}800) + (.4)(\$3{,}000) = 2{,}040$$
$$EC_d = (.2)(\$1{,}500) + (.8)(\$2{,}400) = 2{,}220$$

Now compare the expected costs of nodes *a* and *b* in Figure 3.7. Node *a* is more desirable because its expected cost is lower than that of *b*. We now move to the left in the diagram to determine what decisions have to be made to reach nodes *a* and *b*. At decision square 2_I, decision *C* (costing \$450) leads to node *a* with expected cost of \$1,440 thereafter. The overall

FIGURE 3.7
Decision tree showing expected costs and best decision strategy

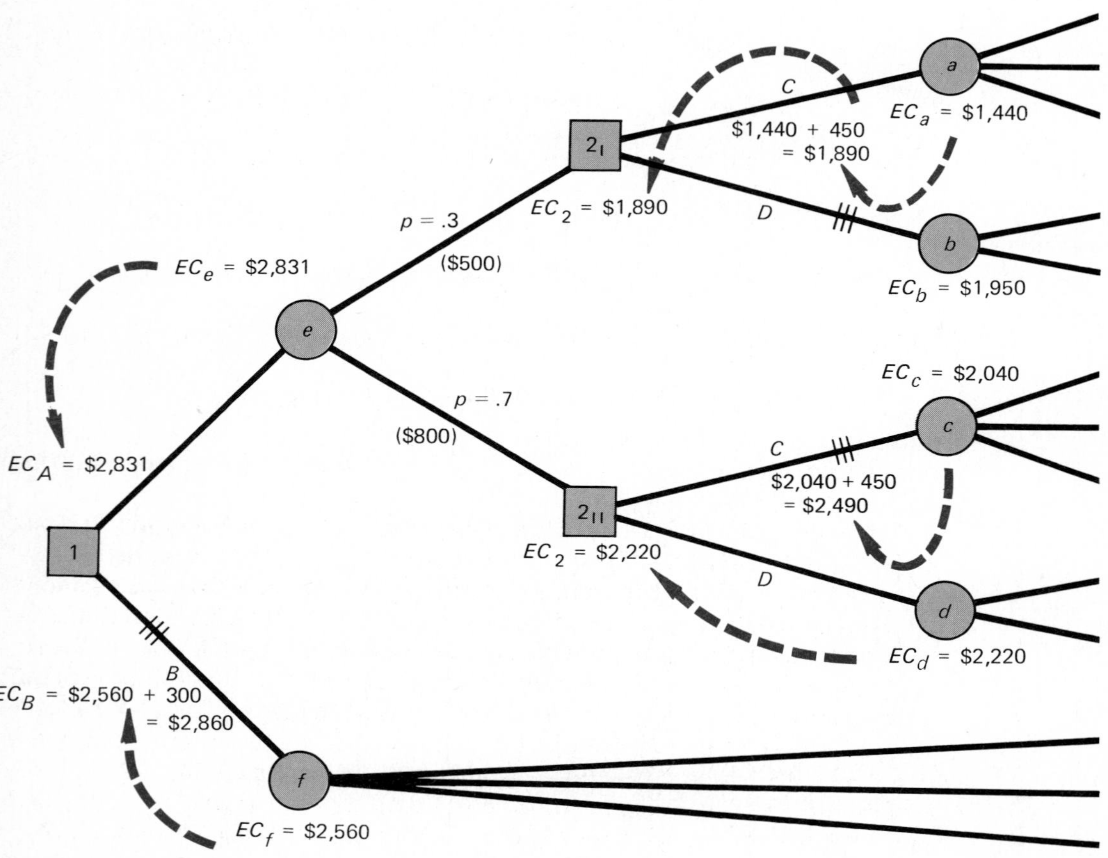

expected cost, then, of C and a is \$1,890. Node b can be reached in only one way, by choosing alternative D at decision square 2_I. Since D has no cost, the overall expected cost of D and b is \$1,950. If you are located at decision square 2_I, which route is more attractive thereafter, C and a or D and b? Using the expected value criterion, you should pick alternative C (expand service), at square 2_I. The expected cost of this best course of action is recorded under decision square 2_I in Figure 3.7. Alternative D has been crossed out, indicating it is less desirable than alternative C. The significance of these calculations is as follows: if the city takes a course of action that results in having to make the decision offered at square 2_I, the best choice is alternative C, which has the minimum expected future cost of \$1,890.

Let us now repeat this analysis for decision square 2_{II}, which involves nodes c and d. Given the choice of nodes c and d, we would prefer d. If we had not expanded service initially and if ridership for years one and two were reduced, we would find ourselves located at decision node 2_{II}. The desired course of action thereafter would be alternative D, which has an expected cost of \$2,220.

Now consider the consequences of being located at node e. There is a .3 chance of sustained ridership for two years with a two-year operating deficit (cost) of \$500, followed by the decision to expand service at an expected cost of \$1,890. There is also a .7 chance of reduced usage costing \$800, after which a "no expansion" decision would be made with an expected cost of \$2,220. The expected cost of node e is calculated as follows:

$$\begin{aligned} EC_e &= (.3)(\$500 + \$1{,}890) + (.7)(\$800 + \$2{,}220) \\ &= 717 + 2{,}114 \\ &= \$2{,}831 \end{aligned}$$

The expected cost for node f is:

$$\begin{aligned} EC_f &= (.2)(\$800) + (.5)(\$2{,}400) + (.3)(\$4{,}000) \\ &= 160 + 1{,}200 + 1{,}200 \\ &= \$2{,}560 \end{aligned}$$

This tells us that if we reach node f, the expected consequences are costs of \$2,560; if we reach node e and select the optimal set of decisions thereafter, the expected consequences are costs of \$2,831. In order to reach node f, decision B must be made initially at an additional cost of \$300. The expected cost of reaching node f is therefore \$300 plus \$2,560 or \$2,860. We have now determined the best course of action for the entire problem. First, the decision should be made to not expand the transit services initially. If the ridership is sustained during the ensuing two years, the system should be expanded. If ridership is reduced during years one and two, service should not be expanded for years three through eight. The expected cost of this course of action is \$2,831 thousands, as shown in Figure 3.7.

BEHAVIOR

Almost by definition, operations analysis requires that paramount consideration be given to models used by the operations analyst. But behavioral considerations play a vital role in operations analysis too, and they raise some important questions. Can formal analysis be beneficial from a behavioral standpoint? What are the advantages and disadvantages of formal analysis when compared to intuitive human judgment?[6] What can the operations manager expect from the analyst?

Characteristics of Intuitive Analysis

In recent years many people have tried to find out how well and why people can perform certain types of analysis. Adams and Swanson, for example, investigated factors that influence how accurately managers can estimate activity durations in a project management setting. The thirty managers' estimation accuracy, overall, was positively related to the amount of information they sought and used. Also, managers' levels of talent and perceived importance of accurate estimates were directly related to the amount of information they sought and processed. The primary conclusion was that estimation accuracy is largely determined by the estimator, even though uncontrollable outside variables affect actual activity duration.[7]

Estimating Probabilities People are not always objective when they estimate probabilities; they tend to overestimate the chances of obtaining a desirable outcome and underestimate the chances of undesired outcomes. A correct analysis, of course, is one in which estimates are made without regard to the desirability of the outcome. Probabilities are needed, you may remember, to perform an expected value analysis. Obviously, if the probabilities are wrong, the expected value will be wrong too. In cases like these, the human behavioral tendency to over- or underestimate probabilities could greatly distort the results of a formal analysis.

Processing Information Another area of study shows that humans tend to be conservative information processors. Given several pieces of information that must be combined into a summary conclusion, people tend to underestimate the amount of information that is present. Suppose you are trying to determine the chances that a decision will lead to a particular outcome. Various pieces of information are given to you. If properly combined, the information should lead to the conclusion that this outcome has a probability of .90 of occurring. People seem reluctant to arrive at such a conclusion. They generally estimate the chances to be much less than .90. A formal analysis using probability and statistical techniques can be helpful in avoiding this sort of inaccuracy.

---

[6]To see how formal analysis can aid in human judgments see "Decisions, Decisions, Decisions," *Dun's Review* (May 1981), p. 99.

[7]J. R. Adams and L. A. Swanson, "Information Processing Behavior and Estimating Accuracy in Operations Management," *Academy of Management Journal* 19, no. 1 (March 1976), pp. 98–110.

Sequential Decisions Potential human inaccuracies may occur in sequential decision problems too. Problems of this type require consideration of several future time periods when a current decision is being made. Research indicates that people do not look far enough into the future when making these decisions; they use an inadequate time horizon. Formal analyses help overcome this inadequacy by identifying the number of future time periods that should be considered.

Interpersonal Relationships Another behavioral aspect of concern is the interpersonal relationships between the analyst and the operations manager. The analyst often spends more time and effort examining a specific problem than does the manager. Consequently, the analyst may observe subtleties or recognize irrelevancies that the manager might not be aware of. The analyst can therefore provide an important service by acting as an information filter, clarifying relevant and irrelevant aspects of the problem for the manager. The relationship between the analyst and the manager depends, of course, on several factors: the personalities of the people involved, the jobs being performed, and the overall organizational climate that exists.

Communication Communication between the analyst and the manager may be the single most important determiner of success or failure of formal analysis efforts in organizations. Most analysts tend to think in terms of models and techniques. In addition, *good* analysts try to blend their thinking into the broader perspective of the organization. Effective analysts have the ability to strip away the elegant technical details of their efforts and present their recommendations to management in understandable ways. The potential communications gap between managers and analysts is an obstacle that should be recognized and dealt with in the organization. Analysis, even if it is accurate, cannot be effective unless it is used to help make decisions—and it won't be used unless mutual respect and understanding exist.

APPLICATION OF MANAGEMENT SCIENCE

Since models and analysis are critical tools in manufacturing and service industries, can we assume they are widely used?[8] How large are the organizations that use models, analysis, management science, and operations research (OR) techniques?

[8]The growing use of mathematical modeling in businesses is discussed in "Industry's Hot New Find: The Mathematician," *Business Week* (July 4, 1983), p. 88. An example of modeling benefits is given in K. Golabi, R. B. Kulkarni, and G. B. Way, "A Statewide Pavement Management System," *Interfaces* 12, no. 6 (December 1982), pp. 5–21. This article won the 1982 Institute of Management Science award for achievement.

Overall Usage of Management Science Techniques

Table 3.2 summarizes the results of several studies on the use of operations research in manufacturing. In each of the first three studies OR was used in only a fraction of the production processes in the organizations surveyed, as indicated in the last column of the table. The Gaither study (1975) surveyed *only* manufacturing firms; 48 percent indicated they used OR techniques. Gaither did not ask about use in production, but we would guess that those firms using the techniques used them heavily in production applications, since they are manufacturing firms. Overall, these studies indicate that somewhere around one-half to two-thirds of firms responding to the surveys use management science techniques. The Gaither study also suggests (Table 3.3) that the larger the firm, the greater the use of OR techniques—although significant usage occurs in all sizes of firms.

Use of Specific Operations Research Techniques

In Chapter 1 we presented a study of the most significant activity areas of production managers. Several other studies have addressed operations managers' use of specific operations research techniques for operations/production problems. One set of results, shown in Table 3.3, indicates that OR techniques are used most frequently for problems of planning and control. The table also shows (across the bottom) the ranking of the five most-used techniques. These same techniques were among those most extensively used in P/OM by 73 of the largest U.S. corporations sampled in one survey, and the 78 respondents in another.[9] These findings are mirrored in functional areas throughout the organization, where OR techniques are also widely used.[10]

TABLE 3.2
The use of operations research (OR) as a percentage of sample size*

Study	Year	Sample size	Use of OR in total organization	Use of OR in production
AMA	1957	631	51%	24%
Hovey and Wagner	1958	90	68	32
Schumacher and Smith	1964	65	75	68
Gaither	1975	275	48	—

*Modified from Norman Gaither, "The Adoption of Operations Research Techniques by Manufacturing Organizations," *Decision Sciences* 6, no. 4 (October 1975), pp. 799 and 803.

[9]W.N. Ledbetter and J.F. Cox, "Are OR Techniques Being Used?" *Industrial Engineering* 19, no. 2 (February 1977), pp. 19-21. T.B. Green, W.B. Newsom, and S.R. Jones, "A Survey of the Application of Quantitative Techniques to Production/Operations Management in Large Corporations," *Academy of Management Journal* 20, no. 4 (December 1977), pp. 669-76.

[10]R.H. McClure and R.E. Miller, "The Application of Operations Research in Commercial Banking Companies," *Interfaces* 9, no. 2, pt. 1 (February 1979), pp. 24-29. G. Thomas and J. DaCosta, "A Sample Survey of Corporate Operations Research," *Interfaces* 9, no. 4 (August 1979), pp. 102-11.

TABLE 3.3
The number of firms applying operations research techniques to manufacturing problems*

Manufacturing problems	Operations research techniques: Linear or nonlinear programming	Computer simulation	PERT, CPM	Exponential smoothing, regression analysis	Queuing theory	Total number of firms	Rank
Production planning and control	41	25	40	23	7	136	1
Project planning and control	1	4	85	1	0	91	2
Inventory analysis and control	20	29	5	22	8	84	3
Analyzing capital investment projects	21	25	5	5	0	56	4
Quality control	15	12	2	27	0	56	4
Maintenance planning	8	5	33	3	2	51	6
Capacity allocation	29	13	0	2	2	46	7
Product mix	31	11	0	2	0	44	8
Material allocation	19	14	1	4	0	38	9
Equipment design analysis	4	21	2	4	1	32	10
Facility location	13	9	6	2	1	31	11
Line balancing	14	6	1	4	6	31	11
Various other	58	46	4	10	37	—	—
Total	274	220	184	109	64		
Rank	1	2	3	4	5		

*Modified from Gaither, p. 809.

The top four techniques in Table 3.3 are discussed in this book: linear programming in Chapters 6 and 7, simulation in the supplement to this chapter, PERT-CPM in Chapter 13, and exponential smoothing in Chapter 5. We discuss these techniques when they naturally apply to a situation in operations, rather than separately as isolated exercises.

Results Achieved and Problems Encountered

Perhaps the question of whether or not to use operations research can be answered by firms that use it. Table 3.4 shows the results of a study of such firms; you can see that the majority felt that the results were either good or excellent. The vast majority (87.1%) of the firms surveyed also believed that the costs of MS/OR are justified by the resulting benefits. Still, many organizations report little or no use of OR—and even when it is used, success is not assured and problems are encountered. Some major difficulties, both technical and behavioral, are summarized in Table 3.5.

TABLE 3.4
Effectiveness ratings and major benefits from implementing management science (MS) and operations research (OR)*

MS/OR effectiveness			
Poor	Fair	Good	Excellent
0%	30.6%	53.3%	16.1%

Major benefit from MS/OR implementation	
The methodology creates useful data	82.3%
Helps define the problem	74.2%
Helps identify relevant policies	61.3%
Provides a useful test laboratory	51.6%

*Modified from G. A. Forgionne, "Corporate Management Science Activities: An Update," *Interfaces* 13, no. 3 (June 1983), pp. 21–22.

TABLE 3.5
Problems encountered in using operations research (OR)*

Benefits of OR are not understood by managers
Managers lack awareness and understanding of OR techniques
Managers are not exposed to OR early in their training
Required data are difficult to quantify or don't exist
Few managers are trained in OR use
Users lack commitment
Change is resisted (from old methods to OR)
OR methods are difficult to sell to management
Time to apply OR to meet decision deadline is inadequate
Poor communication between analyst and management.

*These reasons, commonly cited by managers and OR personnel, are summarized from the following sources: Green, Newsom, and Jones, p. 673; Gaither, p. 811; Thomas and DaCosta, pp. 108–9; H. J. Watson and P. G. Marett, "A Survey of Management Science Implementation Problems," *Interfaces* 9, no. 4 (August 1979), pp. 124–27; and G. A. Forgionne, p. 22.

SUMMARY

This chapter has highlighted the role of analysis in P/OM. Analysis is often needed to solve complex decision problems that arise in managing the conversion process. Relying heavily on the development and use of models, formal analysis requires careful selection of decision criteria. The choice of criteria depends on the type of problem under consideration. Breakeven analysis is helpful in structuring the relationships among volume, costs, and revenues of an organization; decision tree analysis can be used in many multistage problems.

In conclusion, we wish to emphasize that analysis usually does not dictate the final decision. Real problems are so complex that a combination of judgment, experience, and analysis is often necessary to solve them adequately. Practitioners of analysis recommend a formal analysis of subcomponents tempered by real world considerations; such a combination encourages a practical conclusion. Once the conclusion has been reached, managers can decide what criteria to use, what goals to reach for, what plan to follow in future decisions. A plan of action evolves.

Sometimes formal analysis is done by the P/OM manager. In other cases, the analysis effort is so complex that a specialized staff is created to perform it. In these cases, the manager must understand what can be expected from the staff; he or she must guide its overall efforts and evaluate its recommendations from the broader perspective of the total P/OM efforts of the organization.

CASE

Safety Sight Company

Safety Sight Company owns two plants that manufacture bicycle headlights. The Edgewater plant has been fully operational in recent years; the Garland facility has been shut down for the past two years. Management anticipates a large increase in demand for bicycle lights, and future production plans are now being developed. Revenue from the sale of headlights is expected to average $8 per unit over the foreseeable future.

The Edgewater plant has been operating a single shift with fixed costs of $2.5 million and a production capacity of 500,000 units annually. Unit variable costs have been $1.60 for this range of output. Greater output volume could be achieved by starting up a second shift. If that were done, it is estimated that unit variable costs on the new shift would be either $6.3, $5.7, or $5.1 with probabilities of .09, .33, and .58, respectively. Production capacity on the second shift would be 500,000 units annually.

To achieve larger volumes of output, the Garland facility could be reopened. The exact annual fixed cost of operating this facility is unknown. Three recent estimates were: $1.8, $1.65, and $1.55 million with probabilities of .4, .5, and .1, respectively. Unit variable cost for first shift operations is expected to be $1.60, the same as for the Edgewater plant. The first shift capacity of the Garland plant is expected to be 500,000 headlights per year.

Management is considering two alternatives: operate the Edgewater plant on two shifts, keeping the Garland plant shut down; or operate both plants on a single shift. Management is sure either alternative will provide capacity to meet the new expected demand. What should they do?

REVIEW AND DISCUSSION QUESTIONS

1. Discuss the advantages and disadvantages of these models in operations management:
   (a) verbal
   (b) schematic
   (c) iconic
   (d) mathematical
2. The stages of the decision-making process are presented in Figure 3.2. For each stage, identify the roles of the operations analyst and the operations manager.

3. By definition, models are incomplete representations of the things being modeled. Discuss the reasons for this fact and its implications from a mangerial point of view.
4. Develop a model of the operations function of a large apartment complex or a dormitory. Discuss the ways in which your model is useful and the ways it is limited.
5. What criteria do you think should be used to evaluate the operations of a university's school of business?
6. Show the similarities and differences among the criteria you would recommend for evaluating the operations functions in a neighborhood dry cleaning establishment and a toy manufacturing company.
7. Explain in detail the meaning and limitations of the expected value decision criterion.
8. Give examples illustrating personal everyday decision problems under conditions of certainty, risk, and uncertainty.
9. What are the problems of data and information availability you might have in conducting a decision tree analysis?
10. Describe and show differences among: decision, decision alternative, chance event, state of nature, and outcome.
11. How would the results of a decision tree analysis be affected if people made erroneous probability estimates? Demonstrate with an example.
12. In many organizations, operations managers employ an analysis staff that includes operations research specialists.
    (a) What are some potential sources of conflict between manager and analyst?
    (b) What actions could be taken to reduce this conflict?
13. Discuss the role relationships between the operations analyst and various managers throughout the organization.
14. To what extent are management science and operations research used in organizations? What factors tend to encourage or discourage their use?
15. Some managers have expressed disappointment with the results of management science/operations research efforts in their organizations. What might be the causes of these disappointing results?

PROBLEMS

Solved Problems

1. A manufacturer of plastic moldings incurs a material and labor cost of \$1.75 to produce each molding. Fixed costs of operation are \$390,000 per year, and moldings are sold for \$3.10 each. Develop both a schematic and a mathematical model of the volume-cost-revenue relationships. Using both models, determine the breakeven volume of operations.

   The schematic model and its breakeven solution are shown in Figure 3.8.

   Mathematically, total costs and total revenues depend on how many moldings (x) are produced and sold as follows:

$$
\begin{aligned}
TC &= FC + (x)(VC) = \$390{,}000 + (x)(\$1.75) \\
\text{and} \quad TR &= (x)(\$3.10) \quad \text{where} \\
FC &= \text{fixed cost of operation,} \\
VC &= \text{variable cost (material and labor) per molding,} \\
TC &= \text{total cost, and} \\
TR &= \text{total revenue.}
\end{aligned}
$$

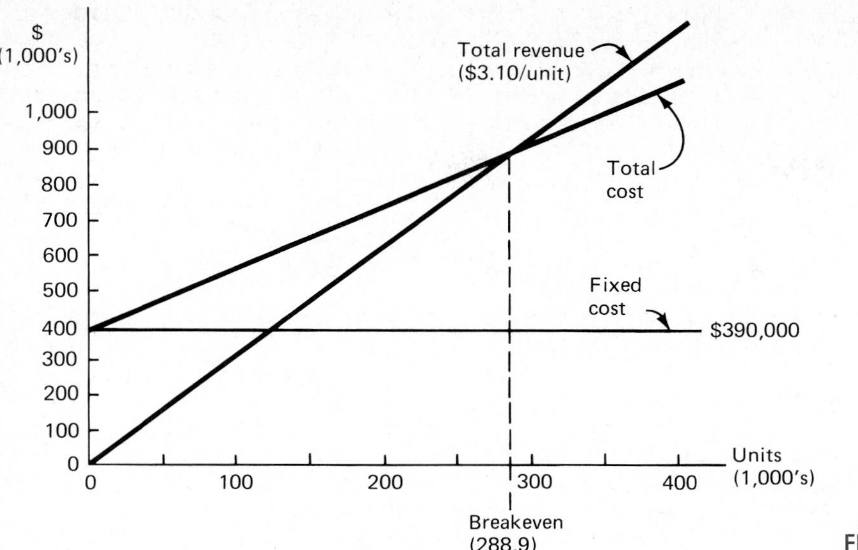

FIGURE 3.8

At the breakeven (BE) volume, TR = TC:

$$(x)(\$3.10) = \$390{,}000 + (x)(\$1.75);$$
$$(x)(\$3.10 - \$1.75) = \$390{,}000; \text{ and}$$
$$x_{BE} = \frac{390{,}000}{1.35} = 288{,}889 \text{ units.}$$

2. Solve the decision tree shown in Figure 3.9, in which costs are shown at the ends of the branches.

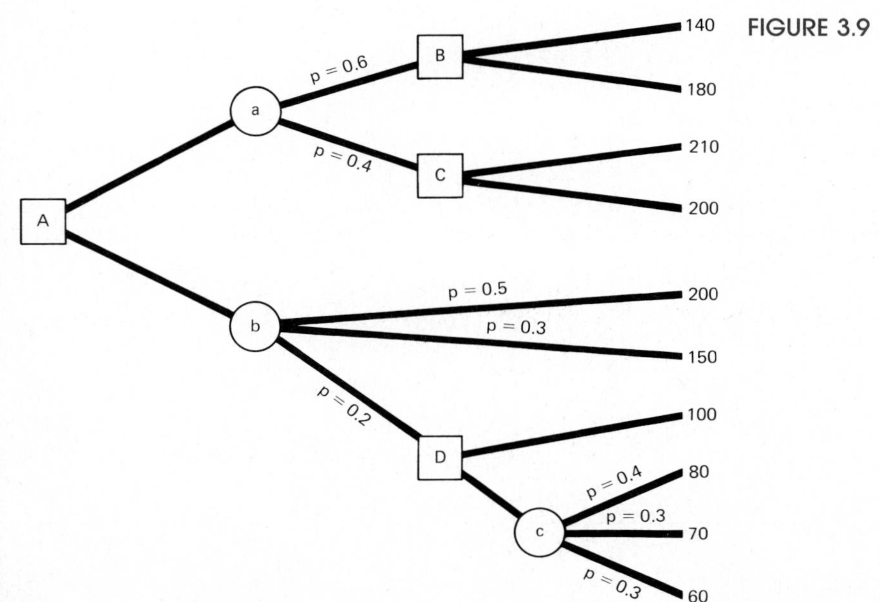

FIGURE 3.9

The solution, shown in Figure 3.10, is found by first eliminating the undesirable alternatives (branches) for decision nodes *B* and *C*. Next, the expected costs of chance-event nodes *a* and *c* are calculated (the resulting expected cost is recorded above each node in the solution diagram). Now the most undesirable alternative for decision node *D* is eliminated and the expected cost of chance-event node *b* can be calculated. Finally, the most desirable alternative at decision node *A* is revealed.

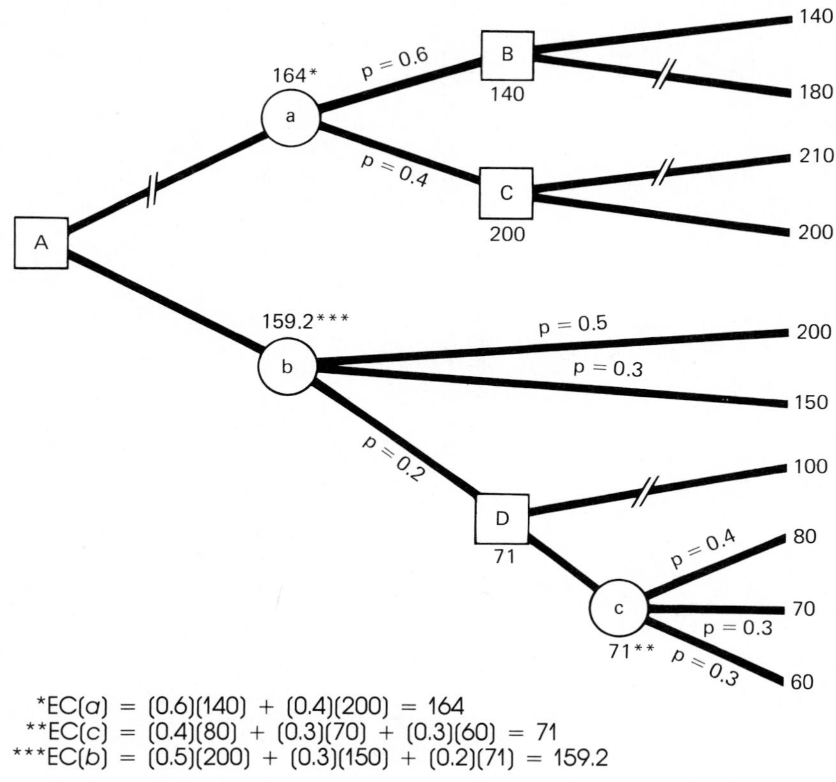

*EC(*a*) = (0.6)(140) + (0.4)(200) = 164
**EC(*c*) = (0.4)(80) + (0.3)(70) + (0.3)(60) = 71
***EC(*b*) = (0.5)(200) + (0.3)(150) + (0.2)(71) = 159.2

FIGURE 3.10

3. A cab company is considering three makes of autos, *A, B,* or *C,* to add to its taxi fleet. The daily operating cost of each make depends on the daily usage rate (demand) as shown below.

Cost per day of operation

	Daily usage rate		
Make	Low	Moderate	High
A	$100	$200	$300
B	190	200	220
C	150	190	230

Which make is best according to the minimax criterion? According to the insufficient reason criterion? If the probabilities of low, moderate, and high usage are 0.5, 0.2, and 0.3 respectively, what is the best make on an expected cost basis?

Since Make *B* offers a lower maximum cost ($220) than the other makes, *B* is best on a minimax basis (the minimum of the maximums). The insufficient reason criterion assigns equal probabilities (0.333) to each usage rate, resulting in expected costs as follows:

$$EC(A) = \$100(0.333) + \$200(0.333) + \$300(0.333) = \$200/\text{day}$$
$$EC(B) = \$190(0.333) + \$200(0.333) + \$220(0.333) = \$203.33/\text{day}$$
$$EC(C) = \$150(0.333) + \$190(0.333) + \$230(0.333) = \$190/\text{day}$$

Alternative *C* is best on the basis of insufficient reason.

If the probabilities stated earlier are available, the expected values, shown below, indicate that make *A* is best:

$$EC(A) = (0.5)(\$100) + (0.2)(\$200) + (0.3)(\$300) = \$180/\text{day}$$
$$EC(B) = (0.5)(\$190) + (0.2)(\$200) + (0.3)(\$220) = \$201/\text{day}$$
$$EC(C) = (0.5)(\$150) + (0.2)(\$190) + (0.3)(\$230) = \$182/\text{day}.$$

Reinforcing Fundamentals

4. A delivery company is considering the purchase of a used truck. Its useful service life is estimated to be 3 years with a probability of 0.1, 4 years with a probability of 0.4, 5 years with a probability of 0.3, and 6 years with probability of 0.2. What is the expected useful life of the used truck?
5. A local entertainment company is contemplating construction of a new theater. Three location sites are under consideration, and their relative attractiveness depends on the number of competing theaters that will be built in the next 5 years. Four possible industry growth rates, their chances of occurrence, and anticipated 5-year profitability (in thousands of dollars) are shown in this table. Which site is best on an expected value basis?

Five-year profitability

	Industry growth rate			
Site	Low	Medium	High	Very high
A	$200	$120	$ 40	$ 8
B	160	240	120	40
C	40	80	200	280
Probability	0.4	0.3	0.2	0.1

6. Four alternative manufacturing methods are being considered for a new product. Profitability, which depends on method of manufacture and level of consumer acceptance, is anticipated as shown here.

Profits (thousands of dollars) from new product

Manufacturing method	Projected consumer acceptance			
	Low	Moderate	High	Very high
I	$100	$200	$300	$600
II	175	300	400	500
III	250	300	350	425
IV	100	300	400	450
Probability	0.25	0.35	0.20	0.20

(a) What is the best manufacturing method according to each of these criteria:
1. expected value
2. maximin
3. maximax
4. insufficient reason

(b) Which manufacturing method should be selected? Why?

7. Which of the decision alternatives in the following table is the most attractive? Why? (Outcomes are expressed in terms of operating costs in thousands of dollars.)

Decision alternatives	Chance event		
	E_a	E_b	E_c
I	$700	$200	$200
II	300	300	300
III	200	100	700
Probability	0.2	0.5	0.3

8. Suresnap fishing reels require variable production costs of $11 per unit. Fixed costs are $250,000 for first shift operations, which have a capacity of 30,000 reels. Distributors purchase reels for $20 each. Suresnap can double capacity by operating a second shift at an additional semi-fixed cost of $80,000, and variable production costs of $12/unit. Using a schematic model, evaluate the alternative levels of plant operation.
9. Evaluate the decision tree shown in Figure 3.11, for which costs are shown at the branch ends.
10. Management, facing a two-stage decision problem, wants to pick a sequence of actions to maximize profits. The first decision (I) has three alternatives: *A*, with a profit of $75; *B*, with a profit of $90; and *C*, with a profit of $110. The chance event following the initial decision has either two or three states of nature, depending on the initial decision. The probability of each state is shown in Figure 3.12 (see page 108.) Thereafter, a second decision, resulting in further profits, must be made. What is the best decision sequence?

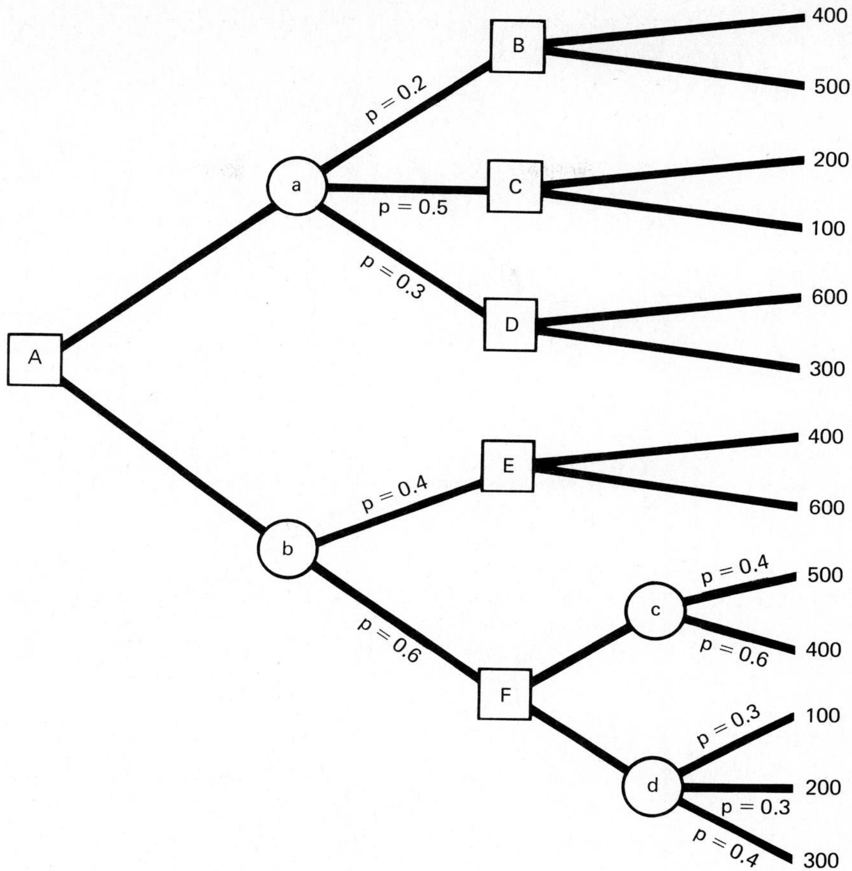

FIGURE 3.11

Challenging Exercises

11. Watersight Tours, Inc. is deciding whether to hire an additional boat mechanic or to just keep their one current mechanic. Their two tourist boats have daily failure probabilities of .04 and .08 respectively. With one boat out of commission the company loses $300 per hour; the operating loss is $800 per hour when both boats are inoperable. The time for a mechanic to repair one boat is 4 hours. Two mechanics, working together, can repair a boat in 3 hours. The second mechanic can be employed at a daily wage of $150. Should Watersight hire the second mechanic? If so, how should the mechanics be used if both boats fail simultaneously?

12. A trucking company has decided to replace its existing truck fleet. Supplier *A* will provide the needed trucks at a cost of $700,000. Supplier *B* will charge $500,000, but its vehicles may require more maintenance and repair than those from supplier *A*. The trucking company is also considering modernizing its maintenance and repair facility either by renovation or renovation and expansion. Although expansion is generally more expensive than renovation alone, it enables greater efficiency of

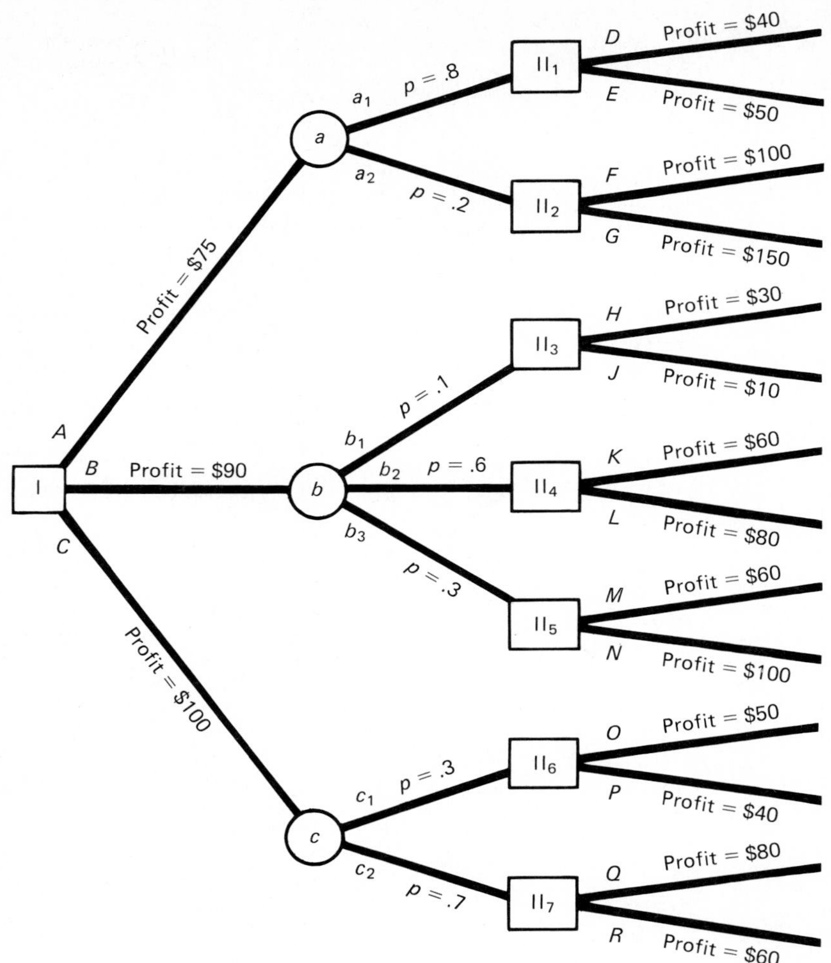

FIGURE 3.12
Two-stage decision problem

repair and therefore reduced annual operating costs of the facility. The estimated costs of renovation alone and renovation and expansion, as well as the ensuing operating costs, depend on the quality of the trucks that are purchased and the extent of the maintenance they require. The trucking company has therefore decided on the following strategy: purchase the trucks now; observe their maintenance requirements for one year; then make the decision as to whether to renovate or to renovate and expand. During the one-year observation period, the company will get additional information about expected maintenance requirements during years 2 through 5.

If the trucks are purchased from supplier *A*, first year maintenance costs are expected to be low ($30,000) with a probability of 0.7 or moderate ($40,000) with a probability of 0.3. If they are purchased from supplier *B*, maintenance costs will be ($30,000) with a probability of 0.3, ($40,000) with a probability of 0.6, or high ($50,000) with a probability of 0.1. The costs of renovation, shown here, depend on the first year's maintenance experience.

One-year maintenance requirements	Renovation costs	Renovation and expansion costs
Low	$150,000	$300,000
Moderate	200,000	500,000
High	300,000	700,000

Expected maintenance costs for years 2 through 5 can best be estimated after observing the maintenance requirements for the first year.

Maintenance costs for years 2 through 5

		Renovate		Renovate and expand	
Supplier	First year maintenance	Maintenance years 2 through 5		Maintenance years 2 through 5	
		Low	Moderate	Low	Moderate
A	Low	$100,000	$150,000	$40,000	$60,000
	Moderate	100,000	150,000	40,000	60,000
		Moderate	High	Moderate	High
B	Low	150,000	200,000	50,000	90,000
	Moderate	150,000	200,000	50,000	90,000
	High	250,000	300,000	70,000	100,000

Probabilities of various maintenance levels in years 2 through 5 depend on the types of trucks selected and the maintenance experience during year 1:

Probabilities of maintenance effort, years 2 through 5

Supplier	First year maintenance	Maintenance level, years 2–5		
		Low	Moderate	High
A	Low	.7	.3	—
	Moderate	.4	.6	—
B	Low	—	.5	.5
	Moderate	—	.4	.6
	High	—	.3	.7

Use decision tree analysis to determine the decision strategy that minimizes expected costs.

13. Scott is thirteen years old and in algebra class in junior high. He wants to mow lawns this summer, but he needs to repair his father's old mower for $50 or buy a new mower for $200 in order to do so. It takes about one-half gallon of gasoline (which costs $1.40 per gallon) to mow a lawn. Scott believes he can average in revenue $10 per lawn mowed and wants to mow one, two, or three lawns throughout the summer. He figures he can mow a yard twelve times. Scott knows he should be able to solve this problem with algebra, but would rather just get two lawns and buy a new mower than try to figure it out. Use decision trees and breakeven to explain to Scott his economic alternatives.
14. Two engineering students from State University have formed a company, Technological Systems, Inc. (TSI). TSI is considering development of a perpetual motion machine (PMM) or an air fueled internal combustion engine (AFICE). TSI wants to decide which project to start now. If it develops PMM, the first-year development costs are expected to be low ($15,000) with a probability of .5 or moderate ($20,000) with a probability of .5. If TSI develops AFICE, first-year development costs are expected to be low ($15,000), moderate ($20,000), or high ($40,000) with equal probabilities of each. Depending upon first-year development costs, the company will continue the initial project or drop it and start a new project. In either case, some immediate one-time expenses are expected:

First-year development costs	Decision to continue only PMM or AFICE	Decision to start new projects
Low	$10,000	$15,000
Moderate	15,000	20,000
High	20,000	25,000

All second-year development costs for PMM or AFICE are expected to be $20,000. In year two the new project can expect low development costs of $10,000 with .2 probability or high development costs of $30,000 with a .8 probability. Set up a decision tree for TSI's situation. Which product development strategy is best?

15. Life Long Support Systems (LLSS) is considering adding a second and third shift to meet expected increases in demand this year. Fixed costs are estimated to be:

Shift	Total capacity	Fixed costs
One	100,000	$200,000
Two	200,000	250,000
Three	300,000	325,000

Further, accounting has estimated variable costs and marketing estimated demand as:

Variable unit cost	Probability of that cost	Demand (units)	Probability of that demand
$ 5	.05	50,000	.2
15	.30	100,000	.3
20	.30	150,000	.3
25	.30	200,000	.1
35	.05	250,000	.1

The unit selling price is $50 for all volumes.

(a) Calculate the breakeven volume(s) and interpret for management.

(b) Recommend to management the number of shifts it should schedule. Justify your choice, indicating expected profit for your decision.

GLOSSARY

Algorithm A procedure consisting of a series of steps that result in achieving a goal.

Breakeven analysis Graphical or algebraic representation of the relationships among volume, cost, and revenues in an organization.

Certainty In decision problems, a condition in which the state of nature is known for sure for each alternative.

Chance event A happening with several possible outcomes, one of which will occur; the decision maker has no knowledge of or control over which outcome will occur.

Criterion Measure of desirability used to distinguish between good and bad alternatives.

Decision tree Device used to structure and analyze a decision problem; used to lay out systematically the sequence of decision points, alternatives, and chance outcomes in diagram form.

Expected value Averaging technique in which each possible outcome is weighted by its chances of occurring.

Experimentation Systematic manipulation of variables used to establish cause-effect relationships.

Heuristic algorithm Simplification procedure in which a set of rules is systematically applied in order to find a satisfactory problem solution.

Iconic model A scaled physical replica of an object or process.

Management science Scientific approach to the study of management, often using a mathematical modeling orientation; frequently used interchangeably with "operations research".

Model A representation of something real; it shows relationships among variables and can be used to predict or explain.

Operations research An interdisciplinary approach to the systematic research of operations.

Optimization algorithm Solution procedure that ensures finding the best solution to an optimization model.

Relevant variables System components, the values of which will be changed depending on the decision that is made.

Risk In decision problems, a condition in which the ultimate state of nature is not known for sure, but probabilities are known for each state of nature.

Schematic model Pictorial or graphical representation of an object or system.

Sequential decision problem Decision problem consisting of a series of interrelated decisions.

States of nature In decision problems, different conditions that can occur as a result of an uncontrollable chance event.

Uncertainty In decision problems, a condition in which the probabilities of the states of nature are not known.

Validity In modeling, the process of assuring that the model adequately reflects the system being studied.

SELECTED READINGS

Adams, J. R. and L. A. Swanson. "Information Processing Behavior and Estimating Accuracy in Operations Management." *Academy of Management Journal* 19, no. 1 (March 1976), pp. 98–110.

Bass, B. M. *Organizational Decision Making*. Homewood, Ill.: Richard D. Irwin, Inc., 1983.

Ebert, R. J. and T. R. Mitchell. *Organizational Decision Processes: Concepts and Analysis*. New York: Crane, Russak and Co., Inc., 1975.

Fishburn, P. C. "Decision Under Uncertainty: An Introductory Exposition." *The Journal of Industrial Engineering* 17, no. 7 (July–August 1966), pp. 341–53.

Forgionne, G. A. "Corporate Management Science Activities: An Update." *Interfaces* 13, no. 3 (June 1983), pp. 20–23.

Gaither, Norman. "The Adoption of Operations Research Techniques by Manufacturing Organizations." *Decision Sciences* 6, no. 4 (October 1975), pp. 797–813.

Green, T. B., W. B. Newsom, and S. R. Jones. "A Survey of the Application of Quantitative Techniques to Production/Operations Management in Large Corporations." *Academy of Management Journal* 20, no. 4 (December 1977), pp. 669–76.

Huber, G. P. *Managerial Decision Making*. Glenview, Ill.: Scott, Foresman and Company, 1980.

Ledbetter, W. N. and J. F. Cox. "Are OR Techniques Being Used?" *Industrial Engineering* 19, no. 2 (February 1977), pp. 19–21.

McClure, R. H. and R. E. Miller. "The Application of Operations Research in Commercial Banking Companies." *Interfaces* 9, no. 2, pt. 1 (February 1979), pp. 24–29.

Michael, G. C. "A Review of Heuristic Programming." *Decision Sciences* 3, no. 3 (July 1972), pp. 74–100.

Morris, W. T. "On the Art of Modeling." *Management Science* 13, no. 2 (August 1967), pp. 707–17.

Rosenzweig, J. E. "Managers and Management Scientists (Two Cultures)." *Business Horizons* 10, no. 3 (Fall 1967), pp. 79–86.

Thomas, G. and J. DaCosta. "A Sample Survey of Corporate Operations Research." *Interfaces* 9, no. 4 (August 1979), pp. 102–11.

Watson, H. J. and P. G. Marett. "A Survey of Management Science Implementation Problems." *Interfaces* 9, no. 4 (August 1979), pp. 124–27.

SUPPLEMENT TO CHAPTER 3

COMPUTER SIMULATION

Simulation is a commonly used technique in operations analysis.[1] Our purposes in this section are to present some fundamental simulation terminology and to introduce the "Monte Carlo" technique, which is used extensively in computer simulations.

EXAMPLE

The manager of a drive-in banking facility is concerned about complaints from customers regarding the length of time they must wait to complete their transactions. A management consultant has offered a proposal that promises

[1]The use of simulation to improve efficiency, productivity, and sales in Burger King Corporation's restaurants is described in W. Swart and L. Donno, "Simulation Modeling Improves Operations, Planning, and Productivity of Fast Food Restaurants," *Interfaces* 11, no. 6 (December 1981), pp. 35–47.

to speed up services. For a fee of $5,000, the consultant will analyze the job content of the bank teller and retrain the teller. He promises this will reduce average time to service a customer by at least 10 percent. The manager of the bank feels that this expenditure is not warranted unless it results in reducing average customer waiting time by at least 15 percent, and she assigns an analyst the task of determining whether or not the consultant should be hired.

The first step taken by the analyst is to decide what *components* of the system to include in a model. In this case, the analyst selects three basic components, one representing customer arrivals, one representing teller services to customers, and one representing customer departures. These are shown in Figure S3.1.

FIGURE S3.1
Components of a drive-in subsystem

Using this simplified representation of the bank, the analyst:

1. builds a model that includes the components of Figure S3.1,
2. gathers appropriate data to represent the behavior of arrivals and services as they now exist,
3. runs the model to ensure that the average simulated waiting time closely approximates the current real average waiting time,
4. modifies the "teller services" component of the model to reflect the improvement in teller service time that is expected from the consultant's proposal,
5. reruns the simulation under these new conditions to measure average waiting time, and
6. compares the average customer waiting times under the existing and new service time conditions.

Model Building

The model begins to operate at a reference point called *time zero,* the arrival time of the first imaginary customer. The simulator records the time of this arrival. Since no other customers are being serviced, the new arrival does not have to wait, and service begins immediately. How long will it take? The simulator generates a representative service time (we will discuss this shortly). When the service time has elapsed, the customer leaves the system. While the first customer was being serviced, however, a second or even a third customer may have arrived. If so, they would have had to wait in line while the first customer was being serviced. The simulator keeps track of waiting times for each customer. Figure S3.2 illustrates a flow of arrivals and services on a time scale similar to that used in the simulator.

This figure shows that the first customer arrived at time zero, did not have to wait for service to begin, and ended the transaction at time 2.5. The

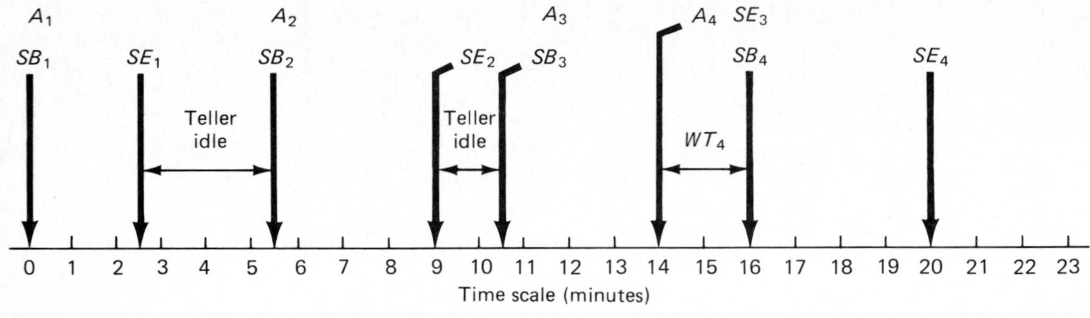

A_i = Time of arrival of customer i	SE_i = Time at which service ends on customer i
SB_i = Time at which service begins on customer i	WT_i = Length of waiting time before service begins for customer i

FIGURE S3.2
Flow of simulation events: time-phased

second customer did not arrive until time 5.5. Service was begun immediately and was completed at time 9. At time 10.5, the third customer arrived and began a transaction at the teller's window. Meanwhile, at time 14 customer four arrived and had to wait in line. At time 16, customer three left, and customer four began a transaction. Customer four had to wait two minutes before beginning the transaction with the teller. At time 20, customer four was served and the queue (waiting line) was empty again. Using this general approach, the analyst intends to simulate many (say 2,000) customer arrivals and services, always recording and accumulating waiting times. At the conclusion of the simulation, the analyst can calculate the average waiting time per customer.

How does the simulator generate arrival times and service times for each simulated customer? The analyst must build into the model a procedure based on real world arrival and service data. Since we want a simulated pattern of the real drive-in window, the analyst sets up a procedure for observing a large sample of customers (say 1,000) at the actual drive-in facility. He records the elapsed time between arrivals of successive customers, the length of time required to service each customer, and customer waiting times. The results of part of this data-gathering effort are shown in Figure S3.3.

Although time between arrivals varied widely, the analyst groups the data into only seven classification intervals and uses the midpoint of the interval to represent the entire class. The same is true for the observed service times. The two resulting relative frequency distributions (frequency is symbolized $f(x)$ on the figures) are expected to provide adequate approx-

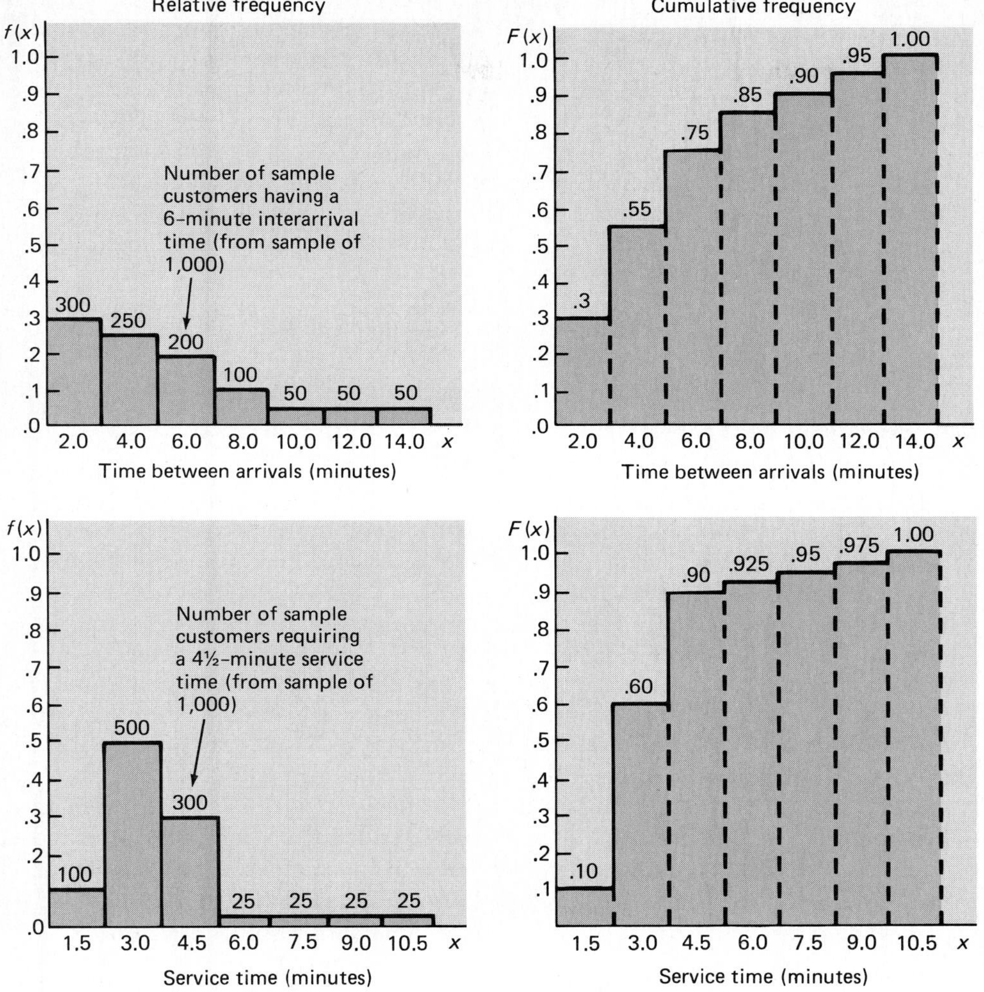

FIGURE S3.3
Relative and cumulative frequency distributions for arrivals and service times

imations of arrival and service patterns. These distributions are built into the simulation model. They are used in the model to generate the arrival time and the time required to service each customer by a procedure known as the Monte Carlo technique.

Monte Carlo Technique

The objective of the Monte Carlo technique is to have the simulator select service times (and arrival times) that fall into a specified pattern. We want the service time for our next simulated customer, for example, to be randomly selected from the service time relative frequency distribution in Figure S3.3. If we randomly select service times for each of many simulated customers, the simulator will replicate the pattern of service times that occurs in the real system. We do not know in advance whether the next service time will be 1.5, 3, 4.5, 6, 7.5, 9, or 10.5 minutes. Any of these is possible, but we want some to be selected randomly more often than others because some occur in real life more often than others. In fact, we want our simulator to have a .1 chance of selecting a 1.5 minute service time, a .5 chance of a 3 minute service time, and so on. The Monte Carlo technique accomplishes this goal in two steps:

1. the relative frequency distribution is converted into a *cumulative* frequency (shown as $F(x)$ in Figure S3.3), and
2. uniformly distributed random numbers are used to enter the cumulative distribution.

A cumulative distribution for service time and one for time between arrivals are shown on the right side of Figure S3.3. Notice that the vertical axis of each cumulative distribution has a maximum value of 1.0 and a minimum value of 0.0. This range of values is subdivided among the various classification intervals in proportion to their chances of occurrence. Look at the cumulative frequency distribution for service time, for example. All the values on the vertical axis from 0.01 to 0.10 are associated with a service time of 1.5 minutes. This range of values (0.01 to 0.10) represents 1/10 (or 10 percent) of all possible values on the vertical axis. Similarly, all the values from 0.11 up to 0.60 on the vertical axis are associated with a service time of three minutes. This range of values (0.11 to 0.60) represents 5/10 (50 percent) of all possible values on the vertical axis. Continuing in this manner, we can see that each possible service time has been allocated a range of vertical axis values in proportion to its chances of being selected as the next service time. These allocations are listed in Table S3.1.

TABLE S3.1
Proportions of probabilities allocated to service times

Service time (minutes)	Range of vertical axis values	Percent of total vertical axis values
1.5	0.001–0.100	10.0
3.0	0.101–0.600	50.0
4.5	0.601–0.900	30.0
6.0	0.901–0.925	2.5
7.5	0.926–0.950	2.5
9.0	0.951–0.975	2.5
10.5	0.976–0.999 and 0.000	2.5
Total		100.0

The next step in the Monte Carlo technique involves the use of random numbers. In most computers, there are standard procedures for obtaining random numbers, and they are also readily available in tables (see Appendix D). Random numbers are uniformly distributed, each with an equal chance of occurring. For our example, we want to use random numbers between 0.000 and 0.999. Since 10 percent of the random numbers have values between .001 and .100, there is a 10 percent chance of drawing a random number between .001 and .100. Likewise, the chances of getting a random number whose value lies between .101 and .600 are 50 percent. This is fortunate because the total range of uniform number values coincides with the values on the vertical axis of the cumulative distribution. By randomly selecting one number from the uniform distribution, we can find the corresponding value on the vertical axis of the service time cumulative distribution. Then we can identify the service time associated with this value. Thus we have randomly selected the length of service time for the next customer. This procedure can be repeated with the cumulative distribution of time between arrivals to generate the time that will elapse between the arrivals of the last customer and the next customer. *This is the Monte Carlo method for generating random occurrences from a probability distribution.*

Let's examine the use of this technique by simulating the arrival and servicing of six drive-in customers. From a table of uniformly distributed random numbers, we have found the numbers shown below. In Table S3.2 are the calculations for each customer.

Uniform random numbers
.964 .843 .876 .847 .952 .476 .841 .943 .342 .682 .852

TABLE S3.2
Simulation data for six simulated customers

	Customer (i)					
Simulation characteristic	1	2	3	4	5	6
Time between arrivals of customers *i* and *i*-1	—	8.0	8.0	4.0	12.0	6.0
Time of arrival (on simulator clock)	0.0	8.0	16.0	20.0	32.0	38.0
Time when service begins (on simulator clock)	0.0	9.0	16.0	25.0	32.0	38.0
Customer waiting time	0.0	1.0	0.0	5.0	0.0	0.0
Length of service	9.0	4.5	9.0	4.5	3.0	4.5
Time when service ends (on simulator clock)	9.0	13.5	25.0	29.5	35.0	42.5

Total waiting time = 0.0 + 1.0 + 0.0 + 5.0 + 0.0 + 0.0
= 6.0 minutes
Average customer waiting time = 6.0/6 = 1.0 minutes

Begin by assuming that customer number 1 ($i = 1$) arrives at time zero on the simulator clock. We determine the length of time required to service this customer by using the first random number, .964. This number, when used in the cumulative service distribution (Figure S3.3), is associated with a service time of 9 minutes, which has been recorded in Table S3.2 as the length of service for the first customer. Service begins on this customer at time zero (no waiting), assuming no other customers were in the system when the first customer arrived. Service on this customer therefore ends at time 9.0 on the simulator clock. All the entries for customer 1 have now been filled in.

To determine the arrival time of the second customer ($i = 2$), we proceed down the random number list to .843. From the cumulative distribution of time between arrivals we find that .843 is associated with 8.0 minutes. This means that the second customer arrives 8.0 minutes after the arrival of the first customer. Thus, the second customer arrives at time 8.0 on the simulator clock. We can also determine the length of time that will be required to service the second customer by using the next random number, .876, in the cumulative service time distribution. If .876 represents a service time of 4.5 minutes for the second customer, at what time on the simulator clock does service begin? Not until time 9.0, when the teller finishes servicing the first customer. This means that the second customer must wait in line from time 8.0 until time 9.0, an elapsed waiting time of 1.0 minutes. Service to customer 2 is completed at time 13.5 on the simulated clock.

The same procedure may now be repeated for each customer in the simulation. Whenever a new arrival time is needed, the analyst merely selects the next random number on the list and uses it to enter the cumulative "time between arrivals" distribution. Then the next random number is used to generate a service time. The simulator clock is a convenient device for keeping track of the time-phased sequence of events. After simulating any desired number of customer transactions, the analyst can calculate the average waiting time for this system.

Using the Monte Carlo technique and a computer, the analyst in our example simulates 2,000 customers. The logic of the simulation model is shown in the flow diagram in Figure S3.4. The pattern of simulated waiting times closely parallels those that had been observed during the data gathering phase of analysis. The results of the analyst's simulation run (shown later) indicated an average customer waiting time of 4.22 minutes. The analyst concluded, therefore, that the model was a reasonable representation of the real system of drive-in operations. Notice that 4.22 minutes for 2,000 customers is considerably different from our hand calculated figure of 1.0 minutes for 6 customers in Table S3.2. Computers allow us to use large samples and reduce errors resulting from small sample sizes.

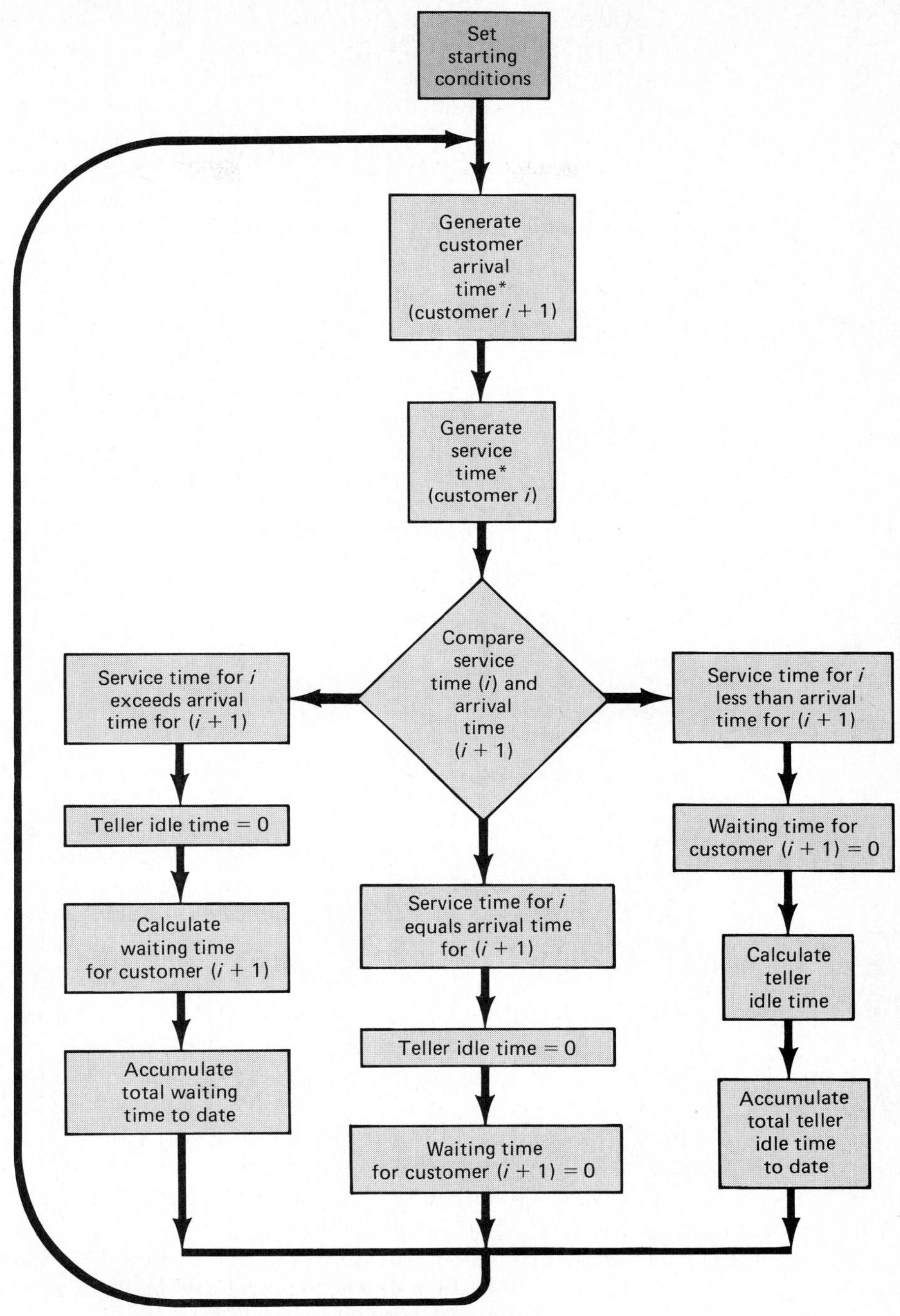

*This step requires use of the Monte Carlo Technique.

FIGURE S3.4
Flow diagram of simulation model logic

Modifying Teller Services and Waiting Times

The consultant's proposal guarantees a 10 percent or more reduction in service time. How would such a reduction affect average waiting time? To estimate the answer, the analyst uses the simulation model. He modifies the old service time distribution to reflect a 10 percent reduction in service times. In the modified distribution, each of the seven possible service times is adjusted to 90 percent of its original value. The modified service time distribution is then used in a new simulation run. Based on a run length of 2,000 customers, average waiting time was found to be 2.43 minutes.

TABLE S3.3
Summary data for 2,000 simulated bank customers

	Run 1 Original service time distribution	Run 2 Reduced service time distribution	Change
Number of simulated customers	2,000	2,000	—
Average waiting time per customer (minutes)	4.22	2.43	−42%
Average idle time of teller per customer served (minutes)	1.04	1.42	+36%

The results of the two simulation runs are summarized in Table S3.3. The analyst compared average customer waiting times under the existing and the proposed systems, and he found that if average service time is decreased by 10 percent, waiting time would be reduced by 42 percent. The analyst therefore recommended that the consultant be hired.

SUMMARY

Monte Carlo simulation involves the following steps:

1. Formulate the problem.
2. Collect and process real world data.
3. Formulate the simulation model.
4. Estimate the model parameters and conditions from the real world data.
5. Test the model. Make an initial evaluation of model adequacy.
6. Formulate a computer program.
7. Validate the model. Compare model results with historical data. Are predictions from the model reasonable?

8. Design and run the experiment to solve the problem formulated in step 1.
9. Interpret, analyze, and utilize the simulation results.

Each of these nine steps was used in the bank teller example. Although most real problems are more complex than the bank manager's, the solution steps are the same, and the Monte Carlo simulation technique can be expanded to handle even very complicated decision problems.

REVIEW AND DISCUSSION QUESTIONS

1. What are "model components" in a simulation model? How does the modeler decide which components to include in a model?
2. Give a detailed description of how the Monte Carlo technique works in a simulation model.
3. Simulation models vary in degree of sophistication, completeness, and detail. Using your own example, show how the sophistication decision affects the amount of real world data gathering effort necessary for using the model.
4. What factors should be considered in deciding on simulation run length?
5. Give an example showing how a simulation model can be developed for experimenting on different operating policies. In your example, describe the situation and identify the data requirements, your procedure for validating the model, and the output measures you have selected.
6. Develop a flow chart showing the logic of the model in question 5.

SELECTED READINGS

Markland, R. E. *Topics In Management Science*. 2nd ed. New York: John Wiley & Sons, 1983.

Meier, R. C., W. T. Newell, and H. L. Pazer. *Simulation in Business and Economics*. Englewood Cliffs, N.J.: Prentice-Hall, Inc., 1969.

Swart, W. and L. Donno. "Simulation Modeling Improves Operations, Planning, and Productivity of Fast Food Restaurants." *Interfaces* 11, no. 6 (December 1981), pp. 35–47.

4 Strategies and Plans for Operations

Westlake Hardware is a service company, a retail hardware chain with stores in five midwestern states. We've grown from an original family store founded in 1905, to ten outlets in 1975, and thirty four outlets by 1985. Our recent expansion rate has forced us to set company objectives to assure that all segments of our business are integrated and striving for the same goals. With thirty four stores and 700 employees spread over a large geographic area and covering diverse markets, it is essential that our operating managers understand our overall company objectives, strategies, and plans, but yet be allowed discretion in adapting to their local situation. This decentralized planning is necessary if we are to react appropriately to local market conditions. Attracting capable operations managers in retailing is essential for both effective planning and the subsequent implementation of those plans in fluid and unique markets.

Scott Westlake
President
Westlake Hardware Supply
Overland Park, Kansas

Planning for operations is the *establishment of a program of action for resource conversion into goods and services.* Before any actual resource conversion takes place, the operations manager identifies what resources will be necessary, determines how the conversion process will have to be designed, and anticipates any problems that may come up in operating the facility and delivering the product or service. He or she should also be alert to ideas for new products or services, remembering that the decision to introduce them is determined by market needs and economic realities. Westlake Hardware provides a good example of how the operating manager must understand the overall company objectives, strategies, and plans, yet be able to react to local markets, costs, and competition.

Once the conversion process has begun, planning must be integrated with the organizing and controlling functions. All are basic to the management process in operations. In their planning efforts, operations managers use modeling approaches and apply behavioral science techniques. The operations manager doesn't devote the first three hours of the day to planning, then two hours to organizing, then five to controlling. Rather, these functions are intertwined throughout the day and week. At one instant the Westlake's manager might be on the store floor taking corrective action to overcome some operating error (controlling). Suddenly he or she may realize the need to develop a better program of action for scheduling jobs (planning). Similarly, when the operations manager is determining the content of jobs (organizing), the need for replanning may be evident. These interfaces of planning, organizing, and controlling are depicted by their overlapping areas in Figure 4.1 (see page 124). Although this chapter concentrates on major planning concepts, you should remember that without careful controlling and organizing, even the best planning would do little good.

As you progress through this chapter, you should note the discussion flowing from the broad, strategic planning level to the more detailed, tactical planning level. After developing strategic planning, we consider such important planning concepts as analysis and standardization of work, and establishment of goals. How operations managers plan products and services is presented. The chapter then specifically relates strategies and planning concepts to the production/operations manager's job, suggesting practical guides to enhance his or her effectiveness.

STRATEGIC PLANNING

Strategic planning is the process of thinking through the current mission of the organization and *the current environmental conditions facing it, then setting forth a guide for tomorrow's decisions and results.* Strategic planning is built on fundamental concepts: that current decisions are based on *future* conditions and results, that strategic planning is a *process,* that it embodies a *philosophy,* and that it provides a *linkage* or structure within the organization.

Strategic Planning for Production and Operations

In the production or operations function, strategic planning is the broad, overall planning that precedes the more detailed operational planning. Executives who head the production and operations function are actively involved in strategic planning, developing plans that are consistent with both the firm's overall strategies and such other functions as marketing, finance-

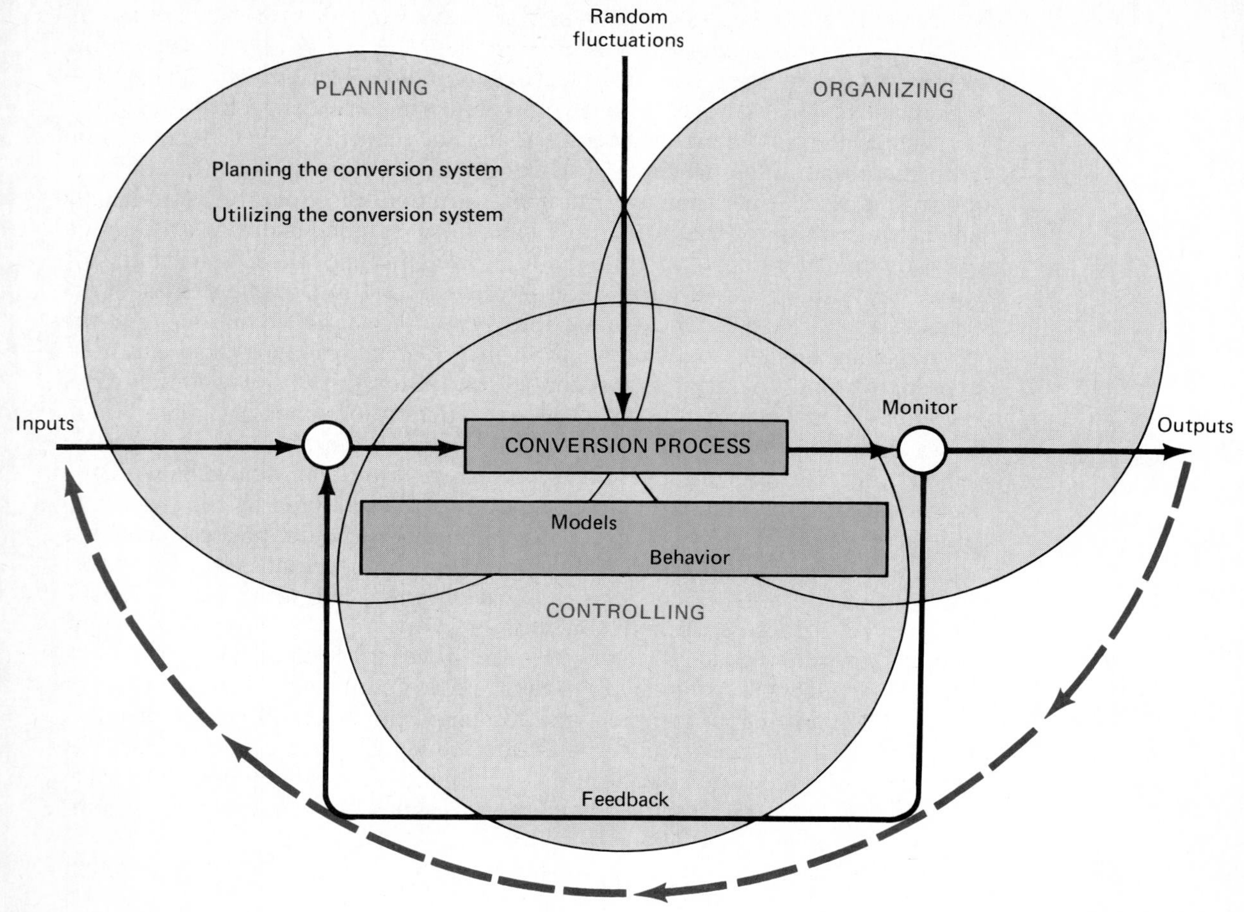

FIGURE 4.1
Major operations planning decisions

accounting, and engineering.[1] Once developed, production and operations strategic plans are the basis for (1) operational planning of *facilities* (design) and (2) operational planning for the *use* of these facilities. In this chapter and book we emphasize these last two planning efforts, but we must also stress that such operational planning should not be done in a vacuum. It must come under the umbrella of effective strategic planning.

[1]Skinner makes this point when he argues that manufacturing and corporate strategy must be linked through an integrating mechanism—manufacturing strategy. See Wickham Skinner, *Manufacturing in the Corporate Strategy* (New York: John Wiley and Sons, 1978), pp. 27–29.

Strategic Planning Approaches for Production/Operations One specialist on strategic planning suggests three contrasting modes of strategic planning: the entrepreneurial, the adaptive, and the planning modes.[2] In the entrepreneurial mode one strong, bold leader takes planning action on behalf of the production/operations function.[3] In the adaptive mode a manager's plan is formulated in a series of small, disjointed steps in reaction to a disjointed environment.[4] The planning model uses planning essentials (which will be discussed in this chapter and book) combined with the logical analysis of management science.[5]

There are many approaches to strategic planning. The key point we want to make is that operations strategies must be consistent with the overall strategies of the firm. Our observations lead us to the conclusion that operations typically utilize the overall corporate approach to strategic planning, with special modifications and, of course, a focus upon operations issues and opportunities. For that reason we want to focus on several general approaches to strategic planning; two forced choice models, the driving force approach, and a growth-market share matrix.

Strategic Planning Models #1 and #2: Forced Choice Models One of many planning models that has been used in strategic planning is a *forced choice* model, shown in Figure 4.2. In group sessions or individually, analysts assess environmental considerations together with the organization's current production/operations position, thus forcing management to develop strategic options for operations. This model is explained in considerable detail, including how to apply it using structured group techniques, elsewhere.[6]

A second forced choice model, one developed explicitly for manufacturing is illustrated in Figure 4.3. In this model, overall company strategy (3), environmental assessment (1, 5, 6), and the organization's position (2, 4) are evaluated (7). The result is a manufacturing strategy, expressed as manufacturing policies (8). Whether management uses this or other meth-

---

[2]Henry Mintzberg, "Strategy-Making in Three Modes," *California Management Review* 16, no. 2 (Winter 1973), pp. 44–53.

[3]See Peter F. Drucker, *Management: Tasks, Responsibilities, Practices* (New York: Harper and Row, 1974), Chapter 10, "Strategic Planning: The Entrepreneurial Skill" pp. 121–29.

[4]See, for example, R. M. Cyert and J. G. March, *A Behavioral Theory of the Firm* (Englewood Cliffs, N.J.: Prentice-Hall, 1963).

[5]See, for example, George A. Steiner, *Strategic Planning: What Every Manager Must Know* (New York, The Free Press, 1979). For a survey of corporate simulation model use in 346 companies, see Thomas H. Naylor and Horst Schauland, "A Survey of Users of Corporate Planning Models," *Management Science 22*, no. 9, May 1976, pp. 927–937.

[6]See Charles N. Greene, Everett E. Adam, Jr., and Ronald J. Ebert, *Management for Effective Performance*, (Englewood Cliffs, N.J.: Prentice-Hall, 1985), Chapter 17, "Strategic Planning."

FIGURE 4.2
A forced choice model of strategic planning for operations
Adapted from: Louis V. Gerstner, Jr., "Can Strategic Planning Pay Off?" *Business Horizons* December 1972.

ods of strategic planning, the point is that successful operational planning is dependent on effective strategic planning.[7]

Strategic Planning Model #3: The Driving Force Tregoe and Zimmerman[8] present a practical and straightforward approach to strategic planning based upon identification of a *driving force* for the organization. Relying on the real life consulting experiences of the authors, this approach looks at the questions executives should be asking in order to understand what their organization is now and what they want it to be in 5 to 10 years. Tregoe and Zimmerman's underlying belief is that an organization is the sum total of the products it offers and the geographic markets, market segments, or customer group it serves. The driving force is the primary determinant of the scope of future products and markets.

They suggest that the driving force comes from one of nine basic strategic areas.[9] All nine areas influence the nature and direction of organiza-

[7]For guides to successful manufacturing strategic planning and case implementation, see Wickham Skinner, *Manufacturing in the Corporate Strategy*. Booze, Allen, and Hamilton have a gap analysis based strategic planning model for production and operations. See Robert J. Mayer, "Applying Manufacturing Strategy Concepts to Practice," *Strategic Management of Operations: Proceedings of the First Annual Winter Conference of the Operations Management Association* (San Francisco, Ca., November 1982), pp. 44–50.

[8]Benjamin B. Tregoe and John W. Zimmerman, *Top Management Strategy: What It Is and How to Make It Work* (New York: Simon and Schuster, 1980).

[9]Ibid., page 43.

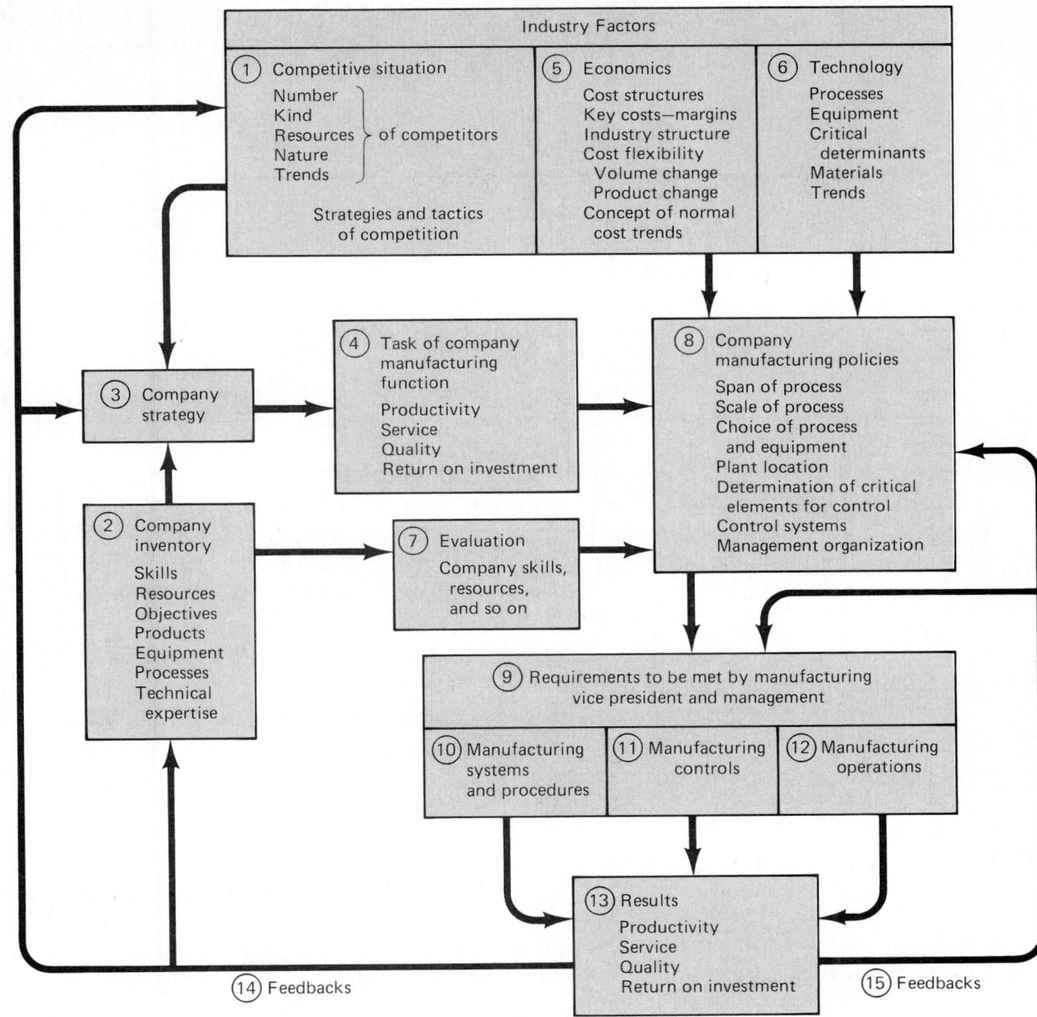

Key

1. What the others are doing
2. What we have or can get to compete with
3. How we can compete
4. What we must accomplish in manufacturing in order to compete
5. Economic constraints and opportunities common to the industry
6. Constraints and opportunities common to the technology.
7. Our resources evaluated
8. How we should set ourselves up to match resources, economics, and technology to meet the tasks required by our competitive strategy
9. The implementation requirements of our manufacturing policies
10. Basic systems in manufacturing (e.g., production planning, use of inventories, use of standards, and wage systems)
11. Controls of cost, quality, flows, inventory, and time
12. Selection of operations or ingredients critical to success (e.g., labor skills, equipment utilization, and yields)
13. How we are performing
14. Changes in what we have, effects on competitive situation, and review of strategy
15. Analysis and review of manufacturing operations and policies

FIGURE 4.3
A strategic planning and policy determination model for manufacturing

SOURCE: Wickham Skinner, *Manufacturing in the Corporate Strategy* (New York: John Wiley & Son, 1978), p. 36.

tions, but the executive team must select one as predominant (driving)—or what they desire to be predominant—for their organization. Strategic areas are:

Category	Strategic area
Products-Markets	Products offered Market needs
Capabilities	Technology Production capability Method of sale Method of distribution Natural resources
Results	Size-growth Return-profit

Each are described in detail with enough examples from company experiences to illustrate their classification. In a final section of the book Tregoe and Zimmerman illustrate how to make strategies happen by focusing on a *critical issues approach;* that is, they suggest that a critical list be prepared and worked which is directed at strengthening the driving force in the organization. Cargill, Inc. explained how this approach worked for them to a group of operations management executives and academics at a strategic planning conference.[10]

Perhaps the greatest value to this approach is in the simplicity of the driving force concept. Others support simplicity too, having found that organizations that perform most successfully strive for a few basic goals that are strongly supported and internalized by the firm's people and processes.[11]

Strategic Planning Model #4: The Boston Consulting Group's (BCG) Growth-Share Matrix The Boston Consulting Group, Inc. has proposed an explanation as to how companies perform based on two simple attributes—growth and market share.[12] In this approach, the *BCG Matrix* shows the results of a firm's strategy placing it in one of four categories, for example, stars, wildcats, cash cows, or dogs (see Figure 4.4.) This analytical approach suggests that a firm will be either (1) in growth markets—with high market share (stars); (2) in growth markets—with low market share (wild-

---

[10]See Sidney G. Burkett, "Using the Driving Force Strategic Concept at Cargill, Inc.," *Strategic Management of Operations: Proceedings of the First Annual Winter Conference of the Operations Management Association* (San Francisco, Ca., November 1982), pp. 39–43.

[11]Thomas J. Peters and Robert W. Waterman, *In Search of Excellence: Lessons from America's Best-Run Companies* (New York: Harper and Row, 1982.)

[12]See B. D. Henderson, *Henderson on Corporate Strategy* (Cambridge, MA: Abt Books, 1979); Donald C. Hombrick, Ian C. MacMillan, and Diana L. Day, "Strategic Attributes and Performance in the BCG Matrix—A PIMS—Based Analysis of Industrial Product Businesses," *Academy of Management Journal 25* no. 3 (September 1982), pp. 510–531; and Arnoldo C. Hax and Nicolas S. Majluf, "The Use of the Growth-Share Matrix in Strategic Planning," *Interfaces 13,* no. 1 (February 1983), pp. 47–60.

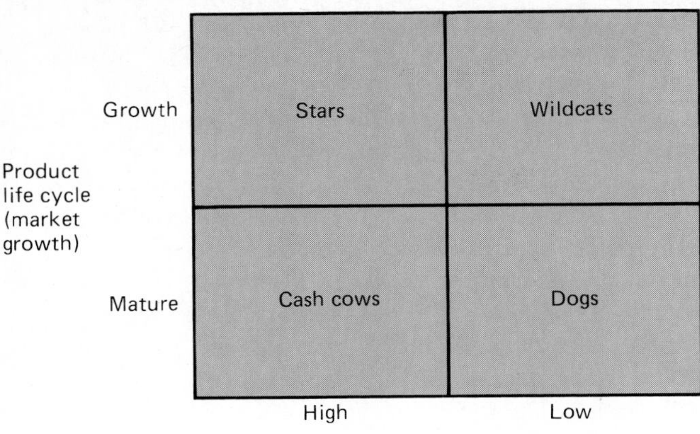

FIGURE 4.4
A market growth–market share matrix.

cats); (3) in mature markets—with high market share (cash cow); or (4) in mature markets—with low market share (dog). The strategy that should emerge is one that would support a firm's move left and upward. The firm would move to the left if it were in mature markets and will go for larger market shares. Additionally, the firm should move upward by developing new products or services to move into growth markets.

The methods of analysis used to characterize a firm and its competitors are analytical evaluation of firm financial characteristics; characteristics such as capacity utilization, new plant and equipment, current assets, capital intensity, R&D expenditures, and marketing expense. These are related to financial performance. Profiles of firms in an industry, for example, are fit into the growth-share matrix. A firm sees where it fits as compared to others and then adjusts its strategies accordingly to enhance performance potential. Although the analytical procedures extend beyond our introductory treatment of strategic planning, we feel that it is important that you be aware of this contemporary approach and how it affects operations.

EXAMPLE

To illustrate application of the BCG method consider this finding from the study by Hombrick, et al. Industrial products companies were analyzed and categorized by the growth-share matrix classification—114 stars, 181 wildcats, 315 cash cows, and 418 dogs. One example finding, "Relative to other cells dogs tend to have dated plant and equipment, medium capital intensity, high inventory levels, low R&D expenses, moderate marketing expenses, narrow domains, low value added, and competitive devices that lag [behind] cow competitors on all fronts.[13]

[13]Hombrick, et al., "Strategic Attributes . . .," p. 529.

Strategic Planning and Operations It is quite refreshing to observe the attention that strategic planning for operations is receiving from businesses and academics. On the one hand we see conceptual articles addressing how operations strategy fits in with other business components. Jelinek and Burstein hypothesize how various production administrative structure choices can fit together with different marketing, production, technology, and organization design choices.[14]

In another study four distinct multiplant strategies prevailing within the nation's largest manufacturing companies were identified and examined. Only one of these strategies is likely to prevail in any single operating division of the corporations investigated; a product responsibility by plant, a market area plant strategy, a process (a segment of the full production process) plant strategy, or a general purpose plant strategy combining any previous strategies. These multiplant strategies govern the charters under which plants operate, thus helping to insure focused factory operations. Using detailed data drawn from over 300 plants, the study reports on the apparent attractiveness of different strategies to different industry groups and singles out those specific plant characteristics which Fortune 500 plants attribute most often to each strategy. This information can aid in the assignment of plant charters within company operating divisions.[15]

Professor Wickham Skinner[16] suggests that the increased attention being given to strategy should be one of the major initiatives under way in operations, a view with which we agree. He perceives manufacturing strategy being addressed to structural decisions—those long-range decisions that lock-in operations well into the future. For example, decisions on technology, plant size, location, and human resource management all have long-term consequences. Skinner also emphasizes the choice of selecting a "key operations task," one that will make or break you with regard to your (the company's) competition. Is it quality? Delivery time? Or, perhaps new products. It takes bold executives to lift their focus above short-term efficiency and productivity goals when planning strategically. That is difficult to do.

Skinner identifies three major roadblocks that must be overcome to effectively change strategies:

1. The short-term financial point of view, focusing on restricted capital investment and immediate operating results.
2. Top management's view of operations as a kind of "productivity machine"

---

[14]Mariann Jelinek and Michael C. Burstein, "The Production Administrative Structure: A Paradigm for Strategic Fit," *The Academy of Management Review* 7, no. 2 (April 1982), pp. 242–252.

[15]Roger W. Schmenner, "Multiplant Manufacturing Strategies Among the Fortune 500," *Journal of Operations Management* 2, no. 2 (February 1982), pp. 77–86.

[16]"Operations Strategy: Past Perspective and Future Opportunity," Wickham Skinner, *Strategic Management of Operations: Proceedings of the First Annual Winter Conference of the Operations Management Association*, (San Francisco, Ca., November 1982), pp. 11–16.

rather than as a potential strategic resource. The focus needs to move from perceiving operations as a means to improved financial performance to operations as a source to make us a stronger competitor.

3. Operations managers need to become better at long-range planning. They need to develop the skills to contribute meaningfully to corporate strategic councils.[17]

The responses to becoming better strategic planners on the part of operations executives is two fold. First, they need to become aware of the challenge and opportunities in planning strategically. Second, they need to learn to perform—to effectively plan strategically. This involves becoming better managers and taking on increasing responsibilities for the overall direction of the firm. The issue here is not technical, but rather managerial—and certainly not totally unique to the operations function in the firm.

Let's now look at some of the shorter-term planning concepts and activities that operations managers are quite good at. Operations has, as we'll see, a rich tradition in intermediate and short-term planning capabilities.

Like most other processes, planning involves a series of steps, distinct phases that follow one another in an ordered pattern. These steps have been discovered and refined over the years by all the major management schools of thought. We have summarized selected concepts from the planning process in Table 4.1, and you may find it helpful to refer to this table and to the chapter glossary as you read the rest of the chapter.

TABLE 4.1
Selected planning concepts

Planning Concept	Management school	Contributor	Brief concept definition
Manager's planning responsibility	Classical	Frederick Taylor	Concern with analysis of the work process and standardization of the work process
Policies and procedures	Classical	Henri Fayol, others	Statements serving as guides to action and rules for specific conditions that lead to action
Work routinization	Classical	Frederick Taylor	Regulation; making work processes habitual and uniform
Goals	Behavioral social system	Chester Barnard	The objectives that the organization seeks to accomplish
Planning time horizon	Modeling decision making	Herbert Simon	Time in future for decision making
Generating alternative programs of action	Behavioral (social system) and modeling (decision-making)	Richard Cyert, James March, Herbert Simon	Searching for alternatives until a satisfactory set is obtained

[17]Wickham Skinner, "Operations Technology: Blind Spot in Strategic Management," *Interfaces* 14, no. 1 (Jan–Feb 1984), pp. 116–125.

Analysis of the Work Process

There is no substitute for knowledge about the work process when one is setting out to plan or develop a program for action. Frederick Taylor emphasized the scientific study of people and machines at work, closely examining the activities being performed on the production (shop) floor. As a result of his observations, he isolated three leading functions of the planning department of an organization:

1. complete analysis of all orders taken by the company for machines or work,
2. analysis of all inquiries for new work received in the sales department and promises for time of delivery, and
3. cost of all items manufactured with complete expense analysis and complete monthly comparative cost and expense exhibits.

These activities are performed in many production/operation processes yet today, and, depending upon the volume and complexity of activities, several different managers and staff specialists often perform them.

Standardization of the Work Process

Organizations are usually dynamic, changing under such pressures as new market demands, new owner demands, new employees, and government restrictions. Often reactions to changes in the environment can result in oscillations that leave the organization unstable—out of control. If decision makers overreact to changes and pressures with erratic or unpredictable decisions, severe mismanagement can result. To minimize this possibility, management attempts to standardize the work process by establishing *policies, procedures,* and *work routinization.*

Policies A *policy is a statement serving as a guide to action.* Policies are somewhat general in nature; they are simply guides for administrators to follow. Since they affect everyone in the organization, policies should be:

1. written down, particularly if they deal with personnel,
2. readily available,
3. understood by managers and subordinates, and
4. general enough to be stable over time.

Policies should also be flexible, comprehensive, and clear, and they should conform to society's canons of ethical behavior. Their purpose is to provide coordination of interrelated subunits.

Suppose that one policy in your organization is: "Schedule jobs in the plant to meet delivery dates." This manufacturing policy reflects the organization's goal of providing good service to customers. Notice that the policy does not state how to accomplish the goal; it provides a guide for selecting scheduling rules, which are much more specific. A scheduling rule reflecting policy goals might be: "Schedule jobs in the stamping department on a due-date basis, with the exception of Jones Printing Company jobs, which should always be scheduled first."

Procedures Work processes are standardized through procedures. *A procedure is a specific rule that must be followed.* One scheduling rule for a stamping department was illustrated in our discussion of policy. The difference between a policy and a procedure can be seen in two statements about hiring. "If one of two or more equally qualified applicants is Mexican-American, and we currently have inadequate minority representation, give preference to the Mexican-American" is a procedure, a specific rule requiring management to achieve an overall ethnic balance. "All personnel selection should be nondiscriminatory" is a statement of policy, a much more general guide from which the procedure was derived.

Work Routinization Work processes are standardized through regulation of activities. *Work routinization is the regulation of habitual uniform work processes.* Variability of work content and behavior is reduced through techniques designed to stabilize the work process. Typical, but certainly not all-inclusive, are these standardizing methods and techniques:

1. *Personnel.* Job descriptions, application forms, testing procedures for selection, personnel evaluation procedures and forms, wage and salary schedules.
2. *Operations.* Automation, job design, work measurement, material handling specifications, quality standards, quantity standards, product design.

As with other concepts we've discussed, Frederick Taylor was among the first to discuss the value of standardized work processes.[18] Many organizations have built on his theories and have found that regulated planning makes for a more efficient operation.

Establishing Goals

The planning function begins with the establishment of goals, objectives the organization seeks to accomplish. Goals give direction to the organization's efforts. But an organization may have many goals, and at times they may conflict. Furthermore, some goals may apply to certain situations and not to others. When goals are established, therefore, careful thought should be given to their *priority, time,* and *structure.*

Priority of Goals An organization must decide which of its goals are primary and which are secondary; secondary goals are derived from and support primary goals. One primary goal of any organization is survival. A secondary goal, such as providing an 8 percent dividend yield to stockholders, is dependent on the primary goal, since an organization obviously cannot provide a dividend if it doesn't survive. At the same time, the secondary goal supports the primary goal; a good dividend helps ensure the organization's survival. Thus the organization's goals, while ordered in

[18]See Frederick W. Taylor, *Shop Management,* p. 111, where he states that the primary functions of the planning department should include time study, line balancing, pay schedules, standards, and systematic part identification.

terms of priority, are complementary. Other secondary goals might include profitability, growth, and quality service.

Timing of Goals Goals can be short-term, intermediate, or long-term. A short-term goal is normally for a year or less, for example to achieve designated sales volumes monthly or annually. Intermediate goals are usually of one to five years' duration, for example to add plant capacity by selecting a new site, purchasing land, and building and staffing the new facility. Long-term goals have longer than a five-year time horizon, for example to establish vertical manufacturing integration.

EXAMPLE

Vertical manufacturing integration was established within AMAX Aluminum Company, where aluminum fabrication operations were purchased and grouped. By becoming a primary aluminum producer in the 1960s and 1970s, AMAX was able vertically to integrate backwards. One interesting side benefit was the possibility of avoiding antitrust action that might have resulted had the integration gone from metal source to purchasing firms for a captive market. AMAX's integration illustrates the pursuit of a long-term goal requiring more than five years. It was supported by intermediate goals and was implemented through a series of short-term goals.

Structure of Goals Structuring goals is the process of breaking them down into units, such as finance, marketing, and production, and assigning goals to each unit. Overall corporate profitability goals, for example, might be translated into cash management goals for the finance department, sales volume goals for the marketing area, and cost control goals for production employees. Structuring according to primary and secondary goals is also effective. Establishing measurable goals that are supportive but not conflicting is both necessary and difficult. In fact, goal formation is one of the most difficult parts of planning.

The Planning Time Horizon

The planning time horizon is that time in the future a decision maker looks forward in evaluating the consequences of a proposed action. Many decisions require managers to look into the future; planning decisions are among them.

Goal setting, budgeting, forecasting, and policy making are all aspects of planning that use a time horizon. Imagine the time horizon as a continuum. At one end is top management, whose involvement in long-term planning often involves a time horizon of five years or more. At the other end of the time horizon continuum are first line supervisors, who are involved in short-term planning, often on a day-to-day basis. In the middle of the time horizon continuum we find people in middle management, who are involved in one- to five-year intermediate planning; they receive inputs from lower managers and review from top management.

What happens if inappropriate planning horizons are used? Consider the following example.

EXAMPLE

In the early 1970s, American and Canadian automobile manufacturers were unable or unwilling to react to consumer demand for small cars and thus lost markets to foreign competition. Perhaps a contributing factor toward the delay was the American/Canadian time horizon for retooling. Although the annual model year time horizon would seem to allow adequate time for market adjustments, major retooling is actually done only every three or four years. Since the automobile companies have such substantial sunk costs in retooling and design, they were unable to respond quickly. Clearly, a shorter planning time horizon and lesser tooling commitment would have been beneficial for the industry. The continued upward price pressures on gasoline and government mileage requirements drastically changed the industry in the late 1970s and early 1980s, making a large car a thing of the past for most drivers.

We can see that using inappropriate time horizons can easily result in excessive costs and lost opportunities for profit. How does a manager avoid this? We know of no simple answer. Perhaps the most important thing the manager can do is to become aware of the concept itself, to recognize that the planning time horizon affects outcomes.

Forecasting Future Events

Planning means considering the future. In order to plan for future events, we must have some idea about what they will be. Just as many of us plan our weekends according to the weather forecast, businesspeople plan future actions according to forecasts of future market conditions. In business, *forecasting is predicting, determining an estimate of future events.* Business forecasts can be derived from intuitive estimation, simple modeling, or sophisticated modeling. As model complexity increases, so do forecasting costs and, usually, forecasting accuracy.

In production/operations, forecasters deal with specification of final product demand, individual component part demand, and technology requirements. Solutions to all these problems are not easily come by, and no one has yet devised a perfect forecaster. Usually we have to rely on a combination of judgment, wisdom, economic indications, and econometric and statistical models. But forecasting is nevertheless a critical phase of planning; good forecasting results in low forecast error, fewer alternatives that must be generated for possible states of nature, and simplified evaluation of alternative programs of action. We will look closely at forecasting in the next chapter, as it is a necessary prerequisite for planning facilities and their use.

Generating Alternative Programs of Action

After possible states of nature have been forecasted, alternative programs of action can be developed. A fundamental question (seldom answered satisfactorily) is: how many alternatives should one generate? How much time, effort, and money should one spend to generate alternatives? The answer is that there is no optimal number of alternatives.

Since it's impossible to find the *optimal* number of alternatives, managers look for a *satisfactory* set. This is especially true for highly complex business problems. *Satisficing,*[19] a term sometimes used to describe behavior that limits the search for alternative solutions, allows managers or administrators to search until a satisfactory alternative is found and then stop. Having found a satisfactory alternative to one problem, they continue on to another. Often, planners don't have the choice of buying additional information or taking the time to develop many alternatives. They must find one good alternative quickly and be satisfied with that.

PLANNING PRODUCTS AND SERVICES

Production and operations managers can become so involved with immediate objectives of delivery, efficiency, and quality that they may ignore product (or service) planning. To do so for extended periods of time could be fatal for the firm and accompanying production processes. Although product or service planning is not necessarily the ultimate responsibility of the production manager, his or her involvement in its design and impact on production processes is significant. The ultimate goal of production is efficient delivery of useful outputs. Figure 4.5 summarizes how product (service) planning decisions affect this objective.

Developing the Product (Service) Concept

Entrepreneurs frequently form new businesses on the basis of a unique product idea or needed service. As competitors infringe and replicate products and services or as the useful product life (to consumers) diminishes, the firm must be prepared to bring new products or services on stream. Product and service ideas come from a variety of sources, including customers, marketing staff, research and development, top management, production staff, engineering, and employees throughout the firm. The successful organization capitalizes on new product or service ideas regardless of their source.

Preliminary Market/Economic Analysis and Product (Service) Selection

Basically, the new product or service decision requires balancing market needs with economic realities. For example, although there might well be a market for large-scale helicopter commuter service between Philadelphia and Washington, D.C., economic realities simply do not support such mass transit with current technology.

[19]James C. March and Herbert A. Simon, *Organization* (New York: John Wiley & Sons, Inc., 1950) and Richard M. Cyert and James C. March, *A Behavioral Theory of the Firm* (Englewood Cliffs, N.J.: Prentice-Hall, Inc., 1963).

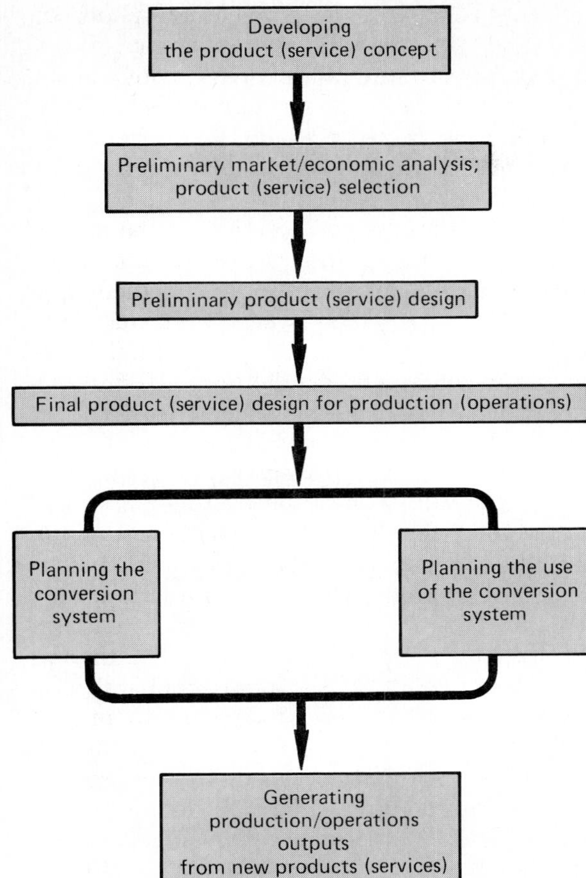

FIGURE 4.5
Product (service) planning for production (operations)

Preliminary market analysis includes sales projections. Economic analysis includes specifying and costing production, adding overhead and profits, and projecting profitability for forecasted volumes. To select the actual products and services, management must balance markets, economic analysis, available technology, and the firm's financial position—all within the framework of the organization's strategic mission. Successful organizations seem to have a high batting average in the product selection ballgame.

Preliminary and Final Product (Service) Design

To determine how feasible a new product or service might be, management needs a preliminary product (service) design. Key elements in the product design process are *function, cost, quality,* and *reliability;* to a lesser degree, such factors as appearance, environmental impact, and product safety should be considered. Marketing, engineering, and production personnel interact to solidify the product (service) concept. Since design is an interactive process, the point at which preliminary design stops and final design emerges is somewhat hazy. Sometimes before a product can be considered final, designers must consider the standardization and interchangeability of parts. Typically, a final design includes drawings and material specifications. Downstream, production planning then translates these specifications into shop floor instructions, identifying materials, pieces of equipment, and personnel required.

In an earlier chapter we discussed the competitive challenges in production and operations. As operations is once again addressed by top managers, after some neglect, there is potential for operations to become too much of a focus. Operations—and the products and services being produced—must fit into the overall strategic plan. As Stobaugh and Telesis state, "Production must be richly and deliberately integrated—both in its appointed tasks and in the ends toward which it is directed—with the product strategies it is to support."[20] International manufacturing has special problems due to the global coordination required and the differing cultures management is expected to transcend.[21] The product selection team and production team, each involved in considerable risk assessment for new products, will want to use the best analysis techniques available to increase the probability of successful product selection, production, and consumption.[22]

Although we cannot cover all the elements in the product design process (function, cost, quality, and reliability), let's take a closer look at *reliability*. A top executive at a major automotive manufacturer recently reviewed what North American consumers want most in their product. Of the five to ten top attributes, reliability was first, ahead of comfort, price, style, and many other important product features. You will note that like most operations topics, reliability blends both quantitative analysis and managerial issues.

Reliability The product's useful life span, or the expected duration of its performance, makes up its reliability. Products like bandages, newspapers, and food are expected to have short lives or to be used only once. Other products, refrigerators, for instance, consist of many subcomponents expected to function in concert over extended time periods. Life expectancies for these products are not left to chance; the products and their subcomponents are designed to meet minimum reliability standards. Once we have

[20]Robert Stobaugh and Piero Telesio, "Match Manufacturing Policies and Product Strategies," *Harvard Business Review* 61, no. 2 (March–April 1983), pp. 113–120.

[21]See Stobaugh and Telesio, op. cit.; and William H. Davidson and Philippe Haspeslagh, "Shaping a Global Product Organization," *Harvard Business Review* 60, no. 4 (July–August 1982), pp. 125–132.

[22]See, for example, Jacob W. Ulvila, Rex V. Brown, and Karle S. Packard, "A Case in On-line Decision Analysis for Product Planning," *Decision Sciences* 8, 1977, pp. 590–615, where a probabilistic discounted earnings model was utilized to evaluate the capital expenditures for new product ventures.

determined the desired reliability for our product, two basic design questions arise: What reliability is required of each of its subcomponents if we wish to achieve the reliability goal for the final product? Which subcomponents should then be selected (used) to most economically meet this desired reliability?

Often a final product does not perform properly unless *all* of its subcomponents function correctly. In cases such as these the reliabilities of individual subcomponents must be greater than the reliability desired for the final product. This situation exists whenever the chances of failure for each subcomponent are independent of each other.

Product reliability is usually expressed in terms of a probability. The probability of the system functioning successfully equals the product of the probabilities of all its subcomponents. Once reliability has been met, we can base subcomponent selection on economic considerations.

EXAMPLE

Suppose we wish to produce a product consisting of two subcomponents. We want the product to have a useful life expectancy of one year with .90 probability. The product functions successfully only as long as *both* subcomponents function. Upon failure of one (or both) subcomponents the product ceases to function. How reliable must each subcomponent be? The table below shows the prices we must pay vendors to supply the two subcomponents for increasing levels of reliability.

Subcomponent	Reliability of subcomponent		
	.90	.95	.98
A	$50	$90	$140
B	$70	$90	$110

Since we want a product reliability of .90, we could select subcomponents each having .90 reliability. The resulting product will meet our reliability standard if both subcomponents *A* and *B* operate successfully for one year. The probability of *both* events occurring is $.90 \times .90 = .81$, which is the reliability of the final product. We see, then, that subcomponent reliability must be greater than the desired reliability of the final product.

The result of using subcomponents *A* and *B* when each has .98 reliability would be $P = .9604$ (or $(.98)(.98)$).

Similarly, for *A* and *B* having .95 reliabilities, $P = .9025$. Both of these options would meet or exceed the desired product reliability.

Which versions of subcomponents *A* and *B* should be used in our product? We answer the question by first identifying all combinations of *A* and *B* that satisfy our overall reliability goal. Then we pick the combination of *A* and *B* that is least costly. Four alternative combinations of *A* and *B* meet or exceed the product reliability goal; five combinations, 5 through 9, are unsatisfactory.

Alternative	Subcomponents		Overall reliability	Cost
	A	*B*		
1	.95	.95	.9025	$ 90 + 90 = $180
2	.98	.98	.9604	140 + 110 = 250
3	.95	.98	.9310	90 + 110 = 200
4	.98	.95	.9310	140 + 90 = 230
5	.90	.90	.8100	
6	.90	.95	.8550	
7	.90	.98	.8820	
8	.95	.90	.8550	
9	.98	.90	.8820	

Overall reliabilities and costs

We would select alternative 1 on the basis of economic criteria.

As you can see, reliability analysis requires probabilities of successful operation of subcomponents. This information, called failure-rate data, is obtained from test results. An evaluation of how subcomponent failures can affect overall system reliability helps in evaluating alternative changes in product design. Let's look now at decisions associated with planning for operations, once a product or service has been specified.

PLANNING FOR OPERATIONS

The fundamentals of planning apply to operations management too. Operating managers in manufacturing, the extractive industries, and the service sector make two sets of planning decisions. If you look at Figure 4.1 again, you'll see that operating managers must make decisions about planning both the conversion system and the use of the conversion system. *Planning the conversion system involves establishing a program of action for acquiring the necessary physical facilities to be used in the conversion process. Planning the use of the conversion process, utilizing the facility, involves establishing programs of action for the actual transformation of the resource inputs into outputs of goods and services, given an existing physical facility.* As Figure 4.1 shows, models and behavioral techniques are applicable to both of these planning areas.

Table 4.2 lists the types of planning decisions that must be made in operations. Our discussion of them in this chapter will be brief and introductory; later, we'll discuss both the planning situations and modeling and behavioral techniques to confront them.

TABLE 4.2
An overview of production/operations management solution procedures*

Planning situations	Solution approaches: Behavior	Solution approaches: Models
P/OM policy	Strategic planning, establishing P/OM goals, establishing procedures, interpreting policy	Economic, cost, and technological analysis of policy alternatives
Planning conversion facilities		
Forecasting	Human intuitive forecasting, predictions, forecast error evaluation	Regression, exponential smoothing, moving averages, adaptive models, Box-Jenkins
Capacity planning	Intuitive evaluation of past, current, and future capacity requirements	Long-run economic capacity planning analysis
Location of facilities	Evaluation of labor markets, unionization, natural resources, tax considerations, environment for quality of living	Economic location models, transportation model of linear programming, computer simulation
Process planning	Participative approach to planning, evaluation of alternative technologies, management/engineering interaction	Assembly charts, route sheets, flow process charts, form charts
Facility layout planning	Mixed layout strategies, layout flexibility desirable, management/engineering interaction, trial and error approaches	Templates, computerized models for layout; heuristics for assembly line balancing
Production planning: research and development	Assessment of technological success, economic success, product and project overall success; R&D management, brainstorming	Net present value, expected value in project selection, project screening models, R&D management models
Utilizing the conversion facility		
Production planning for aggregate scheduling	Information processing, multistage decision making	Linear programming, HMMS model, computer direct search techniques, graphical analysis
Job shop scheduling	Management decision rules, establishing customer priorities, dispatching, corrective action on shop floor control	Priority scheduling rules, assignment method, GANTT chart, minimum flow time, minimum lateness
Production control	Scheduling, supplementary planning, dispatching, corrective action in shop, materials releases, shipping schedules	GANTT charts, MRP, MAPICS
Project planning and scheduling	Activity identification, estimation of activity times, establishing precedence relations among activities, project budgeting and control decisions	PERT, PERT/COST, stochastic PERT, CPM, GANTT charts
Personnel planning	Selection, recruiting, training, establishing personnel requirements, layoff planning, evaluation procedures, discipline, rewards	Human resources accounting, job analysis, job descriptions, wage and salary models, personnel requirements analysis

*Most of these solution procedures are not explained in this chapter; they are used to clarify the behavioral and modeling approaches to planning in P/OM. The solution procedures will be developed in chapters that follow.

Planning Conversion Facilities

Capacity Planning The idea behind capacity planning is to have available the capability to produce a desired number of units of output. The first thing to be done, then, is to convert forecasts of sales demand from dollar amounts into the units the organization provides, whether they are manufactured items, beds occupied in a hospital, or meals served in a cafeteria.

Then the forecasted number of units is compared to existing capability of meeting these demands over time. Management may decide that future demands warrant adding capacity, deleting some capacity, or making no changes in the existing facility.

Location of Facilities Once a need is established for additional capacity, a facility must be designed and a location chosen. The location depends upon a multitude of factors—transportation requirements, necessary delivery times from suppliers and to customers, the labor market, natural resources required for production, utility costs, land availability, and socioeconomic factors in retaining a work force. All these factors help determine the kinds of technological processes that can be handled. Obviously, the location of a TWA overhauling and repair facility would depend on a different set of considerations than would the location of a paper mill for International Paper Company.

Process Planning For any given production/operations process, there are alternative methods of conversion. Management has to decide which plans offer the best hopes of meeting their goals. What degree of automation shall we use? How much capital investment? How shall we use labor?

EXAMPLE

Kawneer Co., Inc., was planning a new aluminum fabrication plant to produce decorative trim parts for the automotive and appliance industry. Process planning resulted in the design and selection of alternative methods of material handling. Suggestions included an overhead crane to move raw materials, an automated run-out for handling hot extrusions, fixed conveyors, mobile conveyors, gravity conveyors, a roof-mounted oven with overhead conveyors, forklift trucks, and a manual transfer system. Kawneer's process planning for material handling required about three months of effort for a 200,000-square-foot plant.

From the various process plans presented to them, management makes process selection decisions, which are usually interactive. Since Kawneer's management, for example, chose the process plan to roofmount a paintbaking oven, they also had to plan for a fixed overhead conveyor to transport parts through the roof and into and out of the oven. They had to eliminate plans that involved manual loading and unloading of the oven. The technical and economic aspects of process planning are often analyzed by an industrial engineering staff or, in their absence, by operations managers.

Facility Layout Planning In layout planning, alternative layouts of equipment and work stations are analyzed and evaluated. How efficiently will work orders flow through different layout configurations? Which one should we select? In facility layout planning, we are concerned with fixing the locations of elements *within* the plant or building walls, unlike capacity planning and plant location, which are concerned with matters external to the actual facility's walls.

Product Planning: Research and Development Product ideas do not just happen; they are planned and developed. For existing products as well as new ones, applied research and development are necessary. Management must plan programs to select, develop, produce, and market their products or services, and they must continually assess the economic and technical risks involved.

Utilizing the Conversion Facility

Forecasting In most operations, future demand for output is not known with certainty. With the help of good forecasts, management can plan for smooth transitions from current output to future output. Accurate forecasting can significantly reduce production variation and thus reduce production costs.

Production Planning for Aggregate Output Once a forecast of aggregate demand in units has been achieved, aggregate (overall) production must be planned. Figure 4.6 illustrates a constant-level production plan for meeting a seasonal demand. This aggregate plan calls for producing 100 units per

FIGURE 4.6
An aggregate forecast and production plan

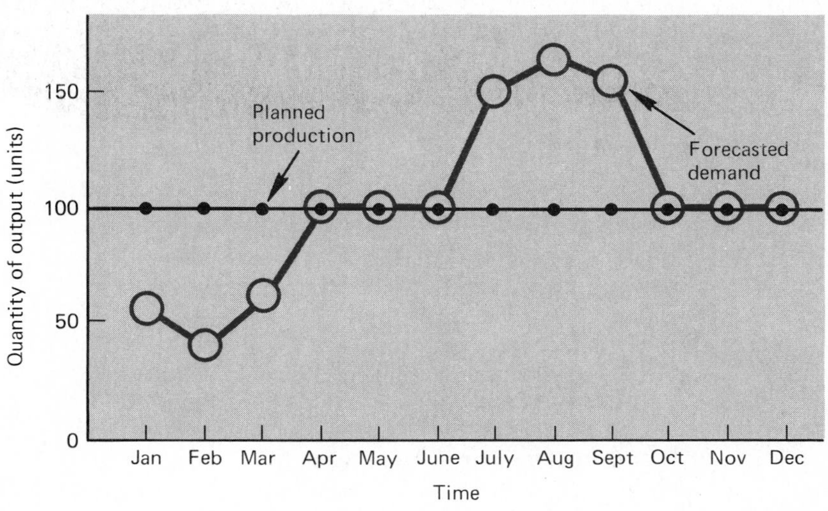

month with a constant work force. Typically, an aggregate plan consists of two basic decisions: establishing the overall production rate and determining the overall number of workers to be employed during each month or period in the chosen planning horizon. To plan for these two decisions, the manager must consider hiring and layoff costs, overtime costs, inventory levels, and similar production-level related costs.

Production Planning for Job Shop Scheduling Besides the broad overall focus of the aggregate planning problem, managers must also plan the more micro problem of job shop scheduling. In a job shop, jobs are basically made to order, and production/operations are intermittent. Because of the diversity of the products they produce, job shops characteristically operate with much shorter planning horizons and face greater uncertainties about demand than do standard product shops. Two short-range tasks must be performed for job shop scheduling: determining which jobs to run first, second, and so on (job scheduling) and determining which machines or work centers should handle which jobs (job assignment).

Production Planning for Production Control Production planning is a prerequisite to effective production control. There are two stages of production planning and control, the preliminary stage and the action stage. In the preliminary, or planning stage, forecasts are converted into a master schedule, supplementary planning is carried out, jobs are assigned to work centers, and jobs are sequenced and scheduled. Work levels are checked to ensure that capacity is not being exceeded. In the action stage, job assignments are released for the first time to shop foremen or operations managers through an activity called *dispatching*. After dispatching, the planning staff continues with instruction, surveillance, and correction; the foremen and operations managers are responsible for conversion in their roles as line supervisors. During conversion, some supplementary planning is carried out by both line and staff personnel; feedback about shop performance comes back to the production planning staff. Since this feedback allows for new programs of action if necessary, it is the essence of the production control activity.

Project Planning and Scheduling If an important one-time major project needs close coordination to be successfully completed, project planning techniques may be useful. They require:

1. identifying and specifying all activities to be performed,
2. establishing the order in which the activities must be performed (precedence relationships),
3. establishing time estimates for the activities, and
4. calculating expected completion times and dates.

Personnel Planning Since most of the jobs in any organization are done by people, personnel planning is vital. Once the facility is ready, workers must be available who can do the specific jobs required by the technology of the conversion process. Personnel (human resource) management, which can be handled by the staff or by the operations manager, prepares job descriptions, recruits and selects employees, provides initial orientation, and often assists in employee evaluation. Furthermore, personnel planners must gather wage and salary surveys and establish wage schedules, and often they must negotiate with unions. Personnel planning is a big job. It must begin early in the planning process, especially for critical technical and professional personnel, and must continue throughout the entire planning process.

Operations Policy Planning all these operations variables is done within the context of P/OM's strategic mission, to ensure that conversion activities are consistent with one another and with the organization's overall strategy. From the statement of strategic mission flow the operations policies, which provide overall guides for such decisions as type of operating technology, quantity and quality standards, service levels, and cost control.

Production/ Operations Objectives

What are the specific goals in production/operations? Some insight can be found in operations managers' answers to survey questions.[23] Most frequently, managers spent time on and stressed labor/industrial relations, cost control, production control (ensuring that adequate quantities are available for delivery on schedule), and quality control. Judging from the surveys and from experience, we can say that primary short-term production/operations objectives are:

1. Establish product (service) characteristics.
2. Establish process characteristics.
3. Deliver the required service to the customer by
   (a) producing quantities to meet expected demand and
   (b) meeting the customer specified delivery date for the goods or services.
4. Produce the goods or services at the desired quality level.
5. Meet the above goals efficiently by
   (a) effective employee relations and labor cost control,
   (b) material cost control, and
   (c) cost control in facility utilization.
6. Maintain adaptability for future survival.

[23]Robert R. Britney and E. F. Peter Newson, *The Canadian Production/Operations Management Environment: An Audit,* School of Business Administration Research Monograph (London, Ontario: University of Western Ontario, 1975), pp. 15–19 and Stephen E. Berry, Hugh J. Watson, and William T. Greenwood, "A Survey as to the Content of the Introductory POM Course," *Academy of Management Journal* 21, no. 4 (December 1978), pp. 699–714.

These short-term objectives support survival of the production process. The long-run production/operations goal is to utilize resources in a manner that meets long-run market demand for the firm. If successful, this process will generate the necessary funds to acquire additional resources, and the cycle of producing to meet market demand can begin again. The production/operations function survives, then, on effectiveness and efficiency criteria, and these criteria are what our objectives are all about.

Models for Planning

It is not surprising to find that planning models are most often presented in verbal or diagrammatic form. Planning requires consideration of so many variables, and interrelationships among them, that precise quantification is almost impossible. This is especially true for strategic planning. Recently, however, researchers have made inroads toward quantifying selected aspects of planning. Two of these quantified approaches are goal programming and the use of a goal consistency model. We won't discuss the technical aspects of these models; our purposes are to point out their existence and to show how they apply to the planning process.

Goal Programming Sometimes multiple goals can lead to goal conflict. After an extensive planning effort you may find, for example, that a marketing subgoal conflicts with one in operations or finance. Similarly, within a single functional area, such as operations, two subgoals may conflict. When resources are limited and all the subgoals cannot be simultaneously accomplished, a method of analysis called *goal programming* can help determine the best course of action. This technique is a special version of linear programming, an optimization method we discuss in the supplement to Chapter 6.

To use goal programming, managers must clearly identify each goal and subgoal. Then each must be given a priority ranking reflecting its relative importance and specifying whether overaccomplishment or underaccomplishment is to be allowed. Finally, limitations of resources necessary for accomplishing the goals must be identified. Having done all this, managers can use the goal programming technique to allocate their resources and meet the priorities they've established. Usually, they will find that some subgoals can be fully accomplished and others can be only partially realized. But managers have the comfort of knowing that although they have been unable to accomplish all goals, they have been able to identify the best uses of limited resources and minimize goal conflict.

Goal Consistency Goal programming prescribes an *optimal* course of action; the goal consistency model does not. Its purpose is to help the planner to be consistent in estimating relationships among elements of a plan.

Most plans begin with rather general goal statements. As the plan is refined and elaborated, its elements become more specific. Ideally, successively detailed elements of the plan are hierarchically linked, ultimately in support of the broadly stated goals that initiated the planning effort in the first place. First the overall goal, such as increasing productive output, is established. Then subgoals that will lead to accomplishment of the overall goal are identified. Next, the planner identifies those policy areas in which decisions can be made to accomplish subgoals. Finally, the plan becomes even more detailed by showing specific action alternatives for each policy area.

After all the subelements of the plan have been listed, the manager assigns numeric importance ratings to them. When all the subelements have been numerically ranked, according to the manager's intuition and judgment, the manager can calculate a goal accomplishment rating for each action alternative and determine which is best. The goal consistency procedure offers several benefits. With it managers can clarify subgoals, examine interrelationships, and uncover sources of plan inconsistency.

PRACTICAL GUIDES IN PLANNING FOR OPERATIONS

Previous sections of this chapter have focused on conceptualizing the planning process. Before we examine the details of operations planning, the subject of the next several chapters, we want to leave you with some practical guides for planning in operations: phases of planning, practical tips, and possible pitfalls. Although there is no one method that is best for planning in every circumstance, *phases of planning* that are often useful include *establishing goals, forecasting events, generating alternatives, establishing policies,* and *operationalizing the plan.*

How important is it to plan? In one study, a questionnaire was administered to some 280 chief executives throughout the world.[24] The executives were asked to rate the relative perceived importance of external relations, meetings, planning, inspection and control, people, personal development, and other activities. Over 65 percent ranked planning first in importance, although they indicated they were not able to spend as much time in planning as they felt its importance warranted. In general, United States executives seemed to stress planning more than executives from other countries.

Suggestions for Effective Planning

Once you understand the general concepts of planning, how do you put them into effect? Here are some practical suggestions:

1. Use planning to increase employees' understanding of their jobs and job responsibilities. Effectively communicated policies will avoid considerable confusion and duplication of individual and group efforts.
2. Encourage participation in establishing goals, especially from subordinates. Although all goals cannot be set with subordinate participation, many can be.

[24]H. Stieglitz, *The Chief Executive and His Job,* Personnel Policy Study No. 214 (New York: National Industrial Conference Board, 1969).

Including subordinates in planning will certainly reduce resistance to change and assist in motivation.

3. Limit arbitrary action of supervisors by effective planning, which establishes guides and encourages rational decisions.
4. Encourage through planning the consideration of many variables and alternatives before action begins. The planning process can lead to better decision making. Good planning should foster contingency decision making.
5. Operationalize plans. Budgets are expectations expressed in quantitative terms; use them. Translate policies into rules and procedures. Establish timetables; completion dates are an important part of operations planning. Establish standards that future performance can be measured against. In general, the planning process should be transferred from the ideal into practical guides.
6. Allow planning to interact with organizing and controlling activities. These functions are not performed in a vacuum; they interact. Feedback from control assists in planning, just as the relationships between jobs and groups of people do in organizations. Effective planning leads to effective organizing and controlling.

Reasons for Planning Failure

Many failures in planning evolve because basic planning concepts have been misapplied or not used at all. A survey of decision making and planning practices in over 350 European and American corporations indicates that most planning failures can be traced to one or more of the following factors:

1. Corporate planning is not integrated into the total management system.
2. Planning is not systematic; there is a lack of understanding of the different dimensions of planning.
3. Various levels of management are not engaged or involved in planning.
4. Responsibility for planning is vested solely in planning departments.
5. Management assumes that because a plan exists it will be put into practice.
6. Too much is attempted at one time.
7. Management "plans its work but fails to work its plan."
8. Extrapolation and financial planning are confused with general planning procedures.
9. Information inputs are inadequate.
10. Too much emphasis is placed on a single aspect of planning.[25]

SUMMARY

The production/operations manager must plan a program of action in advance of actual resource conversion. To do this, the manager must understand strategic planning as well as such classical planning concepts as goal setting, policy making, forecasting, timing, and analysis and standardization of work. The manager should also be alert to ideas for new products or services.

[25]Kjell A. Ringbakk, "Why Planning Fails," *European Business*, no. 29 (Spring 1971), pp. 15–26.

In practice, the operations manager must plan both the conversion process (the facility) and the use of the conversion process. This is done through the wide variety of planning situations illustrated in Table 4.2. Although you are not yet familiar with some of the techniques, you may want to refer to this table as we proceed with our analysis of planning in production/operations management (P/OM). With effective planning, the chances of personal and organizational success increase substantially.

We hope you are now aware of the importance of planning in operations management. Much of your success or failure as an operations manager, and of operations managers who might eventually report to you if you're a general manager, will depend upon your ability to plan effectively.

CASE

Martha's Burger Queen

Martha Thompson, who has worked in restaurants for twenty years, opened her first short-order "Mom-and-Pop" café twelve years ago. She is regarded in her community as an excellent small-business-person. In 1979 she sold her small café and went to work as a professional manager for a fast-food hamburger franchise. In 1981 she resigned and opened Martha's Original Burger Queen. Martha's salary is 25 percent higher than the one she earned as a professional manager. In 1981 her Burger Queen broke even; in 1982 it had a net profit after taxes of $10,000. Martha then opened two more restaurants in the same city. The results of all three restaurants are summarized in the accompanying comprehensive report.

Martha states her strategy: "My restaurant concept is to copy fast-food chains such as McDonalds, Burger King, and Jack-in-the-Box. I've tried parties, soybean burgers, breakfast, and larger sandwiches to increase dollar sales per customer. I believe that I should expand rapidly just as those chains seem to be doing, yet maintain a personable, local operations staff and a 'homey' atmosphere. But I seem to have less efficient operations than we did when I managed for a chain. I think my layout is good, as is my food quality. I can't buy in larger volumes, but do try to turn over my inventory at least weekly. I believe in women employees—especially in management positions. I hire white, black, and Mexican-Americans so no one can say I'm prejudiced."

Martha's response to net income difficulties at the second and third restaurants is, "I need to open more restaurants to spread out my fixed costs. Expansion of operations is my strategy, but I'm finding financing hard to come by now."

Case Questions:

1. Of the various strategic planning modes, which do you believe most typifies Martha's Burger Queen? List characteristics of both the strategy mode and case that support your choice.
2. Examining the comprehensive report, which data (if any) support the idea that Martha needs a change in operations strategy?
3. Set forth what you believe is a good business strategy for Martha. Specify an operations strategy that is consistent with the overall strategy.

Martha's Burger Queen comprehensive report

	Restaurants					
	Martha's original		MBQ2		MBQ3	
	1983	1984	1983	1984	1983	1984
Sales summary						
Revenues	$330,000	$370,000	$210,000	$200,000	$170,000	$150,000
Number customers	132,000	130,00	91,000	90,000	85,000	85,000
Revenues/customer	$2.50	$2.84	$2.30	$2.22	$2.00	$1.76
Expense summary						
Equipment depreciation	$16,500	$16,500	$10,500	$10,500	$8,500	$8,500
Building lease	33,000	33,000	21,000	21,000	17,000	17,000
Operations: Food	82,500	83,400	52,500	52,500	42,500	51,000
Labor	115,500	129,000	73,500	73,500	68,000	68,000
Supplies	16,000	18,000	10,000	10,000	8,500	8,500
Overhead	17,000	17,000	11,000	11,000	8,500	8,500
Gross margin selling and administrative costs						
Advertising	15,000	15,000	12,000	12,000	9,000	9,000
Administration	18,000	18,000	9,000	9,000	8,000	8,000
Net income (loss) before taxes	$16,500	$40,100	$10,500	$500	$0	($28,500)

CASE

Glaskowe Manufacturing, Inc.

Glaskowe Manufacturing, a twenty-year-old firm producing parts for the automotive industry, is headquartered in a midwestern city. About 70 percent of production is sold to Chrysler, Ford, and General Motors. The remaining 30 percent is sold to other automotive, truck, and heavy equipment producers.

Glaskowe has six plants operating in the midwestern and southern United States. The owner and principal stockholder, Thomas Gillet, has approved $4.5 million for a new manufacturing facility to be located near Macon, Georgia. It is currently the fall of 1985, and Mr. Gillet would like the plant to be in operation by September 1, 1986, for the 1987 automotive model year. An experienced process engineer, Tim Anderson, has been working on this project for six months as project director.

A June business school graduate from an eastern university, Cy Wilson, has just been hired by Glaskowe and assigned to Tim Anderson to help see the project through. Tim explains to Cy, "Our responsibility is to have a manufacturing plant and equipment ready for operations September 1, 1986. You and I will not operate it; our Atlanta plant will staff and start up the plant. Since Atlanta is busy with current production, you and I will select, purchase, and coordinate all the plant and equipment necessary for production."

After a couple of days of becoming familiar with Glaskowe operations, Cy gets his first assignment. Tim informs him, "Cy, Monday I want you to go to our

Atlanta plant for a week. Meet the people and spend some time learning our manufacturing technology. Here is a list of things we'll be working on when you return. I want you to size our air compressors and get them on order when you come back. Report to Fred Smith, the plant manager, who is expecting you."

On the airplane to Atlanta, Cy decided he would return with a plan of attack for this project. He didn't believe that buying air compressors was critical right now, nor was he sure at all that the process engineer had all the key activities identified. While in Atlanta, Cy was going to do some real planning for this project.

Macon physical plant

Activity	Project engineer's estimated duration (weeks)
Order equipment	
Conveyors—fixed and variable path	12
Overhead crane	16
Chemical baths	8
250-ton press	32
Stamping presses	16
Chemical storage tanks	8
Air compressors	10
Boilers	12
Schedule construction	3
Oversee construction	26
Finalize facility layout	6
Purchase sprinkler system	8
Hire architect	2
Advertise for personnel	
Maintenance, tool room	8
Manufacturing labor	4
Clerical	4
Foremen and supervisors	8
Select personnel	4
Size boilerroom	3
Select contractor through competitive bids	6
Select products for transfer from Atlanta plant	4

Case Questions:

1. What type of planning problem is this?
2. What general approach might Cy take in formulating a plan?
3. What activities might Cy add or delete?
4. Do you expect a new employee, fresh from college, to have his ideas readily accepted? How should Cy approach Tim?

REVIEW AND DISCUSSION QUESTIONS

1. Explain the differences among the priority, timing, and structuring dimensions in establishing goals.
2. Using the phases of planning as your guide, develop a study plan for a course in production/operations management from a student's perspective.
3. Think of a situation you have observed in which poor planning was evident. Which of the reasons for planning failure were the causes of the situation?
4. Contrast strategic planning and operational planning for increasing football ticket prices at a college, including putting the price increase into effect.
5. Management attempts to standardize the work process by establishing policies, procedures, and work routinization. Explain how management goes about doing this.
6. You are a student confronted with the possibility that on the same day two weeks from now you will have to take one exam in statistics and another in finance. One week from now, the exam schedule will be finalized. What are several alternative actions for and estimated outcomes of this situation? View the situation as a decision theory problem and construct a matrix (table) showing your framework. Which plan would you recommend now? Would you change your plan if you discover next week that your exams are scheduled for different days?
7. (a) Explain the differences between planning the conversion facility and planning the use of the conversion facility.
   (b) Which planning decision situation seems to you to be the most critical? Why?
8. If you were beginning a new venture, opening a wine and cheese shop in a shopping mall, what would your short-term production/operations objectives be?
9. A hospital administrator must plan the use of the conversion process. How would aggregate output planning and personnel planning interrelate in the hospital administrator's specific situation?
10. Explain the different approaches to planning strategically for operations.

PROBLEMS

Solved Problems

1. A commercial airplane manufacturer is concerned over the reliability of the radar sub-system placed in the cockpit of the aircraft. This purchased radar system is used for instrument (automatic) landings. Given the data below, we want to analyze the reliability of a specific purchased radar system currently in use.

   Ten radar systems were operated in the airplane manufacturer's laboratory for 500 flights each. Each simulated flight required use of the radar and the flight landings averaged 20 minutes. Two radar systems failed, one after 121 flights and the second after 273 flights.

   To compute the percentage of radar systems failing,

$$\text{Failures (\%)} = \frac{\text{number of failures}}{\text{number tested}} \times 100\%$$
$$= 2/10 \times 100\% = 20\%$$

   Next, we compute the number of failures per operating hour,

$$\text{Failures/unit-hour} = \frac{\text{number of failures}}{\text{operating time}}$$

$$\begin{aligned}
\text{Total time} &= (10 \times 500 \times 0.33\ \text{Hr}) = 1{,}650\ \text{hrs.} \\
\text{Nonoperating time} &= (1 \times 379 \times .33) + (1 \times 227 \times .33) \\
&= 200\ \text{hours} \\
\text{Operating time} &= (1650 - 200) = 1450\ \text{hrs.} \\
\text{Failures/unit-hr} &= \frac{2}{1450} = .000138
\end{aligned}$$

Examining failures per unit hour operating, the failure rate of 0.000138 seems low. However, it is very likely this is too high for the airplane and airline to have but one radar system in the airplane. The above analysis assumes the airline would not repair or replace the radar system when it failed, which is also quite unlikely. This analysis assumed the 200 down hours were in some 600 flights, flights being flown with a defective radar system. That isn't likely to happen under most airplane maintenance systems. It is likely, however, that the manufacturer would look to another supplier for a more reliable radar system.

Reinforcing Fundamentals

2. A product has two subcomponents, *A* and *B*. Failure of either *A* or *B* results in failure of the product. The probabilities of *A* and *B* performing successfully for 1500 times are .96 and .92 respectively, and are independent.
   (a) What is the probability that the product will operate properly 1500 or more times?
   (b) What is your answer to (a) if the probabilities for *A* and *B* are .85 and .75, respectively?
3. A product has three subcomponents, *A, B,* and *C*. Failure of *A* can cause the failure of the product. Failure of either only *B* or *C* would not cause the failure of the product. However, the product fails if both *B* and *C* fail simultaneously. The probabilities of *A, B,* and *C* performing successfully are 0.95, 0.85, 0.80, respectively.
   (a) Draw a system diagram for this reliability situation.
   (b) What is the probability that the product works successfully?

Challenging Exercises

4. Relectro Corporation produces a miniature electric motor consisting of four basic subcomponents: coil, prime circuit, switch, and simo-wire. Relectro promises its customers a two-year motor life with a probability of .95. Failure of any of the basic components renders the motor useless. Consideration is being given to redesigning the product for purposes of cost reduction. Engineers have gathered the following reliability and cost data for components that could be purchased from new vendors.

Data for existing components

Component	Unit cost	Two-year failure probability
Coil	$17.00	0.01
Prime circuit	8.50	0.03
Switch	1.50	0.05
Simo-wire	4.00	0.01

Data for new vendors

Component	Vendor X Unit cost	Vendor X Two-year failure probability	Vendor Y Unit cost	Vendor Y Two-year failure probability
Coil	$16.25	0.010	$21.00	0.005
Prime circuit	12.00	0.020	15.00	0.001
Switch	2.50	0.030	4.00	0.025
Simo-wire	4.00	0.010	4.50	0.010

Perform a reliability and cost analysis to support your recommendations for redesign of the motor.

GLOSSARY

Forecasting Predicting; determining an estimate of future events.

Goals Objectives the organization seeks to accomplish.

Goal priority The ranking of primary and secondary goals.

Goal structuring Process of breaking goals down into units and assigning goals to each unit.

Goal timing Short-term (one year or less), intermediate (one to five years), or long-term (more than five years) dimension of goals.

Manufacturing policy The overall guides established for converting resources into goods and services.

Planning conversion facilities See "Planning the conversion system."

Planning for operations Establishing a program of action for converting resources into goods or services.

Planning the conversion system Establishing a program of action for acquiring the necessary physical facilities to be used in the conversion process.

Utilizing the conversion process Establishing programs of action for the actual transformation of the resource inputs into outputs of goods and services, given an existing physical plant.

Planning time horizon That time in the future a decision maker looks toward in evaluating the consequences of a proposed action.

Policy A statement serving as a guide to action.

Procedure A specific rule that must be followed.

Project A one-shot set of activities with a distinct beginning and ending.

Scheduling Time sequencing of events.

Strategic planning A process linking the current mission and environment and then setting forth a guide for tomorrow's decisions and results.

Work routinization The regulation of habitual uniform work processes.

SELECTED READINGS

Britney, Robert R. and E. F. Peter Newson. *The Canadian Production/Operations Management Environment: An Audit.* School of Business Administration Research Monograph. London, Ontario: University of Western Ontario, April 1975.

Cyert, Richard M. and James C. March. *A Behavioral Theory of the Firm.* Englewood Cliffs, N.J.: Prentice-Hall, Inc., 1963.

Drucker, Peter F. *Management: Tasks, Responsibilities, Practice.* New York: Harper & Row, 1974.

Fayol, Henri. *General and Industrial Management.* London: Pitman Pub. Corp., 1949.

Gulick, L. and L. Urwick, eds. *Papers on the Science of Administration.* New York: Institute of Public Administration, 1937.

Hax, Arnold C. and Nicolas S. Majluf. "The Use of the Growth-Share Matrix in Strategic Planning." *Interfaces* 13, no. 1 (February 1983), pp. 47–60.

Peters, Thomas J. and Robert W. Waterman. *In Search of Excellence: Lessons from America's Best-Run Companies.* New York: Harper and Row, 1982.

Radford, K. J. *Strategic Planning: An Analytical Approach.* Reston, Virginia: Reston Publishing Company, Inc., 1980.

Ringbakk, Kjell A. "Why Planning Fails." *European Business*, No. 29 (Spring 1971), pp. 15–26.

Schmenner, Roger W. "Multiplant Manufacturing Strategies Among the Fortune 500." *Journal of Operations Management* 2, no. 2 (February 1982), pp. 77–86.

Skinner, Wickham. *Manufacturing in the Corporate Strategy*. New York: John Wiley and Sons, 1978.

______. "Operations Technology: Blind Spot in Strategic Management." *Interfaces* 14, no. 1 (January–February 1984), pp. 116–125.

Steiner, George A. *Strategic Planning: What Every Manager Must Know*. New York: The Free Press, 1979.

Stobaugh, Robert and Piero Telesio. "Match Manufacturing Policies and Product Strategies." *Harvard Business Review* 61, no. 2 (March–April 1983), pp. 113–120.

Taylor, Frederick W. *The Principles of Scientific Management*. New York: Harper & Row, 1911.

______. *Scientific Management*. New York: Harper & Row, 1919.

______. *Shop Management*. New York: Harper & Row, 1911.

Tregoe, Benjamin B. and John W. Zimmerman. *Top Management Strategy: What It Is and How to Make It Work*. New York: Simon and Schuster, 1980.

5 Forecasting

While all elements of operations management are important, I view forecasting as one of the key critical elements in the operations structure. As you study this chapter, which provides an excellent overview of forecasting techniques and models, it will be important to recognize the different models and when to use them based upon your needs.

At Donaldson Company, Inc., we serve a multitude of customers with a wide variety of products ranging from the size of a house to the size of a filter for 3½″ disc drives. We serve our customers through our plants in the United States and throughout the world. The needs of the market are changing for us, and we have to respond more quickly than ever before with product delivery. To do this, we have placed a higher emphasis on forecasting. As this chapter summary says, "Forecasting is the use of past data to determine future events." At Donaldson Company, forecasting is essential to improving our competitive edge.

Richard M. Negri
Vice President and General Manager
Manufacturing Division
Donaldson Company, Inc.
Minneapolis, Minnesota

From this comment by the Vice President responsible for manufacturing at Donaldson Company, Inc., we see how the company must respond quickly to market changes in order to improve its competitive edge. Mr. Negri believes that forecasting enables the company to respond more quickly and accurately than would otherwise be possible. Figure 5.1 shows that forecasting is a sub-

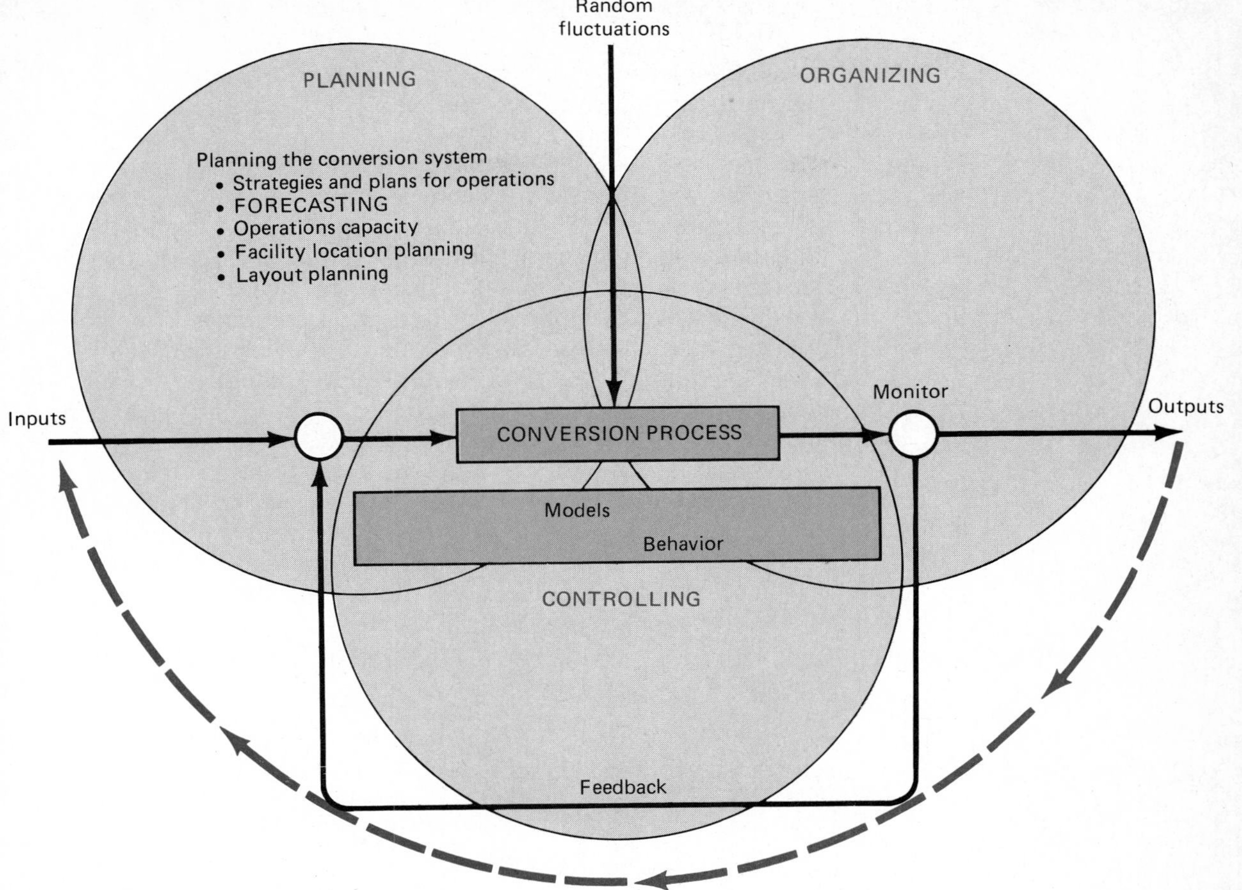

FIGURE 5.1
Forecasting in operations

phase of planning. We have divided planning into two subsegments, both of which require information obtained from forecasts. We will next examine planning *of* the conversion system, its capacity, location, and layout. Then we will consider the second subsegment, planning the use of the conversion system.

We know that in the management process, planning, organizing, and controlling are not independent processes; they interrelate and overlap. If operations have been properly planned and organized, control is easier and smoother. This is where forecasting comes in. It can reduce the costs of readjusting operations in response to unexpected deviations by specifying future demand. Clearly, if future demand for goods and services is accurately estimated, operating efficiency increases. Let's see how successful firms such as Donaldson might use forecasting in operations.

FORECASTING IN OPERATIONS

In a broad sense, forecasting presents a philosophical dilemma. "You can never plan the future by the past," said Edmund Burke; but Patrick Henry disagreed: "I know of no way of judging the future but by the past." Whether and how to use the past to predict the future is a dilemma managers and leaders have confronted for centuries, and it is still unresolved. In operations management, we try to forecast a wide range of future events that could potentially affect success. Most often the basic concern is with forecasting customer demand for our products or services. We may want long-run estimates of overall demand or shorter-run estimates of demand for each individual product. Even more detailed estimates are needed for specific items or subcomponents that go into each product. We want to know, for example, how many subassemblies we'll need, and within the subassemblies, how many screws, nuts, and washers.

We can distinguish among these different kinds of forecasting needs by considering how far into the future they focus. Detailed forecasts for individual items are used to plan the short-run use *of* the conversion system. At the other extreme, overall product demand forecasts are needed for strategies and planning capacity, location, and layout on a much longer time horizon. Different forecasting time horizons must be used to obtain information needed for various types of planning decisions, as Figure 5.2 shows.

FIGURE 5.2
Forecasting requirements in production/operations

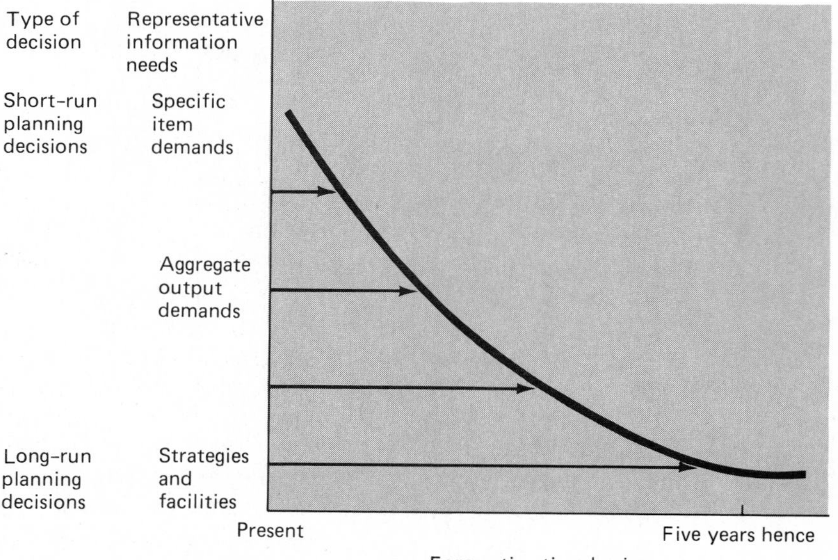

Forecasting Defined

In business, economic, and political communities *forecasting* has various meanings. In operations management, we adopt a rather specific definition of *forecasting*, and we distinguish it from the broader concept of "prediction."

> Forecasting is a process of estimating a future event by casting forward past data. The past data are systematically combined in a predetermined way to obtain the estimate of the future.
>
> Prediction is a process of estimating a future event based on subjective considerations other than just past data; these subjective considerations need not be combined in a predetermined way.[1]

As these definitions make clear, forecasts can only be made when a history of past data exists. An established TV manufacturer, for example, can use past data to forecast the number of coasters required for next week's TV assembly schedule. A fast-food restaurant can use past data to forecast the number of hamburger buns required for this weekend's operations. But suppose the manufacturer offers a new TV model or the restaurant decides to offer a new food service. Since no past data exist to estimate first year sales of the new products, prediction, not forecasting, is required. For predicting, good subjective estimates can be based on the manager's skill, experience, and judgment; but forecasting requires statistical and management science techniques.

In business in general, when people speak of forecasts, they usually mean some combination of both forecasting and prediction. Commonly, forecasting is substituted freely for "economic forecasting," which implies some combination of objective calculations and subjective judgments. We caution students and operations managers to avoid misunderstandings by clarifying what they mean by "forecasting" when they are discussing perceived problems, solution methods, and subsequent actions based on forecasts.

Forecasting and Operations Subsystems

The aggregate demand forecast is normally obtained by estimating expected volumes of sales, expressed in dollars, and then converting these estimates from sales dollars into homogeneous production units. Production units, such items as number of televisions in a plant, number of patients fed in a hospital, number of books circulated in a library, or lots of common stock sold in a brokerage house, can then be subdivided into component parts and converted into estimates of direct labor hours or material requirements. The resulting product forecasts are used as a basis for planning and controlling production subsystems, as shown in Figure 5.3.

In studying forecasting, we must be careful not to immerse ourselves in techniques and lose track of the reasons for forecasting. Forecasting is

[1]R. G. Brown, *Smoothing Forecasting and Prediction of Direct Time Series* (Englewood Cliffs, N.J.: Prentice-Hall, Inc., 1963), p. 2.

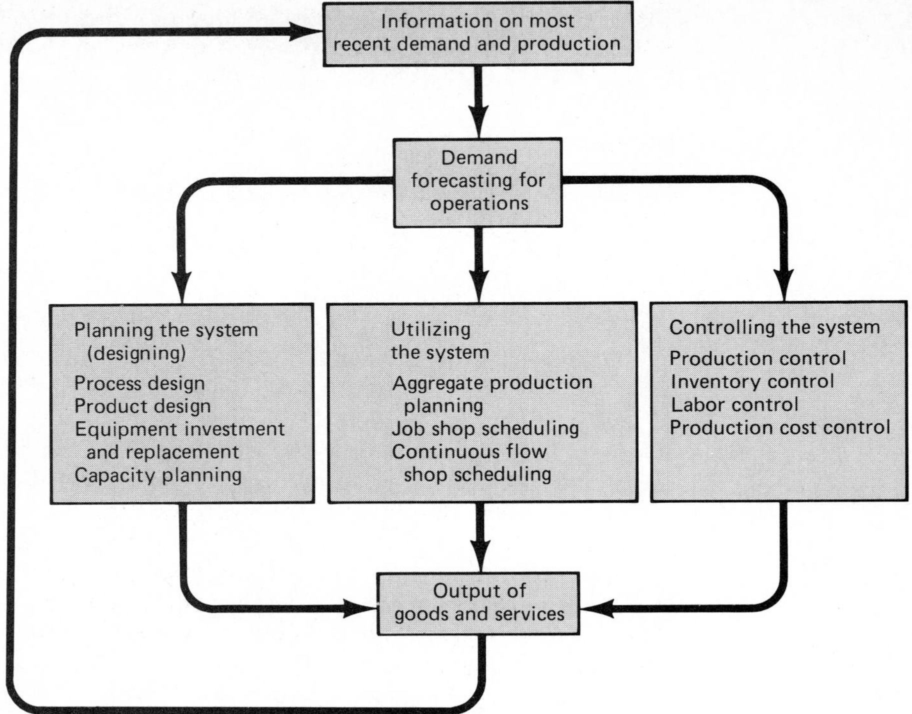

FIGURE 5.3
Demand forecasting and production/operations subsystems

an important component of strategic and operational planning (Chapter 4). It establishes the linkage for planning and control systems discussed in detail throughout this book. Future estimates are necessary for planning the system, planning the use of the system, and controlling the system to facilitate effective and efficient output of goods and services.

Planning (Designing) the System As Figure 5.3 shows, in planning the system we need to know future aggregated demands so that processes can be designed or redesigned to create the product flows necessary to meet demand. The degree to which we automate, for example, depends a great deal upon future product demand. Automated, continuous flows facilitate high production volumes; manual or semiautomated, intermittent flows are generally more economical for smaller production volumes. The demand estimate is critical to this design decision. Once process design, product design, and equipment investment decisions have been made for an anticipated volume, we are locked into a facility of specified capacity. Thereafter wide variations between anticipated demand and actual demand can result in excessive production and operating costs.

These long-run planning decisions require consideration of many factors—general economic conditions, industry trends, likely competitor actions, and overall political climate, among others. Therefore it is not surprising that prediction is used at least as frequently as forecasting in obtaining estimates of long-run future demand.

Capacity planning, which makes use of long-run estimation, is one of the areas in production/operations that is both critical and not well understood or developed. In steel, power generation, and other basic industries, if capacity is not expanded fast enough, both individual firms and the national economy suffer. Particularly during periods of recession, when there is excess capacity, operations managers tend to become overcautious in forecasting and planning additional future capacity. With the costs of excess capacity fresh in their minds, they tend to underestimate future demand.

Utilizing the System For deciding how best to use the existing conversion system, accurate demand forecasts are very important. Management needs intermediate-run capacity forecasts—demand forecasts for three months, six months, and a year into the future. Both current and future work force levels and production rates must be established from these forecasts. Job scheduling in intermittent and continuous operations is more stable if future demand is accurately specified.

Controlling the System As a *production unit basis* for control, forecasting is a short-term problem. Managers need forecasts of demand for operating decisions in production scheduling in job shops and continuous flow shops, for inventory control, production control, labor control, and overall production cost control. Accurate forecasts are needed for the immediate future—hours, days, and weeks ahead. No longer acceptable is an earlier generations' assumption that "all that is produced can be sold." Think about the costs of overproduction of some products and underproduction of others in steel mills, auto manufacturing, and clothing industries. Clearly, survival may depend on production nearing demand in the short run as well as in the long run.

Output of Goods and Services Because of uncertainties in both the environment and the production process, output does not always reach the planned amount, nor does it always correspond with actual demand—even when plans are implemented. Actual demand and output must be monitored, compared with previous plans, and fed back into the demand forecasting decision system so that replanning can be done. As Figure 5.3 shows, the forecasting subsystem is a critical part of the production/operations system. It assists in the interaction among the planning, organizing, and controlling functions so that all the elements can work together for an efficient and effective conversion system.

Characteristics of Demand Over Time

For the systematic analysis of historical data that forecasting problems require, managers commonly use a time series analysis. Analysts plot demand data on a time scale, study the plots, and often discover consistent shapes or patterns. A time series of demand might have, for example, a constant, trend, or seasonal *pattern* (Figure 5.4) or some combination of these patterns (Figure 5.5). A pattern is the general shape of the time series, the general form of its central tendency. Although some individual data points do not fall in the pattern, they tend to cluster around it. To describe the dispersion of individual demands about a pattern, we use the term *noise*. A condition of low noise exists when the points are tightly clustered around the pattern. High noise means the points are highly dispersed. Figure 5.5 shows both high and low noise levels. If you tried to envision the data in Figure 5.5 without the solid line showing the pattern, you might find it difficult to identify the general pattern. Because noise in the demand can effectively disguise the pattern, manual forecasting, and computer modeling as well, can be very difficult; the result can be high forecast errors.

Analysts use the term *stability* to describe a time series's tendency to retain the same general shape over time. The shapes of demand patterns for some products or services change over a period of time, and the shapes for others do not. Future demands are easier to forecast when the pattern is *stationary* (stable) than when it is *dynamic* (unstable). Figure 5.6, taken from a study of demand for frosted microscope slides in a large medical center, shows an example of shifting demand. Examination of the actual demand reveals noticeable upward shifts beginning at about period (week) 150. Later, these shifts become more pronounced. In the study, two forecasting models, simple exponential smoothing and adaptive exponential smoothing, were used to forecast actual demand. These models will be discussed later in this chapter; here we will just observe that one model, the adaptive, responded more quickly to the demand shifts than did the other model.

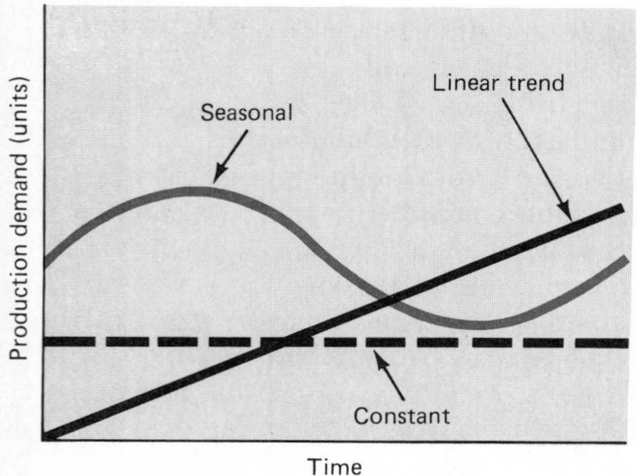

FIGURE 5.4
Demand patterns

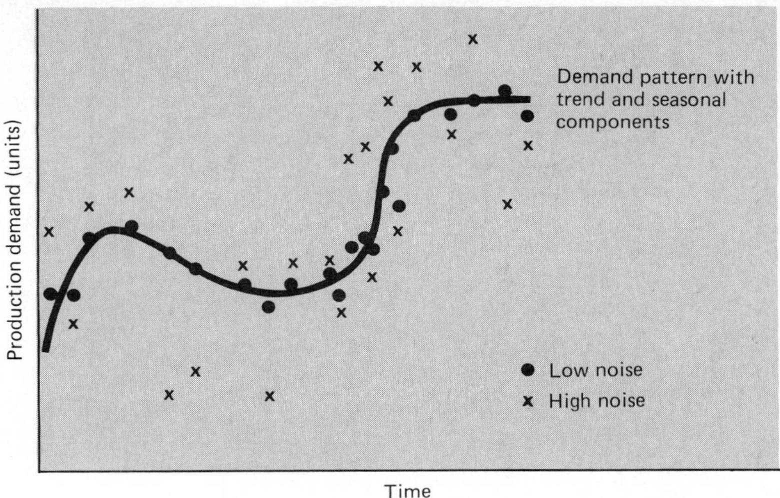

FIGURE 5.5
Noise in demand

Demand can be stationary and demonstrate occasional *outlyers*, points that are not characteristic of the underlying pattern. One bank with multiple branches occasionally and systematically had unusually high daily teller window demand. An investigation found that local industry paydays corresponded to such "spikes." A schedule of industry payroll dates was used to predict outlyers, whereas simple forecasting methods

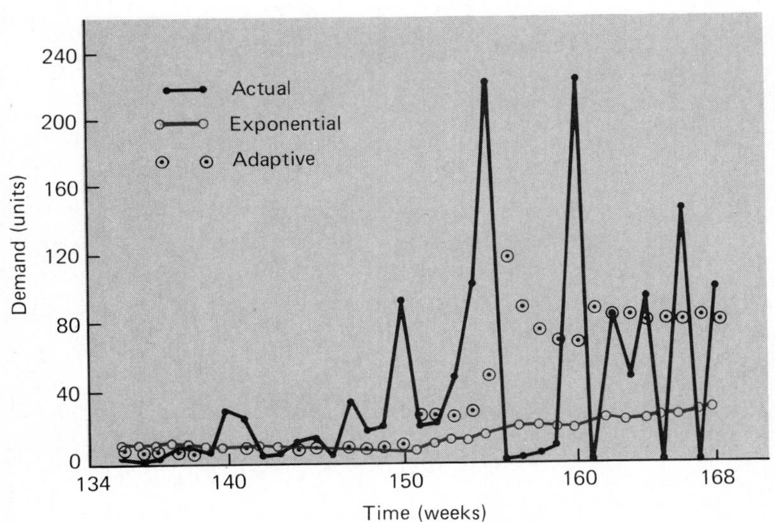

FIGURE 5.6
Frosted microscope slide demand

Source: Everett E. Adam, Jr., William L. Berry, and D. Clay Whybark, "The Hospital Administrator and Management Science," *Hospital & Health Services Administration* 19, no. 1 (Winter 1974), p. 38

were used to forecast the basic demand pattern (once outlyers were explained and treated).[2]

Dependent versus Independent Demand Demand for a product or service is *independent* when it is unrelated to demand for any other product or service. Conversely, *dependent* demand for a product or service occurs when the demand for two or more items interrelates. The dependency may occur when one item demand is derived from a second item (vertical dependency) or when one item relates in another manner to the second item (horizontal dependency). In a movie theater, for example, demand for film postage is independent of demand for popcorn. Vertical dependency might be the relationship between popcorn and theater ticket (patron) demand. Horizontal dependency might be the relationship between popcorn demand and popcorn box demand.

When dependent demand exists in operations management, only the parent item need be forecast; all dependent items can be related to that forecast. If items are independent, there needs to be a forecast for each item. Our discussion in Chapter 16 on material requirements planning (MRP) will further develop this concept.

Later, when we evaluate different forecasting methods, we'll need a measure of effectiveness. Forecast error is the scorekeeping mechanism most commonly used. *Forecast error is the numeric difference between forecasted and actual demand.* Obviously, a method that results in large forecast errors is less desirable than one yielding fewer errors. We'll discuss two measures of error, MAD and Bias.

MAD Equation 5.1 defines a most important error measure, Mean Absolute Deviation (MAD):

$$\text{MAD} = \frac{\text{Sum of absolute deviations for all periods}}{\text{Total number of periods evaluated}} = \frac{\sum_{i=1}^{n} |\text{Forecasted demand} - \text{Actual demand}|_i}{n} \qquad \textbf{(5.1)}$$

In each period (i), you compare the actual demand to the amount you had forecasted. If your forecast was perfect, actual equals the forecasted amount, and there is zero error. As forecasting continues, the degree of error is accumulated and recorded, period by period. After any number of periods (n) has elapsed, you may use equation 5.1 to calculate the average

[2]See William L. Berry, Vincent A. Mabert, and Myles Marcus, "Forecasting Teller Window Demand with Exponential Smoothing," *Academy of Management Journal* 22, no. 1 (March 1979), pp. 129–37 and a related study by Vincent A. Mabert and Arthur V. Hill, "A Combination Projection-Causal Approach for Short Range Forecasts," *International Journal of Production Research* 15, no. 2 (1977), pp. 153–62.

(mean) size of the forecasting error to date. Notice that MAD is an average of several *absolute deviations;* errors are measured without regard to sign. MAD expresses the extent but *not the direction* of error.

There is a relationship between mean absolute deviation and the classical measure of dispersion for forecast error, the standard deviation (σ_e). If the forecast is working properly, forecast errors are normally distributed. When this is so, the smoothed mean absolute deviation (SMAD) is used to estimate the standard deviation. The relationship is:

$$\sigma_e \cong 1.25 \text{ SMAD}$$

Exponential smoothing will be explained later in this chapter; for now you may think of exponentially smoothed MAD as an average MAD over time.

Bias Equation 5.2 is a less commonly used error measure called Bias:

$$\text{Bias} = \frac{\text{Sum of algebraic errors for all periods}}{\text{Total number of periods evaluated}} \tag{5.2}$$

$$= \frac{\sum_{i=1}^{n} (\text{Forecasted demand} - \text{Actual demand})_i}{n}$$

Unlike MAD, Bias indicates the *directional* tendency of forecast errors. If the forecasting procedure repeatedly overestimates actual demand, Bias will have a positive value; consistent underestimation tendencies will be indicated by a negative value.

EXAMPLE

An aluminum extruder estimated demand for a shower stall extrusion to be 500 per month for each of three future months. Later the actual demands turned out to be 400, 560, and 700. His forecast errors, MAD and Bias, are calculated here.

$$\begin{aligned} MAD &= \frac{|500 - 400| + |500 - 560| + |500 - 700|}{3} \\ &= \frac{100 + 60 + 200}{3} \\ &= 120 \text{ units} \\ Bias &= \frac{(500 - 400) + (500 - 560) + (500 - 700)}{3} \\ &= \frac{100 - 60 - 200}{3} \\ &= -53 \text{ units} \end{aligned}$$

As you can see, MAD is 120 units, and Bias is −53 units. Since MAD measures the overall accuracy of the forecasting method, we would conclude that this aluminum extruder does not have a very accurate model. He has a high average absolute error, 24 percent of the forecasted number of shower stall extrusions. The Bias measures *the tendency consistently to over- or underforecast*. In this example, the extrusion forecaster has a tendency to underestimate by 53 units; since actual demand averages 553 units, Bias is, on the average, a 9.6 percent underforecast.

An ideal forecast would have zero MAD and Bias. We find in practice, however, that there is usually a tradeoff between MAD and Bias; in some situations, one must be held low at the expense of the other. If you must stress one at the expense of the other, perhaps MAD should be the focus. Lowering MAD to or near zero will automatically hold Bias low also.

Costs of Errors How important is forecast accuracy? It depends on the situation. Often important decisions are based on forecasted information, and large errors can result in very costly mistakes. Some kinds of estimation errors are more costly than others. In some settings the *direction* of error is critical; in other cases the *magnitude* of error is most important. Although the exact costs of errors are often difficult to determine, forecast errors can and should be converted into costs, even though such a conversion may have to be approximated intuitively.

Equation 5.3 is a general expression showing that operating cost is a function of forecast error:

$$\begin{aligned} \text{Operating cost} &= \text{Function of forecast error} \\ &= [C_1][f(\text{MAD})] + [C_2][f(\text{Bias})] \end{aligned} \qquad \textbf{(5.3)}$$

where:

$$C_1 = \text{relative importance of MAD errors as cost}$$
$$C_2 = \text{relative importance of Bias errors as cost}$$

To avoid a negative cost in the second term above, once f (Bias) is calculated, the absolute value of that function should be computed.

The relative costs of errors of magnitude and direction are not always equal. In the hospital setting in the following example, a slight positive Bias (overproduction) was more acceptable than a negative Bias (underproduction), and it was further desired that MAD be held as near zero as this Bias would allow.

EXAMPLE

In a study in which food service demand was being forecasted at a medical center, dieticians estimated that the cost of underproduction was twice that of overproduction. This was true because the nutritional value of food for patients was important, and the physicians became quite upset when shortages affected their patients. The situation was expressed:

$$\text{Forecast error cost} = C_1\,(\text{Overproduction}) + 2C_1\,(\text{Underproduction})$$

where:

Overproduction occurs when forecast > actual demand
Underproduction occurs when actual demand > forecast

The amount of over- or underproduction is calculated for n periods as follows:

$$\text{Overproduction} = \sum_{i=1}^{n} (\text{Forecast} - \text{Actual})_i$$

$$\text{Underproduction} = \sum_{i=1}^{n} (\text{Actual} - \text{Forecast})_i$$

This set of cost and forecasting relationships was used to select a forecasting model from among several different forecasting models in a 400-bed hospital environment. Since the menu allowed substantial patient selection, eighteen different diets and hundreds of different menu items had to be forecasted daily.[3]

Managers are experiencing continuing difficulty with the accurate forecasts required so that production-inventory systems can be operated at low cost. We now are finding studies directed at investigating the impact of forecast error on production-inventory cost, studies such as the one by Biggs and Campion.[4] They found the critical forecast-error factor to be Bias when evaluating costs in multi-stage (several levels), multi-product, Material Requirements Planning (MRP)-based, production inventory systems. This study illustrates how focusing on forecast error reduction (Bias in this case) can result in lower overall manufacturing costs.

Forecasting in the Service Sector

Traditional production applications are beginning to appear in service sector operations. In 1974 and 1975, the Production/Operations Management Division of the Academy of Management commissioned a study of service sector operations.[5] A questionnaire was distributed to 251 P/OM Division members, primarily to management professors. Responses indicated that of all the traditional P/OM techniques, forecasting is the most frequently ap-

[3]Ann M. Messersmith, Aimee N. Moore, Loretta W. Hoover, "A Multi-Echelon Menu Item Forecasting System for Hospitals," *Journal of the American Dietetic Association* 72 (May 1978), pp. 509–15.

[4]Joseph R. Biggs and William M. Campion, "The Effect and Cost of Forecast Error Bias for Multi-Stage Production-Inventory Systems," *Decision Sciences* 13, no. 4 (October 1982), pp. 570–584.

[5]Everett E. Adam, Jr., John S. Bachman, John S. Fryer, Art Laufer, and Jonathan Rachik, "P/OM Service Sector Study Group Report" (Paper presented at the Academy of Management Conference, New Orleans, Louisiana, August 1975).

plied technique in the service sector. It ranked ahead of many of the other important techniques—systems theory and modeling, job design and work measurement, inventory models, and human behavior models. These results, paired with increased economic activity in the service sector, suggest that the importance of forecasting will continue to increase in the future.

Intuitive or Formal Approaches?

In the practice of operations management today, two fundamental approaches to forecasting are dominant, intuitive estimates of the future and formal statistical modeling. The intuitive approach, which is based on experience, is essentially a summary of a manager's guesses, hunches, and judgments concerning future events. This approach is as much prediction as it is forecasting. The statistical modeling approach systematically combines specific numerical data into a summary value that is then used as a forecast. Within the statistical approach are two basic types of models, which are distinguished by the type of data they use. *Demand-based* models rely solely on historical data about the item that is being forecasted. If we desire a forecast of monthly demand for a lounge chair, for example, our model requires historic monthly demand data for lounge chairs. *Causal* models, on the other hand, may use additional types of data as well. These models might formally relate lounge chair demand to other variables believed to influence demand, such as the number of new housing starts.

A manager must ask several questions when selecting a forecasting approach. First, what is the purpose of the forecast—how is it to be used? Exactly what is being forecasted? Second, the operations manager must ask about the conversion system in which the forecasts will be used. Is this system stable or dynamic, large or small, technologically simple or complex? Finally, the manager must ask how well the past represents the future. What past period to use for future estimates is a difficult decision, and it's the crux of the forecasting dilemma.

Costs and Accuracy There is clearly a cost/accuracy tradeoff in selecting a forecasting approach. The more sophisticated approaches tend to have relatively high costs of implementation and maintenance, but they often provide more accurate forecasts with resulting lower operating costs. Figure 5.7 illustrates one hypothetical cost situation. Note that for any forecasting situation there is an optimal cost region where reasonable accuracy is obtained. Our goal in forecasting for operations is to operate somewhere in this optimal region.

Although this tradeoff generally occurs, there are instances where the more expensive models still do not outperform the less expensive simple models. In one study, causal and econometric models were used to forecast economic time series such as the consumer's price index and gross national product.[6] These forecasts from leading economists were compared to naive

[6]David Ahlers and Josef Lakonishok, "A Study of Economists' Consensus Forecasts," *Management Science* 29, no. 10 (October 1983), pp. 1113–1125.

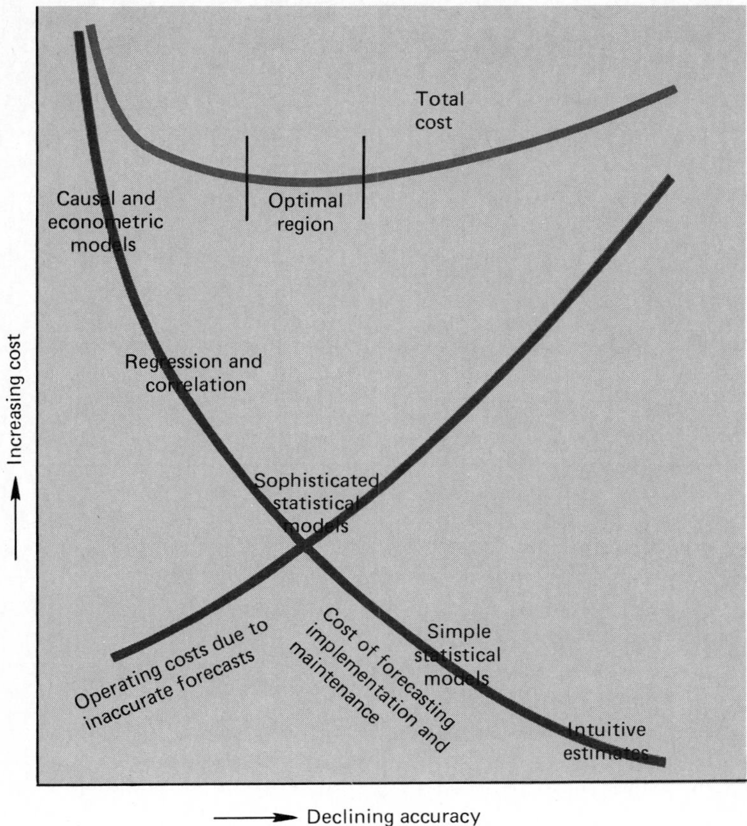

FIGURE 5.7
Cost/accuracy tradeoffs in forecasting

statistical models. The sophisticated models did not outperform the naive models (data from 1947 to 1978), although the sophisticated models did seem to perform better in later years (the 1970s). As a manager, you will want to evaluate carefully the cost of forecasting in relation to the accuracy you are obtaining.

An Overview of Specific Forecasting Methods

We have emphasized that forecasting is a critical part of strategic and operational planning. Others suggest forecasting is a critical component of program planning as well, and they believe that the selection of forecasting techniques depends upon the type of planning that is underway.[7] Rather than get too deeply into specifying types of forecasts for varying situations, we shall summarize: the less analytical, qualitative forecasting methods are

[7]Don Lebell and O. J. Krasner, "Selecting Environmental Forecasting Techniques from Business Planning Requirements," *Academy of Management Review* 2, no. 4 (July 1977), pp. 373–83.

TABLE 5.1
Representative forecasting techniques summarized

Model type	Description
QUALITATIVE MODELS	
Delphi method	Questions panel of experts for opinions
Historical data	Makes analogies to the past in a judgmental manner
Nominal group technique	Group process allowing participation with forced voting
NAIVE QUANTITATIVE MODELS	
Simple moving average	Averages past data to predict the future based on that average
Exponential smoothing	Weights old forecasts and most recent demand
CAUSAL QUANTITATIVE MODELS	
Regression analysis	Depicts a functional relationship among variables
Economic modeling	Provides an overall forecast for a variable such as Gross National Product (GNP)

frequently used for longer-range strategic planning and facilities decisions; the more analytical, time series analysis models are frequently used for operational planning, such as in production and inventory control. Causal forecasting techniques, which are used for a variety of planning situations, are especially helpful in intermediate-term aggregate planning. Let's now look more closely at some of these techniques.

Table 5.1 summarizes modern forecasting techniques. The techniques have been grouped into qualitative methods, naive time series analysis, and causal models. The most frequently used techniques for operations management situations are the qualitative and time series models. The causal models are often more costly to implement and do not offer increased accuracy for short-term item forecasting problems typically faced by the production/operations manager. Even though the qualitative techniques are very popular, they have definite accuracy limitations. We'll limit ourselves to a brief discussion of two qualitative methods and then proceed to some useful time-series models.

Qualitative Techniques

Delphi The Delphi technique is a group process intended to achieve a consensus forecast, often a technological forecast. The process asks a panel of experts from either within or without the organization to provide written comments on the point in question.

The procedure works like this:

1. A question, the situation needing a forecast, is provided in writing to each expert in a general form. Each expert makes a brief prediction.
2. The coordinator who provided the original question brings the statements together, clarifies them, and edits them.
3. The summaries of the experts provide the basis for a set of questions the coordinator now gives to the experts. These are answered.

4. The written responses are brought together by the coordinator and the process repeated until he or she is satisfied with the overall prediction that can be synthesized from the experts.

The key to the Delphi technique lies in the personnel involved. The panel members frequently have diverse backgrounds; two physicists, a chemist, an electrical engineer, and an economist might make up a panel. The coordinator must be talented enough to synthesize diverse and wide-ranging statements and arrive at both a structured set of questions and a forecast.

An advantage of this method is that since direct interpersonal relations are avoided, there are no personality conflicts or dominance by one strong-willed member of the group. The Delphi method has worked successfully for those involved with technological forecasting. For example, a recent study used Delphi to forecast solar electric energy market penetration by the year 2000.[8]

EXAMPLE

At American Hoist and Derrick Company, management felt a need for incorporating its judgments into sales forecasting. Starting with 1975 sales forecasts, management wanted to increase forecasting accuracy to determine just how fast production capacity should be expanded. The Delphi technique was selected to temper historical data with informed judgment. Three rounds of questionnaires were necessary to synthesize judgments of twenty-three key corporate individuals. Previous forecast errors ranged between plus or minus 20 percent. In 1975 the Delphi forecast was \$359.1 million and actual sales \$360.2 million, an error of + 0.3 percent. The 1976 forecast was \$410 million and actual sales \$397 million, an error of − 3.3 percent. The previous forecasting errors were reduced significantly, from 20 percent to less than 4 percent.[9]

Nominal Group Technique The basic assumption behind the nominal group technique is that a structured group of knowledgeable people will be able to arrive at a consensus forecast. The process works like this. Seven to ten people are asked to come to a meeting room and sit around a table in full view of each other, but they are asked not to speak to each other. The group facilitator hands out copies of or writes on a blackboard the question needing a forecast. Each group member is asked to write down ideas about

[8] Rakesh K. Sarin, "An Approach for Long-Term Forecasting with an Application to Solar Energy," *Management Science* 25, no. 6 (June 1979), pp. 543–54.

[9] Shankar Basu and Roger G. Schroeder, "Incorporating Judgments in Sales Forecasts: Application of the Delphi Method at American Hoist and Derrick," *Interfaces* 7, no. 3 (May 1977), pp. 18–27.

the question. After a few minutes, the group facilitator asks each individual in turn to present to the group one idea from his or her list. A recorder writes each idea on a flip chart so that everyone can see it. No discussion takes place in this phase of the meeting; members continue to give their ideas in a round robin manner until all the ideas have been written on the flip chart.

Usually somewhere between fifteen and twenty-five propositional statements result from the round robin, depending upon the question and group composition. During the next phase of the meeting, the members of the group discuss the ideas that have been presented. The facilitator makes sure that all the ideas are discussed; members may ask for clarification of the ideas on the chart. Often similar ideas are combined, and the total number of propositions is reduced. When all discussion has ended, members are asked to vote independently by ranking the ideas, in writing, according to priority. The group decision is the mathematically pooled outcome of the individual votes.

The objectives of the process are:

1. to assure different processes for each phase of creativity,
2. to balance participation among members,
3. to incorporate mathematical voting techniques in the aggregation of group judgment.

The nominal group technique arrives at a forecast, which is the alternative receiving the most votes from the group. Sometimes after the group has been dismissed, several of the high ranking forecasts can be combined into a broader consensus forecast. The keys to the nominal group process are clearly identifying the question to be addressed; allowing creativity; encouraging limited, directed discussion; and ultimately voting.

The nominal group technique can be used for a number of questions besides technological and qualitative forecasting. We have observed, participated in, and conducted nominal group sessions aimed at developing corporate strategies, arriving at a ranking of future scientific research needs, and identifying key quality variables in a quasi-manufacturing and in a service conversion process. The process is not sophisticated; it works; and it leaves group members with a true sense of participation and the organization with tangible outputs.

USEFUL FORECASTING MODELS FOR OPERATIONS

Basic Averaging Models

Many models use historical data to calculate an average of past demand. This average is then used as a forecast. There are several ways of calculating an average; here are a few.

Simple Average *A simple average is an average of past data in which the demands of all previous periods are equally weighted.* It is calculated as follows:

$$\text{Simple Average } (SA) = \frac{\text{Sum of demands for all past periods}}{\text{Number of demand periods}}$$

$$SA = \frac{D_1 + D_2 + \ldots + D_k}{k}$$

where:

D_1 = the demand in the most recent period
D_2 = the demand that occurred two periods ago
D_k = the demand that occurred k periods ago

When simple averaging is used to create a forecast, the demands from all previous periods are equally influential (equally weighted) in determining the average. In fact, a weighting of 1/k is applied to each past demand:

$$SA = \frac{D_1 + D_2 + \ldots + D_k}{k} = \frac{1}{k}D_1 + \frac{1}{k}D_2 + \ldots + \frac{1}{k}D_k$$

Before proceeding further, perhaps we should consider why we are averaging at all. As you may remember from our earlier discussion of "noise" in the demand data, we are trying to detect the underlying general pattern or central tendency of demand. The demand for any one period will probably be above or below the underlying pattern, and the demands for several periods will be dispersed or scattered around the underlying pattern. Therefore, if we average all past demands, the high demands that occurred in several periods will tend to be offset by the low demands in the other periods. The result will be an average that is representative of the true underlying pattern, particularly as the number of periods used in the average increases. Averaging reduces the chances of being misled by a random fluctuation occurring in any single period.

EXAMPLE

At Welds Supplies, total demand for a new welding rod has been 50, 60, and 40 dozen each of the last quarters. The average demand has been:

$$SA = \frac{D_1 + D_2 + D_3}{3}$$

$$= \frac{50 + 60 + 40}{3}$$

$$= 50$$

A forecast for all future periods could be based on this simple average and would be 50 dozen welding rods per quarter.

One advantage of the simple average method is that all past periods' demands enter into the calculation, and thus the effects of randomness are minimized. There is also a major disadvantage, however. If the underlying demand pattern changes over time, the estimate may not be representative of the future. Why? Because although the demands from many periods ago may not be indicative of recent trends, they are still given as much weight as the more recent demands. This difficulty is overcome to some degree by using a simple moving average.

Simple Moving Average *A simple moving average combines the demand data from several of the most recent periods, their average being the forecast for the next period.* Once the number of past periods to be used in the calculations has been selected, it is held constant. We may use a three-period moving average or a twenty-period moving average, but once we decide, we must continue to use the same number of periods. After selecting the number of periods to be used, we weight the demands for each equally to determine the average. The average "moves" over time in that after each period elapses, the demand for the oldest period is discarded, and the demand for the newest period is added for the next calculation.

A simple n-period moving average is:

$$\text{Moving average } (MA) = \frac{\text{Sum of old demands for last } n \text{ periods}}{\text{Number of periods used in the moving average}} \tag{5.5}$$

$$MA = \frac{\sum_{t=1}^{n} D_t}{n} = \frac{1}{n}D_1 + \frac{1}{n}D_2 + \ldots + \frac{1}{n}D_n$$

where:

$t = 1$ is the oldest period in the n-period average
$t = n$ is the most recent period

EXAMPLE

Frigerware has experienced the following product demand for ice coolers this past six months:

Time	Number of ice coolers demanded
January	200
February	300
March	200
April	400
May	500
June	600

The plant manager has requested that you prepare a forecast using a six-period moving average to forecast July sales. It is now July 2nd, and we are to begin our production run on ice coolers July 6th.

$$MA = \frac{\sum_{t=1}^{6} D_t}{6} = \frac{200 + 300 + 200 + 400 + 500 + 600}{6}$$
$$= 367$$

Using a six-month moving average, the July forecast is 367. Now examine the data. Perhaps a three-month moving average might be better than a six-month. If we use three months:

$$MA = \frac{\sum_{t=1}^{3} D_t}{3} = \frac{400 + 500 + 600}{3}$$
$$= 500$$

If we used a one-month moving average, next month's sales is last month's actual demand, and the July forecast is 600.

We must make some recommendation to the plant manager for Frigerware. For now, let's recommend using a three-month moving average of 500 ice coolers for July, since that number looks more representative of the time series than a six-month moving average, and it is based on more data than is the case with a one-month moving average.

Weighted Moving Average Sometimes the forecaster wishes to use a moving average but does not want all n periods equally weighted. *A weighted moving average model is a moving average model that incorporates some weighting of old demand other than an equal weight for all past periods under consideration.* The model is simply:

$$\text{Weighted moving average } (WMA) = \text{Each periods' demand times a weight, summed over all periods in the moving average} \quad \textbf{(5.6)}$$

$$WMA = \sum_{t=1}^{n} C_t D_t$$

where:

$$0 \leq C_t \leq 1.0$$
$$\sum_{t=1}^{n} C_t = 1.0$$

This model allows uneven weighting of demand. If n is three periods, for example, we could weight the most recent period twice as heavily as the other periods by setting $C_1 = 0.25$, $C_2 = 0.25$, and $C_3 = 0.50$.

EXAMPLE

For Frigerware, a forecast of demand for July using a three-period model with the most recent period's demand weighted twice as heavily as each of the previous two periods' demand is:

$$WMA = \sum_{t=1}^{3} C_t D_t = .25(400) + .25(500) + .50(600)$$
$$WMA = 525$$

An advantage of this model is that it allows you to compensate for some trend or for some seasonality by carefully fitting the coefficients, C_t. If you want to, you can weight recent months most heavily and still dampen somewhat the effects of noise by placing small weightings on older demands. Of course, the modeler or manager still has to choose the coefficients, and this choice will be critical to model success or failure.

Exponential Smoothing

Exponential smoothing models are well known and often used in operations management. The reasons for their popularity are two: they are readily available in standard computer software packages, and the models require relatively little data storage and computation, an important consideration when forecasts are needed for each of many individual items. Many computer companies have spent considerable time developing and marketing forecasting software and educating managers in how to use it. In addition, some major professional and trade associations, among them the American Production and Inventory Control Society (APICS), have introduced their members to these techniques.

Exponential smoothing is a specific averaging technique. It is distinguishable by the special way it weights each of the past demands in calculating an average. The pattern of weights is *exponential* in form. Demand for the most recent period is weighted most heavily; the weights placed on successively older periods decay exponentially. In other words, the weights decrease in magnitude the further back in time the data is weighted; the decrease is nonlinear (exponential).

First Order Exponential Smoothing To begin, let's examine the computational aspects of first order exponential smoothing. The equation for creating a new or updated forecast uses two pieces of information: actual demand for the most recent period and the previous (most recent) forecast. As each time period expires, a new forecast is made:

$$\text{Forecast of next period's demand} = \alpha \begin{pmatrix}\text{Most}\\\text{recent}\\\text{demand}\end{pmatrix} + (1 - \alpha) \begin{pmatrix}\text{Most}\\\text{recent}\\\text{forecast}\end{pmatrix} \qquad \textbf{(5.7)}$$
$$F_t = \alpha D_{t-1} + (1 - \alpha)F_{t-1}$$

where:

$$0 \leq \alpha \leq 1.0, \text{ and } t \text{ is the time period}$$

After time period $t - 1$ *ends*, you know the actual demand that occurred (D_{t-1}). At the *beginning* of period $t - 1$ you had made a forecast (F_{t-1}) of what would be demanded during $t - 1$. Therefore, at the *end* of $t - 1$ you have both pieces of information needed for calculating a forecast of demand for the upcoming time period, F_t.

Why is this model called *exponential* smoothing? An expansion of equation 5.7 shows:

Since:

$$F_t = \alpha D_{t-1} + (1 - \alpha)F_{t-1} \tag{5.8}$$

then:

$$F_{t-1} = \alpha D_{t-2} + (1 - \alpha)F_{t-2} \tag{5.9}$$

and similarly:

$$F_{t-2} = \alpha D_{t-3} + (1 - \alpha)F_{t-3} \tag{5.10}$$

We begin expanding by replacing F_{t-1} in equation 5.8 with its equivalent, the right side of equation 5.9:

$$F_t = \alpha D_{t-1} + (1 - \alpha) [\alpha D_{t-2} + (1 - \alpha)F_{t-2}] \tag{5.11}$$
$$F_t = \alpha D_{t-1} + \alpha(1 - \alpha)D_{t-2} + (1 - \alpha)^2F_{t-2}$$

We continue expanding by replacing F_{t-2} in equation 5.11 with its equivalent, the right side of equation 5.10:

$$F_t = \alpha D_{t-1} + \alpha(1 - \alpha)D_{t-2} + (1 - \alpha)^2 [\alpha D_{t-3} + (1 - \alpha)F_{t-3}] \tag{5.12}$$
$$F_t = \alpha D_{t-1} + \alpha(1 - \alpha)D_{t-2} + \alpha(1 - \alpha)^2 D_{t-3} + (1 - \alpha)^3 F_{t-3}$$

Equation 5.12 can be rewritten as:

$$F_t = \alpha(1 - \alpha)^0 D_{t-1} + \alpha(1 - \alpha)^1 D_{t-2} + \alpha(1 - \alpha)^2 D_{t-3} + (1 - \alpha)^3 F_{t-3} \tag{5.13}$$

We have expanded equation 5.8 to obtain equation 5.13. The expansion could be continued further, but it is not necessary for illustrating our point; equation 5.13 shows the relative weight that is placed on each past period's demand in arriving at a new forecast.

Since $0 \leq \alpha \leq 1.0$, the terms $\alpha(1 - \alpha)^0$, $\alpha(1 - \alpha)^1$, $\alpha(1 - \alpha)^2$ . . . are successively smaller in equation 5.13. More specifically, these weights decay exponentially, i.e., they decrease by a constant percentage each period back into the past. The most recent demand, D_{t-1}, is given the most weight, while the older data are weighted less and less heavily. Suppose, for example, that we are using $\alpha = .2$. Then $\alpha(1 - \alpha)^0 = .2$, $\alpha(1 - \alpha)^1 = .16$, $\alpha(1 - \alpha)^2 = .128$, etc., and these are the relative weightings being placed on D_{t-1}, D_{t-2}, D_{t-3}, etc., respectively. Remember, all of this is being accomplished automatically when you use the simple forecasting equation 5.8.

EXAMPLE

Phoenix General Hospital has experienced irregular, and usually increasing, demand for disposable kits throughout the hospital. The demand for a disposable plastic tubing in pediatrics for the last two months has been: September: 300 units and October: 350 units. The old forecasting procedure was to use last year's average monthly demand as the forecast for each month this year. Last year's monthly demand was 200 units. Using 200 units as the September forecast and a smoothing coefficient of 0.7 to weight recent demand most heavily, the forecast for *this* month, October, would have been (t = October):

$$\begin{aligned} F_t &= \alpha\, D_{t-1} + (1 - \alpha)F_{t-1} \\ &= 0.7(300) + (1 - .7)200 \\ &= 210 + 60 \\ &= 270 \end{aligned}$$

The forecast for November would be (t = November):

$$\begin{aligned} F_t &= \alpha\, D_{t-1} + (1 - \alpha)F_{t-1} \\ &= 0.7(350) + (1 - .7)270 \\ &= 245 + 81 \\ &= 326 \end{aligned}$$

Instead of last year's monthly demand for 200 units, November's forecast is for 326 units. The old forecasting method, the heuristic based on a simple average, provided a considerably different forecast from the exponential smoothing model.

Smoothing Coefficient Selection As with other statistical forecasting models, in exponential smoothing we have the problem of parameter selection; that is, we must fit the model to the data. To begin forecasting, some reasonable estimate for an old beginning forecast is necessary. Likewise, a smoothing coefficient, α, must be selected. This choice is critical. As equation 5.7 shows, a high α places heavy weight on the most recent demand, and a low α weights recent demand less heavily. A high smoothing coefficient could be more appropriate for new products or items for which the underlying demand is shifting about (dynamic or unstable). An α of 0.7, 0.8, or 0.9 might be best for these conditions, although we question the use of exponential smoothing at all if unstable conditions are known to exist.

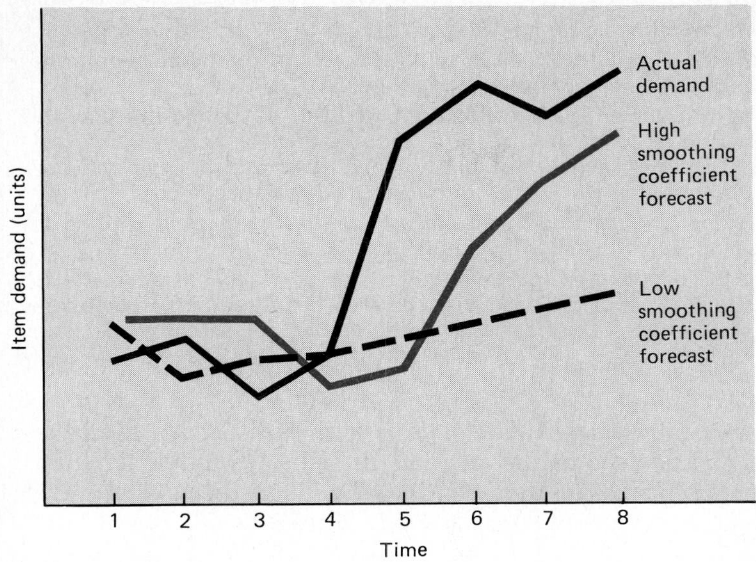

FIGURE 5.8
Selection of smoothing coefficients

If demand is very stable and believed to be representative of the future, the forecaster wants to select a low α value to smooth out any sudden noise that might have occurred. The forecasting procedure, then, does not overreact to the most recent demand. Under these stable conditions, an appropriate smoothing coefficient might be 0.1, 0.2, or 0.3. When demand is slightly unstable, smoothing coefficients of 0.4, 0.5, or 0.6 might provide the most accurate forecasts.

Figure 5.8 illustrates forecasting performance for two different smoothing coefficients for an unstable demand series. The exponential smoothing model with the higher α value performed best; it adapted more quickly to the shift in demand in period 6 than did the lower α value.

Simple exponential smoothing and the other exponential smoothing models share the advantages of requiring that very few data points be stored. To update the forecast from period to period, you need only α, last period's demand, and last period's forecast. Remember, this model incorporates in the new forecast *all past demands*. The model is easy to understand and easily computerized for thousands of part numbers, supply items, or inventory items. The smoothing coefficient can be set for classes or families of items to minimize the cost of parameter selection. We have observed use of the model in both the manufacturing and service sectors. The model's operating simplicity and efficiency for economically obtaining "quick and easy" forecasts are its main advantages.

Selecting Forecasting Parameters and Comparing Models The procedure for selecting forecasting parameters is given in the first four steps that follow; the fifth step is used for comparing and selecting models:

1. Partition the available data into two subsets, one for fitting parameters (the "test" set) and the other for forecasting.
2. Select an error measure to evaluate forecast accuracy of the parameters to be tried. MAD and/or Bias are useful error measures.
3. Select a range of α values to be evaluated. Using one of the α values, apply the forecasting model to the test set of data, recording the resulting forecast errors. Then, selecting a new value for α, repeat the process. Continue this process until representative α values in the selected range have been tested.
4. Select the α value that resulted in the lowest forecast error when applied to the test data. Your model is now fit to the demand data.
5. Forecast with the exponential (or moving average) model that you have fit to test data on the balance of the data. You can also use these data to compare alternative models that have previously been fit to representative demand data.

If you do not intend to compare models, there is no need to partition the data; *all* the data can be used as the test data in steps 1 through 4. Those familiar with computer programming can visualize how using computers can speed computations when this procedure is followed.

Adaptive Exponential Smoothing If the modeler or manager is unsure about the stability or form of the underlying demand pattern, adaptive exponential smoothing provides a good forecasting alternative. In adaptive exponential smoothing, the smoothing coefficient, α, is not fixed; it is set initially and then allowed to fluctuate over time based upon changes in the underlying demand pattern. This method is discussed in the supplement at the end of this chapter.

Regression

Linear Regression Regression analysis is a forecasting technique that establishes a relationship between variables. One variable is known and used to forecast the value of an unknown random variable. From past data a functional relationship is established between the two variables. We will consider the most simple regression situation here, for only two variables and for a linear functional relationship between them.

Our forecast of next period's demand, F_t, is expressed by

$$F_t = a + bX_t \tag{5.14}$$

where F_t is the forecast for period t, given the value of the variable X in period t. The coefficients a and b are constants; a the intercept value for the verticle axis (F axis) and b the slope of the linear line. Often this equation is expressed in the more familiar form

$$Y = a + bX. \tag{5.15}$$

We have substituted F for Y, to indicate F is the forecasted value. In equation 5.14 forecasted demand, F_t, reflects the future. However, to actually find coefficients a and b, old demand is utilized rather than the old forecast. We use D_t to reflect old demand and to find coefficients a and b. Then, once we want to forecast new demand, we use F_t to represent forecasted demand. The coefficients a and b are computed by the following two equations:

$$b = \frac{n\,(\Sigma X_t D_t) - (\Sigma X_t)\,(\Sigma D_t)}{n(\Sigma X_t^2) - (\Sigma X_t)^2} \tag{5.16}$$

$$a = \frac{\Sigma D_t - b\Sigma X_t}{n} \tag{5.17}$$

where:

$$D = a + bX \tag{5.18}$$

EXAMPLE

A paper box company makes carryout pizza boxes. The operations planning department knows that an accurate forecast of pizza boxes for a major customer depends upon the customer's advertising expenditures, which they can receive in advance of the expenditure. Operations planning is interested in establishing the relationship between the pizza company's advertising and sales. Once that is established the pizza boxes ordered, in dollar volume, is known to be a fixed percent of sales.

Quarterly Advertising and Sales

Quarter	Advertising ($100,000)	Sales ($ million)
1	4	1
2	10	4
3	15	5
4	12	4
5	8	3
6	16	4
7	5	2
8	7	1
9	9	4
10	10	2

Computing b and then a, where advertising is X_t for quarter t, sales is D_t for quarter t, and forecast is F_t for future period t,

Quarter	X Advertising	D Sales	X^2	D^2	XD
1	4	1	16	1	4
2	10	4	100	16	40
3	15	5	225	25	75
4	12	4	144	16	48
5	8	3	64	9	24
6	16	4	256	16	64
7	5	2	25	4	10
8	7	1	49	1	7
9	9	4	81	16	36
10	10	2	100	4	20
Σ	96	30	1060	108	328

$$b = \frac{10(328) - (96)30}{10\,(1060) - (96)^2} = 0.29$$

$$a = \frac{30 - .29(96)}{10} = 0.22$$

Thus, the estimated regression line, the relationship between future sales (F_t) and advertising (X_t) is

$$F_t = .22 + .29\,X_t$$

In the example above, the operations planner can now ask for planned advertising expenditures and from that forecast sales. Say, for example, next quarter advertising was expected to be \$1,100,000. Substituting 11 into the above equation for X_t gives

$$F_t = .22 + .29(11) = 3.41$$

Sales are forecast as \$3,410,000. If box orders are 5 percent of sales, the operations planner could expect the total dollar orders to be \$170,500 for the quarter (0.05 × \$3,410,000). Such an estimate can be very helpful in overall operations planning.

Although linear regression methods are computationally more complex than the others we've discussed, they have been found useful in some situations. They may be applied, for example, when a plot of the data suggests that the underlying pattern is a straight line, or nearly so. When data are linear and stable, linear regression can sometimes be used. It requires much data, however, and they can be cumbersome and costly to store. It's also costly to perform the required calculations period by period, often weekly, for thousands of production or operations supply items.

SELECTION OF THE FORECASTING MODEL

We've discussed several statistical forecasting models for demand estimation in planning and control. As a manager, you now have the task of selecting the best model for your needs. Which one should you choose, and what criteria should you use to make the decision?

As we've said before, criteria that influence model selection are *cost* and *accuracy*. Accuracy (forecast error), as measured by MAD and Bias, can be converted into cost (dollars). *Costs to be considered in model selection are implementation costs, systemic costs, and forecast error costs.* Implementation costs include costs of programming and costs of initializing forecasting parameters, training users, and the initial dysfunctional effects of changing from an old forecasting procedure. Systemic costs include costs of monitoring the forecasting system, computer run time or manual computation time, and other costs of maintaining the forecasting system. *Time* required to prepare and implement the forecast is an important criterion. Time could be viewed as a forecasting cost. Nevertheless, quick forecasting procedures are always favored over lengthy (slow) procedures.

Forecast error costs are more complex to evaluate. They depend upon noise in the time series, the form of the demand pattern, the length of the forecasting time horizon, and the measure of forecast error. We can reach one conclusion, however: *forecast error and subsequent model selection are dependent upon the underlying demand pattern.* There is little value in selecting a model that does not correspond to the underlying demand pattern. Errors will be high and costly. A simple moving average model, for example, will always lag a linear trend component, and the result will be high forecast errors, especially if the number of periods used in the average is large. There is no substitute for careful analysis of typical item demands, including plots, when a model is being selected.

Several studies have evaluated and compared the performances of different models. One study considered the effects of differences in level of noise, demand pattern, and time horizon on forecast errors for a limited set of forecasting models. The intent was to identify the better forecasting model under these various conditions. The summary of results is presented as Figure 5.9. Although some of the models that were found to be best are too complex for our introductory treatment (except for double exponential smoothing, which is presented in the supplement to this chapter), you should notice that different models were best, depending on the type of demand pattern, noise level, and length of forecast period, and that several models were usually equally good. It is typical in forecasting to have a choice of several good models for any one demand pattern when the choice is based only on forecast error. *Notice also that double exponential smoothing is among the best for each demand pattern.* This is one of the study's most significant conclusions.

Length of forecast period	1 period ahead					12 periods ahead				
Across all demand patterns and noise levels: best models*	(6), (4), (2)					(6)				
Demand pattern* across all noise levels	1	2	3	4	5	1	2	3	4	5
Best model(s)*	(4), (6) (7), (2)	(6), (2) (4), (1)	(3), (4) (6), (2) (7), (1)	(3), (4) (6), (2) (7), (1)	all	(4), (6) (2), (7)	(6)	(3), (4) (2), (6) (7)	(6)	(3), (6)
Noise level across all demand patterns	Low		High			Low		High		
Best model(s)*	(2), (1), (6)		(4), (6), (3)			(6)		(6), (3), (4), (2)		

*Variable descriptions

Independent variable	Level	Description
Demand pattern	1	Constant
	2	Linear trend
	3	Seasonal
	4	Permanent, seasonal and trend
	5	Linear trend and step function
Forecast model	(1)	Moving average (1 period)
	(2)	Moving average (2 period)
	(3)	Winters' model
	(4)	First order exponential smoothing
	(5)	Second order exponential smoothing
	(6)	Exponential double smoothing
	(7)	Adaptive exponential smoothing

FIGURE 5.9
Forecast model selection based on forecast errors

Source: Adapted from Everett E. Adam, Jr., "Individual Item Forecasting Model Evaluation," *Decision Sciences* 4, no. 4 (October 1973), p. 468, as modified by Dennis W. McCleavy, T. S. Lee, and Everett E. Adam, Jr. "Evaluating Individual Item Forecasting Models," *Decision Sciences* 12, no. 4, (October 1981), pp. 708–714.

Combining Naive Forecasting Models In an application within check processing at Chemical Bank of New York a two-stage forecasting method was developed to estimate daily workloads. Regression and simple exponential smoothing were combined, the combined model outperforming regression used alone, forecast errors 7.5 percent smaller in the combined model.[10]

[10]Kevin Boyd and Vincent A. Mabert, "A Two State Forecasting Approach at Chemical Bank of New York for Check Processing," *Journal of Bank Research* 8, no. 2 (Summer 1977), pp. 101–107.

In a more comprehensive study, Makridakis found that simple average and a weighted average of forecasts from six methods outperformed most or perhaps even all of the individual methods.[11] The six methods being combined as well as sixteen others were estimated as separate forecasting models. This motivated another study by Makridakis and Winkler in which they also averaged several models.[12] They conclude that the forecasting accuracy improves, and that the variability of accuracy among different combinations decreases, as the number of methods in the average increases. Combining forecasting models holds considerable promise for operations. As the authors state, "combining forecasts seems to be a reasonable practical alternative when, as is often the case, a true model of the data generating process or a single best forecasting method cannot or is not, for whatever reasons, identified."[13]

BEHAVIORAL DIMENSIONS OF FORECASTING

To understand some of the dimensions of forecasting you have to consider human behaviors because forecasts are not always made with statistical models. Individuals can and do forecast by intuitively casting forth past data, and they often intervene in other ways in the statistical forecasting procedure as well. A manager may feel that item forecasts generated by models must be checked for reasonableness by qualified operating decision makers. Forecasts generated by models should not be followed blindly; potential cost consequences must be carefully considered. Sometimes the model forecasts will not be changed after review; sometimes they will be adjusted. In making these adjustments, decision makers can take into account qualitative data that are not in the model. (When a change based on other data is made, the forecast becomes a prediction.) Decision makers should use the forecasting model as an *aid* in decision making; they should not rely totally on the forecasting model for all decisions.

Individual Versus Model Forecasting

Many, perhaps most, forecasts for production/operations are individual intuitive forecasts. We have observed intuitive forecasts, for example, in large firebrick manufacturing facilities and in hospitals. One of the problems in implementing item forecasting models lies in convincing the intuitive forecaster that he or she is not doing as good a job as could be done by a model.

[11]Spyros Makridakis, et al., "The Accuracy of Extrapolation (Time Series) Methods: Results of a Forecasting Competition," *Journal of Forecasting* 1 (1982), pp. 111–153.

[12]Spyros Makridakis and Robert L. Winkler, "Averages of Forecasts: Some Empirical Results," *Management Science* 29, no. 9 (September 1983), pp. 987–996.

[13]Ibid., p. 987.

EXAMPLE

For a 400-bed hospital, forecasts of the daily patient load for food services, the daily census, were being made manually. (See Fig. 5.10.) An experienced dietician was making these forecasts, but they incorporated considerable bias, partly because she feared the medical staff if shortages occurred. An adaptive exponential smoothing model improved considerably on the manual procedure, and the resulting implementation considerably reduced food costs from overproduction.

Intuitive Forecasting as a Judgmental Process

Currently, little is known about the relative effectiveness of intuitive forecasting. We can, however, provide a structured approach for examining this area of human behavior by analyzing some of the mental processes involved. A forecast may be regarded as the culmination of a process consisting of several stages, including information search and information processing. It results in human inferences about the future that are based on particular patterns of historical data presented to the forecaster. We can

FIGURE 5.10
Forecasting daily patient census in a hospital: exponential smoothing with tracking vs. manual procedures

Ronald J. Harris and Everett E. Adam, Jr., "Forecasting Patient Tray Census for Hospital Food Service." Reprinted with permission from *Health Services Research* (Winter 1975), p. 384.
Copyright by the Hospital Research and Educational Trust, 840 North Lake Shore Drive, Chicago, Illinois 60611.

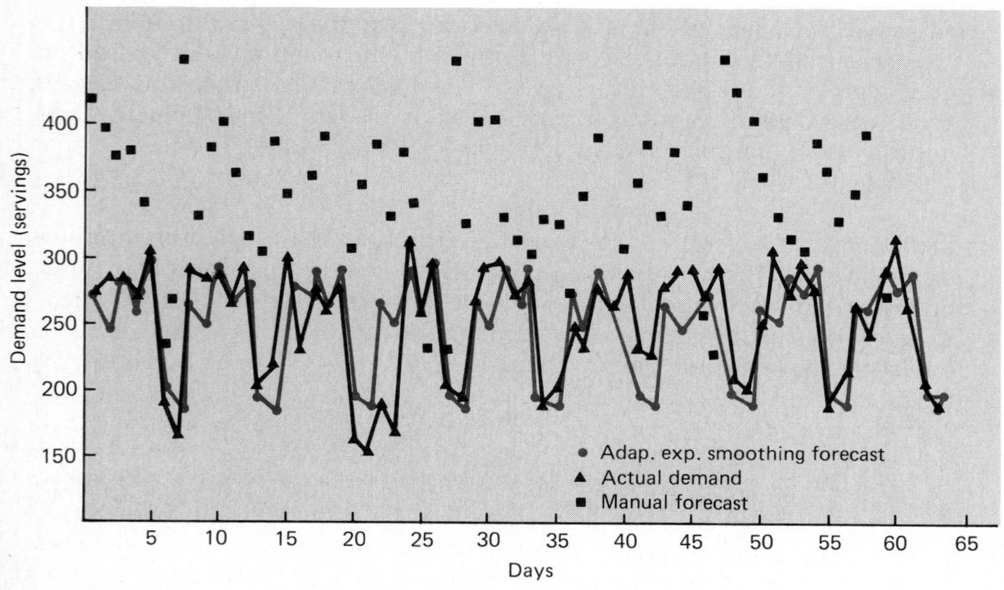

speculate about a number of environmental factors that may affect these mental processes and thereby affect intuitive forecasting performance.

Meaningfulness The forecasting task itself requires the consideration of a restricted set of information cues about historical demand. Although the manner in which these data are utilized to make a "good" forecast may be complex, usually the form and type of information encountered are repetitious. When we discuss job enrichment and job design (Chapter 10), we will find that if repetitious tasks can be made meaningful to the person performing them, positive effects usually result. Therefore, management should make the forecaster aware that his or her efforts are important to the company. If forecasts are accurate, the forecasters should be told that they are, so their behavior is reinforced. Furthermore, the forecaster should know that his or her information will contribute substantially to subsequent decisions affecting the entire organization. Imparting meaningfulness, then, may be expected to affect intuitive forecasting performance; the more meaningful the forecasting task, the more accurate the intuitive forecast.

Pattern Complexity The forecaster may be confronted with any of a variety of demand-generating functions. Previously we mentioned constant, trend, and seasonal effects. Adding two or more components together (adding trend and seasonal components, for example) results in a more complex data generating function than either separately. Pattern complexity, the shape of the demand function, is a critical variable in intuitive forecasting, just as it is in model forecasting.

Some behavioral studies lead us to suggest that intuitive forecasters may perform better on linear than on nonlinear demand patterns. In many instances, when people try to make inferences based on nonlinear data their performance is less accurate than when linear data are present. In addition, people apparently try to use nonlinear data in a linear manner. Intuitive forecasting accuracy is probably lower for nonlinear than for linear demand patterns.

Degree of Noise Given sufficient historical data, the forecasting problems are trivial for most cases without noise. Introducing random variations, however, often brings about a condition psychologists call "cue uncertainty." Cue uncertainty results when noise in the old demand (the cue) hides or masks the basic demand pattern. At one extreme are demand patterns with zero random variability (no noise). Since no randomness is present, the past data provide a clear picture of the basic demand pattern. In other instances, however, the degree of noise is larger, and intuitive forecasting variability increases. Very large noise levels obscure the basis for accurate forecasting, and often the result is lower forecast accuracy.

Meaningfulness, pattern complexity, and degree of noise are three environmental factors that may affect human forecasting. These three factors

TABLE 5.2
Intuitive forecasting mean errors*

Factor	Level (mean error)		
Demand pattern, *A* (pattern complexity)	Trend (18.73)	Trend, low seasonal (17.77)	Trend, high seasonal (24.86)
Meaningfulness, *B*	Meaningful (20.00)	Nonmeaningful (20.91)	
Noise in demand, *C* (cue uncertainty)	High (27.66)	Low (13.25)	

*Source: Everett E. Adam, Jr. and Ronald J. Ebert, "A Comparison of Human and Statistical Forecasting," *AIIE Transactions* 8, no. 1 (March 1976), pp. 120–27. Copyright American Institute of Industrial Engineers, 25 Technology Park/Atlanta, Norcross, Georgia 30092.

were examined in a laboratory study of intuitive forecasting (see Table 5.2). The results indicated that pattern complexity and noise level did significantly affect forecast errors. The lower the mean error, the better that group's forecasting performance. Meaningfulness, as defined in this study, had no effect on forecast error. This result is inconsistent with many other job enrichment studies but concurs with some of the critics of the meaningfulness concept who question whether meaningfulness always uniformly increases performance.

Individual Variability Another finding in this study of intuitive forecasting was the wide variability of performance among the 240 forecasters. There were a few very good forecasters, but there were even more very poor forecasters. If planning and directing production and operations are based on poor intuitive forecasts, these variations in performance can be very expensive.

Individual versus Model Performance In this same study, one-period-ahead forecasts were made for sixty consecutive periods by both human forecasters and several models. The exponential smoothing models, which were fit to the historical demands given to the intuitive forecasters, significantly outperformed group average performance on both period-by-period and overall bases. The findings are illustrated in Table 5.3. Again, the poor forecasters experienced especially high errors compared to the models. Only a few very good intuitive forecasters outperformed the models.

We know that intuitive forecasting and prediction are commonplace. Although models seem to compare favorably to intuitive forecasts, field studies (well-documented real world experiences) are needed to support this contention. Again, as was the case with model selection, the complexity of demand patterns and the noise in the demand patterns are critical to intuitive forecasting performance. The operations manager would be wise to consider models as an alternative to individuals. Models generally are more accurate, and if a large number of items must be forecast, the models are more economical.

TABLE 5.3
Forecasting models vs. human performance*

Experimental condition	Forecast model mean error	Human performance mean error
Across patterns and noise		
First order[1]	17.306	20.460
Winters[2]	14.111	20.460
Patterns (across noise)		
First order		
Trend	12.083	18.737
Trend, low seas.	14.416	17.777
Trend, high seas.[3]	25.416	24.866
Winters		
Trend	11.250	18.737
Trend, low seas.[3]	16.250	17.777
Trend, high seas.	14.833	24.866
Noise (across patterns)		
High Noise		
First order	22.500	27.660
Winters	18.444	27.660
Low noise		
First order[3]	12.111	13.259
Winters	9.777	13.259

*Source: Adam and Ebert, pp. 120–27. Copyright American Institute of Industrial Engineers, 25 Technology Park/Atlanta, Norcross, Georgia 30092.
[1]First order exponential smoothing model.
[2]Winters three factor exponential smoothing with constant, trend, and seasonal factors.
[3]No significant differences between means. All other means were significantly different at $p < 0.001$.

Forecasting, Planning, and Behavior An excellent literature review and evaluation compares many modeling and psychological dimensions of forecasting, planning, and decision-making.[14] Many information processing limitations and biases involving human judgment apply to forecasting and planning as well. Errors found to exist in forecasting procedures include accumulation of redundant information, failure to seek possible disconfirming evidence, and overconfidence in judgment. In addition, insufficient attention has been given to the implications of numerous studies that show that the predictive judgment of humans is frequently less reliable than that of simple quantitative models. Applied studies of forecasting and planning are also reviewed and shown to mirror many of the findings of psychology. Those interested in the behavioral aspects of forecasting or the forecasting and planning interactions will want to examine this comparative analysis more closely.

[14]Robin M. Hogarth and Spyros Makridakis, "Forecasting and Planning: An Evaluation," *Management Science* 27, no. 2 (February 1981), pp. 115–138.

SUMMARY

In operations management, we deviate from the general business concept of business forecasting and define forecasting as the use of past data to determine future events. Prediction, on the other hand, refers to subjective estimates of the future. The skill, experience, and sound judgment of a manager are required for good predictions; often statistical and management science techniques must be used to make reasonable forecasts. Forecasts are a part of planning and subsequently become an input in operations for design, additional planning phases, and control.

There is a cost/accuracy tradeoff in selecting a forecasting approach. Generally, the less expensive the forecasting procedure, the less accurate the results. There are three basic groupings of forecasting techniques: qualitative models, time series analysis, and causal models. The individual item forecasting situation most frequently encountered in production/operations is best approached with time series models.

Research results show that the best forecasting model to use depends upon the forecast time horizon, noise, the measure of forecast error, and, most importantly, the demand pattern. There appears to be no one forecasting model that is best for all demand patterns, although double exponential smoothing does as well as any other.

Often, forecasts are not made with statistical models; individuals can and do intuitively use past data to forecast future events. Generally, individual forecasting performance *decreases* with lack of meaningfulness, increased pattern complexity, and increased cue uncertainty. Generally, forecasting models tend to outperform most intuitive forecasts. There are, however, a few individuals who seem consistently to outperform the models. Since models are generally more accurate and, if a large number of items must be forecasted, more economical than individuals, operations managers would be wise to consider their use.

CASE

Northwestern Hospital Supply, Inc.

Suzi Trotter was hired by a hospital supply company, Northwestern Hospital Supply, Inc., as a salesperson two years ago. Having been successful in developing sales in western Oregon, Suzi has been shifted to operations and is now an operations analyst. She knows that if she can perform well in this job, she will likely be a regional operations manager or an area sales manager in twelve to thirty-six months.

Suzi's first assignment is to recommend an item forecasting procedure for a family of parts that includes orthopedic supplies. The demand for one representative item, burn dressing rolls, is shown in the table below. The current forecasting procedure for this item is an intuitive estimate by an experienced supply clerk. After reviewing class notes from an operations course she took three years ago at Oregon State, Suzi has decided to test a forecasting model, first order exponential smoothing. Her supervisor thinks the data are seasonal and would like a model that reflects seasonality. Suzi would like to use the company's computer to test differing values of the smoothing coefficient, but she is unsure of her programming skills.

After thinking about a forecasting model and selecting parameters (such as starting values and smoothing coefficients), Suzi has decided to use MAD as her primary evaluation mechanism. She has heard of Bias, but remembers nothing of significance that would suggest she should use it.

Burn dressing roll demand

Time period (week)	Sales	Time period (week)	Sales
1	1084	25	964
2	1056	26	936
3	1090	27	970
4	953	28	833
5	868	29	748
6	868	30	847
7	1034	31	905
8	1088	32	968
9	1069	33	861
10	856	34	736
11	876	35	757
12	796	36	752
13	1023	37	903
14	1003	38	883
15	1036	39	916
16	835	40	715
17	747	41	691
18	856	42	736
19	1008	43	888
20	1036	44	908
21	920	45	909
22	805	46	685
23	816	47	696
24	776	48	692

Suggested Case Questions

1. Plot the data and identify any patterns you observe from the plot.
2. Design an analysis procedure for Suzi Trotter. Include forecasting model(s), evaluation measure(s), and the procedure for setting starting values and model parameters for any model to be tested.
3. How could simple moving average and first order exponential models be modified to include adjustments for trend and seasonal data?
4. Carry out the recommended analysis in question 2 above. Using a computer or programmable calculator might be beneficial but is not necessary.
5. Discuss the implementation problems Suzi might encounter once her analysis is complete.

CASE

Spradling Enterprises

Spradling Enterprises manufactures household cleaning products. One product, Stain-ReMover, product number SRM-10, has been difficult to produce in enough volume to sustain inventory between production batches. The table illustrates monthly demand in 24-case lots for the last fifteen months, essentially the total life of SRM-10.

Monthly demand for SRM-10 in 24 case lots

Month	Demand	Month	Demand
December 1984	22	August	57
January 1985	40	September	55
February	32	October	65
March	55	November	73
April	67	December	90
May	53	January 1986	81
June	90	February	93
July	62		

The production manager has asked production control to reexamine the item forecasting procedure for this product. In production control, the initial twelve month forecast from marketing is always used for a new product. In the absence of other instructions, their forecast of 50 lots per month has been used to date for SRM-10.

Spradling Enterprises uses first order exponential smoothing for forecasting item demand for all items after one year of product experience has occurred. Either a slow smoothing (smoothing coefficient of 0.2) or a fast smoothing (smoothing coefficient of 0.7) model is used for each product. The choice of fast or slow smoothing is based primarily on Mean Absolute Deviation (MAD) over the last six periods of data, with some consideration given secondarily to Bias. The initial forecast needed to evaluate fast or slow smoothing for a new product is always the marketing forecast.

The production control manager is concerned about the specific problem of changing the SRM-10 forecast to correspond with current procedures and the more general problem of developing a check list for reviewing the existing forecasting procedure for possible improvement.

REVIEW AND DISCUSSION QUESTIONS

1. Contrast forecasting and prediction and give an example of each.
2. Forecasting is an important information input for operations subsystem decisions. Explain what might be forecast for a supermarket operation and relate that information to Figure 5.3.
3. Explain what the demand noise, pattern, and stability are in time series analysis.

4. Which would you use in evaluating a forecast, MAD or Bias? Why?
5. Present any evidence that suggests forecasting is an important problem in the service sector.
6. Examine Table 5.1, which summarizes modern forecasting techniques. Is there any one best technique? What can be concluded from this table?
7. Contrast the cost/accuracy tradeoffs in forecasting model selection between sophisticated statistical models and intuitive estimates.
8. Explain how the nominal group technique would arrive at a consensus forecast.
9. Explain how the Delphi technique would arrive at a consensus forecast.
10. Individuals forecast intuitively. What are some of the variables that affect the relative effectiveness of those intuitive forecasts?
11. Compare intuitive forecasting to naive statistical forecasting models, citing any relevant research.

PROBLEMS

Solved Problems

1. Demand for part number 2710 has been as shown below. Our forecast for April was 100 units. With a smoothing constant of 0.20 and using first order exponential smoothing, what is the July forecast? What do you think about a 0.20 smoothing constant?

Time	Actual demand
April	200
May	50
June	150

$$F_t = \alpha D_{t-1} + (1 - \alpha)F_{t-1}$$
$$F_{MAY} = .20(200) + (1 - .2)100$$
$$= 120$$
$$F_{JUNE} = .2(50) + (1 - .2)120$$
$$= 106$$
$$F_{JULY} = .2(150) + (1 - .2)106$$
$$= 114.8 \cong 115$$

The July forecast is 115 units (fractional units should be rounded to be realistic). The 0.20 smoothing constant implies that recent demand should not be weighted heavily. This seems appropriate for this data. If demand is unstable, a higher constant should be used. The forecast should react quickly to changes in demand. However, if over a long period demand smooths out, the 0.20 constant may be satisfactory, since it helps to remove noise. It is almost impossible to select a smoothing coefficient with only three periods of data.

2. An ice cream parlor experienced the following demand for ice cream last month. The current forecasting procedure is to use last year's corresponding weekly sales as this year's forecast.

Week	Forecasted demand (gallons)	Actual demand (gallons)
June 1	210	200
June 8	235	225
June 15	225	200
June 22	270	260

Calculate MAD and BIAS and interpret each. Solution:

$$\text{MAD} = |210 - 200| + |235 - 225| + |225 - 200| + |270 - 260|$$
$$= \frac{55}{4}$$
$$= 13.75$$
$$\text{Bias} = (210 - 200) + (235 - 225) + (225 - 200) + (270 - 260)$$
$$= \frac{55}{4}$$
$$= +13.75$$

Since all monthly errors are positive, each error measure gives the same result: the forecasts are consistently high, an average of 13.75 gallons each week.

Reinforcing Fundamentals

3. A Midwestern crop pesticide control manufacturer has experienced the following monthly demand for an environmentally improved pesticide poison.

Month	Demand item #corn-201 (cases)
February	725
March	900
April	810
May	1050
June	1100

(a) Using a simple average, what would the forecast have been for May and June?
(b) What would the three month simple moving average have been for May and June?
(c) Which forecasting method would you recommend? Why?

4. The monthly cost of overstocking crates of bananas in a grocery chain is estimated to be $7.50 times the absolute value of average daily Bias for any one month.
(a) Express this relationship as a cost function.
(b) If daily Bias was a positive 121 crates last month, what was the total cost for that error?
(c) How much should management be willing to spend for a perfect forecast?

5. A hardware chain, Max's, experienced the following demand for paint last month. The current forecasting procedure is to use last year's corresponding weekly sales as this year's forecast. Calculate MAD and Bias and interpret each.

Week	Forecasted demand (gallons)	Actual demand (gallons)
June 1	1,320	1,310
June 8	1,335	1,325
June 15	1,350	1,325
June 22	1,370	1,360

6. A department store analyst is interested in using the *change in price* of sugar in any given month to predict the change in price of candy the following month. She chooses a widely watched exchange and observes the following monthly sequence of *prices* (not price changes):

   80, 82, 85, 81, 80, 80, 80, 84, 88, 89, 90, 88, 84.

   Candy prices in the same months are:

   105, 100, 105, 114, 107, 105, 104, 105, 110, 117, 120, 121, 118

   (a) Construct the appropriate scatter diagram and plot the data.
   (b) Find the estimated regression line.
   (c) What do you conclude about the relationship the analyst is interested in? Might this lead to improved forecasts? How can that help store operations?

7. In finished goods, Blakeman's Supply stocks three horsepower motors. Weekly demand for twelve typical weeks is:

Week	Demand for 3-hp motor	Week	Demand for 3-hp motor
42	20	48	9
43	17	49	4
44	12	50	6
45	14	51	5
46	8	52	4
47	10	53	3

   (a) Calculate a weighted moving average forecast for weeks 54 and 55 using a three-period model with the most recent period's demand weighted three times as heavily as each of the previous two period's demands. After forecasting period 54, actual demand was 6 motors for the period.
   (b) Examining the data visually, what would you suggest as a possible alternative weighted moving average model? Why?

8. A lumber company forecasts demand based on the last two months simple moving average. What would the forecast be for the following items for May? Specify any assumptions you make.

Month	Exterior plywood sheets Demand	Exterior plywood sheets Forecast	B&D saws Demand	B&D saws Forecast	Craft paper rolls Demand	Craft paper rolls Forecast
January	20	25	10	15	2	0
February	missing data	20	10	10	0	1
March	50	—	10	10	1	1
April	60	—	12	10	missing data	1

Does the company need to continue to carry four months of past data for this forecasting model?

9. A Japanese electronics company produces pocket calculators and keeps item demand monthly. The following demand data are for a representative calculator: November, 41; December, 55; January, 67. Using 50 as the first order exponential smoothing forecast for November, forecast February sales.

10. New Cap, a local manufacturing firm, is introducing a new line of men's hunting caps. New Cap wants to forecast component items for these hats with its existing simple exponential smoothing forecasting model. Management has no historical data for these hunting caps.
    (a) What can you recommend to New Cap concerning initialization of parameters and a smoothing coefficient for monthly forecasts for the next six months? Why?
    (b) After four months you have the following data on *actual* demand. Would you agree with New Cap's choice of a smoothing coefficient of 0.3, or would you choose 0.9 the *only* other value it wants to consider for now? Assume that June's forecast was 100.

Month	Caps shipped (doz.)
June	50
July	175
August	225
September	400

11. Mayer Household Cleaning has been experiencing a rapid increase in home cleaning demand, as shown by the weekly demand data below. Staffing is currently based 100 percent on the previous week's demand; Mayer schedules only enough employees to meet that demand.
    (a) Using simple (first order) exponential smoothing, a smoothing constant of 0.4, and a starting forecast for January 15 of 100 homes, forecast demand for the week of February 5.
    (b) Based on Bias, would you favor the exponential smoothing or the old forecasting procedure as a basis for staffing decisions?
    (c) If you could investigate other smoothing coefficient values, would you initially examine values greater or less than 0.4? Why?

Week	Homes demanding cleaning	Week	Homes demanding cleaning
Jan. 1	75	Jan. 22	114
Jan. 8	86	Jan. 29	122
Jan. 15	120	Feb. 5	

12. A company statistician is interested in the relationship between the length (in inches) and the weight (in pounds) of extrusions. Extrusions come in all sizes, shapes, and thicknesses. A random sample of extrusions is taken, with the following results (X = length in inches, F = weight in pounds):

X:	70	75	64	67	71	70	68	76	68	69	70
F:	175	198	156	180	178	182	160	204	167	169	162

    (a) Construct a scatter diagram.
    (b) Find a and b, and draw the estimated regression line of F on X.

(c) Does the use of a linear regression model improve our ability to predict F, given X?
(d) If an extrusion is chosen at random and is 70 inches long, use the estimated regression line to predict weight. Such a "prediction" is different from "demand forecasting," but an important use of regression in operations.

13. Production manager Eric Gates estimates the cost of forecast error to be the absolute value of the multiple; $.50 times the product of Bias and MAD. Using his cost estimate for the item demand below, would you recommend a one- or a two-month simple moving average model? Conduct your analysis forecasting March and April only.

Month	Actual demand
January	100
February	200
March	100
April	300

14. A university central stores experiences demand for staplers which appears to follow this distribution:

Time period	Staplers demanded	Time period	Staplers demanded
10	92	15	138
11	117	16	"182"
12	105	17	"187"
13	135	18	"185"
14	143	19	"210"

We have a forecast of 150 units for period 16. The quotes (" ") mean actual demand is known at the end of that period. Using first order exponential smoothing with a moderately responsive smoothing coefficient of 0.3, forecast demand for periods 17 through 20. Now plot the actual and forecasted values for all periods for which you have data. Recommend to management an improved forecasting method, supporting your recommendation.

Challenging Exercises

15. For the last three years, Professor Gregopolus has been intuitively forecasting the number of students who will enroll in her classes. She really believes that no one knows as much about the value of her classes as she does. Therefore, how could others possibly forecast enrollments better than she? Her forecasts and actual enrollments are given below (rounded to multiples of ten).
(a) What has Professor Gregopolus's accuracy been, based on MAD and Bias? Explain what this means to Professor Gregopolus.
(b) Use 60 students as the forecast for Spring 1982, a smoothing coefficient of 0.2, and MAD to evaluate the model forecast with first order exponential smoothing.
(c) What can you tell Professor Gregopolus about individual intuitive versus modeling as approaches to forecasting?
(d) Based on all of the above, what do you recommend to Professor Gregopolus as a forecasting approach?

Semester	Forecast	Actual	Semester	Forecast	Actual
Fall 1981	—	70	Fall 1983	80	120
Spring 1982	90	60	Spring 1984	120	80
Fall 1982	90	70	Fall 1984	150	60
Spring 1983	100	60			

16. An operations manager is interested in forecasting how training will affect efficiency for production workers assigned to a new job. He gave five different amounts of training, varying from 0.50 day to 4 days. Ten workers took each of the training levels, fifty workers in all. The table below shows each worker's labor efficiency for the first week's work, 100 being the standard or expected output.

	X, training in days				
	0.50	1.00	2	3	4
y, efficiency	117	106	76	125	85
	85	81	88	113	129
	112	74	115	93	90
	81	79	113	89	124
	105	118	108	117	117
	109	110	84	118	121
	80	82	83	81	97
	73	86	81	86	93
	110	111	112	88	122
	78	113	120	120	92

(a) Find the linear regression equation for predicting Y from X.
(b) Plot the linear regression equation, along with the data, on a scatter diagram. What does this mean to the manager?
(c) Calculate the mean and variance for each training group. What can you conclude from comparing groups?

17. Northeastern Electric Company has experienced demand for a transistor, part #7513, as follows:

Period (weeks)	Demand	Forecasted demand
10	200	300
11	300	
12	500	
13	400	
14	300	

(a) Would you recommend first order exponential smoothing with a coefficient of 0.2 or 0.7? Justify your choice based on consideration of MAD.

(b) The inventory control manager of Northeastern Electric believes the most important cost consideration is not to have a stockout of this part. He estimates the cost of forecast error to be equal to the mean absolute deviation of forecast error plus three times the absolute value of Bias. Considering this, would you change your recommendation in (a)? Justify your choice.

(c) If you could direct further study into an overall item forecasting procedure for Northeastern Electric parts, what would you suggest?

18. You are given the following demand for Zeaker's streaker sneakers:

Date	Demand
March 1	30
8	110
15	140
22	85
April 1	45

As a buyer for Bowling Green's largest sneaker outlet, you have been told to forecast streaker sneaker demand weekly in April using first order exponential smoothing.

(a) What smoothing coefficient would you choose? Why?

(b) If the manager's forecast for April 1st was 65, using that as your starting value, what is your forecast for April 8th?

19. Recently, demand for a new carburetor filter stocked by a regional supply house has increased drastically (mechanics and the general public are becoming aware of the filter's fuel economy). Weekly demand is given below.

Week	Actual demand	Week	Actual demand	Week	Actual demand
23	100	31	450	39	927
24	75	32	510	40	950
25	210	33	600	41	945
26	250	34	550	42	1,050
27	350	35	725	43	1,150
28	365	36	775	44	1,200
29	400	37	750	45	1,210
30	425	38	825	46	1,295

(a) Fit a first order exponential smoothing model that minimizes MAD to this data.

(b) Attempt to reduce the overall MAD (for the twenty-four periods of data) by using another model. Feel free to develop a model or to choose a model from a source other than this text. Explain *why* you proceeded as you did.

20. Barfy Burgers, Inc., is a large northeastern hamburger chain that has just completed its fifth year of operation. Every month Barfy must make its meat purchases for the succeeding month. Due to historical demand fluctuations, Buster Barfy, vice-president of operations, has difficulty knowing what future sales to expect. Shown below are the number of pounds of meat demanded during each month of the firm's first five years of operation.

	Jan	Feb	Mar	Apr	May	June	July	Aug	Sept	Oct	Nov	Dec
1981	695	693	714	733	740	684	723	750	790	734	718	730
1982	768	772	765	722	719	777	753	762	732	780	750	705
1983	828	776	823	859	778	776	763	810	759	834	837	786
1984	814	790	841	817	849	769	904	808	809	828	885	849
1985	866	850	869	818	802	754	844	811	811	817	801	810

Based on Barfy's past demand, determine the monthly demand for January 1986.

GLOSSARY

Adaptive exponential smoothing Models in which smoothing coefficient is not fixed but is set initially and then allowed to fluctuate over time based upon changes in the underlying demand pattern.

Bias Forecast error measure that is the sum of actual errors for all periods divided by the total number of periods evaluated; gives the average of the forecast errors with regard to direction; shows any tendency consistently to over- or underforecast.

Causal forecasting models In a formal manner these relate demand to variables that are believed to influence demand.

Demand pattern General shape of the time series; usually constant, trend, seasonal, or some combination of these shapes.

Demand stability Tendency for a time series to retain the same general shape over time.

Exponential smoothing models An averaging method that exponentially decays the weight of an old demand on the current forecast.

Forecast Use of past data to determine future events; an objective computation.

Forecast error The difference between forecasted demand and actual demand.

Intuitive forecasts General approach to forecasting that is essentially the manager's guesses and judgment concerning future events; qualitative forecasting methods.

Mean Absolute Deviation (MAD) Forecast error measure that is the sum of the absolute deviation of actual demand and forecast for all periods divided by the total number of periods evaluated; gives the average of forecast errors without regard to direction.

Noise Dispersion of individual demands about a demand pattern.

Prediction Subjective estimates of the future.

Simple average Average of past data in which the demands of all previous periods are equally weighted.

Simple moving average Average of several of the most recent periods' demand; most recent time periods are added and oldest ones dropped to keep calculations current.

Statistical forecasting models Casting forward past data in some systematic method; used in time series analysis and projection.

Time series analysis In forecasting problems, demand data are plotted on a time scale to reveal patterns of demand.

Weighted moving average Moving average model that incorporates some weighting of old demand other than an equal weight for all past periods under consideration.

SELECTED READINGS

Adam, Everett E., Jr. "Individual Item Forecasting Model Evaluation." *Decision Sciences* 4, no. 4 (October 1973), pp. 458–70.

———, and Ronald J. Ebert. "A Comparison of Human and Statistical Forecasting." *AIIE Transaction* 8, no. 1 (March 1976), pp. 120–27.

Ahlers, David and Josef Lakonishok. "A Study of Economists' Consensus Forecasts." *Management Science* 29, no. 10 (October 1983), pp. 1113–1125.

Biggs, Joseph R. and William M. Campion. "The Effect and Cost of Forecast Error Bias for Multi-Stage Production-Inventory Systems." *Decision Sciences* 12, no. 4 (October 1982), pp. 570–584.

Box, G. E. P., and G. M. Jenkins. *Time Series Analysis, Forecasting, and Control*. San Francisco, California: Holden-Day, 1970.

Boyd, Kevin and Vincent A. Mabert. "A Two Stage Forecasting Approach at Chemical Bank of New York for Check Processing." *Journal of Bank Research* 8, No. 2 (Summer 1977), pp. 101–107.

Brown, R. G. *Smoothing, Forecasting and Prediction of Discrete Time Series*. Englewood Cliffs, N.J.: Prentice-Hall, Inc., 1963.

Dancer, Robert, and Clifford Gray. "An Empirical Evaluation of Constant and Adaptive Computer Forecasting Models for Inventory Control." *Decision Sciences* 8 (1977), pp. 228–38.

Delbecq, Andre, Andrew Van deVen and David Gustafson. *Group Techniques for Program Planning*. Glenview Ill.: Scott, Foresman and Company, 1975.

Harris, Ronald J. and Everett E. Adam, Jr. "Forecasting Patient Tray Census for Hospital Food Service." *Health Services Research* (Winter 1975), pp. 384–93.

Hogarth, Robin M. and Spyros Makridakis, "Forecasting and Planning: An Evaluation." *Management Science* 27, no 2 (February 1981), pp. 115–38.

Kao,, Edward P. C., and Frank M. Pokladnik. "Incorporating Exogenous Factors in Adaptive Forecasting of Hospital Census." *Management Science* 24, no. 16 (December 1978), pp. 1677–86.

Makridakis, Spyros, et al. "The Accuracy of Extrapolation (Time Series) Methods: Results of a Forecasting Competition." *Journal of Forecasting* 1 (1982), pp. 111–153.

Makridakis, S., and S. C. Wheelwright. *Forecasting Methods and Applications*. New York: John Wiley & Sons, 1978.

Makridakis, Spyros and Robert L. Winkler. "Averages of Forecasts: Some Empirical Results." *Management Science* 29, no. 9 (September 1983), pp. 987–996.

Muth, J. F. "Optimal Properties of Exponentially Weighted Forecasts." *Journal of the American Statistical Association* 55, no. 290 (June 1960), pp. 297–306.

Thomopoulos, Nick T. *Applied Forecasting Methods*. Englewood Cliffs, N.J.: Prentice-Hall, 1980.

Wheelwright, S. C. and S. Makridakis. *Forecasting Methods for Management*. 2nd ed. New York: John Wiley and Sons, 1977.

SUPPLEMENT TO CHAPTER 5

ADDITIONAL FORECASTING MODELS

There are many forecasting models other than those discussed in this chapter. We present three models of varying complexity in this supplement. Two models, a linear weighted moving average and double exponential smoothing, are moderately complex, and examples are included. The other model, an adaptive exponential smoothing model, is presented in summary form These models are similar in complexity to regression analysis, which was presented in Chapter 5.

Linear Weighted Moving Average

Another weighted moving average model incorporates linear trends. The model is:

$$\text{Linear moving average (LMA)} = \frac{\sum_{t=1}^{n} D_t}{n} + S(N) \qquad \textbf{(S5.1)}$$

where:

$$S = \text{slope} = \frac{\text{Sum weighted demand}}{\text{Squared weights}} = \frac{\sum_{t=1}^{n} W_t D_t}{\sum_{t=1}^{n} SW_t} \quad \textbf{(S5.2)}$$

$$N_t = \text{number of periods from the base period}$$

EXAMPLE

For the Frigerware ice collers in the two examples in the chapter, it is clear that there is trend in the data. The plant manager realizes this and asks you to compare some trend model to the three-month average model in which you forecasted the July demand of 500, based on a three-month moving average. First, we require an odd number of periods demand; we'll use the most recent five months.

Month	Number of ice coolers demanded	Weighting factor	Weighted demand	Square of weight factor
February	300	−2	−600	4
March	200	−1	−200	1
April	400	0	0	0
May	500	1	500	1
June	600	2	1200	4
	$\Sigma D = 2{,}000$		$\Sigma WD = 900$	$\Sigma SW = 10$

$$\text{Slope } (S) = \frac{\sum WD}{\sum SW} = \frac{900}{10} = 90$$

$$N_t = \textit{Number of months from base, April}$$

$$= 3$$

$$LMA = \frac{\sum D}{n} + S(N_t)$$

$$= \frac{2{,}000}{5} + 90(3)$$

$$= 400 + 270$$

$$LMA = 670$$

The linear moving average forecast for July is 670 ice coolers. When compared with a three-month average forecast of 500, this forecast has picked up the trend in the data and cast it forward.

The model calculates the slope of the trend (S); then it updates the simple moving average (the first term in the model) by multiplying the slope times the number of periods since the base month and adding this result to the base or simple moving average. You must use an odd number of periods for the model to work most effectively; that is, n must be an odd number.

By now, you are probably wondering what will happen to the *LMA* model when ice cooler demand falls off in the fall. That is a good question, and if the trend we've identified is really a seasonal phenomenon, our model will perform poorly. In that case, another moving average model might be best; a one- or two-month simple moving average might be reasonable, for example.

Double Exponential Smoothing

Double exponential smoothing is normally not included in an introduction to operations management. The model does, however, appear to smooth out noise in stable demand series. We are aware of one large pharmaceutical manufacturer who uses this model to forecast item demand for the thousands of drugs produced.

The model is straightforward; it smooths the first order exponential smoothing forecast and the old double exponential smoothing forecast.

$$\text{Forecast next period} = (\alpha)\begin{array}{l}\text{First order}\\ \text{exponential}\\ \text{smoothing}\\ \text{forecast next}\\ \text{period}\end{array} + (1-\alpha)\begin{array}{l}\text{Most recent}\\ \text{double}\\ \text{exponential}\\ \text{smoothing}\\ \text{forecast}\end{array} \quad \textbf{(S5.3)}$$

$$FD_t = \alpha F_t + (1 - \alpha)FD_{t-1}$$

where:

$$0 \leq \alpha \leq 1.0$$

Notice that F_t is the first order exponential smoothing model set forth as equation 5.7 in Chapter 5–and must be calculated *before* FD_t can be found.

EXAMPLE

Milo, Inc., has a first order exponential smoothing model that has provided a forecast of 103,500 bushels for #3 grade wheat in Boone County in July. Last year's June production of #3 grade wheat was 70,500 bushels. We will use that figure as an estimate of the most recent double exponential smoothing forecast. Given that $\alpha = 0.20$ appears to be a good smoothing coefficient for Milo, Inc., calculate a double exponential smoothed forecast for July.

Let t = July; then:

$$\begin{aligned} FD_t &= \alpha F_t + (1 - \alpha)FD_{t-1} \\ &= 0.2(103{,}500) + (1 - .2)(70{,}500) \\ &= 20{,}700 + 56{,}400 \\ &= 77{,}100 \end{aligned}$$

Our forecast for July is 77,100 bushels.

In this example, we see that the difference between first order exponential smoothing and double exponential smoothing is that the appropriate old forecast is smoothed with the *actual demand* in first order and smoothed with the *first order forecast* for this period in double smoothing. Actual demand is in the first order forecast, so that actual demand is in essence smoothed again, or double smoothed. The 103,500 first order forecast was smoothed again with the old second order forecast of 70,500; this resulted in a double exponential smoothing forecast of 77,100 bushels. If the 70,500 were an ongoing forecast, rather than an estimate, it would incorporate all old demand when expanded, just as is the case in first order smoothing.

The strength of double exponential smoothing is to dampen noise by double smoothing old demands. This strength makes the model conservative regarding change; the model is very slow to react to changes in underlying demand patterns.

Adaptive Exponential Smoothing

A simple adaptive model has been developed[1] in which alpha, the smoothing coefficient, is allowed to change plus or minus 0.05 in any one period toward a maximum (say 0.95) or a minimum (say, 0.05). The decision as to whether or not to change alpha is made *each period* based on a comparison of forecast error. Three forecast errors are calculated; forecast error is calculated for the current forecast using α; an error is calculated for a current forecast for $(\alpha + 0.05)$; and an error is calculated for a current forecast for $(\alpha - 0.05)$. The errors for all three forecasts are compared, and the new alpha is set by selecting the current forecast with the lowest error and setting alpha appropriate as α, $\alpha + 0.05$, or $\alpha - 0.05$. There are many more adaptive models and studies comparing adaptive to nonadaptive models, several referenced at the end of this chapter; these studies indicate that some adaptive models are superior to other adaptive and nonadaptive models, especially for unstable demand patterns. The Trigg and Leach adaptive exponential smoothing model shown in Figure 5.6 adapted more quickly to demand for frosted microscope slides in a hospital than did simple exponential smoothing. Note the response of the models about period 150 as demand becomes unstable. A further comparison of the models based on MAD, Bias, and computer time in seconds gave results for simple exponential smoothing of 26.11, −6.58, 3.33 and for adaptive exponential smoothing of 27.40, 1.41, and 3.84. The significant difference was in Bias, favoring the adaptive model.

One should be cautioned that adaptive models react to any change in demand, whether it is a change in *pattern* or *noise*. We like the adaptive feature of changing to changing demand patterns but dislike the feature of "chasing noise around" that adaptive models tend to have. Weaknesses in this concept include the chasing of noise in the series, cost of modeling,

[1]See W. M. Chow, "Adaptive Control of the Exponential Constant," *Journal of Industrial Engineering* 16, no. 5 (1965).

and unwillingness by many managers and administrators to accept reasonably sophisticated models of operating systems. The strengths certainly outweigh the weaknesses for progressive businesses who can overcome most of these weaknesses and apply adaptive models for unstable demand patterns.

PROBLEMS

Reinforcing Fundamentals

1. Smithton Corporation uses a first order exponential smoothing model. For one item, the model provided a demand forecast of 75,500 units. This was used as November's production requirement. Although demand was actually 72,700 units during November, 75,500 units were produced. Calculate a double exponential smoothed forecast for December using 70,000 units as November's double exponential smoothed forecast. All smoothing coefficients are 0.3.
2. A cable television company, Melanie Gates, Inc., is changing its forecasting method to the linear moving average model. Data for a recent period are shown here. What is the forecast for week 18? The company has decided to use four weeks from the base period in its forecast.

Week	Number of cable television installations
11	87
12	95
13	105
14	72
15	110
16	135
17	127

3. Compare first order exponential smoothing and double exponential smoothing over March and April. Minimize the tracking signal (*TS*)

$$TS = \frac{Bias}{MAD}$$

for your recommendation of a model.

Time period	Parts demanded	First order exponential smoothing (smoothing coefficient = 0.4)	Double exponential smoothing (all smoothing coefficients = 0.4)
January	100	120	110
February	"200"		
March	"150"		
April	"120"		

(Note: " " denotes demand at that month's end, after that month's forecast.)

4. E-Z Photocopying Services (EZPS) has experienced weekly demand for photocopying at the university copying center as shown below. Currently, the forecasting procedure is to use last week's average daily demand as next week's daily forecast. Staffing decisions for next week are based on that forecast.

Week	Average daily demand (1,000's)	Week	Average daily demand (1,000's)
Feb. 7	27	March 6	32
Feb. 14	20	March 13	30
Feb. 21	22	March 21	38
Feb. 28	30	March 28	

(a) Find the forecasted demand for the week of March 28th using double exponential smoothing as the forecasting model. Use smoothing constants of 0.2, and February 28th actual demand as the estimate for March 6th forecasted demand required. Forecast for March 28th based on experience in March (that is, do not forecast February at all).
(b) Using MAD as your criterion for evaluation, do you recommend double exponential smoothing or the current forecasting procedure?
(c) What might EZPS management do to further improve forecasting accuracy?

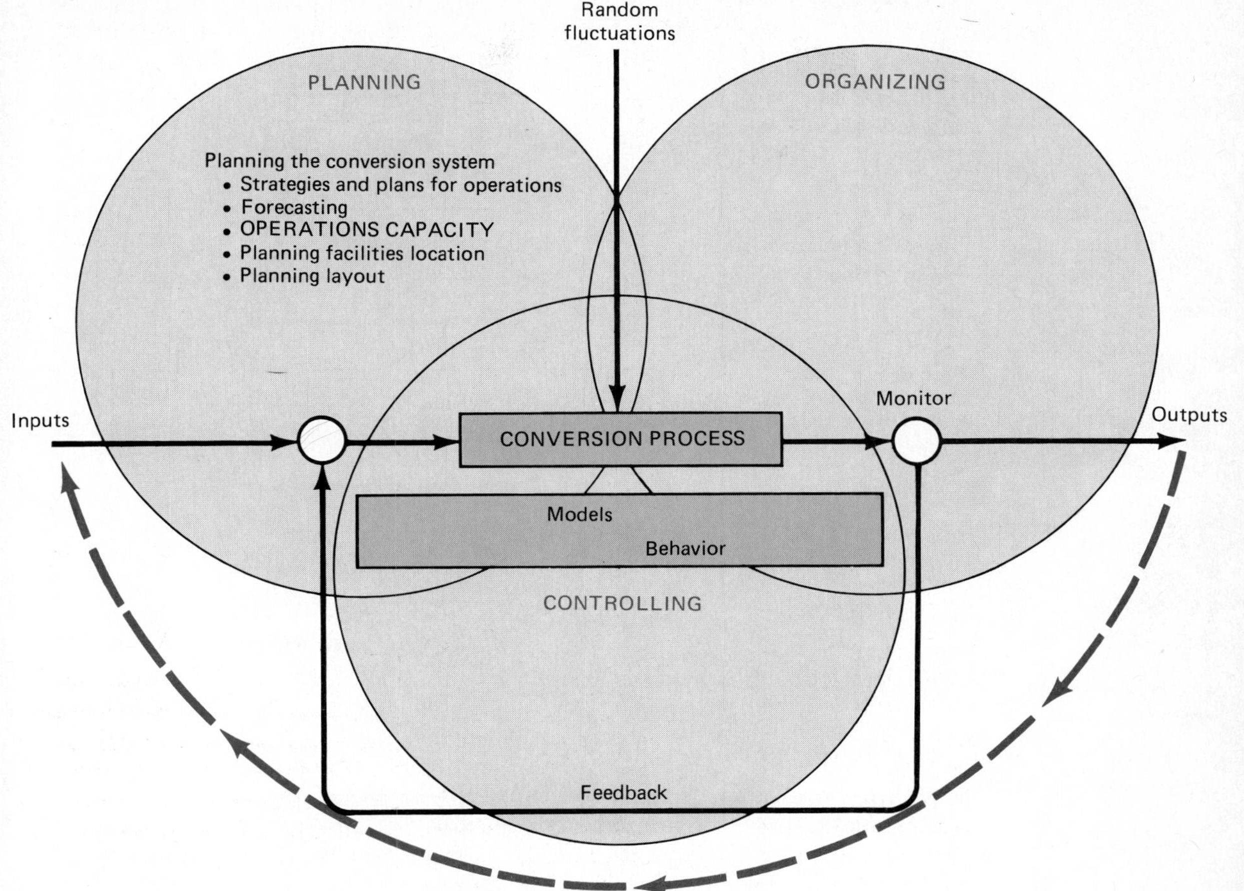

FIGURE 6.1
Production/operations management activities

must be explored, such as temporarily closing, or even selling, facilities. This would not require the sequence outlined in Figure 6.2 as there are no further design decisions in capacity reduction. In such a situation, however, there might be a consolidation that requires some of the Figure 6.2 activities such as relocation, combining technologies, and rearrangement of equipment and process (layout).

Relationship of Capacity and Location Decisions

Often, the capacity decision is inseparable from the facility location decision. This condition exists because demand for many services depends on system location and, of course, desired capacity depends upon demand; therefore, we have a circular relationship. Commercial banks, for example, simultaneously expand capacity and future demand for services by using

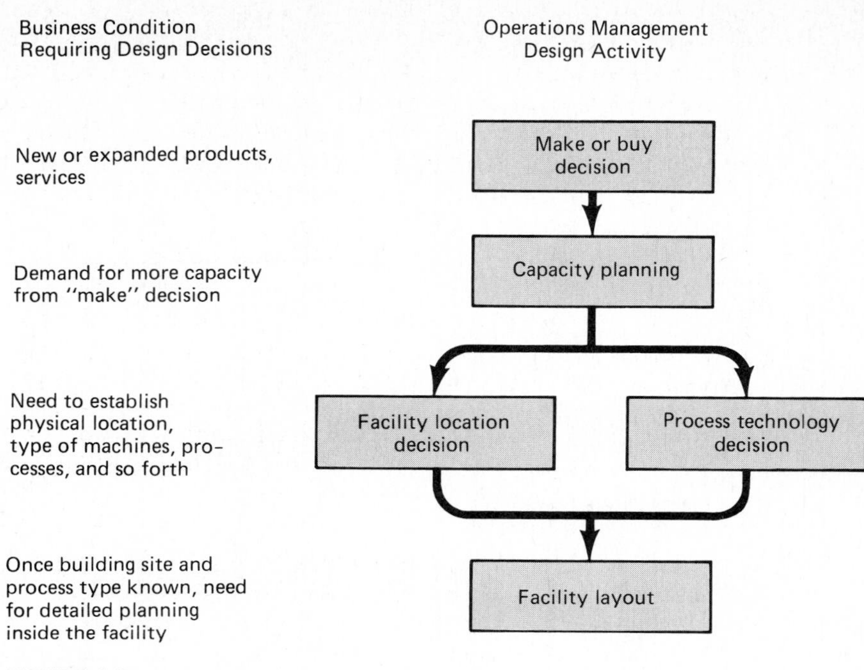

FIGURE 6.2
Conversion system design interactions

branching strategies. Branch location and size decisions are made after management has considered neighborhood population densities and growth projections, geographic locations of market segments, transporation (traffic) flows, and the locations of competitors. The addition of a new branch offers greater convenience to some existing customers and, management hopes, attracts new ones as well. Obviously this decision affects the revenues, operating costs, and capital costs of the organization.

In the public sector, the capacity decision involves similar considerations. Municipalities face ever-increasing demands for public services, strong public sentiment for tightening budgets, and greater performance accountability to a variety of interest groups. Consequently, in recent years officials have increased their efforts to rearrange public resources so they can increase service capacity without increasing costs of operation. Municipal emergency services, for example, are periodically expanded by adding new emergency stations. First, an analysis of the geographic dispersion of demand for services is undertaken to show population growth and shifts. Next, municipal officials plan where to locate new emergency stations, taking into consideration both areas of greatest need and costs of operation and facilities. Although the capacity decision may not involve direct revenues, cost savings for citizens can be considered a form of indirect revenues. These cost savings can result in reduced tax burdens or lower insurance rates in areas with high levels of emergency services.

Modeling techniques, which we will treat later in this chapter, are playing a central role in these planning processes. One study, for example, explains how a computer program allocates police patrol cars by time and geography to meet various service or performance criteria, thereby increasing effective system service capacity.[1] Another study shows how mathematical programming and simulation can be used to analyze urban fire suppression systems, suggesting ways to use existing capacity more efficiently or to reduce the size of operations without diminishing existing service levels, by better deployment of resources.[2] Yet another study demonstrates the value of computer simulation for improving the effectiveness (effective capacity) of urban snow and ice removal systems by varying salt truck routings and salt pile locations.[3] All these examples show how systematic analysis and planning can lead to effective capacity improvement and utilization.

Capacity Planning and Process Technology As a first step in relating process technology to capacity requirements, an audit of existing operations and review of alternatives not being used should be conducted. In this book we have not devoted a chapter to this topic because technology alternatives are situational to an industry. In Chapter 2 we discussed at some length technology and mechanization issues. However, we stopped short of identifying the questions the operations manager or his technical staff should be addressing. Professor Wickham Skinner summarizes this quite nicely in his discussion of design issues and alternative responses. We provide you with his views in Table 6.1. By completing an assessment or audit of equipment and technology needs such as that suggested in Table 6.1, the operations manager will have a profile of needs to guide technology choices.

Capacity Planning Decisions

Toward the conclusion of this chapter we will discuss a practical approach for managing capacity change. Briefly, and as an introduction to the balance of the chapter, capacity planning decisions normally involve these activities:

1. an assessment of existing capacity,
2. forecast estimates of future capacity needs (product, human, and technological) over a selected planning horizon,

---

[1]J. M. Chaiken and P. Dormont, "A Patrol Car Allocation Model: Background," *Management Science* 24, no. 12 (August 1978), pp. 1280–90. J. M. Chaiken and P. Dormont, "A Patrol Car Allocation Model: Capabilities and Algorithms," *Management Science* 24, no. 12 (August 1978), pp. 1291–1300.

[2]D. E. Monarchi, T. E. Hendrick, and D. R. Plane, "Simulation for Fire Department Deployment Policy Analysis," *Decision Sciences* 8, no. 1 (January 1977), pp. 211–27.

[3]T. M. Cook and B. S. Alprin, "Snow and Ice Removal in an Urban Environment," *Management Science* 23, no. 3 (November 1976), pp. 227–34.

TABLE 6.1
Equipment and process technology assessment: developing a profile to guide choices

I. Relative to the industry and stages of existing technology describe the extent to which:
  We are mechanized
  We are ahead or behind competitors in use of latest technology
  We are sharp and aggressive in
    Tooling
    Equipment
    Process/manufacturing engineering
    Industrial engineering

II. Describe key processes on dimensions of:
  Set-up and changeover requirements
  General purpose versus special purpose capability
  Process capability versus product performance and quality requirements
  Mechanization-labor intensiveness
  Skills required
  Maintenance requirements, skills, and costs
  Technology: mature, slow or fast changing, uncertain
  Flexibility for volume changes
  Internal balance of capacities and bottlenecks
  Supervision needed
  Cost of equipment and facilities in P & L (high or low) relative to other costs

III. What does above imply about:
  Competitive ability
  Service levels
  Investment levels
  Production planning and scheduling-inventory management
  Risks
  Quality
  Work force management
  Organizational needs
  Cost structure/break-even curve
  Opportunities
  Ability to meet the manufacturing task

Source: Skinner, Wickham. *Manufacturing in the Corporate Strategy* (New York: John Wiley and Sons, 1978), pp. 112–113.

3. identification of alternative ways to modify capacity,
4. financial, economical, and technological evaluation of capacity alternatives, and
5. selection or choice of a capacity alternative most suited to achieving strategic mission.

Measuring Capacity

For some organizations capacity seems simple to measure. United States Steel can refer to tons of output per year. General Motors Corporation can speak of number of automobiles per year. But what about organizations with more diverse product lines? How do you measure the capacity of a law firm or a veterinary clinic? In part, the answers depend on the diversity of the product mix. Even within General Motors, output consists of automobiles, trucks, and locomotives. When the units of output are identical, or nearly so, a common unit of measure may be selected: megawatts of electricity, tons of gravel, number of autos, or barrels of beer. In these cases, capacity is measured in units of *output*.

On the other hand, when product mix is diverse it is hard to find a common unit of output measure that makes sense. As a substitute, capacity can be expressed in terms of *input* measures. A legal office may express capacity in terms of the number of attorneys employed. A custom job shop or an auto repair shop may indicate capacity by available labor hours and/or machine hours per week, month, or year.

An estimate of capacity, then, may be measured in terms of the inputs or the outputs of the conversion process. Some common examples of capacity measures used by different organizations are shown in Table 6.2. The most common measure of capacity is a *throughput* measure of the organization, a measure closer to output than to inputs. Throughput measures capacity in terms of time—as a *rate* of output or input per *time unit*.

Capacity Defined *Capacity is the maximum theoretical rate of productive or conversion capability for the existing product mix of an organization's operations*. Capacity incorporates the concept of rate of conversion within an operations setting. A change in product mix can change unit output capacity.

It's often difficult to get a realistic measure of capacity because of day-to-day variations. Employees are sometimes absent or late, equipment breakdowns occur, facility downtime is needed for maintenance and repair, machine setups are required for product changeovers, and vacations must

Table 6.2
Measures of operating capacity

Organization	Measure
Output	
Automobile manufacturer	Number of autos
Brewery	Barrels of beer
Cannery	Tons of food
Steel producer	Tons of steel
Power company	Megawatts of electricity
Input	
Airline	Number of seats
Hospital	Number of beds
Job shop	Labor and/or machine hours
Merchandising	Square feet of display or sales area
Movie theater	Number of seats
Restaurant	Number of seats or tables
Tax office	Number of accountants
University	Number of students and/or faculty
Warehouse	Square feet or cubic feet of storage space

be scheduled. Since all these uncertainties and variations cause "true" capacity to vary from time to time, they must all be considered in any estimate of capacity. You can see, then, that the capacity of a facility can rarely be measured in precise terms. Such measures as are used must be interpreted cautiously.

Estimating Future Capacity Needs

Capacity requirements can be evaluated from two extreme perspectives, short-term and long-term.

Short-term Requirements Managers often use forecasts of product demand to estimate the near-term work load the facility must handle. These estimates are obtained from the forecasting techniques presented in Chapter 5. By looking ahead up to twelve months, we can anticipate output requirements for our different products or services. Then we can compare requirements to existing capacity and detect when capacity adjustments will be needed. A company making two products, for example, may observe that one has a seasonal pattern with low demand in winter and higher demand in early spring and summer. The other product may show a steady upward (or downward) trend. Is existing capacity adequate for meeting *overall* demand? If not, what adjustments in capacity can be made? We will answer these questions shortly.

Long-term Requirements Longer-term capacity requirements are more difficult to determine because of uncertainties in future market demand and technologies. Forecasting five or ten years into the future is a risky and difficult task. What products or services will be we producing then? Today's product may not even exist in the future. Demand for products changes with time; to describe the chronological stages of demand for a product, we use the term *product life cycle* (see Figure 6.3). Planners attempt to answer questions about future demand and capacity for their product by identifying future stages of its life cycle. What new products do we think will be adopted in the future, and what are their expected or planned growth rates? It is obvious from these questions that capacity requirements are dependent on marketing plans and forecasts.

Changes in *processing* technology must also be anticipated. Even if our products remain unchanged, the methods for generating them may change dramatically. The development of the digital computer exemplifies a technology change that dramatically increased information processing capacity. Although changes in technology are difficult to anticipate, their consequences can be so dramatic that planners make great efforts to forecast them. Just as capacity requirements depend upon market plans and forecasts, capacity depends upon technology plans and forecasts.

Strategies for Modifying Capacity

After existing capacity has been measured and future capacity requirements assessed, alternative ways of modifying capacity must be identified. Planners must devise both short-run and long-term modification strategies.

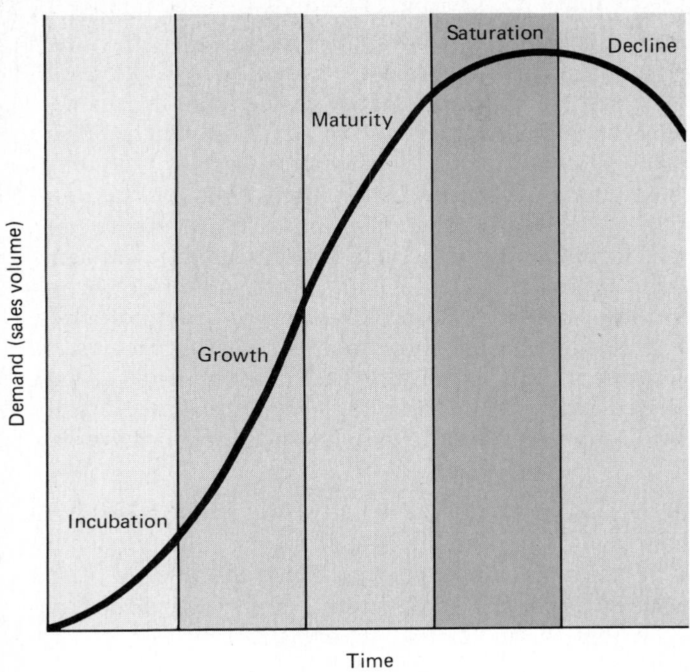

FIGURE 6.3
Stages of a product life cycle

Short-run Responses For short-run periods of up to one year, the fundamental capacity of the conversion process is of fixed size. Major facilities are seldom opened or closed as a regular monthly or yearly practice. Many short-run adjustments for increasing or decreasing capacity are possible, however. Which adjustments to make depend on whether the conversion process is primarily labor or capital intensive and whether the product is one that can be stored in inventory.

Capital-intensive processes rely heavily on physical facilities, plant, and equipment for performing the conversion operations. Short-run capacity can be modified by operating these facilities more or less intensively than normal. The problem with modifying short-run capacity is that temporary changes of this type can be very expensive. The costs of facility setup, changeover, maintenance, procurement of raw materials, manpower procurement, scheduling, and inventory management can all be increased by such capacity changes.

Labor-intensive conversion processes are dominated by human skills rather than by such physical resources as plant and equipment. In labor-intensive processes, short-run capacity can be changed by laying off or hiring people or by having employees work overtime or be idle. These alternatives are also expensive, though, since hiring costs and severance pay may be necessary, premium wages may have to be paid, and the risk of losing scarce human skills may increase.

Present strategies for changing capacity also depend upon the extent to which the product can be stored in inventory. For products that are perishable (raw foods) or subject to radical style changes, finished goods inventories may not be feasible. Also in this category are nonstandard or custom-made products whose specifications are not known in advance. This is particularly true for many service organizations offering such products as insurance protection, emergency operations (fire, police, etc.), and taxi and barber services. In these cases, finished goods cannot be produced and stored in inventory prior to demand; the service is consumed at the same time it is generated. Instead, *input* resources can be expanded or shrunk temporarily in anticipation of demand. Several of the most common strategies are summarized in Table 6.3. Combinations of these strategies, as used by manufacturing firms producing multiple end products and product families, must be evaluated when "rough cut capacity" and "capacity requirements planning" techniques are employed. These techniques are discussed in Chapter 11.

Long-run Responses: Expansion From World War II through the 1960s, the U.S. economy was one of abundance and growth. Since the decade of the 1970s, we have encountered problems of resource scarcity and economic shrinkage. While some sectors of the economy grow, others diminish. Organizations today cannot be locked into thinking only about *expanding* the resource base; they must also consider optimal approaches to *contracting* it. Let's consider the first of these long-run responses, expansion.

EXAMPLE

A warehousing operation foresees the need for an additional 100,000 square feet of space by the end of the next five years. One option is to add an additional 50,000 square feet now and another 50,000 square feet two years from now. Another option is to add the entire 100,000 square feet now.

Estimated costs for building the entire addition now are $16 per square foot. If expanded incrementally, the initial 50,000 square feet will cost $18 each. The 50,000 square feet to be added later are estimated at $24 each. Which alternative is better? At a minimum, the lower construction costs plus excess capacity costs of total construction now must be compared to higher costs of deferred construction. The operations manager must consider the costs, benefits, and risks of each option.

The costs, benefits, and risks of the expansion alternatives pose an interesting decision problem. By building the entire addition now, we avoid higher building costs; we avoid the risk of accelerated inflation (and

TABLE 6.3
Temporary capacity changes

Capacity change	Operations manager's activity
Inventories	Finished goods may be stockpiled during slack periods to meet later demand.
Backlogs	During peak demand periods, customers may be willing to wait some time before receiving their product. Their order request is filed, and they receive their product after the peak demand period.
Employment levels	Additional employees are hired and employees are laid off as demand for output increases and decreases.
Work force utilization	Employees work overtime during peaks and are idle or work fewer hours during slack demand periods.
Employee training	Instead of each employee specializing in one task, each is trained in several tasks. Then, as skill requirements change, employees can be rotated among different tasks. This is an alternative to hiring and layoffs for getting needed skills of specific types.
Process design	Sometimes job content at each work station can be changed to allow productivity increases. Work methods analysis can be used to examine and redesign jobs.
Subcontracting	During peak periods, other firms may be hired temporarily to make the product or some of its subcomponents.
Maintenance deferral	Under normal conditions the facility may be shut down at regular intervals to perform preventive maintenance on facilities and equipment. During peak periods, such maintenance programs are temporarily discontinued. Thus the facility can be operated when it would, without preventive maintenance, have had to be idle.

even higher future construction costs); and we avoid the risk of losing additional future business because of inadequate capacity. But there may also be disadvantages to this alternative. First, our organization may not be able to muster the large financial investment initially needed. Second, if we expand now we may find later that our demand forecasts were bad; we may find that ultimate demand is lower than expected and we have overbuilt. Finally, even if forecasted demand is ultimately realized, it may not fully materialize until the end of the five-year planning horizon. If so, we will have invested in an excess capacity facility on which no return is realized for several years. Since our funds could have been invested in some other ways during this time, we have foregone the opportunity of earning returns elsewhere on our investment. Should we overbuild? Should we expand in one lump or in increments? These questions are good examples of why we develop strategic plans, including identification of the operations mission, which guide our capacity choices.

EXAMPLE

Extol Corporation's competitive strategy capitalizes on its superior nationwide marketing and distribution system and its reputation for high-quality home electronics equipment. Extol chooses to not be a product innovator; hence, it avoids the major costs of extensive product research and development activities. Instead, Extol rapidly adopts new product developments by competitors and quickly adapts its production capabilities, which are dominantly labor-intensive, to introduce quality products during the growth and maturity phases of the product life cycle. Handsome financial returns can be realized with this strategy—but everything depends on the timing of product introduction and availability in the marketplace. Accordingly, Extol intentionally overbuilds its physical facilities by 20 percent of expected capacity to avoid lost sales, which are likely to be far more costly than the incremental cost of the additional 20 percent of capacity.

When an organization is undertaking a capacity expansion today, the decisions involve much more than considering economies of scale. Modern manufacturing capability implies the ability to remain flexible, provide rapid response, have greater control, reduce waste, have greater predictability, speed up throughput, and provide distributed processing capability. These are new or refined capabilities that traditionally have been thought of as conflicting and unattainable. However, we now find progressive firms defining the scope of their manufacturing activities to fulfill these requirements.[4]

The general patterns of capacity utilization costs and incremental expansion can be seen in Figure 6.4. The first curve shows the minimum cost output rate, p_1^*, for an existing productive facility at time one. Production can fall temporarily to a lower level, p_1^-, but if it does, machine and labor resources will be underutilized and unit costs will therefore increase. Output could be increased to higher levels, such as p_1^+, but then unit costs would increase because of excessive overtime, inadequate preventive maintenance, and higher congestion in existing facilities.

If we anticipate that demand will be permanently higher, then the facility could be expanded to reap the benefits of economies of scale offered by a larger facility. Typically, expansion occurs in increments over time rather than in a single lump. The series of curves shows optimum output rates for each stage of expansion as permanent demand increases. Capacity could be expanded in one step, from p_1^* to p_4^*, but in that case the risks of overexpanding would be increased.

[4]See Joel D. Goldhar and Mariann Jelinek, "Plans for Economies of Scope," *Harvard Business Review* vol. 61, no. 6 (Nov-Dec 1983), pp. 141–48.

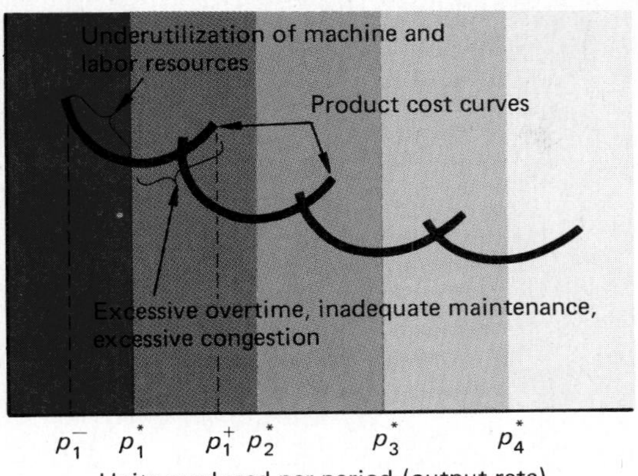

FIGURE 6.4
Product costs related to facility capacity

Long-run Responses: Contraction and Constant Capacity Sometimes long-range planning indicates that future capacity requirements are lower than existing capacity can already produce. When this happens, we can either reduce capacity or find new ways of using what exists. Capacity contraction most often involves selling off existing facilities, equipment, and inventories and firing employees. As serious declines in demand occur, we may terminate operations gradually. Since large sums of money are often involved, present value and capital investment analyses can be useful in guiding our contraction decisions.

Organizations permanently reduce capacity or shut down facilities only as a last resort. Instead, they seek new ways to maintain and use existing capacity. Why? Because a great deal of effort, capital, and human skills have gone into building up a technology. Often this technology and skill base is transferable to other products or services.

EXAMPLE

In a visit to the Davenport, Iowa, manufacturing facility of Ralston Purina we found brand-labeled cereals for grocery chains being made in one area, Purina Dog Chow being made in another area, and a large distribution warehouse in yet another area. All manufacturing involved conversion of grains into foods, and the entire facility was under one operations manager.

As one product reaches the decline phase of its life cycle, it can be replaced with others without increasing capacity (Figure 6.5). This phasing in and out of new and old products does not occur accidentally; it requires planning. Research and development departments and market research

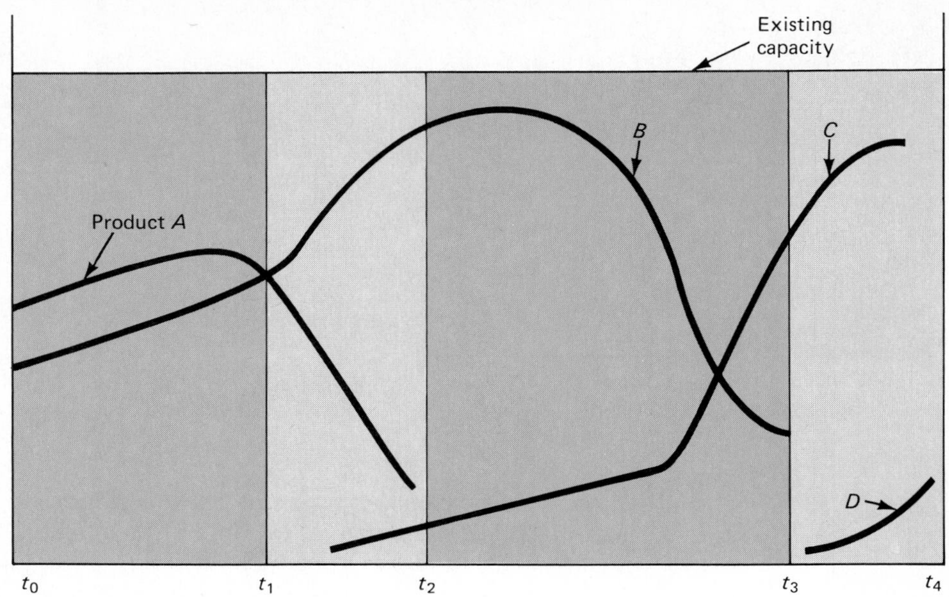

FIGURE 6.5
Ideal use of existing capacity by time-phasing products

groups assess the potential of new product proposals. All these efforts are intermeshed in long-range planning to determine how existing capacity can be used and adapted to meet future product demand. After identifying future capacity requirements, managers should evaluate various ways of modifying capacity. For analyzing alternatives, production/operations managers have found models to be useful.

CAPACITY PLANNING MODELING

Modeling Alternatives

What models are available to assist in capacity planning? *Present value analysis* is helpful whenever the time value of capital investments and funds flows must be considered. (This will be covered in Chapter 19.) *Aggregate planning models* are useful for examining how best to use existing capacity in the short run. (These models are presented in Chapter 11.) *Breakeven analysis,* discussed in Chapter 3, can provide the breakeven volumes required as a minimum when various expansion alternatives are being costed against projected revenues. In the following pages we present two useful models for evaluating short-run capacity utilization: *linear programming* and *computer simulation*. Then we'll apply a *decision tree analysis* to the long-run capacity problem of facility expansion. Although we could discuss even more models, these last three serve to illustrate the diversity of capacity-related problems confronting the operations manager.

Linear Programming Applied to Product Mix and Capacity

Our first example of model applications will illustrate the difficulties of measuring capacity in a multiproduct firm. As we discuss MultiBand's situation, we'll show you a way of finding the best use of capacity during a short-run planning horizon.

EXAMPLE

MultiBand Enterprises manufactures two products, a portable radio (PR) and a citizens' band (CB) radio. The marketing manager states, "We can sell all that can be produced in the near future." She then asks the operations manager, "What is your production capacity per month?" The operations manager replies that his output capacity depends on which product is produced. "Three kinds of labor are required for making our products: subassembly, assembly, and inspection labor. The two products require different amounts of each kind of labor, so our capacity for next month depends on which products we produce. Next month we will have 316 hours of subassembly labor available, 354 hours of assembly labor, and 62 hours of inspection labor." The operations manager knows that each CB radio requires .4 hours of subassembly labor time, .5 hours of assembly labor, and .05 hours of inspection. A portable radio can be produced using .5 hours of subassembly labor, .3 hours of assembly labor, and .10 hours of inspection labor.

The vice-president says, "We know that each CB that we produce and sell contributes $50 towards profit and overhead. Each PR has a $40 contribution margin." What is MultiBand's output capacity, and what mix of CBs and PRs should be manufactured next month?

The *product mix problem*, as it's called, is faced whenever a firm has limited resources that can be used to produce any of several combinations of products. MultiBand's product mix problem is summarized in Table 6.4.

What is MultiBand's output capacity? It depends on the product mix. If all resources next month are devoted to producing CBs, there will be enough subassembly time to produce (316 hours) ÷ (.40 hours/unit) = 790

Table 6.4
Available resources and possible uses by MultiBand

Resource	Amount of resource needed to produce one unit of product (hours)		Total amount of resource available (hours)
	CB	PR	
Subassembly labor	.40	.50	316
Assembly labor	.50	.30	354
Inspection labor	.05	.10	62

units; enough assembly time to produce 354 ÷ .50 = 708 units; and inspection time for 62 ÷ .05 = 1,240 CBs. Since a salable CB requires all three kinds of labor, the maximum number of CBs possible is the smallest of these quantities, 708 units. On the other hand, we could produce only PRs. If each resource is devoted totally to PRs, there will be enough subassembly, assembly, and inspection time for producing 632, 1,180, and 620 PRs; the maximum number of completed PRs is 620.

We can summarize MultiBand's capacity utilization alternatives like this:

1. 708 CBs can be produced; this would use all available assembly time; *or*
2. 620 PRs can be produced; this would consume all available inspection time; *or*
3. some combination of PRs and CBs can be produced during the month.

What is the *best* mix of CBs and PRs to produce? In other words, what is the best way to use existing capacity in the short run? This question can be answered by using a linear programming model, which is described and applied to the MultiBand problem in the supplement to this chapter. Several steps must be taken before this method can be applied.

First, the decision variables must be identified. For MultiBand there are two decision variables, the number of CBs and the number of PRs to be produced next month. Usually in production/operations management applications of linear programming, the decision variables are the products.

Second, some criterion for choice must be specified to indicate (and measure) the "goodness" or "badness" of each decision alternative. Multiband's criterion is total contribution margin, as shown in equation 6.1.

$$\text{Total contribution margin} = \text{Contribution margin from all CBs produced} + \text{Contribution margin from all PRs produced} \qquad (6.1)$$

$$TCM = \$50\ CB + \$40\ PR$$

The value of the criterion, *TCM*, depends on how many CBs and PRs we decide to produce. We wish to select values for CB and PR so that *TCM* is as large as possible; that is, we wish to maximize *TCM*.

Third, the restrictions limiting the number of products that can be produced must be identified. These are shown below for CBs and PRs.

Resource (labor)	Amount of resource used (hours)	Amount of resource available (hours) (resource restriction)	
Subassembly	.40 CB + .50 PR	≤ 316	(6.2)
Assembly	.50 CB + .30 PR	≤ 354	(6.3)
Inspection	.05 CB + .10 PR	≤ 62	(6.4)

The subassembly resource consists of 316 total hours that can be used to make either CBs or PRs. Each CB consumes .40 hours, and each PR consumes .50 hours. The subassembly resource restriction reflects the fact that no more than 316 hours are available for whatever mix of CBs and PRs the manager selects. The other two restrictions are interpreted the same way.

Fourth, a systematic procedure to evaluate possible combinations products must be applied. The combination that results in the highest value of TCM is the one that's selected. By applying a linear programming procedure, we find that the optimal solution for MultiBand is to produce 632 CBs and 126 PRs (approximately) next month. This will result in a contribution margin of:

$$\begin{aligned} TCM &= \$50(632) + \$40(126) \\ &= 31{,}600 + 5{,}040 \\ &= 36{,}640 \end{aligned}$$

This product mix will consume all available subassembly and assembly hours, will result in about eighteen hours of unused or idle inspection time, and will provide a higher total contribution margin than any other combination of CBs and PRs. Since it represents optimal use of existing capacity, this product mix illustrates the most powerful feature of linear programming; *an optimal allocation of resources to maximize profits or minimize costs is always guaranteed.*

Computer Simulation Used to Evaluate Capacity

In many systems, proper scheduling of the conversion facilities can lead to better utilization of existing capacity. Sometimes a careful analysis reveals that a greater output rate exists than was thought possible. Such an analysis was performed at the University of Massachusetts Health-Service Outpatient Clinic.[5] During the first year of this study, the average number of patients seeing a physician each day was about 180. The clinic rotated twelve physicians throughout an eight-hour day, but no more than seven doctors could be made available at any given time. A total of 52 physician-hours was available daily. The facility experienced overcrowding and confusion in waiting rooms, and the professional staff felt overworked and harassed. During the day, when few walk-in patients came and when appointment patients failed to appear, physicians were sometimes idle. Often, physicians were still seeing patients up to an hour past closing time.

A team of analysts set out to find better ways to use the existing capacity and resources of the clinic. Their strategy was to build a Monte Carlo simulation model (Chapter 3) of the clinic and to use the model experimentally to improve the clinic operations. First they examined clinic records to estimate the demand on the system—the number of patient visits per week

[5]This case history is based on the study by E.J. Rising, R. Baron, and B. Averill, "A Systems Analysis of a University-Health-Service Outpatient Clinic," *Operations Research* 21, no. 5 (September–October 1973), pp. 1030–47.

during regular clinic hours. Patients were one of two types, walk-in or appointment. The historical pattern of patient arrivals was examined by day of week and by time of day.

The average number of patients seeing physicians daily were: Monday, 219; Tuesday, 190; Wednesday, 170; Thursday, 162; and Friday, 169. Existing demand patterns seemed to be both stable and predictable, and they revealed that every day uneven demand resulted in both occasional slack periods and periods of very high patient loads. The analysts used the simulation model to test experimentally the effects of various patient scheduling policies. The simulation showed the extent to which the outpatient system could be improved if appointment patients were scheduled during days and hours in which low numbers of walk-in patients were expected.

The recommendations of the simulation experiment were actually implemented at the clinic during the following year, and several improvements in its operation resulted. Customer (patient) service was improved—patient waiting time was reduced; the number of patients seen by physicians was increased more than 13 percent; and the average time that a patient spent with a physician went up by 5 percent. The total number of physician hours allocated to patients decreased by 5 percent; less overtime was required; and the doctors' morales improved. Clearly, the clinic's existing capacity was increased because resources were scheduled and used more wisely. Just as clearly, a simulation model of other kinds of organizations could result in better uses of resources and increased output for them too.

Computer simulation has also been used to explore the capacity decision of an airline system.[6] The purpose was to identify and evaluate alternative ways of modifying capacity, rather than to find the best way of using existing capacity. Thus, the simulation addresses a comprehensive problem and illustrates the variety of capacity factors that should be considered. Scale of operations, for example, should be selected so as to accomplish some higher level system goal, such as maximizing net earnings or return on investment. Earnings, in turn, depend on revenues and costs. Thus, we need estimates of passenger demand for different possible levels of airline service and estimates of revenues and costs associated with alternative ways of providing different levels of service. In an airline system there are at least two ways of modifying capacity on a route, by increasing flight frequency or by increasing the seating capacities on existing flights. The capacity decision, then, involves consideration of fleet size and the mix or types of vehicles in the fleet. These options have implications for operating costs, passenger demand, and revenues, all of which must be related in the model to net earnings. The various options can then be used to aid in the airline's capacity decision.

[6]See the simulation study reported by W. Gunn, "Airline System Simulation," *Operations Research* 12, no. 2 (March–April 1964), pp. 206–29.

Decision Tree Analysis and Facility Expansion

The linear programming and computer simulation models focused on the short-run question of how to use existing capacity; but the planner also faces long-run decisions. One such decision has to do with facility expansion; for analyzing expansion decisions, we often use decision tree analysis, as described in Chapter 3. As you may recall, the procedure involves:

1. laying out decision alternatives,
2. identifying chance events and their probabilities of occuring,
3. identifying monetary consequences of decisions and chance events,
4. calculating the expected value of each decision alternative, and
5. selecting the alternative that has the most attractive expected value.

Let's use an example to help make this risky, long-run decision about how to expand the capacity of an existing facility.

EXAMPLE

The Advance Storage Company has a large warehousing operation. As it develops long-range plans, it is considering expansion of storage service capacity. Estimates of future storage demand, associated revenues, and costs of construction and financing for expansion have been obtained for the five-year planning horizon. Management has narrowed the expansion alternatives to three choices: (1) expand now by adding 100,000 square feet of storage space; (2) add 50,000 square feet now and 50,000 square feet two years later; (3) do not expand.

If the entire expansion is done now, construction costs will be lower than they will be later. Further, there will be a greater chance for higher business revenues, since enough space will be added to take in new business. There is a chance, however, of overexpanding; if the entire expanded facility is not needed, the company will have idle capacity and associated financing, insurance, and maintenance costs. These are the risks of investing funds in an idle, overexpanded facility. On the other side of the decision, however, are the risks of limited storage capacity, which may result in lost opportunities for more business. Estimates of relevant factors for this decision are shown in Table 6.5.

For years one through five, it is estimated that the probability of high annual demand is 0.6; the probability of low demand is 0.4.

Figure 6.6 shows Advance's initial decision tree. The time sequence flows from left to right; three decision alternatives appear at the far left at stage t_0. This decision is followed by a chance event, high or low demand in years one through five, at stage t_1. Stage t_2 represents all the six possible eventual outcomes of the decision problem.

First we calculate the cash flows for *each of the end branches only*, (1) through (6). Factors determining net changes in cash flows include revenues from storage service, costs of operation, costs of financing, mainte-

TABLE 6.5
Data for expansion decision of Advance Storage Company

Decision alternative	Cash outlays for expansion: Expansion cost now	Cash outlays for expansion: Expansion cost two years from now	Expected increase in after-tax cash flow per year: Years 1–2, If demand is high	Years 1–2, If demand is low	Years 3–5, If demand is high	Years 3–5, If demand is low
Full expansion now	100,000 sq ft @ $15/sq ft = $1,500,000	0	$700,000	$ – 50,000	$700,000	$ – 50,000
Expand 50,000 feet now and 50,000 feet in two years	50,000 sq ft @ $17/sq ft = $850,000	50,000 sq ft @ $19/sq ft = $950,000	$400,000	$10,000	$700,000	$ – 50,000
No expansion	0	0	$100,000	$30,000	$100,000	$30,000

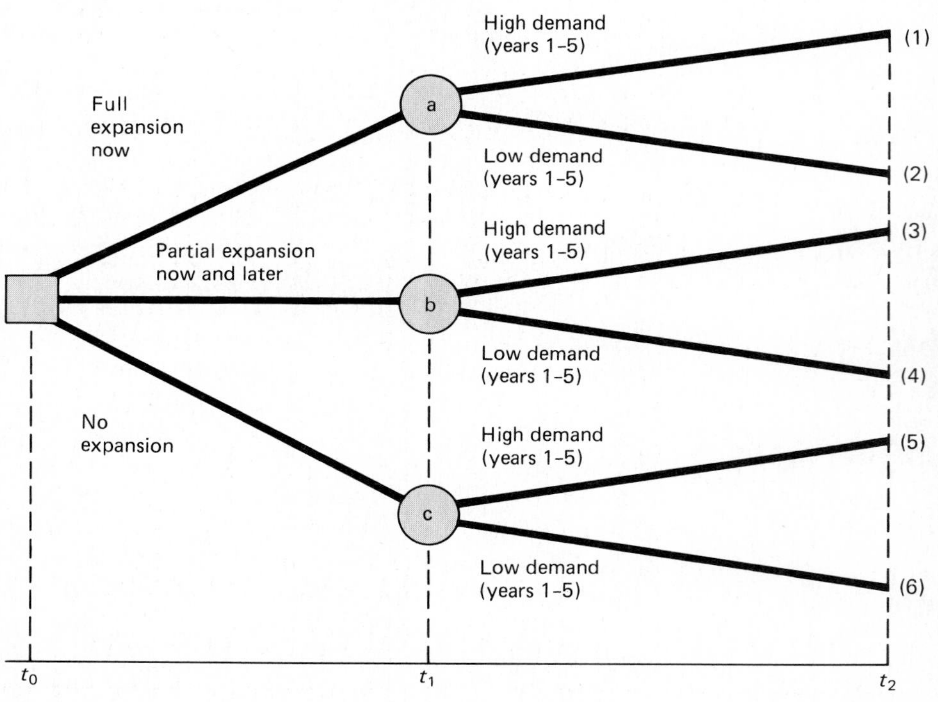

FIGURE 6.6
Decision tree for Advance Storage Company expansion

TABLE 6.6
Calculation of net cash flow values for end branches

Branch	Annual Cash Flow		Number of Years		Total Cash Flow Value for Branch
(1)	$700,000	X	5(years 1–5)	=	$3,500,000
(2)	−50,000	X	5(years 1–5)	=	−250,000
(3) (i)	400,000	X	2(years 1–2)		
(ii)	700,000	X	3(years 3–5): (i) + (ii)	=	2,900,000
(4) (i)	10,000	X	2(years 1–2)		
(ii)	−50,000	X	3(years 3–5): (i) + (ii)	=	−130,000
(5)	100,000	X	5(years 1–5)	=	500,000
(6)	30,000	X	5(years 1–5)	=	150,000

nance, taxes, and insurance. Branch (1) represents five years of high demand with incremental cash inflows of $700,000 per year (see Table 6.5). The total cash flow is 5 × $700,000 = $3,500,000. By similar calculations, we have arrived at the cash flow values for all six end branches shown in Table 6.6.

Moving left in Figure 6.6 to stage t_1, we now calculate the expected value of each chance node *a*, *b*, and *c*. First consider node *a*. If our decision process ever leads us to node *a*, what expected cash inflow would result thereafter? We will attain either outcome (1), with probability 0.6, or outcome (2), with probability 0.4. The *expected* cash inflow is the sum of the possible inflows, each weighted by its chances of occurrence. The expected value for each node at stage t_1 is calculated in Table 6.7.

Continuing backwards to stage t_0 in Figure 6.6, the decision maker has choices leading to node *a*, *b*, or *c*. The first choice, full expansion, requires an outlay of $1,500,000 and will lead to node *a*, which provides an expected net cash flow of $2,000,000. There is therefore an overall expected

TABLE 6.7
Calculation of expected values for nodes *a*, *b*, and *c*

Node	Possible outcome branches	Net cash flow for branch	Probability of this branch	Cash flow X probability	Expected net cash flow for node
a	*a*–(1)	$3,500,000	0.6	$2,100,000	$2,000,000
	a–(2)	−250,000	0.4	−100,000	
b	*b*–(3)	2,900,000	0.6	1,740,000	1,688,000
	b–(4)	−130,000	0.4	−52,000	
c	*c*–(5)	500,000	0.6	300,000	360,000
	c–(6)	150,000	0.4	60,000	

TABLE 6.8
Determination of best decision alternative

Decision alternative	Expected net cash[‡] flow from chance event		Expected cash[†] outlays		Total expected net cash flow	Best decision choice(*)
Full expansion	(node *a*) $2,000,000	−	$1,500,000	=	$500,000	*
Incremental expansion	(node *b*) 1,688,000	−	1,800,000 (850,000 + 950,000)	=	−112,000	
No expansion	(node *c*) 360,000	−	0	=	360,000	

[†]From Table 6.7
[‡]From Table 6.5

value of $500,000 ($2,000,000 − 1,500,000) for this choice. Using this procedure, we can evaluate the alternatives available at the decision point, as we have done in Table 6.8. These calculations indicate that full expansion now is the preferred alternative.

Many decision problems are much more complicated than our example might indicate. We could, for example, have included more decision alternatives, a larger number of possible levels, or more complex probability estimates.[7] A more realistic analysis would also consider the time value of money, using the present value methods discussed in Chapter 20 to account for the timing of funds inflows and outlays. Nevertheless, our example illustrates how decision tree analysis can be useful in evaluating some of the financial and other risky aspects of the long-run capacity determination problem. Top management must now combine the results of such analysis with other considerations as they seek to implement plans to accomplish the organization's strategic mission.

MANAGING CAPACITY CHANGE

Capacity planning, as we've seen, involves much more than answering questions such as: "How much space do I need for product X manufacturing? How much space do I need to provide service Y?" There are questions of measurement, estimating requirements, alternative short-term and long-

[7]A Bayesian analysis could be used to introduce revised probabilities based on additional information. For examples see H. Bierman, Jr., C.P. Bonini, and WH. Hausman, *Quantitative Analysis for Business Decisions*, 5th ed. (Homewood, Ill.: Richard D. Irwin, Inc., 1977).

term responses, and alternative economic models to use. Yet we still have come a little short of developing a practical guide for managing capacity change, the purpose of this section.[8]

The Elusive Nature of Capacity

It is important again to emphasize that managing capacity requires a good understanding of the environment within which the organization is operating. This requires both hard work to understand current demands and existing operations, and a lot of thought to develop a vision regarding future business conditions.

We believe that the effective manager will keep the following very general guidelines in mind when planning capacity changes.

1. *Stretching Output.* Output can be "stretched" to provide rather quick increases in capacity. It is useful to keep in mind the benefits and costs of overtime, extra shifts, part-time help, subcontracting, and using inventory intended to buffer against unusual demands.
2. *Shrinking Output.* Some alternatives exist for reducing output to reduce capacity quickly. Hiring freezes, employee lay-offs, dismissals, terminating rent agreements and leases, and selling pieces of equipment and properties all tend to reduce capacity.
3. *Product Mix.* Product mix is a function of actual orders forecast item-by-item or by service demand, and of forecast accuracy, willingness to take risk in deviating from orders, setup costs, lot sizes, and make or buy decisions. Product mix is a key *management variable,* one that can be controlled somewhat in the short-run and one that certainly must be understood when managing capacity. A management audit of how various product mixes have historically affected shipments (or customers served), percent utilization of facilities, labor utilization, and costs can be extremely beneficial in understanding the impact of product mix on capacity. Capacity is a function of product mix. Therefore the wise manager will understand the operations impact of alternative product mixes.
4. *Permanent Capacity Change.* There are obvious permanent changes that can be made. These often have far reaching strategic implications and should be considered carefully in relation to markets, the financial position of the firm, and technology alternatives. Equipment investment, new plants or service centers, product re-design, process modifications, management innovations—all interact with and determine the *technology* the organization possesses. In turn, individually and collectively, these changes do affect capacity.

Managing Capacity Change: The Process

The following seven-step procedure is suggested as a guide for managing capacity change. It is written for additions to capacity but can be altered for subtractions from capacity.

1. Measure *current output per time* period (volume), and estimate or document the maximum output per time period *(current capacity).*

---

[8]For other discussions of capacity change see David A. Schilling, "Strategic Facility Planning: The Analysis of Options," *Decision Sciences* 13, no. 1 (1982), pp. 1–14; Roger W. Schmenner, *Production/Operations Management: Concepts and Situations,* Science Research Associates (1981), pp. 297–332; and Roger G. Schroeder, *Operations Management: Decision Making in the Operating Function,* McGraw-Hill (1981), pp. 239–40.

2. *For any new business, estimate the required change in capacity.* To do this the manager must
   - define a product mix
   - develop a forecast
   - convert the "scenario for new business" (the mix and forecast) into *gross units,* into the *lowest* possible *expected work area* (a plant, work center, or machine), and finally into the *capacity change required.*
3. Add the new capacity required from the expected new business, the result being *expected required capacity.*
4. *Estimate how to best add the new capacity,* examining both short-term and long-term capacity change choices. Modeling might be useful, but at the very least, alternative total cost scenarios should be developed and evaluated for capacity change alternatives. Useful tools and techniques are: process identification techniques (see Chapter 10); capital investment techniques (to be discussed in Chapter 19); accurate forecasting; break-even analysis; decision-tree analysis; and evaluation of economics of scale.
5. Consider the qualitative factors that will result from a capacity change so that each may be overcome or addressed. These factors include: the impact upon people in existing operations; staffing the new addition; the competitive reaction in the industry to this change; and the impact of this change upon the flexibility required to meet overall objectives.
6. *Establish the location of the new capacity.*
7. Answer "*When* should the new capacity be added?" The disfunctional consequences upon existing operations should be minimized while the capacity change moves forward in a timely manner.

BEHAVIOR CONSIDERATIONS IN CAPACITY PLANNING

Post-Keynesian economic theory has stressed the relationship between business executives' expectations about the future of the economy and their subsequent investment in plant and equipment. Favorable expectations result in increased investment in plant and equipment, and thus capacity is increased. Unfortunately, the psychology associated with the interpretation of economic data by individual businesspeople is difficult to measure, and tracing subsequent behavior to changes in beliefs about the future is similarly difficult to document. Surveys by purchasing agent associations do, however, lend some support to the argument that expectations affect investment. They indicate that as expressed attitudes change over time, so do capital goods purchases, lead times, and subsequent capacity.

In the United States, individuals and groups—both within and without official government channels—are involved in establishing policy. One particularly important policy to businesspeople has to do with the investment tax credit, a tax incentive to induce increased expenditures for plants and equipment. If tax incentives are granted, new and modernized facilities are built, and capacity duly increases. The President, members of the Council of Economic Advisors, members of Congress, and constituents all exert influence on the congressional committee establishing tax policy. The behavioral overtones of all this political-economic activity affect policy outcomes, and policy outcomes directly affect the operations manager's capacity planning decisions.

For any one organization, behavioral considerations receive only minor emphasis in our coverage of operations capacity planning. The main reason for this is that capacity decisions are dominated by considerations of product characteristics, economic factors, and processing technology. At this broad level of planning it is difficult to show how specific aspects of employee behavior relate to the capacity decision in any precise way. This situation changes, however, with two other aspects of operations planning, facility location and layout. We shall discuss them in the chapters that follow.

SUMMARY

Capacity is the maximum rate of productive or conversion capability of an organization's operations. Capacity planning decisions involve assessing existing facilities, estimating future needs, identifying alternatives (strategies), evaluating alternatives, and selecting a capacity alternative.

Capacity is usually measured in terms of an output rate. For some companies with diverse products and for service organizations, however, about the only measure of capacity becomes the maximum inputs rather than outputs. Sometimes throughput, which measures capacity in terms of rate of output or input per time unit, is used instead.

In both estimating future capacity needs and evaluating strategies for modifying capacity, short-term and long-term time horizons must be considered. To assist in reaching an acceptable capacity decision, such modeling approaches as linear programming, computer simulation, and decision tree analysis are helpful. Although modeling should not totally overshadow the behavioral implications of reaching a capacity decision, the fact remains that capacity planning benefits most significantly from the logical analysis implicit in modeling. Product characteristics, economic factors, and processing technology are paramount in the capacity planning process.

CASE

Paradise Land Management Company

Paradise Land Management owns and operates hotels and apartment complexes near a major metropolitan area. They wish to expand operations in the near future, the goal being to increase net earnings before taxes. Two alternative expansion opportunities are under consideration, the Densmore complex and the Highgate project. Both projects involve the purchase of land on which apartment buildings would be constructed and operated.

The site for the Densmore complex is situated in a respected, quiet, sparsely populated residential neighborhood. The building site for the 70-unit complex can be purchased for $60,000. Building costs are estimated at

$1,680,000. Annual maintenance costs would amount to $30,000. Apartment units would rent for $410 per month. Nearby, Paradise plans to construct a recreation facility. It would cost $100,000 and would service both Densmore residents and the residents of Paradise West, the only existing apartment complex in the neighborhood. Paradise West, with 120 units renting for $290 per month, has had an average occupancy rate of 84 percent for the past three years. The addition of Densmore and the recreation facility are expected to increase Paradise West's occupancy rate to 90 percent with probability of 0.6, or to 95 percent with a probability of 0.4. Densmore's occupancy rate is expected to be 90 percent (probability of 0.5), 85 percent (probability of 0.3), or 80 percent (probability of 0.2).

The Highgate project calls for 400 units to be constructed on a site costing $220,000 in a high density population neighborhood with many competing apartments. Building costs would be $4,200,000. Rental revenue per unit would be $240 per month; annual operating costs would be $150,000. The probability of a 90 percent occupancy rate is 0.2, of an 80 percent rate 0.5, and of a 70 percent rate 0.3.

What factors should be analyzed in making this capacity decision?

REVIEW AND DISCUSSION QUESTIONS

1. Define and give examples of these measures of capacity:
   (a) normal
   (b) maximum
   (c) throughput
2. Define and describe the operating capacity of a college of business administration. How should its capacity be measured?
3. Discuss the fundamental differences in short-run versus long-run capacity decisions. What are the major considerations in each?
4. Outline the merits and drawbacks of incremental capacity changes and large lump changes.
5. Create an example illustrating how the product life cycle concept can be helpful in planning for capacity utilization of a manufacturing company.
6. How is product mix related to the capacity utilization decision?
7. What costs would be affected if you closed one of several warehouses (capacity contraction) in a distribution system? How might revenues be affected?
8. What analytical approaches and models are useful in aiding capacity decisions? Under what circumstances would each model be most beneficial relative to the others?
9. Capacity will be modified in response to demand. Demand will be modified in response to capacity. Which of those two statements is correct? Why?
10. Suppose you were considering expansion of your local fire fighting system. Show what factors should be considered and how you would relate them to one another in your analysis.
11. Explain the relationship between capacity planning and location planning. To illustrate, select a service business and explain the relationship for that business.
12. Explain the conversion system design interactions of Figure 6.2 for a new franchise you have received in your home town, to sell yogurt through one outlet.
13. Briefly describe a practical approach toward managing capacity change. Would

it be important for a person wanting to be a general manager, not an operations manager, to understand this process? Why or why not?

PROBLEMS

Solved Problems

1. Annual demand for a manufacturing company is expected to be as follows:

Units demanded:	8,000	10,000	15,000	20,000
Probability:	0.5	0.2	0.2	0.1

Revenues are \$35 per unit. The existing manufacturing facility has annual fixed operating costs of \$200,000. Variable manufacturing costs are \$7.75 per unit at the 8,000 unit output level, \$5.00 at the 10,000 unit level, \$5.33 at the 15,000 unit level, and \$7.42 at 20,000 units of output.

An expanded facility under consideration would require \$250,000 fixed operating costs annually. Variable costs would average \$9.40 at the 8,000 unit level, \$5.20 at the 10,000 unit level, \$3.80 at the 15,000 unit level, and \$4.90 for the 20,000 level.

If we wish to maximize net earnings, which size facility should we select?

Expected net revenue of existing facility

$$\text{Expected variable cost} = [(\$7.75)(8{,}000)(0.5) + (\$5.00)(10{,}000)(0.2) + (\$5.33)(15{,}000)(0.2) + (\$7.42)(20{,}000)(0.1)] = \$71{,}830$$

$$\text{Expected total cost} = \text{fixed cost} + \text{variable cost} = \$200{,}000 + \$71{,}830 = \$271{,}830$$

$$\text{Expected revenue} = \$35\,[(8{,}000)(0.5) + (10{,}000)(0.2) + (15{,}000)(0.2) + (20{,}000)(0.1)] = \$385{,}000$$

$$\text{Expected net revenue} = \$385{,}000 - \$271{,}830 = \$113{,}170$$

Expected net revenue of expanded facility

$$\text{Expected variable cost} = [(\$9.40)(8{,}000)(0.5) + (\$5.20)(10{,}000)(0.2) + (\$3.80)(15{,}000)(0.2) + (\$4.90)(20{,}000)(0.1)] = \$69{,}200$$

$$\text{Expected total cost} = \$250{,}000 + \$69{,}200 = \$319{,}200$$

$$\text{Expected net revenue} = \$385{,}000 - \$319{,}200 = \$65{,}800$$

The existing facility maximizes expected net earnings.

2. Corn-Gas-A-Hol (CGAH) is considering adding a second and a third shift to meet expected increases in demand this year. Current fixed costs are \$50,000 per year for one shift production. A second shift would increase fixed costs \$25,000, a third shift another \$50,000. Capacity is 400 barrels per shift. Accounting estimates:

Processing variable unit cost	Probability of that variable unit cost
\$15	0.20
20	0.30
25	0.30
30	0.15
35	0.05

The unit price for CGAH's product is \$200 per barrel. What is the breakeven volume(s) for CGAH? Interpret your answer for management.

$$\text{Expected unit variable cost} = (\$15)(0.20) + (20)(0.30) + (25)(0.30) + (30)(0.15) + (35)(0.05) = \$22.75$$

Breakeven is that volume x (number of barrels) where TR = TC.

$$\text{One shift: } (\$200)(x) = \$50{,}000 + \$22.75x$$

$$x = \frac{50{,}000}{177.25} = 282.20 \text{ barrels}$$

$$\text{Two shifts: } x = \frac{75{,}000}{177.25} = 423.13 \text{ barrels}$$

$$\text{Three shifts: } x = \frac{125{,}000}{177.25} = 705.21 \text{ barrels}$$

Interpreting, the breakeven for one shift is 282.2 barrels. With a 400 barrel capacity on this shift, a profit could be expected if demand exceeded 282.20 barrels. A profit could also be made with two shifts because breakeven is 423.13 barrels and capacity is 800. Similarly, a profit could be made on three shifts. If full capacity could be sold, then management can maximize profit with three shifts, selling 1,200 barrels.

[Note: the variable costs for Corn-Gas-A-Hol seem *very* low. Perhaps this could be achieved using a low cost by-product as the energy source for conversion operations.]

Reinforcing Fundamentals

3. A manufacturer of dishware is considering three alternative plant sizes. Demand depends upon the selling price of the product; costs of manufacture also depend on the size of the plant selected. Demand is expected to be:

Demand probabilities

Annual demand (sets of dishware)	Selling price per set of dishware $40	$37	$35
10,000	0.2	0.1	0.05
20,000	0.4	0.4	0.25
30,000	0.3	0.4	0.40
40,000	0.1	0.1	0.30

Anticipated operating costs for the three plant sizes for different levels of operation are:

Variable manufacturing costs per unit

Level of plant operation (units of output)	Small	Plant size Medium	Large
10,000	$21	$25	$32
20,000	16	14	18
30,000	19	13	12
40,000	26	18	14
Annual fixed cost of operation	$300,000	$420,000	$500,000

Which alternative is most attractive on the basis of annual net earnings?

4. How would your answer to problem 3 change if variable manufacturing costs were changed to those shown next?

Variable manufacturing costs per unit

Level of plant operation (units of output)	Small	Plant size Medium	Large
10,000	$21	$20	$25
20,000	19	16	18
30,000	19	15	10
40,000	23	18	12

5. Suppose that for the first solved problem above annual demand expectations were as follows:

Units demanded:	8,000	10,000	15,000	20,000
Probability:	0.25	0.25	0.25	0.25

   Is the best alternative under these conditions the same as the best in the original problem? Explain.
6. Nitelite Taxi Company is considering two alternative methods of expanding services. One proposal would add four new taxis and drivers to the fleet during the prime daytime hours. This would increase annual fixed operating costs $40,000. Variable operating cost per passenger would average $.50; revenue would average $4.20 per passenger.

   The second proposal would add only two new taxis and drivers to work overtime as demand dictates. Fixed operating costs for this alternative are $30,000. Total variable costs are expected to average $1.00 per passenger up to the point where 10,000 customers have been served. If more than 10,000 passengers are served during the year, total variable costs (*TVC*) will be

$$TVC = (\$.0002)(x - 10{,}000)^2 + 1.0x$$

   where x is the number of passengers served during the year. Evaluate and discuss the merits of both alternatives.
7. Annual demand for a carpet cleaning company that specializes in small home jobs is expected to be as follows:

Units demanded:	6,000	10,000	12,000	15,000
Probability:	0.4	0.3	0.2	0.1

   Revenues are $42 per unit. The existing company has annual fixed operating costs of $400,000. Variable manufacturing costs are $5.00 per unit at the 6,000 unit output level, $4.00 at the 10,000 unit level, $5.25 at the 12,000 unit level and $6.00 at 15,000 units of output.

   An expanded fleet (capacity) under consideration would require $50,000 fixed operating costs annually. Variable costs would average $6.50 at the 6,000 unit level, $5.20 at the 10,000 unit level, $4.00 at the 12,000 unit level, and $3.85 for the 15,000 level.

   If we wish to maximize net earnings, which size company should we select?
8. Workman's Bank is considering adding a second and a third shift to meet expected increases in consumer check processing increases this year. Current fixed costs are $50,000 per year for one shift production. A second shift would increase fixed costs $35,000, a third shift another $25,000. Capacity is 500 check trays per shift. Accounting estimates:

Processing variable unit cost	Probability of that variable unit cost
$20	0.20
25	0.20
30	0.30
35	0.20
40	0.10

The unit price for processing a tray is $225.00. What is the breakeven volume(s) for Workman's? Interpret your answer for management.

9. A plant manager is attempting to determine whether his firm should purchase a component part or make it at its own facilities. If it purchases the item, it will cost the company $2 per unit. The company can make the item on an assembly line at a variable cost of $0.50 per unit with a fixed cost of $4,000. Or it can make it at individual stations at a variable cost of $1.00 per unit with a fixed cost of $2,000. Determine which alternative the plant manager should select; expected demand is as shown below.

Units Demanded	Likelihood of this demand
4,000	0.20
4,500	0.50
5,000	0.30

Challenging Exercises

10. Micro Distributors is considering an addition of 500,000 square feet of warehouse space to an existing facility during the next two years. Three expansion proposals are being considered: (1) add 100,000 square feet now and 400,000 square feet two years from now, (2) add 200,000 square feet now plus 300,000 square feet in two years, or (3) do the entire addition now. Construction estimates show considerable cost savings for making the additions as soon as possible.

Construction Estimates

	Now		Two years from now	
Alternative	Amount of expansion (thousands of square feet)	Cost ($million)	Amount of expansion (thousands of square feet)	Cost ($million)
1	100	1.00	400	3.2
2	200	1.75	300	2.6
3	500	3.30	—	—

Micro's marketing personnel suggest a wait and see approach with incremental expansion; they favor alternatives 1 and 2. Although expansion is expected to create additional demand, other forces outside Micro's control may result in lower demand, in which case Micro would be left with excessive, unproductive warehousing capacity. A mild expansion now would permit a two-year observation of demand before deciding on additional expansion.

A ten-year planning horizon was chosen. These estimates of demand and net operating revenues were obtained:

Estimates for First Two Years

	Alternative 1		Alternative 2	
Level of demand	Low	High	Low	High
Total net operating revenue ($million)	1.0	1.3	0.8	1.4
Probability	0.4	0.6	0.3	0.7

Estimates for Years 3–10

	Alternative 1				Alternative 2			
	If expanded after 2 years		If not expanded after 2 years		If expanded after 2 years		If not expanded after 2 years	
Level of demand	Low	High	Low	High	Low	High	Low	High
Total net operating revenue ($million)	2.4	7.2	3.8	5.8	2.4	7.2	3.2	6.4
Probability (if demand was high in years 1 and 2)	0.2	0.8	0.3	0.7	0.2	0.8	0.3	0.7
Probability (if demanded was low in years 1 and 2)	0.3	0.7	0.8	0.2	0.4	0.6	0.7	0.3

For alternative 3, ten-year operating revenue is estimated at $9,000,000 with probability of 0.5; $6,000,000 with probability of 0.3, and $2,000,000 with probability of 0.2. Which alternative is best? Justify your recommendation.

11. The Reliable Storage Company has a large warehousing operation. In developing long-range plans, they are considering expansion of storage capacity. Estimates of future storage demand, increased revenues, and costs of expansion have been obtained for the ten-year planning horizon. Management has narrowed the expansion alternatives to three choices: (1) expand now by adding 100,000 square feet of storage space, (2) add 40,000 square feet now and 60,000 square feet three years later, (3) add 40,000 square feet now and nothing later.

If the entire expansion is done now, construction costs will be lower than they will be later. Further, there will be a greater chance for higher business revenues since enough space will be added to take in new business. There is a chance, however, of overexpanding; if the entire expanded facility is not needed, idle capacity will result. The more conservative alternatives are to expand modestly now, wait and see if demand continues to increase as expected, and expand or do not expand accordingly. This approach reduces the risk of investing funds in an idle, overexpanded facility. However, the "wait and see" alternatives have two disadvantages. First, limited storage capacity in the first three years may result in lost opportunities for more business. Second, future construction costs are expected to be considerably higher than those at present levels. Estimates of relevant factors for this decision are shown in Table 6.9.

TABLE 6.9
Data for expansion decision of Reliable Storage Company

	Cash outlays for expansion		Expected after-tax cash flow per year			
			Years 1–3		Years 4–10	
Decision alternative	Expansion cost now	Expansion cost three years from now	If demand is high	If demand is low	If demand is high	If demand is low
Full expansion now	100,000 sq ft @$16/sq ft = $1,600,000	0	$180,000	$90,000	$240,000	$120,000
Expand 40,000 feet now and 60,000 feet in three years	40,000 sq ft @ $18/sq ft = $720,000	60,000 sq ft @ $24/sq ft = $1,440,000	75,000	36,000	210,000	120,000
Expand 40,000 feet now; no further expansion	40,000 sq ft @ $18/sq ft = $720,000	0	75,000	36,000	75,000	36,000

For years one through three, it is estimated that the probability of high annual demand is 0.7; the probability of low demand is 0.3. For years four through ten, the probability of high demand is 0.6, and the probability of low demand is 0.4. Which decision is best?

12. A manufacturer has received the following estimates of daily demand for a product for each of the next two years.

	Demand per day (units)						
	100	*120*	*140*	*160*	*180*	*200*	*220*
Probability (year 1):	0.10	0.20	0.40	0.10	0.10	0.06	0.04
Probability (year 2):	0.02	0.10	0.23	0.30	0.20	0.10	0.05

Three plant capacities (*A, B,* and *C*) are under consideration. For each plant size, operating costs per unit of output are estimated for various output rates as follows:

	Daily output level (units)						
Plant Size	*100*	*120*	*140*	*160*	*180*	*200*	*220*
A	$2.40	$2.20	$2.60	$3.00	—	—	—
B	4.30	3.40	2.70	2.10	2.30	2.80	—
C	6.50	5.00	4.00	3.20	2.50	1.90	2.00

What plant size (daily output capacity) will minimize expected operating costs per unit for the two-year period if we produce to meet demand?

13. United American Savings and Loan has three processing centers (Newburg, Central, and Wilmont) for twenty-seven branch locations. A sudden increase in demand for item processing has come about due to a new service—a customer draft on account, which is similar to a personal checking account in a commercial bank.
United American had closed the Newburg processing center since the facili-

ties at Wilmont and Central had enough capacity on one shift to handle demand. Now either the Wilmont facility must go to a second shift or the Newburg facility must be reopened. Revenue is expected to average $.20 per item processed at each facility.

The Wilmont facility has been operating with fixed costs of $500,000 and variable costs of $.10, with an annual first shift capacity of 10 million items. Starting a second shift would increase variable costs for items processed on that shift to either $.12 or $.14, with probabilities of 0.6 and 0.4 respectively. Second shift annual capacity would be 10 million items.

The Newburg facility can be reopened for fixed costs of either $100,000 or $50,000, with probabilities of 0.3 and 0.7 respectively. Unit variable costs are expected to be $.12, and capacity is 7 million items annually.

As vice president of operations, you must *prepare a recommendation* for expanding capacity for an upcoming meeting with the president. In your analysis, *prepare a decision tree* for the president depicting this situation and a *rough graph* of costs and revenues for various volumes.

GLOSSARY

Capacity Productive capability of a facility, usually expressed as volume of output per time period; maximum rate of productive or conversion capability of an organization's operations.

Linear programming Mathematical technique that guarantees the optimal allocation of resources to maximize profits or minimize costs.

Present value analysis Method for measuring the worth of an investment in which future cash inflows (and outlays) are converted into an equivalent present value.

Product life cycle Concept used to describe the chronological stages of demand for a product.

Product mix problem Decision situation involving limited resources that can be used to produce any of several combinations of products.

Technology of operations Physical, human, and/or mental processes that are required by the organization to convert input resources into products or outputs.

Throughput Capacity measurement in terms of rate of output or input per time unit.

Useful economic life Potential productive capacity of a facility.

SELECTED READINGS

Bierman, H., Jr., C. P. Bonini, and W. H. Hausman. *Quantitative Analysis for Business Decisions.* 5th ed. Homewood, Ill.: Richard D. Irwin, Inc., 1977.

Chaiken, J. M. and P. Dormont. "A Patrol Car Allocation Model: Capabilities and Algorithms." *Management Science* 24, no. 12 (August 1978), pp. 1291–1300.

Cook, T. M. and B. S. Alprin. "Snow and Ice Removal in an Urban Environment." *Management Science* 23, no. 3 (November 1976), pp. 227–34.

Erlenkotter, D. "Capacity Expansion With Imports and Inventories." *Management Science* 23, no. 7 (March 1977), pp. 694–702.

Goldhar, Joel D. and Mariann Jelinek. "Plan for Economies of Scope." *Harvard Business Review* 61, no. 6 (November–December 1983), pp. 141–148.

Manne, A. S., ed. *Investments for Capacity Expansion.* Cambridge, Mass.: The M.I.T. Press, 1967.

Markland, R. E. "Analyzing Geographically Discrete Warehousing Networks by Computer Simulation." *Decision Sciences* 4, no. 2 (April 1973), pp. 216–36.

Monarchi, D. E., T. E. Hendrick, and D. R. Plane. "Simulation for Fire Department Deployment Policy Analysis." *Decision Sciences* 8, no. 1 (January 1977), pp. 211–27.

Scherer, F. M. "The Determinants of Industrial Plant Size in Six Nations." *Review of Economics and Statistics* 55, no. 2 (May 1973), pp. 135–45.

Schilling, David A. "Strategic Facility Planning: The Analysis of Options." *Decision Sciences* 13, no. 1, (1982), pp. 1–14.

Schmenner, Roger W. *Production/Operations Management: Concepts and Situations.* Science Research Associates, 1981, pp. 297–332.

Schroeder, Roger W. *Operations Management: Decision Making in the Operating Function.* McGraw-Hill, 1981, pp. 239–40.

Skinner, Wickham. *Manufacturing in the Corporation Strategy.* Wiley, 1978, pp. 111–113 and 121–122.

Woodward, J. T. "Capital Expenditure Programs and Sales Expectations for 1975." *Survey of Current Business* 55, no. 3 (March 1975), pp. 11–17.

Supplement to Chapter 6

LINEAR PROGRAMMING: THE GRAPHICAL AND SIMPLEX METHODS

The purpose of this section is to present a mathematical optimization technique called linear programming. We'll consider three linear programming (LP) methods: graphical, simplex, and transportation. The graphical method is of limited practical value but is helpful for visualizing the underlying concepts of LP. The simplex method can be used to solve any LP problem. The transportation (or distribution) method can be used only on a special type of problem with particular characteristics; it is presented as a supplement to Chapter 7. When such a problem is identified, the transportation method is computationally more convenient to use than the simplex method.

In general, linear programming can be applied to decision problems with these characteristics:

1. *Decision variables.* The numeric values of two or more decision variables are to be determined. (Decision variables are factors under the decision maker's control that, if modified, result in outcomes different from each other.)
2. *Goal.* The goal is to find the best decision values, those that will maximize (or minimize) the objective function.
3. *Objective function.* The objective (criterion) function is a mathematical equation that measures the outcome of any proposed alternative. In LP, the objective function must be linear, as you will see below.
4. *Restrictions.* The values that can be chosen for decision variables are restricted (constrained); complete freedom of choice does not exist. Allowable (feasible) values of decision variables are defined by linear constraint equations.

The General Linear Programming Problem

The general linear programming problem can be stated in any of several forms. Although you cannot be expected to understand this section until after you have read the graphical method and perhaps even the simplex method, we believe it is helpful to state the problem without explaining it at this point. That way we'll have a clear idea of where we're headed.

The following three forms are equivalent statements of the linear programming problem; your understanding of one or more of the forms will depend upon your background in mathematics.

1. *Maximize*

$$Z = C_1X_2 + C_2X_2 + \ldots C_nX_n \text{ where the } X_1, X_2 \ldots, X_n$$

is a set of variables whose values are to be determined. The C_1, C_2, . . . , C_n are value coefficients reflecting the contribution each unit of the corresponding variables makes to the objective function. Notice that Z is a linear function of the variables X_i; when X_i increases by one unit, the value of Z increases by an amount C_i.

Subject to

$$\begin{array}{llll} A_{11}X_1 & + A_{12}X_2 & + \ldots A_{1n}X_n & \leq B_1 \\ A_{21}X_1 & + A_{22}X_2 & + \ldots A_{2n}X_n & \leq B_2 \\ \vdots & \vdots & \vdots & \vdots \\ \vdots & \vdots & \vdots & \vdots \\ \vdots & \vdots & \vdots & \vdots \\ A_{m1}X_1 & + A_{m2}X_2 & + \ldots + A_{mn}X_n & \leq B_m \\ X_1X_2, \ldots, X_n \geq 0 & & & \end{array}$$

Where each equation is a constraint imposed on the value of the variables, the A_{11}, A_{12}, . . . , A_{mn} are coefficients, and the B_1, B_2, . . . , B_m are initial amounts of resources available. Notice that each constraint is a linear function; when X_j increases by one unit, A_{ij} units of resource B_i are consumed.

2. *Maximize*

$$\sum_{j=1}^{n} C_jX_j$$

Subject to

$$\sum_{j=1}^{n} A_{ij}X_j \leq B_i \qquad i = 1, 2, \ldots, m$$

$$X_j \geq 0 \qquad j = 1, 2, \ldots, n$$

3. *Maximize*

$$\mathbf{CX}$$

Subject to

$$\mathbf{AX} \leq \mathbf{B}$$
$$\mathbf{X} \geq 0$$

where you find a $(n \times 1)$ matrix **X**
when **C** is a $(1 \times n)$ matrix,
A is a $(m \times n)$ matrix, and
B is a $(m \times 1)$ matrix.

Graphical Method

The purpose of the graphical method is to provide an intuitive grasp of the concepts that are used in the simplex technique. The general procedure is to convert a descriptive situation into the form of a linear programming problem by deciding what all variables, constants, objective functions, and constraints are for the situation. Then the problem is graphed and interpreted. To use the graphical method, one must:

1. identify the decision variables,
2. identify the objective (or criterion) function,
3. identify resource restrictions (constraints),
4. draw a graph that includes all restrictions,
5. identify the feasible decision area on the graph,
6. draw a graph of the objective function and select the point on the feasible area that optimizes the objective function, and
7. interpret the solution.

In explaining these steps we refer to the case of MultiBand Enterprises that was used in Chapter 6. For your convenience the situation is repeated here.

EXAMPLE

MultiBand Enterprises manufactures two products, a portable radio (PR) and a citizens band (CB) radio. The marketing manager states, "We can sell all that can be produced in the near future." She then asks the operations manager, "What is your production capacity per month?" The operations manager replies that his output capacity depends on which product is produced. "Three kinds of labor are required for making our products: subassembly, assembly, and inspection labor. The two products require different amounts of each kind of labor, so our capacity for next month depends on which products we produce. Next month we will have 316 hours of subassembly labor available, 354 hours of assembly labor, and 62 hours of inspection labor." The operations manager knows that each CB radio requires .4 hours of subassembly labor time, .5 hours of assembly labor, and .05 hours of inspection labor. A portable radio can be produced using .5 hours of subassembly labor, .3 hours of assembly labor, and .10 hours of inspection labor.

The vice-president says, "We know that each CB that we produce and sell contributes $50 towards profit and overhead. Each PR has a $40 contribution margin." What is MultiBand's output capacity, and what mix of CBs and PRs should be manufactured next month?

Step 1: Identify Decision Variables Citizens band (CB) radios and/or portable radios (PR) can be manufactured by MultiBand. *These are the two decision variables.* The problem is to decide how many CBs and PRs to produce.

Step 2: Identify Objective Function Each CB will provide $50 contribution to profit and overhead, and each PR will contribute $40. MultiBand's total contribution gain will be

$$TC = (\$50)(CB) + (\$40)(PR) \qquad \textbf{(S6.1)}$$

This *linear* objective function states that total gain (or total contribution, *TC*) depends on the decision as to how many CBs and PRs to produce. MultiBand would like total contribution to be as large as possible; it wishes to *maximize* TC.

Step 3: Identify Resource Restrictions To produce radios, MultiBand needs three types of labor: subassembly, assembly, and inspection. The available quantities of these three resources are 316 employee hours of subassembly labor, 354 hours of assembly labor, and 62 hours of inspection labor. A CB radio requires 0.4 hours of subassembly labor, 0.5 hours of assembly time, and 0.05 hours of inspection. The manufacture of a PR requires 0.5 hours of subassembly labor, 0.3 hours assembly time, and 0.1 hours of inspection. Thus we have three restrictions, one for each labor resource. The total number of CBs and PRs that can possibly be produced is limited by the amounts of resources that are available. The restrictions on the use of these three resources are expressed as linear inequalities.

Resource (labor)	Resource consumption		Resource availability (hours)
Subassembly	0.4 CB + 0.5 PR	≤	316
Assembly	0.5 CB + 0.3 PR	≤	354
Inspection	0.05 CB + 0.1 PR	≤	62

Step 4: Draw a Graph of All Restrictions Look at Figure S6.1. The horizontal axis of the graph shows various quantities of CBs that could be produced. The vertical axis shows quantities of PRs. The *solution space* (the part of the graph where the answer to the problem can be found) consists of all points on or to the right of the vertical axis; and on or above the horizontal axis, since negative values of CBs or PRs have no meaning. Each point in this space represents some combination of PRs and CBs.

Let's draw the line for the subassembly labor restriction. If the entire 316 subassembly hours were devoted to producing CBs, how many could be produced? Since each CB requires 0.4 hours, then 316 hours ÷ 0.4 subassembly hours per CB = 790 CBs. This combination of producing zero PRs and 790 CBs is plotted as point *a* on the graph. Another alternative is to produce no CBs. In that case, we have enough subassembly labor to produce 316 hours ÷ 0.5 subassembly hours per PR = 632 PRs. This combination of products (zero CBs and 632 PRs) is represented by point *b* on the

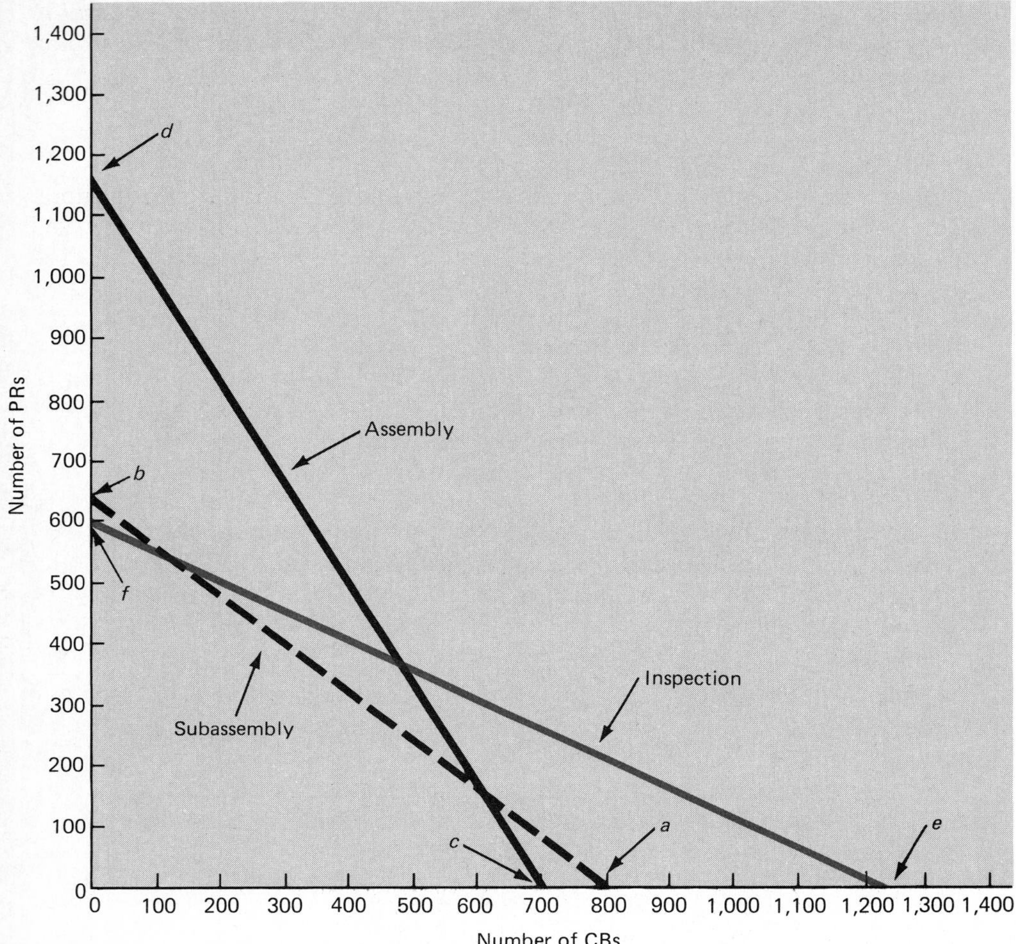

FIGURE S6.1
Restrictions for MultiBand Enterprises

graph. Now, since all restrictions are linear, the line can be drawn connecting points *a* and *b*. Each point on this restriction line represents some combination of CBs and PRs, and each point totally consumes all existing subassembly labor time. In linear programming, all restrictions must be represented by straight lines, never by curves. This is what we mean by a linear function. Points falling above or to the right of line *ab* are *infeasible* combinations of CBs and PRs, since they require more than 316 hours of subassembly.

In a similar manner, we can draw the line representing full use of assembly labor. If no PRs are produced, there is enough assembly labor to produce 708 CBs (354 hours ÷ 0.5 assembly hours per CB). This product mix, zero PRs and 708 CBs, is shown as point *c* in Figure S6.1. If no CBs are produced, 1,180 PRs can be made with available assembly labor (point *d*). Line *cd* is the assembly labor restriction line. Similarly, line *ef* is the restriction line for inspection labor.

Step 5: Identify Feasible Decision Area When management decides how many PRs and CBs to produce, they cannot abide by just one or two of the restrictions. They must adhere simultaneously to all three relevant restrictions. The feasible points that satisfy all these restrictions lie within the white area in Figure S6.2. This feasiblity area is bounded by the corner points 0, *f*, *g*, *h*, and *c*.

FIGURE S6.2
Area of feasible solutions for MultiBand Enterprises

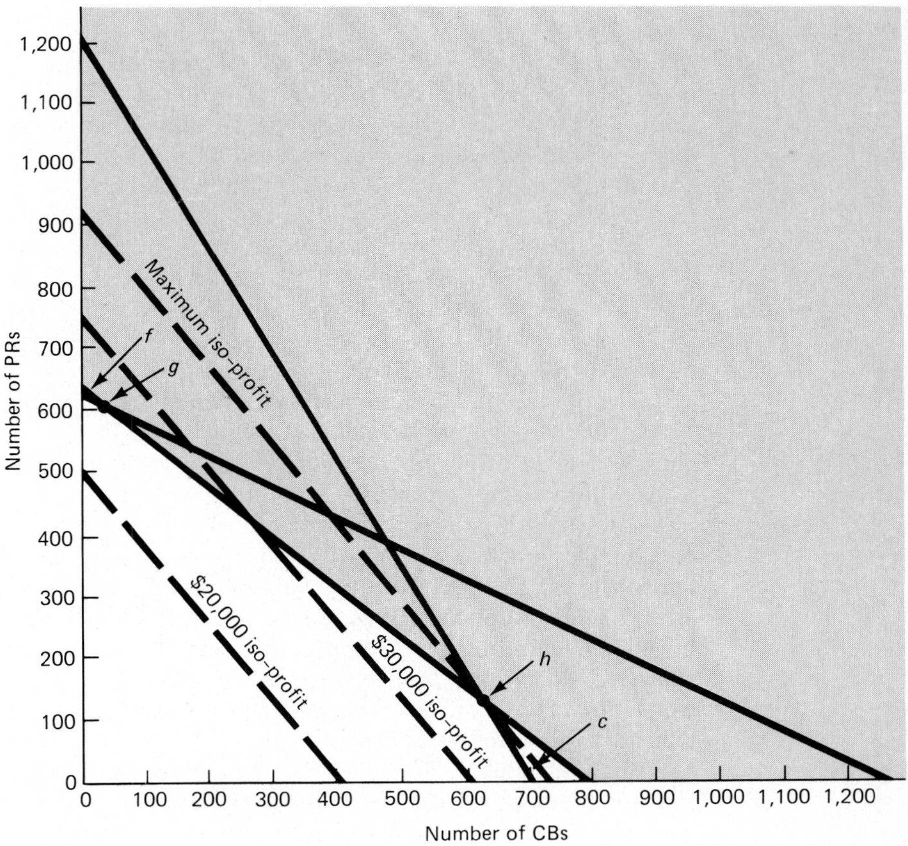

Step 6: Draw Objective Function and Select the Optimum Point Although all points in the bounded area are *feasible* decision alternatives, they are not all equally attractive. Some provide a greater total contribution than others. At point *c* (708 CBs, zero PRs), for example, total contribution is (\$50)(708) + (\$40)(0) = \$35,400. But 300 CBs and 300 PRs would only give a total contribution of (\$50)(300) + (\$40)(300) = \$27,000. We must now pick out the *best* point from among the infinite number of points in the feasible area. Our task is simplified, however, because *the best point will lie at one of the corner (extreme) points of the feasible area*. Therefore, one of points 0, *f*, *g*, *h*, or *c* is optimal. We could calculate the total contribution for each of these five points and select the one that has the highest value.

A graphical procedure also exists for finding the best point. It requires adding one more line to the graph, an *iso-profit*, or *constant-profit*, line. On an iso-profit line, all the points give the same profit. Suppose we want to find the iso-profit line representing a \$20,000 contribution. Using equation S6.1, we find:

$$\$20{,}000 = (\$50)(\text{CB}) + (\$40)(\text{PR})$$

Many combinations of CBs and PRs, all lying on the same line, provide this contribution. On Figure S6.2, we have drawn a dotted line connecting all the points at which a \$20,000 profit would be contributed. You can see, for example, that a combination of zero CBs and 500 PRs would contribute \$20,000. So would a combination of zero PRs and 400 CBs. All the points that fall on this dotted line fall in the feasible area, so it is clearly possible for MultiBand to realize a \$20,000 profit. In fact, even greater profits can be achieved. Look at the \$30,000 iso-profit line. Some of the points on this line fall outside the feasible area and thus are not legitimate alternatives. Other parts of the line, however, fall in the white area. A \$30,000 contribution is therefore attainable.

Two features of these iso-profit lines are particularly noteworthy. First, they are parallel to one another. Second, the farther the lines are removed from the origin of the graph, the greater their contribution. Since all the lines have the same slope, our final step is to continue constructing iso-profit lines that are successively farther away from the origin. This procedure stops when any further movement away from the origin would cause the iso-profit line to lie entirely outside the feasible area. In our example, such a line would pass through point *h*. This point gives the *maximum* contribution; it is the *optimal* decision. When the problem is to maximize the objective function, the iso-profit curve should be the furthest from the origin; when the problem is to minimize, the iso-cost curve should be the closest one to the origin.

The optimal decision at point *h*, interpolated from the graph, calls for the production of about 630 CBs and 125 PRs. The approximate value of this decision is

$$TC = (\$50)(630) + (\$40)(125) = \$36{,}000$$

A more precise evaluation of the solution is obtained by noting the characteristic of the optimal point h. This point lies simultaneously on two restriction lines, the subassembly labor line and the assembly labor line. By using simultaneous linear equations, we find the values for PR and CB that satisfy both equations. This occurs when PR = 126.15 and CB = 632.31. The value of this decision is

$$TC = (\$50)(632.31) + (\$40)(126.15) = \$36{,}661.06$$

Step 7: Interpret the Solution The optimal number of PRs and CBs is now known. How much of our three resources will be used for this product mix? Will any of the resources be unused? We can answer these questions both graphically and algebraically. Observation of the graph shows that the optimal point (h) lies on the subassembly and assembly labor restriction lines, which represent the *maximum* amounts of these resources that are available for use. Therefore, the maximum amounts of these two resources are being used in the optimal solution. There is no unused subassembly or assembly labor. Now consider the usage of inspection labor. The optimal solution falls below the inspection labor line. This means that all available inspection labor is not used in the optimal solution; some amount of inspection labor will be unused or idle. We can algebraically compute the unused labor:

$$
\begin{aligned}
\text{Unused inspection labor} &= \text{Available inspection labor} - \text{Used inspection labor} \\
&= 62.0 \text{ hours} - [(0.05 \text{ hours/CB})(632.31 \text{ CBs}) + (0.10 \text{ hours/PR})(126.15 \text{ PRs})] \\
&= 62.0 - [31.62 + 12.62] \\
&= 17.76 \text{ hours}
\end{aligned}
$$

Similarly, we confirm that subassembly and assembly labor are fully utilized:

$$
\begin{aligned}
\text{Unused subassembly labor} &= \text{Available subassembly labor} - \text{Used subassembly labor} \\
&= 316.0 \text{ hours} - [(0.4 \text{ hours/CB})(632.31 \text{ CBs}) + (0.5 \text{ hours/PR})(126.15 \text{ PRs})] \\
&= 316.0 - [252.92 + 63.08] \\
&= 0.0 \text{ hours}
\end{aligned}
$$

$$
\begin{aligned}
\text{Unused assembly labor} &= \text{Available assembly labor} - \text{Used assembly labor}\\
&= 354.0 \text{ hours} - [(0.5 \text{ hours/CB})(632.31 \text{ CBs}) + (0.3 \text{ hours/PR})(126.15 \text{ PRs})]\\
&= 354.0 - [316.16 + 37.84]\\
&= 0.0 \text{ hours}
\end{aligned}
$$

With the graphical method, we can determine what the different coefficients and variables represent and how the constraints and objective function interact. It allows us to see that the optimal solution will always be at an extreme point. The method can be used for problems with two or three decision variables. Since most operations management applications involve larger problems, the graphical method is of limited utility; it is useful, however, for visualizing the basics of linear programming.

Simplex Method

The simplex algorithm is a mathematical procedure for finding the optimal solution to a linear programming problem. It begins with an initial solution, which is progressively improved in a series of stages. To use this procedure, the analyst should:

1. set up the problem in a linear programming framework,
2. create an initial solution,
3. evaluate the existing solution,
4. evaluate variables that could be introduced to improve the solution,
5. select the most advantageous variable to introduce,
6. determine which variable is to leave the solution,
7. revise the solution matrix, and
8. repeat steps 3–7 until no further improvement is possible.

Step 1: Setting Up the Problem A standard format, a statement of the objective function and constraints, is used to set up the problem. In general form, the LP model is a maximization problem of n variables and m restrictions set up as follows:

To Maximize:

$$Z = C_1X_1 + C_2X_2 + \ldots + C_nX_n$$

Subject to Constraints:

$$
\begin{aligned}
A_{11}X_1 &+ A_{12}X_2 + \ldots + A_{1n}X_n \leq B_1\\
A_{21}X_1 &+ A_{22}X_2 + \ldots + A_{2n}X_n \leq B_2\\
&\vdots\\
A_{m1}X_1 &+ A_{m2}X_2 + \ldots + A_{mn}X_n \leq B_m
\end{aligned}
$$

The above restrictions are stated as *inequalities*. The simplex procedure requires that each restriction be converted into an *equality*. This is accomplished by adding a *slack* variable (S_i) to each restriction.

$$\begin{array}{lllllll} A_{11}X_1 & + A_{12}X_2 & + \ldots & + A_{1n}X_n & + S_1 & = B_1 \\ A_{21}X_1 & + A_{22}X_2 & + \ldots & + A_{2n}X_n & + S_2 & = B_2 \\ \vdots & \vdots & & \vdots & \vdots & \vdots \\ A_{m1}X_1 & + A_{m2}X_2 & + \ldots & + A_{mn}X_n & + S_m & = B_m \end{array}$$

S_1 is the slack variable representing the unused or idle quantity of the first resource. It is that portion of B_1 which is not devoted to real products X_1 . . . X_n. Similarly, S_2 is the amount of resource two that is not used. One slack variable is uniquely associated with each resource that was converted from an inequality to an equality. In the simplex procedure these slack variables, S_i, are treated in the same manner as the original variables, X_i. However, each slack variable has a zero coefficient in the objective function. In the above formulation, therefore, the problem has a total of $n + m$ variables.

In formulating the problem, the conventional practice is to restate the objective function and restrictions so that each includes all of the slack variables. Let's express the MultiBand Enterprises problem in the format described below.

To Maximize:

$$Z = (\$50)\text{CB} + (\$40)\text{PR} + \$0S_1 + \$0S_2 + \$0S_3$$

Subject to:

$$\begin{array}{lllllll} \text{Subassembly labor} & (0.4)\text{CB} & + (0.5)\text{PR} & + 1S_1 & + 0S_2 & + 0S_3 & = 316 \\ \text{Assembly labor} & (0.5)\text{CB} & + (0.3)\text{PR} & + 0S_1 & + 1S_2 & + 0S_3 & = 354 \\ \text{Inspection labor} & (0.05)\text{CB} & + (0.1)\text{PR} & + 0S_1 & + 0S_2 & + 1S_3 & = 62 \end{array}$$

The restriction inequalities have been converted to equalities by inserting the slack variables S_1, S_2, and S_3. Every variable (real and slack) appears in all the equations. Later, when we get to a final solution, S_1 will represent the number of subassembly labor hours not used for the real products CB and PR, S_2 will represent unused assembly hours, and S_3 will represent unused inspection hours.

Step 2: Creating an Initial Solution An initial solution is created by forming the matrix (table) shown in Table S6.1. We begin at the origin, with no real variables and only the slack variables in solution.

TABLE S6.1
Initial solution matrix for MultiBand Enterprises

C_j	In solution	\$50 CB	\$40 PR	\$0 S_1	\$0 S_2	\$0 S_3	Production
\$0	S_1	0.4	0.5	1.0	0.0	0.0	316
0	S_2	0.5	0.3	0.0	1.0	0.0	354
0	S_3	0.05	0.1	0.0	0.0	1.0	62
	Z_j	\$0	\$0	\$0	\$0	\$0	\$0
	$C_j - Z_j$	50	40	0	0	0	

(Annotations: X_j points to CB, PR, S_1; A_{ij} points to coefficients; B_i points to production values.)

Within the dotted rectangle are the coefficients, A_{ij}, of the variables in the restriction equations, i referring to a row and j to a column. The coefficients are arranged in rows and columns just as they appear in the constraint set for the MultiBand problem. At the top of each column is the decision variable, X_j or S_j depending upon the column, to which the coefficients in that column apply. For example, the variable CB has coefficients 0.4, 0.5, and 0.05 in restriction equations one, two, and three, respectively. In the first row of the dotted rectangle are the coefficients of the five variables in the first restriction equation. Notice the zero coefficients for S_2 and S_3 in the first row. These mean that S_2 and S_3 do not consume any subassembly labor, since they are slack variables for assembly and inspection.

Around the outer perimeter of the dotted rectangle we find some additional notation. The "in solution" column lists *the variables that are in the initial or firststage solution. The number of variables in solution is equal to the number of restrictions.* This will also be true for each succeeding stage of the problem. The production column shows the quantity of each variable that is in solution. Thus, the initial solution shows 316 units of S_1, 354 units of S_2, and 62 units of S_3 being produced. Since those are fictitious variables, nothing is really being produced. The next step will clarify this point.

Step 3: Evaluating the Existing Solution Refer again to Table S6.1 and find the C_j values representing the objective function coefficients of each variable. These are used to evaluate the existing solution. The value of the objective function for the existing solution is

$$\begin{aligned} Z &= (\$50)(0) + (\$40)(0) + (\$0)(316) + (\$0)(354) + (\$0)(62) \\ &= \$0 \end{aligned}$$

This initial solution leaves all three resources idle, since none of the resources is used for real products. The economic value of this solution is recorded at the bottom of the production column.

Step 4: Evaluating the Effects of Introducing other Variables into Solution Is it possible to improve upon the initial solution? It might be if a new variable is introduced into the solution. Before introducing a new variable, however, we need a procedure for evaluating the economic effects of each variable that could be introduced. This is the purpose of the Z_j and $(C_j - Z_j)$ rows of Table S6.1. C_j represents the amount of *increase* in the objective function if one unit of variable j is added into solution. Z_j represents the amount of *decrease* in the objective function if variable j is introduced. $(C_j - Z_j)$ is the net increase. At the bottom of Table S6.1, beneath each variable, the $(C_j - Z_j)$ for each variable is recorded. The C_j values are obtained readily from the objective function, but determination of the Z_j values requires some explanation.

Z_j is obtained by considering the *substitution* rates between variable j and the variables that are currently in solution. These substitution rates are given by the coefficients under variable j in Table S6.1. Consider the CB radio column. If one CB is introduced, then 0.4 subassembly hours, 0.5 assembly hours, and 0.05 inspection hours can no longer be idle. Each unit of CB that is added requires "giving up" 0.4 of an S_1, 0.5 of an S_2, and 0.05 of an S_3 that is currently being produced. If we give up the production of S_1, S_2, or S_3, how would the value of the objective function be changed? Since \$0 is contributed by each unit of S_1, S_2, and S_3, the amount of decrease in the objective function is

$$Z_{CB} = (\$0)(0.4) + (\$0)(0.5) + (\$0)(0.05) = \$0$$

In a similar manner, the Z_j and $(C_j - Z_j)$ values for all variables in the MultiBand problem are calculated in Table S6.2. These same values were recorded at the bottom of Table S6.1.

Step 5: Selecting a New Variable By examining the $(C_j - Z_j)$ row of the solution matrix, we see that further improvement is possible. If we add a unit of CB into the solution, the objective function will be increased by \$50. Or, if we add a unit of PR, the solution will improve by \$40. Additional units of S_1, S_2, or S_3 will have no effect on the objective function, since each has a $(C_j - Z_j)$ value of zero. At each stage of the problem, we can introduce only one new variable. Each new variable must be evaluated so that the most attractive one can be chosen. In this case, CB is the most advantageous variable on a per unit basis, so it is the one that should be selected.

TABLE S6.2
Calculation of Z_j and $(C_j - Z_j)$ for MultiBand Enterprises

	If CB is introduced	If PR is introduced	If S_1 is introduced	If S_2 is introduced	If S_3 is introduced
Decreased use of S_1: (a)	0.4	0.5	1.0	0.0	0.0
Decrease in value of objective function:	0.4 × $0 = $0	0.5 × $0 = $0	1.0 × $0 = $0	$0 × $0 = $0	$0 × $0 = $0
Decreased use of S_2: (b)	0.5	0.3	0.0	1.0	0.0
Decrease in value of objective function:	0.5 × $0 = $0	0.3 × $0 = $0	0 × $0 = $0	1.0 × $0 = $0	0 × $0 = $0
Decreased use ofS_3: (c)	0.05	0.1	0.0	0.0	1.0
Decrease in value of objective function:	0.05 × $0 = $0	0.1 × $0 = $0	0 × $0 = $0	0 × $0 = $0	0 × $1.0 = $0
Z_j = Total decrease in value of objective function (a) + (b) + (c)	$Z_{CB} = \$0 + \$0 + \$0 = \$0$	$Z_{PR} = \$0 + \$0 + \$0 = \$0$	$Z_{S1}\ \$0 + \$0 + \$0 = \$0$	$Z_{S2} = \$0 + \$0 + \$0 = \$0$	$Z_{S3}\ \$0 + \$0 + \$0 = \$0$
C_j	$C_{CB} = \$50$	$C_{PR} = \$40$	$C_{S1} = \$0$	$C_{S2} = \$0$	$C_{S3} = \$0$
$C_j - Z_j$	$C_{CB} - Z_{CB} = \$50 - \$0 = \$50$	$C_{PR} - Z_{PR} = \$40 - \$0 = \$40$	$C_{S1} - Z_{S1} = \$0 - \$0 = \$0$	$C_{S2} - Z_{S2} = \$0 - \$0 = \$0$	$C_{S3} - Z_{S3} = \$0 - \$0 = \$0$

Step 6: Determine which Variable Is to Leave Solution In this problem we can have only three variables in solution at one time, one per constraint equation. If a new variable is introduced, an existing variable must leave solution. Since we wish to introduce CB, either S_1 or S_2 or S_3 must leave. To find the variable that should leave solution, we focus on the substitution rates between CB and S_1, S_2, and S_3 (the variables in solution). The relevant portion of the solution matrix is shown in Table S6.3.

By introducing *one* unit of CB, we increase the objective function by $50. Since we're trying to maximize, we wish to add as many units of CB as resources will allow. We must therefore determine how many CBs can

TABLE S6.3
Determining which variable is to leave solution

In solution	Pivot column CB	Production	Maximum number of CBs that can be added
S_1	0.4	316	316 ÷ 0.4 = 790
S_2	0.5	354	354 ÷ 0.5 = 708
S_3	0.05	62	62 ÷ 0.05 = 1,240

be introduced. Each CB requires giving up 0.4 S_1. There are 316 S_1s available to give up. If we consider only subassembly labor, then, a maximum of 790 CBs can be introduced. If we consider assembly labor, a maximum of (354)/(0.5) = 708 CBs can be put into solution. There are enough idle inspection hours (S_3) to allow 1,240 CBs to be introduced. Since *all* restrictions must be met, we can see that available resources are adequate for adding 708 units of CB into solution. If we do this, all assembly labor will be used for producing CBs; none will be idle. Thus, assembly labor is the resource that keeps us from introducing more than 708 CBs; it is the *limiting* resource at this stage.

Let's summarize. We will add 708 units of CB into solution. To do this, we must give up all 354 units of S_2; that is, we give up all the S_2s that were formerly in solution, and S_2 is the variable that leaves solution. In the revised solution, we will be producing 708 CBs and no PRs. Graphically, this is shown as point *c* in Figure S6.2.

Step 7: Revise the Solution Matrix After introducing a new variable into solution, we must go back to Table S6.1 and revise each row of the solution matrix to reflect the changes we have made. The column headings will be the same, but the row headings, restriction coefficients, and production quantities must be changed. In technical terms in the graphical procedure, we are now moving *from the origin to an adjacent extreme point.*

First, we identify the *pivot element,* the coefficient at the intersection of the column entering solution and the row leaving solution. (See Table S6.4, part *a*). The row and column containing this pivot element are called the *pivot* row and the *pivot* column.

TABLE S6.4
Pivot element and calculation of new coefficients for entering variable

(a) Pivot element in initial matrix

	CB	Production	
S_1	0.4	316	
S_2	(0.5)	354 ←	Variable leaving solution
S_3	0.05	62	
	↑ Variable entering solution		

(b) Coefficients for new row

In solution	CB	PR	S_1	S_2	S_3	Production
S_1						
CB	1.0	0.6	0.0	2.0	0.0	708
S_3						

Next we calculate the coefficients for the entering row CB (part *b* of Table S6.4). This is done by dividing each of the old coefficients of the pivot row, S_2, by the pivot element. The old S_2 (pivot) row coefficients (including Production) are 0.5, 0.3, 0.0, 1.0, and 354. Dividing each by the pivot element (0.5), we get the resulting row coefficients: $0.5 \div 0.5 = 1$; $0.3 \div 0.5 = 0.6$; $0. \div 0.5 = 0$; $1. \div 0.5 = 2$; $0. \div 0.5 = 0$; and $354. \div 0.5 = 708$. These results are summarized in part *b* of the table.

The new coefficients must now be found for the first and third rows of the matrix. These rows did not include the pivot element, so they are called *nonpivot* rows. The rule for modifying a nonpivot row is: *From each old nonpivot row coefficient, subtract the product of the corresponding pivot row coefficient and the pivot ratio.* The *pivot ratio* is formed by dividing the old nonpivot row coefficient in the pivot column by the pivot element. This rule can be expressed as an equation:

$$\begin{aligned}\text{New row coefficient} &= \text{Old row coefficient} \\ &- (\text{Corresponding pivot row coefficient} \times \text{Pivot ratio})\end{aligned} \qquad \textbf{(S6.2)}$$

where:

$$\text{Pivot ratio} = \frac{\text{Old nonpivot row coefficient in pivot column}}{\text{Pivot element}}$$

For old row S_1 (Table S6.1), the pivot ratio is calculated as follows:

$$\text{Pivot ratio} = \frac{0.4}{0.5} = 0.8$$

Using equation S6.2, we have calculated the new row coefficients for row S_1 in Table S6.5.

To calculate new row coefficients for row S_3, we use the pivot ratio $.05 \div 0.5 = 0.1$. The new coefficients, calculated by the procedure described above, are recorded in the second simplex tableau (Table S6.6).

This second-stage solution calls for using the three resources as follows: use enough of the three types of labor to produce 708 CB radios; allow 32.8 hours of subassembly labor to be idle; and permit 26.6 hours of inspection labor to be idle. The overall result of doing this is a gain in contribution to profit and overhead of $35,400, a considerable improvement over the initial solution. In Figure S6.2 in the graphical method, we now are at point *c*.

So far we have made one complete cycle through the simplex procedure. Now we can return to step 3 ("evaluate the existing solution") and repeat the entire process. The existing solution in Table S6.6 becomes the starting point. Can this solution be improved? To answer this, we calculate the Z_js as before; they are recorded in Table S6.6.

TABLE S6.5
Calculation of new row coefficients for row S_1

(a) Old row coefficient	0.4	0.5	1.0	0.0	0.0	316
(b) Corresponding pivot row coefficient	0.5	0.3	0.0	1.0	0.0	354
(c) Pivot ratio	0.8	0.8	0.8	0.8	0.8	0.8
(d) (b) × (c)	0.5 × 0.8 = 0.4	0.3 × 0.8 = 0.24	0 × 0.8 = 0	1.0 × 0.8 = 0.8	0 × 0.8 = 0	354 × 0.8 = 283.2
(e) (a) − (d) = New row coefficient	0.4 − 0.4 = 0	0.5 − 0.24 = 0.26	1.0 − 0 = 1.0	0 − 0.8 = −0.8	0 − 0 = 0	316 − 283.2 = 32.8

$$
\begin{aligned}
Z_{CB} &= (\$0)(0) + (\$50)(1.0) + (\$0)(0) = \$50 \\
Z_{PR} &= (\$0)(0.26) + (\$50)(0.6) + (\$0)(0.07) = \$30 \\
Z_{S1} &= (\$0)(1.0) + (\$50)(0) + (\$0)(0) = \$0 \\
Z_{S2} &= (\$0)(-0.8) + (\$50)(2.0) + (\$0)(-0.1) = \$100 \\
Z_{S3} &= (\$0)(0) + (\$50)(0) + (\$0)(1.0) = \$0
\end{aligned}
$$

Interpreting the $(C_j - Z_j)$ row, we find that no change in the objective function will occur by adding into solution a unit of CB, S_1, or S_3. Adding a unit of S_2 into solution will cause the objective function to *decrease* by $100, an undesirable change. PR, however, can be introduced; the objective function will be increased by $10 for each PR that is added. Therefore, we introduce PR, and the PR column becomes the new pivot column.

TABLE S6.6
Second simplex tableau (solution matrix) for MultiBand Enterprises

C_j	In solution	$50 CB	$40 PR	$0 S_1	$0 S_2	$0 S_3	Production
$0	S_1	0.0	0.26	1.0	−0.8	0.0	32.8
$50	CB	1.0	0.6	0.0	2.0	0.0	708.0
$0	S_3	0.0	0.07	0.0	−0.1	1.0	26.6
	Z_j	$50	$30	$0	$100	$0	($0) × (32.8) + ($50) × (708.) + ($0) × (26.6) = $35,400
	$C_j - Z_j$	0	10 ↑	0	− 100	0	

TABLE S6.7
Determining which variable is to leave solution when PR is added

In solution	Pivot column PR	Production	Maximum number of PRs
S_1	0.26	32.8	32.8 ÷ 0.26 = 126.15
CB	0.6	708.0	708.0 ÷ 0.6 = 1,180.0
S_2	0.07	26.6	26.6 ÷ 0.07 = 380.0

How many PRs can be added? This question is answered by repeating step 6, as we did before. Consider the substitution rates between the entering column PR and the variables in solution (S_1, CB, and S_3). Each PR requires giving up 0.26 of an S_1, 0.6 of a CB, and 0.07 of an S_3. The maximum number of these variables available to be replaced is calculated in Table S6.7. The maximum number of PRs that can be added is the smallest of (126.15, 1180.0, 380.0). Thus, 126.15 PRs can be added, and when it is, S_1 will go to zero and leave solution. Therefore S_1 becomes the pivot row in the second simplex tableau.

Step 7, revising the solution matrix, proceeds as previously described. The pivot element, 0.26, is found at the intersection of the PR column-S_1 row in Table S6.6. Each coefficient in the pivot row is divided by the pivot element, and the row coefficients for the new PR row are: $0 \div 0.26 = 0$; $0.26 \div 0.26 = 1$; $1.0 \div 0.26 = 3.846$; $-0.8 \div 0.26 = -3.077$; $0 \div 0.26 = 0$; and $32.8 \div 0.26 = 126.15$. These results are recorded as the PR row coefficients in the third simplex tableau in Table S6.8.

Next, the coefficients are calculated for the first of the *nonpivot* rows, CB. The pivot ratio is $0.6 \div 0.26 = 2.308$. Equation S6.2 is now used to calculate the new CB row coefficients in Table S6.9. Using the same pro-

TABLE S6.8
Third simplex tableau (solution matrix) for MultiBand Enterprises

C_j	In solution	\$50 CB	\$40 PR	\$0 S_1	\$0 S_2	\$0 S_3	Production
\$40	PR	0.0	1.0	3.846	−3.077	0.0	126.154
50	CB*	1.0	0.0	−2.308	3.846	0.0	632.298
0	S_3	0.0	0.0	−0.2692	0.1154	1.0	17.77
	Z_j	\$50	\$40	\$38.44	\$69.22	\$0	(\$40) × (126.154) + (\$50) × (632.298)
	$C_j - Z_j$	0	0	−38.44	−\$69.22	\$0	+ (\$0) × (17.77) = \$36,661.06

*Row coefficients obtained from Table S6.9.

TABLE S6.9
Calculation of new row coefficients for row CB

(a) Old row coefficient	1.	0.6	0.	2.	0.	708.
(b) Corresponding pivot row coefficient	0.	0.26	1.	−0.8	0.	32.8
(c) Pivot ratio	2.308	2.308	2.308	2.308	2.308	2.308
(d) (b) × (c)	0. × 2.308 = 0	0.26 × 2.308 = 0.6	1. × 2.308 = 2.308	−0.8 × 2.308 = −1.846	0. × 2.308 = 0	32.8 × 2.308 = 75.702
(e) (a) − (d) = New row coefficient	1. − 0. = 1	0.6 − 0.6 = 0	0. − 2.308 = −2.308	2. −(−1.846) = 3.846	0. − 0. = 0	708. − 75.702 = 632.298

cedure on nonpivot row S_3 results in the coefficients in Table S6.8. The pivot ratio for row S_3 was 0.07 ÷ 0.26 = 0.2692. After calculation, the new row coefficients, the C_j, and $(C_j - Z_j)$ values were calculated and recorded in the third simplex tableau. The $(C_j - Z_j)$ row reveals that the objective function cannot be increased any further. When all of the $C_j - Z_j$ row cells are zero or negative, the optimum solution has been reached. Adding additional units of CB, PR, or S_3 will result in no change in the objective function. If either S_1 or S_2 is added into solution, the value of the objective function will decrease. We have therefore found the optimal solution that maximizes contribution to profit and overhead: to produce 126.15 PRs, 632.30 CBs, and allow the remaining 17.77 hours of inspection labor to be idle (S_3). This solution corresponds to point *h* on the graph in Figure S6.2.

Some Additional Considerations

Minimization For purposes of illustration, we have used a maximization problem to present the simplex method. *Minimization* problems are also frequently encountered, and the same basic procedure is applied. The $(C_j - Z_j)$ values in step 4, however, have the reverse meaning in minimization problems; that is, as long as a negative $(C_j - Z_j)$ exists, further improvement is possible. The variable having the largest negative value is selected for introduction into solution. When all $(C_j - Z_j)$ are zero or positive, no further minimization is possible.

An alternative way to solve minimization problems is to multiply all C_j coefficients by − 1 and then use the same maximizing procedure that was used for maximization LP problems.

Artificial Variables Another circumstance arises when the problem restrictions are not of the "less-than-or-equal-to" variety used in our example. Two other types of restrictions are commonly encountered. First is the equality of the form:

$$A_1X_1 + A_2S_2 = B_1$$

In this case, a slack variable need not be added since an equality already exists. However, a different kind of variable, an artificial variable, must be added to the left side:

$$A_1X_1 + A_2X_2 + A = B_1$$

The purpose of the artificial variable is to create an identity matrix in the initial tableau. It is undesirable to have the artificial variable appear in the final solution. Therefore, the coefficient of A in the objective function is made to be an arbitrarily large positive value in a minimization problem or an arbitrarily large negative number in a maximization problem. This assures that A will be driven out of solution by the simplex procedure.

Surplus Variables Another type of restriction is the "greater-than-or-equal-to":

$$A_1X_1 + A_2X_2 \geq B_1$$

Both a surplus (negative slack) and an artificial variable must be added. The surplus variable converts the expression into an equality:

$$A_1X_1 + A_2X_2 - S = B_1$$

Then, since S has a coefficient of − 1, an artificial variable must be added to the left side to create an identity matrix:

$$A_1X_1 + A_2X_2 - S + A = B_1$$

Once all the restrictions have been converted into appropriate form by adding the necessary artificial and slack variables, the previously described simplex procedure can be applied.

The Power of Linear Programming

The power of linear programming lies in the fact that *an optimal solution is guaranteed—and guaranteed in a finite number of steps.* Since only extreme points are compared, the simplex procedure starts at the origin and checks adjacent extreme points until profits fall or costs rise with a further step (iteration). At that point the optimal has been found. The number of iterations required to solve an LP problem roughly equals the number of constraints. LP is a powerful resource allocation technique, a technique that is often used to approximate nonlinear functions by embedding the simplex technique into nonlinear solution procedures.

There are several basic operations research and management science texts, some devoted entirely to linear programming. They can provide details on problem formulation, solution, and economic interpretation of linear programming problems. Also, computer packages are readily available for solving large scale linear programming problems.

REVIEW AND DISCUSSION QUESTIONS

1. Of what value is the graphic method of LP?
2. Define and illustrate:
   (a) a linear objective function
   (b) a linear constraint
   (c) a nonlinear objective function
   (d) a nonlinear constraint
3. What is meant by the term "feasibility area" (region of feasibility) in a linear programming model? What is the significance of the corner points?
4. In the simplex method, what is the "standard format" of problem formulation? Give an example.
5. What is a "slack variable"? Why is it used? How many will there be in an LP problem?
6. How many variables will be in solution at any stage of an LP problem?
7. What is the significance of the

   $$C_j - Z_j$$

   row of the LP solution matrix?
8. After determining which variable to introduce next into solution, how do you determine how many units of that variable to introduce?
9. In the simplex method, what indicates that an optimal solution has been reached?
10. Define and illustrate:
    (a) artificial variable
    (b) surplus variable
11. Under what conditions would an LP problem use artificial, surplus, and slack variables? Give examples of each.

PROBLEMS

1. Consider the following LP problem:
   Minimize $C = 16x + 10y$
   Subject to: $12x + 4y \geq 24$
   $6x + 12y \geq 36$
   (a) Using the graphic method, find the optimal solution.
   (b) If the objective function is changed to $C = 16x + 4y$, what is the optimal solution:

2. Solve the following problem using the graphic method of LP.
Maximize $P = 2A + 2B$
Subject to: $2A + 3B \leq 16$
$2A + B \leq 8$
If the objective function is changed to $P = 2A + 5B$, what is the optimal solution?

3. Product *A* offers a profit of $4 per unit; product *B* yields $2.50 profit per unit. To manufacture the products, leather, wood, and glue are required in the amounts shown below.

Resources required for one unit

Resource	Product *A*	*B*
Leather (lbs)	½	¼
Wood (board ft)	4	7
Glue (oz)	2	2

The resources on hand include 2,000 pounds of leather, 28,000 board feet of wood, and 10,000 ounces of glue.
(a) State the objective function and constraints in mathematical form.
(b) Find the optimal solution graphically.
(c) Which resources are fully consumed by the optimal solution?
(d) How much of each resource remains unused in the optimal solution?

4. Fatten Fast Feed Company produces a hog feed made from two basic ingredients, *X* and *Y*. A ton of *Y* can be purchased for $120; a ton of *X* costs $80. Each ingredient contains three types of nutrients, *A*, *B*, and *C*.

Nutrient content (units per ton)

Ingredient	Nutrient A	B	C
X	450	73	69
Y	257	61	208

A ton of hog feed must contain at least 360 units of nutrient *A*, 65 units of nutrient *B*, and 125 units of nutrient *C*. What proportions of *X* and *Y* should be selected to minimize the cost of hog feed?

5. Quick Copy Service has a large backlog of printing jobs to be done. There are 10,000 standard lots of class *A* jobs and 18,000 standard lots of class *B* jobs. The cost of processing a standard class *A* job is $.82, of a class *B* job, $.40. The manager wishes to minimize processing costs for the coming month; however, some constraints must be met. First, the marketing department has requested that a minimum of 80 percent of the class *A* jobs and 60 percent of the class *B* jobs be completed this month. Second, wage payments are already committed for 6,000 direct labor hours for next month in the processing center. A class *A* job consumes .26 labor hours, and a class *B* job requires .33 labor hours. The manager wishes to fully utilize the direct labor during the month. How many jobs of each class should be processed?

6. Real Deal Distributors packages and distributes merchandise to retail outlets. A standard shipment can be packaged in small, medium, or large containers. A standard shipment of small containers yields a profit of $4; medium containers yield

a profit of $12, and large containers yeild a profit of $16. Each shipment is prepared manually, requiring packing materials and time. Each shipment must also be inspected.

Resource requirements per standard shipment

Container size	Packing time (hours)	Packing material (lbs)	Inspection time (minutes)
Small	1.0	2.0	1.5
Medium	2.0	4.0	3.0
Large	4.0	7.0	3.0
Total amount of resource available	1,200	2,400	1,200

(a) Formulate this problem in a simplex format.
(b) What is the optimal number of each container size to produce?

7. Maxim, Inc. sends sales representatives to call on three types of clients: retail, industrial, and professional. Sales revenues of $3,000 result from calling on a retail client, $5,000 from an industrial contact, and $15,000 from each professional client. This month a total of 3,200 hours of sales representative time is available for calling on customers, and $10,000 is available for travel expenses. Management will not allow more than 20 percent of total sales force time to be devoted to retail clients, and they will not allow more than 30 percent of the travel expense budget to be used for calling on professional clients. Six hours of travel and selling time are required to call on a retail client, 11 hours for an industrial client, and 25 hours for a professional client. Travel expenses are $10 for each retail contract, $14 for each industrial client, and $35 for each professional call. What is the optimal client mix for the coming month?

8. The Farmers Cooperative Oil Company produces two lines of motor oil and a special engine additive called New Motor. All three products are produced by blending two components. These components contribute various properties, including viscosity. (Viscosity is the thickness or tendency to flow.) The viscosity in the product is proportional to the viscosities of the blending components. The pertinent data appear in the table below. Assume no limitation on demand. Set this up as a linear programming problem to determine how many barrels of each oil product Farmers should produce each week. Clearly define all variables. (Do not solve for the optimal solution.)

Blending component	Viscosity	Cost per barrel ($)	Availability per week
1	30	10.50	8,000
2	55	14.00	3,000

Product	Viscosity required	Profit contribution per barrel
30W oil	30	$15
40W oil	40	17
New Motor	50	22

9. Greenthumb Landscape Company employs senior and junior tree specialists who are assigned to various landscaping jobs. Daily wages are $70 for each senior specialist and $45 for each junior specialist. Working alone, a senior specialist processes an acre of work in four days. A junior specialist requires seven days to process one acre. However, if both types of workers are assigned to a project, two days of senior work and three days of junior work will complete one acre. Greenthumb receives $600 revenue for each acre it processes. Supervisory requirements depend on the type of tree specialist assigned to a project; .8 days of supervisor time is required for each acre processed by a senior specialist; 1.0 days of supervision is needed for an acre processed by a junior specialist; and 2.0 supervisor days per acre are needed for projects using both junior and senior specialists. In total, 450 work-days of supervision, 1,200 work-days of junior specialist labor, and 1,000 work-days of senior specialist skills are available. How should the work force be utilized to maximize the profit?

10. Given the following simplex tableau:

C_j	In solution	P_1	P_2	P_3	P_4	P_5	Production
		1	0	1	0	0	4
		0	1	0	1	0	6
		3	0	0	-2	1	6
	Z_j	0	5	0	5	0	30
	$C_j - Z_j$	3	0	0	-5	0	-30

(a) What variables form the basis solution? That is, what variables are "in solution?"
(b) What are the values of $C_1, C_2, \ldots C_j$?
(c) Is this the optimal solution? Explain.
(d) Regardless of your answer in (c) above, *assume* this is the optimal solution. Your supervisor says we *must* produce 2 units of P_1. What effect would this have on the above objective function value of 30 units?

11. Betherton Furniture Manufacturing has always used an outside carrier to make its deliveries. It is now investigating purchasing trucks and making its own deliveries. Betherton has available 220 man-days which it can use for the trucking operation and $800,000 to invest in trucks. Due to loading restrictions and an unwillingness to become a totally owned private carrier, Betherton will purchase a maximum of forty trucks; outside carriers will still be used a great deal. The three types of trucks under consideration have characteristics as shown below. Formulate, but do not solve, Betherton's situation as a linear programming problem.

Truck type	Delivery capacity (ton-miles per day)	Operator requirements to meet delivery capacity (man-days per vehicle)	Purchase cost
A	7,300	3	$16,000
B	9,000	6	26,000
C	13,010	6	30,000

SELECTED READINGS

Anderson, D. R., D. J. Sweeney, and T. A. Williams. *An Introduction to Management Science*. St. Paul, Minn.: West Publishing Co., 1976.

Cabot, A. V. and D. L. Harnet. *An Introduction to Management Science*. Reading, Mass.: Addison-Wesley Pub. Co., Inc., 1977.

Dantzig, G. B. *Linear Programming and Extensions*. Princeton, N. J.: Princeton University Press, 1963.

Wagner, H. M. *Principles of Management Science*. Englewood Cliffs, N.J.: Prentice-Hall, Inc., 1970.

7 Facility Location Planning

In the truckload transportation business, profit margins are relatively thin. We must therefore manage capital very efficiently in order to earn an adequate return on investment. Since physical facilities require significant expenditures of capital, we like to keep the number of facilities to a minimum. However, carriers generally will have a substantially higher market share in territories near their physical facilities, and certain expenses increase as the distance between customers, drivers, and our physical facilities increase. Therefore, the strategic location of an optimal number of physical facilities is vital to success in our business.

Michael L. Lawrence
President and Chief Executive Officer
Burlington Northern Motor Carriers, Inc.
Fort Worth, Texas

Mr. Lawrence has identified a key strategic problem in the motor carrier industry—how many facilities should we have and where should they be located? This problem is encountered by service and goods-producing organizations in both the public and private sectors. Banks, restaurants, recreation agencies, and manufacturing companies are all concerned with selecting locational sites that will best enable them to meet their long-term goals. Facility location is clearly an important part of operations planning.

Facility location planning may be viewed as a part of planning the conversion system, as we show in Figure 7.1. The success of this planning activity will both affect and be affected by organizing and control activities. Since the operations manager fixes

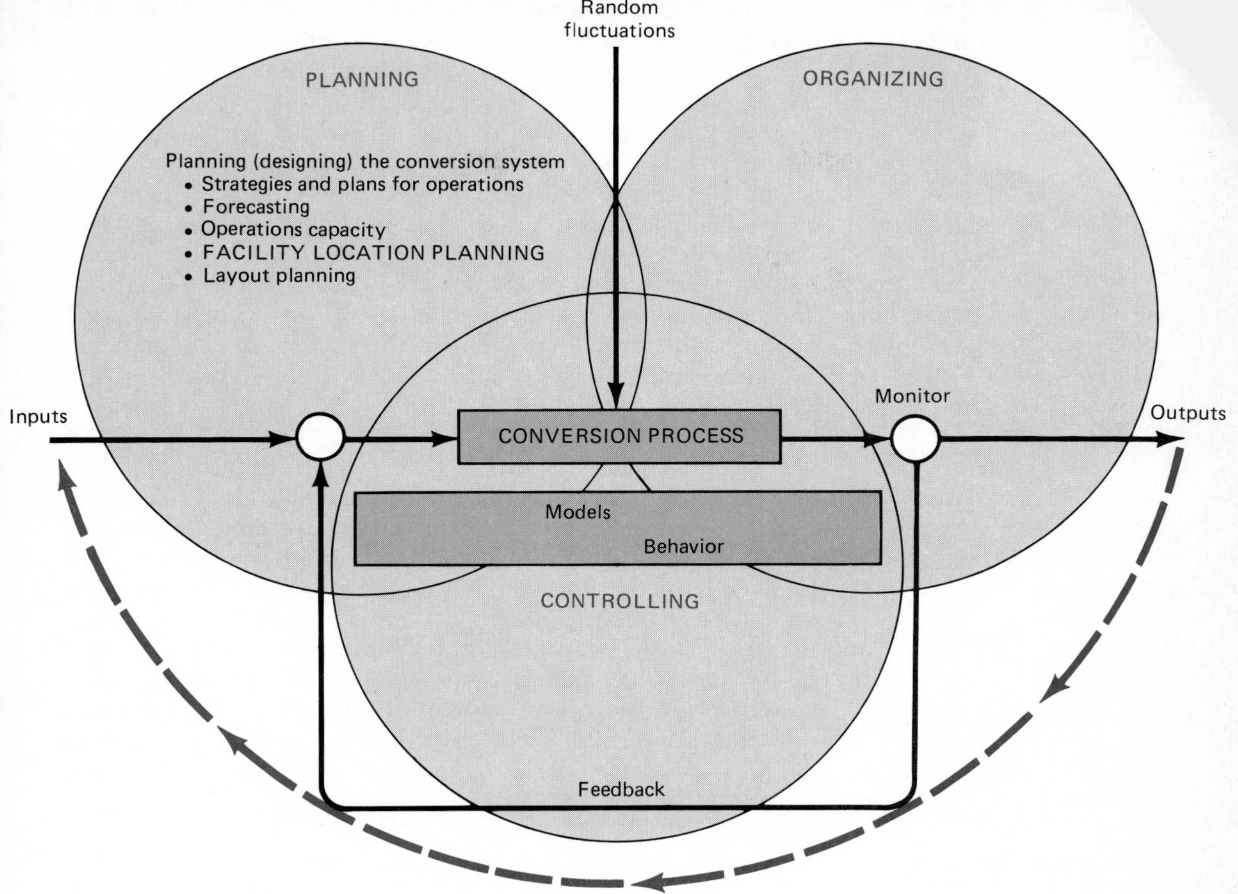

FIGURE 7.1
Production/operations management activities

many costs with the location decision, both the efficiency and effectiveness of the conversion process are dependent upon location. Leading to this decision are analyses with both modeling and behavioral dimensions. Let's examine the facilities location activity in more detail.

NEED FOR FACILITY LOCATION PLANNING

Location Effects on Costs and Revenues

Public and private organizations are concerned with revenue and cost behavior, both of which can be affected by location. We need to understand how each of these profitability components depends on where the facility is situated.

Revenues In some industries, revenues depend on having the facility near potential customers. For manufacturing firms that supply customers (who are often themselves manufacturers and assemblers), delivery time can be a crucial component of the strategic mission.[1]

In service industries, the situation is somewhat different. For *stored services,* those not directly consumed, location is not so important. Federal Reserve banks, automotive repair shops, and manufacturers who repair appliances are often quasi manufacturers in the conversion process, and they don't necessarily have to be located near consumers. On the other hand, for firms that offer *directly consumed services,* location can be critical. Movie theaters, restaurants, banks, apartments, dry cleaning stores, and even public recreation areas obviously must be located at sites that are convenient to the public; if they aren't, consumers will go somewhere else, and revenues will decline.

Fixed Costs New or additional facilities entail fixed initial costs, usually incurred only once, which must be recovered out of revenues if the investment is to be profitable. Acquisition of new and additional facilities involves costs for new construction, addition to existing facilities, purchase and renovation of other existing plants, or rental. And once they're acquired, more money must be spent on equipment and fixtures. The magnitude of these costs may well depend on the site that is selected. A choice merchandising corner location in downtown Washington, D.C. requires a totally different capital outlay from one in Greencastle, Indiana. Construction costs also vary greatly from one place to another.

Variable Costs Once built, the new facility must be staffed and operated, and these costs depend on location. For labor-intensive conversion processes, labor availability and local wage structures are major concerns. Management must also consider proximity to raw materials sources (inputs) and to finished goods markets (outputs), either of which can cause transportation and shipping costs to go up or down.

Seldom does an organization find a single site that is best in terms of all revenue and cost variables. The location offering the highest revenue potential may also incur higher variable costs of operation. Tradeoffs must be made among fixed costs, variable costs, and revenue potential; the final locational choice should be the one that offers the best overall balance toward achieving the organization's mission.

---

[1]For a discussion of locational considerations in multiplant manufacturing strategies, see R. W. Schmenner, "Look Beyond the Obvious Plant Location," *Harvard Business Review* 57, no. 1 (January–February 1979), pp. 126–32.

EXAMPLE

Suppose you are selecting a location for a new apartment building. Choosing a site near existing apartments may result in high initial property costs and stiff competition. On the other hand, future costs of advertising vacancies may be substantially lower because apartment seekers are already drawn to the area, and revenues may be high because of existing shopping, barber, and similar services in the area. How do you decide?

Manufacturing industries face many similar decisions. Companies may be attracted to a new geographic location by more favorable labor rates. This happened in textile and other manufacturing industries, and they shifted from the northern U.S. to the South and from the U.S. to foreign locations. Sometimes these relocations require great capital investment in equipment and processing technology to overcome the scarcity of speciality skills and to sustain the overall rate of output.

In evaluating any potential site, then, we must consider all these principal revenue and cost factors, perhaps using a breakeven analysis (see Figure 7.2). For location *a*, fixed costs are low, variable operating costs are high, and expected revenue per unit is low because of locational inconvenience to the customer. The high fixed cost of location *b* is offset by low

FIGURE 7.2
Breakeven analysis for overall comparison of two alternative sites

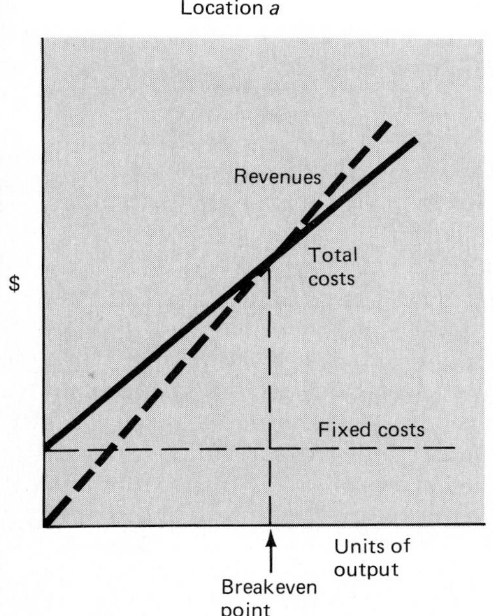

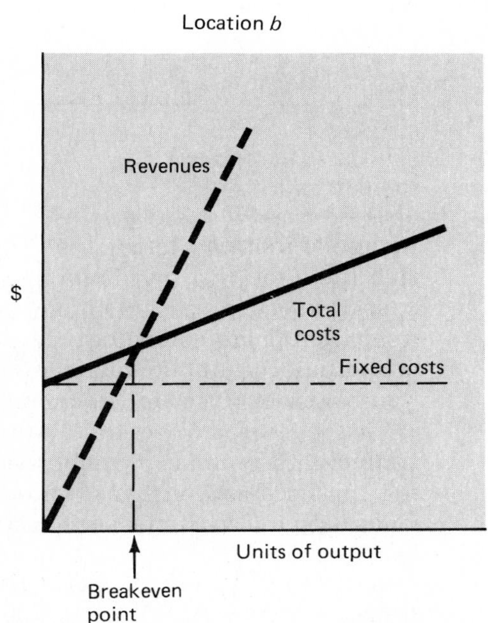

variable costs and the greater revenue per unit that can be commanded for locational convenience. In spite of high fixed costs, then, the breakeven volume is substantially lower for location *b* than it is for *a*.

Reasons for Locational Changes

In addition to the need for greater capacity, there are other reasons for relocating old facilities or locating new ones:

1. Changes in input resources may occur. The cost or location of labor, raw materials, and supporting resources (such as subcontractors) may change.
2. Shifts in geographical demand may occur. As product markets change, it may be desirable to change facility locations to provide better service to customers.
3. Mergers of companies may result in redundant facilities, some of which must be phased out.
4. The introduction of new products may necessitate locational changes, so that new input resources and product markets can be reached more economically.

GENERAL PROCEDURES FOR FACILITY LOCATION PLANNING

The Preliminary Study

A screening study is usually initiated early in the planning process to identify feasible sites. For some kinds of facilities, particular environmental or labor considerations are crucial. Breweries, for example, require an adequate supply of clean water. Aircraft manufacturers must be located near a variety of types of subcontractors; primary aluminum producers need substantial amounts of electrical power. Some main resources and local factors that must be considered are listed here.

Resources	Local conditions
Labor skills and productivity	Community receptivity to business
Land availability and cost	Construction costs
Raw materials	Organized industrial complexes
Subcontractors	Quality of life: climate, housing, recreation, schools
Transportation facilities (highways, rail, air, water)	Taxes
Utility availability and rates	

Sources of Information After identifying several key factors, management undertakes a search to find alternative geographic locations that seem consistent with general requirements. Obviously inappropriate alternatives are eliminated from further consideration. Where does all this information come from? Local chambers of commerce provide literature promoting expansion possibilities in various state and local communities. The *Wall Street Journal* and numerous trade publications contain advertisements placed by cities and communities wishing to attract new commerce. The

National Industrial Conference Board, federal Departments of Commerce, the Small Business Administration, and the U.S. Census of Manufacturers are among the many sources that provide both general and detailed information for location of facilities. These data include geographic breakdowns of labor availability, population, transportation facilities, profiles of existing types of commerce, and similar information.

Detailed Analysis

Preliminary screening usually narrows serious alternative sites to just a few. At this stage a more detailed analysis ensues. At each potential site a labor survey may be conducted to assess the availability of local skills. Where community reaction remains a serious uncertainty, or where the strength of local consumer response is questionable, pilot studies or systematic surveys may be undertaken. Community response is important, for example, in deciding where to locate a nuclear reactor, a recreation area, a commercial bank, a state prison, or a restaurant. For assessing existing attitudes and for developing strategies to gain favorable acceptance in the community, survey research techniques can be very helpful.

Factor-Rating Systems Factor ratings are frequently used for overall evaluations of location alternatives because: (1) their simplicity facilitates communications about why one site is favored over another; (2) they enable managers to bring diverse locational considerations (factors) into the evaluation process; and (3) they foster consistency of judgment when evaluating the relative merits of the alternatives prior to final site selection. Typically, the first step is to list the site characteristics (factors) that are most relevant in the location decision (column one in Table 7.1). Next, each characteristic is assigned a numeric weighting, say from 1 (very low) to 5

TABLE 7.1
Factor ratings for location alternative A

Characteristic (factor)	Factor weighting (importance)	Ratings for location A	Evaluation for location A
Tax advantages of state and community	4	8	32
Suitability of labor skills	3	2	6
Proximity to customers	3	6	18
Proximity to suppliers	5	2	10
Adequacy of water	1	3	3
Community receptivity	5	4	20
Quality of educational system	4	1	4
Access to rail and air transportation	3	10	30
Climate	2	7	14
Availability of power	2	6	12
		TOTAL SCORE =	149

(very high), reflecting its relative importance in the current site location decision (column two in Table 7.1). Then, each location under consideration is rated, say on a scale from 1 (very low) to 10 (very high), for its merits on every characteristic (column three in Table 7.1). Finally, the importance weighting is multiplied times the merit rating for each characteristic (column four in Table 7.1), and the sum of the resulting numbers yields the total evaluation score for that location. The total scores, comparatively, indicate which alternative locations, on balance, are most promising in consideration of all the various locational characteristics.

When the few remaining location alternatives are about equally attractive, for many industries the final decision hinges on transportation costs. A facility located far from its raw materials or product markets will have to invest in truck fleets and/or will incur higher daily operating costs for transportation. Analysis of transportation costs has been the main area in which models have been applied to the location problem.

FACILITY LOCATION MODELS

Various quantitative models are used to help determine the best locations of facilities. Sometimes, models are tailor-made to meet the specific circumstances of a unique problem. In New York City, for example, a mathematical model was developed for use as a policy tool for determining the best locations of fire companies.[2] Public officials wish to balance available fire fighting service to reduce risks of property damage and fatalities. Among the regions of the city are different compositions of residential and commercial structures, alarm rates, hazard ratings, and street configurations. Furthermore, since many of these characteristics change with time, the problem is dynamic; a good location pattern now may not be so good in future years. The mathematical model for evaluating fire company locations takes into account many of these factors. The expected travel times (to be minimized) of fire companies are related mathematically to all these characteristics of regions in which they might be located: size of the area to be serviced, number of fire companies in the region, average alarm density in the region, street configuration, and travel characteristics of the fire company. This specialized model may be highly effective for locating emergency services in an urban setting.

There are some widely known, general models that can be adapted to the needs of a variety of systems. In the sections below we briefly introduce three types of models that have had application to the location problem: the "simple median model," linear programming, and simulation. All these models focus on transportation costs, although each considers a different version of the basic problem.

[2]This model is reported by K. L. Rider, "A Parametric Model for the Allocation of Fire Companies in New York City," *Management Science* 23, no. 2 (October 1976), pp. 146–58.

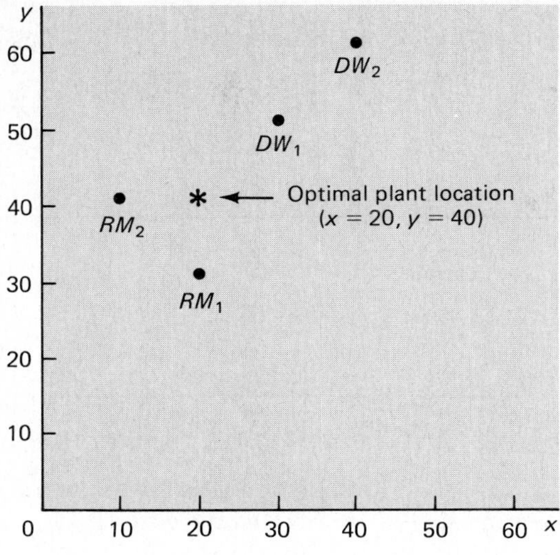

FIGURE 7.3
Existing raw materials sources and distribution warehouses (locations shown on a coordinate system with arbitrary origin)

Simple Median Model

Suppose we wish to locate a new manufacturing plant that will annually receive shipments of raw materials from each of two existing sources, RM_1 and RM_2. The plant will create finished goods that must be shipped to each of two existing distribution warehouses, DW_1 and DW_2. Given these four existing facilities, shown in Figure 7.3, where should we locate the new plant so as to minimize annual transportation costs of the entire network of facilities?

The simple median model can help answer this question. This model considers the volume of loads transported on *rectangular* paths.[3] All movements are made in east-west and/or north-south directions; diagonal moves are not considered. The simple median model provides an optimal solution.[4]

Table 7.2 shows the number of loads, L_i, to be shipped annually between each existing facility and the new plant; it also shows the x and y coordinates (location) of each existing facility.

The Model Let's assume that the transportation cost to move a standard load a unit-distance is represented by C_i. Then overall transit cost is measured by adding the number of loads times the distance each is moved times the unit distance cost per load:

$$\text{Transportation cost} = \sum_{i=1}^{n} C_i L_i D_i \tag{7.1}$$

[3]See. R. C. Vergin and J. D. Rogers, "An Algorithm and Computational Procedure for Locating Economic Facilities," *Management Science* 13, no. 6 (February 1967), pp. 240–54.

[4]An alternative procedure, the center of gravity method, provides an approximate (but not necessarily optimal) solution and can be found in J. J. Coyle and E. J. Bardi, *The Management of Logistics*, 2nd ed. (St. Paul, MN: The West Publishing Co., 1980).

TABLE 7.2
Locations of existing facilities and number of loads to be moved

Existing facility (i)	L_i Annual number of loads moved between facility i and new plant	C_i Cost to move a standard load one unit-distance	Coordinate location of existing facility i	
			X_i	Y_i
(1) RM_1	700	\$1	20	30
(2) RM_2	900	1	10	40
(3) DW_1	400	1	30	50
(4) DW_2	500	1	40	60
	2,500			

In equation 7.1, L_i is the number of loads to be moved between the new plant and existing facility i. In our example there are $i = 4$ existing facilities. D_i represents the distance between the new plant and facility i. This, the distance each load is to be moved, depends on our location choice. We then add together the number of loads times the distance they are moved times the cost of moving such a load from each existing site. The answer represents the cost of all movements in the system.

Since all loads must be on rectangular paths, total distance of a load is measured by its length of movement in the x direction and in the y direction:

$$D_i = |x - x_i| + |y - y_i| \qquad [7.2]$$

The variables x and y in equation 7.2 represent the coordinates of any proposed location for the new plant. Once a location is specified, the distance for all load movements (D_i) can be calculated. What we wish to do is find the values for x and y (new plant) that result in minimum transportation cost. We use these three steps:

1. identify the median value of the total number of loads moved,
2. find the x-coordinate value of the existing facility that sends (or receives) the median load, and
3. find the y-coordinate value of the existing facility that sends (or receives) the median load.

The x and y values found in steps 2 and 3 define the desired location for the new facility.

Application of the Model Let us apply these steps to the data in Table 7.2

1. *Identify the median load.* Total number of loads moved to and from the new plant will be 2,500. The *median* number of loads is that value above which half the number of loads lie and below which the other half

lie. If the total number of loads is odd, the median load will be the middle load. If the total number of loads is even (for example 2,500), the median loads will be the two middle loads. For 2,500 loads, the median loads are the 1,250th and 1,251st loads, since 1,249 loads lie above and below these amounts.

2. *Find x-coordinate of the median load.* First we consider movement of loads in the x-direction. Beginning at the origin of Figure 7.3 and moving to the right along the x-axis, observe the number of loads moved to or from existing facilities. Loads 1–900 are shipped by RM_2 from location $x = 10$. Loads 901–1,600 are shipped by RM_1 from location $x = 20$. *Since the median loads (1,250, 1,251) fall in the interval 901–1,600, $x = 20$ is the desired x-coordinate location for the new plant.*

3. *Find y-coordinate of the median load.* Now consider the y-direction of load movements. Begin at the origin of Figure 7.3 and move upward along the y-axis. Movements in the y direction begin with loads 1–700 being shipped by RM_1 from location $y = 30$. Loads 701–1,600 are shipped by RM_2 from location $y = 40$. *Since the median loads (1,250, 1,251) fall in the interval 701–1,600, $y = 40$ is the desired y-coordinate for the new plant.*

The optimal plant location, $x = 20$ and $y = 40$, results in minimizing annual transportation costs for this network of facilities. To calculate the resulting cost, we substitute equation 7.2 into equation 7.1:

$$TC = \sum_{i=1}^{n} C_i L_i (|x - x_i| + |y - y_i|) \qquad \textbf{(7.3)}$$

Total cost, \$44,000, is shown in Table 7.3

TABLE 7.3
Calculation of total cost for optimal plant location ($x = 20$, $y = 40$)

(1) Existing facility i	(2) x_i for existing facility	(3) x for new plant	(4) Distance loads move in x-direction $\|x - x_i\|$	(5) y_i for existing facility	(6) y for new plant	(7) Distance loads move in y-direction $\|y - y_i\|$	(8) Total distance x cost (C_iD_i) loads move (4) + (7) (\$1)($\|x - x_i\| + \|y - y_i\|$)	(9) Number of loads L_i	(10) Number of loads times distance x cost moved (8) × (9) $C_i \times D_i \times L_i$
1	20	20	0	30	40	10	\$10	700	\$ 7,000
2	10	20	10	40	40	0	10	900	9,000
3	30	20	10	50	40	10	20	400	8,000
4	40	20	20	60	40	20	40	500	20,000

Total cost $= \sum_{i=1}^{4} C_iL_iD_i =$ \$44,000

Some concluding remarks are in order. First, we have considered the case in which only one new facility is to be added.[5] Second, you should note an important assumption of this model: any point in the $x - y$ coordinate system is an eligible point for locating the new facility. The model does not consider road availability, physical terrain, population densities, or any other of the many important locational considerations. The task of blending model results with other major considerations to arrive at a reasonable locational choice is a major managerial responsibility.[6]

Linear Programming

Linear programming may be helpful after the initial screening phase has narrowed the feasible alternative sites to a finite number. The remaining candidates can then be evaluated, one at a time, to determine how well each would fit in with existing facilities, and the alternative that leads to the best overall system (network) performance can be identified. Most often, overall transportation cost is the criterion used for performance evaluation. A special type of linear programming called the *distribution* or *transportation* method, has been found to be of particular usefulness in location planning.[7] It has been applied in the simplified example that follows. The mechanics of this technique are omitted in the example but are demonstrated in the supplement to this chapter. Our example shows how to conceptualize and set up the problem in a linear programming framework. It also shows the end result, or optimal solution, of the analysis.

EXAMPLE

Alpha Processing Company has three midwestern production plants located at Evansville, Indiana; Lexington, Kentucky; and Fort Wayne, Indiana. Plans being developed for operations five years hence will require that 200 shipments of raw materials be delivered annually to the Evansville plant, 300 shipments to Lexington, and 400 shipments to Fort Wayne. Currently, Alpha has two sources of raw materials, one at Chicago, Illinois, the other at Louisville, Kentucky. The Chicago source will be capable of supplying 300 shipments per year; Louisville has a 400 shipment capacity. An additional source of raw materials must therefore be opened to meet the anticipated raw material needs of the plants. Preliminary screening by Alpha has narrowed the choice to two attractive alternatives, Columbus, Ohio, and St. Louis, Missouri. Each of

---

[5]For adding multiple facilities, see R. A. Johnson, W. T. Newell, and R. C. Vergin, *Operations Management: A Systems Concept* (Boston: Houghton Mifflin Co., 1972).

[6]For a successful application that blends model results with other qualitative factors, see A. A. Aly and D. W. Litwhiler, Jr., "Police Briefing Stations: A Location Problem," *AIIE Transactions* 11, no. 1 (March 1979), pp. 12–22.

[7]The simplex method of linear programming has also proved useful in location analysis. For an example of implementation for locating two new industrial production facilities, see R. F. Love and L. Yerex, "An Application of a Facilities Location Model in the Prestressed Concrete Industry," *Interfaces* 6, no. 4 (August 1976), pp. 45–49.

these sites would be capable of supplying 200 shipments annually. Alpha has decided to make its selection on the basis of minimizing transportation costs. Estimates of the cost per shipment from each source to destination are shown in the cells of the matrix in Table 7.4.

The cost analysis for Alpha Company proceeds in two stages. Stage one finds the lowest cost obtainable if the Columbus source were added to the existing network. Stage two determines the minimum cost possible if the St. Louis source were chosen. The results of these two analyses are compared, and the most favorable alternative is then selected. A final solution of this analysis for Alpha is shown in Figure 7.4.

If Columbus is selected, minimum annual shipping costs will be \$120,000. This occurs if 100 shipments go from Chicago to Evansville (costing \$200 each), 200 shipments from Chicago to Fort Wayne (costing \$200 each), 100 from Louisville to Evansville (\$100 each), 300 from Louisville to Lexington (\$100 each), and 200 shipments from Columbus to Fort Wayne (\$100 each). These optimal shipment quantities are shown in part (*a*) of Figure 7.4. This shipping plan satisfies the raw material needs of all three plants and fully uses the capacities of all three raw materials sources. Any different patterns of source-to-destination shipments will result in higher annual shipping costs.
costs.

Part (*b*) of Figure 7.4 shows that if St. Louis is selected, the minimum cost shipping pattern will incur \$140,000 of annual costs. Columbus is therefore the preferred raw materials location site.

TABLE 7.4
Sources, destinations, and costs of raw material shipments

Source	Evansville	Lexington	Fort Wayne	Number of shipments available from source
Chicago	\$200	\$300	\$200	300
Louisville	100	100	300	400
Columbus	300	200	100	200
St. Louis	100	300*	400	200
Number of shipments needed by destination	200	300	400	

*Cost to transport one shipment from St. Louis to Lexington

(a)
If Columbus is selected destination

Source	Evansville	Lexington	Fort Wayne	Shipments available
Chicago	$200 100	$300	$200 200	300
Louisville	$100 100	$100 300	$300	400
Columbus	$300	$200	$100 200	200
Shipments needed	200	300	400	

Minimum total annual cost = $120,000

(b)
If St. Louis is selected destination

Source	Evansville	Lexington	Fort Wayne	Shipments available
Chicago	$200	$300	$200 300	300
Louisville	$100	$100 300	$300 100	400
St. Louis	$100 200	$300	$400	200
Shipments needed	200	300	400	

Minimum total annual cost = $140,000

FIGURE 7.4
Evaluation of system transportation costs for two raw materials sources

Notice that the linear programming formulation differs from the previous simple median model approach in two fundamental ways:

1. Number of alternative sites. The median model assumes that all locations in geographic space are eligible for selection as the new location. Linear programming, in contrast, considers only a finite number of alternative sites that are preselected from preliminary feasibility studies.
2. Direction of transportation movements. The simple median model assumes that all shipments move on retangular coordinates. The LP procedure does not.

Simulation

Although several quantitative models like the ones we've discussed can handle location problems of limited scope, many real world problems are more complex than our examples. Some systems have multiple sources shipping to numerous plants; they in turn ship finished goods to warehouses from which further shipments are made to retailers. A multiechelon (multilevel) system such as this is shown in Figure 7.5. Even with the simplest revision of this system, adding or deleting one network component, the combinational aspects of the problem make it computationally difficult to evaluate. More realistically, we may wish to consider more drastic changes, such as a total revision of the warehousing network. With problems of this complexity, no optimal solution is possible. Instead, approximation techniques like computer simulation are used.

The grocery products division of Ralston Purina, for example, decided to evaluate the effects of deleting various warehouses in ten midwestern

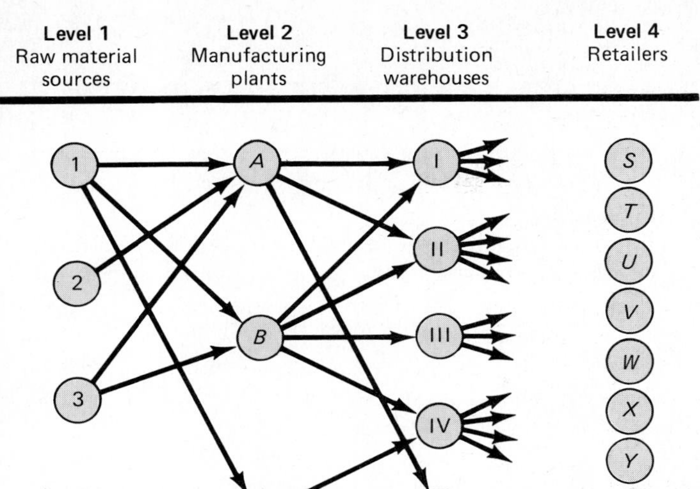

FIGURE 7.5
Multiechelon production-distribution system

states.[8] To do this, they built a simulation model of a system similar to the one we've shown in Figure 7.5. By examining many warehouse locational patterns, the simulation analysis showed that distribution costs could be lowered by reducing the existing five warehouses to a three warehouse configuration. Although the simulation model cost more than $50,000 to build, the company had made a good investment, because closing two warehouses produced an annual savings of $132,000, several times the cost of the simulation. The simulation was used for other analysis purposes as well.

BEHAVIORAL IMPACT IN FACILITY LOCATION

Because they can involve many different consequences for the organization, location decisions are difficult and complex.[9] Our previous discussions of models focused on the *cost* consequences. But costs are not the whole story, and models must be interpreted with caution because model results are deceptively precise. No matter how exact, models are inadequate; they simply don't consider any aspects of a problem that are non-

[8]This simulation study is reported by R. E. Markland, "Analyzing Geographically Discrete Warehousing Networks by Computer Simulation," *Decision Sciences* 4, no. 2 (April 1973), pp. 216–36.

[9]A substantial portion of this section is taken from R. J. Ebert and E. E. Adam, Jr., "The Human Factor in Facilities Location Planning," *Business Horizons* 20, no. 5 (November 1977), pp. 35–42. Copyright, 1977, by the Foundation for the School of Business at Indiana University. Reprinted by permission.

quantifiable. New locations require that organizations establish relationships with new environments and employees, and adding or deleting facilities requires adjustments in the overall management system. The organization structure and modes of making operating decisions must be modified to accommodate the change. These hidden "system costs" are usually excluded from quantitative models, and yet they are very real aspects of the location decision.

Our coverage of behavioral dimensions of location planning includes three considerations: cultural differences in the location decision, job satisfaction of employees, and consumer dimensions of location.

Cultural Differences

The decision to locate a new facility usually means that employees will be hired from within the new locale. It also means that the organization must establish appropriate community relations to "fit into" the locale as a good neighbor and citizen. To be successful at these endeavors, the organization must recognize the differences in the way people in various ethnic communities, and urban, suburban, and rural areas react to new businesses. Managerial style and organizational structure must adapt to the norms and customs of local subcultures.

At the heart of environmental influences are four social institutions that provide an individual's value systems: the family, religion, the school, and the state. Differences in subcultures are ultimately reflections of influences from these sources. The individual's disposition toward accepting responsibility, exercising independence of thought and initiative, style of interpersonal interaction with others, and lifelong goals and aspirations are tempered by environmental elements. Family structures and role relationships, for example, can mold one's views on the "proper" roles of men and women. These views are carried over into the workplace and affect employees' attitudes toward men or women occupying certain occupational roles. Employee acceptance of superior-subordinate relationships and varying degrees of authoritarianism may vary with subcultures in which family relationships are male-dominant, female-dominant, or egalitarian.

Within the United States, employees from a midwestern rural setting are likely to adhere to a middle-class value system, including a strong influence of the Protestant ethic, the belief that each person is responsible for his own situation instead of being compelled by forces beyond his control. Hard work is generally valued for its own sake, as is occupational achievement. In an urban setting, on the other hand, less uniformity exists. Various ethnic groups and social classes contribute to heterogeneous value systems reflected in diverse life goals, beliefs about the role of work, career aspirations, and perceptions of opportunity, which result in different on-the-job behaviors and talents. Such differences have implications not only for managerial style but for staffing, training, and job mobility as well.

Age distributions often vary from one geographical location to another, and workers' ages can affect on-the-job behavior too. When the Vega plant in Lordstown, Ohio, faced a pervasive labor problem several years ago, management found that within the plant the general age of the work force determined the intensity of labor's protest—the lower the age, the likelier the outcries. During the dispute UAW vice-president Ken Bannon commented, "The traditional concept that hard work is a virtue and a duty, which older workers have adhered to, is not applicable to younger workers, and the concepts of the younger labor force must be taken into account."[10]

At the international level, there are even greater cultural differences. Compare, for example, the Japanese work tradition with that of Western industrial society:

> Japanese workers are hired for life. They are practically never fired. Promotions go largely by seniority even at managerial levels. The incompetent executive moves up with advancing years to positions with titles appropriate to his age—even when this means devising types of duties that will keep him from interfering with the progress of the firm. The pay of workers bears no relation to their productivity. The pay envelope is the sum of a complex set of factors, in which length of service and number of dependents figure prominently. All management decisions are made on a group basis—at least normally. If an individual were credited with a certain decision that turned out to be unwise, then the individual would lose face. To spare management people from such humiliation, to all appearances the group as a whole shares responsibility in all decisions.[11]

Obviously operations managers in Japan face a very different set of managerial problems than their U.S. counterparts. Wage determination, employee turnover, hiring, and promotion practices are not at all the same.

The need for recognizing international differences in cultural and social systems is illustrated in one study contrasting experiences in the United States and Europe.[12] The European social system has resulted in more of a "managerial elite" in their organizations than in those in the United States. A gap in knowledge, skills, and value orientations exists between upper and lower managerial levels. Because of education, training, and the socialization process, including a lifelong exposure to a relatively rigid class system, lower subordinates have not been prepared to accept participative managerial styles. Further, higher management is not disposed toward creating and using such styles. Thus, social distance and lack of preparation have tended to result in organizational forms that are more authoritarian/centralized than participative/decentralized. Attitudes toward executive mobility in the U.S. and Europe have also differed. A manager's diverse employment and experience background is generally valued in the U.S. In Europe, however, employment diversity is often regarded as indicative of questionable competence or loyalty.

---

[10]"The Spreading Lordstown Syndrome," *Business Week*, no. 2218 (March 4, 1972), pp. 69–70.

[11]William F. Whyte, *Men at Work* (Homewood, Ill.: Richard D. Irwin, Inc., 1961), p. 66.

[12]Fremont E. Kast, "Management Concepts and Practices: European Style," *Business Horizons* 7, no. 4 (Winter 1964), pp. 25–36.

In managerial decision making too, cultural differences are apparent. Like everyone else's, managers' cultural backgrounds determine what alternatives are acceptable to them in a decision situation. Several cross-cultural studies have revealed differences in managerial value systems. One study of the life goals of managers in several countries revealed striking contrasts between those in the U.S. and in Denmark. Danish managers ranked "service" highest and "leadership" eighth from among a list of life goals; U.S. managers expressed almost the opposite rank ordering of these factors.[13]

By recognizing cultural differences, we can anticipate special problems if we decide to locate in another society. It is not simply a matter of duplicating a highly refined manufacturing process from the U.S. somewhere else. In discussing the transfer of technology from developed to less developed countries, one authority points out that ". . . the developed country's class structure, behavior and attitude are often implicitly built into its technology."[14] The productive tools and techniques that are workable and appropriate at home may be unworkable abroad:

> A familiar sight in any less developed economy is the half finished plant, abandoned and idle, or the broken down machine awaiting spare parts, or the huge factory producing at a tenth of its potential capacity. Where four men could do a job at home, twenty-five are required abroad, and often the job cannot be done at all.

Merely transferring tools and equipment is not adequate. To operate the physical facility, managerial techniques and skills, in proper mixture, must be borrowed from the culture, and so must the cultural assumptions that are needed to make them work. Consider the situation depicted in Figure 7.6. The triangle represents the hierarchical mixture of employees needed to operate a facility in an industrialized Western culture. Relatively few people are needed at the top levels of the organization, more in the middle, and even more at the bottom. The society (outlined by the dotted line) has a mixture of available human skills and orientations that are inconsistent with the needs of the technology. This society features a relatively large proportion of people possessing top-level skills (area *a*), few in the middle (area *b*), few at the bottom, and a large number of unemployable persons (area *c*). Where will the skills that are needed to operate the technology come from? It may be necessary to establish schools or training programs, or otherwise to try to change centuries of tradition in order to garner appropriate human resources for successful operation of the facility. Unanticipated disruptions might also arise if local governments put pressure

---

[13]See R. A. Alexander, G. V. Barrett, B. M. Bass, and E. C. Ryterband, "Empathy Projection and Negation in Seven Countries," in *Clinical Psychology in Industrial Organizations*, L. E. Abt and B. F. Reiss, eds. (New York: Grune and Stratton, Inc., 1971), pp. 29–49.

[14]See Richard N. Farmer, "Organizational Transfer and Class Structure," *Academy of Management Journal* 9, no. 3 (September 1966), pp. 204–16.

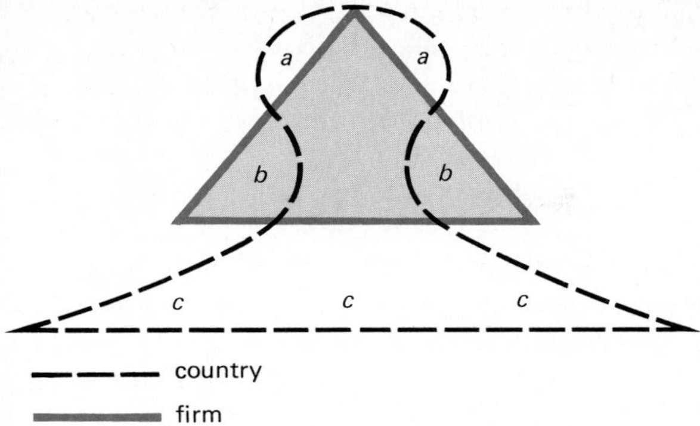

FIGURE 7.6
Technological skill requirements compared to cultural skill availability

Source: Richard N. Farmer, "Organizational Transfer and Class Structure," *Academy of Management Journal 9,* no. 3 (September 1966), p. 211.

on the organization to hire the unemployables so as to raise the local standard of living. Clearly, the economic, political, and cultural makeup of a society has far-reaching effects on the technological and economic success of multinational locational decisions.[15]

Job Satisfaction

In recent years managers have been very concerned about employee job satisfaction because it has an impact on how well the organization operates.[16] Although no consistent overall relationship between job satisfaction and *productivity* seems to exist, other important relationships have been found. As compared with employees with *low* job satisfaction, those expressing *high* job satisfaction exhibit the following characteristics:

1. lower labor turnover,
2. less abesenteeism,
3. less tardiness, and
4. fewer grievances.

These four factors can have substantial impact on both costs and disruptions of operations. But how is job satisfaction related to facility location? There is some evidence that satisfaction is related to community characteristics. One study of female clerical workers, for example, found that job satisfaction was inversely related to community prosperity.[17] Employees in more prosperous communities were less satisfied with their work than those in less prosperous communities. In a similar vein, earlier research showed that employee morale tended to be lower in large industrialized

[15]For issues in international operations see chapters 15–17 of W. Skinner, *Manufacturing in the Corporate Strategy,* (New York: John Wiley & Sons, 1978).

[16]B. K. Scanlan, "Determinants of Job Satisfaction and Productivity," *Personnel Journal* 55, no. 1 (January 1976), p. 12–14.

[17]C. L. Hulin, "Effects of Community Characteristics on Measures of Job Satisfaction." *Journal of Applied Psychology* 50, no 2 (1966), p. 185–92.

metropolitan locations. Studies in other companies have found higher employee satisfaction in small town settings and where there is a lower degree of unionization. Accordingly, a company with facilities in multiple locations can expect variations in employee satisfaction due to attitudinal and value-system variations across locational sites.[18]

Consumer Considerations

For many organizations, location planning must emphasize consumer behavior and proximity to customers. If your primary product is to provide a service to the public, locational convenience for the customer may be the prime consideration. Theaters, banks, supermarkets, and restaurants heavily emphasize customer convenience when choosing a location. In fact, convenience of location itself is often considered to be the product offered by some firms. For these reasons the location decision may be regarded as a marketing function instead of a production/operations responsibility, especially as it affects revenues rather than costs.

SUMMARY

The problems of planning for capacity and location of facilities are interrelated, because the decision to change capacity often involves the location of new facilities or the dislocation of existing ones. Problems of selecting a facility location require careful consideration of how costs and revenues will be affected. Preliminary studies are needed to gather information from many sources and to identify feasible sites. Detailed studies using models enable the operations manager to evaluate cost consequences of alternative locations. Some of these models are simulation models, which can be constructed to include many types of costs in complex multilevel production-distribution systems, and simple median and linear programming models, which are particularly useful when there are substantial transportation costs among multiple facilities in a system.

Throughout the process of identifying and evaluating alternatives, management must consider the behavioral implications of location. The revenues of many service organizations depend upon a location featuring customer convenience and accessibility. Organizations having less direct contact with the consuming public must recognize potential differences in employee behavior that can arise at various locations. In the various regions within a country, different life styles and value orientations are necessarily carried over into the work place, and these differences affect on-the-job behavior and overall organizational performance. Subcultural differences have implications for both job design (conversion technology) and managerial style.

At the international level, cultural differences limit locational alternatives in other countries. At the very least, production/operations managers must recognize that locating in another country usually involves more than a simple transplanting of technology, and they must try to uncover any "hidden" problems. The skills and environmental support required to operate may be scarce or nonexistent, or cultural differences may inhibit efficient operations—to name just a couple of potential difficulties that present quite a complex challenge to the operations manager.

[18] See C. L. Hulin and M. R. Blood, "Job Enlargement, Individual Differences, and Worker Responses." *Psychological Bulletin* 69, no. 1 (1968), pp. 41–55.

CASE

Porta-Putt, Inc.

Porta-Putt, Inc., manufactures and distributes gasoline-powered out-board motors for boats. One of their three plants, the St. Louis assembly plant, is obsolete. The Los Angeles and Chicago assembly plants were recently renovated. Rather than continue operation in St. Louis, management is considering the possibility of finding a new location for the third plant. This is an opportune time, because in two years the new Denver distribution warehouse will be opened. Since the new assembly plant could be the primary supplier of motors to the Denver warehouse, the new plant could be located so as to minimize shipping costs, which are a substantial part of Porta-Putt's operating costs.

Two types of shipping costs are incurred at the St. Louis plant. First, raw materials and subcomponents used in assembling the motors are shipped from Minneapolis and Seattle to the St. Louis facility. Then, after final assembly, the St. Louis plant ships the finished products to the Denver distribution center. Figure 7.7 shows the geographic locations of the three facilities that ship to or from the St. Louis facility. Table 7.5 summarizes the annual number of standard loads shipped between St. Louis and each of the other three sites. The cost of shipping a standard load is estimated to be 10¢ per mile.

FIGURE 7.7
Porta-Putt, Inc.

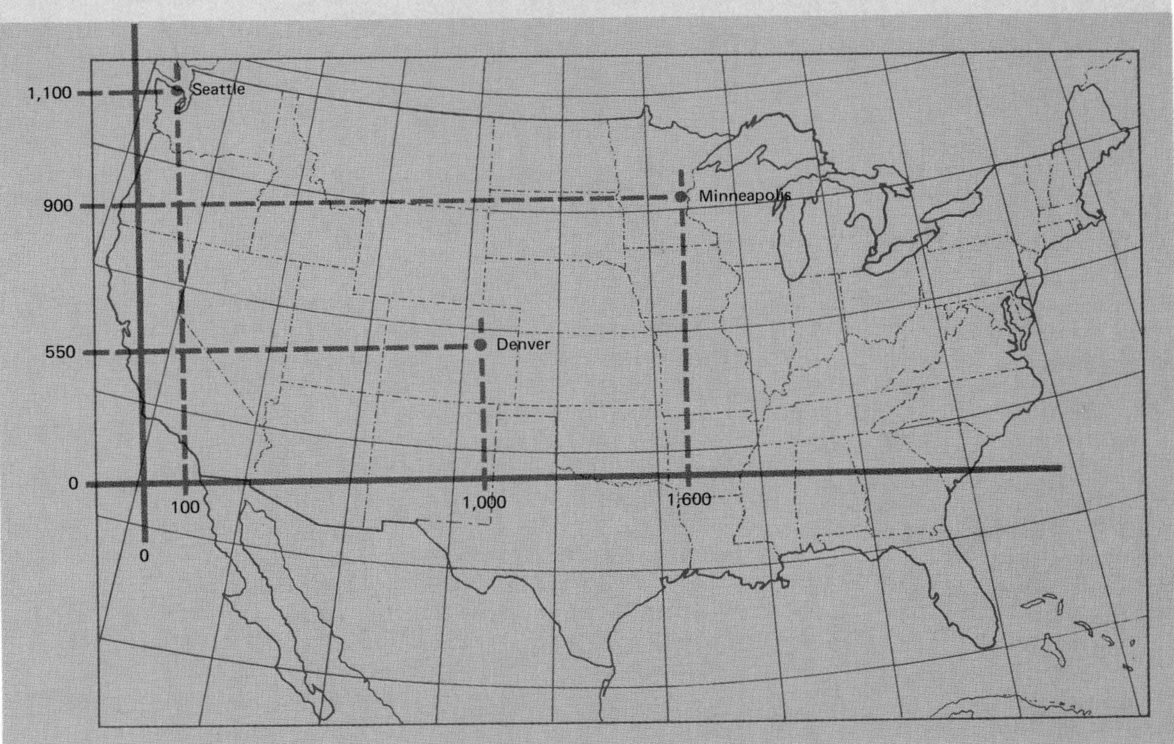

TABLE 7.5
Shipments between the St. Louis plant and other Porta-Putt facilities

Existing facilities	Annual number of standard loads	Coordinates of existing facility x	y
Denver	10,000	1,000	550
Seattle	8,000	100	1,100
Minneapolis	4,000	1,600	900

Management would like to find a location that would minimize the potentially high annual transportation costs. At the same time, however, there is some hesitation about moving away from metropolitan St. Louis, the original assembly facility established thirty-five years ago. Porta-Putt's experienced work force has survived many work-methods and assembly-line changes. From these refinements had evolved an intricate assembly operation that efficiently produced quality motors—until recently, when the plant became technologically obsolete. The vice president, who must make the relocation decision, feels that he should tell the St. Louis employees they might lose their jobs, but so far he has only discussed this possibility with several managers there. When the idea of relocation was introduced, these managers were dismayed at the prospect of leaving the St. Louis area. Present an analysis of the major factors in this decision and recommend a location.

REVIEW AND DISCUSSION QUESTIONS

1. Although facility location is a planning decision, it has implications for decisions in the organizing and controlling subfunctions. Explain.
2. Outline the factors that should be considered in locating a nuclear generating plant. List these factors in order of priority to show each's importance to the decision.
3. Contrast the location problems of a manufacturing firm and a supermarket, showing the relevant considerations they share and those that differ.
4. Discuss the possible reasons for changing the location of an emergency services system, such as an urban fire fighting company.
5. Suppose for economic reasons you wish to locate your manufacturing facility in a small community that currently seems to be unfavorably disposed toward your industry. What strategies might you employ before making your decision?
6. Discuss the primary limitations of the simple median model. How important to the location problem are these limitations?
7. The simple median model is appropriate for some location problems; linear programming is appropriate for others. Identify the conditions of the location problem that would lead you to select one model over the other.

8. In facility location analysis, under what circumstances would computer simulation be preferred over other models?
9. What aspects of different subcultures should be considered in locational analysis?
10. How might subcultural differences at alternative sites affect the organizing and controlling activities in a facility?
11. If you expand your existing company by opening a new division in a foreign country, should the new division be staffed by local personnel or by personnel imported from the parent organization? Explain.
12. Discuss the relationships among job satisfaction, personal value systems, facility location, and productivity.

PROBLEMS

Solved Problems

1. Location *A* would result in annual fixed costs of $300,000, variable costs of $63 per unit, and revenues of $68 per unit. Annual fixed costs at location *B* are $800,000, with variable costs of $32 per unit, and revenue of $68 per unit. Sales volume is estimated to be 25,000 units per year. Which location is most attractive?

   A cost-volume-revenue analysis is helpful for evaluating the two alternatives. The breakeven points are found from

$$BE = \frac{\text{fixed cost}}{\text{revenue per unit} - \text{variable cost per unit}}$$

$$BE_A = \frac{\$300{,}000}{\$68 - 63} = 60{,}000 \text{ units}$$

$$BE_B = \frac{\$800{,}000}{\$68 - 32} = 22{,}222 \text{ units}$$

   At the expected demand of 25,000 units, profits (loss) for the alternatives are:

	Alternative	
	A	B
revenue	$1,700,000	$1,700,000
costs		
total variable	1,575,000	800,000
total fixed	300,000	800,000
total costs	1,875,000	1,600,000
profit (loss)	(175,000)	100,000

   Location *B* is most attractive, even though annual fixed costs are much higher than for *A*.

2. A site is sought for a temporary plant to supply cement to three existing construction sites: downtown, at a mall, and at a suburb. The locations of the existing sites and the loads to be delivered to each are as follows:

Delivery site	Grid location (miles)		Number of loads required	Delivery cost per load per mile
	east	north		
downtown	20	10	22	$10
mall	10	40	43	$10
suburb	40	20	36	$10
			total = 101	

Find the best site for the cement plant. What total shipping cost will result?

Using the simple median model, the median load is 51. To find the best east location we begin at mile zero on the grid and proceed eastward to the location that receives the 51st load. At the first grid location used (mile 10), 43 loads go to the mall. At the next location eastward (mile 20), 22 loads go to downtown and at this location the median (51st) load will have been delivered. Hence, the optimal east location (E^*) is mile 20. In a similar fashion the median load in the northern direction is delivered at mile 20 to the suburb site ($N^* = 20$). The resulting shipment costs, $22,300, are shown in the following table:

Delivery site	Distance (miles) from cement plant $\|E - E^*\|$	$\|N - N^*\|$	Total (D_i)	Cost per mile per load (C_i)	Number of loads (L_i)	Cost $C_i x L_i x D_i$
mall	$\|10 - 20\| = 10$	$\|40 - 20\| = 20$	30	$10	43	$12,900
downtown	$\|20 - 20\| = 0$	$\|10 - 20\| = 10$	10	10	22	2,200
suburb	$\|40 - 20\| = 20$	$\|20 - 20\| = 0$	20	10	36	7,200
					total =	$22,300

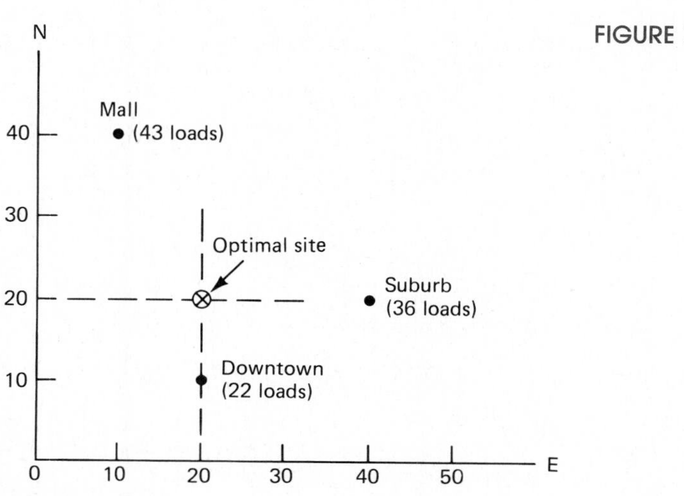

FIGURE 7.8

Reinforcing Fundamentals

3. Bubble Breweries has two distribution warehouses on Highway 70. Warehouse *A*, located at mile zero, receives 3,000 standard beer shipments annually from the brewery. Warehouse *B*, located at mile 1,200, receives 1,000 standard shipments annually from the brewery. For these shipment patterns, what would be the better brewery location for minimizing annual transportation costs to warehouses?
4. Ontario Dairies, Ltd., is considering where to locate dairy processing centers to pre-prepare milk products for regional markets in Canada. Locations and milk volumes are given below. Transportation costs, $0.50 per mile per 100 lbs., are uniform throughout the area. Use the simple median model to find the best location. *Show Your Work.*

Location	Coordinate* location (Miles)	Milk processing (100,000 lb. units)
London, Ont.	*N/S/E/W* = O	300
Cochrane, Ont.	*W* = 20, *N* = 400	800
Toronto, Ont.	*E* = 120, *N* = 20	200
Montreal, Queb.	*E* = 340, *N* = 80	200

**N* is North, *S* is South, *E* is East, *W* is West

5. Bigtown is trying to find the best location for a master solid waste disposal station. At present, four substations are located at the following coordinate (*X*, *Y*) locations: station 1 (40, 120), station 2 (65, 40), station 3 (110, 90), and station 4 (10, 130). The number of loads hauled monthly to the master station will be 300 from station 1, 200 from station 2, 350 from station 3, and 400 from station 4. Use the simple median model to find the best location.
6. Bigtown public officials (see problem 5) are puzzled because of adverse public reaction to the proposed location of a master solid waste disposal station. The public works manager has determined that locations in the area from *X* = 30 to *X* = 140 and *Y* = 5 to *Y* = 120 are not feasible location sites. The city engineer proposes two new alternatives, one at (*X* = 25, *Y* = 50), the other at (*X* = 100, *Y* = 150). Which is the best site for the master disposal station?
7. Can Bigtown's problem of locating the solid waste station (problem 5) be set up in a linear programming framework? Explain.
8. First National Bank is considering the location of a branch central processing facility (CPF) to perform check processing and other paperwork operations for four existing branch banks in its northeastern market area. This new facility will not be open to the public. Figure 7.9 shows the current facilities' proximity to the existing main bank (which is shown as zero on the axis). The monthly volume to be processed from each branch bank is shown in the following table:

Bank	Volume (1,000 items)
A	80
B	60
C	30
D	70

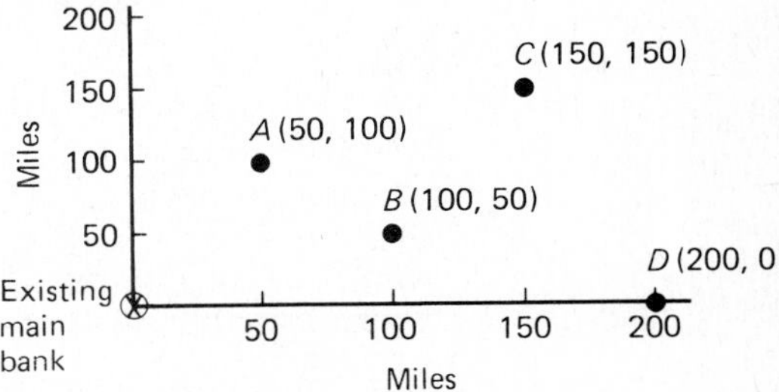

FIGURE 7.9

The existing main bank wants to move all of this dollar volume to the new CPF location.

(a) Locate the CPF using the simple median model. Show the CPF on the above graph. Show your work.

(b) The actual cost of transportation is $100 per 1,000 items processed per mile. What will be the cost savings for processing branch C work at the CPF rather than at the existing main bank?

9. The University of Missouri is considering the location of a food processing center to pre-prepare food for all four campuses. Campus locations and food volumes are given below. Transportation costs are one dollar per mile per 100 pounds and are uniform throughout the state. Use the simple median model to find the best location. *Show Your Work.*

Campus	Coordinate* location (miles)	Food processing (100 lbs. units)
UMSL (St. Louis)	$N/S/E/W = 0$	600
UMR (Rolla)	$W = 90, S = 50$	300
UMC (Columbia)	$W = 120, N = 10$	800
UMKC (Kansas City)	$W = 240, N = 20$	200

**N* is North, *S* is South, *E* is East, *W* is West.

Challenging exercises:

10. A company has conducted a comprehensive study of five cities, one of which will be selected as the site for a new facility. Annual operating costs for each city are estimated as follows:

Annual operating costs ($millions)

City	Labor	Transportation	Local taxes	Power	Other
1	.90	.10	.17	.21	.16
2	1.10	.08	.20	.29	.11
3	1.20	.07	.25	.25	.12
4	.85	.12	.19	.18	.16
5	.75	.14	.17	.23	.18

For each community, the company compiled subjective ratings of several important attributes:

Attribute

City	Community receptivity	Labor availability	Transportation quality	Quality of life
1	very good	good	fair	acceptable
2	fair	very good	acceptable	fair
3	good	fair	outstanding	good
4	fair	outstanding	acceptable	very good
5	very good	acceptable	fair	outstanding

(a) On the basis of annual operating costs, which site is best?

(b) Devise a method for quantifying the intangible factors, and integrate them with the cost data into overall evaluation measures. Which site is best now?

11. Highline Enterprises manufactures its products at plants in Los Angeles and Chicago. Shipments are then sent to customers in Denver, Seattle, and New York. The Los Angeles plant produces a maximum of 50 shipments annually, and the Chicago plant produces a maximum of 70 shipments. Costs per shipment from Los Angeles are $1,000 to Denver, $900 to Seattle, and $1,600 to New York. A shipment from Chicago costs $800 to Denver, $1,300 to Seattle, and $1,000 to New York. Next year, demand is expected to be for 60 shipments at Denver, 40 at Seattle, and 80 at New York. Highline will build a new plant at either Dallas or Knoxville, and the plant will have an annual capacity of 60 shipments. At Dallas, manufacturing costs would average $100,000 per shipment; the manufacturing cost at Knoxville would be $80,000. Shipment cost from Dallas is $600 to Denver, $1,000 to Seattle, and $1,400 to New York. From Knoxville a shipment to Denver is $900, to Seattle $1,200, and to New York $700.
    (a) Set up this problem in a linear programming framework.
    (b) Outline the specific kinds of information you would expect from the linear programming model.
    (c) What relevant information for this decision would not be provided by the model?

12. Wilmont Trucking is considering the location of a new terminal to process some of the freight now handled in its Jacksonville, Florida, terminal (*J*). Some freight also will come from terminals in Tampa (*T*), Mobile, Alabama (*M*), and Atlanta, Georgia (*A*). Figure 7.10 shows the distance of the facilities from Jacksonville (shown as zero on the axis). The annual volume expected to be transferred from each terminal is shown in the following table.

Terminal	Volume (truckloads)
J	1000
T	200
M	100
A	800

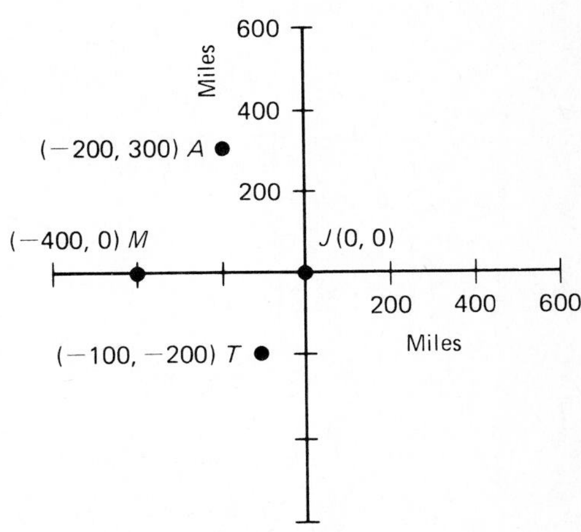

FIGURE 7.10

    (a) Locate the new terminal using the simple median model.
    (b) The actual cost of transportation is $200 per load per 100 miles. Currently, Jacksonville is a "break-bulk" facility, handling all shipments in the southeastern United States. If Atlanta were allowed to ship direct to the new location rather than through Jacksonville, how many dollars could be saved next year?
    (c) It is likely the new facility will not be located in a metropolitan area. Some behavioral dimensions cannot be incorporated in a model. Which of these might have some impact on location decisions?

13. Revise the simple median model to reflect differences in transportation cost rates for loads flowing between the new facility and several existing facilities.

14. A company has three existing warehouses to which it will ship furniture from a new factory whose location must be decided. The factory will receive raw materials from its wood supplier and its fabric supplier. The annual number of shipments, shipment costs, and the locations of the suppliers and warehouses are shown below. Where should the factory be located to minimize annual transportation costs?

Existing Facility	Number of loads per year to or from factory	Cost ($) per load per mile	Coordinate location (miles)	
			X	Y
wood supplier	120	$8	100	400
fabric supplier	200	6	800	700
warehouse #1	60	5	300	600
warehouse #2	40	5	200	100
warehouse #3	70	5	600	200

GLOSSARY

Consumer behavior The acts and decisions of individuals in obtaining and using goods and services.

Culture Socially shared and transmitted knowledge, beliefs, customs, and morals.

Job satisfaction Employee perceptions of the extent to which their work fulfills or satisfies their needs.

Labor turnover A measure of the stability or change in the organization's work force; the net result of employee terminations and entrances.

Location of a facility Geographic site at which a productive facility is situated.

Simple Median Model A mathematical procedure for finding a facility location that minimizes transportation costs of a network of facilities.

Subculture Regional or ethnic variations of a culture.

Value system Individual's beliefs or conceptions of what is desirable, good, and bad.

SELECTED READINGS

Aly, A. A. and D. W. Litwhiler, Jr. "Police Briefing Stations, A Location Problem." *AIIE Transactions* 11, no. 1 (March 1979), pp. 12–22.

Cole, J. J. and E. J. Bardi. *The Management of Logistics*, 2nd ed. St. Paul, MN: The West Publishing Co., 1980.

Farmer, R. N. "Organizational Transfer and Class Structure." *Academy of Management Journal* 9, no. 3 (September 1966), pp. 204–16.

Hulin, C. L. "Effects of Community Characteristics on Measures of Job Satisfaction." *Journal of Applied Psychology* 50, no. 2 (1966), pp. 185–92.

Hulin, C. L. and Mr. R. Blood. "Job Enlargement, Individual Differences and Worker Responses." *Psychological Bulletin* 69, no. 1 (1968), pp. 41–55.

Kast, F. E. "Management Concepts and Practices: European Style." *Business Horizons* 7, no. 4 (Winter 1964), pp. 25–36.

Love, R. F. and L. Yerex. "An Application of a Facilities Location Model in the Prestressed Concrete Industry." *Interfaces* 6, no. 4 (August 1976), pp. 45–49.

Schmenner, R. W. "Look Beyond the Obvious in Plant Location." *Harvard Business Review* 57, no. 1, (January–February 1979), pp. 126–32.

Skinner, W. *Manuacturing in the Corporate Strategy*. New York: John Wiley & Sons, 1978.

Sweeney, D. J. and R. L. Tatham. "An Improved Long-Run Model for Multiple Warehouse Location." *Management Science* 22, no. 7 (March 1976), pp. 748–58.

Vernon, R. and Wells, L. T., Jr. *Manager in the International Economy*, 4th ed. Englewood Cliffs, NJ: Prentice-Hall, 1981.

Whyte, W. F. *Men at Work*. Homewood, Ill.: Richard D. Irwin, Inc., 1961.

SUPPLEMENT TO CHAPTER 7

LINEAR PROGRAMMING: THE TRANSPORTATION METHOD

The transportation (or distribution) method is a special form of the general linear programming problem and must meet the general characteristics noted in the supplement to Chapter 6. Additionally, the transportation method is applicable to problems with the following characteristics:

1. *Sources*. A quantity of resources exists at a finite number of "sources," and these resources are available for allocation.
2. *Destinations*. A finite number of "destinations" exists, each of which needs to be supplied with a specified quantity of resources that are available from the sources.
3. *Homogeneous units*. From the viewpoint of the destinations, the available resources are homogeneous; that is, a unit of resource supplied by one origin (source) is equivalent to a unit supplied by any other origin.
4. *Costs*. The cost of allocating a unit of resource from each origin to each destination is known and constant.

Although problems meeting the above conditions can be formulated and solved by the simplex method, the transportation method is less cumbersome. We'll first explain the procedure in general terms and then apply it to the Alpha Processing location problem from Chapter 7.

The transportation format consists of a source-destination matrix, as shown in Figure S7.1. There are m distinct sources (rows), each of which has RA_i units of resource available. The RA_i are usually not numerically equal. There are n destinations, each in need of RN_j units of resource. The cost of allocating one unit of resource from source i to destination j is C_{ij}. The problem is to allocate resources from sources to destinations so that the total cost of allocations for the system is minimized. The restrictions are:

1. all destination needs must be met,
2. no source may allocate more units than it has available, and
3. negative quantities cannot be allocated.

The objective, then, is to minimize total cost

$$
\begin{aligned}
TC = {} & C_{1A}X_{1A} + C_{1B}X_{1B} + \ldots + C_{2A}X_{2A} \\
& + C_{2B}X_{2B} + \ldots + C_{mA}X_{mA} + C_{mB}X_{mB} \\
& + \ldots + C_{mn}X_{mn}
\end{aligned}
$$

where X_{ij} is the number of units allocated from i to j, subject to the above restrictions (constraints).

	Destination (j)				
	A	B	-----	n	Units of resource available from source i
Source (i) 1	C_{1A}	C_{1B}		C_{1n}	RA_1
2	C_{2A}	C_{2B}		C_{2n}	RA_2
⋮					
m	C_{mA}	C_{mB}		C_{mn}	RA_m
Units of resource needed at destination j	RN_A	RN_B		RN_n	ΣRA_i / ΣRN_j

FIGURE S7.1
Transportation LP matrix

The Transportation Method

See the Alpha Processing Company example (page 274), which we will use to illustrate the transportation method.

Alpha Processing's two raw material sources send shipments as needed to the various plants. The addition of a new raw material source at Columbus, Ohio, is being considered. We will focus on that one alternative. Management would like to know how to allocate raw materials from the three sources to the plants so that annual transportation costs of the system are minimized. Shipment costs, plant requirements, and source availabilities are summarized in Figure S7.2.

A five step procedure will be used to find the set of allocations that minimize total shipment costs:

1. frame the problem such that the total number of shipments available equals the number of shipments needed,
2. create an initial feasible solution,
3. evaluate the existing solution for possible improvement,
4. modify the existing solution, and
5. repeat steps 3 and 4 until no further improvement is possible.

Cost per shipment is the dollar amount in each cell

Raw material source	Plant (destination) P_1	P_2	P_3	Number of shipments available annually from source i
RMS_1	\$200	\$300	\$200	300
RMS_2	\$100	\$100	\$300	400
RMS_3	\$300	\$200	\$100	200
Number of shipments needed annually at plant j	200	300	400	900 / 900

FIGURE S7.2
Transportation matrix for Alpha Processing Company, adding the Columbus raw materials source (RMS_3)

1. Ensure that Availability Equals Requirements. In Figure S7.2, the number of shipments available at the three sources (900) is equal to the number needed by the destinations. Later we will show how to adjust the matrix when this equality does not exist.

2. Create an Initial Feasible Solution. A *feasible* solution is one in which the needs of all destinations are filled and the capacities of all sources are fully used. Many initial solutions are possible. By convention, we will use the Northwest Corner Rule to create an initial solution here. Allocate as many shipments as possible into the northwest cell of the matrix. In this example, 200 units can be allocated from RMS_1 to P_1. Thereafter, allocations are made to adjacent cells to the east or south of the northwest corner. As shown in Figure S7.3, the next allocation would be 100 shipments from RMS_1 to P_2. At this stage the requirements of P_1 have been met and the shipping capacity of RMS_1 has been fully utilized. The third assignment will be 200 shipments from RMS_2 to P_2. Next, 200 shipments go from RMS_2 to P_3. Finally, 200 shipments are assigned from RMS_3 to P_3. These shipments are recorded beneath the diagonals in the appropriate cells. Overall, the pattern of shipments in the matrix flows generally from the northwest to southeast. All of this was done without regard to the costs involved. The resulting initial solution is feasible because all restrictions in the problem have been met. If this pattern of shipments was used, the annual cost would be as follows:

$$TC = (\$200) \times (200) + (\$300) \times (100) + (\$100) \times (200) + (\$300) \times (200) + (\$100) \times (200) = \$170{,}000$$

Destination

Source	P_1	P_2	P_3	Shipments available
RMS_1	\$200 / 200	\$300 / 100	\$200	300
RMS_2	\$100	\$100 / 200	\$300 / 200	400
RMS_3	\$300	\$200	\$100 / 200	200
	200	300	400	900 / 900

FIGURE S7.3
Initial feasible solution for Alpha Processing Company

3. Evaluate the Existing Solution. Would a different shipping pattern reduce total cost? This question can be answered by using the "stepping stone" procedure for evaluating alternative solutions.

First, the number of used cells in the existing solution must be considered. These are the cells in which shipping assignments have been made. In general, the stepping stone procedure requires that there be $(m + n - 1)$ used cells, where $m + n$ equals the number of row and column constraints, respectively. In Figure S7.3, there are three row restrictions (one for each source) and three column restrictions (one for each destination), for a total of six. Therefore, $(m + n - 1)$ requirement is met and we can proceed with the stepping stone procedure. Later we will consider how to proceed if the number of used cells is not equal to $(m + n - 1)$.

The only way to generate alternative solutions is by making some shipments in cells that are currently unused. This is the purpose of the stepping stone procedure. Using the existing solution as a starting point, we evaluate the unused cells one at a time to see how the costs would be changed. If several of these cells offer cost improvements, the most attractive *one* is selected, and the existing solution is modified accordingly. If none of these cells offers a cost improvement, the existing solution is optimal and the analysis ends.

We will begin by evaluating the unused cell RMS_2 to P_1. If one shipment is allocated to this cell, the shipments in cell RMS_1 to P_1 must be reduced to 199. Otherwise, the P_1 column restriction (200 shipments) would be violated. Next, shipments from RMS_1 to P_2 must be increased from 100 to 101 so that the RMS_1 row restriction is met. Finally, the shipments from RMS_2 to P_2 must be reduced from 200 to 199. By making these changes, we have fully satisfied the row and column restrictions. It is important to notice what has happened from a *systems* viewpoint. By making a change in allocations to *one* cell (RMS_2 to P_1), we needed to make subsequent adjustments in *other* cells in the network so that the overall system adhered to the constraints. The cells requiring adjustment are shown in part (*a*) of Figure S7.4. The arrows indicate the *path* of cell adjustments for the four affected cells. Notice the pattern of alternating pluses and minuses from cell to cell throughout the path. A minus indicates that shipments were reduced in that cell; a plus means that shipments were increased to balance the network. This evaluation path was not arbitrarily selected; it is *unique*.

FIGURE S7.4
Evaluating unused cells

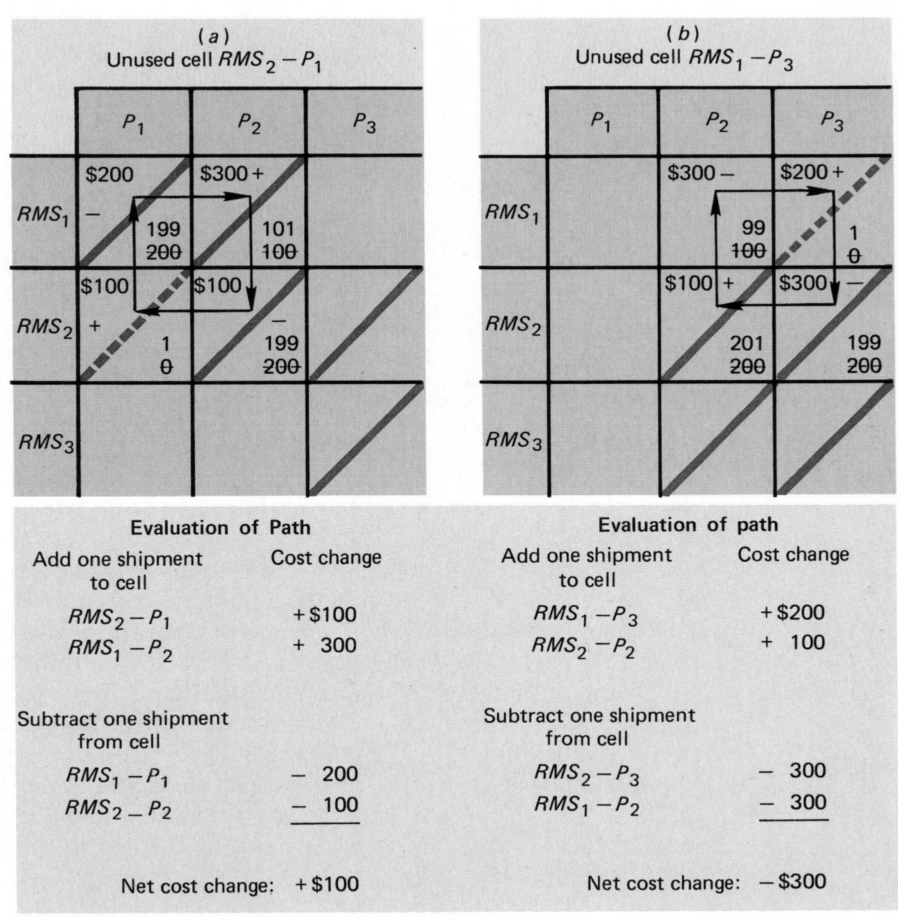

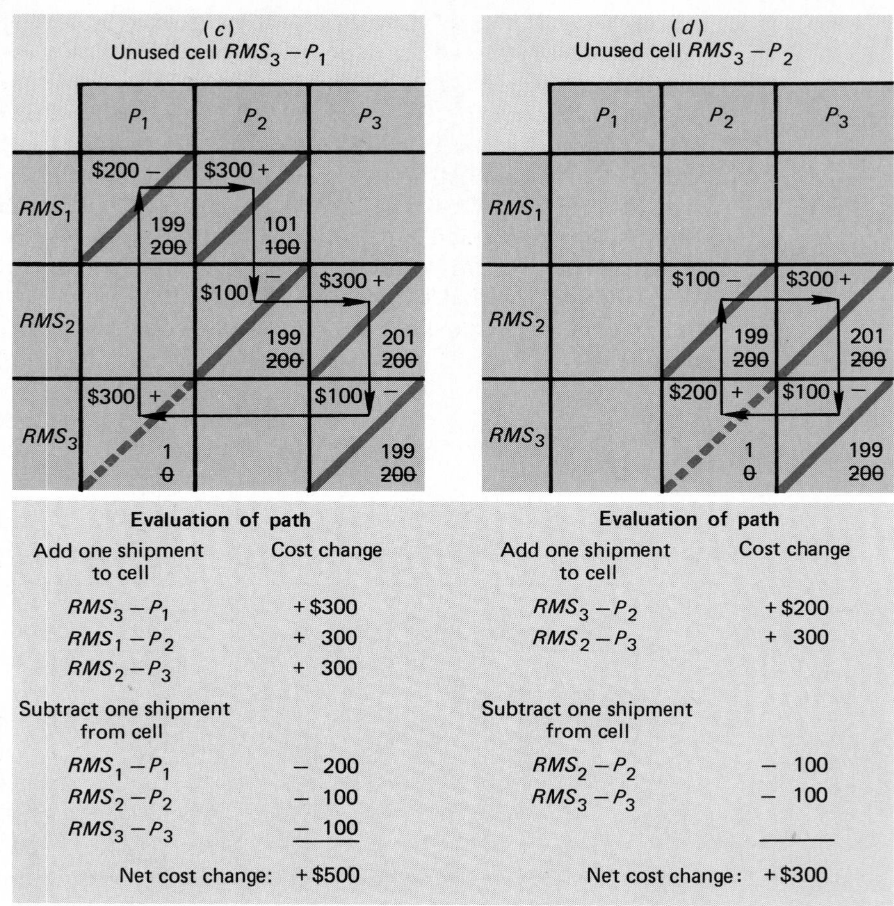

FIGURE S7.4
(cont.)

When the number of used cells in the existing solution equals $(m + n - 1)$, there is a unique evaluation path for each unused cell in the matrix. The evaluation path *always* consists of one unused cell and several used cells. The used cells in the path are called the stepping stones.

How does one find the unique stepping stone path? Beginning in the unused cell (to be evaluated), move onto any used cell (call it stepping stone number one, SS_1). Then rotate 90 degrees from SS_1 onto SS_2. From SS_2 rotate 90 degrees onto SS_3, and continue this process until a 90 degree rotation from SS_i leads back to the original unused cell from which the movements began. This series of rotations is clearly portrayed as a square path for cell $RMS_2 - P_1$.

If these changes were made, how would costs be affected? Relative to the existing solution, costs would be affected as follows: costs would increase by \$100 since a new shipment is made into cell $RMS_2 - P_1$; costs in cell $RMS_1 - P_1$ would decrease by \$200 since one less shipment is made here; an additional shipment is made to cell $RMS_1 - P_2$, thus raising costs by \$300; and costs in cell $RMS_2 - P_2$ would decrease by \$100. Adding together all the increases and decreases, the overall net effect would be a cost increase of \$100. This cell evaluation, summarized in part (*a*) of Figure S7.4, shows that this cell is unattractive and does not offer a desirable alternative solution. We now proceed to evaluate the other unused cells.

The stepping stone path for evaluating unused cell $RMS_1 - P_3$ consists of $(RMS_1 - P_3) \rightarrow (RMS_2 - P_3) \rightarrow (RMS_2 - P_2) \rightarrow (RMS_1 - P_2)$. The clockwise direction of movement on this path (part (*b*) of Figure S7.4) is irrelevant; it could just as well have been counterclockwise. This unique path shows that overall costs would be *reduced* by \$300 if a shipment were made from RMS_1 to P_3. Instead of changing the existing solution to obtain this cost savings, we will first evaluate all other unused cells to see if even greater cost savings may be possible.

The stepping stone paths have been evaluated for each of the two remaining unused cells. Parts (*c*) and (*d*) show that costs would increase if shipments were made to either $RMS_3 - P_1$ or $RMS_3 - P_2$.

As you can see, only one of the four unused cells in the original solution, cell $RMS_1 - P_3$, offers any cost reduction.

4. Modify the Existing Solution. The original solution will be modified by allocating shipments into cell $RMS_1 - P_3$. Furthermore, since \$300 of cost savings result for each shipment, we will allocate as many as possible. Examination of part (*b*) of Figure S7.4 reveals that 100 shipments, at most, can be allocated, since no more than 100 can be removed from cell $RMS_1 - P_2$. Therefore, 100 units will be added to $RMS_1 - P_3$, and appropriate adjustments will be made in cell shipments on the rest of the evaluation path. This course of action will result in a cost savings of (\$300/shipment) × (100 shipments) = \$30,000. The modified solution is shown in Figure S7.5, part (*a*).

5. Reevaluate and Modify. The first revised solution is now treated as a new problem in which steps 3 and 4 are repeated. Applying the stepping stone procedure, we find that only one cell ($RMS_2 - P_1$) offers any cost reduction. This desirable change is highlighted in Figure S7.5, part (*b*). Therefore, a second revised solution is created by allocating as many shipments as possible, 100, into $RMS_2 - P_1$ (see Figure S7.6).

Evaluation of the unused cells in Figure S7.6 shows that no further cost reduction is possible; adding shipments to any of the unused cells will cause total costs to increase (as shown by the positive cell evaluations in parentheses). The optimal solution has been found. If the Columbus, Ohio,

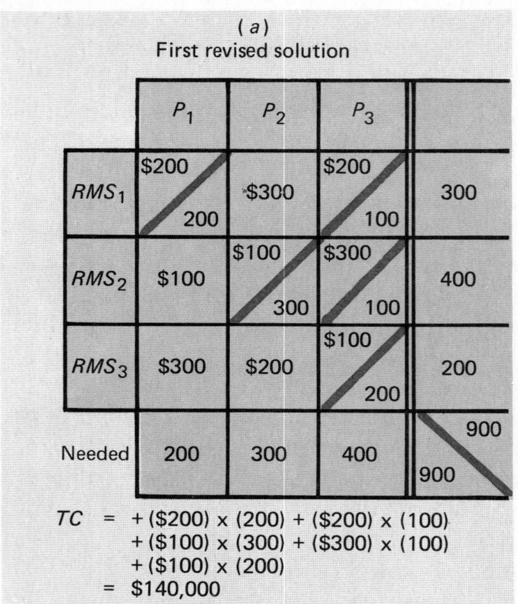

(*a*)
First revised solution

	P_1	P_2	P_3	
RMS_1	\$200 / 200	\$300	\$200 / 100	300
RMS_2	\$100	\$100 / 300	\$300 / 100	400
RMS_3	\$300	\$200	\$100 / 200	200
Needed	200	300	400	900 / 900

TC = + (\$200) x (200) + (\$200) x (100)
+ (\$100) x (300) + (\$300) x (100)
+ (\$100) x (200)
= \$140,000

(*b*)
Evaluation of unused cells in first revised solution

	P_1	P_2	P_3	
RMS_1		+ \$300		
RMS_2	–\$200			
RMS_3	+ \$200	+ \$300		

FIGURE S7.5
Assignment revisions for Alpha Processing Company

	P_1	P_2	P_3	Available
RMS_1	\$200 / 100	\$300 (+\$100)	\$200 / 200	300
RMS_2	\$100 / 100	\$100 / 300	\$300 (+\$200)	400
RMS_3	\$300 (+\$200)	\$200 (+\$100)	\$100 / 200	200
Needed	200	300	400	900 / 900

TC = (\$200) x (100) + (\$200) x (200) + (\$100) x (100) + (\$100) x (300) + (\$100) x (200)
= \$120,000

FIGURE S7.6
Second revised (optimal) solution for Alpha Processing Company

raw material source is added to the existing network, the best shipping pattern is to send 100 shipments from RMS_1 to P_1, 200 from RMS_1 to P_3, 100 from RMS_2 to P_1, 300 from RMS_2 to P_2, and 200 from RMS_3 to P_3 when RMS's were respectively Chicago, Louisville, and Columbus, and P's were Evansville, Lexington, and Fort Wayne.

Some Additional Considerations

Inequality of Availability and Requirements We said earlier that the transportation method can be applied only when the resources available equal the resources required. In the Alpha Company example, 900 shipments were needed and 900 were available. If the problem had originally stated that only 800 shipments were required by the destinations, an additional fictitious destination would be created and added to the matrix. This new dummy plant, P_4, would become a column with a requirement of 100 shipments, and the adjustment would provide the necessary equality. A zero cost coefficient would be inserted in each cell of the dummy column to reflect the fact that assignments in these cells are fictitious, having no real cost. The use of a dummy row or column, whichever is needed, is equivalent to the use of slack variables in the simplex method.

Degeneracy A condition called degeneracy exists in a transportation problem when the number of used cells is less than $(m + n - 1)$. Degeneracy can occur at the initial or at intermediate stages of the problem. When degeneracy exists, it means that a unique stepping stone path cannot be identified for evaluating an unused cell. A standard procedure for overcoming degeneracy calls for placing an arbitrarily small, fictitious assignment called *theta* (Θ) in one of the currently unused cells. The cell with *theta* is then treated as if it were a used cell during this stage of the problem. *Theta* is not, however, a real assignment, and it does not result in any real cost.

To illustrate the use of *theta*, suppose we had the intermediate solution shown in Figure S7.7 (*a*). The four used cells are not adequate for evaluating the unused cells, since $(3 + 3 - 1) = 5$ used cells are needed. A *theta* must be added—but where? The choice is arbitrary, but time can be saved by adding *theta* to an empty cell that will allow as many unused cells as possible to be evaluated. In this example, *theta* is added to $\text{RMS}_2 - \text{P}_1$ in part (*b*) of the figure. This cell then becomes one of the stepping stones for evaluating $\text{RMS}_1 - \text{P}_1$, $\text{RMS}_3 - \text{P}_2$, and $\text{RMS}_3 - \text{P}_3$. The evaluation path for $\text{RMS}_3 - \text{P}_3$ is traced out in the figure. *Theta* remains in the matrix until it is subtracted out, or until a real allocation is made into its cell. It then disappears from the problem.

Maximization Problems Sometimes the problem has a maximization rather than minimization objective. The same procedure is used in either case. In a maximization problem, the cell evaluations have a reverse interpretation. When maximizing, a positive cell evaluation indicates that further improvement is possible in that cell. A negative evaluation indicates that the cell offers an undesirable change.

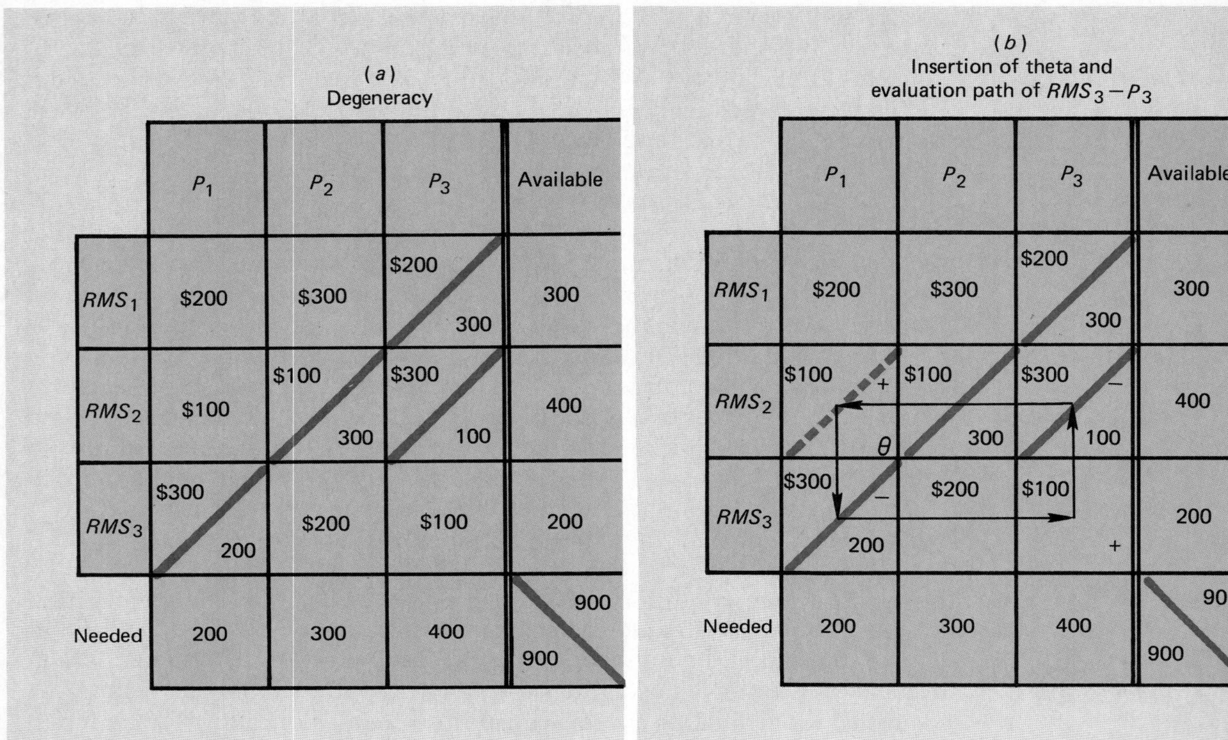

FIGURE S7.7
Degenerate solution for Alpha Processing Company

Alternative Optimal Solutions The final optimal solution may not be unique. Alternative optimal solutions exist whenever any unused cells have zero cell evaluations. A zero evaluation means that although the existing solution mix can be changed, the criterion value will not change.

REVIEW AND DISCUSSION QUESTIONS

1. In general, how do you decide which cost elements to include in or exclude from the cells of a transportation LP problem?
2. What problem characteristics must exist to enable the use of the transportation method of LP?

3. Explain what is happening when you use the stepping stone procedure for cell evaluation.
4. What is meant by the property of "homogeneity"? Why is it important?
5. Identify the similarities and differences of the transportation and simplex methods of LP.
6. What is the significance of having $(m + n - 1)$ used cells in solution? Will an optimal solution have $(m + n - 1)$ used cells?
7. Describe the northwest corner rule as a method for obtaining an initial feasible solution. Are there other ways of getting an initial feasible solution? Explain.
8. What conditions must exist to enable you to know an optimal solution has been found? That an alternative optimal solution exists?
9. If total resources available are unequal to the total required, what adjustments must be made in formulating the problem?
10. Why are dummy cells assigned a cost coefficient of zero? Can non-zero cost coefficients be used? Explain.
11. For an optimal solution matrix, give an economic interpretation of the cell evaluations.
12. What is the significance of degeneracy in transportation LP problems?
13. What types of locational problems can be aided by the transportation method of LP?

PROBLEMS

Reinforcing Fundamentals

1. Consider the following problem, in which costs are recorded for allocating one unit from each source to each destination:

Source	Destination *A*	*B*	*C*	Maximum units available
1	$1	$3	$2	300
2	2	4	1	300
3	3	2	3	300
Minimum units requested	355	395	150	

(a) Use the northwest corner rule to obtain an initial feasible solution.
(b) What is the cost of this initial solution?
(c) Find the minimum cost solution.
(d) What is the optimal allocation pattern, and what is its cost?
(e) Is there an alternative optimal solution?

2. Suppose the data matrix in problem 1 contained profit figures rather than costs. Find the profit maximizing solution.
3. The costs of shipping a unit from each source to each destination, along with the rim requirements, are shown below.

Source	Destination A	B	C	D	Source availability (units)
1	$7	$5	$8	$5	728
2	6	4	9	7	475
3	3	6	10	8	775
Destination requirements (units)	226	675	351	455	

(a) Develop an initial feasible solution using the northwest corner rule.
(b) Find the optimal solution.
(c) Interpret the optimal solution.

4. Following are the source availabilities, destination requirements, and the costs of assigning a unit from each source to each destination:

Source	Destination A	B	C	Source availability (units)
1	$4	$7	$3	250
2	5	6	2	150
3	3	7	5	250
4	6	1	4	200
Destination requirements (units)	350	300	200	

Develop an initial feasible solution using the northwest corner rule, and find the optimal solution.

5. Bill's Gravel Company operates three gravel pits from which loads of gravel are shipped to various construction sites. Pit 1 has a monthly capacity of 100 loads; 85 loads can be delivered from pit 2, and pit 3 can supply 145 loads each month. Requests for deliveries next month have come from four construction sites, *A* (121 loads), *B* (87 loads), *C* (59 loads), and *D* (94 loads). Bill's profits depend on which pit is used to supply each construction site:

Profit per load of gravel From pit	Construction site A	B	C	D
1	$24	$30	$27	$32
2	29	19	21	36
3	26	29	20	18

What should Bill do?

Challenging Exercises

6. Set up problem 1 in a simplex format.
7. Refer to problem 11 at the end of Chapter 7. Solve the problem using the transportation method. Which site should be selected, Knoxville or Dallas? Explain.
8. A company has factories at cities, *V*, *W*, and *X*. Management will add an additional plant at city *Y* or *Z*, with an annual capacity of 500,000 units of output. Capacities of existing plants are 702,000 at *V*, 520,000 at *W*, and 818,000 at *X*. City *Y* is attractive

because labor costs will average only \$5.10 per unit, compared to \$5.40 at city *Z*. Unit labor costs are \$5.25 at *V*, \$6.30 at *W*, and \$5.70 at *X*. The factories annually ship output to wholesalers in cities *A* (615,000 units), *B* (961,000 units), and *C* (914,000 units), with shipping costs as follows:

From factory	Average cost of shipping one unit to wholesaler *A*	*B*	*C*
V	\$1.00	\$1.50	\$1.25
W	1.25	1.30	1.10
X	.90	1.15	1.35
Y	1.05	.95	1.00
Z	.95	.80	1.10

Which site, *Y* or *Z*, is most attractive?

SELECTED READINGS

Anderson, D. R., D. J. Sweeney, and T. A. Williams. *An Introduction to Management Science*. 2nd ed. St. Paul, Minn.: West Publishing Co., 1979.

Bierman, H., Jr., C. P. Bonini, and W. H. Hausman. *Quantitative Analysis for Business Decisions*, 5th ed. Homewood, Ill.: Richard D. Irwin, Inc., 1977.

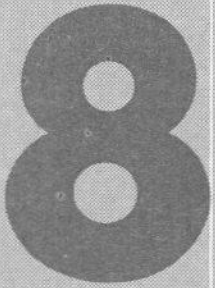

Layout Planning

Layout planning and machine or assembly line balancing have always been given priority in our operations.

World competition and technological advancements have forced significant changes in our layout planning process. We are utilizing computer aided layouts for increased productivity and alternate design analysis. Computer software packages are used to determine total cost relationships, for example, the materials department's most effective combination of "move and stores" and reduction of in-process material cost.

Participative management processes and employee involvement have become an integral part of effective layout planning.

"Selling" new projects and effective implementation are the results of sound layout practices reflecting the everchanging workplace environment.

Utilization of the tools for layout planning discussed in this chapter are basic to understanding and optimizing the operations layout function.

William W. Willoughby
Manager, Engineering Support
BOC Powertrain
General Motors Corporation
Flint, Michigan

Mr. Willoughby's comments demonstrate that successful internal operations depend upon the physical layout of facilities. Materials flows, productivity, and human relationships all are involved in a changing environment. Planning for these changes is

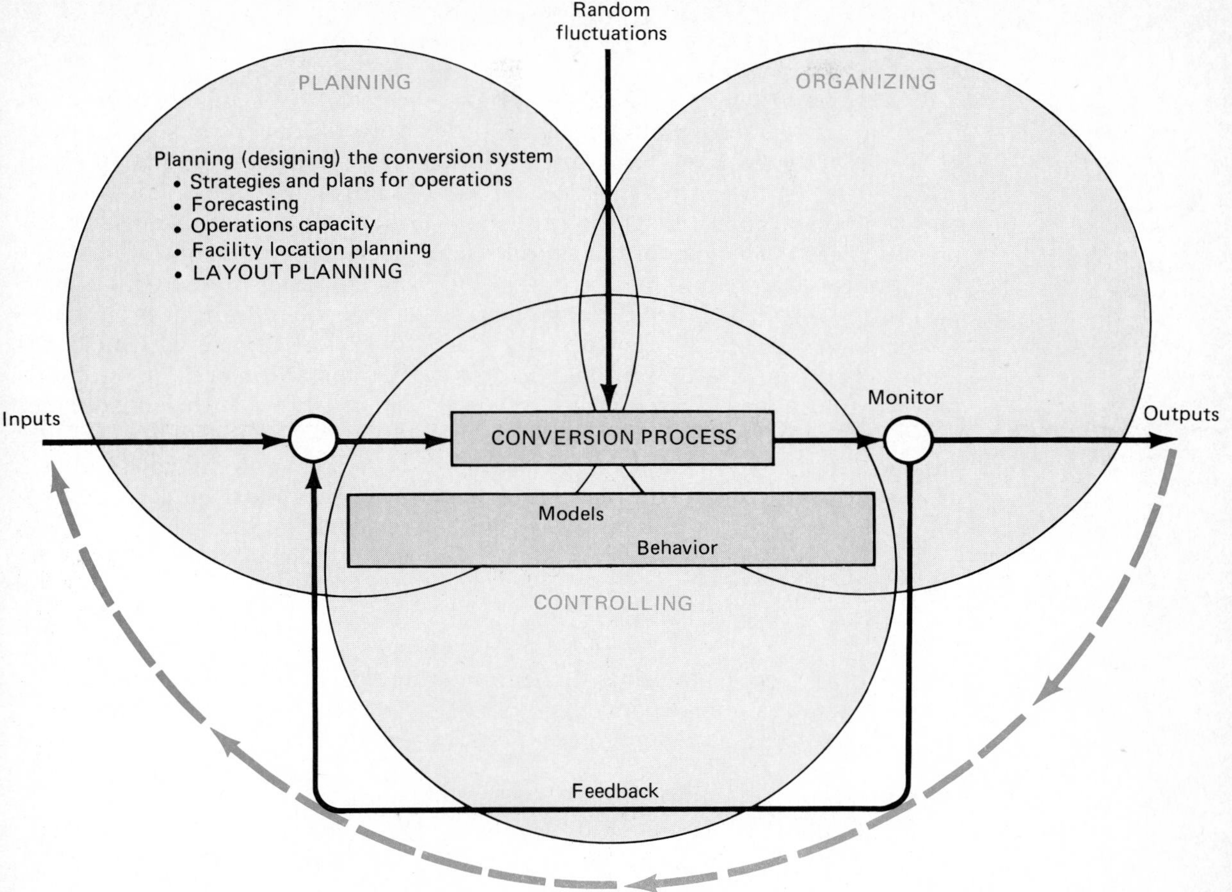

FIGURE 8.1
Production/operations management activities

an important part of the design process in operations management. In Chapters 6 and 7, we focused on two aspects of conversion process design—establishing capacity and facility location. We continue our emphasis on planning now by considering the internal arrangement of the conversion facility. Figure 8.1 shows how layout planning fits into our production/operations model; it also stresses the importance of modeling and behavioral considerations in layout planning.

Layout design interrelates with the capacity decision and the processing technology, both of which dictate some spatial requirements on the facility. On the input side of operations, for example, capacity and technology require that certain quantities of raw materials be on hand, stored in appropriate places, to allow subsequent operations to flow smoothly. The sizes and locations of these storage and work-in-process areas must be considered in layout.

The locations of various departments must also be decided. Equipment maintenance departments may have to be located near some especially breakdown-prone departments to ensure continuous, uninterrupted work flows. At the output side of conversion, finished goods storage areas and the conveyances for getting finished products into storage must both be considered. The size of the product and the volume of output will dictate storage area requirements; but so will our shipping plans, which are part of the physical distribution system. Large volumes of output produced to order may be transported directly from the end of the conversion line and packed into nearby railroad cars for immediate shipment. Or outputs may go into a large warehouse area, to be loaded after a future customer order has been received. The design of the system will determine costs of storage and materials handling. As we shall see, some modeling techniques are useful for layout planning, and behavioral factors must be considered too. Let's begin by finding out just what layout planning is.

LAYOUT CONCEPTS

To see how layout planning affects operating costs and effectiveness, we have to examine layout concepts—particularly how different types of layout designs apply in different situations.

Types of Manufacturing and Service Operations

The operations function in both manufacturing and service organizations can be divided into two basic types, intermittent and continuous, depending on the degree of product standardization and volume of output.

Intermittent Operations Intermittent manufacturing is conversion with production characteristics of low product volume, general purpose equipment, labor-intense operations, interrupted product flow, frequent schedule changes, large product mix, and made-to-order products. Services with these same characteristics (automobile repair facilities, for example) are also classified as intermittent conversion operations.

Continuous Operations Continuous conversion operations are featured by high product volume, special purpose equipment, capital-intense operations, uninterrupted product flow, few schedule changes, small product mix, and standardized products made to inventory. As was the case with intermittent operations, services with characteristics similar to those in continuous manufacturing operations are also classified as continuous conversion operations. Because of the frequent labor intensity of service operations, however, most service conversion processes are intermittent rather than continuous.

Basic Layout Designs

A layout design is the location or configuration of departments, work stations, and equipment that constitute the conversion process. It is the spatial arrangement of the physical resources that are used to create the product.

We will discuss three basic layout designs: process-oriented, product-oriented, and fixed-position. These designs are differentiated by the types of work flows they entail; the work flow, in turn, is dictated by the nature of the product.

Process Layout Process-oriented layouts are appropriate when work flows are not standardized for all units of output, a condition that is found in intermittent manufacturing. Unstandardized work flows occur either when a variety of different products is produced, or when one basic type of product with many possible variations is made. *In a process layout, the processing components (work centers or departments) are grouped together according to the type of function they perform.* Distribution warehouses, hospitals and medical clinics, universities, office buildings, and job shop facilities are often designed in this manner. Figure 8.2 shows a process layout for a medical clinic. Another characteristic of process layouts is the grouping of similar types of machines so that the product can travel to the machines required by the operation (see Figure 8.3).

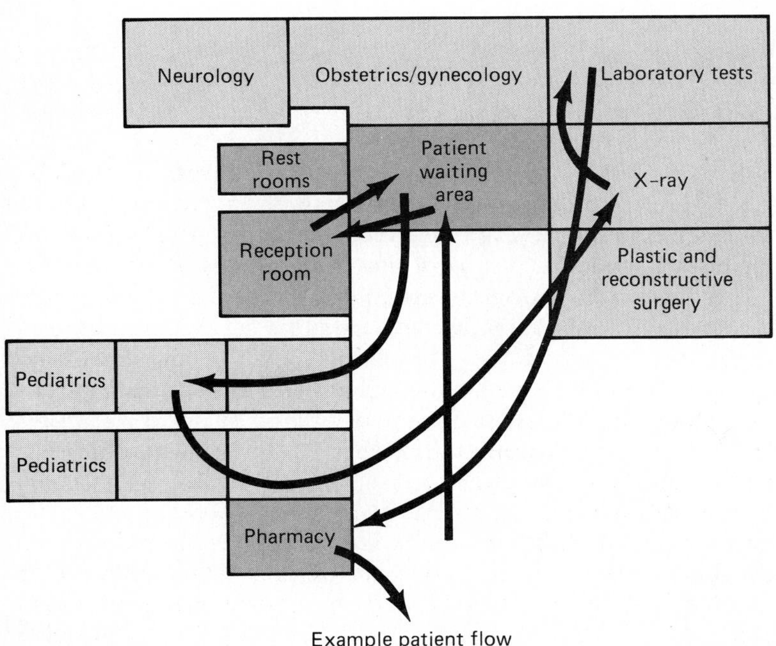

FIGURE 8.2
Process layout for medical clinic

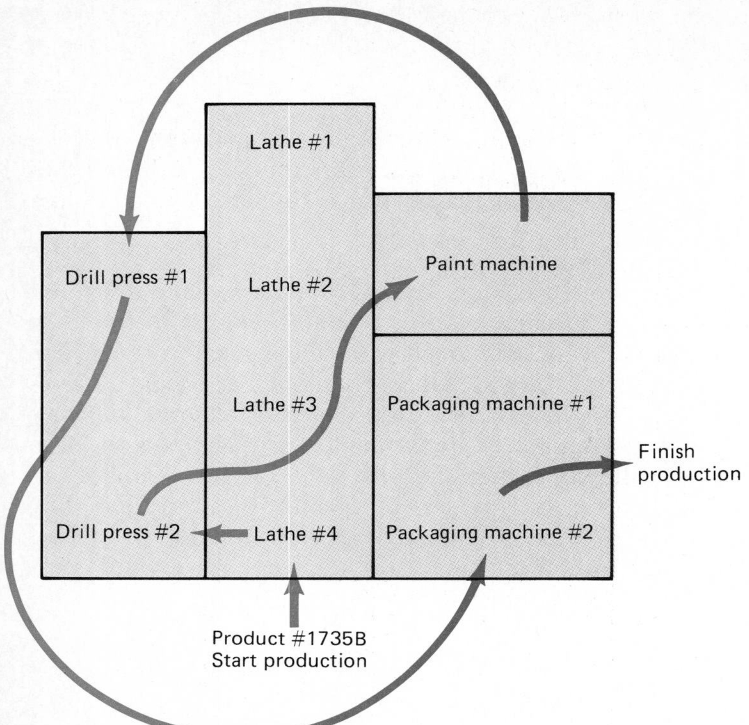

FIGURE 8.3
Process layout in manufacturing

Product Layout Product-oriented layouts are used when one standardized product is being produced, usually in large volume (a characteristic of continuous or repetitive manufacturing). Each of the units of output requires the same sequence of operations from beginning to end. *In product layout, work centers and equipment are therefore ideally arranged in a line to provide the specialized sequence of operations that will result in product buildup.* Each work center may provide one highly specialized part of the total buildup sequence. Automatic car washes, cafeteria serving lines, mass medical exams for military recruits, automobile assembly, and beverage bottling plants use product-oriented layouts. Figure 8.4 illustrates a product layout organized to provide the necessary sequence to build up, from beginning to end, a manufactured product. Figure 8.5 illustrates a familiar product layout, an automated carwash.

Fixed-position Layout Fixed-position layouts are necessary when, because of size, shape, or any other characteristic, it isn't feasible to move the product. *In fixed-position layout, the product remains in one location; tools, equipment, and human skills are brought to it, as needed, to perform the*

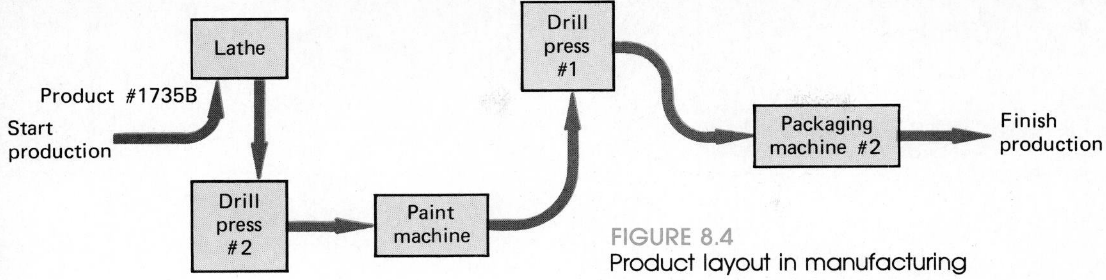

FIGURE 8.4
Product layout in manufacturing

appropriate stages of buildup. Layouts for building ships, locomotives, and aircraft are often of this type, as are agricultural operations, in which plowing, planting, fertilizing, and harvesting are performed as needed in the fields. A home plumbing repair operation in which resources are brought to the service site is illustrated in Figure 8.6.

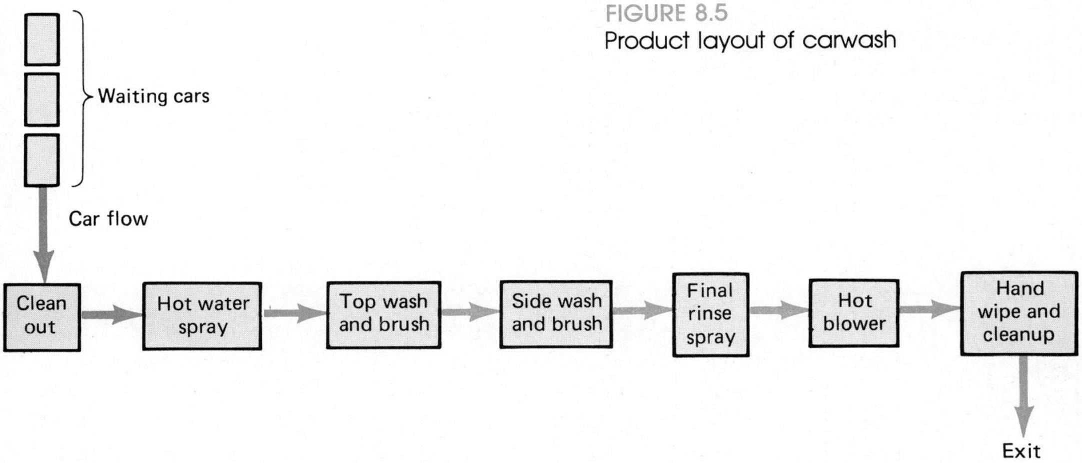

FIGURE 8.5
Product layout of carwash

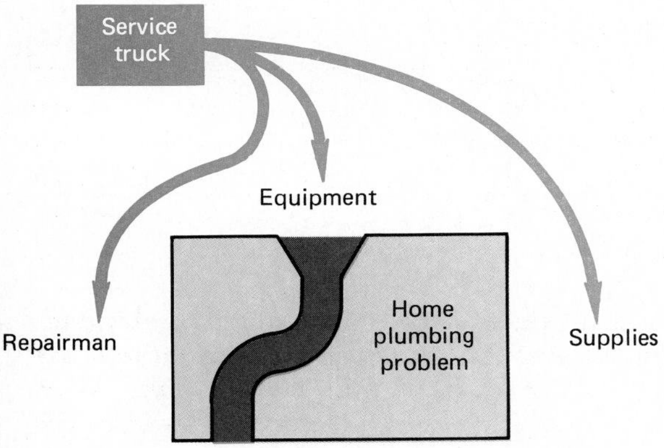

FIGURE 8.6
Fixed position layout for plumbing repair service

TABLE 8.1
Characteristics of layout designs

Aspect of the conversion process	Product-oriented	Process-oriented	Fixed-position
Product characteristics	Layout geared to producing a standardized product, in large volume, at stable rates of output	Layout for diversified products requiring common fundamental operations, in varying volume, at varying rates of output	Low volume, each unit often unique
Product flow pattern	Straight line flow of product; same sequence of standard operations on each unit	Diversified flow pattern; each order (product) may require unique sequence of operations	Little or no product flow; equipment and human resources brought to site as needed
Human skills requirement	Tolerance for performing routine, repetitive tasks at imposed pace; highly specialized work content	Primarily skilled craftsmen; can perform without close supervision and with moderate degree of adaptability	High degree of task flexibility often required; specific work assignments and location vary
Supporting staff	Large administrative and indirect support staff for scheduling materials and people, work analysis and maintenance	Must possess skills for scheduling, materials handling, and production and inventory control	High degree of scheduling and coordinating skills required
Material handling	Material flows predictable, systematized and often automated	Type and volume of handling required is variable; duplication of handling often occurs	Type and volume of handling required is variable, often low; may require heavy-duty general purpose handling equipment
Inventory requirements	High turnover of raw material and work-in-process inventories	Low turnover of raw material and work-in-process inventories; high raw materials inventories	Variable inventories due to lengthy production cycle can result in inventory tieups for long periods
Space utilization	Efficient utilization of space, high rate of product output per unit of space	Relatively low rate of output per unit of facility space; large work-in-process requirements	For conversion within the facility, a low rate of space utilization per unit of output may occur
Capital requirements	High capital investment in equipment and processes that perform very specialized functions	Equipment and processes are general purpose and feature flexibility	General purpose equipment and processes that are mobile
Product cost components	Relatively high fixed costs; low unit direct labor and materials costs	Relatively low fixed costs; high unit costs for direct labor, materials (inventory) and materials handling	High labor and materials costs; relatively low fixed costs

Combination Layouts Often pure layouts do not exist, and a combination layout must be used. This is most common for process and product combinations.

EXAMPLE

Refrigerator manufacturers use a process-oriented arrangement to produce various parts and subcomponents. Metal stamping may be consolidated into one department, all types of welding in another, and various heat-treating processes grouped into yet a third work center. At the same time, all these components are brought together in assembly operations, especially for final assembly of the product. The final assembly operations are designed on a product flow or product-oriented basis.

Differences Among Basic Layout Designs

Does it really matter what type of basic design is selected? Yes. The appropriate layout depends upon many factors: anticipated volume, degree of product standardization, physical characteristics of the product, available alternative technologies, and the availability of adequate long-term and short-term financial resources. Table 8.1 summarizes some ways in which basic layouts differ from one another.

For some products, only one type of conversion process may be technologically feasible. In those cases, the process will dictate the type of layout design. But sometimes several methods of conversion may exist. Then the choice of layout design should be based on relative economic advantages and the availability of financial resources. Behavioral and modeling techniques are also important for evaluating design alternatives in both product and process layouts. Let's begin examining modeling and behavioral techniques that are applicable to process layout.

DEVELOPING THE PROCESS LAYOUT: MODELS AND BEHAVIOR

Process Layout Models

Many kinds of models are useful in layout planning. Mathematical analysis can help managers conceptualize the problem; computer models can provide quick approximations of good layouts; and physical models (templates and scale models, among others) can help us visualize the physical aspects of layouts.

EXAMPLE

In designing and constructing a new manufacturing facility in Kentucky, an initial task was to list all equipment to be placed into a boiler room, which was to be attached to the main building. This task had to be done first, because only after the room had been sized could the price be negotiated with the general building contractor. First, the floor dimensions and heights of all boilers, air compressors, water pumps, and similar equipment were obtained. Second, templates were cut to scale. Third, alternative layouts were tried until a reasonable layout was found. Upon review, an experienced maintenance foreman pointed out that to "rod-out" (clean) the boilers, a wall would have to be knocked out. To avoid having to knock a wall out, the boilers were turned in another direction on the template; but this increased the space requirements. After review by several technical people, a reasonable layout and size were decided upon and the boiler room constructed accordingly.

Graphic and Schematic Analysis Perhaps the most common layout technique is the use of templates, two-dimensional cutouts of equipment drawn to scale. These cutouts are moved about by trial and error within a scaled model of the walls and columns of the facility. This technique is used for all three types of layouts, process, product, and fixed. Similarly, microcomputer graphics can visually display tentative layouts on a cathode-ray tube and modifications can be made by keyboard manipulations. The basic procedures for such analyses have been summarized:

> The most familiar tools utilized for the solution of layout problems have been graphic and schematic models, particularly two- and three-dimensional templates, assembly charts, operation process charts, and product flow process charts.
>
> Recent improvements in graphic and schematic layout techniques include "link analysis," "travel charting," and "operations sequence analysis." These techniques utilize data collected on the amount of materials flowing from each department to every other department for some time period. The data are accumulated into a matrix form which is frequently referred to as a "from-to chart," "cross chart," or "flow matrix." The methodology for reducing materials flow is to locate departments in such a way as to minimize the volume of nonadjacent departmental flow.[1]

Although some of these techniques are beyond the scope of this book, we will be encountering some product and process charts in a future chapter on job design and work measurement.

A Load-distance Model In a process-oriented facility, diversified products are processed, work flows in various day to day patterns, and a relatively high amount of material must be handled. The flow path of a product through successive stages of buildup reveals many movements from one work center to another. An outpatient of a medical clinic may move through as many as six different work centers for treatment. The manufacture of a special-order tool may require that it move through as many as

[1]Thomas E. Vollmann and Elwood S. Buffa, "The Facilities Layout Problem in Perspective," *Management Science* 12, no. 10 (June 1966), pp. B451–52.

twenty different work centers as buildup progresses from raw materials to finished form. Although the flow path in each case depends upon the particular needs of the individual product, each product must be transferred or moved among many work centers. All this movement costs money. People and equipment must be on hand, and space must be available for storing the product while it awaits its turn in the next work center. Since transporting per se adds no direct value to the product, it is a wasteful expenditure. Managers of process-oriented facilities therefore seek layout designs that will reduce or minimize unnecessary flows among departments.

The most commonly used quantitative model for process layout considers not only the *number* of interdepartmental moves of a product but also the *distances* over which the moves are made. A long move is usually more costly than a short move. In this model, we try to minimize the criterion (C) that considers both the number of loads and distances moved. Minimize C where

$$C = \sum_{i=1}^{N} \sum_{j=1}^{N} L_{ij} D_{ij} \tag{8.1}$$

where N = the number of work centers,
L_{ij} = the number of loads or movements of work between work centers i and j, and
D_{ij} = the distance between work centers i and j

The criterion (C) being minimized may be viewed as a cost by assuming all load-distance moves have constant unit costs. If unit costs are unequal, equation 8.1 could be modified by multiplying $L_{ij}D_{ij}$ by K_{ij}, where K_{ij} is the cost to move a unit load a unit distance between work centers i and j.

We must begin by estimating the number of loads, L_{ij}, expected to be moved among all pairs of departments during an appropriate planning horizon, say one year. These estimated annual volumes of movements can be summarized in a flow matrix like that in Table 8.2.[2] Estimates can be obtained from past records in production control, work flow analysis, or aggregate production schedules.

The next step is to determine the distances, D_{ij}, among all pairs of departments. These will depend on the relative locations you assign to the departments in your layout design. You begin the design process by proposing an initial layout configuration; departments are assigned to avail-

[2]The flow matrix in Table 8.2 is appropriate when the *direction* of flow between departments is immaterial. In some situations, however, a load from i to j may be more or less costly than a load moving from j to i. In those cases, an expanded flow matrix must be developed so as to identify the direction of flow. For a discussion of this expanded treatment, see Richard A. Johnson, William T. Newell, and Roger C. Vergin, *Operations Management: A Systems Concept* (Boston: Houghton Mifflin Co., 1972).

TABLE 8.2
Flow matrix showing estimated number of loads, L_{ij}, per planning period among all pairs of departments

		Department				
		1	2	3	4	5
	1	—	220	130	400	370
Loads moved between depts. 1 and 2 (→ 220)	2		—	0	400	470
	3			—	150	400
	4				—	100
	5					—

able spaces. Then, using equation 8.1, you measure the effectiveness of the initial configuration. Finally, you modify the initial layout so that you can increase effectiveness by reducing transport costs. Repeat this process until you can find no further improvement.

Actually, the cost effectiveness of each possible design need *not* be fully calculated with equation 8.1. Although many different designs are possible, many of them are equivalent, or nearly so, from a transport cost viewpoint, and they need not be calculated separately. Consider the situation shown in Figure 8.7: six work centers could be assigned to six available areas in these four different ways, among others. From a geometric viewpoint, the four configurations are nearly equivalent. In each design, these pairs of departments are located as close to one another as is possible: 1–2, 2–3, 4–5, 5–6, 1–4, 2–5, 3–6. Further redesigns cannot reduce transport costs of flows between these work centers. Therefore, the evaluation criterion needs to consider only the flows between *nonadjacent* departments, 1–3, 1–6, 3–4, 4–6. *This means that the* L_{ij} D_{ij} *computations following the initial evaluation for a layout design can be reduced just to those with nonadjacent flows.* The procedure is directed trial and error, and optimality is not guaranteed. We will illustrate these concepts with a simplified example. After reading it, you should be able to do a simple layout analysis.

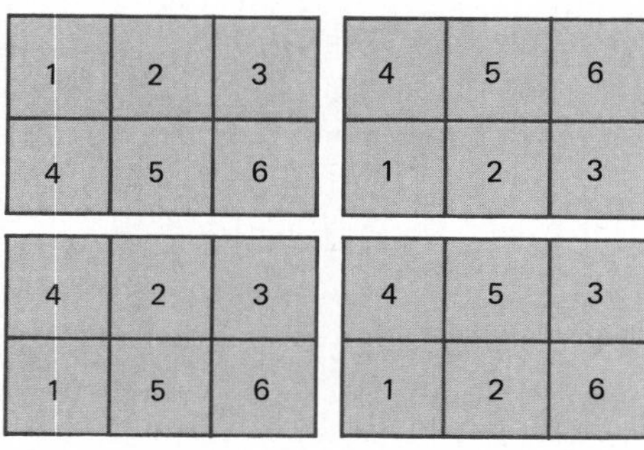

FIGURE 8.7
Four different but equivalent layout configurations

EXAMPLE

Greenwich Supply Company is a wholesale warehouse distribution facility. It receives orders from building contractors for kitchen cabinets and appliances. Inventories of various products are stored in the warehouse and retrieved, as needed, to fill each order. All products for an order are transported by forklift truck to a centralized packing area where they are packaged for shipment to the contractor. Each completed order is then moved by forklift from the packing area to the shipping and receiving dock. We will evaluate the warehouse layout to see if it can be modified to reduce materials handling costs.

The existing facility layout is diagrammed in Figure 8.8. Section 1 is the shipping and receiving dock, and section 9 is the current packing area. The other fourteen sections are storage areas for different types of appliances and cabinets.

Materials handling flows occur between the packing area and the other fifteen sections. Loads are hauled to area 1 from only one source, section 9. All other loads flow from the remaining sections *into* section 9. In this illustration, no flows occur between storage areas. The location of the shipping and receiving dock is fixed; it cannot be relocated. All other sections are eligible for relocation.

An examination of records for the last two years reveals that the average annual load flows from departments 2 through 8 to department 9 are: 2–500, 3–80, 4–320, 5–140, 6–150, 7–160, and 8–330; from departments 10 through 16 to 9 are: 10–250, 11–100, 12–140, 13–240, 14–100, 15–240, and 16–500. The load flow from department 9 to department 1 is 2,500. We now use equation 8.1 to calculate the effectiveness of the existing layout for this representative flow pattern. Table 8.3 shows the calculations for both adjacent and nonadjacent loads. The existing layout has a load distance rating of 12,300.

To improve the layout, we try to move those departments with heavy load flows closer together. Departments 8 and 9, for example, can be exchanged, thus moving the packing area closer to the shipping dock. We could also relocate department 16 closer to the packing area, and department 14 could be relocated to a more remote setting. A revised layout incorporating these and other changes is shown in Figure 8.9.

This process is then repeated to obtain a second revised layout, also shown in Figure 8.9. Overall, the layout analysis has reduced load movements by 34 percent. If the new layout is implemented, material handling costs are expected to be reduced by about this same amount. In addition to these direct cost savings, we expect that day-to-day congestion will be reduced in the order filling operation.

Some Limitations Since many vital aspects of the real layout problem are not considered in our example model, it may not yield a realistic design. At best, our analysis provides a starting point, a layout that can be modified to account for additional complexities. Often the sizes and/or shapes of all departments cannot be uniform. Special restrictions may be imposed by aisle requirements, limited access to work areas, different types of materials handling methods, and electrical and plumbing requirements. Other

	2	3	4	5	6
1 Shipping and receiving	7	8	9 Packing area	10	11
	12	13	14	15	16

FIGURE 8.8
Existing layout of Greenwich Supply Company's relative locations of product storage areas (aisles omitted)

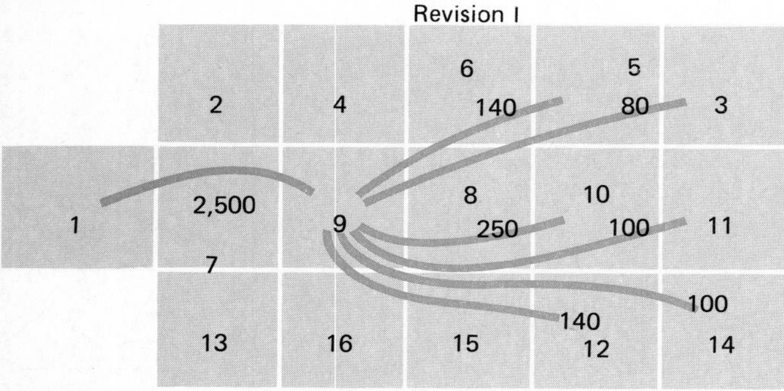

Effectiveness			
Adjacent departments		Nonadjacent departmen1	
Departments	$L_{ij}D_{ij}$	Departments	$L_{ij}D_{ij}$
2-9	500	3-9	240
4-9	320	5-9	280
6-9	150	10-9	500
7-9	160	11-9	300
8-9	330	12-9	280
13-9	240	14-9	300
15-9	240	9-1	5,000
16-9	500		
Subtotal = 2,440		Subtotal = 6,900	
Total effectiveness = 2,440 + 6,900 = 9,340			
Improvement over initial layout = 24%			

FIGURE 8.9
Two revised layouts with effectiveness ratings computed

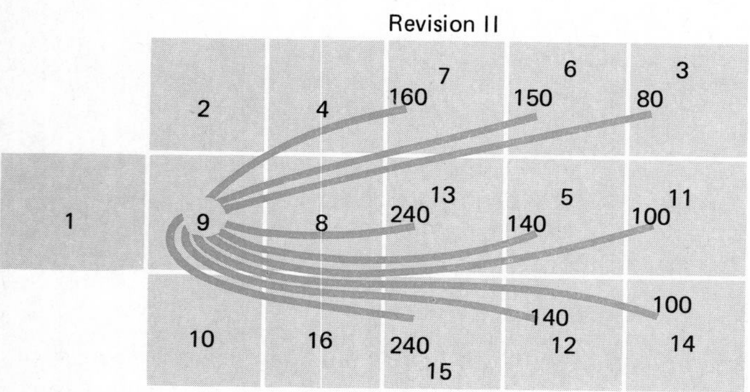

Effectiveness			
Adjacent departments		Nonadjacent departments	
Departments	$L_{ij}D_{ij}$	Departments	$L_{ij}D_{ij}$
9-1	2,500	3-9	320
2-9	500	5-9	420
4-9	320	6-9	450
8-9	330	7-9	320
10-9	250	11-9	400
16-9	500	12-9	420
		13-9	480
		14-9	400
		15-9	480
Subtotal = 4,400		Subtotal = 3,690	
Total effectiveness = 4,400 + 3,690 = 8,090			
Improvement over initial layout = 34.2%			
Improvement over Revision I = 13.4%			

TABLE 8.3
Calculation of existing layout effectiveness

Adjacent departments			
Adjacent departments	Unit distance between departments (D_{ij})	Number of loads between departments (L_{ij})	Loads times distance ($L_{ij}D_{ij}$)
3–9	1	80	1 × 80 = 80
4–9	1	320	1 × 320 = 320
5–9	1	140	1 × 140 = 140
8–9	1	330	1 × 330 = 330
10–9	1	250	1 × 250 = 250
13–9	1	240	1 × 240 = 240
14–9	1	100	1 × 100 = 100
15–9	1	240	1 × 240 = 240

$$\sum_{i=1}^{N}\sum_{j=1}^{N} L_{ij}D_{ij} \text{ for}$$

movements between adjacent departments = 1,700

Nonadjacent departments			
Nonadjacent departments	Unit distance between departments (D_{ij})	Number of loads between departments (L_{ij})	Loads times distance ($L_{ij}D_{ij}$)
2–9	2	500	500 × 2 = 1,000
6–9	2	150	150 × 2 = 300
7–9	2	160	160 × 2 = 320
11–9	2	100	100 × 2 = 200
12–9	2	140	140 × 2 = 280
16–9	2	500	500 × 2 = 1,000
9–1	3	2,500	2,500 × 3 = 7,500

$$\sum_{i=1}^{N}\sum_{j=1}^{N} L_{ij}D_{ij} \text{ for}$$

movements between nonadjacent departments = 10,600
Total effectiveness for all departments = 1,700 + 10,600 = 12,300

unique process considerations may require, for example, that noisy operations not be adjacent to audio-testing areas sensitive to noise, or that operations that create contaminants should not be near expensive instruments sensitive to dirt or dust. In addition, the model we have used can require lengthy computational efforts, particularly when the number of departments and combinations of interdepartmental flows become large. For these reasons, alternative types of layout analysis are often used.

Computer Models Many computer based layout models have been developed. We will briefly discuss only one of them, CRAFT, the Computerized Relative Allocation of Facilities Technique.[3] CRAFT is a heuristic procedure (one in which a set of rules is systematically applied); it rearranges departmental locations in an attempt to find configurations that reduce the materials handling costs of the facility. The user has no assurance that the *best* (least cost) possible configuration will ever be found. Instead, the idea is to obtain a *satisfactory* layout design. CRAFT can help you avoid tedious hand calculations by evaluating thousands of alternative layout patterns quickly on a computer.

CRAFT can handle facilities consisting of up to forty work centers of different shapes and sizes, and individual work centers that are either movable or immovable for purposes of relocation. These features take into account realistic restrictions imposed by the construction of buildings. CRAFT also considers differences in types and costs of materials handling among work centers. To use CRAFT, the analyst must provide certain types of input information:

1. An initial layout configuration showing the overall size (square feet) of the facility, and the number, location, and size of each department.
2. A load matrix identifying the volumes of materials flows among all departments.
3. A transport cost matrix identifying the cost of transporting a load for one unit distance between departments with interchanges of materials.

The evaluation procedure uses a criterion similar to equation 8.1. After calculating the effectiveness of the initial layout, CRAFT exchanges pairs or triplets of departments. The effectiveness of each exchange is evaluated, the best of these exchanges is adopted, and the entire process is repeated. When total materials handling costs can be reduced no further or when a specified number of repetitions has been reached, the best available solution is printed out. The output consists of a layout in the form of a block diagram and a statement of the associated material handling costs.

Many limitations exist in the final design obtained from CRAFT. It provides a starting point, but further modification is required to get a realistic design. Human judgment, based on both future plans and knowledge of past difficulties, must be applied to the layout design.

A more recent version of CRAFT, CRAFT-M, produces a layout that incorporates department move costs and material handling improvement factors in the analysis.[4] This modification attempts to overcome some of CRAFT's earlier limitations.

---

[3]Elwood S. Buffa, Gordon C. Armour, and Thomas Vollmann, "Allocating Facilities with CRAFT," *Harvard Business Review* 42, no. 2 (March–April 1964), pp. 136–58.

[4]Philip E. Hicks and Troy E. Cowan, "CRAFT-M for Layout Rearrangement," *Industrial Engineering* (May 1976), pp. 30–35.

Behavioral Aspects of Process Layout

Operations managers must consider individual and group behavior when planning a process-oriented layout. Why? For several reasons. The layout specialist's problem-solving ability, which is necessary for developing the final design, is a form of individual behavior. Also, the layout design, once implemented, can affect both employee relationships and group behavior and customer behavior and satisfaction.

Behavior in Layout Design Until recently, the graphic and systematic techniques we've described were used almost exclusively by layout designers. But within the last twenty years, the designer's role seems to have changed with the introduction and increasing use of computer heuristics. Contemporary writings seem to assume that these computer approaches are superior to the traditional designs that people developed. But are they? Some studies suggest that they may not be.[5] The Scriabin and Vergin study found that people developed more economical designs to reduce materials handling costs than did three of the more widely publicized computer-based design models. This was true for both large and small layout problems. Although modern technologists have assumed that computer models would be superior to humans' designs, especially as the size (number of departments or work centers) of the layout problem increases, the experimental results did not support this assumption. The researchers offer the following possible explanation of their findings:

> It may well be that in problems of larger size the ability of man to recognize and visualize complex patterns gives him an edge over the essentially mechanical procedures followed by the computer programs. Such an explanation is supported by experience in other types of problem solving . . . (179)

We can draw two conclusions from the results of this study. First, we must not be too hasty in adopting computer-based models at the expense of human experience and problem-solving skills until the question of relative superiority is answered. Second, some combination of human and computer interaction may lead to even better results. The researchers have stated the case for human involvement:

> If the computer algorithms do not afford a significant advantage in terms of results, that is, if certain persons can compete effectively with the computerized algorithms, then it stands to reason that those same persons could do even better in the overall layout problem, where they can apply their experience, concurrently taking into account other considerations (other than just materials handling costs) such as noise levels, ventilation, future expansion plans, and so on. (173)

[5]Michael Scriabin and Roger C. Vergin, "Comparison of Computer Algorithms and Visual Based Methods for Plant Layout," *Management Science* (October 1975), pp. 172–81. For different results and conclusions, see Thomas W. Trybus and Lewis D. Hopkins, "Human Vs. Computer Algorithms for the Plant Layout Problem," *Management Science* 26, no. 6 (June 1980), pp. 570–74.

Individual and Interpersonal Behavior of Employees We know that our environment affects how people feel about themselves and react toward others. The layout design can either help or hinder employees' relationships with each other. We don't know enough about this phenomenon yet to give precise design guidelines, but some initial efforts have been made to identify the impact of spatial arrangements on employee satisfaction, internal motivation, and performance.[6] The operations manager should keep abreast of new information about the impact of layout changes on human behavior.

Process layouts result in departmentalization of activities according to skills. Each skill or craft group establishes norms, agreements about behavior, that determine the kinds and amounts of productive effort its members make. Often these norms are compatible with official standards set by management, but at other times they are not. Group members often develop great pride in their craft specialties and strong feelings of group affiliation. A redesigned layout may inadvertently disrupt existing group relationships. If the relayout causes a group to be disbanded and its members reassigned to newly formed work centers, some time will have to elapse before new group structures fully develop. Employee reactions to these changes may be adverse, and absenteeism, employee turnover, and labor relations problems may all increase.

Another implication that stems from strong group affiliations has to do with the types of managerial skills that will be needed. Physical proximity and occupational similarities among members in a work center result in group interest and loyalty that are more inner-directed than outer-directed. Group loyalties can lead to conflicts among groups. As a result, *the manager of the entire operation must be particularly skilled at intergroup coordination.*

A different type of difficulty arises in the layout of facilities for service-producing organizations. Management may wish to locate departments so as to maximize professional interaction among specific types of employees rather than by process flows. When interaction between two departments is necessary, perhaps they should be located side by side, even though that may increase overall interdepartmental movements of records, paperwork, and people. Recently office layout designers have been paying greater attention to this behavioral element. In one study, a state government layout used three interlocking computer programs to place individuals who interact often next to one another; the goal was to maximize effectiveness. In a second similar study, linear programming was used in the layout of the College of Administration at The Ohio State University. In

---

[6]Randall S. Schuler, Larry P. Ritzman, and Vicki Davis, "Merging Prescriptive and Behavioral Approaches for Office Layout," *Journal of Operations Management* 1, no. 3 (February 1981), pp. 131–42.

this study, decision makers interacted with those undertaking modeling and programming efforts.[7]

Customer Behavior Process layout is frequently used when orders are taken to customer specifications and most orders are different from one another. For some organizations, this customer-producer interaction creates special problems, especially when the customer is present in the facility and takes part in the conversion process. In medical, dental, and legal facilities, welfare agencies, supermarkets, and banking businesses, individual customers (clients) have differing needs, and they may be "processed" through different departments accordingly. The layout can affect not only the quality and speed of service, but customer satisfaction as well. In these cases, layout is not just an operations problem, but also at least partially a marketing function. The layout of a full-service bank facility, for example, must be based on several criteria. Facilities for such daily transactions as withdrawals, deposits, and money orders must be conveniently located for quick processing of walk-in customers. At the same time, areas for loan applications must be both quickly accessible and private. Data processing facilities and maintenance and administrative offices can be placed in more remote locations. Overall, the facility must provide a balance between easy, quick service and customer convenience and satisfaction on the one hand and efficient flows of materials and information for internal operations on the other.

Materials handling efficiency, inventory minimization, and other such criteria, while of primary concern in warehousing and industrial facilities, may play very minor roles in deciding layout designs in some other organizations. Retail establishments like supermarkets and department stores rely on layout as a chief means of facilitating customer purchases. The decisions as to which products to group together and the amount of store space to allocate to each should be based on consumer behavior and preferences, not on internal operating measures like materials handling costs and so on. The data for determining good layouts often come from marketing research studies of consumer tastes, preferences, and expectations. Management determines locations of displays and products to aid the consumer and promote sales; this may require duplication of inventories to achieve logical clusters of individual products.

Measuring Subjective Criteria One of the primary parameters of layout design is flexibility, especially for organizations with a recent history of growth and change. In some organizations space changes occur frequently,

[7]Robert Jacobs, John Bradford, Larry Ritzmann, and Randall Schuler, "An Office Space Planning System: Application and Theoretical Foundations" (Working Paper, Management Sciences Department, The Ohio State University, October 1978); and Larry Ritzmann, John Bradford, and Robert Jacobs, "A Multiple Objective Approach to Space Planning for Academic Facilities," *Management Science* 25, no. 9 (September 1979), pp. 895–906.

and high costs of construction and reconstruction result. To offset these costs, in recent years open design strategies have been used increasingly. Basically, one massive room is subdivided into offices and work areas separated by movable panels, with special attention given to the acoustical properties throughout the structure. This arrangement retains a suitable degree of privacy and also provides flexibility at a reasonable cost.

Although a single effectiveness criterion sometimes may not apply, we may nevertheless be able to use a revision of our previous layout criterion. In equation 8.1, L_{ij} could be used as a subjective priority indicator instead of the number of loads between two departments. Early in the design phase of layout, management can use an arbitrary scale, say between 1 and 10, to rate the importance of having two departments located close together. A rating of 10 indicates the most importance, 1 the least importance. After rating the importance of proximity for all pairs of departments, management can summarize the resulting priorities in a matrix. This L_{ij} matrix can then be used in equation 8.1, and the layout procedure can proceed as we described it earlier. This procedure provides a systematic way of using subjective priorities, including behavioral phenomena, in layout analysis.

DEVELOPING THE PRODUCT LAYOUT: ASSEMBLY LINE MODELS AND BEHAVIOR

Organizations that produce large volumes of a single product can gain economic benefits from a product-oriented (assembly line) layout. Early in the twentieth century, Henry Ford revolutionized an industry and the U.S. economy by mass producing automobiles. Since each car was identical, the entire buildup sequence could be studied in careful detail. All work requirements were subdivided into smaller and smaller tasks that, when performed in proper sequence on each car, resulted in a large volume of finished cars each day. Each task was minutely studied by engineers and managers to find ways to do it more quickly and at lower cost. (This is called *job analysis*.) Better work methods, specialized equipment and tools, and extensive employee training were used to reduce performance times. Although many workers were required for the entire line, each one did his job so well that large volumes of cars flowed off the end of the line at a price that millions of people could afford. This, then, was the basic concept of the Ford assembly line. These fundamental concepts, including the product layout, are as applicable today as they were in 1913. Later, we shall examine some contemporary behavioral considerations that were of minor concern at the beginning of the century.

Product Layout Models

Graphic and Schematic Analysis Assembly lines are most often designed and laid out by industrial engineers. Historically, they have used trial-and-error manual techniques and templates, drawings, and graphical procedures to develop initial designs and then improve them. Unfortunately, for large facilities with many tasks and work stations we have no mathematical procedures for ensuring that the best possible design has been found. The quality of the design therefore depends upon the experience and judgment of qualified designers. Substantially the same graphic and schematic techniques are used as those we discussed for process layout.

Heuristics in Product Layout Mathematical and computer-based heuristic models can offer some assistance in obtaining a quality design. Applied to product layout, heuristics are logical sets of rules that help the layout analyst rapidly identify and evaluate many alternative designs, far more than could be evaluated manually or intuitively. These rules are developed as much by observation and experimentation as they are by theory, and they are often specially adapted to the specific problem at hand.

Defining the Design Problem The fundamental problem of layout planning for assembly lines is to find the number of work stations (workers), and the tasks to be performed at each station, so that a desired level of output is achieved. All of this is to be accomplished in such a way that excessive input resources are minimized.

Notice several important points in this definition. First, the design focuses on achieving a desired level of productive capability (output capacity). Second, if tasks are to be assigned to work stations, the *sequence* of tasks must be considered. Which tasks must be done first, and which ones may follow? Finally, the definition emphasizes our concern with attaining desired output *efficiently*, without using unnecessary input resources.

Capacity, Sequencing, and Efficiency Let's illustrate these ideas by using an example.

EXAMPLE

A manufacturer is developing plans for a facility to make aluminum storm windows. The desired minimum output capacity is 320 windows per day. The operations manager has obtained the tentative assembly line layout design shown in Table 8.4 and Figure 8.10. The manager wishes to know if this is a good design and if better designs are possible.

This is a good design if:

1. it meets the desired output capacity,
2. the sequence is technically feasible, and
3. it is an efficient line.

TABLE 8.4
Initial assembly line design for assembly of aluminum storm windows

Work station	Preceding work station	Task to be performed at work station	Task definition	Task time (seconds)
1	—	A	Assemble and position frame	70
2	1	B	Install rubber molding	80
3	2	C	Insert frame screws	40
		D	Install frame latch	20
4	3	E	Install frame handle	40
		F	Install glass pane	30
5	4	G	Cover frame screws	50
6	5	H	Inspect and pack window unit	50
				380

1. Is Capacity Adequate? Capacity is determined by the longest time required from among all the work stations. From Table 8.4, we know that the work done at station 1 requires 70 seconds, and station 2 requires 80 seconds. Station 3 consists of two tasks, inserting frame screws (*C*) and installing the frame latch (*D*). Thus, the work done at station 3 requires 60 (40 + 20) seconds. The times required for stations 4, 5, and 6 are 70, 50, and 50 seconds. The longest time, then, is needed at station 2 (80 seconds), since a unit spends fewer than 80 seconds at every other station. Since every unit passes through all stations, and each must spend 80 seconds at station 2, station 2 is the *bottleneck* operation, the station that restricts the rate of flow off the line. A finished window assembly will flow off the end of the line every 80 seconds. This length of time is called the *cycle time* of the line. It is the shortest elapsed time between successive units being completed by the entire line.

With a cycle time of 80 seconds, how many windows will be produced daily? It depends on the length of a working day. If the operation

FIGURE 8.10
Diagram for storm window assembly line

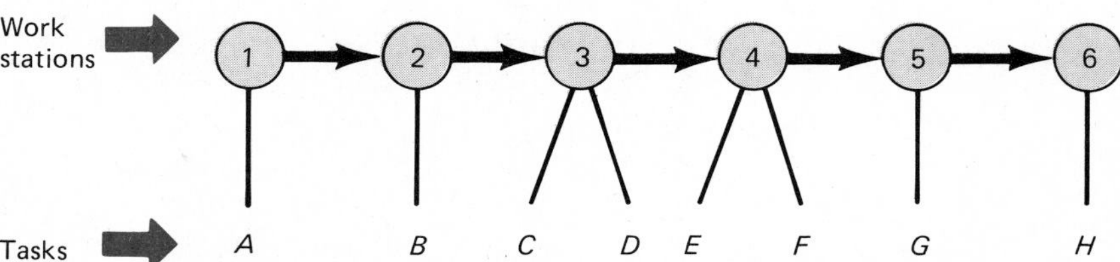

runs for one 8-hour shift each day, then the available productive time each day is 28,800 seconds (8 hours × 3,600 seconds per hour). Therefore, maximum daily output can be determined by calculating as follows:

$$\text{Maximum daily output (number of units)} = \frac{\text{Available time per day}}{\text{Cycle time required per unit}}$$

$$\text{Maximum daily output} = \frac{28{,}800 \text{ seconds/day}}{80 \text{ seconds/unit}}$$

$$= 360 \text{ units/day}$$

We see, then, that since it can generate more than the required 320 units daily, this assembly line design provides adequate output capacity.

There is an alternative method for determining whether capacity is adequate. We can calculate the *maximum allowable cycle time* if desired capacity (320 units per day) is to be achieved.

$$\text{Maximum allowable cycle time to meet desired capacity} = \frac{\text{Available time per day}}{\text{Desired number of units per day}}$$

$$= \frac{28{,}800 \text{ seconds/day}}{320 \text{ units/day}}$$

$$= 90 \text{ seconds/unit}$$

This calculation shows that any design with a cycle time of 90 seconds or less will provide the desired capacity. Designs with cycle times in excess of 90 seconds will not be of adequate capacity.

2. Is the Sequence of Tasks Feasible? We will assume that the proposed sequence of tasks is feasible. We will return to this question soon.

3. Is the Line Efficient? The proposed design has six stations, each manned by one employee. All six workers are paid daily wages for eight hours. How wisely are we utilizing this available resource in the proposed design? How much of our employees' time is spent on productive effort and how much on idleness? It depends on the pace of the line that management selects. The pace can be set anywhere between the cycle times of 80 and 90 seconds. A pace greater than 90 seconds per cycle will slow the line so much that the line will not achieve desired capacity. A pace below 80 is not possible because of the bottleneck operation at station 2. In Table 8.5, we have calculated the efficiency of labor utilization for cycle times of 90 and 80 seconds.

As you can see idleness is higher for the 90-second cycle, and labor utilization is more efficient for the 80-second cycle. We can further calculate the number of daily hours of idleness for each cycle.

TABLE 8.5
Calculation of labor utilization efficiency for proposed 80- and 90-second lines

	Station 1	2	3	4	5	6	Total time per cycle	Utilization of employees (efficiency)
			Efficiency for 90-second cycle time (seconds)					
Productive time (task time) expended each cycle	70	80	60	70	50	50	380	380/540 × 100 = 70.4%
Available employee time each cycle (cycle time)	90	90	90	90	90	90	540	—
Idle time each cycle	20	10	30	20	40	40	160	160/540 × 100 = 29.6
			Efficiency for 80-second cycle time (seconds)					
Productive time (task time) expended each cycle	70	80	60	70	50	50	380	380/480 × 100 = 79.2
Available employee time each cycle (cycle time)	80	80	80	80	80	80	480	—
Idle time each cycle	10	0	20	10	30	30	100	100/480 × 100 = 20.8

$$\text{Daily labor hours idle} = \frac{(\text{Idle seconds/cycle})(\text{Cycles/day})}{(\text{Seconds/hour})}$$

$$\begin{array}{l}\text{Daily labor hours idle}\\ \text{(90-second cycle)}\end{array} = \frac{(160)\left(\dfrac{28{,}800}{90}\right)}{3{,}600} = 14.2 \text{ hours}$$

Similarly, for an 80-second cycle, daily labor idle time is 10 hours.

If the hourly wage is \$5, then \$50 is paid each day for idleness on the 80-second line. On the 90-second line, \$71 is paid daily for idleness. These excessive costs would eventually have to be passed on to the customer by appropriate price setting. Clearly, an efficient layout design has long-run importance for both the company and the consumer.

Balancing the Line How can the cost of idleness be reduced? The most common way is to redefine the work content at each station. Perhaps the eight elementary tasks (A to H in Table 8.4) can be reassigned in different ways, and we can come up with work assignments that are more evenly distributed in terms of time. If productive times required at all stations were equal, we could have no idle time, and the line would be perfectly balanced. *The design problem of finding ways to equalize performance times at all stations is called the line balancing problem.* Our procedure for improving the design uses six steps:

1. define elemental tasks,
2. identify precedence requirements,
3. calculate the minimum number of work stations needed,

4. apply an assignment heuristic for specifying the work content at each station,
5. calculate effectiveness and efficiency, and
6. seek further improvement.

For the example aluminum storm window facility, we have already taken the first step, defining elemental tasks, and shown them in Table 8.4. In general, we use job analysis (also called *work content analysis*) to subdivide the total work into subtasks. There is a limit, however, to how far this subdividing can go. An elemental task is the smallest work task that can reasonably be assigned to a work station. Tasks *A* through *H* are examples.

The second step tells us that elemental tasks cannot be done in just any order. The nature of the product and the processes for producing it require that some tasks be done before others. Certainly the window units, for example, cannot be packed until they are completely assembled. Production designers must specify which tasks must precede other tasks.

These precedence relationships can be summarized in a diagram like the one in Figure 8.11. Arrows are used to show only the required *direction* of flow; arrow length has no meaning. The nodes are the tasks. The diagram shows that task *A* must be done *before* we can do tasks *B*, *C*, *D*, or *E*. *F* cannot be done until *B* and *C* are completed. *G* cannot be done before *C* is completed, and *D*, *E*, *F*, and *G* must precede *H*. The diagram also implies that *B*, *C*, *D*, and *E* can be done in any order. *F* and *G* may either precede or follow *D* and *E*.

It is usually helpful to know how many work stations will be needed. Once the desired line output is specified, we can calculate the *theoretical minimum number of stations* that will be required, the third step in our procedure. From this calculation the planner has an idea as to the *least* number of stations needed:

$$\begin{aligned}\text{Theoretical minimum number of stations} &= \frac{\begin{pmatrix}\text{Total work content}\\ \text{(time) per unit}\end{pmatrix}\begin{pmatrix}\text{Desired number of}\\ \text{units per day}\end{pmatrix}}{\begin{pmatrix}\text{Total productive time available}\\ \text{per day}\end{pmatrix}}\\ &= \frac{\text{(380 seconds/unit)(320 units/day)}}{\text{(28,800 seconds/day)}}\\ &= 4.22 \text{ stations}\end{aligned} \tag{8.2}$$

The total work content (time) that goes into the manufacture of one window is the sum of the task times for tasks *A* through *H*, 380 seconds of labor content. A minimum of 4.22 stations will be required. Since we are dealing in whole stations, at least five stations will be needed. The *actual* design may use more than the minimum number of stations; it depends on the types of precedence relationships that exist in the problem. The initial design in Table 8.4 used six stations.

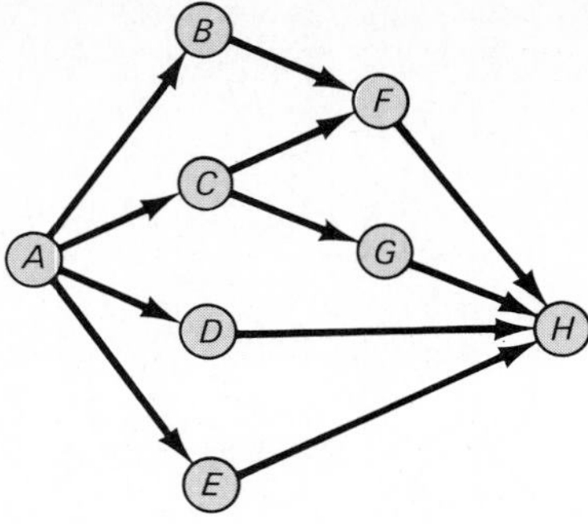

FIGURE 8.11
Precedence relationships for window assembly

The fourth step involves applying an assignment heuristic. The designer must now assign eight tasks to five or more stations. The performance times for tasks assigned to each station cannot exceed the 90-second maximum cycle time. Furthermore, tasks must be assigned in compliance with the precedence relationships. Several combinations of task-to-station assignments meet these requirements. For larger problems with thousands of tasks and hundreds of stations, there are enormous numbers of feasible designs. To trim such problems down to reasonable size, we often use heuristics. Although heuristics do not guarantee that the best solution to a problem will be found, they do help simplify complex problems and may lead to satisfactory solutions. We will apply a "longest-operation-time" rule to the line balancing problem. First we will find a balance to achieve the maximum allowable cycle time (90 seconds), and then we will balance to achieve the minimum possible cycle time (80 seconds).

The steps in the *longest-operation-time (LOT) rule* are:

LOT 1. Assign remaining tasks to the next station according to the length of task operation time; the eligible task with the longest time is assigned first. Maintain precedence relationships.

LOT 2. After assigning a task to a station, determine how much unassigned time remains at the station.

LOT 3. Determine whether other eligible tasks can be assigned to the station. If so, make the assignment. Maintain precedence relationships. If not, return to step 1 and add a new station. Continue until all tasks have been assigned to stations.

To apply the rule, we first array the tasks in descending order of operation time. Task sequence with operation times parenthetically in seconds is: *B* (80), *A* (70), *G* (50), *H* (50), *C* (40), *E* (40), *F* (30), and *D* (20).

In step LOT 1 we try to assign *B* to station 1, since *B* has the longest time. However, *B* is ineligible because it must follow *A* (precedence requirement). In fact, *A must* be assigned to station 1 before any other task becomes eligible for assignment. After A is assigned to station 1, 20 seconds of unassigned time remains (LOT 2). Using LOT 3, we see that *D* is

TABLE 8.6
Assigning tasks to stations using the longest-operation-time heuristic achieving a 90-second cycle time

Heuristic steps	Station	Eligible tasks	Task selected for assignment	Task operation time (seconds)	Unassigned time remaining at station (seconds)	Remaining eligible tasks for this station
1	1	A	A	70	20	D
2	1	D	D	20	0	none
3	2	B,C,E	B	80	10	none
4	3	C,E	C	40	50	E,F,G
5	3	E,F,G	G	50	0	none
6	4	E,F	E	40	50	F
7	4	F	F	30	20	none
8	5	H	H	50	40	none

the only eligible task that can be assigned to this station. *B*, *C*, and *E* all meet the precedence requirements, but their operation times exceed the unassigned time (20 seconds) at station 1. Therefore, station 1 consists of tasks *A* and *D* for a total of 90 seconds operation time.

Now we add station 2. *B* has the longest operation time (80 seconds) among the eligible unassigned tasks. *B* is therefore assigned to station 2. Using LOT 2, we find that 10 seconds (90 − 80 = 10) of unassigned time remain at this station. Since all other tasks require more than 10 seconds, none is eligible to be added to station 2.

To the third station we may assign *C* or *E*. We arbitrarily select *C*, with an operation time of 40 seconds. Remaining unassigned time at station 3 is therefore 50 seconds (90 − 40 = 50). Then *E* and *G* become eligible at this station. Since *G* has the longest operation time, it is assigned. Thus station 3 consists of tasks *C* and *G* with a total performance time of 90 seconds (40 + 50 = 90).

This entire process, carried to completion, is summarized in Table 8.6. The procedure has resulted in a five-station assembly line consisting of the work elements shown in Figure 8.12.

FIGURE 8.12
Revised diagram for storm window assembly

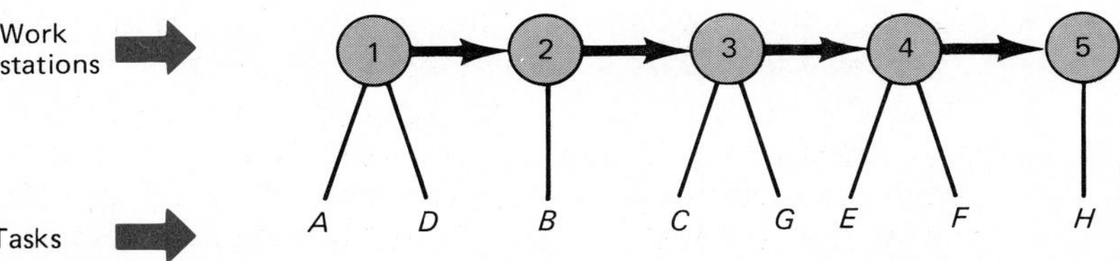

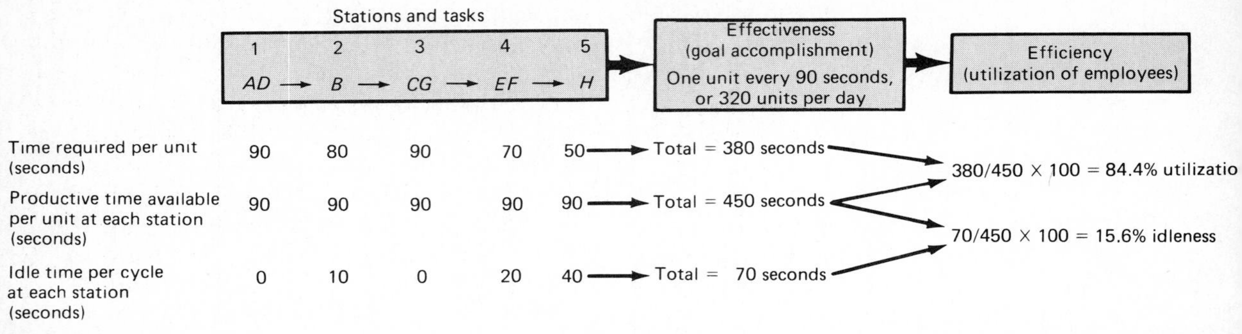

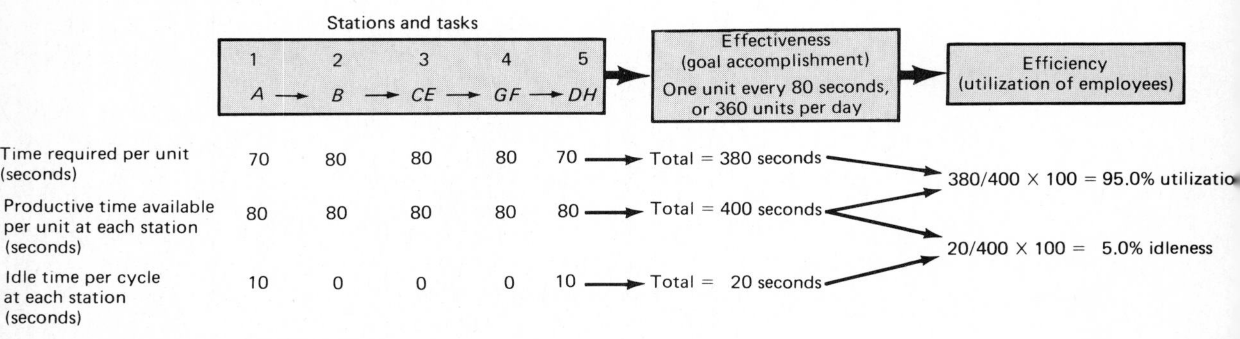

FIGURE 8.13
Assembly line designs for 90-second and 80-second cycles

The design is *effective* if it meets the desired capacity—if the output goal is accomplished. Its *efficiency* is measured by the labor utilization measure we described earlier. In the fifth step, we want to check both measures of performance. In the previous section, we balanced to achieve the maximum allowable cycle time (90 seconds). We have also obtained a balance to achieve the minimum possible cycle time (80 seconds), although the analysis is not shown here. Both designs are shown in Figure 8.13, along with calculations of efficiency and effectiveness. Both of these designs are more efficient than the ones presented to the operations manager in our example earlier in this chapter.

At this stage, we may be able to improve a design by trial and error, step 6 of our procedure. In addition, many other heuristics may be used instead of the longest-operation-time approach. Several computerized heuristics are available, and since different heuristics can lead to different designs, you may wish to try more than one approach. How well do computerized heuristics compare with individual intuition? Generally, heuristics compare favorably. However, one study illustrates that human-computer interaction on the assembly line balancing problem was superior to four common computer heuristics used alone.[8] This is consistent with the recent study we cited in process layout; human performance was better than computer heuristics in that case too.

There are occasions when output capacity and efficiency can be increased by deviating from the procedures we have presented. "Task sharing," for example, occurs when there are three stations, each manned by one operator, all of which have some idleness each cycle. By eliminating one operator, we can reduce idleness by letting the remaining two take turns doing the task at the third station. Other improvements are possible if more than one person can be assigned to a single work station. Finally, if the desired output level exceeds the line capability, further work analysis may be helpful. Bottleneck operations may be reexamined by time study, or methods improvements may be sought to reduce task time. These topics are covered more fully in a future chapter.

Behavioral Aspects of Product Layout

The major behavioral issues in product-oriented layouts revolve around employee satisfaction, motivation, boredom, and productivity. Historically, the assumption has been that ever-increasing job specialization would lead to increased labor productivity. Experience has shown this assumption to be true up to a point. In some cases in which productivity has increased, however, there have also been some unexpected costs. Sometimes routinization leads to job dissatisfaction, absenteeism, and higher employee turnover. Often employees feel that as jobs become more highly specified, something gets "lost"; the work tends to become meaningless. When this happens, productivity may decrease. Responses to these problems include quality circles and job enlargement, enrichment, and rotation, all of which are discussed more thoroughly in Chapter 10.

COMPARATIVE APPROACHES TO REPETITIVE MANUFACTURING: IMPLICATIONS FOR LAYOUT

The preceding forms of layout reflect the approach to operations that has dominated manufacturing thought in Western societies for decades. More recently, however, a different approach by the Japanese has proven its competitive effectiveness in repetitive manufacturing and, consequently, is receiving considerable attention by Western firms as they seek to regain their competitive positions today.

[8]Victor B. Godin, "Interactive Scheduling: Historical Survey and State of the Art," *AIIE Transactions* 10, no. 3 (September 1978), pp. 331–37.

Repetitive Manufacturing: Push or Pull?

Repetitive manufacturing processes are those that produce many units of one product or many of several models of one basic product. This occurs commonly in such industries as appliances, toys, and automobiles.[9] Many units of a given model can be visualized as progressing in a flow-oriented process through stages of product buildup. It may begin with fabrication of the basic components that are then built into subassemblies that are, in turn, combined in final assembly into the finished product units. The decisions of when and how many units to produce at each stage of processing vary considerably depending on the choice of a "push" versus a "pull" system for planning and control.

Push Versus Pull[10] The traditional Western approach emphasizes a "push" orientation toward getting production through the manufacturing system. This basic orientation emphasizes nonstop adherence to a predetermined production schedule derived from anticipated demand for the product. We preplan when final assembly will occur and, working backwards toward earlier stages, we identify when subassemblies, fabricated parts, and purchased materials will occur to provide the ingredients for the scheduled quantity of finished outputs. Then, assuming that this schedule will be met, we control the progression of activities, ensuring that each stage completes its obligations by providing the required quantity of parts at the specified time so that the next stage can execute its obligations. Thus, once the schedule is set into motion, the work at each stage proceeds in large lots or batches and, when completed, the subcomponents are either sent to the next department or are delivered to a storage area (inventory) where they wait for retrieval when needed by the users at the next stage of processing. After a work center has met the schedule, its obligation to succeeding stages is fulfilled. Its subsequent activities are relatively independent of the other work centers because of the cushion of inventories it has provided. Thus the units progress in batches which are pushed through successive stages of buildup until, finally, the required quantity of completed product units is fulfilled.

The "pull" system of planning and control, popular in Japanese manufacturing, is quite different. It emphasizes simplicity, flexibility, and close coordination among work centers in repetitive manufacturing. Although final assembly schedules are developed, the manufacturer recognizes that actual demand will vary from what was anticipated and, consequently, is prepared to adapt production as these variations occur. The Japanese orientation is toward "assembly-to-order" rather than "assembly-to-schedule." The upstream activities (subassembly, fabrication, purchasing of materials)

---

[9]For a discussion of repetitive manufacturing see Richard J. Schonberger, "The Transfer of Japanese Management Approaches to U.S. Industry," *Academy of Management Review* 7, no. 3 (July 1982), pp. 479–87.

[10]Push versus pull systems are discussed in greater detail in Robert W. Hall, *Zero Inventories* (Homewood, Ill.: Dow Jones-Irwin, 1983).

are geared to match the final assembly needs. Consequently, the what and when of production in upstream departments is highly variable and is governed by what the downstream departments need. The subassemblies and component parts are thus "pulled" through the system by actual end-item demands in the specific models, sizes, or color combinations of the product demanded by consumers. The idea is that if units aren't needed now, then don't produce them now or ahead of time; when they are needed, be prepared to create them rapidly in the required quantity.

This austere vision of inventory is exemplified by the Toyota Kanban (card) system.[11] Here, inventory is closely controlled at minimum levels by using a manual two-card system. One kind of card (conveyance kanban), similar to a requisition, authorizes the withdrawal of a container of materials from a supplying work center to a using work center. A second card (production kanban) authorizes production of a container of materials to replace those that were withdrawn earlier. Each item of material in the production process has a prescribed number of containers in circulation at any one time. In addition, a container has in it a prescribed quantity (say four units) of its designated material. By choosing the number of containers and the standard quantities in them, inventories are carefully and visibly controlled on the shop floor. By reducing the number of cards circulating between two interacting work centers, in-process inventories approach zero and the needed parts arrive just in time. As a result there is an absence of inventories (raw materials, component parts, final products); stockless production is a major feature of the "pull" system of planning and control.

Although the differences between the push and pull approaches seem straightforward, they have rather dramatic implications for almost every aspect of operations design and management. Let's briefly examine some of their implications, especially those involving facility layout.

Operations Characteristics in Push Versus Pull Systems

The design and operation of a conversion system takes on quite a different flavor depending upon whether it is geared toward a push or a pull orientation. The two approaches impose different types of equipment, machinery, and maintenance policies, as well as inventory postures, worker skills, support staffs, and management abilities. For each of these areas, the push versus pull contrasts are summarized in Table 8.7.

Push System To accomplish its scheduled production in nonstop flows, the push system emphasizes predesigned and relatively fixed assembly line balances using dedicated single-purpose machines with high output capabilities. Abundant supplies of work-in-process inventories between stages facilitate nonstop production runs once they're started in downstream de-

[11]The kanban system is discussed in Richard J. Schonberger, *Japanese Manufacturing Techniques* (New York: The Free Press, 1982). See also Robert W. Hall, *Zero Inventories* (Homewood, Ill.: Dow Jones-Irwin, 1983).

partments. Materials handling equipment shuttles parts and components to work areas from supplying departments or storage depots when scheduled by the materials control staff. The workers at receiving stations perform their specialized tasks repetitively on all units in the production lot. Work center management focuses on ensuring that the station is manned, has materials available, and on motivating employees to meet scheduled output commitments.

The plant layout typically involves a combination of process-oriented departments (Figure 8.3) for fabricating components and subassemblies in batches, and product-oriented assembly lines (Figure 8.4) for final assembly. Inventory storage areas are created as needed between departments. Furthermore, the assembly line is usually a straight-line configuration with substantial spaces between work stations for materials storage. Often, each product model has a dedicated production line on which only that model

TABLE 8.7
Characteristics of contrasting approaches to repetitive manufacturing

Operations Characteristics	Push System (U.S.)	Pull System (Japan)
Major orientation	Balanced nonstop flows to meet predetermined schedule.	Flexibility and simplicity in responding quickly to actual demand.
Machines	Use single specialized machines with production capacities in excess of anticipated needs. Large capital investment in machine and special tooling to perform a single purpose repeatedly.	Multiple copies of smaller, simpler, less expensive, and perhaps slower machines with specially developed flexible tooling to facilitate shutdown, startup, and changeovers to different product models. Tools and attachments located conveniently at machine site to simplify setups and changeovers.
Material handling equipment	Extensive reliance on elaborate devices to move large lots or batches of raw materials, components and subassemblies between work stations and inventory storage areas.	Minimal use of conveyance equipment. Frequent use of manual transfer of components from worker to worker by locating work stations close together and producing in small batches or one at a time.
Inventory posture	Extensive work-in-process inventories accumulate between work stations and stages of production. Produce large runs of components to spread high setup costs across many units, to avoid expensive changeovers, to hedge against equipment failures, and to compensate for defective components.	Avoid excessive inventories. In general, the prevailing view is that inventories are dysfunctional because they mask or hide production problems. Produce only what is needed as it is needed. Instead of producing ahead of need, produce just in time in small batches (or one at a time) as frequently as necessary.
Relationships with suppliers	Supply contracts often awarded on basis of price competition among suppliers who are geographically dispersed. Relationships between buyer and suppliers is transient. Materials purchased and delivered in large quantities and stored until used.	Close, long-lasting, and team-like supplier-buyer relationships. Close purchase-delivery coordination, frequently on short notice in variable quantities, with suppliers located near customer's facility.

TABLE 8.7 (cont.)
Characteristics of contrasting approaches to repetitive manufacturing

Operations Characteristics	Push System (U.S.)	Pull System (Japan)
Manpower utilization	Features task specialization and strict division of labor in fixed work assignments with limited task scope. Limited transfer of employees across jobs with different work content and variety. Employees oriented toward performing specialized tasks on many units of one product with emphasis on keeping the line running.	Flexible labor oriented toward a broader scope and view of work responsibilities. Concerned with discovering and correcting process weaknesses to ensure error free production of every unit of product. Make equipment changeovers and setups of their own work stations as needed to produce varieties of product models. Limited hiring and layoffs by transferring employees to diverse jobs as demand at their own workplace fluctuates. Production lines stop until any problems are corrected through efforts and ingenuity of workers.
Support staff	Extensive investment in staff personnel for pre-production design of equipment, facilities, line balancing to a planned output rate, and job design for efficiency. Attempt to design production problems and bottlenecks out of the system to meet anticipated output levels. Extensive use of staffs for planning and controlling inventories, materials flows, and product quality during production. Foremen on production lines that are dedicated to a single product model ensure that each work station has the materials and people to meet the scheduled output. Foremen responsible for motivating a large number of employees.	Emphasis on improving production processes during as well as before production. Joint problem solving by engineering, workers, and managers as needed to address and resolve each problem as it arises. Foremen provide floor-level leadership for problem-solving and frequent rebalancing of lines in response to variable demands for mixed models of product. Constant emphasis on improving quality and reducing inventories and setup times. Strive for a single production line that can produce mixed models by rapid changeovers to meet market demand.

is produced; this avoids the expensive setup and changeover costs of running mixed models on any single line.

Pull System Emphasizing flexibility and simplicity, the pull system aims toward producing variable quantities (including small amounts) of the models *when they are needed*. Accordingly, less expensive, smaller, adaptable machines are adopted rather than one big one. Attention is given to the design of intricate tools and attachments to permit rapid equipment changeovers as required for different models at each work station. The goal of lotless (stockless) production in assembly is reflected in the closeness of work stations; this permits each unit of product to be passed to the next station when it is completed, rather than accumulating in large batches after each stage. This gives station-to-station visibility of work progress and it eliminates in-process inventories, inventory storage areas, inventory conveyance equipment, and materials control staff.

Since small quantities of various models are being produced from hour-to-hour at each work station, the work content is highly variable and the individual product units must be completed properly at every stage of product buildup. Accordingly, diligent workers are the preeminent resource in the system. In addition to making the product itself, these workers adjust their own equipment for quick changeovers to different models. When low product demand warrants the shutdown of their production line, they will be reassigned to other lines, or work on redesigning their own work stations and equipment to improve the production process or to do preventative maintenance. The pull system also demands more floor-level leadership from its foremen, who must exercise problem-solving skills in balancing and rebalancing production-line work daily to meet frequent demand variations rather than adhering to nonstop predetermined schedules.

Workplace Layout: The U-Shape The emphasis on flexibility in pull systems is exemplified by the use of U-shaped, as opposed to straight-line, layouts. Consider, for example, the 13-station production work center in Figure 8.14. Suppose incoming materials are available to produce a small batch, say five units, of one product. If the thirteen stations are positioned compactly, one or two workers can quickly set up all the machines without much wasted travel time between stations. Once production begins on the 5-unit lot, the worker at location *A* can perform operations 1–3 and 11–13 on all the units while the worker at *B* performs operations 4–10. As you can see, the U-shape offers more options for flexible work assignments than

FIGURE 8.14
U-shape layout for a work station

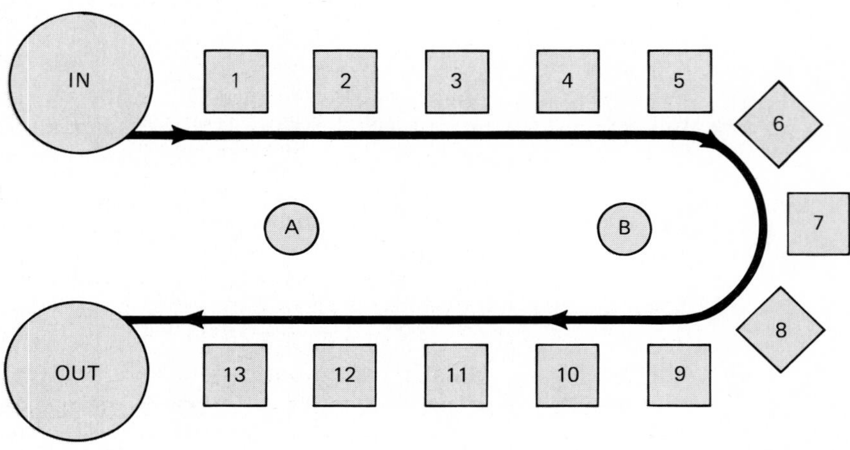

does a straight-line layout. A worker can operate both sides of the parallel legs or adjacent stations. When the demand for this work center's output declines, one operator alone can do the work at all 13 stations. When demand rises, the lone worker can be joined by another to respond rapidly with more output. The trick is to decide how many workers to use, how to distribute the workload, and what size the small batches to be produced in each lot should be.

Relationship to Competitive Focus and Strategy

On the basis of competitive experience during the past decade, Japanese successes with the pull system are vivid evidence of its effectiveness as a competitive weapon. Its dominant success has been in situations that feature the repetitive manufacturing of a relatively modest variety of models, sizes, styles, or color combinations of one basic product. By intensively focusing their manufacturing skills on a limited product line they develop fast and flexible responses to market demand, high product quality, and reduced inventory costs, all with lower investments in plant facilities and equipment. This exemplifies how the production function can be designed and focused to provide an advantage in a company's competitive strategy.

SUMMARY

Layout decisions are made only periodically. Since they have long-run consequences, they must be planned carefully. The layout design ultimately affects the cost of producing goods and delivering services for many years into the future. We have discussed three traditional, basic layout formats: process, product, and fixed-position. Process layouts are arranged in such a way that work centers or departments are grouped together according to the type of function they perform. Product layouts arrange work centers and equipment in a line so that a specialized sequence of operations will result in product buildup. In a fixed-position layout, the product remains in one location, and resources are brought to it.

For process and product (assembly line) layouts, the design begins with a statement of the goals of the facility. Layouts are designed to meet these goals. After initial designs have been developed, improved designs are sought. This can be a cumbersome and tedious task because the number of possible designs is so large. For this reason, quantitative and computer-based models are often used to assist the designer. The models for process and product layouts are distinctly different: process models generally minimize load (volume)-distance moved relationships, and product models generally focus on minimizing idle labor time through line-balancing techniques.

Aside from the traditional views, a newer orientation in facility layout has emerged from the Japanese success with "pull" rather than "push" production systems for repetitive manufacturing. The layout implications of these two orientations were contrasted, along with some other characteristics of the production system. These comparisons illustrate how different layout designs are appropriate for different production systems, depending upon the organization's chosen focus and competitive strategy.

CASE

Sonographic Sound Systems, Inc.

SSS is a small local manufacturer of high-quality phonographs. For two years, SSS has produced its most popular portable phonograph on an eight-hour shift at a rate of 84 units per day. Management is satisfied with existing plant capacity but is concerned about the labor efficiency of its main assembly line. Fred Regos, operations manager, has asked his industrial engineer to recommend a redesign of the existing assembly line, because the vice president has established a goal of increasing labor utilization without decreasing output rate. This goal is consistent with the broader goal of a cost reduction of 10 percent for the production facility.

The assembly line currently has seven stations in which a total of ten tasks are performed. The task descriptions, times, and precedence relations are as follows:

Task	Description	Must follow (predecessor)	Task time (minutes)
A	Load chassis frame	—	1
B	Insert gear assembly on frame	A	2
C	Install electric motor on frame	A	4
D	Assemble turntable stem to gear assembly	B	2
E	Install rubber bearing assembly onto gear assembly	B	1
F	Mount, fit, and fasten turntable mechanism to stem	D	5
G	Interconnect gear and motor assemblies	C and E	1
H	Install turntable	F and G	3
I	Install tone arm assembly	G	4
J	Install and fasten cover	H and I	3

The existing assembly line and personnel are:

Station	1	2	3	4	5	6	7
Work content	A and B	D and E	C and G	F	H	I	J
Worker	Alice	Tom	Bill	Debbie	Sam	Clorice	Ike

All employees have been with SSS two years or more. Tom finds that he has time on his hands and enjoys chatting with Alice. In all his time at SSS, Sam has never worked at another station. Although Bill doesn't like to perform task G, he takes great pride in his skill at doing C. Clorice and Ike agree that their jobs tend to get boring.

What changes would you recommend to Fred Regos? What reactions to these changes would you expect from the line employees?

REVIEW AND DISCUSSION QUESTIONS

1. Give examples of organizations that have predominantly product, process, and fixed-position layouts.
2. Compare and contrast the characteristics of intermittent and continuous conversion operations.
3. Describe and illustrate the significant relationships among the capacity and layout decisions.
4. What relationships exist between the layout and location decisions?
5. To what extent do the quantitative layout models consider behavioral factors?
6. Compare the manual and quantitative models for product-oriented (assembly line) layout design. What are the advantages of each kind of model?
7. Identify and describe the different models used to assist the layout designer.
8. Identify the primary behavioral factors involved in process-oriented layout design. Give examples.
9. Explain the essential features of CRAFT, a computerized layout model.
10. Identify the primary behavioral factors involved in product-oriented (assembly line) layout design. Give examples.
11. Compare the manual and quantitative models for process layout design. What are the advantages of each kind of model?
12. Compare differences in design strategies for developing an initial layout design (for a new facility) and for developing a revised layout design (for an existing facility).
13. Some would contend that employees generally should not have a major voice in layout design. Others argue that the layout should be developed in a participative manner, with major involvement by employees. Discuss this issue.
14. Explain how and why the push versus pull system for planning and control affects facility layout design.
15. Compare and contrast major aspects of employee behaviors under push versus pull systems for repetitive manufacturing.

PROBLEMS

Solved Problems

1. The assembly line design shown in Figure 8.15 provides the desired output rate for an eight-hour shift. Calculate the following: total work content; maximum eight-hour output; theoretical minimum number of stations; efficiency and idleness of the line.

FIGURE 8.15

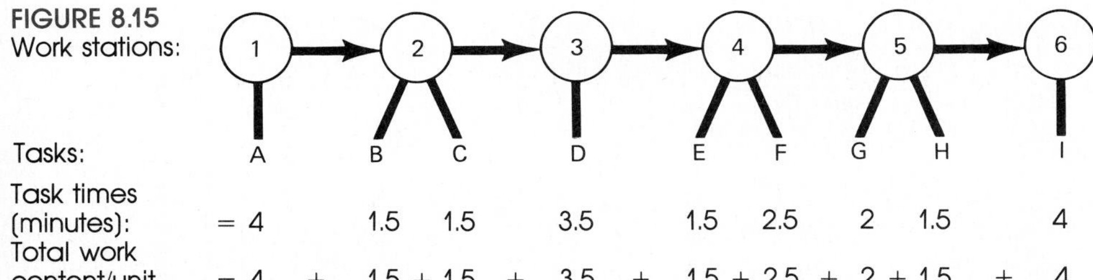

$$= 22 \text{ minutes/unit}$$

$$\text{Maximum daily output} = \frac{\text{available time/day}}{\text{cycle time/unit}} = \frac{480 \text{ minutes/day}}{4 \text{ minutes/unit}} = 120 \text{ units/day}$$

$$\text{Theoretical minimum number of stations} = \frac{\begin{pmatrix}\text{work}\\ \text{content/unit}\end{pmatrix}\begin{pmatrix}\text{desired}\\ \text{units/day}\end{pmatrix}}{\begin{pmatrix}\text{total productive time}\\ \text{available/day}\end{pmatrix}} = \frac{(22)(120)}{480} = 5.5 \text{ (or 6 whole stations)}$$

$$\text{Efficiency/cycle} = \frac{\text{productive time/cycle}}{\text{available time/cycle}} = \frac{22 \text{ minutes}}{6 \text{ stations} \times 4 \text{ minutes/station}} = \frac{22}{24} = 91.6\%$$

$$\text{Idleness/cycle} = \frac{\text{idle time/cycle}}{\text{available time/cycle}} = \frac{0 + 1 + .5 + 0 + .5 + 0}{24} = \frac{2}{24} = 8.4\%$$

2. Seven departments (see Figure 8.16) will receive incoming parts from the factory's receiving dock which can be located at either position A or position B in the facility. The number of loads per month is shown in parentheses. Which position is best, A or B?

FIGURE 8.16

A	1 (90)	B
2 (60)	3 (30)	4 (50)
5 (40)	6 (90)	7 (70)

Departments 1, 3, and 6 are ignored in the analysis since each of them is equidistant from A or B.

For A:

Receiving department	Unit distance from A	Number of loads	Loads times distance
2	1	60	60
4	2	50	100
5	2	40	80
7	3	70	210
		Total =	450

For B:

Receiving department	Unit distance from B	Number of loads	Loads times distance
2	2	60	120
4	1	50	50
5	3	40	120
7	2	70	140
		Total =	430

The B location offers lower cost.

Reinforcing Fundamentals

3. A vacuum cleaner manufacturing company incurs a variable cost of $58 per unit produced and receives revenues of $80 per unit. Two alternative layout designs are being considered for finished goods storage and shipment. The first alternative would involve loading the products directly into trucks for shipment at a large loading facility near the end of the assembly lines. Annual fixed costs of operation of the large truck fleet would be $400,000; materials handling costs would be $200,000.

   The second alternative, a large warehouse near the assembly area, would result in a truck fleet costing $190,000 annually, average additional inventory carrying costs annually of $170,000, $50,000 each year to manage and maintain inventories, $25,000 damage to products annually, and $15,000 per year to load, operate, and maintain the conveyance equipment from the assembly area to the warehouse.

   Existing fixed costs of operation (in addition to the two layout alternatives) are $450,000 per year. What impact, if any, do the layout designs have on the company's breakeven volume of operation?

4. The university library is considering a new location for department 6, the Book Purchase Processing Department. Libary staff would like to change departments 6 and 2, 2 being the social science reference staff. Given estimates as shown, what would be the impact of this change?

Effectiveness (Monthly book loads)

Department	Department					
	1	2	3	4	5	6
1	—	100	0	100	200	0
2	—	—	0	0	0	0
3	—	—	—	10	100	0
4	—	—	—	—	0	100
5	—	—	—	—	—	0
6	—	—	—	—	—	—

Current layout

1	2	3
6	5	4

5. Work centers *A* through *L*, tentatively located as shown, have the load shipments in the load-flow chart.

Inter-department flows (units/year)

From	To				
	D	G	H	I	J
A	300	600	—	—	200
B	200	—	—	—	500
C	600	300	200	—	600

Layout (tentative)

A	*B*	*C*	*D*
E	*F*	*G*	*H*
I	*J*	*K*	*L*

   (a) Assuming $1 transportation cost per unit distance for each load, find a good layout.

   (b) Suppose cost per unit-distance is $4 for each load from work center *B* and is $1 for each load from *A* and *C*. Find a good layout.

6. A small printing shop wishes to locate its seven departments in a one-floor building that is 40 units wide and 50 units long. Department sizes are:

Department	Length (units)	Width (units)
Layout	10	10
Cutting	20	10
Shipping	10	10
Supply storage	20	15
Printing	25	20
Binding	20	20
Art	20	20

The average annual number of loads flowing between departments is expected to be:

Annual number of loads among departments

	To department						
From department	Layout	Cutting	Shipping	Supply storage	Printing	Binding	Art
Layout	—	—	—	—	—	—	—
Cutting	—	—	—	100	—	400	—
Shipping	—	—	—	500	—	—	—
Supply storage	—	600	100	—	400	100	—
Printing	—	—	—	—	—	1,200	100
Binding	—	100	1,000	—	200	—	—
Art	—	100	—	—	100	—	—

What is your layout recommendation?

7. In considering a new office layout, a designer obtained importance ratings for locating service groups near one another. On a scale of 1 (low importance) to 10 (high importance), service group proximity ratings were as shown in the table on page 343.
   Assume the overall space is 3 units wide and 3 units long; all service group areas are of equal size, 1 unit by 1 unit. What is your recommended layout design?
8. Given the following tasks and requirements for an assembly line, what is the maximum daily output and efficiency?

Task	Performance time (minutes)	Must follow
A	5	*F*
B	2	*F*
C	3	*E*, *G*
D	7	*A*, *B*
E	8	*D*, *H*
F	4	—
G	6	*D*
H	3	*D*

Importance of close proximity among service groups

Service group	Maintenance	Library	Design	Estimating	Accounting	Computer	Records	Sales engineers	Management
Maintenance	—	—	—	—	—	—	—	—	—
Library	—	—	9	—	—	—	—	2	—
Design	—	—	—	8	—	8	7	10	7
Estimating	—	—	—	—	4	—	2	8	4
Accounting	—	—	4	—	—	9	10	5	3
Computer	—	—	—	—	—	—	2	6	3
Records	—	—	—	—	—	—	—	5	—
Sales engineers	—	—	—	—	—	—	—	—	8

9. Consider the following production line in which work elements *A-H* must be performed in alphabetical order:

Work station:	1	2	3	4	5	6
Work elements:	*A, B*	*C*	*D, E*	*F*	*G*	*H*
Element time (minutes):	2, 1.5	4	2, 2	3	2.5	3

   (a) Identify the bottleneck operation.
   (b) What is the minimum cycle time?
   (c) Assuming an eight-hour work day, what is the maximum daily output?
   (d) If the line uses one employee per station, how many hours of idle time exist daily? How many hours of productive time?
   (e) Calculate the efficiency of the line.

10. For a food processing plant, the following data on the task precedence relationships exist. Assume the tasks cannot be split.
   (a) What is the theoretical minimum cycle time?
   (b) Balance the line using the "longest-operation-time" rule. Use the theoretical minimum cycle time.
   (c) Calculate the efficiency of the balanced line.

Task	Performance time (minutes)	Must follow
A	3	—
B	6	*A*
C	7	*A*
D	2	*A*
E	2	*A*
F	4	*C, B*
G	5	*C*
H	5	*D, E, F, G*

Challenging Exercises

11. A group of physicians is considering forming a new medical clinic in a single-story facility in a suburban area. Although design plans are just underway, they have decided to have service departments with these relative sizes (space requirements):

Service department	Size (sq ft)
Laboratory	1,200
Plastic surgery	600
Patient waiting area	600
Ob./gyn.	800
Neurology	600
Pediatrics	1,800
Pharmacy	400
X-ray	600

The number of patients flowing among pairs of departments during each month is expected to be:

Number of patients flowing between departments

Department	Lab	Plastic surgery	Waiting	Ob./gyn.	Neurology	Pediatrics	Pharmacy	X-ray
Lab	—	200	50	100	80	200	—	200
Plastic surgery	—	—	70	—	10	—	20	5
Waiting	—	—	—	400	200	900	—	50
Ob./gyn.	—	—	—	—	—	50	40	50
Neurology	—	—	—	—	—	10	20	80
Pediatrics	—	—	—	—	—	—	150	200
Pharmacy	—	—	—	—	—	—	—	30

The physicians are not yet concerned with the overall configuration of the building, just so all departments are on one floor. There is a direct relationship between number of patients and patient walking distances. What relative department locations do you recommend for minimizing patient flows (walking distances)?

12. An assembly line must be established to include these tasks:

Task	Time (seconds)	Must follow
A	120	—
B	50	*A*
C	40	*B*
D	80	*C, F*
E	100	*A*
F	20	*E*
G	90	*H*
H	60	*A*
I	30	*A*
J	60	*D, G, I*

(a) Construct a precedence diagram for the tasks.
(b) To balance the line to a 120-second minimum cycle time, what is the theoretical minimum number of work stations?
(c) Use the longest-operation-time rule to balance the line to a 120-second cycle.
(d) What is the efficiency of the line?

13. For the data in problem 12, redo parts (c) and (d) using the shortest-operation-time rule. Using the largest-number-of-follower-tasks rule.
14. A toy company, Electro-Play, Inc., is interested in balancing a production line that will manufacture an electronic football game to compete with the successful pocket-calculator size model of Mattel. Tasks, performance times, and precedence relationships are shown:

Task	Performance time (seconds)	Must follow
A	40	—
B	20	*A*
C	15	*B*
D	60	—
E	50	*D*
F	10	*C*
G	25	*C*
H	10	*E*
I	20	*E*
J	5	*F, G, H, I*
K	10	*J*

(a) Construct a precedence diagram for the tasks.
(b) To balance the line with a 60-second minimum cycle time, what is the theoretical minimum number of work stations? A seven-hour day is worked.
(c) Balance the line with the longest-operation-time (LOT) rule, balancing to a 60-second cycle.
(d) What is the efficiency of the line?
(e) Many of the behavioral problems in assembly line balancing also apply to the more general problem of job design. What suggestions might you offer if you wanted to incorporate job enlargement/enrichment into the above balanced line?

15. Able Manufacturing has an opportunity to bid on a contract to produce an electronic assembly. Able could use excess assembly capacity at its main production facility. The contract would require delivery (within two years) of 30,000 units. Able's methods engineers suggest an assembly line consisting of nine tasks:

Task	Performance time (minutes)	Must follow
A	4	*G*
B	6	*G*
C	2	*B, D*
D	5	*A, F*
E	3	*D*
F	4	*G*
G	3	*I*
H	2	*C, E*
I	4	—

Assembly would occur on one shift with average productive time of 7½ hours per employee daily (allowances for breaks, fatigue, shutdowns, etc.). There would be twenty-two productive days monthly. Direct labor costs are \$11 per hour; variable overhead is estimated at 10 percent of direct labor; direct materials are \$18 per unit; initial tooling for the project is \$150,000 and semifixed costs of manufacturing for the assembly line are estimated at \$8,000 per month. Able desires a 15 percent profit margin on selling price for such contractual commitments. Should Able submit a bid and, if so, at what selling price?

GLOSSARY

Bottleneck operation Of all assembly line work stations, the one that requires the longest operation time.

Cycle time Elapsed time between completed units coming off the end of an assembly line.

Elemental task The smallest work task that can be assigned to a work station.

Fixed-position layout Facility arrangement in which the product remains in one location; resources are brought to the product location to perform the appropriate stages of buildup.

Heuristic Simplification procedure in which a set of rules is systematically applied; results in the discovery of a satisfactory problem solution.

Job analysis Minute study of a task in an effort to eliminate unnecessary activity and find ways to do the task faster and cheaper.

Kanban A card system used for controlling the movement and production of materials on the shop floor in a stockless manufacturing system.

Layout design Location or configuration of departments, work stations, and equipment that constitute the conversion process; spatial arrangement of the physical resources used to create the product.

Line balancing Assigning tasks to assembly line stations so that performance times are equalized as much as possible.

Norms Agreements as to how group members should behave.

Process layout Arrangement of facility so that work centers or departments are grouped together according to the type of function they perform.

Product layout Arrangement of facility so that work centers and equipment are in a line; provides specialized sequence of operations that will result in product buildup.

Pull system A manufacturing system that makes parts only when needed by the users of those parts; thus the parts and materials are drawn or pulled through the system by user demand for them.

Push system A manufacturing system that makes parts to meet a predetermined schedule and then sends them forward to the next stage or to inventory storage to await further processing.

Repetitive manufacturing Processes that produce many discrete (whole) units of one product or many discrete units of different models of a basic product.

Stockless production Manufacturing systems that strive to operate without work-in-process inventories; also referred to as lotless production and just-in-time systems.

SELECTED READINGS

Buffa, Elwood S., Gordon C. Armour, and Thomas Vollmann, "Allocating Facilities with CRAFT." *Harvard Business Review* (March-April 1964), pp. 136–58.

Chase, Richard B. "Strategic Considerations in Assembly-Line Selection." *California Management Review* (Fall 1975), pp. 17–23.

Francis, Richard L. and John A. White. *Facility Layout and Location*. Englewood Cliffs, N.J.: Prentice-Hall, 1974.

Hall, Robert W. *Zero Inventories*. Homewood, Illinois: Dow Jones-Irwin, 1983.

Hicks, Philip E. and Troy E. Cowan. "Craft-M for Layout Rearrangement." *Industrial Engineering* 8, no. 5 (May 1976), pp. 30–35.

Ignall, Edward J. "A Review of Assembly Line Balancing." *Journal of Industrial Engineering* (July-August 1965), pp. 244–54.

"In McDonald's Offices, Everyone is Out in the Open." *The Office* 84, no. 3 (September 1976), pp. 115–19.

Ritzman, Larry, John Bradford, and Robert Jacobs. "A Multiple Objective Approach to Space Planning for Academic Facilities." *Management Science* 25, no. 9 (September 1979), pp. 895–906.

Schonberger, Richard J. *Japanese Manufacturing Techniques*. New York: The Free Press, 1982.

Schonberger, Robert J. "The Transfer of Japanese Manufacturing Management Approaches to U.S. Industry." *The Academy of Management Review* 7, no. 3 (July 1982), pp. 479–87.

Schuler, R. S., L. P. Ritzman, and V. Davis, "Merging Prescriptive and Behavioral Approaches for Office Layout." *Journal of Operations Management* 1, no. 3 (February 1981), pp. 131–42.

Scriabin, Michael and Roger C. Vergin. "Comparison of Computer Algorithms and Visual Based Methods for Plant Layout." *Management Science* (October 1975), pp. 172–81.

Trybus, Thomas W. and Lewis D. Hopkins. "Human Vs. Computer Algorithms for the Plant Layout Problem." *Management Science* 26, no. 6 (June 1980), pp. 570–74.

Vollmann, Thomas E. and Elwood S. Buffa. "The Facilities Layout Problem in Perspective." *Management Science* 12, no. 10 (June 1966), pp. B450–58.

Information Systems and Operations

The General Electric Company is a leading developer and producer of jet engines for both military and commercial applications.

Development, evaluation testing, and production of a modern jet engine is a lengthy and complex cycle which totally depends on high technology management information systems. Engineering analysis of increasingly complex components requires computers which use programs such as finite element analysis and advanced heat transfer to design the thousands of components used in a jet engine.

Use of Computer Aided Design and Computer Aided Manufacturing transfers the engineer's ideas into hardware in the minimum amount of time and with the minimum amount of errors. This is extremely important when engine development costs are measured in hundreds of millions of dollars and one malfunctioning part may lead to an engine failure and possible program delays.

Once the design has been established, the process of buying, manufacturing, and assembly of the various components and raw material commences. Decisions to "make or buy" are based on available facilities, required investment, technology required, schedules, etc., and must be integrated into a Material Requirements Planning System. This system insures that the castings, forgings, fabrications as well as the finished parts arrive in the correct quantity and sequence to be transformed into an engine.

Any problems which impede or delay the manufacture or delivery of a component must be dealt with swiftly since the non-availability of only one part can hold up delivery of the engine.

Therefore, continous feedback and schedule monitoring is necessary in an efficient and workable MRP System.

The on-time delivery of a quality product to our customer is the final step in an engineering and manufacturing process that is becoming more integrated, more technologically complex, more productivity oriented, and more and more dependent upon the use of management information systems.

J. W. Tucker
General Manager
Product Design & Operations Control
General Electric Company
Cincinnati, Ohio

FIGURE 9.1
Production/operations management activities

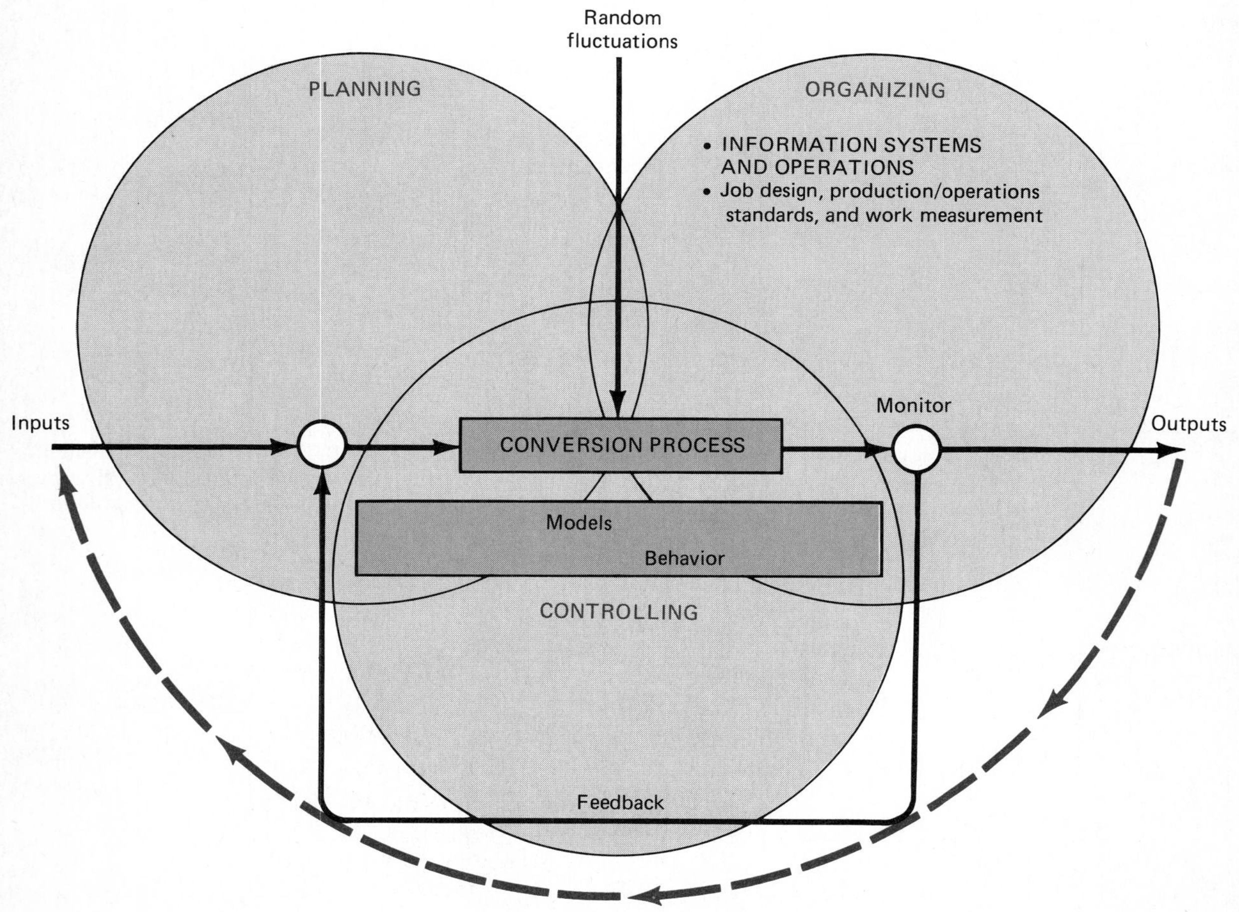

Mr. Tucker's comments show the competitive importance and the complexity of information systems in managing manufacturing operations. His situation is not unusual; information management is a major concern in the organizing function of nearly every operations management setting. *Organizing is the means by which individuals, groups, and facilities are combined in a formal structure of tasks, authority, and information relationships.* Through its information structure, the organization provides a means for people, equipment, and facility to work together so that they can achieve the organization's goals. As Figure 9.1 indicates, information systems, what they are and how they facilitate operations, is the topic of this chapter. We will begin with some basic information-system terminology followed by an overview of computers and their characteristics. Then, after examining some information system structures and their applications in operations, we will explore some emerging systems for improving operations-decision effectiveness.

MANAGEMENT INFORMATION SYSTEMS (MIS)

The invention and continually increasing sophistication of the computer represent a profound technological breakthrough; its usefulness to the organization and its impact on operations management have been equally profound. With computer-based information systems, managers efficiently conduct organizational activities of such complexity that were inconceivable as recently as two decades ago. Today's operations manager must have a basic understanding of computer information systems and their role in organizations.[1] In our discussion, we will treat "management information systems" (MIS) and "computer-based information systems" as synonomous, interchangeable terms.

Definition of MIS

For the present, we adopt the following operational definition of a management information system:

> . . . an integrated, man/machine system for providing information to support the operations, management, and decision-making functions in an organization. The system utilizes computer hardware and software, manual procedures, management and decision models, and a data base.[2]

Purpose of MIS

The purpose of a management information system (MIS) is to help management make effective decisions about problems in the organization. Because it costs money to create, maintain, and use the MIS, the system should justify that cost by providing specific, identifiable benefits.

[1]The basics of management information systems are presented comprehensively in G. B. Davis, *Management Information Systems* (New York: McGraw-Hill Book Company, 1974) and J. G. Burch, Jr., and F. R. Strater, Jr., *Information Systems: Theory and Practice* (Santa Barbara, California: Hamilton Publishing Company, 1974).

[2]G. B. Davis, *Management Information Systems*, p. 5.

Basic Elements of a MIS

A MIS consists of five basic elements: (1) people, (2) machines, (3) procedures, (4) a data base, and (5) control.

People The most important element, people, play many roles at various levels throughout the system. Managers and staff personnel are the prime beneficiaries of the system, which is designed to meet identifiable managerial needs.[3] Systems designers and technical support staff are essential; they cause the system to come into being, make sure it operates to meet its intended purpose, and revise it to accommodate new needs and capabilities.

Machines For centuries organizations have used machines for processing, manipulating, and operating on data to obtain information. Such mechanical devices as adding machines and cash registers were succeeded by electromechanical technologies, which were followed by electronic computers. Today's MIS is distinguished by the presence of the computer—a digital, electronic data processing system. People are as critical to computer-based systems as they were to precomputer information systems. Their roles, however, have shifted in emphasis from calculating to making decisions based on system inputs and outputs.

Procedures *Procedures* in the system involve the use of both computer-based and noncomputer-based knowledge, models, and personnel to ensure that proper data and models get to the computer and are then properly transformed, outputted, and used.

Within the information system, procedures can be classified as either *external* or *internal* to the computer. External procedures include all processing and information-flow activities involved in the problem area or subsystem. In a materials control information system, for example, there are external procedures for ordering, receiving, inspecting, invoicing, storing, costing, counting, and disbursing materials. Each procedure describes one of these many activities—who performs it and when, why, where, and how it is performed. In this sense the procedure is both an instructional reference guide and a communication link among personnel and activities.

Usually, internal (to the computer) procedures in the information system are in the form of computer programs and program specifications. Computer programs are detailed procedures, logically related, that are executed on the computer in a logical sequence. Additional procedures identify the various computer programs, their purposes and authorized use, when they are to be used, and how they relate to other programs. There are also procedures instructing users how to access, maintain, and modify computer programs.

[3]Crucial aspects of user needs that should be considered in designing information systems are presented in R. L. Daft and N. B. MacIntosh, "A New Approach to Design and Use of Management Information," *California Management Review* 21, no. 1 (Fall 1978), pp. 82–92.

Database At the heart of information systems are the processes of collecting, storing, and processing data so it can be used for making decisions. In a computer-based system, these data must be accessible to and compatible with the computer. The database is the foundation upon which the information system is built.[4]

An organization's database consists of information stored in such various media as card files, record cabinets, memoranda, etc. Some of these are computer-accessible; others are not. When computer-accessible data are stored in numerical, alphabetical, or other special form and are maintained in a logical structure, they make up the computer data base. The smallest data element in this database, called a *field*, consists of one or more characters. "Item number," for example, might be the name of a field, and the contents of that field might be the identification number of an inventory item: "PS 106." A group of fields that are logically related comprises a *record*. A product record, for example, may contain the following fields: item number, item description, item location, quantity of item available, quantity needed of item, item procurement lead time, item cost, etc. A data *file* is a collection of data records that are logically related. The following data records, for example, may form a data file: product record, sales record, vendor record, purchases record, accounts payable record, etc. The aggregation of all the related data files is the *database*. The sizes of the fields, records, files, and database are determined by the limitations of the hardware and software of each particular computer system. Reports are generated from the database for various management levels. For these reports to be useful, the database must be accurate and complete.

Control Central to every MIS is an emphasis on control, which permeates all the other basic elements—people, machines, procedures, and data base—to ensure that they interact in ways that result in a cost-effective system. This emphasis on control will become evident later when we review some information system designs.

The Computer System and Characteristics

Since the computer is so prominent in today's MIS, let's consider briefly some of its important elements. The computer is a technological device that accepts data, processes them, and provides results in some form of output. The *central processing unit* (CPU) is the "nerve center" that orchestrates all the activities of the data processing system (see Figure 9.2).

The CPU receives data inputs in numerical, alphabetical, or other symbolic form. These symbols can either be recorded on some input *medium* (magnetic tape, hard disk, floppy disk, punched cards, punched paper tape, and the like), or they can be input directly into the computer with a key console. When processing is completed, the finished results are deliv-

[4]The need for and structuring of an organizational data base is presented in G. M. Scott, "A Data Base for Your Company?" *California Management Review* 19, no. 1 (Fall 1976), pp. 68–78.

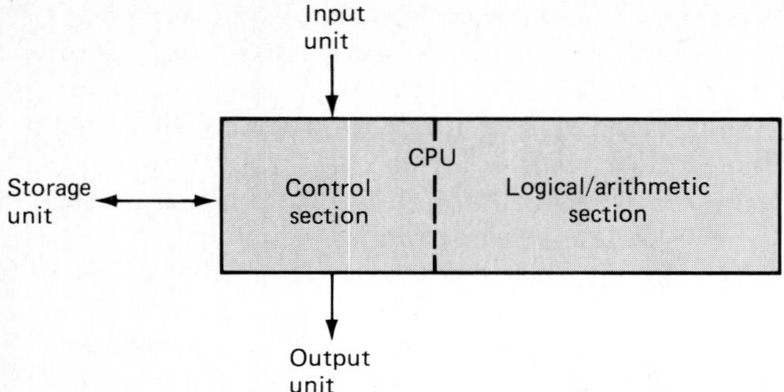

FIGURE 9.2
Structure of central processing unit (CPU)

ered through some output medium such as a video display or high speed printout on paper. The processed information also can remain available in the computer on disks or tapes for further processing if necessary.

Main system storage, usually called *core storage,* is the computer memory in which entering data are stored before processing. Each storage location is assigned an address; data are indexed and available for rapid accessing. In addition to input data, such other information as programmed instructions, intermediate results, and other records and tables can be assigned storage locations with specific addresses. These enable the computer to find the information it needs to create the desired results. The size (capacity) of the storage unit determines how much information can be held in the system. Expensive, powerful computers with large core capacities can hold megabytes (billions of characters) of data. Main storage must have enough capacity to hold the data and all the processing instructions. The speed of the computer system depends on how fast the computer can retrieve information from storage and transfer it to other parts of the computer.

Between the input and output stages, the computer processes information in a predetermined sequence of operations, which are prescribed by a series of instructions, the *program.* The programmer must create this set of instructions in a form that is understandable (in computer language) to the computer. Processing can require such operations as analyzing, sorting, arithmetic calculating, testing for various conditions, and shifting from one set of instructions or data to another. These operations are carried out rapidly in the logical/arithmetic section of the CPU as called for by the stored program.

The control section of the CPU coordinates all of the operations involving input, storage, arithmetic/logical, and output activities. It directs and synchronizes the entire system according to the instructions it receives from the system programmers and operators. The control section is the "operations manager" of the subelements within the computer.

Hardware/Software Computer hardware is the physical equipment and devices used for the input, processing, and output functions of the system. Equipment that is in direct communication with the CPU is called an *online* device. In a mainframe system, for example, remote terminals (when turned on) are online devices. Similarly, microcomputers with modem connections to a mainframe are online devices. With online processing, the computer can perform two functions simultaneously: it can operate the input/output devices controlled by the CPU and process data at the same time.

Some of the major hardware elements are the central processing unit and storage devices. Main (core) storage temporarily holds data and instructions until processing is completed. Before and after processing, these data and instructions are stored in secondary storage devices, the most common of which is the hard disk. To gain more secondary storage capacity, devices such as magnetic tape (for mainframe computers) and floppy disks (for microcomputers) provide large volume storage backups for the system.

Software includes computer programs written for a particular system and all the routines, subroutines, compilers, and assemblers that extend the computer's capabilities. Computer programs come in a range of types (or levels), which vary in speed and flexibility. The highest level programs, *operating system* (OS), feature high speed and flexibility. OS programs are system-oriented, instructing the CPU how to interact with other devices—for example, to monitor and direct other programs in queue awaiting processing. At the intermediate level are *application* programs, which are written to do a specific job. Application programs can be written in several languages. A computer simulation program, for example, may be written in a language such as FORTRAN, PL 1, or COBOL. Lower level programs, which can be slower and less flexible, come in *program packages*, which allow a novice user to interact with the package and obtain a specific desired result. These packages, which are very user oriented, have revolutionized computing into a practical and useful tool for millions of users. Database packages, electronic spreadsheets, word processing, and graphics packages provide off-the-shelf utility for many applications. Today, software can extend the capabilities of computer systems even more than hardware. Our ability to supply useful computer system applications in the production operations environment depends largely on the availability of skilled computer programmers who can write appropriate software programs.

MIS Structures

To design and implement information systems, one must consider the basis for structuring the system configuration. Decisions must be made about the managerial/organizational focus and about the degree to which the information systems should be consolidated.

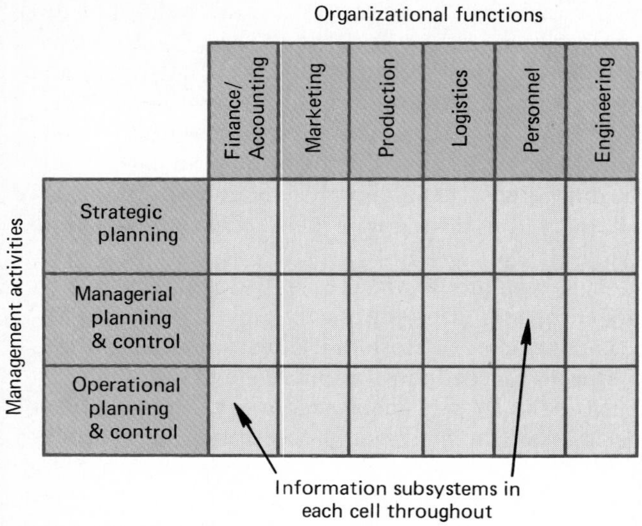

Organizational functions

	Finance/ Accounting	Marketing	Production	Logistics	Personnel	Engineering
Strategic planning						
Managerial planning & control						
Operational planning & control						

Management activities

Information subsystems in each cell throughout

FIGURE 9.3
Organizational functions/management activities interfaces and information subsystems

Managerial/Organizational Focus Most information systems are, in reality, a federation of information subsystems scattered among such *organization functions* as finance and accounting, marketing, production, logistics, and engineering. Each function has primary problems, decision responsibilities, and particular data and information needs.

In addition, information systems frequently focus on the types and hierarchical levels of *management activities* being performed, such as strategic planning, managerial planning and control, and operational planning and control.[5] Whereas strategic planning, for example, uses inputs and models for long-run market and economic forecasts, operational planning and control may be more concerned with an item's on-hand inventory level or the status of today's in-process orders.

By observing management activities within various functional areas (Figure 9.3), we can identify information subsystem needs and configurations that emerge in organizations. Each of the cells in Figure 9.3 represents one or more information subsystems designed to effectively serve a management need area. At the same time, however, many of these areas share common input, processing, and output data; others are relatively independent and unrelated. One reason for performing a systems analysis is to determine the areas of shared need and purpose. This is taken into account in the design.

[5]Chapter 4 of this book discusses various planning levels in operations. For an overview of different information systems geared to meet the decision needs of various levels of management and operations see R. H. Sprague, Jr. and H. J. Watson, "Bit by Bit: Toward Decision Support Systems," *California Management Review* 22, no. 1 (Fall 1979), pp. 60–68.

Degree of Consolidation The fact that there are areas with shared needs suggests that it might be possible to consolidate or integrate information subsystems within the organization. Indeed, much discussion today centers on this question. At an extreme, at least conceptually, is the vision of a totally centralized and integrated (monolithic) system, as opposed to a more decentralized, distributed (modular) system.[6] Several aspects of an information system can be centralized, and to varying degrees; these areas include responsibility for the data processing function and personnel, physical location and use of equipment in the system, and data base. The advantages and disadvantages of highly integrated and distributed systems are summarized in Table 9.1.

Overall, the popularity of distributed systems has increased in recent years. This is due, in part, to significant breakthroughs in the development of relatively low-cost microcomputers and telecommunications, providing substantial computing power and flexibility at a reasonable cost to individual users for tailor-made applications. Still, there is a strong sentiment for the potential advantages offered by more integrated systems. This dilemma of integrated versus distributed systems has resulted in a wide variety of system configurations as we see next.

Computer-User Configurations Various designs of computer systems and their use have emerged, sometimes haphazardly and at other times systematically, in diverse organizations. Some typical computer-user configurations are depicted in Figure 9.4. In configuration 1 the users have a large mainframe computer and each functional department (user) maintains and controls the use of its own data files. Although the computer system is consolidated, the organization's information system is not integrated by the computer itself (although it may be integrated by some other means). When the user files are combined into an integrated data base (configuration 2), multiple users can access and share all the data, thus providing both a consolidated computer system and, potentially, an integrated information system. In either case a common arrangement is for remote terminal access by the user on a time sharing basis that restricts when or for how long access is available. In configuration 3 the adoption of microcomputers, due to their low cost, ease of accessibility, and user-friendly software, provides another layer to the system.[7] Here, the user's access to the mainframe is supplemented by the more personalized flexibility of one or more standalone micros. The fourth configuration, without a mainframe, depicts independent microcomputers dedicated to each user. Here the computer resources are not consolidated nor is there an integrated information system.

---

[6]Distributed systems using minicomputers are discussed in S. L. Mandell, "The Management Information System Is Going to Pieces," *California Management Review* 17, no. 4 (Summer 1975), pp. 50–56.

[7]See S. Wiltsie, "Microcomputers in Manufacturing," *P&IM Review and APICS News*, January 1983, pp. 27–29. See also B. A. Chartier, "Microcomputers = Productivity Power," *P&IM Review and APICS News*, January 1984, pp. 32–61.

TABLE 9.1
Major possible advantages/disadvantages of integrated and distributed systems

Integrated system	
Potential advantages	**Potential disadvantages**
(1) Reduction of inefficiencies from duplication of equipment, data base, processes, and support activities.	(1) Individual departments and units relinquish control over data processing to a central authority.
(2) Increased standardization of processes, procedures, methods and equipment.	(2) Absence of top management support and total organizational commitment of extensive resources for long-term development and implementation pose financial and technical risks.
(3) Increased justification for acquiring more competent data processing specialist skills.	(3) Individual organizational units may experience difficulty getting their needs satisfied.
(4) Increased direct control over the security of and access to the common data base.	(4) Breakdown of the central system can cause extensive disruption throughout the organization.
(5) Provides multiple individual organizational units access to a centralized system that these units might not be able to support individually.	

Distributed system	
Potential advantages	**Potential disadvantages**
(1) User has high degree of direct control over the system.	(1) Increased duplication of equipment, processes, data and personnel.
(2) Greater flexibility and ease of adjusting the system to meet unique user needs.	(2) Can result in nonstandardized procedures and processes within the organization in reporting, editing, etc. of information.
(3) Breakdown of system does not have extensive and pervasive consequences as in integrated system.	(3) Can be difficult to coordinate information-related activities among organizational units.
(4) Less expensive equipment, processes, and software can be used independently of a central system.	
(5) Does not require an extensive, expensive high-risk commitment.	

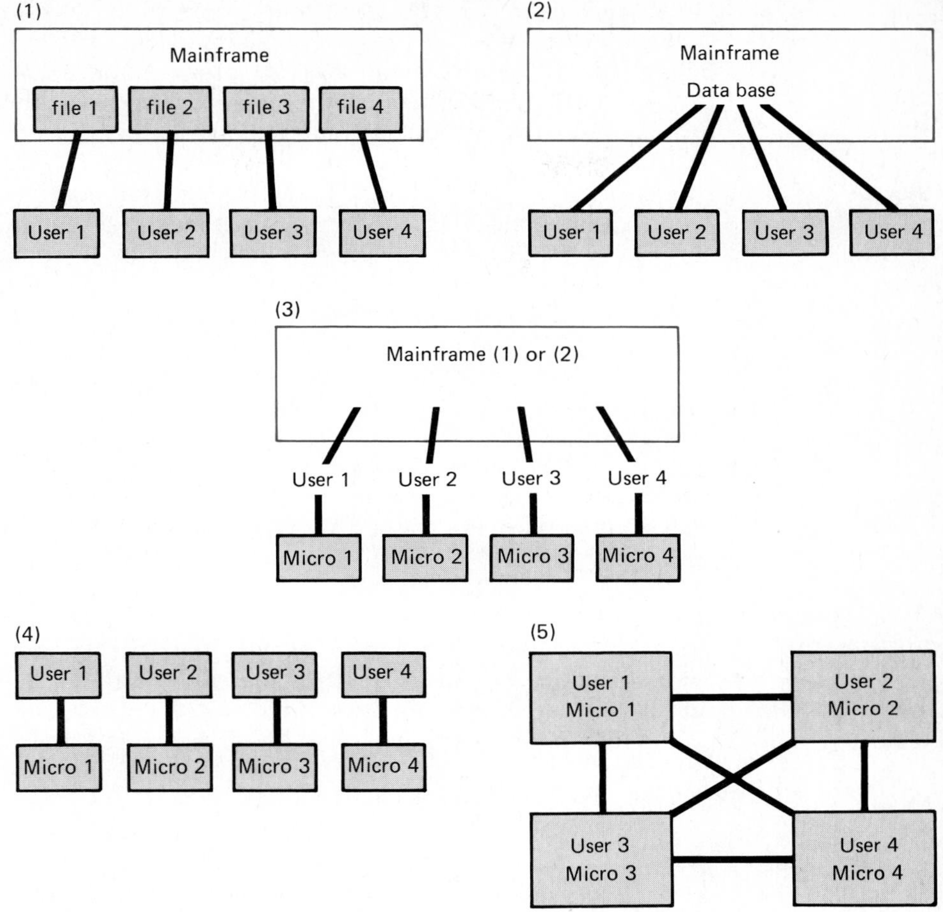

FIGURE 9.4
Computer-user system configurations

The fifth configuration is a network of integrated microcomputers with direct communications linkages that permit an integrated information system. These five configurations, along with others, provide MIS applications of various types as we see next.

MIS APPLICATIONS

Computer-based information systems have a proven record of productivity enhancement and, for the future, their use will expand in both manufacturing and service organizations. The progression of these developments is illustrated below as first we discuss MRP, a manufacturing planning and control system that has been widely adopted since the decade of the 1970s. Then, computer-integrated manufacturing, a more advanced-level system, is discussed. Finally, we briefly review office automation as an emerging application area for information systems.

Material Requirements Planning Systems

Material requirements planning (MRP) is a computerized information system that integrates the scheduling and the control of materials for manufacturing. The MRP system shows what materials procurement actions are needed and when, so that the desired quantities of end products are completed as needed during the planning horizon.

The MRP environment is usually an assembly, fabrication, or combination assembly-fabrication manufacturing situation where the various end products are produced from many subcomponents, assemblies, and materials, for which the sequence of product buildup is known. Thus, the management problem involves both material control and planning; the many component parts must be delivered on time in the right quantities at all stages of product buildup. MRP is the means for coordinating all these efforts.

MRP System Components

Figure 9.5 shows the basic components of an MRP system. Three major information elements are mandatory in the MRP system: a master production schedule, an inventory status file, and a bill of materials file for product structure. Using these three information sources, the MRP processing logic (computer program) provides three kinds of information outputs

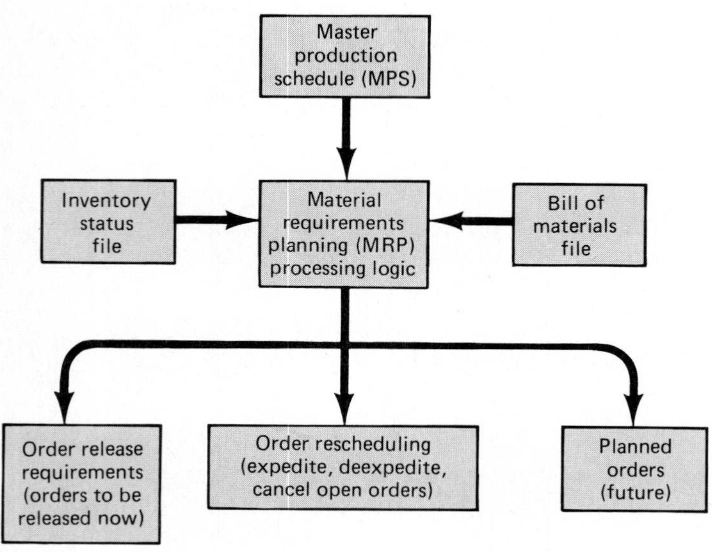

FIGURE 9.5
Material requirements planning system

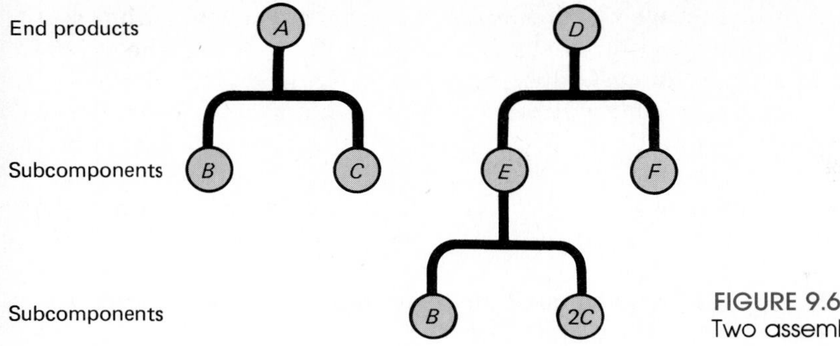

FIGURE 9.6
Two assembled products

about each product component: order release requirements, order rescheduling, and planned orders. Let's examine each of these elements in more detail.

Master Production Schedule (MPS) The MPS is initially developed from firm customer orders or from forecasts of demand before the MRP system begins to operate; it becomes an input to the system. Designed to meet market demand, the MPS identifies the quantity of each end product (end item) and when it needs to be produced during each future period in the production planning horizon. The MPS provides the focal information for the MRP system; it ultimately governs the MRP system's recommended actions on the timing of materials procurement and subcomponents buildups, which are geared to meeting the MPS output schedule.

Bill of Materials (BOM) The BOM identifies how each end product is manufactured, specifying all subcomponent items, their sequence of buildup, their quantity in each finished unit, and which work centers perform the buildup sequence in the facility. This information is obtained from product design documents, work flow analysis, and other standard manufacturing and industrial engineering documentation.[8]

The primary information to MRP from the BOM is the *product structure,* an example of which is shown in Figure 9.6. One unit of end product *A* requires one unit each of subcomponents *B* and *C*. The product structure for end Product *D* requires one *E* and one *F*. Subcomponent *E* is created from one *B* and two units of item *C*.

In MRP terminology, *A* and *D* are "upper-level" end items, while the subcomponents are "lower-level" items. By precisely identifying the levels

[8]The central role of the bill of materials in MRP is discussed in Joseph A. Orlicky, George W. Plossl, and Oliver W. Wight, "Structuring the Bill of Material," *Production and Inventory Management* 13, no. 4 (1972), pp. 19–42.

in the product structure, we clearly show the relationships among the component items in all our end products. Each item in the product structure is given a unique identification number. Since product design changes occur periodically, we must be able to change the BOM file to accurately reflect the current product structure. This is a must in MRP systems. Subsequently, by knowing the master schedule for end items, MRP can schedule and time-phase the orders for lower-level component items in the product structure.

Inventory Status File The system must retain an up-to-date file of the inventory status of each item in the product structure. This file provides accurate information about the availability of every item controlled by MRP. The system uses this information to maintain an accurate accounting of all inventory transactions, both actual and planned. The inventory status file contains the identification number, quantity on hand, safety stock level, quantity disbursed (allocated), and procurement lead time of every item. The time needed to procure an item, once an order for it is initiated, is taken into account when deciding when to place an order for that item.

The MRP Processing Logic The MRP processing logic accepts the master schedule for end items and determines the components schedules for successively lower-level items throughout the product structures. It calculates for each of the time periods (typically one-week periods) in the scheduling time horizon how many of that item are needed (gross requirements), how many units from existing inventory are already available, the net quantity we must plan on receiving in new shipments (planned order receipts), and when orders for the new shipments must be placed (planned order releases) so that all materials arrive just when needed. This data processing continues until it has determined the requirements for all items that will be used to meet the master production schedule. Then, the updated plans are available to managers throughout the manufacturing and procurement system.

Management Information from MRP The MRP output gives a report, similar to the example in Figure 9.7, for each item in the product structure. The example report shows that 400 units of this item are needed (gross requirements) in week 4 and another 500 are needed in week 8. No outstanding orders were previously placed so there are no units of this item scheduled for receipt as of this time. There are, however, 50 uncommitted units of the item already available in inventory and these will go toward meeting the week 4 requirements. Consequently, there are net requirements of 350 units for week 4 and 500 units for week 8. To meet these net requirements, the report indicates we should plan on receiving 350 units in week 4 and a 500-unit order in week 8. Since this particular item has a 3-week procurement leadtime, the first order must be placed (released) in week 1 and the second order in week 5.

Item identification: #3201—Mounting Bracket
Lead time: 3 weeks
Report date: week 0

	Week 1	Week 2	Week 3	Week 4	Week 5	Week 6	Week 7	Week 8
Gross requirements				400				500
Scheduled receipts								
Available for next period	50	50	50					
Net requirements				350				500
Planned order receipts				350				500
Planned order releases	350				500			

FIGURE 9.7
An MRP report for one item

This report clearly identifies what procurement actions are required to keep production on schedule. It also gives suppliers advanced notification of the demands that will be placed on them in the future. As end-item demands change with the passage of time, modifications in the master schedule will dictate corresponding adjustments of lower-level requirements. Weekly updating, for example, will revise the previous schedules and may indicate that an order must be received earlier (expedited) or that a previously placed order can wait until later (deexpedited) or even be cancelled. As you can imagine, this information system is especially valuable when there are many end items with hundreds or thousands of related subcomponents that must be coordinated among numerous suppliers and departments.

While more details of MRP are discussed later in Chapter 16, we wish to note here that the effectiveness of MRP, like any other information system, relies on its people, machines, procedures, and data base, as outlined in the following example.

EXAMPLE

People are involved in many ways in the MRP information system. Members of *management* must prescribe what they require of the MRP system and must commit resources to accomplish its purpose. They must decide, for example, whether or not to include capacity requirements planning, how frequently the master production schedule should be updated, and which products in the product mix should be included in the MRP system. *Staff personnel* must identify data input requirements, obtain the data, and convert data into system-compatible and user-needed form for storing, updating, processing, and reporting. People with technical skills are needed to create software (the MRP logic), to maintain system hardware, and to design system procedures.

Appropriate *machines* must be selected, acquired, and maintained. Professionals must ensure that the capacity, speed, and flexibility of the system's input, storage, processing, and output units are cost effective for materials management.

Procedures are necessary to control access to the MRP system. The accuracy and integrity of the system require decisions about who, how, and when it will be used, updated, and modified. Data involving bills of materials, inventory status, materials purchases and lead times, end-item forecasts, and master production schedules must come from designated authorized sources, and they must be incorporated into the system through prescribed procedures.

The MRP *data base* consists of all the inventory status and bills of materials files that are logically related in the system. The organization must make provisions for updating these files to incorporate new products, product structure modifications from engineering changes, and revised inventory data.[9]

Historically, most MRP information systems were developed on a modular (distributed) basis, rather than as part of a highly integrated information system. More recently, however, other information subsystems throughout the organization have been logically related to the MRP system. Bills of materials data, for example, could be shared with an engineering information system data base; order release and order receipts data could be shared by the order billing and accounts payable information systems; and inventory status data from MRP could become part of marketing and/or purchasing information systems. This type of information integration, in fact, is exactly the impetus for MRPII, the new generation of manufacturing planning and control systems.

Manufacturing Resource Planning (MRPII) Manufacturing resource planning (or "closed loop" MRP) is an integrated information system that steps beyond first-generation MRP to synchronize all the aspects (not just manufacturing) of the business. The MRPII system coordinates sales, purchasing, manufacturing, finance, and engineering by adopting a focal production plan and by using one unified data base to plan and update the activities in all the systems.[10]

As shown in Figure 9.8, the process involves developing from the overall

---

[9]Data base structure, organization, and access as applied to MRP systems is analyzed in R. H. Bonczek, C. W. Holsapple, and A. B. Whinston, "Aiding Decision Makers with a Generalized Data Base Management System: An Application to Inventory Management," *Decision Sciences* 9, no. 2 (April 1978), pp. 228–45.

[10]See V. Chopra, "Productivity Improvement Through Closed Loop MRP (Part One)," *Production & Inventory Management Review and APICS News,* March 1982, pp. 18–21. See also V. Chopra, "Productivity Improvement Through Closed Loop MRP (Part Two)," *Production & Inventory Management Review and APICS News,* April 1982, pp. 49–51.

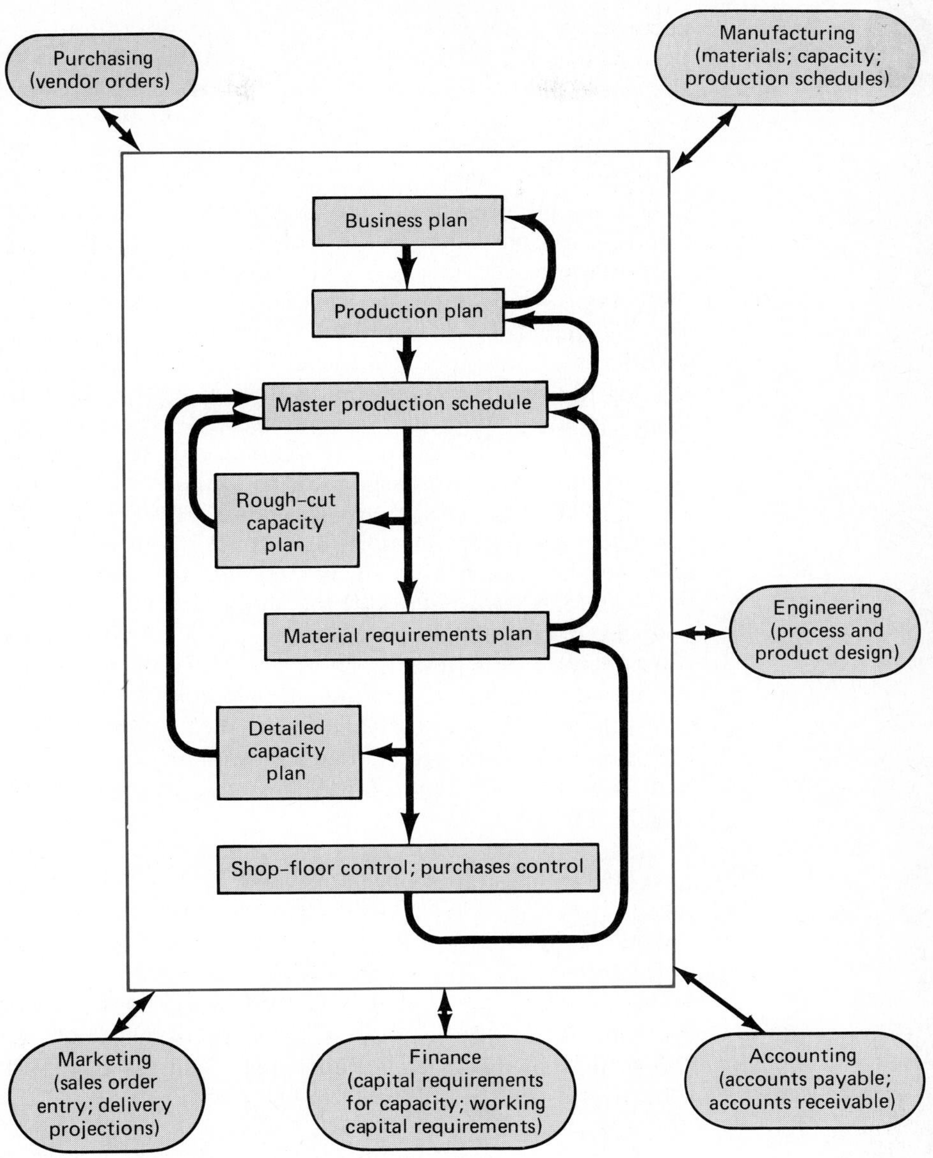

FIGURE 9.8
MRPII: An integrated system for planning and control

business plan, a production plan that specifies, generally, monthly levels of production for each product line over the next one to five years. Since this production plan affects all the functional departments, it is developed by the consensus of executives for whom it subsequently becomes the "game plan" for company operations. Production is then expected to produce at the committed levels, the sales department is expected to sell at these levels, and finance will ensure adequate financial resources. Guided by the production plan, the master production schedule specifies the weekly quantities of specific products to be built. At this point a check is made to determine whether or not the capacity available is roughly adequate to sustain the proposed master schedule. If not, either the capacity or the master schedule must be changed. Once settled, the master schedule is used in the MRP logic, as previously described, to create materials requirements and priority schedules for production. Then, a detailed capacity requirements evaluation determines whether or not the necessary capacity exists for producing the specific components at each work center during the scheduled time periods. If not, the master schedule is revised to reflect the realities of the limited available capacity. After a realistic, capacity-feasible schedule is developed, the emphasis shifts to *execution* of the plan; purchase schedules and shop schedules are generated. From these schedules, work center loadings, shop floor control, and vendor followup activities can be determined to ensure that the master schedule is implemented.

The feedback from MRPII is valuable in two respects. First, it keeps all relevant departments informed about operations progress, enabling them to adjust harmoniously to deviations from the plan. Thus, a delinquent vendor delivery, a machine breakdown, or a customer's request for quicker delivery of an order can be fed back into the requirements planning system so that all the schedules for related subcomponents can be modified.

A second use of the MRPII system is to evaluate various business proposals. The computer program can be used to simulate the effects of "what if" questions about business operations. If, for example, the output of product X were to increase by 20 percent in weeks 15 to 20 and that of Y decrease by 15 percent in weeks 10 to 15, how would operations and profitability be affected? The system will show how purchases and, hence, accounts payable are affected, when deliveries to customers and accounts receivable will occur, what capacity revisions are needed, and so on. The company-wide implications of the proposed change can be evaluated and the actions of the various departments can be coordinated toward a common purpose.

Computer-Integrated Manufacturing

Computer-integrated manufacturing (CIM), while not yet a reality, is a vision of things to come.[11] Some elements of the CIM concept are operational in many companies today and the impetus is toward a computer-based sys-

[11]See W. H. Slautterback and W. B. Werther, Jr., "The Third Revolution: Computer-Integrated Manufacturing," *National Productivity Review* 3, no. 4 (Autumn 1984), pp. 367–374.

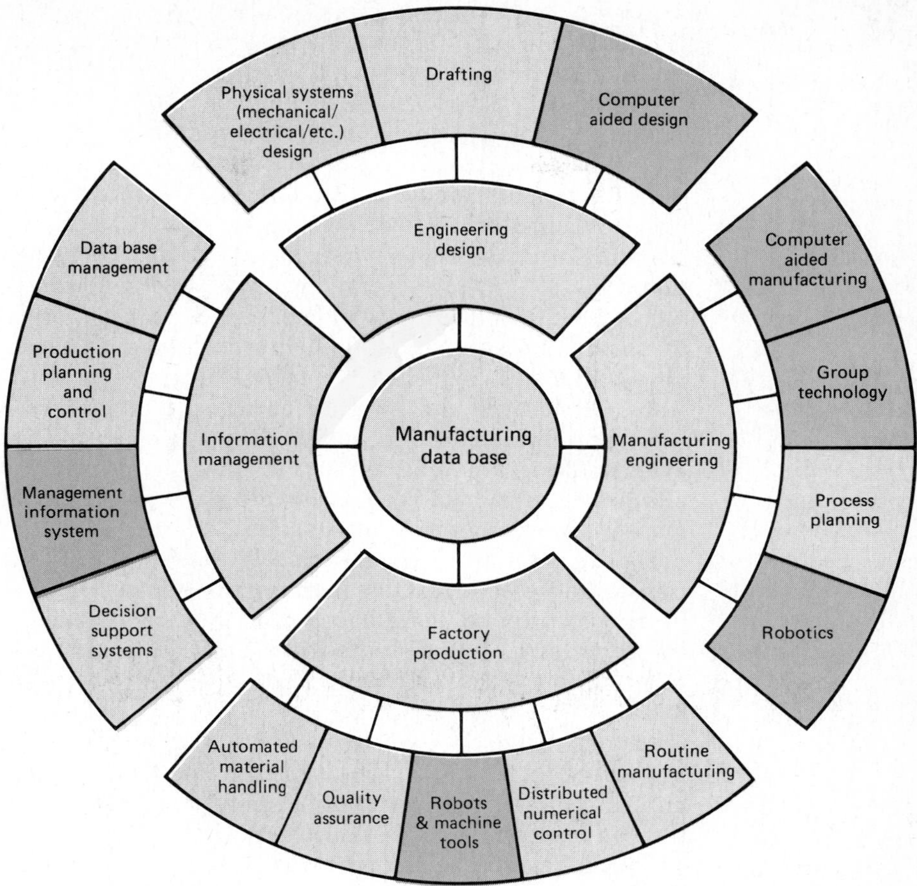

FIGURE 9.9
Computer integrated manufacturing sub-functions

tem that more fully integrates the entire concept-to-market process. In a sense, then, the "manufacturing" label (in CIM) is a misnomer because the system involves engineering (of products and processes) as well as production. As shown in Figure 9.9 and discussed in Chapter 2, CIM centers around a manufacturing database that contains all product and process-related information for producing the company's products. The database is built on data from engineering design, manufacturing engineering, factory production, and information management which, in turn, draw upon the database for information to conduct their functional activities. This interactive sharing is the glue that synchronizes the four activity areas into a unified whole and, thereby, offers potential productivity gains. As we review CIM, you'll see some of the problems of implementing the concept, especially in the information and database management areas on the left side of Figure 9.9.[12] Each of the six shaded subfunctions are discussed next to illustrate how they tie together in the CIM system.

Computer-Aided Design (CAD) New products and components begin with a design concept that, eventually, is translated into specifications to provide the desired functional and aesthetic characteristics. The design process traditionally has been an iterative one in which product specifications are refined in successive stages based upon the designer's experience, computations, sketches, and drawings. CAD, using computational and graphics software, has substantially enhanced design productivity. The geometry of the component can be graphically displayed and manipulated easily on video monitors. Alternative designs can be evaluated more quickly and some of the time and expense of physical mock-ups, models, and prototypes are eliminated. Furthermore, by accessing the data base, an already-existing design may be found and, thereby, duplicative design efforts are eliminated. These reductions in design costs and lead times are supplemented by savings in other operational areas as well. Once a satisfactory design is determined, for example, it is stored in the database and can be transmitted electronically; it is rapidly accessible to manufacturing engineering, production, and purchasing. And, as the component is redesigned, the new design is transmitted in a timely and accurate manner that eliminates erroneous use of obsolete designs.

Computer-Aided Manufacturing (CAM) Computer-aided manufacturing systems control the operations of machine tools on the shop floor. The machines typically can perform a variety of operations, not just one, and the machine memory receives instructions from a computer on the sequence and specifications of its operations. CAM offers several production benefits: the machine operations are usually more reliable than those by skilled operators; product quality is more consistent from unit to unit; closer tolerances can be obtained; and labor costs are lower because less operator time is needed. These benefits, of course, don't come free of costs. Manufacturing engineering must create the equipment and software that governs machine operation. They work closely with engineering design to ensure a workable, affordable matchup of the manufacturing processes and the design of the products and components. Further, from production's standpoint, the equipment and software must provide changeover capabilities for flexible production runs and reliable performance to meet production schedules for various components and products. The computer programs can be stored in the manufacturing database, retrieved, updated, and revised as components are added or redesigned, accessed as needed by pro-

---

[12]See D. Gerwin and J. C. Tarondeau, "Case Studies of Computer Integrated Manufacturing Systems: A View of Uncertainty and Innovation Processes," *Journal of Operations Management* 2, no. 2 (February 1982), pp. 87–99.

duction, and can be transmitted electronically in-house or, externally, by satellite to other divisions and facilities.

Group Technology (GT) Group technology is especially useful where up to hundreds of thousands of parts and components are active in the production process. GT is a classification and coding scheme for grouping parts into families with similar characteristics. To be operational, GT requires a database retrieval system with software that calls out and sorts large listings on the key characteristics of interest to the user. I might, for example, wish to identify all the various steel mounting brackets that are smaller than six inches in width. You, in contrast, may want a similar list but sorted by strength rating rather than by type of material or size. Obviously, extensive software development is involved in designing a functional, user-oriented GT system to meet the diverse needs of engineering designers, process planners, and inventory control personnel. Once developed, GT offers several benefits to the manufacturing system by identifying unwanted parts redundancies. Rather than designing a new bracket, for example, engineering may find a suitable substitute that was designed earlier for another application. Components simplification and consolidation eliminates excessive inventories and simplifies inventory control, quality assurance, and vendor relationships.

Robotics and Robots The benefits of robots have been widely publicized. They replace humans in some very heavy, dirty, dangerous, or unpleasant tasks. They also provide consistent quality and, although they're often slower than humans, they are highly reliable and can sustain a steady pace for long periods of time. Reprogrammable robots can perform a variety of specialized tasks and task sequences to precise specifications and they require less plant space than do alternative production processes.

As our experience with robots increases, we're finding out that they affect other functional areas in some unanticipated ways. In spot-welding metal components, for example, engineers traditionally have overdesigned manufacturing specifications by calling for more welds than were really needed, anticipating that the human welder would miss one or two welds with the onset of fatigue or distractions on the job. Robots, in contrast, never miss a weld and consequently, engineers are rethinking their traditional overdesign practices. While the robot's computer programs and operational specifications do not reside in the manufacturing database of most organizations today, the computer-integrated manufacturing concept is aimed toward doing so in the future.

Management Information System The computer integrated manufacturing system is a network of information for enhancing organizational effectiveness. Suppose for illustrative purposes it includes MRPII among its other management information systems. Then, the manufacturing database contains the master production schedule, inventory status files for components, and bills of materials for the various product structures. It also contains order release information and production schedules that reflect engineering and production lead times within manufacturing's capacity and process capabilities. Before this system can become an operational reality, it is obvious that some substantial problems, primarily in database management and software development, must be resolved. Methods are needed to integrate vast quantities of diverse kinds of data into forms that are compatible and accessible to numerous users at remote locations. Additional considerations involve deciding who should have access to the system and under what circumstances in order to preserve the integrity of the database, to protect proprietary and experimental design developments and, at the same time, provide high utility to the users. These and related design dilemmas are being addressed today in the emergence of computer integrated manufacturing.

Office Automation

The vast numbers of people employed in services, as opposed to manufacturing, indicate that substantial productivity potential exists in our office operations, public agencies, and private sector service industries. Indeed, some service industries, most notably commercial banking and insurance, have realized healthy productivity gains while others have not. In each instance where improvement has occurred, it is associated with how information is managed. Consequently, information is perhaps the key resource in the white collar environment. There is a growing emphasis on managing information just as we do other resources such as money, equipment, personnel, and raw materials.

Office automation (OA) is a computer-based system for managing information resources including activities such as word processing, report generation, and data handling of clerical, professional, and management personnel. As stated by one source,

> Office automation (OA) may be defined as the use of integrated computer technology to help maximize the productivity of office resources.[13]

OA's most distinctive feature is the emphasis on *integrated* automation:

> The goal of the integrated electronic office is to connect every piece of office equipment—mainframes, personal computers, photocopiers, and other devices—to every other, not only in one location but in company branches and in suppliers' and customers' offices throughout the world. . . .[14]

---

[13]J. C. Crawford, "Successfully Evaluating and Implementing Office Automation," *CA Magazine*, August 1984, p. 106.

[14]M. Hart, "How the Office of the Future is Shaping Up," *CA Magazine*, August 1984, p. 72.

Highly integrated systems are feasible today due to the abundance of affordable, advanced telecommunications and electronics technologies. These devices have changed white collar job content and capabilities, streamlining the flows of communications among work stations and people. Information is created and transmitted more rapidly and directly than in pre-OA systems. Desk-top terminals provide easy data entry, either by voice or keyboard, for messages to be transmitted directly to the recipient's terminal. Photocopies or facsimilies of the message can be produced quickly on equipment that is directly integrated with the sender's or receiver's terminal. Teleconferencing through terminals provides direct communications among executives in remote locations, thus avoiding mail delays or traveling costs for meeting together at one location. User-friendly word processing systems provide a faster, more accurate means of producing letters, reports, and other documents than do earlier types of equipment. Electronic spreadsheets, database software, and graphics software enable professionals and executives to retrieve and manipulate data for problem analysis, decision making, and reporting.

In observing the evolution of office automation we can trace its upward progression beginning with clerical tasks (data processing for bookkeeping; word processing for typing) and extending into managerial and executive applications (teleconferencing and decision aiding). A transition is underway today in this latter area, managerial and executive decision aiding. It is the center of attention in decision support systems, the newest development in information systems, as we see next.

DECISION SUPPORT SYSTEMS

Decision support systems (DSS) are the newest generation of developments in the evolution of information systems. With them, we seem headed toward a new plateau in our concept of the computer's potential for management decision making.

> A decision support system is an interactive system that provides the user with easy access to decision models and data in order to support semistructured and unstructured decision-making tasks.[15]

DSS extends MIS with an emphasis on providing more decision-making support; it ". . . shifts attention from the level of operations (an information system for job order status or accounts receivable) toward the issues of managerial problem solving."[16] This distinction between classical MIS

[15] H. J. Watson and M. M. Hill, "Decision Support Systems or What Didn't Happen with MIS," *Interfaces* 13, no. 5 (October 1983), p. 82.

[16] P. G. W. Keen and M. S. S. Morton. *Decision Support Systems*. Reading, Mass.: Addison-Wesley Publishing Company, 1978, pp. 57–58.

and DSS is more substantial than it may appear at first glance. For although we may have intended MIS to be an information system for managers, DSS advocates Keen and Morton note that: ". . . many practicing managers argue that this is not so. They claim to be uninfluenced by computer-based information systems although they willingly grant that the organization under them has been considerably affected."[17]

Why have these systems not lived up to their potential? Part of the answer resides in the way they were introduced and used in organizations during the formative years of computers; some early, limited perceptions from those days linger still. Another factor is our growing awareness of management science-computer potential from recent advances in modeling and computer technologies. Both factors, the historical use and our views of the technologies involved, are evident in the evolution of information systems.

Stages in the Evolution of Information Systems

We can trace three distinct stages in the evolution of information systems (Figure 9.10). The first, electronic data processing (EDP), was focused on exploiting the high computational speed and large memory capacity of a centralized computer. Huge data files could be stored, repetitive computations performed, transactions processed, and summary reports created. The information for management described past and current operational status. Data processing efficiencies were quickly realized and the status-transaction reports benefited first-line managers in their day-to-day planning and control decisions. They were not very helpful, however, for the unstructured decisions facing higher-level managers.

In stage two, the MIS era, the information focus was redirected more toward the tactical matters of middle management. Systems were designed and structured to provide pre-identified flows of information, usually organized according to business function (for example, marketing, personnel, and finance). Using an integrated database and specific-purpose models for selected problem areas, users could initiate inquiries and receive reports. Thus, for example, the model for projecting cash flows, or the one for projecting materials requirements for planned production, or the model for estimating six-month sales revenues could be activated. When a particular problem arose, the user searched the system for the appropriate model (if it existed).

In stage three, decision support systems offer an even higher level of assistance. DSS are decision-focused and, accordingly, they emphasize flexibility, adaptability, and quick response; they are user-initiated and controlled.[18] DSS design emphasizes support for the personal decision-making

---

[17]Op. cit., p. 54.

[18]R. H. Sprague, Jr. and E. D. Carlson. *Building Effective Decision Support Systems.* (Englewood Cliffs, N.J.: Prentice-Hall, Inc., 1982), p. 7.

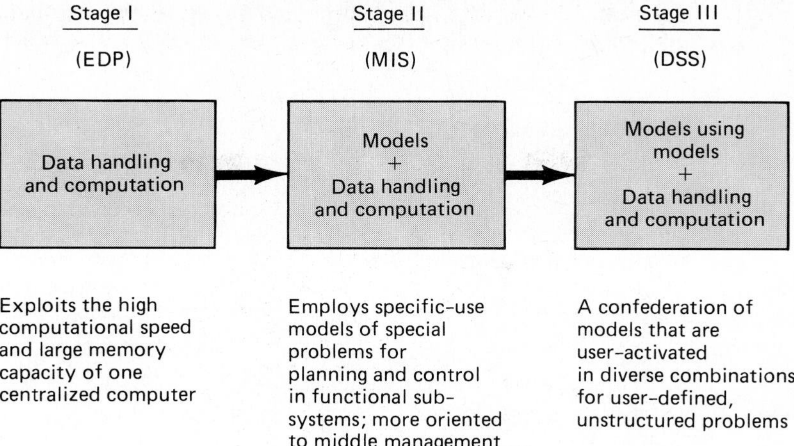

FIGURE 9.10
Evolutionary stages of information systems

styles of individual managers. We can understand from these features why DSS have been characterized as ". . . *interactive* computer-based systems that *help* utilize *data* and *models* to solve *unstructured* problems."[19] These features open the doors of information systems to the needs of higher-level decision makers. These sentiments are reflected by three prominent DSS advocates:

> Whereas early efforts dealt with modeling one or another particular problem area within an organization, present-day emphasis is upon a coordinated modeling of several problem areas. This integration of models is necessary if support of high-level decision making is to be enhanced, since high-level decision-making (for example, strategic planning) involves many problem areas.[20]

The Manager-Model-Machine Interface

Today's concept of DSS includes an array of management science models, rather than isolated ones, that are combined into a single system with which managers can directly communicate. Depending on the type of problem the user specifies, different combinations of the models are integrated with one another and with the database. This provides a rich domain of problem inquiries and information. The choices of inquiry and resulting

[19]Op. cit., p. 4.

[20]R. H. Bonczek, C. W. Holsapple, and A. B. Whinston, "The Evolving Roles of Models in Decision Support Systems," *Decision Sciences* 11, no. 2 (April 1980), p. 345.

information reports are determined uniquely by the user, rather than being rigidly prespecified by the system designer.

EXAMPLE

In 1973, Ronald Seaberg and Charlotte Seaberg revealed a corporate decision-aiding system developed for Xerox of Canada Limited (XCL). It was, in the words of its developers, ". . . a family of timeshared models, developed . . . in an effort to link the functional areas for communication, planning, and control purposes. Using the approaches of statistical forecasting, heuristics, and simulation, the XCL Decision System assists and guides management all the way from deriving product demand forecasts to simulating the day-to-day operations of the firm to formulating divisional financial statements to preparing corporate operating and medium-range plans. Developed in a short time span and at low cost, the system is used extensively in Canada and has been adopted, in part, by U.S. Corporate and regional offices."[21]

What does a system like this involve? The primary ingredient is a more refined concept of manager-model-machine interactions, depicted in Figure 9.11. The user can invoke a command (arrow *a* in the diagram) to Model I or to the data base (arrow *b*) to receive a model response or data as in conventional systems. In addition, however, Model I itself may become a user (arrow *c*) of the data base if so directed by the decision maker. Using a simple command language, Model I can be invoked to explore and compute results for a variety of data conditions. It may be, for example, a cash-flow prediction model, reporting results for past, current, or future data. Used in this fashion it is a rather typical stand-alone model.

The DSS concept, however, expands this to a confederation of models, rather than just one, that perform different functions. Although each of them has stand-alone capabilities (as in conventional MIS), they also can be used together in various combinations. Companion models become users of other models. Thus, Model I, when activated, can itself activate Model II (arrow *d*), which can access data (arrow *e*). The subsequent output report of Model II becomes the input report for Model I. Then the overall results from Model I are reported to the decision maker.

When the system contains several models, not just two, you can envision the variety of information combinations that become accessable for the diverse interests of the users. Its flexibility and adaptability are highly utilitarian for addressing complex decision problems. Xerox's Decision

[21]R. A. Seaberg and C. Seaberg, "Computer Based Decision Systems in Xerox Corporate Planning," *Management Science* 20, no. 4 (December, Part II, 1973), p. 575.

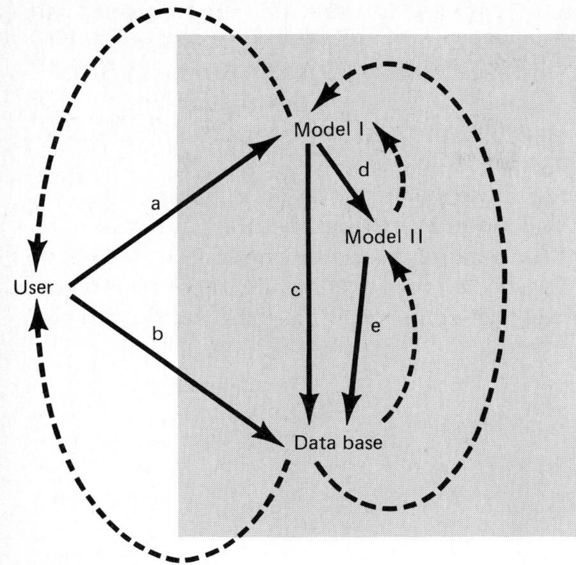

FIGURE 9.11*
Man-machine-model interrelationships in DSS

*Adapted from R. H. Bonczek, C. W. Holsapple, and A. B. Whinston, "The Evolving Roles of Models in Decision Support Systems," *Decision Sciences* 11, no. 2 (April 1980), p. 339.

System, outlined above, is an example. It enables management to gain a better grasp on its plans and actions for the future. Adopting a 12-month forward look at the business, it examines the combined effects of marketing, finance, service, manufacturing, and distribution. The inputs include assumptions and strategies that are manager-controlled. The input variables include various fixed and variable costs, trade assumptions, inventory parameters, and growth rates. The output from the system's equations include variables such as sales orders, revenues, inventory levels, expenses, manpower requirements, and net profit.[22]

The system allows managers to conveniently investigate "what-if" questions like the following:

- If the compensation plan is changed, what is the most likely effect on salesperson performance and productivity?
- Based on current sales trends, what is the 12 month profit picture? How will profitability change if the product-pricing structure is modified? Or, what if I increase the sales force by five percent?
- How should the manufacturing mix of production be adjusted to achieve the profit plan for current and projected sales?[23]

[22]Op. cit., pp. 577–78.

[23]Op. cit., pp. 577–78.

The Xerox experience is no longer an isolated case but, instead, it marked a beginning. Since then, DSS applications have become rather widespread. Along with fast-moving technologies, we're becoming better informed about the human and organizational variables that influence the acceptance and use of these systems.[24] If they are to become truly effective decision aids, system technologies must be reconciled with the changing needs of managers. Used properly, these systems can be a major asset. Effective information systems depend upon the skills, abilities, and commitment of employees throughout the organization and should be designed with those factors in mind. Carelessly employed, they can become a major liability—a liability so burdensome that some organizations should clearly stay with manual information systems.

SUMMARY

Information management is a major concern in organizing the production-operations system. Through its information structure, the organization provides the means for synchronizing its people, equipment, and facilities toward achieving its goals. Management information systems provide this formal structure and they do so by capitalizing on the powerful computational capabilities of computers. Computer-based systems are created to support decision-making functions; they consist of five basic elements: people, machines, procedures, a database, and control. Some basic characteristics and terminology, essential for understanding these systems, were presented.

Several MIS applications revealed how they enhance productivity in both manufacturing and service environments. One production application, the MRP information system, is especially helpful in materials management where operations managers are confronted with considerations of inventory, forecasting, procurement, and detailed production scheduling involving vast amounts of data and information. With MRP, managers can make timely decisions that shorten delivery lead times to customers and reduce inventory levels. Manufacturing resource planning, computer-integrated manufacturing and office automation provided examples of more highly integrated information systems.

Finally, three stages of evolution in information management—electronic data processing, management information systems, and decision support systems—reveal how decision-aiding has advanced in recent years. The decision support systems have opened the doors of information assistance to the needs of higher-level managers. As these technologies develop, we are becoming more aware of the sensitive balance among manager-model-machine interrelationships. This awareness is an important step toward enhancing effective management.

---

[24]See W. L. Fuerst and P. H. Cheney, "Factors Affecting the Perceived Utilization of Computer-Based Decision Support Systems in the Oil Industry," *Decision Sciences* 13, no. 4 (October 1982), pp. 554–69. See also C. R. Adams, "How Management Users View Information Systems," *Decision Sciences* 6, no. 2 (April 1975), pp. 335–45.

CASE

Computers Talk to Computers*

Background

The health care industry is growing faster than any other industry in the United States. With the possible exception of defense, it is the largest industry, with nearly 10 percent of the GNP directly or indirectly related to health care.

Most U.S. residents are insured in one way or another. The largest insurance agency is Blue Cross-Blue Shield. A major portion of the industry's activity is done in hospitals and medical centers. These facilities deliver services and then collect money from the patients and/or their insurance company. The information system of the health care system is very complex and it is distributed in the following locations:

1. Physicians' offices
2. Facilities' offices (hospitals, clinics)
3. Insurance companies
4. State and local health offices and agencies
5. Federal health offices and agencies
6. Vendors (e.g., hospital supply companies, contractors for services)
7. Health research institutions

The amount and complexity of health information is rapidly increasing due to government regulations and controls, improvements in medicine and research, and legal requirements (regarding malpractice). As a result, the expense of information handling has sharply escalated. It has been estimated as high as 40 percent of any hospital's total expenses[1].

The Case of Sunshine Hospital

In an attempt to deal with these problems, there has been an increased use of computers at all levels and locations. For example, Sunshine Hospital increased the number of CRTs from 2 to nearly 300 in less than 10 years. Nearly 70 percent of all the hospital employees use the computer on a day-to-day basis. Furthermore, the hospital owns two large computers and several mini- and microcomputers, all tied together in one system.

The hospital billing subsystem is tied electronically with Blue Cross.[2] The hospital claims are transmitted by Sunshine's computer, through regular telephone lines, to the State's Blue Cross-Blue Shield computer center. This tie-in allows Blue Cross to process claims rapidly and accurately. It also allows Blue Shield to perform a wide range of statistical and quantitative analyses. In addition, Blue Cross management is provided with information required for planning, control, and marketing research.

The hospital computer is tied to several computers located in physicians' offices. Thus information regarding admission of patients, required tests, and other hospital work on patients is transformed directly to the hospital.

Finally, the hospital computer system is tied to the computer of its major supplier. Orders are transmitted automatically to the supplier, and bills are received electronically.

*Source: E. Turban in *Cases and Readings in Management Science*, E. Turban and N. P. Loomba (eds.) (Plano, Texas: Business Publications, Inc., Rev. ed., 1982), pp. 345–47.

Blue Cross publishes various valuable reports on the status of health care. Some information in its database is directly available to Sunshine. The hospital has access to the data bank at any time, to receive statistical data, comparative information and interpretation of rules and regulations.

In an attempt to take advantage of this situation, the management of Sunshine decided to develop a decision-support system. The following decision areas are especially important to management:

1. Rate setting (How much to charge? What will be accepted by Blue Cross? Are rates compatible?)
2. Forecasting of demand
3. Long-range planning (required for accreditation)
4. Budget planning and control
5. Inventory control
6. Employees scheduling
7. Allocation of resources to departments
8. Scheduling of the operating rooms

Case Questions

You are called in as a consultant to help the hospital in constructing a DSS; also, top management would like to use more management science techniques.

1. Outline the steps necessary to build the DSS.
2. Discuss the implications of the tied-in computers.
3. The hospital would like to know the feasibility of an in-house development versus purchasing packaged software (available from shared medical systems). Compare the alternatives.
4. Discuss how behavioral and organizational considerations may influence your analysis.
5. In what ways can DSS help in the implementation of quantitative analysis in the hospital?
6. In what ways can DSS improve the efficiency and effectiveness of the hospital's decision making?

Case References

[1]Veazie, S. "Information Systems: In the Cost Containment Battle," *Hospitals,* April 1, 1978.

[2]Elliot, J. O., and G. E. Tucker. "Electronic Billing Saves Time, Money," *Hospital Financial Management,* January 1979.

REVIEW AND DISCUSSION QUESTIONS

1. Clearly demonstrate why a computer-based information system is necessary for MRP.
2. Outline the purposes of MRP and explain how an MRP system can achieve these purposes.

3. Outline the data contents of an MRP information system database. Identify other organizational information systems that would most likely benefit from sharing this database.
4. Identify and discuss difficulties and problems that can arise in implementing an integrated information system.
5. An information system in support of a day-to-day management control activity will differ from one designed to support a high-level management activity. Give an example activity of each of these two management levels and describe key differences in their associated information systems.
6. Explain the role of the master production schedule and how it relates to the other elements of an MRP system.
7. Provide an outline of and explain the MRP processing logic for an end item and its subcomponents.
8. Compare and contrast the purposes and uses of MRP versus MRPII.
9. Some authorities contend that MRPII is a decision support system while others argue that it is not. Resolve this issue.
10. The designers of a computer-integrated manufacturing system must consider its people, equipment, procedures, database, and control requirements. Develop an initial set of specifications for each of these five areas.
11. Select an unstructured operations decision problem and outline the design of a decision support system that will assist you in resolving the problem.
12. Finance, marketing, and production decisions often involve overlapping or commonly-shared data. Identify specific examples of these shared data needs and illustrate how they can be combined and used in an integrated database.

PROBLEMS

Reinforcing Fundamentals

1. Product 601 is made from three 740 subassemblies, two 810 subassemblies, and one 900 subassembly. A 740 subassembly consists of one 309 component and two units of part 207. The 900 subassembly is made from two units of component 400 and one unit of part 782. An 810 subassembly consists of one 309 component, one 721 component, and two 682 subassemblies. A 682 subassembly is made from one unit of component 400 and one unit of part 207. Create a product structure tree for product 601 and determine how many units of each component are required to produce 100 units of product 601.
2. Determine the net requirements for items *x* and *y*, below:

	Item x	Item y
Gross requirements	600	50
Scheduled receipts	100	0
Available	0	50
Planned order receipts	0	50
Planned order releases	700	0

3. Consider the following MRP situation:

Product component flow table

Part # PBZ-701

LEAD TIME—2 weeks	Week									
	1	2	3	4	5	6	7	8	9	10
Gross requirements		60				80			40	
Scheduled Receipts										
Available (Stock on Hand)	80	20	20	20	20					
Net Requirements						60			40	
Planned order receipts						40			40	
Planned order releases				60				40		

What changes, *if any,* are required to have a correct product component flow table for part number PBZ-701? Gross requirements are correct.

Challenging Exercises

4. Carcord, Inc., has received an order for 100 units of product 501 with the product structure shown in Figure 9.12. The quantity in parentheses is the number of units of that component that is required by its parent item. There is no stock on hand (available) and none on order. Determine the order release data for all necessary orders.

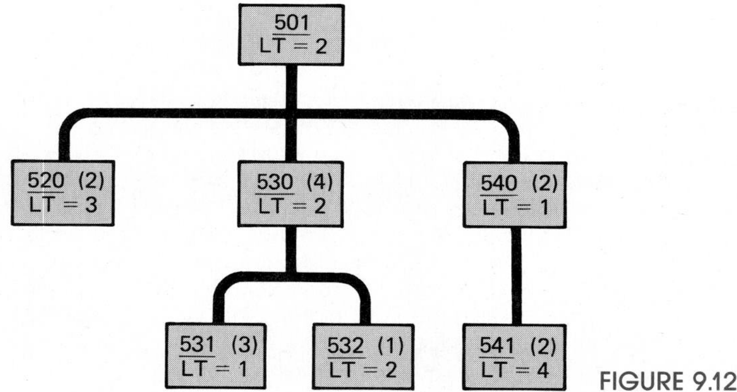

FIGURE 9.12

5. Ambrex, Inc., has received an order for 70 units of product 20 and 50 units of product 40, to be delivered in twelve weeks. The product structures for products 20 and 40 are shown in Figure 9.13. The quantity in parentheses is the number of units of that component that is required by its parent item. Ambrex has on hand (available) 300 units each of components 31 and 37; there is no stock on hand or on order for other components. Determine the sizes and timing of planned order releases necessary to meet delivery commitments for products 20 and 40.

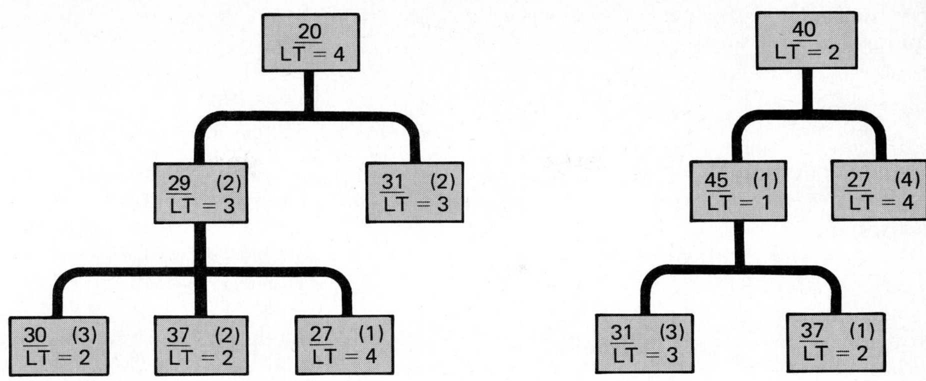

FIGURE 9.13

6. After planning for the conditions stated in problem 5, Ambrex receives a request for an additional order for 50 units of product 40. The Ambrex sales representative wants to know if she can promise delivery within ten weeks, or earlier if possible, to the potential customer. As the production planner, realizing that your assembly operation can, at most, work on assembling 50 units of product 40 at any given time, what is your response to the sales representative's inquiry?

GLOSSARY

Bill of materials Describes product buildup details of an item, including all subcomponent items, their buildup sequence, the quantity needed for each, and the work centers that perform the buildup sequence.

Central processing unit (CPU) Computer component that directs all activities (including data acceptance, processing, and output) of the data processing system.

Computer program Detailed procedures, executed by the computer, that logically sequence and relate data for a specified purpose.

Core storage Main computer memory in which system data are retained.

Database Aggregation of all data files in a system.

Detailed capacity planning Iterative process of modifying the master production schedule and/or planned resources to create consistency between capacity and the production schedule.

Distributed system Information system in which personnel, physical and organizational location, equipment, and database are decentralized.

Field Smallest data element in a database.

File A collection of logically related data records.

Gross requirements Overall quantity of an item needed in each future time period to meet planned output levels. Planned output for end items is obtained from the master production schedule. Planned output for lower-level items is obtained from the MRP system.

Hardware Physical equipment and devices used for the input, processing, and output functions of the computer system.

Information system An integrated network of people, procedures, equipment, models, database, and control that support decision making; modern information systems evolved through three stages—electronic data processing, management information systems, and decision support systems.

Integrated system Information system in which the database and equipment of users are interrelated into a common network.

Inventory status file Complete documentation of the inventory status of each item in the product structure, including item identification, on-hand quantity, safety stock level, quantity allocated, and lead time.

Master production schedule Describes the quantity and timing of each end product to be pro-

each future period in the production ...g horizon.

...equirements Net quantity of an item that ...st be procured to meet the scheduled output ...r this period. It is calculated as "gross requirements" minus "scheduled receipts" for the period minus "available" from the previous period.

Offline Equipment not connected to the computer system.

Online Equipment directly connected to the computer system.

Part-period method A nonoptimal lot-sizing policy that generates varying order sizes by considering holding versus ordering costs.

Planned order receipts Quantity of an item that is *planned* to be ordered so that it will be received in this time period to meet "net requirements" for this period. The order has not yet been placed.

Planned order release Quantity of an item that is *planned* to be ordered, and the planned time period for releasing this order, that will result in the order being received when needed. It is the "planned order receipt" offset in time by the item's lead time. When this order is placed (released), it becomes a "scheduled receipt" and is deleted from "planned order receipts" and "planned order releases."

Product structure A product tree showing the levels and quantities of subcomponent relationships constituting an end item.

Record A grouping of logically related data fields.

Rough-cut capacity planning The level of planning that evaluates the feasibility of the proposed master production schedule within existing capacity.

Scheduled receipts Quantity of an item that will be received from suppliers as a result of orders that have been placed (open orders). The order has already been placed.

SELECTED READINGS

Adams, C. R. "How Management Users View Information Systems." *Decision Sciences* 6, no. 2 (April 1975), pp. 337–45.

American Production and Inventory Control Society, *Capacity Planning and Control*. Washington, D.C.: APICS 1979.

Berry, W. L. and D. Clay Whybark. "Research Perspectives for Materials Requirements Planning Systems." *Production and Inventory Management* 16, no. 2 (1975), pp. 19–25.

Bonczek, R. H., C. W. Holsapple, and A. B. Whinston. "Aiding Decision Makers with a Generalized Data Base Management System: An Application to Inventory Management." *Decision Sciences* 9, no. 2 (April 1978), pp. 228–45.

Bonczek, R. H., C. W., Holsapple, and A. B. Whinston. "The Evolving Roles of Models in Decision Support Systems." *Decision Sciences* 11, no. 2 (April 1980), pp. 337–56.

Burch, J. G., Jr. and F. R. Strater, Jr. *Information Systems: Theory and Practice*. Santa Barbara, California: Hamilton Publishing Company, 1974.

Daft, R. L. and N. B. MacIntosh. "A New Approach to Design and Use of Management Information." *California Management Review* 21, no. 1 (Fall 1978), pp. 82–92.

Davis, G. B. *Management Information Systems*. New York: McGraw-Hill Book Company, 1974.

Keen, P. G. W. and M. S. S. Morton. *Decision Support Systems*. Reading, Mass: Addison-Wesley Publishing Company, 1978.

Mandell, S. L. "The Management Information System Is Going to Pieces." *California Management Review* 17, no. 4 (Summer 1975), pp. 50–56.

Miller, Jeffrey G. and Linda G. Sprague. "Behind the Growth in Material Requirements Planning." *Harvard Business Review* 53, no. 5 (September-October 1975), pp. 83–91.

Orlicky, Joseph A. *Material Requirements Planning*. New York: McGraw-Hill Book Co., 1975.

———, George W. Plossl, and Oliver W. Wight. "Structuring the Bill of Material." *Production and Inventory Management* 13, no. 4 (1972), pp. 19–42.

Scott, G. M., "A Data Base for Your Company?" *California Management Review* 19, no. 1 (Fall 1976), pp. 68–78.

Seaberg, R. A. and C. Seaberg. "Computer Based Decision Systems in Xerox Corporate Planning." *Management Science* 20, no. 4 (December, Part II, 1973), pp. 575–84.

Sprague, R. H., Jr. and E. D. Carlson. *Building Effective Decision Support Systems*. Englewood Cliffs, N.J.: Prentice-Hall, Inc., 1982.

Sprague, R. H., Jr. and H. J. Watson. "Bit by Bit: Toward Decision Support Systems." *California Management Review* 22, no. 1 (Fall 1979), pp. 60–68.

Note: The views expressed by Mr. Tucker in his introductory comment are his own and do not necessarily express the position of General Electric Company.

10 Job Design, Production/Operations Standards, and Work Measurement

Job design, job standards, and work measurement have always been important to 3M Company. Job design in particular is becoming ever more important and, I believe, is the most critical.

In 3M, the behavioral human factors element of job design is gaining in recognition and has resulted in the creation of a separate human factors resource group for the corporation. I am glad to see that this chapter recognizes the importance of this factor. Job design must also be considered in the very beginning of product design, for we have too often designed products for end users without much thought for good manufacturability and resultant consistent quality.

In 3M Company, we have found that in labor intensive areas work standards and work measurement together increase productivity approximately 20%. As the chapter points out, many companies overlook or neglect this important element of operations. While money has to be spent to *develop* standards and measure the work, and money must continue to be spent to *maintain* these standards and measurement, 3M has found that this always pays off. The return on investment is generally more than 3:1. Work standards and work measurement must be evaluated carefully for their effect on quality—factors often overlooked in the past.

A challenge for operations management in the future is to develop effective design, standards, and measurement for white-collar jobs. Although difficult, this is not impossible. Because of automation and other productivity measures, the percentage of blue-collar workers in 3M, and in business as a whole, is gradually declining. As a result, improvement of white-collar productivity is becoming increasingly important and needs to be seriously addressed. I believe much can be accomplished in this area through applying the principles and methods described in this chapter.

C. W. Pipal
Staff Vice President
3M Company
St. Paul, Minnesota

The framework for production/operations management shown in Figure 10.1 reviews for us the relationship of organizing to the planning and control functions and reminds us that models and behavior are also vital in organizing for conversion. As we employ this framework in studying the concepts and techniques relating to jobs in an organization, we'll discuss the traditional systematic approaches for establishing job standards, work measurement, and job design and examine some contemporary behavioral contributions directed at improving jobs.

It is encouraging to see a successful, established company like 3M benefit so much from applying the essentials of this chapter. Although we know many companies utilize traditional engineering approaches with contemporary behavioral modifications, the productivity increases of 20 percent and return on investments of up to 3:1 cited by Mr. Pipal are eyecatching. We hope this encourages you to grasp the fundamental issues and techniques we are discussing here.

This chapter focuses on people at work. The basic building block in a manufacturing or service organization is the job, a group of related tasks or activities that need to be performed to meet organizational objectives. Jobs are then grouped into larger units called departments, and departments are grouped into such basic functions as marketing, engineering, and production. Consider an example. The elements of placing a washer on a bolt, placing a nut on a bolt, and tightening the nut firmly with an automatic wrench constitute a *task*. Repeating this and similar tasks constitutes a *job* in the motor assembly *department,* which is in the *production function* of an organization that finances, markets, and produces washing machines. As we focus on people at work in this chapter, we'll use a narrow approach, examining in detail tasks and jobs in production and operations management.

Two basic developments have characterized organizations in modern industrialized societies. First and most significant was scientific management's focus on the logic of the production process, particularly people and machines at work on a job. This follow-up of Adam Smith's concept of labor specialization has led to establishment of logical approaches to job design, individual and group standards for performance, and techniques for measurement of work. A good bit of the development in industrial engi-

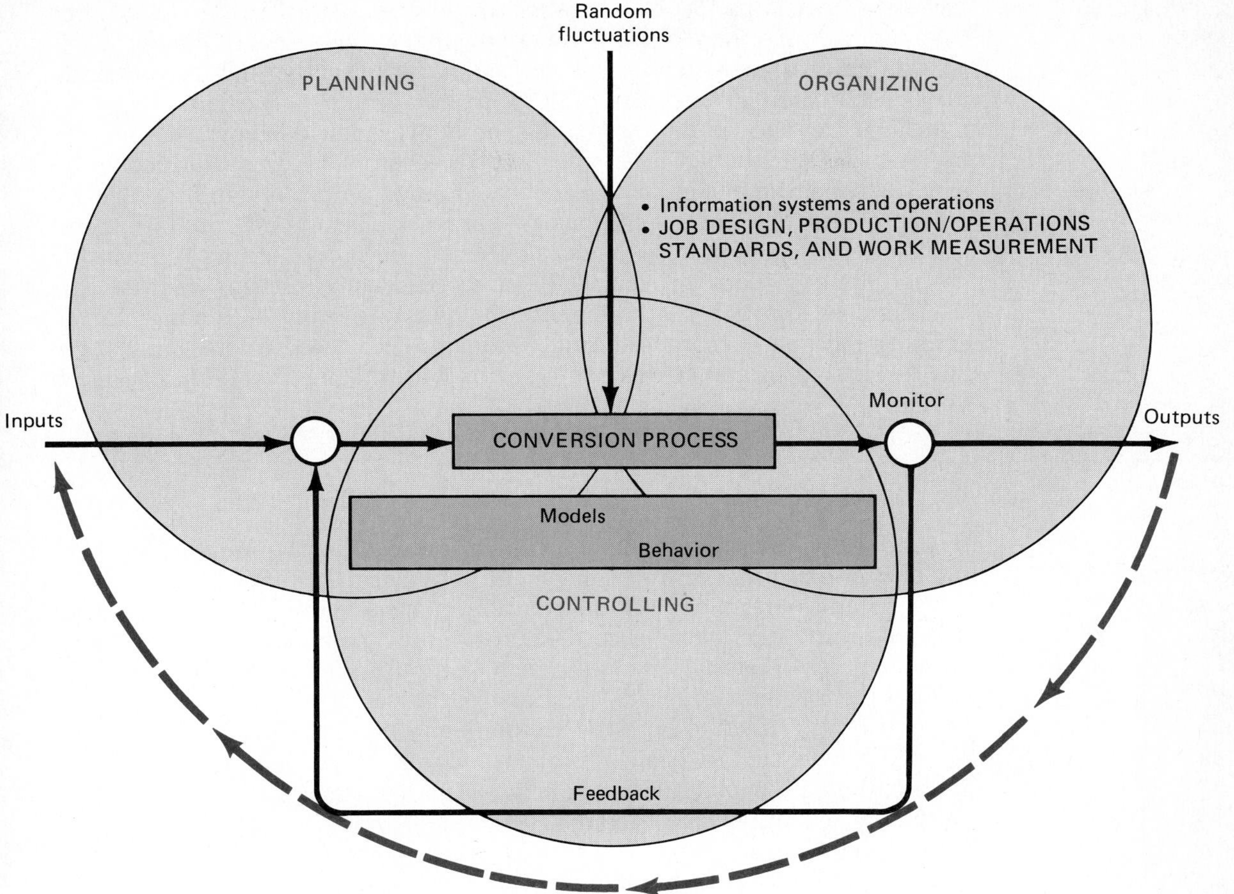

FIGURE 10.1
Production/operations management activities

neering over the last century has been devoted to this rational, scientific, logical approach to job analysis.

More recently, human relations and behavioral science studies of jobs have come about. The development of the behavioral approach has tended to moderate scientific management's rational approach to jobs. The behavioral approach has provided clear evidence that people have multiple needs, feelings, and personal goals that are not always consistent with job designs, standards, and performance measures obtained from using traditional rational techniques. Clearly, the modern production and operations manager must be aware of and respond to the worker as an individual. The manager must moderate logical approaches and consider such alternatives as worker participation in job decisions. Sometimes workers can become involved through job redesign, job enlargement, and job enrichment.

In job design, we use methods analysis to establish the general work flow in the facility. Once the general work flow has been established, specific jobs can be detailed. After the jobs have been designed, a standard needs to be established to ensure that the jobs are being performed properly. Establishing a standard, however, requires an understanding of work measurement. We want to emphasize that work measurement *follows* methods analysis. Only after we have established the proper method for getting the job done (job design) can we be concerned about measuring it (setting the standard through measurement). Obviously, setting a standard for an existing job and then redesigning it constitutes wasted effort. Let's begin our discussion of these three related areas with the one that comes first, job design.

JOB DESIGN

In production and operations, job design follows the planning and designing of product, process, and equipment. Job design specifies the content of each job and determines the distribution of work within the organization. Just as an architect can build (design) a house many different ways with many different materials, so can a manager build (design) a job with many different parts (elements). A combination of creativity and adherence to basic goals is critical to both the architect and the manager.

Although the two basic approaches to job design were developed separately, they are not mutually exclusive. The first, the micro approach, scientifically examines each detail of the job so that wasted effort is eliminated and output is raised. The second, more recent, approach to job design is behavioral. In it, psychological and socio-psychological considerations encourage job enlargement, job enrichment, and employee participation in job design. Under certain conditions, it too can result in improved output.

Traditional Engineering Dimensions of Job Design

Often managers, responsible for many subordinates and equipment, feel overwhelmed by details. Couldn't we be more efficient if we improved our jobs? But how can we improve them when we hardly know what the jobs consist of? One answer to the managers' dilemma is offered by the scientific approach. It urges managers to:

1. Identify the general operations problem area and the jobs that seem to be contributing to or causing the problem.
2. Carefully analyze and document how the work is currently being performed. (Established industrial engineering techniques are available to assist in analysis and documentation.)
3. Analyze the content of individual jobs and job elements.
4. Develop and implement new work methods.

Often jobs can be broken apart, separated into elements. If the elements are assigned to different workers, each worker can perform fewer elements, but he can perform them faster and perhaps under more specialized conditions (with special tools or work benches, for example). This basic concept, *specialization of labor,* has been very effective in increasing operating efficiency in manufacturing; it has been less effective, however, in the service industries.

To help the manager or a staff analyst study a job once a problem has been identified, certain techniques have been developed. One of these uses *operation charts* to analyze the job into elementary motions of the right and left hands—reaching, carrying, grasping, lifting, positioning and releasing, for example. Often a time scale is placed in the middle of the operation chart so that it is clear how much time is taken by each hand to perform the associated motion. Operation charts are appropriate for routine, repetitive, short cycle tasks performed on low to moderate production volumes. Figure 10.2 shows a right hand-left hand operation chart for assembling

FIGURE 10.2
Left-hand right-hand operations chart

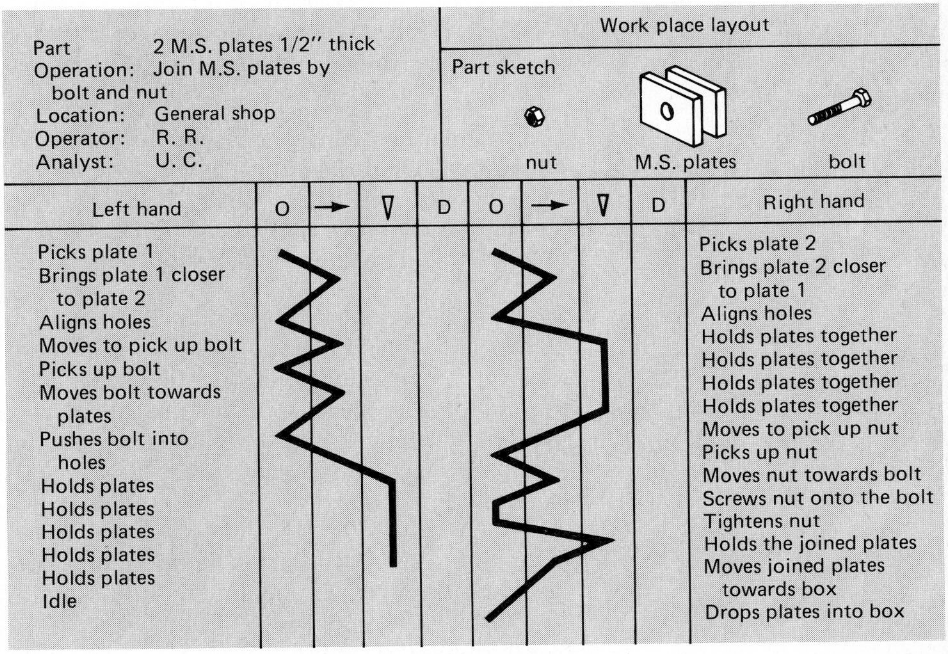

Part: 2 M.S. plates 1/2″ thick
Operation: Join M.S. plates by bolt and nut
Location: General shop
Operator: R. R.
Analyst: U. C.

Work place layout
Part sketch: nut, M.S. plates, bolt

Left hand	O	→	∇	D	O	→	∇	D	Right hand
Picks plate 1 Brings plate 1 closer to plate 2 Aligns holes Moves to pick up bolt Picks up bolt Moves bolt towards plates Pushes bolt into holes Holds plates Holds plates Holds plates Holds plates Holds plates Idle									Picks plate 2 Brings plate 2 closer to plate 1 Aligns holes Holds plates together Holds plates together Holds plates together Holds plates together Moves to pick up nut Picks up nut Moves nut towards bolt Screws nut onto the bolt Tightens nut Holds the joined plates Moves joined plates towards box Drops plates into box

Method summary

		LH	RH
O	Operation	4	6
→	Transport	3	4
∇	Holds	4	5
D	Delay	....	....
	Total	11 sec	15 sec

two mild steel (M.S.) plates. In this chart, there is no time scale, but you can see the standard process chart symbols.

Activity charts divide operations into the major task segments performed by the worker and the machine and separate them by a vertical time scale. In this way, the analyst can easily compute the percentages of productive and idle time and concentrate on methods of reducing idle time for the worker and/or the machine. Activity charts are appropriate for routine, repetitive tasks with worker-machine interaction. The activity chart in Figure 10.3 illustrates how a punched deck of computer cards is loaded and unloaded by a card reader. In this example, the analyst might improve efficiency by focusing on the first 10 seconds of idle machine time, the second 10 seconds of idle worker time, and the last 3 seconds of idle machine time.

Flow process charts analyze interstation activities, attempting to portray the flows of the overall production process. To capture this flow, analysts classify each movement of the product through the conversion process into one of five standard categories: operation, transportation, storage, inspection, or delay. Flow process charts are appropriate for visualizing the sequential stages of the conversion process. They help reveal unnecessary product movements or duplication of effort whose elimination would improve efficiency. Flow process charts provide a broader level of analysis than the preceding methods; many jobs are examined, but none in depth. The five categories of product movement are:

○ *Operation:* the work performed in manufacturing the product; usually assigned to a single work station.

⇨ *Transportation:* any movement of the product, or any of its parts, among various locations in the production process.

▽ *Storage:* intervals during which the product, or any part of it, waits or is at rest. Often a *T* inside the triangle is used to designate temporary storage, when the product is stored for a short time before the conversion process has been completed, and a *P* inside the triangle is used to indicate permanent storage, when the completed product waits in a storage facility more than a day or two.

□ *Inspection:* all activities performed to verify that the product meets mechanical, dimensional, and operational requirements.

D *Delay:* temporary storage before or after a production operation. When the temporary storage symbol is used, this category is often omitted.

Product:	Punched cards	Operator: D.V.	
Process:	Read in a deck of cards in an IBM 370 card reader	Charted by: U.C.	
Time (seconds)	**Employee**	**Machine**	**Time (seconds)**
0			
2	Removes rubber band from deck of cards		
4	Picks up weight from the hopper		
6	Places deck in the hopper	Idle	
8	Replaces weight on the deck		
10	Pushes start button		
		Card reader reads the deck of cards	12
			14
	Idle		16
			18
20	Picks up deck from the output stacker	Idle	
22	Replaces rubber band on the deck		

Summary

	Employee Time (sec)	Employee %	Machine Time	Machine %
Work	14	63.6	8	36.4
Idle	8	36.4	14	63.6

FIGURE 10.3
Employee-machine activity chart

EXAMPLE

A study was conducted to document current library operations in the technical processing function of a major resource library.[1] The purpose of the study was to provide a basis for specification of computer automation systems in technical processing. Figure 10.4 is a typical product process chart. The following excerpt from the report illustrates this service sector application of traditional job design techniques.

Materials Flows and Procedures. This section presents the operations of the University of Missouri-Columbia Elmer Ellis Library's Technical Services Division in considerable detail. Because of the extensiveness of this description, a summary of the processing of materials is presented. . . . The summary takes the form of "product process charts" and "floor diagrams" describing the general operations and movements undergone by the broader categories of library materials. The "station" identifiers heading each column of the process charts refer to desk locations as marked on the accompanying floor diagrams.

Product process charts are in common use for describing processing of industrial materials, and they provide a convenient means of summarizing the numerous flow diagrams. . . . The charts are easy to read once the following symbols and corresponding meanings are understood:

◎ Point of origination

◯ Operation performed on an item or group of items

○ Movement of an item or group of items from one location to another

▽ Delay

◇ Verification or check of some aspect of the item against a standard or other information

The flow process charts presented technical procedures in enough detail that computer systems programmers could proceed with programming procedures for computers rather than continue with manual operations.

[1]S. Craig Moore, Everett E. Adam, Jr., Edward P. Miller, Daniel W. Doell, and Louis E. Fruend, *Library Studies Project:* Volume I, *Project Summary,* and Volume II, *Technical Services in the UMC Library System* (Columbia: University of Missouri, 1973). See pp. 12–15, Vol. II.

These three traditional techniques, operation charts, activity charts, and flow process charts, facilitate intrajob analysis (at the individual job station) and interjob analysis (between job stations). After systematically studying existing job content, engineers and technicians can often find means of improving jobs that have been overlooked by foremen and managers. To reduce idle time, they may recommend eliminating unnecessary elements or modifying the sequence of elements.[2]

In Table 10.1, we summarize the application of these techniques to various kinds of work activities. In the table, two terms are mentioned for the first time: *gang process charts*, which trace the interaction of several workers and one machine, and *principles of motion economy*. Principles of motion economy are general guidelines for analyzing and improving work arrangements, the use of human hands and body, or the use of tools to increase efficiency and reduce fatigue. Table 10.2 lists several principles of motion economy, many of which can be applied to both shop and office work.

---

[2]See, for example, Donald L. Gochenour, Jr., Edward L. Fisher, and Harry G. Gibson, "IE Principles Applied to Forest Conservation," *Industrial Engineering* 12, no. 1 (January 1980), pp. 14–19.

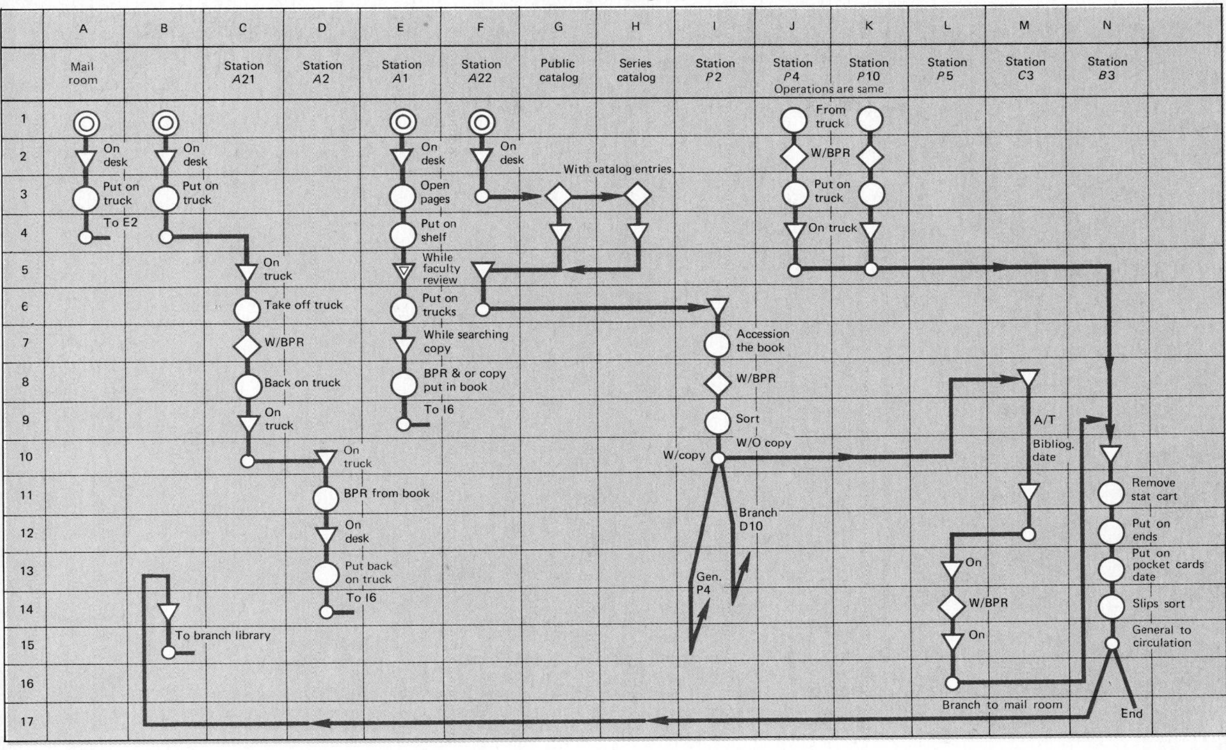

FIGURE 10.4
Product process chart of library operations

TABLE 10.1
Traditional engineering work methods aids in job design

Activity	Analysis method
Routine, repetitive tasks with short cycle times and low to moderate production volumes; stationary worker at a fixed work place	Operations charts, principles of motion economy
Routine, repetitive tasks with long cycle times and moderate to high production volumes; worker interacts with equipment or other workers	Activity charts, worker-machine charts, gang process charts
Overall conversion process; interactions of workers, work stations and work units; flow of work	Process charts, flow diagrams

Table 10.2
Principles of motion economy

Using the human body the way it works best	Arranging the work place to assist performance	Using mechanical devices to reduce human effort
1. The work should be arranged to provide a natural rhythm which can become automatic. 2. The symmetrical nature of the body should be considered: a. the motions of the arms should be simultaneous, beginning and completing their motions at the same time b. motions of the arms should be opposite and symmetrical. 3. The human body is an ultimate machine and its full capabilities should be employed: a. neither hand should ever be idle b. work should be distributed to other parts of the body in line with their ability. c. the safe design limits of the body should be observed d. the human should be employed at its "highest" use. 4. The arms and hands as weights are subject to the physical laws and energy should be conserved: a. momentum should work for the person and not against them b. the smooth continuous arc of the ballistic is more efficient c. the distance of movements should be minimized d. tasks should be turned over to machines. 5. The tasks should be simplified: a. eye contact should be few and grouped together b. unnecessary actions, delays and idle time should be eliminated c. the degree of required precision and control should be reduced d. the number of individual motions should be minimized along with the number of muscle groups involved.	1. There should be a definite place for all tools and materials. 2. Tools, materials, and controls should be located close to the point of use. 3. Tools, materials, and controls should be located to permit the best sequence and path of motions. 4. Gravity feed bins and containers can deliver material close to the point of use. 5. The work place should be fitted to the task and to the human.	1. Vises and clamps can hold the work precisely where needed. 2. Guides can assist in positioning the work without close operator attention. 3. Controls and foot-operated devices can relieve the hands of work. 4. Mechanical devices can multiply human abilities. 5. Mechanical systems should be fitted to human use.

Barnes, Frank C. "Principles of Motion Economy: Revisited, Reviewed, and Restored." *Proceedings Southern Management Association Annual Meeting,* (Atlanta, 1983), p. 298.

Worker Physiology Over the years considerable effort has been devoted to studying people's physiology as it relates to their work. Statistics on reaching range, grip strength, lifting ability, and many other physiological factors have been reasonably well documented. Work place arrangements, job design, and equipment design all require consideration of physiological factors. An industrial engineering handbook is a good source of information on the physiological capabilities of workers.

Working Environment The working environment is extremely important in designing jobs. Temperature, humidity, and air flow all affect work. One classic study in Britain illustrates the effects of temperature on performance.[3] Before the experiment began, testing identified "good" and "average" performers. High and low incentives were used with each group, and temperatures of the workers' rooms were changed from day to day. The results of this study are shown in Figure 10.5. As you can see, performance (amount of work done) decreased for all workers as temperatures increased. The most work was performed at temperatures of about 60 degrees Fahrenheit; as temperatures increased to 80, 85, and 90 degrees, work accomplishment dropped off substantially. Although this study concentrated on workers performing physical tasks, the same principle holds for clerical workers. Optimal temperatures for work that is not physically demanding varies from 68 to 72 degrees; as temperatures increase, performance decreases.

If you've ever tried to mow grass or move furniture on a hot, humid day, you know how much harder high temperatures make your job. The same is true for less physically demanding work—typing, writing, and studying, while easier at temperatures a little warmer than those that are best for manual tasks, are harder when temperatures are very high than when temperatures are moderate.

The Occupational Safety and Health Act

Just as noise, airflow, light intensity, and many other environmental variables affect productivity, they also affect health and safety. Recognizing the lack of national uniformity in working conditions, Congress passed the Williams-Steiger Occupational Safety and Health Act of 1970 (OSHA). The Act, which covers every employer with one or more employees in a business concerned with commerce, establishes strict health and safety standards by encompassing existing codes and adding to them. Publications describing the program are available from local OSHA area directors; they describe the Act's purpose like this:

> . . . to assure as far as possible every working man and woman in the Nation safe and healthful working conditions and to preserve our human resources . . . .
> How is OSHA to implement this mandate? Congress was specific:

[3] N. H. Mackworth, "High Incentives versus Hot and Humid Atmospheres in a Physical Effort Task," *British Journal of Psychology* 38 (1947), pp. 90–102.

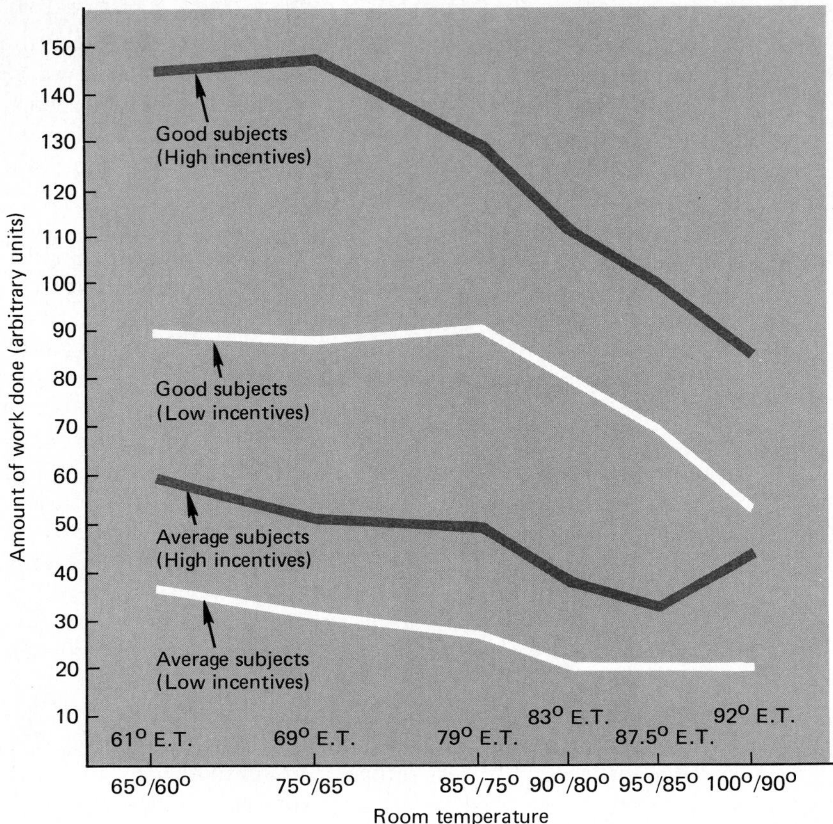

FIGURE 10.5
Level of ability and the effects of stronger incentives in hot and humid atmospheres

Source: N. H. Mackworth, "High Incentives versus Hot and Humid Atmospheres in a Physical Effort Task," *British Journal of Psychology* 38 (1947), pp. 90–102. Reprinted by permission of Cambridge University Press © The British Psychological Society, 1947.

- by encouraging employers and employees to reduce hazards in the workplace, and start or improve existing safety and health programs;
- by establishing employer and employee responsibilities;
- by authorizing OSHA to set mandatory job safety and health standards;
- by providing an effective enforcement program;
- by encouraging the states to assume the fullest responsibility for administering and enforcing their own occupational safety and health programs that are to be at least as effective as the federal program; and
- by providing for reporting procedures on job injuries, illnesses, and fatalities.[4]

---

[4]U.S. Department of Labor, Occupational Health and Safety Administration, *All About OSHA*, OSHA publication No. 2056, p. 3.

Although the program's success depends significantly on voluntary compliance, OSHA does provide enforcement measures and information to employers to help them understand and obey the law. OSHA inspectors now have the capability of identifying employers with the "worst" safety records and inspecting those locations first.[5] OSHA officials have accepted a "worst-first" scheduling rule. As best we can judge, inspections are based on a combination of worker complaints, target industries, random inspection, and worst-first analysis.

Behavioral Dimensions of Job Design

In the past, industrialized societies have used economic criteria as their primary guides in designing jobs. Traditional job design emphasizes specialization, task repetition, and reduction of skill requirements to minimize the impact of the individual worker on the production process. Jobs have been designed to minimize immediate cost and maximize immediate productivity. We agree that economic criteria are still paramount. We mustn't forget, though, that behavioral implications in job design can and do influence performance. To ignore these concepts is to bypass the opportunity to add further economic benefits to those we obtain through traditional approaches. After World War II managers and behavioral scientists, developing an interest in industrial jobs in which workers had the "blue collar blues," developed *job rotation* and *job enlargement* techniques as responses to an overemphasis of scientific management. More recently *job enrichment* and the *redesign of job characteristics* have added to our abilities to improve jobs. Keeping in mind that our goal is to add further economic benefits, let's examine each of these behavioral ideas.

Job Rotation

Sometimes we cannot eliminate undesirable aspects of a job by redesigning or automating it. An excellent way to approach such a job is to move employees into it for a short period of time and then move them out again.

Have you ever worked the graveyard shift (from midnight until 8:00 AM)? Many people find it undesirable. Such service organizations as police and fire departments and hospitals, however, must have people on duty around the clock, and workers are moved into and out of the graveyard shift. Just as employees can move in and out of a shift that is undesirable, *they can be rotated in and out of jobs that are undesirable*. Even though there is no change in job content, rotating employees among different jobs can reduce boredom and monotony by exposing the employee to a broader perspective of the entire production process. Although the ability to use

[5]For initial development of the "worst-first" scheduling concept, see Everett E. Adam, Jr., "Priority Assignment of OSHA Safety Inspectors," *Management Science* 24, no. 15 (November 1978), pp. 1642–49. Target industry analysis based on accident frequency and severity is reported in Emil A. Thies and Everett E. Adam, Jr., "Establishing Target Industries for OSHA Inspections," *Proceedings 1979 National American Institute for Decision Sciences*, (New Orleans, Louisiana: November, 1979).

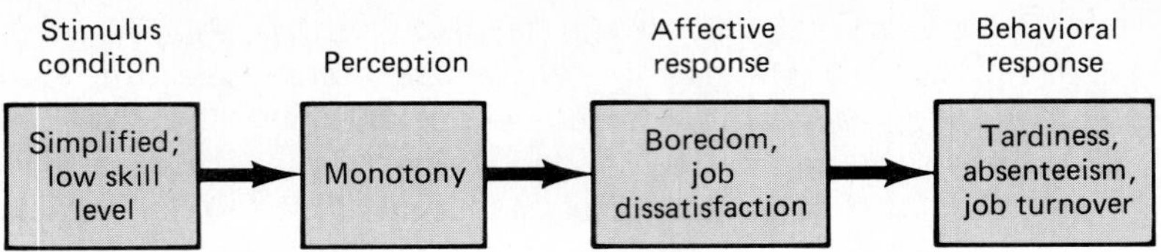

FIGURE 10.6
Assumptions behind job enlargement

rotation is often restricted by the seniority system in both union and non-union shops, the technique has been successful in many situations, and we suspect that it will continue to be used.

Job Enlargement We can think in terms of jobs being composed of tasks, each of which is performed by a worker. With each task is associated a set of stimuli, auditory, visual, and/or tactile. As the worker performs the tasks, he or she receives various stimuli, cues. The number and kinds of stimuli depend on the nature of the tasks. A job consisting of many varied tasks provides varied stimuli; a job with routine, repetitive tasks usually provides few stimuli.

Job enlargement proponents argue that we have simplified and routinized jobs to the point where they are so specialized that workers perceive them to be monotonous; workers are bored and dissatisfied. Because of boredom and job dissatisfaction, many workers withdraw from the organization, which has high levels of tardiness, absenteeism, and turnover. If managers would enlarge jobs by adding tasks, additional stimuli would reduce the ill effects of too simplified, too specialized jobs. Figure 10.6 illustrates the assumptions behind job enlargement.

Our conceptualization of an enlarged job offers the employee four opportunities:

1. variety, the opportunity to use a variety of skills;
2. autonomy, the opportunity to exercise control over how and when the work is completed;
3. task identity, the opportunity to be responsible for an entire piece or program of work; and
4. feedback, the opportunity to receive on-line information.[6]

Thus job enlargement is the procedure of redesigning jobs or modifying work so that employees can feel more involved in and responsible for what they do.

---

[6] J. R. Hackman and E. E. Lawler, "Employee Reactions to Job Characteristics," *Journal of Applied Psychology*, Monograph 55 (1971), pp. 259–86.

The nature and content of a job may be changed through job enlargement in two basic ways. First, more tasks of a similar nature and skill level can be added. If a job consists of tightening one nut on one bolt, for example, it could be redesigned to consist of tightening four different nuts on four different bolts. The job would then be enlarged horizontally. Second, other tasks of a different nature but similar skill level may be added. Instead of tightening one nut on one bolt, the worker could assemble two pieces of metal and a piece of plastic, tighten a nut and bolt to hold the assembly together, and walk to a storage area to get more nuts and bolts. The job would then be enlarged vertically.

EXAMPLE

In a regional library, a job analysis was performed on all positions. The five circulation clerks' duties included working at the circulation desk, shelving books, and maintaining a particular part of the general collection (records, films, or young adult periodicals). The analyst discovered that the clerks found maintaining part of the collection the most rewarding and important part of their jobs. The routine, repetitious duties consisted of merely receiving and checking out books.

After their jobs had been redesigned, circulation clerks continued to perform their old duties of shelving books and maintaining a special part of the general collection, but they also began to perform some of the duties formerly done by a page. Time at the circulation desk was not allowed to exceed two hours at any one time, and total time at the desk was normally no more than four hours a day. This essentially vertical redesign resulted in increased job satisfaction and reduced job turnover.

Job Enlargement at AT&T Much research has been done on job enlargement.[7] We will discuss one of the broader studies, which reports on job enlargement programs within AT&T.[8] To date, there have been some eighteen studies in AT&T contrasting enlarged jobs with control groups in which jobs were unchanged. Table 10.3 shows the extensiveness of the enlargement studies. The study found that the jobs that were most successfully enlarged were in the treasury and commercial departments; improvements in traffic, plant, and engineering jobs were modest, and in one job enlargement group there was no change at all in performance. Table 10.4 shows the savings resulting from one of the more successful attempts at job enlargement, the shareholder correspondents' jobs.

[7] An excellent review of the literature of job enlargement can be found in C. C. Hulin and M. R. Blood, "Job Enlargement, Individual Differences, and Worker Responses," *Psychological Bulletin* 69 (1968), pp. 41–55.

[8] R. N. Ford, *Motivation Through the Work Itself* (New York: American Management Association, 1969).

TABLE 10.3
Bell system job enlargement studies*

Department	Job	Location	Enlarged jobs
Treasury	Shareholder correspondent	New York City	28
Commercial	Service representative	Toronto	50
		Montreal	75
		Chicago	40
		Illinois—suburban	25
		Northern Massachusetts	70
		Rhode Island	60
		Maryland	65
Traffic	Toll operator	Saginaw, Michigan	250
		New York City	350
Plant	Installer	California—large urban	45
		Chicago	30
	Frame cross-connection	New York City	40
Comptroller's	Service order reentry clerk	Los Angeles	30
	Service order transcription clerk	Atlanta	20
	Key puncher	Minnesota	13
Engineering	Equipment engineer	Detroit	30

*Reprinted by permission of the publisher from *Motivation Through the Work Itself* by R. N. Ford, © 1969 by American Management Association, pp. 48–49.

TABLE 10.4
Saving over an 18-month period from enlarging shareholder correspondent job*

Activity	Reduction
Twenty seven percent drop, turnover, nonsupervisory specialists	$245,000
Investigation and file clerks—salaries, annual (force reduced from 46 to 24 clerks, three management jobs eliminated)	135,000
Correspondents' group—salaries (five management, four verifier jobs eliminated)	76,000
Stock transfer group—salaries eliminated	40,000
Merger of employee stock—pension unit and dividend reconciliation unit—salaries eliminated	100,000
Improved productivity (not priced)	
Improved service indexes (not priced)	
Improved tone of exit interviews (not priced)	
Personnel section, job rearrangements (not priced)	
Offset—half salary, six employees working on job enlargement program part-time	(38,000)
Total cost reduction	$558,000

*Reprinted by permission of the publisher from *Motivation Through the Work Itself* by R. N. Ford, © 1969 by American Management Association, p. 44.

Some cautionary words are in order, however. Although the Bell System reported much success with job enlargement, even in that extensive program not every enlargement resulted in increased performance. Further, the jobs selected for enlargement in these studies were routine, repetitive jobs with high probabilities of success. The Bell System found limited success with enlarging the jobs of managers and professionals. In general, it appears that jobs performed by some blue-collar workers offer maximum potential for performance gains from enlargement.

It is very difficult to make a strong generalization about applying job enlargement. We do know that managers and professionals tend to respond favorably to more responsibility and are likely to accept jobs that are even broader than we might think. Attempts to enlarge blue-collar jobs, however, provide mixed results. It seems clear that for routine, repetitive jobs with total job cycle times below one and one-half to two minutes, there is some chance of improved performance through job enlargement.[9] One study reported that when foremen were given broader responsibilities, quality increased, cost decreased, and there was no change in organizational withdrawal. Other studies have reported improved satisfaction from job enlargement without performance changes. Perhaps these job satisfaction gains, which quite frequently result in decreased organization withdrawal, will turn out to be the primary, or at least the most consistent, benefit that can be attained from systematic job enlargement programs.

Job Enrichment Job enrichment presumes that many jobs are so highly specialized that operative workers can no longer visualize how their work contributes to the organization goals. The worker tightening a nut on a bolt all day long loses sight of the fact that because that nut helps hold a wheel on a new car, the safety of a family might well depend on how diligently he does his job.

EXAMPLE

A manufacturing vice president for a leading foods manufacturer visited a class in beginning operations management and explained how job enrichment worked at his organization. The company was brand labeling corn flakes for a larger grocery chain, and the buyers were at the corn flakes plant for the day. Two production workers were selected and brought directly into a conference room where boxes of both competitors' and the company's corn flakes were available. These workers were asked, "Why are our corn flakes as good or better than others?" They answered by crunching various brands on the table and explaining in detail their jobs and quality control.

[9] Maurice Kilbridge and Leon Webster, "An Economic Model for the Division of Labor," *Management Science* 12, no. 6 (February 1966), pp. B255-69.

Two benefits resulted from this. First, the buyers were impressed with the workers' knowledge. Second, and most important, the workers returned to the work place enthused about their contribution, and they spread this enthusiasm to other workers in their group. They related their contribution in "selling the product." The operative workers' jobs were more meaningful to them, and their attitudes toward their jobs were improved.

Job enrichment not only provides satisfaction, however; it can also make the organization more efficient. Many managers feel that the goals of job enrichment and increased efficiency are not only compatible; they are necessary partners. They argue that it's impossible to sustain productivity without the conscious satisfaction that job enrichment helps create.

Two conditions need to be established for effective job enrichment:

1. Management must supply information on goals and performance that previously was not available to the workers.
2. A proper *organizational climate* has to be established for success. Primarily, this climate does not imply excessive control of individual behavior in the organization.

These two conditions can be met by reorienting traditional management thinking:

1. Every employee must be viewed as a manager. Each must get involved in the management activities of planning, organizing, and controlling his or her own job. This is the basic goal of job enrichment.
2. The organization should strive to make work like play—to make the job fun. If a worker's job can be designed so that it offers the rewards that a game does—visible and meaningful goals, immediate feedback, group cohesiveness, and people who are there because they want to be—then workers will enjoy their jobs. We've designed too many of these rewards out of jobs; we can design them back in.[10]

Job Enrichment at General Foods The manufacturing vice president in the previous example told our class that his company's interest in job enrichment stemmed directly from a competitor's experience. In 1968 General Foods (the competitor) built a pet food plant in Topeka, Kansas, with the intent of emphasizing new behavioral techniques that would develop skills, create challenging jobs, and encourage teamwork. The new job design focused on several basic features: autonomous work groups, challenging job assignments, job mobility and learning rewards, information availability, self-government, status symbols, and evaluation.[11]

---

[10]M. Scott Myers, *Every Employee a Manager* (New York: McGraw-Hill Book Co., 1970), pp. 47–49 and 70.

[11]R. E. Walton, "How to Counter Alienation in the Plant," *Harvard Business Review* (November-December 1972), pp. 70–81.

There were some start-up pains, but the first eighteen months of the job enrichment effort generally yielded positive results. Fixed overhead costs were 33 percent lower than existing plants'; quality rejects were reduced by 92 percent; the safety record was outstanding compared to other company plants; morale was high; absenteeism was 9 percent below the industry norm; and turnover was far below average.

Job Design in Sweden Two well-known Swedish automobile manufacturers introduced significant job design efforts, in which teams participated in redesigning their own jobs. In the late 1960s and early 1970s, Saab and Volvo experimented with varying degrees of job enlargement, job rotation, job enrichment, and production team procedures. The results, though mixed, were generally positive.[12] At one Volvo automobile assembly plant, for example, management combined job rotation and enrichment by having workers follow the same auto body through several work stations. The job cycle time was increased six- or sevenfold, to some twenty minutes. Job turnover, the primary target for reduction, was in fact reduced from 40 percent to 25 percent. Absenteeism, however, nearly doubled. Increased absenteeism was attributed to government legislation enacted during Sweden's then current economic slowdown; it allowed workers to stay off the job with little or no effect on salary.

Partial Solutions in Job Design Although not every job can be enriched, there are many partial solutions for jobs that are hard to enrich, particularly routine, boring, and otherwise undesirable jobs. Table 10.5 offers a few suggestions.

As is true with job enlargement, studies of job enrichment aren't conclusive. Those that have been done have generally concentrated on jobs lending themselves to enrichment. It is clear that if pay or supervision is a source of dissatisfaction, job enrichment likely will fail.[13] Some workers don't accept the middle-class values and goals inherent in job enrichment; they "don't want to be a manager." For some workers, enrichment might reduce social interaction, a result many workers would find undesirable. And many employees prefer a low level of required competency, high security, and relative independence to the increased responsibility and growth that job enrichment implies.

Job enrichment does have promise, though, and has been successful in some situations. We simply want to caution you against accepting this

---

[12]Andrew S. Szilagyi, Jr. and Marc J. Wallace, Jr., *Organization Behavior and Performance,* 2nd ed. (Santa Monica, California: Goodyear Publishing Co., 1980), pp. 173–77; W. F. Dowling, "Job Design in the Assembly-Line: Farewell to the Blue Collar Blues?" *Organizational Dynamics* (Spring 1973), pp. 51–67; and C. H. Gibson, "Volvo Increases Productivity Through Job Enrichment," *California Management Review* (Summer 1973), pp. 64–66.

[13]Raymond J. Aldag and Arthur P. Brief, *Task Design and Employee Motivation* (Glenview, Illinois: Scott, Foresman and Company, 1979), p. 101.

TABLE 10.5
Partial job design solutions for jobs that cannot be enlarged or enriched

Job characteristics	Partial solutions to job design
Routine, repetitive, boring, hot, noisy, generally undesirable	Use the job as an entry job in the organization, with the understanding that the employee will be there only a short time. Occasionally a worker might even want to remain in the job. Post the job daily. Often you will get a few daily volunteers who are looking for a change but don't want the job permanently. Employ the mentally handicapped, fitting them carefully to these types of jobs. They often make excellent employees when adequately trained and properly matched to a job. Employ part-time workers. Especially if full-time work is not available, part-time workers are often happy to do work that they would dislike on a full-time basis.

behavioral technique *in place of* sound work measurement and traditional job design procedures. A possible supplement? Yes. A replacement? We think not.

Redesign of Job Characteristics Recent research in job design suggests that certain *core dimensions* of jobs can be redesigned to improve performance. These include task variety, task identity, task significance, task autonomy, and feedback. Conceptually, we can redesign these core dimensions so that they allow for individual differences in people's reactions to and feelings about their jobs. Researchers have not yet been able to answer some basic questions about job redesign. How do we identify and measure individual characteristics? Can we directly relate these characteristics to observed (not perceived) job performance? Research is still preliminary—but it does suggest that *individual differences* have a significant impact on the effectiveness of any job redesign effort.[14]

Participation in Job Design There is very little in life that people feel more strongly and possessive about than their jobs. In later chapters, we will discuss change and resistance to change in detail; we'd like to point out now, however, that when jobs are redesigned, you should expect resistance

[14]See Andrew D. Szilagyi, Jr. and Marc J. Wallace, Jr., *Organizational Behavior and Performance,* 2nd ed. (Santa Monica, California: Goodyear Publishing Co., 1980), pp. 160–68; Raymond J. Aldag and Arthur P. Brief, *Task Design and Employee Motivation* (Glenview, Illinois: Scott, Foresman and Company, 1979), pp. 81–105; Jon L. Pierce and Randall B. Dunham, "Task Design: A Literature Review," *The Academy of Management Review* 1, no. 4 (October 1976), pp. 83–97; and J. Richard Hackman, Greg Oldham, Robert Janson, and Kenneth Purdy, "A New Strategy for Job Enrichment," *California Management Review* 17, no. 4 (Summer 1975), pp. 57–71.

to change of some magnitude and intensity. Employees have seen far too many changes for the sake of change in their organizations. It sometimes seems to them that every new manager brings new procedures and programs that upset their established patterns and, at least in the short run, make their jobs more difficult. The general feeling is, "I know this job better than you do; who are you to be changing it?" It is much easier to bring about meaningful change in jobs if you involve the workers, or at least give them the opportunity to participate, in the change process. If they're involved, they can learn the changed job more easily than they could otherwise because they have a positive attitude. It really doesn't take much effort or time to explain the goals of the new job and ask for suggestions. We suggest you try it.

EFFECTIVE JOB DESIGN: COMBINING ENGINEERING AND BEHAVIORAL APPROACHES

On the one hand we have suggested traditional industrial engineering techniques for designing jobs, techniques that are an outgrowth of the scientific management approach. Yet on the other hand we suggest behavioral approaches to job design, most of these having been developed as a part of more recent organizational behavior research. What, then, is best? Let's try to relate these two approaches conceptually by looking at Figure 10.7.

As you study Figure 10.7, you will see that *both* traditional engineering and behavioral job design techniques are used to obtain the expected outcomes, accomplishment, and positive employee feelings. But no matter how well engineering and behavioral job design is done, the outcomes depend upon the external environment, the actual organization, and individual employee characteristics. These variables moderate or intervene between *job design* and *desirable outcome,* thus making effective job design highly complex as Figure 10.7 suggests.

PRODUCTION AND OPERATIONS STANDARDS

Let's say that you've used the available charts, examined environmental impacts and followed the guidelines established in OSHA, made changes through enlargement or enrichment, and finally completed the job design. Now you need a performance standard to be sure the job is being done properly. Let's see how standards are established in production and operations.

In the conversion process, a product or service is produced as output. To produce this good or service effectively and efficiently, management must establish goals for evaluating actual performance before the conversion process begins. These goals are translated into standards. A produc-

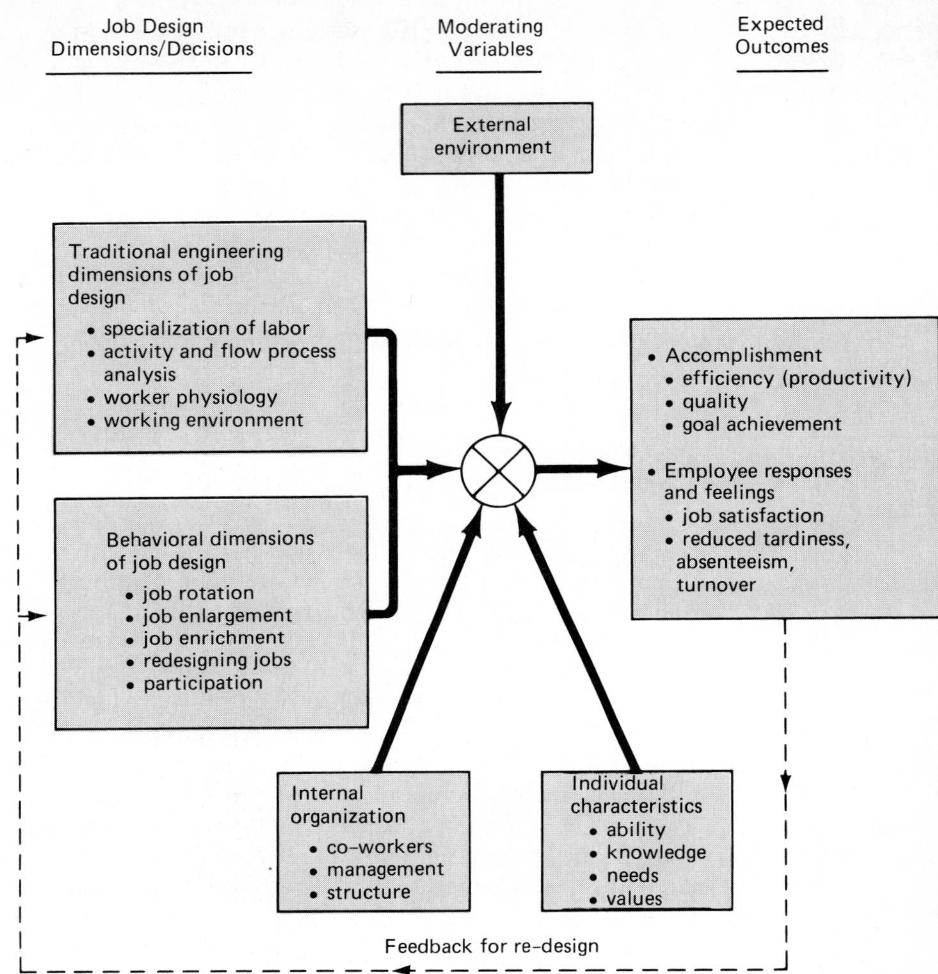

FIGURE 10.7
Effective job design

tion and operations standard is a criterion established as a basis for comparison in measuring or judging output. The standard can be set for quantity, quality, cost, or any other attribute of output, and it is the basis for control. Without established, measurable standards, there is no way to compare actual performance with planned performance and, therefore, no way to take corrective action through the control function if necessary.

At what levels in the organization should standards be set? Are standards static or dynamic? What are the uses of standards? How are they actually established? It is to these and similar questions that we turn now.

Standards at Various Levels in the Organization

Individual Job Standards The terms *standard, labor standard, production standard,* and *time standard* are used interchangeably in operations management. A labor standard is simply what is expected from an average worker under average working conditions for a given time period. It is the concept of a "fair day's work." A standard set at the lowest level within the organization is expressed in terms of production time required per unit of output or, conversely, output per unit of time. A candy-making operation, for example, in which coconut is sprinkled on soft chocolate might have a standard of .01 minutes per piece or 100 pieces per minute.

Departmental Standards Several workers may perform as a unit, thus forming a team assembly operation. These teams and the equipment they use may have one group standard for the team output. By adding all the individuals and teams together, managers can set department standards for quality, quantity, costs, and delivery dates.

In production/operations, one of the basic units of accountability is the department; the foreman or supervisor of the department is often evaluated in terms of his or her ability to manage the department efficiently. Frequently this evaluation is made against an expectation to operate at or near 100 percent labor efficiency. (Labor efficiency is the comparison of "actual" labor hours to "standard" labor hours.) In other words, for every actual labor hour used directly in operations, an expected number of pieces should be produced; this expected number is the standard. If the expected number is attained, 100 percent of standard is earned. If more pieces are produced, a greater than 100 percent efficiency occurs, and if fewer pieces are produced, a less than 100 percent efficiency is earned.

Plant Standards At the plant, works, or comparable service level unit (such as a hospital or a school), quantity and labor standards are maintained as a goal just as they are at the department level. At this level, however, more standards are added, and some of them conflict. Cost standards, for example, are critical at this level. The problem is that operations managers face certain conflicting constraints. A specified volume of goods or services must be produced; labor, materials, and overhead standards must be maintained, and at the same time their costs must be controlled. If you are familiar with cost accounting systems, you realize the need for accurate cost systems for labor, materials, and overhead. Likewise, quality levels must be maintained commensurate with product objectives. The point is clear—operations managers have multiple goals, and they must react to them with multiple standards.

Surprisingly, labor time standards are used much less uniformly in the service sector than they are in hard goods manufacturing. Since the service sector is generally more labor intense, it could benefit most from labor time standards. If you, as an emerging operations manager, find yourself employed in the service sector, you have an opportunity to bring great benefits to the largest labor sector of the economy by applying these scientific management techniques.

Uses of Standards

As a basis for making operating decisions, (labor) time standards are used to evaluate the performance of workers and facilities and for predicting, planning, and controlling operations. (See Table 10.6) Standards established by industrial engineering are used in production control, cost accounting, and many other departments or work units. They play an important overall role in the product pricing decision. The time standard is a key communication device between those involved in the actual conversion activities and those planning, organizing, and controlling those activities.

Consider two uses of time standards in Table 10.6, formulating standard costs and cost estimating. Standard costs are computed in accounting as:

$$\text{Standard cost} = \text{Standard usage} \times \text{Standard labor rate} \quad \textbf{(10.1)}$$

The standard usage is the industrial engineering established time (labor) standard; the standard labor rate is the accepted labor rate for the labor force that will be performing the work. If the standard usage, the labor standard, is incorrectly established, the standard cost will be in error. Standard costs are compared to actual costs giving a labor efficiency variance where:

$$\text{Actual costs} = \text{Actual usage} \times \text{Standard labor rate} \quad \textbf{(10.2)}$$

and

$$\text{Labor efficiency variance} = \text{Standard costs} - \text{Actual costs} \quad \textbf{(10.3)}$$

Key operation management performance evaluation decisions are based on labor efficiency variances, so it is important for data in calculating the var-

TABLE 10.6
Uses of time (labor) standards

Evaluating performance	Predicting, planning, and controlling operations
Evaluating individual performance; subsequent compensation	Aggregate planning of work force levels and production rates
Evaluating department performance; subsequent supervisor compensation	Capacity planning and utilization
Evaluating process design, layout, and work methods	Scheduling operations; time sequencing jobs
Estimating expense and revenue streams in equipment evaluation as alternatives are compared	Cost estimating of products and production lots
Formulating standard costs	Planning types of labor skills necessary and budgeting labor expenses

iance to be correct. The following example illustrates how an error in establishing the labor standard carries through to the labor efficiency variance.

EXAMPLE

A manufacturing firm introducing a new product set a preliminary labor standard at 10 units per hour. The standard labor rate is \$4 per hour in the plant where the part is to be produced. During the third month of production, 800 units were produced using 90 labor hours. The labor efficiency variance is calculated as

$$\begin{aligned}\text{Standard cost} &= (.10\ \text{hr/unit})\ (800\ \text{units})\ (\$4/\text{hr}) \\ &= \$320 \\ \text{Actual cost} &= (90\ \text{hrs})\ (\$4/\text{hr}) \\ &= \$360 \\ \text{Labor efficiency variance} &= \$320 - \$360 = \$-40\end{aligned}$$

Management was somewhat concerned about the negative variance but decided to have industrial engineering thoroughly check the labor standard before taking corrective action. Engineering recommended the standard be established at 12 units per hour; this was done. The labor efficiency variance was recalculated as:

$$\begin{aligned}\text{Standard cost} &= (0.0833\ \text{hr/unit})\ (800\ \text{units})\ (\$4/\text{hr}) \\ &= \$266.56 \\ \text{Labor efficiency variance} &= \$266.56 - \$360 = \$-93.44\end{aligned}$$

The labor standard was in error by 20 percent (from 10 to 12 units per hour). This resulted in more than doubling the unfavorable variance (from \$−40 to \$−93.44). Management now set out to find causes for the more unfavorable variance.

Formal and Informal Standards

One approach to cost estimation for products and services is to use the standard usage (the labor standard) and standard labor rate to compute a standard labor cost. In costing the product or service, the standard labor cost can be used directly, or it can be adjusted to reflect historical performance. The ultimate cost estimate will incorporate the standard labor cost with material and overhead costs. This cost estimate is used in the product or service pricing decision. If the labor standard is in error, the standard labor cost, the cost estimate, and the ultimate product or service price will all be in error.

The actual work standard may vary considerably from the scientifically established industrial engineering standard. There is no escaping the impact of the informal organization, with its own communication network, system of authority, leaders, and work standards. Operations managers should not ignore the informal organization. Rather, they must attempt to influence the informal organization to communicate its work standards and at the same time attempt to influence the acceptance of formal standards by the informal work group. A classic example of how to use the informal work group is found in the Harwood Manufacturing "participation" studies (to be discussed in detail in Chapter 19). Job standards for a job redesign were set informally by participating workers. When checked against previous performances and industrial engineering standards, the informal standards were perfectly acceptable. Management received an unexpected side benefit from operative workers' participation in change: quickly established, acceptable standards.

WORK MEASUREMENT

A labor standard tells what is expected of an average worker performing under average job conditions. The critical questions in establishing a labor standard are:

1. How do we determine who is an "average" worker?
2. What is the appropriate performance dimension to be measured?
3. What scale of measurement should be used?

After answering these questions, you can use work measurement techniques to establish labor time standards. *Work measurement is the determination of the degree and quantity of labor in production/operations tasks.*

The Average Worker

People vary not only in such physical characteristics as height, arm span, and strength, but in their working pace as well. To determine a labor standard, we need to find an "average worker"—but how do we do that? If we choose one typical worker, he or she may not be typical in every respect. Usually, the best thing to do is observe several workers and estimate their average performance. We need to trade off the costs of sampling and the costs of inaccurate standards. The total cost of establishing a standard is increased by the number of workers sampled and studied in depth. If we study each of seven workers one hour rather than each of three workers for an hour, the cost of studying performance (the sampling cost) more than doubles. The tradeoff is that the more workers sampled and studied, the closer the performance standard should be to true "average" performance. There are also costs associated with inaccurate standards; they can lead to tolerating inefficiencies, result in distorted product costs, and affect all the uses of standards we listed in Table 10.6. We can't guarantee an accurate

TABLE 10.7
Distribution of 100 workers sampled

Number of workers sampled	Performance in units per hour	Frequency of total workers	Cumulative frequency of workers	Complementary cumulative frequency of workers
5	10–14	0.05	0.05	0.95
20	15–19	0.20	0.25	0.75
45	20–24	0.45	0.70	0.30
25	25–29	0.25	0.95	0.05
5	30–34	0.05	1.00	0.00

standard, but if we increase the number of workers studied, we can reduce the total costs of inaccuracy. In trading off the costs of sample size and the costs of inaccuracy, we can find a range of reasonably low total costs.

The concept of an average worker brings up yet another point. Once average performance rates have been determined, the performance standard remains to be set. Should the standard be set at the average of total performances for the group, or at a level at which almost all the group can be expected to reach the standard? Table 10.7 and Figure 10.8 show a hypothetical situation in which workers are divided into five performance cate-

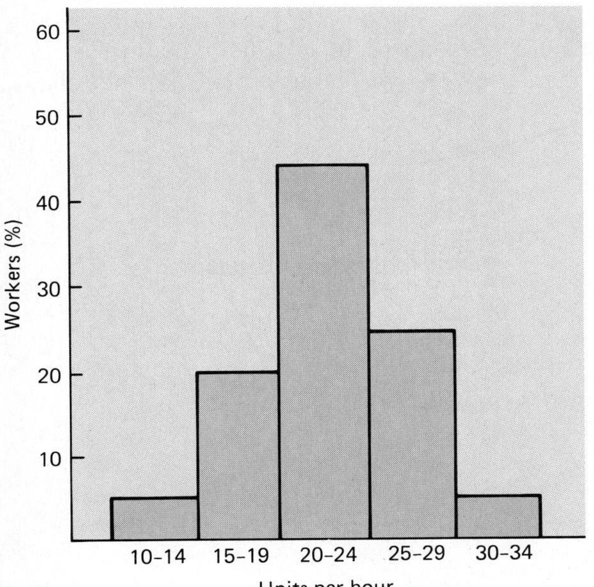

FIGURE 10.8
Frequency distribution of workers sampled

gories. Should the standard be set at 22.25 units per hour, the mean, or at 14 units per hour, a number that 95 percent of the workers can be expected to reach? Arguments for both sides are obvious. Some engineers feel that quoting a minimum standard, the second choice, encourages poor performance. They prefer to have about one-half the workers seeking but not attaining 100 percent of the standard; that is, they suggest setting the standard at the mean performance. Others feel that standards should be attainable by 90 to 95 percent of the workers. Both approaches can be used effectively.

Performance Dimensions

When establishing work standards, management generally considers quantity to be the primary performance to be measured and quality the secondary standard. Quantity is usually measured as pieces per time period in manufacturing and service units per time period in service industries. A lumber sawing operation, for example, might have standard performance set at 1,200 pieces sawed per hour; a bank teller might have standard performance measured and set at 24 customers served per hour. Quality standards are often set as a percent defective—defective units divided by total units, all multiplied by 100. The sawing operation might have a quality standard of 1.0 percent allowable defective units, and the teller operation might allow a 0.05 percent error in counting coins. The key points in determining dimensions of performance are:

1. The dimension must be specified before the standard is set.
2. The standard and subsequent actual performance dimension must both be measurable.

Measurement Scales

Our discussion of work measurement will use a scale in which the normal performance is scaled at 100 percent. This scale is illustrated in Figure 10.9. If performance is 25 percent above normal, the worker is producing

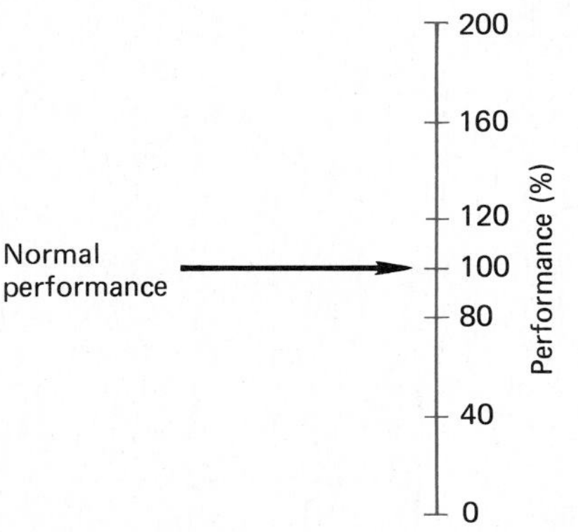

FIGURE 10.9
Most common work measurement scale

at 125 percent of the normal scale. You can find a more detailed discussion of scaling in many industrial engineering texts.

Accuracy

How accurately can a work standard be set? Obviously, experienced raters can set a standard more accurately than can inexperienced raters. Although even experienced raters make errors, the standards they set are generally found to have lower variability than standards set using only historical data. We recommend that you use raters for work measurement, although you must be aware that because setting a standard is not a finely developed scientific procedure, there are bound to be some errors.

Work Measurement Techniques

There are six basic ways of establishing a time (work) standard:

1. ignoring formal work measurement,
2. using the historical data approach,
3. using the direct time study approach,
4. using the predetermined time study approach,
5. using the work sampling approach, and
6. combining approaches 2 through 5.

Ignoring Formal Work Measurement For many jobs in many organizations, especially in the labor-intense service sector, formal labor standards are simply not set at all. The issue of a fair day's work for a fair day's pay is ignored. The result is poor management or ineffective administration. Even though there is no explicit basis for criticism, workers may be blamed for poor performance and inefficiency. If workers are given no specific, understandable goals, poor labor efficiency can easily result. Often because management has not established a work (time) standard, some informal standard is established by default. Since this informal standard generally compares unfavorably with those set by other techniques, we do not recommend ignoring formal work measurement.

Historical Data Approach This method assumes that past performance represents normal performance. In the absence of other formal techniques, some managers use past performance as their main guide in setting standards.

What are the advantages of this method? Basically, it is quick, simple, inexpensive, and probably better than ignoring the questions of establishing a work standard at all. The major disadvantage, as you have observed, is that the past might not at all represent what an average worker could perform under average working conditions. Some of the historical data may reflect unusual working conditions or the performances of unusually capable or incapable workers. Unless management intuitively adjusts past performance data upward or downward before applying it as a standard, the historical approach may misrepresent average performance. In spite of these weaknesses, however, many companies and government agencies have used the method successfully to achieve goals of profitability, growth, and survival over extended periods of time.

Direct Time Study Approach Often called a time study, a stopwatch study, or "clocking the job," this technique is certainly the most widely used method for establishing work standards in manufacturing. Perhaps you have observed a job being studied by an industrial engineer, clipboard and stopwatch in hand.

How does direct time study work? We won't go into the fine points here, but basically there are six steps in the procedure:

1. Observe the job being timed. This technique depends upon direct observation and is therefore limited to jobs that already exist. The job selected should be standardized, in terms of equipment and materials, and the operator should be representative of all operators.
2. Select a job cycle. Identify the work elements that constitute a complete cycle. Decide how many cycles you want to time with a stopwatch.
3. Time the job for all cycles. Workers behave in varying ways when their performances are being recorded; common reactions are resentment, nervousness, and slowing the work pace. To minimize these effects, repeated study, study across several workers, and standing by one worker while studying a job somewhere nearby, perhaps in another department, can be helpful.
4. Compute the normal time based on the cycle times.
5. Determine allowances for personal time, delays, and fatigue.
6. Set the performance standard (standard time) as the sum of observed normal time and determined allowances (the sums of steps 4 and 5).

Another way to state step 6 in the above procedure is:

$$\text{Standard time} = \frac{\text{Normal time}}{1 - \text{Allowance fraction}} \qquad \textbf{(10.4)}$$

where

$$\text{Normal time} = (\text{Average cycle time}) \times (\text{Rating factor}) \qquad \textbf{(10.5)}$$

$$\text{Average cycle time} = \frac{\Sigma \text{ Time recorded to perform an element}}{\text{Number of cycles observed}} \qquad \textbf{(10.6)}$$

$$\text{Allowance fraction} = \text{Fraction of time for personal needs, unavoidable work delays, fatigue}$$

and

$$0 \leq \text{Allowance fraction} \leq 1.0$$

EXAMPLE

The time study of a machinery operation yielded cycle times of 8.0, 7.0, 8.0, and 9.0 minutes. The analyst rated the worker observed as 90 percent. The firm uses a 15 percent allowance factor. Computing the standard time,

$$\text{Average cycle time} = \frac{8.0 + 7.0 + 8.0 + 9.0}{4} = 8.0 \text{ minutes}$$

$$\text{Normal time} = (8.0)(.90) = 7.2 \text{ minutes}$$

$$\text{Standard time} = \frac{7.2}{(1 - 0.15)} = \frac{7.2}{.85} = 8.47 \text{ minutes}$$

The standard time for this machinery operation would be set at 8.47 minutes, which is greater than the average cycle time observed adjusted for the rating factor (90 percent) and the allowance fraction (15 percent).

Industrial engineers frequently use a rating factor when timing jobs. In essence the engineer is judging the worker as 85 percent normal, 90 percent normal, or some other rating depending on his or her perception of "normal." Obviously, ratings of this kind depend on subjective judgments.

EXAMPLE

A laboratory research study required that a routine, repetitive task be designed so that quantity and quality could easily be measured.[15] A collating task similar to such industrial jobs as collating sheets of paper for a promotional mailing, interleaving ash trays and paper in a packing operation, or collating papers for filing by an office file clerk was devised. For this collating task, a male worker took an IBM data processing card from each of six boxes, examined each card for keypunching errors, and sequenced the cards in order, one from each box. A sequence of six good cards made one good units. The worker then stepped to another table and placed the unit in a box of good units. If an error card was found, the worker placed the error card in an error box and returned to obtain a good card from the box in which he had found the error card. The study required that he repeatedly collate good units of six cards for several hours.

A time study was made by observing five different workers for twenty cycles each. A cycle consisted of starting at box one, completing a unit, and returning to box one. The average time for each worker is expressed as an observation and shown in the table. Workers were observed without their knowledge; the average overall cycle time was 0.2247 minutes per cycle. (Another way of stating the standard would be at 4.4503 units per minute or, more commonly, 267 units per hour.)

[15] Everett E. Adam, Jr., "An Analysis of the Change in Performance Quality Employing Operant Conditioning Procedures," *Journal of Applied Psychology* (December 1972).

Direct time study for the quantity standard (expressed in minutes per cycle)

Observation	Single card	Six cards	Average time
1	.0286	.1610	.1966*
2	.0255	.1540	.2287
3	.0166	.2089	.2804
4	.0276	.1616	.1831
5	.0292	.2096	.2345
Average	.0255	.1790	.2247

*Average of performance times for twenty cycles.

One question arises from this example. Why was the sample made up of five workers and twenty cycles? It was judged that this sample was of sufficient size to give a reasonably accurate estimate of average time at a reasonable cost; in direct time study there is an accuracy/cost tradeoff.

Predetermined Time Study Approach For jobs that are not currently being performed but are being planned, the predetermined time study approach is helpful in setting standards. Predetermined time studies can also be applied to existing jobs as an alternative to using direct time study methods. The bases of this technique are the stopwatch time study and time study from films. Historical data for tens of thousands of people making such basic motions as reaching, grasping, stepping, lifting, and standing have been accumulated. These motions have been broken down into elemental actual times, averaged by industrial engineers into predetermined standards, and published in table form. The procedure for setting a predetermined time standard is:

1. Observe the job or think it through if it is yet to be established. If you are observing the job, it is best to use a typical machine, representative materials, and an average worker performing the job correctly.
2. Record each job element. Do not be concerned about elemental times; just thoroughly document all the motions performed by the worker.
3. Obtain a table of predetermined times for various elements and record the motion units for the various elements. Motion units are expressed in some basic scale (a Therblig scale is often used) that corresponds to time units.
4. Add the total motion units for all elements.
5. Estimate an allowance for personal time, delays, and fatigue in motion units.
6. Add the performance motion units and allowance units for a standard job motion unit together and convert these motion units to actual time in minutes or hours. This total time is the resulting predetermined time standard.

This procedure is illustrated by reexamining the collating task we discussed earlier.

EXAMPLE

For the collating job, a predetermined time standard was set. Table 10.8 shows the motions of the right and left hands, provides a code, and shows the TMU (Time Measurement Unit) motion units. This technique is called Methods Time Measurement (MTM) and is a widely accepted predetermined time study approach. The MTM procedure allows one to observe the task, breaking it down into movements that have been studied in depth and that have a predetermined average time. The MTM chart in Table 10.8 was broken into several blocks for clarity.

Notice toward the bottom of Table 10.8 the error allowance (placing an error card in the error box) and the allowance for personal needs (fatigue and unavoidable delay). The time allowance for personal needs, fatigue, and unavoidable delays is a standard industrial engineering allowance. Fifteen percent, a widely used allowance, is assumed for this task.

Since one TMU equals 0.00001 hours, the total MTM time per cycle, 397.9 TMU, is converted directly to .23874 minutes per cycle. This is 4.188 units per minute, or 251 units per hour.

TABLE 10.8
Methods time measurement chart for the quantity standard

Right hand	Code	TMU	Code	Left hand
		14.2	R12D	Reach to cards
		3.5	G1B	Grasp a card
		10.6	AP2	Apply pressure to separate
		3.5	T45S	Turn card
		13.4	M12B	Move to focus eyes
Transfer card from other hand	G3	5.6		
Subtotal		50.8		Subtotal
Multiplied by 6		304.8		Multiplied by 6
		5.6	G3	Transfer cards from other hand
		13.4	M12B	Move to final box
		4.0	D1E	Disengage cards
		15.0	WP(1)	Walk to start again
Subtotal		342.8		Subtotal
Error allowance		3.2		Error allowance
Subtotal		346.0		Subtotal
		51.9		15 percent personal, fatigue, and delay allowance
Total TMU		397.9		Total TMU

The primary advantage of predetermined time studies is that they eliminate nonrepresentative worker reactions to direct time studies. Workers don't slow the pace or get nervous, because the standard is set away from the workplace in a logical, systematic manner. Since the workers aren't anxious, disruptions on the shop floor are less severe with this technique than with direct time studies. The basic disadvantage of this technique is encountered early in its use. If some job elements are not recorded, or if they are recorded improperly, future timing won't be accurate. If job elements can't be properly identified and set forth in a table, they must be evaluated with the direct time study approach.

Work Sampling Approach Work sampling, which was pioneered in the 1930s, is the most recently developed technique of those discussed here. Work sampling does not involve stopwatch measurement, as do many of the other techniques; instead, it is based on simple random sampling techniques derived from statistical sampling theory. Its purpose is to estimate what proportion of a worker's time is devoted to work activities. It proceeds along these steps:

1. Decide what conditions you want to define as "working" and what conditions you want to define as "not working." Not working consists of all activities not specifically defined as working.
2. Observe the activity at selected intervals, recording whether a person is working or not.
3. Calculate the proportion of the time a worker is engaged in work (P) with this formula:

$$P = \frac{x}{n} = \frac{\text{Number of observations in which working occurred}}{\text{Total number of observations}} \quad \textbf{(10.7)}$$

With this calculation the manager can estimate the proportion of time a worker is engaged in work activity; this proportion can then be used as a performance standard.

EXAMPLE

A library administrator was concerned about the percent of time that a circulation clerk spent with patrons at the desk. Circulation activity included only those times when a clerk was engaged in assisting a patron at the circulation desk. The information clerk working at a nearby desk was asked to record once every half-hour for a week whether or not the circulation clerk was "working." Results were as follows:

Day	Number of observations	Number of circulation (working) observations
Monday	16	8
Tuesday	15	8
Wednesday	20	12
Thursday	16	10
Friday	16	10
Total	83	48

The proportion of the time spent in the circulation activity, as defined by the administrator, was

$$P = \frac{x}{n} = \frac{48}{83} = .578$$

The administrator concluded that the proportion was low enough to add other clerical activities to this job.

Work sampling can also be used to set production standards; the procedure is similar to the one used in direct time studies. We can determine normal times as shown below (equation [10.8]) and calculate standard times according to equation 10.4.

$$\text{Normal time} = \frac{(\text{Total study time}) \times \left(\begin{array}{c}\text{Percent of time}\\ \text{employee observed}\\ \text{working}\end{array}\right) \times \left(\begin{array}{c}\text{Performance}\\ \text{rating}\\ \text{factor}\end{array}\right)}{\text{Number of pieces produced}} \tag{10.8}$$

The work sampling approach to job measurement is particularly adaptive to service sector jobs—jobs like those in libraries, banking, health care, insurance companies, and government. A good deal of the accuracy of this technique depends upon sample size. As is the case with any sampling procedure, there is a tradeoff between larger sample size and increased accuracy versus the cost of increasing the sample size. Reliability and precision are the key statistical concepts; if you're interested, a basic statistics book can assist you in setting the sample size for various reliability levels.

By including a concept called *rating* or *leveling performance*, you can extend work sampling to include output standards. Once a job has been studied, the analyst must decide whether the worker's performance was average, above average, or below average. If the analyst decides performance was average, no adjustment is made. If the analyst decides the worker is above average (measured as units/time period), his or her rate is multiplied by a factor less than one; if the employee was working below average, the rate is leveled to average by multiplying the observed performance by a factor greater than one.

The accuracy of performance leveling depends, in large part, upon the industrial engineer's judgment and talent. Thus, the technique may lack objectivity, and results may be uneven from study to study. Another disadvantage is that the study must be limited to few workers. Further, "working" is a broad concept, not easily defined with precision. There are, however, some obvious advantages with work sampling. It is simple, easily adapted to service sector and indirect labor jobs, and an economical way to measure performance. In short, work sampling is a useful work measurement technique if it is used with discretion.

Combining Work Measurement Techniques Which work measurement technique should you use? In practice, they are used in combination, as crosschecks. One common practice is to observe a job, write down in detail all the job elements, and set a predetermined time standard. Then one can check the history of performance on this or similar jobs to verify that the predetermined standard is reasonable. To provide a further check, the job by elements and in total can be time studied. The point is clear; no one work measurement technique is totally reliable. Because of the high skill level required in setting the standard, we recommend a cross-check whenever possible.

EXAMPLE

For the collating task we discussed earlier, the predetermined time standard was .2383 minutes per collation cycle. This was cross-validated by direct time study, which provided a standard of .2247 minutes per cycle. Finally, according to a previous study that used this task but under slightly different working conditions, actual historical times in the similar task were .1954 minutes per cycle. The first two times cross-validated quite closely, and the historical standard was reasonably close, so the predetermined time standard was adopted.

An apparent oversite in the direct time study is the ommission of the 15 percent allowance used in the predetermined method. If this allowance were deleted from the predetermined method, the predetermined time would be .2076, which is similar to the historical time.

Work Measurement for White-collar Workers Among the work measurement techniques presented, which appear most suitable for white-collar workers? Since white-collar jobs are typically labor intense and minimally automated, the same measurement techniques employed in the service sector would seem appropriate. We suggest a combination of historical data and

TABLE 10.9
How standards are established

Technique	Percent of time used
Time study	89.5
Predetermined approaches	
Standard data	61.4
Predetermined time standard system	32.2
Estimate based on historical experience	44.2
Work sampling	21.3
Others	3.0

Source: Robert S. Rice, "Survey. . .," page 21. Reprinted with permission from *Industrial Engineering* magazine, July 1977. Copyright Institute of Industrial Engineers, 25 Technology Park / Atlanta, Norcross, GA 30092.

work sampling.[16] When predetermined time study can be used—on more routine white-collar jobs—it can be a useful approach too.

Current Usage of Work Measurement A comprehensive 1976 survey of United States and Canadian industries asked a simple question, "Are you using work measurement and, if you do, for what purposes?"[17] This study was compared to a similar survey *Factory* magazine had conducted in 1959, seventeen years earlier. Of the nearly 1,500 usable responses to the 1976 study, 89 percent reported they were using work measurement. This contrasts sharply with the 1956 survey, in which only 71 percent of the 785 respondents reported using work measurement. Correspondingly, the later study found 53 percent of the respondents used work measurement to measure employee performance, compared with only 20 percent in the earlier study. In the 1976 study, work measurement was also used for estimating and costing (89 percent), establishing wage incentives (59 percent), and production scheduling (55 percent). As the study makes clear, this traditional scientific management technique is by no means "dead" or "outdated" in industry; rather, it is apparently quite useful.

Another dimension of the more recent survey involves setting standards. The question was asked "What conditions trigger revision of a standard?" The most frequent reasons were changes in methods and materials (75 percent of respondents checked), low performance due to a tight standard (65 percent checked), and high performance due to loose standards (54 percent checked). The respondents were also asked "How are standards established?" From Table 10.9 we see time study to be the most popular technique (used 89.5 percent of the time). The percentages will not add to

[16]See, for example, R. Keith Martin, "Don't Overlook Clerical Productivity," *Industrial Engineering* 9, no. 2 (February 1977), pp. 28–33.

[17]Robert S. Rice, "Survey of Work Measurement and Wage Incentives," *Industrial Engineering* 9, no. 7 (July 1977), pp. 18–31.

TABLE 10.10
Obstacles to increasing applications of work measurement

Obstacle	Percent respondents indicating
Not enough industrial engineering personnel	43
Uneconomical to measure	28
Impractical to measure	25
Management not interested	21
Employee and/or union resistance	9
Don't know how to measure	7
Other obstacles	1

Source: Robert S. Rice, "Survey . . .," page 31. Reprinted with permission from *Industrial Engineering* magazine, July 1977. Copyright Institute of Industrial Engineers, 25 Technology Park / Atlanta, Norcross, GA 30092.

100 percent since often more than one technique is used to set a standard, as we advised earlier.

As each work measurement technique was discussed, we addressed its advantages and disadvantages. In light of the apparent advantages why aren't all organizations using work measurement? We find the answer in the opinion of the 1500 survey respondents in Table 10.10, 43 percent of whom listed shortage of qualified specialists as an obstacle. There is a career opportunity here for those interested in work measurement.

SUMMARY

A key function in production/operations management is organizing work. This requires the manager to design jobs, establish job standards, and perform work measurement. In practice, methods analysis (job design) is followed by work measurement (establishing the job standard through measurement).

Traditional engineering approaches to job design have emphasized the use of operation charts, activity charts, flow process charts, and principles of motion economy. Consideration must also be given to worker physiology and environmental conditions as these affect job design. Such behavioral concepts as job rotation, enlargement, enrichment, and redesign of job characteristics can enhance productivity and satisfaction. If managers use both traditional modeling and contemporary behavioral concepts in designing jobs, the results may be more efficient and effective performance than could be provided by either alone.

After the job has been designed, individual, department, and plant job standards must be established. Standards are used for evaluating the performance of employees and facilities and predicting, planning, and controlling operations.

Although work measurement techniques do not provide perfect accuracy, they are considerably more accurate than other alternatives, including total reliance on management's judgment. Methods of work measurement vary; they include using historical data, direct time study, predetermined time study, and work sampling. In practice, several techniques are used in combination to cross-validate the work that is measured.

CASE

Sediment Oil Company

Sediment Oil Company is a regional independent company that distributes gasoline and oil products in sixteen western states. Distribution is divided by market area, and an operations manager is responsible for about twenty-two retail service stations, all of which are company owned and operated. Each station has a manager, an assistant manager, and from one to six additional employees.

Todd Smith is a new operations manager with six years' experience in retail clothing. He has been assigned a district that has nineteen service stations. The district is not profitable as a whole and is experiencing high job turnover. Upon investigation, Todd finds the high job turnover to be in the job performed at the pump, the attendant position. Further, when reviewing profitability overall and at individual stations, Todd finds that labor costs are excessive compared to more profitable company operations.

Todd is determined to focus on the attendant position for improvement. He remembers the typical attendant pumping gasoline, servicing vehicles at pump islands, and waiting for vehicles when doing neither of these tasks. Todd has noticed that both credit card and cash sales are handled by either the manager or the assistant manager. This seems unusual to him; it is unlike his experience in retail clothing. Likewise, the manager, assistant manager, or a mechanic do all the mechanical work, from repairing tires to tuning engines. Stations are not equipped for full-line auto mechanic work, but they do provide limited services with proven profitability.

Todd has decided to analyze closely the work of the station attendant, but he is not sure how to document or measure the current situation. Todd believes that he can redesign the job to cut down on labor and decrease job turnover. The state manager, to whom Todd reports, will be spending two days traveling with Todd at the end of next week. Todd hopes to have a detailed plan for measuring and redesigning the attendant's job for approval by the state manager, but he is having problems preparing a plan.

CASE

First National Bank

Lock-box operations in a large commercial bank process accounts receivable for customers. First National Bank has a major commitment to lock-box operations and is currently the regional processor for several major oil companies and national retailers, one of the larger credit card companies, and dozens of smaller regional companies. Customers of these companies mail their payments directly to First National, using a special zip code. Theoretically, First National is able to intercept the payment (shorten the mail time), process the paperwork, and credit the firm's account—all within a day from the time it receives the payment.

Lock-box operations are becoming a problem for First National. Every day it receives thousands of bills and payments for hundreds of accounts. Over the last few months, there have been as many as three days' backlog in work-in-process. First National is in jeopardy of losing two national accounts to competitor regional banks, which are out-performing it (a typical major oil company might use four banks geographically dispersed about the country). First National has assigned a "breakthrough" team to set performance standards and study jobs within this department.

The key employee appears to be the account processor, a person who opens incoming mail, verifies payment with the bill, records payment by account number, separates payments and bills, and delivers each for further processing. The account processor must also encode the payments (usually checks) and send them to check processing so that they can clear the bank and First National can receive credit for the money it has credited to the national account customer.

The team performed both a direct time study and work sample for the account processor job, with the results shown below. The bank uses a 15 percent allowance factor in all clerical jobs.

Management is concerned that setting a standard now will further damage performance. In fact, the day after the direct time study, fourteen of the thirty-five second-shift workers were absent, a number much higher than the normal 10 percent. Jan Holms, an informal group leader who was one of the workers studied, told the analyst the company would "pay for this pressure." She was one of those absent the next day.

Frank Waring, the operations vice president, would like to change the entire work flow orientation, dissolving the lock-box department as it is now organized and grouping lock-box and other operations functions by customer rather than product. Frank's counterpart at Citibank recently wrote an article for the Harvard Business Review explaining that bank's success with a customer account focus, and Frank was most impressed. Although this seems like an appropriate time to consider such a move, Frank is not gathering the support he had anticipated from his team of management subordinates.

Direct time study data—processor job

	Cycle time (minutes) Processor # 1	# 2	Number times observed Processor # 1	# 2
	0.5	0.5	1	2
	0.7	0.7	3	4
	1.0	1.0	5	3
	1.3	1.5	2	1
	1.5	2.0	1	1
Performance ratings:	Worker 1	85%		
	Worker 2	80%		

Work sampling data—processor job

	Worker 1	Worker 2
Number payments processed	322	296
Length of time observed	8 hours	8 hours
Performance rating	85%	80%
Idle time	25%	30%

REVIEW AND DISCUSSION QUESTIONS

1. Explain the difference between job design and production/operations standards.
2. Discuss the relationship between work measurement and methods analysis. Which typically follows the other? Why?
3. Contrast operation charts, activity charts, and flow process charts.
4. Each of us realizes that such environmental variables as temperature and noise affect our work. What empirical evidence can you cite that supports the impact such environmental variables have on output?
5. What is OSHA? What might the Act do for the employer and employee?
6. Contrast job enlargement and job enrichment. Are they mutually exclusive?
7. Discuss the assumptions behind job enlargement.
8. Explain how departmental and plant standards differ from individual job standards. Provide an example of each from an organization of your choice.
9. Select two uses of time (labor) standards. Explain how the time standard could help a municipal police department in a city of 40,000 persons for the two uses you have selected.
10. Discuss the essential features and findings of each of the following studies: the Bell System job enlargement studies, job enrichment at General Foods, and job design in Sweden.
11. Explain the predetermined time study approach to work measurement.
12. Why would combinations of work mearsurement approaches be a good strategy in establishing a standard?
13. Explain how you would proceed to set a standard for a group of seven draftsmen in a large architectural firm.
14. Why are production/operations standards important?

PROBLEMS

Solved Problems

1. In a candy factory a direct time study was made of the chocolate melting and pouring operation. Two inexperienced industrial engineers and one experienced engineer each made the study simultaneously. They agreed precisely on cycle times (shown below) but varied on rating the work, the experienced engineer rating the worker 100 percent and the other engineers rating the worker 80 percent and 110 percent. The firm uses a 15 percent allowance factor.

Cycle time (minutes)	Number times observed
25	1
29	2
30	2
31	1

(a) Determine the standard time using the experienced industrial engineer's judgments.

(b) Find the standard times using the data of each inexperienced engineer. What is your interpretation when compared to (a)? Are you sure the experienced engineer is correct? What could be done to enhance consistency in analyst "performance ratings"?

Rating the worker at 100%:

$$\text{Normal time} = \frac{25 + (29)(2) + (30)(2) + 31}{6} = 29 \text{ minutes}$$

$$\text{Standard time} = \frac{29}{1-.15} = 34.12 \text{ minutes}$$

Rating the worker at 110%:

$$\text{Normal time} = 29 \times 110\% = 31.90 \text{ minutes}$$

$$\text{Standard time} = \frac{31.90}{1-.15} = 37.53 \text{ minutes}$$

Rating the worker at 80%:

$$\text{Normal time} = 29 \times 80\% = 23.20 \text{ minutes}$$

$$\text{Standard time} = \frac{23.2}{1-.15} = 27.29 \text{ minutes}$$

Obviously, considerably different standard times are derived for different ratings. Although an experienced engineer could be wrong, we have more confidence in an experienced person. We could enhance consistency by training. Training films and short courses are available for use.

2. As a cargo loader for Southeastern Airlines, you are charged with the responsibility of setting a time standard (in minutes) for uploading refrigerated unitized loads. The following study was conducted over a period of 300 hours with 900 uploading performed.

Composite performance rating	Activity	Number of observations
80	Manually check and lift unitized load onto trailer.	100
100	Tow loaded trailer with tractor to aircraft.	300
120	Check electrical contacts holding pins and safety wires (called "wiring out"; this time will be reduced by 50 percent by an additional inspection during manufacture of the containers).	400
90	Correct any malfunctioning observed during wiring out.	100
110	Load unitized load into plane bay with automatic lift.	400
140	Return tractor and trailer to warehouse.	300
	Personal or idle time.	400

Official Southeastern personal time allowance is 10 percent of total eight-hour work day *unless otherwise stated;* it is not otherwise stated here.

$$\text{Avg. observed time/uploading} = \frac{300 \text{ hrs.}}{900 \text{ uploading}} \times 60 \text{ min/hr}$$
$$= 20 \text{ min/uploading}$$

$$20 \text{ min} \times \frac{100}{2000} \times .80 \qquad = \frac{\text{Normal minutes/uploading}}{.8 \text{ min}}$$

$$20 \text{ min} \times \frac{300}{2000} \times 1.00 = 3.0$$

$$20 \text{ min} \times \frac{400}{2000} \times 1.20 \times \frac{1}{2} = 2.4$$

$$20 \text{ min} \times \frac{100}{2000} \times .90 = .9$$

$$20 \text{ min} \times \frac{400}{2000} \times 1.10 = 4.4$$

$$20 \text{ min} \times \frac{300}{2000} \times 1.40 = \underline{4.2}$$

Total normal time minutes/uploading 15.7 min

$$\text{Standard time} = 15.7 \text{ min/uploading} \times \frac{100}{100 - 10} = 17.44 \text{ min/uploading}$$

$$= .29 \text{ hrs/uploading}$$

Reinforcing Fundamentals

3. An experienced industrial engineer conducted a direct time study for an acid mixing operation. The analyst found cycle times as shown below, rated the worker observed as 90 percent, and used the firm's 10 percent allowance factor. Determine the standard time.

Cycle time (minutes)	Number times observed
1.7	3
1.7	4
1.9	2
2.1	1
2.2	1

4. A speciality wood products company in eastern Kentucky manufactures handmade miniature wooden dogs. This Dandy Dogie product line is hand carved, varnished, labeled, and boxed, all by the same person. But there are wide variances in quality and performance times, which management is no longer willing to accept. In the hope of establishing a standard time, management has done a direct time study focusing on the two-inch walnut beagle. The results are shown below. For now, carving is being eliminated from the study. The firm's allowance factor is 10 percent. Establish a standard time for the remainder of the job.

Job element	Cycle observed (minutes) 1	2	3	4	Performance rating
(a) Varnish	5	4	5	4	105%
(b) Label	0.5	0.4	0.3	0.5	95%
(c) Box	2	2	1	2	95%

5. American Commerce's labor standard for over-the-road truck drivers is 320 miles per eight-hour shift. Current wages are $8 per hour under a nationwide contract. The assigned drivers from the Cleveland terminal logged 31,525 miles the first week of April and recorded 822 hours of work. A no overtime policy is in existence for Cleveland-based drivers.
   (a) What is the labor efficiency variance for the first week of April?
   (b) The American Commerce shop steward (driver union representative) contends that since the drivers log primarily noninterstate miles, the standard should be 10 percent less, or 288 miles per day. Operating management would like a comparative labor variance for the first week in April. What do these labor variances actually mean to management?
6. A farming conglomerate has a large cow-calf operation. The manager expects the hay crew to place 1,750 bales of hay in the barn daily during harvest. The contract costs for labor only are $180 per day (for a crew of four). In the past four days 8100 bales have been harvested. What is the farm manager's labor efficiency variance for the hay crew? Would you suggest any action based on this figure?
7. Direct time study for a task resulted in the following times, expressed in minutes per cycle.

Observation	Average time
1	1.321
2	1.411
3	1.704
4	1.175

   A predetermined time standard was set at 2,128 TMU per cycle, which converts to 1.275 minutes per cycle. What time standard would you recommend? Justify your choice.
8. Develop an employee-machine activity chart to show how a multipage term paper should be copied on a coin-operated photocopy machine. Use a layout diagram. Assume there are ample coins and that the stack of pages is prepared (unstapled) at the start of the task.
9. Develop a left-hand right-hand operation chart for: (a) manually stuffing, sealing, and stamping an envelope for mailing—assume that the preaddressed envelope is to contain a one-page letter that must be folded before it is inserted into the envelope; (b) opening mail that was just received. Each envelope must be opened and the contents removed, unfolded, and placed on a desk. A knife-like letter opener is used.
10. Job analysis and methods study reveal that during an eight-hour workday a man-machine operation typically experiences various unavoidable delays totaling 40 minutes and one equipment setup changeover of 20 minutes. Operators need 20 minutes for personal time and take two 15 minute coffee breaks. Standard time per operation cycle (to produce one unit) is 10 minutes. How many units are produced by an operator who produces at 85 percent of standard? At 115 percent of standard?
11. A student is facing midterm exams and decides to start the semester's first real studying. After one day in the library, the student is dismayed to find that at the rate of present studying, he will not be ready to take the exams until four days after they are over. A friend volunteers to do a work sampling study and finds the following:

Two-hour time period	Number of observations	Number of studying observations
1	12	9
2	21	10
3	9	4

As a percentage, what is the proportion of time spent studying?

12. A work-sample study conducted over forty hours of a one-week period yielded the following. An operator produced 135 parts and was performance rated as 115 percent. The operator's idle time was 12 percent; the company established allowance was 15 percent for this job class and part. Determine the standard time for this part.
13. Filing clerks in a state department of welfare were considered to be filing any time they had a paper in their hands. The following seven days of observations were selected at random over the past month. What proportion of the time is spent in filing? What work measurement approach is this? How might one alternatively define filing?

Day	Number of observations	Number of filing observations
1	12	8
2	19	12
3	10	5
4	23	14
5	15	10
6	12	9
7	17	11

Challenging Exercises

14. Several laboratory technicians in a hospital are primarily responsible for running the highly automated "Chemistry 12" blood profile test. An experienced technician was work sampled on this job over a two-week period (seventy hours). The lab technician produced 412 blood samples. The analyst studying the job found that the technician was working 60 percent of the time and idle the rest. Some idleness was due to waiting for the automated equipment to complete analysis. The performance rating was 85 percent, but the analyst was uncertain about this because of the automated equipment. Allowances are set at 10 percent.
    (a) Determine a standard time for a standard blood profile.
    (b) How could the analyst be more certain about the performance rating?
15. A manufacturer is considering the purchase of one of two types of equipment, type *A* or type *B*, to perform an operation. Initial equipment cost is $10,000 for either *A* or *B*. Operating costs are estimated as follows:

	A	*B*
Maintenance (per month)	$750	$500
Supplies (per unit)	—	.052
Operator (per, hour)	9	9

The equipment manufacturers both arranged for experimental demonstrations, in which stopwatch time studies of operator/machine performance for five cycles were measured. Demonstrations revealed the following time in minutes:

	Cycles for A					Cycles for B				
Activity	*1*	*2*	*3*	*4*	*5*	*1*	*2*	*3*	*4*	*5*
Load machine	0.32	0.29	0.28	0.31	0.30	0.30	0.27	0.25	0.22	0.21
Machine time (machine paced)	2.73	2.61	2.68	2.71	2.63	2.62	2.57	2.59	2.51	2.54
Unload machine	0.14	0.10	0.09	0.12	0.11	0.12	0.09	0.10	0.11	0.09
Inspect product	1.21	1.08	1.29	1.15	1.20	0.92	0.94	0.86	0.79	0.87
Apply label to product*	—	—	—	—	—	0.05	0.04	0.05	0.05	0.04

*Label application is automatic for *A* and manual for *B*.

The time study expert rated the operator as performing at 115 percent of normal on *A* and 110 percent of normal on *B* during the observation cycles. It is estimated that operators will receive two 15-minute coffee breaks daily. Unavoidable delays are estimated to be 40 minutes for *A* and 25 minutes for *B* during an eight-hour day. Evaluate the two alternatives and justify your recommendation of *A* or *B*.

16. A post office mailroom receives mail and cancels the postage stamps. After the application of appropriate work simplification techniques, you take a direct time study of the simplified job and obtain the following elemental times in minutes:

	Job Element	Cycle 1	2	3	4	5
Empty mail bags	1	.16	.31	.14	.15	.16
Straighten mail	2	.60	.60	.60	.60	.60
Carry trays to reader	3	.34	.36	.35	.37	.38
Cancellation machine	4	.50	.50	.50	.50	.50
Empty trays	5	.24	.24	.48	.27	.25

You further determine the following information about this job.

(1) Job elements 2 and 4 are machine-controlled and cannot be speeded up by the operator.
(2) You observed two irregular occurrences while timing the job. These are the elemental times, which vary from the average of all readings by more than 20 percent of each element's average.
(3) You rated the operator at 120 percent when he was working.
(4) Management and the worker's union have negotiated the following allowances for this job.

Personal—30 minutes a day
Unavoidable delay—40 minutes a day
Fatigue—10 percent of the normal time.

(5) An operator on this job earns $5 per hour.
(6) Material cost per unit is $.50.
(7) Total overhead cost is added in at a rate of 150 percent of the sum of direct labor and material cost.

(a) How many pieces should each operator produce during an eight-hour shift?
(b) What is the total standard cost per piece?

17. Assume you, as a bank officer, have your bank tellers count out $100 in denominations of six $10 bills, seven $5 bills, and five $1 bills. The purpose of this operation is to supply your bank's night teller IV service with this bankpack. Suppose a continuous stopwatch time/study yielded the following data:

	Cycle (minutes, cumulative)								Performance rating
Element	1	2	3	4	5	6	7	8	
(1) Count 6–$10	.12	.66	1.24	1.95	3.26	3.91	4.52	5.05	110
(2) Count 7–$5	.27	.84	1.40	2.12	3.41	4.08	4.66	5.21	115
(3) Count 5–$1	.38	.96	1.51	2.20	3.52	4.18	4.74	5.29	105
(4) Count $100	.56	1.09	1.80	2.41	3.80*	4.36	4.94	5.48	110
(5) Place stocks in chute**	—	—	—	3.13	—	—	—	—	90

*Teller had to recount because of error.
**Occurs about once every ten cycles.

The allowances for this job are set at 15 percent of the work day (eight hours).

a) What is the normal time for this job?
b) What is the standard time for this job?
c) What is the standard output in terms of $100 bundles/hour?
d) How long (in terms of man hours) would it take to package 500 packs, if the tellers assigned to the job worked at a 115 percent pace on the average?

18. Pimola Olive Stuffers (the Pride of Sicily) has been in business for many years. It is an old family concern in which Papa Pimola even gets in and stuffs a few olives once in a while just for old times' sake. One of the policies of Papa Pimola has been to provide cigars and vino free at the three "rest" breaks each day. Pressed by modern business methods of other olive stuffers, Papa Pimola has hired a work measurements expert to monitor his operation and see if it is operating efficiently.
Listed below are the facts the work measurements expert came up with.

Number of observations	Activity	Performance rating
100	Pick up olive	90
100	Pit olive	110
100	Pick up pimento	90
150	Roll pimento	120
250	Stuff olive	130
200	Insert olive in jar	110
100	Idle time	

Papa Pimola has a work crew of five, each being paid $2.50/hour. They take three 20-minute rest breaks for cigars and vino each day—free from Papa Pimola. The above figures were taken during a 40-hour workweek in which 5,000 jars of olives (20 olives/jar) were produced.

(a) What is the weekly output in jars of olives if the crew works at a normal pace?
(b) What is the labor cost per 1,000 jars if the crew works at a 110 percent pace?

GLOSSARY

Activity chart Divides operations into major task segments performed by workers and machines; times them to determine idle and productive times; appropriate for routine, repetitive tasks with worker-machine interaction.

Direct time study A work measurement technique that involves observing the job, determining the job cycle, stopwatch timing the job cycle, and computing a performance standard.

Flow process chart Analyzes interstation activities to capture the flows of products through the overall production process.

Gang process chart Traces interaction of several workers and one machine.

Job Group of related tasks or activities that need to be performed to meet organizational objectives.

Job design Specifies the content of each job and determines the distribution of work within the organization.

Job enlargement Procedure of redesigning jobs or modifying work content to provide greater stimulus variety, autonomy, task identity, and feedback for the worker.

Job enrichment Procedure of redesigning work content to give more meaning and enjoyment to the job by involving employees in planning, organizing, and controlling their work.

Job rotation Movement of employees into a job for a short period of time and then out again.

Operation chart Analyzes and separates the motions of the right and left hands to determine how much time is taken by each hand for a job; appropriate for routine, repetitive, short cycle tasks.

OSHA Williams-Steiger Occupational Safety and Health Act of 1970; develops standards, penalties and enforcement procedures for job-related safety and health.

Predetermined time study A work measurement technique that involves observing or thinking through a job, recording job elements, recording preestablished motion units, and computing a performance standard.

Principles of motion economy General statements focusing on work arrangements, the use of human hands and body, and the use of tools.

Standard A criterion established as a basis for comparison in measuring or judging output.

Work measurement The determination of the degree and quantity of labor in product tasks.

Work sampling Work measurement technique that involves defining the condition "working," sampling the activity over time, and computing proportion of time the worker is engaged in "work".

SELECTED READINGS

Aldag, Raymond J. and Arthur P. Brief. *Task Design and Employee Motivation*. Glenview, Illinois: Scott, Foresman and Company, 1979.

Barnes, Frank C. "Principles of Motion Economy: Revisited, Reviewed, and Restored." *Proceedings Southern Management Association*. Atlanta, 1983, pp. 297–299.

Barnes, R. M. *Motion and Time Study: Design and Measurement of Work*. 6th ed. New York: John Wiley & Sons, Inc., 1968.

Ford, R. N. *Motivation Through the Work Itself*. New York: American Management Association, Inc., 1969.

Hackman, J. R. and E. E. Lawler. "Employee Reactions to Job Characteristics." *Journal of Applied Psychology*. Monograph 55 (1971), pp. 259–86.

Hulin, C. C. and M. R. Blood. "Job Enlargement, Individual Differences, and Worker Responses." *Psychological Bulletin* 69 (1968), pp. 41–55.

Nadler, Gerald. *Work Design: A Systems Concept*. Rev. ed. Homewood, Ill.: Richard D. Irwin, Inc., 1970.

Pierce, Jon L. and Randall B. Dunham. "Task Design: A Literature Review." *The Academy of Management Review* 1, no. 4 (October 1976), pp. 83–97.

Rice, Robert S. "Survey of Work Measurement and Wage Incentives." *Industrial Engineering* 9, no. 7 (July 1977), pp. 18–31.

Szilagyi, Andrew S., Jr. and Marc J. Wallace, Jr. *Organizational Behavior and Performance*, 2nd ed. Santa Monica, California: Goodyear Publishing Co., 1980.

U.S. Department of Labor. Occupational Health and Safety Administration. *All About OSHA*. OSHA publication No. 2056.

11 Scheduling Systems and Aggregate Planning

Because the aircraft manufacturing industry is highly sensitive to fluctuating demands, and to the corresponding cost impacts of these fluctuations upon the production environment, a thorough knowledge of the fundamentals of scheduling systems and operations by management is essential to our competitive position. A stable work staffing level is a major goal of our aggregate planning process because of the added costs associated with erratic variation of these levels. Even minor changes resulting in job transfers multiply to many changes in a highly skilled and unionized environment. McDonnell Douglas Canada Ltd. utilizes several methods to maintain the delicate balance between the flexibility required with regard to market schedule demands and long-term production planning to maintain competitive cost. The use of suitable long-term planning horizons, effective use of inventories, reassignment of employees, and level loading through finite capacity planning are some of the methods used to temper the impact of changes.

In an industry in which as many as 20,000 different parts (some of them used in large quantity multiples) are incorporated into a single aircraft component with very long detailed part flow times relative to other industries, a disciplined approach to planning and scheduling systems is required.

Garret G. Ackerson, President
McDonnell Douglas Canada Ltd.
Toronto, Ontario
Canada

Imagine yourself in charge of a large facility, such as McDonnell Douglas Canada Ltd., that houses many types of equipment and people. How should you use these potentially productive resources during the next six months, year, or even longer? Your answer to this question, as indicated in Mr. Ackerson's introductory comments, will directly affect the success of your organization. You must establish a program of action for guiding the utilization of these productive resources. One source of guidance is provided through operations planning and scheduling systems.

Keep in mind that our major focus is on *planning* the use of the existing fixed-capacity conversion processes. Remember also that these planning processes, including their modeling and behavioral aspects, are related to the organizing and controlling activities of operations management, as we show in Figure 11.1. You will see these relationships in this chapter when we present an overview of operations planning and scheduling systems. Then we will concentrate on two of its elements, aggregate planning and master scheduling, showing how they are used in both manufacturing and service operations.

OPERATIONS PLANNING AND SCHEDULING SYSTEMS

Operations planning and scheduling concerns the volume and timing of outputs, the utilization of operations capacity, and balancing outputs with capacity at desired levels for competitive effectiveness. The management systems for doing all of this involve various hierarchical levels of activities that fit together from top to bottom in support of one another, as shown in Figure 11.2, so that overall plans become a reality in the marketplace.

As you will see, the time orientation ranges from long to short as we progress from top to bottom in the hierarchy. Also, the level of detail in the planning process ranges from broad at the top to detailed at the bottom.[1] Although each firm has its own unique variations, the general processes and steps in our system apply to both goods-producing and service operations, and to repetitive manufacturing, job-lot (intermittent), and assembly line operations.

In this chapter we will give a brief overview of each level in the overall process. Then we will focus on the aggregate production and capacity plan and its decomposition down to the level of master production scheduling and roughcut capacity planning. The remaining levels are covered in detail in subsequent chapters; material requirements planning and detailed capacity planning are discussed in Chapter 16 in conjunction with other

[1]Hierarchical planning and decisions are discussed in H. C. Meal, "Putting Production Decisions Where They Belong," *Harvard Business Review* 62, no. 2 (March–April 1984), pp. 102–111.

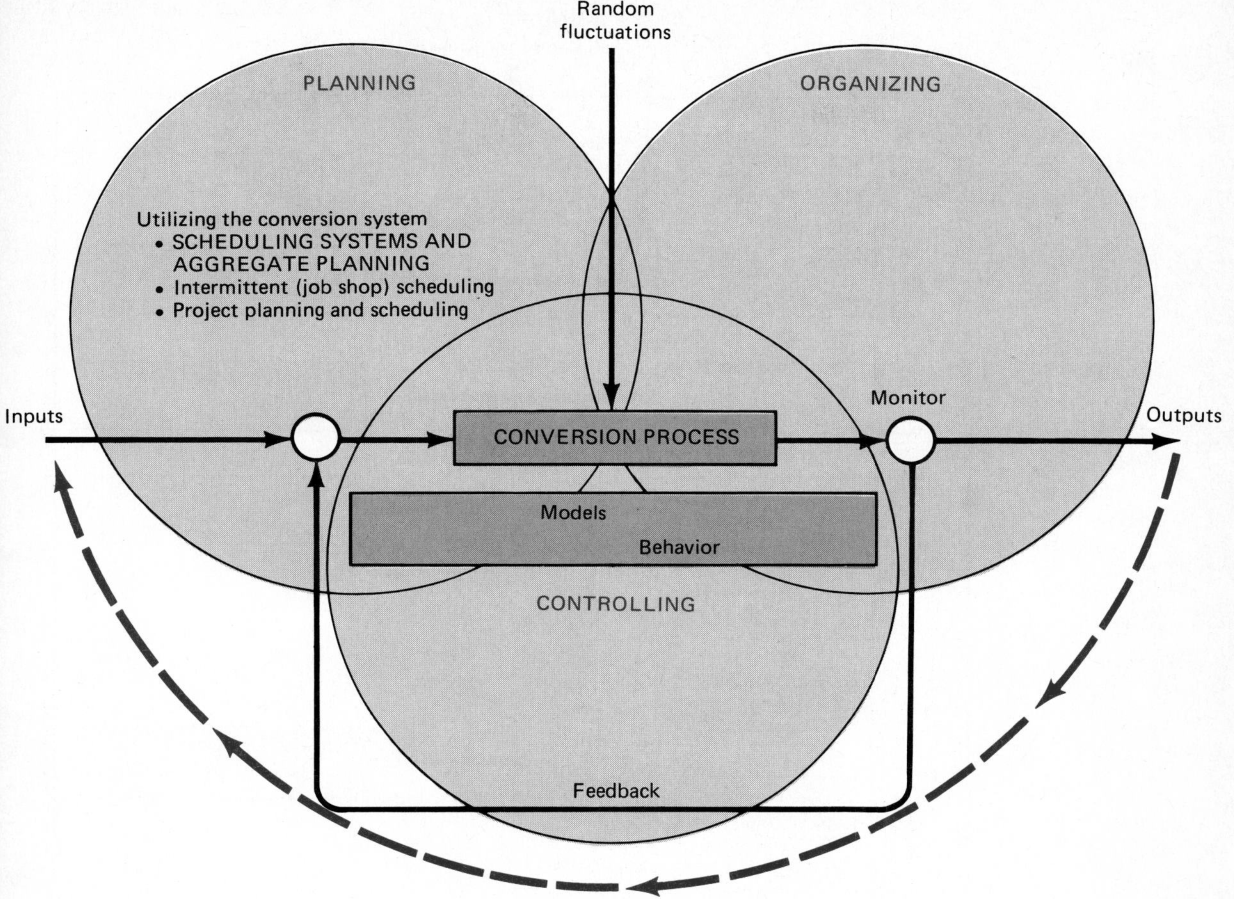

FIGURE 11.1
Production/operations management activities

inventory and materials planning procedures, while shop floor control is presented in Chapter 12 in the context of intermittent (job-lot) production.[2] Let's begin with an overview of the entire system.

Overview of the Operations Scheduling and Planning System

The Business Plan The business plan is a statement of the organization's overall level of business activity for the next 6–18 months. Developed at the top executive level, the plan is based on forecasts of general economic conditions, anticipated conditions of the industry, and competitive considerations; it reflects the company's strategy for competing during the coming

[2]Although shop floor control is discussed in Chapter 12 in the context of intermittent production, it applies to repetitive and continuous processes as well.

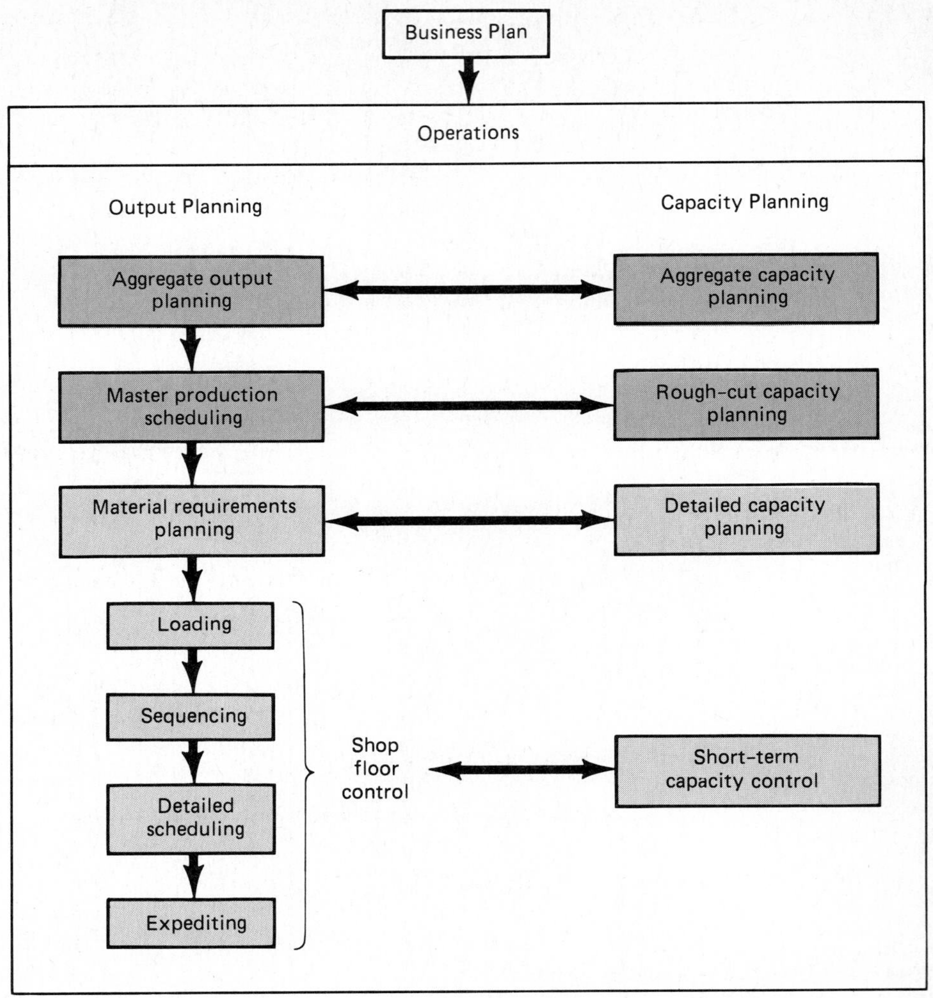

FIGURE 11.2
The operations planning and scheduling system

year(s). It is usually expressed in terms of outputs (dollar volume of sales), quarterly or sometimes monthly, for each of its broad product groups but not for the specific items or individual products within each group. It also may specify the overall inventory and backlog levels to maintain during the planning period.

The business plan, in a sense, is an agreement between all functional areas—finance, production, marketing, engineering, R&D—as to what level of business activity and product groups they will be committed to support. It is not, at this level, concerned with all the details and specific timing of the actions for executing the plan but, instead, it determines a feasible general posture for competing to achieve its major goals. The resulting plan guides the lower-level, more detailed decisions that are needed to make the business plan materialize, week-by-week, during the months ahead.

Aggregate Production (Output) Planning This plan is the production portion of the business plan and addresses the *demand* side of its overall activities by showing the outputs it will produce, expressed in numbers of units of its product groups or families. Since various product groups may be produced at diverse plants, facilities, or manufacturing divisions, each of them needs its own production plan. The division's aggregate output plan covers the next 6–18 months on a weekly or monthly basis and reflects its share of the higher-level business plan. Aggregate plans are developed from forecasts of product group demands (demands for product families) which are usually estimated by marketing. Planned output levels are then determined, month-by-month, to blend with anticipated demand throughout the planning horizon. The planning process at this level ignores such details as how many of each individual product, style, color option, or model to produce. In meeting anticipated demand, the plan is constrained by the division's existing fixed capacity and by the company's overall strategies and policies for maintaining inventories and backlogs, employment stability, and subcontracting. Consequently, a feasible, realistic aggregate plan recognizes fixed capacity limitations and adopts temporary (short-term) capacity adjustments to provide the overall inventory and employment postures dictated by competitive conditions.

Capacity Planning Any statement of output intentions isn't useful unless it is workable and feasible. This is the role of aggregate capacity planning—to keep capacity utilization at desired levels and to test the feasibility of planned output against existing capacity. Thus, it addresses *supply*-side questions of the division's ability to meet the demand; the two, capacity and output, must be in balance as indicated by the arrow between them in Figure 11.2. Capacity planning translates production output plans into *input* terms to *approximate* how much of the division's production capacity will be needed and consumed. A product group, for example, usually consumes or shares some logical blocks of capacity such as labor hours of assembly, fabrication, and subassembly, or machine center hours, or number of machine cycles. Although their basic capacities are fixed, management can manipulate the short-term capacities of these blocks by the ways they deploy their workforce, by subcontracting, or by using multiple work shifts to adjust the timing of overall outputs. As a result, the aggregate planning process is an interactive evaluation of tentative output balanced against fixed capacity constraints and temporary capacity adjustments until a feasible aggregate plan is determined that meets demand and utilizes capacity at desired levels during the coming months. The resulting plan sets limits on the master production schedule.

Master Production Scheduling (MPS) The purpose of master scheduling is to meet the demand for individual products in the product group. This more detailed level of planning is a qualitative departure from higher levels in two respects: (1) forecasts of and customer orders for *individual* products, rather than product groups, are considered; and (2) the overall plan for product groups is *disaggregated* into individual products and when they'll be produced. The master schedule shows week-by-week (or even daily) how many units of each item or end product are due for completion. The schedule is the anticipated build plan and it provides an important linkage between marketing and production. If properly executed, the MPS shows when incoming sales orders can be scheduled into production and, upon completion, when each shipment is scheduled to the customer. Thereby, it can provide realistic order-promising that takes into account backlogs of existing orders when new sales orders are booked.

Rough-Cut Capacity Planning (RCCP) Rough-cut capacity planning (sometimes called resource requirements planning) is done in conjunction with the tentative master schedule to test its capacity feasibility before the MPS is finally settled. This step ensures that a proposed MPS doesn't inadvertently overload any key department, work center, or machine, prohibiting the MPS from being implemented. Although the check can apply to all work centers, it typically is performed on the critical ones that are most likely to pose bottlenecks in the manufacturing process. Standard or historical performance data for individual departments or work centers are matched against the shop workload for end items from the MPS. It may show discrepancies between the capacity requirements (in direct labor hours for example) of the MPS and available capacity. If so, either the capacity can be temporarily adjusted or the MPS can be adjusted until the two are synchronized. This provides only a "rough" check because it makes some simplifying assumptions; it doesn't take into account existing finished parts or work-in-process inventories, nor does it consider the time-phased requirements of lower-level items in the product structure. Nonetheless, it provides quick, inexpensive approximations of shop-level capacity requirements for the MPS during the weeks or months ahead.

Material Requirements Planning (MRP) The master schedule is the driving force for the material requirements planning (MRP) system or any other type of materials and inventory planning system. As previously introduced in Chapter 9 and discussed in Chapter 16, MRP explodes the bills of materials for scheduled end-items and shows the time-phased requirements for materials order releases and receipts.

Detailed Capacity Planning (DCP) Detailed capacity planning, also called capacity requirements planning, is a companion process used with MRP to identify in detail the capacity required to execute the material plan. Again, as was the case with rough-cut planning and master scheduling, if capacity requirements and capacity availabilities don't correspond, the material plan will be poorly executed. With capacity requirements planning, however, substantially more detail is possible because of additional information from the MRP system including time-phased planned orders, open shop orders (scheduled receipts), and component inventory availabilities at each work center. At this level, more accurate comparisons of available and needed capacity for scheduled workloads are possible.

Shop Floor Control All of the preceding steps are for *planning* the output and capacity of operations; the next steps are for executing and controlling shop operations. Here, the emphasis is on weekly and day-to-day actions that get the jobs done, as nearly as possible, in accordance with the plans. Individual jobs are assigned to machines and work centers (loading), the sequence of processing the jobs for priority control is determined, start times and job assignments for each stage of processing are decided (detailed scheduling), and materials and work flows from station-to-station are monitored and adjusted (expediting). Coordinating all of these activities into smooth flows, especially when unplanned delays and new priorities arise, often calls for last-minute adjustments of outputs and capacities (short-term capacity control). In doing all this we can evaluate and monitor the compatibility between short-term output and capacity by using input-output control procedures.

With this background on the entire production planning and scheduling process, let's take a closer look at aggregate planning and master scheduling.

BASIC CONCEPTS IN THE AGGREGATE PLANNING PROCESS

Developing an aggregate production plan involves four basic considerations: the concept of aggregation; the goals of planning; using forecasts of aggregate demand; and the options for adjusting short-run capacity.

Concept of Aggregation

To develop an aggregate plan, you must first identify a meaningful measure of output. This presents no problem for organizations with a single product because their outputs are measured directly by the number of units they produce. Most organizations, however, have several products, and a common denominator for measuring total output may not be so easy to find. A brewery manager, for example, can plan in terms of gallons of beer-producing capacity of his or her facility, ignoring for the moment how that capacity will be subdivided among various types of beer and packaging alternatives. A steel producer can use "tons of steel," and a paint producer may use "gallons of paint." Service organizations such as urban transit systems may use "passenger miles" as a common measure; health care facilities use "patient visits"; and educational institutions often use "faculty-to-student contact hours" as a reasonable measure.

A meaningful measure usually can be found by identifying product groups or families of individual products that, although different from one another, share common production processes or consume similar basic resources. Five models of electronic pocket calculators or six models of outboard boat motors are examples of two such product groups. In these cases it may be reasonable to plan in terms of producing so many units of "the representative" calculator or of maintaining inventories of so many units of "the typical" outboard motor in the product group. You can see, then, that each organization strives for an overall measure of output that makes sense in the context of their unique production process and product mix.

Goals for Aggregate Planning

The aggregate plan must satisfy simultaneously a number of goals. First, it has to provide the overall levels of output, inventory, and backlogs that are dictated in the business plan. If the business plan calls for inventory buildups in anticipation of a major promotional campaign, the aggregate plan should offer the appropriate production support. Similarly, the plan must respond to seasonal sales variations or reductions of order backlogs if called for by the business plan.

A second aggregate planning goal is to use the facility's capacity in a manner consistent with the organization's strategy. Underutilized capacity can be an expensive waste of resources. Similarly, any attempt to overutilize normal capacity can lead to poor (late) delivery performance and expensive capacity adjustments such as multiple work shifts, subcontracting, and so on. Therefore, many firms seek a balanced aggregate plan with a level production rate close to full capacity for efficient operations. Other companies, however, (those competing on the basis of superior product quality or flexible service to customers) will keep a cushion of excess production capacity for quick reactions to sudden surges in market demand. We can see then how the aggregate plan should provide some desired level of capacity utilization over the coming months.

Finally, the plan should be consistent with the company's goals and policies regarding its employees. A firm may emphasize employment stability, especially where critical job skills are scarce, and therefore be reluctant to hire or lay off employees. Other firms, without such goals, will change employees freely as the output level is varied throughout the aggregate planning horizon.

Forecasts of Aggregate Demand

The benefits to be gained from aggregate planning efforts depend on forecasting capabilities. You may remember that in Chapter 5, we presented various models that can be used to forecast demand for individual products (outputs) for the planning horizon. These same models can forecast product-group rather than individual product demands. These forecasted patterns of aggregate (group) demand are necessary information inputs to aggregate planning. It is the month-to-month demand *fluctuations* that really create the output planning problem. If monthly demand did not fluctuate, if it were constant, the difficulties of output planning would be substantially reduced.

Interrelationships Among Decisions

Often plans for aggregate output are developed for periods of six to eighteen months into the future. As we shall see later, however, these plans are generally put into action much more frequently than this, on a weekly or monthly basis. If the implementation occurs over such short time intervals, why does the plan cover such a long time span? Because week-to-week and month-to-month actions are not independent of one another. In fact, they are closely interrelated, since management actions and decisions in one month determine which alternatives will be available in subsequent months. This is what happens with a multistage, or sequential, decision problem. If monthly decisions are evaluated as if they were simply a sequence of independent, single-stage decisions, very costly consequences can result. Managers must consider the future consequences of current decisions.

EXAMPLE

As manager of a refrigerator manufacturing facility, you wish to plan the level of output for February. At the end of January you observe 100 finished refrigerators left over in inventory. Twenty assemblers were on the payroll in January, each earning a salary of $1600 per month. On average, each assembler is capable of producing 10 refrigerators per month. You have just been informed that 200 refrigerators will be demanded by customers during February. Since you already have 100 units in inventory, you decide to produce exactly 100 more units during February so you can meet the February demand of 200 units. Since only 10 assemblers will be required to produce February's planned output, you lay off 10 assemblers at an average layoff cost of $400 per worker. One month later you face a similar decision. Consumer demand for refrigerators in March is estimated to be 300 units. Since no refrigerators are left in inventory from February, the entire 300 units for March must be produced during March. To accomplish this, you must hire 20 additional assemblers at the beginning of March so that the work force (30 assemblers) can produce the required 300 units. The cost of hiring and training assemblers averages $300/assembler, and inventory costs are assumed to be negligible.

This is an example of planning with a one-month time horizon. If each month is treated separately and independently for planning purposes, what costs would result? Table 11.1 shows us.

Now suppose you had used a two-month planning horizon. At the end of January you find out that demand is expected to be 200 units in February and 300 units in March. With this information you develop the plan (in

TABLE 11.1
Total cost using a one-month planning horizon

Planned decisions and costs	February	March	Total
Number of employees	10	30	40
Units of output	100	300	400
Wages (costs)	10 × \$1,600 = \$16,000	30 × \$1,600 = \$48,000	\$64,000
Layoff (costs)	10 × 400 = 4,000	0	4,000
Hiring (costs)	0	20 × 300 = 6,000	6,000
Total (costs)	\$20,000	\$54,000	\$74,000

Table 11.2) for both February and March. This plan calls for retaining all 20 assemblers for February and March and thereby avoiding the layoff and hiring costs of the first plan. This cost savings was accomplished by looking into the future and considering not only next month's expected demand but the demand for the following month as well. Now compare the February costs for the two plans. In the best plan (using a two-month horizon) we intentionally incur more costs in February than we would had we used the one-month horizon plan. But by so doing, we reduce the total cost for the entire planning horizon. This type of sacrificing strategy is a common phenomenon in multistage decision problems. As you can see, selecting an appropriate time horizon is very important for planning. Aggregate plans should be developed not to minimize costs in each individual period but overall, since minimizing costs in the short run can turn out to be a *suboptimal* plan in the long run.

We have seen that short time horizons can be undesirable. Can we select a horizon that is too long? From a practical standpoint, the answer is yes. By enlarging the planning horizon, we increase dramatically the

TABLE 11.2
Total cost using a two-month planning horizon

Planned decisions and costs	February	March	Total
Number of employees	20	20	40
Units of output	200	200	400
Wages (costs)	20 × \$1,600 = \$32,000	20 × \$1,600 = \$32,000	\$64,000
Layoff (costs)	0	0	0
Hiring (costs)	0	0	0
Total (costs)	\$32,000	\$32,000	\$64,000

number of possible alternative plans. If each of these many plans is evaluated so that the best plan can be selected, the costs of computation (and the time required) can become prohibitive. Also, forecasts of future demand usually become less accurate as we look farther into the future, and plans based on highly inaccurate forecasts may be of little value.

STRATEGIES FOR DEVELOPING AGGREGATE PLANS

An Aggregate Plan for a Manufacturer

Let's apply these basic concepts to develop an aggregate output plan using a simple graphical or manual approach. The goal is to find a cost-effective plan that meets expected demand over a twelve-month horizon.

EXAMPLE

Go-Rite Company is a make-to-stock wagon manufacturer whose primary product group consists of three models of wagons. The annual business plan, based on marketing's sales forecasts, calls for wagon sales totaling $6,840,000, with quarterly sales as follows in row 1:

	Quarter			
	1	2	3	4
Forecasted sales ($) for product-group	$1,080,000	2,640,000	1,960,000	1,160,000
Units (# of wagons)	27,000	66,000	49,000	29,000
Labor hours	21,600	52,800	39,200	23,200

The business plan was translated into manufacturing terms (units and labor hours) using historical conversion factors. First, the typical wagon contributes $40 to sales revenue so the approximate number of wagons per quarter is shown in row two. Since output on average is 10 wagons per day for each production employee (or 0.8 labor hours per wagon), the estimated labor-hour requirements are shown in row three. Forecasts of product-group demand (Figure 11.3) reflect a major peak in the spring and a minor peak in the fall. Lowest demand occurs during the winter months.

The first step in the analysis is to determine the productive requirements this demand pattern places on the facility. At first glance, May appears to be the peak month, with 24,000 units demanded. The actual number of available productive days must also be considered, however. Because of an annual vacation shutdown, for example, August has only eleven productive days. If our plans were to produce each month the number of wagons demanded, considerable fluctuation in output rate would result. This

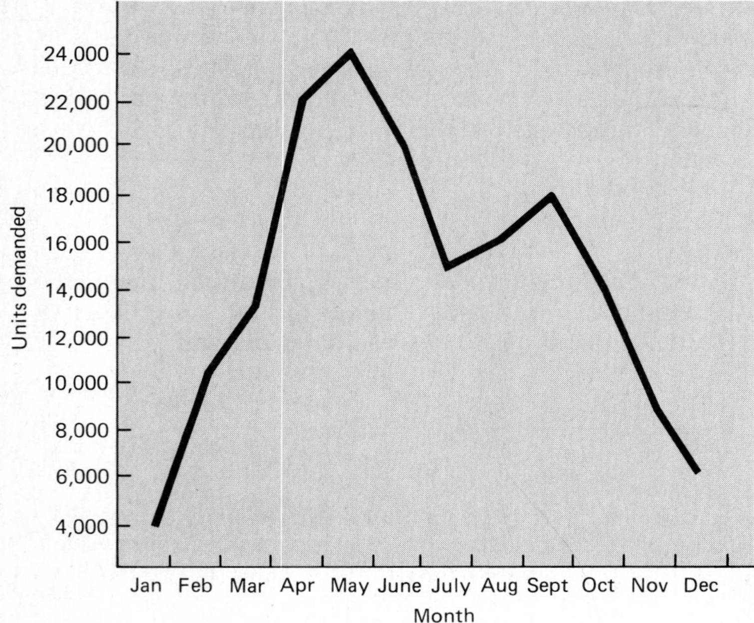

FIGURE 11.3
Product-group demand forecasts for the coming year

fluctuation is shown in Figure 11.4, where output rate is measured in units per available productive day.

Were it to produce the indicated number of units daily, the company would just meet its anticipated monthly demand. But the changes in output rate from month to month are large and can be very costly. Let's examine three "pure strategies" that the planner could use to cope with the wide swings in monthly demand.

Three Pure Planning Strategies

Several short-term capacity adjustments can be used to absorb monthly demand fluctuations. Common in make-to-stock organizations are three of these adjustments: work force size, inventories, and work force utilization. Any one of these can be varied to meet demand variations without consideration of the other two (thus they can be called "pure" strategies). Usually, however, some combination of the three is better than using just one. In addition to these three internal adjustments, manufacturers often have opportunities to employ additional external resources. The use of subcontractors, rented or leased equipment, and other external resources is useful for responding to periods of heavy demand.

Strategy 1: Vary the Number of Productive Employees in Direct Relation to Monthly Output Requirements From historical data, management can estimate the average productivity per employee and thus determine the number of employees needed to meet each month's output. When required

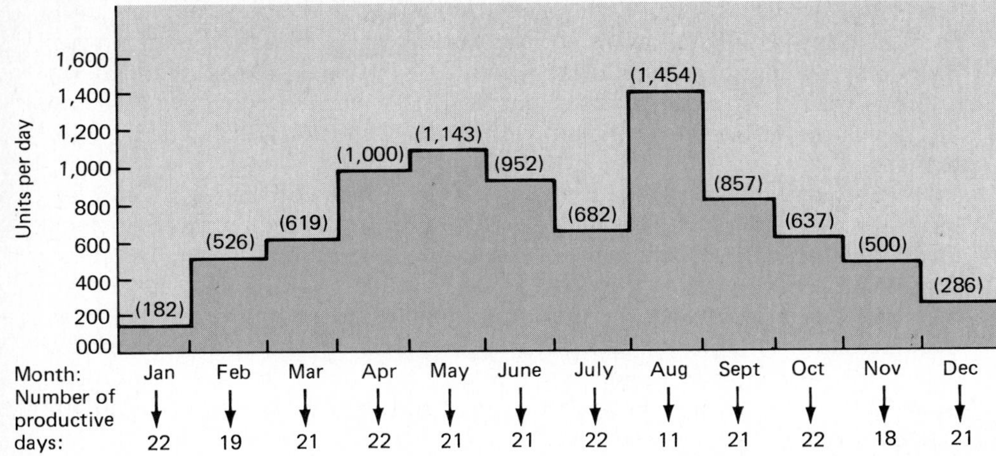

FIGURE 11.4
Output rate per productive day when monthly production meets monthly demand

monthly output declines, employees can be laid off. As monthly demand increases, the work force can be increased accordingly. In our example, output average per employee is 10 wagons per day. Therefore about 18 employees would be needed in January, 53 in February, 62 in March, and so on.

Several disadvantages are obvious in this strategy. The wide swings in employment levels cause very high hiring and layoff costs. Also, indirect costs of training new employees, decreases in employee morale during periods of layoff, and the like are common. In addition, required work skills may not be readily available when they are needed. When fairly long lead times are needed to procure special employee skills, these hiring lead times and training periods must be accounted for in the planning horizon. Furthermore, sometimes community reactions to such a strategy are negative. Companies are known in the community by the employment practices they follow. Some industries are well-known for long histories of wide employment fluctuations. Usually, employees prefer to obtain employment with companies having more stable employment practices. Finally, this strategy is not feasible for companies with guaranteed wage and other hiring and layoff agreements with unions.

Strategy 2: Maintain a Constant Work Force Size but Vary the Rate of Work Force Utilization Suppose for example we chose the strategy of employing 70 workers per month throughout the year. On an average, this work force would be capable of producing 700 wagons each day. During the lean months (January, February, March, July, October, November, December) the work force would be scheduled to produce only the amount forecasted.

Since the employees are capable of producing more than the forecasted amount, they would therefore be idle during some working hours. During high-demand months (April, May, June, August, September), overtime operations would be needed to meet demand. The work force would therefore be intensely utilized during some months and underutilized in other months.

A big advantage of this strategy is its avoidance of the hiring and layoff costs associated with strategy 1. But other costs are incurred instead. Overtime, for example, can be very expensive, commonly 50 percent higher than regular-time wage rates. If overtime requires working on weekends or holidays, wage rates may be as much as 200 percent above regular rates. Furthermore, there are both legal and behavioral limits to the amount of overtime that can be worked. When employees work extensive amounts of overtime, they tend to become inefficient, productivity diminishes, and job-related accident rates increase.

Idle time also has some subtle drawbacks. During slack periods, employee morale can diminish and employment uncertainties increase, especially if the idle time is perceived to be a prelude to future layoffs. Opportunity costs also result from idle time. When employees are forced to be idle, the company forgoes the opportunity of getting units of output that could have been produced. Although wages are paid, output is not received. Some potential output has been lost forever.

Strategy 3: Allow Inventories to Fluctuate in Response to Demand Variations

Finished goods inventories in make-to-stock companies can be used to cushion the response to demand fluctuations. A fixed number of employees, selected so that little or no overtime or idle time is incurred, can be maintained throughout the planning horizon. Producing at a constant rate, output will exceed demand during slack demand periods, and finished goods inventories will accumulate. During peak periods, when demand is greater than productive capabilities, the demand can be supplied from inventory. This planning strategy results in fluctuating inventory levels throughout the planning horizon.

EXAMPLE

In Figure 11.4, there are 241 available productive days in which to produce 171,000 wagons. Therefore we can produce an average of about 710 wagons per day throughout the year to meet this total demand. This can be done during regular working hours by employing 71 workers (each producing an average of 10 wagons per day).

By following this level production strategy, we can determine how our inventory of finished goods will fluctuate during the year. We have done this in Table 11.3 and Figure 11.5. If we use strategy 3, inventories accumulate during the first three months of the year. After that, April demand exceeds productive capacity. Part of April's demand must therefore be supplied from accumulated inventories. Similarly, inventories are further depleted in May. During June, finished goods inventories are totally depleted, and customer backorders (unfilled demand) result. Backorders accumulate to a maximum of 14,200 wagons as of the end of September. In October and November, expected demand is less than productive capacity, and backorders are "worked off" (reduced). Finally, December planned production is sufficiently larger than demand, and inventory returns to near zero at the end of the planning horizon.

The comparative advantages of strategy 3 are obvious: stable employment, no idle time, and no expensive overtime. What about disadvantages? First, inventories of finished goods (and other supporting inventories) are not cost-free. Inventories tie up working capital that could otherwise be earning a return on investment. Materials-handling costs, storage space requirements, risk of damage and obsolescence, clerical efforts, and taxes all increase with larger inventories. Backorders can also be costly. Customers may not be willing to tolerate backordering, particularly if alternative sources of supply are available; sales may be lost, and customer ill will may negatively affect future sales potential. In short, there are costs for carrying too much or too little inventory.

TABLE 11.3
Production plan for strategy 3

Month	Productive days	Planned output (units)	Expected product-group demand (units)	Net additions (subtractions) to inventory (units)	End-of-month cumulative inventory to date (units)
Jan	22	15,620	4,000	11,620	11,620
Feb	19	13,490	10,000	3,490	15,110
Mar	21	14,910	13,000	1,910	17,020
Apr	22	15,620	22,000	(6,380)	10,640
May	21	14,910	24,000	(9,090)	1,550
June	21	14,910	20,000	(5,090)	(3,540)
July	22	15,620	15,000	620	(2,920)
Aug	11	7,910	16,000	(8,190)	(11,110)
Sept	21	14,910	18,000	(3,090)	(14,200)
Oct	22	15,620	14,000	1,620	(12,580)
Nov	18	12,780	9,000	3,780	(8,800)
Dec	21	14,910	6,000	8,910	110
	Total = 241 days		Total = 171,000 units		

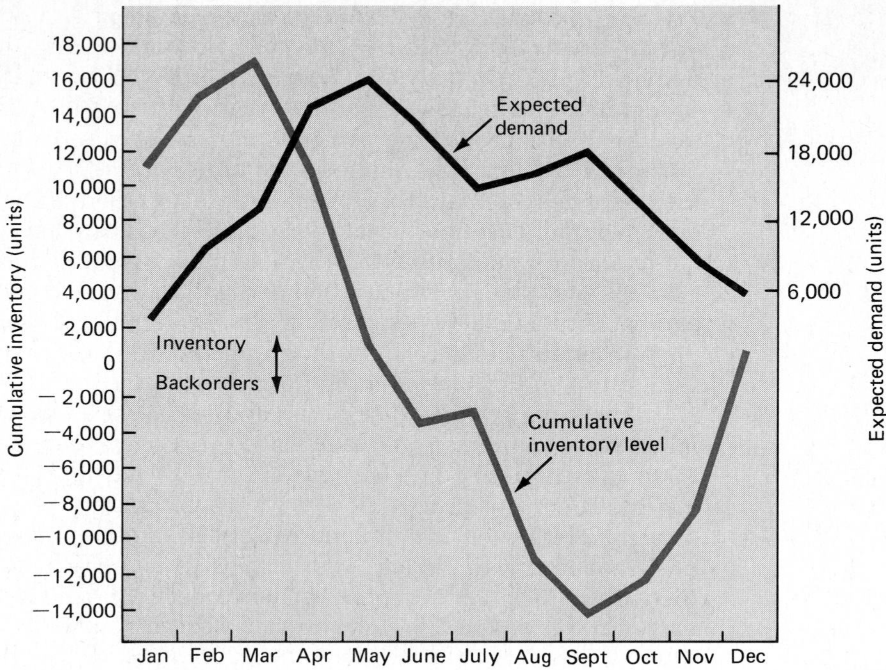

FIGURE 11.5
Cumulative inventory for strategy 3

A Graphical Method for Aggregate Output Planning

Usually, none of the pure strategies is best by itself; a mixture of two or three is better. There is a large number of alternative plans or "mixtures" to choose from and these choices involve tradeoffs. One way to develop and evaluate these alternatives is by using a *graphical* planning procedure. The graphical method is convenient and relatively simple to understand, and it requires only minor computational effort. To use the graphical method, follow these steps:

1. Develop a graph showing cumulative production days for the entire planning horizon on the horizontal axis and cumulative units of product on the vertical axis. Plot the cumulative demand data (forecasts) for the entire planning horizon.
2. Select a planning strategy, and determine the proposed production output for each period in the planning horizon. Calculate and plot on the graph the cumulative output for this tentative plan.
3. Compare expected demand and proposed output; plot both on the same graph. This comparison identifies periods of excess inventories and periods of inventory shortages, and it essentially evaluates the tentative plan.
4. Calculate the costs for this plan.
5. Modify the plan, attempting to meet aggregate planning goals by repeating steps 2 through 4 until a satisfactory plan is established.

We will demonstrate steps 1 through 4 for three different aggregate plans. The fifth step, additional modification, is left for you to do as an exercise. Since step 4 requires cost data, the following cost estimates have been obtained from Go-Rite's accounting and engineering departments:

EXAMPLE

Inventory carrying costs are $1.00 per unit for each month that the wagon is carried in inventory. Inventory costs are based on the average level of inventory for the month. Costs are incurred for changing the company's production rate. When the production rate is increased, additional employees must be hired and trained. When the production rate is reduced, some employees must be laid off and/or idle time occurs. The larger the change in production rate (increase or decrease), the greater the cost incurred. Table 11.4 shows the costs of changing production rates by different amounts. Production rates are expressed in terms of units (wagons) per day. It is assumed for initial planning purposes that daily production rate, once selected, will be used every day for the entire month. The company places a high cost on backorders and lost sales, a cost so high that management wants a plan in which cumulative output at least meets expected demand throughout the planning horizon. The facility's maximum capacity is 100 employees (1,000 wagons per day) on a single shift. Capacity can be temporarily increased by using overtime with additional costs of $4/unit.

A Plan with Level Production We'll develop a plan that meets all the above requirements and that does so by using a constant output (production) rate with no hiring, layoffs, idletime, or overtime. Step 1 of our procedure, plotting cumulative forecasted demand, is done in Figure 11.6.

For step 2, we have specified a planning strategy consisting of a constant average production rate for each day. If we were to plot cumulative production day by day for this strategy, it would appear as a straight line on the graph in Figure 11.6. The line would begin at the origin (zero units

TABLE 11.4
Estimated cost for changing production rates from month to month

Change in daily production rate from previous month in units (increase or decrease)	Estimated cost of changing production rate
1–200	$ 4,000
201–400	10,000
401–600	18,000
601–800	28,000

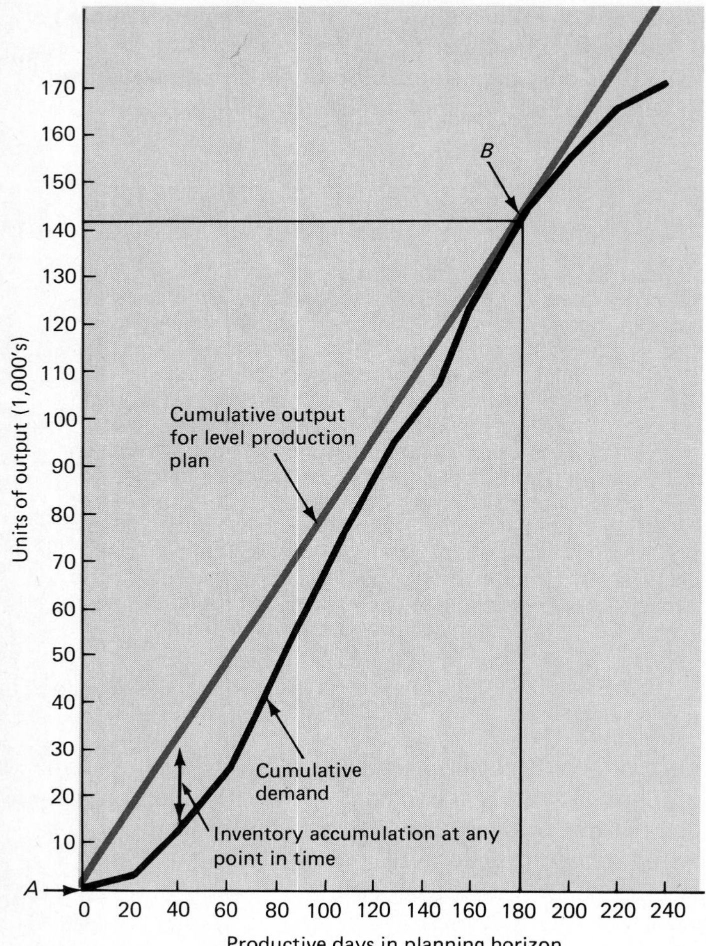

FIGURE 11.6
Aggregate output plan and forecasted demand

of output) and rise steadily to the right as cumulative output increases. The higher the production rates, the steeper the line would be. What slope should be selected? Go-Rite's cumulative output line should be steep enough always to meet or exceed cumulative demand requirements throughout the entire planning horizon. In this way, the plan meets the goal of avoiding lost sales and backorders. If the production curve is too steep, however, excessive inventories are accumulated. The desired production is found by passing a line through the origin (point *A*) and the outlying point (point *B*) on the cumulative demand curve.[3] The cumulative

[3]Passing the line through point A assumes no beginning inventory exists. If there are finished units on hand at the beginning of the planning horizon, the amount should be marked on the vertical axis and that mark, rather than point *A*, is the beginning point of the output line on the graph.

production output described by this line meets our planning requirements: beginning on the first day production commences at a constant daily rate and total output exceeds total demand until the end of September (point *B*). At the end of September, units produced to date equal the total demanded to date. Thereafter, output exceeds expected demand for the remainder of the planning horizon. What is the daily production rate? Point *B* represents 180 cumulative days of production and 142,000 cumulative units of output (from Table 11.3). Thus:

$$\frac{142{,}000 \text{ units}}{180 \text{ days}} = 790 \text{ units/day (approximately)}$$

Since we know the daily production rate, we can now develop a plan for each month. The monthly plans are shown in Table 11.5. Since 790 units are produced each day, and since each employee can average 10 units per day, 79 employees will be needed.

Finally we can determine the cost of this plan. Since the daily production rate is unchanged from month to month, there are no production rate change costs. Table 11.5 shows average monthly inventories totaling 120,405 units for the year. Therefore, inventory costs will be about $120,405 ($1 per unit per month).

A Plan that Closely Follows Demand One alternative to producing at a constant rate is a plan in which monthly output is geared to meeting expected monthly demand. This is sometimes called a *chase* plan because the output

TABLE 11.5
Monthly plan for level production rate

Month	Days	Output rate/day	Output	Demand	Beginning inventory	Net additions (subtractions) to inventory	Ending inventory	Average monthly inventory (beginning and ending)/2
Jan	22	790	17,380	4,000	0	13,380	13,380	6,690
Feb	19	790	15,010	10,000	13,380	5,010	18,390	15,885
Mar	21	790	16,590	13,000	18,390	3,590	21,980	20,185
Apr	22	790	17,380	22,000	21,980	(4,620)	17,360	19,670
May	21	790	16,590	24,000	17,360	(7,410)	9,950	13,655
June	21	790	16,590	20,000	9,950	(3,410)	6,540	8,245
July	22	790	17,380	15,000	6,540	2,380	8,920	7,730
Aug	11	790	8,690	16,000	8,920	(7,310)	1,610	5,265
Sept	21	790	16,590	18,000	1,610	(1,410)	200	905
Oct	22	790	17,380	14,000	200	3,380	3,580	1,890
Nov	18	790	14,220	9,000	3,580	5,220	8,800	6,190
Dec	21	790	16,590	6,000	8,800	10,590	19,390	14,095
								120,405

rate is chasing (closely following) the demand rate. In this case, the cumulative output curve coincides with the cumulative demand curve. Therefore, we plan to produce 4,000 units in January, 10,000 in February, 13,000 in March, and so on. Since the number of days per month is known, the daily output rate for each month is easily approximated. In January, for example, 22 productive days are available. Since we propose producing 4,000 units in January, the daily production rate is:

$$\frac{4{,}000 \text{ units}}{22 \text{ days}} = 182 \text{ units/day (approximately)}$$

Using this procedure for each month results in the plan shown in Table 11.6. Since monthly inventories are trivial, inventory costs for this plan are very low. A positive net inventory is retained for each time period; that is, backorders or stockouts are not permitted. The daily production rate is changed each month. February's rate is 345 units per day greater than January's; from Table 11.4, we know that the cost of this increase is approximately \$10,000. Similarly, we can calculate the cost of changing output rates for all the months in the planning horizon (see Table 11.7). Further costs are incurred for overtime work in May and August when production exceeds the fixed capacity of 1000 units per day.

An Intermediate Plan As we have seen, excessive inventories and changes in production rates can be costly. Let's develop a plan that changes production rates only occasionally instead of every month. The plan in Table

TABLE 11.6
Monthly plan for variable production rate (chase plan)

Month	Days	Change in production rate	Output rate/day	Output	Demand	Beginning inventory	Net additions (subtractions) to inventory	Ending inventory	Average inventory
Jan	22		182	4,004	4,000	0	4	4	2.0
Feb	19	+345	527	10,013	10,000	4	13	17	10.5
Mar	21	+ 92	619	12,999	13,000	17	(1)	16	16.5
Apr	22	+381	1,000	22,000	22,000	16	0	16	16.0
May	21	+143	1,143	24,003	24,000	16	3	19	17.5
June	21	−191	952	19,992	20,000	19	(8)	11	15.0
July	22	−270	682	15,004	15,000	11	4	15	13.0
Aug	11	+772	1,454	15,994	16,000	15	(6)	9	12.0
Sept	21	−597	857	17,997	18,000	9	(3)	6	7.5
Oct	22	−220	637	14,014	14,000	6	14	20	13.0
Nov	18	−138	499	8,982	9,000	20	(18)	2	11.0
Dec	21	−213	286	6,006	6,000	2	6	8	5.0
									139.0

TABLE 11.7
Costs of changing production rates for plan that closely follows demand

Months	Change in daily production rate (from previous month)	Estimated cost of change
Jan to Feb	+345	$ 10,000
Feb to Mar	+ 92	4,000
Mar to Apr	+381	10,000
Apr to May	+143	4,000
May to June	−191	4,000
June to July	−270	10,000
July to Aug	+772	28,000
Aug to Sept	−597	18,000
Sept to Oct	−220	10,000
Oct to Nov	−138	4,000
Nov to Dec	−213	10,000
Total		$112,000

11.8 calls for a constant production rate of 548 units per day during January, February, and March. This rate is boosted to 1,000 units per day from April through July. Output is then decreased to 689 units per day for the remainder of the year. The inventory cost of this plan would be $1 per unit inventoried, or $67,276. Production rate changes would cost $18,000 for

TABLE 11.8
Intermediate plan

Month	Days	Change in production rate	Output rate/day	Output	Demand	Beginning inventory	Net additions (subtractions) to inventory	Ending inventory	Average inventory
Jan	22		548	12,056	4,000	0	8,056	8,056	4,028
Feb	19		548	10,412	10,000	8,056	412	8,468	8,262
Mar	21	+452	548	11,508	13,000	8,468	(1,492)	6,976	7,722
Apr	22		1,000	22,000	22,000	6,976	0	6,976	6,976
May	21		1,000	21,000	24,000	6,976	(3,000)	3,976	5,476
June	21		1,000	21,000	20,000	3,976	1,000	4,976	4,476
July	22	−311	1,000	22,000	15,000	4,976	7,000	1,976	8,476
Aug	11		689	7,579	16,000	11,976	(8,421)	3,555	7,776
Sept	21		689	14,469	18,000	3,555	(3,531)	24	1,790
Oct	22		689	15,158	14,000	24	1,158	1,182	603
Nov	18		689	12,402	9,000	1,182	3,402	4,584	2,883
Dec	21		689	14,469	6,000	4,584	8,469	13,053	8,818
									67,276

TABLE 11.9
Operating costs for three plans

Type of cost	Plan		
	Level production rate	Variable production rate (chase)	Intermediate
Overtime	$ 0	$ 31,988*	$ 0
Inventory	120,405	139	67,276
Production rate change	0	112,000	28,000
Total cost	$120,405	$144,127	$95,276

*May: 143 units/day × 21 days × $4/unit = $12,012.
August: 454 units/day × 111 days × $4/unit = $19,976.

the March–April change and $10,000 for the July–August change, for a total of $28,000.

Comparing the Plans Now we can evaluate the three plans on the basis of total cost for the planning horizon. We have done this in Table 11.9. The level production plan has high inventory costs and no overtime or rate change costs. The plan that varies production rate to meet demand has negligible inventory costs, high rate change costs, and some overtime costs. These plans exemplify two of the pure strategies discussed earlier. The third (intermediate) plan incurs substantial costs of inventories and rate changes but has the lowest total cost. This plan reflects a mixed strategy, using moderate (not extreme) amounts of inventory and production rate changes to absorb demand fluctuations. Moderate inventories are accumulated in January, February, and December. Average inventories for the year are far lower in this plan than in the level production plan. These moderate inventory levels allow us to be selective in changing the production rate, and we can avoid the high costs of frequent and extreme changes.

In our example, we "smoothed" production fluctuations. This is why the aggregate planning process is sometimes called "production smoothing." As demand decreases to lower levels, it is cheaper to decrease production rates (occasionally) than to continue to build up excessive inventories. If there is any one generalization that can be made about aggregate planning, it is this: *when planning production, smooth out the peaks and valleys to meet uneven demand because extreme fluctuations in production are generally very costly.*

Capacity Planning

In evaluating the capacity *feasibility*, we see differences among Go-Rite's three aggregate plans. Neither the level plan nor the intermediate plan exceeds the facility's maximum capacity of 1,000 units per day. The chase plan, however, exceeds maximum capacity in May and August and, accordingly, overtime or second-shift operations would be needed.

In terms of capacity *utilization,* the level plan consistently uses 79 percent of maximum capacity. The chase plan's utilization, in contrast, varies from only 18 percent up to 145 percent during the year. The intermediate plan uses 55 to 100 percent of maximum capacity. If these levels of utilization are unsuitable, then either the demand for its products must be stimulated (to gain higher capacity utilization) or the capacity must be adjusted.

MASTER SCHEDULING AND ROUGH-CUT CAPACITY PLANNING

The next step in the planning process is master production scheduling that translates the aggregate plan into operational production schedules for individual products. As we illustrate the master scheduling concepts, we'll use the intermediate aggregate plan (Table 11.8) for the Go-Rite Company.

Disaggregation of Aggregate Plans

As contrasted with aggregate plans, the master schedule is more detailed—it deals with individual products (not just product groups) and when they'll be produced week-by-week. How should our aggregate output be subdivided among each of the products we produce? What mix of these products should comprise our aggregate inventories? This process of translating aggregate plans into plans for individual products is called *dissaggregation,* a problem that has received surprisingly little formal attention until recently.[4] As a result, the dominant practice today involves disaggregation by cut-and-fit or trial-and-error procedures. Using forecasts of individual product demands, trial amounts of each product are scheduled week-by-week. The resulting weekly totals of output are then compared against aggregate requirements and checked for their capacity feasibility. Then, the initial schedule is adjusted until the proposed quantities of all products give a suitable balance between the overall output level and the amount of capacity utilization. You can see all of these steps in the discussion below as we develop a master schedule for the Go-Rite Company.

Developing a Trial Master Production Schedule

The master scheduler in our Go-Rite example has obtained forecasts of weekly demands for the three wagon models (A, B, C). These forecasts, coupled with known customer orders, resulted in the "forecasted" demands shown in Table 11.10 (forecasts beyond 16 weeks are omitted here

[4] A review of the status of disaggregation is given in L. J. Krajewski and L. P. Ritzman, "Disaggregation in Manufacturing and Service Organizations: Survey of Problems and Research," *Decision Sciences* 8, no. 1 (January 1977), pp. 1–18.

for brevity). Each of the 16 weeks is five working days and thus, the forecasts (44,970 wagons) cover the next 80 days and match closely with the aggregate plan's overall demand of 45,000 wagons.

Next, a trial master production schedule was developed (Table 11.11) for Go-Rite's three wagon models during each of the next 16 weeks (only 16 weeks are shown here although the MPS may be developed for the entire year). We can see that some of all three models are scheduled for production during the first week since no beginning inventories are available and Go-Rite's aggregate plan calls for no stockouts. After week one, the master scheduler has settled on a general pattern of producing wagons A and C in the same weeks while B is often produced alone. Through experience, by trying various combinations, the scheduler hopes to meet product demand, avoid excessive production setup costs, maintain appropriate aggregate inventory levels, and do all of this within planned capacity levels.

How well does this MPS match up with the aggregate plan? If implemented the schedule will result in cumulative production output levels that exceed cumulative demands, as shown in Table 11.12, throughout the 16 weeks. In addition, aggregate inventories after 8 weeks and 16 weeks closely parallel the levels sought in the aggregate plan. Thus, the MPS is feasible insofar as the aggregate plan is concerned.

Rough-Cut Capacity Planning

Is the MPS feasible from the standpoint of Go-Rite's production capacity? Will adequate labor be available to produce the mix of wagons scheduled for each week? Let's make some rough (approximate) checks to answer these questions.

We can check overall labor-hour requirements using accounting and engineering data. Suppose Go-Rite's labor standards (standard hours per unit) are 0.88, 0.66, and 1.08 hours for products A, B, and C respectively.[5] Applying these standards to the 16 week (80 day) schedules, we see in Table 11.13 that the required labor hours are reasonably close to the planned available labor hours, overall, if employees work at the standard rates.

Going beyond the *overall* requirements, let's estimate the *weekly* labor-hour needs; they can differ from week-to-week depending on the mix of products scheduled for production. In Table 11.14 the MPS has been converted into labor-hour requirements by using the standard labor hours for each type of wagon. Weekly total requirements vary from 1,808 hours to 3,696 hours. The available labor hours (from the aggregate plan) are shown in the bottom row of the table. We see that planned capacity is

[5]The labor standards for the three types of wagons, when weighted by their historical proportions of total sales, result in an overall standard of 0.8 labor hours per wagon. The proportions of sales for the wagons are 35%, 50%, and 15% for models A, B, and C respectively: $(.35 \times .88 + .5 \times .66 + .15 \times 1.08 = .8)$.

TABLE 11.10
Forecasts of weekly demands (units) for individual products

	Week																
Product	1	2	3	4	5	6	7	8	9	10	11	12	13	14	15	16	Totals
A	160	160	160	160	500	735	735	735	890	930	930	930	1300	1545	1545	1545	12,960
B	295	295	295	295	940	1370	1370	1370	1625	1690	1690	1690	2420	2910	2910	2910	24,075
C	455	455	455	455	500	525	525	525	485	475	475	475	495	545	545	545	7,935
Totals	910	910	910	910	1940	2630	2630	2630	3000	3095	3095	3095	4215	5000	5000	5000	44,970

TABLE 11.11
Master production schedule (trial): units of output for each product

	Week															
Product	1	2	3	4	5	6	7	8	9	10	11	12	13	14	15	16
A	540	1740	1740				1740	1740			1740	1740		1800	1800	1800
B	1200			2740	2740	1740			2740	2740			3096	3200	3200	3200
C	1000	1000	1000			1000	1000	1000			1000	1000	1000			

TABLE 11.12
Cumulative demand and output after 8 weeks and 16 weeks for trial MPS

Product	cumulative	Week 1	2	3	4	5	6	7	8	Ending Inventory Week 8		16	Ending Inventory Week 16
A	demand	160	380	420	640	1,140	1,875	2,610	3,345	4,155		12,960	3,420
	production	540	2,280	4,020				5,760	7,500			16,380	
B	demand	295	590	885	1,180	2,120	3,490	4,860	6,230	2,190		24,075	2,521
	production	1,200			3,940	6,680	8,420					26,596	
C	demand	455	910	1,365	1,820	2,320	2,845	3,370	3,895	2,105		7,935	1,065
	production	1,000	2,000	3,000			4,000	5,000	6,000			9,000	
Scheduled ending inventory from MPS:										8,450			7,006
Desired ending inventory from aggregate plan:										8,468			6,976

TABLE 11.13
Rough-cut capacity test: overall MPS labor requirements versus planned capacity

	Labor-hour requirements (80 days) from MPS		
Product	(1) Units scheduled	(2) Standard hours/unit	(3) = (1) × (2) Total labor hours required
A	16,380	0.88	14,414
B	26,596	0.66	17,553
C	9,000	1.08	9,720
Total MPS requirement = 41,687 hours			
Available labor (from aggregate plan) = 41,581 hours*			

*(548 units/day × 62 days × 0.8 hours/unit + 1,000 units/day × 18 days × 0.8 hours/unit = 41,581 hours)

adequate for requirements in weeks 4, 5, 9, 10, and 13 through 16, but not for the other eight weeks.[6]

The discrepancies between available and required capacities must be reconciled. One option is to revise the MPS, perhaps so that A and C wagons (the highest labor consumers) are not produced together during so many of the weeks. Instead, try producing more Bs and Cs or, similarly, more A and B models in the same week. Another alternative, less desirable, would retain the current MPS, using overtime during the high-need weeks and allowing some idleness during low-need weeks.

In summary, we can see how the goals of master scheduling and capacity planning become balanced by the process we've described. Capacity planning keeps capacity utilization at desired levels while master scheduling meets product demand.

AGGREGATE PLANNING FOR SERVICE ORGANIZATIONS

Service organizations can also use aggregate planning. The typical service operation, however, is a make-to-order rather than a make-to-stock situation. Consequently, finished goods are not available for responding to demand fluctuations. Instead, backlogs of jobs can be increased or decreased to utilize capacity at desired levels.

[6]Further methods for rough-cut capacity planning are available in T. E. Vollmann, W. L. Berry, and D. C. Whybark, *Manufacturing Planning and Control Systems* (Homewood, Ill.: Richard D. Irwin, Inc.), 1984. See also D. W. McLeavey and S. L. Narasimhan, *Production Planning and Inventory Control* (Boston: Allyn and Bacon, Inc.), 1985.

TABLE 11.14
Rough-cut capacity test: weekly MPS labor requirements versus planned availability

	Labor hour requirements for MPS															
	Week															
Product	1	2	3	4	5	6	7	8	9	10	11	12	13	14	15	16
A	475[a]	1531	1531				1531	1531			1531	1531		1584	1584	1584
B	792			1808	1808	1148			1808	1808			2043	2112	2112	2112
C	1080	1080	1080			1080	1080	1080			1080	1080	1080			
Weekly requirements:	2347	2611	2611	1808	1808	2228	2611	2611	1808	1808	2611	2611	3123	3696	3696	3696
Available (from aggregate plan):	2192[b]	2192	2192	2192	2192	2192	2192	2192	2192	2192	2192	2192	3277[c]	4000[d]	4000	4000

[a]540 units of A × 0.88 standard hours/unit = 475 standard hours
[b]548 units/day × 5 days/week × 0.80 planned standard hours/unit = 2,192 planned standard hours
[c](548 units/day × 2 days + 1,000 units/day × 3 days) × 0.8 planned standard hours/unit = 3,278 planned standard hours
[d]1,000 units/day × 5 days/week × 0.80 planned standard hours/unit = 4,000 planned standard hours

Consider a city government's public works department, which is responsible for maintaining streets and roads throughout the year. Its "products" are:

1. repairing existing streets and roads (gravel, asphalt, concrete) and drainage systems,
2. building new roads, and
3. removing snow and ice.

The department cannot build up inventories of these finished products. It can, however, retain the resources that are necessary for providing the products. The proper mixtures of skilled labor, unskilled labor, equipment, supplies, and the use of subcontractors must all be selected to meet the demand for various "products" (services).

EXAMPLE

In the past, the public works department has had an experienced work force of about 400 people and, with an emphasis on stable employment, the director is reluctant to change the number of regular employees. The workers average 2,000 road miles of service per month. This figure is used to estimate the expected productivity of five road miles per employee per month, or .24 miles per employee per day. Three sources are available for meeting excess demand:

1. The regular work force can work overtime. The overtime premium is 50 percent of the regular $1,500 monthly wage.
2. Subcontracting to private firms is available at an average cost of $400 per road mile. Contracts for these services must be arranged several months in advance.
3. Supplementary labor, up to a maximum of 100 workers, is available from May to September at a salary of $1,200 per month. Hiring and layoff costs average $100 per supplementary employee.

Among the three types of services, snow removal is given top priority due to its public safety implications. Second priority is on new road construction because the department's crews work closely with subcontractors and the work has to occur under favorable weather conditions. Road repair and maintenance is somewhat variable and less weather-dependent. As the third priority service it is used to absorb variations in the overall workload as long as the repair backlog doesn't get out of hand.

Currently, the director is evaluating three alternative plans for aggregate output and is dually concerned about their cost and service implications. Although cost minimization is important, effective service to the public is a major concern in this highly visible operation.

Using "road miles" as the common unit of measurement, the director has obtained last year's aggregate (product group) demand and the de-

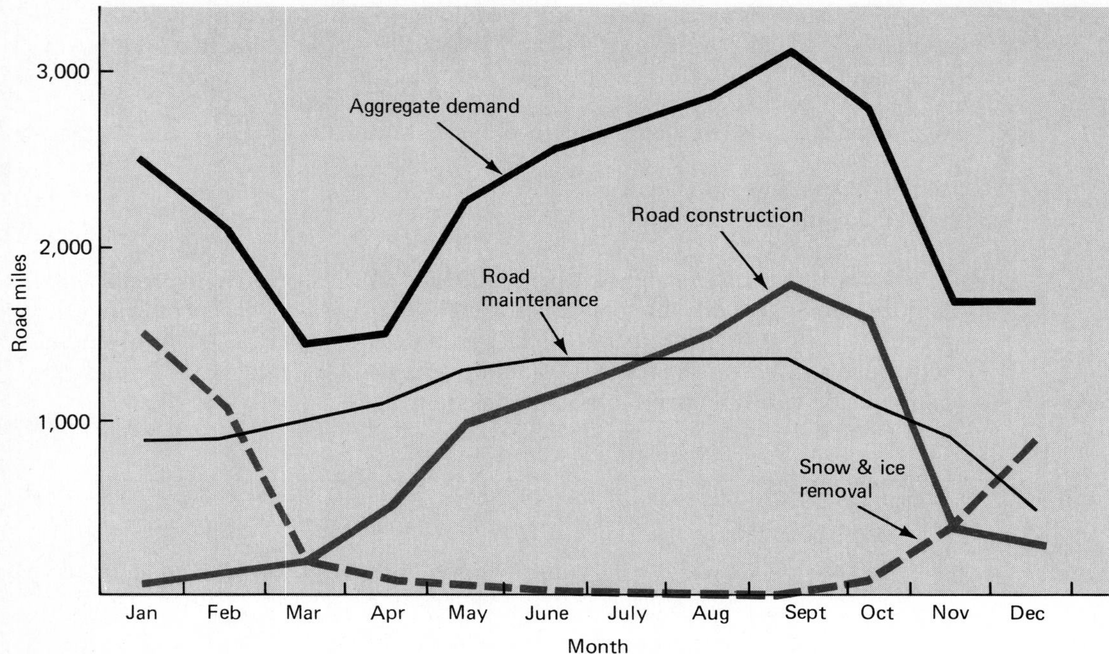

FIGURE 11.7
Aggregate demand for road and street services

mands for each type of service (see Figure 11.7). These data are then used to see how each alternative plan would have performed, in terms of job backlogs and costs, if the plans had been in effect last year.

Alternative Plans for Services

The first alternative, Plan A, would employ the 400 full-time employees throughout the year. In addition, subcontracting would provide additional capacity for the peak loads from early summer through fall. In this plan the 400 employees provide an average output capacity of 96 road miles per working day. Using a five-day work week, regular time output capacity for each month is shown in Figure 11.8.

Table 11.15 shows that the 400 employees would have provided enough capacity (column 4) for snow removal and new construction (column 3) in every month. Road repair and maintenance (column 2), the lowest priority service, cannot be accomplished and a backlog develops (column 5) during nine of the months. By the end of the year, if no subcontracting is used, the backlog accumulates to more than two months worth of work. By subcontracting in May through November, the 4,172

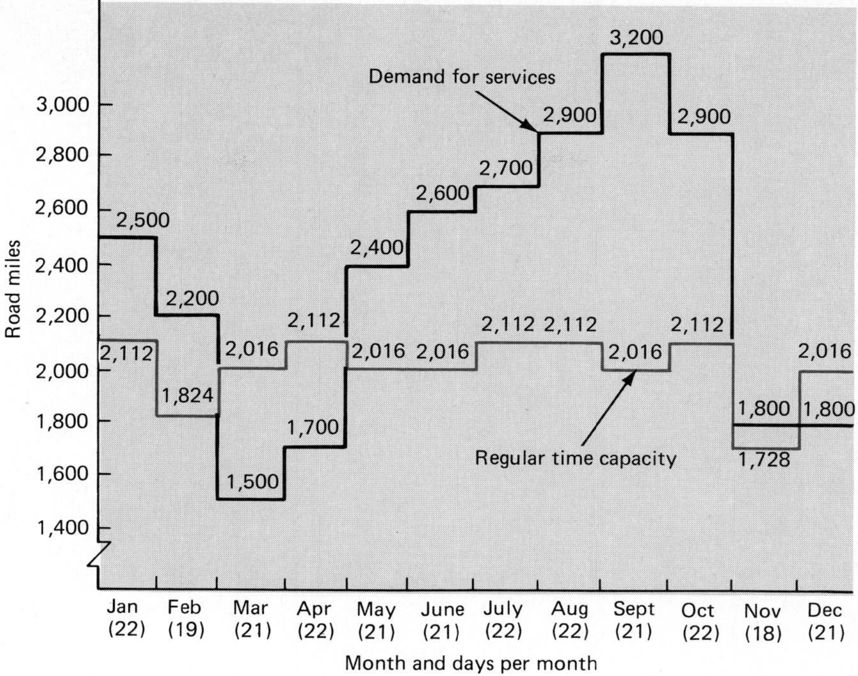

FIGURE 11.8
Monthly demand and capacity for road services

miles of year-end backlogs could have been eliminated. The winter backlog (January through March) of repair work, however, would not be worked off until April.

The second alternative, Plan B, would increase the work force to 480 full-time employees throughout the year. This provides a capacity of 115.2 road-miles per day and, without subcontracting, would have resulted in smaller backlogs than Plan A. As shown in Table 11.16, the March and April capacity is highly underutilized. However, the backlog at year-end is smaller—less than one-half of one month's work. The ending backlog (967 road models) could be avoided by subcontracting during June through October.

Plan C proposes 400 full-time employees and 100 supplementary workers during May through September, along with subcontracting in the peak months. The supplementary capacity for May through September (Table 11.17) would have reduced peak-season backlogs and left less than one month of unmet demand at year end. Subcontracting for 1,724 road-miles

TABLE 11.15
Capacity evaluation for Plan A

Month	(1) Total demand (road-miles)	(2) Repair & maintenance (road-miles)	(3) Snow removal & new construction (road-miles)	(4) Capacity (road-miles)	(5) Backlog (−) from capacity shortage versus excess capacity (+) without subcontracting (road-miles)	(6) Cumulative backlog (road-miles)
Jan.	2,500	850	1,650	2,112[a]	−388[b]	−388
Feb.	2,200	870	1,330	1,824	−376	−764
Mar.	1,500	1,000	500	2,016	+516	−248
Apr.	1,700	1,150	550	2,112	+412	0
May	2,400	1,300	1,100	2,016	−384	−384
June	2,600	1,350	1,250	2,016	−584	−968
July	2,700	1,350	1,350	2,112	−588	−1,556
Aug.	2,900	1,350	1,550	2,112	−788	−2,344
Sept.	3,200	1,300	1,900	2,016	−1,184	−3,528
Oct.	2,900	1,150	1,750	2,112	−788	−4,316
Nov.	1,800	800	1,000	1,728	−72	−4,388
Dec.	1,800	600	1,200	2,016	+216	−4,172

[a]400 employees × 0.24 road-miles/employee/day × 22 days = 2,112 road-miles
[b]2,112 capacity miles (col. 4) − 1,650 miles (col. 3) − 850 miles (col. 2) = −388 road-miles (backlog of repair and maintenance for month)

TABLE 11.16
Capacity evaluation for Plan B

Month	(1) Total demand (road-miles)	(2) Repair & maintenance (road-miles)	(3) Snow removal & new construction (road-miles)	(4) Capacity (road-miles)	(5) Backlog (−) from capacity shortage versus excess capacity (+) without subcontracting (road-miles)	(6) Cumulative backlog (road-miles)
Jan.	2,500	850	1,650	2,534[a]	+34	0
Feb.	2,200	870	1,330	2,189	−11	−11
Mar.	1,500	1,000	500	2,419	+919	0
Apr.	1,700	1,150	550	2,534	+834	0
May	2,400	1,300	1,100	2,419	+19	0
June	2,600	1,350	1,250	2,419	−181	−181
July	2,700	1,350	1,350	2,534	−166	−347
Aug.	2,900	1,350	1,550	2,534	−366	−713
Sept.	3,200	1,300	1,900	2,419	−781	−1,494
Oct.	2,900	1,150	1,750	2,534	−366	−1,860
Nov.	1,800	800	1,000	2,074	+274	−1,586
Dec.	1,800	600	1,200	2,419	+619	−967

[a] 480 employees × 0.24 road-miles/employee/day × 22 days = 2,534 road-miles

TABLE 11.17
Capacity evaluation for Plan C

Month	(1) Total demand (road-miles)	(2) Repair & maintenance (road-miles)	(3) Snow removal & new construction (road-miles)	(4) Capacity (road-miles)	(5) Backlog (−) from capacity shortage versus excess capacity (+) without subcontracting (road-miles)	(6) Cumulative backlog (road-miles)
Jan.	2,500	850	1,650	2,112[a]	−388	−388
Feb.	2,200	870	1,330	1,824	−376	−764
Mar.	1,500	1,000	500	2,016	+516	−248
Apr.	1,700	1,150	550	2,112	+412	0
May	2,400	1,300	1,100	2,520[b]	+120	0
June	2,600	1,350	1,250	2,520	−80	−80
July	2,700	1,350	1,350	2,640	−60	−140
Aug.	2,900	1,350	1,550	2,640	−260	−400
Sept.	3,200	1,300	1,900	2,520	−680	−1,080
Oct.	2,900	1,150	1,750	2,112	−788	−1,868
Nov.	1,800	800	1,000	1,728	−72	−1,940
Dec.	1,800	600	1,200	2,016	+216	−1,724

[a]400 employees × 0.24 road-miles/employee/day × 22 days = 2,112 road-miles
[b]500 employees × 0.24 road-miles/employee/day × 21 days = 2,520 road-miles

during June through November would have satisfied the demand for services by year end.

Comparing the Plans

The costs of the three plans are compared in Table 11.18. Plan C is the lowest-cost alternative and, like Plan A, it accumulates some backlogs of road repair and maintenance in the early months of the year. Plan B is more costly and avoids backlogs in the early months. It is risky, however, because it adds full-time employees who may have to be released later if future workloads should diminish.

By now the fundamental considerations of the public works department should be clear. See if you can find a good aggregate plan for their operations to assure yourself that you understand this planning procedure.

Additional Models for Aggregate Planning

The graphical technique (model) has the advantages of simplicity, understandability, and no requirement of any special equipment. It can be done easily on a computer or manually. Its primary drawback is that the planner has no assurance that a "best" plan has been developed. How good is the plan we come up with? Experience and judgment are the only bases for answering this question. Some models, many beyond the scope of this book, have also been developed to judge aggregate plans. Sophisticated or simple, all these models share several features. First, they all require the user to specify a planning horizon and obtain aggregate demand forecasts. Second, in every model the decision variables must be explicitly identified. (Decision variables are the factors that can be varied to generate alternative plans—size of work force, production rate, overtime/idle time, inventory level, subcontracting, etc.) Third, the relevant costs must be identified. When decision variables are modified, some costs increase; others decrease. Those costs that change for different plans are called relevant costs; they include costs of wages, hiring/layoff, overtime, inventory, subcontracting, and so on.

TABLE 11.18
Annual costs for three plans

Cost component	Plan A	Plan B	Plan C
Full-time employee wages	$7,200,000	$8,640,000	$7,200,000
Seasonal wages	—	—	600,000
Hiring/layoff	—	—	10,000
Subcontracting	1,668,800	386,800	689,600
Total	$8,868,800	$9,026,800	$8,599,600

Optimal Models for Aggregate Planning

Linear Programming It is possible to formulate aggregate planning in a linear programming framework.[7] The linear programming procedure then identifies the *optimal* plan for minimizing costs. Not a trial-and-error procedure like the graphical method, this plan specifies the number of units of output to produce in each time period, how many shifts the manufacturing facility should operate each time period, and how many units of inventory should be carried each period. It does all of this by taking into account the operating capacity of the facility. One limitation of linear programming is its assumption of linear costs. As we shall see later, linear cost relationships are not always accurate representations of actual costs.

Linear Decision Rules A well-known mathematical modeling approach identifying the *optimal* aggregate plan can be applied to various organizations. This procedure results in a set of equations that can be used to calculate the best work force size, production rate, and inventory level for each time period in the planning horizon. This set of equations has become known as the Linear Decision Rules (LDRs).[8] The advantages of this procedure are that, like linear programming, it guarantees an optimal solution and saves trial and error computations. In addition, it recognizes that some cost relationships may be nonlinear rather than linear. Examples of some of these nonlinear costs are shown in Figure 11.9. Notice that regular wage costs are linear; each additional unit of work force costs a constant amount. The other three cost functions are *non*linear; they are quadratic in form. The overtime cost, for example, rises much faster than do linear costs. Ten hours of overtime cost far more than ten times the cost of one hour of overtime. You may remember that linear programming uses only linear cost functions. The LDR model has an advantage, then, since it can use both linear and quadratic (nonlinear) cost relationships.

A disadvantage of the LDR model is that it must be tailor made for each organization. The procedure requires a careful study of a company's cost structure, which must then be expressed in mathematical form. Next, a rather extensive mathematical analysis must be made to come up with the proper Linear Decision Rules for that particular company. Whenever the company's cost relationships change, for example when salaries increase, the mathematical derivation of the LDRs must be redone.

---

[7]The application of linear programming to aggregate planning was pioneered by E. H. Bowman, "Production Scheduling by the Transportation Method of Linear Programming," *Operations Research* 4, no. 1 (February 1956), pp. 100–103. An application of the simplex method to production planning by a truck manufacturer is given by J. A. Fuller, "A Linear Programming Approach to Aggregate Scheduling," *Academy of Management Journal* 18, no. 1 (March 1975), pp. 129–36.

[8]The procedure for developing the LDRs is demonstrated by C. C. Holt, F. Modigliani, J. F. Muth, and H. A. Simon, *Planning Production, Inventories, and Work Force* (Englewood Cliffs, N.J.: Prentice-Hall, Inc., 1960).

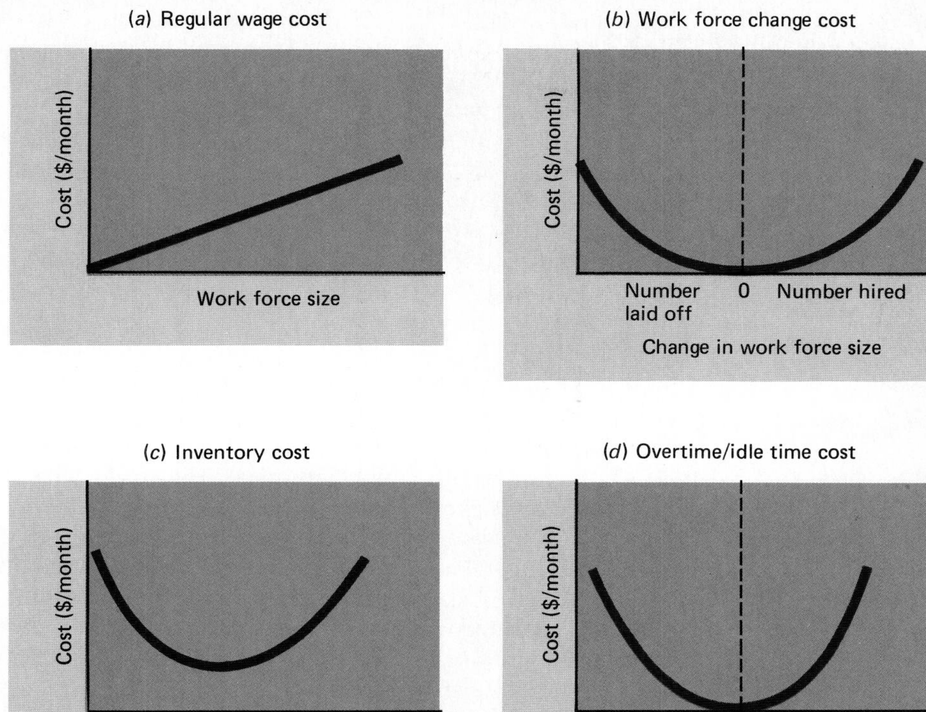

FIGURE 11.9
Example cost relationships used in linear decision rules

Heuristic Approaches for Aggregate Planning

A final class of aggregate planning models has evolved in recent years. These methods apply in situations in which management has done aggregate output planning on an intuitive basis.

Management Coefficient Model This procedure requires obtaining records of past work force, production, and inventory decisions. These data are analyzed by multiple regression techniques to find those regression equations that best fit the historical data. These regression equations are then used to make *future* planning decisions in much the same way that the LDRs are used.

Parametric Production Planning In this heuristic approach, a rough estimation is made of four variables. These four variables are searched in combination to provide a least-cost decision combination. Since the four variables are inserted into work force and production rate decision rules for actual planning, this approach approximates the firm's aggregate planning environment.[9]

The advantages of these heuristic models are that they are easy to obtain if sufficient historical data are available and that by reducing the variability in decision making, they can reduce costs. They must be applied, however, with great caution. The fact that *past* decision-making tendencies have been successful does not necessarily mean they will be successful when they are applied mechanically to *future* circumstances. Furthermore, this procedure may provide plans that are nowhere near optimal.

Search Procedures

Often it is possible to have a computer search for optimal aggregate plans. The computer does this by trying many combinations of work force and production rate for each period in the planning horizon. Although it explores many possible combinations of these variables, it does not do so randomly. Very specific rules are built into the search procedure to guide the search in a systematic way. Work force and production rate, in combination, are increased and/or decreased. These variations result in cost changes. When a cost improvement is found, the computer attempts to make further improvements. The search continues until no further improvement results or until a specified amount of search has been reached.

A disadvantage of computer search is the possibility of obtaining a nonoptimal plan. The search guidelines, heuristics, are fallible. Although they explore and evaluate a large number of plans, they do not examine *all* possible plans. Thus unlike the mathematical optimization models, the best plan may not be discovered by computer search.

Computer search is probably the most flexible of the optimum-seeking aggregate planning models. Cost functions need not be linear or quadratic, nor do they need to be unchanging over time. Various types of costs and operating constraints can be incorporated in the model. When the tradeoffs for cost and accuracy are considered, the computer search procedures are very attractive approaches to aggregate planning.

Selecting an Aggregate Planning Technique

Few studies have compared the various solution techniques that range from simple graphical techniques to more complex mathematical models. The primary reason for a lack of comparative studies is the modeling costs involved in collecting data, fitting models, and comparing the models over time in the context of a real firm. A notable exception is the work of Lee and Khumawala.[10]

---

[9]E. S. Buffa and J. G. Miller, *Production-Inventory Systems: Planning and Control,* 3rd ed. (Homewood, Ill.: Richard D. Irwin, Inc., 1979).

[10]W. B. Lee and B. M. Khumawala, "Simulation Testing of Aggregate Production Planning Models in an Implementation Methodology," *Management Science* 20, no. 6 (February 1974), pp. 903–11.

TABLE 11.19
Comparative profit performance of selected aggregate planning models*

Aggregate planning model	Annual profit
Company decisions	$4,420,000
Management Coefficients Model	4,607,000
Linear Decision Rule	4,821,000
Parametric Production Planning	4,900,000
Search Decision Rule	5,021,000

*Source: William B. Lee and Basheer M. Khumawala, "Simulation Testing of Aggregate Production Planning Models in an Implementation Methodology," *Management Science* 20, no. 6 (February 1974), p. 906.

Lee and Khumawala compared four models with company decisions for an aggregate planning situation in a capital goods firm having an $11 million annual sales volume. The plant was a typical job shop manufacturing facility in which parts were produced for inventory and then assembled into the final product. A computer simulation was developed that closely followed the firm's operations and allowed the models to be compared. Models compared in the study are listed in Table 11.19. As you can see, comparative profits clearly favor each model over the existing company decisions. The Management Coefficients Model showed the least improvement, $187,000 (4 percent); the Search Decision Rule showed the greatest improvement, $601,000 (14 percent).

This comparative study illustrates that considerable absolute dollars can be turned into profits through effective aggregate planning. We recommend that graphical techniques be used, at least as an aid in aggregate planning. If the firm in this study used some graphical approach (a reasonable assumption), more complex and costly models might improve performance even futher.

IMPLEMENTING AGGREGATE PLANS AND MASTER SCHEDULES

Unplanned Events

Once the aggregate plan is developed, it serves as a guide for making operating decisions. The plan must be continually updated as time elapses. Furthermore, it must be revised to take into account unplanned occurrences. Although January's forecasted demand may have been 4,000 units, at the end of January we may find that actual demand was above or below the forecasted amount, and ending inventory for the month may be at some level other than what we expected. Therefore, the original plan must be modified. Other unexpected events can also disrupt plans. Perhaps the planned output level for the month was not achieved, or perhaps the work force did not produce at its average capability. In any event, unplanned events must be taken into account by replanning for subsequent time periods. To replan, we simply reuse the aggregate planning methods we used before, except that we now use actual conditions, instead of planned conditions as input data to the model.

When aggregate plans are updated we can expect corresponding changes will be needed in the master production schedule. In fact, MPS changes are needed even when the aggregate plan remains fixed. MPS transactions, records, and reports are updated and reviewed periodically as forecasts of individual item demands change, when methods improvements or engineering changes modify the production process and performance times, and when materials delays or equipment failures occur. This periodic review and updating process, called *rolling through time,* exemplifies the dynamic nature of the planning and scheduling activities in operations management.[11]

Behavioral Considerations

Behavioral considerations enter into aggregate planning and scheduling both in the planning process itself and in attempting to implement the plan.

Behavior in the Planning Process

Some important behavioral factors arise from the extreme complexity of the planning problem and the capacity limitations of the person who must resolve the planning problem. Theoretically, the number of possible planning alternatives is infinite. But people do not possess sufficient mental capacity to deal with such vast ideas. Our integrative abilities, memory, and objectivity are limited.[12] Consider the time horizon that should be used for optimal planning. In some situations a long horizon is required, and problem complexities increase accordingly. Do planners adopt a long enough horizon? Some experimental research reveals that they do not.[13] Although "short-sighted" plans based on judgment and experience result in operating costs that are higher than they need to be, the use of longer horizons apparently poses a difficult mental task. Fortunately, today's abundance of computers and software offers inexpensive, powerful assistance. Microcomputers with database software and electronic spreadsheets permit desktop convenience for exploring complex planning

---

[11]"Rolling through time" is discussed in T. E. Vollmann, W. L. Berry, and D. C. Whybark, *Manufacturing Planning and Control Systems* (Homewood, Ill.: Richard D. Irwin, Inc.), 1984, Chapter 7.

[12]Human capacity limitations are analyzed in R. J. Ebert and T. R. Mitchell, *Organizational Decision Processes: Concepts and Analysis* (New York: Crane, Russak & Company, Inc., 1975).

[13]Time horizon and the effects of irrelevant information in intuitive planning are presented in the study by R. J. Ebert, "Environmental Structure and Programmed Decision Effectiveness," *Management Science* 19, no. 4 (December 1972), pp. 435–45.

and scheduling problems quickly, and they're often used to supplement the human elements of the planning process.

Behavioral Considerations in Implementation The implementation of a plan can affect organizational behavior in several ways. It signals the need for actions by other parts of the organization. Purchasing must plan to acquire necessary materials and resources. Arrangements may have to be made for retaining the services of subcontractors. Changes in work force must be closely coordinated with the personnel department so that appropriate human resources are available when needed. In short, the adoption of an aggregate plan initiates decision-making activities throughout the organization.

Implementation of a plan may also affect the organizational climate. Both motivation and job satisfaction can be affected. If the work force is decreased in successive time periods, morale can diminish, and productivity may decrease. Suppose an aggregate plan calls for fluctuating work force levels in response to demand variations. Such a plan often calls for periods of high employee layoffs. When layoffs occur, or are anticipated, job security is threatened, and both morale and job satisfaction decrease. This is true not only for operative employees but on all levels throughout the organization.

In concluding this section we wish to emphasize the interdependence of the planning and organizing functions in P/OM. Consider the seemingly unrelated areas of job design (Chapter 10) and aggregate planning. If job design decisions are made independently of aggregate planning and scheduling decisions, the result can be conflict and contradiction. Suppose that specific job design goals include both meeting output requirements and enhancing job satisfaction. At the same time an aggregate planning strategy might call for high layoff levels, a strategy that could lead to deterioration of job satisfaction. In a situation like this, different parts of the organization could be working at cross-purposes. Coordinating the efforts of organizational subunits and activities is a difficult but necessary part of the operations manager's job.

SUMMARY

Operations planning and scheduling systems give coherence to production activities and, overall, direct them toward enhancing the organization's competitive effectiveness. These systems involve various hierarchical levels of activities that fit together from top to bottom in support of one another. The aggregate output plan identifies the level of production activity for the next 6 to 18 months, expressed in quantities of product groups, in support of the overall business plan. Aggregate capacity planning emphasizes the availability of resources for implementing planned output and the two—planned output and capacity—must be balanced at the aggregate level of analysis.

Master production scheduling deals with output and capacity questions in more detail. The master schedule shows week-by-week how many units of each item or end product are due for completion, based on customer orders and short-term forecasts of demand. To ensure its feasibility, the MPS is developed in conjunction with rough-cut capacity planning. If scheduled production and capacity are mismatched, either the schedule must be modified or the capacity must be temporarily adjusted. Once settled, the master schedule will be consistent with the aggregate plan from above and will also guide the more detailed scheduling activities that are undertaken later in the production process.

CASE

Chemtrol Pharmaceutical

Forecasts of Chemtrol Pharmaceutical's primary product show seasonality of monthly demand as follows (units per month): 400, 300, 500, 600, 500, 600, 500, 400, 200, 200, 300, 300. Currently, 300 units are on hand in finished goods inventory. Historically, the highly skilled work force has averaged one-half unit per person daily when 38 to 48 employees are operating. Average productivity drops to .416 units per person when fewer than 38 employees are working, and it averages .446 units per person with more than 48 employees. Standard materials cost $30 per unit. Chemtrol's policy of producing 300 units per month during September through February and 500 units per month from March through August has led to predictable employment patterns for the local labor force. Wage rates average $10 per hour, and the company operates an eight-hour shift on each of the twenty working days each month. Costs of hiring and training a new employee are estimated at $2,000; a layoff costs $1,000 per employee. Finished goods are costed at 4 percent of the value of an item in inventory per month. Backorders are estimated to cost $15 per unit per month.

Arlin Sprang, production manager, has been requested to find ways to reduce operating costs by at least 10 percent as part of Chemtrol's overall cost reduction program. He wants to consider what possible efficiencies might result from alternative production scheduling policies.

REVIEW AND DISCUSSION QUESTIONS

1. Identify the relevant costs that should be considered in developing a plan for aggregate output and capacity.
2. Compare and contrast rough-cut with aggregate capacity planning. How are they similar and different?
3. What factors should be considered in selecting a planning horizon? Explain.
4. Outline the advantages and disadvantages of the three pure strategies of aggregate planning.
5. Compare and contrast three different methods of aggregate planning: graphical, linear programming, and a heuristic approach.
6. What role does forecasting play in the aggregate planning process?
7. Aggregate plans and master production schedules are developed on the basis of demand forecasts. But after the forecasts have been made, actual demand often

deviates from the forecasted amount. Explain how the aggregate planning process continues when this happens.

8. Explain how aggregate plans and master production schedules serve as initiators of action in other functional activities of the organization.
9. Demonstrate how aggregate planning and scheduling costs are affected by forecast errors.
10. Discuss similarities and differences in the aggregate planning problems facing service organizations and goods-producing organizations.
11. What problem characteristics cause the master production scheduling problem to be so complex?
12. How might aggregate planning affect job satisfaction?
13. What problem characteristics cause the aggregate planning problem to be so complex?

PROBLEMS

Solved Problems

1. A manufacturer has the following information on its major product:

   Regular-time production capacity = 2,600 units per period.
   Overtime production costs = $12 per unit.
   Inventory costs = $2 per unit per period (based on the ending inventory).
   Backlog costs = $5 per unit per period.
   Beginning inventory = 400 units.

Period	Demand (units)
I	4,000
II	3,200
III	2,000
IV	2,800

Develop a level production plan that yields zero inventory at the end of period IV. What costs result from this plan?

Period	Demand	Production	Ending inventory	Regular production	Overtime production
0			400		
I	4,000	2,900	−700	2,600	300
II	3,200	2,900	−1000	2,600	300
III	2,000	2,900	−100	2,600	300
IV	2,800	2,900	0	2,600	300
Average = 3,000					

$$\begin{aligned}\text{Total cost} &= \text{overtime} + \text{inventory} + \text{backlogs}\\ &= (300 \times 4 \times \$12) + (0 \times \$2) + (1{,}800 \times \$5)\\ &= \$23{,}400\end{aligned}$$

2. A chair manufacturer who produces three different models (A, B, and C) has developed a master production schedule for the next five weeks. Historically, worker

productivity has averaged 8 units per week for each employee based on the "typical mix" of chairs. The company employs 50 workers. The standard labor hours for chairs are 1.0, 2.0, and 1.5 hours for models A, B, and C respectively.

	Master production schedule (units)				
	Week				
Chair	1	2	3	4	5
A	200		200		100
B				200	100
C	100	300	100		

Evaluate the capacity utilization of the MPS.

	Schedule of labor hours				
	Week				
Chair	1	2	3	4	5
A	200		200		100
B				400	200
C	150	450	150		
Total requirements (hrs.)	350	450	350	400	300
Total hrs. available	400	400	400	400	400

Capacity is underutilized in weeks 1, 3, and 5; capacity is inadequate in week 2.

Reinforcing Fundamentals

3. Refer to the data for "solved problem" number 1, above. If you could adjust the beginning inventory (400 units) to any level you choose, what beginning level would minimize the annual operating costs?
4. Refer to the data for "solved problem" number 2, above. Develop a master schedule that improves the capacity utilization under the following conditions: production during the 5-week horizon must include 500, 300, and 500 units of chairs A, B, and C, respectively, and no more than two types of chairs can be scheduled in any week.
5. Reconsider the aggregate planning problem of the Go-Rite Company example that was presented in this chapter. If the beginning aggregate inventory is 15,000 units (instead of zero), develop a good aggregate plan that uses a level production rate. How would the costs of your plan compare with those of the previous level plan in Table 11.9?
6. Reconsider the aggregate planning problem of the Go-Rite Company example that was presented in this chapter. If the beginning aggregate inventory is 15,000

units (instead of zero), develop a good aggregate plan that uses a "chase" strategy. How would your plan's costs compare with those of the "chase" plan in Table 11.9?

7. Referring to the data in problem 6, evaluate the capacity feasibility and utilization of the new "chase" plan.
8. Randolf Corporation has estimated its aggregate demand for the coming year as follows:

Month	Productive days	Demand (units)
Jan	22	8,000
Feb	19	12,000
Mar	21	18,000
Apr	22	20,000
May	21	28,000
June	21	25,000
July	22	26,000
Aug	11	16,000
Sept	21	18,000
Oct	22	14,000
Nov	18	9,000
Dec	21	7,000

Currently, there are 100 employees with normal productivity of 12 units daily per employee. Daily capacity can be increased by up to 30 percent by working overtime at an additional cost of $2 per unit. Regular time salaries average $30 daily per employee. Costs of storing units in inventory are $2 per unit per month. Inventory shortages cost $10 per unit short. Costs of hiring and training a new employee are $300, and a layoff of an employee costs $200. Additional capacity is available by subcontracting to a local manufacturer at a cost of $8 per unit. Currently, Randolf has 5,000 units in inventory. Develop a good plan for next year's aggregate output.

9. An office equipment repair company has sales/service offices throughout North Carolina. The company services such products as typewriters, dictating equipment, photocopiers, and small computers. The following is the demand forecast for the next year in bimonthly groups.

Period	Forecasted demand (standard units of work)
Jan–Feb	210
Mar–Apr	245
May–June	260
July–Aug	250
Sept–Oct	235
Nov–Dec	220

(a) Prepare a graph of cumulative service units demanded vs. cumulative service days, assuming that each two-month period has forty-three working days.

(b) Assume that an employee contributes 344 working hours each two months and that each unit requires thirty standard hours to produce. Assuming no overtime or part-time employees, calculate the number of employees required each period.

(c) The company staffs to meet peak demand without overtime, hiring, or firing to meet demand changes. With a current labor rate of $8.25 per hour, what will be the bimonthly and annual labor costs? What is the extra cost incurred for this policy?

(d) Cost out an alternative aggregate plan that allows hiring or firing a maximum of twice during the year. For this plan assume hiring costs equal firing costs and are $2,300 per employee hired or fired. Would you recommend this plan over (c) above?

10. Reconsider the three aggregate plans that were developed for the public works department example in this chapter. Prepare for the director your recommendation for a better aggregate plan.

11. Reconsider the master production schedule for the Go-Rite example (Table 11.11) in this chapter. Suppose the standard labor hours per unit are 0.80, 0.75, and 0.97 for models A, B, and C, respectively. Perform rough-cut capacity tests of the MPS under these new conditions and compare your results to those in Tables 11.13 and 11.14.

Challenging Exercises

12. Reconsider the Go-Rite Company example in this chapter. Assume that customer backorders are now allowed and the backlog cost in $2 per unit per month. Develop a good aggregate plan for wagon production.

13. Reconsider the Go-Rite Company example in this chapter. Suppose three months have elapsed since the initial aggregate planning, and during that time actual demand was 5,000 units in January, 12,000 in February, and 14,000 in March. New sales forecasts for April through December are 24,000; 25,000, 21,000; 16,000; 16,000; 18,000; 14,000; 10,000; and 7,000. Develop a revised plan to take into account this recent information.

14. Reconsider the aggregate planning problem of the Go-Rite Company in this chapter, and do the following:
    (a) Develop a good plan for the first three months of the year, ignoring the remaining months.
    (b) Develop a good plan for the first six months of the year, ignoring the last six months.
    (c) Assuming your six-month plan in part (b) is fully implemented, develop a good plan for the final six months of the year.
    (d) Compare the costs of the three-month, six-month, and twelve-month plans. Explain any differences among them.

15. A manufacturing firm is trying to schedule production for the coming three months. Product demand for each of the next three months is forecasted as 300, 250, and 325 units respectively. Currently, 95 units are on hand and available in finished goods inventory at the factory. At the end of the three month scheduling period, the company wants to have 120 finished units available for future demand, and it wants to have supplied enough units to meet all demand (backorders are not allowed). Regular shift operations are capable of producing 200 units per month at a cost of $10 per unit. Overtime operations can supply up to 100 units monthly at $15 cost per unit. Inventory carrying costs are $2 per unit per month for finished goods. Structure this scheduling problem in a transportation linear programming format. Create and interpret an initial feasible solution.

16. Reconsider the master production schedule for the Go-Rite Company (Table 11.11) example in this chapter. The master scheduler wishes to do a more detailed job of rough-cut capacity planning to see if the trial schedule is feasible in Go-Rite's four major work centers. The planned labor availability is as follows:

Work center	Days 1 through 62		Days 63 through 80	
	Number of people	Standard hours/week	Number of people	Standard hours/week
Fabrication	19	760	35	1,400
Welding	16	640	30	1,200
Paint	6	240	10	400
Assembly	14	560	25	1,000

Each wagon is processed through all the work centers and, historically, the total work content in a "typical wagon" is distributed as follows: 35 percent in fabrication, 30 percent in welding, 10 percent in painting, and 25 percent in assembly. Evaluate the capacity feasibility and utilization in the work centers for the trial MPS.

GLOSSARY

Aggregate capacity planning The process of testing the feasibility of planned output (aggregate) against existing capacity and evaluating overall capacity utilization.

Aggregate output planning The process of determining output levels (units) of a product group over the next 6 to 8 months on a weekly or monthly basis; it identifies the overall level of production outputs in support of the business plan.

Backorders Outstanding or unfilled customer requests for output.

Blocks of capacity Clusters of key resources in the facility that are consumed during the production process; examples include machine time and labor time.

Business plan A statement of the organization's overall level of business activity for the next 6 to 18 months, usually expressed in terms of dollar volume of sales for its various product groups.

Disaggregation The process of translating aggregate plans for product groups into detailed operational plans for individual products.

Graphical method of aggregate planning Two-dimensional model showing the time phasing of demand against aggregate output rates and aggregate capacity.

Linear Decision Rules (LDRs) Set of equations determining optimal work force and production decisions for aggregate output.

Master production schedule (MPS) Shows week-by-week how many of each end product are due for completion; developed from customer orders and demand forecasts for each product.

Mixed strategy Aggregate scheduling strategy that incorporates or combines some elements from each of the "pure" aggregate planning strategies.

Product group (family) A set of individual products that share or consume common blocks of capacity in the manufacturing process.

Pure strategy Aggregate planning strategy using just one of several possible means to respond to demand fluctuations.

Relevant costs Those costs that change, or potentially change, depending upon the decision alternative selected.

Rough-cut capacity planning The process of assessing the capacity feasibility of master production schedules.

Shop floor control Activities that execute and control shop operations; includes loading, sequencing, detailed scheduling, and expediting jobs in production.

Work force utilization Extent to which existing work force resources are over-or underutilized relative to their regular time availabilities.

SELECTED READINGS

Bowman, E. H. "Consistency and Optimality in Managerial Decision Making." *Management Science* 9, no. 2 (January 1963), pp. 310–21.

Buffa, E. S. "Aggregate Planning for Production." *Business Horizons* 10, no. 3 (Fall 1967), pp. 87–97.

——— and J. G. Miller, *Production-Inventory Systems: Planning and Control*. 3rd. ed. Homewood, Ill.: Richard D. Irwin, Inc., 1979.

Ebert, R. J. "Environmental Structure and Programmed Decision Effectiveness." *Management Science* 19, no. 4 (December 1972), pp. 435–45.

———. "Time Horizon: Implications for Aggregate Scheduling Effectiveness." *AIIE Transactions* 4, no. 4 (December 1972), pp. 298–307.

——— and T. R. Mitchell. *Organizational Decision Processes: Concepts and Analysis*. New York: Crane, Russak & Co., Inc., 1975.

Holt, C. C., F. Modigliani, J. F. Muth, and H. A. Simon. *Planning Production, Inventories, and Work Force*. Englewood Cliffs, N.J.: Prentice-Hall, Inc., 1960.

Krajewski, L. J. and L. P. Ritzman. "Disaggregation in Manufacturing and Service Organizations: Survey of Problems and Research." *Decision Sciences* 8, no. 1 (January 1977), pp. 1–18.

Lee, W. B. and B. M. Khumawala. "Simulation Testing of Aggregate Production Planning Models in an Implementation Methodology." *Management Science* 20, no. 6 (February 1974), pp. 903–11.

McLeavey, D. W. and S. L. Narasimhan. *Production Planning and Inventory Control*. Boston: Allyn and Bacon, Inc., 1985.

Meal, C. H. "Putting Production Decisions Where They Belong." *Harvard Business Review* 62, no. 2 (March–April 1984), pp. 102–111.

Taubert, W. H. "Search Decision Rule for the Aggregate Scheduling Problem." *Management Science* 14, no. 6 (February 1968), pp. 343–59.

Vollman, T. E., W. L. Berry, and D. C. Whybark. *Manufacturing Planning and Control Systems*. Homewood, Ill.: Richard D. Irwin, Inc., 1984.

12 Intermittent (Job Shop) Scheduling

First Express, a division of First Tennessee Bank, N.A., provides payment system services to financial institutions and corporations located nationwide. Each night, all across the nation, Federal Express airplanes fly to Memphis and while Federal Express employees are sorting packages, First Express employees are sorting checks. Upon completion of the process and according to schedule the airplanes fly from Memphis back to the originating cities and both the checks and packages are delivered to their appropriate destinations.

First Express provides this service because of the time value of money. When a check drawn on a Miami bank is deposited in a Seattle bank, the check must be sent from Seattle to Miami. The time the check is in transit is called float. Reducing the float time creates opportunities for a financial institution to produce additional business or produce income for itself. Let's assume the above mentioned check is for $10 million and normally it takes two days from the time it is deposited in the Seattle bank until it is paid by the Miami bank. If a service can clear the check in one day, rather than two, the real value at today's rates is nearly $2,700. To the Seattle bank, this could be income that flows directly to the bottom line.

First Express provides this service. Intensive job shop and work center scheduling is required by many different organizations if the desired results are to be achieved. The financial institution in Seattle must process and deliver the check to Federal Express before the plane departs. The plane must arrive in Memphis on time and be off-loaded rapidly.

First Express's operation consists of receiving, sorting, reject processing, outbound packaging, and reconciling. The inbound area requires more manpower initially as the boxes arrive quickly and receive priority sequencing at this point. This heavy workload moves to other departments as the evening progresses. Consequently, work schedules must accommodate each work center's highs and lows. Personnel on the inbound side are cross trained and shifted to outbound later in the work cycle. Each step of this process is dependent on the successful completion of the preceeding one. We have a narrow processing window; slackness in one area cannot be made up in another. With such little room for error, our employees must work quickly and accurately.

Packages arrive at First Express from 11:00 P.M. till 1:30 A.M. and begin to leave our facility at 2:05 A.M. The packages are loaded into the Federal Express airplanes and flown to the destination city. Upon arrival in the city, a Federal Express employee immediately delivers the package to our clearing bank. The delivery must occur before that bank's deposit deadline or the "speed up" in the availability of funds will not occur.

Many variables must be appropriately managed to provide our service. Every night, First Express puts into practical operation the concepts provided in this chapter.

Walter W. Stafeil
Senior Vice President & Manager
First Express
Memphis, Tennessee

As Mr. Stafeil's comments indicate, the operations at First Express have direct and visible consequences for their customers. Success at First Express depends on the ability to manage complex intermittent operations systems. Intermittent, or job shop, conversion systems are commonly encountered in business and governmental organizations. These systems present different types of management problems than do assembly-type and continuous flow systems. In this chapter we examine the nature of intermittent systems and introduce some concepts, models, and behavioral considerations that enter into planning their use. Figure 12.1 shows how job shop scheduling relates to the overall framework of the book. Although scheduling is a planning subfunction, we'll also have some discussion of control because planning and controlling are so closely interrelated in job shop systems.

WHAT ARE INTERMITTENT SYSTEMS?

Conversion systems can be broadly classified as either continuous or intermittent, depending on the characteristics of the conversion process and the product or service. A continuous or assembly type system is one in which

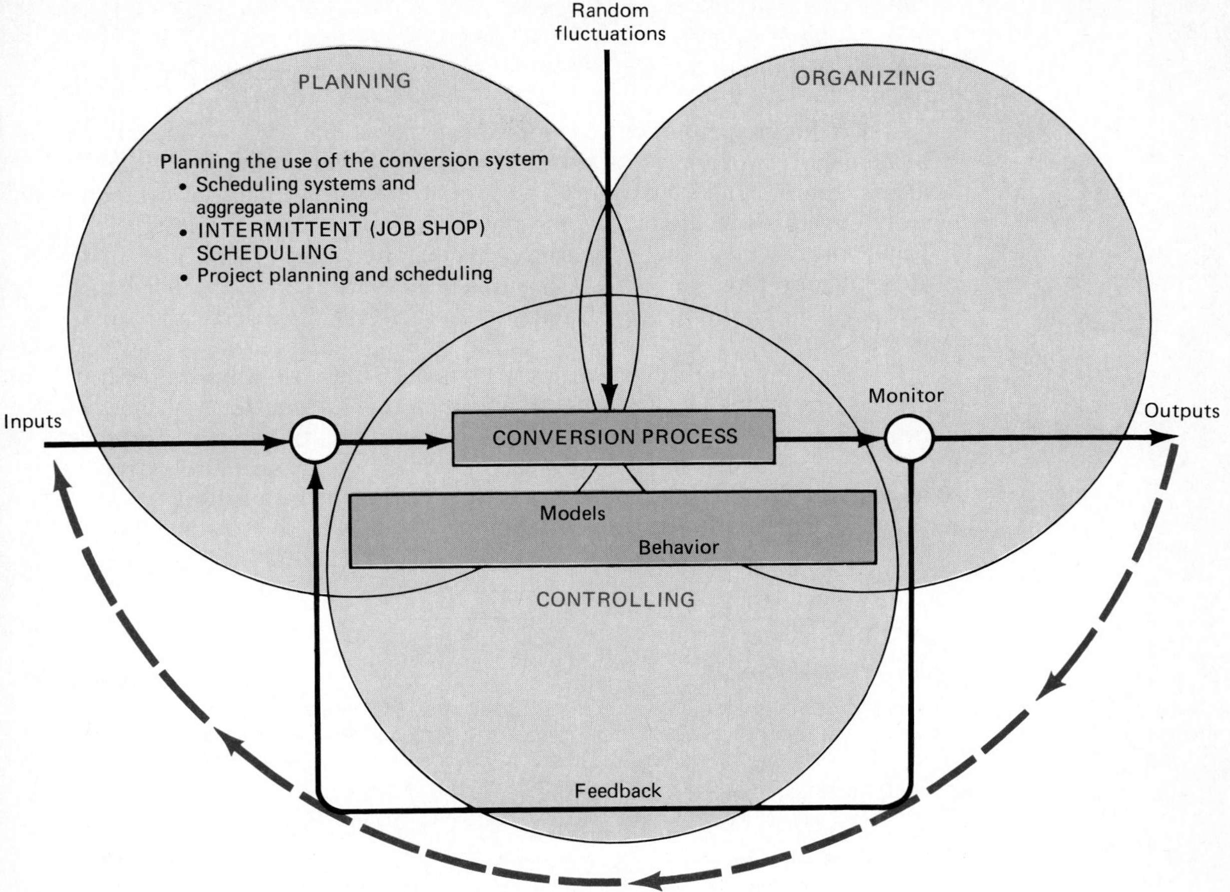

FIGURE 12.1
Production/operations management activities

a large or indefinite number of units of a homogeneous product is being produced. Intermittent systems, on the other hand, produce a variety of products one at a time (in which case they are custom made) or finite numbers of different products in batches to customer order. Many conversion facilities are neither strictly intermittent nor solely continuous but a combination of both.

In Chapter 8 we observed the features of process-oriented layouts for intermittent systems. As you may remember, processing stations (work centers) are grouped together according to the type of function they perform. Each work order may travel through a unique flow path of work centers to meet the customer's requirements. Since the product specifications for each order are different, a separate routing through the system must be developed for each one. Separate records must be kept on each job, and the progress of jobs must be closely monitored. In short, each job may differ in completion schedule, routing, input materials, type of transformation, and due date.

In a manufacturing context, intermittent systems are traditionally referred to as job shops. As work orders arrive, the work load on the facility increases. Some work centers may be idle at the same time that others are severely overloaded. A work center may experience a large buildup of "to-be-done" orders awaiting processing. When one order is completed, the equipment may have to be reset or adjusted before the next order can be processed. The challenge is to manage these flows of orders through the shop.

The *sequence* in which waiting jobs are processed is important in determining the efficiency and effectiveness of the intermittent system. Sequencing determines the amount of job lateness, costs incurred for setup and changeover, delivery lead times, inventory costs, and the degree of congestion in the facility. Indeed, the scheduling of intermittent systems poses a challenging problem for operations managers.

EXAMPLE

As manager of Matchless Machining Company, you are responsible for processing jobs requiring metal fabrication and forming to customer order. Some jobs, such as thread cutting on metal pipe, are simple. Other jobs are more complex and require intricate metal machining in many stages at different work centers. Your facility consists of 200 work centers specializing in various aspects of machining and supporting services. Ten foremen and 150 skilled employees provide the human resources for your operation. An average of 100 new customer orders arrives daily. On average, a job spends forty-five days in the shop. You wish to process the jobs in such a way that customers' orders are finished on time and that Matchless Machining achieves its profit objectives.

Since new orders arrive at irregular rates and consist of different requirements, work loads are seldom evenly distributed across the various work centers; while lengthy delays are occurring in some, others are idle. Of the thousands of jobs in the system, which should you give top priority? For each job, how do you select the sequence in which its various operations are to be performed? Who keeps track of its current status? How do you decide when to switch labor skills from one area to another?

The decisions you make are important because they determine the quality of service to your customers and the costs you incur for processing orders. These decisions affect the average number of jobs in the system and hence the amount of in-process inventories on hand. In addition to inventory costs, your decisions affect the efficiency of work force utilization. Further, the sequence in which jobs are processed through the work stations can result in high setup costs. In some instances, setup costs are negligible, but in other situations they are significant.

Intermittent systems exist in goods-producing and in service organizations. Intermittent service systems frequently offer "provided-to-order" services. In restaurants offering meals served to customer order and in watch repair shops, for example, conversion systems are similar in concept to those in manufacturing job shops.

INTERMITTENT SCHEDULING CONCEPTS AND PROCESSES

As with continuous and assembly-type operations, the overall stages of planning in Figure 12.2 apply to job shop operations as well. Guided by the business plan, aggregate planning reveals overall levels of planned output and capacity utilization as we discussed in Chapter 11. Then, customer orders and forecasts for specific products are incorporated into a master production schedule for the weeks and months ahead. This master schedule feeds the material requirements planning system (discussed in Chapters 9 and 16), or any other type of materials planning procedure, that identifies when the products and components are due for completion. Then a transition occurs in the planning process; its emphasis shifts to even more detailed, day-to-day scheduling and control activities called shop floor control. As we discuss these activities in the context of job-shop operations, you'll see how they supplement the production plans and how they direct shop operations toward desired results.

Overview of the Scheduling and Control Process

After production plans reveal when specific items and products are needed, there still remain some tasks for translating them into operational terms for their implementation on the shop floor. Included among these are loading, sequencing, detailed scheduling, expediting, and input/output control.

Loading Each job may have its unique product specification and, hence, its routing through various work centers in the facility. As new job orders are released, they are assigned or allocated among the work centers, thus establishing how much of a load each work center must carry during the coming planning period. This assigning of jobs to work centers and the committing of work centers to jobs is known as *loading* (sometimes called *shop loading* or *machine loading*). "The following fifteen jobs will be processed on work center x during the coming month" is a loading statement. Notice that only the due date of the jobs (one month hence) is specified; the job release statement has not specified in what sequence the awaiting jobs will be processed through the work center.

Sequencing This stage establishes the priorities for jobs in the queues (waiting lines) at the work centers. Priority sequencing specifies the order in which the waiting jobs will be processed; it requires the adoption of a priority sequencing rule, a concept we'll discuss later.

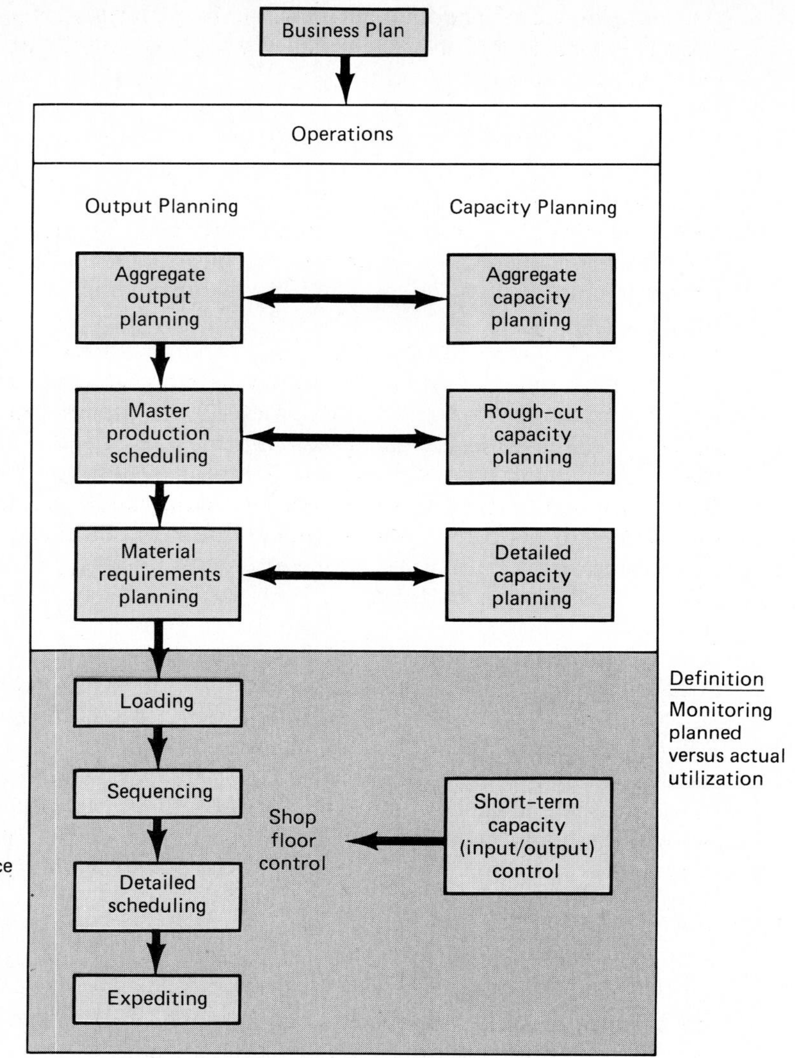

FIGURE 12.2
The operations planning and scheduling system

Detailed Scheduling Calendar times are specified when job orders, employees, and materials (inputs), as well as job completion (outputs), should occur at each work center. This scheduling supplements preceding scheduling; detailed dates and times are usually not specified until loading and sequencing have been completed. After the priority sequencing rule has been applied, the sequence for processing waiting jobs can be determined.

Using estimates of processing durations and due dates for all jobs, schedulers can establish their beginning and ending dates and develop the detailed schedule.

Expediting In tracking a job's progress, special action may be needed to keep it moving through the facility on time. Production disruptions—equipment breakdowns, materials inavailabilities, last-minute priority changes—that cause deviations from plans and schedules will sometimes necessitate expediting an important job on a "special-handling" basis.

Input-Output (Short-term Capacity) Control Production plans and schedules call for certain levels of capacity and output for a work center, but its actual utilization may differ from what was planned. We can monitor actual versus planned utilization by using input-output reports and, when discrepancies exist, we can make adjustments to control the utilization at desired levels.

Let's take a closer look at each of these activities to see what they involve and how they relate to one another.

LOADING

Given the existence of several work centers capable of processing new customer orders, which jobs should be assigned to which centers? We know from the production schedule what products are due for completion and when. Furthermore, we have each item's routing so we know which work centers might be involved. If we have only one work center that meets the technical processing requirements of a specific job order, we have no choice. In other instances, several work centers may be able to meet the job requirements, and we have to decide which to use. So, procedures are required to match up the jobs with the work centers and, thus, the loads are created. Although even the best production schedule creates imbalanced loads, either too heavy or too light, we can still manipulate and manage them at reasonable levels. Two basic approaches for doing so, infinite and finite loading, are in use today. Let's look first at infinite loading, the predominant approach, and then we'll review finite loading.

Infinite Loading

With *infinite* loading systems, jobs are allocated to work centers without regard to the work center's capacity; jobs are loaded from the production schedule into the work center as if its capacity were unlimited. With either manual or computer-based systems, Gantt charts and visual load profiles can be helpful for evaluating the current loadings.

The Gantt Load Chart This graphical procedure is shown in Figure 12.3. The aircraft repair facility has four work centers through which five jobs (open orders) must be processed. Aircraft *A*, *B*, *C*, *D*, and *E* require sheet

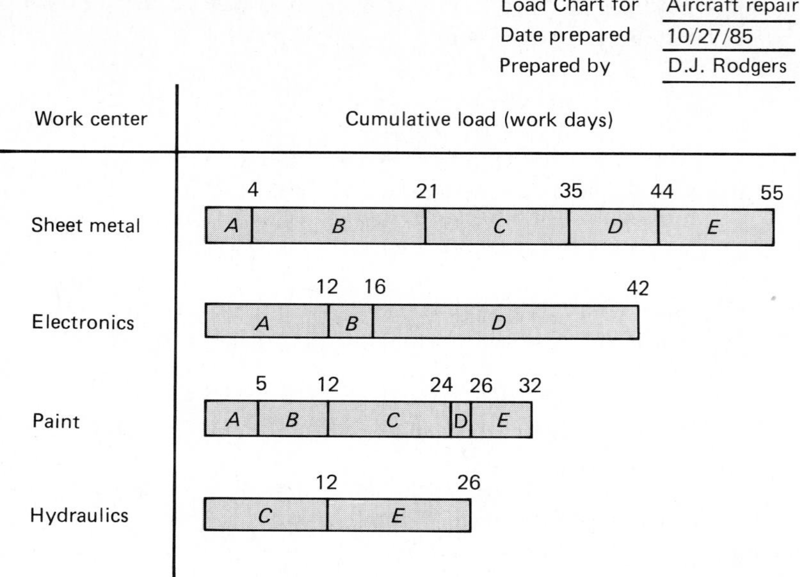

FIGURE 12.3
Gantt load chart for aircraft repair facility

metal work; *A*, *B*, and *D* are the only aircraft needing electronics work. The chart shows the total estimated work load that the open orders require at all work centers. Thus, fifty-five days of cumulative work lie ahead of the sheet metal center; the paint center faces a thirty-two day load, and so on. The chart does not specify which job will be completed at which time, nor does it show the sequence in which the jobs should be processed.

The Gantt load chart offers the advantages of ease and clarity in communicating important shop information. It does have some important limitations, however. Since the chart is a deterministic device, it does not convey the variabilities of task duration, equipment (including breakdowns), and human performance times, any of which can cause the estimated load to be inaccurate. Also, the chart is static and must be updated periodically to account for new job arrivals and revised time estimates for existing jobs.

The Gantt chart, whether applied to several departments, machines, or facilities, clearly displays the relative work loads in the sytem. It signals the need for reassigning resources when the load at one work center becomes too large. Employees from a low load center may be temporarily shifted to high load areas, or, alternatively, excessive load buildup may be alleviated by temporarily increasing the size of work force. Multipurpose equipment can be shifted among work centers. If the waiting jobs can be processed at any of several work centers, some of the jobs at high load centers can be reassigned to low load centers. Later we will show how the Gantt chart can be applied to detailed scheduling as well as to loading.

Visual Load Profiles Open job orders are assigned completion dates from the production schedule and, with infinite loading, they're loaded into the work center according to their due dates. Since loading ignores its capacity, the work center can be underloaded or overburdened with waiting jobs in future periods. A visual load profile, like those shown in Figure 12.4, reveals the matchup between the workload and the capacity.

For a manual scheduling system (in part a. of the figure), the load consists of open orders that have been released to the work center. The load for week 1 exceeds capacity but the future loads are well within weekly capabilities.

In a computer-based scheduling system, such as time-phased MRP, planned order releases and scheduled receipts, in addition to open orders, can be projected into the load profile (part b. of the figure). Doing so, we see that projected loads for weeks 3, 4, and 6 exceed capacity even though the loads for the open orders are feasible.

The load report provides useful information; it identifies when and how much conflict exists between workloads and capacity and it signals the need for action. When confronted with critical overloads any of several steps can be taken. We can try to shift some of the overload to alternative work centers or routings. Or, we can use *lot-splitting,* whereby a job order is split and only part of it is processed now and the rest is deferred until

FIGURE 12.4
Infinite loading for a work center: visual load profiles

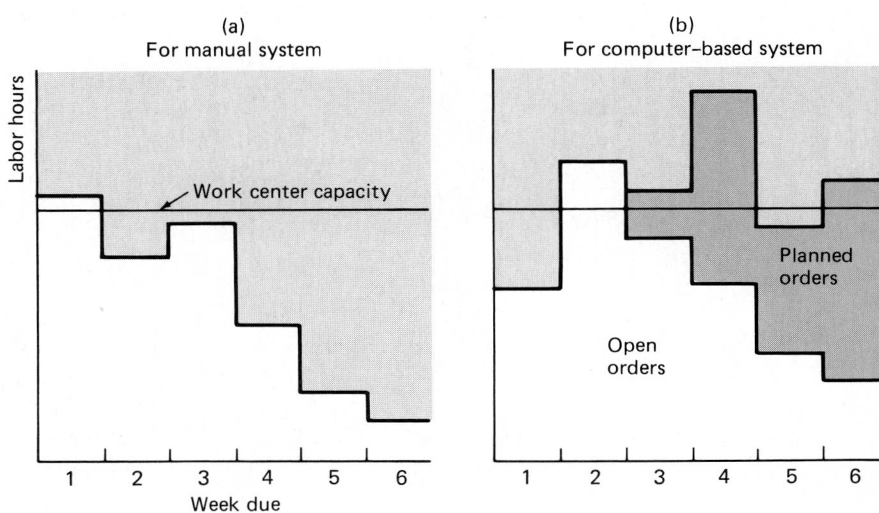

later. Still another alternative is *operations splitting;* part of the job is processed at this work center and the rest is done in another, similar work center.

Loading with the Assignment Algorithm Sometimes the loading process is assisted by mathematical models to achieve a desired economic or performance goal in the facility. The assignment algorithm, for example, may be helpful for the special case where the number of jobs to be loaded equals the number of work centers or machines on which the jobs can be processed.

EXAMPLE

The metalworking work center of a job shop has been assigned the task of processing four orders. Four machines in the work center are all capable of processing any of the orders. The foreman must decide which job to allocate to each machine.

This method requires that each machine be assigned one and only one job. Furthermore, some criterion must be chosen to evaluate the "goodness" of the assignments that will eventually be made. The foreman may wish to assign in such a way that profit is maximized, operating cost is minimized, or completion time is minimized.

EXAMPLE

Suppose the foreman wishes to minimize total processing time in the work center. The estimated days required to process each job on each machine are recorded in the matrix.

Job	Machine			
	1	2	3	4
1	13	16	21	14
2	17	13	19	14
3	12	16	20	16
4	20	12	17	11

For job 3, machine 1 is preferred, because the processing time is only 12 days. However, machine 1 is also preferred for job 1 because this job can be processed fastest on that machine. Since machine 1 can be assigned only one job, a conflict exists.

The assignment algorithm for resolving this problem is a special case of linear programming. It identifies the desired criterion and considers opportunity costs of different possible assignments. The optimal assignments for our example are shown here. This example is presented here to clarify the type of problem to which the assignment algorithm is applicable. For details of the algorithm, refer to the supplement to this chapter.

Optimal assignments and times		
Job	Machine	Time (days)
1	4	14
2	2	13
3	1	12
4	3	17
		56

Limitations of the Algorithm The applicability of this procedure has some limitations. First, if the number of jobs is not equal to the number of machines, certain adjustments must be made (these are beyond the scope of this book). Second, this approach does not consider that new jobs, with their loading decisions, may arrive continually; it is a *static* approach. Suppose this algorithm is applied weekly to all new jobs arriving during that week. Over a series of weeks, a heavy work load may accumulate at one machine and a relatively low load at another. A simple updated Gantt chart could detect when the loads are becoming unbalanced. Depending upon the due-dates of the individual jobs, reassignments of jobs to machines may be necessary to even out the loads. Finally, it is commonly found that all jobs cannot be processed on all machines in intermittent systems. Some jobs can be done on only a particular machine or by only one process. When this is the case, no choice exists, and the algorithm cannot be applied.

As the loading process proceeds, by whatever method, the resulting work loads often present conflicts; jobs are competing for the work center's capacity and these conflicts are normally resolved by assigning priorities to the jobs and then sequencing them in priority order as we see next.

PRIORITY SEQUENCING

When jobs compete for a work center's capacity, which job should be done next? Priority sequencing rules are a shop floor control tool for handling this problem on a routine basis. With any given rule, a priority measure is applied to all jobs awaiting in the queue. Then, when the work center becomes open for a new job, the one with the highest priority is processed next.

Choosing the Right Sequencing Rule

Many different sequencing rules are available as we'll soon see, and the logical questions are "Which one should I select?" and "What difference does it make?" Your choice is important because a sequencing rule that performs well on one dimension, say on minimizing inventories, may not do so well on another dimension such as minimizing production setup costs. So, your choice should be guided by the importance you place on various performance criteria. Some major criteria are the following:

- Setup costs.
- In-process inventory costs.
- Idle time, percent.
- Percentage of jobs late.
- Average job lateness.
- Standard deviation of job lateness.
- Average number of jobs waiting.
- Average job completion time.
- Standard deviation of job completion time.

Three of the criteria (setup costs, in-process inventory costs, and station idle time) are primarily concerned with internal facility efficiency. The more these are minimized without jeopardizing service to customers, the better the use of limited resources and chances for improved profitability. Three of the criteria (percentage of jobs late, average job lateness, and variance of job lateness) are more customer-/or service-oriented than internally oriented. To the extent that these criteria increase, service to customers deteriorates. Finally, three of the criteria (number of jobs waiting, average job completion time, and variance of job completion time) reflect both a customer service and internal efficiency orientation that are hard to separate.

It is difficult, if not impossible, to find a sequencing rule that best satisfies all these criteria simultaneously. Therefore, when selecting a sequencing rule, the operations manager must carefully consider the criteria's relative importance to the organization's goals and competitive strategy.

Some Priority Sequencing Rules

The following rules are representative of the many that are used today in manufacturing and service industries:

- First-come-first-served (FCFS). As its name suggests, incoming jobs or customers are processed in their order of arrival using this rule. It is commonly applied in service industries such as banks, supermarkets, etc.
- Earliest due date (EDD). Top priority is assigned to the awaiting job that has the earliest due date. This rule ignores when the jobs arrive and the amount of operation time each of them requires.
- Shortest processing time (SPT). The job that can be completed in the shortest time at this work center is processed next. The jobs' due dates and order of arrival are immaterial.

- Truncated shortest processing time (TSPT). This rule is the same as the SPT rule, except that the jobs that have waited longer than some designated truncation time are given highest priority and are processed next.
- Least slack (LS). This rule calculates the slack of each awaiting job and gives highest priority to the one having the least slack. Slack is the time remaining until its due date minus the duration of the operation time for the job. The order of arrival is ignored with this rule.
- Critical ratio (CR). This is a dynamic rule that updates priorities as time elapses using the following comparative ratio for each job:

$$CR = \frac{\text{time remaining}}{\text{work remaining}} = \frac{\text{due date} - \text{today's date}}{\text{days needed to complete the job}}$$

A low critical ratio indicates a high urgency (priority) for processing the job to avoid getting further behind schedule.

Let's examine some of these rules to illustrate how they work and to become more familiar with their terminology. We'll apply them to the five job orders awaiting sheet metal operations in the aircraft repair facility we discussed earlier. Customers submitted these job orders during the past week. As sheet metal supervisor you must decide on the processing sequence through your department. Rather than evaluating all of the 5! or 120 different possible sequences for these five jobs, you've decided to evaluate the sequences created by the FCFS, SPT, and CR rules.

First-come-first-served (FCFS) Sequencing In a sense of fairness to the customers, you decide to use a first-come-first-served (FCFS) sequencing rule. Say that job orders arrived alphabetically, and that customers requested that their sheet metal work be completed at the times listed under "due date" in Table 12.1.

TABLE 12.1
Sequencing data for a first-come-first-serve (FCFS) priority rule

Job sequence	Job operation time (days)	Job flow time	Job due date
A	4	4	6
B	17	21	20
C	14	35	18
D	9	44	12
E	11	55	12
	55		

The "job flow time" for this processing sequence measures the length of time each job spends in the system to complete that job. Thus, flow time includes waiting time and processing time for each unit. Job *B*, for example, waits 4 days while *A* is being processed and then takes 17 days operation time itself. Job *B* is therefore to be completed in 21 days, its flow time.

Our FCFS sequencing rule will result in the following:

1. *Total completion time.* All jobs will have been completed in 55 days.
2. *Average completion time.* The average number of days a job spends in the system is 31.8. This figure is calculated by summing the flow times for all jobs and dividing by the number of jobs:

$$(4 + 21 + 35 + 44 + 55)/5 = 31.8$$

3. *Average number of jobs in the system.* The average number of jobs in the system from the beginning of the sequence through the time when the last job is finished is 2.89. For the first 4 days, 5 jobs are in the system; for the next 17 days, 4 jobs are in the system; for days 22 to 35, 3 jobs are in the system, and so forth. There are 55 total days for the sequence. Hence,

$$[5(4) + 4(17) + 3(14) + 2(9) + 1(11)]/55$$
$$= 2.89 \text{ jobs per day in the system}$$

4. *Average job lateness.* The average lateness of the jobs is 18.6 days. The lateness for each job is obtained by comparing its flow time with its due date. Thus, job *A* is completed at day 4; since its due date is day 6, there's no lateness. Job *B* is completed at day 21, and its due date is day 20; this job is one day late. Similarly, lateness for jobs *C*, *D*, and *E* is 17, 32, and 43 days. Average lateness is:

$$(0 + 1 + 17 + 32 + 43)/5 = 18.6 \text{ days}$$

The FCFS sequencing rule has the advantage of simplicity, and in some respects it provides a sense of "fair play" from the customer's viewpoint. However, some other rules are more desirable from the productive system's viewpoint.

Shortest Processing Time (SPT) Consider the "shortest processing time" (SPT) rule: sequence the orders according to processing time, and assign highest priority to the order with the shortest processing time.

The SPT rule yields the data in Table 12.2 and the following performance by using the sequence *A, D, E, C, B:*

1. *Total completion time.* All jobs will have been completed in 55 days.
2. *Average completion time.* The sum of flow times is (4 + 13 + 24 + 38 + 55) = 134. Average completion time is 134/5 = 26.8 days.
3. *Average number of jobs in the system.* Over the entire span of 55 days, 5 jobs are in the system (waiting or being processed) for 4 days while job *A* is being

TABLE 12.2
Sequencing data for a shortest processing time (SPT) priority rule

Job sequence	Job operation time (days)	Job flow time	Job due date
A	4	4	6
D	9	13	12
E	11	24	12
C	14	38	18
B	17	55	20

processed; 4 jobs are in the system while job *D* is being processed for 9 days, and so on. Thus, the average number of jobs in the system each day is:

$$[5(4) + 4(9) + 3(11) + 2(14) + 1(17)]/55$$
$$= 2.44 \text{ jobs}$$

4. *Average job lateness.* The days late for each job in this sequence are 0, 1, 12, 20, and 35 days, respectively. Average lateness is:

$$(0 + 1 + 12 + 20 + 35)/5 = 13.6 \text{ days}$$

When we compare the performance of the two rules, we see that SPT is superior. Although total completion time is 55 days for both sequences, SPT offers a lower average completion time. This means that inventories are tied up to a lesser extent, and quicker service can be provided to customers. With SPT, the average number of jobs in the system is reduced; this reduction can lead to less shop congestion and lower inventory levels. Finally, since average lateness in deliveries to customers is reduced, overall service is improved.

The superior performance of the SPT rule in our example was not an accident. For jobs to be processed in one work center, it is consistently superior to other rules; it is optimal for minimizing average completion time, average number of jobs in the system, and average job lateness.

Critical Ratio (CR) In comparison with the previous rules, the critical ratio rule has two distinguishing features: 1. it considers job due dates, and 2. the priorities are dynamic—they change daily. The dynamic priorities are apparent in Table 12.3 where the CR rule has been applied at two points in time.

The CR calculations at time 0 gave top priority to job *E* and, after completing that job on day 11, priorities were recalculated for the remaining four jobs. Notice that the sequences of the remaining jobs have changed

TABLE 12.3
Critical ratio sequences at two points in time

Time 0 (now):

Job	(1) Operation time	(2) Due date	(3) Time remaining (due date − today's date)	(4) Critical ratio: (3) ÷ (1)	(5) Sequence
A	4	6	6	1.500	5
B	17	20	20	1.176	2
C	14	18	18	1.286	3
D	9	12	12	1.333	4
E	11	12	12	1.091	1*

*next job to be processed (estimated completion = day 11)

Time 11:

Job	(1) Operation time	(2) Due date	(3) Time remaining (due date − today's date)	(4) Critical ratio: (3) ÷ (1)	(5) Sequence
A	4	6	−5	− 1.250	1*
B	17	20	9	0.529	4
C	14	18	7	0.500	3
D	9	12	1	0.111	2

*next job to be processed (estimated completion = day 15)

during this lapse of time. If we continue to update the priorities in this manner after completing the most urgent job at each stage, the jobs finally would be processed as shown in Table 12.4.

Characteristics of the Rules Among the six rules cited earlier, only three—EDD, LS, CR—are *due date* based. This feature is especially useful in MRP scheduling systems because the MRP outputs identify scheduled receipts in weekly or even daily time periods that become the due dates for batches of component items. Furthermore, the CR rule's dynamic feature is compatible with the frequent updating that occurs in MRP-based systems; when schedules are updated, MRP determines new due dates of the related subcomponents and, accordingly, their priorities change at the various work centers. The current priorities can be disseminated on daily dispatch sheets at relevant work centers throughout the manufacturing facility.

Sequencing Through Multiple Work Centers

Our discussion of sequencing, up to this point, has focused on processing jobs through a single work center and, for this simple problem, optimal analytical solutions are possible. Most facilities, however, aren't faced with having several jobs to be processed at a single work center; they have many jobs to be done on multiple (often as many as a hundred) centers. Further, not all jobs are going to follow identical routings; some pass through a few

TABLE 12.4
Sequencing data for critical ratio (CR) priority rule

Job sequence	Job operation time	Job flow time	Job due date
E	11	11	12
A	4	15	6
D	9	24	12
C	14	38	18
B	17	58	20

Total completion time: 55 days
Average completion time: 28.6 days
Average number of jobs in system: 2.6 jobs/day
Average job lateness: 15.2 days

work centers, but others pass through many. As jobs arrive at facilities in a variety of patterns, they are routed diversely. Thus the composition of waiting jobs at a work center may change continuously, and priority sequencing becomes a dynamic ongoing process.

For instances like these, optimal analytic solution procedures do not exist. One approach by mathematicians and operations researchers has been to apply queueing theory to jobs as they form waiting lines (queues) in advance of being served (processed). The strength of queueing theory is that it provides optimal solutions. Application of queueing theory is severely limited because the mathematical complexity becomes insurmountable once such assumptions as arrival times and service times are relaxed from a few well-known distributions (exponential and Poisson, for example) to more realistic empirical distributions. Queueing theory is not advanced enough to handle the complex job shops encountered in reality. Instead computer simulation techniques have been used to test the effectiveness of various sequencing rules in these complex situations.

Simulation of Intermittent (Job Shop) Systems

The basic procedures of simulation we discussed in the supplement to Chapter 3 can be used to evaluate various sequencing rules in job shop facilities. The following outline shows the components and procedures that would be included in a simulation approach to modeling an intermittent system.

1. *Shop configuration.* The number of work centers in the shop must be specified in the model.
2. *Job arrivals.* One segment, or module, of the model is needed to generate the arrivals of new jobs entering the system. The pattern and timing of simulated arrivals can be based on historical patterns previously experienced by the

facility. During the simulation, the Monte Carlo technique can be used to select at random the time of the next job arrival based on the data pattern supplied by the simulation designer.

3. *Job classification*. Once a new job arrives, its processing requirements or routing must be established. Again, historical data can reveal patterns of processing (routing) requirements that may be built into the model. When a new simulated job arrives, its routing is determined in the simulator, using the Monte Carlo technique.
4. *Processing times*. In the simulator, the time required to process a job at a work center can be determined based on historical service time patterns supplied by the simulation designer. Often, the service (processing) time for a job is randomly selected from a service time distribution that is representative of that work center. The Monte Carlo technique is used for this purpose.
5. *Specification of shop performance parameters*. The designer specifies the shop performance characteristics of interest. Such statistics might include percent of idle time at each center, length of job queues throughout the system, average waiting times for jobs, value of inventories in process, measures of job lateness, and measures of job flow times through the system.
6. *Specification of sequencing rule*. The priority sequencing rule to be tested is selected and built into the model.
7. *Simulation*. The simulation is conducted over time (this is called a simulation run). It is executed by generating new job arrival times, determining their routings, loading them to the appropriate work centers, sequencing them by use of the priority rule, and creating the representative service times for each job at each center. This simulation is done for a large number of job arrivals, say 10,000 or more. When a job is finished at one center, it is placed in the waiting line at the next center in its routing to await processing there. When a work center finishes one job, it is free to begin servicing one of the jobs in its waiting line. The awaiting job with highest priority (based on the sequencing rule) is selected for processing next on the open work center.
8. *Recording shop performance parameters*. After all jobs have been processed, the resulting shop performance statistics are recorded and saved for later evaluation and comparison. The simulation run has been completed.
9. *Replication*. At this point, the original sequencing rule can be replaced with an alternative rule in the model. Then, with all other model components unchanged, the simulation can be repeated. The shop performance characteristics from the second run can be compared with those of the first run to determine which of the two sequencing rules performs better. Systematic replications can be made for any number of different rules.

Simulation offers advantages for evaluating system performance as compared to tampering directly with the job-shop itself. First, live testing of a priority rule in a real-world system would require that it be used for an extensive period of time, for months or even years. To test several rules, one would need a prohibitive length of time for valid comparison. Computer models can simulate many years of operation in a matter of seconds or minutes. Second, if different priority rules were studied in the real system for long periods of time, it would be difficult to determine the effects of the different rules. Why? Because the performance characteristics of a real system could be caused by many factors and events other than just the priority rule. Variations in people, equipment, communications systems, organizational structure, and numerous other elements cause system performance to change from time to time. If such factors cause performance to improve, the change might be erroneously interpreted to be the result of a newly implemented priority rule. Simulation models help avoid such misinterpretations by controlling for these extraneous factors. The only variable that changes from one simulation run to the next is the priority rule being used. Thus, any differences in performance are due solely to the priority rules.

Let's briefly review some simulation results for complex intermittent systems in which various sequencing rules were evaluated for job completion time, job lateness, and inventory levels.

Simulation Results for Job Completion Time One study tested ten different priority dispatching rules in six different job shop configurations using computer simulation.[1] The results are based on processing over two million simulated jobs through the system. Our main interest in the results has to do with the *job completion* characteristics of the rules, an important concern to shop managers.

Job completion time is commonly measured in two ways: as the *average* processing or flow time of jobs through the system; and as the *dispersion* of job flow times through the system (measured by a standard deviation or variance). Ideally, one would desire a system with small measures on both dimensions. This would mean that a given volume of jobs would pass quickly through the system, giving good customer service, reducing in-process inventories, and freeing the facility for processing a larger volume of new customer orders.

The simulation study found, among the ten rules that were tested, that average (mean) flow time per job was lowest (0.99) for the SPT rule, and for the other rules it was as high as 2.54. The standard deviation of flow time ranged from 1.55 to 5.43 for the various rules. Although the standard deviation of flow time was lower for two of the other rules, SPT did well on this dimension also. These results are not surprising when you consider how the SPT rule works. Since the job selected for processing next is the one with the smallest expected completion time, this job doesn't have to wait long in the queue; its flow time (waiting plus processing time) is low. After all the low-time jobs are processed, those with intermediate times are processed. As you can see, jobs with long processing times are continually given low priority and consequently have long waiting times. Eventually, after the quicker jobs are processed, the jobs with long processing times are worked off, but only after considerable waiting time. As a result of these long waits, some of these jobs accumulate a very long flow time. Overall, then, this causes a somewhat higher standard deviation of flow times than

[1]See Y. R. Nanot, "An Experimental Investigation and Comparative Evaluation of Priority Disciplines in Job Shop-Like Queueing Networks" (Ph. D. diss., UCLA, 1963).

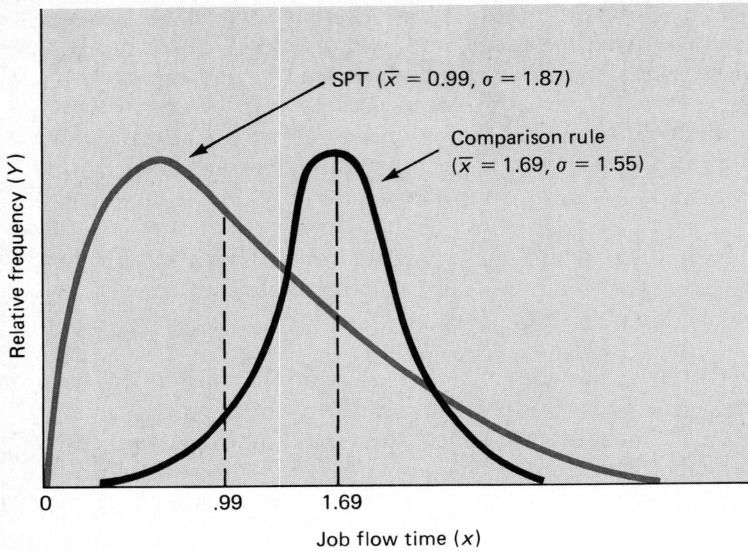

FIGURE 12.5
Comparative forms of flow time distributions for SPT rule and a comparison rule

might be desired. This system behavior is portrayed visually in Figure 12.5. In the figure, two good rules are compared. SPT has the lower mean flow time but a higher variance as is shown by the standard deviation about the mean (the wider distribution).

An additional result from the study is the flow time of the first-come-first-served (FCFS) rule that is often used in service facilities. In a sense, FCFS offers "fairness" to the customer. The results indicate, however, that it leads to higher average flow times and a higher dispersion as well, so the customer doesn't fare so well as one might think.

In another simulation study, the truncated SPT was tested in an attempt to overcome SPT's high dispersion of flow times.[2] The analysts proposed and tested truncation rules as follows: "Apply the SPT rule as usual unless a job ends up waiting longer than x time periods to be processed; then give that job top priority." The value for x is set by management. What this does is to interrupt occasionally the normal SPT processing sequence to "work in" jobs that would otherwise continue to wait in line. It helps to avoid the otherwise extremely long flow times possible with the simple SPT. What happens as a result? The standard deviation of flow time gets smaller, as expected. However, average job flow time becomes longer, an undesirable feature in many shops. This result suggests that in choosing between the simple and truncated SPT, the operations manager should consider which is most desired, low average flow time or low dispersion of flow time.

---

[2]This work is reported by R. W. Conway and W. L. Maxwell, "Network Scheduling by the Shortest Operation Discipline," *Operations Research* 10, no. 1 (1962), pp. 51–73.

Simulation Results for Job Lateness and Work-in-process Inventories Using a computer simulation, another researcher examined how well thirty-nine different priority rules performed in terms of job lateness and in-process inventories in the facility.[3] We merely summarize some of the major results here. In terms of percentage of jobs late (that is, jobs not completed by due date), SPT performed far better than most other rules tested. Occasionally, under a few selected conditions, another rule was slightly better than SPT, but overall, SPT was better than the others.

There are several ways of measuring work-in-process. The total number of jobs in the shop is sometimes used as a measure. Another is the total work content, the sum of all processing times for all jobs in the shop. Using several measures of work-in-process, this same study found that the SPT rule was not optimal for minimizing work-in-process, although its performance was still relatively good. The optimal rules are called "compound rules." They require somewhat more complex calculations than does the SPT rule. These compound rules are a weighted combination of the SPT and other rules, all combined into one.[4] In short, the SPT, although not optimal, performed well, and it did so without requiring the extensive calculations necessary in the more complex rules.

Sequencing Procedures for Other Criteria

Some additional sequencing procedures are available for more specialized situations. First we'll examine sequencing for situations where setup costs are the primary consideration; then we'll look at a procedure that minimizes the completion time for the last job through two successive work centers.

Setup Dependence Sometimes the dominant consideration at a work station is the setup, or changeover, cost for processing the different jobs.

Our previous examples assumed these costs to be negligible or independent of the job sequence. But this is not always the case. If a substantial setup cost is incurred, the scheduler will consider this factor, because minimizing overall setup costs for the sequence may be a major goal.

Table 12.5 shows that overall setup costs for the aircraft repair facility depend on the sequence in which the five jobs are processed. These data show the setup cost when job j is processed after job i. It assumes that job A is already being processed and jobs B, C, D, and E remain to be done.

---

[3]See R. W. Conway, "Priority Dispatching and Job Lateness in a Job Shop," *Journal of Industrial Engineering* 16, no. 4 (July–August 1965), pp. 228–37, and "Priority Dispatching and Work-in-Process Inventory in a Job Shop," *Journal of Industrial Engineering* 16, no. 2 (March–April 1965), pp. 123–30.

[4]For examples of combination rules see E. LeGrande, "The Development of a Factory Simulation Using Actual Operating Data," in *Readings in Production and Operations Management*, ed. E. S. Buffa (New York: John Wiley and Sons, Inc., 1966); also J. C. Hershauer and R. J. Ebert, "Search and Simulation Selection of a Job-Shop Sequencing Rule," *Management Science* 21, no. 7 (March 1975), pp. 833–43.

TABLE 12.5
Matrix of setup costs

		Follower Job j				
		A	B	C	D	E
Predecessor Job i	A	\$0	\$29	\$20	\$18	\$24
	B	0	0	14	19	15
	C	0	35	0	37	26
	D	0	15	10	0	10
	E	0	18	16	40	0

If we choose job B to follow A, a high setup cost (\$29) is incurred. If job D follows A, the setup cost is only \$18. Which sequence of all jobs minimizes total setup costs?

Although optimal solution techniques exist for solving small-scale problems of this type, they are often not feasible for larger size real-world problems. Of more practical value are some heuristic approaches.

The Next Best Rule (NB) One such heuristic, the "next best rule" (NB) states, "Given that job i is being processed, select next the unassigned job j for which setup cost is minimum." For example, if job A is currently being processed, job D would be selected next, since it has the lowest setup cost following job A. After job D, job C or E (\$10 setup cost) would be selected next. The NB rule would yield two sequences:

Sequence	Cost
NB_1: A–D–C–E–B	\$18 + 10 + 26 + 18 = \$72
NB_2: A–D–E–C–B	\$18 + 10 + 16 + 35 = 79

NB_1 is preferred, since its cost is lower than NB_2. This NB_1 sequence is not optimal. An enumeration of all 24 possible sequences shows that the optimal sequence is $A - D - E - B - C$, with a cost of \$60. However, NB_1 may be considered *satisfactory*, especially if we were dealing with larger problems for which complete enumeration of all alternatives was not feasible.

In this example, sequence NB_2 happens to be identical to the SPT (shortest processing time) sequence. In general, however, the NB and SPT sequences are not expected to coincide. If they do not, you must choose between the two rules. Your choice will depend on the relative importance you place on costs of machine setup (NB) as opposed to the value of gaining overall shop effectiveness (SPT).

Sequencing Through Two Work Centers Imagine that you have a set of awaiting jobs, all of which have to be processed through two successive work centers. If you wish to sequence the jobs so as to minimize the completion time for the last job through the process, an optimal procedure for doing so is available.

Suppose the five jobs, *A* through *E*, in the aircraft repair facility must each pass through the sheetmetal center and then through the paint center. We wish to find the sequence that minimizes completion time of the last job. The processing time (PT) for each job in each center is shown in Table 12.6.

Since there are five jobs, there will be five positions in the processing sequence. These steps tell how to allocate the jobs to the five positions in the sequence:

1. Determine the minimum of all the processing times, PT_{ij}.
2. If the minimum PT_{ij} is associated with work center 1, place the corresponding job in the earliest available position in the sequence; if the minimum PT_{ij} is associated with work center 2, place the corresponding job in the latest remaining position in the sequence.
3. Cross out both times of the job just assigned to omit that job from further consideration. Cross out the PT_{ij} for the job i just assigned, across all work centers, j.
4. Now return to step 1 and repeat the procedure by identifying the minimum of all remaining PT_{ij}.

Using the data from Table 12.6, the assignments proceed as follows:

1. PT_{D2} is the minimum, 2 days.
2. Since PT_{D2} is associated with center 2, job *D* is assigned to the last (5th) position in the sequence.

TABLE 12.6
Processing times (in days) for jobs in 2 work centers*

Job	Work center 1 (sheet metal)	Work center 2 (paint)
A	4	5
B	17	7
C	14	12
D	9	2
E	11	6

*PT_{ij} = processing time of job i in center j, where i = A, B, C, D, E and j = 1, 2.

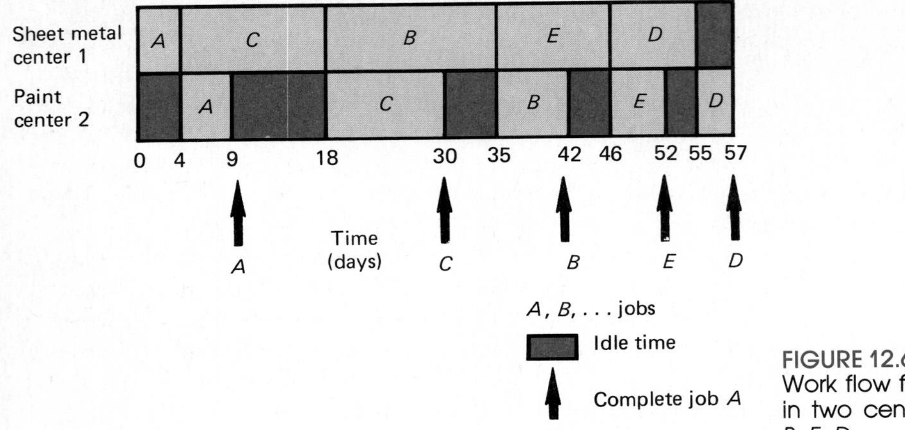

FIGURE 12.6
Work flow for sequencing five jobs in two centers in sequence A–C–B–E–D

3. Since job D has been assigned, its times are crossed out and only jobs A, B, C, and E require further consideration.
4. (Return to step 1). Of the remaining eight PT_{ij}, $PT_{A1} = 4$ is the smallest. Since it is associated with center 1, job A is assigned to position 1 in the sequence. Then the times for job A are crossed out, and only jobs B, C, and E have yet to be assigned to remaining positions 2, 3, and 4 in the sequence.
5. (Repeat). Of the remaining six PT_{ij}, $PT_{E2} = 6$ is minimum. Since it is associated with center 2, job E is assigned to the last available position in the sequence (position 4).

Continuing in this manner, we find that the desired sequence turns out to be $A - C - B - E - D$. The time-phased flow of this job sequence is shown graphically in Figure 12.6. Completion of job D, the last job in the sequence, occurs in 57 days, the minimum.

It is important to remember that this rule applies when all jobs must be processed *in the same order on both work centers*, first on center 1, then on center 2.

In concluding our coverage of sequencing, you should note two of its overriding features. First, an abundance of sequencing methods is available and they can affect shop performance in different ways. Second, in choosing among these methods you should carefully evaluate them in terms of the criteria that are of greatest importance for your organization's competitive posture.

DETAILED SCHEDULING

Having discussed the loading and sequencing levels of intermittent systems scheduling, let's now examine how the supplementary scheduling is accomplished. This process provides the detailed schedule required by operating personnel so that they know when to start what job and when it should be finished. This involves a myriad of daily, hour-by-hour, and minute-by-minute activities to initiate machine setups and changeovers, make job assignments to workers, keep track of actual starts and completions before reassigning workers, and otherwise adjusting resources to compensate for late arrivals of subcomponents, equipment failures, or poor quality. To help handle some of this confusion, many practitioners find that simple graphical scheduling aids, such as the Gantt chart, are beneficial.

Gantt Scheduling Charts We previously showed a Gantt load chart. Another version of the Gantt chart can be helpful for visualizing detailed scheduling of orders. Figure 12.7 is an example; it shows one possible processing schedule for jobs *A* through *E* in the aircraft repair facility. Each pair of brackets denotes on the time scale the estimated beginning and ending of the activity enclosed within it at each work center. The solid bars beneath the brackets show the cumulative work loads that currently exist at each work center. The hydraulics center, for example, has a scheduled load of 26 days of work, 12 days for job *C* and 14 days for job *E*. The sheet metal center faces the heaviest scheduled load, 55 days. This 55-day load, however, is spread over a time span of 76 days. Why? First, because job *D* cannot be started in sheet metal until it is finished in electronics on day 67. Thus, days 49 through 67 are currently scheduled to be idle, or open and available for new jobs, in the sheet metal center. Second, two days of setup or changeover time are scheduled in sheet metal. After job *A* is com-

FIGURE 12.7
Gantt chart for order scheduling (job sequence: *A–C–B–E–D*)

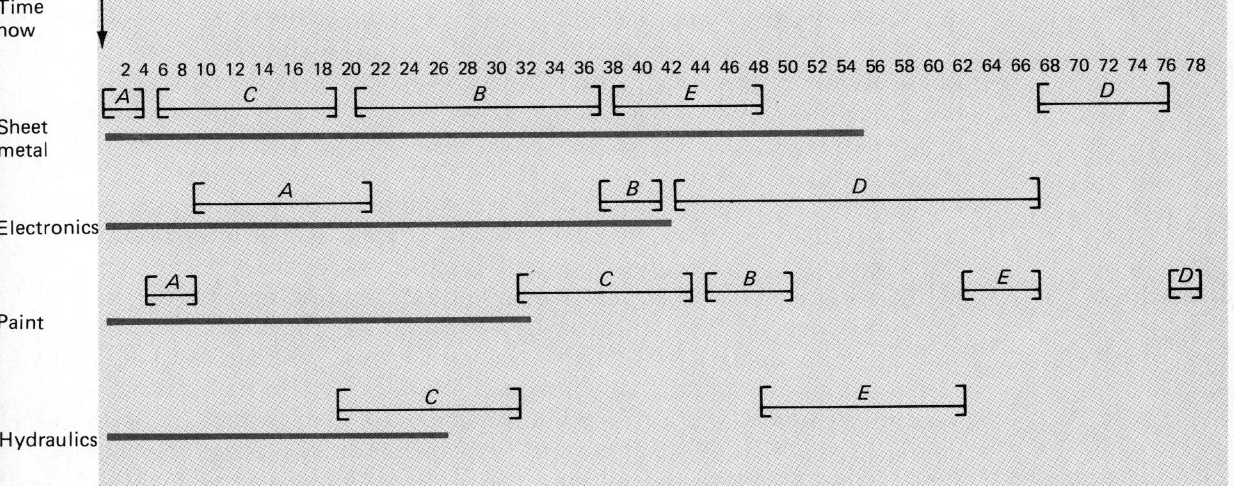

pleted, one day of setup is required in preparation for job C. Overall, then, 55 days of job processing, two days of setup, and 19 days of idle time constitute the 76-day sheet metal schedule. As work is completed, the "Time now" arrow moves to the right, and a heavier or color-coded line may be used between the schedule brackets to denote work actually accomplished. Scheduled and completed work can thus be compared.

In practice, many refinements of this charting procedure are used. The chart may be updated daily to show which orders are behind, ahead of, or on schedule, and why. Updating assists in monitoring the progress of orders, points out bottleneck operations, records reasons for progress interruptions (lack of appropriate materials, delays due to tool trouble, delays from improper operator performance, and so on), provides a basis for accurate progress reports to customers, in some situations indicates the need for last-minute shifting of work loads from some departments to others, and signals the need for working overtime when completion schedules do not conform to requirements.

FINITE LOADING

Finite loading is an alternative scheduling technique that combines into a single system the loading, prioritizing, and detailed scheduling activities that we discussed individually above. In contrast to infinite loading, finite loading systems start with a specified capacity level for each work center and a listing of potential work orders (jobs). The work center's capacity is then allocated unit-by-unit (e.g., labor hours) to the work orders by simulating job starting times and completion times. Thus, the system creates a detailed schedule for each job order and each work center based on the centers' finite capacity limits. Jobs are allocated to the centers according to their capacities hour-by-hour and day-by-day into the future. The resulting finite capacity load profile would resemble the one shown in Figure 12.8.

The priority sequencing rule is built into the simulator. Since inputs to the simulator (say, from an MRP system) specify job due dates (not start times nor completion times), the jobs can be loaded using either a forward or a backward scheduling procedure, as we see next.

Forward Scheduling

Forward (or set forward) scheduling is commonly used in job shops where customers place their orders on a "needed as soon as possible" basis. Forward scheduling determines start and finish times for the next priority job by inserting it into the *earliest* available time slot and, from that time, determines when the job will be finished in that work center. Since the job and its components start as early as possible, they will typically be completed before they are due at subsequent work centers in the routing. Consequently, the set-forward procedure accumulates in-process inventories that sit throughout the facility until they're needed at subsequent stations. While these excessive inventories are a drawback, forward scheduling is

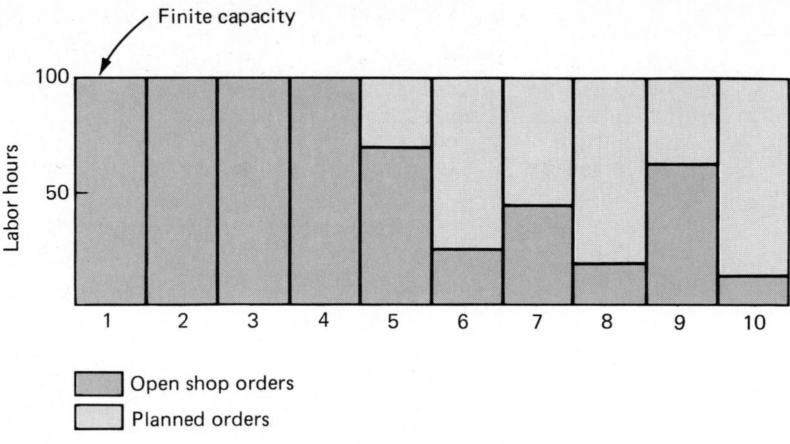

FIGURE 12.8
Finite capacity load profile

simple to use and it gets jobs done in shorter leadtimes, overall, than does the backward scheduling procedure.

Backward (Set Backward) Scheduling

Another method, often used in assembly-type industries and in job shops that commit in advance to specific delivery dates, is the backward scheduling procedure. It inserts the next priority job into the *latest* open time slot that will enable its completion just when it is due, but not before. Then the job's start time is determined by setting back from this finish date. By scheduling jobs and parts as late as possible, the backward procedure minimizes inventories since the components aren't produced until they're needed by subsequent work stations. To gain these inventory efficiencies, however, a price is paid; bills of materials and leadtime estimates must be accurately maintained for all work centers or else the system breaks down—due dates are violated and delivery service to customers deteriorates.

EXAMPLE

The Hi-speed Machining Company has received two job orders, A and B, both of which require processing at machines I and II. The first-come-first-served rule is used to assign priorities to jobs which are coded alphabetically as to their order of arrival. The operations sequences are given below in the routings for the two jobs, both of which are due after 8 hours. Each machine is available for 8 hours every day and no other jobs are currently scheduled on them. Develop schedules for the jobs using the forward and backward procedures.

Route sheet: Job A			Route sheet: Job B		
Operations sequence	Machine	Operation time (hours)	Operations sequence	Machine	Operation time (hours)
1	I	2	1	I	2
2	II	3	2	II	3
3	I	1			

The forward technique first schedules top-priority job A as early as possible; its first operation is for 2 hours on machine I (as circled in Figure 12.9). Then it is scheduled in hours 3 to 5 on machine II. Job A finishes on machine I in hour 6, its earliest possible finish time. Next job B is scheduled into the remaining open times as early as possible. First it goes into machine I in hours 3 and 4. Then its second operation, on machine II, is scheduled for hours 6 through 8.

The backward technique starts by scheduling the highest priority job so that it finishes at its due time. Therefore, job A's latest operation is scheduled into machine I for hour 8. Then its preceding operation is scheduled as late as possible, hours 5 through 7 in machine II. Similarly, operation 1 is scheduled for hours 3 and 4 in machine I for job A. Now job B is scheduled for its last operation, at machine II, in hours 8, 4, and 3. Its first operation is then assigned to machine I for hours 1 and 2.

You can see that the two procedures yielded entirely different sched-

FIGURE 12.9
Forward and backward schedules for Hi-speed Machining Company

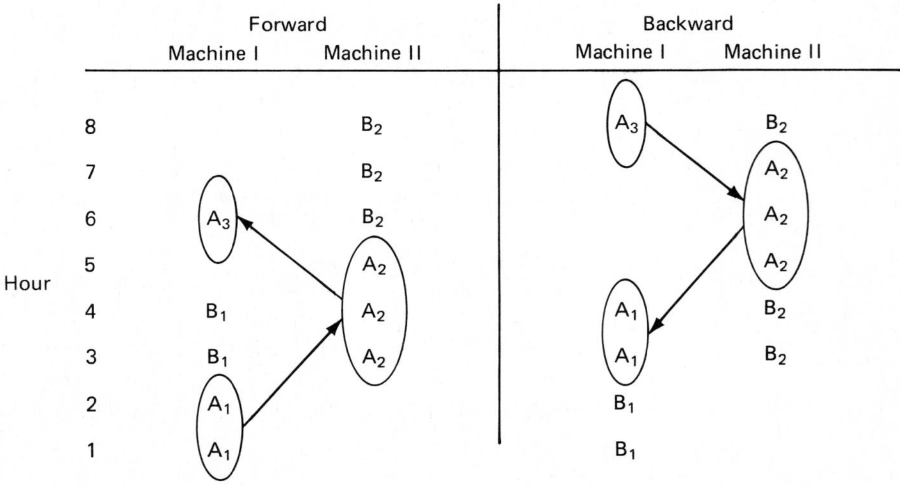

ules for the two machines. In this example both jobs can be completed by their due times but this often won't be the case and job lateness, especially for lower-priority jobs, will be the result. In our forward schedule, excess inventories accumulate; job A finishes two hours early and the first operation on job B finishes one hour before it is needed at machine II. In the backward schedule job B is interrupted at machine II after hour 4 to allow the higher-priority job A to pass through. Then job B resumes in hour 8.

Using Finite Versus Infinite Loading

Finite loading has some drawbacks that lead its critics to conclude that it is an inappropriate shop floor control technique. Its planned schedules for the work centers often become obsolete from unanticipated materials delays and inaccurate processing time estimates at feeder work centers. Consequently, the finite loading simulation has to be rerun (updated) frequently and these run costs are much greater than the low costs of sequencing by priority rules for infinite loading systems. Advocates of finite loading, however, claim they get more accurate capacity load estimates for the very short term, the next few days, than they get from the infinite loading-sequencing-detailed scheduling procedure.

EXPEDITING

Let's say that we have accomplished all the activities we've discussed so far. We have finished loading, sequencing, and detailed scheduling. But we are not done yet. Disruptions may prohibit our plans from being implemented to some extent. Necessary materials or manpower may not be available at the right times as planned; equipment may break down; a particularly important customer may desire special treatment. Any of these and other contingencies may cause disruptions and result in rescheduling, a form of corrective action that is part of the *control* process.

Often, the progress and status of each job are monitored as it flows through the system. If the progress of a job is unsatisfactory, the job may be *expedited*. Special attention is devoted to it, and priorities may be shifted at work centers to "hustle the job through" ahead of others. Supervisors are notified in advance that the job is coming and is to be given special treatment. Materials needed to do the job may be obtained from suppliers on a special-order basis instead of waiting for receipt of a routine shipment. All this monitoring, special procurement, and advance notification of shop personnel is often done by one person, the expeditor, who is responsible for seeing this particular job through to completion. Certainly expediting is sometimes necessary; but caution should be exercised lest it tend to be overused. Some intermittent shops have been known gradually to increase the use of expediting to the point where most of the jobs are considered "hot jobs" requiring expediting, and attention is given only to "hot hot" lists. Confusion, shop congestion, and inefficiencies are magnified as a result.

INPUT-OUTPUT (SHORT-TERM CAPACITY) CONTROL

Control reports from input-output analysis are helpful for monitoring each work center's performance. It enables us to evaluate over time how well the available capacity is being utilized. In Table 12.7, labor-hour requirements for new jobs into the work center for each week were recorded in the first row as "planned input." Management planned to place these new demands on the work center based on the scheduling system's planned orders and scheduled receipts. After four weeks of operation we see that the actual inputs of new jobs turned out to coincide with the planned amounts.

The work center's "planned output" is the weekly work rate (hours of capacity to be expended) that was chosen by management. In Table 12.7 we see that planned outputs exceed planned inputs, reflecting management's intentions to decrease the work center's backlog, week-by-week, from the beginning level of 300 units at week 0 down to 100 units (labor hours) by week 4.

Actual output has deviated from the planned amounts in each week; this is normal. The deviations may occur for such reasons as poor product quality, low or high productivity, materials shortages, equipment breakdowns, and so on. As a result, we see that the actual backlogs deviate somewhat from the planned levels, but they are reasonably on target. With this input-output monitoring we can evaluate the matchup of input and output rates and adjust them to achieve the desired backlog levels.

TABLE 12.7
Input-output report for work center 100 (report prepared after week 4)

	Standard hours per week				
	1	2	3	4	5
Planned input	400	350	350	300	300
Actual input	400	350	350	300	
Cumulative deviation (actual-planned)	0	0	0	0	
Planned output	450	400	400	350	300
Actual output	440	410	405	330	
Cumulative deviation (actual-planned)	− 10	0	+5	−15	
Planned backlog	250	200	150	100	100
Actual backlog	260	200	145	115	

Backlog at time 0 = 300 units

OPTIMIZED PRODUCTION TECHNOLOGY

An alternative to the production planning and scheduling approaches previously presented in this chapter is OPT (Optimized Production Technology). OPT is a computer-based system for planning production, materials needs, and resource utilization. It was first introduced in the United States in 1979 by Creative Output Inc., a consulting firm in Milford, CT.[5] The key feature of OPT is its emphasis on carefully utilizing bottleneck work centers (people or machines) in shop operations. The OPT philosophy recognizes that managing bottlenecks is the key to successful performance; total system output can be maximized and in-process inventories can be reduced.

The OPT software consists of four modules: (1) BUILDNET; (2) SERVE; (3) SPLIT; and (4) OPT. The starting module, BUILDNET, creates a product network that identifies the shop situation. It includes definitions of how each product is made (its buildup sequence, bill of materials, and routing through the shop), the product's time requirements (setup, runtime, schedule delay), the capacity availability of each resource (work center, machine, worker), and the order quantities and due-dates of work orders in the shop.

The initial purpose of SERVE is to create a tentative processing schedule for the awaiting jobs in the shop; later, it creates a more refined schedule. Using the data from BUILDNET, SERVE's initial analysis uses a backward scheduling procedure, assuming infinite resource capacity, based on the due-dates of job orders. The crucial information obtained from this initial schedule is an estimate of the percentage utilization of the various shop resources.

The SPLIT module separates critical from noncritical resources based on their percentage utilizations in the initial schedule. Resources that are near or above 100 percent utilization are the bottleneck operations. These bottlenecks, and the operations that follow them in the product buildup sequence, are the "critical" operations; all others (those with lower percentage utilizations) are "noncritical."

The OPT module re-schedules the critical part of the network using a forward scheduling procedure that considers the finite capacities of resources. This reveals when the various jobs and materials should be available at the critical work stations.

After the critical part of the network is scheduled (in the OPT module described above), the procedure cycles back to the SERVE module to reschedule the noncritical resources (work centers or machines). Now, how-

[5]See F. R. Jacobs, "OPT Uncovered: Many Production Planning and Scheduling Concepts Can be Applied With or Without the Software," *Industrial Engineering* (October 1984), pp. 32–41. See also R. E. Fox, "OPT—An Answer for America—Part IV," *Inventories & Production* 3, no. 2 (March/April 1983).

ever, SERVE schedules the noncritical activities to meet the due-times that were determined by OPT for the critical activities. This ensures that the supporting, noncritical activities are finished in time to keep the critical activities moving along as scheduled. The feeder activities and safety stocks are geared to supply adequate materials flows without delays in order to fully utilize critical operations. The orientation is towards careful use of critical activities first and, thereafter, the use of noncritical activities to serve and support the critical ones.

One special feature of the OPT procedure is its use of variable batch sizing to schedule production through critical work centers. Each job order (lot) is broken into several smaller lots called "transfer" batches. Once a transfer batch is processed, it can be sent on to the next operation without having to wait for completion of the original, larger job order. Succeeding operations can progress and idleness is avoided. This lot-splitting and overlapping of batches yields high (100 percent) utilization of bottleneck operations and lower variability in operation times. Then, when multiple transfer batches of the same job order arrive at the bottleneck, they can all be run together to save the cost of multiple setups.

The OPT package consists not just of software, but of consulting services and training for implementation as well. The specific details of the procedure, especially of SERVE and OPT (the detailed scheduling modules), are proprietary (not published and available to the general public). Consequently, detailed comparative evaluations of its performance with that of other systems are not available. However, claims of success by Creative Output Inc. and an increasing number of users indicate that OPT is a useful, state-of-the-art system that will see more widespread applications in the future.

SELECTED BEHAVIORAL ELEMENTS IN INTERMITTENT SYSTEMS

Operations managers are keenly aware of some prominent behavioral considerations in intermittent systems. These factors are *part of* the system, and they arise from two sources: the sheer technical complexities of having large numbers of jobs at various stages of completion, and the organization of and role relationships in the system. Although these two sources of behavioral considerations are interrelated, we will consider them separately.

Complexity of Job Status

When you must decide how to process a few jobs through a small number of work centers, your problem is manageable. When the number of jobs increases to hundreds or thousands, each with different routings among hundreds of processing stations, however, your problems are magnified many times. Not only must you process all these jobs, you want to satisfy customers with on-time deliveries, and you want to do so smoothly and efficiently. A single individual is incapable of accomplishing all this. Our limited mental capacities prohibit total awareness of current job status and how that status changes over time. For these reasons, the tools presented earlier have great value to managers of intermittent systems. Gantt load charts and scheduling charts, although simplistic in concept and appearance, serve as memory supplements. They graphically portray the load on the system (and system subcomponents) and the current and projected status of individual job orders.

For decision making, priority sequencing rules play a similar role. The existence of so many jobs and the enormous number of their possible processing sequences pose an unmanageable and continual decision-making problem for people's limited capabilities. We need a simplification process to reduce this decision problem to manageable proportions. By systematically applying priority rules, we get the simplified process we need. Although the rules do not ensure optimal system performance, they do help achieve satisfactory performance, and they are usually better than alternative approaches, including human intuition.

System Organization and Role Relationships

A more pervasive set of problems emerges when one considers the entire intermittent system and the relationships among its subcomponents. The behaviors of individual employees, groups, and work centers or departments must all be integrated in an effective system. Some factors affecting these behaviors can be identified.

Individual Characteristics You may remember that intermittent systems, as compared to continuous flow systems, contain a high degree of task variety. Different types of employee skills and work orientations are necessary. Generally, jobs in intermittent systems are already "enlarged"; work content varies, and a higher degree of employee responsibility is emphasized in executing the tasks. Viewed another way, the variety of tasks in intermittent systems is a form of built-in job rotation, one of the methods proposed to enhance employee satisfaction. In hiring, managers seek employees who have high skill levels and who can work independently without a great deal of supervision. Once employees who are highly skilled and oriented with values of responsibility and occupational achievement have been hired, management must establish a working environment to encourage these individual orientations. Through monetary reward systems, by facilitating group relationships, and through various methods of allocating work among employees, management can create a working environment that enhances the security and fulfills the social needs of its employees. Fulfilling these needs increases motivation in job performance.

Group Characteristics In discussing facility layout (Chapter 8), we pointed out that intermittent systems consist of departments or work centers sharing common processes. A facility might have three departmental groupings consisting of machining, painting, and photography, for example. In these different departments are found different skill or craft groups, and group affiliations are often established. There are three reasons for these group affiliations: command structure, physical proximity, and shared craft interest. As a *formal* basis for group affiliation among machinists, for example, the organizational structures may specify that all machinists report to a machining foreman. Departmental members must communicate and interact with one another to some extent in accomplishing departmental tasks. Second, the physical proximity of machinists in the facility, since they usually work near one another, tends to facilitate interaction and communication, both work-related and personal. Since this is likely to occur on a regular basis, strong group bonds may form. Finally, the existence of an important shared interest, the craft or skill of the department employees, provides a basis for interaction. Unions facilitate this last affiliation; it is likely that in a unionized facility of any size, more than one union will represent differing groups of employees.

The existence of a work group has significant implications for the operations of the system. Although the employees in a group usually adopt a set of shared norms and strive toward satisfying member needs, the group goals may or may not be consistent with organizational goals. Group norms can strongly influence the kinds and amounts of productive activities of its members, especially in highly cohesive groups. When the goals of these cohesive groups are consistent with management's goals, the groups tend to produce at higher levels.[6] When group and management goals are at odds, however, lower productivity can be expected. The relationship between group goals and productivity is not so strong for groups with low cohesiveness.

Centralized versus Decentralized Decision Making An interesting question about employee motivation arises when we consider decentralized planning and scheduling systems versus those that are more centralized. The decentralized system provides an important dimension of managerial discretion for the first-line supervisor: *the supervisor decides which employees will work on which job orders.* This type of action prerogative doesn't exist in more centralized systems. In an environment in which wages are hourly and fixed, the decentralized system might be one of the few devices directly available to the supervisor for rewarding and motivating employees. In the more centralized systems, job assignments are often made on a relatively depersonalized basis by the production control center. Any gains from better interdepartmental coordination could be offset by losses in intradepartmental dissatisfaction and/or productivity.

A potential advantage of decentralized systems is the first-line supervisor's awareness of the local situation and how it might be matched with the work load. The supervisor is aware of employee and equipment capa-

[6]Stanley E. Seashore, *Group Cohesiveness in the Industrial Work Group* (Ann Arbor, Mich.: University of Michigan, Institute for Social Research, 1954).

bilities, individual needs, and group norms and values. Employees are easily motivated if their supervisor assigns them to jobs that fulfill their needs. In many companies, bargaining between subordinates and foremen for job assignments is a traditionally accepted interpersonal process. Without it, the prestige attributed to the supervisors' role and the respected craftsmen's esteem may both diminish. Unless other adjustments are made, the diminution of the process could lead to frustration and defensive behavior by supervisors and subordinates alike. Failure to recognize and incorporate behavioral dimensions like these into the design of the intermittent system can seriously damage its chances for efficient and effective operation.

SUMMARY

Intermittent systems have several distinctive characteristics. The types of processes, job orders, work flows, and human skills contrast sharply with those of continuous, or mass-production, systems. Generally, intermittent systems have to deal with diversified customer requests and irregular work flows. The intermittent scheduling process involves aggregate planning, master scheduling, materials planning, loading, priority sequencing, detailed scheduling, expediting, and input-output control.

Concentrating on shop floor control, we showed how infinite loading systems allocate incoming jobs to work centers and how Gantt charts and visual load profiles help evaluate current loadings. The assignment algorithm also was presented for loading in special circumstances. Then, the question of how to sequence jobs through the loaded work centers was considered. Some representative priority sequencing rules illustrated the sequencing problem and how the rules work, and clarified the terminology of sequencing. In addition, some techniques were given for sequencing in specialized situations. Simulation was discussed as a more general approach for evaluating alternative sequencing rules prior to selecting one for actual application. We saw how some rules performed well on selected dimensions but not so well on others. Then, the processes of detailed scheduling, expediting, and input-output control were described and linked together with the sequencing and loading processes.

Finite loading systems, those having integrated loading, sequencing, and detailed scheduling processes, were presented as an alternative to infinite systems. Finally, we concluded with some behavioral considerations of both individuals and groups for intermittent systems operation.

CASE

Newtone

In 1962 Bill Withers began to make custom furniture full time in his garage. Bill's work had been admired by friends and neighbors, who often asked him to make special pieces for them. In 1965, he leased a previously used facility and expanded his operations by hiring two additional craftsmen, a woodworker and a leather specialist. By 1968, Newtone was incorporated and had eleven employees.

Today, Newtone serves a custom furniture market covering the northwestern region of the United States. Bill Withers, the president, has a staff of thirty-seven employees. Custom made furniture is the sole product line, and the company has prided itself on high quality and timely delivery services. Organizationally, Newtone has sales, purchasing, shipping, and design departments. Internal processing departments include wood framing, wood preparation, wood finishing, metal finishing, leather, glass, plastics, and cloth fabrics.

This past year anywhere from 250 to 300 jobs were processed in the facility on any given day. Although product quality remains high, on-time deliveries have deteriorated; the average job seems to be four to seven weeks late. Bill Arnold, an employee since 1967 and a special assistant to the shop manager, does the shop loading. His job also includes coordinating the overall shop efforts with those of the sales and design departments. He recently compiled data (shown in the table below) on waiting job orders for a typical day.

Detailed scheduling of orders has always been the responsibility of the three shop foremen. Larry Cline is foreman of the wood preparation, framing, and finishing departments. Isaac Trumbolt has the leather department and cloth fabrics. Willie Heft is foreman of three departments: metal, glass, and plastics.

Bill Withers is concerned about job lateness. He feels deteriorating customer service might well affect future sales. He has requested George Herring, whose primary experience has been coordinating a new physical distribution system, to analyze the current situation and recommend changes. George is uncertain which factors he should consider and how to proceed with the problem.

Work center	Number of orders waiting to be processed	Number of shop operations required on waiting orders: 3	4	5	6	7	8	Lateness status of waiting jobs: on time or ahead (# of jobs)	lateness (weeks): 1–2	3–5	6 or more
Wood framing	314	63	69	47	44	44	47	261	44	9	—
Wood preparation	409	98	86	74	45	57	49	61	147	119	82
Wood finishing	223	65	60	45	29	20	4	22	34	78	89
Metal finishing	71	—	7	32	25	7	—	55	16	—	—
Leather	157	—	—	44	61	23	29	135	19	3	—
Glass	63	19	22	16	6	—	—	63	—	—	—
Plastics	106	48	37	21	—	—	—	106	—	—	—
Cloth fabrics	198	—	41	74	53	30	—	133	45	20	—

REVIEW AND DISCUSSION QUESTIONS

1. What is a job shop (intermittent system)?
2. Outline and describe the critical parameters of the job shop scheduling problem.
3. Identify elements of human behavior that are affected by job shop scheduling.
4. Is job shop scheduling a planning activity or a control activity? Explain.
5. Four levels of the shop floor control are loading, sequencing, detailed scheduling, and input-output control. What are the distinctions among these four activities?
6. What are priority sequencing rules? Why are they needed?
7. Discuss the advantages and limitations of using the Gantt load chart and visual load profiles.
8. Discuss the significance of maintaining data integrity in computerized scheduling systems.
9. How does a Gantt chart for detailed scheduling differ from a Gantt load chart?
10. Why do most organizations settle for priority rules yielding satisfactory, rather than optimal, system performance?
11. Employee skills and orientation in intermittent systems differ from those in continuous flow systems. Identify some of these differences. Why do the differences exist?
12. Outline and discuss major differences between finite and infinite loading.
13. Compare and contrast visual load profiles for infinite versus finite loading systems at a work center.

PROBLEMS

Solved Problems

1. Five jobs await processing on a machine and the setup costs, shown below, depend on the sequence in which the jobs are processed. Apply the next-best rule to determine the sequence for these jobs if job I is processed first.

Setup Costs (Dollars)

Predecessor job	Follower job				
	I	II	III	IV	V
I	—	1,300	100	900	300
II	1,000	—	200	700	600
III	100	500	—	1,100	900
IV	500	800	900	—	400
V	800	200	600	300	—

Sequence: I-III-II-V-IV
Cost: \$100 + 500 + 600 + 300 = \$1,500

2. Jobs A, B, and C arrived in alphabetical order and are given priority on a first-come-first-served basis. The routings and operation times are shown below. Develop schedules for the jobs on the machines using the forward scheduling procedure.

Operations sequence	Route sheet: job A		Route sheet: job B		Route sheet: job C	
	machine	time (hours)	machine	time (hours)	machine	time (hours)
1	I	2	II	2	I	3
2	II	3	III	1	III	4
3	III	1	I	3	II	1

		Forward schedule: machine		
		I	II	III
hour	13		C	
	12			C
	11			C
	10			C
	9			C
	8	C		
	7	C		
	6	B		A
	5	B	A	
	4	B	A	
	3	C	A	B
	2	A	B	
	1	A	B	

Reinforcing Fundamentals

3. Jobs arriving at Joanna's Downtown Upholstery Shop are processed and due as shown.

Waiting orders (in order of arrival)	Estimated processing time (days)	Due date (days from now)
#317	12	20
#318	11	20
#319	14	18
#320	2	8

(a) How many processing sequences are available for these four jobs?
(b) Apply the first-come-first-served priority sequencing rule, calculating average job lateness. Now apply the shortest processing time rule and find the average job lateness. Which rule is better for average job lateness? Will that always be the better rule for any data?

4. Given the following data for jobs awaiting processing at a work center, calculate system performance using first-come-first-served, last-come-first-served, and shortest processing time sequencing rules.

Waiting orders (in order of arrival):	*P*	*Q*	*R*	*S*	*T*
Processing time (days) :	10	4	16	8	7
Due date (days from now) :	20	14	26	18	17

5. Suppose, for the waiting jobs in problem 4., setup costs are incurred for processing the next job after finishing any other job at the work center.

Setup Costs (dollars)

Predecessor job	Follower job				
	P	*Q*	*R*	*S*	*T*
P	—	120	90	80	30
Q	100	—	20	70	60
R	10	50	—	100	80
S	50	90	80	—	40
T	80	70	60	60	—

Assuming job *P* is being processed now, apply the next best (NB) sequencing rule and determine the resulting total setup cost. How does this setup cost compare with that of the SPT rule?

6. Arline Industries is an intermittent manufacturing facility, processing jobs to customer order. Currently, eight open orders are awaiting processing. All jobs must be processed at the same facility.

Waiting orders (in order of arrival) :	*A*	*B*	*C*	*D*	*E*	*F*	*G*	*H*
Processing time (days) :	27	14	7	31	9	27	3	21
Due date (days from now):	32	33	17	40	28	52	9	44

(a) Develop a Gantt load chart for the facility.
(b) How many different processing sequences are possible?
(c) Develop a visual load profile for infinite loading; the work center's capacity is five days of processing per week.

7. (a) Apply the first-come-first-served (FCFS) priority sequencing rule to the Arline facility in problem 6. Calculate total completion time, average completion time, average number of jobs per day in the system, and average job lateness.
(b) Apply the shortest processing time (SPT) rule and perform the same calculations as in part (a).

8. Apply the last-come-first served (LCFS), earliest due date (EDD), and least slack (LS) rules to the Arline facility in problem 6. Compare these results to those in problem 7.

9. Data Systems, Inc., processes all incoming jobs through two successive work centers, *A* and *B* (each job goes first through *A*, then through *B*). Five jobs await processing.

Job:	*S*	*T*	*U*	*V*	*W*
Processing time in *A*:	14	3	22	31	7
Processing time in *B*:	8	9	4	17	12

Assign a job sequence that minimizes the completion time of the last job processed. What is the total flow time for this sequence?

10. At McFilly Corporation, eight jobs await processing at a single facility. After one job is finished, facility setup costs are incurred before the next job can be processed. Setup costs depend on the processing sequence.

Waiting orders :	*A*	*B*	*C*	*D*	*E*	*F*	*G*	*H*
Processing time (days) :	23	16	5	31	11	20	2	27
Due date (days from now):	28	35	15	40	30	45	8	50

Facility Setup Costs (dollars)

Predecessor job	Follower job							
	A	*B*	*C*	*D*	*E*	*F*	*G*	*H*
A	—	15	15	20	10	25	15	20
B	15	—	5	10	20	15	5	10
C	5	20	—	30	15	10	10	10
D	25	10	15	—	25	5	5	15
E	20	25	15	30	—	10	30	20
F	30	15	20	25	35	—	10	15
G	15	30	5	10	25	5	—	35
H	10	5	15	20	10	25	10	—

(a) Assuming job *G* is currently being processed, determine the minimum cost sequence for processing the remaining jobs.

(b) For the sequence obtained in part (a), calculate total completion time, average completion time, average number of jobs per day in the system, and average job lateness.

(c) Assuming job *G* is processed first, calculate setup costs for the processing sequence obtained by applying the SPT rule to the remaining jobs.

11. Ten new projects await processing by Environmental Impact Affiliates. Each job requires an empirical research evaluation before it can be assessed by the legal advisor. All projects must be evaluated empirically and legally. Estimates of processing times (days) for the empirical and legal phases are:

Project :	*A*	*B*	*C*	*D*	*E*	*F*	*G*	*H*	*I*	*J*
Empirical phase:	23	16	5	31	11	20	2	27	14	24
Legal phase :	7	21	36	9	12	17	8	22	17	12

(a) Develop a Gantt load chart for the work centers (empirical and legal).

(b) Find the processing sequence that minimizes the completion time of the last project processed.

(c) Draw the Gantt chart for order scheduling based on the results for part *(b)*.

(d) What is the completion time of the last project to be processed?

12. Jobs A, B, and C arrive at a work center in alphabetical order and are given priorities on a first-come-first-served basis. The routings and estimated operation times through this work center's three machines are shown below. Develop schedules for the jobs on the machines using the forward and the backward scheduling

procedures. The jobs' due times are hour 10 for A, hour 16 for B, and hour 14 for job C. How much job lateness results? How much excess inventory results?

	Route sheet job A		Route sheet: job B		Route sheet: job C	
Operations sequence	machine	time (hours)	machine	time (hours)	machine	time (hours)
1	I	3	II	3	I	4
2	II	3	III	2	III	4
3	III	2	I	2	II	2

Challenging Exercises

13. Reconsider problem number 12, above. Now, however, suppose job priorities are based on the SPT rule (not on the FCFS). Develop forward and backward schedules and compare the results to those for problem 12. Now, instead of the SPT priorities, use earliest due date (EDD) priorities to develop forward and backward schedules; compare these results with your earlier results.
14. Suppose, for the data in problem 11, that each project must pass through both processing phases but does not have to be processed through them in any particular order. A project may go through either the empirical or the legal phase first, and then go through the other phase. Assume the projects were received in alphabetical order. Job due dates are: 60 for *A*, 75 for *B*, 32 for *C*, 85 for *D*, 70 for *E*, 95 for *F*, 25 for *G*, 110 for *H*, 130 for *I*, and 97 for *J*. Determine the processing sequence for the projects using the following sequencing heuristic:
    1. Assign an awaiting project to a work center whenever the work center becomes available.
    2. If both work centers become available simultaneously, the next assignment is made to the empirical research phase.
    3. At each work center, unstarted projects have priority over projects that have completed one phase of processing.
    4. Awaiting projects are assigned to work centers on a first-come-first-served basis.

    (a) Determine the sequence in which projects are processed and completed.

    (b) Calculate total completion time, flow times, average completion time, and average job lateness for the sequence obtained in part *(a)*.

    (c) Determine the sequence in which projects are processed and completed, using the following sequencing heuristic:

    1. Assign a project to a work center whenever the work center becomes available.
    2. If both work centers become available simultaneously, the next assignment is made to the empirical research phase.
    3. Projects are assigned to work centers on the basis of processing time; the awaiting project with the shortest processing time (SPT) is given highest priority, regardless of whether or not it has completed one phase of processing.

    (d) For the sequence obtained in part *(c)*, calculate total completion time, flow times, average completion time, and average job lateness.

    (e) Compare the results of parts *(b)* and *(d)*.
15. Referring to the data in problem 10, above, suppose the eight open job orders are prioritized according to the critical ratio (CR) rule. Determine the job sequence, assuming that the estimated processing times materialize. Determine the resulting setup costs. Compare these results to those for problem 10.

GLOSSARY

Assignment algorithm A particular version of linear programming used to assign jobs to facilities such that a specific criterion is optimized.

Detailed scheduling Determining start times, finish times, and worker assignments for all jobs at each work place.

Expediting Tracking a job's progress and taking special actions to move it through the facility.

Flow time Total time that a job is in the system; the sum of waiting and processing times.

Gantt chart A graphical procedure showing work loads and/or scheduled activities on a time scale.

Input/output control A procedure for monitoring actual versus planned utilization of a work center's capacity.

Load Cumulative amount of work (open orders or planned orders) currently assigned to a work center for future processing.

Queue A waiting line.

Routing The processing steps or stages needed to create a product.

Sequence rule A systematic procedure for assigning priorities to jobs, thereby determining the sequence in which jobs will be processed.

Setup cost Cost of revising and preparing a facility or department for processing a job.

Shop floor control Procedures for the detailed execution of production plans for jobs at work centers on the shop floor.

Visual load profile A graph showing the time-phased load from open or planned job orders on the work center.

Work center A facility, set of machines, or work station that provides a service or transformation needed by a job or a customer order.

SELECTED READINGS

Conway, R. W., W. L. Maxwell, and L. W. Miller. *Theory of Scheduling*. Reading, Mass.: Addison-Wesley Pub. Co., Inc., 1967.

Gavett, J. William. "Three Heuristic Rules for Sequencing Jobs to a Single Production Facility." *Management Science* 11, no. 8 (June 1965), pp. B166–76.

Hershauer, James C. and Ronald J. Ebert. "Search and Simulation Selection of a Job-Shop Sequencing Rule." *Management Science* 21, no. 7 (March 1975), pp. 833–43.

McLeavy, D. W. and S. L. Narasimhan. *Production Planning and Inventory Control*. Boston: Allyn and Bacon, Inc., 1985.

Nanot, Y. R. "An Experimental Investigation and Comparative Evaluation of Priority Disciplines in Job Shop-Like Queueing Networks." Ph.D. diss. UCLA, 1963.

Seashore, Stanley E. *Group Cohesiveness in the Industrial Work Group*. Ann Arbor: University of Michigan, Institute of Research, 1954.

Vollman, T. E., W. L. Berry, and D. C. Whybark. *Manufacturing Planning and Control Systems*. Homewood, Ill.: Richard D. Irwin, Inc., 1984.

Weeks, J. K. and J. S. Fryer. "A Methodology for Assigning Minimum Cost Due-Dates." *Management Science* 23, no. 8 (April 1977), pp. 872–81.

SUPPLEMENT TO CHAPTER 12

LOADING WITH THE ASSIGNMENT ALGORITHM

Occasionally a special case of the linear programming algorithm can be useful for assisting in the loading problem. It can be used when the number of jobs equals the number of work centers or machines on which the jobs must be processed.

This method requires that each machine be assigned one and only one job. Furthermore, some criterion must be chosen to evaluate the "goodness" of the assignments. The person loading may wish to assign in such a way that profit is maximized, operating cost is minimized, or completion time is minimized.

Often there are conflicts, in that there is not always a best load center (such as a machine) for each job. Perhaps two jobs could best be run on one load center, but the load center can only process one job. The assignment algorithm is used to resolve this problem. It involves four simple steps that consider the *opportunity* costs of different assignments.

1. *Column reduction.* Subtract the lowest cost in each column from every cost element in that column. Do this for every column. This new matrix of *opportunity* costs is now used in the next step.
2. *Row reduction.* Subtract the lowest cost in each row from every cost element in that row. Do this for every row. This new matrix of opportunity costs is now used in the next step.
3. *Cover the zeros.* Cover all the zero elements in the matrix with horizontal and/or vertical lines. Find the *minimum* number of lines necessary to cover all zeros. If the number of lines required is equal to the number of machines available, an optimal solution has been reached. The optimal assignments are found by examining the zero elements in the matrix. If the number of lines is fewer than the number of machines, go to step 4.
4. *Create new zeros.* Begin with the matrix and the lines from step 3. Find the smallest uncovered cost element (not covered by a line) and *subtract* it from all uncovered cost elements, including itself; add it to all cost elements at the line interections. All other cost elements remain unchanged. Now erase all horizontal and vertical lines and return to step 3.

The following example illustrates that the assignment algorithm can be used for service sector application. Gantt chart loading is also applicable in the service sector. Just remember to make analogies to the machine (server) and job (item or person processed). These processes could also be used in assigning jobs to typists in a word processing center, assigning inspection tasks to inspectors in a government health service inspection unit, and assigning farm workers to farm work centers that have varying machine/labor skill requirements.

EXAMPLE

For the Beef Eater Restaurant, management must decide how to direct different types of customers into different waitress service areas. Management knows that various customer types/waitress combinations will result in different service costs because of varying customer traits and waitress' skills and personality traits. Let's use the assignment technique to illustrate how a satisfactory loading can be arranged when costs for Beef Eater are given in the following matrix.

Customer type	Sally	Waitresses Wanda	Bertha
1	$12.90	$11.90	$12.10
2	15.30	15.50	14.30
3	13.90	13.90	13.00

Our first matrix would be for column reduction, the second for row reduction.

	S	W	B			S	W	B
1	0	0	0		1	0	0	0
2	2.40	3.60	2.20	→	2	0.20	1.40	0
3	1.00	2.00	0.90		3	0.10	1.10	0

The minimum number of lines required to cover all zeros is 2, a number that does not equal the number of servers. (Servers are analogous to machines and customers to jobs in the algorithm.) We proceed to step 4.

	S	W	B
1	0	0	0.10
2	0.10	1.30	0
3	0	1.00	0

The minimum lines now equal the number of servers and the optimal solution is:

Customer type	Waitress	Cost
1	Wanda	$11.90
2	Bertha	14.30
3	Sally	13.90
		$40.10

PROBLEMS

1. Verify the solution to the assignment situation of four jobs to four machines given on pages 488–89. As you apply each step, write out each of the four steps in the solution procedures. By developing the solution with written procedures, you should create a good example for future reference.
2. The costs of processing each of five jobs on five different machines are shown here. Use the assignment algorithm to determine the job-to-machine assignments that will minimize costs.

Job	A	B	Machine C	D	E
1	$100	$ 75	$ 70	$110	$120
2	120	130	115	90	100
3	90	90	110	115	115
4	60	65	40	80	70
5	140	150	170	160	155

3. Architectural Design Associates has six jobs to be assigned to six architects. The expected effectiveness of each architect on each job has been estimated on a rating scale from 1 to 100; a rating of 1 is high effectiveness, and 100 represents low effectiveness. Make the six assignments that will maximize overall effectiveness.

	Effectiveness Ratings					
Job	Louise	William	Ken	Mary	Carl	Patricia
1	33	40	19	24	58	36
2	57	61	8	29	3	24
3	25	56	12	20	10	14
4	44	72	22	37	47	27
5	62	42	31	20	10	33
6	49	33	30	15	22	41

4. First National Bank has four new tellers with varying skills who are to be assigned to the main bank or one of the branches. The criterion for assigning tellers to locations is minimized customer waiting time. An index of customer waiting time is shown in the table below for each of four locations and varying teller skills. Make teller assignments, using the assignment technique, that will minimize the index of overall waiting time. What is the total waiting time for the optimal assignment?

Location	Teller			
	1	2	3	4
Main Bank	40	60	30	90
Southwest Branch	60	30	60	60
Clearwater Branch	80	60	40	40
Northgate Branch	70	50	60	40

13 Project Planning and Scheduling

In Prentice-Hall's college production department our products are books, complicated books, books headed for the college market. Each book is a "project" which appears on the production editor's desk as a large pile of manuscript pages, a combination of typed copy, tear sheet copy of art and text from previous editions, figures drafted by the author, other illustrations, and front and back matter material. These disparate elements are sent off in different directions for various treatments, and must appear bound within covers and ready for sale approximately ten months later.

Planning for the production of a college text involves decisions about the book's specifications (size, color, paper, covers); design (complexity and level, typefaces, art); permissions (where and in what languages the book will sell); composition (setting the type); printing; and binding. Scheduling involves overlapping time frames so that some tasks can be done at the same time (editing and establishing costs, for example), while other tasks that depend on prior events occur later (paging and indexing, for example); and the schedule must end at a time advantageous to sales. Planning and scheduling for a specific book takes place at a launch meeting, where activities are identified, the sequencing is established, and a time is set for each activity within the overall ten month limit. The book's advance through the schedule is recorded and adjustments made as necessary. The production editor at Prentice-Hall is able to carry a considerable number of books at the same time, very efficiently, thanks to the production schedule.

Susan J. Fisher
College Book Editorial Production
Prentice-Hall
Englewood Cliffs, New Jersey

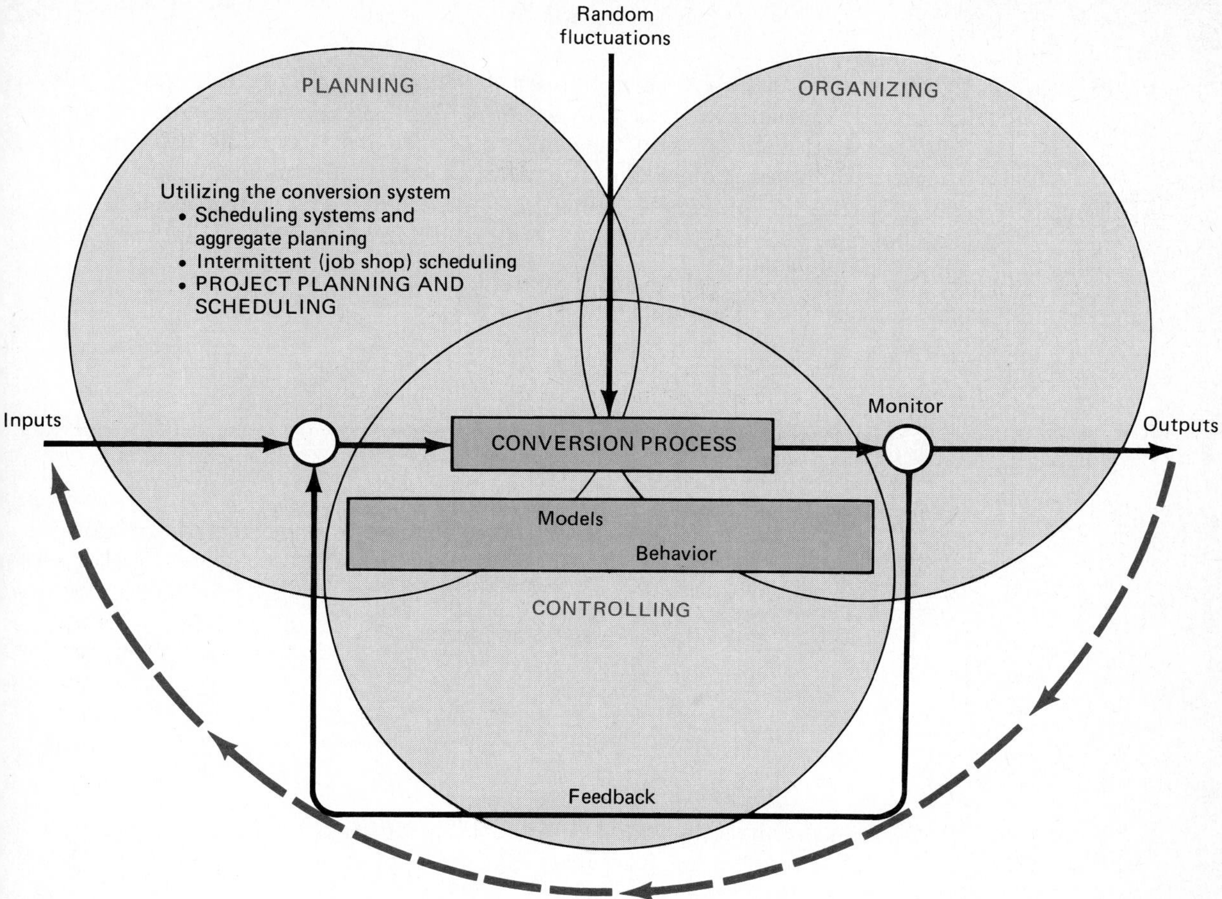

FIGURE 13.1
Operations management activities

Ms. Fisher's commentary on book production emphasizes a project orientation for creating and launching Prentice-Hall's new products into the marketplace. The production editor plans, organizes, and controls the progress of each project (book) according to its unique production requirements. Project management in this environment is a way of life that calls for the coordination of numerous and diverse activities. Figure 13.1 reminds us that these activities are all interrelated. Project planning and scheduling, like aggregate planning and scheduling and job shop scheduling, is part of the general process of planning the use of the conversion facilities. Like other planning functions, it affects organizing and controlling, and like them it requires certain behavioral considerations.

PROJECT PLANNING

Project Defined

A project is a one-shot set of activities with a definite beginning and ending point. The activities must be done in a particular order (they have precedence relationships), and they take place in real time. The key concept that differentiates project planning from other types of planning and scheduling is that the project is a one-time occurrence, an occurrence that will not be repeated daily, weekly, or monthly in converting resources into goods and services.

EXAMPLE

First Christian Church has an annual Sunday School picnic in June. This year the men's club is the host organization. The picnic has been set for Sunday, June 14, and will begin at 4:00 P.M. and end at 9:00 P.M. Activities that must be planned for this project include publicity; providing ice cream, soft drinks, games, and prizes; arranging for a potluck meal; obtaining a facility (location); and coordinating the evening's activities.

Project Planning: A Special Case of General Planning

In general, planning includes all those activities that result in developing a course of action. In project planning, these planning activities guide the manager in future decision making about a specific project. *Goals* for the project, including resources to be committed, completion times, and results, must be set and their priorities established. Actual work responsibilities must be identified and assigned. Time estimates and resources required to perform the work activities must be *forecast*. *Budgets* are as useful in planning projects and in controlling their costs as they are in any other operations management activity. Finally, the project manager must make *policies* to determine which activities are most critical for project completion, how resources should be used, and how additional monies for "crash" completion, should that course of action become necessary, should be spent.

Project *planning*, which includes all the managerial activities that result in developing a course of action, is broad in scope. Project *scheduling* is more specific. It establishes times for the various phases of the project. In project scheduling, the manager considers the many activities of an overall project, the tasks that must be accomplished, and relates them coherently to one another and to the calendar.

EXAMPLE

Slick Wilson, a first-semester freshman at State, is receiving advice from his sophomore roommate on how to study for finals, which start in two weeks. Slick, who has ignored the entire problem until now, is advised to list all his courses and estimate how much time he needs to study for the final in each course. Next, Slick's roommate suggests, he should look in the final exam schedule. When he has determined the order in which he must take his finals, Slick should study for the first one first, the second one next, and so on until he has prepared for all his exams. Slick follows this advice, and he decides that upon completion of the last final, he will throw the schedule away, and forget about finals, school, and his introduction to project scheduling.

What is the *project* in this example? To study for finals. What were the *beginning and ending points* of Slick's project? The ending point is clear: when Slick steps in to take the last final. The beginning point is not so clear. Since Slick has started planning and scheduling for finals so late, the starting point is now, two weeks before his first final. What are the *activities?* The project activities are studying for various courses. These activities must be *time sequenced against each other,* so that Slick can be prepared for his finals in the order he has to take them, and they also have to be *time sequenced against a calendar.* Had Slick failed to ask his roommate's advice, another week might have slipped by before he started hitting the books for finals. Viewing final exam preparation as a project, how could you improve the scheduling of your study time at the end of this semester (or term)?

We might reason that the project planning situation, since it occurs infrequently and for only one time, is not worth the effort of modeling. This is not the case. When a project misses a completion date and overruns budget, cost consequences can be high indeed.

PROJECT SCHEDULING MODELS

There are various methods for scheduling projects. *Mathematical* models can schedule projects using probability and network theory; these might be applied if resource commitments are high and the project consists of hundreds or even thousands of activities. Schematic models are the most common and perhaps the most useful methods of analyzing a project and establishing a schedule to be used as a guide in directing and controlling project progress.

In this section we will look at two simple project scheduling models, Gantt charting and the Program Evaluation and Review Technique (PERT). Both are schematic models, but PERT also has some mathematical model adaptations.

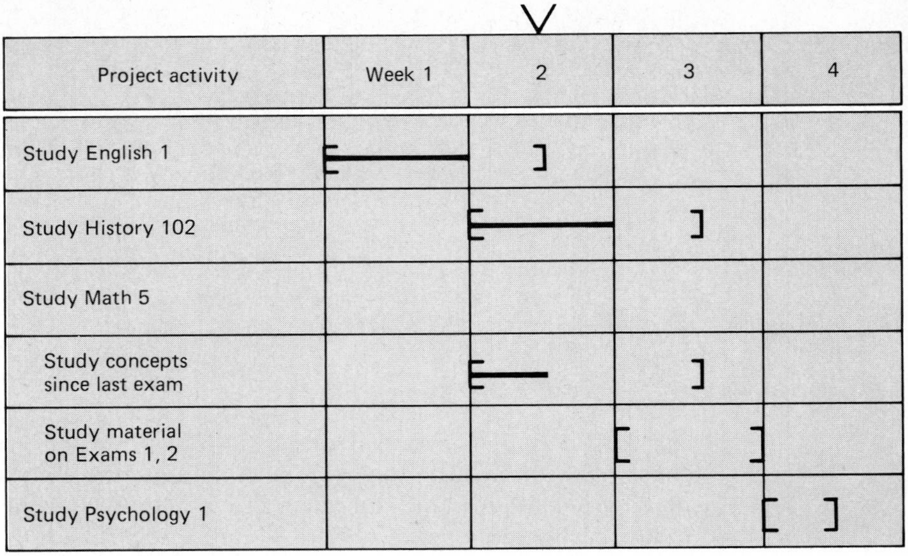

Project activity	Week 1	2	3	4
Study English 1	[————	]		
Study History 102		[————	]	
Study Math 5				
Study concepts since last exam		[——	]	
Study material on Exams 1, 2			[	]
Study Psychology 1				[ ]

FIGURE 13.2
Gantt chart for project scheduling

Gantt Charts

A Gantt chart, as you may remember from Chapter 12, is essentially a bar chart that shows the relationship of activities over time. Project activities are listed down the page and time across the page.

Figure 13.2 shows a Gantt chart developed for a student preparing for final exams. The project activities are studying for exams in English, history, math and psychology. Math is broken into two subactivities, studying new concepts since the last exam and studying material on exams one and two for review. By examining the horizontal time axis we see that all activities must be completed in three and a half weeks.

Table 13.1 shows some common Gantt chart symbols. Opening a bracket indicates the scheduled start of the activity, and closing a bracket indicates the scheduled completion. Studying English 1, for example, is

TABLE 13.1
Gantt chart symbols

Symbol	Symbol meaning
[	Start of an activity
]	End of an activity
[——]	Actual progress of the activity
v	Point in time where the project is now

scheduled to start at the beginning of week 1 and end after one and a half weeks. The heavy line indicates the currently completed portion of the activity. For English 1, one of the one and a half weeks of studying has been completed. Finally, the caret at the top of the chart indicates current time on the time scale. In Figure 13.2, calendar time is at the end of one and a half weeks.

How is this student doing on his studying? What adjustments should he make if he is to meet his schedule? To answer these questions, look down the activities at the point of the arrow. As we've observed, he is behind one-half week in studying English 1. He is also ahead one-half week in studying history and right on schedule in math. He should stop studying history the next half-week and put that time into catching up in English—assuming the English exam is yet to come.

One of the strengths of project scheduling with Gantt charts is the simplicity of the schematic model. In the construction example below, contractors, foremen, and company management could readily read and understand the model.

EXAMPLE

A new manufacturing facility, which required an expenditure of about $2 million in plant and equipment, was built in Kentucky. The general contractor was a local, nonunion contractor who had had previous project experience; but the largest of his projects had been about half this size. The contractor, a competent builder, had never used formal scheduling techniques. To help him, the company representative, with the cooperation of the general contractor, drew up Gantt charts. These charts included both an overview chart listing major general and subcontractor activities and more detailed charts for critical activities from the overview chart. The charts forced the general contractor to plan in a way he hadn't done before. Later, the company representative saw the contractor using the charts to communicate with his foremen and subcontractors.

The Gantt charts were also valuable for the company representative, a recent civil engineering and business school graduate. The process of constructing the chart provided him with an understanding of project activities, their precedence relationships, and how in real time the project would be completed by the target date. The charts were, for him, a critical model for subsequent project control.

Network Modeling

Many production/operations management problems, including project scheduling, lend themselves to network modeling. Although network models are based on rigorous theory and precise definitions, we will touch on only a few terms and concepts here. Network modeling allows us to address project scheduling a little more formally than we can with the Gantt chart.

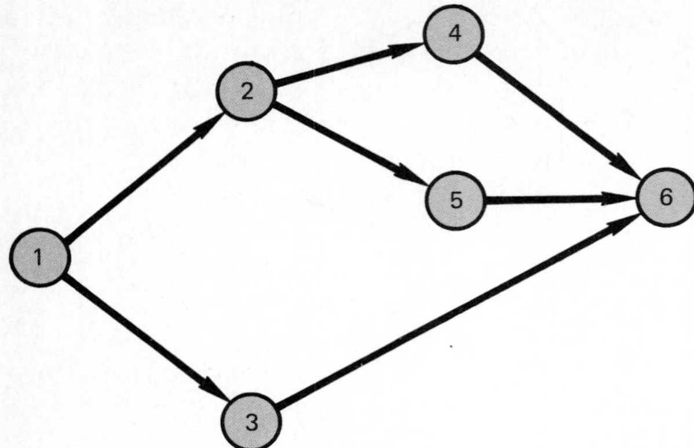

FIGURE 13.3
Network of nodes and arcs

Figure 13.3 illustrates the essential features we want to cover in network modeling. *A node is a circle on the graph that designates the beginning and/or ending of an arc;* there are six nodes in Figure 13.3. *An arc is the arrow that begins at one node and ends at another;* arcs in Figure 13.3 are 1–2, 1–3, 2–4, 2–5, 4–6, 5–6, and 3–6. On an arc, the arrowhead defines direction; the head is at the ending point. Arc 1–2, for example, begins at node 1 and is completed at node 2. By convention, the diagram is constructed to flow generally from left to right, but arrow *length* is of no significance.

The purpose of the diagram is to depict precedence relationships among the arcs. Some arcs must occur before others. *Precedence is indicated at each node; all arc arrowheads (which lead into the node) must be completed before new arcs may begin (before an arrow from the node can begin).* In Figure 13.3, for example, arc 1–2 precedes arcs 2–4 and 2–5 but does not precede arc 1–3. Arcs 1–2 and 1–3 are parallel arcs with no precedence relationship. All these network concepts will be used when we discuss PERT.

Program Evaluation and Review Technique (PERT)

Development of PERT Program Evaluation and Review Technique (PERT) is a project scheduling technique that is an application of network modeling. PERT was developed for the U.S. Navy in 1958 for planning and control of the Polaris project. The results of using PERT in that application, in which some 3,000 contractors were involved, is generally reported to have reduced by two years the project completion time for the Polaris nuclear submarine project. In both government and industry today, PERT is widely used. The Defense Department, the National Aeronautics and Space Administration, and other government agencies require a PERT analysis for companies now doing project work with them.

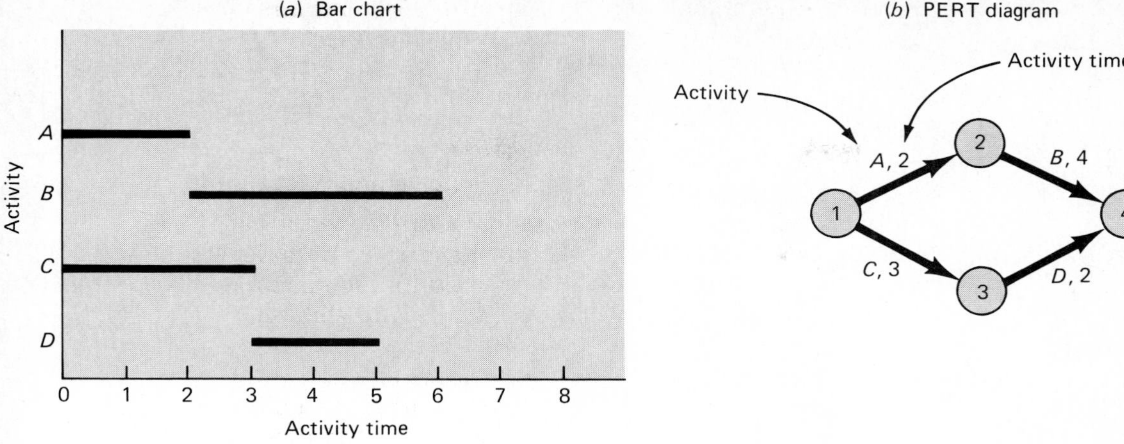

FIGURE 13.4
Bar chart and PERT diagram comparisons

A similar modeling approach called the Critical Path Method (CPM) is also used by business and government. Since CPM and PERT are nearly equivalent, we will concentrate on only one of the two, PERT.[1]

Bar Charts and PERT PERT can be viewed as an extension of a simple bar chart. Consider the illustration in Figure 13.4. The bar chart (part (*a*)) shows that all activities in this project can be completed by time 6. Activity *B* does not start until activity *A* has been completed, and activity *D* does not start until activity *C* has been completed. Activities *A* and *B*, however, can take place at the same times that *C* and *D* are taking place as long as the *B* to *A* and *D* to *C* precedence relationships are maintained.

The corresponding PERT diagram is illustrated in part (*b*). Note that the diagram is constructed so that all precedence relationships are maintained. Each activity is represented by a unique arc. The time scale in the bar chart is absent in the PERT diagram; the times are recorded directly on the activity arcs (arrows). Thus, the lengths of the arrows are meaningless; the arrows portray sequential relationships only.

Application of PERT First we should clarify when PERT may be used. If your situation lacks the following features, PERT application will have little benefit. First, the scheduling problem must be a project with identifiable

[1]Characteristics of twenty major computer software programs for network analysis are compared in Larry A. Smith and Peter Mahler, "Comparing Commercially Available CPM/PERT Computer Programs," *Industrial Engineering* 10, no. 4 (April 1978), pp. 37–39.

activities. Second, the project and activities must all have clear starting and ending points. Third, PERT is most beneficial for projects that are complicated by having many interrelated tasks. Fourth, PERT is good for projects with alternative possible arrangements and sequences of activities and time durations.

The Language of PERT Basically, the PERT language is an interpretation of simple symbols. Table 13.2 explains the symbols and terms that make up PERT's vocabulary. Key symbols include the *activity* designation, the *event* designation, and the *critical path*. Since the critical path requires the long-

TABLE 13.2
PERT glossary

Symbol	Term	Meaning
	PERT	Program Evaluation and Review Technique
→	Activity	A work component needed to be accomplished; a task within the overall project that has a definite beginning and ending point. The activity consumes time. The length of the arrow representing the activity has no meaning.
○	Event	A node in the network that designates the beginning and/or ending of activities. A point in time.
○→○	Network	Combination of nodes and arcs that describes the logic of the project. There is one definite starting and ending point for the entire project.
	Critical path	The path through the network consisting of several activities whose total activity times are the longest of any path through the network. The most pressing, dangerous, risky path through the network. Usually denoted by heavy lines or dashed lines through the activities on that path.
	Critical path time	Total time of all activities on the critical path.
t_e	Expected time of an activity	Expected completion time of an activity. The time estimate with a 50-50 chance of being over-or underachieved. The mean time for the activity.
t_o	Optimistic time	Time estimate for fast activity completion. There is very little chance (say 1 in 100) of completing the activity in less than that time. Will occur only under rare favorable conditions.
t_p	Pessimistic time	Estimated time in which there is very little chance (say 1 in 100) of completing the activity in more than that time. Will occur only under rare unfavorable conditions.
t_m	Most likely time	Estimated time that is the single best guess for activity completion. The "mode" of the distribution of activity times; the most likely time.
T_E	Earliest expected time	Summation of t_e times up to that event. Calculated at an event. Earliest time expected to complete all previous activities.
T_L	Latest allowable time	Latest time an activity can be started that still allows the project to be completed on time. Calculated at an event that designates the start of an activity.
T_s	Slack time	Difference between T_E and T_L; the amount of freedom or latitude available in deciding when to start an activity without jeopardizing the timely completion of the overall project. $T_s = T_L - T_E$.
	Dummy activity	A fictitious activity with no actual time. Necessary occasionally to preserve network logic.

est time through the network, management should watch it most closely to avoid unnecessary project delays. This path is therefore critical, because it threatens on-time project completion.

Logic of PERT How does PERT work? It works by following these steps:

1. All activities in the project must be clearly identified.
2. The sequencing requirements among activities must be designated.
3. A diagram reflecting the sequence relationships must be constructed. (See Table 13.3 for typical sequence relationships.)
4. Time estimates for each activity must be obtained.
5. The network is evaluated by calculating the critical path and similar management decision variables. The evaluation creates the schedule and plan for subsequent control.
6. As time passes and actual experience is recorded, the schedule is revised and reevaluated.

Necessary time estimates are obtained from either past data or the experience of those responsible for completing a particular activity. In some instances, the times will simply be educated guesses by management. Optimistic (t_o), pessimistic (t_p), and most likely (t_m) times must be estimated so that the expected (average) activity time can be calculated from this equation:

$$t_e = \frac{(t_o + 4t_m + t_p)}{6} \qquad (13.1)$$

TABLE 13.3
Precedence relationships in PERT

Network	Meaning
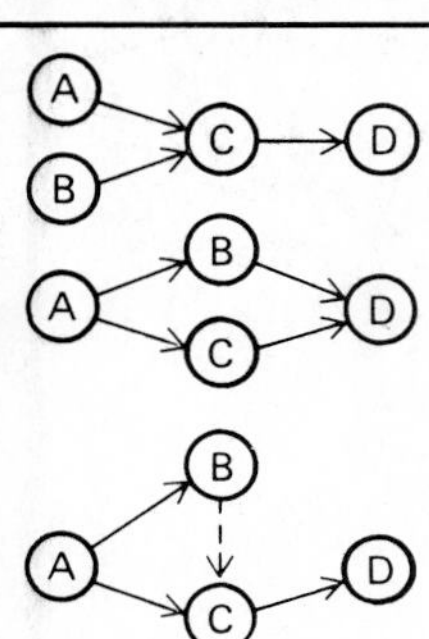	Represents activities *AC, BC,* and *CD,* where activity *CD* may not begin until both *AC* and *BC* have been completed. Activities *AC* and *BC* may occur concurrently and are called *parallel activities.*
	BD may not begin until *AB* is completed. *CD* may not begin until *AC* is completed. *AB–BD* and *AC–CD* are *parallel paths.* However, *AC* does not have to begin at the same instant that *AB* begins, although it *may.* Similarly, *BD* does not have to be completed at the same instant that *CD* is completed, although it may. Similarly, *BD* may be completed before *AC* is completed.
OR 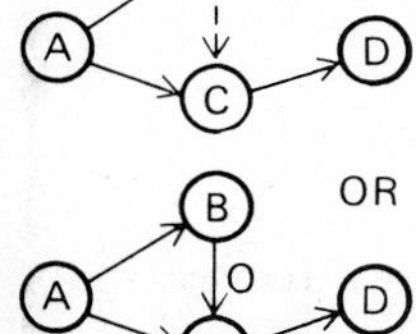	*BC* is a *"dummy"* activity, used when necessary to preserve the logic of the network. It may be represented in two ways, as shown. A dummy activity requires no time. The use of a dummy allows all activities to have unique identities. Activity *CD* cannot begin until activities *AB* and *AC* are completed. This network has two paths: *AB–BC–CD* and *AC–CD.*

Calculating t_e in this manner is common practice. As you can see, the most likely estimate is given four times more weight than the most optimistic and pessimistic times.[2] This equation allows us to consider a *distribution* of times for any one activity rather than just a single time estimate (t_m). If we wanted to calculate the variances of the activity times, we could use equation 13.2.

$$\sigma_e^2 = \left(\frac{t_p - t_o}{6}\right)^2 \tag{13.2}$$

Generally speaking, at least the critical path, critical path time, and event slacks are calculated in the analysis step for scheduling, planning, resource allocation, and control. Let's use the five PERT steps in an example.

EXAMPLE

The Long-Term Care situation. Long-Term Care, Inc., is a Professional II nursing home aspiring to become a Professional I nursing home. It wants to provide the ultimate in nursing care for patients, but because of recent federal regulations it will need a new, specially designed facility. The administrator at Long-Term Care, Inc., has been so busy with current operations that she has not had time to generate an overall project schedule.

The first thing the administrator must do is to identify all activities. Let's presume that as consultants we assist the administrator in doing so.

EXAMPLE

Long-Term Care activities. The administrator prepares this list of activities:

A. Perform pilot services for 6 patients in new facility.
B. Build the facility.
C. Install all equipment and furnishings.
D. Recruit nursing home staff.
E. Train nursing home staff.
F. Pass safety inspection of Municipal Building Authority.

[2]Equation 13.1 is an approximation of the Beta distribution, as is the variance calculation discussed next. Although these equations approximate the Beta distribution, we are unaware of empirical evidence suggesting that activity times on projects are Beta distributed. We accept these formulas based on practices and intuitive appeal, rather than evidence concerning the actual distribution of activity times.

These activities are very general, which is acceptable, but are they in the proper sequence? As consultants, we encourage the administrator to establish precedence relationships. After some thought she identifies the necessary sequence of activities shown here.

EXAMPLE

Long-Term Care sequencing of activities. The sequencing, predecessor activities, and time estimates are:

Activity	Predecessor activity	Time estimates (weeks) t_o	t_m	t_p
B. Build facility	None	20	24	30
F. Safety inspection	*B*	2	3	4
C. Install equipment	*B*	8	16	20
D. Recruit staff	None	2	2	3
E. Train staff	*D*	4	5	6
A. Perform pilot	*C, E, F*	4	5	9

Figure 13.5 accomplishes step 3, diagramming the sequence relationships. Then an arbitrary coding scheme was adopted to create node identification numbers. Note that there must be a node to *begin* (node 10) and to *end* (node 60) the project.

A dummy activity is required in the diagram because activity *A*, which also can be called activity 50–60, must be preceded by activities *E*, *C*, and *F*. The only way we can logically arrange those precedents and have unique arc identities is to use the dummy activity, 40–50. Look at node 50. Before activity 50–60 can begin from the node, activities 20–50, 30–50, and 40–50 must be completed. All arrowheads coming into a node must be completed before new arrows may leave the node. This assures that the dummy activity is completed. If we didn't use the dummy, activities *C* and *F* would both begin at node 20 and end at node 50; they would not have unique identities.

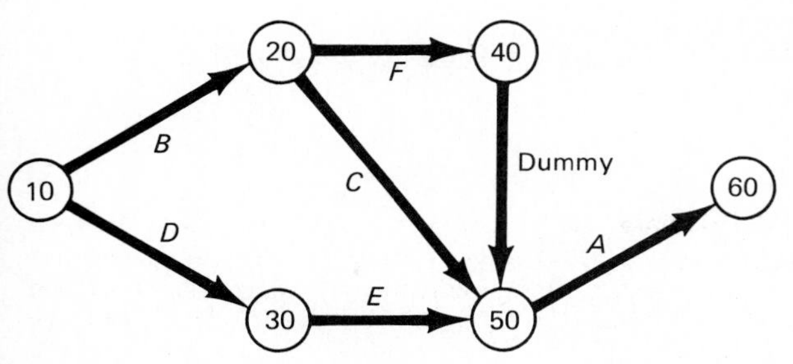

FIGURE 13.5
PERT diagram for Long-Term Care, Inc.

Our next step is to get the administrator to establish time estimates for each activity. Where can she find these times? She can ask building contractors, equipment manufacturers, and her own staff for their estimates of recruitment, training, and pilot program times. Time estimates are provided above.

Next we perform step 5, finding the critical path, critical path time, and slack times. First we must calculate, using equation 13.1, the expected time, t_e, for each activity. For activity 10–20 (activity B) this calculation is:

$$t_e = \frac{(t_o + 4t_m + t_p)}{6}$$

$$= \frac{(20 + 4(24) + 30)}{6} = \frac{(20 + 96 + 30)}{6}$$

$$t_e = 24.3 \text{ weeks}$$

Similar calculations are made for each activity, and the expected times are shown in Figure 13.6.

The critical path is the path with the longest time through the network. There are three paths, 10–20–40–50–60, 10–20–50–60, and 10–30–50–60. The total expected time for the first path is (24.3 + 3.0 + 0 + 5.5), or 32.8 weeks; for the second path is (24.3 + 15.3 + 5.5), or 45.1 weeks; and for the third path is (2.1 + 5.0 + 5.5), or 12.6 weeks. Therefore, the critical path is 10–20–50–60, and the critical path time is 45.1 weeks. The administrator had better focus her attention on activities on the critical path and allow for a completion time of 45.1 weeks. In Figure 13.7, we have shown the critical path on the PERT diagram.

Figure 13.7 also shows the earliest expected times (T_E) and latest allowable times (T_L) *at each event,* allowing us to calculate the *event slack,* the extra time available at each event if we arrive as soon as possible and leave as late as possible and still be able to finish the Professional I nursing home facility on time. First we calculate the earliest expected time (T_E) for each node in the network beginning with node 10. To calculate T_E for a node, sum all previous t_e's up to that node on that path. T_E for node 10, set for convenience to time zero, will occur when the project starts. At node

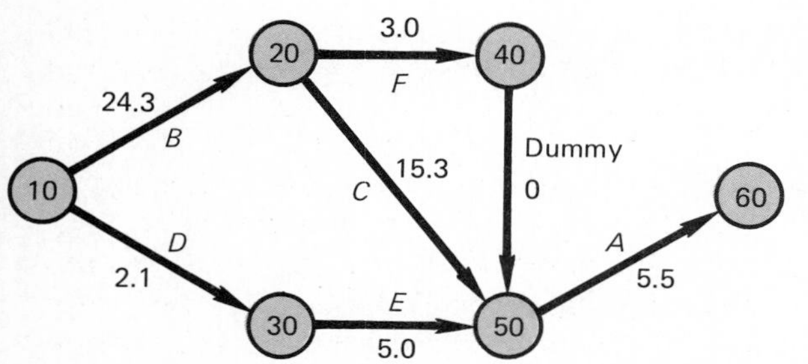

FIGURE 13.6
Expected activity times (in weeks) for Long-Term Care, Inc.

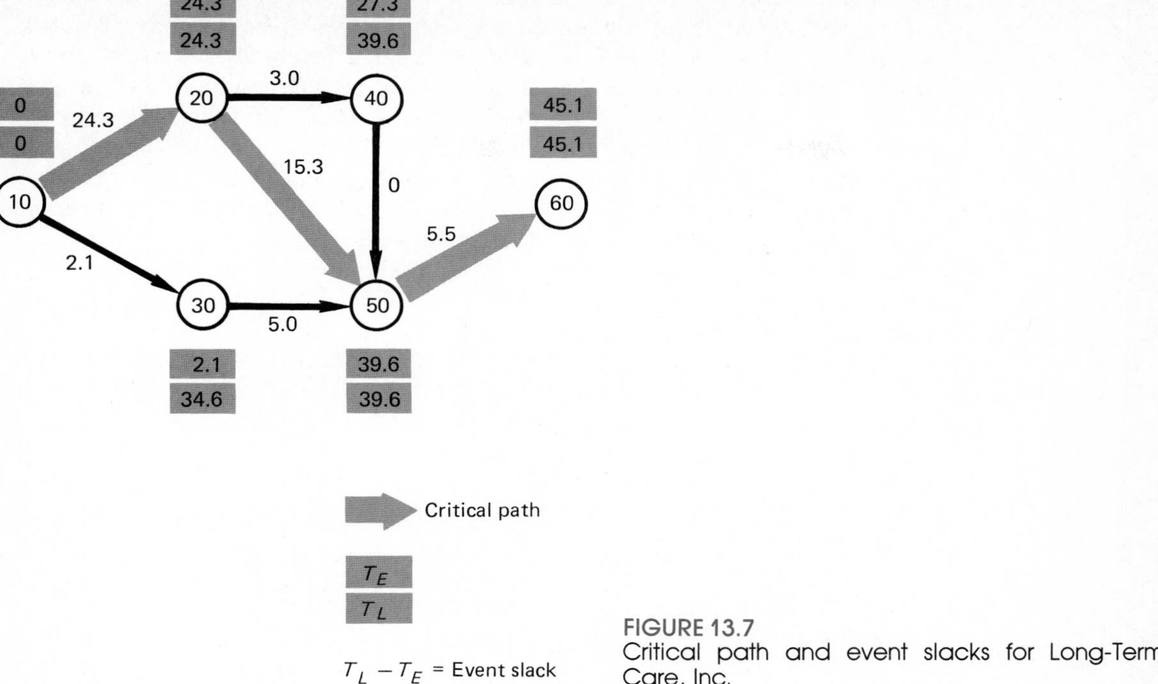

FIGURE 13.7
Critical path and event slacks for Long-Term Care, Inc.

20, T_E is equal to the preceding T_E plus the t_e of activity 10–20 (24.3 weeks). Thus, T_E at node 20 is (0 + 24.3), or 24.3. At node 40, T_E is 27.3 weeks, the sum of t_e's for activities 10–20 and 20–40; alternatively, T_E at node 40 is the sum of T_E at node 20 and the t_e of activity 20–40, or (24.3 + 3.0). Notice that T_E at event 50 is 39.6. The sum of t_e's for the path 10–20–40–50 is 27.3, and the sum of t_e's for path 10–30–50, an alternative way to get to event 50, is 7.1. The sum of t_e's for the other alternate path, 10–20–50, is 39.6. Since T_E represents the earliest expected completion time of *all* activities up to that node, it must be 39.6 weeks until we arrive at event 50, rather than 7.1 or 27.3 weeks. Continuing in this manner, T_E for event 60 is 45.1 weeks, the earliest expected completion time for the entire project. As we have shown, T_E calculations begin at the front end (the source) of the network and continue on through until all T_E's for the entire network have been determined.

The reverse procedure is used for the T_L calculations; we begin at the end of the network and proceed backwards, node by node, to the beginning. First consider node 60. Its earliest expected completion time is 45.1. If it can be completed in that time, we conveniently designate 45.1 as the *latest* permissible finish time. This is recorded as T_L for node 60 in Figure 13.7. Next we work backwards to node 50. Since activity 50–60 will require

5.5 days, event 50 must occur no later than time 39.6 if event 60 is to occur by time 45.1. The latest allowable time for node 40 is T_L for node 50 less t_e for activity 40–50: (39.6 − 0), or 39.6 weeks. Similarly, at node 30, T_L equals T_L at node 50 minus t_e of activity 30–50: (39.6 − 5.0), or 34.6 weeks. T_L for node 20 requires special consideration; two activities must be considered, 20–40 and 20–50. First let's consider activity 20–40. T_L for node 20 equals T_L for node 40 minus t_e of activity 20–40: (39.6 − 3.0) or 36.6 weeks. Next, for activity 20–50, T_L for node 20 equals T_L for node 50 minus t_e of activity 20–50: (39.6 − 15.3), or 24.3 weeks. The *smaller* of these two T_L choices for node 20 is selected. Thus, T_L for node 20 is 24.3 weeks. Had we chosen T_L of 36.6, event 50 could not occur by its latest permissible time of 39.6. Following the same logic, we find T_L for node 10 is zero.

Now we can calculate the event slack, which is $T_L - T_E$, for each event. If we look at Figure 13.7, we see that event slack is zero for most events. Event 30, however, has slack of (34.6 − 2.1), or 32.5 weeks, and event 40 has slack of (39.6 − 27.3), or 12.3 weeks. Why is slack zero at events 10, 20, 50, and 60? *Because slack will always be zero on the critical path*. That is why that path is critical; there is no "fool-around," or slack time.

At event 30 we may recruit workers (10–30) as soon as we start the building (10–20). If we start then, in 2.1 weeks we can expect to be finished recruiting workers. What is the very latest we need to start training the workers (30–50)? We must have the project completed in 45.1 weeks less 5.5 weeks for pilot runs and 5.0 weeks for training. Therefore, we must begin training no later than at (45.1 − 5.5 − 5.0), or 34.6 weeks. *The slack time at event 30 is therefore the difference between latest start and earliest start (34.6 − 2.1), or 32.5 weeks*. Since management attention and resources may be shifted to the critical path from paths that have a good bit of slack, this is an important concept. There is also slack time for activity 20–40. See if you can identify the amount of slack and explain its implications for project management.

PERT Scheduling Once a PERT analysis has been completed, the project manager has data for scheduling the activities, focusing particular attention on the critical path. The first activity on the critical path is scheduled first, the second critical path activity scheduled second, and so on until all critical path activities have been sequentially scheduled.

After the critical activities are scheduled, the project manager returns to the beginning of the network and schedules the remaining activities, considering each activity's latest allowable time—the latest time an activity can be started and still allow the project to be completed on time. The manager works from the start (source) toward the end (sink) of the network so that precedence relationships among noncritical path activities can be maintained.

Time/cost Tradeoffs In network scheduling models, managers often want to reduce critical path times, even if it costs extra money to make the reductions. PERT/COST procedures, formal approaches to reducing critical path times, can be used, but they are very expensive and therefore appropriate only for complex projects with tremendous resources. Although we won't discuss these formal methods here, we will consider basic time/cost tradeoff concepts.

In projects that need time reduction, there are two costs. *Indirect project costs* include costs of overhead, facilities, and resource opportunity costs that can be eliminated if the project is shortened. Monthly overhead costs of maintaining a house trailer at a construction site, for example, might be $1,100 per month for heat, light, telephone, clerical help, and other *indirect* construction costs.

A second cost is the *activity direct cost* associated with expediting (speeding up) the project. These expediting costs are direct; they include overtime work, hiring extra labor, retaining an expeditor, long-distance telephone calls, and leasing more equipment.

The essence of the time/cost tradeoff in projects is allocating resources (spending money) to reduce project time only to the point where further expenditures equal indirect project costs. Beyond this point, the cost of expediting exceeds the benefit of reduced indirect project costs gained from reducing project times. The procedure we will use for such an analysis in PERT is straightforward:

1. *Obtain costs.* For each activity, determine indirect project costs and expediting costs. Find these costs per time period ($/day, $/week) corresponding to the PERT time scale.
2. *Determine crash times.* For each activity, find the shortest possible activity time.
3. *Identify activities on the critical path.*
4. *Evaluate the PERT network.* Reduce the critical path (CP) activity times observing these restrictions:
   - 4–1. Begin expediting the CP activity with the least expediting cost, continuing to the second least costly, and so on to the most costly, or until
   - 4–2. the target expedited time has been reached, or
   - 4–3. the resources for expediting ($) have been exhausted, or
   - 4–4. the indirect project costs are less than the expediting costs for each activity on the critical path.

In this procedure, you must be careful to keep an eye on the critical path. As the original path is reduced, other paths may also become critical. Should two or more paths have to be expedited simultaneously, the procedure may become too costly. We will go through an example to illustrate this procedure.

EXAMPLE

The facilities manager of Home State Insurance Company's new office wing finds that the air conditioning unit is not functioning after the normal May trial. The compressor is out; the fan is out; and because the system was improperly wired, the manufacturer will not cover any losses. After much discussion, the general contractor has agreed to replace the whole system, the cost to be shared between the general contractor and Home State. Of course, the manager wants to know how quickly the job can be done. He has collected data as summarized in Table 13.4.

The manager has decided that it would be helpful to schedule this project. He intends to construct a PERT diagram to assist in planning the work by finding the critical path and critical path time. He also intends to spend $400 expediting if it is economical to do so.

The facilities manager is experienced in PERT diagramming and constructs the diagram in Figure 13.8. The critical path is comprised of activities *A*, *D*, *G*, *H*, and *I* with a critical path time of 19 days. Steps 1 through 3 have been completed in our cost/tradeoff analysis.

To reduce the critical path time according to step 4-1, the manager can expedite only activities *A* at $50 per day for one possible day and *G* at $120 per day for four possible days. *A* is reduced for one day at a cost of $50. The critical path has still not changed, but project completion time has been reduced to eighteen days. *G* is reduced by two days at a cost of $240. Now two paths become critical: path 1-2-5-6-7-8 and path 1-2-4-6-7-8. Up to this point, project completion time has been reduced to sixteen days. The manager has spent a total of ($50 + $120 + $120), or $290 of the $400 allowable for expediting. To reduce one more day, he must spend $120 on *G* and $80 on *F* (the cheaper of *C* and *F*) simultaneously. To take the fourth day from the project, he must spend ($120 + $80), or $200. He cannot do so; he is constrained by step 4-3 of our procedure. The new PERT diagram (spending $290 and keeping $110) is shown in Figure 13.9.

Probabilistic PERT PERT can be used to estimate the probability of completing a project within some desired length of time. We do this by considering the variance (σ_e^2) as well as the mean (t_e) of the activity times. In using probabilistic PERT, we make the two assumptions that activities are independent and that project completion time is normally distributed. The independence assumption allows us to add the activity variances to obtain a total project variance. The normality assumption lets us use the normal distribution in our analysis.

The mean of the distribution of project completion time is the sum of the individual t_e's on the critical path; it is the expected critical path time. The total variance for the critical path is the sum of the individual critical path activity variances:

$$\sigma_{cp}^2 = \sum_{e=1}^{n} \sigma_e^2 \tag{13.3}$$

TABLE 13.4
Home State Insurance Company data

Activity	Activity identification	Immediate predecessors	Expected duration (t_e) (days)	Standard deviation of duration (σ_e) (days)	Minimum duration (crash time) (days)	Cost per day to expedite
Place order	*A*	—	3	1	2	$ 50
Pull old compressor	*B*	*A*	4	0	2	100
Pull and remove old fan	*C*	*A*	6	0	4	200
Manufacture new unit	*D*	*A*	4	3	4	—
Remove old compressor	*E*	*B*	5	5	2	400
Modify duct work	*F*	*C*	3	2	2	80
Ship new unit	*G*	*D*	7	1	3	120
Install new unit	*H*	*F, G*	3	2	3	—
Start up new unit	*I*	*E, H*	2	1	2	—

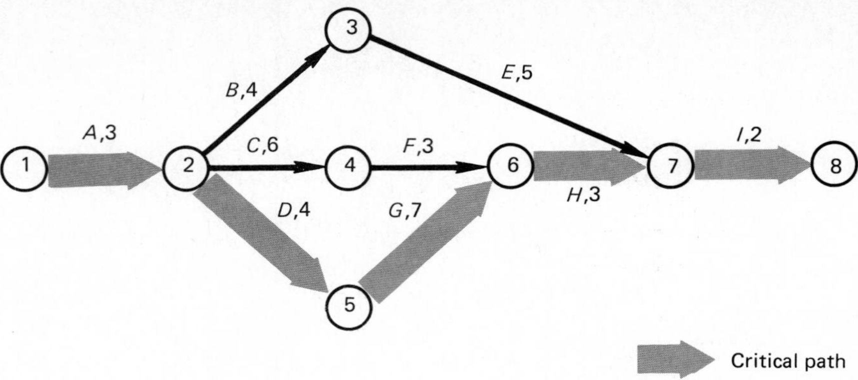

FIGURE 13.8
Home State Insurance Company PERT diagram

Consider the Home State Insurance Company example. In the data for Home State Insurance (Table 13.4), the standard deviations for the critical path activities were 1 for *A*, 3 for *D*, 1 for *G*, 2 for *H*, and 1 for *I*. From equation 13.3, we see the critical path variance (σ^2_{cp}) is:

$$\begin{aligned}\sigma^2_{cp} &= \sum_{e=1}^{5} \sigma^2_e \\ &= [(1)^2 + (3)^2 + (1)^2 + (2)^2 + (1)^2] \\ &= 16\end{aligned}$$

The critical path probability distribution then has a mean (the critical path time) and standard deviation:

$$\mu_{cp} = 19$$
$$\sigma_{cp} = 4$$

Suppose now that the facilities manager wants the project to be completed by July 5th, which is sixteen days away. Using *X* to represent project completion time, he wants to find the probability

$$P(X \leq 16)$$

This is illustrated in Figure 13.10. We can find the standard deviate, *Z*, by:

$$Z = \frac{X - \mu_{cp}}{\sigma_{cp}}$$

$$Z = \frac{16 - 19}{4} = -0.75$$

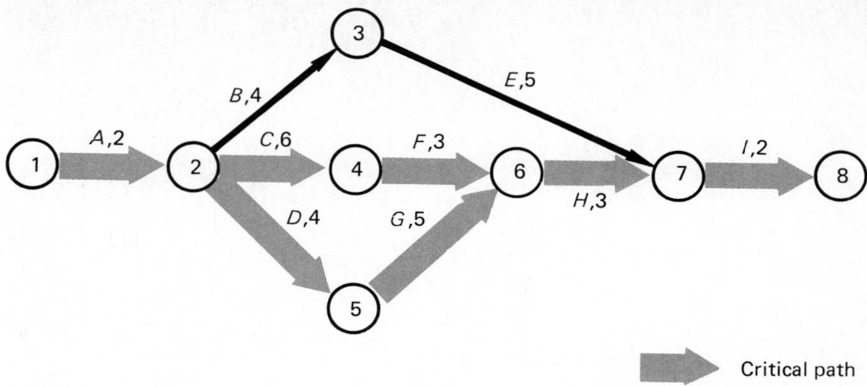

FIGURE 13.9
Home State Insurance Company PERT diagram after expediting

In the normal table in the appendices, we find for $Z = -0.75$ the corresponding probability of 0.2734, which is the $P(16 \leq X \leq 19)$. Subtracting from the mean:

$$\begin{aligned} P(X \leq 16) &= 0.5000 - P(16 \leq X \leq 19) \\ &= 0.5000 - 0.2734 \\ P(X \leq 16) &= 0.2266 \end{aligned}$$

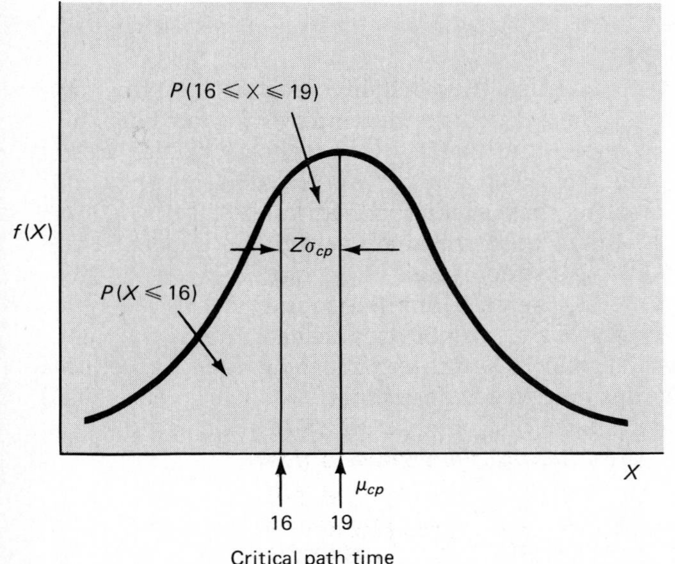

FIGURE 13.10
Critical path time and variance for Home State Insurance Company

The chance of finishing the project by July 5th is only about 22.7 percent. The manager might now want either to expedite or to generate some contingency plan.

Since probabilistic PERT allows managers to use simple statistics to consider a whole range of possibilities, it's a useful procedure. In our example, the manager was able to take advantage of the *shape* of the distribution of activity times as well as the *mean*, the critical path time.

Limited Resources PERT assumes that there are sufficient resources available to complete simultaneously all activities that are scheduled. This is often not the case. If there are conflicts, limited amounts of labor, for example, some rule is needed to allocate resources among competing activities.[3] Although there are models for approaching this problem, we have observed that heuristics are generally used in practice. Some heuristics for limited resources might be:

- Schedule the shortest activity first.
- Schedule the activity with the lowest variance (most certain) first.
- Schedule the jobs for a particular organization unit (division, department) first.
- Schedule the activity with the least amount of total slack first.

MANAGING THE PROJECT

Project management, unlike routine functions that are repeated, presents some special challenges that require somewhat different talents and a unique management style. Getting the project launched and overseeing its completion have both technical and behavioral dimensions as we see next.

Planning and Controlling the Project

In contrast to our previous examples, most major projects are highly complex and, accordingly, they pose real management challenges for their planning, progress monitoring, and control. Determining what activities are required is complicated and time consuming, as are determining their sequences, timing, and ensuring their execution within budget limitations. Project management is assisted in these duties by two methodologies, work breakdown structures and progress reporting.

Work Breakdown Structure The work breakdown structure (WBS) is a methodology for converting a major large-scale project into detailed schedules for the thousands of activities that are involved for project completion. The

[3]For a review of the limited resources case, see E. W. Davis, "Project Scheduling Under Resource Constraints—Historical Review and Categorization of Procedures," *AIIE Transactions* 5, no. 4 (December 1973), pp. 297–313.

WBS is similar in its concept to the bill of materials in an MRP system. It is a level-by-level breakdown of project modules; the overall project is subdivided into major subcomponents that, in turn, are further subdivided into another lower level of more detailed subcomponent activities, and so on. Beginning from the top level, the major subcomponents (activities) are identified, defined, and clarified. This stage of planning is completed when agreement emerges that the scope of the subactivities at this second level indeed will result in successful completion of the project. Then, the planning begins at the next lower level and, of course, involves even more detail. Activities of this third level are identified and defined until their summation covers the scope of the activities at the next higher level. Eventually, all the tasks for every activity are identified, commonalities of detailed activities are discovered, and unnecessary duplication of activities can be eliminated.

After the WBS is developed, it can be used to create segments of the network structure which, ultimately, are combined into the PERT network for the project. Let's examine the WBS methodology in an example.

EXAMPLE

Long-Term Care, Inc. intends to expand into a new, specially designed facility. Now, however, the administrator wants a more realistic project analysis rather than the simplified preliminary analysis shown earlier. Consequently, the consultants developed a work breakdown structure that reveals several types and levels of activities that were omitted in the preliminary study of the project. Figure 13.11 shows selected portions of the WBS; only five of the level 3 activities are shown and all activities below level 3 are omitted from the diagram. Some of the tasks for three of these activities are listed for future reference. In planning for level 2, some new activities were added that had been overlooked in the preliminary study—certification and long-term financing. At level 3, two special equipment needs were identified as were three different kinds of professional staff personnel.

The administrator used the WBS to create segments of the network structure. From level 3, for example, she identified linkages among the tasks for therapist procurement and the installation of the two special equipment systems. As Figure 13.12 shows, the cardio-stress analyzer (2) cannot be calibrated until the hydro-muscular bath (1) is installed because the two systems work together. Similarly, the analyzer (2) must be tested after the bath testing is completed. Although therapists (3) can be recruited earlier, their training cannot begin until the analyzer (2) is fully calibrated; therapist training in this instance is geared toward the special equipment in this facility.

By following the procedure in the example the administrator developed a complete PERT network (not shown) involving some 300 activities for the facility project. Start and finish dates for the activities were estimated along with their costs. From these data she developed project bud-

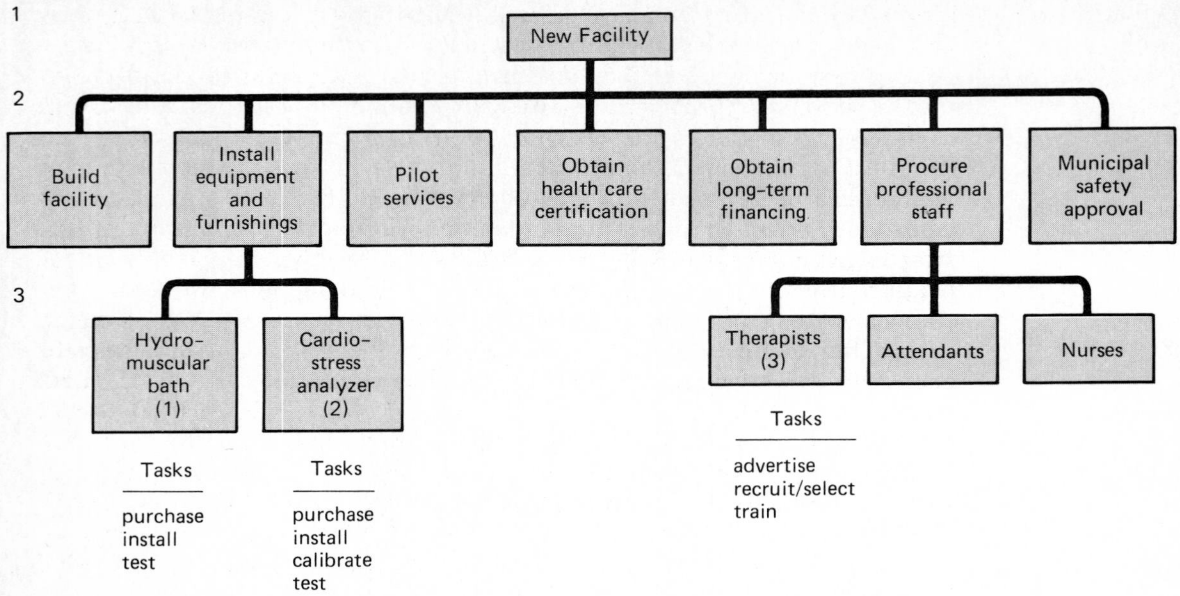

FIGURE 13.11
Work breakdown structure for Long-Term Care project

FIGURE 13.12
Creating network segments from work breakdown structures

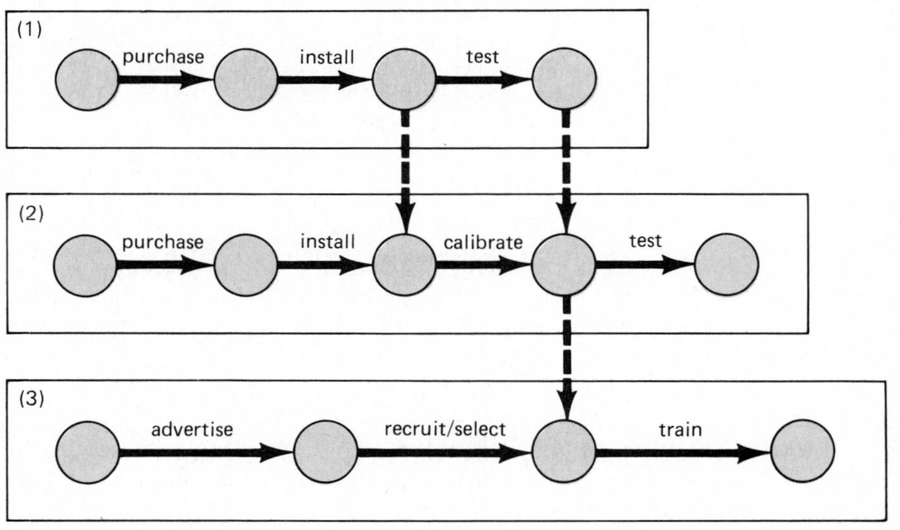

gets which would enable her to monitor the project, stage by stage, as it progressed.

Progress Reporting Project management involves more than just planning; it also requires progress monitoring and taking corrective action when activities deviate from schedules or costs get out of line. Progress reporting assists in these control efforts by showing cost variances (actual versus budgeted) and time variances (actual versus scheduled) during the life of the project. Figure 13.13 shows how these time and cost variances can be consolidated into a visual progress report.

After the project began in January, the actual costs of work completed (ACWC) were tallied, month-by-month, into a cumulative total. As of the end of November (now), actual costs are 365,000 dollars for all work completed. How do the actual costs compare to the budgeted costs for those same activities? The budgeted costs for work completed (BCWC) have been consistently lower than actual costs; cost overruns have been experienced. At the end of June, for example, the cumulative overrun for all work completed was about 60,000 dollars, as indicated by the vertical distance between the ACWC curve and the BCWC curve. Corrective action is needed to contain the high cost variance.

FIGURE 13.13
Progress report for a project

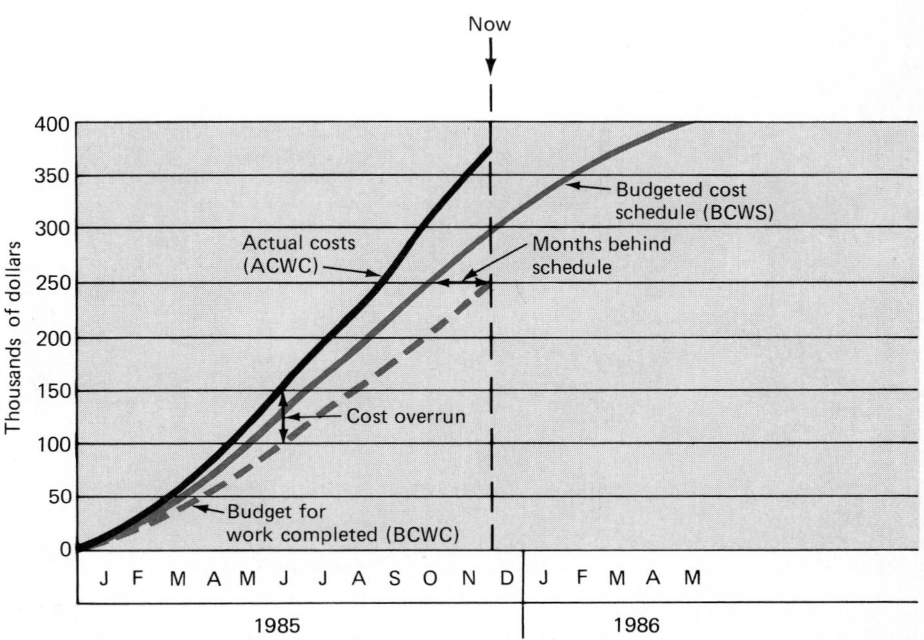

The progress report also shows the budgeted cost for work scheduled (BCWS) in the project. These are the time-phased expenditures that were budgeted when the project was planned. If the activities had progressed as planned, expenditures would have occurred as indicated by the BCWS curve. At the end of November, however, actual progress is lagging behind scheduled progress. The horizontal distance between the BCWS line and the BCWC line indicates the project is nearly two months behind schedule in terms of work completed versus work scheduled to date. Again, adjustments in work progress are required if the project is to be completed on schedule.

Behaviors in Implementation

Aside from the technical aspects of projects, their success usually depends on organizational abilities as well. Some adjustments of the organization's structure are commonplace, as are the behavioral adjustments of managers and subordinates in project settings.

Matrix Organization The matrix organization is a team approach to special projects. When the teams are established, the organization's structure departs from the conventional functional basis for departmentalization. Figure 13.14 illustrates a project organization using this matrix concept. In this example the "home" departments of the various team members are functional: engineering, production, and marketing, depending upon what skills are required for the particular project. Thus the organization's structure becomes a matrix of functional areas (the horizontal dimension of the matrix) and projects (the vertical dimension).

FIGURE 13.14
Matrix (project) organization chart

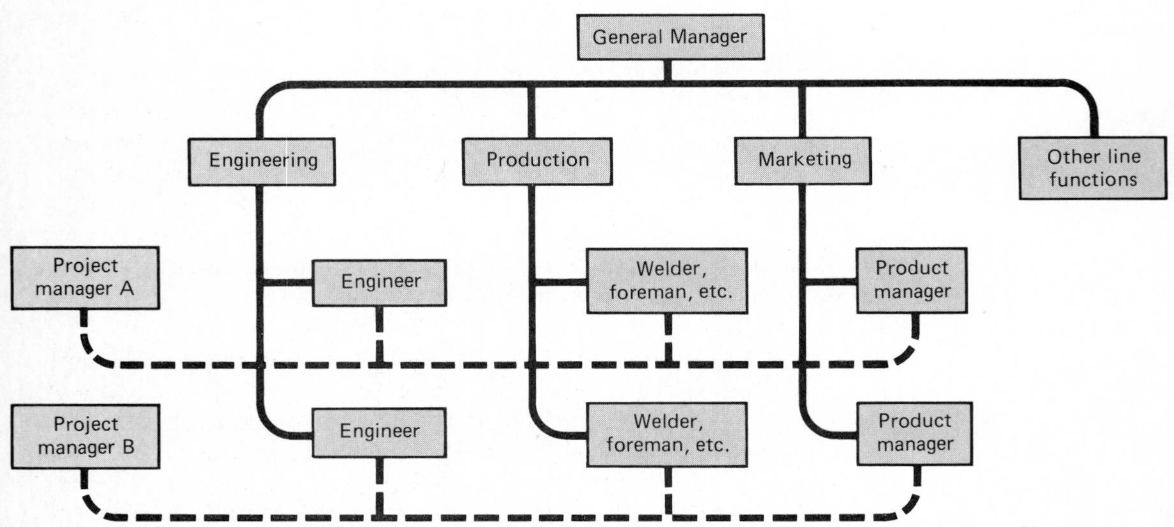

What problems might arise with a matrix organization? A major one is that an employee has two supervisors. Management must consider questions about delegation, responsibility, and authority among the general manager and his or her functional and project managers. Who will evaluate and subsequently reward employees? When the project team is dissolved what new assignments will be given to its members?

When these problems are worked out—and they can be—this form of organization can be very beneficial. Engineers, scientists, technicians, market specialists, and other *existing* skilled personnel can be effectively and efficiently loaned from their "home" organization unit into another unit for periods of time. Because the project can be a part-time or a full-time assignment, management can avoid duplicating skills and save unnecessary costs to the organization.

Although project teams had been used in the Manhattan Project during World War II, it wasn't until the cold war period in the 1950s and 1960s that project teams were used extensively. For the Minuteman, Polaris, and Apollo space flights and later for various defense projects, both the government and American firms have increasingly used project organization. Today, project teams enjoy widespread acceptance in many of our major industries. They are especially effective in large companies that emphasize new product development and rapid launching of new products into the marketplace.

Several factors seem to have been responsible for this trend toward project organization and project management. Rapid technological advances in capabilities and reaction times forced organizations to minimize lead times and avoid obsolescence. Changing theories and philosophies of national defense and prestige and the need to produce project products at minimum expense encouraged project use. The combination of these environmental trends and the one-time characteristic of projects resulted in the need for a kind of organization that could cut across functional areas. The matrix (project) organization fills that need.

Behaviors in a Project Environment

Project managers must have many of the same skills that are exhibited by successful production/operations managers. They must not only be competent technically but must also be skilled in analysis, interpersonal relations, and decision making. Both project managers and production/operations managers (who in some cases are the same person) must act in such a way that their complex projects are completed effectively. Let's briefly examine a few key behaviors within project teams.

Communication Project leaders must be able to communicate freely with both team members and line employees who are not regular team members. Within the immediate project team, communication is frequent and often involves intensive collaboration. Short daily meetings, written correspondence, and one-on-one problem solving sessions are often necessary for the sorts of tasks required of project teams. The nonroutine, diverse, often ill-structured tasks that project teams engage in require flexible relationships and exceptional communication to avoid duplication of effort and costly project delays.

Motivation The several motivators that can be used by a project leader are not substantially different from those available to other managers. Key motivators can be either extrinsic or intrinsic rewards.

Extrinsic rewards come from outside the individual. They include, among others, monetary rewards, fringe benefits, job titles, and project status. Typically, extrinsic rewards can be seen by others. The primary motivator, in our opinion, is a monetary reward. Since money can be used to acquire such a variety of extrinsic rewards, widely different goods and services, we believe it is of paramount importance. Unfortunately, project managers may not have sufficient latitude to give monetary rewards to employees working on the project, particularly employees in line positions. They may be able, however, to see that monetary rewards as incentives for cost control and completion time are given to full-time project team members. Another extrinsic motivator is often competition. When a productivity index is calculated on a departmental basis and posted for everyone to see, less productive departments often complain about the index but try to improve their performance before the next one is posted. Within limits, competition of this sort is healthy for the project.

Intrinsic rewards come from within the individual. These include satisfaction from project tasks accomplished, pride in quality workmanship, pleasure from job flexibility, and pride in the team effort. All of these can be fostered and encouraged by managers in most projects.

Group Cohesiveness When group members are willing to stay together, developing bonds that hold them, the group is cohesive. Group size, goal achievement orientation, group status, members' dependence on the group for satisfaction of their needs, and management demands and pressures all affect group cohesiveness and apply to project teams.

As project team and overall group size increase, group cohesiveness decreases. Groups that have achieved stated goals have more of a tendency to remain together than do project groups or subgroups whose goals are not being realized. The higher a group ranks in organization status (measured by project importance, skills required, and job flexibility) the more cohesive the group tends to be. If group members' social, economic, or psychological needs are met by a group, they tend to feel strong ties to the group. The more a project team fills these needs, the more cohesive the team. Finally, management pressures for group members to work in close proximity to one another under stress conditions usually contribute to group cohesiveness.

Overall, the more cohesive the group the better the chances a project can be completed on budget and on time. Because of both the diversity of team members and the one-shot nature of the project, group cohesiveness is difficult to obtain in project teams. But project teams that exhibit cohesiveness have an increased chance of achieving their primary goals.

Project Organization Advantages and Disadvantages

Perhaps the one overriding advantage of project organization is that by grouping people and tasks, the organization can take on jobs outside the mainstream of its activities. Firms can form interdisciplinary teams to increase their capabilities. Without major reorganization, firms can fix responsibility and centrally control costs.

There are disadvantages too, however. Building and dispersing project teams can be upsetting to the routine of most employees. Furthermore, project managers often feel considerable constraints in having to accept responsibility for completing the project without being given line authority to control it. A final disadvantage is that the matrix (or project) structure can lead to greater organizational complexity:

> While it may be an extreme case (and there may be other contributing factors), one aerospace company found significant changes when it contrasted its organization structure one year before project organizations were established with the structure two years after this form of organization was used initially. While total company employment had declined about 6 percent, the number of departments, the number of managers, and the number of second-level supervisors had about doubled.[4]

SUMMARY

Project planning includes all those activities resulting in a course of action for a one-shot venture with specific beginning and ending points. Project scheduling is the time sequencing of the project activities. It can be viewed as a subphase of overall project planning. In project scheduling, the activities of the project are identified and related to one another and to the calendar.

Techniques for project scheduling include Gantt charts and PERT analysis. Gantt charts are visual aids whose strength lies in their simplicity and ease of understanding. Program Evaluation and Review Technique (PERT) analysis is an application of basic network analysis. Activities, represented as network arcs, are related sequentially to one another and represented schematically. Such statistics as critical path time, critical path variance, and event slack are calculated to enhance the value of PERT analysis as a basis for project control. Other useful variations include cost/time tradeoff analysis and probabilistic PERT.

Planning for and monitoring the project is aided by work breakdown structures and progress reporting. Organizing, by creating a project-oriented organization, focuses on a matrix approach to grouping jobs. In a situation somewhat unique to projects, the project manager assumes responsibility for project goals without commensurate authority over line activities. Thus the project manager needs skills in communication, coordination, motivation, and maintaining a cohesive project work group.

---

[4] Stephen R. Michael and Halsey R. Jones, *Organizational Management: Concepts and Practice* (New York: Intext Publishers Group, 1973), pp. 153–54.

CASE

Electran Manufacturing, Ltd.

Electran Manufacturing, Ltd., is a diversified manufacturer in two primary fields, electronic applications and transportation equipment. In the transportation field, Electran products are in the forefront of technological applications, especially in terms of electrical circuitry and component packages. Electran management takes great pride in its technological leadership and has decided to retain earnings to support a substantial research and development (R&D) effort.

Currently seventy-four persons are employed full-time in the R&D division, and at any one time at least twice that many more are involved to some degree in research or development projects. These employees are assigned primarily to line operations in such functional areas as engineering, finance, marketing, and production.

Electran organizes its R&D effort by functional area within the division. Engineers, scientists, and technicians are grouped separately. Additionally, within each of these technical specialities, employees are grouped and housed together. Electrical engineers, mechanical engineers, and metallurgical engineers, for example, are each grouped and located together. Projects rotate from group to group, depending upon what work needs to be accomplished. There is a department head for each of the engineering, science, and technical support areas, and three additional project managers have individual project responsibility. There is considerable pressure on project managers for project completion, but they have limited control over staff within the R&D division and even less control over the approximately 150 employees who assist in product development on an occasional basis. The R&D division manager has recently read a brief article about matrix organization. He wonders if matrix organization might be helpful in relieving some of the burden from his project managers and in enhancing division productivity.

One of the three project managers is trying to grasp the basis of PERT. He has assembled the following data for a project soon to be started. He wants to establish a PERT diagram for the project, determine the earliest completion date from project start using expected times, and find the minimum cost plan. This project manager doesn't know whether he has enough data to proceed; even if he does have enough data, he doesn't know how to analyze them and apply the results.

Activity	Immediate predecessor	Expected time (days)	Cost per day to expedite
A–B	—	2	$100
A–C	—	4	80
A–D	—	5	70
B–E	*A–B, A–C*	3	100
E–F	*B–E*	6	150
F–H	*E–F*	2	50
D–H	*A–D*	11	100
H–I	*F–H, D–H*	1	100

The project manager has budgeted $200 for expediting should he want to use it.

REVIEW AND DISCUSSION QUESTIONS

1. Differentiate between project and other types of planning.
2. Explain how project planning and project scheduling relate.
3. Provide an example, not given in this chapter, of a project. Describe the project, identifying the beginning and ending points, the activities, and the time sequencing of the activities against each other and the calendar.
4. Discuss how a Gantt chart can be used as a scheduling tool. What type of model is a Gantt chart?
5. PERT has characteristics of both a mathematical model and a schematic model. Explain.
6. Explain how the scheduling and cost performance of a project might be measured. When might such a measure be useful?
7. Discuss the key behaviors that occur within project teams. In your discussion, explain who the people are who exhibit each behavior and explain the possible consequences of such behavior on project goal accomplishment.
8. Contrast the advantages and disadvantages of project organization.
9. Provide the features that a situation should present before PERT may be used.
10. In PERT, the terms are important. Explain the difference between an activity and an event. What is a critical path?
11. Present the logic of PERT. (How does PERT work?)
12. Explain how a time/cost tradeoff could exist in a project involving the construction, staffing, and opening of a new clubhouse at an existing country club.
13. Managers often complain that statistical analysis is too complicated. Suppose that although your supervisor exhibits such an attitude, he likes PERT. In minimally technical terms explain the advantages of probabilistic PERT to your supervisor and try to convince him to accept it.
14. Your project is to design and build an insulated dog house for your favorite Collie. Show how to use a work breakdown structure to develop the project network.

PROBLEMS

Solved Problems

1. Compute the values for the earliest expected times (T_E) and the latest allowable times (T_L) for the network shown in Figure 13.15. The expected time is shown beside each activity.

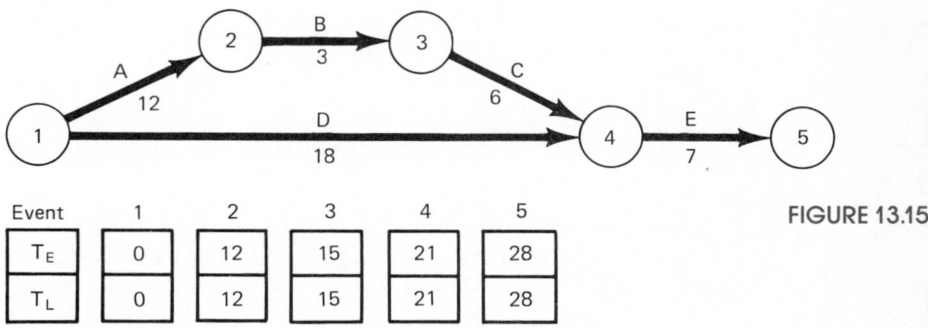

Event	1	2	3	4	5
T_E	0	12	15	21	28
T_L	0	12	15	21	28

FIGURE 13.15

2. Determine the expected completion time and the variance of completion time for the network shown in Figure 13.16 (the optimistic, most likely, and pessimistic time estimates are shown for each activity).

FIGURE 13.16

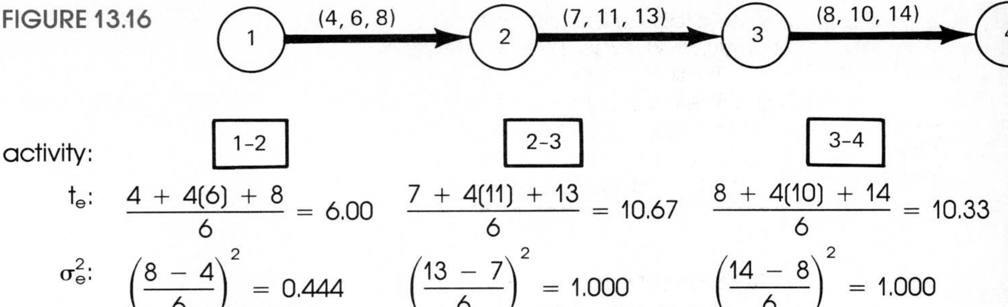

activity: 1-2; 2-3; 3-4

t_e: $\frac{4 + 4(6) + 8}{6} = 6.00$ $\quad \frac{7 + 4(11) + 13}{6} = 10.67$ $\quad \frac{8 + 4(10) + 14}{6} = 10.33$

σ_e^2: $\left(\frac{8 - 4}{6}\right)^2 = 0.444$ $\quad \left(\frac{13 - 7}{6}\right)^2 = 1.000$ $\quad \left(\frac{14 - 8}{6}\right)^2 = 1.000$

network: expected completion time = 27.00 weeks; variance = 2.444.

Reinforcing Fundamentals

3. A veterinarian would like to put drains for collecting animal waste and a septic tank in his animal shelter. He has identified the following activities and estimated their times (in days): planning (4), obtaining contractor (7), excavating (3), laying drainage tile (2), concrete work (4), landscaping (3). All activities are sequential except for laying the drainage tile and concrete work which may be done at the same time but must be done after excavation.
   (a) Prepare a Gantt chart.
   (b) Prepare a PERT chart.
   (c) Which chart do you believe would be most useful on this project? Why?
4. Given the following PERT diagram (Figure 13.17) with times in days:
   (a) Compute the values for the earliest expected times (T_E) and the latest allowable times (T_L).
   (b) Find the event slack at event 2.
   (c) The penalty cost per day for each day over twenty days is $10. The costs of expediting, for those activities that allow it, are:

Activity	Expediting cost per day	Maximum days that can be reduced by expediting
2–4	$ 7	2
3–4	6	1
4–5	15	3

   Which activities (and by how many days), *if any,* would you expedite?
5. Given the following PERT activities (Figure 13.18):
   (a) What is the critical path?
   (b) Construct a Gantt chart for this project.
   (c) Examine the activity variances. Which path through the network would you suggest that the project manager watch most closely? Why?

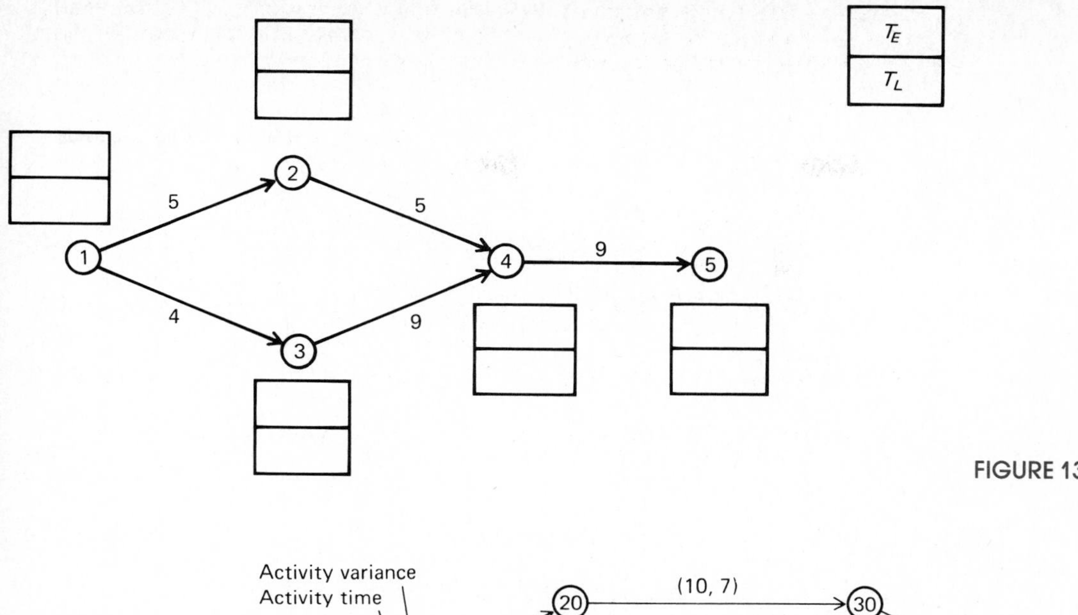

FIGURE 13.17

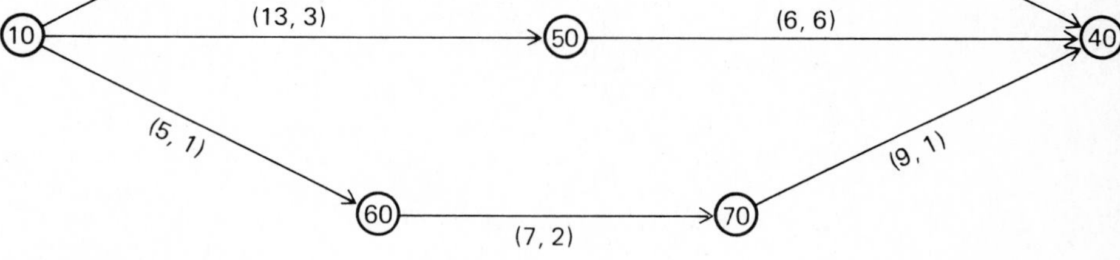

FIGURE 13.18

6. Given the following data (Figure 13.19):

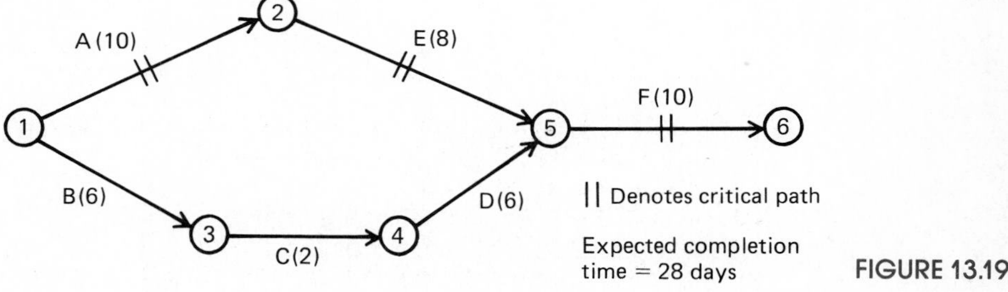

FIGURE 13.19

Activity	Expected duration (days)	Cost ($)/day to expedite	Minimum duration (days)
A	10	$60	6
B	6	$30	3
C	2	—	2
D	6	$50	3
E	8	$80	4
F	10	$100	6

(a) What is the minimum expected completion time of the project (for an "all-crash" solution) and the associated expediting cost?
(b) Identify all activity durations and expediting costs that minimize total expediting costs while still providing the minimum expected completion time for the project.

7. For the data given in problem 6, above, identify all possible expected project durations and the minimum total expediting costs of each. Develop a graph of this relationship, and identify the activity durations and the critical path activities for each point on the graph.
8. Consider the research and development project PERT diagram shown in Figure 13.20.

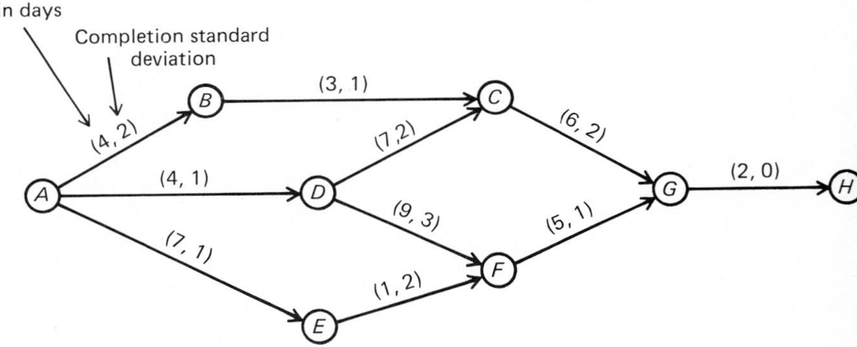

FIGURE 13.20

(a) Find the critical path and critical path time.
(b) What is the probability that the project will take more than twenty-one days to be completed?
(c) A new activity is being considered. The activity, economic evaluations of pesticide application, would precede activity *DC* and follow activities *AB, AD,* and *AE.* Draw the new PERT network. Identify the new activity on your network.

9. A market research project for Trademark Greeting Cards (TGC) is being planned as shown below. For the market research manager:
(a) Construct a PERT diagram.
(b) Explain the critical path concept and what the critical path is for this project.
(c) Analyze costs and recommend action. The project has fixed costs of $100 per day; that is, each day the completion time is shortened from the expected time, the firm saves $100.

Activity	Immediate predecessor activity	Expected completion time (days)	Minimum expedited time (days)	Expedited cost per day
1	—	10	5	$ 80
2	1	20	15	65
3	2	25	15	40
4	2	20	15	70
5	3,4	15	13	90
6	5	15	10	105
7	1	60	45	30
8	6,7	5	4	85

10. A public accounting firm has described an audit program at a bank in terms of activities and events and has calculated the expected activity times (t_e) and their variances (σ_e^2) as shown (for example, activity 10–20 has $t_e = 11$ and $\sigma_e^2 = 3$). The activity times are in days in the PERT network (Figure 13.21).

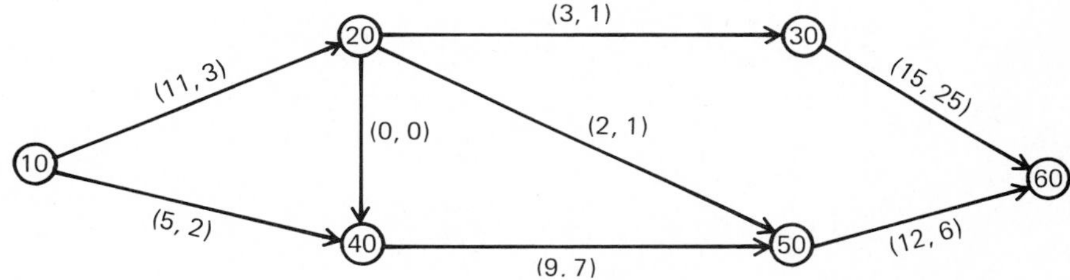

FIGURE 13.21

(a) Find the critical path and the mean critical path time for the audit program.
(b) If activity times are assumed to be independent and normally distributed, what is the probability that the audit is completed in twenty-two days or fewer? Of what value is this information to a partner in the firm?
(c) What can you tell about activity 30–60 as it relates to the critical path?
(d) What is the event slack at event 50? Why?

11. For a Research and Development project, the following PERT network was constructed (Figure 13.22). Activity times are in months.

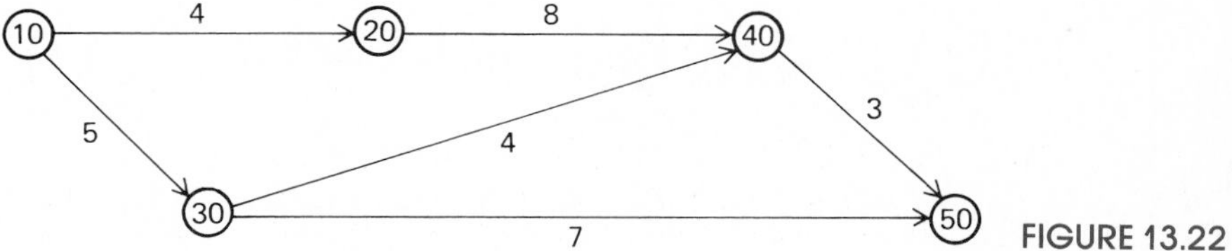

FIGURE 13.22

(a) What is the critical path?
(b) What is the event slack at event 30? What does that mean?
(c) Two activities have to be added due to a change in project definition. An activity of two months must precede the entire project, and an activity of two months must precede activity 10–30. What impact, if any, will this have on the critical path and on the event slack at event 30?

Challenging Exercises

12. A short project has data as shown in the table below.
    (a) Construct a PERT diagram. Calculate the critical path time and clearly designate the critical path.
    (b) Calculate the earliest expected time, the latest allowable time, and slack time at each event. Why is slack time always zero at each event on the critical path?
    (c) Assuming independent activities that are normally distributed, what is the probability of completing the project in nineteen days or fewer?
    (d) If you chose to expedite only one activity, which would you choose? Why?

Activity	Immediate predecessor	Expected time (days)	Variance	Cost per day to expedite	Maximum days that can be expedited
a	—	6	2	$100	3
b	—	11	9	50	1
c	—	13	5	200	2
d	*a*	6	4	—	—
e	*c, f, g*	4	4	300	1
f	*d*	4	1	150	1
g	*b*	7	3	200	2

13. A project manager for Electromagnet, Inc., has constructed the PERT network shown in Figure 13.23.

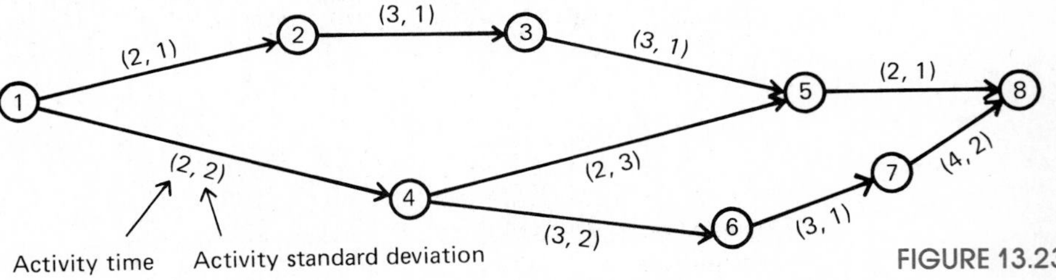

FIGURE 13.23

Assist the manager by determining:
(a) the critical path and critical path time
(b) the probability of completing this project in eleven days or fewer and the probability of completing the project in thirteen days or more (assuming independent activities and normally distributed completion times)
(c) the expected gain (or loss) from this project if completed, given the following payoff table:

	State of nature		
Alternatives	Finish 11 days or fewer	Finish in 12 days	Finish 13 days or more
Complete the project	+$800	+$200	−$100
Don't start the project	$0	$0	$0

14. A computer programming team has divided a project in terms of activities and events and has calculated expected activity times (t_e) and their variances (σ_e^2) as shown in Figure 13.24. (For example, activity 10–20 has $t_e = 10$ and $\sigma_e^2 = 3$.) The activity times are in days in the PERT network.

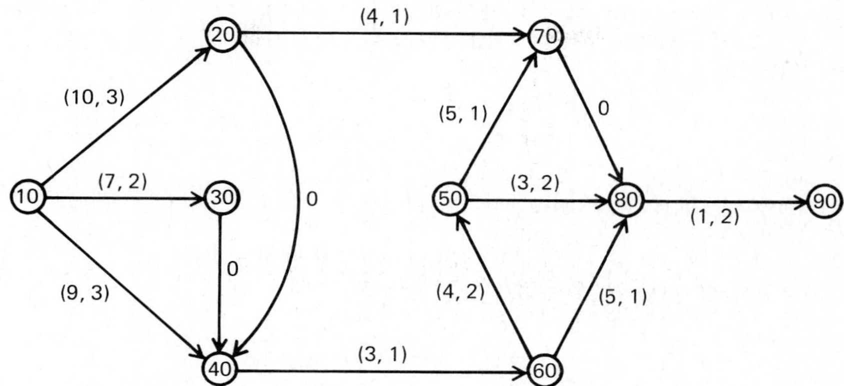

FIGURE 13.24

(a) Find the critical path and the mean critical path time for the project.
(b) If activities are assumed to be independent and normally distributed, what is the probability that all computer programming is completed in twenty days or fewer?
(c) Your goal is a lower project completion time. If you can spend $500 and reduce activity 50–80 one day *or* $600 and reduce activity 60–80 two days, which, if either, should you do?
(d) If the project requires more than 22 days, a penalty of $300 per day is assessed on the programmers. If the project finishes in fewer than 22 days, a bonus of $300 per day is given to the programmers. What is the expected payoff to the programmers?

15. Temple Hospital is designing and implementing a wage incentive program. Included are the activities of this project and other project information. Activity times are independent and normally distributed.
(a) Construct a PERT network and mark the critical path.
(b) What is the probability of completion in more than fifteen weeks?
(c) You have $1,000 to spend expediting. Where would you spend it? Why?

Activity	Immediate predecessor	Expected time (weeks)	Expected standard deviation	Minimum expected time	Cost per week to expedite
Project planning 1–2	—	3	1	3	—
Job analysis 2–3	1–2	5	2	2	$ 500
Performance analysis 2–4	1–2	4	2	2	500
Market wage survey 2–5	1–2	7	3	6	300
Structure internal wage program 3–5	2–3,2–4	3	2	2	1,000
Finalize incentive program 5–6	2–5,3–5	4	2	4	—

GLOSSARY

Arc In networks, the arrow that begins at one node and ends at another.

Matrix organization An organization that combines functional and project bases for groupings of organization units.

Node In networks, a circle that designates the beginning and/or ending of an arc.

PERT Program Evaluation and Review Technique; a project scheduling technique that is an application of network modeling.

PERT activity Work needed to be accomplished; designated by an arc.

PERT critical path The path through the network consisting of several activities whose total activity times are the longest of any path through the network.

PERT event A point in time on the project; designated by a node; designates the beginning and/or ending of activities.

PERT slack time Event slack or time latitude for activity performance that still allows the project to finish on time.

Probabilistic PERT A modification of PERT to consider the variance (σ^2) and the mean (t_e) of the activity times.

Progress reporting A methodology for monitoring the time and cost variances during the progress of a project.

Project A one-shot set of activities, a project venture, with a definite beginning and ending point.

Project planning All activities that result in developing a course of action for a one-shot venture with a specific beginning and ending point.

Project scheduling Time sequencing of activities in a project.

Work breakdown structure A methodology for the level-by-level breakdown of a project into successively more detailed subcomponents.

SELECTED READINGS

Baumgartner, John S. *Project Management*. Homewood, Ill.: Richard D. Irwin, Inc., 1963.

Davis, E. W. "Project Scheduling under Resource Constraints—Historical Review and Categorization of Procedures," *AIIE Transactions* 5, no. 4 (December 1973), pp. 297–313.

Moder, J. J., C. R. Phillips, and E. W. Davis. *Project Management with CPM, PERT, and Precedence Diagramming*. 3rd ed. New York: Van Nostrand Reinhold Co., 1983.

Smith, Larry A. and Peter Mahler. "Comparing Commercially Available CPM/PERT Computer Programs," *Industrial Engineering* 10, no. 4 (April 1978), pp. 37–39.

Weist, J. D. and F. K. Levy. *A Management Guide to PERT/CPM*. 2nd ed. Englewood Cliffs, N. J.: Prentice-Hall, Inc., 1977.

14 Inventory Control Fundamentals

Inventory control is a subject of vital importance to almost every type of business, whether production or service oriented; it touches almost every facet of our water and electric utility. Raw materials such as coal and fuel oil must be scheduled and stockpiled for the production of electricity. Operating supplies such as hydrogen, chlorine, and fireside treatment chemicals must be delivered and on hand in the proper quantities for the operation of the power plant and the water treatment plant. Large stocks of materials such as poles, wire, valves, and pipe must be kept to operate, maintain, and expand the extensive distribution system required to deliver electricity and water to the customer. If the proper materials are not available when needed, construction crews will not be able to extend service to new customers in a timely fashion. During a loss of power or water pressure, the lack of a proper repair part could mean that a customer might be without service for an extended period of time. On a daily basis, even stocks of blank forms and envelopes must be kept on hand for the preparation of monthly bills.

Since the health and welfare of a community is involved, it would be easy to take the approach that large volumes of everything must be kept on hand to insure that there will never be a shortage. But customers also like low rates, and the value of inventory on hand can easily exceed 5 percent of the annual revenues of the utility. Thus the proper balance must be struck to provide proper inventory with the minimum financial impact on the customer.

Richard E. Malon
Water and Light Director
City of Columbia
Columbia, Missouri

Production/operations managers are responsible for operations cost control. One critical cost of operations is investment in raw materials, supplies, work-in-process, and finished products not yet shipped. If this investment becomes excessive, the results are high capital costs, high operating costs, and decreased production efficiency when too much space is used for inventory. Although these costs are apparent for manufacturing, it is easy to believe that service organizations do not have such inventory costs. Electricity is, after all, an "invisible" service we simply use when we turn on a switch. Yet, as Mr. Malon so aptly illustrates, inventory control is crucial to both efficiency and cost control in the generation and delivery of electricity and water to consumers who expect their public utility to provide good service at reasonable rates.

Operations managers usually develop a plan specifying desired levels for materials and they organize jobs to carry out this plan. Because of environmental influences, however, actual performance often does not conform to planned performance, and managers must exercise material (or inventory) control. Operations managers must monitor output, compare actual with planned output, and take corrective action through feedback mechanisms. The basics of inventory control are simply an application of control theory. As we have noted in this discussion and illustrated in Figure 14.1, inventory control relates closely to planning and organizing.

In most other functional production/operations areas, there is more of a balance between modeling and behavioral considerations than there is in inventory control. Inventory theory and modeling have been developed so thoroughly by applied mathematicians that one often is left in awe at the level of model sophistication. In this and the next chapter, we will focus on fundamental modeling, the richest approach for learning the basics of inventory control. In Chapter 16 our focus shifts to computer applications in material control.

Independent and Dependent Demand Previously we made the distinction between independent and dependent demand (Chapter 5). This chapter and the next reflect inventory control systems for independently demanded items, that is for items that are unrelated to one another. In Chapter 16 material requirements planning systems respond to demand where items are dependent upon one another, often the case in demand for assembled items or products. Before we turn to basic inventory concepts, let's briefly examine the elements of a control system in more detail than we have previously. Understanding control is important for managing inventories, but equally so for quality and overall cost control as well.

Elements of a Control System

Controlling is a process by which some aspect of a system is modified to achieve desired system performance. A homeowner, for example, may lower the thermostat setting at night to hold monthly heating bills within a budgeted amount. A manufacturer of luggage may decide to purchase leather from a new supplier when it discovers that present suppliers are

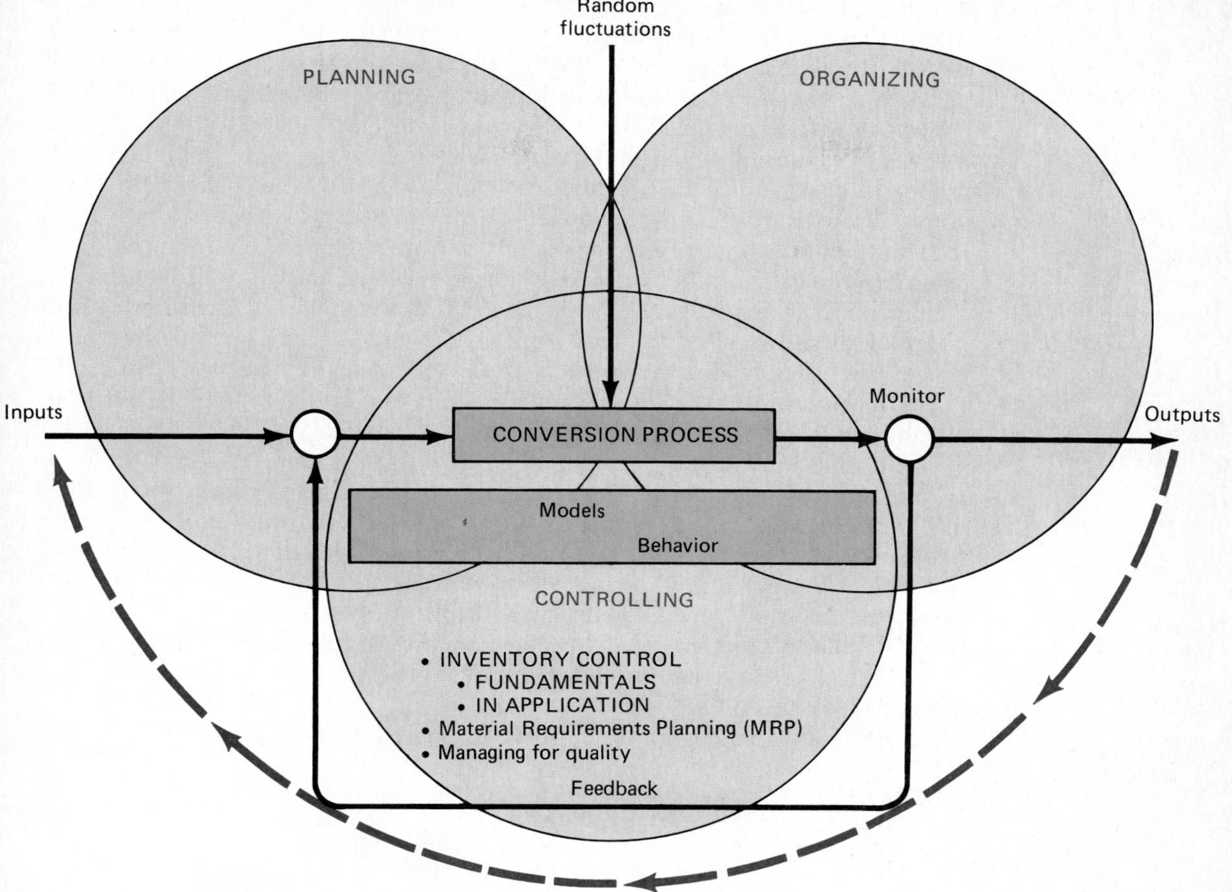

FIGURE 14.1
Production/operations management activities

providing inferior leather. The purpose of the control process is to cause the system to run true to its objectives. Control is not an end itself but rather a means to an end—improving system operation.

Conceptually, many kinds of systems—biological, social, mechanical, political, and economic—have control subsystems that share certain elements. These include system inputs, outputs, a sensor, a comparator, a memory, and an activator. The relationships among these subsystem elements are shown in Figure 14.2

Let's consider some aspects of control in manufacturing luggage. Overall, inputs (such as leather) provided to the conversion system are processed or converted for the purpose of creating desired outputs (luggage).

The outputs (luggage) are monitored and measured by a sensing device (a human inspector and/or test equipment). The resulting measurement (leather thickness or impact resistance) is used in the comparator to detect discrepancies between the measured output and a prespecified standard (luggage design specifications) for output. The performance standard, and allowable ranges of deviation from it, are stored in the memory element (in a book, a chart, blueprints, human memory, or some other form). The activator (foreman, manager, or mechanical device) receives information from the comparator and initiates corrective action when the comparator indicates discrepancies outside the tolerance range. The activator has a memory element containing rules for the type of corrective action ("Call the leather supplier to get a new shipment of leather") and the amount of corrective action (the quality and thickness of replacement leather needed). By modifying (correcting) the system inputs, managers change system output and monitor it again. Thus the entire process is repeated.

Information flows are essential to a control system. Without them, a system simply cannot exist—or if it does, it is certainly inoperable. In Figure 14.2, the information segments (*a*) through (*d*) comprise an information feedback loop. This feedback is the basis for all control systems. Information from the output side of the conversion process is transformed and fed back into the input side in a steady flow. In this way, management is continually able to compare actual performance with planned results.

Although we may be unaware of them, control systems operate around us all the time. When the pupils in your eyes enlarge or contract as light intensity changes, your body is using a control system. When your

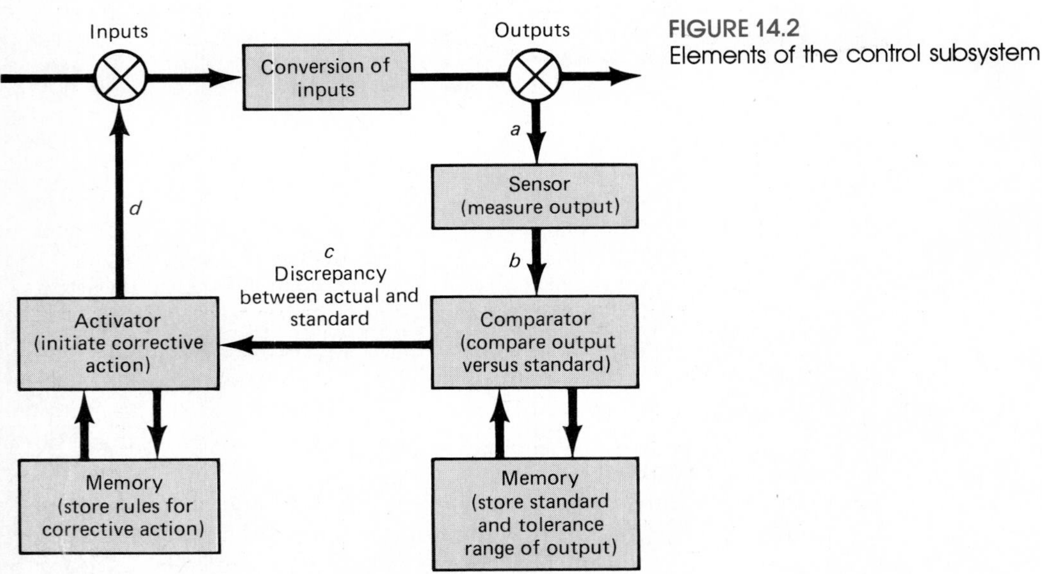

FIGURE 14.2
Elements of the control subsystem

automatic thermostat turns on the furnace because the room is you want it to be, it is operating a control system. Look again a and see if you can identify the subcomponents of these or systems.

INVENTORY CONCEPTS

Inventory Defined

Inventories play a major part in the economy of the United States, as Table 14.1 shows. These data alone suggest that operating managers should find inventory management a fruitful area for cost control. From the firm's viewpoint, inventories represent an investment; capital is required to hold materials at any stage of completion. Inventories should be evaluated in the same manner as other investments available to the firm and should be retained or increased only if they offer a favorable return on invested capital.

Inventory is stores of goods and stocks. In manufacturing, inventories are called stockkeeping items and are held at a stock (storage) point. Stockkeeping items usually consist of:

- raw materials,
- work-in-process,
- finished products, and
- supplies.

Inventory control is the technique of maintaining stockkeeping items at desired levels. Generally, product-oriented manufacturing organizations experience more tangible inventory situations than do labor-intense service-oriented organizations. In manufacturing, since the focus is on a physical product, emphasis is on materials and material control; in the service

TABLE 14.1
U.S. gross national product (GNP) and inventories (billions of 1972 adjusted dollars)

Year	GNP	Inventories	Inventories as a % of GNP
1950	533.5	130.2	24.4%
1960	736.8	171.6	23.2
1970	1075.3	261.3	24.3
1975	1202.3	292.1	24.3
1978	1385.1	318.0	22.9
1982*	1473.9	339.0	23.0

*Annual rate includes fourth quarter 1982 estimate.
Source: 1979 *Economic Report of the President,* pp. 184 and 201; 1982 *Economic Report of the President,* February, 1983, pp. 164, 183.

sector, the focus is on a service, and there is very little emphasis on materials or stocks. In many cases, services are consumed as they are generated rather than stocked for later consumption.

EXAMPLE

First National Bank is a commercial bank with full line services. The typical individual account includes various transactions: checking, savings, lock boxes, and loan transactions. Focusing on the teller operation, one has difficulty distinguishing among raw material, work-in-process, and finished goods inventories. The technical operation is to convert labor and material into the service of caring for money. The service is consumed as it is generated. Such materials as deposit slips, withdrawal slips, and loan payment coupons are more like operating supplies than raw materials. The accounting service depends upon properly completed slips and coupons; they could be viewed as work-in-process. Customer statements awaiting mailing could be viewed as finished goods (services).

EXAMPLE

St. Louis Diecasting Company is an aluminum and zinc diecasting company. It is an intermittent manufacturing company, a typical job shop. This company maintains an inventory mix typical of many firms. *Raw materials* include primary metal alloys of aluminum and zinc in ingot form. This bulk metal is subsequently melted and diecast into parts, and the diecast parts are custom fabricated. *Work-in-process* includes diecastings being transported by automatic conveyers, diecastings sitting idle awaiting fabrication (drilling, deburring, etc.), and diecastings awaiting packing. After packing, *finished goods* inventories are stored in pallets of boxes awaiting shipment to such customers as Caterpiller and General Motors, who use the diecastings in assembly operations. *Supplies* that support manufacturing include gloves, buffer wheels, drill bits, and packing materials.

In service-oriented organizations that are not so highly labor-intense, inventories assume more importance. Community blood banks must keep inventories of blood types; military organizations and transit systems maintain inventories of equipment and replacement parts. In local department stores, inventories must be substantial to encourage sales. Regardless of the specific institutional setting, production/operations management focuses on conversion of inputs into outputs of goods or services. This conversion process is reexamined with emphasis on material input in Figure 14.3. Note that there may be stock points at the input (raw material), conversion (work-in-process), and output (product) stages. Now, think about the definition of inventory control. Perhaps you can visualize a manufacturing or

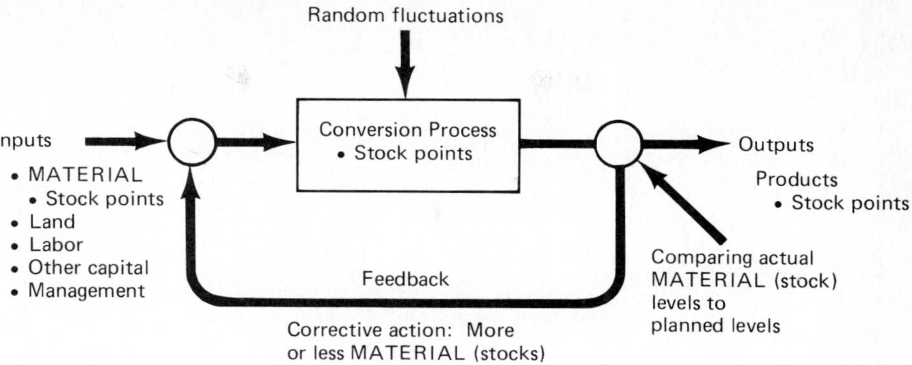

FIGURE 14.3
The conversion process: materials conversion

service facility where you have seen these inventory points and witnessed inventory control.

Why Inventories?

The fundamental reason for carrying inventories is that *it is physically impossible and economically impractical for each stock item to arrive exactly where it is needed exactly when it is needed.* Even were it physically possible for Alcoa to deliver aluminum ingots to St. Louis Diecasting every few hours, for example, it would still be prohibitively expensive. St. Louis Diecasting must therefore keep extra ingots in its supply of raw material inventory for use when they're needed in the conversion process.

Other reasons for carrying inventories are summarized in Table 14.2. Inventory should be viewed as an investment and should compete for

TABLE 14.2
Why organizations carry inventory

Level	Reason
Fundamental (primary)	Physical impossibility of getting right amount of stock at exact time of need Economical impracticality of getting right amount of stock at exact time of need
Secondary	Favorable return on investment Buffer to reduce uncertainty Decouple operations Level or smooth production Reduce material handling costs Allow production of family of parts Price changes (can be disadvantage) Bulk purchases Display to customers

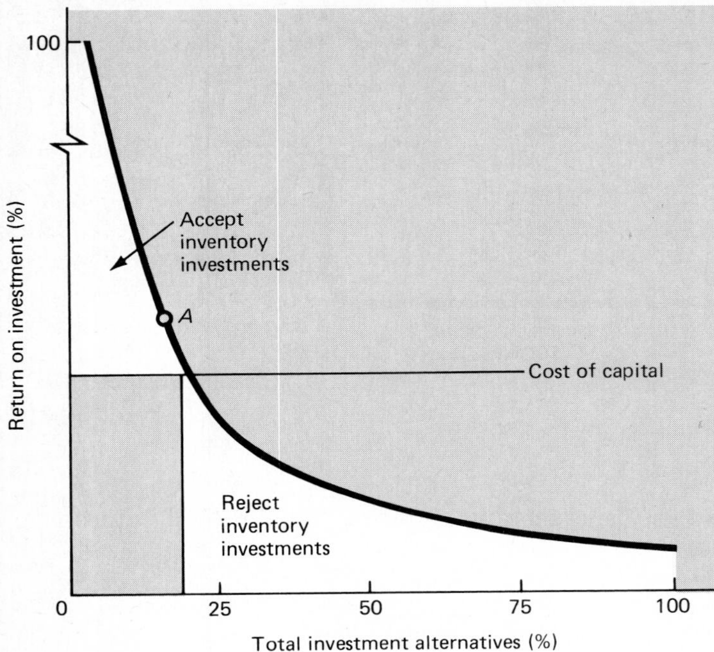

FIGURE 14.4
Typical marginal efficiency of capital curve (MEC)

funds with other investments contemplated by the firm. If you have studied finance, you have been introduced to the concept of the marginal efficiency of capital (MEC). This concept holds that a firm should invest in those alternatives that provide a greater return than capital costs to borrow. Look at Figure 14.4, which shows a marginal efficiency of capital curve. This figure shows the rates of return on various inventory investment alternatives (shown as a percentage of total investment alternatives). The MEC curve for this firm shows that about 20 percent of the inventory investment alternatives will give a return on investment above the cost of capital. That is, about 20 percent of the firm's inventory alternatives will bring the firm more money than it would have to spend if it borrowed money. These 20 percent of investments should be accepted. The 80 percent of the investment alternatives that would bring in less than the cost of capital should be rejected. Inventory investment alternative *A* in Figure 14.4, for example, is an acceptable investment. If inventory cannot compete on this same basis with other uses of funds (plant, equipment, land, advertising, bonds, etc.), then inventory should be reduced until it becomes an attractive alternative for the firm.

Both manufacturing and service firms are interested in return-on-investment or return-on-assets employed. Return-on-assets is profits divided by assets. With a little thought we realize: (profits/assets) = (profits/sales)(sales/assets). Profits/sales is markup and sales/assets is turnover.

Now we see that one way to improve return-on-investment is to increase turnover. We want to sell those assets that are inventory over and over again in a reasonable time frame. One way to do this is to keep the assets in inventory low, thus improving the chance of high inventory turnover.

When demand is unusually high, some protection is needed against the prospects of high stockout costs. Inventory can be used to "buffer" against such uncertainties. Likewise, procurement *lead time,* the time between ordering and receiving goods, is not always constant. Buffer stocks can be used to protect against stockouts from uncertain demand during procurement lead times.

Inventories are also useful when they *decouple* operations, when they break operations apart so that one operation's supply is independent of another's supply. This decoupling function serves two purposes. First, inventories are needed to reduce the dependencies among successive stages of operations so that breakdowns, material shortages, or other production fluctuations at one stage do not cause later stages of operations to shut down. Figure 14.5 illustrates this concept in a diecasting firm. The diagram shows that although the drilling operation has no diecasts stored as in-process inventories, deburring and packing do have inventory waiting for them. Since deburring and packing could continue to operate from inventories should diecasting and drilling be shut down, they can be decoupled from the production processes that precede them.

A second purpose of decoupling through inventories is to let one organization unit schedule its operations independently of another. In automobile manufacturing, for example, engine buildup can be scheduled separately from seat assembly, and each can be decoupled from final automobile assembly operations through in-process inventories.

Inventories can also assist in leveling production. When we examined aggregate planning and scheduling in Chapter 11, we noted that products can be built through slack demand periods and used in peak demand periods. Thus high costs of production rate and work force level changes can be avoided.

FIGURE 14.5
Decoupling of operations by using inventory

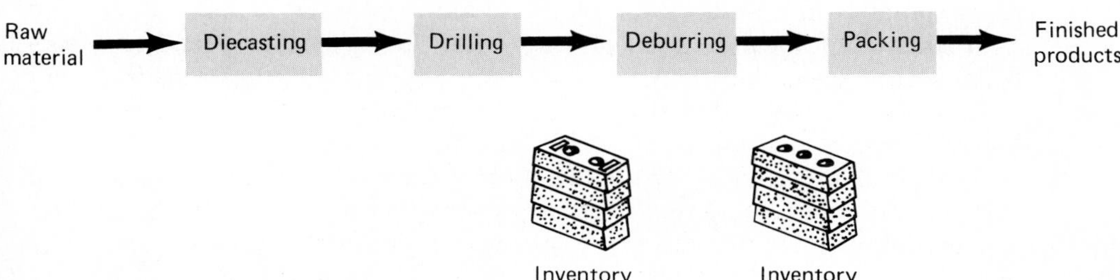

In some manufacturing and service operations, material handling costs can be reduced by accumulating parts between operations. This is particularly true of intermittent systems, since they involve less automation of material handling than do continuous systems. Parts can be accumulated and inventoried in tote boxes or baskets and transported by handjack dollies or fork-lift trucks much more economically than they can be carried by hand. In continuous manufacturing, automated material handling systems, rather than larger work-in-process inventories, are designed to reduce overall handling costs.

Inventories are also useful in the production of similar parts, called a family of parts. Here, inventories enable operations to be conducted more economically.

The strategy in the example shown on the next page obviously increases in-process and finished goods inventories. Since overall savings in setup costs more than offset the added investment in inventories, however, the strategy provides a favorable return on investment.

Inventories can also be carried to take advantage of price changes. With bulk purchases, quantity discounts can be arranged, thus providing a cost advantage of inventories. If firms practice economies of scale in production by producing large volumes, or if a firm's transportation costs are lower for bulk shipments, those firms often offer quantity discounts.

EXAMPLE

In the production of roll-formed aluminum trim pieces for refrigerator shelves, often the only difference among parts is length (various refrigerator models use parts of different lengths). The setup of a rolling machine requires from eight to sixteen hours. Thousands of pieces per hour can be manufactured once a setup has been made. Thirty minutes or less are required to change the cutoff press at the end of the rolling machine for various part lengths. Therefore, for the costs and volumes involved in this low unit cost roll form, it is best to schedule and produce a family of many different parts, perhaps a dozen, for as much as six months ahead of demand at any one setup.

Inventory System Concepts

Multistage Inventories When parts are stocked at more than one stage in the sequential production process, there are multistage inventories. Figure 14.5 illustrated several stages of production in a diecasting facility. Since there is interaction between inventory items in the various stages (raw material, diecastings, drilled parts, etc.), it is a difficult problem to establish balanced inventory levels at each stage and for the system overall. Our treatment in this chapter will focus on inventory at a single stage, with little consideration of interactions of the various stages. Materials requirements for successive stages will be discussed in Chapter 16.

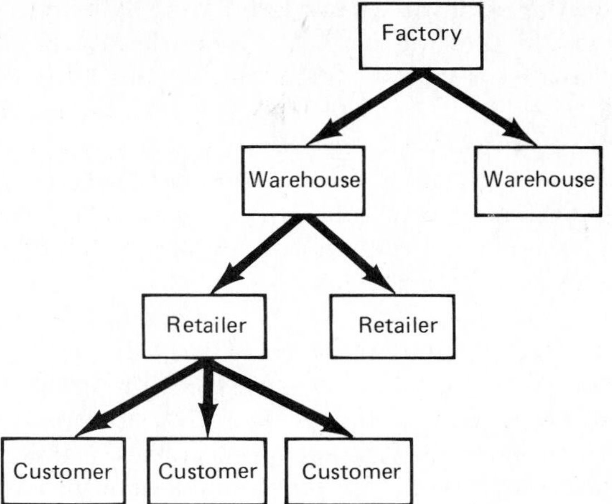

FIGURE 14.6
Multiechelon inventory systems

Multiechelon Inventories In inventory systems, multiple institutional levels are involved in converting raw materials into consumer products. The factory level, for example, supplies products to the warehouse level, and the warehouse supplies the retailer who, in turn, supplies the customer. Each level is called an echelon. Multiechelon inventories, illustrated in Figure 14.6, include products stocked at the various levels in the distribution system. Our introductory discussion will center on inventory problems at individual echelons.

EXAMPLE

In a large medical center composed of a hospital, a medical school, a school of nursing, and auxiliary research units, the annual expenditure for disposable surgical gloves exceeded $75,000. The stores clerk, who set reorder points and stock levels for the gloves, said that she carried high volumes because demand to central stores was erratic, with occasional large withdrawals. Further examination uncovered two additional echelons of glove inventory in the hospital: stocked gloves on the hospital floor or wing housing a surgery room and stocked gloves in the doctors' and nurses' offices and desks. Thus, demand in central stores was buffered by storerooms near surgery, and storerooms were buffered by emergency supplies in offices.

Reaction to Demand Changes The system should not have to react to rising demand by changing inventories in direct proportion to the increase in demand. As the hospital example illustrated, this is sometimes a complication in a multiechelon inventory structure. One statistical study of inventory-sales ratios in selected firms in Australia and the United States concluded that *an increase in demand can be serviced by a less than proportional increase in inventories.*[1] The converse is also true; when demand decreases, inventories cannot be decreased in direct proportion. Many firms became aware of this concept first hand in the 1974–1975 and 1980–1982 recessions. As demand weakened during these periods, many firms reduced their inventories too much and suffered substantial production cost increases as a result.

The Operating Doctrine

Operations managers must make two basic inventory policy decisions: *when* to reorder stock and *how much* stock to reorder. These decisions are referred to as the *inventory control operating doctrine.*

The time to reorder is called the reorder point. A system signal, usually a predetermined inventory level, tells clerical or other responsible personnel when it is time to reorder stocks. The amount that should be reordered is called the order quantity. *The inventory level that signals the need to reorder and the reorder quantity selected are economic decisions at the heart of the operations manager's inventory control function.* Although the manager may not actually operate the control system, he or she is responsible for setting the operating doctrine.

Inventory Systems

Q/R Inventory System One practical way to establish an inventory system is to keep count of every item issued from stores and place an order for more stock when inventories dwindle to a predetermined level, the reorder point. The order is fixed in size (volume), size having been predetermined. Thus, for a quantity-reorder point (Q/R) system, the operating doctrine is established by specifying both when and how much to reorder. Once established, the doctrine is continuously reapplied.

Figure 14.7 illustrates two Q/R inventory systems. In the system on the left, the demand for inventories, the usage rate, is known and constant. Replenishment inventories are assumed to be received at the stock point the moment they have been ordered. Notice that at the beginning of the time axis (far left) an order seems just to have arrived. As time goes by, inventory is steadily depleted until a level of R_1 units is reached. At R_1, the reorder point (also called the trigger level), another order is placed for Q_1 units from the supplier. These units arrive at the instant they are ordered. Procurement lead time is zero. The usage pattern is then repeated, and at level R_2, quantity Q_2 is ordered. In a simple case like this, there would be no need to carry buffer stocks; delivery is instantaneous, and the demand for the inventory item is known for certain. Thus R_1 is set at zero units.

[1]See J. M. Samuels and D. J. Smyth, "Statistical Evidence on the Relationship Between a Company's Sales and Its Inventories," *International Journal of Production Research* 6, no. 3 (1968), pp. 249–56.

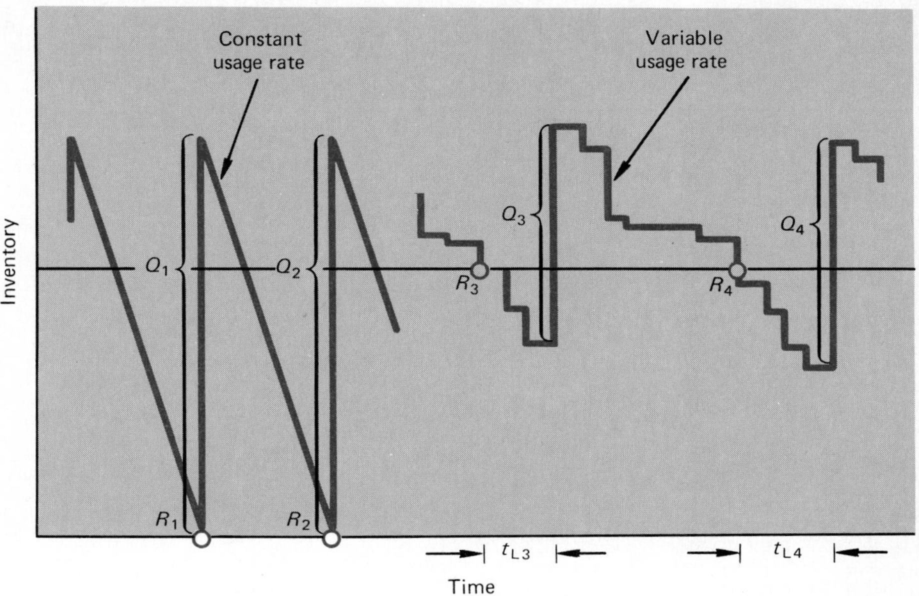

FIGURE 14.7
Q/R inventory systems

In a Q/R system, both the reorder quantity and the reorder point are fixed. For Figure 14.7, then:

$$R_1 = R_2 \text{ and } Q_1 = Q_2$$

A second and slightly more complex inventory situation is shown at the right of Figure 14.7. Usage (demand) is variable; we do not know in advance how rapidly inventory will be depleted. Here again, a reorder quantity and reorder point have been established as the operating doctrine. As before, $R_3 = R_4$ and $Q_3 = Q_4$; however, as you can see, somewhat different procedures are used to determine their values. It is difficult to establish the most economical operating doctrine when demand varies, as it does here, and even more difficult when lead time varies too. Since lead time is the time between placing and receiving an order, it is shown as t_{L3} and t_{L4} on the graph. When either demand or lead time varies, the time interval between orders varies—but the order quantity always remains constant.

Periodic Inventory System Another practical inventory control method is to examine inventories only at set time intervals, periodically, and to then reorder an amount equal to some preestablished base stock level. In peri-

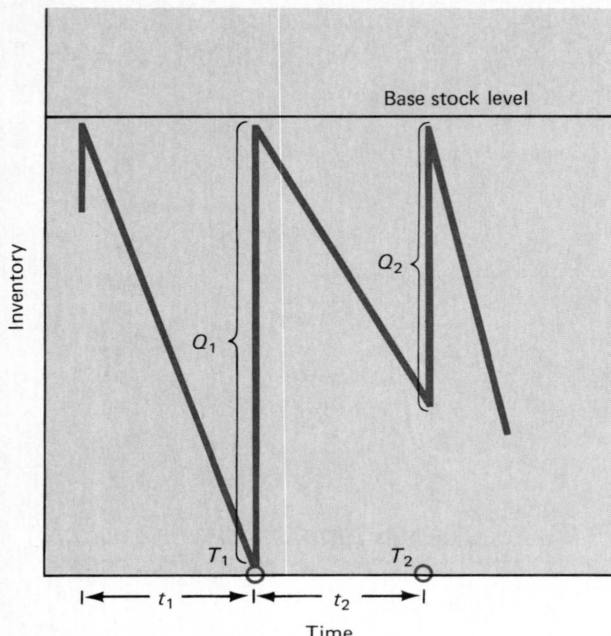

FIGURE 14.8
Periodic inventory system

odic systems the time interval between reviews is always constant, but the order quantity varies. As Figure 14.8 illustrates, the level of inventory is examined at times T_1 and T_2, and orders are placed for quantities Q_1 and Q_2. The base stock level and the time between orders, t_1 and t_2, are set by operations management and comprise the inventory system's operating doctrine. In the periodic system $t_1 = t_2$, but Q_1 does not necessarily equal Q_2. Although Figure 14.8 shows constant demand within any one review period and zero lead time, these conditions could be relaxed and still allow the periodic inventory system concepts to be retained.

In this book, we will emphasize Q/R systems. Although we will concentrate on determining economic order quantities and reorder points, however, remember that the procedures are similar for the periodic system. Economic order quantity in the Q/R system and base stock levels in the periodic system both determine how much to order; reorder point in the Q/R system and time between orders in the periodic system both determine when to order.

INVENTORY COSTS

In operating an inventory system managers should consider only those costs that vary directly with the operating doctrine in deciding when and how much to reorder; costs independent of the operating doctrine are irrelevant. Once the relevant costs have been identified, managers can seek an operating doctrine that will result in cost minimization. Basically, there are five types of relevant costs:

1. the cost of the item itself,
2. the costs associated with procuring the stocks,
3. the costs of carrying the stock items in inventory,
4. the costs associated with being out of stock when units are demanded but are unavailable, and
5. operating costs associated with data gathering and control procedures for the inventory system.

Often these five costs are combined in one way or another, but let's discuss them separately before we consider combinations that may be used in different inventory situations.

Cost of Item

The cost, or value, of the item is the sum paid to the supplier for the item received or the direct manufacturing cost if produced. It is normally equal to the purchase price. In some instances, however, transportation, receiving, or inspection costs, for example, may be included as part of the costs of the item. If the item unit cost is constant for all quantities ordered, the total cost of purchased goods needed during the planning horizon is irrelevant to the operating doctrine. (We show in this chapter's supplement how it drops out of the total cost equation when we model this situation.) If the unit cost varies with the quantity ordered, however, this cost is relevant. Often, in practice, price per unit decreases for larger order quantities; a price reduction called a quantity discount.

Procurement Costs

Procurement costs are those incurred by placing a purchase order or incurred as set-up costs if manufactured. These costs vary directly with each purchase order placed. Procurement costs include costs of postage, perhaps telephone calls to the vendor, labor costs in purchasing and accounting, receiving costs, computer time for record keeping, and purchase order supplies.

Inventory Carrying Costs

Carrying, or holding, costs are the real out-of-pocket costs associated with having inventory on hand. Typical out-of-pocket costs include insurance, warehouse rental, heat, light, taxes, and losses due to pilferage, spoilage, or breakage. Another opportunity cost, while not an out-of-pocket cost, must be considered—the cost incurred by having capital tied up in inventory. If funds are borrowed to finance the inventory purchase, interest payments are direct costs. The size of all these carrying costs usually increases or decreases in proportion to the amount of inventory that is carried.

For example, the high costs of borrowing money in the United States during the first half of 1980 directly affected inventory levels. As the prime interest rate approached 20 percent, the Federal Reserve Bank placed additional margin restrictions on commercial banks to limit spending. Although we were most aware of decreased consumer borrowing and spending on durables and the crunch in automobile and housing industries, pressures were severe on production/operations managers throughout industry to reduce their investment in inventories.

Stockout Costs

Stockout costs, associated with demand when stocks have been depleted, take the form of lost sales costs or backorder costs. When sales are lost because of stockouts, the firm loses both the profit margin on actual unmade sales and customer good will. If customers take their business elsewhere, future profit margins may also be lost.

When customers agree to come back after inventories have been replenished, they make backorders. Backorder costs include loss of good will and money paid to reorder goods and notify customers when goods arrive. At times, the choice is made to incur an expediting cost to avoid a stockout. Special delivery, air freight, or similar costs can be treated as a special stockout cost as are the lost sales or backorder costs.

EXAMPLE

A customer at First National Bank had two unpleasant banking experiences this year. First, he went to a teller to get six rolls each of dimes and quarters. At this drive-in banking facility, the teller was out of rolls of dimes; she substituted two rolls of nickels but could spare no more. This forced the customer to make another stop at a competitor bank. The second experience was an attempt to obtain an $8,000 commercial rate loan to purchase some land. The customer agreed to provide adequate stocks and bonds as collateral but was refused the loan because loan funds were not available, not because he was a bad risk. The customer received the loan at a competitor bank and thereafter did all his banking at the competitor.

As this example shows, stockouts can and do occur in the service industries as well as in manufacturing. Stockouts can result in lost service opportunities, lost interest or profit, and lost customer good will.

Cost of Operating the Information Processing System

Whether by hand or by computer, someone must update records as stock levels change. In those systems in which inventory levels are not recorded daily, this operating cost is primarily incurred in obtaining accurate physical counts of inventories. Frequently, these operating costs are more *fixed* than variable over a wide quantity (volume) range. Therefore, since fixed costs are not relevant in establishing the operating doctrine, we will not consider them further.

Cost Tradeoffs

Our objective in inventory control is to find the *minimum cost operating doctrine* over some planning horizon. We need to consider all relevant costs—the cost of the item, procurement costs, carrying costs, and stockout costs. Using an annual planning horizon, these costs can be expressed in a general cost equation:

Total annual relevant costs	=	Cost of the item	+	Procurement costs	+	Carrying costs • Cycle stocks • Buffer stocks	+	Stockout costs • Lost sales • Backorders	**(14.1)**

Each of the costs in the equation can be expressed in terms of order quantity and reorder point for a given inventory situation. The solution method is then to *minimize* the total cost situation. This can be accomplished graphically; by tabular analysis using trial and error; or by using the calculus, the most accurate method. Using the calculus, operations researchers have developed a wide range of optimal formulas, which vary with changes in the actual inventory situation.

Graphically, the minimization of this equation consists of cost tradeoffs. For a simple model in which costs of purchased goods (items) and stockouts are irrelevant, the tradeoff is between only two cost components, procurement and carrying costs (see Figure 14.9). Notice that annual car-

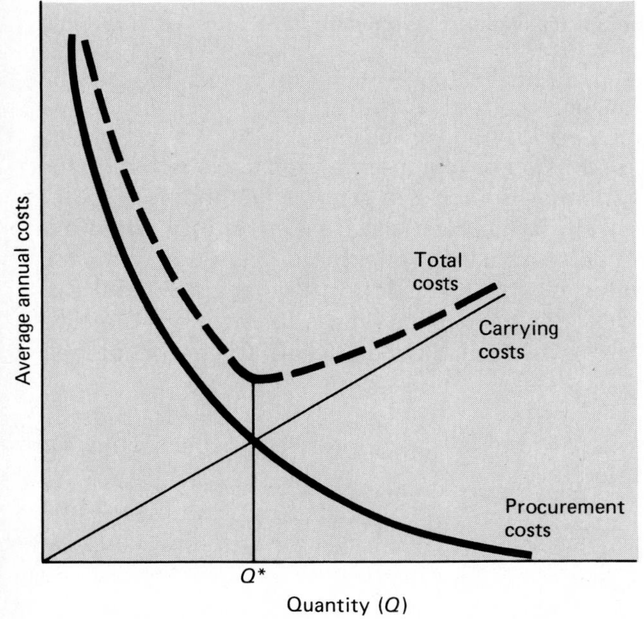

FIGURE 14.9
Cost tradeoffs in inventory control

rying costs increase with larger values of order quantity, Q. This is logical; large values of Q result in large average inventory levels and, therefore, large carrying costs. Likewise, when Q increases, fewer orders must be placed during the year and annual ordering costs decrease. Therefore, as shown in Figure 14.9, procurement costs decrease as carrying costs increase. There is a *cost tradeoff* between the two. If we add the costs graphically, we obtain a total cost curve. The optimal order quantity is the point at which annual total cost is at a minimum, Q^* in this case.

For more complex cost situations, the cost curves become difficult to graph and analyze tabularly, *but the cost tradeoff concepts remain the same*. In practice, although many inventory situations are never formally analyzed, successful operations managers take into account relevant costs and the tradeoffs between these costs as they attempt to control inventory. Intuitive decision makers in inventory control must consider these costs if they are to operate successfully.

INVENTORY MODELING

The methodology for modeling inventory situations is straightforward. The purpose is to derive an operating doctrine, and four simple steps are involved.

1. Examine the inventory situation carefully, listing characteristics and assumptions concerning the situation.
2. Develop the total annual relevant cost equation in narrative.
3. Transform the total annual cost equation from narrative into the shorthand logic of mathematics.
4. Optimize the cost equation, finding the optimum for how much to order (order quantity) and when to reorder (reorder point).

As mentioned in our discussion of inventory systems, we will develop models only for the Q/R system, although the general methodology holds for the periodic system as well. Remember, too, that inventory situations can be classified as either *deterministic* (variables are known with certainty) or *stochastic* (variables are probabilistic). In this chapter we'll discuss two deterministic models, especially the simple lot size formula, saving our discussion of a third deterministic model and stochastic models until Chapter 16.

Variables in Inventory Models

For model development and discussion, we will use the following notation.

D = Annual demand in units
Q = Quantity ordered
Q^* = Optimal order quantity
R = Reorder point

t_L = Lead time
S = Setup or procurement cost per order
I = Carrying charge per unit, expressed as a percentage rate
C = Cost of the individual item; the purchase cost per item
K = Stockout cost per unit out of stock
P = Production rate; units per period of time
d_L = Demand per unit of time during lead time
D_L = Demand during lead time; total demand during lead time

DETERMINISTIC INVENTORY MODELS

The Simple Lot Size Formula

The earliest derivation of what is often called the simple lot size formula was developed by Ford Harris in 1915.[2] Apparently, it was again independently derived by R. H. Wilson, who popularized it. In his honor, it is sometimes referred to as the *Wilson formula.*

This inventory situation assumes that:

1. inventory is being controlled at one point (in a stockroom or in raw materials, for example),
2. demand is deterministic and at a constant known rate per year,
3. no stockouts are allowed,
4. lead time is constant and independent of demand, and
5. the purchase cost per unit is fixed.

To simplify the case even further, lead time can be assumed to be zero; that is, delivery is instantaneous.

What will the total annual relevant cost equation look like? Let's modify equation 14.1 to fit this situation:

$$\begin{matrix}\text{Total annual} \\ \text{relevant costs}\end{matrix} = \begin{matrix}\text{Procurement} \\ \text{costs}\end{matrix} + \begin{matrix}\text{Carrying} \\ \text{costs}\end{matrix} \qquad \mathbf{(14.2)}$$

Stockouts do not occur, and the annual cost of purchased goods is excluded, since the purchase price per unit is fixed. Only those costs that can be affected by our choice of Q are included. Expanding equation 14.2,

$$\begin{matrix}\text{Total} \\ \text{annual} \\ \text{relevant} \\ \text{costs}\end{matrix} = \begin{pmatrix}\text{Cost of} \\ \text{ordering}\end{pmatrix}\begin{pmatrix}\text{Number of} \\ \text{orders} \\ \text{placed/yr}\end{pmatrix} + \begin{pmatrix}\text{Cost of} \\ \text{carrying} \\ \text{one unit}\end{pmatrix}\begin{pmatrix}\text{Average} \\ \text{number of} \\ \text{units carried}\end{pmatrix} \qquad \mathbf{(14.3)}$$

$$TC = S\begin{pmatrix}\text{Number of} \\ \text{orders placed/yr}\end{pmatrix} + IC\begin{pmatrix}\text{Average number} \\ \text{of units}\end{pmatrix}$$

[2]Ford Harris, *Operations and Cost* (Chicago: A. W. Shaw Company, 1915), pp. 48–52.

The number of orders placed per year can be expressed in terms of annual demand and order quantity. Since

$$\text{Annual demand} = \begin{pmatrix}\text{Quantity ordered} \\ \text{in each order}\end{pmatrix}\begin{pmatrix}\text{Number of orders} \\ \text{placed per year}\end{pmatrix} \tag{14.4}$$

then

$$\begin{aligned}\begin{matrix}\text{Number of orders} \\ \text{placed per year}\end{matrix} &= \frac{\text{Annual demand}}{\text{Quantity ordered in each order}} \\ &= \frac{D}{Q}\end{aligned}$$

How can we determine the average inventory per year? Look again at the constant usage situation in Figure 14.7. What is the maximum inventory, the highest that inventory will ever be? It is the order quantity, Q. What is the lowest inventory? Since we reorder when the stock is fully depleted, the lowest is zero. This intermittent pattern, in which inventories vary from maximum to minimum and then back to maximum, is called a cycle. For *any one cycle,* the average inventory would be:

$$\begin{aligned}\begin{matrix}\text{Average inventory} \\ \text{per cycle}\end{matrix} &= \frac{\text{Maximum inventory} + \text{Minimum inventory}}{2} \\ &= \frac{Q + 0}{2} \\ &= \frac{Q}{2}\end{aligned}$$

Think about the several cycles of inventory orders in Figure 14.7. The average for any *one* of these cycles is $Q/2$, but what is the average inventory per year? It is still $Q/2$. *Average inventory is time independent.*

EXAMPLE

Morrison, Inc., orders new trays and issues them to various cafeterias from central stores. If Morrison orders 1,000 trays eight times a year, what is the *annual average inventory* in trays, presuming all the assumptions for the simple lot size formula hold? The average inventory for the first, second, and so on to the eighth cycle would be 1,000/2, or 500. Try to picture the cycling of inventories eight times and the annual effect of this cycling. For the *entire year,* the maximum would be 1,000 and the minimum 0, and the uniform usage would produce an average inventory of 500 new trays.

Substituting our expressions for the number of orders placed per year and average inventory into equation 14.3, our total cost equation becomes

$$TC = S\frac{D}{Q} + IC\frac{Q}{2} \tag{14.5}$$

From this total cost equation evolves the formula for the optimal order quantity:

$$Q^* = \sqrt{\frac{2DS}{IC}} \tag{14.6}$$

What happens was illustrated graphically in Figure 14.9. The total annual costs of this situation involve a tradeoff between annual carrying costs and annual procurement costs. The optimal economic order quantity, Q^*, is located at the low point of the total cost curve, also the point of intersection of the procurement and carrying cost curves.

Since delivery is instantaneous, the reorder point should be set at the lowest point possible, zero, to avoid carrying excess stocks. The operating doctrine, then, is:

$$\begin{aligned} &\text{Order} && Q^* = \sqrt{\frac{2DS}{IC}} \\ &\text{At the point} && R^* = 0 \end{aligned}$$

The calculus is not necessary for understanding the cost tradeoffs illustrated in Figure 14.9 nor for understanding that a low point in the total cost curve is where the optimal order quantity, Q^*, occurs. If you want to see how the calculus is used in this derivation, read the supplement at the end of this chapter.

EXAMPLE

Our Redeemer Catholic Church orders candles periodically, and delivery is essentially instantaneous. Annual demand, estimated to be 180 candles, is constant. Candles cost $8 per dozen; the cost of placing the order is estimated to be $9; and the annual carrying charge is estimated to be 15 percent of the candle cost. What quantity should the priest order, and when should he reorder? Calculate the economic order quantity:

$$Q^* = \sqrt{\frac{2DS}{IC}}$$

$$= \frac{\sqrt{2\left(\frac{180}{12}\right)(9)}}{.15(8)}$$

$$= \sqrt{225}$$

$$Q^* = 15 \text{ dozen}$$

The priest should order 15 dozen. Since delivery is instantaneous, he should order only upon depleting stock, which happens exactly once a year. The operating doctrine is $Q^* = 15$ dozen candles at the point $R^* = 0$.

In our example, the priest is ordering periodically, perhaps intuitively. Possibly he considers that the reasonable cost of candles ($8 per dozen) and the high cost of placing an order ($9) mean that he needn't order very frequently. This raises an important question. How *sensitive* are costs to optimal order quantity? When he's intuitively ordering candles, how far away from optimal order quantity could the priest be and still have relatively low costs? Let's examine the sensitivity of the simple lot size formula.

Model Sensitivity We can compare the sensitivity of total costs (TC) for any operating system with the total costs for an optimal inventory system (TC^*) by using the ratio TC/TC^*. To do this, we compute TC/TC^* as a function of Q/Q^*.

$$\frac{TC}{TC^*} = \frac{S\frac{D}{Q} + IC\frac{Q}{2}}{S\frac{D}{Q^*} + IC\frac{Q^*}{2}} \tag{14.7}$$

Substituting $Q^* = \sqrt{2DS/IC}$ into equation 14.7 and solving algebraically, we find the general relationship

$$\frac{TC}{TC^*} = \frac{1}{2}\left[\frac{Q^*}{Q} + \frac{Q}{Q^*}\right] \tag{14.8}$$

Note that the total cost ratio in this equation is expressed solely in terms of Q and Q^*. If our existing order quantity (Q) is very close to optimal (Q^*), the ratio TC/TC^* is slightly larger than unity. As Q departs farther from Q^*,

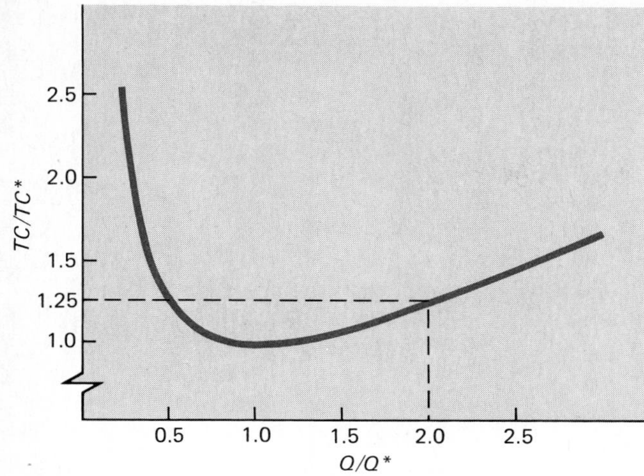

FIGURE 14.10
Inventory sensitivity—simple lot size case

Source: G. Hadley and T. M. Whitin, *Analysis of Inventory Systems* (Englewood Cliffs, N.J.: Prentice-Hall, Inc., 1963), p. 36.

we expect TC/TC^* also to grow. Graphically, the relation between Q/Q^* and TC/TC^* for the simple lot size case (equation 14.7) is shown in Figure 14.10. Note the flatness of the curve around the minimum point, 1.0 on each axis. If actual Q is off from optimal either direction by a factor of two, costs are increased by only 25 percent. This has important practical implications. For cases that fit the assumptions of the simple lot size model, improving ordering rules won't save much money. Correcting an ordering rule, even one far from optimal, might not result in a very large dollar savings.

EXAMPLE

Thompson Tooling has a Department of Defense contract for 150,000 bushings a year. Thompson orders the metal for the bushings in lots of 40,000 units from a supplier. It costs \$40 to place an order, and estimated carrying costs are 20 percent of the item cost, \$.15. Thompson wants to know what the percent variation their order quantity is from optimal and what this variation is costing them, if anything. Finding optimal order quantity:

$$Q^* = \sqrt{\frac{2DS}{IC}}$$

$$= \sqrt{\frac{2(150{,}000)(40)}{.2(.15)}}$$

$$Q^* = 20{,}000$$

Comparing optimal order quantity to current order quantity, Q:

$$\frac{TC}{TC^*} = \frac{1}{2}\left[\frac{Q^*}{Q} + \frac{Q}{Q^*}\right]$$
$$= \frac{1}{2}\left[\frac{20{,}000}{40{,}000} + \frac{40{,}000}{20{,}000}\right]$$
$$\frac{TC}{TC^*} = 1.25$$

This calculation shows that even though order quantity deviates from optimal by 20,000 units, or 100 percent, the costs are only 25 percent higher than optimal. The excess (marginal) costs of the nonoptimal order quantity can be found as follows:

$$\text{Marginal costs} = 0.25\ (TC^*)$$
$$= 0.25\left(S\frac{D}{Q^*} + IC\frac{Q^*}{2}\right)$$
$$= 0.25\left(\frac{40(150{,}000)}{20{,}000} + \frac{.2(.15)(20{,}000)}{2}\right)$$
$$= 0.25\ (300 + 300)$$
$$= \$150$$

Alternatively,

$$TC^* = S\frac{D}{Q^*} + IC\frac{Q^*}{2}$$
$$= \frac{(40)(150{,}000)}{20{,}000} + \frac{(.20)(.15)(20{,}000)}{2}$$
$$= 300 + 300$$
$$= \$600$$

and

$$TC\text{ actual} = \frac{(40)(150{,}000)}{40{,}000} + \frac{(.20)(.15)(40{,}000)}{2}$$
$$= 150 + 600$$
$$= \$750$$

Marginal cost of the nonoptimal policy is \$750 − \$600, or \$150.

Notice from this example that for annual purchases valued at \$22,500, even though order quantity was off *100 percent,* the cost to Thompson Tooling was only an additional \$150. You may also note that for the TC^* calculation, ordering costs are equal to carrying costs, each being \$300. This is just what we illustrated graphically earlier.

In inventory modeling, the manager or inventory clerk is confronted with the issue of rounding numbers. Order quantities, for example, often cannot be a number such as 247.3. Instead, 247 or 248 items must be ordered. (On the computer, the rounding rule that is used manually can be programmed.) Similarly, suppose that an item must be ordered in gross quantities (multiples of 144); then either 144 or 288 must be ordered. Although rounding compromises the optimal solution, this decision is often forced on the manager for practical reasons.

Gradual Replacement Model

Sometimes, part of the delivery is instantaneous upon ordering, but the rest of the units are sent little by little over time. When the order is placed, the supplier begins producing units, which are supplied continuously to the purchaser. While these units are being added into inventory (causing it to grow), customers are drawing units out of inventory (causing it to diminish). Consider the case in which replenishment rate exceeds withdrawal rates. After some time, the order quantity has been produced, and net inventories have increased. The inventory level, however, never reaches the same high level as the simple lot size model, the order quantity. This situation is illustrated in Figure 14.11. During the time t_p, the slope of inventory accumulation is not vertical, as it was in the simple lot size model. This is the case because the entire order is not received at one time. Here, the production rate (ability to supply) must always be greater than the demand rate ($P > D$). This means that during the time t_p, inventory is consumed as well as built up, and this situation continues until the initial order quantity, Q, has been produced and delivered. At that point, inventory is at its maximum. Thereafter, during time t_d, demand occurs while the process used for production is idle or shifts to other jobs. At the end of time t_d, another order for Q is placed, production startup is instantaneous, and the cycle repeats.

As with the simple lot size case, we assume demand is known with certainty, and production (delivery) begins instantaneously upon placing an order. However, the order for the entire lot is filled continuously over time, not immediately as was the case with the simple lot size model.

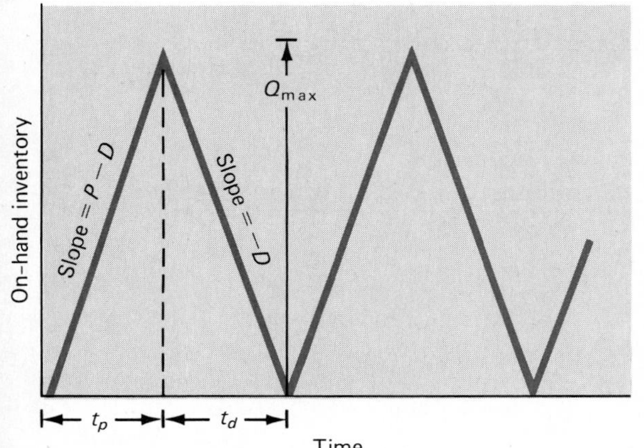

FIGURE 14.11
Gradual replacement (finite production rate) inventory situation

Still applying the other assumptions of the lot size model, the total annual cost equation for this model is the same as equation 14.2:

$$\text{Total annual relevant costs} = \text{Procurement costs} + \text{Carrying costs} \qquad \textbf{(14.2)}$$

It can be written:

$$TC = S\frac{D}{Q} + IC\left(\begin{matrix}\text{Average number}\\ \text{of units}\end{matrix}\right)$$

As we have noted, maximum inventory never reaches Q but is something less. Therefore, average inventory carried will not be Q/2. Realizing that the positive slope of the graph is P − D and the negative slope is −D, we can find the maximum inventory, Q_{max}, from

$$\text{Slope} = \frac{\text{Rise}}{\text{Run}}$$

$$P - D = \frac{Q_{max}}{t_p}$$

But the length of time required to produce a lot is

$$t_p = \frac{Q}{P}$$

Substituting

$$P - D = \frac{Q_{max}}{\frac{Q}{P}}$$

$$Q_{max} = (P - D)\frac{Q}{P} = Q\left(\frac{P - D}{P}\right)$$

Average inventory is then:

$$\text{Average inventory} = \frac{\text{Maximum inventory} + \text{Minimum inventory}}{2}$$

$$= \frac{\frac{Q(P - D)}{P} + 0}{2}$$

$$\text{Average inventory} = \frac{Q}{2}\left(\frac{P - D}{P}\right)$$

The total cost equation to be minimized for the gradual replacement correction case is:

$$TC = S\frac{D}{Q} + IC\left(\frac{Q}{2}\left[\frac{P - D}{P}\right]\right) \tag{14.9}$$

which yields

$$Q^* = \sqrt{\frac{2DS}{IC}\left(\frac{P}{P - D}\right)} \tag{14.10}$$

Since production and resupply begin instantaneously, the optimal reorder point would again be at $R^* = 0$. Note that for this operating doctrine, the formula for Q^* is identical to Q^* for the simple lot size model (equation 14.6) except for the *finite correction factor,* $(P/(P - D))^{1/2}$. Will this finite correction result in Q^* being greater here than in the simple lot size formula? Examine the factor and remember that $P > D$.

In the next example, an order should be placed for 1,414 salads when there are no salads on hand. If salads are served 365 days a year, the daily usage is a little less than 83 salads; production capability is slightly over 123 salads per day. When 1,414 salads are ordered, it takes about 11.5 days to produce them and about 17 days to consume them. A salad may be kept fresh, however, for a maximum of 5.5 days. The manager should therefore question whether it is feasible to meet the restriction. This situation illustrates for us how inaccurate costs or an inappropriate inventory model can distort reality. If a salad *cannot* be kept long enough, something must be changed. Carrying costs may have to be increased; this would force smaller order quantities. Production rates may have to be reduced to be more in line with demand. Or perhaps a more appropriate inventory model should be used to reflect more accurately the cost of perishable goods. We suspect the carrying costs are unrealistically low. This model is valid and the calculations correct for the information given in the illustration. As the example shows, however, you should always make validity checks in applying inventory or other models to production/operations situations.

EXAMPLE

A large hotel serves banquets and several restaurants from a central kitchen in which labor is shifted among various stations and jobs. Salad consumption (demand) is virtually constant and known to be 30,000 salads per year. Salads can be produced at a rate of 45,000 per year. Salads cost \$.40 each, and it costs \$4 to set up the salad line. Carrying costs of salads, high because of spoilage, are estimated to be 90 percent of the cost of a salad. No stock-outs are allowed. The hotel would like to establish an operating doctrine for salad preparation.

First, we can set the reorder point at $R^* = 0$ because labor can be shifted to the salad operation instantaneously, and the production rate is greater than the demand rate. Finding Q^*:

$$Q^* = \sqrt{\frac{2DS}{IC}\left(\frac{P}{P - D}\right)}$$
$$= \sqrt{\frac{2(30{,}000)(4)}{.9(.4)}\left(\frac{45{,}000}{45{,}000 - 30{,}000}\right)}$$
$$= \sqrt{2(10)^6}$$
$$Q^* = 1{,}414$$

Lead Time in Deterministic Models

Deterministic models can easily be adjusted for lead times known with certainty. The reorder point is calculated:

$$R^* = \text{Buffer stock} + \text{Demand during lead time}$$
$$= 0 + (\text{Lead time})\ (\text{Demand per unit time})$$
$$R^* = t_L d_L$$

Reorder point is now set and shown in Figure 14.12. Note that total demand during lead time, D_L, is lead time times demand per unit time. At R^*, an order will be placed for Q^* units. The actual order for quantity Q^*

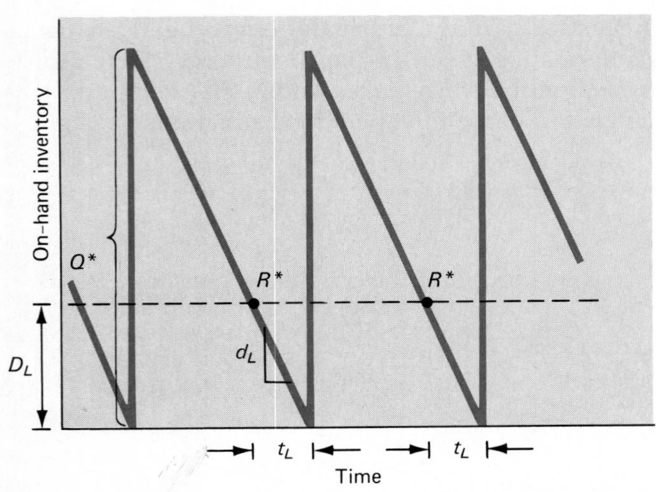

FIGURE 14.12
Reorder points with lead times

will arrive t_L later. During the time between ordering and arrival, d_L units will be demanded, and inventory will be reduced accordingly.

EXAMPLE

A hamburger chain has a local retail outlet that uses 730 cases of six-ounce paper cups annually. Ordering costs are $15; carrying costs are 30 percent of average inventory investment; and a case costs $12. Delivery lead time is known with certainty to be five days. Establishing the optimal operating doctrine:

$$
\begin{aligned}
Q^* &= \sqrt{\frac{2DS}{IC}} = \sqrt{\frac{2(730)(15)}{.3(12)}} \\
&= 77.99 \\
Q^* &= 78 \\
R^* &= t_L d_L \\
&= 5d_L \\
&= 5\left(\frac{730}{365}\right) \\
R^* &= 10
\end{aligned}
$$

The operating doctrine would be to order seventy-eight cases when stocks on hand reach ten boxes.

SUMMARY

Inventories are necessary for a number of reasons, the fundamental one being that it is physically impossible and economically impractical for every stock item to be delivered exactly when it is needed. In controlling inventories it is necessary to establish an operating doctrine, policy decisions concerning *when* to replenish stocks and *how much* stock to replenish.

These decisions are usually made within the framework of either a quantity/reorder inventory system or a periodic inventory system. In the Q/R system, when stock is depleted to an established reorder point, a predetermined quantity is ordered. In the periodic system, after an established time interval has passed, stock is replenished up to a predetermined base stock level.

Inventory costs that are relevant in selecting the operating doctrine are the cost of the item, costs associated with procurement, costs of carrying the item in inventory, and costs associated with being out of stock when units are demanded. Formally or informally, inventory control decisions must consider these cost components and their tradeoffs.

For inventories with deterministic demands and lead times, some helpful models are the simple lot size formula (Wilson EOQ) and the gradual replacement (finite correction) model. When demand and lead times are known, there is no need to carry buffer stock, since stockouts will never occur. This simplifies the models considerably.

REVIEW AND DISCUSSION QUESTIONS

1. Identify and describe the elements of control systems. Use a schematic diagram to assist in your discussion.
2. Give an example of a nonorganizational control system in science or engineering. Identify its goal, its control elements, and its information flows.
3. Give an example of an organizational control system. Identify its goals, its control elements, and its information flows.
4. Differentiate between multistage and multiechelon inventories. Must you have only one or the other? Explain.
5. What is meant by the inventory operating doctrine? In the operating doctrine, why are *two* decisions necessary?
6. Contrast the periodic and quantity/reorder inventory system operating doctrines.
7. Explain the steps in the modeling methodology for inventory situations. Why is the understanding of this methodology important to the practicing manager?
8. Define inventory control in the context of an automobile repair facility employing four mechanics. For any technical terms used in your definition, provide examples.
9. Refer to Figure 14.3 (the materials conversion process). For a general purpose farming operation, provide one example of a material item for each stock point.
10. Why are inventories necessary? Discuss.
11. What kinds of items should be selected when managers are attempting to improve inventory systems? Why?
12. Explain the cost tradeoffs of equation 14.5 in essay form, using a graph if it is helpful.
13. Explain how the finite production (gradual replacement) rate inventory situation differs from the simple lot size situation. What impact does the cost of the item have on each situation? Explain.
14. In deterministic inventory models, total costs are relatively insensitive to deviations from the optimal operating doctrine. Explain.

PROBLEMS

Solved Problems

1. A television manufacturer requires 24,000 two-centimeter-long pieces of wire every month for assembly. Ordering costs are estimated at \$42, and the cost of carrying is 25 percent of the unit price, which is \$.08. Assuming delivery is instantaneous, find the reorder point and economic order quantity.

$$D = (24{,}000)\,(12) = 288{,}000 \text{ pieces/year}$$
$$S = \$42$$
$$I = 25\%$$
$$C = \$0.08$$
$$Q^* = \sqrt{\frac{2DS}{IC}} = \sqrt{\frac{(2)\,(288{,}000)\,(\$42)}{(.25)\,(\$0.08)}} = 34{,}779.3$$

There should be 34,780 pieces per order; $R^* = 0$.

2. The Ohio State University location of McDonald's uses 120 six-ounce paper cups per day. McDonald's plans to be open 360 days per year. The cups cost \$.10 per dozen; ordering costs are \$5 per order; and carrying costs are 50 percent of the item cost (since space is a premium).

(a) Find the economic order quantity if delivery is instantaneous.
(b) Currently, cups are ordered every thirty days. Relate current ordering quantity, optimal order quantity, current total costs, and optimal total costs. What does this mean?

Solution (a) D = (120/12)(360) = 3600 dozen
S = \$5
I = .50
C = \$.10

$$Q^* = \sqrt{\frac{2DS}{IC}} = \sqrt{\frac{2(3600)(\$5)}{.50(\$.10)}} = 848.53 = 849 \text{ dozen}$$

Solution (b) Current order quantity (Q) = 3600/12 = 300 dozen
Current total costs:
Ordering Costs = \$5 × 12 (orders) = \$60
Carrying Costs = \$.05 × 150 (average inventory) = \$7.50
Total Current Costs = \$67.50
Costs when using EOQ:
Ordering Costs = \$5 × (3600/849) = \$21.20
Carrying Costs = \$.05 × 424.5 = 21.225
Total Costs – EOQ method = \$42.425

Obviously, McDonald's can save \$25.075 by using the EOQ method rather than the current operating policy, a savings of more than 37% from current costs.

Reinforcing Fundamentals

3. A local bakery, Harry's, orders 100 fifty-pound bags of flour every three months.
   (a) What is the average inventory for three months (in bags)?
   (b) What is the average inventory for a year (in bags)?
   (c) What is the average monthly inventory (in pounds)?
4. Delicious Donut Shop requires fifty bags of flour every three months. The costs of ordering are \$12 per order placed and a carrying charge of 22 percent of the flour cost. A bag of flour costs \$27. Flour can be delivered virtually instantaneously from a local warehouse. Determine the operating doctrine for a quantity-reorder point inventory system.
5. The owner of Delicious Donut Shop (see problem 4) has been ordering 100 bags of flour at one time.
   (a) What percentage is the owner away from optimal order quantity? How much is this deviation costing per year?
   (b) Considering the total cost of flour per year, what can you conclude about deviations from optimal order quantity? Should the owner continue to investigate similar situations? Why or why not?
6. Use the graphical method to estimate Q^* for the following situation, in which delivery is instantaneous and usage rate is constant throughout the year.

   D = 10,000 units, R = 0 units
   I = .25, C = \$100 per unit
   Procurement cost per order = \$50 + \$0.50 per unit in the order

7. The optimal lot size (using the simple lot size formula) is Q^* = 6,000 for an automobile engine used by Precision Specialties Company. For calculating Q^* the carrying charge per unit (I) was 25 percent. Should this operating doctrine (Q^* = 6,000) be adopted?

8. A textile manufacturer is interested in optimally determined inventories for cutting operations for a children's product line. The production manager would like to establish the optimal reorder point and order quantity for each item in the line. Garment 78A201, a typical product, is demanded uniformly throughout the year, total demand being 14,000 items. The production rate is 2,000 items per month. Sewing, the operation following cutting, is staffed to meet annual demand exactly. Setup costs for cutting are $240, and the cost of carrying one item for a year is $.50. Since cutting and sewing are done in the same plant, delivery of cut items to sewing is essentially instantaneous. Determine the cutting operation operating doctrine for garment 78A201.
9. A missile manufacturer requires a particular electric wired subassembly for final assembly. Annual subassembly demand is 480 "wire bundles"; order costs are $85; carrying costs are 75 percent of average inventory investment; and bundles cost $1,125 each. Delivery time is known with certainty to be twenty-one days. Establish the optimal operating doctrine.
10. Trinidad Co. is interested in the economical order quantity for a production subassembly that is currently purchased from another company. The final assembly made by Trinidad Co. is for a parent company, under an annual contract, with the year's demand set at 50,000 units. Two purchased subassemblies are required for one final assembly. The cost of a subassembly is $10, and the cost of placing an order with the supplier is $3.60. The annual inventory holding charge is $.20. Trinidad currently orders 750 units at one time. Can you save them any money by recommending a new order quantity? If so, how much can they save and what quantity should they order?

Challenging Exercises

11. Ward Paper Box Company supplies a particular candy box to Russell Stover Candy Company, delivering 200 one-pound candy boxes per day. The machine that produces these boxes has a capacity of 1,000 boxes per day. In the past, Ward has always run the machine one day a week to satisfy the weekly demand of 1,000 cartons over a five-day work week (fifty weeks a year). Setup costs are $100 per run and carrying costs 1/20 of a cent per box per day.
    (a) Find the economic order quantity for this candy box.
    (b) What is the cost savings in a year by ordering the economic order quantity rather than following current policy?
12. A fastfood outlet uses 180 breakfast paper cartons per day. The outlet plans to be open 365 days per year. The cartons cost $.20 per dozen; ordering costs are $5 per order; and carrying costs are 70 percent of the item cost (since space is a premium).
    (a) Find the economic order quantity if delivery is instantaneous.
    (b) Currently, cartons are ordered every 14 days. Relate current ordering quantity, optimal order quantity, current total costs, and optimal total costs. What does this mean?
13. A bakery that supplies a large number of retail outlets uses an ingredient at the rate of 2,000 pounds a day, 250 days a year. Delivery is virtually constant and requires five days. A three-day usage of safety stock is set by management and cannot be changed. Ordering costs are $49 per order, and the cost of carrying inventory charge is $0.001 per pound per day. Determine
    (a) the economic order quantity,
    (b) the reorder point,
    (c) the maximum inventory level, and
    (d) the total annual carrying costs.
14. The following equation represents the response behavior of a system:

$$X_{t+1} = 1.4X_t + .1y_t$$

X_{t+1} is a numeric measure of the system's condition in time period $t + 1$. This numeric status depends on two things, the system's status, X_t, in the previous time period and the decision, y_t, made in period t. Hence, the previous status and the current decision determine the next status. The decisions, y_t, can be any positive or negative values you choose. Each time you make decisions to change the status of the system, costs are incurred:

$$C_t = (0.1)(y^2_t + X^2_{t+1})$$

The costs resulting from a decision made in period t are obtained by squaring the numeric decision and squaring the resulting system status, summing these squares, and then multiplying the sum by 0.1.

(a) Using trial and error, make a sequence of ten monthly decisions, trying to minimize costs for the entire ten periods. Assume the initial system status $X_o = 1$.
(b) Repeat part (a); try to improve your initial decisions.
(c) After doing part (b), reflect on the overall process you went through. Which elements of a control system were present in your mental process? Which ones were not present? Identify each as explicitly as possible.

15. Often variances for production are computed and the results are used for subsequent production control.
(a) Compute the raw material price and usage (quantity) variance and the direct labor quantity variance for Milton Industries' key product, shown below. State the variance as favorable or unfavorable.
(b) For each measure in (a), would you take action as a manager? Why or why not?
(c) Write the general formula you used to compute this variance. (Note: We did not provide a formula in this chapter.)

	Standard for 1,000 units	Actual for 1,000 units
Raw materials:		
Price	$1.20 per lb	$1.40 per lb
Quantity	1 lb per unit	1,100 lbs
Direct labor:		
Price	$6.00 per hour	$6.00 per hour
Quantity	2.37 hr per unit	2,172 hrs

16. A missile manufacturer (see problem 9 above) is investigating setting up a "bundle wiring" room and manufacturing the wire bundles for production. This would bring 480 items currently purchased at $1,125 "in-house," generating some $540,000 of business a year. The method of production under investigation produces a maximum of four bundles per day over a 250-day year. Cost per item produced is estimated to remain at $1,125 each but items can be delivered when they are produced rather than in the previously determined lot size (problem 9). Ordering costs are expected to fall to $30 per order, with carrying costs remaining 75 percent of inventory investment. The $1,125 per item cost estimate would cover all fixed costs of the new production line and variable costs for this item only.
(a) For the EOQ of problem 9, find the total annual inventory cost when the items are purchased.
(b) Establish the EOQ for the manufacturer producing the wire bundle "in-house."
(c) For the EOQ in (b), find the total annual inventory cost.
(d) Which do you recommend, purchase or produce? Why? What qualitative factors did you consider in your decision?

GLOSSARY

Buffer stocks Inventories to protect against the uncertainties of unusual product demands and uncertain lead times.

Carrying costs Real out-of-pocket costs associated with having inventory on hand; include opportunity costs, heat, light, breakage, and taxes.

Decoupling Use of inventories to break apart operations so that one operation's supply is independent of another's supply.

Inventory Stores of goods and stocks.

Inventory control Technique of maintaining stockkeeping items at desired levels.

Lead time Time between ordering and receiving goods.

Multiechelon inventories Products stocked at various levels (factory, warehouse, customer) in a distribution system.

Multistage inventories Parts stocked at more than one stage in the sequential production process.

Operating doctrine Basic inventory policy decisions made by operations managers concerning when to reorder stocks and how much stock to reorder.

Periodic inventory system Operating doctrine of replenishing stocks up to a base stock level after an established time period has elapsed.

Procurement costs Costs of placing an order, including postage, telephone calls to vendor, labor, and computer costs associated with purchasing.

Q/R inventory system Operating doctrine of replenishing stocks by ordering an economic order quantity (Q) when the reorder point (R) is reached.

Stockout costs Costs associated with demand when stocks have been depleted; generally lost sales or backorder costs.

SELECTED READINGS

Buffa, E. S. and R. G. Miller. *Production-Inventory Systems: Planning and Control.* 3rd ed. Homewood, Ill.: Richard D. Irwin, Inc., 1979.

Hadley, G. and T. M. Whitin. *Analysis of Inventory Systems.* Englewood Cliffs, N.J.: Prentice-Hall, Inc., 1963.

Harris, F. W. *Operations and Costs.* Chicago: A. W. Shaw Company, 1915.

Magee, J. F. and D. M. Boodman. *Production Planning and Inventory Control.* 2nd ed. New York: McGraw-Hill Book Co., 1967.

Starr, M. K. and D. W. Miller. *Inventory Control: Theory and Practice.* Englewood Cliffs, N.J.: Prentice-Hall, Inc., 1962.

SUPPLEMENT TO CHAPTER 14

OPTIMIZATION AND INVENTORY CONTROL

In this supplement we briefly present several optimization concepts from the calculus and relate them to inventory control. The calculus concepts will not be thoroughly understood by the reader who has never been exposed to the calculus; they are stated to provide a brief review for those understanding the basics of classical optimization.

The only inventory case derived here is the simple lot size formula, the first inventory model presented in the chapter. The derivation is started where the chapter stopped; development of the model terms will not be repeated.

Classical Optimization

The Derivative The concept of a derivative is to differentiate with respect to a variable. Differentials that are required for this supplement are

$$\begin{aligned} d(a) &= 0 \\ d(ax) &= a\,dx \\ d(x + y - z) &= dx + dy - dz \\ d(x^n) &= nx^{n-1}\,dx \end{aligned}$$

where a represents a constant and x, y, and z are variables.

Let's find the first derivative of the expression $y = 3x^2 + x - 3$ with respect to the variable x:

$$\frac{d(y)}{dx} = \frac{d}{dx}(3x^2) + \frac{d}{dx}(x) - \frac{d}{dx}(3)$$
$$\frac{d(y)}{dx} = 6x + 1$$

In this example, each of the differentials was used to find the first derivative, $d(y)/dx$. The second derivative would be found by taking the derivative of the first derivative:

$$\frac{d^2(y)}{dx^2} = \frac{d}{dx}(6x) + \frac{d}{dx}(1)$$
$$\frac{d^2(y)}{dx^2} = 6$$

Optimization In the calculus, the derivative is taken to find the value of the decision variable that will give the largest or smallest value of a criterion function. The general procedure is to take the first derivative of a function with respect to a decision variable and set the result equal to zero. The equation is then solved for the decision variable in terms of the other parameters in the equation. To determine whether the optimal point is a maximum or a minimum, the second derivative is taken. If the second derivative is positive, the optimal point is a minimum. If the second derivative is negative, the optimal point is a maximum. If the second derivative is zero, the point is an inflection point.

In the previous example,

$$\frac{d(y)}{dx} = 6x + 1$$

The optimal value of x is found by setting this equation equal to zero and solving for x:

$$0 = 6x + 1$$
$$x = -\frac{1}{6}$$

When the second derivative was found, it was +6. Therefore, $x = -1/6$ is a minimum point.

Partial Derivatives The object of a partial derivative is to hold all variables as constants except the one that is being differentiated. We partially differentiate, viewing all other variables as constants rather than variables.

For example, if $y = zx^3 - x^2 + 2x$, let's find the first partial derivative of y with respect to x. To do this, we treat z as though it were a constant and differentiate:

$$\frac{\delta y}{\delta x} = \frac{\delta}{\delta x}(zx^3) - \frac{\delta}{\delta x}(x^2) + \frac{\delta}{\delta x}(2x)$$
$$= z\frac{\delta}{\delta x}(x^3) - \frac{\delta}{\delta x}(x^2) + 2\frac{\delta}{\delta x}(x)$$
$$= 3zx^2 - 2x + 2$$

Optimizing the Simple Lot Size Formula The total cost equation for the simple lot size formula was developed to be:

$$TC = CD + S\frac{D}{Q} + IC\frac{Q}{2}$$
$$= CD + SDQ^{-1} + \frac{IC}{2}Q$$

Taking the partial derivative of total cost with respect to order quantity, Q,

$$\frac{\delta(TC)}{\delta Q} = 0 + (-SDQ^{-2}) + \frac{IC}{2}$$

Setting the first derivative equal to zero, and solving for Q:

$$0 = \frac{-SD}{Q^2} + \frac{IC}{2}$$
$$\frac{SD}{Q^2} = \frac{IC}{2}$$
$$Q^* = \sqrt{\frac{2DS}{IC}}$$

Checking the second derivative to assure a minimum of the cost function:

$$\frac{\delta^2(TC)}{\delta Q^2} = \frac{\delta}{\delta Q}\left(-\frac{SD}{Q^2}\right) + \frac{\delta}{\delta Q}\left(\frac{IC}{2}\right) = -(-2)\frac{SD}{Q^3} + 0$$

$$= \frac{2DS}{Q^3}$$

a positive value results, thus assuring a minimum. Notice that the term CD, the item cost, dropped out of the first equation in the first derivative. This illustrates that this cost component is contant with regard to changes in order quantity.

Again, we can see the power of the logic in calculus, but you need not be overwhelmed if you cannot follow all the mathematics. Clearly, the logic of mathematics is useful when applied to the many rational problems in productions/operations.

PROBLEMS

1. For the following total cost (TC), find the optimal order quantity, Q^*. A is a constant. Is this a minimum or a maximum cost point? Why?

$$TC = (27 + A)Q + \frac{100}{Q} + 274$$

2. Given a (Q, R) item control system in which:
   (a) Delivery is instantaneous.
   (b) The vendor quotes a price (c) as twice the variable charge (V) plus the ratio of the fixed charge (F) divided by the order quantity (Q).
   (c) The inventory storage rate (i) is applied to the value of the *maximum* inventory.
   (d) No stockouts are permitted.
   (e) The demand per year (d) and the cost of ordering per order (S) are both known. Define any additional notation used.
   (a) Explain the basic approach one should take in proceeding to analyze this type of system. Determination of the *optimal* operating doctrine is the goal.
   (b) Write a verbal total cost equation for the entire system.
   (c) Solve the system for the optimal operating doctrine (Q^* and R^*).

15 Inventory Control Applications

Stockless production, discussed in part of this chapter, goes by various names, "just-in-time production," "zero inventories," and others. Perhaps all the names are misnomers because the real goal is excellence in manufacturing, and a better description would be Total Production System. Reducing inventory is only one of the methods used to direct constant attention to detailed problems—product engineering, quality, process engineering, layout, setup times, tooling, maintenance and many others. A full review of stockless production is like relearning Manufacturing 101 from a different point of view—problem solving in an atmosphere of constant improvement.

Development through stockless production means taking advantage of every possibility to improve through standard, repetitive operations. A base of knowledge and experience is necessary for this development, just as good fundamentals are important in the development of any athletic team. Developing people takes first priority, followed by development of the production process, and as a result a smooth system of material flow emerges as testimony to a long program of improvement in many areas.

Robert W. Hall
Professor of Operations Management
Indiana University
Indianapolis, Indiana

Professor Hall brings to our attention that applying inventory fundamentals calls on management to become involved in the total production system. Before we examine stockless production and the application issues Professor Hall raises, let's look at a few inventory situations that are slightly more complex and realistic than those in the last chapter. Each of us has purchased consumer goods in larger volumes than immediately needed so that we could pay a lower unit price (dollars per pound, per gallon, etc.). Let's see how that situation, known as the quantity discount case, is formalized.

DETERMINISTIC INVENTORY MODELS

Quantity Discounts

When demand is known for certain, delivery is instantaneous (no stock-outs), and item cost varies with volume ordered, the result is a modified simple lot size situation called the *quantity discount* case. Although the concept of quantity discounts is also applicable to other inventory situations, for our introductory treatment we will modify only the simple lot size situation we discussed in Chapter 14.

Figure 15.1 illustrates the quantity discount concept, the basis of which is examination of price breaks. As volume ordered (Q) increases, the supplier can often produce and ship more economically. To encourage volume purchases, the supplier shares the economies of scale with the customer.

EXAMPLE

Safeway, a grocery store chain, recently advertised grapefruits at the price of twelve for $1.00. Customers could buy grapefruits for $.10 each in quantities fewer than twelve, twelve for $1.00 as advertised up to forty-nine, or in large bags of fifty for $3.50. Thus, unit prices decreased as volume increased ($.10 each for fewer than twelve, 8.33¢ each for twelve to forty-nine, and $.07 each for fifty or more).

In Figure 15.1, the solid lines represent average annual costs for various feasible order quantities. Note, however, that the solid lines are *discontinuous* at the price breaks; for different ranges of Q values, different cost curves apply.

In the operating doctrine for quantity discounts, reorder point is still at zero inventory, since delivery is assumed to be instantaneous. The general procedure for determining the reorder quantity starts by checking the lowest cost curve for an optimal Q. If that is unsuccessful, each higher cost curve is systematically checked until optimal is found. Follow these steps:

1. Calculate the economic order quantity (EOQ) using the simple lot size formula for the lowest unit price.

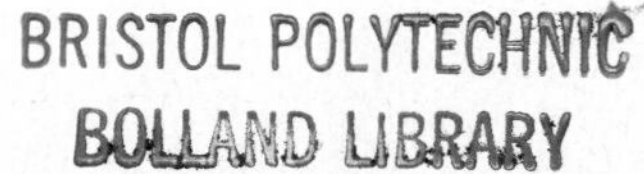

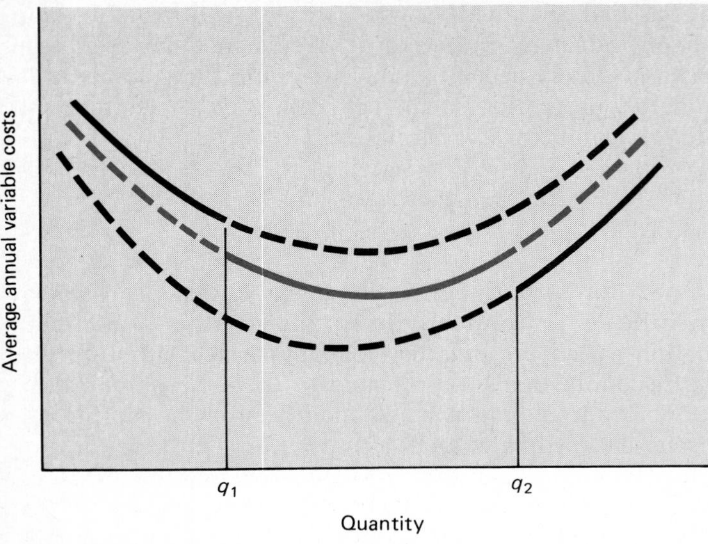

FIGURE 15.1
Quantity discounts

2. Determine if the EOQ in step 1 is feasible by determining whether it is in the quantity range for that price. *If it is feasible,* stop here. Compute the total cost for this quantity, compute the lowest total cost at each price break, and choose the quantity with the lowest total cost.
3. If the EOQ in step 1 is not feasible, compute the total cost for the lowest *feasible* quantity for the lowest unit price.
4. Perform the first and second steps for the next higher unit price. If there is a feasible solution, stop and follow the procedure in step 2. If not, perform the third step. The "best" price/quantity to date will be for the *lowest total cost* of all costs evaluated in step 3.
5. Repeat step 4 until a feasible solution is found or all prices are evaluated. If no feasible optimal quantity is found with the EOQ, choose the price break with the lowest total cost.

Essentially, this procedure finds the lowest cost point on the lowest cost curve, checks feasibility, and if nothing is feasible, computes a cost at the price break that allows a feasible solution. Then we move to the next highest cost curve (see Figure 15.1) and repeat the procedures. In this way, all *minimum cost* EOQ's will be calculated, and all price breaks will eventually be checked, provided an optimal feasible solution is not discovered earlier. As in all inventory operating doctrines, the optimal order quantity is the *quantity that offers the lowest total cost.* An example should help clarify this procedure.

EXAMPLE

Consider an inventory situation in a medical center where disposable sanitary packs are ordered in boxes of five dozen per box. Annual demand is 400 boxes; the cost of placing an order is $12; and the inventory carrying charge is 20 percent. There are two price breaks; price per box is $29 for 1 to 49 boxes, $28.50 for 50 to 99 boxes, and $28 for an order of 100 or more boxes.

To determine the optimal quantity, we begin on the lowest cost curve and compute Q for a price of $28 per unit.

$$Q = \sqrt{\frac{2DS}{IC}} = \sqrt{\frac{2(400)(12)}{.2(28)}} = 41.40$$
$$Q = 41 \text{ boxes}$$

Since 100 or more boxes must be ordered to realize a price of $28 per box, our $Q = 41$ is not feasible. Computing the total cost at the lowest feasible quantity, 100, we get:

$$\begin{aligned} TC &= CD + S\frac{D}{Q} + IC\frac{Q}{2} \\ &= 28(400) + 12\left(\frac{400}{100}\right) + .2(28)\left(\frac{100}{2}\right) \\ &= \$11{,}528 \end{aligned}$$

Moving to the next highest curve,

$$Q = \sqrt{\frac{2DS}{IC}} = \sqrt{\frac{2(400)(12)}{.2(28.5)}} = 41.04$$
$$Q = 41 \text{ boxes}$$

The price of $28.50 is for a volume of 50 to 99 boxes, so $Q = 41$ is not feasible. Computing the total cost at the first feasible quantity (50) in this range:

$$\begin{aligned} TC &= CD + S\frac{D}{Q} + IC\frac{Q}{2} \\ &= 28.50(400) + 12\left(\frac{400}{50}\right) + .2(28.50)\left(\frac{50}{2}\right) \\ &= \$11{,}638.50 \end{aligned}$$

Moving to the next highest and last cost curve:

$$Q = \sqrt{\frac{2DS}{IC}} = \sqrt{\frac{2(400)(12)}{.2(29)}} = 40.68$$
$$Q = 41 \text{ boxes}$$

This is a feasible quantity, since \$29 is the price for a volume of 1–49 units. Now we must compute the total cost for $Q = 41$:

$$\begin{aligned} TC^* &= CD + S\frac{D}{Q^*} + IC\frac{Q^*}{2} \\ &= 29(400) + 12\left(\frac{400}{41}\right) + .2(29)\left(\frac{41}{2}\right) \\ &= \$11{,}835.97 \end{aligned}$$

Comparing all total costs, we see that the lowest total cost is \$11,528 for an order quantity of 100. Therefore the operating doctrine for disposable sanitary packs is:

$$\begin{aligned} Q^* &= 100 \\ R^* &= 0 \\ \text{and } TC^* &= \$11{,}528 \end{aligned}$$

The quantity discount overcame higher carrying costs. The total of ordering and carrying costs were \$328 for $Q = 100$, \$238.50 for $Q = 50$, and \$235.97 for $Q = 41$. However, the quantity discount of \$1 per box for 400 boxes (comparing $Q = 100$ to $Q = 41$) overcame the additional \$92.03 in ordering and carrying costs, making $Q = 100$ the more attractive choice.

In Chapter 14 and in the quantity discount situation above, we explained several deterministic models. In reality we rarely encounter the simplified conditions shown in these models. Let's now relax the deterministic conditions and examine some models of a more practical nature, stochastic inventory models. We'll also consider some practical applications for reducing inventory costs to the organization.

STOCHASTIC INVENTORY MODELS

Variable Demand, Variable Lead Time, Variable Demand During Lead Time

Variable Demand For simple inventory models, we assumed that future demand is known with certainty. Generally, however, this is not the case; demand must be estimated. The most common way to estimate demand is to collect data about past experiences and forecast future demand based on that data. Here is a summary of the most recent seven days' demand for a part used in manufacturing:

Actual daily demand (units)	Number of occurrences (days)	Relative frequency of occurrence
1–200	3	42.8%
201–400	2	28.6
401–600	1	14.3
601–800	1	14.3
	7	100.0%

In the conventional method for measuring usage, we

1. calculate the average usage rate from historical data, and
2. calculate the standard deviation of usage about the average.

In the data for the manufacturing part, the usage rate intervals are very wide; each interval covers a 200-unit range. To obtain some very approximate indicators of the demand pattern, we calculate the mean and standard deviation of these data using only the midpoints of the intervals. Average, or expected, demand is calculated as follows:

$$\begin{aligned}\text{Expected demand} &= \frac{100(3) + 300(2) + 500(1) + 700(1)}{7}\\ &= 300 \text{ units per day}\end{aligned}$$

We find the variability in demand by computing the standard deviation of demand about the mean:

$$\begin{aligned}\text{Standard deviation of demand} &= \sqrt{\sum_{i=1}^{n} \frac{(\text{Demand}_i - \text{Expected demand})^2}{n}} \qquad \textbf{(15.1)}\\ &= \sqrt{\frac{3(100 - 300)^2 + 2(300 - 300)^2 + (500 - 300)^2 + (700 - 300)^2}{7}}\\ &= 214 \text{ units}\end{aligned}$$

Finally, we get a visual portrayal of usage and its variability by constructing a relative frequency distribution of daily demand as shown in Figure 15.2. As you can see, lower levels of usage have a greater chance of occurring than do higher levels.

Lead time Like demand, lead time is often uncertain rather than constant. If it is uncertain, the length of lead time takes on some distribution. Extending our manufacturing part example, we find that the lead time distribution is:

Actual lead time (days)	Number of occurrences	Relative frequency of occurrence
2	2	28.6%
3	3	42.8
4	2	28.6
	7	100.0%

The expected lead time and standard deviation of lead time are found like this:

$$\text{Expected lead time} = \frac{2(2) + 3(3) + 4(2)}{7} = 3 \text{ days}$$

$$\begin{aligned}\text{Standard deviation of lead time} &= \sqrt{\sum_{i=1}^{n} \frac{(\text{Lead time}_i - \text{Expected lead time})^2}{n}} \qquad \textbf{(15.2)} \\ &= \sqrt{\frac{2(2-3)^2 + 3(3-3)^2 + 2(4-3)^2}{7}} \\ &= 0.75 \text{ days}\end{aligned}$$

FIGURE 15.2
Relative frequency distribution of daily usage and lead times

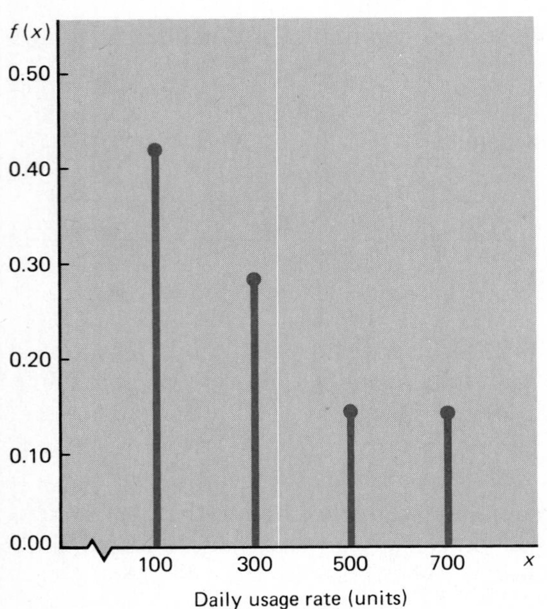

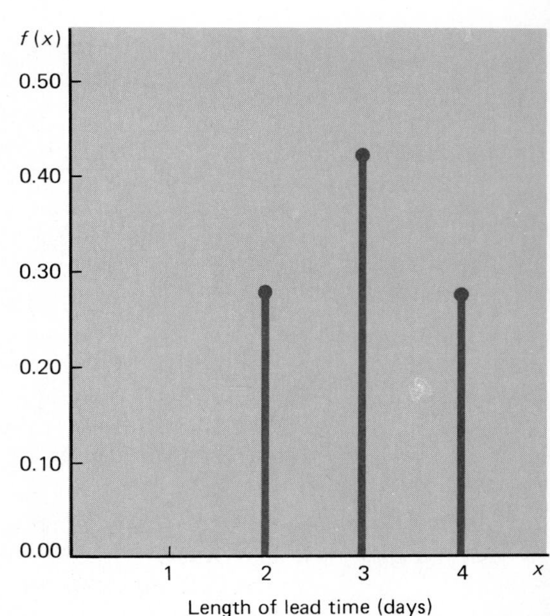

We can describe the lead time distribution in terms of its mean, three days, and standard deviation, 0.75 days. A relative frequency distribution of lead time duration is also shown in Figure 15.2.

Demand During Lead Time The two sources of demand variation during lead time, the length of lead time itself and the demand per time period of lead time, interact to determine *demand during lead time.* For our example we can determine "expected demand during lead time" (average demand). For the manufacturing part:

$$\begin{array}{c}\text{Expected demand}\\\text{during lead time}\end{array} = (300 \text{ units/day})\ (3 \text{ days}) = 900 \text{ units}$$

If we had the lowest demand for each day of the shortest lead time, we would have a low demand of:

$$\begin{array}{c}\text{Lowest demand}\\\text{during lead time}\end{array} = (100 \text{ units per day})\ (2 \text{ days per lead time})$$
$$= 200 \text{ units}$$

Likewise, if the most demanding condition prevailed, highest demand per day and longest lead time, then:

$$\begin{array}{c}\text{Highest demand}\\\text{during lead time}\end{array} = 700(4)$$
$$= 2{,}800 \text{ units}$$

As you can see, between these extreme points, there can be various levels of demand. We can calculate all possible combinations of lead time duration and daily demand, and see what values are possible for demand during lead time. We can also calculate the probabilities of these demands and use them to construct a probability distribution of demand during lead time. For larger problems involving many classification intervals of demand and lead time, hand calculations become tedious. An alternative method for generating the distribution of demand during lead time is to *simulate* the operation of the inventory system over time on the computer. By drawing a lead time, drawing a demand, computing a demand during lead time, and repeating the process dozens of times, we could classify the data into a distribution of lead time demands and compute a mean and standard deviation to describe that distribution.

Figure 15.3 illustrates how inventory levels are affected by variations in lead time demand. After the first reorder point, R_1, expected demand and expected lead time occur. After R_2, the second lead time, t_{L_2}, *occurs. Although* t_{L_2} is shorter than expected, daily demand during the lead time is considerably greater than expected; thus, overall lead time demand is greater than expected. At R_3, both lead time, t_{L_3}, and daily demand are

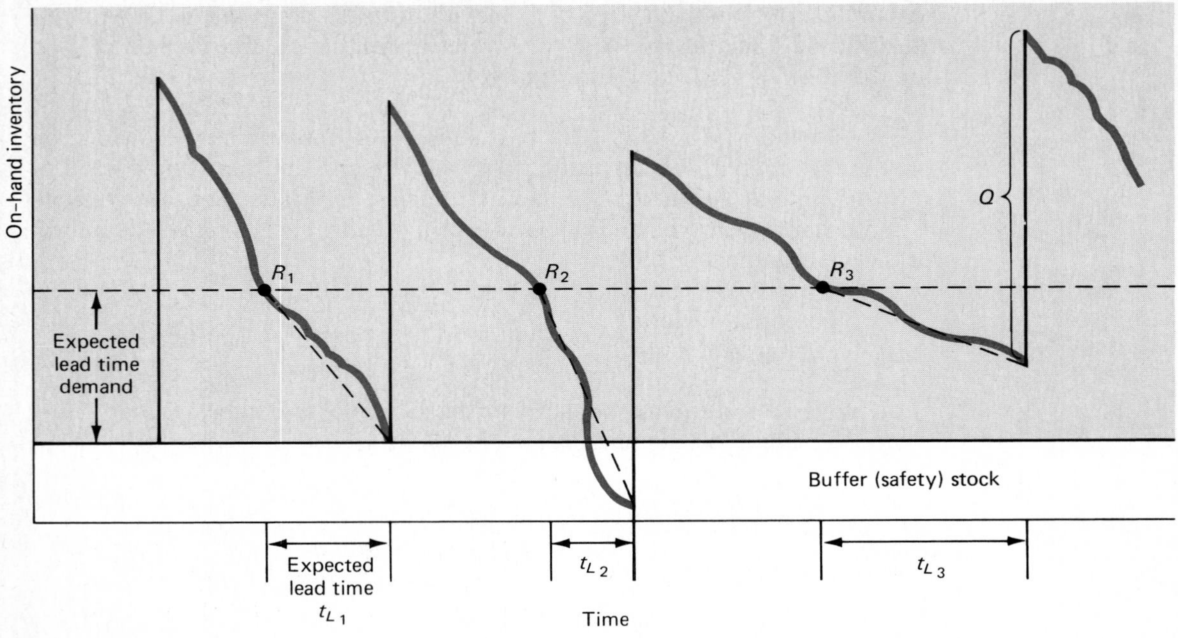

FIGURE 15.3
Q/R model with varying demand and lead times

different from what was expected; demand is much lower than expected, and lead time is much greater than expected. As the figure shows, the two random variables, demand and lead time, interact. This interaction is common in actual inventory situations.

A Model for Variable Demand and Constant Lead Time, with Specified Service Level

Now let's examine a moderately complex quantity-reorder point model in which lead time does not vary, but demand is variable. In this model, we want to find an operating doctrine that takes into account the possibility of a stockout. We want to establish buffer stocks that are adequate for providing a specified level of protection for service to customers when demand is uncertain.

We'll define a few additional variables to those defined in the previous chapter:

$$\mu = \text{random variable representing demand during lead time}$$

$$\sigma_\mu = \text{standard deviation of demand during lead time}$$

$$\bar{\mu} = \text{expected lead time demand}$$

$$\bar{d} = \text{average daily demand}$$

$$\sigma_d = \text{standard deviation of daily demand}$$

$\overline{D}$ = expected annual demand

B = buffer stock

z = number of standard deviations needed for a specified confidence level

Look closely at the first cycle in Figure 15.3. Several relationships exist. First, we can see that the expected lead time demand ($\overline{\mu}$) plus the buffer stock (B) equals the reorder point (R_1). This general relationship holds:

$$R = \overline{\mu} + B \tag{15.3}$$

Second, we know that if lead time (t_L) is constant, which it is for the model being developed, expected lead time demand is expected demand times lead time:

$$\overline{\mu} = \overline{d}t_L$$

We also know that the buffer stock is the *protection* for the service level specified, $z\sigma_\mu$ units. Buffer stock is z standard deviates of protection for a given *variability* of demand during lead time. Substituting, the reorder point for our operating doctrine is now:

$$\begin{aligned} R &= \overline{\mu} + B \\ R^* &= \overline{d}t_L + z\sigma_\mu \end{aligned} \tag{15.4}$$

The order quantity is simply the simple lot size formula with expected annual demand substituted for annual demand:

$$Q^* = \sqrt{\frac{2\overline{D}S}{IC}} \tag{15.5}$$

The use of average demand in equation 15.5 is appropriate for this model regardless of the shape of the demand distribution. Because of its variable nature, demand may take on many shapes. It may be a very unconventional empirical distribution, or it may be normally distributed, Poisson distributed, or negatively exponentially distributed. You may not be familiar with all of these distributions; we mention them only because they have been found to be reasonable representations of demand at various levels of production-wholesale-distribution systems. There is some evidence, for example, that the normal distribution describes many inventory situations at the production level; the negative exponential describes many of the wholesale and retail levels; and the Poisson describes many retail situations.[1]

[1]J. Buchan and E. Koenigsberg, *Scientific Inventory Control* (Englewood, Cliffs, N.J.: Prentice-Hall, Inc., 1963).

EXAMPLE

Daily demand for product EPD101 is normally distributed with a mean of 50 units and a standard deviation of 5. Supply is virtually certain with a lead time of six days. The cost of placing an order is $8, and annual holding costs are 20 percent of the unit price of $1.20. A 95-percent service level is desired for the customers who place orders during the reorder period. Backorders are allowed; once stocks are depleted, orders are filled as soon as the stocks arrive. There are no stockout costs. We can assume sales are made over the entire year.

Determining the operating doctrine, we calculate order quantity to be:

$$Q^* = \sqrt{\frac{2\bar{D}S}{IC}} = \sqrt{\frac{2(50)(365)(8)}{.2(1.20)}}$$
$$= 1{,}103$$

From the normal distribution, a 0.95 confidence level gives $z = 1.645$ (see Appendix A). Thus

$$R^* = \bar{d}t_L + z\sigma_\mu$$
$$R^* = 50(6) + 1.645\sigma_\mu$$

From statistics, we know that for an independent variable the total variance is the sum of the individual variances. The variance of demand during lead time is:

$$\sigma_\mu^2 = \sum_{i=1}^{6}\sigma_i^2 = 6(5)^2$$
$$\sigma_\mu = \sqrt{6(5)^2} = 12.2$$

Therefore:

$$R^* = 50(6) + 1.645(12.2)$$
$$= 300 + 20 = 320 \text{ units}$$

Our operating doctrine is to order 1,103 units when we reach an order point of 320.

In our example for product EDP101 the operating doctrine accomplishes two things. First, it results in economical levels of cycle stocks because our choice of Q^* provides a proper balance between ordering costs and inventory carrying costs throughout the year. Second, it provides the desired level of customer service during lead times while we are waiting to receive a replenishment order from our suppliers. As illustrated in Figure 15.4, the 320 units we have on hand when we place an order provide a 95 percent assurance of being able to meet customer demand until the new shipment is received. We expect only 300 units to be demanded, but we carry an extra 20 units of buffer stock to provide the desired service level. How much do we pay to obtain this extra level of production? Our average

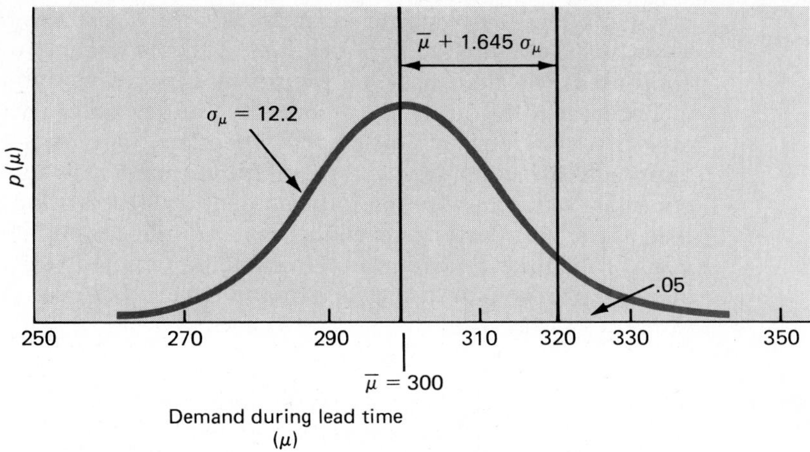

FIGURE 15.4
Distribution of demand during lead time when lead time is six days and daily demand is normally distributed with mean of 50 units and standard deviation of 5 units.

inventory levels for the year are 20 units higher than they otherwise would have been. Therefore, the annual cost of carrying buffer stock is:

$$\begin{aligned} BIC &= (20 \text{ units})(.20)(\$1.20 \text{ per unit}) \\ &= \$4.80 \end{aligned}$$

Expected Stockout Cost and Expected Number of Stockouts At times demand is expressed as an empirical distribution, and lead time is constant. When this is the case, the density function ($f(x)$), the cumulative function ($F(x)$), and the complementary cumulative function ($1-F(x)$) can readily be found. *The complementary cumulative function is also the probability of a stockout if that demand occurs.* The expected stockout cost, a key calculation in the total inventory cost, would be the expected probability of a stockout times the stockout cost for stockout costs that are incurred regardless of the number of units short. The concept of the complementary cumulative can also be used to set buffer stocks for the allowable number of stockouts per year. The expected number of stockouts for any demand level is found by multiplying the number of orders in a year (D/Q) times the probability of a stockout. If the stockout cost is per unit short, then the calculation of stockout costs is more complex.

Variable Demands and Lead Times The basic procedure for finding operating doctrines when *both* daily demands and lead times vary is a convergence procedure; we use directed trial and error. For the quantity-reorder point model, we compute an order quantity assuming constant demand. Then we calculate a reorder point using the order quantity we have just computed. We then use this reorder point to revise the previous estimate of order quantity and recalculate the reorder point. Eventually, the order quantity and reorder point converge upon their optimal values. Another approach for considering two distributions is an analytical calculation: complete enumeration of a joint probability distribution for demand during lead time. Similarly, one could use computer simulation to generate the joint probability distribution.[2] Although a detailed treatment of these models is beyond our introductory treatment, we believe you should be aware of their existence.

A Single Period Model for Perishable Products and Services

Products News vendors, produce managers, and owners of meat markets all must face the question "How much should I order, given that the product is perishable?" When the ordering situation is for the next period only, the critical costs are the costs of being understocked (C_u) and the costs of being overstocked (C_o). C_u is a shortage cost. The news vendor, manager, or owner is faced with minimizing overall costs when demand is not known with certainty.

Equation 15.6 suggests that the person ordering a perishable product or service should stock at that fractile (portion) of demand, the critical fractile (CF), where the ratio of the shortage cost to the sum of shortage and overstock costs is met.

$$CF = \frac{C_u}{C_u + C_o} \tag{15.6}$$

The critical fractile, CF, is the service level that will maximize profits for the perishable goods case.

EXAMPLE

A magazine shop owner has four different retail locations. A popular monthly magazine varies uniformly from 500 to 1200 copies for demand at all stores combined. Ordering is centralized and magazines can be moved easily from store to store. The magazines cost $125 per hundred and sell for $2.25 each. When purchased in lots at this price the publisher accepts no returns. What should be the ordering quantity for the next period?

$$CF = \frac{C_u}{C_u + C_o}$$

[2] See Jack R. Meredith and Thomas E. Gibbs, *The Management of Operations* (New York: John Wiley and Sons, 1980), pp. 437–44 for generating joint probability distributions.

$$= \frac{(\$2.25 - \$1.25)}{(\$2.25 - \$1.25) + \$1.25}$$

$$= \frac{1.00}{1.00 + 1.25} = \frac{1.00}{2.25}$$

$$CF = 0.444$$

The manager would experience a loss in profit of $1.00 ($2.25 − $1.25) if he orders too few, but a loss of $1.25 if he orders too many. He should stock at 0.444 of the difference between 500 and 1200 copies.

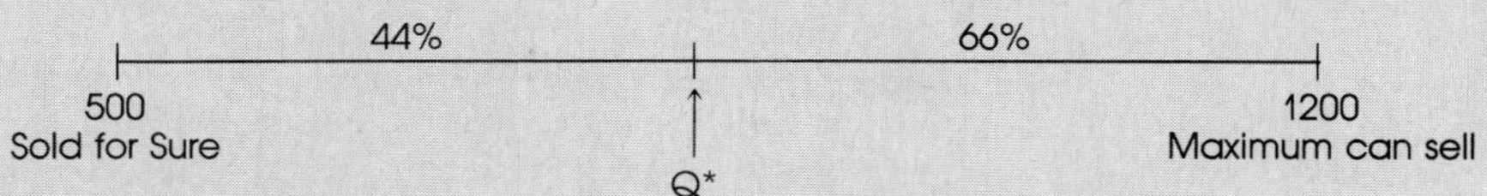

The economic order quantity (Q*) is then

$$Q^* = 500 + .444\ (1200 - 500)$$
$$= 500 + 310.8 = 810.8$$

Since orders must be in lots of 100, the closest to optimal would be to order 800 copies of the magazine for next month.

Services This ordering rule holds for single service orders, just as for products. Consider, for example, the capacity planning question for service vendors such as accountants, cleaning services, and hotels. "How much capacity should be ordered for next period, if we know past demands, costs, and profits?" The assumption is that demand cannot be stored, just as in the perishable good case.

EXAMPLE

A motel with 32 rooms is trying to determine whether to build an addition or incur stockouts, referring customers to competitors when demand exceeds supply. The cost of maintaining a hotel room averages $15.00 per day. A typical room rents for $45.00 per night. Capacity is currently thirty-two rooms. During the last six months, demand has averaged as follows:

Daily rooms demanded	Number of occurrences (days)
0–20	90
21–30	50
31–40	32
41 or more	10
	182 days

The critical fractile, or optimal service level, is calculated

$$CF = \frac{(\$45.00 - \$15.00)}{(\$45.00 - \$15.00) + (\$15.00)} = \frac{\$30}{\$45} = .667$$

The demand distribution should be met up to the 0.667 fractile of the distribution to optimize profit. The fractiles are:

Demand	Number of occurrences	Cumulative number of occurences	Cumulative fractile
0–20	90	90	0.494
21–30	50	140	0.769
31–40	32	172	0.945
41 or more	10	182	1.000
	182		

It is optimal to have a capacity of rooms that falls between 0–20 rooms and 21–30 rooms (0.667 is between 0.494 and 0.769). If 20 rooms were available, that demand would be met 49.4 percent of the time; if 30 rooms were available, that demand would be met 76.9 percent of the time. Since the motel currently has 32 rooms, it should not add capacity.

From the above examples, for both products and services, we can see that is important to understand the concept of inventory situations for single periods. This type of inventory planning is critical to the success of a business. We suspect that most successful business owners understand the economics of such situations, although they might not be able to explain their decisions in such precise terms.

INVENTORY CONTROL IN APPLICATION

Concepts for the Practitioner

Dynamic Inventory Levels The simple lot size formula

$$Q^* = \sqrt{\frac{2DS}{IC}}$$

illustrates that the relationship between demand (D) and order quantity (Q^*) varies with the square root of demand. Table 15.1 illustrates this relationship for several demand levels. Note that as demand increases 100 percent, inventory order quantity, and subsequently maximum inventory levels, increase only 41 percent. *Demand changes should not cause rapid, wide fluctuations in inventory.* If operations managers find in application

TABLE 15.1
Relationship between demand and order quantity in the simple lot size situation: example demands

Demand	Change in demand	Order quantity	Change in order quantity
1,000	—	$31.62\sqrt{2S/IC}$	—
1,500	50%	$38.73\sqrt{2S/IC}$	22%
2,000	100	$44.72\sqrt{2S/IC}$	41
3,000	200	$54.77\sqrt{2S/IC}$	73
4,000	300	$63.24\sqrt{2S/IC}$	100

that work-in-process and finished goods inventories are building rapidly, the problem may very well be caused by scheduling and loading difficulties, not by increases in demand.

Service Level Service levels, treatment policies for customers when there may be stockouts, can be established and measured in several different ways. In this chapter we have focused on one measure, the probability that there will be a stockout (of any size) during a leadtime or cycle. Firms utilize at least two more common measures, which are

1. the ratio of the number of *customers* receiving the product to the number of customers demanding the product, and
2. the ratio of the number of *units* supplied to the number of units demanded.

Suppose four customers each demanded 100 units and demand was met. When a fifth demanded 200 units, however, demand was not met. Service level as a customer ratio in this case is 4/5, or 80 percent serviced; service level as a unit ratio is 400/600, or 67 percent serviced. Our example in Figure 15.4 used the number of units as the service level criterion. Whether a firm uses a customer or a unit ratio depends on what use management wants to make of buffer stocks. As an operations manager, you must make sure that marketing and general management understand the way service level is being measured so that internal disagreements can be minimized.

Inventory as a System Input Because demand is not always certain but must be projected in some way, forecasting is a requirement for inventory systems. Similarly, inventory levels established with the operating doctrine are necessary inputs for production/operations management decisions in many other functional areas. Table 15.2 illustrates some of the production/operations management activities that depend heavily upon inventory levels in operations. As you can see, inventory control and other major planning and control activities interact in operations. Poor inventory con-

TABLE 15.2
Inventory as a system input

Production/operations management activity	Role in inventory
Aggregate output planning	Input to establish work force levels and production rates
Material requirements planning	Input to establish on-hand inventories preceding ordering
Physical distribution	Input as actual finished goods stocks; the basis for shipping schedules
Scheduling and loading operations	Input to determine *net* production requirements

trol, whether it allows rapidly changing inventory levels or fails to account accurately for inventories, results in wide variations in other operations subfunctions.

Saving Money in Inventory Systems

Suppose your first assignment on your first job is to evaluate the current inventory system and procedures at a major distribution center for a national company. Where would you begin? What would you do? In this section, we hope to provide you with a general guide toward saving money in inventory systems. As you read it, remember that this is a general guide, not a solution procedure for all inventory problems. With that in mind, we suggest you consider these possible cost saving areas.

ABC Classification When an organization's inventory is listed by dollar volume, generally a small number of items account for a large dollar volume, and a large number of items account for a small dollar volume.

The ABC inventory concept divides inventories into three groupings, an *A* grouping for those few items with large dollar volume; a *B* grouping for items with moderate unit and dollar volume; and a *C* grouping for the large number of items accounting for a small dollar volume. The *A* group might contain, for example, about 15 percent of the items, the *B* group 35 percent, and the *C* group 50 percent.

Table 15.3 lists a number of stock items according to decreasing dollar usage, and Table 15.4 groups these items into an ABC classification. The *A* items comprise 79.5 percent of the total dollar volume, the *B* items 17.6 percent, and the *C* items only 2.9 percent. Notice, however, that the *A* items are only 22.2 percent of the total items, the *B* items 22.2 percent, and the *C* items 55.6 percent. Figure 15.5 graphically illustrates the dollar value classification for this example.

If you are trying to reduce costs in an inventory system, which class would you concentrate on? The high dollar volume group, the *A* class, should receive your attention first; one of the major costs of inventory is

TABLE 15.3
Example annual usage of inventory by value

Item stock number	Annual dollar usage	Percent of total value
2704	$125,000	46.2
1511	90,000	33.3
0012	32,000	11.8
2100	15,500	5.8
0301	6,200	2.3
0721	650	0.2
8764	525	0.2
7402	325	0.1
3520	300	0.1
	$270,500	100.0

annual carrying costs, and your money is invested largely in class *A*. Tight control, sound operating doctrine, and attention to security on these items would allow you to control a large dollar volume with a reasonable amount of time and effort. Items in this class are usually either high unit cost items or high volume items with at least moderate costs.

A good start in examining an inventory system is to make an ABC classification and focus initially on the *A* items—unit cost/volume combinations that account for high dollar volumes. Class *C* items, the bulk of all items, should have carefully established but routine controls.

Blanket Rules When blanket rules, general rules, are being used in inventory systems, they are often good places to investigate for cost savings. Such rules as "always carry a month's supply on all items," "reorder when you take out the last case of any item," and "don't order any inventory that won't fit in this stock room" almost always provide an opportunity for cost

TABLE 15.4
Example ABC grouping of inventory by value

Classification	Item stock number	Annual dollar usage	Percent of total dollar usage	Number of items	Percent of total number of items
A	2704, 1511	$215,000	79.5	2	22.2
B	0012, 2100	47,500	17.6	2	22.2
C	0301, 0721, 8764, 7402, 3520	8,000	2.9	5	55.6
Totals		$270,500	100.0	9	100.0

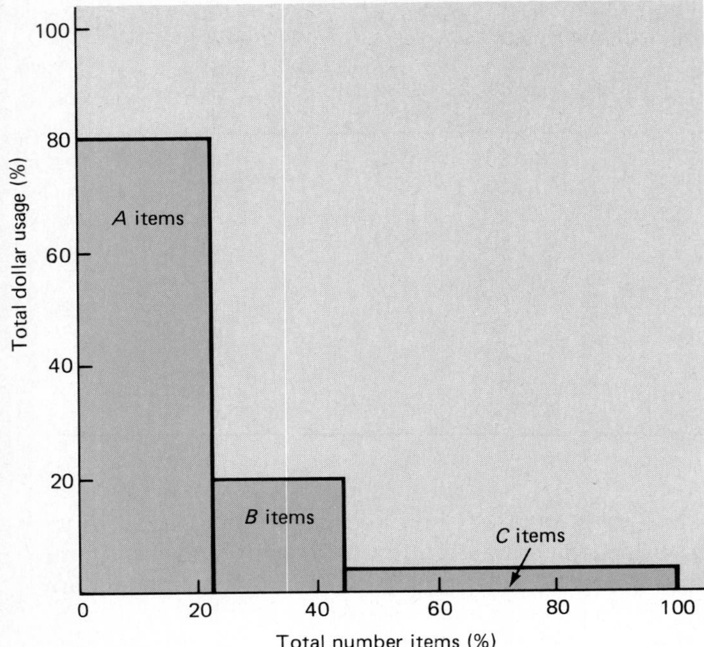

FIGURE 15.5
Example ABC inventory classification: percent inventory value vs. percent of items

savings. Try to think of individual items and families of parts that by violating the rule would reduce costs. Sometimes comptrollers send such directives as "Reduce all inventories 33 percent" to operations managers. If you can prove that current inventories costs are reasonable by justifying inventory as a return on investment (see Chapter 14), you may be able to challenge such a directive successfully.

Stochastic Demand and Lead Time It is very unlikely that you will observe many situations in which the deterministic simple lot size formula applies. Even if it does apply, you probably will not save much money; stock clerks can be off on order quantities a good bit without incurring excessive costs. Nevertheless, you can use your understanding of the modeling approach and cost tradeoffs to attack situations with these characteristics:

1. High variability in demand. It is likely that with wide variations in demand, systematic evaluation and buffer stock calculations can reduce the erratic reactions to demand that result in repeated overstock and understock situations.
2. High variability in lead times. Essentially, the same is true for lead times; we want to have good estimates of the mean and variability of demand during lead time in our inventory system to reduce overstock and understock situations.

High Stockout Costs When stockout costs are high, buffer stocks should be increased accordingly. It is costlier for stockouts in some items than it is in others. Focus on items that have high cost consequences to the organization when they are out of stock. For these high stockout cost items, examine the operating doctrine to see how buffer stocks are set and see that inventories are adequate.

Safety Stocks Evaluate safety stock levels to be sure that they relate to the variability of demand and lead time and to the costs of stockouts. If demand variability, lead time variability, and stockout costs are not high, buffer stocks are unnecessary. Remember, buffer stocks should be demand and cost dependent; they should not be set intuitively.

Decoupling Operations One common use of inventories is to decouple operations. This use of inventories can become excessive, however, if work-in-process continues to rise at the expense of inadequate finished goods inventories and shipments. There are several ways to reduce excessive buildups and reduce costs. MRP systems (Chapter 16) are especially effective in this respect.

Raw Material and Finished Goods Inventory Excessive inventories at the beginning or the end of the production process can lead not only to high carrying costs but also to increased risk of obsolescence. Furthermore, when physical inventory records are collected for tax and auditing purposes, as they are periodically, it is unpleasant and embarrassing to have accountants and marketing staff find that you are carrying obsolete raw material or finished goods. Such a situation shows that control is poor and often results in a write-off against production/operations' profitability.

Table 15.5 summarizes some practical ways managers can save money in inventory control.

Inventory Control Procedures

Inventory control procedures vary in complexity and accuracy from the absence of any noticeable control to computerized systems for distribution and production. In between these extremes are simple visual controls, the two-bin system, and cardex systems. We'll briefly examine two of the systems, a cardex file and IBM's computerized MAPICS system. Then in a following section we will discuss the Japanese just-in-time and kanban systems. The two-bin system, which needs no extended explanation, consists simply of filling two bins with units of the same item. One bin is used first; when it is empty, the quantity necessary to replenish the empty bin is reordered, and stock from the second bin is used.

Cardex File System The cardex file system has variations, but the essential features are:

1. There is a card for every stock item; the cards are filed on a rotating drum or file cabinet in a central location.

TABLE 15.5
A general guide for saving money in inventory control

Inventory situation	Operating guides
No priority for inventory items	Classify by ABC; examine high dollar volumes first, low dollar volumes last.
Blanket rules applied	Challenge on cost basis by examining items and families of parts; justify by return on investment.
Stochastic (variable) demand and lead times	Obtain estimates of mean and variance of demand, lead time, and especially demand during lead time; adjust buffer stocks, reorder point, and order quantity to avoid continued overstock or understock situations.
High stockout costs	Identify high stockout cost items by questioning staff; adjust buffer stocks on cost tradeoff basis.
Safety stocks	Evaluate reasons for safety stocks; levels should be based on demand, lead times, and cost tradeoff among ordering, carrying, and stockout costs; do not set intuitively.
Decoupling operations	Justify in-process inventory levels as basis for cost reductions and efficiency in operations; reduce levels if too much inventory results in inefficiencies due to space limitations.
Raw material and finished goods inventory	Examine physical inventories carefully; accept obsolescence write-offs but reduce future obsolescence through more careful scheduling and control; coordinate closely with purchasing on raw materials and marketing on finished goods inventories.

2. On the top of each card is the computed operating doctrine. For a Q/R system, the economic order quantity and reorder point are listed. For a periodic system, the time between orders and the base stock level are listed. The supply source (vendor) may be listed here also.
3. A ledger comprises the balance of the card. It states beginning inventory, orders placed, orders received, issues from stores, and current inventory levels. Each time a transaction is made, an entry with the corresponding date is recorded. When physical inventories are taken, cards are adjusted to reflect current actual inventories.

Table 15.6 shows a cardex file card for one stock item.

The primary advantage of this procedure is simplicity. Because records are on hand, any part may be checked quickly. This procedure is especially good for inventory situations that do not have more than 500 or 1,000 items. A primary problem with the cardex file is the validity of the data; it's difficult to ensure that *all transactions* are recorded and current levels computed accurately. If withdrawals are made when the stock clerk is either absent or busy, the transaction may not be recorded, and the records are invalid. Furthermore, it can become expensive both to maintain credibility in the data and, for large inventory situations with many items, to maintain the system itself.

Cardex file card for one inventory item

ARTOTURF, INC.							
PART #:3799 ITEM DESCRIPTION: Vinyl back artificial turf					UNITS: Square yard COST: $16.25/sq yd		
					Adjustments		
Date	Invoice #	Purchases	Sales		Dr.	Cr.	Balance (sq yd)
11/15 85	Beg inventory						256172
11/15	3033, 3035		3767				
11/16	3039		3424				
11/17	3041, 3042, 3049		14040				
11/18	3047, 3048		11618				
11/19	3050		8547				
11/22	3051, 3052		10354				
11/23	3053, 3054, 3056, 3062		13854				190568
11/24	3064		4933				
11/29	3066, 3068, 3069		10459				
11/30	3077		11467				163709

Recently, remote terminal access computer facilities with central processing capabilities have made this cardex procedure obsolete for multilocation distribution and manufacturing firms. Computers are less costly than cardex systems. Cardex files are still useful, however, for small and medium-sized organizations with limited computer access, even though microcomputers offer a good alternative for the progressive small businessperson.

IBM's MAPICS The Manufacturing Accounting and Production Information Control System (MAPICS) is a series of modules for information and control in manufacturing.[3] Modules include financial, order processing and accounting, and manufacturing applications as well as a guide for implementation planning. The key module for control is that on manufacturing applications. It includes product data management, material requirements planning (MRP), inventory management, and production costing and control applications. Figure 15.6 illustrates how the manufacturing applications would work for an order flowing through the manufacturing process. Note the frequency of the material requirements planning (MRP) module and the inventory management (IM) module.

IBM suggests that the benefits of the inventory management application include improved plant productivity, reduced time required by inven-

[3]This section is based on IBM's *Manufacturing Education Guide*, GH30-0241-0, and the *MAPICS Features Education Manual*, SR30-0369-1 (Atlanta, Ga., 1979).

Business Activity		Manufacturing Applications Support
Set product schedule	↓	Material Requirements Planning (MRP)
Generate the needs for component parts based on the bill of materials	↓	MRP and Product Data Management
Plan orders, based on inventory	↓	MRP and Inventory Management (IM)
Release orders and identify shortages	↓	IM
Monitor the released orders and accumulate labor and material costs	↓	Production Control and Costing
Adjust orders to meet changing conditions	↓	IM and MRP
Close out orders and stock/ship orders		IM and Order Entry and Invoicing

FIGURE 15.6
MAPICS manufacturing applications for an order flowing through the manufacturing process
Source: IBM's *MAPICS* Features Education Manual, SR30-0369-1 (Atlanta, Ga., 1979), p. 4–2.

tory personnel, reduced inventory investment and storage space, improved customer service, and establishment of the basic inventory data and status reports as required for successful application of MRP. Several other available computerized inventory systems are not discussed here. Production/operations managers will find computer firms' representatives and software companies eager to help them find a system that will fit their needs.

Quantity-Reorder Versus Periodic Inventory Systems

To practice independent demand item inventory control, production/operations managers must select either a quantity/reorder (Q/R) system or periodic inventory system. The following points might assist you in making that decision.

1. The *periodic system requires less manpower to operate than the Q/R system.* In the Q/R system, each item must be counted as it is issued or demanded. This requires a person to record the transaction. In the periodic system, no person is required in the inventory area except at the end of the period, when a physical inventory must be taken. The periodic is especially good for raw

material and supply inventory systems for which tight security is not necessary.

2. *The periodic system requires less calculating time than the Q/R system.* In the Q/R system, each issue or demand from stock must be subtracted to obtain net inventory. If this is not done, a reorder point might be skipped. Use of the computer for receiving data on issued items and for making the calculation of on-hand inventory can greatly reduce this clerical time in the Q/R system and largely cancel out the advantage of the periodic. *Systemic costs,* the costs of running the system, are generally less with the periodic system.
3. *The periodic system may require more buffer stock to protect against uncertainties of demand and lead time.* If the quantity-reorder point and corresponding base stock level-reorder time are set mathematically, in a minimum cost framework, there is no advantage to one system over the other. However, often in the periodic system, the reorder time is set to correspond with a nonoptimal weekly or monthly physical inventory resulting in higher costs.
4. *The periodic system can result in more stockouts when unusually high demand occurs.* When one or more successive unusually large demands occur, because the Q/R system keeps track of a net inventory with each unit demanded, it can react more quickly.

The tradeoffs among these advantages and disadvantages are unique to any one application. Within any one medium or large organization (a hospital, a steel fabricator, an automotive dealer, or a nursery, for example), more than likely both periodic and Q/R systems are useful for different inventory situations.

THE JAPANESE APPROACH TO INVENTORY MANAGEMENT

The Japanese have experienced substantial gains in overall manufacturing productivity during the past twenty-five years (see Chapter 2) and those gains have come in part from their approach to inventory management. It is quite difficult to explain Japanese manufacturing techniques without considering automation, behavior, inventory, process design, quality, and scheduling. We will try to summarize succinctly what others believe to be the inventory concepts the Japanese follow and how they make these concepts work to reduce costs.[4] But let's start with a brief review of the principles underlying their approach to manufacturing.

Japanese Manufacturing and Inventory

Professor Robert W. Hall, Indiana University, suggests these cornerstones to the Japanese manufacturing system.

1. Produce what the customer desires.
2. Produce products only at the rate the customer wants them.

[4]This section on Japanese inventory systems relies on a number of sources, major sources being Robert W. Hall, *Zero Inventories,* © 1983, Dow Jones-Irwin, Homewood, IL; and Richard J. Schonberger, *Japanese Manufacturing Techniques: Nine Hidden Lessons in Simplicity* (The Free Press, 1982).

3. Produce with perfect quality.
4. Produce instantaneously—with zero unnecessary leadtime.
5. Produce with no waste of labor, material, or equipment; every move has a purpose so there is zero idle inventory.
6. Produce by methods that allow for the development of people.[5]

Quite similarly, Professor Richard J. Schonberger, University of Nebraska, identifies nine simple—yet hidden—lessons from the Japanese.[6] These lessons focus on management technology, just-in-time production, total quality control, plant configurations, flexibility, purchasing, self-improvement of work quality, and striving for simplicity in all things.

How Japanese Manufacturing Ideally Works Throughout this book, we have made recommendations for approaching these aspects of operations management in the United States. With the exception of managing for quality (Chapter 17), you now have the background to understand and evaluate what follows. Although our example is oversimplified, the Japanese approach to manufacturing would ideally be as follows.

First, identify the customer's needs. Find out what the customer requires in terms of quantity, quality, and schedule. Know as much about the customer's needs as he or she does. Second, obtain the exact amount of material needed for today and process it piece-by-piece. The first person in the manufacturing process must perform his or her job and hand the piece to the next person. The piece must be correct or there will be delays all the way down the line. If there is an error and the next person can't use the piece, it should be handed back with admonishment; it should be clear, though, that there is a willingness to help solve any problems so this won't happen again. There is no in-process inventory. Everything currently being made is needed by the customer, so no finished-goods inventory exists.

Quality is perfect. Waste cannot be hidden—poor products that are 2, 3, or 4 percent defective cannot be made and put in storage to be sorted later. Finally, everyone is expected to be involved in discovering how to simplify the job, and management strives to aid all employees in accomplishing this goal. Cooperation, teamwork, and a striving for consensus in all decisions are foremost in management's mind.

Stockless/Just-in-Time Production It is suggested the key element in Japanese manufacturing is "stockless" production. Everything is ordered, made, and delivered just when needed. Production is "just-in-time."[7] There is a

---

[5] Hall, *Zero Inventories*, p. 2.

[6] Schonberger, *Japanese Manufacturing Techniques*, 1982. Each lesson is a chapter in the book.

[7] For a synopsis of stockless/just-in-time systems, see Richard A. Schonberger, "Some Observations on the Advantages and Implementation Issues of Just-in-Time Production Systems," *Journal of Operations Management* 13, no. 1 (November 1982), pp. 1–11; and Jinichiro Nakane and Robert W. Hall, "Manufacturing Specs for Stockless Production," *Harvard Business Review* 61, no. 3 (May–June 1983), pp. 84–91.

TABLE 15.7
Results of stockless production programs in Japan

Company	Duration of program	Inventory reduction (percent of original value)	Throughout time reduction (percent of original value)	Labor productivity (percent increase)
A	3 years	45%	40%	50%
B	3 years	16	20	80
C	4 years	30	25	60
D	2 years	20	50	50

This data was collected in late 1981 by Professor Jinichiro Nakane, Waseda University, Tokyo. The companies did not wish to be identified. The figures represent rough management estimates, as the rounded figures suggest. Labor productivity is estimated as sales in yen adjusted for inflation divided by *total* employees.

The superior progress of Company B may be somewhat illusory, since it was thought to be in the worst condition when starting stockless production.

None of these companies had more than two months in raw material plus work-in-process inventory when they began the program. All had some version of quality circles and quality improvement programs in place when they began, so the measurements of improvement have a high base point from which to index improvement.

Improvements are still taking place at each of these companies, and all of them are perhaps Class B at this point. Stockless production is a condition of constant improvement. All the companies anticipate more and more progress on these goals unless overtaken by a business disaster.

Source: Hall, 1983, p. 24.

necessary linkage between stockless production and quality—every item must be made correctly just-in-time and every time. This is a key element in productivity gains. There is no waste. Therefore labor, material, and tools are all used productively.

What can this stockless production do for a company? Table 15.7 illustrates that the results are spectacular for four selected companies; benefits include savings in inventory, improvement in meeting schedules, and increased labor productivity.

The concept of zero inventories is very appealing, but we know that this approach is not always economically or practically feasible. Consider, however, the results of moving closer to this goal. Figure 15.7 illustrates how removing in-process inventory is much like dredging a channel in a river—the level of the water is reduced. There are no deep pools anymore. Protection is gone, but the flow is much smoother, ideally reaching a situation similar to the ideal presented in Figure 15.7.

Kanban Kanban (pronounced kahn-bahn) literally translated means "visible record."[8] Generally we think of kanban as a card. In manufacturing, it is a card that is attached to a basket or container containing an order for

[8]For details on kanban, see Schonberger's "The Kanban System," (Appendix), *Japanese Manufacturing Techniques* 1982, pp. 219–238.

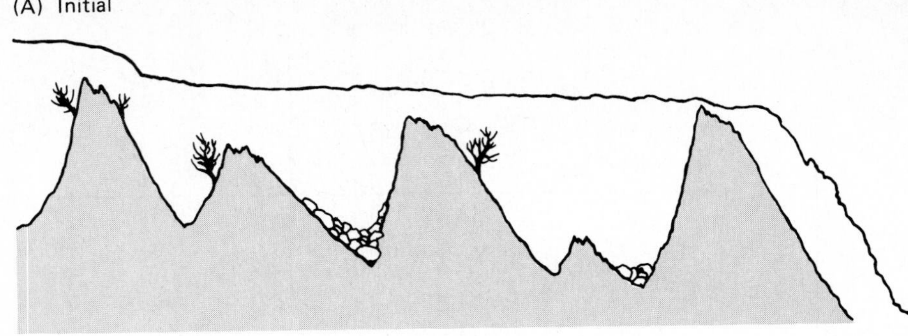

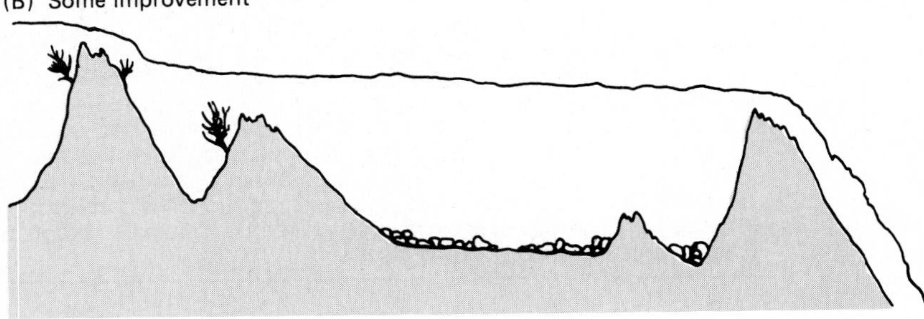

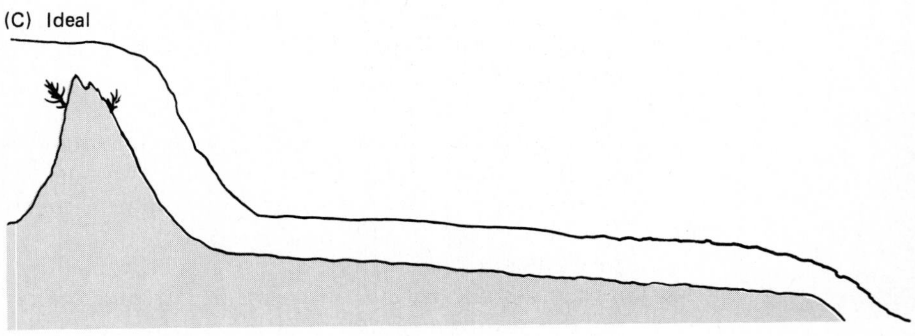

FIGURE 15.7
A material flow and water flow analogy

production. What is produced fits into that container—no more, no less—and is always of excellent quality. The container card is the scheduling system and this card system "pulls" manufacturing parts through the plant. The traditional United States and European inventory system is a schedule-based system. The order release "pushes" items through the plant. With kanban the customer's order is filled without guesswork or excesses.

Schonberger explains what is needed to make kanban work:

> Kanban provides parts when they are needed but without guesswork and therefore without excess inventory resulting from bad guesses. But there is an important limitation to the use of kanban. Kanban will work well only in the context of a just-in-time (JIT) system in general, and in the context of the setup time/lot size reduction feature of JIT in particular. A JIT program can succeed without a kanban subsystem, but kanban makes no sense independently of JIT.[9]

Inventory Turnover One method of judging the effectiveness of an inventory system is to measure inventory turnover—the number of times total inventory turns over (is sold) in a time period. As discussed earlier, when we examined "Why have inventories?", this straight-forward calculation (cost of goods sold/average dollar inventory) assists the manager. Generally speaking, the more rapidly inventory turns, the more profitable is the firm. This is true until some minimum inventory level, which is necessary to support sales, is reached. This minimum inventory will vary; it is higher for a retail sale outlet than a custom machinery manufacturer.

To illustrate how inventory turnovers vary, consider a 1982 survey of forty U.S. high technology companies with $25 million to $2 billion in annual sales.[10] Across all forty companies, annual inventory turns for 1982 averaged 2.91. This ranged from 2.72 for the computer systems companies to 3.72 inventory turns for telecommunication companies. Individual companies varied from 0.96 to 5.61 inventory turns for all companies in the survey. Examining five years of annual survey data, the authors found the higher growth firms (in annual sales dollar increases) had slightly higher inventory turns. Companies with higher sales backlogs also experienced higher inventory turns, as might be expected.

Although we cannot make a direct comparison with foreign competitors for the above survey, a Japanese survey suggests that, based on annual inventory turnover, American competitors are being outperformed. As Table 15.8 indicates, the Japanese firms are turning inventory 50–78 times while their American competitors are in the 6–25 range; this is indeed a substantial difference.

Jidoska Kiki Company Ltd. Professor Hall provides an excellent set of examples from Japanese manufacturing companies. Although Toyota is perhaps the most documented success story, we believe Jidoska Kiki Company Ltd. also provides a good example. In the data of Table 15.9 note how inventory, productivity, quality, and setup times all improve together. We

---

[9]Schonberger, p. 221.

[10]Pittiglio, Rabin, Todd, and McGrath Consulting Company, "Inventory Performance for High Technology Industries-1982," *Production Inventory Management Review* 3, no. 6 (June 1983), pp. 27–30.

TABLE 15.8
Comparison of manufacturing inventories*

Company	Days on hand	Annual§ turnover
Toyota Motor Company† (1980)	4.0	62
Tachikawa Spring Company‡ (1982)	3.3	75
Jidosha Kiki‡ (1982)	3.2	78
Kawasaki Motorcycle—Japan (1981)	3.2	78
Kawasaki USA (active parts—1982)	5.0 est.	50 est.
Tokai Rika†,‡ (1982)	3.7	68
American competitors (1981)	10–41	6–25 est.

*Manufacturing inventory is defined as raw material, parts, and work in process. It does not include finished goods. The companies using stockless production typically count the manufacturing inventory at the end of each month. Estimates of the American companies were made by materials managers of the companies at a meeting of the American Production and Inventory Control Repetitive Manufacturing Group in June 1981. The estimate of days on hand at Kawasaki USA was made by the inventory manager.
†Figures include inventory on consignment at small suppliers.
‡These companies are among the larger suppliers of the Japanese auto industry.
§Annual turnover and days on hand are related by

$$\text{Turnover} = \frac{\text{(250 Days per year)}}{\text{(Days on hand)}}$$

The Japanese companies typically state inventory in days on hand, the American ones by a turnover ratio. American reaction at first is that the amount of money required for inventory is minuscule. That is true, but recall that inventory levels are really an indicator of the degree to which the production process itself has become flexible and free of breakdowns and rework. The financial impact of that is enormous, but it is not explicitly identified as a separate item in the financial statements.

Source: Hall, 1983, p. 31.

certainly have a great deal to learn from Japanese inventory management and we encourage those interested in manufacturing management to pursue this topic more thoroughly.

BEHAVIORAL PITFALLS IN INVENTORY CONTROL

Rational Decision Making Establishing the inventory operating doctrine involves a decision process that is rational, logical, and unemotional. This decision, based on cost tradeoffs, is typical of the decisions Frederick Taylor thought managers should make. But Taylor believed that people are rational and unemotional, and we know that such is not always the case. As operations managers, you should be aware that people making inventory decisions interject their own biases and individual traits into the decision-making process from time to time. The people you work with are complex, with wants and desires of their own, and they should not be expected to behave like machines. The inventory management *process* is rational, but the people involved in the process are not always rational.

TABLE 15.9
Development of stockless production at Jidosha Kiki Company Ltd.

	Start of program 1976	1981	
Inventory (days on hand)			
Raw material	3.1	1.0	
Purchased parts	3.8	1.2	
Work-in-process	4.0	1.0	
Finished goods	8.6	3.7	
	19.5	6.9	
Productivity index	100	187	
Defect rates			
From suppliers	2.6%	.11%	
Internally (cumulative)	.34%	.01%	
Setup times			
Over 60 minutes	20%	0%	
30–60 minutes	19%	0%	
20–30 minutes	26%	3%	
10–20 minutes	20%	7%	
5–10 minutes	5%	12%	Single-digit setups
100 seconds–5 minutes	0%	16%	Single-digit setups
Under 100 seconds	0%	62%	One-touch setups

These data were taken from a briefing by Jidosha Kiki executives during a visit July 2, 1982. Jidosha Kiki, which supplies brakes and steering gear to the auto industry, learned its methods from Toyota, and their system is very similar. They began a very clear conversion to this kind of thinking with a "revolution" in 1976, and the results have been very good for them. Jidosha Kiki has a few large presses. Most of the rest of their equipment is small, light, flexible metalworking equipment.

The extremely low amount of raw material, purchased parts, and finished goods results from the truck delivery system of Japan, described later. Jidosha Kiki executives were unsure if these levels would be further reduced, but they were certain that additional in-plant improvement could further reduce work in process to 0.5 days on hand.

Source: Hall, 1983, p. 30.

Feedback Operations managers must monitor inventory levels and make adjustments within the production planning and control process when they discover that actual output deviates from planned output. These adjustments might well involve decisions to build inventory, reduce inventory, or change inventory procedures and operating doctrines. There can be no *control* in inventory without three activities:

1. monitoring of performance and inventory levels,
2. feedback to decision makers comparing actual performance and material usage with planned performance and usage,

3. adjustment of inputs to the conversion process, especially the capital inputs of inventory.

Feedback should include status reports, prepared manually or by the computer, as well as visual feedback obtained by touring the facility. There is no good substitute for walking through the conversion process yourself—whether your organization is a bank, a restaurant, a school, or a manufacturing facility. When you see the conversion process yourself, you can compare your first-hand observations with planned conditions and quickly make adjustments for discrepancies you may find.

Inventory Policy Often, top management adjusts aggregate inventory levels. These manufacturing and operations policy decisions should be well grounded in cost analysis. The policy decisions about aggregate levels of inventory changes should then be converted to specific items by middle management, first-line management, and clerical personnel. Again, we need to emphasize the dynamic nature of inventory. Overreacting to a problem by changing inventory levels can result in higher costs in aggregate planning, material requirements planning, physical distribution, and scheduling. We caution top executives against making frequent and drastic inventory policy changes, as they might inadvertently increase overall production costs.

Individual Risk-taking Propensity As you probably know from your own experience, people vary considerably in their tendencies to take chances. Some people thrive on taking risks; others are risk-averse. Any banker can tell you that among checking account customers are a certain percentage who keep far too many cash reserves in low interest-bearing accounts because they are afraid of future uncertainty. Operating managers can also be risk-averse. In their overreactions to the possibility of a stockout, they may carry excessive buffer stocks.

On the other hand, some people are high rollers, risk takers. As operations managers or supervisors, people who take excessive risks are just as damaging to inventory control as are people who are too risk-averse. They may allow inventory levels to vary drastically and cause stockouts, high costs, and adverse effects in other operations subsystems. Individual propensity to take risks within the organization's inventory control procedures should be assessed carefully. Extreme behaviors are costly to operations.

SUMMARY

Stochastic (variable) inventory models are required when demand, lead time, or both are variable. The operations manager is most interested in the distribution of demand during lead time; this is a critical factor in establishing buffer stocks and the reorder point.

Money can be saved in inventory systems by evaluating the ABC classification, blanket rules, stochastic demand and lead times, high stockout cost items, safety stocks, decoupled operations, and raw material and finished goods inventory.

There are numerous inventory control procedures for practical application, among them the cardex file system and IBM's MAPICS. The cardex file system is a manually operated system in which an inventory card represents each stock item and transactions are kept on the card. The MAPICS system is a manufacturing information and control system, inventory management being an important system module.

The Japanese stockless production concept (just-in-time) seems to work well in reducing inventories. One feature, kanban, provides discipline to shop-floor control of inventories, a continuing problem in any inventory system.

Primarily, inventory control is a rational process that lends itself to logical procedures. Behavioral pitfalls in inventory control involve the irrationality of decision makers, lack of control, poorly established inventory policies, and the variability in people's propensity to take risks.

CASE

Good Shepherd Home

The Good Shepherd Home is a long-term care facility with an eighty bed capacity located in San Mateo, California. Mr. Scott, the administrator, is concerned about rising food costs. He questions whether administration is as efficient as it might be and realizes that food, a "raw material" for his food services, has increased in price significantly. Mr. Scott decides to investigate food services more closely.

Analyzing last month's purchased items, Mr. Scott summarizes a random selection of items. Mr. Scott wonders what interpretation he should make about these typical items. He has looked at 100 stock items and is considering tighter controls on the forty stock items that resulted in 400 quantities (dozen, cases, pounds, etc.) being ordered.

Good Shepherd typical inventory items

Number of stock items	Quantity ordered	Total cost	Average inventory
3	50	$3,500	$1,200
12	150	2,500	900
20	200	1,500	600
40	400	2,000	200
25	200	500	100

Of particular interest is a problem with a perishable good, bread. Since the home has residents from independent living units eating at the home irregularly, bread demand is uneven. Bread is delivered daily and is used that day for table meal service only; the day-old bread is salvaged for dressing and similar items. Scott estimates the cost of bread to be $.75/loaf and the cost of day-old bread to be $.25/loaf. Scott says, "We should not be out of fresh bread at the table. Although man cannot live by bread alone, it is very important to our residents. I put a high cost on being out of bread—considerably more than the cost of a loaf. In fact, I think every time we run out of bread, it costs a dollar per loaf short in good will lost from our residents." Knowing he feels this way, the food services supervisor has a standing order for thirty loaves per day and twice that amount on Sunday. The demand for bread the last two weeks is shown below.

Good Shepherd bread demand

Week 1		Week 2	
Day	Bread demand	Day	Bread demand
Mon	20	Mon	19
Tue	15	Tue	27
Wed	21	Wed	20
Thu	30	Thu	32
Fri	31	Fri	27
Sat	19	Sat	16
Sun	42	Sun	39

In conversation with Mr. Scott, the supervisor says, "I recently heard about cost tradeoffs in food service inventory. I don't really see what item cost, carrying cost, ordering costs, and stockout costs have to do with proper nutrition. I try to buy good quality foods and spend less than $5 per day per resident on food. That's my objective." Mr. Scott has heard about cost tradeoffs too, but he wonders what they mean and how they could assist in a nursing home environment. To try to understand this better he talked to his bookkeeper. The supervisor says that she knows with certainty that demand for hamburger over a menu cycle is 200 pounds. Further, the bookkeeper estimates it costs $12 to place an order and 20 percent of the hamburger cost to carry hamburger in inventory. Hamburger costs $1.55 per pound. The dietitian says a menu cycle lasts 2 weeks, and Good Shepherd currently orders hamburger every week. Mr. Scott is puzzled by all this.

REVIEW AND DISCUSSION QUESTIONS

1. Explain three common ways to measure and establish service levels, giving an example of each.
2. What is meant by the ABC classification? How might an organization's inventory be analyzed using the ABC classification?
3. In Figure 15.1, why are the lines dotted? Will the optimal cost always be at the lowest point on a cost curve? Why or why not?
4. Inventory control is a rational process in which decisions are often made irrationally. Explain.
5. Given a probability distribution of demand and a distribution of lead time, what alternatives exist for finding the probability distribution of demand during lead time? Select one alternative and explain how it works. Why is the distribution of demand during lead time important?
6. For Figure 15.3, explain how lead time and demand vary. What impact does such variation have on buffer stocks, if any?

7. Suppose a directive comes to a manufacturing facility from the controller strongly suggesting a 35 percent across the board reduction in inventory levels. The plant manager asks you to assist him in explaining the need for inventories in manufacturing. What points would you make in favor of having inventories to assist the plant manager in answering the controller?
8. Select two general areas in which money might be saved in inventory control and explain how you would plan a cost study for each.
9. Discuss the advantages and disadvantages of the periodic inventory system compared to the quantity-reorder inventory system.
10. Explain the concept of inventory turnover. How do American companies compare to Japanese companies based on inventory turnover? Discuss.
11. A nonbusiness student comments, "What is the big deal about Japanese manufacturing? I like their products, they do what I want done. Are they really different in their manufacturing ways than American companies?" How would you respond? Explain.
12. In Japan manufacturing setup time, inventory, quality, and the way employees behave all interact. Explain why this is so.
13. Compare the U.S. "push" scheduling/inventory system to the Japanese "pull" system. What is the role of kanban in the Japanese system?
14. Relate individual propensity for risk taking to decision making in inventory control.
15. Explain how an order might flow through a manufacturing process, stressing the impact on inventory management. Prepare your discussion based on a real situation, such as an order of Colonel Sanders' fried chicken for a large sorority picnic.

PROBLEMS

Solved Problems

1. Actual daily demand and lead time distributions are given below. What is expected demand during lead time? What is the minimum that demand during lead time will ever be?

Actual daily demand (units)	Number of occurrences	Actual lead time (days)	Number of occurrences
1–5	2	2	2
6–10	6	3	3
11–15	2	4	2

To find expected demand during lead time we need first to find expected demand and expected lead time.

$$\text{Expected demand} = \frac{3(2) + 8(6) + 13(2)}{10} = 8 \text{ units per day}$$

$$\text{Expected lead time} = \frac{2(2) + 3(3) + 4(2)}{7} = 3 \text{ days}$$

$$\text{Expected demand during lead time} = 8 \times 3 = 24 \text{ units}$$

The minimum that demand during lead time will ever be is 3 units per day × 2 days = 6 units (not using mid-points for daily demand it *could* be 1 × 2 = 2 units).

2. Daily demand for mini wheels, a popular toy, is normally distributed with a daily mean of 60 cases and a standard deviation of 10 cases. Supply is virtually certain, with a lead time of three days. The cost of placing an order is \$6, and annual holding costs are 20 percent of the unit price of \$1.20. We want a 90 percent service level at our warehouse for customers who place orders during the reorder period. Service level is the probability that there will be a stockout of any size during lead time. Backorders are allowed; once stocks are depleted, orders are filled as soon as the stocks arrive. We can assume orders arrive 200 days throughout the year. Determine the operating doctrine for mini wheels.

   $\bar{d}$ = 60 cases per day t_L = 3 days
   S = \$6 σ_d = 10 cases
   I = .20 Z = 1.282 for 90% service level
   C = \$1.20

   Orders arrive 200 days throughout the year.

$$Q^* = \sqrt{\frac{2DS}{IC}} = \sqrt{\frac{2(60)(200)(\$6)}{.20(\$1.20)}} = 774.59 = 775 \text{ cases}$$

$$\sigma\mu = \sqrt{3(10)^2} = 17.32$$

$$R^* = \bar{d}t_L + Z\sigma\mu = 60(3) + 1.282(17.32) = 180 + 22.20 = 203 \text{ cases}$$

   The operating doctrine for mini wheels is to order 775 cases when the on hand inventory reaches 203 cases.

3. A Christmas tree supplier has evaluated weekly demand for November–December over the last 7 years. Demand appears normally distributed with a mean of 350 trees demanded weekly and a standard deviation of 200. To assure a fresh supply and maintain a reputation for quality, trees are cut weekly in anticipation of demand. A Christmas tree sells for an average \$6.00 wholesale locally and can be salvaged, if not sold locally, by shipping out-of-state at an average revenue of \$2 per tree (sold "not freshly cut"). Cost to raise and harvest a tree is \$3.75. What should be the weekly ordering (harvesting) quantity for the upcoming Christmas season?

$$CF = \frac{C_u}{C_u + C_o}$$

   If understocked, the lost sale cost is revenue less harvesting, \$2.25, (\$6.00 − \$3.75). If overstocked, the cost is harvesting less salvage, \$1.75, (\$3.75 − \$2.00).

$$CF = \frac{2.25}{2.25 + 1.75} = \frac{2.25}{4.00} = 0.5625$$

   The optimal harvesting level will have 56.25 percent of the normal curve to the left of this stocking level. From Appendix A, we find that the area of the normal curve to be at $Z = 0.157$. Shown graphically in Figure 15.8, we need to find x, the ordering level.

$$\begin{aligned} x &= u + Z\sigma \\ &= 350 + 0.157\,(200) = 350 + 31.4 = 381.4 \end{aligned}$$

   The supplier should harvest 381 trees a week, given these data, to optimize profits.

Reinforcing Fundamentals

4. A bookstore orders blue books (exam booklets) in boxes of one gross. Annual demand is even throughout the year and known with certainty to be 600 boxes. Lead

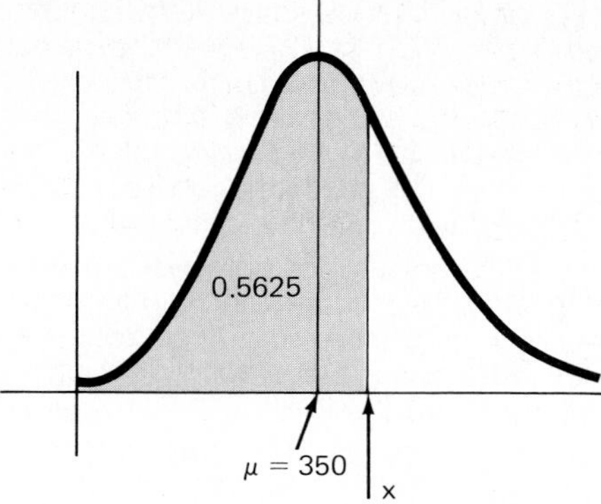

FIGURE 15.8

time is known to be exactly one month. The cost of placing an order is $16, and annual carrying charges are 36 percent. The wholesaler gives the bookstore a quantity discount as follows:

Quantity (boxes)	Price per box
1–49	$7.50
50–99	7.35
100 or more	7.00

Establish the economic operating doctrine.

5. Actual daily demand and lead time distributions are given below. What is expected demand during lead time? What is the minimum that demand during lead time will ever be?

Actual daily demand (units)	Number of occurrences	Actual lead time (days)	Number of occurrences
10–20	4	1	3
21–30	3	3	2
31–40	3	4	2

6. An electrical motor housing has an annual usage rate of 75,000 units per year, an ordering cost of $20, and annual unit carrying charge of 15.4 percent of the unit price. For lot sizes of fewer than 10,000 the unit price is $.50; for 10,000 or more the unit price is $.45. Delivery lead time is known with certainty to be two weeks. Determine the optimal operating doctrine.
7. Daily demand for a manufactured part is normally distributed with a daily mean of 80 cases and a standard deviation of 30 cases. Supply is virtually certain, with a lead time of three days. The cost of placing an order is $15 and annual holding costs are 20 percent of the unit price of $6.50. We want a 90 percent service level at our warehouse for customers who place orders during the reorder period. Service level is the probability that there will be a stockout of any size during lead time. Backorders are allowed; once stocks are depleted, orders are filled as soon as the stocks arrive. We can assume orders arrive 200 days throughout the year. Determine the operating doctrine for this part.

8. The daily demand for a component assembly item is normally distributed with a mean of 80 and standard deviation of 7. Further, the source of supply is reliable and maintains a constant lead time of four days. If the cost of placing the order is $30 and annual holding costs are $.60 per unit, find the order quantity and reorder point to provide a 80 percent service level. Service level is the probability that there will be a stockout of any size during lead time. Unfilled orders are filled as soon as an order arrives. Assume sales occur over the entire year.
9. A florist orders flowers weekly. Demand for carnations varies uniformly from 8 to 20 dozen a week. Carnations cost $6 a dozen and sell for an average price of $12 a dozen, some sold individually and some sold in arrangements. Salvage is virtually zero after a week's storage. Establish the ordering quantity for carnations. Explain your results in terms the florist will understand.
10. Daily demand for pickles for a local chain of fast food restaurants is normally distributed with a mean of 30 jars and a standard deviation of 7. Supply is virtually certain with a lead time of two days; the cost of placing an order is $2.50, and annual holding costs are 80 percent of the unit price of $.60 per jar. A 98-percent service level is desired. Service level is the probability that there will be a stockout of any size during lead time. The restaurant chain serves 365 days a year.
    (a) Determine the operating doctrine for ordering pickles.
    (b) Construct graphs similar to Figures 15.3 and 15.4 to portray this situation.
    (c) What is the annual cost for pickle buffer stocks? Does this cost seem reasonable for a 98-percent service level?
11. For the fast food restaurant chain in problem 10, suppose that exactly the same situation exists for coffee as did for pickles, except that coffee costs ten times as much per can as do pickles per jar.
    (a) What is the operating doctrine for coffee?
    (b) What is the annual cost for coffee buffer stocks?
    (c) What conclusions can you reach concerning the effect price has on operating doctrine and buffer stocks (by comparing your answer to problem 10)?
12. For the fast food restaurant chain in problem 10, suppose that exactly the same situation exists for chocolate syrup as did for pickles, except that chocolate syrup demand is 30 cans per day with a standard deviation of 28 cans.
    (a) What is the operating doctrine for chocolate syrup?
    (b) What is the annual cost for chocolate syrup buffer stocks?
    (c) What impact does the variability of demand (the standard deviation) seem to have on buffer stocks (by comparing your answer to problem 10)?
13. Bilson, Inc., purchases all metal needed in bar stock form. With an annual demand of 4,000 units, a purchase ordering cost of $80, and storage costs of 20 percent of the unit cost, what is the optimal order quantity given these price breaks:
    (a) 0–299, $50 per unit
    (b) 300–499, $40 per unit
    (c) 500 or more, $30 per unit.

Challenging Exercises

14. The demand per period for an important inventory item seems to have the following probability distribution:

Demand *(D)*	Probability of demand occurring
5	0.4
6	0.2
7	0.1
8	0.3

All stock to meet the demand for a period must be acquired at the start of the period. The product costs \$5 per unit and sells for \$8 per unit. Any leftover at the end of a period must be disposed of as "seconds" at a selling price of \$4 per unit. On the other hand, if the stock becomes depleted, there is no cost associated with the shortage.

(a) Under the above conditions, will it be more profitable to stock six or seven units at the start of each period?

(b) If there were a cost associated with a shortage and a probability of a shortage for each demand level, how would you modify part *(a)*?

15. Demand for the local daily newspaper at a newsstand is normally distributed with a daily mean of 210 copies and standard deviation of 70. A newspaper sells for twenty-five cents and costs twenty cents to purchase. Day-old newspapers are very seldom requested and therefore destroyed upon receipt of the next day's paper. What should the newsstand's daily order be to maximize profits?

16. A bank purchases promotional ball-point pens for \$4 each. The company that supplies the pens suggests that if the imprinted pens were ordered in twice the quantity, a 25 percent discount could be arranged. At present the bank orders 100 pens every two months. Ordering costs are \$12, and the bank's cost of money is 15 percent. What ordering policy should be followed? Show your analysis to support your decision.

17. A family of products in the Economize line of a hardware producer are so similar that they are grouped and viewed as one product. Daily demand for this group is normally distributed with a mean of 20 and a standard deviation of 10. Supply is virtually certain with a lead time of five days. The cost of placing an order is \$27.50, and holding costs are 20 percent of the group product price of \$94. Management wants a 90 percent service level for customers who place orders during the reorder period. Service level is the probability that there will be a stockout of any size during lead time. Back orders are allowed; once stocks are depleted, orders are filled as soon as the stocks arrive. Assume sales are made over the entire year.

    (a) Find the reorder point.

    (b) Draw an on-hand inventory versus time graph of this inventory situation, placing the correct reorder point on the graph and identifying data given or calculated where possible.

18. At McDonald's on the Ohio State University campus, six-ounce paper cups are used at a rate of 120 cups per day and are ordered in lots of 850 dozen. McDonald's is open 360 days a year. After several months on the job, a business school student (employee) finds that lead time is virtually a constant three days, not instantaneous as was previously assumed, and that daily demand varies with a mean of 120 cups and a variance of 36 cups. The manager desires to run out of cups once every six months or less (an average of two times a year). Establish an operating doctrine for management.

19. You find yourself, as operations manager of a group of stock market analysts for a small brokerage firm, faced with the following problem. The company's market research group suggests you "follow" (analyze) some "risky" stocks, as some customers desire this kind of investment. They estimate maximum demand from any one "high risk taker" to be in any one month:

Number of risky stocks demanded	Probability of this number being demanded
2	0.30
4	0.20
5	0.10
6	0.30
8	0.10

They also assess a cost associated with not having the number of risky stocks demanded to be \$100 (loss of customer possibilities). Further, you know that your unit costs per month (C) to "follow" stocks are

$$C = \begin{cases} \$25D \text{ for } D \leq 4 \\ \$15D \text{ elsewhere} \end{cases}$$

where D is the number of risky stocks demanded. How many risky stocks should you "follow" each month?

20. Grab-A-Snack is interested in the inventory of chickens, a raw material ordered in lots of a dozen at a fixed price of \$30 per lot. It costs \$60 to place an order. The cost of carrying chickens is \$80 per lot per year. Expected demand is 10 lots per week, 52 weeks per year.
    (a) If delivery is instantaneous, what are the economic order quantity and reorder point?
    (b) Upon further analysis, demand is found to vary according to the normal distribution, the mean remaining 10 lots per week with a variance of 9 lots per week. Lead time has slipped to one week but is known to be certain. Management desires a 98 percent service level on chickens. Service level is the probability that there will be a stockout of any size during lead time. What is the optimal operating doctrine for Grab-A-Snack now?
    (c) After a year of operation, with variable demand (as in (b)), management was able to leave the retail business and supply cooked chickens to a captive market, reverting to a constant and known demand situation (as given initially in the problem). Now, however, lead time varies by the distribution below. What is the economic ordering doctrine for a 98 percent service level?

Lead time	Number of occurrences	Probability of lead time
1 week	5	0.25
2 weeks	10	0.50
3 weeks	5	0.25

21. A bank is evaluating teller capacity. Daily demand for teller services is as shown below. The cost of not serving a customer or having the customer leave angry because of a long wait is estimated to be high and should be avoided. The cost of having a teller and facility is \$75 per day. A teller typically generates \$250 per day in revenue. Develop a decision rule for the bank to follow in comparing current capacity to the most economical capacity.

Daily average number of tellers busy (demanded)	Number of occurrences observed
0	0
1–2	13
3–4	21
5–6	10
7 or more	6

22. You have a product with average weekly sales of 600 units. By looking at past demand records, you find that the demand pattern has followed the distribution below:

Demand above	Percent of the time
400 units/week	100
450	90
500	79
550	64
600	50
650	22
700	8
750	3
800	0

The cost of carrying an item on inventory for one year is $1.30. There is a fixed cost of ordering of $72 for every order placed. Lead time is constant at one week. The stockout policy has been set to allow two stockouts per year on average. Determine the order quantity and the safety stock that will minimize the variable costs.

23. Wendy's is interested in analyzing the ordering policy for some perishable items, including tomatoes. The daily demand for crates of tomatoes is shown below.

Daily demand tomatoes (crates)	Probability this number being demanded
2	0.3
4	0.4
6	0.1
7	0.1
9	0.1

This cost of ordering tomatoes is small, estimated to be $.25 for a crate; a crate costs an average of $24. If we carry tomatoes, our cost of capital is 20 percent of the item cost. The average shelf life to us of tomatoes is one day with zero salvage value. If a crate that is not on hand is demanded, the cost of being out of tomatoes is estimated to be $100. Lead time is known with certainty to be one day. To simplify ordering, management will only order lots of 2, 4, 6, 7, or 9 crates. Establish an optimal operating doctrine for Wendy's, which operates 365 days a year.

GLOSSARY

ABC classification Inventory division with three groupings, an *A* grouping for a few items with a large dollar volume, a *B* grouping for items with moderate volume and moderate dollar volume, and a *C* grouping for items with a large volume and small dollar volume.

Bill of materials A listing of all materials required to produce a part.

Cardex file Manually operated system when an inventory card represents each stock item with transactions kept on the card.

Individual risk taking propensity Degree to which individuals tend to take or avoid chances.

Lead time demand Units of stock demanded during lead time; can be described by a probability distribution in stochastic situations.

MAPICS Manufacturing and Accounting Production Information Control System; IBM's computerized common data base manufacturing information system.

Master schedule The conversion of customer orders and/or forecasts into time phased quantities due.

MRP Material Requirements Planning; a computerized data information system that can support scheduling and inventory manufacturing functions.

Quantity discounts Policy of allowing item cost to vary with the volume ordered; usually the item cost decreases as volume increases due to economies of scale in production and distribution.

Service level Treatment policy for customers when there are stockouts; commonly established either as a ratio of *customers* served to demanded or a ratio of *units* supplied to demanded.

SELECTED READINGS

Brown, R. G. *Decision Rules for Inventory Management*. New York: Holt, Rinehart and Winston, 1967.

Buchan, J. and E. Koenigsberg, *Scientific Inventory Control*. Englewood Cliffs, N.J.: Prentice-Hall, Inc., 1963.

Buffa, E. S. and J. G. Miller, *Production-Inventory Systems: Planning and Control*. 3rd ed., Homewood, Ill.: Richard D. Irwin, Inc., 1979.

Green, James H. *Production and Inventory Control Systems and Decisions*. Rev. ed. Homewood, Ill.: Richard D. Irwin, Inc., 1974.

Hadley, G. and T. M. Whitin. *Analysis of Inventory Systems*. Englewood Cliffs, N.J.: Prentice-Hall, Inc., 1963.

Hall, Robert W. *Zero Inventories*. Homewood, Ill.: Dow Jones-Irwin, 1983.

IBM. Manufacturing Accounting and Production Information Control System (MAPICS). Manufacturing Education Guide and MAPICS Features Education manual. (Order numbers GH30-0241-0 and SR30-0369-1). Atlanta, Ga., 1979.

Magee, J. F. and D. M. Boodman. *Production Planning and Inventory Control*. 2nd ed. New York: McGraw-Hill Book Co., 1967.

Meredith, Jack R. and Thomas E. Gibbs. *The Management of Operations*, New York: John Wiley & Sons, 1980.

Sasser, W. E., R. P. Olson, and D. D. Wyckoff. *Management of Service Operations*. Boston: Allyn and Bacon, 1978.

Schonberger, Richard J. *Japanese Manufacturing Techniques: Nine Hidden Lessons in Simplicity*. New York: The Free Press, 1982.

Starr, Martin K. and D. W. Miller. *Inventory Control: Theory and Practice*. Englewood Cliffs, N.J.: Prentice-Hall, Inc., 1962.

Stevenson, William J. *Production/Operations Management*. Homewood, Ill.: Irwin, 1982.

16 Material Requirements Planning

As a real life practitioner I can assure you that you are about to enter one of the most exciting chapters in this book. MRP has become a centerpiece for all manufacturing systems. The key to successful production and operations management in a manufacturing company is the balancing of requirements and capacities. It's that simple and yet very challenging.

We at Hallmark Cards produce hundreds of products. About half of our annual sales volume consists of cards and the other half a wide variety of "social expression" products ranging from party goods, puzzles, pens and pencils to mugs and stickers. In our card area, we produce 32 million cards a week. Without MRP we would be totally out of control. This informative chapter will be one of the keystones of your professional career. To understand it is essential and to practice it can be a lot of fun. Remember what you are trying to do: Meet the needs of your customers—How? By having the product available when it is wanted. In production management, we do this by knowing in advance what our requirements are now and in the future and planning ahead to have the capacity available. We at Hallmark know this and practice it. It's not a theory—it's the real world.

Al Sondern
Corporate Vice President
Hallmark Cards, Inc.
Kansas City, Missouri

Mr. Sondern's remarks give clear evidence that managing conversion systems effectively entails attention to materials management, including materials procurement, coordinating materials availability, inventory control, and controlling materials utilization. As a practitioner he is keenly aware that the complexities of producing numerous different products can cause confusion, inefficiencies, and inferior customer service in any organization. Management is better able to control in such an environment if it gets the timely and accurate information it needs. A Materials Requirements Planning (MRP) system, the topic of this chapter, can provide this vital information.

PLANNING FOR MATERIALS NEEDS

In recent years materials planning systems (e.g., MRP) have replaced reactive inventory systems (discussed in Chapters 14 and 15) in many organizations. Whereas the older systems asked, "What should I do *now?*," the new systems look ahead and ask, "What will I be needing in the *future?* How much and when?"

It may seem like a subtle difference between the two but, in fact, this reorientation represents a whole new way of thinking about materials management. The *reactive* system (the old way) was simpler to manage in many respects but it had serious drawbacks, especially its high inventory costs and low production delivery reliability. The new way, the *proactive* system, is more complex to manage, but it offers numerous advantages. It reduces inventories and their associated costs because it carries only those items and components that are needed—no more and no less. It permits better control over materials flows and, by looking ahead to ensure that all materials are available when needed for product buildup, it reduces order processing delays. By setting realistic job completion dates, it gets jobs done on time, order promises are kept, and production lead times are shortened. This better customer service and inventory cost reduction, along with reduced expediting efforts, come at a cost. They require an information system with accurate inventory and product buildup information. They also require a planning orientation and a realistic master production schedule (MPS) to specify when various quantities of end items will be completed. Finally, and perhaps most important, they require a certain *discipline,* a commitment by schedulers, supervisors, managers, and shop floor employees to make the system work. Once MRP job priorities and schedules are set, they must be adhered to; inventory records must be accurately maintained; physical counts on the shop floor and in storage must conform to the inventory records; transactions on job order progress and materials must be accurately maintained; and, when discrepancies between planned progress and actual job progress arise, actions are needed to adjust the system and cause the plans to materialize. If they can't, and this happens sometimes, then replanning of the system is necessary. The key to getting this employee commitment resides in the honesty of the system—keeping it accurate and believable.

As we examine these materials planning systems you'll see that a pre-

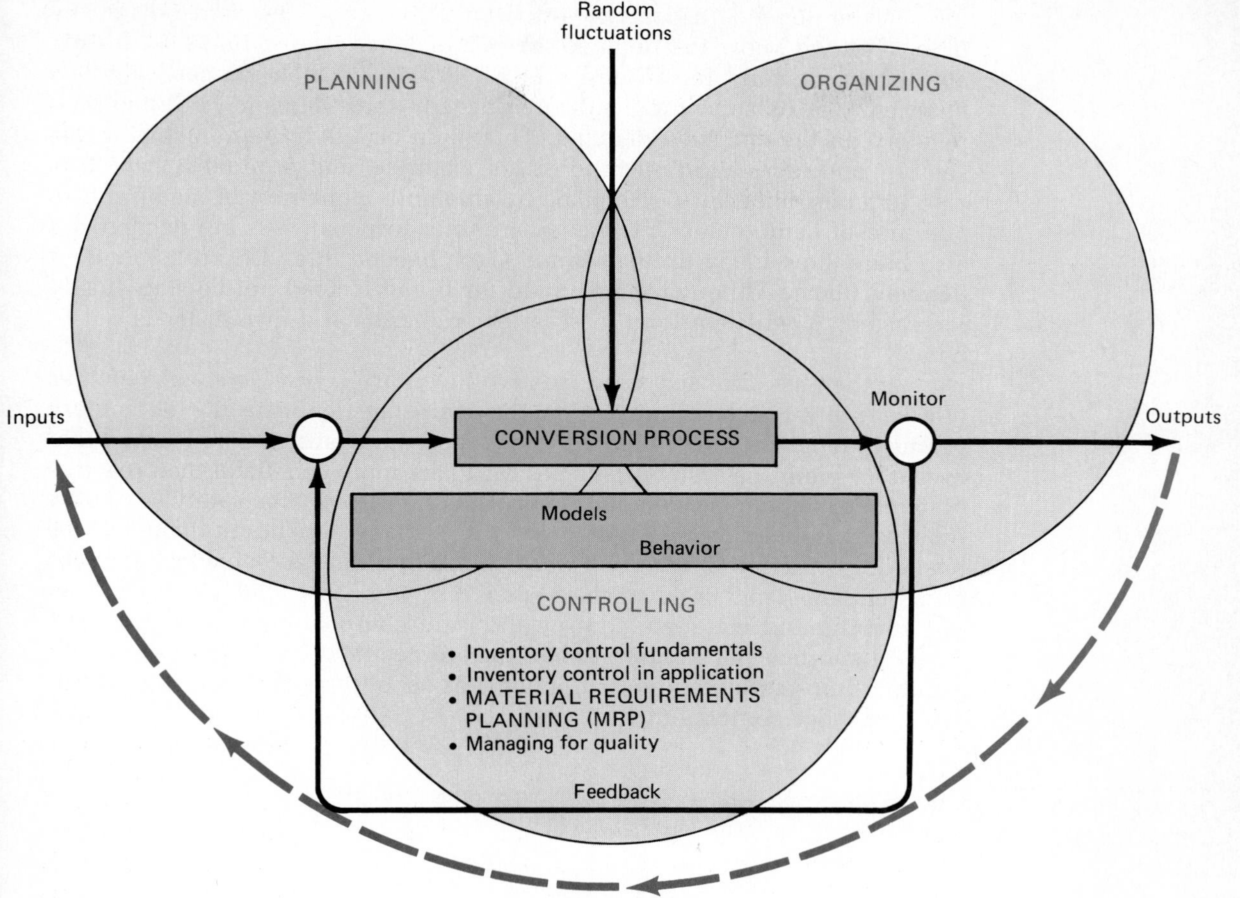

FIGURE 16.1
Production/operations management activities

requisite for them is the concept of dependent versus independent demand for products and their subcomponents. Let's review this important concept to prepare for our discussion of MRP.

Demand Dependency

We need to distinguish between independent-demand and dependent-demand items because the appropriate inventory control system for one is inappropriate for the other. Demand dependency is the degree to which the demand for some item is associated with the demand for another item. With *independent demand,* demand for one item is unrelated to the demand for others. We attempt to estimate or predict independent item demand with various forecasting methods. For most organizations, end products offered to customers are independent demand items.

In the *dependent demand* situation, if we know the demand for one item, then we know the demand for one or more related items. If, for example, the demand for an end product is known, then we can calculate how many of its subcomponents are needed—their demand is directly dependent on the end item demand. This often occurs in manufacturing, assembly, and fabrication operations. For example, end product A, which is sold to a customer, may be created by assembling one unit of material B to one unit of component C. Once we are told how many As are needed, we also know how many units of B and C are needed. B and C are dependent demand items. Although the demand for B and C need not be statistically forecasted, A will require a forecast or prediction if a firm order is not in hand.

In the past, industry used reactive inventory control systems (such as reorder point-reorder quantity) as the mainstay, ignoring the dependent versus independent distinction. More recently, however, we've learned that inventory planning systems (such as MRP) are more beneficial than reactive systems for dependent demand items. We don't need large safety stocks for them because usually we know exactly how many dependent items will be needed. Furthermore, we don't need to accumulate excessive cycle stocks of dependent items in advance of when they're needed. With accurate record keeping and materials control, the right components can be available without shortages or excesses when they're needed. Our MRP systems use accurate information about components as substitutes for excessive inventories of those components.

THE ROLE OF MRP IN THE OPERATIONS SCHEDULING SYSTEM

In Chapter 9 we discussed MRP from an information systems perspective. Now we shall concentrate on MRP from the standpoint of operations planning and scheduling, as a technique for scheduling the time-phased materials requirements for production operations. As such, it is geared towards meeting the end-item outputs prescribed in the master production schedule as shown in Figure 16.2. It also provides outputs, such as due dates for components, that are subsequently used for shop floor control. Once these MRP outputs are available, they enable us to estimate the detailed capacity requirements for the production work centers. MRP's role in these activities becomes evident as we examine its objectives and structure in greater detail.

MRP Objectives and Methods

MRP systems are intended to provide the following:

1. reduced inventory requirements,
2. reduced production lead times and delivery lead times to customers,
3. realistic delivery commitments to customers,
4. increased operating efficiency.

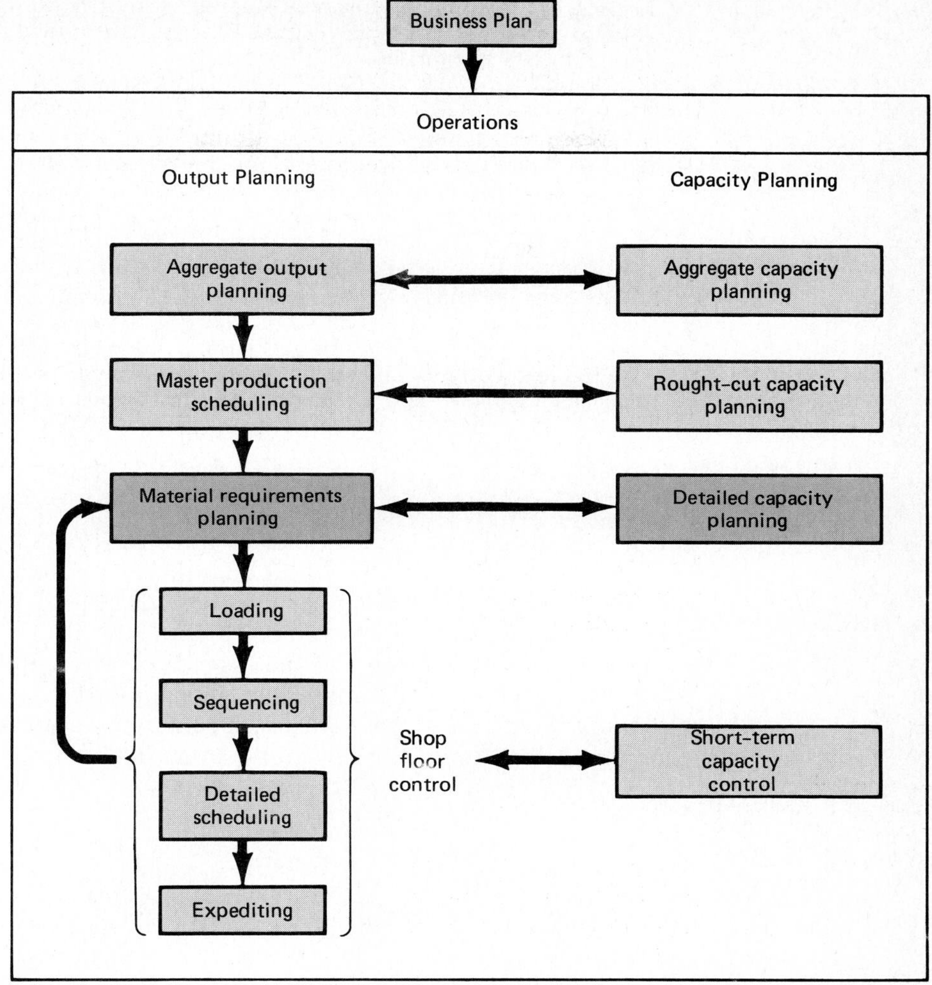

FIGURE 16.2
The operations planning and scheduling system

How does MRP accomplish these objectives?

1. *Inventory reduction.* MRP determines how many of a component are needed and when to meet the master schedule. It enables the manager to procure that component as it is needed, thereby avoiding costs of continuously carrying it and excessive safety stocks in inventory.
2. *Reduction in production and delivery lead times.* MRP identifies which of many materials and components needs (quantity and timing), availabilities, and actions (procurement and production) are needed to meet delivery dead-

lines. By coordinating inventories, procurement, and production decisions, it helps avoid delays in production. It prioritizes production activities by putting due dates on customer job orders.

3. *Realistic commitments.* Realistic delivery promises can enhance customer satisfaction. By using MRP, production can give marketing timely information about likely delivery times to prospective customers. Just how does this happen? The MRP system contains the bill of materials, inventory status, lead time (production and procurement) information, and a schedule of the existing production load. Potential new customer orders can be added to the system to show the manager how the revised total load can be handled with existing capacity. The result can be a more realistic delivery date.
4. *Increased efficiency.* MRP provides close coordination among various departments and work centers as product buildups progress through them. Consequently, production can proceed with fewer indirect personnel, such as materials expeditors, and with fewer unplanned production interruptions because MRP focuses on having all components available at appropriately scheduled times. The information provided by MRP encourages and supports production efficiencies.

MRP System Structure

Figure 16.3 shows the basic components of an MRP system as they were introduced in Chapter 9. The first of three major information inputs, the *master production schedule* (MPS), identifies how many of each end product (item) are needed during the time periods (usually weeks) in the planning horizon. The *bill of materials* (BOM) identifies the buildup sequence of an end product by specifying its successive stages (component levels) from raw materials, fabrication, and subcomponents through final assembly, including the leadtimes and work centers for each operation. The third source of information, the *inventory status file,* contains the current avail-

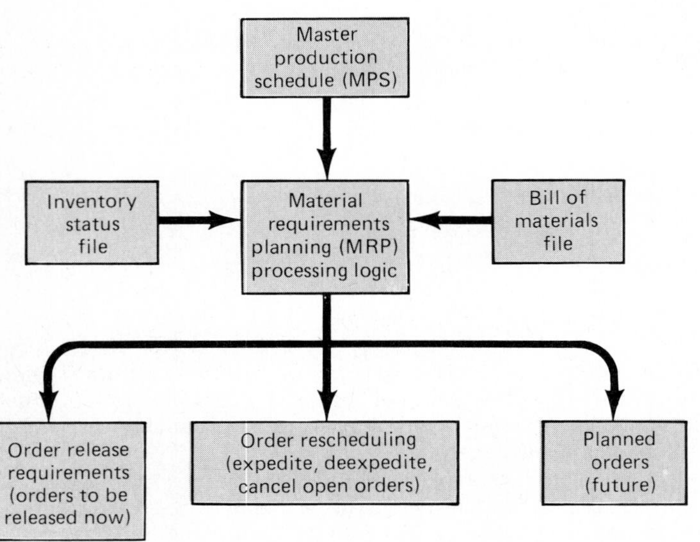

FIGURE 16.3
Material requirements planning system

Lead time: 1 week Standard order quantity: 10 units		Week 1	2	3	4	5	6	7	8
Gross requirements		50	50	80	80	70	70	70	70
Scheduled receipts		100							
Available	30	80	30	50	70		30	60	90
Planned order releases			100	100		100	100	100	

FIGURE 16.4
MRP record for motor cover

abilities of every item controlled by MRP: quantity on hand, safety stock level, and quantity allocated to various job orders.

The major output document from MRP is a time-phased component record for each item, level by level, in the product structures of end items in the MPS. The example in Figure 16.4 for just one component (motor cover) identifies its gross requirements, scheduled receipts, units available, and planned order releases. The top row in this record shows the *time buckets* (weeks in this example) in which future activities are planned. By convention, the current time is the beginning of the first period. Whenever there is a planned order release in the current period, it is referred to as the *action bucket* (signifying that action is imminent in the current time period). Table 16.1 defines some of the key terminology used in the MRP system and its components records.

The MRP Processing Logic

The MRP computational procedure uses the input information to calculate the current records for each component and item as illustrated in the following example.

EXAMPLE

Consider a company that makes kitchen chairs. Their simplest chair, model H, has two frame components, one for the seat and the front legs and another for the backrest and rear legs. To assemble the seat to the front legs, a worker needs four fasteners (see Figure 16.5). Similarly, to assemble the backrest and rear legs, a worker needs four more fasteners. The two frame subassemblies (F and G) are then attached to each other with four more fasteners. When the two subassemblies are combined, the chair assembly is complete.

Figure 16.6 shows the *product structure tree* and component information including item identification, requirements for one parent item, lead time, and description. Each item in the product structure is categorized by a *level code*.

The completed chair, item H, is the high-level item (level 0). Level 1 items are those whose parent is item H; these include items E, F, and G. Items A, B, C, D, and E are the individual components in level 2. Finally the lowest level (level 3) items are raw materials (RM) for the level 2 components.

Figure 16.7 shows a material requirements plan for shipping of 500 chairs in eight weeks, and fifty units each of items A and D in three weeks for replacing and repairing chairs in the field (raw materials have been omitted from the figure).

Without concerning ourselves with how this plan was developed, for the moment, let's concentrate on the information available at the current time for each item. We see that 100 units of H, finished chairs, are on hand prior to week 1. However, we need a safety stock of fifty for unexpected demand. Thus, the net available for meeting the 500 requirement in week eight is fifty. Similarly, 200 units of G are on hand, but thirty units are for safety stock and sixty units were previously allocated to other job orders. Therefore, 110 units are currently available for future allocation.

MRP System: Information Processing Sequence

The MRP processing logic is applied first to the high-level items (end products) in the product structure, then it proceeds to the next lower-level items. It continues downward, level by level, until it has determined the

TABLE 16.1
Selected terminology of inventory status file and MRP processing logic

Allocated: The quantity of an item's on-hand inventory that has been committed for use and is not available to meet future requirements.

Gross Requirements: The overall quantity of an item needed at the end of each future time period to meet planned output levels. Planned output for end items is obtained from the Master Production Schedule. Planned output for lower-level items is obtained from the MRP system.

Scheduled Receipts: The quantity of an item that will be received at the beginning of a time period from suppliers as a result of orders that have already been placed (open orders).

Available: The quantity of an item expected to be available at the end of a time period for meeting requirements in future time periods. This includes "scheduled receipts" plus "planned order receipts" minus "gross requirements" for the period, plus "available" from the previous period.

Net Requirements: The net quantity of an item that must be acquired to meet the scheduled output for this period. It is calculated as "gross requirements" minus "scheduled receipts" for the period minus "available" from the previous period.

Planned Order Receipts: The quantity of an item that is *planned* to be ordered so that it would be received at the beginning of this time period to meet "net requirements" for this period. The order has not yet been placed.

Planned Order Release: The quantity of an item that is *planned* to be ordered and the planned time period for releasing this order that would result in the order being received when needed. It is the "planned order receipt" offset in time by the item's lead time. When this order is placed (released), it becomes a "scheduled receipt" and is deleted from "planned order receipts" and "planned order releases."

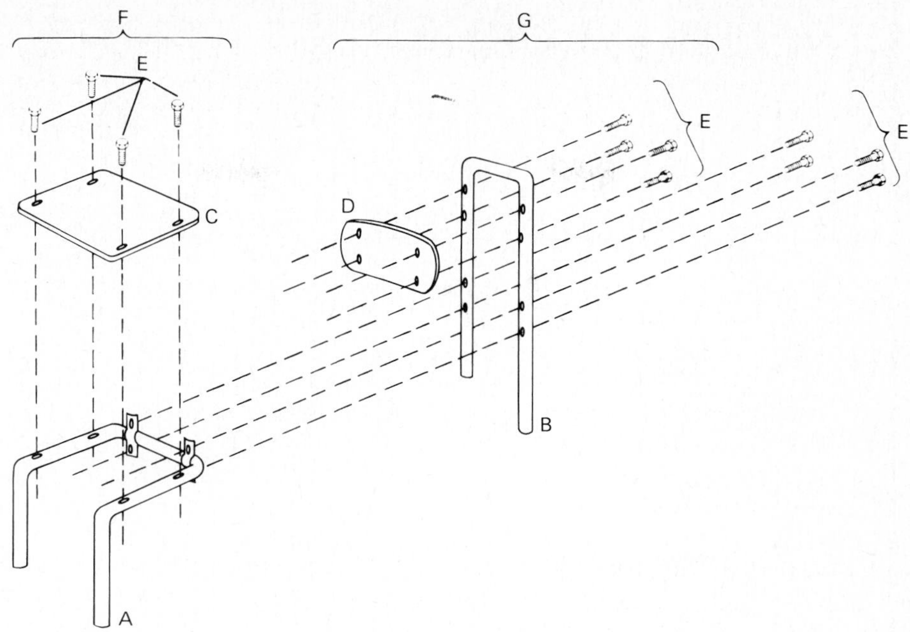

FIGURE 16.5
Assembly diagram for chair model H

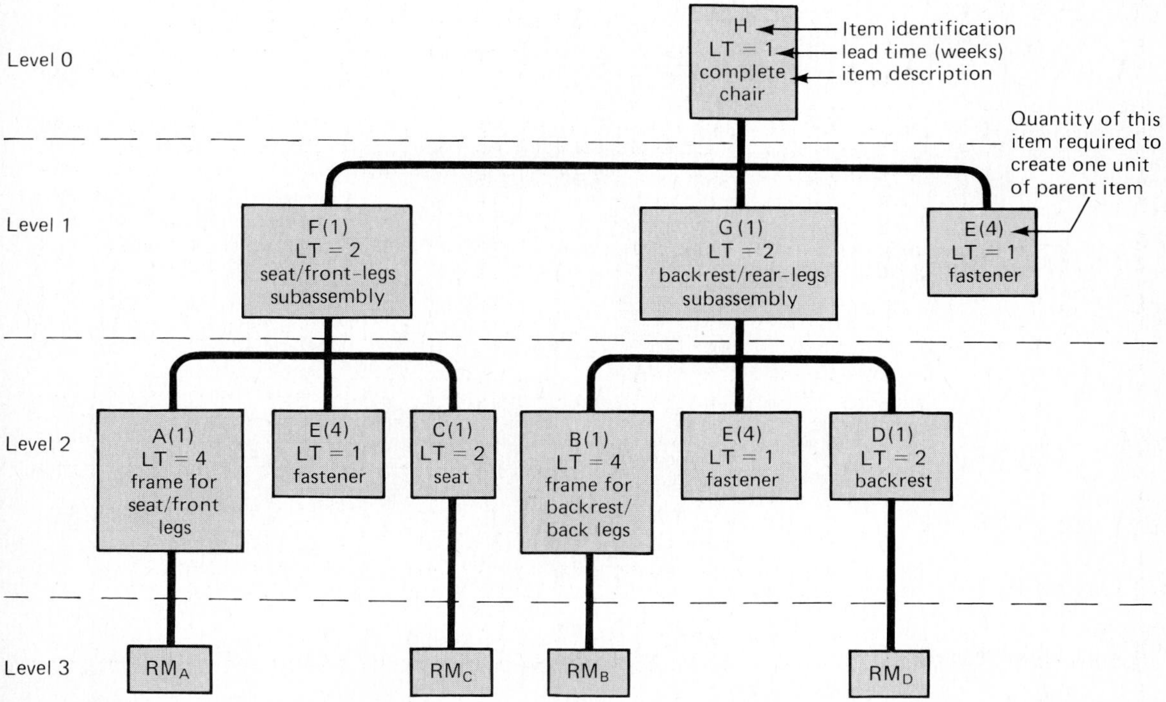

Level 0

H
LT = 1
complete chair

Item identification
lead time (weeks)
item description

Quantity of this item required to create one unit of parent item

Level 1

F(1)
LT = 2
seat/front-legs subassembly

G(1)
LT = 2
backrest/rear-legs subassembly

E(4)
LT = 1
fastener

Level 2

A(1)
LT = 4
frame for seat/front legs

E(4)
LT = 1
fastener

C(1)
LT = 2
seat

B(1)
LT = 4
frame for backrest/back legs

E(4)
LT = 1
fastener

D(1)
LT = 2
backrest

Level 3

RM_A

RM_C

RM_B

RM_D

FIGURE 16.6
Product structure tree and item information

(Assumes lot-for-lot ordering)

Item ID	Low level code	Lead time (weeks)	On hand	Safety stock	Allocated			Week 1	Week 2	Week 3	Week 4	Week 5	Week 6	Week 7	Week 8	
H	0	1	100	50	0	Gross requirements									500	from MPS
						Scheduled receipts										
						Available	50	50	50	50	50	50	50	50	0	
						Net requirements									450	
						Planned order receipts						lead time offset			450	
						Planned order releases								450		
G	1	2	200	30	60	Gross requirements								450		
						Scheduled receipts										
						Available	110	110	110	110	110	110	110	0		
						Net requirements								340		
						Planned order receipts						lead time offset		340		
						Planned order releases						340				
F	1	2	52	30	20	Gross requirements								450		
						Scheduled receipts										
						Available	2	2	2	2	2	2	2	0		
						Net requirements								448		
						Planned order receipts								448		
						Planned order releases						448				
A	2	4	50	20	30	Gross requirements				50		448				
						Scheduled receipts				50			replacement parts ordered from field			
						Available	0	0	0	0	0	0				
						Net requirements				0		448				
						Planned order receipts						448				
						Planned order releases		448						from F		
C	2	2	60	20	30	Gross requirements						448				
						Scheduled receipts										
						Available	10	10	10	10	10	0				
						Net requirements						438				
						Planned order receipts										
						Planned order releases				438						
B	2	4	150	20	30	Gross requirements						340		from G		
						Scheduled receipts										
						Available	100	100	100	100	100	0				
						Net requirements						240				
						Planned order receipts						240				
						Planned order releases		240								
D	2	2	52	20	30	Gross requirements				50		340		from G		
						Scheduled receipts							replacement parts ordered from field			
						Available	2	2	2	0		0				
						Net requirements				48		340				
						Planned order receipts				48		340				
						Planned order releases		48		340						
E	2	1	500	300	150	Gross requirements						3152		1800	from H×4	
						Scheduled receipts								from G×4 + F×4		
						Available	50	50	50	50	50	0	0	0		
						Net requirements						3102		1800		
						Planned order receipts						3102		1800		
						Planned order releases					3102		1800			

FIGURE 16.7
Material requirements plan

requirements for all items in the product structure that will be needed to meet the master production schedule. In the chair assembly example, the completed chair (H) is the "level 0" (high level) item requiring 500 completed units in week eight; this information was an input from the MPS to the MRP processing system. All subsequent information processing is geared toward honoring this schedule. The inventory status file tells us that fifty units of *H* are currently available from existing inventory; these fifty units are carried forward as available at the end of week seven, resulting in a "net requirements" of 450 additional units of *H* in week eight. The MRP processing logic then calculates a "planned order receipt" to occur in week eight (at the time needed) for 450 units of *H*. When must this order be placed (released) so that it arrives when it is needed? The processing system answers this question by "offsetting" by the length of the lead time, one week, as indicated in the Inventory Status File for item *H*. This process is called "lead time offsetting." The result is the "planned order release" at the beginning of week seven, which, after the one week lead time, will result in a receipt of 450 units at the beginning of week eight.

Having determined requirements for all "level 0" items, processing commences on the next lower-level items, either *F* or *G* in the product structure (item *E* at level 0 is a special case to be discussed soon). Level 1 items are considered next, because they are the only items needed to produce the level 0 item. The "gross requirements" for components *G* and *F* are determined by the "planned order releases" of the higher-level item *H*, 450 units in week seven. In general, the "gross requirements" for a lower-level item must include the "planned order releases" of the parent item for that time period. Then "net requirements" for each of *F* and *G* can be determined, and "planned order receipts" can be determined for the period. As was done for *H*, lead times are "offset" for *F* and *G* to determine "planned order releases." The processing logic now proceeds to the next lower level of the product structure and determines requirements for each of items *A–E*. Then, raw materials requirements would be determined.

Indented Bill of Materials To do its level-by-level calculations the MRP processing logic obviously needs accurate, concise information about an end item's relationship to all its subcomponents. The indented bill of materials provides this information. Our model H chair (the end item) has an indented bill of materials (see Table 16.2) with the same information as its product structure tree, except it's now in a convenient computational format. We can see quickly how many of which components are required at each level for one complete chair.

TABLE 16.2
Indented bill of materials for model H chair

Level	Quantity	Part ID	Description
1	1	F	Seat/front-leg subassembly
2	1	A	Seat/front-leg frame
2	4	E	Fastener
2	1	C	Seat
1	1	G	Back/rear-leg subassembly
2	1	B	Back/rear-leg frame
2	4	E	Fastener
2	1	D	Back
1	4	E	Fastener

Product Explosion To create a parent item we often need multiple units of a lower-level item. One unit of *H*, for example, requires four units of *E*. Hence, the "planned order releases" of 450 *H* in week seven must be multiplied by four ($4 \times 450 = 1{,}800$) to determine the "gross requirements" of *E* for week seven. This process is called "product explosion" or "bill of materials explosion."

Low Level Coding Often a single item exists in the product structures of multiple end items, or it exists in several levels of one product structure. Item *E*, for example, exists at both levels 1 and 2. To avoid duplicate or multiple requirements calculations for such an item, MRP by convention assigns the item to the lowest coding level in which it occurs in the product structure. Thus, *E* is treated as a level 2 item; "gross requirements" are determined from the "planned order releases" of its parents, items *F*, *G*, and *H*.

Service Components Periodically, assembled products in use by customers need replacement (service) components, so service agencies in the field occasionally place orders for replacement parts and subcomponents. A subcomponent of our end product, from both the service agency's and the MRP system's viewpoint, can thereby become an independent demand end item. Such orders are scheduled in the Master Production Scheduling process and given as inputs to the MRP system. In our example, fifty units each of items *A* and *D* have been so scheduled or planned for completion in week three. An order was released two weeks ago (not shown in Figure 16.7) for fifty *A*s, resulting in "scheduled receipts" of fifty units in week three. For item *D*, the "planned order release" for forty eight units in week one should result in "order receipts" necessary to meet "net requirements" of *D* in week three.

Using MRP Outputs to Control

From Figure 16.7 we see that to maintain the planned production schedule, "planned order releases" for items *A*, *B*, and *D* must be acted on in the current week. These cells are the "action buckets." The action is to release an order for the quantities in the planned order release/period 1 cell. MRP merely indicates what actions are needed to meet the MPS goal; now management must act to "make things happen"—to cause (control) the productive system to execute so that it gets the results it wants.

Keeping MRP Current in a Changing Environment

MRP is not a static system; it is responsive to new job orders from customers and current shop conditions, as well as changes anticipated for the future. Consequently the MRP system must be updated with current information and, at the same time, it must facilitate stable production operations in the face of continual change. Four aspects of MRP—pegging, cycle counting, updating, and times fences—are vital elements in this dynamic environment.

Pegging Various disruptions occur in materials plans—operations are delayed at some stages, physical inventory counts reveal unanticipated parts availabilities or shortages, the MPS is revised—and the materials plans must be updated accordingly. *Pegging* is a procedure for identifying which components are affected when a change occurs in any single item. Pegging shows the level-by-level linkages of components and their time-phased status in the MRP records. Figure 16.8 is an example; it shows the current records for end item A and for subcomponents B and C at two lower levels in the product structure.

If we discover that the 20 units of C (scheduled receipts) for period 1 cannot be completed, then plans for B and A are affected. The planned order release for B (20 units in period 1) should be cancelled because its supporting materials (C) won't be available. Consequently, the planned order release for 20 units of A in period 2 will be futile and should be cancelled unless special action is taken now to obtain the 20 units of B that are required for week 2.

Similarly, if the master scheduler increases week 7's gross requirements for A from 10 to 30 to meet a special customer order, the pegging procedure traces down through the records to identify associated changes at lower levels. The planned order release for A in week 6 is raised from 20 to 30, and the associated requirements for B and C are changed accordingly. The pegging procedure shows exactly which items' plans must be changed.

Cycle Counting Accurate data records are a must in MRP; otherwise, production schedules can't be maintained, deliveries will be missed, and labor and equipment inefficiencies will result. *Cycle counting* is a procedure for ensuring that on-hand physical inventories correspond to the quantities shown in the MRP records. With cycle counting, components are monitored and counted, including deductions for defective units, at each stage

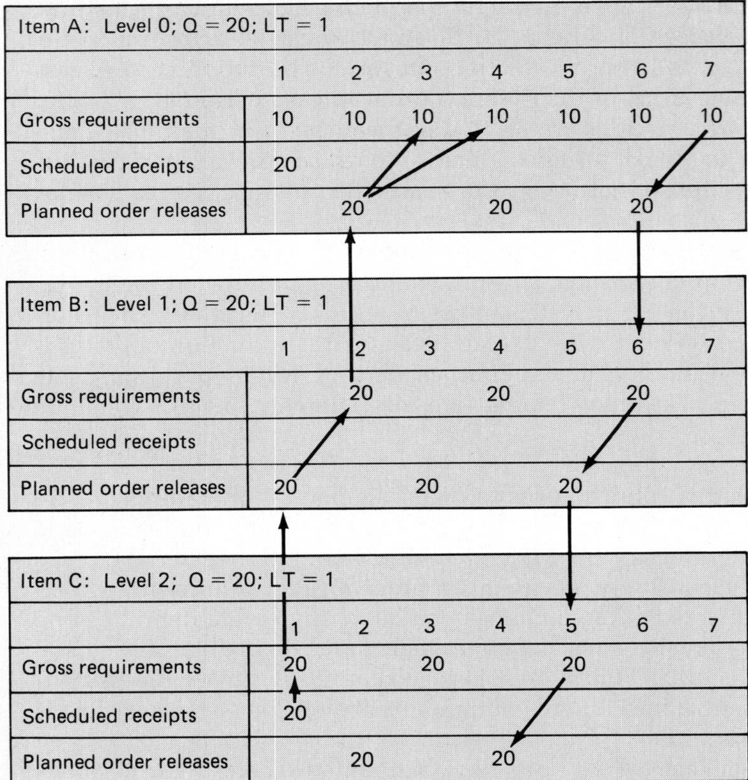

Item A: Level 0; Q = 20; LT = 1							
	1	2	3	4	5	6	7
Gross requirements	10	10	10	10	10	10	10
Scheduled receipts	20						
Planned order releases		20		20		20	

Item B: Level 1; Q = 20; LT = 1							
	1	2	3	4	5	6	7
Gross requirements		20		20		20	
Scheduled receipts							
Planned order releases	20		20		20		

Item C: Level 2; Q = 20; LT = 1							
	1	2	3	4	5	6	7
Gross requirements	20		20		20		
Scheduled receipts	20						
Planned order releases		20		20			

FIGURE 16.8
Pegging the MRP records

of production and in storage areas on a regular basis. Then the MRP records are updated, weekly or daily, to reflect these actual inventory counts. The subsequent updated records will indicate where special adjustments are warranted in production schedules due to excesses and shortages of components at different work centers.[1]

Updating the MRP System When job orders and other shop transactions occur, the MRP system must be updated. The existing plan must be updated when there are changes in the master production schedule or the inventory status file (such as revised lead times), or when engineering changes or product redesign modify product structures. Two updating approaches are available—the *regenerative* and the *net change* methods—and they differ in updating frequency. The regenerative approach completely reprocesses the entire set of information and recreates the requirements

[1]Various methods for cycle counting are described in T. E. Vollmann, W. L. Berry, and D. C. Whybark, *Manufacturing Planning and Control Systems* (Homewood, Ill.: Richard D. Irwin, Inc.), 1984, Chapter 3.

plan from beginning to end. It reprocesses the production plan at regular intervals, often weekly, and produces a complete, updated plan.

Net change systems, on the other hand, reprocess only those portions of the previous plan that are directly affected by informational changes. They update the production plan each time a change is posted and exploded throughout the system. The updated output contains those parts of previous plans that have changed. To do this, net change systems can require substantial computer access and rather elaborate computer programs. The net change systems do not seem to be as well received by users.

Time Fence As you can see, the dynamics of the MRP environment create potential confusion; if left unchecked, the changes can lead to unstable and irratic shop operations ("system nervousness"). Stability is gained by using *time fences* in the MRP system. The time fence is incorporated into the MPS and is the shortest lead time from raw material to finished production for an end item. Within this time fence, the MPS is fixed; rescheduling is not allowed, except under unusual circumstances.[2] Thus, for the Model H Chair (Figure 16.6), the time fence can be found by using the longest normal lead time at each level of its product structure plus the longest lead time for purchased materials (not shown in Figure 16.6). The longest lead times at levels 0, 1, and 2 are 1, 2, and 4 weeks respectively, so the time fence will be 7 weeks plus the raw materials lead time. Within this time fence, the MPS becomes "frozen" and the associated order releases are called "firm planned orders."

Lot Sizing

The MRP system generates planned order releases, which trigger purchase orders for outside suppliers or work orders for internal subcomponent production. Associated with each order is a "setup cost"—all the costs of placing and receiving an order. This raises the question of how much to order; one must consider the tradeoff of ordering costs and holding costs. Various lot sizing policies are possible. In our example for the model H chair, we assumed *lot-for-lot ordering;* order size equals net requirements for a given period. In MRP systems, economic considerations often result in order quantities that are larger than a single period's net requirements so that holding and ordering costs will balance out. The *EOQ technique, the Wagner-Whittin algorithm* (an optimal procedure), and others can be used, some of which are more elaborate and expensive than others.[3]

---

[2]System nervousness and time fences are discussed in D. W. McLeavy and S. L. Narasimhan, *Production Planning and Inventory Control* (Boston: Allyn and Bacon, Inc., 1985), Chapter 8.

[3]See William A. Ruch, "Economic Lot Sizing in MRP: The Marriage of EOQ and MRP." (Paper presented at the 19th Annual Conference, American Production and Inventory Control Society, Atlanta, Georgia, October 1976). See also Harvey M. Wagner and Thomson M. Whitin, "Dynamic Version of the Economic Lot Size Model," *Management Science* 5, no. 1 (October 1958), pp. 89–96. A comparative evaluation of various lost sizing and sequencing rules is given in Joseph R. Biggs, "Heuristic Lot-Sizing and Sequencing Rules in a Multistage Production-Inventory System," *Decision Sciences* 10, no. 1 (January 1979), pp. 96–115. See also E. Steinberg and H. A. Napier, "Optimal Multi-Level Lot Sizing for Requirements Planning Systems," *Management Science* 26, no. 12 (December 1980), pp. 1258–71.

One lot sizing method, the *part-period method*, does not provide an optimal lot size, but it is a low-cost method that approaches optimality.[4] It generates various order sizes by considering holding versus ordering costs. In the top half of Table 16.3 we see a series of net requirements for an item; in lot-for-lot ordering, this would result in seven separate orders. Assume that ordering cost (setup) per order is $100 and holding cost is $0.50 per part per period, based on ending inventory for that period. Using lot-for-lot orders, the total ordering cost for the horizon is $700, and, if the item is ordered and received at appropriate times, holding cost is zero as shown in the lower half of the table.

Looking at the part-period method, we know that an order must be placed to meet the net requirement of fifty units for week one. If we increase this order size to include the eighty units needed in week two, we incur a holding cost of $40 (80 units × $0.50/week) to store the eighty units from week one until they are used in week two. This larger batch is less costly than the alternative of placing two separate orders ($200 ordering costs), so the order size should be increased from fifty to 130 units. Should it be increased even further? If it also included the forty units needed for period three, the additional holding costs of $40 (40 units × 2 periods × $0.50/unit/period) would raise cumulative holding costs to $80 for this order. Since this cumulative cost is less than the $100 additional ordering cost, the order size should increase to 170 units. Increasing the order size by still another ninety units (required for week four) would require carrying these ninety units for three extra weeks at a cost of $135 (90 units × 3 periods × $0.50/unit/period), which would raise cumulative holding costs to $215. Since this $135 exceeds the $100 ordering cost, we cannot economically justify including these 90 units in the order to be received in week one. We therefore order 170 units to be received in week one, and this order meets our requirements for weeks one, two, and three. We must place a subsequent order to meet the requirements of week four and future weeks, and that order must be economically justifiable. Table 16.3 shows the order receipts pattern of the part-period method and its resulting costs, as compared with the lot-for-lot method for the example situation. Note that the part-period rule out performed the lot-for-lot rule by $220 in this example.

DETAILED CAPACITY PLANNING

Each time the MRP system is updated we face the question of whether or not shop capacity is sufficient to implement the current plans. *Detailed capacity planning* is a technique that addresses this question and it does

[4]See W. L. Berry, "Lot Sizing Procedures for Requirements Planning Systems: A Framework for Analysis," *Production and Inventory Management* 13, no. 2 (1972), pp. 19–34, and H. M. Wagner and T. M. Whitin, op. cit.

TABLE 16.3
Reordering patterns and inventory-related costs for two lot sizing rules

Inventory situation (patterns)									
Period (week):	1	2	3	4	5	6	7	8	
Net requirement:	50	80	40	90	0	60	120	80	
Units in order received: (part-period rule)	170	0	0	150	0	0	200	0	
*Inventory-related cost for two rules**									*Total cost*
Lot-for-lot rule									
Holding cost	0	0	0	0	0	0	0	0	$700
Ordering cost	$100	$100	$100	$100	0	$100	$100	$100	
Part-period rule									
Holding cost	$60	$20	0	$30	$30	0	$40	0	$480
Ordering cost	$100	0	0	$100	0	0	$100	0	

*Ordering cost per order = $100; holding cost per item per period = $.50

so in more detail than the rough-cut method we presented in Chapter 9. You may recall that rough-cut planning approximates the overall capacity required by the proposed (or trial) master production schedule. Once this master schedule is processed by MRP, however, the new information from MRP permits some refinements that were unavailable at the rough-cut level. Let's see how this MRP information is used in detailed capacity planning (also called capacity requirements planning).

Reconsider the chair manufacturer that was discussed previously; we'll do a detailed capacity analysis for component A (the frame for seat/front legs) shown in the product structure tree, Figure 16.6. A route sheet (Table 16.4) has been developed for component A; it lists the operations sequence, the work centers, the lead times in each center, as well as

TABLE 16.4
Component A: route sheet

			Standard times (hours)	
Operation number	Work Center	Lead time (wks)	Setup time/batch	Operation run time/unit
1	metal cutting	1	1 hours	.05 hours
2	metal forming	1	3 hours	.20 hours
3	drilling	1	.5 hours	.04 hours
4	finishing	1	2 hours	.15 hours

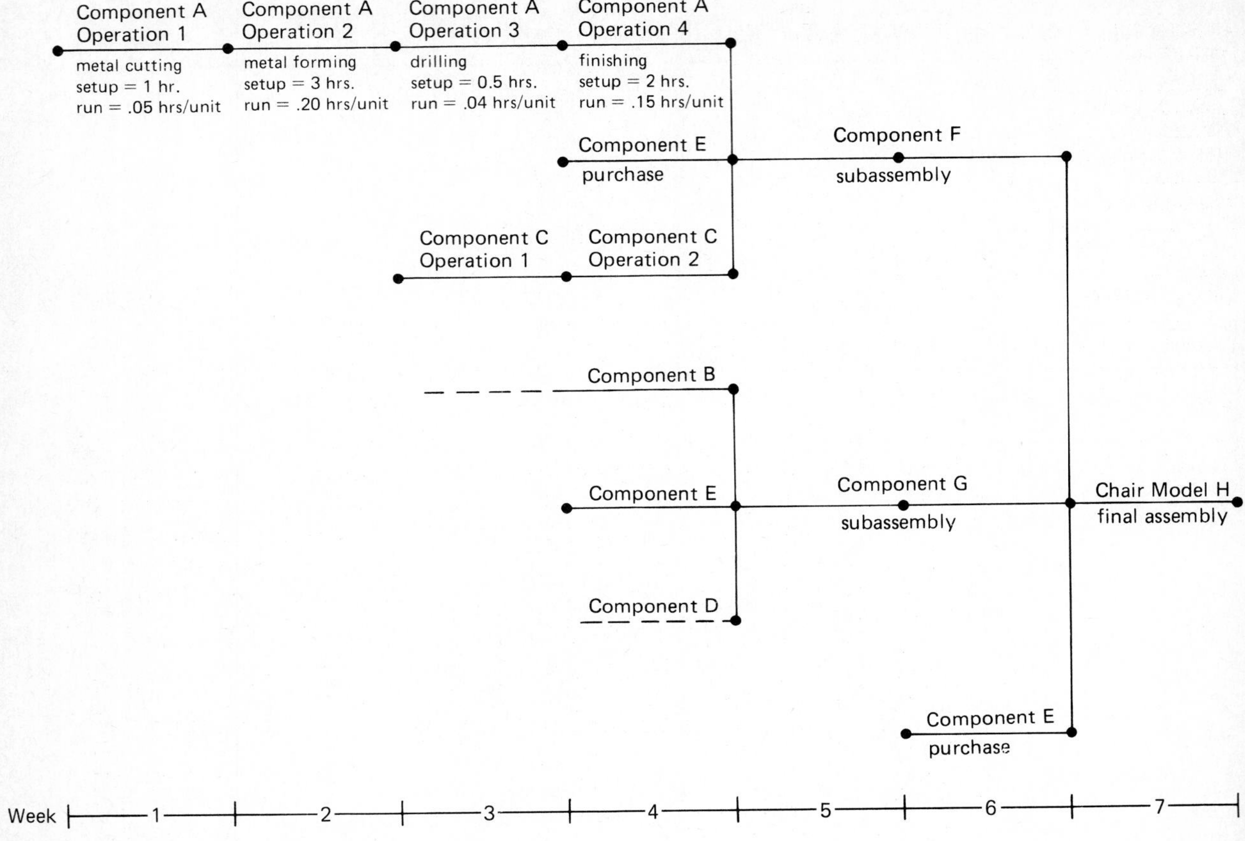

FIGURE 16.9
Partial operation set-back chart for chair model H

the standard setup and run times. This routing information, obtained from engineering and production records, will be used for evaluating the capacity requirements for item A.

To visualize the time-phased capacity requirements we first construct the *operation set-back chart* for the end item, chair model H.[5] The abbreviated chart in Figure 16.9 shows details from the route sheet only for component A; details for the other components are omitted.

We can see from the set-back chart that the future capacity demands on the four work centers by component A depend on the planned order releases of its parent item, component F. It also depends on how many component A's, if any, are already finished and available in inventory. This

[5]Set-back charts are described in T. E. Vollman, W. L. Berry, and D. C. Whybark, op. cit., Chapter 4.

Component A (seat/front frame) LT = 4		period 1	2	3	4	5	6	7	8
Gross requirements		80	90	90	90	70	70	70	80
Scheduled receipts		70	70	70	80				
Available	70	60	40	20	10	0	—	—	—
Net requirements		—	—	—	—	60	70	70	90
Planned order receipts						60	70	70	90
Planned order releases		60	70	70	90				

FIGURE 16.10
Current MRP record: component A

information is provided in the current MRP record for component A, shown in Figure 16.10. The gross requirements for A were calculated from the planned order releases of its parent item, component F (not shown). We see that planned order receipts for A are desired in weeks 5 through 8 and their planned release times are weeks 1 through 4. Each work center's labor-hour requirements (capacity) created by these planned orders are calculated from the standard time data (Table 16.4) and recorded in Table 16.5.

The resulting capacity requirements take into consideration the projected availability of 10 units per component A for week 5; only 60 net units in week 5, rather than the gross requirement of 70, require metal cutting capacity in week 1. Additional capacity requirements in these same four work centers will arise from component B, the back frame, and from other chair models in the product line. By combining all the requirements from all sources (products) detailed capacity planning provides accurate estimates of the time-phased capacity demands on the work centers.

TABLE 16.5
Capacity requirements (hours) for four work centers

Work center	Week 1	2	3	4	5	6	7
Metal cutting	4.0*	4.5	4.5	5.5			
Metal forming		15.0	17.0	17.0	21.0		
Drilling			2.9	3.3	3.3	4.1	
Finishing				11.0	12.5	12.5	15.5

*1 hour setup + .05 hours per unit × 60 units = 4.0 hours

LIMITATIONS AND ADVANTAGES OF MRP

The limitations of MRP have to do primarily with the assumptions that must be met before it can be used. A computer is necessary; the product structure must be assembly oriented; bill of materials and inventory status must be assembled and computerized; and a valid master schedule must exist. This last assumption, a required master schedule, is neither new nor unique to MRP systems. Converting customer orders and/or forecasts into a master schedule is a key part of any manual or computerized production-inventory control system. *The master schedule is dependent on good forecasts or firm orders for future demand.* Another source of difficulty has to do with data integrity. Unreliable inventory and transactions data from the shop floor can wreck a well-planned MRP system. Training personnel to keep accurate records is not an easy task, but it is critical to successful MRP implementation. In general, the system must be believable, accurate, and useful to its users or else it will become an expensive ornament that is bypassed in favor of informal, ad hoc systems.

MRP has several potential advantages, many of which we have previously discussed. Its overriding virtue is its ability to coordinate diverse production activities in a large-scale, complex manufacturing environment. This coordination can bring greater effectiveness and efficiency even though market and shop conditions are continually changing.

The dynamic nature of the MRP system is a vital advantage. It reacts well to changing conditions; in fact, it thrives on change. Changing conditions from the master schedule for several periods into the future can affect not only the final required part but also hundreds, even thousands, of component parts. Because the production-inventory data system is computerized, management can make a new MRP computer run and it can revise production and procurement plans based on this new information. Since runs typically take several hours of computer time for reasonably complex manufacturing environments, and since computer costs are high, the MRP system usually is updated only once a week. Even so, this is a vast improvement over most informal systems and, with a dedicated computer of high priority processing, the MRP system reacts quickly to changes in customer demands as reflected in the master schedule.

MRP User Experiences[6]

In 1979, Anderson and Schroeder reported preliminary results of an MRP user study sponsored by the University of Minnesota and the American Production and Inventory Control Society (APICS). Questionnaires were

[6]The data in this section are from John C. Anderson and Roger G. Schroeder, "A Survey of MRP Implementation and Practice." (Paper presented at the 10th Annual Conference, American Institute for Decision Sciences, New Orleans, November 1979) and an earlier paper, "A Survey of MRP Implementation and Practice." (MRP Implementation Conference sponsored by the Twin Cities APICS Chapter and the University of Minnesota, Minneapolis, Minnesota, September 1978). See also J. C. Anderson, R. G. Schroeder, S. E. Tupy, and E. M. White, "Material Requirements Planning Systems: The State of the Art," in D. W. McLeavey and S. L. Narasimhan, *Production Planning and Inventory Control* (Boston: Allyn & Bacon, Inc., 1985), pp. 277–291.

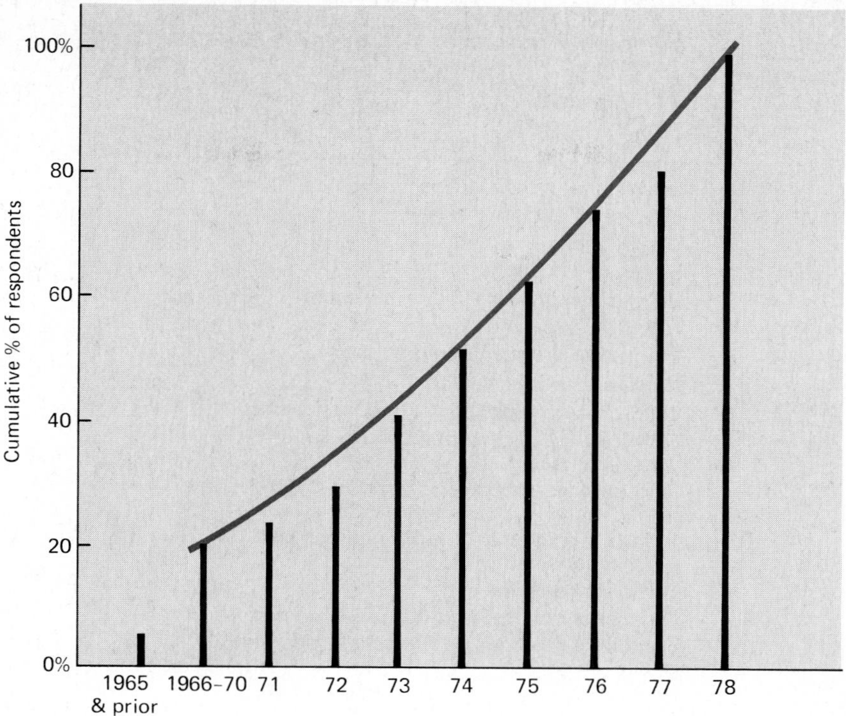

FIGURE 16.11
Pre-MRP year as reported by users

Source: Data for this graph were obtained from John C. Anderson and Roger G. Sroeder, "A Survey of MRP Implementation and Practice." Paper presented at the 10th Annual Conference, American Institute for Decision Sciences (New Orleans, November 1979)

mailed to 1,700 managers; of the 679 responses, 433 were using MRP systems. Respondents, industrial production/inventory control managers, indicated when they started an MRP system. Clearly, MRP is a recent phenomenon whose use has grown exponentially (see Figure 16.11).

Respondents' ideas about some major characteristics, problems, and benefits of MRP systems are shown in Table 16.6. Some users reported implementation problems—lack of communications about MRP within the company, lack of company expertise, and inadequate support from marketing and manufacturing personnel—all of which were viewed as more severe than computer hardware/software problems. When asked for *the* major problem in implementing MRP in their firm, the two most frequent answers were "education of personnel" and "top management support."

Production/inventory control managers rated the accuracy of information in their production processes. These managers felt the least accurate information they had, overall, was on capacity (and capacity planning),

TABLE 16.6
Selected MRP system and environment characteristics (based on user responses)

Characteristic of system/environment	Representative measure of this characteristic for all respondents
Use regenerative updating method	70%
Use weekly updating of MPS	57%
Use pegging	55%
Use cycle counting	61%
Have automatic lot sizing by computer	45%
Employ *weekly* time bucket	70%
Initiated MRP system after 1971	76%
Number of weeks in MPS	40 (average)
Installation cost (exclusive of operating cost)	$424,000 (average)
Estimated eventual system cost (exclusive of operating cost)	$715,000 (average)
Product data: produce both made to order and to stock	70%
Type of manufacturing: both assembly and fabrication	83%
Number of end items (per plant)	1,546 (average)
Number of parts and components (per plant)	12,445 (average)
Number of levels in Bill of Materials (per plant)	6.2 (average)

Source: Anderson and Schroeder, "A Survey of MRP Implementation and Practice."

market forecasts, and shop floor control. Their most accurate information was bill of materials records; this was followed by master production schedule and inventory records.

Users estimated present and future benefits of MRP as well. They cited greater inventory turnover, reduced delivery lead time, increased success in meeting delivery promises, reductions in internal production adjustments to compensate for unavailable materials, and reductions in the number of materials expediters. These benefits coincide with MRP objectives and are most likely to be found in an appropriate application environment.

It is evident from the results of this study that MRP is an improvement over previous production planning and control systems for many users. Its applications are growing as operations managers continue to improve their competitive effectiveness.

SUMMARY

Material requirements planning is a materials management information system that enables managers to improve operations efficiency, shorten delivery lead times to customers, and reduce inventory levels in many organizations today. MRP is applicable in environments where end products are produced from many demand-dependent subcomponents, assemblies, and materials with a known and stable sequence of product buildup. With information inputs from bills of material, inventory status files, and the master production schedule, the MRP processing logic provides time-phased plans for materials procurement and utilization. For each component in the product structure, MRP shows current and planned activities—open shop orders, planned order releases, scheduled receipts—for each period in the planning horizon.

MRP is especially useful in complex operations where new customer orders are arriving for a variety of products and where shop orders for various parts and components are in different stages of completion. The numerous transactions are accommodated through periodic system updating with accurate shop status data. To facilitate stable production operations in the face of these continual changes, MRP systems adopt procedures such as pegging, cycle counting, and time fences. This enables easy tracing of which components are affected by a change, ensures that actual materials availabilities coincide with planned amounts, and freezes the near-term production plans so that imminent shop schedules are more predictable.

Each time the MRP system is updated the question of capacity sufficiency arises; are we overutilizing or underutilizing our productive shop capacity? Detailed capacity planning is a technique used in conjunction with MRP to answer this question. The MRP planned order releases, open shop orders, and inventory information are converted into time-phased capacity requirements at each work center. Then, discrepancies between desired and actual capacity can be resolved for better capacity management.

CASE

Solar Fabricators, Incorporated

Solar Fabricators, established in 1975, specializes in manufacturing components and supplies for residential construction. Its most successful product line is Solar Seal Window Assemblies, which consists of two independent products, a "main module" (one large standard-size window assembly) and the "secondary module" (a smaller standard-size window assembly). These and the other Solar products, including replacement subcomponents for field servicing, are sold directly to large building and construction contractors throughout the sunbelt states. The master production schedule for these products calls for gross requirements of 2,000 units in week 12 and 3,000 units in week 16 for the main module; 1,600 units in week 11 and 2,500 units in week 16 for the secondary module; 400 units in week 7 for the installation tool for field needs of the main module, and 600 units in week 4 for the measurement fixture for field needs of the secondary module. For all items, scheduled receipts, available units, safety stock, on-hand units, and allocated units are zero. Solar Fabricators wishes to know which of two lot sizing methods, lot-for-lot ordering or the part-period method, would be most advantageous for its material requirements planning efforts. Production data are given in the accompanying table.

Main Module

Item ID	Item Level	Item Description	Parent	Quantity required/unit of parent item	Source of supply	Procurement lead time (weeks)	Setup or* ordering cost order	Holding cost/unit/week
A	0	Packaged window set ready for shipping			SFI**	1	$400	$1.00
B	1	Packing container	*A*	1	OS	2	100	0.10
C	1	Window set	*A*	1	SFI	3	2,100	0.80
D	2	Measurement fixture	C	1	OS	3	1,800	0.10
E	2	Installation tool	C	1	OS	2	200	0.05
F	2	Framed window	C	1	SFI	3	1,600	0.60
G	3	Frame screw	*F*	4	OS	1	300	0.10***
H	3	Rubber gasket seal	*F*	1	OS	3	700	0.10
I	3	Glass panel	*F*	2	OS	4	1,200	0.30
J	3	Metal frame	*F*	1	OS	2	600	0.20

*Includes all costs of placing, processing, setup, and receiving an order. A purchase order for multiple items from a single supplier results in a 20 percent reduction of ordering costs per order.
**SFI: produced internally by Solar Fabricators; OS: purchased from outside supplier. Items *B* and *BB* are purchased from one supplier. Items *D* and *DD* are purchased from one supplier. All other items are supplied by different suppliers.
***Cost/week for holding 10,000 frame screws in inventory.

Secondary Module

Item ID	Item Level	Item Description	Parent	Quantity required/unit of parent item	Source of supply	Procurement lead time (weeks)	Setup or* ordering cost order	Holding cost/unit/week
AA	0	Packaged window set ready for shipping	—	—	SFI	1	$350	$0.80
BB	1	Packing container	*AA*	1	OS	2	100	0.10
CC	1	Window set	*AA*	1	SFI	2	700	0.60
DD	2	Measurement fixture	*CC*	1	OS	3	1,800	0.10
E	2	Installation tool	*CC*	1	OS	2	200	0.05
FF	2	Framed window	*CC*	1	SFI	2	1,400	0.50
G	3	Frame screw	*FF*	4	OS	1	300	0.10***
HH	3	Rubber gasket seal	*FF*	1	OS	3	900	0.10
II	3	Glass panel	*FF*	2	OS	4	1,400	0.20
JJ	3	Metal frame	*FF*	1	OS	2	500	0.20

***Cost/week for holding 10,000 frame screws in inventory.

REVIEW AND DISCUSSION QUESTIONS

1. Discuss the appropriateness of statistical forecasting to demand-dependent and independent-demand items.
2. Identify the basic issues involved in capacity management and describe how these are treated in detailed capacity planning.
3. Find or create example data illustrating inventory-related cost advantages of part-period versus lot-for-lot sizing policies.
4. Compare the cost tradeoffs involved in choosing among the following lot sizing rules: lot-for-lot, EOQ, and the part-period method.
5. Explain the role of the master production schedule and how it relates to the other elements of an MRP system.
6. What is cycle counting? Explain how and why it is used in MRP systems.
7. Consider a product structure consisting of four levels. Suppose, for one of the lowest level items in the structure, that a cycle count reveals that 10 fewer units are available than is shown in its current MRP record. Show how pegging is a useful procedure for this situation. Why?
8. Identify the pros and cons of frequent versus infrequent updating of MRP systems. What variables should the system designer consider in selecting an updating cycle?
9. How many time periods should be included in the time fence for an end item? Under what conditions should the time fence be violated by master production scheduling changes?
10. What information is needed for detailed capacity planning? Where does this information come from? Show how it is used in a capacity analysis.
11. Of what use are route sheets and operation set-back charts in MRP systems?
12. Within the context of overall planning and scheduling systems for operations, explain the role of MRP.
13. In what ways do materials planning systems differ from reactive materials systems? Describe the advantages and limitations of each of these two types of systems.
14. Explain how a discontinuous or lumpy demand pattern can exist for a subcomponent of a parent item, even though the parent item has a smooth demand pattern.

PROBLEMS

Solved Problem

1. The product structures for end items A and S are shown in Figure 16.12. All items have a one-week lead time. Currently, there are 20 units of A available, 15 units of S, and 90 of C. The standard lot sizes are 50 for A, 35 for S, and 100 for C. The

FIGURE 16.12

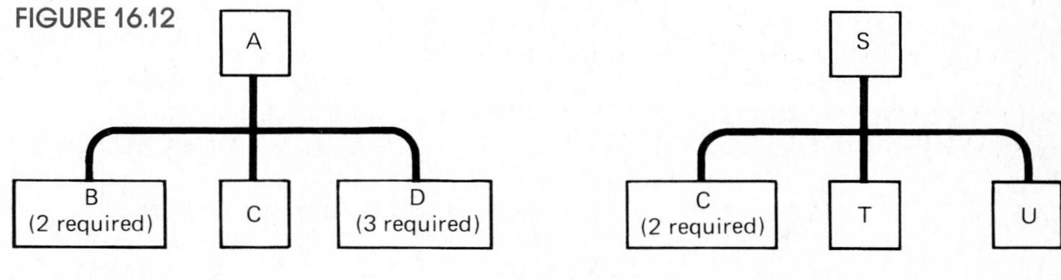

master production schedule calls for 20 units of item A and 15 units of item S for each of the next 5 weeks. An open order for 100 units of item C is scheduled for receipt in week 1. Create the MRP records for items A, S, and C.

		Week				
Item A		1	2	3	4	5
Gross requirements		20	20	20	20	20
Scheduled receipts						
Available	20	0	30	10	40	20
Planned order releases		50		50		
Item S		1	2	3	4	5
Gross requirements		15	15	15	15	15
Scheduled receipts						
Available	15	0	20	5	25	10
Planned order releases		35		35		
Item C		1	2	3	4	5
Gross requirements		120		120		
Scheduled receipts		100				
Available	90	70	120	70		
Planned order releases			100			

Reinforcing Fundamentals

2. Creative Wood Products manufacturers interior accessories for homes. One of their products, the Trophy Rack, is shown in Figure 16.13. Draw the product structure diagram of the Trophy Rack, label it, and identify the low-level codes for its items.
3. Product 800 is made from two 801 subassemblies, three 802 subassemblies, and two 803 subassemblies. An 801 subassembly consists of two units of component 406 and two units of part 407. The 802 subassembly is made from two units of component 205 and one unit of part 603. An 803 subassembly consists of one part 407, one 950 component, and three 747 subassemblies. A 747 subassembly is made from six units of item 910, three units of item 205, and one unit of 942. Create a product structure tree for product 800 and determine how many units of each component is required to produce 100 units of product 800.
4. Create an indented bill of materials for product 800 using the data in problem number 3, above.
5. Given the product structure diagram shown in Figure 16.14 complete the MRP records for items X and Z.

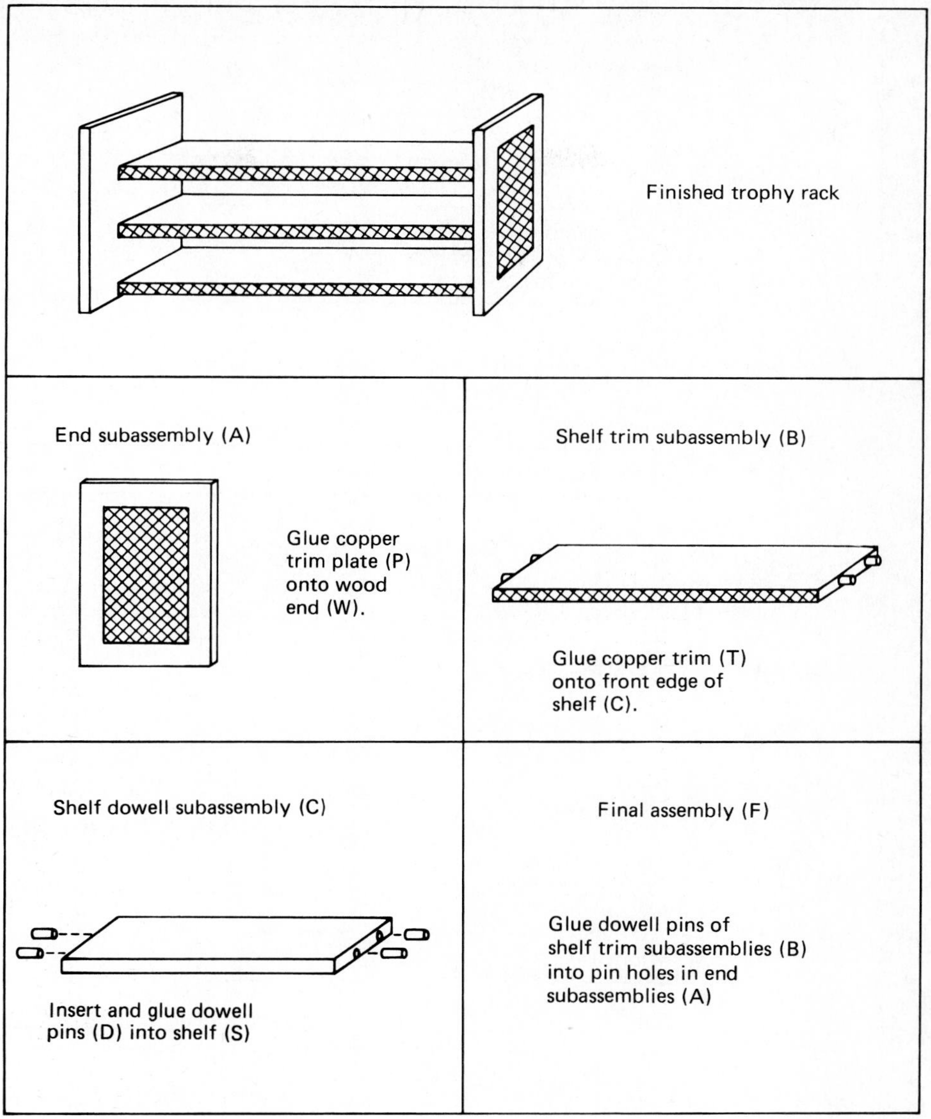

Finished trophy rack
End subassembly (A)
Glue copper trim plate (P) onto wood end (W).
Shelf trim subassembly (B)
Glue copper trim (T) onto front edge of shelf (C).
Shelf dowell subassembly (C)
Insert and glue dowell pins (D) into shelf (S)
Final assembly (F)
Glue dowell pins of shelf trim subassemblies (B) into pin holes in end subassemblies (A)

FIGURE 16.13

X
Y
Z
(2 required)

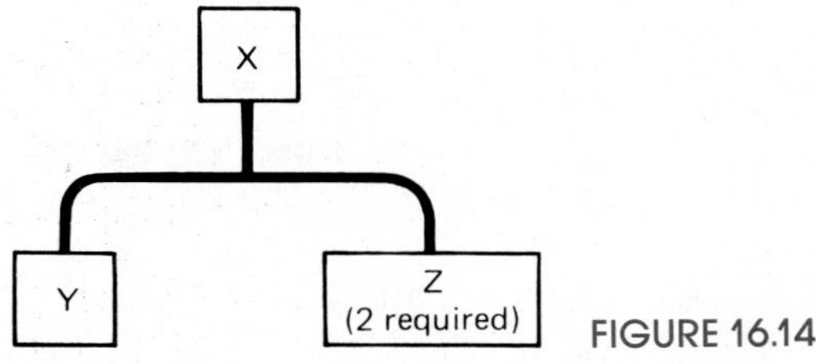

FIGURE 16.14

Item X:

Lead time = 1 week
Standard order quantity = 40

		Week					
		1	2	3	4	5	6
Gross requirements		25	30	20	15	15	20
Scheduled receipts							
Available	30						
Net requirements							
Planned order receipts							
Planned order releases							

Item Z:

Lead time = 2 weeks
Standard order quantity = 80

		Week					
		1	2	3	4	5	6
Gross requirements							
Scheduled receipts		80					
Available	90						
Net requirements							
Planned order receipts							
Planned order releases							

6. Route sheets for components A and B are shown below. Planned order releases at the beginning of the current week are 60 units for item A and 40 units for item B. Each work center has an 8-hour capacity each day (5 days per week).
   (a) Create an operations set-back diagram for components A and B.
   (b) Determine the capacity requirements of the planned order releases for the current week.
   (c) In what sequence should the jobs be scheduled at each work center?

Route sheet: Component A Lead time = 1 week				
			Standard times (hours)	
Operation sequence number	Operation work center	Lead time (days)	Setup time/batch	Operation run time/unit
1	100	1	2	.1
2	200	1	1	.05
3	100	1	1	.05
4	300	1	2	.15

Route sheet: Component B Lead time = 1 week				
			Standard times (hours)	
Operation sequence number	Operation work center	Lead time (days)	Setup time/batch	Operation run time/unit
1	200	1	2	.15
2	100	1	1	.05
3	300	1	1	.10

7. As a production planning analyst, you are given the current Material Requirements Planning (MRP) record shown below:

Item #203B On Hand—50
Lead Time—2 Weeks
Safety Stock—10
Allocation—20

	Week 1	2	3	4
Gross requirements				100
Available	20	20	20	0
Net requirements				80
Planned order receipts				80
Planned order releases		80		

(a) Is the record correct? If not, what changes need to be made?
(b) For the correct record, what would be the impact of an additional order for 50 units of item #203B required in week 3 *and* a reduction in requirements in week 4 to 80 units? Show the new record.

8. You are given the following current record for an item in an MRP system. All gross requirements are correct.

On Hand—100
Safety Stock—100
Item #3715
Lead Time—2 Weeks
Order Quantity—100

	Week 1	2	3	4	5	6
Gross requirements			1400			100
Scheduled receipts		1000				
Available	300	300	1300	0	0	0
Net requirements			100			100
Planned order receipts			100			100
Planned order release	100			100		

(a) Indicate what corrections, if any, are necessary in the record.
(b) Separate from (a) above, assume that the *economic* order quantity is found to be 50. What changes, if any, should be made in the record?

9. Patterson Assemblies has a gear assembly that requires part #GA211, with material requirements scheduled as shown below. Average demand is 83 units per week, the cost of placing an order (setup) is \$200, and the inventory carrying charge is \$1.50 per unit per week. Holding costs are calculated assuming that average inventory is centered within each week.

Week number	0	1	2	3	4	5	6	7	8
Requirements	—	20	120	80	0	160	194	20	70
Quantity ordered	—								
Beginning inventory	0								
Ending inventory	0								

Using the lot-for-lot ordering rule, complete the MRP record for part #GA211. What action needs to be taken if it is now the beginning of period 1? Calculate the total of ordering and holding costs over eight periods.

10. Refer to the data in problem 9. Using the Wilson EOQ formula (deterministic case), complete the MRP record. Calculate the total of ordering and holding costs over eight periods. What assumption is violated by using the EOQ formula in this case?

11. Refer to the data in problem 9. Using part-period total cost balancing as an ordering rule, complete the MRP record. Calculate the total of ordering and holding costs.

12. Compare the total costs from the results of problems 9, 10, and 11 above. Which rule appears best? Examining the cost components for each rule, briefly explain the difference in the behavior of the various rules.
13. Carcord, Inc., has received an order for 300 units of product G to be completed eight weeks from now. The product structure diagram is shown in Figure 16.15. There is no stock on hand (available) and none on order. Determine the order release data for all necessary orders.

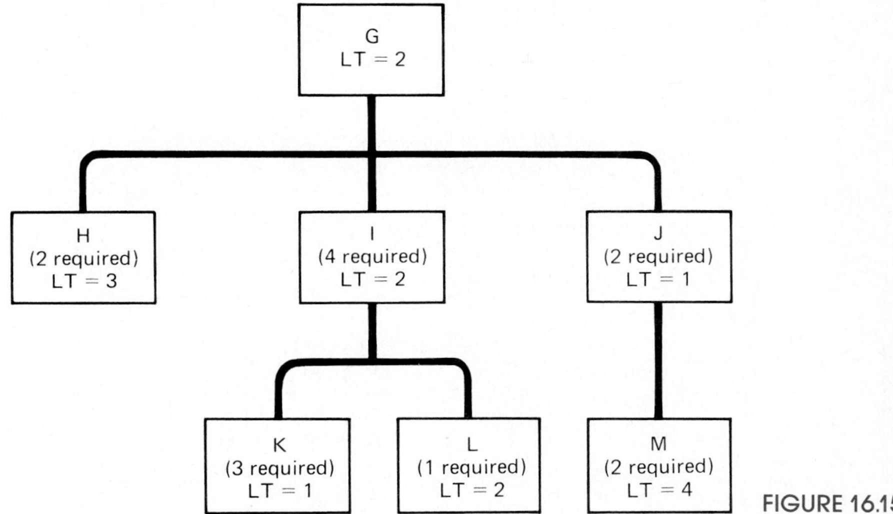

FIGURE 16.15

14. For the situation in problem 13, Carcord has just been advised by the supplier of component L that a delivery delay of two extra weeks is expected because of an equipment breakdown. What impact will this delay have on Carcord's deliveries of product G?

Challenging Exercises

15. Components A and B are level-2 items in the product structure of the chair shown in Figure 16.6 in this chapter. Their route sheets are shown below along with their current MRP records and status reports on open orders.

Route sheet

Component A: Frame for seat/front legs

			Standard times (hours)	
Operation number	Work Center	Lead times (wks)	Setup time/batch	Operation run time/unit
1	metal cutting	1	1	.05
2	metal forming	1	3	.20
3	drilling	1	.5	.04
4	finishing	1	2	.15

Route sheet

Component B: Frame for back-rest/back legs				
			Standard times (hours)	
Operation number	Work Center	Lead times (wks)	Setup time/batch	Operation run time/unit
1	metal cutting	1	1	.07
2	metal forming	1	1	.15
3	drilling	1	1	.07
4	finishing	1	2	.12

Current MRP records:

	Week							
Component A	1	2	3	4	5	6	7	8
Gross requirements	200	240	240	240	170	170	170	230
Scheduled receipts	170	190	200	230				
Available 140								
Planned order releases								

Lead time = 4 weeks
Lot-for-lot ordering

	Week							
Component B	1	2	3	4	5	6	7	8
Gross requirements	200	240	240	240	170	170	170	230
Scheduled receipts	190	200	240	240				
Available 50								
Planned order releases								

Lead time = 4 weeks
Lot-for-lot ordering

Status of open orders:

Orders scheduled for receipt in week	Operations completed as of now	Operations remaining
Week 1	1, 2, 3, 4	none
Week 2	1, 2, 3	4
Week 3	1, 2	3, 4
Week 4	1	2, 3, 4

(a) Complete the MRP records for items A and B.
(b) Prepare a capacity requirements report covering the next seven weeks for the four work centers.

16. Foley, Inc., has received an order for 70 units of product A and 50 units of product S, to be delivered in twelve weeks. The product structures for products A and S are shown in Figure 16.16. Foley has on hand (available) 300 units each of components C and E; there is no stock on hand or on order for other components.

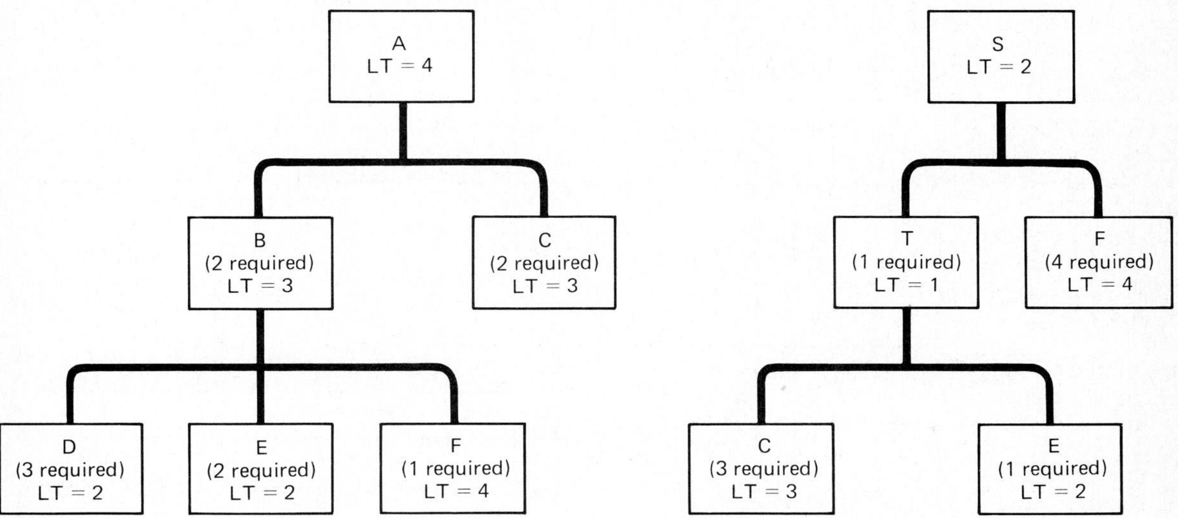

FIGURE 16.16

(a) Determine the planned order releases for products A and S.
(b) After planning for the conditions stated above, Foley receives a request for an additional order for 50 units of product S. The Foley sales representative wants to know if she can promise delivery within eleven weeks, or earlier if possible, to the potential customer. As the production planner, realizing that your assembly operation can, at most, work on assembling 50 units of product S at any given time, what is your response to the sales representative's inquiry?

GLOSSARY

Available Quantity of an item expected to be available at the end of a time period for meeting requirements in future time periods. This includes "scheduled receipts" plus "planned order receipts" minus "gross requirements" for the period, plus "available" from the previous period.

Bill of materials Describes product buildup details of an item, including all subcomponent items, their buildup sequence, the quantity needed for each, and the work centers that perform the buildup sequence.

Dependent demand Relationship between the demand for two or more items; when the demand is known for one item, the relationship tells us the demand for the other item(s).

Detailed capacity planning Iterative process of modifying the master production schedule and/or planned resources to create consistency between capacity and the production schedule.

Gross requirements Overall quantity of an item needed in each future time period to meet planned output levels. Planned output for end items is obtained from the master production schedule. Planned output for lower-level items is obtained from the MRP system.

Inventory status file Complete documentation of the inventory status of each item in the product structure, including item identification, on-hand quantity, safety stock level, quantity allocated, and lead time.

Item level Relative position of an item in the product structure; end items are high-level; preliminary items in the product structure are lower-level.

Lead time offsetting Process of determining the timing of a planned order release; backing off from the timing of a planned order receipt by an amount equal to the lead-time length.

Lot-for-lot ordering Lot sizing policy in which order size equals net requirements for the period.

Master production schedule Describes the quantity and timing of each end product to be produced in each future period in the production planning horizon.

Net change system MRP system in which updating the plan involves reprocessing only those portions of the previous plan directly impacted by informational changes.

Net requirements Net quantity of an item that must be procured to meet the scheduled output for this period. It is calculated as "gross requirements" minus "scheduled receipts" for the period minus "available" from the previous period.

Part-period method A lot-sizing policy that generates varying order sizes by considering holding versus ordering costs.

Planned order receipts Quantity of an item that is *planned* to be ordered so that it will be received in this time period to meet "net requirements" for this period. The order has not yet been placed.

Planned order release Quantity of an item that is *planned* to be ordered, and the planned time period for releasing this order, that will result in the order being received when needed. It is the "planned order receipt" offset in time by the item's lead time. When this order is placed (released), it becomes a "scheduled receipt" and is deleted from "planned order receipts" and "planned order releases."

Product explosion Determination from the product structure and planned order releases the needed quantities of all subcomponent items.

Product structure A product tree showing the levels and quantities of subcomponent relationships constituting an end item.

SELECTED READINGS

American Production and Inventory Control Society, *Capacity Planning and Control.* Washington, D.C.: APICS 1979.

Anderson, John C., Arthur V. Hill, Roger G. Schroeder, and Janice I. Degross. *Proceedings of the Material Requirements Planning Implementation Conference.* Twin Cities APICS Chapter and University of Minnesota. Minneapolis, Minnesota, September 1978.

Anderson, John C. and Roger G. Schroeder. "A Survey of MRP Implementation and Practice." Paper presented at the 10th Annual Conference, American Institute for Decision Sciences. New Orleans, November 1979.

Berry, W. L. and D. Clay Whybark. "Research Perspectives for Materials Requirements Planning Systems." *Production and Inventory Management* 16, no. 2 (1975), pp. 19–25.

"Computer Takes on MRP, Savings Multiply." *Industrial Engineering* 11, no. 3 (March 1979), pp. 26–27.

McLeavey, D. W. and S. L. Narasimhan. *Production Planning and Inventory Control.* Boston: Allyn & Bacon, Inc., 1985.

Miller, Jeffrey G. and Linda G. Sprague. "Behind the Growth in Material Requirements Planning." *Harvard Business Review* 53, no. 5 (September–October 1975), pp. 83–91.

Orlicky, Joseph A. *Material Requirements Planning.* New York: McGraw-Hill Book Co., 1975.

Peterson, L. D. "Design Considerations for Improving the Effectiveness of MRP." *Production and Inventory Management* 16, no. 3 (1975), pp. 48–68.

Ruch, William A. "Economic Lot Sizing in MRP: The Marriage of EOQ and MRP." Paper presented at the 19th Annual Conference, American Production and Inventory Control Society. Atlanta, Georgia, 1976.

Vollmann, T. E., Berry, W. L., and D. C. Whybark. *Manufacturing Planning and Control Systems.* Homewood, Ill.: Richard D. Irwin, Inc., 1984.

Wagner, Harvey M. and Thomson M. Whitin. "Dynamic Version of the Economic Lot Size Model." *Management Science* 5, no. 1 (October 1958), pp. 89–96.

Whybark, D. Clay and J. Gregg Williams. "Material Requirements Planning Under Uncertainty." *Decision Sciences* 7, no. 4 (October 1976), pp. 595–606.

17 Managing for Quality

At Ford Motor Company we have adopted an operating philosophy to establish and maintain an environment which will result in never-ending improvement in the quality and productivity of products and services throughout the Company, its supply base, and its dealer organizations. The new philosophy requires that the Company improve the quality and productivity of every element of the business from planning through field service. This includes—but is not limited to—all products and services, people relationships, attention to customers' needs, profits, shareholders' investments, and management approaches. In the final analysis, we are "Customer-Driven."

MISSION

Our mission is to continually improve our products and services to meet our customers' needs, allowing us to prosper as a business and to provide a reasonable return for our stockholders, the owners of our business.

VALUES

- *People:* Our people are the source of our strength. They provide our corporate intelligence and determine our reputation and vitality. Involvement and teamwork are our basic human values.
- *Products:* Our products are the end result of our efforts, and they should be the best in serving our customers world-wide. As our products are viewed, so are we viewed.
- *Profits:* Profits are the ultimate measure of how efficiently we provide customers with the best products for their needs. Profits are required to survive and grow.

GUIDING PRINCIPLES

- *Quality Comes First:* To achieve customer satisfaction the quality of our products and services must be our number one priority.
- *Customers Are the Focus of Everything We Do:* Our work must be done with our customers in mind, providing better products and services than our competition.
- *Continuous Improvement Is Essential to Our Success:* We must strive for excellence in everything we do: in our products, in their safety and value—and in our services, our human relations, our competitiveness and our profitability.
- *Employee Involvement Is Our Way of Life:* We are a team. We must treat each other with trust and respect.
- *Dealers and Suppliers Are Our Partners:* The Company must maintain mutually beneficial relationships with suppliers, dealers, and our other business associates.
- *Integrity Is Never Compromised:* The conduct of our Company worldwide must be pursued in a manner that is socially responsible and commands respect for its integrity and for its positive contributions to society. Our doors are open to men and women alike without discrimination and without regard to ethnic origin or personal beliefs.

The overall effort must mobilize the entire workforce in the pursuit of specific Company goals aimed at satisfying customer requirements for quality, value, and delivery.

John A. Manoogian
Executive Director—Product Assurance
North American Automotive Operations—Ford Motor Company
Dearborn, Michigan

Performance quality is crucial to the long-term survival of most businesses and government organizations. Each of us is aware, in varying degrees, of the international challenge to the North American automobile industry and the impact on quality and value. We thought it appropriate, therefore, to ask Mr. John Manoogian to comment on Ford Motor Company's quality, as he had a significant hand in developing quality strategies and supporting improvement in the 1980s at Ford. It is interesting that he chose to comment on quality in the context of Ford's mission, values, and guiding principles (the first of which is quality). We wanted to share his entire comment as our introduction to Chapter 17, "Managing for Quality." His introduction illustrates that quality is a major part of Ford's business objectives.

MANAGERIAL RESPONSIBILITY IN MANAGING FOR QUALITY

The National Association of Broadcasters participates actively in the Broadcasting Industry Council to Improve American Productivity. In 1984 a brief study was conducted in Philadelphia, utilizing a focus group to assist in establishing themes for a national media campaign directed at quality. Perhaps you have since seen some of the short spots narrated by Mr. Howard K. Smith on television, heard messages on the radio concerning quality, or seen advertisements in the printed media. The following example summarizes this initial study.

EXAMPLE

Discussion groups, commonly known as "focus" groups, were conducted in Philadelphia in June 1984 with a target of having 10 middle managers in each group, each group equally divided between manufacturing and services. The purpose of this research study was to identify the key *motivating* factors for a manager to want to learn the necessary philosophies and methods to improve quality and to uncover *predispositions* in the minds of management that might get in the way of successful implementation of a quality program. The media campaign could then be targeted to respond to these feelings and beliefs.

Findings from the group discussions were:

1. There seemed to be a roundly shared awareness of the importance of increasing productivity in American business, but quality assurance aspects of productivity were not so broadly comprehended. Managers were generally unaware of worker involvement in solving quality problems.
2. When the importance of quality was acknowledged, the idea of "doing it right the first time" as the key to quality improvement was not widely understood.
3. The key motivators for training to learn how to improve quality were self-centered; first job security and second becoming a more competent manager. Least motivating was the concept of national pride.
4. Expected barriers to receipt of a new quality emphasis include 1) "that is for manufacturing—I'm in services," 2) "I don't need it," 3) "unions will get in the way so why bother?" 4) "The expense will be too high to the company, so why bother?"[1]

[1]"Productivity Campaign Focus Group Study," Research Report of The Broadcasting Industry Council to Improve Productivity, June, 1984.

Managing for Quality, the subject addressed in this chapter, begins and ends with managerial responsibility. If we accept the above focus groups' views, we see that there is no burning desire on the part of managers to improve quality. Managers seem to be unaware of the urgency of the situation. Nationally, the need for a quality improvement effort seems to go unrecognized; in fact, there are many barriers to such efforts. In this chapter we want to increase your *awareness* as to the importance of performance quality in operations and to provide you with some alternative *analysis and program choices for improvement*. Should you become involved in, or responsible for, an operations function the material in this chapter will help you in your decision making. You will be aware of the alternatives available to you and your organization in seeking quality improvement.

How important is quality to an organization or nation? Peters and Waterman, in the popular management book *In Search of Excellence*, identify quality as a characteristic repeatedly identified in excellent corporations throughout the United States.[2] What about quality in other nations? In thinking about this issue, we return to the Japanese experience since World War II and ask many questions. How can a country of 100 million people achieve world-wide leadership in automobile manufacturing, steel production, shipbuilding, and consumer electronics? How can this be accomplished on an island the same size as California with no national resources except labor? What qualities do consumers admire in Japanese products? The answer is generally the same to these and similar questions—the Japanese understand and provide quality and value in their products.[3] Let's first briefly discuss the quality concept and then focus on managing for improving quality.

PRODUCT QUALITY

Product (Output) Quality

As Figure 17.1 illustrates, managing for quality involves the conversion process operated to produce outputs, often a product. However, in any one conversion process we do not produce just any product, but one possessing specific characteristics. The product's important characteristics are specified when it is designed prior to its manufacture. These characteristics are called the *design specifications*. After the product has been produced, we can observe the extent to which it conforms to or deviates from the design specifications. *Product (output) quality is the appropriateness of design specifications to function and use as well as the degree to which the product conforms to the design specifications*. Service (output) quality is similarly defined. As you know, output quality can apply to either products or

[2]Peters, Thomas J. and Robert H. Waterman, *In Search of Excellence: Lessons from America's Best-Run Companies*, (New York: Harper and Row, 1982).

[3]See Chapter 2 of this book, the sections on productivity and quality and on international productivity; Richard Tanner Pascale and Anthony G. Athos, *The Art of Japanese Management*, (New York: Warner Books, 1981); Robert W. Hall, *Zero Inventories*, (Homewood, Ill.: Dow-Jones Irwin, 1983); and Richard J. Schonberger, *Japanese Manufacturing Techniques: Nine Hidden Lessons in Simplicity*, (The Free Press, 1982).

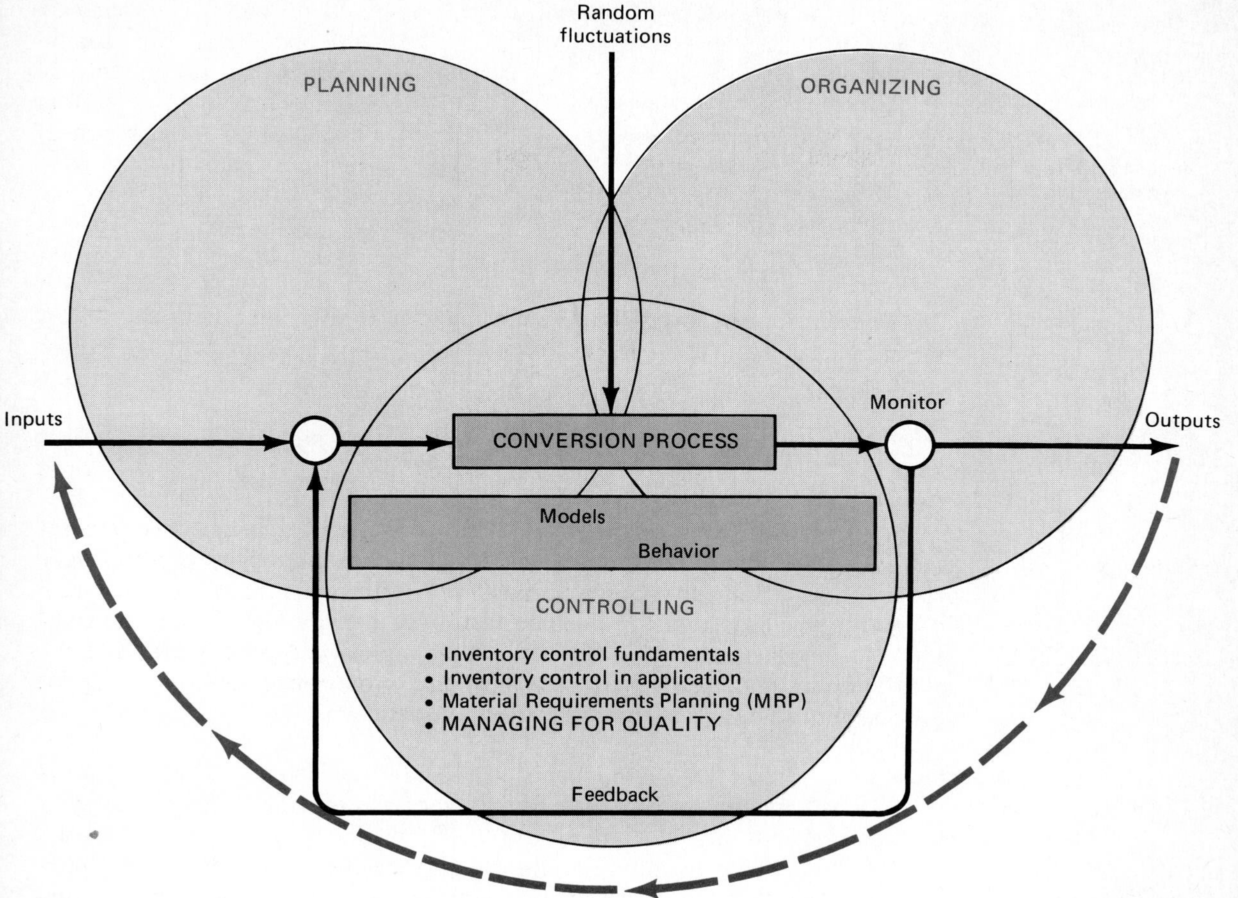

FIGURE 17.1
Production/operations management activities

services. We will ask you to make inferences from the discussion of products to service quality in this chapter.

Previously we focused on product and process design. In production and operations, we often have limited affect on design. This is unfortunate, because the job of production focuses on output conformance to design. For the most part, our discussion of quality in this chapter will be about the somewhat narrower operations perspective involving conformance to a design. When there is close conformance between design and output characteristics, there is a high degree of product (output) quality. When there are important discrepancies, there is a low level of quality. Product quality can be seen to fall on a continuum ranging from very low to very high, as Figure 17.2 shows.

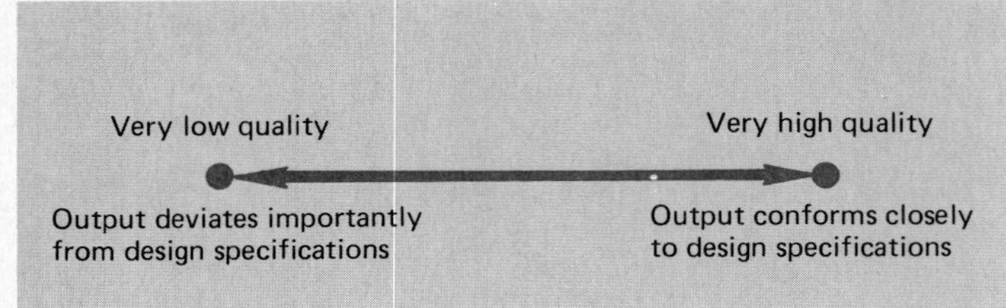

FIGURE 17.2
Degrees of output quality

There are popular alternative concepts of quality, among these

- "Quality is fitness for use."
- "Quality is doing it right the first time—and every time."
- "Quality is the customer's perception."
- "Quality provides a product or service at a price the customer can afford."
- "You pay for what you get (quality is the most expensive product or service)."

Although we find each of these views to have merit, they have shortcomings as well. Our judgment is that little is accomplished by arguing over precise quality definitions or slogans. The key to managing for quality lies first in the awareness of the need to improve, and then selecting improvement techniques with the best chance for success. An understanding of product characteristics, product design, and process capability will assist us in becoming aware of quality issues in operations.

Product Characteristics All aspects of the product are not equally important to our customers. Usually, only some of them need be considered when assessing the level of quality. But which aspects are most important? Weight? Size? Shape? Color? Functional performance? *The important product characteristics are determined by the specific market goals of the organization and by the technical requirements of the important stages of the conversion process.* Often we must compromise between these two sources of quality requirements.

EXAMPLE

Not all financial institutions, magazines, or automobiles are similar in product quality or *market goals.* Credit unions, for example, provide financial services to a different market from that serviced by banks and savings and loan institutions. *Playboy* magazine was designed to appeal to readers with a different set of interests from those who read *Mechanics Illustrated.* Likewise, Mercedes automobiles appeal to a market segment distinctly different from the one Volkswagon aims at. The *technical requirements* of financial institutions are generally less demanding than automotive manufacturers, each conversion process distinctly shaping product characteristics.

Design Of two firms producing the same product, one may have to pay high costs to maintain an acceptable quality level, while its competitor can maintain the same quality at a much lower cost. The difference is often a result of the emphasis placed on quality considerations in the design phases of product development, prior to full-scale production. The old adage, "quality is *designed into* the product," holds true. Seemingly minor modifications in product design can dramatically increase ability to reach desired output quality once production has begun. The number of stages in the conversion process, the types of input resources needed, and the types of technical processes required to produce the output are all largely determined in the product design phase.

Process Capability A maximum quality level, or upper capability limit, can be established for every technical process. If the operations manager can select the best material and the best operator in the plant and arrange for all the equipment to be properly set up and operated, output can be produced under carefully controlled, ideal conditions. Say that under these conditions, output averages 1 percent defective (1 percent of the units produced are unacceptable). In this case, 1 percent defective is the upper bound on quality level; it is the *process capability*. Two things are important to remember about process capability. First, in general there are errors in conversion operations because of the random variability of materials, people, and equipment. Process capability is *not* necessarily zero errors. Second, the process capability is not necessarily the most efficient level of production. In fact, most processes should be priced and operated for a higher quantity and lower quality level than the process capability. Statistical control charts, which will be presented later in this chapter, occasionally show process capability as separate control limits on the chart. Also, process capability should not remain fixed. As the manager and employee strive for *continuous improvement*, process capability should change as well.

Of course product-and-process design does not end when production begins. Design often continues throughout the product life in the form of various redesign activities. These redesign needs are signaled by reliability studies, quality assurance programs, warranty costs, and customer complaints.

MANAGING FOR QUALITY PRODUCTS AND SERVICES

Now that we have an awareness of the quality concept, let's ask how managers actually go about—or should go about—establishing and reaching the quality levels desired. There are several significant steps in effectively managing for quality products and services, as illustrated in Figure 17.3. We have summarized the activities that operations managers must perform in order to establish an overall quality framework, as well as in carrying out the details to achieve the planned level of quality.

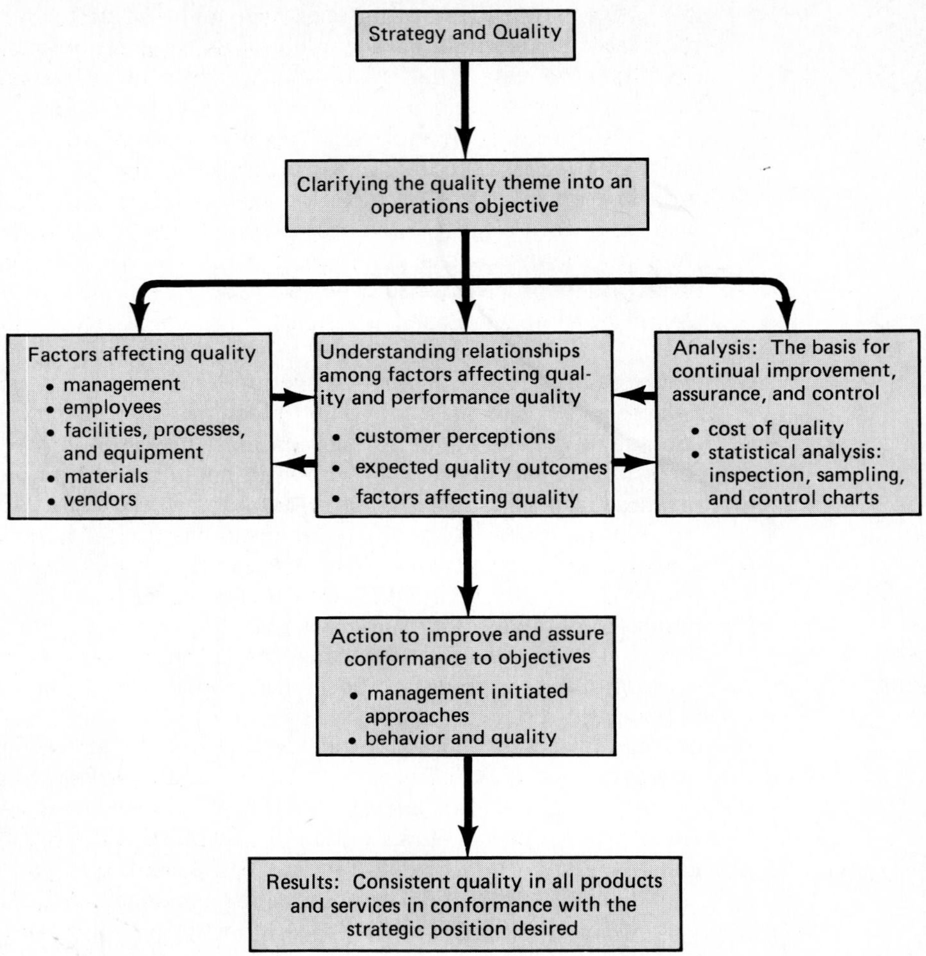

FIGURE 17.3
Managing for quality products and services

The manager must first determine how quality fits into the overall organizational strategy. Then, more specifically, he or she must determine the role that quality will play in the manufacturing (or operations) strategy; the approach used in production or operations should complement the overall strategy of the organization. Once this is accomplished, the quality theme must be clarified; it is essential that individuals at all levels within the organization comprehend quality goals.

For any organization there are key elements that affect quality. The effective manager must be able to identify these aspects—they typically include people, facilities, and materials—and seek to understand how they interact in his or her firm.

Once a strategy is developed and communicated and the key variables affecting quality are understood, then the conversion function takes place. Products are manufactured. Parts are made. Services are generated. Customers are served. But, how do we know if we *are* conforming to plan? Are we seeking the continual quality improvement desired? With respect to quality, are processes under control? Are quality costs in line with expectations? Fortunately, there is a rich and thorough set of analysis techniques to assist the operations manager in answering these questions. Effective managers have found that statistical techniques, in particular, can be quite useful; these methods will be stressed in this chapter.

Upon completing analysis to identify potential areas for quality improvement, it is necessary to take action and give specific directions to assure performance quality. A variety of programs and techniques exist to help bring behaviors and processes into conformance with expectations. We will survey several major programs in this chapter. Finally, we can observe the long-term results: consistent quality in all products and services in conformance with the strategic position desired. Let's now address each major block of Figure 17.3, with particular attention to the quality analysis and action (programs) issues; both are extremely significant in day-to-day operations management.

Strategy and Quality

Long-term planning within an organization should encompass the operations function; it should also specify a strategy that can be understood by production and operations executives. Typically, market potential (demand) is related to operations capability. As product or service ideas emerge, a general production approach and sales plan are formed. The desired quality level for the product or service is defined. Executives must develop a quality expectation to guide the organization. The quality expectation must be consistent on all levels—it should be specified by the top executives and clearly understood by top managers in the marketing and operations functions. In fact, a quality standard should be set for all activities that support the primary business goals—activities in accounting, finance, engineering, distribution, and administration—as well as for products and services directly consumed by the ultimate customer.

This linkage of strategy with quality is crucial if the firm is to have a consistent purpose. Let's look at a few examples of organizations that understand the importance of this connection.

EXAMPLE

Japanese manufacturing firms have developed company-wide quality control (CWQC) that has evolved from inspection-oriented quality control (prior to 1945), through a statistical quality control growth phase (1945–1955), through a total quality control growth phase (1955–1970), into what is now CWQC with rapid growth (1970-present). The thrust in a typical Japanese firm is to implement a "process" to promote never-ending improvement in the effectiveness and efficiency of all elements of a business. The goal of CWQC is to mobilize the entire work force in a pursuit of specific company goals aimed at satisfying customer requirements for quality, price, and delivery. The strategy used by an organization accepting CWQC is to improve the effectiveness and efficiency of every element in the business through the use of statistical thinking, managing with facts, and defect and error prevention. Japanese firms accepting CWQC stress these six elements in their approach:

1. Quality is first in all business thinking and action.
2. Assure the quality of new product development.
3. Quality must be customer oriented, not producer oriented.
4. Consider the next step in any process as the customer.
5. Use a continuing "plan, do, check, action cycle" in all business elements.
6. Respect humanity.[4]

[4]"Company-Wide Quality Control (CWQC)," Report of the NAAO Product Assurance Committee, February 13, 1984.

In the United States, we see variations of the Japanese theme as companies react to world-wide quality competition. Some remarks by chief executive officers (CEOs) illustrate this strategic thrust.

EXAMPLE

In a booklet directed at involving all Packaging Corporation of America employees toward quality improvement, President Monte R. Hayman states,

> We have embarked on a course to make Quality a fundamental part of our long-term strategy. We have committed to extensive time, management effort and monies in an effort to have PCA meet the ever increasing demands for Quality products and service.
>
> The goal of this Quality process is to get each of us, managers, office workers, professional or production operators, to do our job right the first time. Any job done wrong will spoil every subsequent job that depends on it, whether our job is taking a phone message correctly, taking the time to be courteous and helpful, typing a letter, or preparing a report or a customer proposal.
>
> Quality is not something a committee can create nor a president can order. It is the cumulative result of everyone caring about his or her work and wanting to build a respected, secure, profitable company in which to work.
>
> We are committed to excellence in all that we do at PCA. Quality performance is the process by which this will be achieved.
>
> Thank you for your personal effort in making our company a success.[5]

[5]Monte R. Hayman, "PCA Quality," Packaging Corporation of America, 1984.

EXAMPLE

J. Fred Bucy, President and CEO, Texas Instruments, Inc., made the following statement concerning TI's quality philosophy and policy. "Quality is the cornerstone of TI's People and Asset Effectiveness program and the personal responsibility of each TIer. . . . TI's quality policy is this: *For every product or service we offer, we shall define the requirements that solve the customers' problems, and we shall conform to those requirements, without exception. For every job each TIer performs, the performance standard is: 'Do it right the first time.'* This policy applies to all our products and services. The word 'requirements' in our policy means the specifications and delivery schedules that our products and services must meet to satisfy our customers' needs. But in order for our end products to meet our customers' requirements, all the intermediate requirements or steps necessary for a finished product must be met also."[6]

[6]J. Fred Bucy, "Quality." Statement released by Texas Instruments, Inc., October 1982.

There are certainly many companies that stress quality as a corporate strategy, among them Boeing, Caterpillar, Hewlett Packard, and IBM. For example, a survey of CEOs by a major business publication asked the CEOs for their perception of the American companies with the highest quality products or services. Boeing was the top-rated company by these executives.

Clarifying the Quality Theme

A key to successful quality is first to set a strategy, and then effectively communicate this strategy as a theme to employees and customers. We have seen from several of the above examples the effort CEOs are taking in stressing a theme. As consumers we've seen the media presentations for products: Hallmark's "Mark of Excellence," Ford's "Quality Is Job #1," and General Electric's "Quality Is Our Most Important Product," to name but a few.

Companies also go to great lengths to stress the theme, goal, or quality thrust to employees. Some of the alternative definitions we explored stress this communication issue. Let's consider Caterpillar, a producer of technically sophisticated and expensive products. Managers at Caterpillar communicate their message to employees at all levels by emphasizing a statistical approach. They do this in an effort to seek continuous improvement, as the following comment to stockholders explains.

EXAMPLE

Continued quality and technological leadership is a vital part of Caterpillar's long-range business strategy.

Our experienced, knowledgeable, and dedicated work force has developed state-of-the-art products, made in the most modern and best-equipped facilities in the industry. In recent years, we've made sizable technological advancements in manufacturing, including patented processes and apparatus. Manufacturing patents range from new ways to treat molten iron at the Mapleton, Illinois, foundry, to an isothermal metal-forming apparatus developed at our Solar subsidiary.

Advancements like these are allowing us to achieve higher levels of consistent quality and reliability. Moreover, using advanced technology to improve quality is having a favorable impact on costs.

Ongoing efforts aimed at achieving a continuous improvement in quality were augmented during 1983 with the launching of a new companywide quality improvement program based on a systematic, statistically oriented plan.[7]

[7]Comments to the shareholders, Lee L. Morgan, Chairman, and Robert E. Gilmore, President, Caterpillar Tractor Co. Annual Report 1983, p. 5.

Key Elements Affecting Quality

A systems viewpoint helps us understand the key elements affecting quality. When we view the organization as a system that interacts externally with customers and vendors, we identify two key factors that specify and affect quality at the boundaries of the firm. Customers' desires should be the basis for organization quality objectives. Often in service-oriented companies, customers also participate in generating the service—setting quality standards and making sure they are met. Examples include joint participation at self-service gasoline stations, cafeterias, and discount department stores. A customer, to a great extent, serves oneself—and quality can vary widely from individual to individual. It becomes a challenge to design service systems to meet a particular quality level in such a shared labor situation.

Vendors are very important, especially to organizations purchasing a high percentage of their products. Progressive firms are moving toward vendor certification as a means of eliminating incoming inspection. In essence, certification makes the vendor a part of the company team.

Within an organization we find that management, employees, material, facilities, processes, and equipment all affect quality. Dr. Joseph Juran and Dr. W. Edwards Demming, specialists on Japanese quality, suggest that as much as 85 percent of the quality problems are *management* problems. Their view is that management, rather than employees, has the authority and tools to correct most quality ills.

As *employees,* most of us have had opportunities to affect quality within an organization. Similarly, as students and professors, we daily see variations in quality. We know that some differences are individually determined. In a production environment, *materials* vary; high-quality materials are easier to work with than low-quality materials, and they often result in a labor savings. The key factor in production is often the degree of *variation*—there should be piece-to-piece consistency within a material lot, and in subsequent lots. This is true for material used (inputs) as well as for products and services produced (outputs).

How do *facilities, processes,* and *equipment* affect quality? Tools wear out and break. Roofs sometimes leak and require fixing. Equipment needs to be in good repair so parts are made the same every time. Consider the importance of reliable processes in the following service company.

EXAMPLE

In Burger King's operating manual, quality is stressed throughout. Key elements at Burger King are quality raw ingredients, standard preparation procedures, and equipment repair and preventive maintenance to assure consistency. Procedures are specified as a response to these *key elements* in their food service system—materials, people, and processes.

Understanding Relationships Among Factors Determining Quality

Customer Perceptions A progressive organization should have a well-established strategy for quality; one that is based upon customer perceptions regarding quality. After products are made and services delivered, customer perceptions should be measured systematically, just as outgoing quality is actually measured. Customer service after the sale of a product is often as important as the quality of the product itself. A customer service audit is one way of identifying customer perceptions concerning quality. In the audit, questions can be asked about the product, its function, the customer service function, and overall satisfaction. The questions can be written, asked by telephone, or asked face-to-face. This approach is equally meaningful for services and products. It is also useful for all services performed internally (for others in the firm). The following example illustrates how Caterpillar emphasizes quality from a customer perspective.

EXAMPLE

Elements of Caterpillar Tractor Company's quality program include:

- conducting two customer satisfaction surveys following each purchase, one after 300 hours of product use and the second after 500 hours of use;
- maintaining a centrally managed list of product problems as identified by customers from around the world;
- analyzing warranty and service reports submitted by dealers, as part of a product improvement program;
- asking dealers to conduct a quality audit as soon as the products are

received and to attribute defects to either assembly errors or shipping damages;

- guaranteeing 48-hour delivery of any part to any customer in the world;
- encouraging dealers to establish side businesses in rebuilding parts to reduce cost and increase the speed of repairs.[8]

[8]Hirotaka Takeuchi and John A. Quelch, "Quality Is More Than Making a Good Product," *Harvard Business Review* 61, no. 4 (July-August, 1983), 139–145.

Expected Quality Outcomes Throughout this book we have emphasized that people, materials, and processes are blended together to provide products and services for customers. These products and services have a quality attribute, the conformance to expectations. We've emphasized that these expectations should be customer based rather than manufacturing or engineering based.

In reality, manufacturing and operations attempt to conform to internally (engineering or manufacturing) set specifications. The design must ensure that these internally set specifications are consistent with customer expectations. Further, design must also assure that specifications are accurately translated into the language of manufacturing and operations—bills of materials, drawings, route sheets, procedures manuals, job descriptions, and so forth. In manufacturing, this is the work of manufacturing engineering. There must be a customer-product or customer-service linkage, a well-managed interface with clear instructions and feedback to operations (where the work is actually performed). This is equally important for services and manufacturing organizations.

Factor Relationships It is necessary to be more specific than simply stating that people, materials, and processes are interrelated in producing quality products and services. What are the key variables in operations that affect product or service quality?

Although our general answer is "it depends upon the manufacturing or service situation," we need to clarify. The way resources are blended (technology), the relative emphasis of one resource over another (cost structure), and the skills and abilities of people are all crucial. Competition, pride, knowledge, . . .; the list can go on and on as to what contributes to quality performance.

We've discussed the Japanese attention to quality. Why are they so effective? There appears to be no one simple answer. Some suggest that the nation rallied about a common cause during the post-World War II years to rid the image of shoddy workmanship and products. Others say the reason is cultural—the nature of the Japanese people—while others attribute quality success to statistical methods and thinking by all workers in the firm.

Similarly, within any firm worldwide, it is ambiguous how all of the people, materials, and processes blend for a given quality level. Figure 17.4

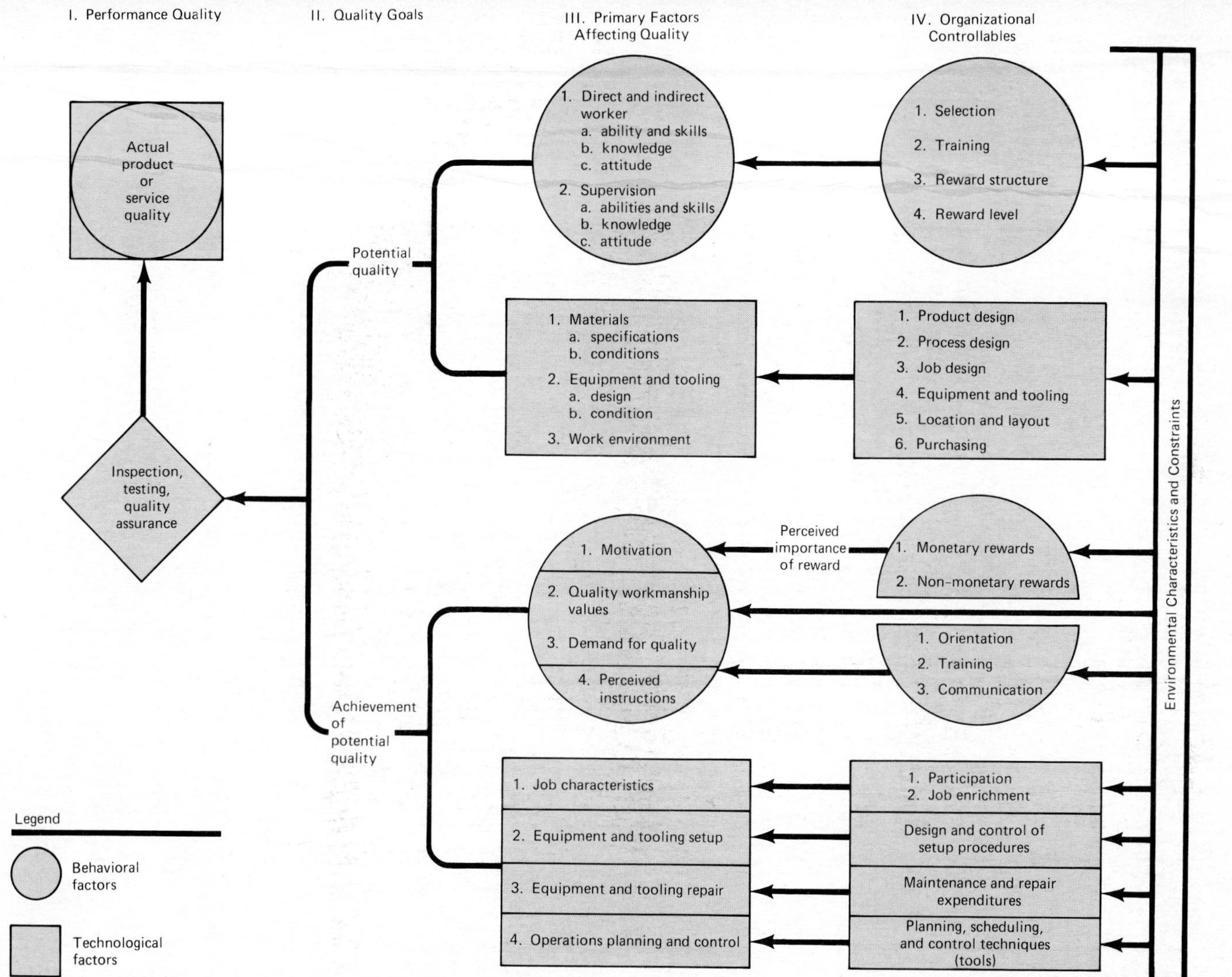

FIGURE 17.4
Behavior-technology model of factors affecting quality

Source: Everett E. Adam, Jr., James C. Hershauer, and William A. Ruch, *Productivity and Quality: Measurement as a Basis for Improvement,* (Englewood Cliffs, N.J.: Prentice-Hall, 1981), pp. 162–63.

shows one set of hypothesized relationships. This is a model of how variables might relate in general. Note that in this figure the authors suggest that *potential quality* and *achievement of potential quality* are separable goals, each with primary factors contributing to quality. Also, this model separates behavioral and technological factors contributing to quality. The circles represent behavioral factors, while the squares indicate technological aspects.

In the remainder of this chapter we will examine closely three issues: (1) analysis techniques, particularly statistical techniques, that affect quality; (2) current management-initiated approaches for bringing about organizational change to improve quality; and (3) behavioral factors that affect performance quality for both individuals and groups. Figure 17.4 could be modified to include explicit analysis techniques and organization change programs by adding each to the organizational controllable column (far right). Many key behavioral variables—such as rewards, participation, and job enrichment—are already included.

It is our opinion that statistical thinking, planned change, and selected behavioral interventions hold the most promise for contemporary operations managers attempting to improve quality. We have formed this opinion after seeking advice from many experienced operations and quality assurance executives; we have also had a number of experiences as quality professionals, reviewed extensive research on quality, and simply examined our own beliefs on this subject.

ANALYSIS FOR IMPROVEMENT, ASSURANCE, AND CONTROL

The Cost of Quality

If organizations were to examine systematically the cost of poor quality, they would be amazed at how expensive it is. As a percentage of total cost of goods sold, poor quality is often well in excess of 20 percent of sales. There are big dollar savings for the organization that is willing to improve quality systematically.

Where are such high costs located? How can one document these costs? Why haven't otherwise successful companies reduced such costs? These and similar questions can be addressed by examining four broad cost categories: prevention, appraisal, internal failure, and external failure.

Internal failure costs are perhaps the most commonly found and easiest costs to document. Accounting systems support scrap, rework, and similar costs. To a large extent, appraisal costs can also be estimated. In the traditional quality organization in the U.S., much of the inspection process is staff and can be accounted for. This task is more difficult in a progressive, quality-oriented firm where every employee inspects his or her work as part of a job responsibility. However, even in this type of situation, costs can be estimated.

Prevention costs are more difficult to assess. Training, planning, measurement, vendor certification, equipment maintenance, and similar prevention activities can, however, be estimated. External failures—failures of the product or service after it leaves the facility and is being used or consumed—are much more difficult to assess. Field service costs, warrantee claims, and lost sales are all very real.

Although it may be a major effort for the accounting system to construct a cost estimate, the results of such an effort are usually worthwhile. Sampling procedures can be used. For example, a product may be traced throughout for all quality costs for a particular time period. That data could be extrapolated to all or similar products to get an estimate of the total cost of poor quality to the firm. Regardless of the data collection method, *top management will certainly stop and pay attention to a well-constructed and reasonably documented total-cost-of-quality estimate.* It is an effective *analysis tool* to gain support for quality improvement efforts and expenditures. Evaluating the components of total quality costs can provide the astute operations manager with insight into areas with high potential for improvement.

Quality Costs and Assurance Quality assurance programs commonly involve systematic efforts to assess the overall level of output (final product) quality. They determine current quality levels and trends in these levels, and they make comparisons with the quality levels of competitors. This information is used in product and process redesign, market strategy, and product pricing decisions. Organized information sources for assurance may include:

- product life tests, or accelerated life tests that can include destructive testing,
- analysis laboratories for determining the causes of product failures,
- sampling of finished products to detect deficiencies,
- establishment of field representatives to examine "in-use" product performance.

After product standards have been set by management, they must be checked. Since these product standards involve so many aspects of quality control, the costs of quality assurance are high. Prevention, appraisal, and internal and external failure costs, outlined in Table 17.1, are all quality assurance costs.[9]

Another way to visualize costs of quality assurance is in terms of cost tradeoffs. These are similar to total cost and cost components tradeoffs in inventory control. There is a basic tradeoff between *control costs* (those in Table 17.1) and the *cost of undetected defects.* Although operations man-

[9]Also see Lee Blank and Jorge Solorzano, "Using Quality Cost Analysis for Management Improvement," *Industrial Engineering* 10, no. 2 (February 1978), pp. 46–51.

TABLE 17.1
Costs of quality assurance

Prevention (costs associated with design and planning of a quality control (QC) program)	Appraisal (costs involved in the direct appraisal of quality both in the plant and in the field)	Internal failure (costs directly related to the occurrence of defective production within the plant)	External failure (costs associated with the failure of a product or service in the field)
■ QC administration and systems planning ■ Quality training ■ Quality planning (QC engineering work) Incoming, inprocess, final inspection Special processes planning Quality data analysis Procurement planning Vendor surveys Reliability studies ■ Quality measurement and control equipment ■ Qualification of material	■ Testing ■ Inspection ■ Quality audits ■ Incoming test and inspection and laboratory acceptance ■ Checking labor ■ Laboratory or other measurement service ■ Setup for test and inspection ■ Test and inspection material ■ Outside endorsements ■ Maintenance and calibration ■ Product engineering review and shipping release ■ Field testing	■ Scrap, at full shop cost ■ Rework, at full shop cost ■ Scrap and rework, fault of vendor ■ Material procurement ■ Factory contact engineering ■ QC investigations (of failures) ■ Material review activity ■ Repair and troubleshooting	■ Complaints and loss of customer good will ■ Warranty costs ■ Field maintenance and product service ■ Returned material processing and repair ■ Replacement inventories ■ Strained distributor relations

Adapted from J. W. Gavett, *Production and Operations Management* (New York: Harcourt Brace Jovanovich, Inc., 1968), pp. 401–402.

agers may not have precise cost data, they will have at least a rough idea of how these costs behave.

Organizing and Controlling for Quality

Often, quality control in manufacturing firms is organized in a way distinctly different from the way it is organized in service organizations. Usually, quality control in manufacturing is a staff function established to monitor, police, and assist in corrective action. Within a quality control group we typically find a manager, quality assurance engineers, quality technicians, and an inspection function. One survey of practices in quality control had 173 firms responding.[10] Firms were rather uniformly represented by size (number of employees), except for the 30 percent of respondents with 1,001 to 5,000 employees. Two sizes of quality control departments predominated, 36 percent of the respondents having zero to nine employees and 34 percent having more than fifty employees. Other department

[10]Erwin M. Saniga and Larry E. Shirland, "Quality Control in Practice . . . A Survey," *Quality Progress* 10, no. 5 (May 1977), pp. 30–33.

sizes were rather equally distributed. Quality control responsibilities are usually separated from line production responsibilities so as to obtain unbiased assessments of product quality. Consequently, conflict sometimes arises between quality control and production personnel. When this happens it's the plant manager's responsibility to manage and mediate the conflict situation. Whether the plant manager can maintain a proper balance between product quality and production quantity in these conflict situations depends to a large extent upon the person.

It would be best, in our judgment, if quality control departments were to be deemphasized and eventually disappear. As employees who produce goods and services are trained in statistical processes, and given the tools to improve and control their own outputs, they should be accountable for quality. This shifts the responsibility directly to the source of good quality (as well as errors)—the operative employee and his or her management. With this shift must come management support. The result of this change will be inspection at the source of production by the participant in operations. There will no longer be a need for large quality control and assurance departments.

Controlling Of all the problems facing the operations manager, none is more demanding than product quality control. Why? Because control is an action process, and deciding when and how to activate this process requires astute judgment.

Try to recall the basic elements of a control process (Figure 14.2). Suppose we were concerned with a product characteristic—length, for example. Quality control would involve several steps. Once the desired length has been specified (in the design) and outputs are occurring, we measure those outputs. We can measure length in feet, inches, or centimeters. This measurement tells us how long the product actually is. Next we enter a comparison phase, in which we compare the actual length with the desired length. If the length measurement conforms satisfactorily to product standards (length specifications), we transmit the conformance information to those operating the conversion process and no action follows. On the other hand, if there are deviations between what actually exists and what is desired, we need to take further action.

All these preliminary phases lead up to and support the action phase. When the conversion process is operating, product quality always exists. It may be very high, low, or intermediate, but it is always there. Quality *control,* however, exists only when *deliberate action* is undertaken to cause output characteristics to conform to desired levels.

Measurement and Analysis Measurement plays an important role in quality analysis and control. In our example, we could check the length of the product in two ways: we could measure and record actual length, or we could test to see if actual length falls within upper and lower limits. If we measure by actual length, we measure by *variable;* variable measurement requires some specified scaled physical dimension—weight, volume, length, or sound. If we test to see whether length falls within upper and lower limits, we measure by *attribute*. When we measure by attribute, the product is either good or bad; either it falls within the limits, or it doesn't. With attribute measurements, we have only two choices, accept or reject; with variable measurement, we have a wide continuum of choices. Deciding whether to measure by variable or by attribute depends on matters we will discuss later, when we consider control charts. The kind of measurement we use determines the kind of control chart we select.

Measurement of Services Generally, service characteristics are more complex than product characteristics. They are harder to identify and measure. Consequently, measuring and subsequently controlling quality are frequently ignored in services. Although service quality is important, the characteristics that determine customer acceptance are often intangible, complex customer perceptions—such as timeliness, employees' attitudes toward customers, and the physical environment where the service is delivered.

One study has been directed at measurement in services.[11] It describes a measurement procedure that was developed and tested in the Federal Reserve Banking System (summarized in Table 17.2). The procedure is participative; quality measures are developed by those involved in the delivery of services. A good bit of the overall effort centers on definition—definition of process (system) boundaries, process components, and sources of variation (deviations). Measures are both *quality indicators* (such as number of errors or percent defective) and conceptually innovative *quality productivity ratios* (relating outputs to resources inputs for quality). This measurement procedure has been used in a variety of service functions—personnel, check processing, transfer of funds (banking), data processing, and production planning. Several large and medium-sized commercial banks and manufacturers, including Honeywell, Inc., have reported applications.[12]

In a previously cited survey of quality control in practice, the most frequently mentioned problem associated with the use of quality control techniques was the "lack of education/knowledge about quality control techniques by line supervisors/production managers/management/and other nonquality control individuals."[13] The purpose of this book's treatment of

[11]Everett E. Adam, Jr., James C. Hershauer, and William A. Ruch, *Measuring the Quality Dimension of Service Productivity,* National Science Foundation Grant No. APR 76-01740, University of Missouri-Columbia, 1978.

[12]See Everett E. Adam, Jr., James C. Hershauer, and William A. Ruch, *Productivity and Quality: Measurement as a Basis for Improvement* (Englewood Cliffs, N.J.: Prentice-Hall, 1981) for details of the procedure, case applications, references for personnel and check processing studies, and related studies.

[13]Saniga and Shirland, p. 32.

Table 17.2
A quality measurement procedure summary*

Activity sequence	Activity	Participant	Estimated activity time	Estimated elapsed calendar time
1	Top management decision to measure productivity	Organization management	one-half day	one–two weeks
2	Select project coordinators	Organization management	one-half day	one–two weeks
3	Familiarize with system (function)	Project coordinators	one–two days	one week
4	Select participants; divide into groups	Project coordinators and top management (group A)	two–three hours	two days
5	Define system and establish boundaries	Project coordinators in consultation with top management	two hours	one day
6	Determine unit operations	Supervisors and technicians (group B) with project coordinators	four hours	one day
7	Generate deviations; select and rank deviations	Group *B*	three hours	one-half day
8	Finalize key quality deviations	Project coordinators and possibly technical facilitator	two hours	one-half day
9	Generate key quality deviation measures	Groups *A* and *B*	three hours	one-half day
10	Collect technology and system inputs data	Group *B*; individual experts	two hours	one day
11	Transform measures into productivity ratios and indicators	Project coordinators or analyst	one day	two days
12	Rank productivity measures	Project coordinators or analyst develop questionnaire; group *A* ranks	two–three days	two weeks
13	Select final quality productivity measures	Organization management	one day	one week

*Adam, Hershauer, and Ruch, *Productivity and Quality: Measurement as a Basis for Improvement,* pp. 39–88.

the most used techniques in analysis—inspection, sampling, and control charts—is to help you avoid this deficiency in your potential role as a production/operations manager.

Inspection

Inspection of raw material, work-in-process, and finished products provides the basic data needed for the comparison phase of the control process. Inspection is the observation and measurement of the conversion process outputs and inputs. Inspection can be done either visually or mechanically; its purpose is to see whether the physical characteristics of the good or service conform with specifications. Inspection is commonly divided into three areas: receiving inspection, work-in-process inspection, and finished goods inspection.

Receiving Inspection The quality of outputs from a conversion process can be no better than the inputs from which they are generated, unless excessive costs are first incurred to modify the inputs. Inputs are often built up, over a succession of stages, into the final product. At the end of this progression, we sometimes find that defective inputs used in initial stages result in an unacceptable final product. This requires subsequent costly repair, which could have been avoided. Therefore, management often establishes programs to monitor the inputs prior to their use. At *receiving inspection,* incoming shipments of raw materials subcomponents from vendors or other inputs are observed and evaluated against predetermined quality standards. These materials are often physically separated from work-in-process materials and are only released to operations after passing the initial inspection. It is best to eliminate this activity, moving inspection to the vendor's facility if that close a working relationship and trust can be established.

Work-in-process Inspection When there is a felt need for someone other than the line production employee to inspect work, often management inserts special inspection points between successive stages of the conversion sequence; this is called *work-in-process inspection.* The outputs of one or more stages are screened before they are used in subsequent operations. The intensity of inspection depends on the volume of output, the cost of inspecting, and the cost consequences (in subsequent stages) of not inspecting.

An important decision for the operations manager is how many inspection stations to have and where to locate them. A very simple heuristic can be used to help make this decision. Two key factors must be considered, the *percent of defective* output expected at each stage of the conversion process and the *cost* of inspection. Ideally, you would want to inspect at locations where inspection costs are low and percent defective is high. This would give a low cost of inspection per percent defectives detected. We can use a simple three-step procedure for selecting the locations of inspection stations:

1. Identify all stages of the conversion process that are potential locations for inspection stations. Estimate the inspection costs and gather historical percent defective information for these stations.
2. Compute the critical ratio for each potential inspection station:

$$\text{Critical ratio} = \frac{\text{Cost of inspection}}{\text{\% defective}} \tag{17.1}$$

3. Rank the inspection stations by critical ratio. The lowest critical ratio is the most desirable location, the second lowest critical ratio second most desirable, etc. With limited resources, locate inspection stations until funds are depleted.

EXAMPLE

A process has three possible location sites for inspection, *A*, *B*, and *C*. Process percent defectives are 10 percent for site *A*, 5 percent for site *B*, and 6 percent for site *C*. The cost of inspection at *A* is \$150, at *B* is \$200, and at *C* is \$100. Critical ratios are

$$A = \frac{\$150}{.10} = \$1{,}500$$

$$B = \frac{\$200}{.05} = \$4{,}000$$

$$C = \frac{\$100}{.06} = \$1{,}667$$

Inspection stations should be located first at station *A*, second at station *C*, and finally at station *B*. If funds are limited, locate in that order until funds for inspection are depleted.

Finished Goods Inspection For conversion processes that produce identifiable final products (such as physical goods), finished goods inspection is often used. Various testing procedures can be used to determine whether the final product conforms to functional and appearance standards. If it does not, sources of discrepancy must be identified, and corrective measures must be initiated. Finished goods inspection should be a verification stage as the management focus should be *prevention* early in the operations process, not detection at this stage.

Sampling Plans

Sampling is a process of selecting representative observations from a population to make inferences about the population. We sample to tell us about the output quality and the process that produced it. *Sampling plans* assist us in output variation; *control charts* help in process variation. Both are widely used in practice.[14] Sampling plans are an important statistical application in quality control. These modeling procedures are often used to monitor the quality of incoming materials and parts and for final acceptance sampling of finished goods. They help us make judgments about output quality in an economical manner.

[14]See Saniga and Shirland, p. 32, who found that over 70 percent of responding firms used sampling and control charts. About a third of the respondents judged quality control techniques moderately useful, a third fairly useful, and a third of great consequence. Few rated the techniques of little consequence.

We'll focus on sampling plans as they might apply to receiving inspection. When a large shipment of a purchased item arrives, someone must decide whether to accept or reject the shipment. We have a range of choices from inspecting all units in the shipment to systematically sampling a few units. A systematic sampling can provide the information needed for the accept/reject decision for the entire shipment. Thus the time, effort, and cost of more extensive inspection are avoided. Of course, there are some risks involved because of possible sampling errors.

Two kinds of errors can result from sampling. A shipment of good quality can be mistakenly rejected if a disproportionately large number of defective units from the shipment is selected at random. It is also possible to select at random mostly good units from a shipment of poor quality overall. The first type of risk is α, the "producer's risk"; the second is β, the "consumer's risk." We want a sampling procedure that assures that each of these risks is no greater than a specified chosen level.

For large shipments consisting of many units, say 5,000, we must determine a sample size (n) and an acceptance number (c) such that we obtain satisfactory assurance that our accept/reject decision, based on the sample, is correct. The n and c determine the characteristics of our sampling plan. First, randomly select n units from the shipment and determine the quality of each unit. If the quality of more than c of the units is incorrect, reject the entire shipment. If the quality of c or fewer of the units is incorrect, accept the shipment.

Standard procedures are available for determining the sampling plan parameters, n and c, that will meet the performance requirements specified by the user. The details of these procedures are presented in the supplement to this chapter.

EXAMPLE

A large medical clinic purchases quantity shipments of pregnancy test kits (PTKs). A shipment contains 10,000 PTKs. It is important that the chemical composition of the PTK shipment be evaluated so that prescribing physicians are assured of valid tests.

Physicians have found in the past that a shipment is of good quality if no more than 2 percent of the PTKs in it are of incorrect chemical composition. They consider shipments with 5 percent or more defectives to be an extremely bad quality shipment. We want a plan that has a .95 probability of accepting good shipments but only a .10 probability of accepting extremely bad shipments. These performance specifications for the sampling plan are summarized on the left side of Table 17.3. A sampling plan was derived to meet these performance requirements. The plan calls for 308 PTKs to be sampled from each shipment (right side of Table 17.3). If more than ten of these are defective, the entire shipment is rejected. If ten or fewer defectives are found, the shipment is accepted. In this way shipments consisting of 2 percent defectives have only five chances out of 100 of being rejected, while shipments with 5 percent defectives have only ten chances out of 100 of being accepted. This sampling plan includes procedures for determining the probability of accepting the shipment if percents defective are between 2 and 5. These probabilities are shown in Figure 17.5.

The solid curve in Figure 17.5, called the "OC curve" (operating characteristics curve), reveals how a sampling plan will discriminate when used on incoming shipments. If a shipment is of high quality (low percent defectives), a good sampling plan gives us a high probability of accepting the shipment. Shipments of poorer quality (high percent defectives) have a lower probability of being accepted by the plan.

You can see from the solid OC curve in Figure 17.5 that the desired probabilities of accepting good and bad PTK shipments have been obtained. The second sampling plan, $n = 154$ and $c = 5$, will not meet desired performance specifications. The supplement to this chapter presents the details of how the desired plan was found.

General Effects of *n* and *c* Each sampling plan consisting of n and c has a unique OC curve. Sampling plans with large sample sizes are more discriminating than plans with smaller sample sizes. Figure 17.5 shows OC curves for two sampling plans with different sample sizes and acceptance numbers. For both plans the acceptance number, c, is in constant proportion to n. For plans with larger n's the probability of accepting good quality lots is higher than for plans with smaller n's. Also, for bad quality lots, the probability of acceptance decreases when n is larger. Of course, these benefits are not obtained without incurring the higher inspection costs associated with larger sample sizes.

The effect of increasing the acceptance number (for a given value of n) is to increase the probability of accepting the shipment for all levels of

TABLE 17.3
Sampling plan and specifications for PTKs

Performance specifications	Parameters of sampling plan
Good quality = 2% or fewer defectives	
Desired probability of accepting a good quality shipment = .95	n = 308
Risk: proability of α errors = .05	c = 10
Bad quality = 5% or more defective	
Desired probability of accepting a bad quality shipment = .10	
Risk: probability of β errors = .10	

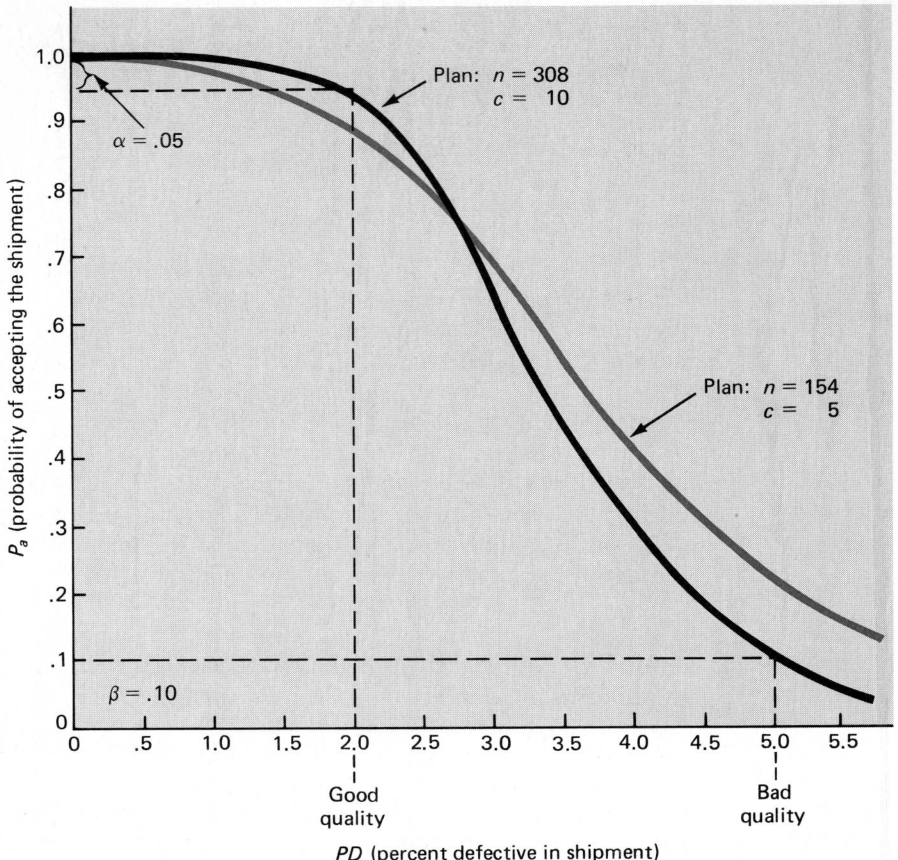

FIGURE 17.5
Probability of accepting a PTK shipment (OC curve)

percent defective other than zero (Figure 17.6). By using a larger c, we allow shipments with more defectives to pass inspection. As c is decreased, the inspection plan becomes tighter.

In general, higher values of c allow for "looser" performance, increasing the probability of accepting a shipment with a given level of defectives. Increasing n results in greater confidence that we have correctly discriminated between good and bad shipments. However, inspection costs are also increased with larger values of n. The task of quality management is to find the proper balance between the costs and benefits of alternative sampling plans.

From a practical standpoint, as an operations manager you will not have to develop sampling plans. Your quality control technician, or you in

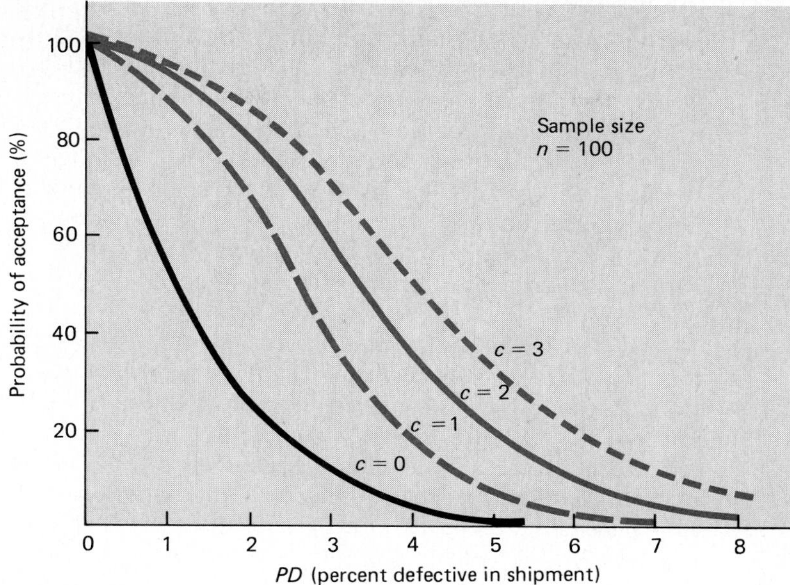

FIGURE 17.6
Effect of variations in C

his or her absence, can refer to *Military Standard 105 (MIL-STD-105D)*, a widely accepted manual of sampling plans. For most applications this manual specifies both sample size and rejection and acceptance levels. You need only be an informed user—not a statistician—to use statistical quality control techniques.

Establishing Policies on Good and Bad Quality Choosing what percents defective constitute good and bad quality is a vital management decision. The sampling plan is designed around this decision. If managers are too stringent in defining good quality, the costs of obtaining (purchasing) such high quality shipments can become exorbitant. At the other extreme, a high percent defective can result in conversion disruptions, high scrap and rework costs, and higher costs of customer ill will. If it's possible to negotiate good and bad quality levels when you're purchasing shipments from suppliers, you can arrange for the vendor's finished goods inspection to have the same sampling plan that the customer's receiving inspection uses. Such a procedure can simplify matters considerably, and we recommend it.

Quality Control Charts

In Chapter 14 we discussed control as a process by which some aspect of a system is modified to achieve desired system performance. Detecting shifts when they occur is a major difficulty in the surveillance of process and product characteristics. When a conversion process begins to shift out of control, we would like to know as soon as possible so we can initiate corrective action. Although one would think it would be a simple matter to detect a shift by observation, it usually isn't. Occasionally, random variability in the process may make it seem that process output is bad when actually there has been no basic change. At other times, real shifts are mistakenly attributed to random variability. If a basic change occurs we want to detect and correct it so we can avoid costs of producing faulty products. On the other hand, we do not want to waste resources trying to correct a process that is already operating properly. To help avoid interpretative errors and detect when real shifts have occurred, quality control charts are very useful.

Control charts are used in some form in many manufacturing facilities. We have seen them in automobile manufacturing, appliance production, diecasting operations, pet food production, metal stamping, and petroleum refining. More recently, service industries have adopted this useful technique in various settings; accident rates provide measures of goodness of traffic control processes, numbers of robberies as a measure of public safety systems, sickness rates as measures of health care systems, and accident rates as measures of safety in ski slope recreation systems. Banks, hospitals, and other service organizations make use of them too.

The basic idea behind a quality control chart is that one can measure what is happening regarding quality. As more output is produced, the future should always be like the past. A quality attribute is identified and it is noted when quality is good or satisfactory. Then, when it is measured in the future, the quality attribute should be the same. If not, the process has changed and we say the process is different than in the past—or out of control. The manager then investigates to find the cause.

Control charts are based on the statistical concept of the *central limit theorem*. This theorem allows us the convenience of using the standard normal distribution in making judgments about changes in the process we are monitoring. With it, we can conveniently determine the chances that some important characteristic of our process has changed, and we can express these chances explicitly. To use this theorem, we take a randomly selected sample of several units of output from some stage of the conversion process. For each unit sampled we measure the critical characteristic, say its length, and compute the arithmetic average of the observed lengths. We then use this *average* to make our judgments regarding *system performance*. The central limit theorem specifies that if we compute many such averages, they will be approximately normally distributed regardless of the shape of the distribution of individual lengths, and this approximation to normality improves as the size of our sample is increased.

A control chart is unique to the operation that it is describing. Figure 17.7 shows a control chart for the temperature of a chemical plating operation. This chart has three important parameters, which were determined from historical data: mean (average) temperature, upper control limit (UCL), and lower control limit (LCL). In the past, the mean, or average,

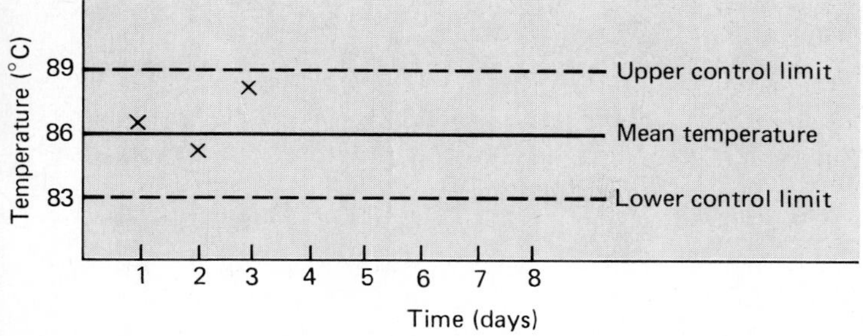

FIGURE 17.7
Example control chart

temperature for the process has been 86°C. The upper and lower control limits have been set at 89° and 83°. After the chart had been constructed, three more days of operation transpired. Sample temperature readings for these days were measured and then recorded on the chart. Temperature averages for the first two days were near the mean; the third sample average was near the upper control limit. An operations manager could glance at this chart and say, "The process is in control based upon the last three days' performance." With this overview of what control charts are, let's outline the steps for constructing and interpreting them. A more detailed presentation is given in the supplement to this chapter.

Here are the steps in developing quality control charts:

1. Determine whether *measurement* in the process is by variable or attribute. The type of measurement dictates which calculating formulas to use.
2. Partition the *historical data.* A control chart is constructed from historical data; current or future performance is compared with this past performance. You must have two distinctly different data sets, one for control chart *construction* and a second to reflect most recent performance.
3. Using the data for control chart construction, *calculate* a process mean and upper and lower control limits.
4. *Graph* the control chart. The chart will be some measurement (on the y-axis) versus time (on the x-axis).
5. *Plot* current or most recent performance on the graph.
6. *Interpret* the chart to see if (a) the process is in control and no action is required, (b) the process is out of control and an assignable cause should be sought, or (c) the process is in control but trends are occurring that should alert the manager to possible out-of-control conditions.
7. *Update* the control chart. After a reasonable period of time, often a month, the control chart is reconstructed by returning to step 2 above. You can repartition the data by discarding the oldest historical data and replacing it with historical data collected since the last updating.

Look at step 3. After a mean has been calculated, management must decide how certain we want to be that when the process appears out of control, it really is out of control. Managers may desire different degrees of certainty based upon their knowledge of the importance of an error in the

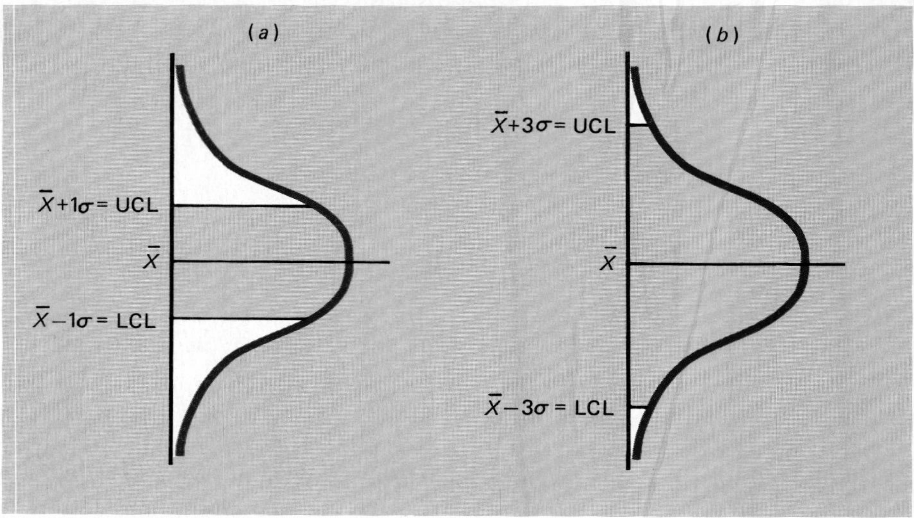

FIGURE 17.8
Probabilities of α error for control limits set at 1 standard deviation (a) and 3 standard deviations (b)

process. Three of the many choices available in setting the control limits are to set the limits at ± 1, 2, or 3 standard deviations from the mean. These choices are expressed in terms of standard deviations (σ) of the bell-shaped unit normal curve shown in Figure 17.8. With narrow control limits ($\bar{x} \pm 1\sigma$), there is a reasonable chance that when the process appears to be out of control it may not actually be out of control (probability .317, i.e., 1 − .683). This probability is equal to the shaded area in part *(a)*. With wide control limits ($\bar{x} \pm 3\sigma$), there is little chance of a sampling error (probability .003) from the producer's viewpoint (type I error). This is the shaded area in part *(b)*; when a sample mean falls outside these limits, the process is very likely out of control.

The selection of control limits involves tradeoffs between two types of risks. With the first type, α, the *producer's risk,* there is a possibility of concluding that the process is out of control when it is actually in a state of statistical control. (This is the same terminology used in sampling plans.) The producer's risk is reduced by using wide control limits; it is increased by using narrower control limits. The second type of risk, β, the *consumer's risk,* describes the situation in which an out-of-control process is mistakenly adjudged to be in control. This risk increases as the control limits are widened and decreases as they are narrowed. Ultimately, the choice of control limit width must be based on these risks and the costs associated with them. If the costs of undetected shifts are extremely high relative to the costs of correcting the process, narrow limits (lower consumer risk) are appropriate. If the costs of restoring the process to the desired state are very high compared to the costs of producing defective output, wider limits (lower producer's risk) are appropriate.

In the next section we discuss control charts for attributes. Control charts for variables are discussed in the supplement to this chapter.

Control Charts for Attributes When sample units are classified into one of two categories (good or bad, success or failure, etc.), measurement is by attribute. Suppose we observe a sample of units from some process and classify each as either defective or acceptable. We can calculate the fraction of defective units in the sample and compare it to the historical fraction defective in the process. If the sample fraction defective (p) deviates widely from the historic process fraction defective ($\overline{p}$) we may conclude that some change in the process has occurred, that the current fraction defective is either higher or lower than usual. Attributes control charts are used for this purpose. If the process is under control, the sample fraction defective (p) is an estimate of the underlying process fraction defective. Several such sample estimates tend to be normally distributed, and the control chart has the form shown in Figure 17.9.

To construct an attribute control chart, we begin by inspecting a sample of n units to determine what fraction of those units is defective. We do this with equation 17.2, where x is the number of defective units:

$$p = \frac{x}{n} \tag{17.2}$$

If this process is repeated, say m times, we get several estimates of fraction defective. Then, using these m estimates of p, we calculate the historical *average* fraction for the process using equation 17.3.

$$\overline{p} = \frac{\sum_{i=1}^{m} p_i}{m} \tag{17.3}$$

FIGURE 17.9
Attribute control chart

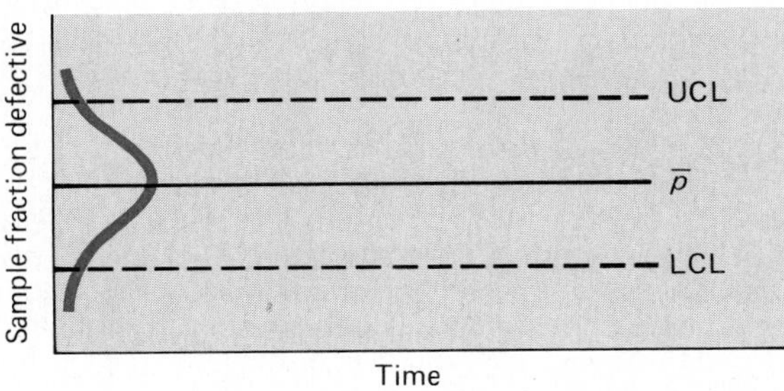

The central limit theorem applies for attribute or proportion charts (p-charts) in that a relative frequency distribution of a sample of p values would look something like the normal distribution. The standard deviation is given by equation 17.4. In this equation, $\overline{p}$ is the average fraction defective, and n is the sample size used in each sample that was taken.

$$\sigma_p = \sqrt{\frac{\overline{p}(1 - \overline{p})}{n}} \tag{17.4}$$

If we want a small α error, the control limits might be set at three standard deviations:

$$\begin{matrix}\text{Control limits} \\ \text{(UCL and LCL)}\end{matrix} = \overline{p} \pm 3\sigma_p$$

for a process in which we desire reasonably tight control.

In the example below, and for most end-of-chapter problems, we use a small number of samples (five below) to limit computations. In practice, twenty or more samples would typically be collected.

EXAMPLE

A visual inspection for scratches (each unit is judged good or bad) on a decorative paint trim operation produced the following data for last week.

Day	Number of units samples	Number defective
Mon	30	3
Tue	30	10
Wed	30	6
Thurs	30	2
Fri	30	3

This week we have worked two days, Monday and Tuesday, and thirty pieces were sampled each day. Six pieces were found defective Monday and nine Tuesday. As operations manager, you are wondering if the process is in control this week.

To find a solution, construct a fraction defectives control chart based on last week's typical process performance. Last week's data are used to calculate average fraction defective ($\overline{p}$), the standard deviation of average fraction defective (σ_p), and the control limits (UCL and LCL). Then you can plot the percent defective for this week's Monday (p_m) and Tuesday (p_t) against last week's control chart. The required calculations are shown here.

$$\bar{p} \text{ (for last week)} = \frac{\Sigma x}{\Sigma n} = \frac{24}{150} = .16$$

$$\sigma_p = \sqrt{\frac{\bar{p}(1 - \bar{p})}{n}} = \sqrt{\frac{.16(1 - .16)}{30}} = .067$$

$$\text{UCL} = \bar{p} + 3\sigma_{\bar{p}} = .16 + 3(.067) = +.361$$

$$\text{LCL} = \bar{p} - 3\sigma_{\bar{p}} = .16 - 3(.067) = -.041$$

Since fraction defective cannot be less than zero, the LCL will be set at zero.

$$\text{Sample defectives: Monday } p_m = \frac{6}{30} = 0.20\text{; Tuesday } p_t = \frac{9}{30} = .30$$

Now you can construct the resulting control chart:

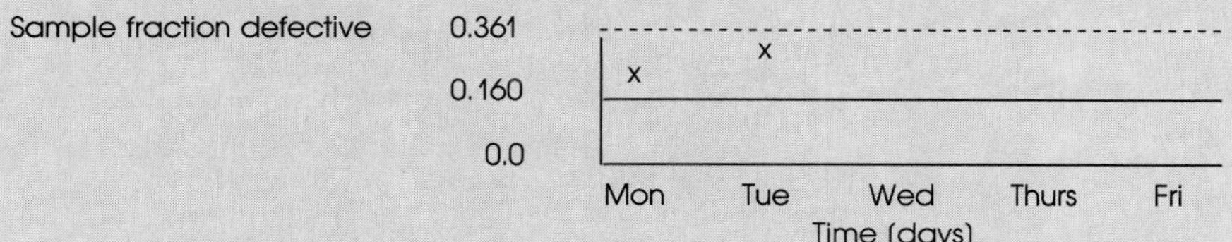

Monday's fraction defective is close to the historical process average. Tuesday's sample indicates that the process is still in a state of control. If a future sample falls outside the control limits, the operating manager can be quite confident (99.7 percent) that he or she should look for an assignable cause.

Control Charts for Variables When measurement is by length, weight, or any continuous variable, a different set of statistical formulas are used to establish the control chart. These are presented in the supplement to this chapter. Charts that focus on variability, the process variation or standard deviation, are also available. Perhaps the most common of those are R-charts, which focus on measuring the range.

We have presented p-charts because of their simplicity, yet there is user evidence from the Saniga and Shirland study referenced at the end of this chapter that, of the dozen or so most used control chart techniques, the top three are first variable ($\bar{x}$) charts, then range (R) charts, and then attribute or proportion (p) charts.

Other Control Chart Considerations As Figure 17.10 shows, control chart data can form many configurations. Notice that in "normal behavior," sample observations are randomly scattered around the central value of the

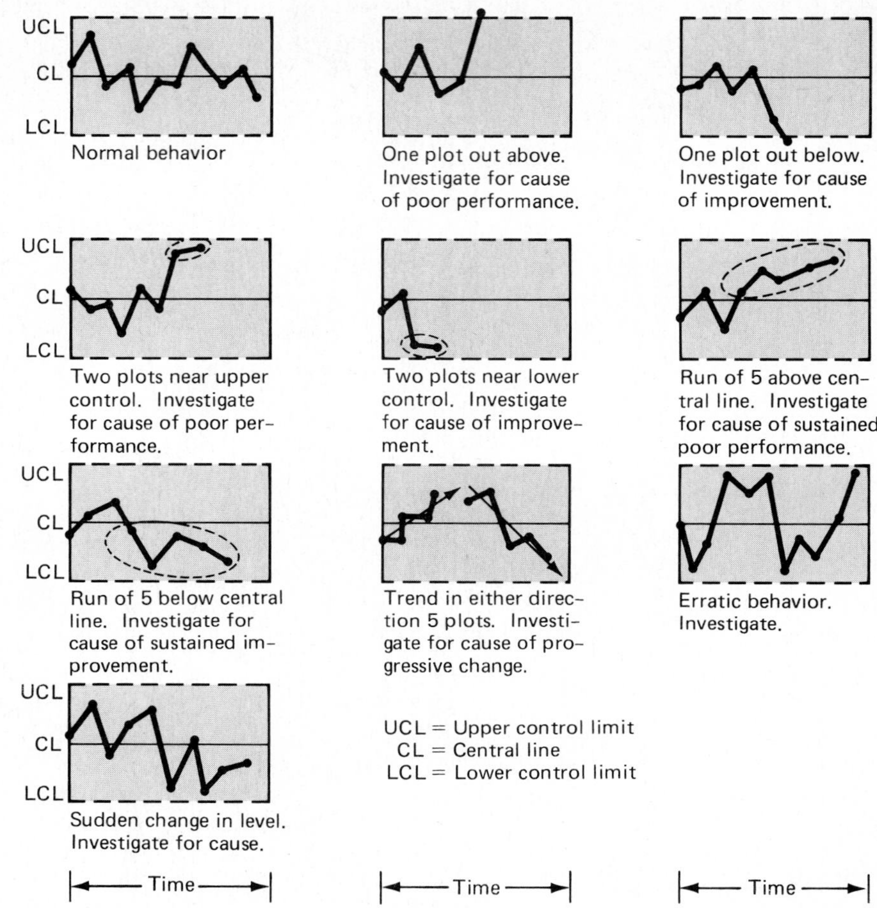

FIGURE 17.10
Control chart evidence for investigation

Source: B. L. Hansen, *Quality Control* (Englewood Cliffs, N.J.: Prentice-Hall, Inc., 1973).

chart. When successive sample points form an identifiable pattern or fall outside the control limits, very likely something other than random effects is in operation. Subsequently management should launch an investigation to determine the cause of this nonrandom behavior.

Step 7 in the construction of control charts, you may remember, is updating the charts. When the charts are periodically updated, they become dynamic rather than static. The control limits and/or the central tendency of the chart change as the process changes over time. Look at Figure 17.11. During June and July, the UCL and the LCL were updated daily. August and September's control limits were not updated daily, but September's control limits and central tendency were determined from the behavior that was experienced in August. The point is that over four months, the process changes, in this case stabilizes. Since the control charts simply reflect process performance, they change too; in this case they get narrower.

After we have identified the product (or process) characteristic to be controlled, we must resolve a number of other design questions. What sample size should be used? How often should a sample be taken? What control limits should be selected? To what degree do we want to emphasize

FIGURE 17.11
Control chart for percent defective—four months' production of an electrical device

Source: Eugene L. Grant, *Statistical Quality Control,* 3rd ed. (New York: McGraw-Hill Book Co., 1964).

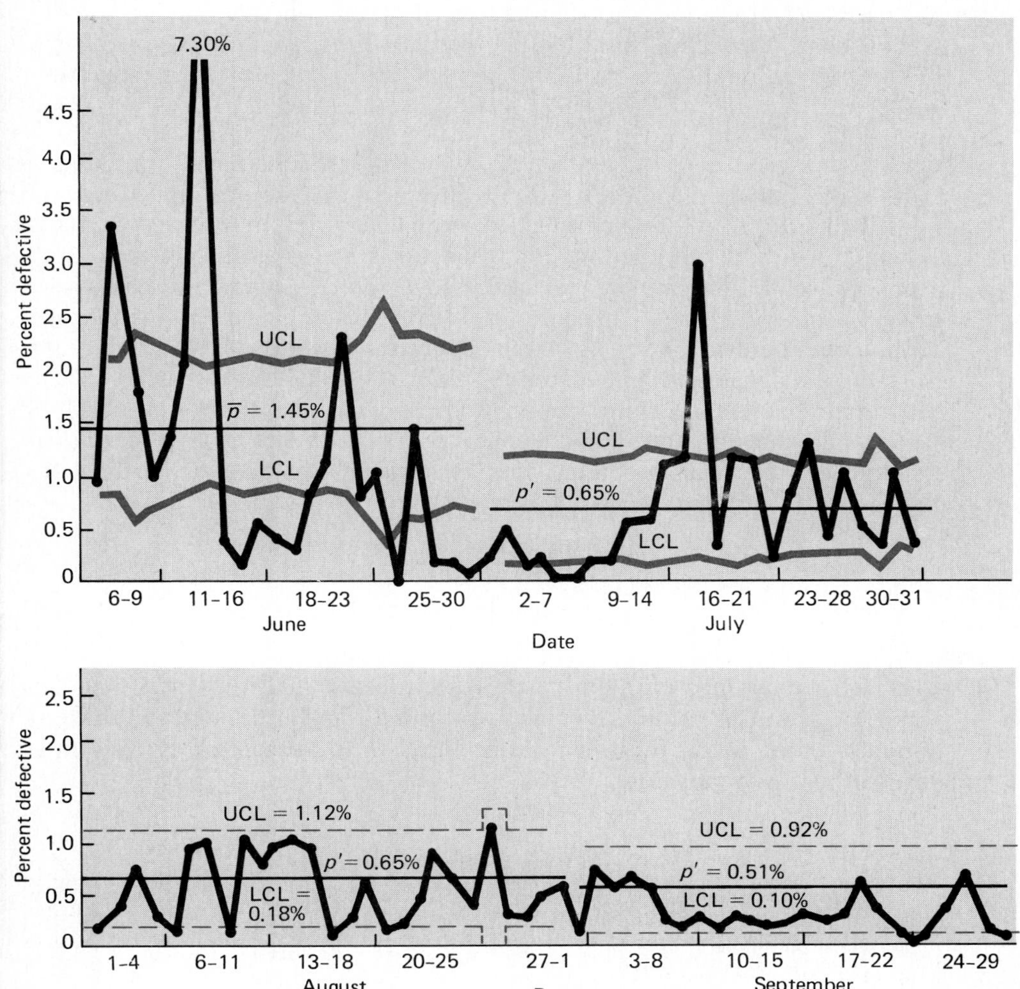

detection and control versus prevention? The answers to these and other design questions are important because they determine both the effectiveness and the cost of the control process. Specific answers to these design questions depend to a great extent on the specific organization, on the nature of its processes and products. In general, choices among alternative design parameters involve tradeoffs among opposing costs and risks, and these economic design considerations must be evaluated.

Specification Versus Control Limits One final point needs to be made in our discussion of control charts. Control limits on a control chart reflect actual quality performance. *Specification* limits, on the other hand, are statements of what the product characteristics should be. Thus, product specification limits might be less than, equal to, or greater than the quality control limits. We want to caution you to distinguish between the concepts of quality *control* chart limits and quality *specification* limits, much as you distinguish between quality control chart limits and quality process capability limits.

Japanese Analysis—A Lesson in Simplicity The Japanese have applied several simple statistical procedures in addition to inspection, sampling, and control charts. These procedures are straightforward in concept and extremely useful in application. Japanese firms stress graphs, pareto diagrams, cause-and-effect diagrams, check sheets, histograms, and scatter diagrams. Most of these are common techniques learned in elementary mathematics and statistics. A pareto diagram is simply a bar chart with grouping by cause and phenomenon—similar to the one we used in the ABC inventory classification application. A cause-and-effect diagram is a "fish-bone" diagram developed by Dr. Ishikawa. It is a graph, simple in construction and interpretation, that is a schematic diagram with statements about cause and effect. (It is not a graph with numbers.)[15]

MANAGEMENT-INITIATED APPROACHES AND ACTIONS TO IMPROVE QUALITY

American companies are taking action to improve quality. Upon what research or premises are these firms developing their approaches? What actions are being taken by leading-edge firms to increase quality? We now turn to these two questions.

[15]For summary and application see "The Quest for Higher Quality: The Deming Prize and Quality Control" (Fairfield, N.J.: Ricoh of America, 1984), 27 pages, and Dr. Kaoru Ishikawa, *Guide to Quality Control* (Tokyo, Japan. Asian Productivity Organization, 1976) (Eleventh Printing, 1983).

Contemporary Management-Initiated Approaches to Improving Quality

The most popular approaches to increasing quality awareness and improvement in the United States are based upon the teaching, writing, and consulting of Dr. W. Edwards Deming, Dr. Joseph M. Juran, and Philip B. Crosby. Let's briefly discuss each, providing references for the interested reader to pursue further.

Deming's Statistical Thinking

Dr. Deming has worked closely with the Japanese since 1950. Rarely has an American received such respect in Japanese business circles. His approaches to quality improvement, analysis, and statistics are widely accepted by Japanese business. In fact, the highest quality award in Japanese industry, the Deming Prize, carries his name. What, then, does he propose?

Dr. Deming lays responsibility for quality improvement at management's doorstep. The *system* is generally the cause for inefficiency and low quality, according to Deming, and it is management's responsibility to *work on the system* (as workers work in the system). Deming's fourteen principles stress design of product, specification of the service offered, measurement by simple statistical methods, and action on the causes identified by these methods. He stresses variation as a major manufacturing problem and proposes the use of control charts to assist in evaluating variation. Students of operations management can learn about Deming's philosophy by studying a set of video training tapes offered by the Massachusetts Institute of Technology's (MIT) Center for Advanced Engineering Study.[16]

Juran's Management Processes Through Quality

Dr. Juran is a popular author, lecturer, and consultant. For decades, he has presented his views to American managers on management's role regarding quality improvement. Juran has an international background and his message is managerial in nature. He addresses American management on issues such as rationality, analysis, and management processes in order to get at problems in quality. Although he uses statistical analysis freely, his primary objective is to get top management to help the company's management team develop the *habit of annual improvement.* In Juran's approach, continuing improvement is supplemented with a "breakthrough" sequence, essentially an organized approach to problem identification, analysis, and change based on this analysis.

Juran has published a number of books, contributed freely to professional quality journals, and developed a set of lectures and video tapes to explain his approach. We've had the opportunity to sample each and have found his message to be well thought out and presented in a lively way.

---

[16] W. Edwards Deming, "On Some Statistical Aids Toward Economic Production," *Interfaces* 5, no. 5 (August 1975), pp. 1–15; Myron Tribus, "Deming's Way," (MIT Center for Advanced Engineering Study, April 1982), 8 pages; Myron Tribus, "Deming's Redefinition of Management," (MIT Center for Advanced Engineering Study, Working Paper).

The key to the Juran message, again, is that management can and must seek continual improvement. In doing so, quality will improve, along with other performance dimensions. Because competition with other firms and nations is so great, *annual improvement, hands-on management,* and *training* to institutionalize improvement must all fit together in order to meet the competition for quality products and services.[17]

Phil Crosby's Concept of Free Quality As an experienced executive who for fourteen years was corporate vice-president and director of quality for ITT, Mr. Crosby was involved in the initial phases of "zero defects" programs (presented later in this chapter). He is an active consultant, lecturer, and author of a popular quality book, *Quality Is Free.* The concept of this book, which explains his overall approach, is that

> Quality is free. It is not a gift, but it is free. What costs money are the unquality things—all the actions that involve not doing jobs right the first time. Quality is not only free, it is an honest-to-everything profit maker. Every penny you don't spend on doing things wrong, over, or instead becomes half a penny right on the bottom line.[18]

Phil Crosby Associates (PCA) in Winter Park, Florida, has been involved in educating 20,000 executives from throughout the world concerning quality awareness as a means for improvement. The focus of this training is on conformance to requirements, prevention, the proper attitude toward quality, and measuring quality as a cost of quality. These "absolutes" are put together in an effective presentation package for corporations. Crosby's approach is based on attitudes and awareness; he focuses on management's role in using this approach to improve quality. Whereas Deming and Juran use analysis as a basis for their philosophies, Crosby's approach is behavioral. Evidently, his methods are quite effective. We are aware of individual quality assurance executives, as well as major corporations such as IBM, who have had good success with Crosby's approach.

Experiences of Leading-Edge Firms

Although we know of the strides forward made in quality by such companies as Armco, Firestone, Hewlett Packard, Honeywell, IBM, and McDonnell Douglas Corporation, it is difficult to obtain documented and published details of successful corporate-wide quality programs. However, we do have a few well-documented examples; we will now take a closer look at some organizations that have achieved high quality.

---

[17] J. Juran, *Upper Management and Quality,* 4th ed. (New York: Juran Institute, Inc., 1983); idem, *Management of Quality,* 4th ed. (New York: Juran Institute, Inc., 1981); idem, *Quality Control Handbook,* 3rd ed. (New York: McGraw-Hill, 1974); idem, *Quality Planning and Analysis* (New York: McGraw-Hill, 1980).

[18] Philip B. Crosby, *Quality Is Free* (New York: Mentor, 1979), p. 2. Also see Jay W. Leek, "Quality in Review, the PCA Experience," *Proceedings the World Quality Congress 1984* (Brighton, England, June 1984).

TABLE 17.4
Number of annual proposals by workers at Toyota

Year	Total number of proposals	Number of proposals per person	Acceptance rate
1965	9,000	1.0	39%
1970	40,000	2.5	70
1973	247,000	12.2	76
1975	380,000	15.3	83
1976	463,000	—	83
1977	454,000	—	86
1978	528,000	—	86
1979	576,000	—	91
1980	859,000	18.7	94

Source: Robert W. Hall. *Zero Inventories,* (Homewood, Ill.: Dow Jones-Irwin, 1983), p. 27.

Toyota Motor Company Toyota has been a pacesetter for automotive companies throughout the world as a consistently low-cost, high-quality producer. The Toyota concept of stockless production provides high inventory turnover: an annual turnover of working assets of 62 times in 1970, compared to an annual turnover of less than 10 times for typical U.S. firms.[19] Toyota also has several important quality features, including: (1) involvement of the work force in quality and productivity suggestions (quality circles), (2) inspection of supplier plants, and (3) the use of statistical methods and analysis at all levels in the company.

The involvement of the work force can be seen in Table 17.4. Professor Hall notes that the great increase in 1973 resulted from a need to react effectively to the oil crisis. This event jolted Toyota into greater action. Managers should keep in mind that many small savings add up, and some proposals may lead to large savings. Project-by-project teams, often in the form of quality circles, account for many of the formal proposals and implementations.

Professor Hall raises the question as to whether too much pressure is being put upon the low-level Japanese worker at Toyota. We do not perceive this type of pressure as a problem in American industry. We suggest instead that the American worker simply doesn't have the opportunity or the perceived incentive to improve his or her own work. From our understanding of Toyota, it is clear that management must provide that environment.

Toyota and Nissan regularly inspect supplier plants. This practice is now being followed by U.S. auto manufacturers,[20] as we'll see as we look

[19]Robert W. Hall, *Zero Inventories,* (Homewood, Ill.: Dow-Jones, Irwin, 1983), p. 26.

[20]Richard J. Schonberger. *Japanese Manufacturing Techniques.* New York: Free Press, 1982, p. 58.

at Ford in the next section. Toyota, like many Japanese firms, depends upon workers at all levels to use statistical thinking (as Deming proposes). This is the third characteristic we've identified as leading to their high quality position in the automotive industry.

Ford Motor Company In addition to employing Dr. Deming as a consultant, Ford has actively pursued the Japanese—and in general the foreign car—quality lead in automobile production. Ford has developed an integrated business strategy to (1) actively pursue product quality improvement, adopting many Japanese quality techniques, and (2) promote and advertise both the commitment to quality and any actual achievements due to product improvement. Quality improvement is stated as the number one business priority at Ford.

Regarding the first part of Ford's strategy, we have had numerous conversations with top Ford executives. They have provided us with materials reflecting Ford's commitment to quality.[21] Ford is in the process of renewing its use of statistical management methods in order to improve productivity and quality. Ford Chairman Donald E. Peterson has endorsed Dr. Deming's 14 points as the foundation for Ford's goal of never-ending improvement in quality and productivity. Activities that are now underway are summarized for us by Ford and presented in Table 17.5.

The results of Ford's efforts are now being recognized by consumers. In 1985 Ford advertised that they are number 1 in quality among American automobile manufacturers; they cited independently collected data to support their claim.

Xerox Corporation The segment of Xerox that produces copiers and duplicators has met extremely quick foreign competition—especially from Japanese manufacturers. This competition is directed at gaining market share with low-cost, high-quality products.[22] Xerox's response has been to

- completely reassess the way they have been doing business,
- learn to deal with issues involving quality and productivity in a different way,
- implement a number of new approaches that will enable long-term competitiveness.

Xerox, unique in its industry because it developed the product line that formed the industry, now has a basis for comparison with very *real*

[21]The authors are particularly indebted to Ford executives John A. Manoogian, Executive Director Product Assurance, North American Automotive Operations and Dick Smith of his staff; James K. Bakken, Corporate Vice-President, Operations Support Staff; and William W. Scherkenbach, Director Statistical Methods.

[22]This section based on Frank J. Pipp, "A Management Commitment to Quality" (The keynote speech to the 37th Annual Quality Congress, American Society for Quality Control, May 1983).

⁊.5
ıtegrated quality program: key features

Management Commitment
ket Research made it abundantly clear that Ford customers wanted quality products and services. In turn, orate management established quality improvement as the No. 1 priority. "Quality is Job #1" is a long-term itment supported by a specific written Corporate policy. This was followed by the establishment of long- t-In-Class" quality goals for all vehicle lines.

Awareness and Involvement
quality information is being communicated to all personnel from top management to the production emplo a continuing basis. A number of statistical seminars are available to all employees and suppliers conducte selected statistical experts. These include Dr. W. Edward Deming's three-day seminar. An approved list o nsultants is also available to assist with specific statistical applications. All employees are encouraged to participate in Employee Involvement (EI) programs where they can work together and make suggestions to improve working conditions as well as product quality. Today, virtually all facilities have EI teams, and the majority of employees have received EI training.

3. *Training*
Keeping abreast of advances in skills, knowledge, and opportunities and assuring that employees are properly trained in the latest procedures is a continuing long-term effort. Statistical training is emphasized for all employees from top management to production people on the plant floor. The training is tailored to meet the needs of the employees and carefully constructed to train them in only those tasks that are necessary for improving their job performance. All work areas must be considered, including Planning, Engineering, Manufacturing, Finance, Administration, Marketing, Sales, and Service. All phases starting with awareness training, and progression through rudimentary and advanced techniques are included. Also, retraining is in place to assure a thorough and continuous approach. Seminars and courses, including workshops with practical applications, are convenient to all employees and available during regular working hours whenever possible.
4. *Teamwork*
In addition to the Employee Involvement teams, Ford has adopted the use of reliability and quality teams that involve Planning, Design, Manufacturing, Supplier, Financial, Services, Sales, and Marketing personnel. These teams have been established for each vehicle and its major component parts to assure a strong interaction during the development process.
5. *Designing Quality Into All New Products*
Designing-in quality is part of the prevention process and is directed toward meeting customer expectations and ease of manufacture. Important disciplines include:
   - determining customer expectations,
   - developing customer acceptance criteria,
   - examining historical and potential failure modes,
   - analyzing manufacturing data,
   - testing, evaluation, and verification of the final product.
6. *More Tolerant Product Designs*
Ford is asking itself, "Can we make the product more tolerant to production variability?" We are investigating an approach that explores ranges of nominal or target values of product dimensions and other characteristics far beyond those normally considered. In turn, we search for values that will result in less variation in the performance of the product for the same variation in the characteristics.
7. *Building Quality Into the Manufacturing and Assembly Processes*
Building-in quality again emphasizes prevention through process capability and control rather than after-the-fact inspection. Ford's programs to assure built-in quality include:
   - increased applications of high-technology processes,
   - elimination of historical failure modes,
   - determination of process capability prior to parts being made ready for production,
   - assuring acceptable quality prior to high-volume production through OK-to-build and OK-to-ship approvals at the manufacturing and assembly plants by top management personnel,
   - continuous reduction in parts variability to improve product consistency. As parts are made more nearly alike and closer to nominal values, the fit and function more nearly approaches the desired ideal levels. This is being achieved through a transition from inspection to statistical process control of manufacturing and assembly operations,

TABLE 17.5 (Cont.)

8. *Monitoring Quality and Customer Service*
Monitoring provides the feedback necessary for evaluating current quality performance and for continual updating of design and test standards, methods, and procedures to be responsive to changing customer requirements. This allows prevention of problems at the source rather than detecting and fixing them later.
9. *Outside Supplier Self-Control of Quality*
Suppliers are involved early in feasibility feedback, development, and evaluation processes and are being trained in techniques such as statistical process control to enable them to improve their capability and "self-certify" their parts.
10. *QI Preferred Quality Supplier Program*
It is Ford's policy to do business with suppliers who continually strive to improve quality and productivity. To recognize quality suppliers, Ford developed the QI Preferred Quality Supplier Program. Criteria includes use of statistical process controls, high success rate on initial samples and first production shipments, outstanding ongoing quality performance at the Ford using location, an absence of significant field problems, commitment from supplier management, and the ability and willingness to conduct manufacturing feasibility studies.
11. *Technology*
Technological advances that include CAD/CAM, automation, robotics, and flexible manufacturing systems offer opportunities to reduce variability and probability for error. Today, we can go from design to tool and die manufacturing on outer body panels, for example, entirely by using the CAD/CAM concept. In addition, Ford has over 2500 robots in use world-wide; and laser welding systems are being used in our new high-tech four-speed transaxle. New technology will be successful in improving quality and productivity when it is supportive of our defect prevention philosophy.

Source: Provided by Mr. John A. Manoogian, Ford Motor Company, and published with Ford's permission.

competitors who once did not exist. Xerox has three major phases underway:

1. *Competitive benchmarking*. Developing and implementing a continuous process of measuring Xerox products and services against the best and toughest competitors in the world—the best in any industry, not just copiers and duplicators. This led to action resulting in a 21 percent gain in satisfaction in 1982.
2. *Employee involvement*. Getting the best from the minds and talents of Xerox employees at all levels. Problem-solving teams, quality circles, changing management style—over one-fourth of Xerox employees are now involved in team activities aimed at improvement.
3. *Leadership through quality*. Exposing the very top executives to the work of Drs. Juran and Deming, and attending Phil Crosby's Quality College in Winter Park, have led to the beginning of a total quality control process in all aspects of the corporation. Top management credibility has been established at Xerox.

From the reaction of Xerox, we see how a U.S.-based company prepares to meet the quality-productivity challenge. We see in Toyota, Ford, and Xerox several similar ideas—and a return to the basic concepts and principles of leading world-wide quality experts. Why? World-wide competition in terms of quality products and services, seems to be the driving force.

BEHAVIOR AND QUALITY

When quality levels fail to meet specifications, the quality control technician knows to look for some "assignable cause." By the time an error has been detected by internal inspection efforts, from customer complaints, or from product failure, it is possible that a large number of similarly defective units has also been produced. Clearly, a fundamental limitation of statistical quality control is its historical orientation. Inspection involves examining products or services *after* they have been produced. The quality level is put there by operating line personnel. Thus, the attainment of suitable quality depends upon appropriate human performance when the product is being made.

In recent years much effort has been devoted to instilling a "quality orientation" in the people who work in the conversion process. Behavioral change procedures directed at changing performance quality *before* rather than after the fact, however, have met with limited success. We will discuss some of these attempts and the inherent behavioral problems that relate to quality in the following few paragraphs.

Quality/Quantity Tradeoffs

Few studies have specifically investigated the relationships between quantity and quality of output. A popular view supported by Dr. Deming and Dr. Juran is that any decrease in quantity would be more than offset by the reduction in waste due to correct performance the first time. A review of the literature suggests there is no simple inherent relationship between these two factors. Especially for such routine, repetitive tasks as typing, bank proofing, or collating, operators tend to emphasize one over the other. If quality improves, quantity decreases; if quantity goes up, quality suffers. For tasks involving more complex and diverse physical and mental processes, the relationships between quantity and quality are not nearly so clear. In these more complex tasks, when does the operator emphasize quality at the expense of quantity? When does the reverse occur? There is no simple answer to our questions. The quantity/quality tradeoff is usually determined by how the conversion processes are designed, staffed, and managed.

Zero Defects

Zero Defects programs, which attempt to improve quality by changing workers' attitudes, were particularly popular in the 1960s and 1970s. Their theme, "Do it right the first time," stresses error-free performance. Unfortunately, however, production/operation processes inevitably result in some undesirable output. Error-free performance is, for most processes, economically and practically infeasible. Although many people assume that errors are made because employees are not conscientious enough about their work, attempts to change employee attitudes have met with very limited success. Banners, slogans, Zero Defect days, and the like generally im-

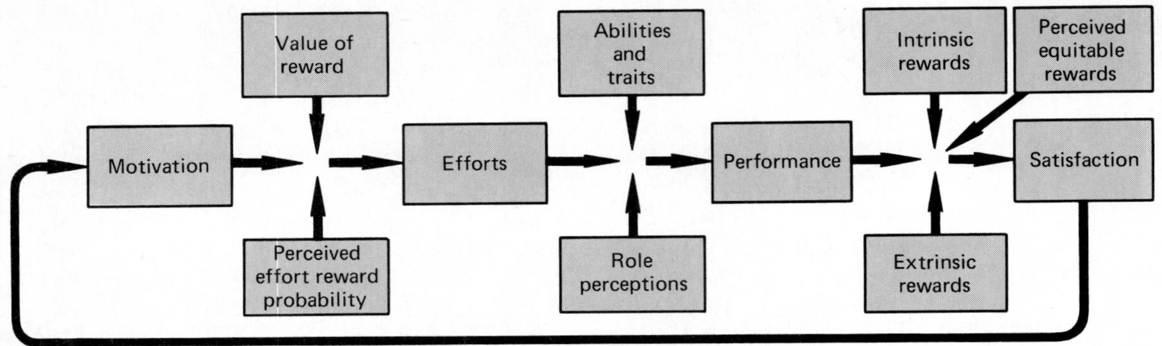

FIGURE 17.12
Expectancy model of motivation

From D. A. Nadler, J. R. Hackman, and E. E. Lawler III, *Managing Organizational Behavior.* Copyright © 1979 by David A. Nadler, J. Richard Hackman, and Edward E. Lawler III. Reprinted by permission of Little, Brown and Company.

prove performance only temporarily; in about six months, employees' performance returns to its previous level.[23] Nevertheless, this sort of approach has some value. "Quality motivation" focuses the organization's attention on the human variable in product quality; it attempts to influence, rather than simply report, behavior that affects quality.

Quality Motivation

The American Society for Quality Control's *Quality Motivation Workbook* stresses some basic concepts for motivating employees. The idea is to apply techniques of motivation and management to obtain improved product quality.

To supplement this booklet, managers should try to be familiar with other systematic ways of thinking about the many factors that determine employees' performance. Consider the basic expectancy model in Figure 17.12. This model suggests that effort leads to performance, which, in turn, leads to satisfaction. Satisfaction then leads to future efforts. Basic to the individuals' efforts are their perceptions of how much they will be rewarded—and the chances of their being rewarded—for their efforts. Effort, together with abilities and role perceptions, leads to performance, or accomplishment. Individuals are rewarded according to their performance. The rewards, and how equitable they seem to the employees, determine their satisfaction; the degree of satisfaction then affects how much effort individuals will expend in the future. How could all this apply to the quality of an individual's work performance? Let's look at an example.

[23]See Everett E. Adam, Jr., "An Analysis of Changes in Performance Quality with Operant Conditioning Procedures," *Journal of Applied Psychology* 56, no. 6 (1972), pp. 480–86, for a review of studies about Zero Defects by quality control specialists.

EXAMPLE

A student working as a stock clerk for a grocery chain can exercise some control over the quality of his work by checking prices before stocking, cleaning shelves, facing groceries properly (labels out) when stocking, and being friendly and courteous with customers. The degree to which this PERFORMANCE QUALITY is attained is a function of his abilities, role perception, and the effort he extends. The effort he extends may be a function of how much he needs money (reward) to continue his education and the relationship he perceives between his effort and rewards. If the stock clerk notices, for example, that the manager gives more hours of work to clerks who extend the greatest effort, he may extend more effort himself. Performance leads to money (extrinsic reward) and to the satisfaction of looking at full, clean shelves and pleased customers (intrinsic rewards). If the rewards seem equitable to the stock clerks, if wages are fair and just, job satisfaction is likely. The result of these behavioral processes is a positively motivated stock clerk.

Behavioral Modification in Quality Control

There have been several attempts to influence performance quality on routine repetitive tasks by employing operant conditioning procedures.[24] Operant conditioning assumes that behavior can be modified by a series of rewards. People act as a result of habits, built-up associations between a particular situation or set of circumstances and the response it generates. When faced with a situation, people react predictably because of the response they have received in the past. If the response is changed, behavior can be changed. Studies in the behavioral laboratory and in organizations provide some generalizations about influencing performance quality with behavior modification procedures. First, it appears that performance *quality* is more difficult to change than performance *quantity*. Second, it is clear that financial rewards more often result in improved quality than nonfinancial rewards. Once reasonable quality performance levels have been reached, however, continued financial rewards do not obtain significant additional quality improvement. Third, actual behavior is influenced more greatly by direct rewards than by attitude change procedures. We should be aware, finally, that these procedures provide, at best, mixed results.

---

[24]See Everett E. Adam, Jr., "Behavior Modification in Quality Control," *Academy of Management Journal* 18, no. 4 (December 1975), pp. 662–79. This work provides references to the related works of George A. Johnson, William A. Ruch, William E. Scott, Jr., and James B. Shein, all of whom have contributed to recent quality motivation research. Also see David A. Sprague, Barry Zinn, and Robert Kreitner, "Improving Quality Through Behavior Modification," *Quality Progress* 9, no. 12 (December 1976), pp. 22–24.

EXAMPLE

In an attempt to influence quality in a diecasting department of some 36 men, one company succeeded in obtaining a significant quantity increase but no significant change in quality. Figure 17.13 shows weekly changes in the department as the result of a formal program involving weekly individual meetings between the supervisor and each employee. Quantity is measured as percent of standard, and quality is measured by percent defective. Overall, the company, with a $73,000 first-year cost reduction in this department, judged the program successful and implemented it in other departments. The fact remains, however, that quality did not improve, even though emphasis was given to performance quality at least weekly.

Quality Circles

Quality circles (QCs) were initially developed in Japan as employee participative programs to identify the quality variations and then with management to eliminate the source of those deviations. To understand how these work, we need to be familiar with the following cultural conditions in which they were developed: (1) lifetime employment with one firm, (2) a cooperative labor-management team, (3) a culture of trust and support, and (4) employees willing to take work-related problems outside the office or factory in an attempt to further resolve them.

Quality circles in Japan are essentially small groups of employees (perhaps six to twelve) who meet informally, often in an employee's home to resolve quality-related problems from work. Ideas for solutions are suggested to management and they work as a team to implement the changes. Employees at all levels in the firm are trained in the basic skills of data charting, sampling, and control. These analytical and statistical skills have

FIGURE 17.13
Weekly diecasting quality (percent scrap) and quantity (percent performance) performance

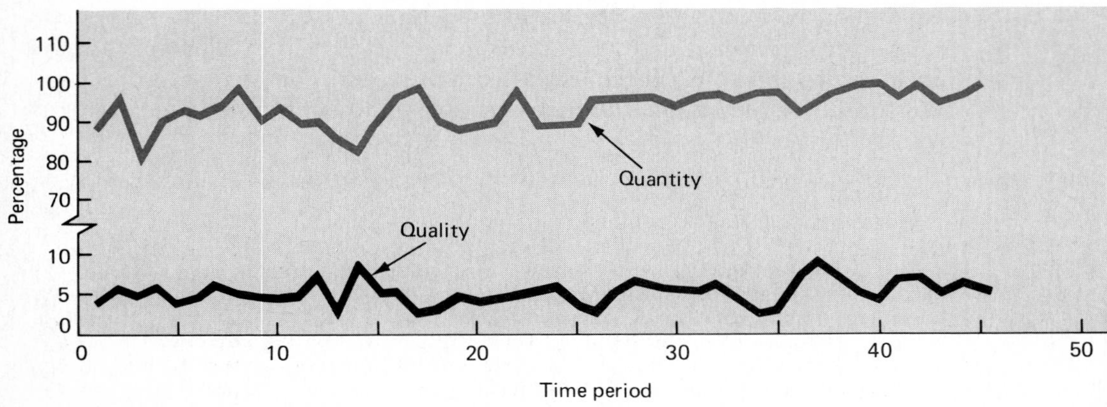

become a part of the Japanese general education curriculum and are widely reinforced by industry usage at the level of the operative worker. In 1980, quality control experts estimated that just under a million workers were involved in quality circles in Japan, but only as few as a hundred thousand workers were taking part in the programs in the United States.[25] Those numbers are certainly larger now, as reflected by the increasing interest in the International Association of Quality Circles. The 1984 membership in that organization was estimated at 3500 quality circle facilitators, primarily from the United States.

Within the United States quality circles have evolved into participative productivity improvement programs which focus on both performance quantity and quality. As in Japan, participation is voluntary. Employees are paid while participating during regular working hours or on overtime. A group leader is selected and trained for the leadership role by the organization. Then the participating group receives training in the methods of problem solving, analysis, and reporting. The group begins meeting to identify problems, collect and analyze the data, recommend solutions, and carry out management-approved changes. Many companies are testing this participative technique in a few locations with an eye toward wider application.[26]

The key feature of quality circles in the United States is that real participation of hourly employees in productivity improvement is actively sought and utilized. Many managers, owners, and academics believe that the hidden resource in the United States is the untapped mental facilities of operative workers. Management has not always structured jobs so that operative workers could use their minds as well as their hands to improve performance. The adversary relationships between ownership (and their management) and labor cannot be changed overnight by any one program, but perhaps the quality circle trend is a step in the right direction.

There are very few evaluations of quality circle performance. Most organizations report savings to costs in a range of 3:1 to 6:1, clearly favoring the programs. Others simply accept quality circles as a management

---

[25]Source of Japanese estimate: "If Japan Can Do It . . . Why Can't We?" *NBC White Paper*, 1980; and R. E. Cole, *Work, Mobility and Participation: A Comparative Study of American and Japanese Industry*, (Berkeley, CA: University of California Press, 1980); Cole estimates 840,000 members take part in Japan. Source of United States estimate: William Werther, "Quality Circles in the United States," 1981 American Institute for Decision Sciences Conference, Boston, November 1981.

[26]For example discussions of Quality Circles and their applications see: A. V. Feignbaum, "The Internationalization of Quality," *Quality Progress* 12, no. 2 (February 1979) pp. 30–32; Gerald E. Swartz and Vivian C. Comstock, "One Firm's Experience with Quality Circles," *Quality Progress* 12, no. 9 (September 1979) pp. 14–16 (Westinghouse's experience); Charles A. Aubrey II and Lawrence A. Eldridge, "Banking on High Quality," *Quality Progress* (December 1981), pp. 14–19 (Continental Bank's experience); George Munchus, III "Employer-Employee Based Quality Circles in Japan: Human Resource Policy Implications for American Firms" *Academy of Management Review* 8, no. 2 (April 1983) pp. 255–261; and John D. Blair and Kenneth D. Ramsing, "Quality Circles and Production/Operations Management: Concerns and Caveats," *Journal of Operations Management* 4, no. 1 (November 1983), pp. 1–10.

participative philosophy without documenting savings. One field study, however, did systematically evaluate QC's effectiveness.[27] In this study empirical investigation of effective and less-effective quality circles was conducted in nine manufacturing plants of a large, midwestern company. Subjects consisted of 457 employees who were organized into 44 QCs. Effectiveness was defined as (1) the number of quality improvements adopted and (2) average member satisfaction. Variables measured by questionnaire for each group were average age; age range; tenure; cohesion; performance norms; satisfaction with leader, job, and coworkers; intrinsic satisfaction; extrinsic satisfaction; self-esteem; self-monitoring; and perceptions of the organization's commitment to the QC concept. Significant differences among several key variables were found between the effective and less-effective QCs. Effective QCs reported higher cohesion, performance norms, job satisfaction, intrinsic satisfaction, satisfaction with coworkers, self-esteem, self-monitoring, and organization commitment than did the less-effective groups. If an organization values the group's suggestions and values member satisfactions and feelings, then the results of this study indicate that quality circles will be effective.

Management Style and Quality Control

Several writers suggest that a participative management style best enhances quality control and improvement efforts.[28] Focusing on the individual, these efforts—many of which are in services—emphasize involvement in setting quality goals, establishing quality measures, and designing jobs for enhanced quality. A panel of experts selected the twelve studies that contributed most to productivity improvement from among the hundreds published in the management and behavioral sciences during the 1970s. Two studies involved quality and productivity, one focusing on behavior modification and the other employee participation. In the first, Shaw and Capoor stress a management style of participation that enhances productivity and quality. In the second, Hostage explains Marriott management's successful incentive program, which involves managers and workers in delivering quality services. We have found managers to be increasingly interested in quality, especially in *management techniques* to improve quality. Perhaps this managerial awareness is increasing because of the difficulties encoun-

---

[27]Ricky W. Griffin and Sandy J. Wayne, "A Field Study of Effective and Less Effective Quality Circles," *Academy of Management Proceedings 1984*, pp. 217–221.

[28]See John R. Hinrichs, *Practical Management for Productivity* (New York: Van Nostrand Reinhold Company, 1978). Hinrichs returned to field sites and interviewed participants in quality improvement studies (see Chapter 2, "Enhancing Product Quality," the original study by E. E. Adam, Jr., and Chapter 6, "Building a Participative Management System to Enhance Product Quality," the original study by F. B. Chaney and K. S. Teel). Also see John C. Shaw and Ram Capoor, "Quality and Productivity: Mutually Exclusive or Interdependent in Service Organizations?" *Management Review* (March 1979), pp. 25–28 and 37–39; G. M. Hostage, "Quality Control in a Service Business," *Harvard Business Review* 53, no. 4 (July–August 1975), pp. 98–106; and A. V. Feigenbaum, "Quality and Productivity," *Quality Progress* 10, no. 11 (November 1977), pp. 18–21.

tered recently by such basic United States industries as steel and automobiles—international competitors have challenged and sometimes outperformed U.S. productivity and quality in these areas.

EXAMPLE

The 1983 White House Conference on Productivity was established by the United States Congress to address productivity decline in the United States. Government, labor, and private enterprise presented recommendations on a wide variety of variables that affect productivity and the competitive posture of American industry. Several recommendations were keyed to performance quality and the quality of U.S. products and services. We had the opportunity to work with three other academics and some fifteen to twenty top quality executives from various companies in the United States to recommend (1) a national quality awareness campaign; (2) that private sector organizations develop strategies for quality and productivity improvement; (3) that these organizations work actively to help integrate quality education into the American educational system; (4) the establishment of a national quality association; and (5) implementation of awards, recognition, and incentives for quality at all levels.[29] As academics we are encouraged by the dedication, insight, energy level, and national loyalty and concern expressed by these executives individually and collectively. In continuing with an American Productivity Center-sponsored computer interactive network with an expanded set of managers and executives, we find that they are energetically addressing implementation of these recommendations in 1984 and 1985. There is an increasing quality *awareness* and we see *managerial action* within individual companies directed toward quality improvement.

[29]*Computer Conferences on Productivity. A Final Report for the White House Conference on Productivity.* American Productivity Center, (Washington, D.C., September, 1983).

Several other important quality-related behavioral problems remain unsolved. Human error in inspection is a common occurrence. A 100 percent inspection certainly does not mean that *all* defective parts are observed and discarded by the inspector. Another difficulty arises from ambiguous quality standards (specifications) in some monitoring tasks. Our previous examples assumed that standards were clear and unambiguous, and that a unit of output could be adjudged either definitely suitable or definitely unsuitable (defective). In many real situations, however, precisely defined standards do not exist. Product characteristics must sometimes be evaluated against *general*, rather than specific, criteria, particularly in the service sector.

Another quality problem is often found in group situations. If several inspectors are all monitoring the same items, there may be a "group effect." In such settings, group norms often emerge, and group members apply sanctions to obtain compliance with these norms. From the organization's viewpoint it is desirable for the group norm to coincide with the desired or intended quality standard. The problem for the manager is to detect the group standard and direct it toward the desired standard. By instituting surveillance programs, employee training, group discussion, and methods of clarifying and communicating desired standards, the operations manager may be able to favorably influence behavior.

SUMMARY

In this chapter on managing for quality, we have discussed concepts of product quality; factors affecting quality; analysis useful in quality control, including inspection, sampling, and control charts; contemporary management approaches to improving quality; and behavioral dimensions in quality. Quality improvement, assurance, and control can be facilitated by management's planning and organizing efforts. Operations managers should set up inspection stations and sampling plans, and should construct control charts. However, they must be aware that all of these control procedures are used by people. Quality motivation and behavioral modification techniques are some methods operations managers can use to encourage employees to improve quality. The Japanese have taught us a good bit about high quality—both in analysis and managing people.

It is our belief that the most important aspects of an introduction to quality are understanding concepts in quality, being able to apply basic control models, and understanding that quality control is not totally a statistical problem. If you have mastered these concepts, you have a grasp of the fundamentals of quality control.

CASE

Hydrolock, Inc.

In 1978 George Thrall founded Hydrolock, Inc., a manufacturing company producing small rubber gaskets used in hydraulic systems. His gaskets were simple in design and relatively easy to produce in large quantities. In 1985, gross sales from servicing customers throughout North America with large quantity shipments reached $8 million. A very autocratic management style exists throughout the company.

Demand for Hydrolock products has increased so rapidly that the manufacturing facility is constantly under pressure to increase output around the clock. Customers and sales personnel in the field often call the home facility to determine estimated lead times for prospective orders and estimated delivery times for existing orders. In response, production foremen have increasingly emphasized to employees the need for increasing output to meet demand.

In late 1985, George Thrall began experiencing a new problem, an increase in customer complaints about the quality of shipments being received. Plant supervision insisted the problem was twofold and that nothing could be done about either: (1) workers were asked to produce at maximum efficiency, so quality suffered; and (2) workers had absolutely no motivation for high quality performance. George decided to add a quality control analyst to the Hydrolock staff in hopes of finding and correcting the sources of customer dissatisfaction.

In his first two weeks the quality analyst uncovered some data that a production foreman had recorded two years previously.

Data for gasket YB4 (1984)

Sample number	Sample size	Number of defective gaskets in sample
1	40	6
2	40	1
3	40	0
4	40	2
5	40	1
6	40	4
7	40	3
8	40	2
9	40	6
10	40	0
11	40	3
12	40	2

The analyst began gathering data on current production of the same gasket. Samples were taken once each day for five consecutive work days with these results.

Data for gasket YB4 (1986)

Sample number	Sample size	Number of defective gaskets in sample
1	40	4
2	40	8
3	40	6
4	40	2
5	40	8

If you were the new analyst, what ideas would you entertain for getting to the bottom of George Thrall's quality problem? Of what value are the data at hand? Does management have a style and outlook toward employees that enhances quality performance? What would you recommend?

REVIEW AND DISCUSSION QUESTIONS

1. If you were to design a portable radio, what product characteristics would you specify as critical for enhancing sales? What characteristics are less important?
2. What product characteristics and quality analysis procedures are important in a dormitory cafeteria? Which of these is most important? Which is least important?
3. Discuss the roles of the cost of quality assurance in quality planning.
4. In some organizations, quality control responsibilities are separated from line production responsibilities; in other organizations they are not separated. Why?
5. Identify different types of inspection and discuss their roles in the quality assurance and control process.

6. What are the distinctions between inspection and sampling?
7. How does inspection by variables differ from inspection by attributes?
8. What is an acceptance sampling plan? How does it work, what factors must be considered in designing it, and what costs are incurred in using it?
9. What is an OC curve?
10. How do control charts differ from acceptance sampling plans? Under what circumstances is each appropriate?
11. Give examples of control chart patterns that would lead you to conclude that control action may be warranted.
12. Explain how strategy and quality interrelate.
13. Explain the interactions among the components in Figure 17.3, "Managing for quality products and services."
14. "If our employees are requested to increase output quality, the quantity of output is going to suffer." Discuss this statement.
15. Discuss the relative importance of intrinsic and extrinsic rewards in the expectancy model of motivation (Figure 17.12) as they relate to the quality goals of the organization.
16. Is operant conditioning an effective management technique for quality motivation in nonroutine, nonrepetitive tasks?
17. In this chapter the manager is asked to become proficient in quality analysis techniques, and is also expected to understand contemporary improvement programs and behavior. Are these expectations inconsistent? Explain.

PROBLEMS

Solved Problems

1. An attribute control chart exists (Figure 17.14) for part #223B with average fraction defective 0.125, upper control limit 0.200, and lower control limit 0.050. The chart is based on two months of daily data. Twelve units were sampled each day for the past six days with defectives, 2, 1, 2, 0, 3, and 3.

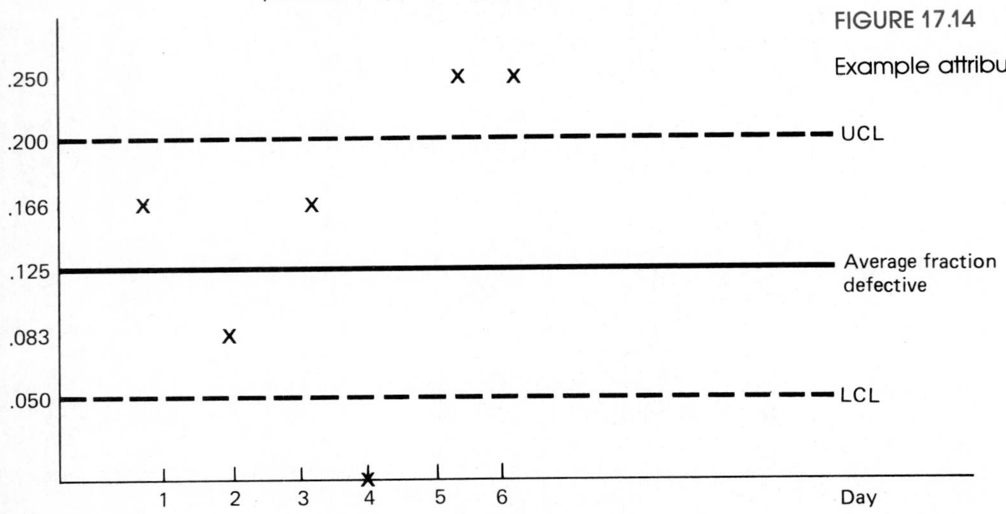

FIGURE 17.14

Example attributes control chart

(a) Construct a control chart for management, carefully labeling the chart, and interpret it for management.
(b) What is the significance of day four being below the lower control limit—which was set by the quality control technician?
Solution (a) The solution for (a) is shown in Figure 17.14. Fraction defective for the past six days:

$$\frac{2}{12} = .166, \frac{1}{12} = .083, \frac{2}{12} = .166, \frac{0}{12} = 0, \frac{3}{12} = .250, \frac{3}{12} = .250$$

The processs is out of control on days four, five and six.
Solution (b) The control limits should be set in such a way that any outcome out of the limits is regarded as a warning signal. Why is the perfect sampling outcome of day four regarded as out of control? There likely is no reason for it. The lower control limit for "fraction defective" is useful because exceptionally careful work might be accompanied by lower output. On the other hand, exceptionally low fraction defective might be accompanied by higher output, truly improved overall performance, and a cause for rejoicing.

2. An electronics manufacturer has a station that always uses a sample size of ten products and has a record for the past 100 samplings of:

Number of defective products	Total products examined
150	1000

The system is believed to have been under normal operating conditions.
(a) Construct a control chart with control limits such that 95 percent of the products under normal process conditions would fall within the control limits.
(b) Suppose we find the number of defective products over the next five samplings were: 3, 4, 2, 0, and 7. What can you tell about the process now? Why?

Solution (a)

$$\overline{P} = \frac{150}{1000} = .15$$

$$\sigma_{\overline{P}} = \sqrt{\frac{\overline{P}\,(1 - \overline{P})}{n}} = \sqrt{\frac{(.15)(.85)}{10}} = 0.113$$

For 95% confidence interval, Z(95%, two-tail) = 1.96

$$\text{UCL} = \overline{p} + Z\sigma_{\overline{p}} = .15 + (1.96)\,(.113) = .371$$
$$\text{LCL} = \overline{p} - Z\sigma_{\overline{p}} = .15 - (1.96)\,(.113) = -.071$$

Solution (b)

Sampling	Fraction Defective
1	3/10 = .3
2	4/10 = .4
3	2/10 = .2
4	0/10 = 0
5	7/10 = .7

Two of five samplings fell above the UCL, hence the process is out of control. We are 95% sure for any one point that is out of control. (See Figure 17.15.)

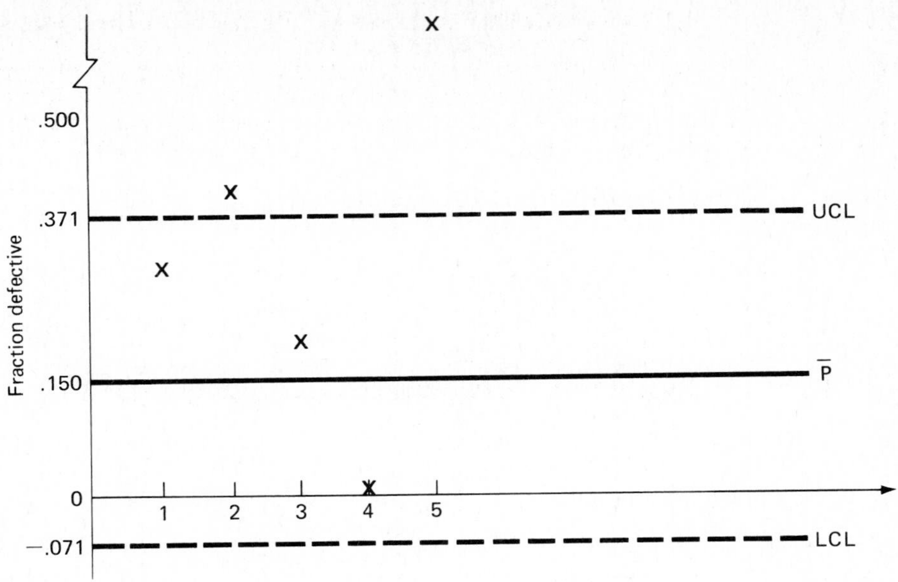

FIGURE 17.15
Electronics attribute control chart

Reinforcing Fundamentals

3. Instrumentation, Inc., has been examining a lens during production for scratches. If there are, in the inspector's opinion, too many scratches, the lens is "bad" and rejected. Otherwise the lens is good. Construct a control chart for last month's inspected lenses.

Last month	Pieces inspected	Pieces rejected
Week 1	60	10
2	60	12
3	60	6
4	60	8
5	60	9

4. An attribute control chart exists for a manufactured part with average fraction defective 0.250, upper control limit 0.450, and lower control limit 0.050. The chart is based on two months of daily data. Ten units were sampled each day for the past six days with defectives 2, 4, 2, 0, 3, and 3.
   (a) Construct a control chart for management, carefully labeling the chart, and interpret it for management.
   (b) A foreman doesn't like the sixth day's results and wants you to re-sample. What is your response? Why?
5. A relatively new test, a Gravindex Test, has been used by our lab for the past ten weeks. This test indicates pregnancy by determining whether hormones are present

in the urine. If hormones are present, the test is positive; in the absence of hormones, the test is negative. We want to establish some means of checking *future* test results to see if the test appears to be staying in control. Each time the test is run, a known positive and known negative test are also run. Data below are for the "known positive" control test, i.e., ninety-five times were "good" and five times were "bad." Our results to date, using a sample size of ten tests each week, are:

Negative	Positive	Total tests
5	95	100

(a) Construct a control chart for this test.
(b) Suppose we collect the following data over the *next* four weeks for our "known positive" Gravindex Test.

Week	Negative results	Positive results
1	0	10
2	1	9
3	2	8
4	3	7

Is the process (test) in control during these four weeks? If not, what do you do?

6. An optics lens manufacturer has a station that always uses a sample size of 12 products and has a record for the past 100 samplings of:

Number of defective products	Total products examined
103	1200

The system is believed to have been under normal operating conditions.
(a) Construct a control chart with control limits such that 97 percent of the products under normal process conditions would fall within the control limits.
(b) Suppose we find the number of defective products over the next five samplings were: 1, 2, 5, 0, and 1. What can you tell about the process now? Why?

Challenging Exercises

7. In conjunction with a class assignment, two industrious operations management students decided to study book returns to the campus library by library users. The students collected their data by sitting on the library steps several days and watching books being returned. They observed the following:
Wednesday: 32 people entered the library, 5 of whom were returning books
Thursday: 55 people entered the library, 15 of whom were returning books
Friday: 27 people entered the library, 6 of whom were returning books
These students need your help in constructing a control chart of this "process." After hearing about this, you go over on two successive Mondays and observe:
Monday: 10 people enter the library, 3 of whom are returning books
Monday: 10 people enter the library, 5 of whom are returning books
What inferences can you make concerning your observations based on the data of your fellow students? What, if any, criticism would you make concerning the sampling procedures?

8. We have a manually operated hydraulic press that forms refractory bricks. There seems to be some concern over the lengths of the bricks being stamped. We know that for an 8.00-inch brick, product specifications are 8.00″ ± 0.10″; the press manufacturer guarantees the press to hold a setting of ± 0.15″ when brick length is between 5″ and 10″; and our Quality Control Department informs us that process capability on an 8.00″ brick shows a UCL = 8.25″ and an LCL of 7.90″. We observe samples over each of the last six hours (of size five) and find the average lengths to be: 8.00″, 8.12″, 8.05″, 8.17″, 7.99″, and 8.10″. We noted while sampling that the press appeared to be properly set up to stamp an 8.00″ brick. From this information: (a) Do we have a problem here and if so, what is it? (b) What action can you recommend, if any, based on this information?
9. An appliance manufacturer has just hired you to evaluate and set up a quality control program in their manufacturing facility that supplies their anodized aluminum decorative trim parts. You report in a staff capacity to the plant manager. In-process inspection and finished goods inspection are currently being performed by some thirty inspectors in a facility employing 500; but little is being done with this data other than recording pieces sampled, number defective, and reasons for defects by employee and job.
   (a) What type of information might you want to gather to assess current quality levels?
   (b) What variables do you want to measure and start systematically providing to supervisors throughout manufacturing? (Example: Provide OC curves or plant percent defective.)
   (c) How would you implement your program?
10. A manufacturing facility consists of three work stations for which there are currently no inspection stations. You have estimated the cost of adding inspection stations and gathered some additional information summarized below.

Work station	Output per day (units)	Average percent defective	Estimated inspection cost per day	Estimated cost of each undetected defective
A	1,000	5%	$20	$6
B	1,000	10	30	4
C	1,000	3	25	2

   (a) As quality manager your limited budget will allow you to add only one inspection station in your conversion process. Which location would you select from the three possible locations?
   (b) What would be your choice if the output rates at *A*, *B*, and *C* were 1,000, 1,500, and 2,000 units per day, respectively?
   (c) Develop a heuristic for inspection station selection that considers all of the variables in the problem.
11. The production manager for the only facility of a small manufacturer of kitchen appliances is interested in getting management's attention on quality issues. He has allies in the marketing manager and accountant, but little interest from the president and the primary owner, both of whom are interested in production efficiency, sales volume, short-term profits, and growth. The production manager and his allies have the following data, but don't know how to organize it into an effective presentation. From this information, put together the best case possible to impress management that quality is important and should be stressed.

Data Item	Value (last year)
1. Customer responses to questions about top-selling product last year	a. style—good b. price—excellent c. reliability—poor d. would recommend to friend—no
2. Quality training costs	$1200
Vendor qualification program	500
Field testing	3,500
Purchase quality measurement (calipers, etc.)	400
Scrap, full cost less scrap value	475,000
Inspection in plant	85,000
Field maintenance	15,000
Rework, at full shop cost	1,200,000
Warranty costs	45,000
Returned material processing & repair	375,000
Laboratory testing	3,700
3. Sales	$10,000,000
Total cost of goods sold	7,000,000
Selling and administrative expenses	1,300,000
Total assets in business	3,500,000
4. Percent defective for top-selling product last year	
a. fabrication	7.2%
b. assembly	11.5%
c. finished goods	9.8%
5. Estimated cost due to loss of good will with distributors	
a. late deliveries	$50,000
b. poor quality	200,000

12. The control charts in Figure 17.16 were attached to an extrusion machine at the facility of a major dog chow manufacturer's production facility. This extruding machine combined inputs of various grains, heat, and water, put the mixture under pressure and extruded ("squeezed out") dog chow that was put into chunks upon extrusion. This is the key machine in the production process and, as shown, three variables are constantly watched and recorded hourly. Realizing the actual charts are incomplete in labeling and detail, answer the following questions as best you can.
    (a) The day shift started at 7 A.M. and ended at 2 P.M. Then operators changed. Did the second shift operators make any significant changes in inputs?
    (b) Which, if any, attributes being measured are out of control on the first shift (7 A.M.–2 P.M.)?
    (c) What can the shift foreman do when he observes the control chart during period 1 (1 P.M.)?

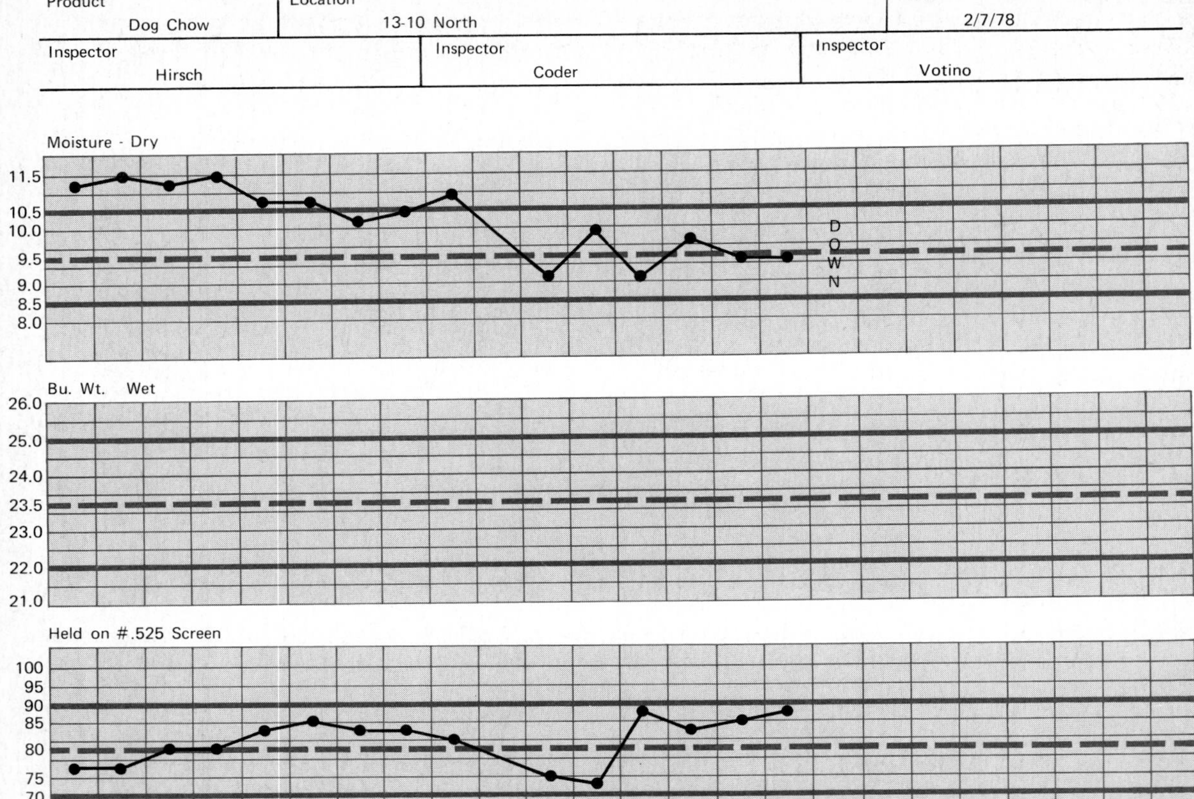

FIGURE 17.16

GLOSSARY

Acceptance number One parameter of a single sampling plan; the largest number of defectives allowed in the sample that still permits acceptance of the shipment.

Attributes measurement Type of measurement in which a product characteristic is classified into one of two categories: success or failure, accept or reject, etc.

Consumer's risk Probability of concluding that a poor quality shipment of inputs is of good quality.

Control chart A graphical device, based on sampling results, used to make inferences about the control status of a process.

Control limits Upper and lower bounds of a control chart; used to indicate the control status of the productive process.

Design specifications Detailed requirements of a product specifying its important desired characteristics.

Inspection Observation and measurement of conversion inputs and outputs.

OC curve Operating characteristics curve; the relationship of acceptance probability to level of incoming quality for a specified sampling plan.

Process capability Maximum level of output quality performance of a productive process that can occur under ideal operating conditions.

Producer's risk Probability of concluding that a good quality shipment of inputs is of poor quality.

Product quality The appropriateness of design specifications to function and use, as well as the degree to which the product conforms to design specifications.

Quality motivation Application of management motivation techniques to workers to improve quality.

Receiving inspection Inspection subfunction that focuses on assessing the quality of conversion inputs.

Sampling Process of selecting representative observations from a population.

Sampling plan Specific procedure that incorporates sampling to permit inferences to be made about some population characteristic.

Specification limits Boundaries that define the limits of variation for a product characteristic; any output outside these boundaries is unacceptable.

Variables measurement Type of measurement in which a product characteristic is classified according to its degree of conformance on some measurement scale.

Zero Defects Formal programs adopted by organizations to change worker attitudes toward quality improvement.

SELECTED READINGS

Adam, E. E. "Behavior Modification in Quality Control." *The Academy of Management Journal* 18, no. 4 (December 1975), pp. 662–79.

———, J. C. Hershauer, and W. A. Ruch. *Productivity and Quality: Measurement as a Basis for Improvement.* Englewood Cliffs, N.J.: Prentice-Hall, Inc., 1981.

Aubrey, Charles A. II and Lawrence A. Eldridge. "Banking on High Quality." *Quality Progress* (December 1981), pp. 14–19.

Blair, John D. and Kenneth D. Ramsing. "Quality Circles and Production/Operations Management: Concerns and Caveats." *Journal of Operations Management* 4, no. 1 (November 1983), pp. 1–10.

Cole, R. E. *Work, Mobility and Participation: A Comparative Study of American and Japanese Industry.* Berkeley, CA: University of California Press, 1980.

Computer Conferences on Productivity, A Final Report for the White House Conference on Productivity, American Productivity Center, Washington, D.C., September 1983.

Crosby, Philip B. *Quality is Free.* New York: Mentor, 1979.

Deming, W. Edwards. "On Some Statistical Aids Toward Economic Production." *Interfaces* 5, no. 5 (August 1975), 1–15.

Dodge, H. F. and H. G. Romig. *Sampling Inspection Tables.* New York: John Wiley & Sons, Inc., 1959.

Duncan, A. J. *Quality Control and Industrial Statistics.* 3rd ed. Homewood, Illinois: Richard D. Irwin, Inc., 1965.

Grant, E. L. *Statistical Quality Control.* 3rd ed. New York: McGraw-Hill Book Company, 1964.

Griffin, Ricky W. and Sandy J. Wayne. "A Field Study of Effective and Less Effective Quality Circles." *Academy of Management Proceedings 1984,* pp. 217–221.

Hinrichs, John R. *Practical Management for Productivity.* New York: Van Nostrand Reinhold Company, 1978.

Hostage, G. M. "Quality Control in a Service Business," *Harvard Business Review* 53, no. 4 (July–August 1975), pp. 98–106.

Ishikawa, Kaoru, *Guide to Quality Control.* Tokyo, Japan: Asian Productivity Organization, 1976 (Eleventh Printing, 1983).

Juran, J. *Upper Management and Quality.* New York: Juran Institute, Inc., 4th ed., 1983.

Juran, J. *Quality Planning and Analysis.* New York: McGraw-Hill, 1980.

Munchus, George III. "Employer-Employee Based Quality Circles in Japan: Human Resource Policy Implications for American Firms." *Academy of Management Review* 8, no. 2 (April 1983), pp. 255–261.

Saniga, Erwin M. and Larry E. Shirland. "Quality Control in Practice . . . A Survey," *Quality Progress* 10, no. 5 (May 1977), pp. 30–33.

Takemchi, Hirotaka and John A. Quelch. "Quality Is More Than Making a Good Product," *Harvard Business Review* 61, no. 4, (July–August 1983), pp. 139–145.

SUPPLEMENT TO CHAPTER 17

CONSTRUCTING SAMPLING PLANS AND CONTROL CHARTS

The purpose of this supplement is to present briefly the more detailed aspects of sampling plans and control charts and to identify some underlying concepts and techniques.

Sampling Plans

The sampling plans discussed in this book are based on the Poisson approximation to the binomial probability distribution. We assume a random sample of size n is taken from a Poisson population that has an average number of defective units, p', in a standard sample size. Then we use tables or graphs to calculate the probability of obtaining c or fewer defectives in the sample or of obtaining more than c defectives. This general approach is adopted here to derive a sampling plan.

First, let's summarize again the process of acceptance sampling. We wish to make an accept/reject decision about the overall quality of a large shipment of items. To avoid the high costs of 100 percent inspection, we devise a systematic sampling procedure in which only a randomly selected subset of the total shipment is inspected. The sampling plan consists of a sample size (n) and an acceptance number (c), and it is designed to provide us the level of risk protection that we desire. As we shall see, our choices of n and c are very important.

To determine suitable values for n and c, we need four additional items of information: *AQL*, *LTPD*, α, and β. *AQL* is conventional notation meaning "acceptable quality level," or "good" quality. *LTPD* is "lot tolerance percent defective," or "poor" quality level. Assigning numeric values to these four parameters is largely a matter of managerial judgment. As soon as their numeric values have been decided, values for n and c can be determined.

After we have specified what constitutes good and poor quality, we must specify acceptable degrees of risk for each type of error in our sampling plan. Alpha (α) is used to represent the probability we will tolerate for rejecting good (*AQL*) shipments. An $\alpha = .05$, for example, might be selected. Similarly, we specify a probability for the risk that our sampling plan will accept shipments of poor (*LTPD*) quality. This probability is represented by β; assume for this example that $\beta = .10$. The values of α and β are often negotiated but are commonly assumed to be .05 and .10.

Repeating the previous (Chapter 17) example for the pregnancy test kits (PTKs), let's derive the sampling plan that eventually called for $n = 308$, $c = 10$. First, the design parameters are identified: $AQL = .02$, $\alpha = .05$, $LTPD = .05$, $\beta = .10$.

TABLE S17.1
Factors for selecting a sampling plan (n and c) that approximates the desired *AQL* and *LTPD* when $\alpha = 0.05$ and $\beta = 0.10$*

c	$p'n_{0.95}$	$p'n_{0.10}$	$p'n_{0.10}/p'n_{0.95}$ = *LTPD/AQL*
0	0.051	2.30	45.10
1	0.355	3.89	10.96
2	0.818	5.32	6.50
3	1.366	6.68	4.89
4	1.970	7.99	4.06
5	2.613	9.28	3.55
6	3.285	10.53	3.21
7	3.981	11.77	2.96
8	4.695	12.99	2.77
9	5.425	14.21	2.62
10	6.169	15.41	2.50
11	6.924	16.60	2.40
12	7.690	17.78	2.31
13	8.464	18.96	2.24
14	9.246	20.13	2.18
15	10.04	21.29	2.12

*Source: Frank E. Grubbs, "On Designing Single Sampling Inspection Plans," *The Annals of Mathematical Statistics* (1949), p. 256.

Approximate values for n and c are found by calculating the desired ratio, *LTPD/AQL*, which in our example is $.05/.02 = 2.5$. From Table S17.1 (column 4) we find that $c = 10$ gives the desired ratio. Having found $c = 10$, we now find the desired sample size n. This is done by making two calculations using columns 2 and 3 of Table S17.1. First, the value of $p'n_{0.95}$ for $c = 10$ must be divided by *AQL*: $6.169/.02 = 308$, the suggested sample size n. What are we doing when we are making this calculation? We are finding a sample size n that gives a 0.95 probability of accepting a shipment that contains an *AQL* percent defective when $c = 10$. In Table S17.1, the values of $p'n_{0.95}$ have been precalculated from a Poisson probability chart, which will be shown below. The calculation made above is really $p'n_{0.95}/p' = n_{0.95}$ when p' is chosen to be at the *AQL* level.

The second required calculation is similar to the previous one, except that column 3, $p'n_{0.10}$, is used with *LTPD*. The value of $p'n_{0.10}$ for $c = 10$ is divided by *LTPD*: $15.41/.05 = 308$, the suggested sample size. This shows that a sample size of 308 gives a 0.10 probability of accepting a shipment that contains an *LTPD* (10 percent) percent defective when $c = 10$.

In our example, we were fortunate that both calculations led to a sample size of 308 units for $c = 10$. Often it is impossible to find one set of n and c that simultaneously satisfies all the desired design parameters α, *AQL*, β, and *LTPD*. In such cases we must be willing to sacrifice (modify)

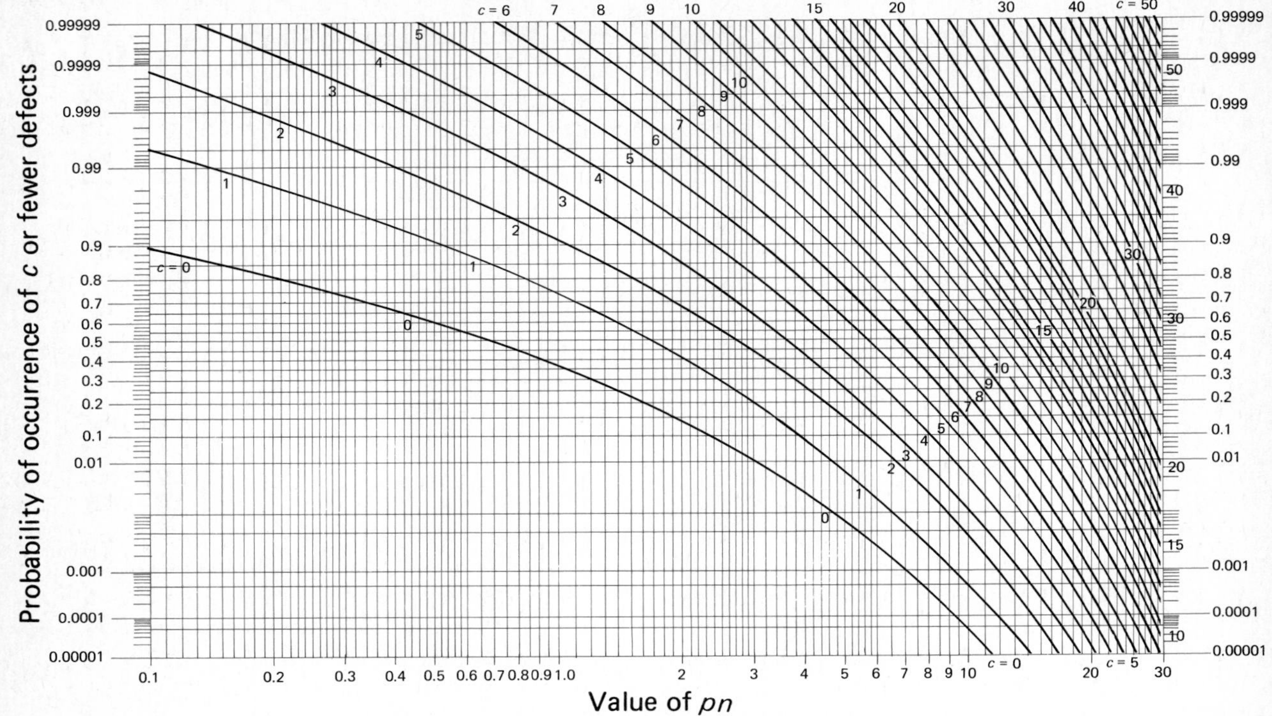

FIGURE S17.1
Probability curves for Poisson distribution

Source: H. F. Dodge and H. G. Romig, *Sampling Inspection Tables* (New York: John Wiley & Sons, Inc., 1959).

α or β, and the calculations become somewhat more tedious. If α or β is modified, we can no longer rely on the tabulated values in Table S17.1, since these apply only for $\alpha = 0.05$, $\beta = 0.10$. Instead we must use the Poisson probability chart, Figure S17.1. Let's use another example to illustrate.

Suppose we want a plan that satisfies the following: $AQL = 0.02$, $\alpha = 0.05$, $LTPD = 0.06$, $\beta = 0.10$. The desired ratio, $LTPD/AQL$, is $.06/.02 = 3.0$. From Table S17.1 (column 4) we find that the desired ratio falls between $c = 6$ and $c = 7$. Now we must evaluate four sampling plans that will come close to our desires. These are summarized in Table S17.2.

In plan 1, for $c = 6$, β is held at the desired value of 0.10, but the desired α is not obtained. In plan 2, α is held at the desired value of .05, but β deviates from the desired level. Corresponding conditions exist in plans 3 and 4, except that $c = 7$. For each plan an approximate sample size was obtained from the appropriate value in column 2 or 3 of Table S17.1.

TABLE S17.2
Four alternative sampling plans that approximate desired specifications

If $c = 6$		If $c = 7$	
Plan 1 $\beta = 0.10$ α modified	Plan 2 $\alpha = 0.05$ β modified	Plan 3 $\beta = 0.10$ α modified	Plan 4 $\alpha = 0.05$ β modified
$n = \frac{p'n_{0.10}}{LTPD}$ $= \frac{10.53}{.06}$ $= 175$	$n = \frac{p'n_{0.95}}{AQL}$ $= \frac{3.285}{.02}$ $= 164$	$n = \frac{p'n_{0.95}}{LTPD}$ $= \frac{11.77}{.06}$ $= 196$	$n = \frac{p'n_{0.95}}{AQL}$ $= \frac{3.981}{.02}$ $= 199$

Since either α or β has been modified in each plan, we must determine how much they have been changed. For example, plan 1 calls for $c = 6$ and $n = 175$. What value of α results? The answer can be found by calculating $p'n$ and entering this value in Figure S17.1. In this case $p'n = (AQL)\ (175) = (.02)(175) = 3.50$. After entering 3.50 at the bottom of the chart, we proceed upward until intersecting the curved line for $c = 6$. To the far left of this intersection we can read the probability of acceptance, 0.94. Hence, the α risk is $1.00 - 0.94 = .06$ for this plan. In a similar manner the unknown α or β for each plan has been calculated and summarized in Table S17.3.

Although all four plans come close to meeting desired specifications, none meets them exactly. As manager, you must choose the plan you feel is most suitable.

TABLE S17.3
Calculation of unknown α or β for each of four sampling plans

Plan 1	Plan 2	Plan 3	Plan 4
$\beta = 0.10$: determine α for $c = 6, n = 175$ $p'n = (AQL)\ (n)$ $= (.02)\ (175)$ $= 3.50$ Probability* of acceptance = .94 $\alpha = 0.06$	$\alpha = 0.05$; determine β for $c = 6, n = 164$ $p'n = (LTPD)\ (n)$ $= (.06)\ (164)$ $= 9.84$ Probability* of acceptance = .14 $\beta = 0.14$	$\beta = 0.10$: determine α for $c = 7, n = 196$ $p'n = (AQL)\ (n)$ $= (.02)\ (196)$ $= 3.92$ Probability* of acceptance = .955 $\alpha = 0.045$	$\alpha = 0.05$: determine β for $c = 7, n = 199$ $p'n = (LTPD)\ (n)$ $= (.06)\ (199)$ $= 11.94$ Probability* of acceptance = .095 $\beta = 0.095$

*Probability obtained from Figure S17.1.

Control Charts for Variables

In some situations we're interested in obtaining actual measurements of lengths, weights, or volumes. In these cases we use control charts for variables. Our discussion focuses on charts for controlling the process *average*.

Let x_i be the measured value for the ith unit in a sample of size n, and $\bar{x}$ be the average value of these n measurements. Now instead of sampling only once, suppose we sample m times and obtain m sample averages always picking samples of size n. Each sample average is then denoted as $\bar{x}_j$. We can then calculate the average and standard deviation of these sample averages. Equations S17.1 through S17.4 are the fundamental equations used for constructing a variables control chart.

$$\bar{x} = \frac{\sum_{i=1}^{n} x_i}{n} \quad \textbf{(S17.1)}$$

$$\bar{\bar{x}} = \frac{\sum_{j=1}^{m} \bar{x}_j}{m} \quad \textbf{(S17.2)}$$

$$s_{\bar{x}} = \sqrt{\frac{\sum_{j=1}^{m} (\bar{x}_j - \bar{\bar{x}})^2}{m - 1}} \quad \textbf{(S17.3)}$$

$$\text{Control limits (UCL and LCL)} = \bar{\bar{x}} \pm 3s_{\bar{x}} \quad \textbf{(S17.4)}$$

The control chart takes the form shown in the example below.

EXAMPLE

Micron Distribution Center, Inc., packages imported cameras in cartons for shipment to retailers throughout the United States. They wish to use adequate packing materials in each carton to minimize shipping and handling damage, but they do not want to overpack the cartons. Management has decided that current packing procedures are desirable and wants to document the current packing process for future comparisons. A control chart will be constructed given the following data, obtained by sampling the current packing process. Note that measurement is by variables (interval scaled data). We first find the sample averages when $\bar{x}_i = \Sigma x_i/n$, as shown in column 3.

Packing date	Ounces of packing material per carton (x_i)	Sample average ($\bar{x}_i$)
May 1	8, 7, 5, 9, 11	40/5 = 8.0
3	8, 8, 7, 7, 5	35/5 = 7.0
4	8, 4, 7, 13, 8	40/5 = 8.0
5	10, 12, 8, 9, 11	50/5 = 10.0
7	9, 9, 10, 9, 8	45/5 = 9.0

Then we find:

$$\bar{\bar{x}} = \frac{\Sigma \bar{x}_j}{m} = \frac{8.0 + 7.0 + 8.0 + 10.0 + 9.0}{5} = 8.4$$

$$s_{\bar{x}} = \sqrt{\frac{\Sigma(\bar{x}_j - \bar{\bar{x}})^2}{m - 1}} = \sqrt{\frac{(8.0 - 8.4)^2 + \ldots}{4}} = 1.2$$

$$UCL = \bar{\bar{x}} + 3s_{\bar{x}} = 8.4 + 3(1.2) = 12.0$$

$$LCL = \bar{\bar{x}} - 3s_{\bar{x}} = 8.4 - 3(1.2) = 4.8$$

Our packing material control chart, which can be used to plot future daily performance, is:

Sample average (ounces)		
	12.0	UCL
	8.4	$\bar{\bar{x}}$
	4.8	LCL

Time (days)

REVIEW AND DISCUSSION QUESTIONS

1. How does one's choice of AQL, LTPD, α, and β affect the cost of acceptance sampling?
2. How is the OC curve affected by changes in n and c?
3. Discuss the cost tradeoffs involved in selecting the control limits of a variables control chart.

PROBLEMS

1. Thompson Metal Works manufactures metal screws. The following shows the diameters for part #2735, a standard metal screw, the last time the part was produced two months ago.

Date	Screw diameters (cm)
8/5	0.5, 0.6, 0.4, 0.3
8/6	0.5, 0.5, 0.4, 0.6
8/7	0.7, 0.5, 0.5, 0.6
8/8	0.5, 0.5, 0.5, 0.5

   (a) Construct a control chart for the last production run.
   (b) A sample was taken today, the first day of production in two months on this part. Metal screws diameters were 0.5, 0.9, 0.5, 0.9. Based on the control chart developed above, what can you tell the general foreman about his process?

2. Your reputation as an analyst has gained widespread acclaim in the Allstate University athletic department. The basketball coach asks you to help him with the following problem. Coach Stewart believes that the lack of success of the team in

conference play has been because of the way nonconference foes defensed Smith (games 4–8) and the way conference foes defensed him (games 9–13). He gives you the following data concerning the average of Smith's first 11 shots of each game:

Game	Sample mean of distance from basket	Game	Sample mean of distance from basket
4	6.0	9	6.0
5	8.0	10	8.0
6	5.0	11	5.0
7	4.0	12	9.0
8	7.0	13	10.0

You are asked to apply what you have learned in quality control, viewing Smith's performance as a process. Provide Coach Stewart with an answer as to whether Smith's conference performance is in control based upon his performance during nonconference games.

3. The results of four samples concerning a shaft diameter were taken three weeks ago when our process was running smoothly ($n = 3$). It is shown here. Since then we have experienced a labor strike, and some business school students are running our production line. Results of two samples taken today are: sample 1—2.30, 2.15, and 1.91; sample 2—1.85, 1.87, 1.78. What can we tell our plant manager about the process today compared to our previous base? What does this mean he should now do? Support your decision with analysis.

Sample	Diameter (inches)		
1	2.10	2.08	1.96
2	1.97	1.98	2.05
3	1.95	1.91	1.98
4	2.07	2.08	2.03

4. As area coordinator of technical services in a large hospital, you notice the laboratory seems to have problems with a Serum Calcium Test, which is used to indicate a tendency for kidney stones. We are quite proud of the consistency of our tests but are not so sure about this test and would like to "track" our performance on it. We know our recent test results for five tests each day are:

Test date	Milligrams per 100 cc of Serum				
May 1	9,	8,	6,	8,	10
3	8,	8,	5,	7,	5
4	7,	3,	6,	12,	7
5	10,	8,	9,	8,	10
7	9,	9,	7,	9,	8

We know that doctors say the expected range is 8.5 to 10.5 milligrams per 100 cc of serum for healthy adults. Construct a control chart reflecting historical performance. How might you explain this control chart to laboratory technicians so they can benefit from it in the future (that is, explain the *interpretative value* of this tool to them)?

5. Peanuts, Inc., has asked you to check the automatic temperature control of its main baking oven; manufacturing personnel claim the control is broken. Having a business school background (and not an electrical engineering background), you have decided to approach the problem from a statistical quality control standpoint. You have gathered the following data.

Date	Sample mean of three temperature readings	Date	Sample mean of three temperature readings
6/1	120° F	7/26	125° F
6/2	122° F	7/27	127° F
6/3	116° F	7/28	128° F
6/4	118° F	7/29	131° F
6/5	124° F	7/30	131° F

Specifications:

Manufacturer's guarantee on equipment is for any setting between 100° F–150° F with a variance of ± 7° F from the setting.

Product (peanut) specifications are 120° F ± 5° F.

Specifically, you have been asked to determine as of 7/31 if Peanuts, Inc., has a baking oven problem. If so, what do you recommend?

6. Construct OC curves for the following sampling plans:
(a) $n = 100, c = 1$
(b) $n = 200, c = 2$
(c) $n = 300, c = 3$

7. Construct OC curves for the following sampling plans:
(a) $n = 100, c = 1$
(b) $n = 100, c = 2$
(c) $n = 100, c = 3$

8. Find an acceptance sampling plan that meets the following specifications:

$$\alpha = .05 \qquad AQL = .01$$
$$\beta = .10 \qquad LTPD = .08$$

9. Find an acceptance sampling plan that meets the following specifications:

$$\alpha = .03 \qquad AQL = .01$$
$$\beta = .05 \qquad LTPD = .08$$

18 The Conversion Process in Change

With vast reserves of coal in the United States amounting to over a 300-year supply at today's consumption rates, and with domestic oil reserves being used faster than they were being replaced, an economical method of utilizing coal as a fuel, with minimal environmental impact, was a goal sought by many. This "external" need caused "internal" reaction at Texaco, Inc.

Texaco research studied ways to utilize the energy from this traditionally dirty fuel in a clean, environmentally acceptable manner. A new "Alternate Energy" department was formed to evaluate all forms of non-petroleum energy, but primarily to commercialize Texaco's proprietary coal gasification technology, and to develop new business opportunities based on this clean, competitive process.

The Texaco gasification process is capable of producing a clean synthesis gas from a number of different coal feed stocks. The most recent commercial venture using coal gasification was with Southern California Edison Company, located in the Mojave Desert at Daggett, California. Called the "Cool Water Coal Gasification Program," it brought in additional participants to help design and construct the facility, such as General Electric Company, Electric Power Research Institute, Bechtel Power Corporation, Japan Cool Water Program Partnership, and others. The Cool Water facility was completed in 1984, ahead of schedule and under budget, and began the production of electricity as the nation's first such commercial-scale power plant. This 120-megawatt plant is capable of serving the energy needs of about 100,000 households.

Indeed, external forces can, and do, create internal reactions.

S. Keith McSpadden, Director, Human Resources
Texaco, Inc., White Plains, New York

Organizations and their conversion subsystems are dynamic. Both because there always seems to be room for further improvement and because new demands are placed on the organization from various sources, managerial processes and actions are continually in motion. At Texaco, the external need for clean coal gasification brought about change of considerable magnitude. Managerial action prompted new research, the formation of a new department, and the development of new business opportunities for Texaco. To make improvements and meet new demands, managers must make changes. Whether large or small, changes are the rule rather than the exception. A continual process, change becomes a way of life in the organization. Because it is so pervasive and has important effects on system operation and output, change deserves special consideration by the manager.

Open Versus Closed Systems

Both "closed" and "open" systems concepts have been used in our coverage of P/OM. Conceptually, a closed system is a self-contained entity within a definable boundary. Within the boundary are the interrelated subcomponents of the system. Since it is self-contained, the system does not depend on exchanges of inputs and outputs with its environment. It is sealed off from environmental encroachments. In introducing the operations subsystem, we have often treated it as if it were a *closed* system consisting of many separate subcomponents. In this way we have been able to concentrate on basic concepts of selected problems faced by the operations manager and to learn about these problems in an uncomplicated manner.

The open system, on the other hand, exchanges energy and/or matter with its environment. Although it retains its unique wholeness, it is an integral part of the larger environment; its continued viability requires that the system adjust to the varied energy inputs from the environment. All organizations can realistically be viewed as open systems—systems that are integral parts of larger social systems. In Figure 18.1, our general framework, inputs, outputs, and random fluctuations are the only representations of environment/subsystem exchanges.

In this chapter the emphasis shifts from analysis to synthesis. We wish to emphasize the dynamics of operations that arise from system interrelationships and to stress the openness of the operations subsystem to the environment. We hope to enable you to recognize how the need for change occurs and why adjustments in the subsystem are necessary for survival.

SYSTEM INTERRELATIONSHIPS

Change's ultimate effects on the organization revolve around the interrelationships inherent in such systems. Three types of interrelationships are readily apparent: the subfunctions of the management process, the functional areas of the organization, and the basic operations problems.

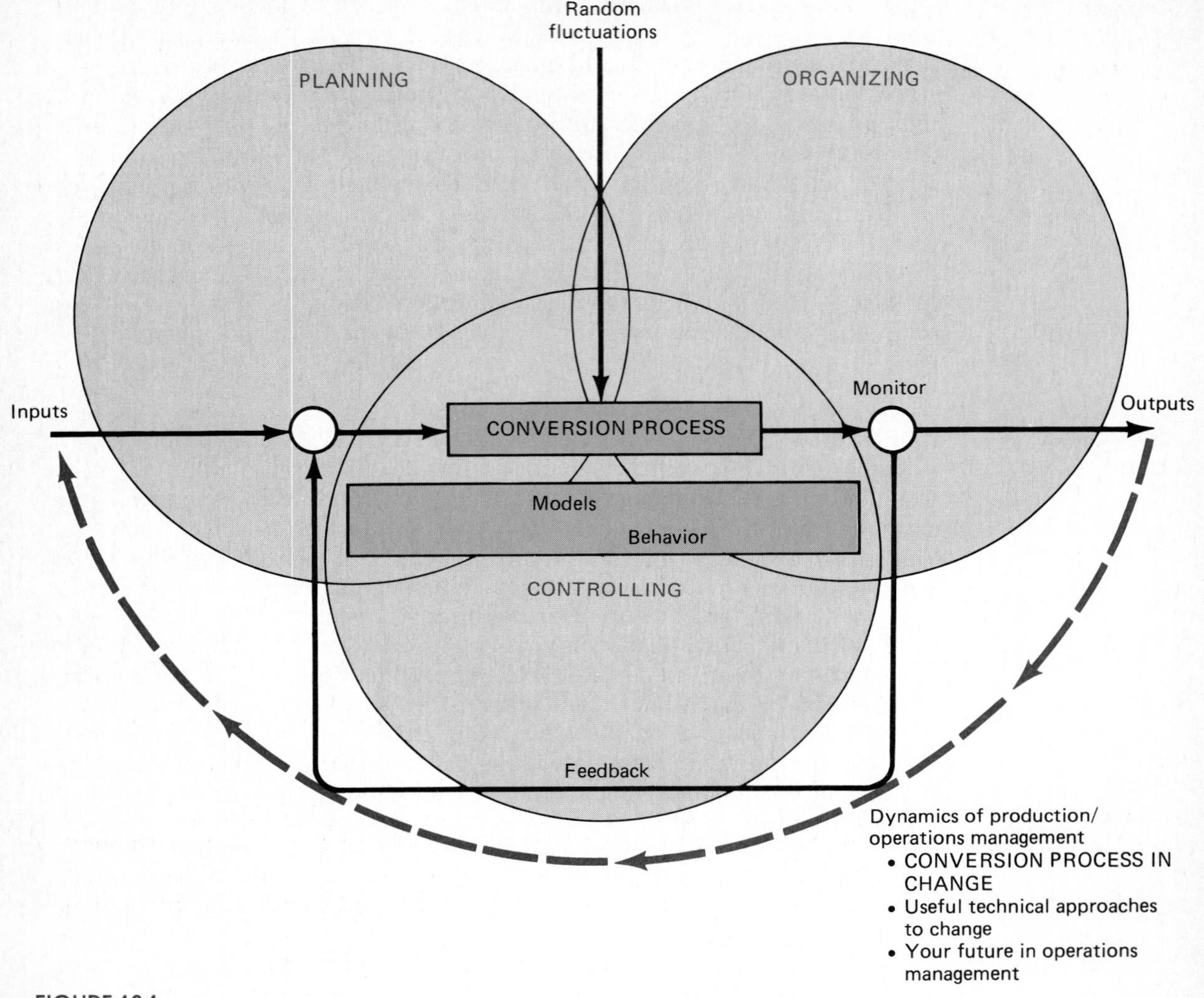

FIGURE 18.1
General model for production/operations management

Subfunctions of the Management Process

Throughout this book we have emphasized the planning, organizing, and controlling subfunctions of the managerial process and their interrelationships. Since these are complementary activities, changes in any one can cause corresponding adjustments in the others. New control procedures necessitate replanning and possibly reorganizing. Changes in plans necessitate reallocating resources, which involves reconsideration of authority/responsibility relationships and the design of control processes. A change in one subfunction introduces the prospect of changes in the others.

Functional Areas of the Organization

In the production/operations subsystem, we cannot overemphasize our interdependence with the other subsystems, including marketing and finance. Consider the implications of a major marketing decision, the introduction of a new product or service. This change introduces accompanying changes in operations; changes in the conversion process, including job design and the organization structure, must be made. These conversion changes then necessitate further changes in the finance subsystem, because sources of capital and credit must be arranged and working capital and cash flow requirements must be estimated.

When new processing innovations occur, they cannot be adopted unilaterally within the operations subsystem. The decision to change must be made jointly after management has ascertained that the necessary investment meets the organization's return requirements and that the financial resource requirement is feasible.

For manufacturing firms that produce several products, there are efficiency advantages to producing large quantities of one before changing over to produce another. When the operations manager decides to deviate from past changeover practices, the effects are felt in the marketing and finance areas. The marketing and distribution function may find shortages of some products and excess quantities of others relative to market demand. Similarly, a new promotional campaign by marketing may necessitate that traditional production schedules be revised so that output is coordinated with anticipated market response. In these and many other ways, changes in one functional area can have an impact on others.

Basic Operations Problems

Because the basic operations problem areas are interrelated within an operations subsystem, changes in one facet stimulate changes in others. New inventory control doctrines result in output scheduling changes. New location decisions affect procurement and delivery lead time requirements and may result in new transactions patterns among units in the production/distribution system. Changes in product quality specifications may mean that employees must be retrained, jobs redesigned, equipment and processes renovated, and inventory control doctrines changed. Let us consider an inventory/scheduling example to illustrate how a change in one area can affect changes in others.

EXAMPLE

An assembly department uses component part number *X*131, which is manufactured in the fabrication department. Historically, the assembly department supervisor orders an optimal quantity (Q^*) of 10,000 units and uses them at a constant rate of 200 units per day (d). The fabrication department requires a five-day lead time (after receiving the request) before it can begin producing and supplying the units at a continuous rate of 500 units per day (p). Thus, the assembly department uses a reorder point of 1,000 units, just enough to meet its assembly needs for five days until the new shipment begins to arrive from fabrication. This same pattern of ordering and replenishment, shown in Figure 18.2, has existed for several years. Because of changes in inventory-related costs, the assembly supervisor has decided to begin using a new optimal order quantity of 15,000 units.

Historically, the fabrication supervisor has been accustomed to twenty days of productive time being devoted to manufacturing component *X*131. During the remaining thirty days of the cycle, the fabrication department is scheduled to work on jobs for other customers. How is the fabrication schedule affected by the assembly supervisor's revision of order quantity? The new order quantity (15,000 units) will require thirty instead of twenty days of productive time in fabrication. Since annual demand for *X*131 is unchanged, the number of orders placed per year will be smaller than they were, but the run lengths will be longer. Because established scheduling patterns have been disrupted, the fabrication supervisor must determine

FIGURE 18.2
Existing inventory pattern for component *X*131 in assembly department

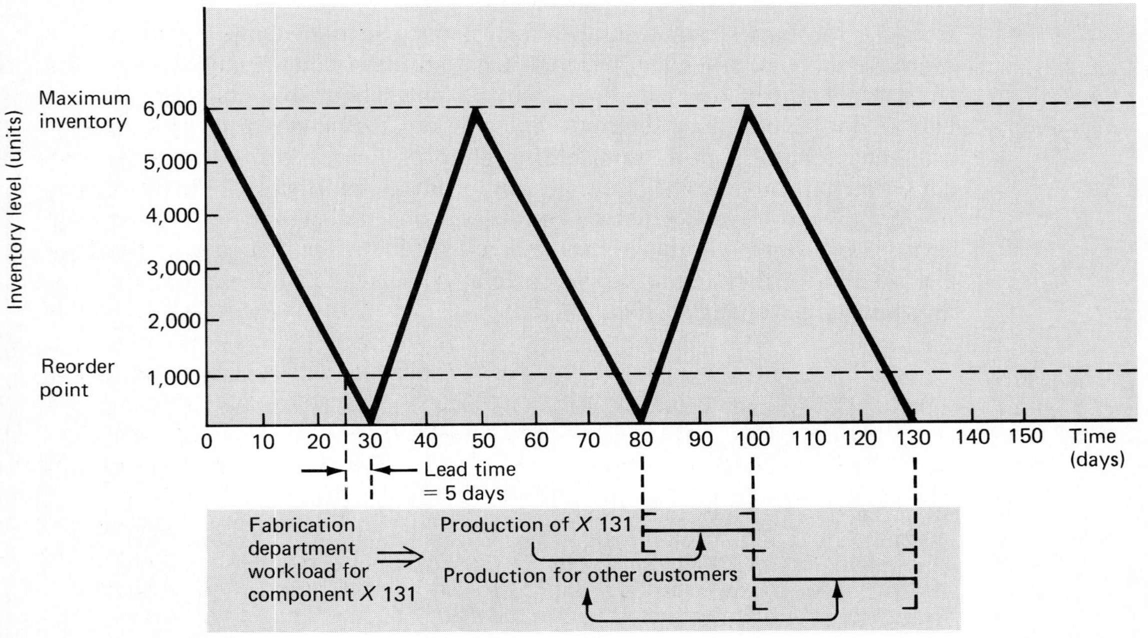

how to schedule other jobs through the department so that a smooth, efficient overall flow of jobs will result. You can think of the impact of this change on the functional areas of finance and marketing as well.

Japanese manufacturing firms emphasize Just-in-Time (JIT) production where the *exact* product quantity demanded by the customer is manufactured *just-in-time* for consumption. This dictates ever decreasing production lot sizes. JIT manufacturers suggest a lot size of one as their goal and, for all practical purposes, set the *maximum* lot size as one-tenth of a day's production. This forces rapid response at a low change-over cost to manufacturers. Clearly, the fabrication supervisor in our example above would be faced by tremendous changes, as would his company, were JIT procedures adopted by the firm.

In light of the many considerations we've discussed, it is no surprise to find that organizations are often hesitant to change; sometimes they avoid dramatic change until it becomes an absolute necessity. It is more comfortable to live with established relationships than to face the uncertainties that accompany change. Most managers give careful consideration to the types of interrelationships we've discussed before they initiate change.

DYNAMICS OF PRODUCTION/OPERATIONS MANAGEMENT

Changes in the conversion process do not occur one at a time. Usually, multiple changes of various magnitudes are occurring simultaneously. Further, these changes are not independent of one another; changes in one part result in changes in other parts. Some of these "ripple" effects are predictable; others are not. In short, organizational change can rapidly become a "can of worms" if not approached cautiously. The complexities of change present a management dilemma. Management desires a predictable or stable conversion process that allows the goal of economic efficiency to be met; nevertheless, as an open system we must recognize the need for changes in order to remain a viable organization. As a production/operations manager, you must strike a proper balance between stability and adaptability in your organization. If you understand the dynamics of organizational change, you may be able to balance stability and adaptability in a more enlightened way. For these reasons we suggest a somewhat systematic approach to studying the dynamics of the conversion process. The framework we suggest is shown in Figure 18.3, in which the broad dimensions of change flow from left to right. Recognition of the need for change, targets for change, the change process, and the desired results of change are distinct phases usually identifiable in any change situation. In Figure 18.3 we have shaded behavioral targets for change, as these targets will be discussed later in this chapter.

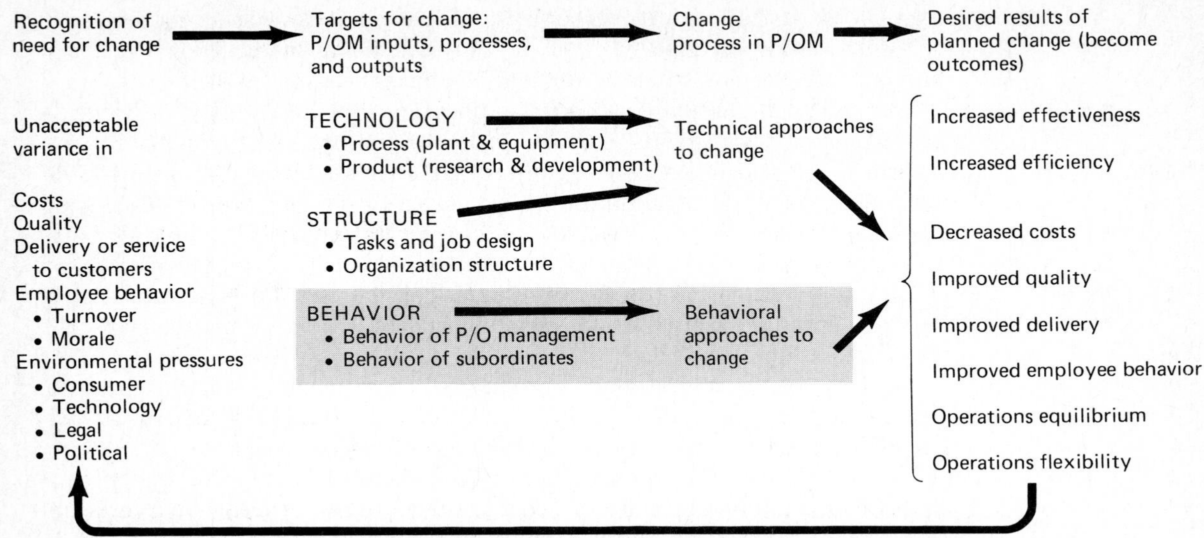

FIGURE 18.3
Dynamics of production/operations management: the conversion process in change

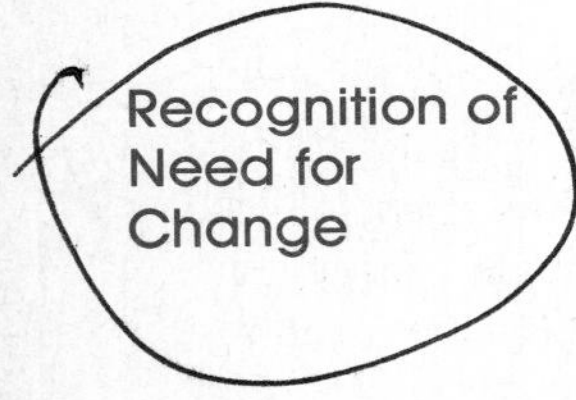

Recognition of Need for Change

Before we can plan and initiate change, we have to recognize that a change is needed, and we have to know why it is needed. Indicators that change is needed can come from internal sources or from sources that are external to the organization. Random fluctuations, unplanned and/or uncontrollable environmental influences that tend to cause actual output to differ from planned output in the conversion process, are necessary in our model because they happen so often in reality. We may have to make changes to meet existing organizational goals; or it may be necessary to change the goals themselves.

Internal Indicators The conversion process operates to meet predetermined goals and sets performance standards that are consistent with goal attainment. Most commonly, management establishes goals for profitability, product quality, customer service, and commitments to employees. It is not surprising, then, that measures that are closely related to these goals are the primary internal indicators of the need for change. Some of the most commonly used indicators are:

- costs
- product quality
- delivery or service to customers
- employee behaviors

Some of these indicators are readily quantifiable; others are not. Reports of direct and indirect labor expenses (costs), scrap rates (quality), and employee absences and quitting rates (employee behaviors), for example, are usually reported periodically in standard report forms. These can easily be compared against performance standards, and deviations can be noted and investigated. Some indicators are much more subtle, however. Not all costs are recognized; some aspects of product quality or customer service are not conveniently measurable; and employee dissatisfaction may surface in nonquantifiable form. When the indicators are subtle, formal change may not occur until the underlying problem magnifies itself. By this time, remedial changes may be very costly to implement, much more so than if the indicators had been recognized earlier. Sometimes the change is made even though the need for it is not formally recognized.

EXAMPLE

Operations employs a major, if not majority, portion of the employees in a typical business or governmental unit. Employee absenteeism is a major, largely unresolved, business problem and therefore a major operations management problem. Other cultures, such as the Japanese, are less permissive than North American companies, demanding a commitment to the firm that results in docking pay and quick dismissal for absenteeism. British and other European firms tend to approach North American permissiveness regarding absenteeism and productivity suffers.

Studies estimate absenteeism to equate to a cost of 1.75 times the average daily pay, $150/employee per percent absent per year (1972 dollars), or $66 per day (1977 dollars) per person-day of absenteeism. A recent study traces the impact of absenteeism on added overtime costs, carrying extra employees and inventory quantity, schedule upheavals, and other operating charges.[1] In a representative, but hypothetical, example for a company with $6.5 million in annual sales, 100 employees, a $7.0/hour wage rate, and a 5 percent absenteeism rate, absenteeism costs totaled $154,385 for the year. These costs totaled 12.5 percent of total direct labor costs, $1543 per direct employee, $140.35 cost per day per employee, 2.5 times average daily pay, and 0.64 percent of total production costs.

[1]Ken Kivenko, "Employee Absenteeism—The Deterioration of Productivity," *Production and Inventory Management Review* 4, no. 5 (May 1984), pp. 52–55 and p. 70.

What is the point of all the absenteeism statistics above? Our point is that an internal indicator, like 5 percent absenteeism, can have far-reaching operations cost consequences that are not normally quantified in day-to-day reporting. A need for change can exist, in this case a behavioral need, and it can gradually increase in significance without management action. The astute operations manager must pick up on such indicators and express them as costs that upper management can understand, and therefore gain support for the needed change.

External Indicators In general, the conversion process is designed to enable efficient operation shielded from external impingements. The system can never be totally closed, however; as the external environment changes, it imposes changes on internal operations. An obvious example is the change in consumer tastes and desires in a competitive market. If video recorders and players are the rage, organizations with the technological and financial capability will begin producing video units if they wish to establish or improve their market position.

In some instances, external indicators arise in a more direct way. This is particularly true in service industries making products to suit the needs of particular customers. Here a close degree of customer-supplier cooperation results in new product designs. Changes in products or processes are often made on a regular basis.

Besides consumer tastes and technological innovations, there are other significant environmental sources of change. Broad societal changes in values are often reflected in new laws and governmental regulations that require compliance. Today's concern over environmental pollution has a direct impact on the internal operations of most organizations. Scarce energy resources force changes that have been of little concern to operations managers in the past. Legal and political pressures for changes are also evident to the perceptive production/operations manager.

Targets for Change

Once the need for change has been recognized, the manager can identify one or more aspects of the conversion process that must be modified, including the technology, the organization structure, or employee behavior in the conversion process.

Technology The technology consists of the physical or mental processes by which conversion from inputs to outputs is accomplished. The technology for manufacturing refrigerators is dominated by cutting, forming, and assembling of sheet metal, manufacturing electronic and mechanical components, assembly (including the compressors and refrigeration components), painting, and packing. The technology of an automatic car wash includes soap and water sprays, roller brushes, chain drives, and blower-dryers.

In dental clinics, the human components of the technology are more directly visible. Knowledge and skills of dentists and technicians are directly witnessed by the customer (patient). The physical aspects of the dentist's technology range from materials used in treating the patient (drilling equipment, teeth-cleaning preparations, and so on) to elaborate laboratory equipment never seen by the patient.

Changes directed primarily toward the technology often involve redesign of plant and equipment to process existing products as new processes or materials are developed. The development of plastics, for example, resulted in displacement of many refrigerator components formerly made of metals. This necessitated the replacement of metal rolling and forming with plastics extrusion processes. The decision to switch from one processing technology to another can be analyzed in part from an engineering/economic viewpoint. Some methods for doing this will be presented in the next chapter.

Often, the basic product itself must be modified to meet changing consumer needs or to comply with external requirements. The annual model changes and new product introductions practiced by many industries are examples. In fact, one way to compete in some industries is to be effective in quick development, manufacture, and delivery of new products (operations flexibility). The product line, consequently, is very volatile. In the manufacturing equipment industry, it is not unusual for customer-supplier cooperation to produce new designs, features of which will be incorporated in future editions of the supplier's "regular" products. In these cases operating system effectiveness is measured in terms of flexibility, the ability to work with product and customer engineers to develop and manufacture unique products that, in some cases, are later produced in volume. Often, then, new products and processes are necessary from a strategic viewpoint.

Structure Sometimes the organization structure, tasks and jobs within the oranization, become the targets for change. When costs, quality, or employee satisfaction indicates that changes are warranted, individual jobs may be redesigned. Job analysis and work methods studies may reveal that some job elements should be eliminated, others simplified, and still others expanded. Task redesign may also be appropriate when new products and processes are developed. Unless the new product is very similar to the old one, old tasks cannot simply be reapplied to new products.

At a broader level, the entire organizational structure may need changing. If goals are not met, new departments and divisions may be formed and old ones dissolved. Perhaps the quality control function may be reassigned from the manager of manufacturing to the vice-president of operations to obtain higher level control. Job shop scheduling and dispatching may be centralized to improve overall shop throughput; or a new customer relations department may be created to improve service to customers.

New products and technological changes may also necessitate structural adjustments. Many manufacturing organizations have created environmental engineering groups to redesign conversion processes and facilities so that environmental contamination is reduced. The computer expertise developed by many organizations has led to computer services departments that serve not only the operations function but the other functional areas of the organization as well.

As companies grow and product markets expand, structures are changed accordingly. Organizations may diversify along product lines to gain greater efficiencies; others may decentralize as a means of developing future managerial skills and experience. In Chapter 19 we will show how "system dynamics" models can be used to evaluate the effects of structural changes like these.

Behavior From the operations manager's viewpoint, behavior is a third target for change. Very often, goal attainment is possible by modifying employee behavior rather than by changing the technology or the structure of the conversion process. Product quality and efficiency goals may be enhanced through on-the-job training of operative employees. These training efforts are designed to modify behavior in favorable directions. Similarly, managerial effectiveness can be improved by development and training programs in such areas as decision making, leadership, and employee/supervisor relationships.

When behavior is the primary target for change the manager may use several change strategies. How successful the change is depends upon human learning capabilities and the reinforcement/reward procedure that is used. These procedures and the methods by which change is introduced affect how readily change is accepted or resisted in the organization.

The Change Process in Production/Operations

Obviously, the three targets for change are not independent of one another. Of the three, behavioral change is the most pervasive. It is difficult to conceive of technological and structural changes that do not also result in the need for behavioral change. Consider the computerized checkout systems in many large hardware stores and supermarkets. The technological change from the old system to the new one brought about the need for modified skills and behaviors of employees, particularly as they relate to inventory procedures. Previously, inventory counts of shelf items were periodically updated by hand. In the computer-based system, each transaction is recorded by stock number at the cash register, where inventory levels are updated and reordering may be automatic. Store managers and other employees now focus their skills and efforts on other tasks than counting stock items. Certainly some retraining and reorientation of work behavior are required when such a change is made. Because the behavioral process involved in change has special overall importance, we will discuss it next in some detail.

The Behavioral Change Process

As shown in Figure 18.3, the behavioral change process includes:

1. Recognition of the need for change.
2. Identification of the behavioral targets for change by production/operations managers and/or their subordinates.
3. Decision to change in a certain way.
4. Strategy for change; the behavioral approach toward change.
5. Implementation of the behavioral change; the actual changing of behaviors of participants in the production process.

We have already pointed out how to recognize the need for change. Let's examine steps 2 through 5 of the behavioral change process, concentrating not only on the process itself but on dealing with resistance to it and management's role in changing behavior for the good of the organization. But before we do, let's look at one alternative change model.

Thaw-Move-Refreeze An alternative change model that is perhaps the most widely accepted model of the change process in management involves thawing (or unfreezing) current activities, moving (or changing) to the desired activities and resulting outcomes, and then refreezing activities so the changes will be permanent.[2] This model is not inconsistent with the planned change model of Figure 18.3 and the behavioral change process above. Key differences are the need to soften or *thaw* (a way to get the change process ready to take), and the idea of *refreezing*. We'll discuss reinforcement processes directed at this refreezing. The idea that changes must be institutionalized as a regular way of behaving and operating is an excellent concept for operations managers to grasp.

Behavioral Targets for Change

Consistently, experienced P/O managers find that *it is the reblending of behaviors—the behaviors of labor (the operative worker) and management (operations managers at all levels)—that is the most difficult and challenging of all change problems.* Typical engineering problems faced by production managers can be approached on the basis of scientific and economic rationality. Behavioral change problems, however, are an altogether different story. Behavioral change involves people, and people have emotions. Futher, we often find that in order for managers to change their subordinates, they must change themselves first. Therefore, as production and operations managers, you must think of behavioral change in terms not only of your subordinates but of yourselves as well.

Strategies for Behavioral Change

Three distinct strategies have been suggested for changing behavior.[3] As we discuss them, remember that they may help managers change the behaviors of both supervisors and operative workers.

Empirical-rational Strategies Empirical-rational strategies assume that people are rational, that they will act in their own self-interest. If managers wish to advance change, they should show employees that the change is not only desirable for the organization but for the employees' self-interest too. When employees understand that change will benefit them, they will change their behavior.

Assume, for example, that a line foreman is personally rewarded when the production costs of his unit are acceptable. If the foreman is shown rework and scrap cost reports indicating that his department ex-

---

[2]For a more complete discussion of this change model see Charles N. Greene, Everett E. Adam, Jr., and Ronald J. Ebert, "Organization Change and Development," *Management for Effective Performance* (Englewood Cliffs, N.J.: Prentice-Hall, Inc., 1985), Chapter 14.

[3]Robert Chin and Kenneth D. Benne, "General Strategies for Effecting Changes in Human Systems," in *The Planning of Change,* 3rd ed., Warren G. Bennis, Kenneth D. Benne, Robert Chin, and Kenneth E. Corey, eds. (New York: Holt, Rinehart, and Winston, Inc., 1976), pp. 22–45. Alternative strategies are identified by Greene, Adam, and Ebert that relate the change strategy to change interventions. Ibid., Chapter 14, Figure 14.6.

ceeds plant average, he will logically decrease his costs by improving quality because it is in his own self-interest to do so. How will he do this? By explaining to subordinates that it is in their self-interest to improve quality; that is, by using the same empirical-rational approach with them that was used with him.

Normative-reeducative Strategies Normative-reeducative strategies build upon the empirical-rational strategies. Besides assuming that workers are rational, these strategies presume that people act as a result of attitudes and values they have acquired over time. Thus changing behavior involves not only presenting people with facts in their own self-interest but changing their attitudes, skills, and relationships as well.

Suppose that a foreman, for example, has long believed that quantitative analysis is useless for managing product quality. Under this strategy, the foreman might be sent to a series of application sessions teaching the essentials of sampling and statistical inference. If in these sessions the foreman's own data were used to make up control charts and demonstrate sampling, he might begin to change his attitude toward quantitative analysis.

Power-coercive Strategy This strategy is based on the concept of the application of political, economic, or some other form of power. Power can be legitimate (the proper use of delegated authority), or it can be informal (without formal organization sanction). Often, power is simply the effective use of leadership and position in the organization. In other cases, power may be brought to bear on individuals from peer groups, informal leaders, economic realities, or fear (fear of job loss, for example). Whatever its form, the result is the same; power can be a very effective way to bring about changes in individual and group behavior.

One good example of power to bring about change in production/operations management is in the collective bargaining process. The production/operations manager has the economic power to bring about change in seniority and management rights, among other things. The union, through the threat of collective withdrawal of labor, has the power to bargain for higher wages and improved fringe benefits, should they elect to do so, at the expense of seniority and management rights.

The Learning Process

Employee behaviors evolve in the learning process with the adoption of new skills, attitudes, and experiences. Given a new task, employees will learn. The question is whether they will adopt behaviors that are beneficial to the organization or behaviors that are disruptive.

Reinforcement In the learning process, the critical determinants of adopted behaviors are the *environmental consequences of those behaviors*. These consequences are called reinforcers.

Positive reinforcers are pleasant, rewarding, and satisfying; they serve to increase the probability that the behavior (response sequence) will occur again. Negative reinforcers are usually unpleasant, undersirable, and even painful. Generally, behaviors with positive consequences tend to be repeated when the situation reoccurs; behaviors with negative consequences tend to be abandoned.

Behavioral Effects of Reinforcement Schedules Not only the reinforcement itself but also its timing are important. One study notes:

> The effectiveness of a given reinforcer will depend upon its magnitude, its quality, the degree to which it has been associated with other reinforcers, and the manner in which it is scheduled. As a matter of fact, the effectiveness will depend as much upon its *scheduling* as upon any of its other features.
>
> A schedule of reinforcement is a more-or-less formal specification of the occurrence of a reinforcer in relation to the behavioral sequence to be conditioned. It is fairly easy, even for individuals with a minimum of training, to follow specified schedules of reinforcement in order to generate predictable behavioral patterns.[4]

Schedules of reinforcement may be either continuous or intermittent. Continuous reinforcement occurs after every response sequence that has been chosen for conditioning. Consider a new employee on a mass production line who completes hundreds of units daily. Although many units are assembled correctly, others are not. Under continuous reinforcement, a foreman would observe every unit and provide either a positive or a negative reinforcer. This rarely, if ever, occurs in production/operations because of time and resource limitations. More often, reinforcement is intermittent, occurring occasionally after the response sequence (the behavior). Under continuous reinforcement conditions, although learning takes place more quickly, so does extinction (forgetting the response and reinforcement relationship) once the reinforcement is withdrawn.

Intermittent reinforcement schedules are grouped into fixed interval, variable interval, fixed ratio, or variable ratio classifications. Interval schedules are tied to a time dimension; ratio schedules are tied to the number of responses. In *fixed interval* schedules, reinforcement occurs regularly after a fixed period of time has elapsed. In *variable interval* schedules, the time interval between reinforcements varies. *Fixed ratio* schedules provide reinforcement after a fixed, preplanned number of responses, after each one hundred units of output, for example. *Variable ratio* reinforcements are staggered to occur after various numbers of responses have been made.

Typically, production/operations managers reinforce and are themselves reinforced on variable rather than on fixed schedules. Because of the time pressures in operations, managers can't be committed to fixed reinforcement schedules. In fact, this is all to the good, because when reinforce-

[4]Everett E. Adam, Jr., and W. E. Scott, "The Application of Behavioral Conditioning Procedures to the Problems of Quality Control," *The Academy of Management Journal* 14, no. 2 (June 1971), pp. 175–93.

ment schedules are variable, behavior patterns, once they have been learned, tend to persist.

Since our interest is changing behavior, we can draw several conclusions from what we've discussed so far. First, new behavior patterns are learned fastest with continuous, or nearly continuous, reinforcement schedules. Second, behavior patterns that have been learned under variable intermittent reinforcement schedules are the most difficult to change. Third, negative reinforcement, when properly administered, can be effective. When punishment (the infliction of pain or discomfort) is administered, however, the consequences can be disastrous. Let's look a little closer at punishment and its consequences in operations.

Punishment There is research to suggest that punishment, under differing circumstances, may increase occurrences of undesirable behavior, cause it to last longer, be a short-lived deterrent, cause people to vary their behavior but be unable to control the direction of the new behavior, and arouse negative feelings. On the other hand, mild punishment may help improve behavior by at least providing negative feedback on performance.[5] Since the effects of punishment are unpredictable and often adverse, we think it might be better to use positive reinforcement instead.

EXAMPLE

Two foremen in the same production facility employed different reward systems, each beyond normal organizational rewards. The first foreman seemed always upset and irritated at his subordinates, verbally admonishing them for any small reason, often hours or days after the behavior. His employees tended to ignore his behavior and react neither negatively nor positively over time. The second foreman administered praise and/or candy to his workers intermittently. He was very careful and always praised or offered a piece of candy after outstanding behavior. He was one of the most highly thought of, successful foremen in the facility, and his department was very productive.

Now, of course we aren't recommending that every foreman lay in a supply of candy. The success of the second foreman's reward system resulted not from the magnitude of the reward but from its *systematic administration*. He almost always reinforced acceptable behavior, and often in the presence of others. The real reward was recognition. This is not to say that punishment never brings about beneficial change; but dysfunctional consequences are also a distinct possibility.

---

[5]See Timothy W. Costello and Sheldon S. Zalkind, *Psychology in Administration* (Englewood Cliffs, N.J.: Prentice-Hall, Inc., 1963), pp. 215–16.

Extinction Much of the research in behavior modification suggests that desirable behaviors should be rewarded and undesirable behaviors ignored. When positive reinforcement is withdrawn, behaviors supposedly extinguish—but often only after an initial increase in the response that is seeking the old reinforcement. If the employee is unaware that the old response-reinforcement contingency has ended, he may continue, even intensify, the old response. This might occur, for example, when rewards to the employee come from the task itself. These intrinsic rewards are part of the task being performed. One of these, the "batch traction," is the worker's feeling that he should finish a group of units or a specific part of a task before he takes a voluntary rest period. Seeing a task through to completion results in a pleasant, positive reinforcement. At times, these kinds of intrinsic reinforcements can conflict with extrinsic reinforcements.

EXAMPLE

Although a manager stresses quality on a daily basis to employees, the employee also enjoys the batch traction effect of seeing quantities of finished products pile up in front of him. As the "to-be-done" pile diminishes and the "finished" pile builds up, the employee tends to let quality slip at the expense of quantity for the final units in the lot. This quality/quantity tradeoff exists for many routine, repetitive tasks.

Resistance to Change

We suggest that you change behavior by altering positive reinforcers and placing behavior under positive control. The potential for conflict among positive reinforcers suggests that it is important for management to communicate *current* response-reinforcement contingencies clearly.

There are all sorts of reasons why people are reluctant to change. Positive reinforcers for current behavior patterns encourage us to continue acting as we are. Perhaps we're afraid of failing at something new. People like the stability afforded by established patterns of relationships in their personal and professional lives. The security we feel from orderly and familiar ways of doing things can be threatened by change, and so can our status, authority, autonomy, and discretion. Change sometimes makes old skills obsolete and requires us to develop new skills. In general, there are four basic reasons for resisting change:

1. Economic factors—a threat to economic security, such as losing a job.
2. Inconvenience—a threat of making life more difficult, such as having to learn new ways of doing things that were formerly done routinely.
3. Uncertainty—a threat of not knowing the implications of forthcoming change.
4. Interpersonal relationships—a threat of disrupting or destroying customary social relationships, group standards, or socially valued skills.

If training for change disrupts the current work flow, resistance to change is intensified. Work will be initially disrupted, and higher operating costs can be expected temporarily. The initiator of change must be prepared to accept these added costs. Employee resistance is high at these initial stages; often the employee does not clearly perceive the need for change in the first place. All he knows is that he is now further behind in his work.

Resistance behaviors may take a variety of forms, including aggression, withdrawal, or regression. These manifest themselves in higher absenteeism, requests for transfer, sabotage, or a series of emotional outbursts. To illustrate resistance, let's look at a classic research study. Although conducted in the 1940s, the study is still valid for today's organizations.

Harwood Manufacturing Company The study site was the main plant of the Harwood Manufacturing Company, which produced pajamas.[6] Harwood employed some 500 women and 100 men. The purpose of the research was to investigate two questions. Why do people resist change so strongly? What can be done to overcome this resistance?

The plant had an outstanding personnel program with minimal labor unrest and no movement toward unionization. The company worked hard to maintain good employee relations at all levels. Payment was on an incentive system, with an allowance for changing to a new job to offset decreased efficiency during the learning period. Despite this allowance, however, attitudes toward job change in the factory were negative. Turnover was high for employees who were changed to another job; they quit rather than learn a new set of tasks. Among employees who were transferred and remained, these feelings were standard:

> In addition to resentment against the management for transferring them, the employees typically show feelings of frustration, loss of hope of ever regaining their former level of production and status in the factory, feelings of failure, and a very low level of aspiration. In this respect, these transferred operators are similar to . . . chronically slow workers . . .

The researchers felt that the most appropriate methods for overcoming resistance to change would be group methods. Therefore, they designed several experiments. The first experiment involved three degrees of participation among groups to be transferred to new jobs:

1. No participation in planning changes; this group was simply told that its members would be transferred to new jobs.
2. Participation through representation; this group selected one member to help design the new jobs.
3. Total participation by all group members in designing their new jobs.

[6]Lester Coch and John R. P. French, Jr., "Overcoming Resistance to Change," *Human Relations* 1 (1948), pp. 512–32.

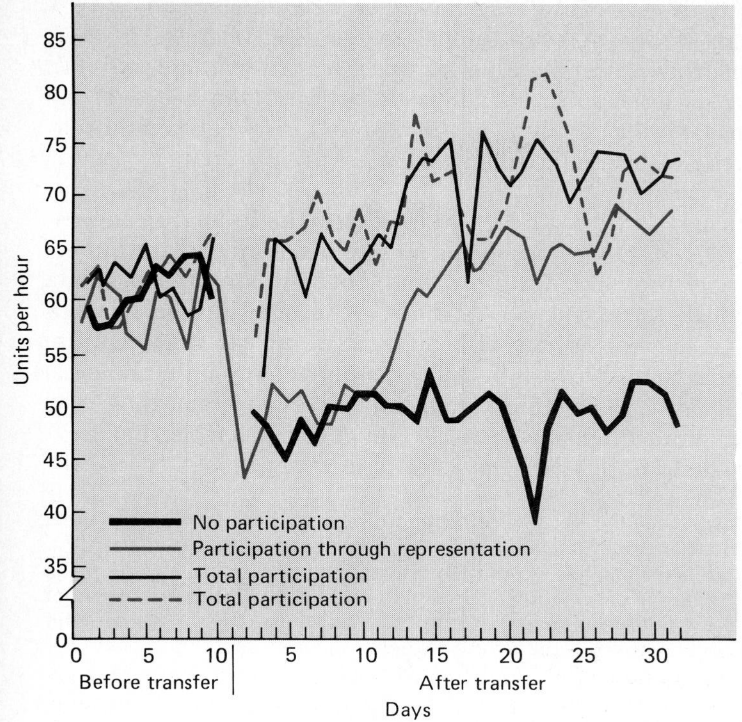

FIGURE 18.4
Effects of participation through representation and of total participation on recovery after an easy transfer

Source: Lester Coch and John R. P. French, Jr., "Overcoming Resistance to Change," *Human Relations* 1, no. 4 (1948), pp. 512–32, fig. 4.

Two groups were given treatment 3, total participation.

Results of this experiment are shown in Figure 18.4. Output was substantially lower for the no participation group (1) after the transfer than for the three participation groups. There was also a substantial difference in attitude among the three groups. After forty days, 17 percent of the employees in group 1 quit. Many of the members of this group felt hostility, and several filed grievances about the new rate. Group 2, which enjoyed limited participation, had a substantially better learning curve than did group 1. But the two total participation groups showed even better results. Furthermore, in none of the three participation groups (groups 2 and 3) had anyone quit; they showed no signs of aggression or hostility at all.

Then the researchers devised a second experiment, which involved only the members of the no participation group. After the initial thirty-two-day study period, the remaining members of this group were dispersed to new jobs throughout the factory for seventy-five more days. Then they were brought back together and transferred to a new job, but this time they were allowed to participate in the job design. The results were in sharp contrast to their previous behavior. Output was 35 percent higher than it was before; no one showed any signs of aggression or hostility; and not a single person had quit after nineteen days on the new job.

Clearly, participation in designing new jobs overcomes many of the frustrations and aggressions that are typical in resisting change. Further, and most important from a cost standpoint, units of output increased and turnover decreased under conditions of participation. This piece of research has been a basic building block in the foundation of participation as a strategy to overcome resistance to change.

Overcoming Resistance to Change As you look over the following suggestions for overcoming resistance to change, remember that each is only a partial solution to the problem. Unfortunately, there is simply no single way to break down all the resistance barriers.[7] You should also keep in mind that resistance to change may appear throughout the organization, from the highest to the lowest levels. Because people occupying high levels within the organization have benefited from the existing system, they may resist changes even more intensely than people at lower levels. Let's examine some factors that are related to resistance to change.

1. *Peer group influences.* Peer groups often encourage group members to meet the job standards that they participate in establishing. Peer groups have influences where there is a strong sense of belonging to the group and a perception that the group is superior to others. Groups significantly influence member behavior, and the effective manager attempts to influence the group directly or indirectly through the informal group leaders.
2. *Group discussion.* Participation is most effective if the needs for change are clearly communicated to the group at a level the group members understand, employees want to get involved in the change, and a group meeting is held to encourage discussion and consideration of ideas and suggestions.
3. *Suggestions from employees.* Some employee suggestions should be implemented and the implementation brought to the attention of participants. A superficial "sense of participation" that merely covers an autocratic manager's actions will soon be understood by employees to be no participation; behaviors will adjust accordingly.
4. *Manager's job security.* P/O managers can provide a sense of job security for subordinate supervisors. If supervisors feel that their jobs are secure, they will not perceive employee participation as a threat to their own positions.
5. *Sensitivity (T-Group) training.* Sensitivity training is a group therapy session designed to increase individual awareness of others and to stress authentic relations with others. We question the application of this technique by nonprofessional leaders. Leaders should have strong therapeutic backgrounds in clinical psychology, a background that is missing from most practicing managers. Transactional analysis, a somewhat similar technique, emphasizes self-awareness. We mention these techniques more to caution against quick adoption than to recommend their value. Research results suggest that such

---

[7]James H. Donnelly, James L. Gibson, and John M. Ivancevich, *Fundamentals of Management,* rev. ed. (Dallas, Texas: Business Publications, Inc., 1975), p. 287, and John B. Miner, *The Management Process: Theory, Research, and Practice* (New York: Macmillan Pub. Co., Inc., 1973).

groups may destroy employees' value structures and provide nothing to replace them, the result being dysfunctional job behaviors.

6. *Terminology*. Using certain words, "change," for example, can arouse aggressive behaviors unnecessarily from employees whose behavior you want to modify. Further, any reference that infers manipulation of an individual is likely to arouse anxieties and create resistance to change. Once the employee becomes defensive, communication is nearly impossible.

Planning for Behavioral Change

Planning for behavioral change can be helpful in two ways: it forces careful consideration of the implications of change, and it can facilitate the transition during change. After recognizing the need for change and identifying the goals to be accomplished, you can anticipate potential resistance and develop ways to overcome it. To do this, you must have a clear understanding of whom the change will affect and how, how the change might be resisted, and the resource restrictions with which you are faced.

One useful approach for systematically clarifying potential pitfalls in change is to construct a simple "people-change" matrix like the one in Table 18.1. The left side of the matrix lists all people who will be affected by the change alternative under consideration. Across the top are listed all job-related characteristics that may be modified if the change is adopted. These characteristics are the potential sources of resistance.

Within each cell is the manager's assessment of the importance, to the person affected, of changing each of the job characteristics. Your ability to fill in this matrix depends on your awareness of the needs, desires, capabilities, and aspirations of the people on the left side of the matrix. It also depends on your insights about the potential impact of the change alternative on the various job characteristics. Once you have filled in the matrix, you can begin identifying likely sources of resistance, the reasons for this resistance, and ways of overcoming it. Methods such as these can be very helpful in planning for change.

TABLE 18.1
An example "people-change" matrix for one change alternative

	Job characteristic affected by change					
People affected	Job skills	Work content	Superior/ subordinate relationship	Work group relationships	Informal relationships	Potential for career mobility
Brown	high	low	high	low	low	medium
Smith	low	low	medium	medium	medium	low
Green	low	low	high	low	high	high
Watts	medium	low	high	medium	low	high
Hone	low	medium	medium	high	low	high

Organization Development Organization development (OD) is a broad term used in management to describe organizational change through the application of knowledge from the behavioral sciences—psychology, sociology, and cultural anthropology for example. A consultant, often a full-time employee, acts as a change agent to facilitate this change process. Our understanding of OD is that it involves the entire planned change process that we've been discussing, but here we will focus on interventions specifically applied to production and operations processes. Let's see how the operations manager can actively participate in this change process.

The Production Operations Manager as Change Agent In behavioral change procedures, it is generally agreed, there are *facilitators* and *learners* of change. In our discussions of the learning process and overcoming resistance to change, we have stressed the production/operations manager's role in initiating change. Essentially, P/O managers are the *facilitators* of change; they are the *change agents*. Production/operations managers continually face the situation of getting changes accomplished through others; operative workers continually face the situation of learning these changes.

Role of Top Management If top management does not support change programs at lower levels, change simply will not occur. Management's support must be strong and consistent. We have observed "partial support of change" in management training seminars. Let's look at a case in which top management initially believed that the management training program developed especially for the company did not apply to themselves.

EXAMPLE

A medium-sized corporation instituted a training program that consisted of twenty two-and-a-half day sessions spanning about six months. Top management initially insisted on participating only in a synopsis of the program, which lasted half a day. All 400 managers at other levels took the full training program, and many began implementing changes as a result. About midway through the program—about three months after its inception—top management decided they were missing something and needed the entire program, so they were scheduled as a group for a full two-and-a-half day session at the end. Several times during this session, top-level executives commented on changes their subordinates were implementing. They could now see where the impetus for the changes had originated and commented that they would be even more supportive in the future. There was a general feeling from subordinate managers that by having implemented the training program at all, top management showed themselves to be interested in improvement and change. After top management went through the entire program, their support was even clearer.

Several studies indicate that unless top management supports new managerial techniques and approaches, even people exposed to training will continue their old behavior. This is the case because top management continues to reinforce old behavior. In fact, under these conditions, training programs can even make matters worse. At one organization, managers were trained to use a human relations approach to dealing with people. At the end of the program, the managers accepted the idea and decided to use it. After a few months, however, those same managers were found to have become even more autocratic than they had been in the first place. Why? Because top management, uninvolved in the program, continued to reinforce autocratic behavior, and subordinate managers, who had learned through the program to emulate top management's style, had actually learned to be more autocratic than they had been before the program.

Production/Operations Changes

Processes change, plants and physical facilities wear out—in short, manufacturing and operations facilities go through a life cycle just as products do.[8] Changes brought on by deterioration or by the desire for improvement have been successfully carried out in organizations and documented through company records, reports at professional meetings, and professional publications. Many of you have had work experience in complex organizations. In light of our discussion in this chapter, can you think of a successful or an unsuccessful change that you've observed? What was the need for the change? Who effected the change? Was there resistance to the change? What strategy led to the success or failure of the change? Consider these questions as we examine an example that is concerned with a production scheduling problem, in which the author focused on the change process that led to implementation of a model.[9]

EXAMPLE

A Production Scheduling Change at Baumritter The Baumritter Corporation is a furniture manufacturer selling primarily under the Ethan Allen brand name. In 1970 sales were approximately $65 million, with manufacturing in eighteen factories. The author and several colleagues at the University of Rhode Island have had a five-year research affiliation with Baumritter; the primary orientation is on the process of major system design and implementation. Baumritter has been deeply involved in a system to control materials throughout the organization.

---

[8]Roger W. Schmenner, "Every Factory Has a Life Cycle," *Harvard Business Review* 61, no. 2 (March–April, 1983), pp. 121–129.

[9]Excerpted from Thomas E. Vollman, "A User Oriented Approach to Production Scheduling" (Paper presented at the 3rd Annual American Institute for Decision Sciences Conference, St. Louis, Missouri, 1971). This company, Baumritter, is the source of several excellent change examples beyond those described here. See Thomas E. Vollman, William L. Berry, and D. Clay Whybark, *Manufacturing Planning and Control Systems* (Irwin, 1984).

Aggregate Capacity Planning One facet of the research led to the conclusion that a critical need for aggregate capacity planning existed and that Baumritter personnel did not fully comprehend the problem. It was felt that this situation represented a fertile opportunity for the design of an implementation-oriented model. The intent was to plant a seed in the Baumritter system that could be nurtured on a cooperative basis, the research team's relative role decreasing over time. The model was built and demonstrated to the vice president of manufacturing, assistant vice president of manufacturing, plant managers, assistant plant managers, other manufacturing executives, and systems analysts working on the materials flow system.

The reaction of these people was highly positive; their recognition of the seriousness of this problem was improved, and the research team expected that cooperative implementation would take place shortly. However, no amount of prodding on their part caused this to happen.

There is a moral to be learned from this story: the top down approach of selecting the most critical problem first is conceptually elegant, but the bottom up approach of finding a problem of present concern will usually produce implementable results. The place to be studied was a large factory in Orleans, Vermont.

Production Scheduling The process of scheduling assembly lines at Orleans was somewhat chaotic. All the parts for a complete item were simultaneously started at the cutoff saws, with the expectation that the item would be ready for assembly eight weeks later. As time elapsed, however, the standard eight-week lead time from cutoff saw to the start of final assembly was often missed. Although the stated goal was to assemble an entire manufacturing lot size upon completion, this goal was rarely met. "Hot list" requirements, poorly constituted finished goods inventories, marketing demands, and pool car shipments all led to sizable variation in the quantities being assembled.

Three of the key manufacturing executives at Orleans attempted to design an assembly schedule on the basis of smaller lot sizes than the cutting lot sizes. They attempted to determine what items to make week-by-week for the next seven or eight weeks on each major assembly line. The effort involved one or two days, or about five labor days per week. The procedure was to arrange pieces of paper on a long table; each piece of paper represented a particular assembly lot of an item. Demand forecasts, standard assembly times, part availabilities, pool car requirements, and dollar output objectives were used.

The actual output from the assembly lines was at considerable variance with what the schedule had predicted. As one week's output was off, corrective actions were taken in subsequent weeks; this made the validity of estimates for future time periods ever more dubious.

At this time the author and his colleagues proposed that the production scheduling process be attacked with a time-shared computer model. The reaction to this suggestion was overwhelmingly negative. Comments included: "The computer is no substitute for manufacturing judgment"; "Go back to your Ivory Tower"; "You are wasting your time, and I will not permit anyone in my organization to waste his time by cooperating with you." No Orleans employee was forbidden to work with us on the project, but no one was encouraged to do so, either.

Implementation The strategy for designing a model that would be implemented in this environment forced consideration of the relative strengths of insiders, or users who understood the goals, criteria, constraints, and data inputs; and outside experts or designers who have model building skills.

The approach to the problem was to send a research assistant to the factory to stay until someone could be convinced. The entree had to be through an individual who could be convinced that the programs could help *him* solve problems with which *he* was personally involved. Finding this kind of individual and getting him on your side is essential.

The individual at Orleans was one of the three men involved in the major assembly scheduling process. His job in the organization was industrial engineer—time study man—assistant to the assistant plant manager. He had had two years of college and no exposure to computers. He didn't see how he could participate in the development of a computer model, nor did he understand why it was necessary for him to be involved. Convincing him of the necessity for his involvement was a key step in the implementation process.

When the inside man or user became convinced that the effort was worth trying, he received a substantial amount of personal harassment from his fellow workers. Some were friendly: "I always knew you was a college professor at heart"; but others were more substantive; he was essentially told that no company time was to be devoted to this project. He did it largely on his own time.

As the model was being developed, people around the plant showed considerable interest. Most of the interest was negative, and when the first run produced results that were clearly wrong, many individuals had a good time saying I told you so. The user, however, expected the first run to be invalid. He also expected the reason for the lack of validity to be apparent; this proved to be correct. His fellow workers only saw the invalid model, not the glaring inconsistencies that could be remedied. The model's requirement for explicitness quickly pointed out major inconsistencies in data inputs, criteria, and the process of scheduling itself. Within a month these inconsistencies were largely removed, and the model was generating valid assembly schedules eighteen weeks into the future.

Once the model became operational at Orleans and actual results began to match the schedule, people who had been openly hostile became believers virtually overnight. There was no arguing with success, and the amount of managerial talent freed up to work on other activities was significant. News of the success quickly spread through other Baumritter factories, and the author and his colleagues were besieged with requests for the scheduling model.

The approach to these requests was to promote the original user to the status of expert major assembly scheduling model builder with the job of transplanting the model to other locations. The researchers helped him in the first two or three transplantations, with their role gradually diminishing. He was thereafter able to implement the system in several factories by himself. Interestingly enough, the problems experienced by Orleans were largely universal, and the model did fit in most other applications. In some of these other applications, new problems were uncovered; at least one of these problems was found also to exist at Orleans. The model went through several stages of generalization, but most of this work was accomplished by Baumritter employees.

Benefits The benefits from the production scheduling model are somewhat difficult to tie down explicitly. Companies that implement a good system of production planning and inventory control often achieve a 10 to 20 percent increase in productivity due to better utilization of equipment, reduced expediting, etc., and productivity has indeed increased in Baumritter plants since the scheduling system was put in. In addition, major assembly scheduling became so predictable in all factories that order acknowledgment was changed and is now based upon the production schedule. An anticipated problem with filling railway cars did not matter, since improved scheduling allowed for much better planning of railway car needs. Purchasing activities were similarly made easier with a clearer understanding of needs. However, the most fundamental benefit coming from major assembly scheduling model was the clearly perceived need for rationalizing the rest of the production planning and inventory control-materials flow system.

Perhaps most interestingly of all, about a year after major assembly scheduling was working, the vice president of manufacturing became convinced that his most significant problem was aggregate capacity planning; the systems approach had now evolved the problem definition to where the author and his colleagues had seen it two years earlier.

Assessing the Overall Effects of Change

We have discussed some key issues in changing behaviors, technologies, and structures of organizations. At the present time, the change process is more an art than a science. Although managers attempt to be systematic and rational in planning for change, complete rationality is not possible, and no one can accurately predict all the effects of change. At best, we can be aware of some general concepts and procedures to help smooth out the transitions that occur in organizations. In advance of the change, we can make rough estimates of its potential effects by asking some "what if" questions about system behavior and economic consequences. Management used to rely on intuition and experience to assess and prepare for the impacts of change. Now there is a better way. Recently, computer simulations have begun being used to explore the implications of proposed changes in a more explicit manner. Let's briefly examine this approach.

SYSTEM DYNAMICS

The examination of overall system behavior is important for two reasons. First, many individuals make changes in various parts of the organization. The *combined* effects of these changes determine overall system performance. Second, any decision or policy should be judged on how it affects the system over time rather than on its effects at one point in time. While static modeling emphasizes one point in time, dynamic modeling focuses on changes over time. Although we are ultimately interested in the steady-state performance after a change, we are interested in the transient system behavior as well. Since implementing changes takes time, their significant effects are usually not realized immediately. Similarly, the reactions of interrelated system subcomponents may not be visible immediately.

System dynamics is a term for a computer-based simulation methodology that attempts to meet these two needs. Pioneered by Professor Jay W. Forrester at M.I.T., system dynamics is a quantitative methodology for developing and analyzing models of systems and their behavior.[10] We won't concern ourselves with the technical details of system dynamics but discuss instead its general potential for management.

An Example System Dynamics Study

In our discussion, we'll outline a research report that illustrates both the general form of simulation results from system dynamics models and the artificiality of system boundaries chosen for purposes of analysis and decision making.[11] It will help you see the advantages of viewing an organization as an open system rather than as a closed system. In this example, internal organizational changes acting through external organizations result in smoother overall operations. As we discuss the example, we will relate it to our model for change, Figure 18.3.

The system under consideration is an industrial components manufacturer with no formal production-inventory-employment control system. Internal operating policies and decision rules are made on the basis of managerial intuition and experience. Adjustments of production rates, inventory levels, and employment levels are primarily reactive. When customers periodically complain about slow deliveries, for example, management reacts by hiring more production employees, increasing production rate, and thereby increasing inventory levels and improving deliveries to customers. Customer complaints are an external indicator of the need for change; behavior and/or structure are the targets for change; improved deliveries are the desired result of change. On other occasions, when bad financial reports show excessive inventories, management reacts by reducing employment levels, reducing production, and thereby reducing inventories to more favorable levels. When this occurs, the financial reports are the internal indicators of need for change, and internal behavioral changes are directed toward the end result of decreasing operating costs. This mode of operation is not unusual.

A system dynamics model of this situation was constructed; it included representations of incoming customer orders, manufacturing rates, employment changes, inventory levels, and product deliveries of the components manufacturer. A computer program was developed reflecting the logic of what actually happened in the firm. A computer simulation run of this model was conducted, and system performance was recorded on the following dimensions: on-hand inventory level, manpower (employment) levels, volume of incoming customer orders, and backlog of customer orders. The resulting system performance is shown in Figure 18.5 *(a)*.

Let us examine and interpret these results. First, system performance is recorded over 300 simulated weeks. Incoming customer orders declined during the initial twenty weeks, increased during the next twenty weeks,

[10]Jay W. Forrester, *Industrial Dynamics* (Cambridge, Mass.: The M.I.T. Press, 1961).

[11]See Edward B. Roberts, "Industrial Dynamics and the Design of Management Control Systems," *Management Technology* 3, no. 2 (December 1963), pp. 100–118.

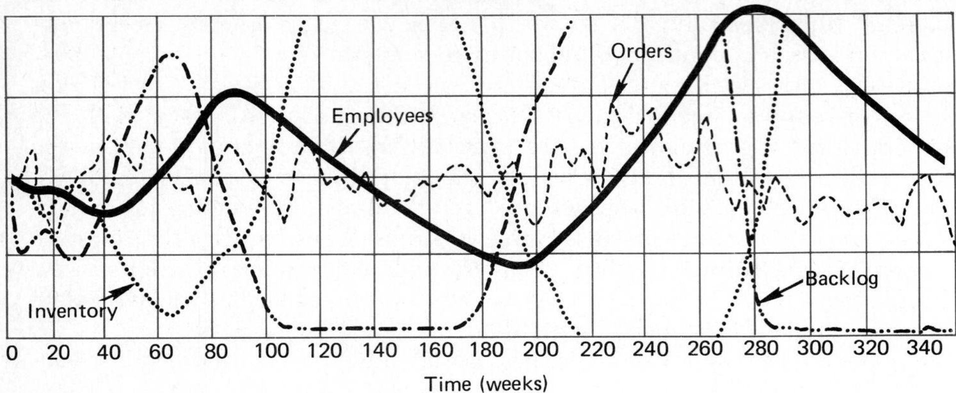

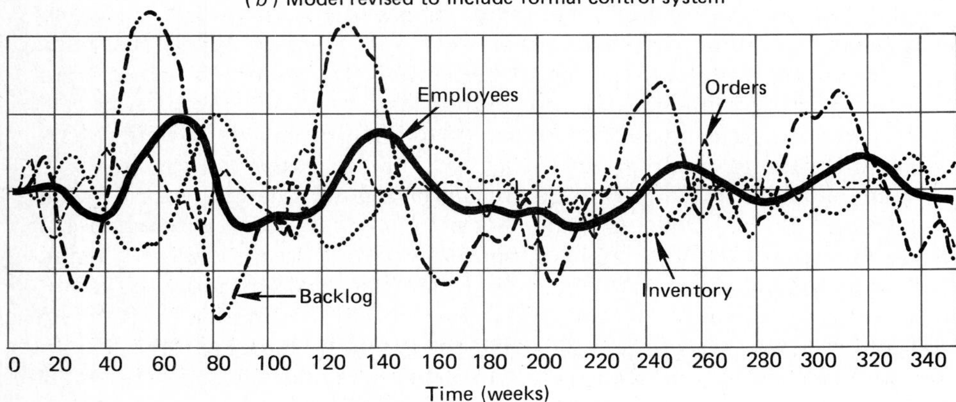

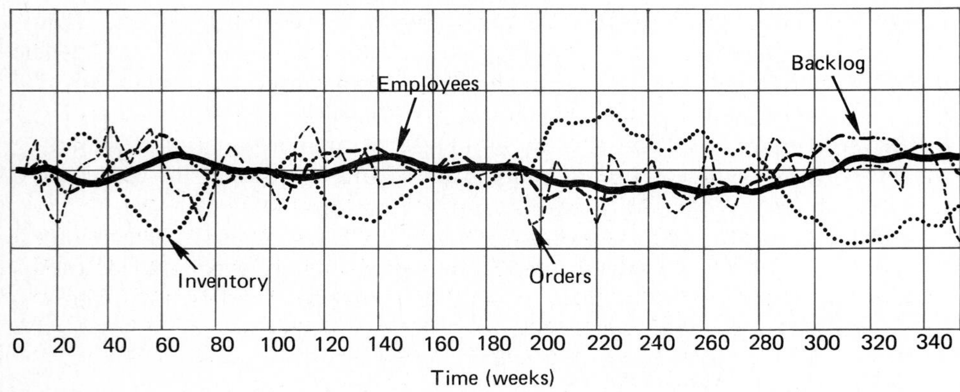

FIGURE 18.5
Results of three system simulation runs

Source: Edward B. Roberts, "Industrial Dynamics and the Design of Management Control Systems," *Management Technology* 3, no. 2 (December 1963), pp. 109 and 113. Printed by permission from *Management Science*.

and continued to show considerable variability for the remainder of the simulation run. The variations in employment, inventory, and backlogs were even more dramatic. Notice that as inventories decline, employment increases, but with a lag; as inventories increase, employment decreases. Further, as time passes, the amplitudes (heights of peaks and depths of valleys) of employment, inventory, and backlogs increase substantially. These wide variations can be very costly, and there is obviously room for considerable improvement. Goals of operations equilibrium, reasonable costs, and customer deliveries are not being met. The system performance is a further indicator of the need for change.

A new, more formal management control system was proposed for the components manufacturer, with the goal of reducing existing wide variations. Its primary features were designed to:

- gather better information on sales,
- smooth the sales estimates, thereby reducing the chances of direct factory responses to random sales variations,
- periodically review inventories and implement reordering policies that would bring actual inventories into line with target inventory levels,
- monitor order backlogs so they don't drift afar from normal levels, and
- adjust work force to meet the desired production rate in consideration of current sales volume and manufacturing backlog conditions.

This proposal involves changes in managerial technology and structure (targets) to achieve operations equilibrium, lower costs, and improved deliveries (desired results). From the manufacturer's viewpoint, all these changes can be accomplished internally within the manufacturing system. Would this new management control system improve the manufacturer's performance? To find out, the analyst revised the previous model, incorporating the features under consideration. The revised model was then run over 300 simulated weeks with the results shown in part *(b)* of Figure 18.5. As you can see, system performance has generally improved; variations in employment, inventory, and backlogs are substantially reduced. Still, the basic dynamic pattern remains—the sales fluctuations are followed by even larger fluctuations in inventories, employment, and backlogs. These results are an indicator of need for further change.

At this point, management considered adding to the model a representation of the consumer sector of the industry (the addition of an external factor). The customers of this components manufacturer are themselves manufacturers of military and other consumer electronics products. It seemed appropriate to consider the consumer sector because fluctuations in incoming consumer orders seemed to be the driving force behind the other fluctuations in the manufacturer's system. A better understanding of consumer ordering practices might be worthwhile. An investigation revealed that consumer ordering practices were related to the manufacturer's delivery lead time. On this basis the consumer sector, including representations of the consumer's components inventory, production rate, engineering evaluation process, and order release policies, was added to the simulation model. While developing these new additions to the model, management discovered that the customer's rate of releasing new orders (to the manufacturer) is affected by the manufacturer's delivery delay (to the customer), and the manufacturer's delivery delay is influenced by the rate of new orders received from customers. The revised model incorporated this interrelationship and was tested over 300 simulated weeks. Performance of the manufacturing system under these conditions was improved, as shown in Figure 18.5 *(c)*. Overall, the dynamic behavior of the system under these conditions is much more stable than it was under the previous two conditions.

The results indicate that the greatest improvement in the manufacturer's system performance could be obtained by adjusting the factory lead time for deliveries. This is an *internally* controllable parameter of the manufacturer. Even more noteworthy, however, is the thought process necessary to recognize the significance of this parameter. *This awareness occurred only after someone was willing to look at environmental elements, in this case the structure of consumer policies, outside the system of immediate concern.* Thus, a useful internal change was identified when management took an "open" systems approach to the problem.

SUMMARY

Since organizations and their conversion subsystems are dynamic, open systems in constant interaction with their environments, changes of varying magnitude are constantly occurring. Managers must be aware of the process of change and its role in the organization.

Several aspects of change must be understood if change is to be successfully managed. First, one must recognize the need for change as signalled by either internal or external indicators. Next, the targets for change—technology, structure, and behavior—must be identified. Any or all of these are directly involved in the organizational change process.

The behavioral change process involves recognition of the need for change, identification of the behavioral targets for change, decisions to change a certain way, accepting a strategy for change, and implementing the behavioral change.

Strategies for change may be one or a combination of an empirical-rational strategy, a normative-reeducative strategy, or a power-coercive strategy. Regardless of the strategy, the production/operations manager cannot expect a 100 percent behavioral change in subordinate managers and workers.

It is up to the production/operations manager to facilitate learning of behaviors that are supportive of operations goals. Positive rewards should be used intermittently to support (reinforce) worker behaviors that the manager wants continued. The manager must correctly evaluate what reinforcement the worker is currently receiving for undesirable behaviors so that the reinforcements can be withdrawn.

Managers and their subordinates will resist change, some more than others. Worker participation can help reduce the barriers to change. Several other partial solutions exist that can help reduce resistance to change.

The unpredictable nature of the overall effects of change arise from three sources of complexity. First are those arising from interrelationships among the subfunctions of the management process (planning, organizing, and controlling). Second are those stemming from the interactions among functional areas (operations, finance, and marketing, for example). Third, complexities arise from the inherent interrelationships among operations subproblems (scheduling, layout, location, and inventory).

Since many simultaneous decisions are ultimately interrelated, it is difficult to predict in advance their overall effects. Consequently, some systemic methods are desirable for assessing proposed changes. System dynamics is one methodology for accomplishing this. Still, the state of the art remains relatively underdeveloped, and managerial intuition and experience remain the main means used for predicting the overall effects of change.

CASE

Education Copy Services

Before August 1985, two photocopy machines were available for use by the faculty and secretarial staff of the School of Business. This resource provided easy, quick, and convenient service to faculty in reproducing materials related to personal, teaching, research, and service activities. In an effort to reduce the high copying cost, a new policy was implemented. All copying for small jobs was to be done by the secretarial staff, and automatic devices were installed to monitor and count all copies made. The machine would not operate without one of these devices, preset with a department charge account. Some faculty found that access to copying was considerably less convenient than it had been in the past. It was harder to get last-minute service, and they needed a longer planning horizon for copied material. Secretaries found that they had to make many special trips to the machines, which interrupted their typing and other office responsibilities.

Then it was announced that as of November 26, 1985, the number of machines would be reduced from two to one. Small jobs (fewer than eleven copies) would continue to be run by secretaries on the one machine. Jobs of eleven or more would be transported across campus to Quick Copy Service for reproduction. This change was to be on a trial basis and offered a handsome cost savings to the college. All indications were that copy service to faculty would be at least as good as they had experienced since August.

The management department chairman and secretarial staff thought about the potential implications of the new system. They decided to send a memo to faculty identifying some things that could be done to enhance the service from the new system. The essential points presented to the faculty were:

1. Jobs requiring more than ten copies will be sent to Quick Copy.
2. Generally, the secretarial staff will mail or deliver jobs to Quick Copy twice daily, once in the morning, once in the afternoon.
3. Quick Copy will deliver the finished jobs back to the departmental office.
4. The secretarial staff will continue to process small jobs on the machine here in the building. This will be done once in the morning and once in the afternoon. This will enable the secretaries to perform their other obligations to faculty more effectively.

5. As a result of these four steps, the faculty is reminded that some lead time will be necessary for getting the jobs done. The necessary lead time is not expected to be any greater, in general, than it was under the old system. If we allow Quick Copy two to three days lead time, they will be able to get us special emergency service on those exceptional occasions when it is needed.

After thinking about the new system and the memo, the chairman wondered about faculty reaction. The new system seemed to have implications for changes in traditional patterns of behavior. What reactions would you expect if you were chairman? What actions should be taken to ensure smooth adaptation to these changes?

REVIEW AND DISCUSSION QUESTIONS

1. In some situations it is useful to view operations as a closed subsystem, while in other situations an open system view is more useful. Give examples of both.
2. Reliable National Bank is considering the installation of automatic teller units at several locations throughout the city. What indicators of the need for change and what desired results led to considering this change?
3. Suppose you are requested to predict the results of Reliable National Bank's contemplated change (see question 2). Outline your approach for making such a prediction, including a list of the main factors that must be considered.
4. Identify two organizations for which external indicators of the need for change are of minimal importance. List two others for which external indicators are dominant.
5. Identify and discuss the behavioral implications of decisions to change job shop priority rules, facility layout, and facility location.
6. Give examples showing how changes in the finance and marketing subsystems necessitate changes in the operations subsystem of the organization.
7. Facility location is a major planning decision in operations management. Show how it is interrelated with organizing and controlling of operations.
8. Colleges and universities are often bureaucratic in dealing with students. Faculty and staff may be abrupt, inconsiderate, and outright wrong in their behaviors. Think of one experience you've encountered when that was so. Placing yourself in the role of a university operations administrator, use the steps in the behavior change process to show how such an experience could be avoided in the future.
9. State the strategies for behavioral change and briefly explain each. In answering question 8, which strategy for behavior change were you suggesting?
10. Contrast positive reinforcement, negative reinforcement, and punishment. Which holds the most promise for behavioral change in production/operations management? Why?
11. An owner/production manager offers criticism when he observes a mistake, offers praise only at the end of a day, pays for performance weekly on an incentive plan, and provides medical benefits whenever a valid claim occurs. For each of these actions, explain the reinforcement schedule. Utilize continuous-intermittent, fixed-variable, and interval-ratio dichotomies in your answer.
12. Contrast the thaw-move-refreeze change model to the planned change model of Figure 18.3.
13. A claims processing clerk is fearful of losing her job when the new computer system

is installed. She has been most reluctant to help the system designers understand her current duties. In fact, she has hidden some of the complex tasks from them. Which of the four basic reasons for resisting change is most prevalent here? Why?

14. Explain the experimental design of the Harwood Manufacturing study that dealt with resistance to change. What were the results in comparing the "no participation" group to the "total participation" groups? Why are the results of this study from the 1940s still of value to operations managers?
15. Explain the role of top management in bringing about change in the organization.
16. Consider the production scheduling change at Baumritter presented in the chapter. Answer these questions, which were posed at the beginning of that section for the Baumritter situation:
    Can you identify successful or unsuccessful changes?
    What was the need for change?
    Who was the change agent?
    Who were the learners?
    Was there resistance to the change?
    What strategy led to the success or failure of the change?

GLOSSARY

Analysis Process of decomposing a "whole" into separate subparts to permit a better understanding of the individual subcomponents.

Change agent The facilitator of change; the role the production/operations manager takes in bringing about behavioral change in subordinates.

Closed system A self-contained entity within definable boundaries; a system that has no exchanges (inputs or outputs) of energy with its environment.

Empirical-rational change strategy Strategy assuming that presented with facts, knowledge, and information, people will act in their own self-interest and rationally change behaviors to that end.

Extinction Ignoring, by withdrawing positive reinforcements, unacceptable behaviors in hopes they will diminish and eventually disappear.

Extrinsic rewards Social or economic incentives that are external to the task being performed.

Intrinsic rewards Internal incentives that are psychologically part of the task being performed; satisfaction inherent in the task.

Learning Having a goal, responding to obtain the goal, obtaining feedback from the response, making additional responses, adjusting the responses or goal until the goal is met.

Normative-reeducative change strategy A strategy assuming that people have attitude and value systems; when presented with facts, knowledge, and information directed at attitudes and values, people will change behaviors as they change their attitudes and values.

Open system A system that is an integral part of a larger system; its viability depends upon successful adjustments to varied inputs from and outputs to its environment.

Participation Approach to overcoming resistance to change through employee involvement in planning and implementing the change.

Power-coercive change strategy Use of political, economic, or some other form of influence to force change in the behavior of others.

Punishment The infliction of pain or discomfort.

Reinforcement Environmental consequences of behavior.

Reinforcement schedules More or less formal specification of the occurrence of a reinforcer in relation to the behavioral sequence to be conditioned; can be continuous or intermittent; intermittent can be interval or ratio and fixed or variable.

Synthesis Process of constructing or reconstructing the "whole" by combining various subparts; attempts to understand how the "whole" will behave once it has been created from interrelated subcomponents.

System dynamics A computer-based simulation methodology for developing and analyzing models of systems and their behavior.

SELECTED READINGS

Abernathy, W. J. "Production Process Structure and Technological Change." *Decision Sciences* 7, no. 4 (October 1976), pp. 607–19.

Adam, E. E. "An Analysis of the Change in Performance Quality Employing Operant Conditioning Procedures." *Journal of Applied Psychology* 56, no. 6 (December 1972), pp. 480–86.

______and W. E. Scott. "The Application of Behavioral Conditioning Procedures to the Problems of Quality Control." *The Academy of Management Journal* 14, no. 2 (June 1971), pp. 175–93.

Bandura, A. *Principles of Behavior Modification*. New York: Holt, Rinehart and Winston, Inc., 1969.

Bennis, Warren G., Kenneth D. Benne, Robert Chin, and Kenneth E. Corey. *The Planning of Change*. 3rd ed. New York: Holt, Rinehart and Winston, Inc., 1976.

Chin, Robert and Kenneth D. Benne. "General Strategies for Effecting Changes in Human Systems." In *The Planning of Change*, Warren G. Bennis, Kenneth D. Benne, Robert Chin, and Kenneth E. Corey, eds. 3rd ed. New York: Holt, Rinehart and Winston, Inc., 1976.

Coch, Lester and John R. P. French, Jr. "Overcoming Resistance to Change." *Human Relations* 1 (1948), pp. 512–32.

Forrester, Jay W. *Industrial Dynamics*. Cambridge, Mass.: The M.I.T. Press, 1961.

Greene, Charles N., Everett E. Adam, Jr., and Ronald J. Ebert. *Management for Effective Performance*. Englewood Cliffs, N.J.: Prentice-Hall, Inc., 1985.

Kivenko, Ken. "Employee Absenteeism—The Deterioration of Productivity." *Production and Inventory Review* 4, no. 5 (May 1984), pp. 52–55 and 70.

Lee, J. A. "Leader Power for Managing Change." *Academy of Management Review* 2, no. 1 (January 1977), pp. 73–80.

Miner, John B. *The Management Process: Theory, Research, and Practice*. New York: Macmillan Pub. Co., Inc., 1973.

Roberts, Edward B. "Industrial Dynamics and the Design of Management Control Systems." *Management Technology* 3, no. 2 (December 1963), pp. 100–118.

Schmenner, Roger W. "Every Factory Has a Cycle." *Harvard Business Review* 61, no. 2 (March–April 1983), pp. 121–129.

Slocum, J. W., Jr. and D. Hellriegel. "Using Organizational Designs to Cope With Change." *Business Horizons* 22, no. 6 (December 1979), pp. 65–76.

Student, K. R. "Managing Change: A Psychologist's Perspective." *Business Horizons* 21, no. 6 (December 1978), pp. 28–33.

Vollman, Thomas E. "A User Oriented Approach to Production Scheduling." (Paper presented at 3rd Annual American Institute for Decision Sciences Conference. St. Louis, Missouri, 1971).

Vollman, Thomas E., William L. Berry, and D. Clay Whybark. *Manufacturing Planning and Control Systems*. Irwin, 1984.

19 Useful Technical Approaches to Change

This chapter describes techniques for measuring and evaluating purposeful change in an operations context. The techniques generally quantify the results of estimates about the future. Thoughtful development of such inputs is of great importance. The end result of the technique is perhaps best viewed as an aid to business judgment rather than a substitute for it.

At Travelers, we operate a $12½ billion portfolio of real estate investments through a regionalized, nationwide professional staff of over 200 people. Many of the techniques described in this chapter are indispensable elements in our annual transaction volume of $3 billion. We reorganized this operation two years ago and have since had extensive experience with the learning curve, although the nature of our operation makes it difficult to quantify.

The economics of change are properly addressed in this chapter on a straightforward economic basis. In many firms, however, the accounting effects of purposeful change may significantly impact shareholder or creditor relationships. It is not uncommon that the ultimate change will be the best economic choice that does not disrupt these important external relationships.

The old saying that "nothing is as certain as change" remains true. The ability to recognize the need for change, then plan and change to get the desired results, is one of top management's greatest challenges.

Robert W. Lisle
Senior Vice President
The Travelers Corporation
Hartford, Connecticut

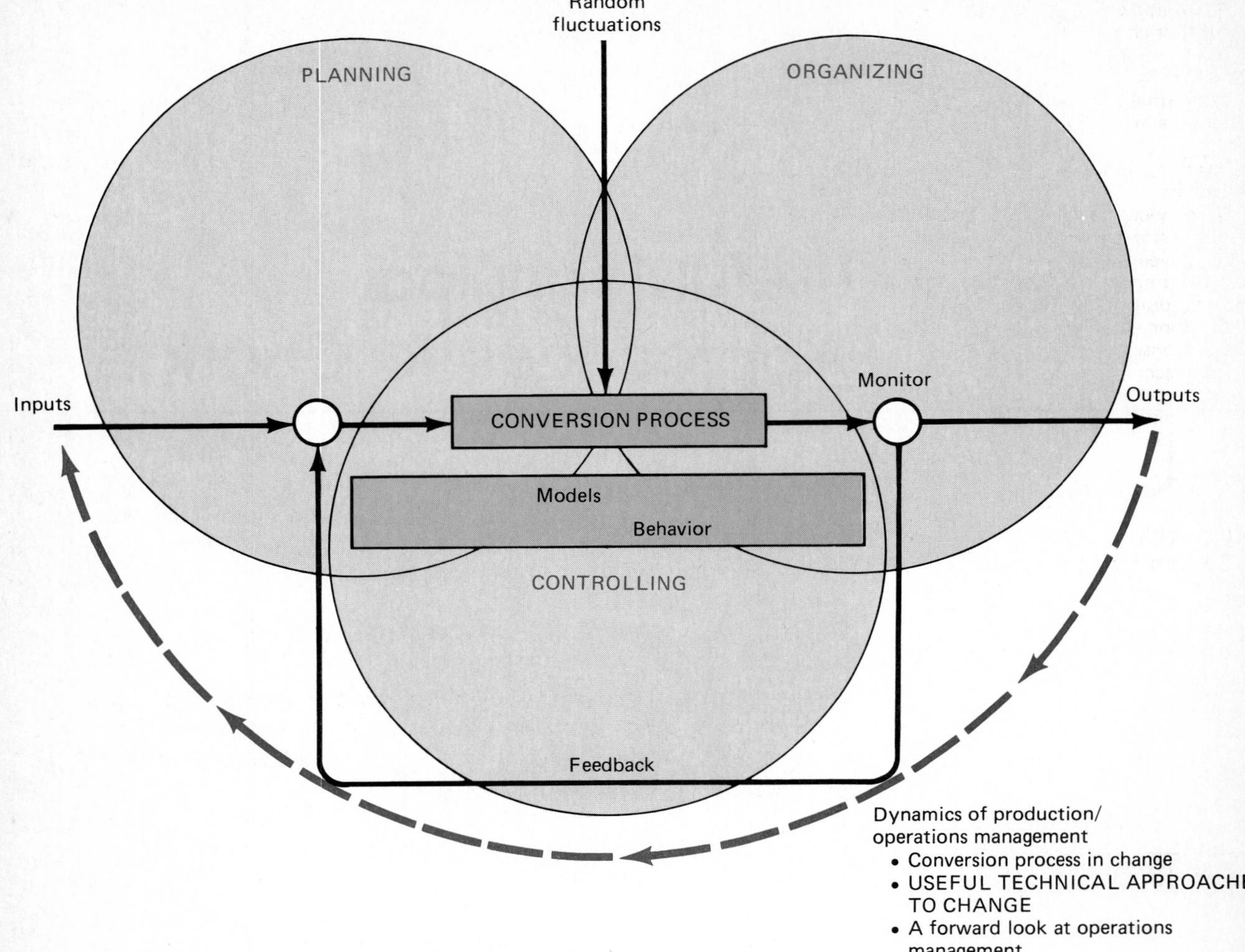

FIGURE 19.1
General model for production/operations management

Managers of organizations must expect change. The question is not whether change will be necessary but how to deal with it. In Chapter 18, we considered three target areas for change, technology, structure, and behavior, as we put the process of change into an overall, integrative framework. In this chapter, we'll discuss useful technical approaches to change in technology and structure. As Figures 19.1 and 19.2 show, change is a necessary part of all conversion processes, and learning to deal with change in a rational way is an important managerial task. It is clear from Mr. Lisle's comments that

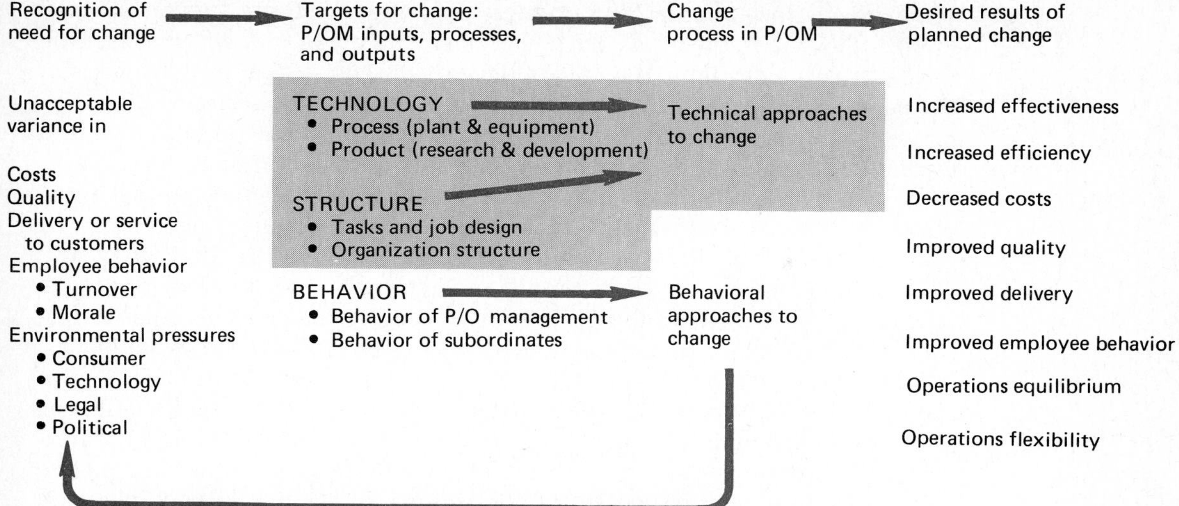

FIGURE 19.2
Dynamics of production/operations management: the conversion process in change.

the management at Travelers Corporation uses rational, technical approaches to help them arrive at judgments which will guide change in their organization. We will first look at rationality and then apply it to operations change.

THE ROLE OF RATIONALITY

Managerial intuition, judgment, and experience play major roles in change decisions. Whether these decisions are based on hunch or thoughtful analysis, the full effects of significant change are usually unpredictable to some extent. But managers need not be discouraged by the absence of complete predictability; we can take some careful, systematic steps to increase predictability somewhat and help ourselves cope with change.

One procedure that lends rationality to the change process is the scientific approach to decision problems. Six steps in this approach are:

1. problem recognition and definition,
2. statement of objectives,
3. formulation of alternative solutions,
4. data collection,
5. evaluation of alternatives,
6. decision or choice.

We can recognize and define a problem only after the indicators of the need for change have appeared. Then we state our objectives in terms of the desired results of planned change (Figure 19.2). It is the final four steps of the scientific approach to change that we want to emphasize in this chapter. As managers learn to formulate alternative solutions, collect data, and evaluate alternatives, they become better able to make rational decisions.

By a "rational" approach, we mean the process of carefully identifying change alternatives, analyzing their effects from a financial, economic, or other logical point of view, comparing the alternatives on this basis, and identifying the best of the alternatives. Typically, this kind of approach involves quantitative analysis. Thereafter, additional nonquantifiable factors can be introduced and considered before the final choice is made.

When technology is the target, changes in products, processes, equipment and/or facilities are considered. Ordinarily, formal or rational analysis in these instances is of a financial or engineering nature. When organizational structure or policy is the target, some attempts are made to measure change in financial terms, but to a lesser extent; the impact of these changes can't always be captured in financial terms. Nevertheless, the rational approach is still applicable. We are generally forced to employ nonfinancial measures of system performance, however; changes in crime rate, service to customers, reduction in procurement lead times, and similar patterns often reflect system performance. Let's begin our discussion of changes in conversion technology with a look at financial and economic analysis.

FINANCIAL AND ECONOMIC ANALYSIS IN OPERATIONS

To almost every organization in both the public and private sectors, financial analysis is vital. Public agencies operating on limited budgets want to provide as much service as possible to the public. Private firms strive to provide suitable returns on capital invested by their owners. Whenever proposals are made to change products, processes, equipment, or facilities, some financial implications must be considered. Operations managers are concerned with proposals for revising facility layouts, changing the system capacity, deciding facility location, revising inventory systems, and so on. Proposals for change are almost always made in the hope that some benefits will result; but the benefits can't be realized unless the necessary resources are committed first. Are the anticipated benefits of change worth the anticipated costs? This is the central question of financial and economic analysis.

Terminology and Concepts

Although it's not always possible to do so, decision makers try to evaluate alternatives logically and comparably. Toward this end, economic analysis borrows some standard terminology from finance and accounting.

Cost and Revenues When considering existing or prospective equipment and facilities, the manager is interested in the costs associated with their ownership and operation. This information is needed, for example, to decide whether old equipment should be retained or replaced by newer models. What is the old equipment worth? Although sometimes the relevant information can be obtained from accounting data, often it cannot be. Frequently, accounting cost data are not relevant for use in investment decisions because they are historic rather than current. By reflecting what has occurred in the past in a standard, orderly fashion, they give some measure of current operating status. They do not reflect changes in market values of existing equipment or the costs of replacing old equipment and facilities with new. For financial analyses of investment proposals, accounting costs play a secondary role. *The costs that are used in economic analysis are current costs, actual costs.* Let's examine a few costs that become important to us in analysis.

Opportunity costs are the returns that are lost or forgone as a result of selecting one alternative instead of another. The amount of the opportunity cost is determined by comparing the benefits or advantages of a choice with those of the best alternative. Selection of one alternative usually involves forgoing the opportunity of gaining benefits offered by other alternatives.

EXAMPLE

Suppose you wish to sell your car and person *A* offers you \$900. Then a friend, person *B*, offers \$800. If you select alternative *A*, you must forgo the \$800 offered by *B*. If you select alternative *B*, you must forgo the \$900 offered by *A*. Thus alternative *A* offers a \$100 net advantage. Stated otherwise, should you choose *B*, the loss from passing over alternative *A* is a \$100 opportunity cost to you. If you wish to maximize your dollar return, you would select alternative *A*, thereby minimizing the opportunity loss for this decision.

Sunk costs are past expenditures that are irrelevant to current decisions. Suppose a company purchased a special piece of equipment one year ago for \$10,000. Since the purchase is a past event, the cost of \$10,000 should not be considered in future choices. Before the investment, up to the time when the decision was made to buy the equipment, the \$10,000 purchase price was a relevant consideration. Thereafter, it became irrelevant for any future decisions. Should you now be interested in replacing the piece of equipment, its salvage value is important, but the initial sunk cost of \$10,000 is not.

The salvage value of facilities and equipment is a relevant revenue (a negative cost), since existing assets that are abandoned or replaced may be saleable. The income received from an asset sale is the *salvage value*. Thus, when a decision alternative involves income from the sale of existing assets, salvage value is a relevant consideration. Salvage value is a market value, similar to the concept of current, actual costs.

Salvage value provides a good example of how accounting records can be inappropriate for financial decision making. The book value of an asset, in an accounting sense, is usually not an accurate indicator of the asset salvage value. Although the company's book value may be thousands of dollars, the market value may be higher, lower, or even zero. The market or salvage value, not the book value, is relevant for decision analysis.

To assist in decision analysis, current and future salvage values are estimated for the asset under consideration. A schedule of salvage values, an example of which is shown in Table 19.1, shows the estimated salvage value for an existing piece of equipment that is being considered for replacement. Current salvage value is $10,000; year-end salvage values are shown for each of three succeeding years. Suppose the company is examining the financial impact of selling the equipment now versus selling it at the end of each of the three ensuing years. Notice that salvage value is expected to decrease annually and that opportunity costs can be calculated for each of the decision alternatives. From the viewpoint of salvage income, the best alternative is to sell now; current salvage value is highest, and the proceeds can be invested during year 1 at 8 percent for an additional $800 in income. By selling at the end of year 1, the company forgoes $2,000 of salvage income and the $800 interest income. Compared to selling now, the total first year opportunity cost is $2,800. Of course, other relevant costs besides those associated with salvage value must also be considered, and so should the revenues that can be generated each year with the equipment.

Depreciation is an accounting concept for recovering outlays (expenditures) for assets over their lives. Depreciation, a bookkeeping concept, does not reflect current market values. Since we are interested only in market values, of what value is depreciation to the economics of change (re-

TABLE 19.1
A schedule of estimated salvage value of an existing piece of equipment

		Annual opportunity costs		
Sell at end of year	Expected salvage value at year end	Income lost due to decrease in salvage value from previous year	Income lost from not investing salvage funds at 8% during succeeding year	Total lost income
0(now)	$10,000	$ 0	$ 0	$ 0
1	8,000	2,000	800	2,800
2	5,000	3,000	640	3,640
3	1,000	4,000	400	4,400

placement)? Depreciation is important only in that the depreciation schedule affects income tax rates, and income taxes affect actual cash flows. The higher the depreciation in any one period, the lower the taxes paid and the greater the cash flows (revenues less expenses). Although we will cover depreciation and taxes in some detail in the supplement to this chapter, for our purposes here we will simplify matters by ignoring them both.

Incremental Cash Flows When we evaluate and compare investment opportunities, we have to consider the alternatives' incremental cash flows. When we do a cost comparison of two alternatives, we are interested only in the cost differences, or increments, between them; obviously, cost elements that are shared in common are irrelevant.

Cash flows are of central interest in evaluating any investment proposal. What are all the cash flows associated with an alternative? Some involve only outlays of funds with no anticipated additional revenues. If we assume, for example, that new and old equipment generates the same revenues, investing in replacement equipment involves only outlays of funds. Other proposals offer both new revenues and outflows. If we decided to open a wine and cheese shop at a new shopping center, we could expect both new cash outflows and inflows. All inflows and outflows that result from adopting an alternative should enter into the analysis, including not only initial outlays but also ongoing outlays expected throughout the asset life. Anticipated costs of owning, operating, and maintaining the asset should therefore be considered. To determine incremental cash flows, we must also consider expected revenue from sales and possible salvage decisions. Also important are the *magnitude* (size) of cash flows, the *direction* (revenue or expense) of cash flows, and the *patterns* (exactly when) cash flows take place over the life of the asset.

Life of the Asset

There are several ways of viewing the life of an asset. Consider the life of a piece of equipment. First, we can determine its *accounting life*, the life used to develop a depreciation schedule. Second, we can consider its *machine life*, the length of time the machine could actually function. At the end of the machine life, there might or might not be some salvage value. Machine life typically is of secondary interest to us in economic analysis. We are primarily interested in *economic life*, the period of time the asset performs its useful economic service to the organization. These three measurements may be widely divergent.

EXAMPLE

A national diamond wholesaler, who considers it absolutely necessary for his firm to convey a prosperous image, requires his salespeople to drive either Lincoln Continentals or Cadillacs. He has established a policy of purchasing only new automobiles and retaining them for two years. At the end of that time, the economic usefulness of the luxury car ends. The accounting department, on the other hand, sets up a depreciation schedule based on a three-year life; and the automobile manufacturers' data suggest that properly maintained Continentals and Cadillacs should last ten years. For these cars, then, machine life is ten years, accounting life three years, and economic life two years. When management undertakes an economic analysis of fleet replacement, economic life is critical.

Time Value of Money

When analysts speak of the time value of money, they mean the revenues that may be received for money over time. A sum of money held as cash may either depreciate or appreciate in value over time, but it will not earn any revenues unless it is invested. If the same sum of money is invested over time for a specified amount with a guarantee of repayment of the principal, the original sum of money has value over time. This idea of money having value over time is an important consideration in evaluating proposed changes.

EXAMPLE

Suppose you are given \$100 as a birthday gift. You decide to invest now for two years in a bank paying 8 percent annual interest. At the time of initial investment, time zero for purposes of analysis, the bank owes you \$100. After one year, the bank owes you not only the initial amount but 8 percent of that amount as well. At the end of year one, the amount due you is \$108, or \$100 + (.08)(\$100). Thus, at the beginning of year two you have an investment of \$108, which will remain in the bank during year two. At the end of year two, the bank owes you not only the \$108 you had at the beginning of that year, but also an additional 8 percent of that amount, interest on your investment during the second year. At the end of year two, the amount owed you is \$116.64, or \$108 + (.08)(\$108). Your savings have been *compounded.*

Income and Expense Patterns and Associated Compound Interest Factors

Income and Expense Patterns In equipment and operations replacement situations, there are six basic patterns of income and expense flows. Figure 19.3 shows three of these flow patterns, and since each pattern has a reverse flow as well, there are six possible cash flows. The three not shown (given P to find S, given P to find R, and given S to find R) would have the same graphical patterns as their counterparts, except that the cash flows would be reversed.

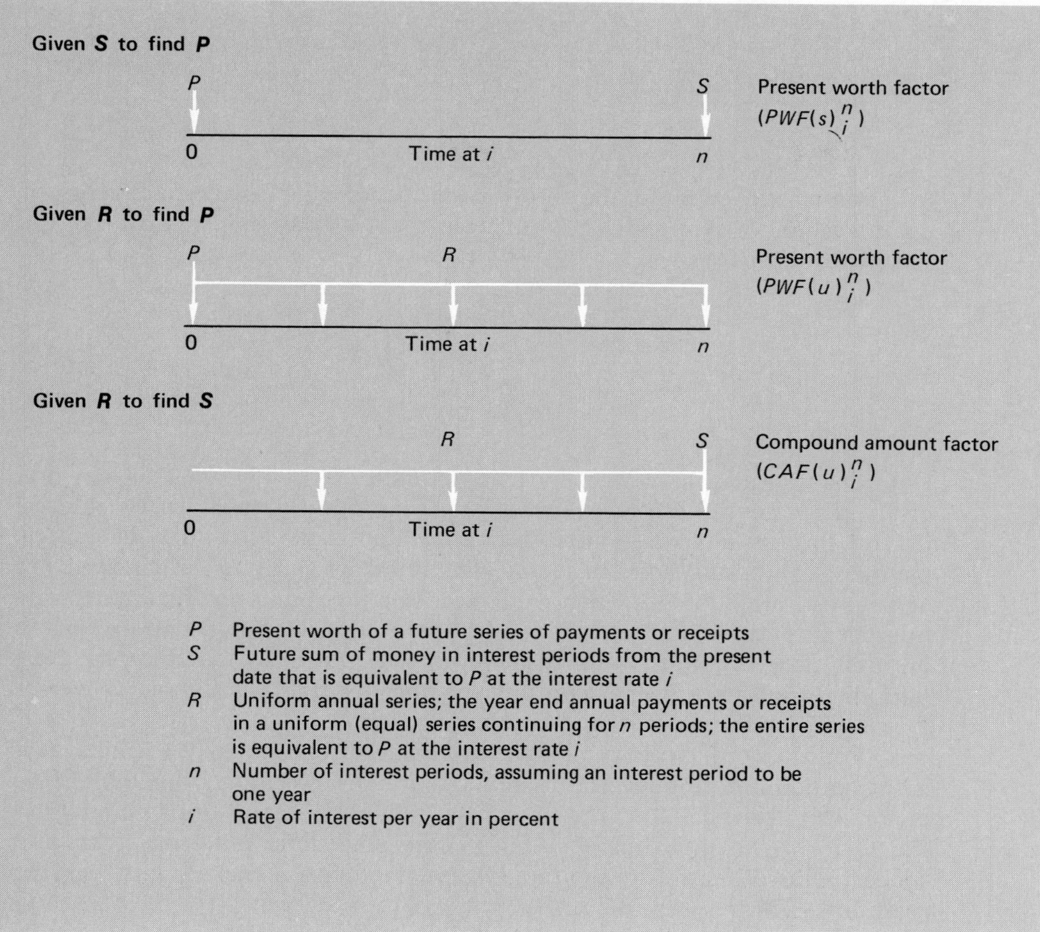

FIGURE 19.3
Income and expense flow patterns and compound interest factors

Compound Interest Factors Which income flow pattern applies to our birthday gift example? Given a present sum of money (P), find a future sum of money (S) after n periods. If we consider the time value of money at interest rate i over the n years, we have the concept of a compound interest factor. Let's call this particular factor a single payment compound amount factor. It could be defined as $CAF(s)_i^n$ and illustrated:

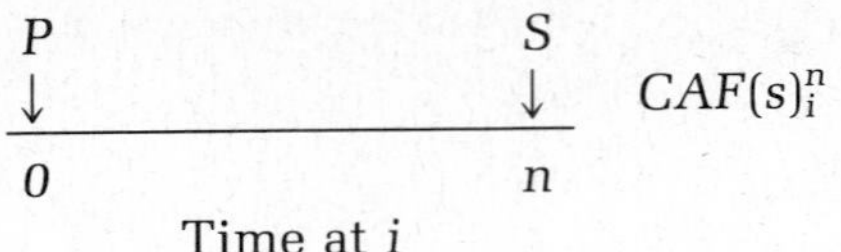

In terms of our example, the future sum of money, S, is found by looking up the factor in Appendix B (appendices are at the end of the text) and solving for S as follows:

$$\begin{aligned} S &= P(CAF(s)_i^n) \\ &= \$100\ (CAF(s)_{.08}^2) \\ &= 100\ (1.166) \\ &= \$116.60 \end{aligned} \tag{19.1}$$

Note that the answer we get by using equation 19.1 ($116.60) is not precisely the same as the answer we got by computing each year's interest ($116.64). This is because the factor is rounded in the appendix. The single payment compound amount factor was found by going to Appendix B for an interest rate, i, of 8%. Then we look in the n column for the appropriate number of periods, in this case 2. Next we find the column that applies to our cash flow situation, in this case given P to find S. By matching the time periods (2) with the proper column, we find that 1.166 is the factor we are looking for, and we use it in our calculation.

You do not have to remember the name of the factor (the single payment compound amount factor) nor the interest formula from which the factor was derived ($(1 + i)^n$) to use the table. *You need only understand the logic of the investment situation, the cash flow patterns given and sought.* The different compound interest factors associated with varying cash flows are:

Cash flow	Factor name	Factor symbol
given S to find P	present worth factor	$PWF(s)_i^n$
given P to find S	compound amount factor	$CAF(s)_i^n$
given R to find P	present worth factor	$PWF(u)_i^n$
given P to find R	capital recovery factor	CRF_i^n
given R to find S	compound amount factor	$CAF(u)_i^n$
given S to find R	sinking fund factor	SFF_i^n

Note that (s) refers to a single payment and (u) to a uniform annual series for the various factors. Can you find each factor in Appendix B?

Now let's illustrate another factor.

EXAMPLE

Your brother promises to give you \$116.64 two years from now. If money earns 8 percent interest, what is the *present* value to you? This is a cash flow situation in which *S* is given, *P* must be found.

$$\begin{array}{ccc} P & & S = \$116.64 \\ \downarrow & & \downarrow \\ 0 & \text{———} & 2 \end{array}$$

$$n = 2$$
$$i = .08$$

Solving for P,

$$\begin{aligned} P &= S \text{ (given } S \text{ to find } P \text{ factor)} \\ &= S(PWF(s)_i^n) \\ &= \$116.64\ (PWF(s)_{.08}^2) \\ &= 116.64\ (.8573) \\ &= 99.995 \\ P &\cong 100.00 \end{aligned}$$

This is the reverse of our previous example, in which \$100 invested for two years equaled \$116.64. The present value of \$116.64 in two years at 8% is \$100.00.

Choosing a Discount Rate The importance of the time value of money is reflected in the choice of *i* in the compounding and discounting process. How should the value of *i* be chosen? What should it represent? These questions are not always simple to answer for investment decisions. For some organizations, *i* represents the interest rate charged by lending institutions that loan the money needed to make the investment in plant or equipment. Many companies interpret *i* as the "cost of capital," the cost to them of procuring the funds necessary to finance an investment. Some companies, in choosing *i*, think in terms of opportunity costs—"If I invest in project x it had better offer at least a rate of return of *i* because an alternative investment offers rate *i*." Finally, some firms have a blanket investment policy—"No investment will be made unless it offers at least a return of *i* percent per year." Many of these interpretations will be used as we discuss methods of investment evaluation.

Methods of Evaluation

There are several formal financial methods of evaluating proposed operations changes, and they vary in the degree of simplicity and the type of information they provide. We will focus on the equipment replacement problem, one of several rational operating change problems faced by management. We will choose one model that is simple to calculate, the payback method, and one model that is not as simple to calculate but is often more informative, *net present value*.

Payback One of the most commonly used methods of evaluating investment proposals is to calculate the payback period of the investment as follows:

$$\begin{pmatrix}\text{Payback}\\ \text{period}\end{pmatrix} = \frac{(\text{Net investment})}{\begin{pmatrix}\text{Net annual income}\\ \text{from investment}\end{pmatrix}}$$

Net investment, in dollars, includes the purchase and installation cost less anticipated future salvage value of the asset under consideration. Net annual income is the annual financial benefit (excess of income over expenses) expected from using the asset. The payback period, then, measures the length of time required to recover one's investment. Organizations may be interested in recovering their investment quickly so that they may use the funds for reinvestment in other alternatives. In these cases, payback periods can be calculated for each alternative, and the one offering the quickest turnover of funds (shortest payback period) can be selected.

For several reasons, the payback criterion should be used with caution. First, it does not consider the time value of funds. Second, uneven expense and revenue flow patterns cannot be considered. Finally, it ignores all inflows that occur after the payback period. On the other hand, it has the advantages of simplicity and ease of communication. We recommend it not be used as the sole basis of decision but in conjunction with, or as a supplement to, the other methods of analysis.

EXAMPLE

Two different orange pickers are being considered by Arizona Orchards, Inc., to assist in harvesting the orange crop at the Chandler, Arizona, farm. Alternative *A* requires a net investment of \$10,000 and is expected to return \$2,500 in net annual income per year. Investment *B* is slightly more expensive, \$12,000, but is expected to return \$2,750 per year in income. Calculating the payback period,

$$\text{Payback } A = \frac{\$10{,}000}{\$\ 2{,}500/\text{yr}} = 4 \text{ yr}$$

$$\text{Payback } B = \frac{\$12{,}000}{\$\ 2{,}750/\text{yr}} = 4.36 \text{ yr}$$

Alternative *A* has the shorter payback period.

Net Present Value Net present value considers all cash flows associated with an investment, discounts each unique flow (revenue or expense) back through time to its current equivalent value by using the appropriate compound interest factor, and then sums the net value of all discounted flows at the present time. The result is a net *present* value:

$$\text{Net present value} = \sum \left\{ \begin{pmatrix}\text{Periodic} \\ \text{revenue}\end{pmatrix} - \begin{pmatrix}\text{Periodic} \\ \text{expense}\end{pmatrix} \right\} \left\{ \begin{matrix}\text{Compound} \\ \text{interest} \\ \text{factor}\end{matrix} \right\} - \text{I} \quad \textbf{(19.2)}$$

$$NPV = \sum_{1}^{T} (v_t - c_t)\,(PWF(s)_i^t) - \text{I} \quad \textbf{(19.3)}$$

where

i = rate of interest per year in percent
I = initial investment made at present time
T = life of investment
v_t = income or receipts occurring in period t, where $t = 1, 2, \ldots, T$
c_t = expenses or disbursements made in period t, where $t = 1, 2, \ldots, T$

The procedure for using net present value is:

1. Separate all data by alternatives. Repeat each of the following steps for each alternative.
2. Identify the cash flows. (A diagram of cash flow might be helpful.) On the diagram identify the interest rate and time periods.
3. Write a total net present value equation in words to reflect the situation, the cash flow patterns.
4. Substitute the appropriate dollars and compound amount factors for each flow in the equation.
5. Find the compound amount factors in the Appendices and solve, finding the net present value for each alternative.
6. Choose the alternatives with the *greatest* net present value.

Once you have solved a few problems, you'll probably be able to shortcut this procedure considerably. To simplify *NPV* analysis we assume that cash flows that occur throughout the year always occur at year end. Let's take one example through the complete procedure. This example involves existing equipment that is deteriorating and must be replaced to sustain operations. The manager can compare decision alternatives on a present value basis using the organization's cost of capital as the discounting rate.

EXAMPLE

Fireway Company must purchase a piece of replacement equipment and is considering models offered by two competing equipment manufacturers. Both models have a useful life expectancy of six years (no expected salvage value), and Fireway has a cost of capital of 10 percent for its investments. Each model provides an income of $4,000 annually. Alternative *A* requires an initial outlay of $10,000 and requires maintenance expenditures of $1,000 annually. Alternative *B*, a deluxe model, requires an initial outlay of $12,000 and annual maintenance costs of $500. Which alternative is less costly? The first step has been completed as the data are already organized according to investment alternative. The cash flows are:

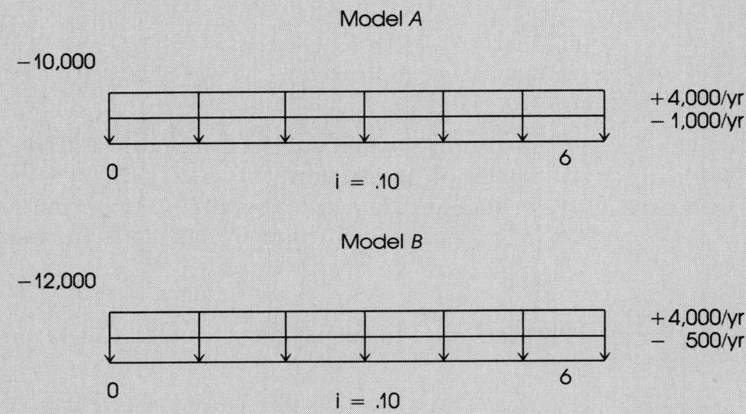

The net present value equation for *A* would be:

$$
\begin{aligned}
NPV(A) &= \text{Sum for each of six years (revenue} - \text{expense)(factor)} - I \\
&= (4{,}000 - 1{,}000)(\text{given } R \text{ to find } P) - I \\
&= (4{,}000 - 1{,}000)\ PWF(u)^{6}_{.10} - 10{,}000 \\
&= 3{,}000(4.355) - 10{,}000 \\
&= 13{,}065 - 10{,}000 \\
NPV(A) &= +\$3{,}065
\end{aligned}
$$

Similarly, the net present value for *B* would be:

$$
\begin{aligned}
NPV(B) &= (4{,}000 - 500)\ (\text{given } R \text{ to find } P) - 12{,}000 \\
&= 3{,}500\ PWF(u)^{6}_{.10} - 12{,}000 \\
&= 3{,}500\ (4.355) - 12{,}000 \\
&= 15{,}242 - 12{,}000 \\
&= +\$3{,}242
\end{aligned}
$$

Choose *B* over *A* because $3,242 > $3,065.

As you might have figured out, another method of solution could also be used. With this method, use separate present worth factors for each of the six periods and sum the six amounts and the initial investment at the current time, time zero. The answers should be equivalent or nearly so using the rounded table factors with those we calculated above for alternatives *A* and *B*. Let's look at a more complex example.

EXAMPLE

Hopi Trucking has just paid $16,000 cash for a new truck. Hopi management estimates that the useful life of the truck is four years. At the end of four years, the estimated salvage value will be $2,500. Maintenance and other operating costs are expected to be $10,000 per year for three years and $12,000 in the fourth year. Assuming we can replace the truck in four years for the same price, how much money must be generated each year from this investment to have at least enough to purchase another truck in four years? Money is worth 8 percent to Hopi, and revenues flow in uniformly to the firm.

First, we must recognize that we are being asked for a dollar amount four years hence, not at the present time. Second we should realize that the $16,000 truck we now have is a sunk cost. Since we are not considering depreciation and taxes, they will not influence our decision. Let *X* be the dollars of revenue required each year to cover expenses and provide $16,000 at the end of four years. Our problem then is as follows.

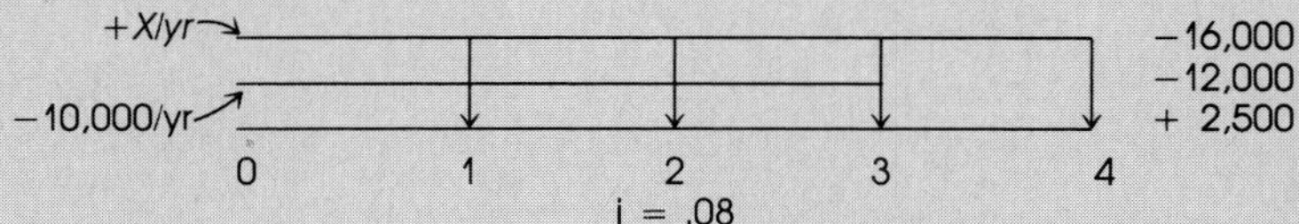

We have −$10,000 per year occurring for three years and, at the end of the fourth year, −$12,000 for expenses. We also have $16,000 for a new truck and +$2,500 for salvaging our old truck. The cash inflow we are looking for is *X* per year for four years. This can be expressed *at year four:*

$$
\begin{aligned}
NPV &= -10{,}000\,(R \text{ to find } P)_{\substack{n=3\\ i=.08}}\,(P \text{ to find } S)_{\substack{n=4\\ i=.08}} \\
&\quad + X(R \text{ to find } S)_{\substack{n=4\\ i=.08}} - 16{,}000 - 12{,}000 \\
&\quad + 2{,}500 \\
&= -10{,}000\,(PWF(u)^3_{.08})(CAF(s)^4_{.08}) \\
&\quad + X(CAF(u)^4_{.08}) - 25{,}500 \\
&= -10{,}000\,(2.577)(1.360) + 4.506\,X - 25{,}500 \\
&= 4.506\,X - (35{,}047 + 25{,}500) \\
NPV &= 4.506\,X - 60{,}547
\end{aligned}
$$

Setting $NPV = 0$ (the breakeven for sales and expenses at four years) and solving for X gives:

$$0 = 4.506\,X - 60{,}547$$
$$X = 60{,}547/4.506$$
$$X = \$13{,}437$$

Annual sales revenue will have to be \$13,437 to cover expenses and provide \$16,000 cash at the end of four years.

With this example, we have solved a problem with a more complex cash flow and an unknown value other than the net present value. Notice that the three-year annual operating expense was brought back to time zero as an annuity and then carried forward four years as a single payment. Although this process was computationally more efficient than taking the \$10,000 forward to the fourth year each of three times, the result would be the same in either case.

What should we do if the investment alternatives have *unequal lives*? Clearly, we can't compare them directly. Let's assume that like-for-like replacement can occur at the end of the life of each asset and use the least common multiple of lives over which to compare the investment. If one alternative has a three-year life and one a two-year life, we would make the comparison over six years. We are assuming, then, that the first alternative would have two exactly similar (like-for-like) investments and the second alternative three exactly similar investments.

EXAMPLE

Yardcare, a lawn company, can purchase an inexpensive lawn mower for \$80 that lasts one year or a more expensive mower for \$120 that lasts two years. Neither mower requires maintenance the first year, but in the second year the more expensive mower will require \$40 worth of maintenance. Both are essentially worthless at the end of one and two years respectively. Money is worth 10 percent to Yardcare. Currently, Yardcare purchases about thirty mowers every two years with no guiding investment replacement principle. What should it do in the future?

Let the inexpensive model be *I*, the more expensive *E*. We need to compare over equal lives, the least multiple being two years. Comparing for one mower, we assume that *I* is replaced at the end of year one with another *I*. The patterns and solutions for each are:

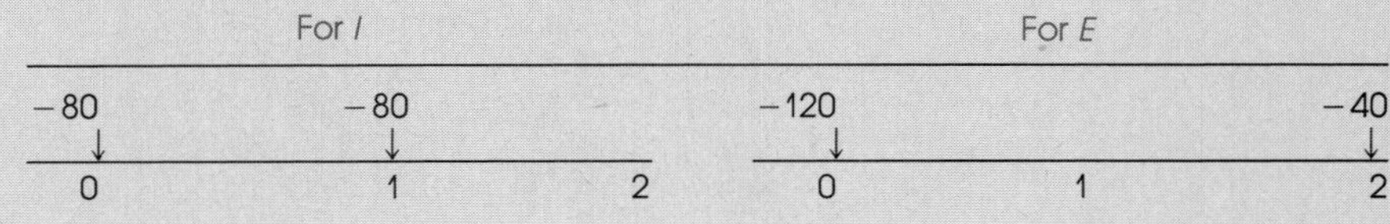

$$NPV(I) = -80 - 80\ (S \text{ to find } P) \quad n = 1,\ i = .10$$
$$= -80 - 80\ (.9091)$$
$$= -80 - 72.72$$
$$NPV(I) = -\$152.72$$

$$NPV(E) = -120 - 40\ (S \text{ to find } P) \quad n = 2,\ i = .10$$
$$= -120 - 40\ (.8264)$$
$$= -120 - 33.05$$
$$NPV(E) = -\ \$153.05$$

Based on present value, the inexpensive model is favored; the cost is \$0.33 less per mower (\$153.05 – \$152.72). For all practical purposes, Yardcare would be indifferent about the choice. The money saved every two years, 30 times \$0.33, or \$9.90, is negligible, and it is doubtful cost data used in the analysis are completely accurate. Errors in data concerning maintenance and purchase prices are always likely.

At times, organizations want investments to meet a minimum rate of return. If the *net* present value at that rate of return is positive, the investment provides greater returns than would the rate used in determining the present value. The investment is made. On the other hand, if the present value is negative, the return is less than that provided by the interest rate used, and the investment is unattractive.

EXAMPLE

XYZ company is considering adding one truck to its fleet of delivery trucks. The truck can be obtained at a cost of \$18,000 if it is purchased for cash now. It is estimated that this used truck will have a useful service life of three years but will require year-end maintenance expenditures of \$3,000 each year. As a result of expanded delivery service, management estimates that annual net revenues will be increased by \$10,000 per year for each of three years. XYZ requires a minimum rate of return of 10 percent and does not wish to make investments that do not offer at least a 10 percent return. The cash flows are:

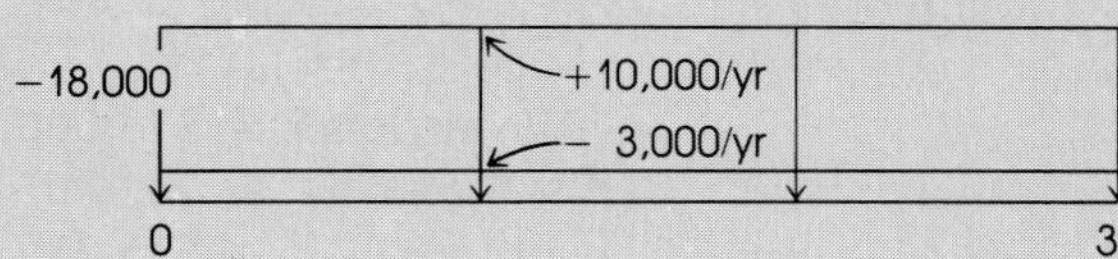

The net present value is calculated:

$$NPV = -18{,}000 - 3{,}000\ (\text{given } R \text{ to find } P)\ + 10{,}000\ (\text{given } R \text{ to find } P)$$
$$n = 3,\ i = .10 \qquad n = 3,\ i = .10$$
$$= -18{,}000 - 3{,}000(PWF(u)^{3}_{.10}) + 10{,}000\ (PWF(u)^{3}_{.10})$$
$$= -18{,}000 + 7{,}000(PWF(u)^{3}_{.10})$$
$$= -18{,}000 + 7{,}000(2.487)$$
$$NPV = -\$600$$

The net present value is −$600. The negative sign indicates that the proposed investment will not meet XYZ's requirement of a 10 percent return on investment. The investment should not be made.

We could expand this analysis to include the effects of depreciation and taxation. Furthermore, if salvage is expected after the project's useful life, the salvage value should be treated as a future inflow.

Internal Rate of Return Suppose you have identified the inflows and outflows of an alternative and wish to determine the rate of return it offers. In this case, i is not prescribed but is a variable whose value you are seeking for this alternative. *The internal rate of return is the discount rate i at which net cash flows for the alternative equal zero.* In other words, the process for finding the internal rate of return involves finding the value of i for which the present value of outflows equals the present value of inflows. The resultant value of i is called the internal rate of return; it is determined by process of trial and error.

We have analyzed XYZ Company's truck purchase proposal and found it had a negative net present value for $i = .10$. What is the internal rate of return offered by this proposal? We know it is less than 10 percent, so we first try something less, say 8 percent. In Appendix B, the annual series present value factor for three years and 8 percent is 2.577. The proposal's present value for $i = .08$ is then:

$$\begin{aligned} PV \text{ inflows} &= (\$10{,}000)(2.577) \\ &= \$25{,}770 \end{aligned}$$

and

$$\begin{aligned} PV \text{ outflows} &= \$18{,}000 + (\$3{,}000)(2.577) \\ &= 18{,}000 + 7{,}333 \\ &= \$25{,}730 \end{aligned}$$

Since inflows exceed outflows on a present value basis, we know the rate is between 0.08 and 0.10 but very close to 0.08. Although we could interpolate to find the exact rate, the net present value of $40 is so close to zero for 8 percent that we will call the internal rate of return 8 percent for this investment alternative. As manager, you may wish to compute this rate of return for all alternatives and choose the one offering the highest return if it exceeds your cost of capital.

Model Selection We recommend again that you use payback in conjunction with net present value in financial change analysis. In the supplement to this chapter, we'll show you why we recommend using payback with either the risk analysis model, a modification of NPV, or the present value model.

Frailties of Estimation

As manager, you will want to take into account some of the assumptions used in financial analysis of investment proposals. You should recognize, however, that several estimates enter into the analysis, and they may turn out to be erroneous. Actual salvage values, useful lives, and applicable interest rates (costs of capital) may be different from the values assumed at the time of analysis. This is especially true for long-term alternatives. How can we know the salvage value twenty years from now? What difference does it make to the current decision?

One approach to these questions is to perform a multiple analysis of each alternative. Instead of performing one present value analysis for alternative *A* using a salvage value of $2,000, two or more analyses may be done. The first might be based on a very pessimistic estimate of salvage value, a second on a very optimistic estimate, and the third might incorporate a most likely estimate. Analysis results can then be compared with one another and with those of other alternatives as well. It may turn out that alternative *A*, even under the most pessimistic conditions, is still better than other alternatives. This is a useful piece of information for decision purposes. The risk analysis procedure discussed in the supplement illustrates another approach to solving the estimation problem.

PLANNED CHANGE IN PRODUCTS AND PROCESSES

In Chapter 18 we observed that recognition of the need for change can be either voluntary or imposed by a variety of forces acting on the organization. Historically, many organizations have found it beneficial to deal with technological change proactively rather than reactively. If we defer action until the legal, social, or competitive environments demand a change in products and conversion processes, we may lose opportunities. A proactive posture recognizes not only that change is going to occur in the future but that organizational efforts and resources can be used to guide the direction and timing of change to some extent. In other words, we can plan for change so that the results are compatible with system goals. With ample awareness of impending change, we can make transitions with fewer disruptions and at lower cost than we can if we wait passively for change to overtake us.

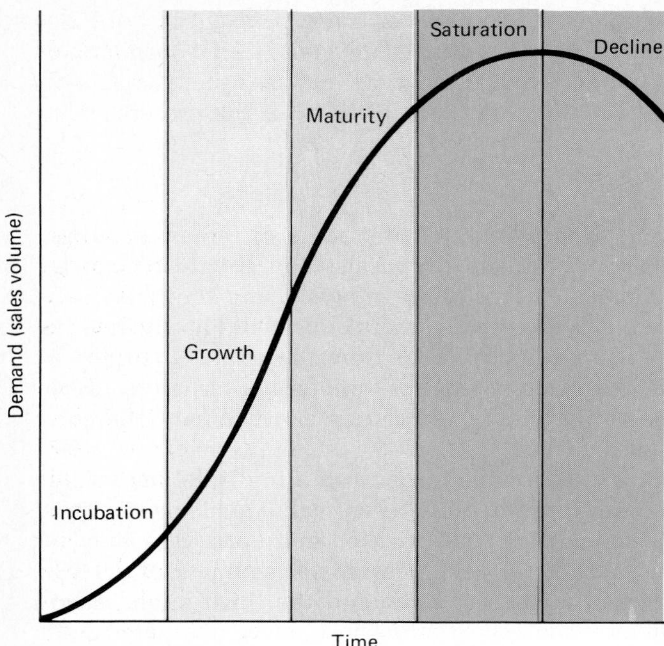

FIGURE 19.4
Stages of a product life cycle

Product and Process Life Cycles

The demand for a product, its market acceptance, generally tends to follow a predictable pattern.[1] Shown in Figure 19.4 the product life cycle has some important ramifications for managers as they attempt to deal with change in their organizations.

The pattern suggests that most products do not have indefinite lives; they arise from meager beginnings, and they reach ultimate peaks at which the level of demand is substantially higher than it was at the initial stage. The time span over which the stages occur is not specified; it varies considerably across industries. For many novelty products, the time from birth to death may be very short, perhaps a matter of weeks or months. For other products, the life cycle may span many years or even decades. In any case the very nature of this pattern raises significant questions for management. When will the various stages occur? What can we do to influence their occurrence? What facilities, materials, and labor are optimal for meeting the anticipated demand? What should be done with existing facilities and conversion processes as demand declines and the product's life ends?

[1]For an empirical approach to evaluating product life cycles, see Cornelis A. deKluyver, "Innovation and Industrial Product Life Cycles," *California Management Review* 20, no. 1 (Fall 1977), pp. 21–23. Process and facility life cycles are discussed in Roger W. Schmenner, "Every Factory Has a Cycle," *Harvard Business Review* 61, no. 2 (March–April, 1983), pp. 121–129.

Some of these questions are not solely the concern of the operations subsystem; they are an integral part of the marketing and finance subsystems as well. They require coordinated actions by the entire organization.

Phasing Multiple Products A general strategy of phasing new products in and old products out is often used to sustain existing processing technology. This concept was previously discussed in Chapter 6 and shown in Figure 6.5. As existing products are demanded less during the later stages of their life cycles, new products are developed and produced. In this way, output capacity can remain stable. While one product goes through saturation and begins the decline stages another product may complete the incubation stage. Similarly, other products are initiated later as earlier products decay, so as to maintain constant capacity requirements.

Of course, actual transitions are not nearly so smooth as in our simple ideal example. Rarely does capacity remain constant; the technologies needed to produce different products are not identical, and at least some changes are almost always necessary. Organizations do not always have a new product waiting for introduction at the precise moment that an existing product begins to decline. Furthermore, the rates of growth and decline may not be highly predictable. With marketing promotional efforts, however, rates of growth and decline can sometimes be influenced. IBM, an expert at planned change, has introduced new computer lines since the late 1950s. Phasing new computers into and old ones out of its basic product line, IBM plans for the changes in its market.

Research and Development

Many organizations, especially larger ones, do not leave the development of new products and processes to chance. They direct formal concerted efforts toward creating new products, finding new uses for existing products, and developing new processes that will reduce capital or manufacturing costs. These are the objectives of research and development (R&D).[2]

A new successful product or process does not happen overnight. Most often it occurs over a succession of steps and involves the talents and expertise of many people, especially in the initial phase. Consider, for example, a relatively new process for tagging salmon used in wildlife management. Historically the process involved catching the fish, physically handling it, tagging, and physically releasing the fish. The new process consists essentially of "tagging" by remote laser beam, thus eliminating the need for physically catching, tagging, and releasing. Now think of the research and development efforts that were required to bring about this new process. Many years ago the theories of physics underlying the laser were conceptualized. Later, developmental research in physics and electronics resulted in a working laser beam. Since then many scientists and engineers

[2]The role of R&D in organizational change is discussed by Neil V. Hakala, "Administration of Industrial Technology," *Business Horizons* 20, no. 5 (October 1977), pp. 4–10.

have developed applications of laser beams in space explorations, health, science, industry, and other settings. Only recently, with the help of fish biologists, has this new tagging process been brought into use. Overall we can identify fundamentally different stages of innovation.

Stages of Innovation There are four generic stages of technological innovation: basic research, applied research, development, and implementation.

Basic research: Research projects that represent original investigation for the advancement of scientific knowledge and that do not have specific commercial objectives. They may, however, be in the field of present or potential interest of the company.

Applied research: Research projects that represent investigation directed toward the discovery of new scientific knowledge. They have specific commercial objectives for either products or processes.

Development: Technical activities concerned with nonroutine problems that are encountered in translating research findings into products or processes.

Implementation: Once the other stages have been completed, the innovation process involves building pilot models, designing and building the necessary equipment and facilities, and initiating the marketing channels necessary for dissemination of the product or process.

Who Pays for Research and Development? In the years 1965 to 1975, the federal government was expending funds at the rate of some $16 billion and private industry was expending about $20 billion annually on research and development.[3] Of this, basic research was receiving about $2 billion of federal and less than $1 billion of industry monies. Applied research received about $3 billion of federal and $3 billion of industry funds. The overwhelming amounts, $11 billion federal and $16 billion industry, were allocated to development. By 1984 the federal R&D expenditure rate was estimated to reach $45 billion, which, due to inflation, did not represent a real increase over the earlier period. Of this $45 billion, $6 billion went to basic research, $8 billion to applied research, and $31 billion to development.[4]

A survey of federal programs and practices as they affect manufacturing technology illustrates that the government is contributing minimally toward developing new manufacturing technology.[5] Manufacturing produc-

---

[3]U.S., National Science Foundation (NSF 78-320), *An Analysis of Federal R&D Funding by Function: Fiscal Years 1969–1979* (Washington, D.C.: Surveys of Science Resources Series, 1978).

[4]U.S. National Science Foundation (NSF 83-319), *Federal Funds for Research and Development Fiscal Years 1982, 1983, and 1984*, pp. 14–15 (Washington D.C.: Superintendent of Documents, 1984).

[5]William A. Hetzner, Louis G. Tornatzky, and Katherine J. Klein, "Manufacturing Technology in the 1980's: A Survey of Federal Programs and Practices," *Management Science* 29, no. 8 (August 1983), pp. 951–961.

tivity is part of the broader question of technological innovation and the international technological competitiveness of U.S. industry. Of the thirteen federal programs evaluated, virtually all have been established for a reasonable period of time (85 percent established five years or longer). In summary, the bulk of the federal presence in manufacturing technology is concentrated in a relatively few mission agencies, which emphasize short-term, user-oriented, relatively small scale, hardware technologies. The programs have limited impact on longer term, large scale systems technologies. They also tend to direct themselves to their user firms with little or no direct contact with others. In short, the federal research programs concerned with manufacturing technology have minimal effect, leaving the competitive challenge to the private sector.

Private funds have been paid mainly by larger firms in high technology industries with relatively rapid product turnover. Chemical, electronics, aerospace, and transportation industries, unlike such relatively dormant industries as canning and mining, expend great efforts in research and development. In the more dynamic industries innovation is accepted as an inherent characteristic of organizational life, and R&D is a vital part of it. Annual budgetary allocations are made on a regular basis, often as a percent of sales.

The costs of R&D are typically very high. It requires investment in such facilities as laboratories with highly specialized, expensive equipment for experimentation and testing. Scientific, engineering, and technical expertise must be procured. Technical libraries and computing facilities are a necessity. In addition, a supporting staff, including research administrators, is required. Often it is difficult to see the tangible contributions of R&D to corporate goals. Especially for basic research, R&D contributions are infrequent or irregular. In light of the high costs and infrequency of tangible results, it is no wonder that many firms are hesitant to engage in extensive R&D efforts. Consequently, many "research" departments are actually almost completely concerned with development. In fact, a good number of these hardly even concern themselves with development, concentrating instead on *innovation,* which involves simply putting a new twist on an old product.

Organization of R&D In most companies R&D is a staff function located at either the corporate or divisional level. Three examples of R&D organizational structure are shown in Figure 19.5. In part (*a*), R&D is centrally located. From this location, R&D can economically serve the needs of all divisions and avoid duplication of effort. A disadvantage is that the R&D unit may be geographically and organizationally remote from the immediate needs of the various divisions. This difficulty is overcome by decentralized R&D (*b*). This structure, however, can tend to raise the overall corporate costs of the R&D effort insofar as duplication across divisions may result. Decentralization is well suited to companies in which applied research and development dominate the overall R&D effort, particularly when the prod-

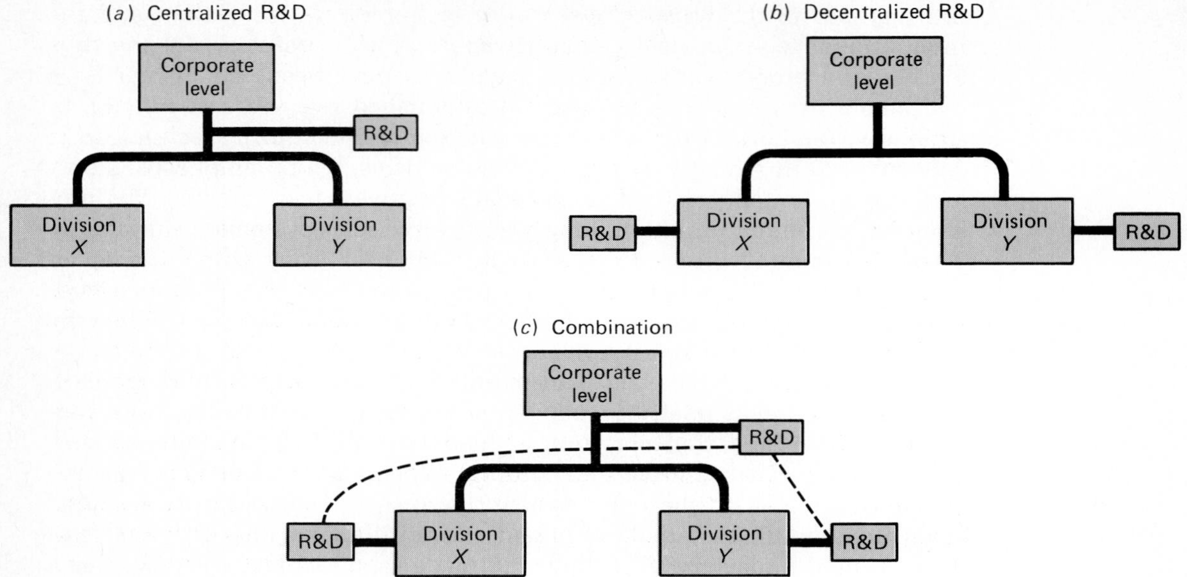

FIGURE 19.5
R&D location in organization structure

ucts and processes have a high degree of technological differentiation along divisional lines. Here the development efforts are specialized, tailored to the nature of each specific division.

The combination structure, (*c*), attempts to reap the best of the benefits offered by both centralization and decentralization. R&D units at divisional levels can be specialized toward the special needs at that level, especially in the developmental and applied areas. Some of the applied research and perhaps all of the basic research may be centralized at the corporate level. Development and innovation frequently occur at the divisional level. The dotted lines among the three R&D units reflect subsidiary relationships among them; relevant results of basic or applied research at one level are transferred to the others. On occasion, the progress of development efforts at a divisional level may be impeded because further applied research is needed. If the corporate R&D unit, for example, is the only one prepared to work in the necessary applied area, the problem must then be referred to it until a solution is reached.

Project Adoption and Change From the R&D process emerge new concepts, ideas, potential projects, and technologies. Then management must decide which potential R&D projects should be adopted within the limited budget in each of the R&D units. As existing products and processes reach new stages in their life cycles, R&D efforts are directed toward bringing new products and processes onstream so that desired overall levels of organizational output can be sustained with minimal disruption.

CHANGES IN ORGANIZATION STRUCTURE, TASKS, AND POLICIES

Thus far we have discussed two useful technical approaches to change, investment analysis and research and development of products and processes. Now we must consider changes that occur in organization structure, tasks, and policies. Are rational approaches available for these types of changes? Yes, with two qualifications. First, the effects of policy and structural changes are less predictable because of their potentially widespread influence throughout the organization and because they can affect organization performance in so many diverse ways. Second, the research methodologies for studying policy and structural changes are relatively new and are not yet highly developed or widely used. We will present two methodologies for studying the effects of change, learning curve analysis and system dynamics. These two methodologies differ substantially in focus and orientation. Learning curve analysis is one way of evaluating the effects of changes in tasks; it is based on traditional industrial engineering techniques. In contrast, system dynamics is applicable to a broader range of potential changes in organizational structure and policy. Both methodologies are helpful for identifying and evaluating change alternatives, and they can play an important role in the scientific approach to problem solving.

Learning Curve Analysis

When a new model of an existing product is introduced, especially if the work content is similar, learning curve analysis can be helpful in its manufacture.[6] As an organization gains experience in manufacturing a product, the resource inputs required per unit of output diminish over the life of the product. The hours of labor that go into manufacturing the first unit of a new commercial aircraft are typically much higher than those needed for the one-hundredth unit, for example. As the cumulative output of the model grows, the labor inputs continue to decline. As you know, if you repeat a new task continually, your performance improves. The performance time drops off rather dramatically at first, and it continues to fall at some slower rate until a performance plateau, a leveling off, is reached. This learning phenomenon occurs for groups and organizations as well as for individuals. Furthermore, performance data from many companies show that this learning pattern is often regular and predictable. The general form of this pattern, called the learning curve, is shown on arithmetic co-

[6]For a review of learning curve development, see Louis E. Yelle, "The Learning Curve: Historical Review and Comprehensive Survey," *Decision Sciences* 10, no. 2 (April 1979), pp. 302–28.

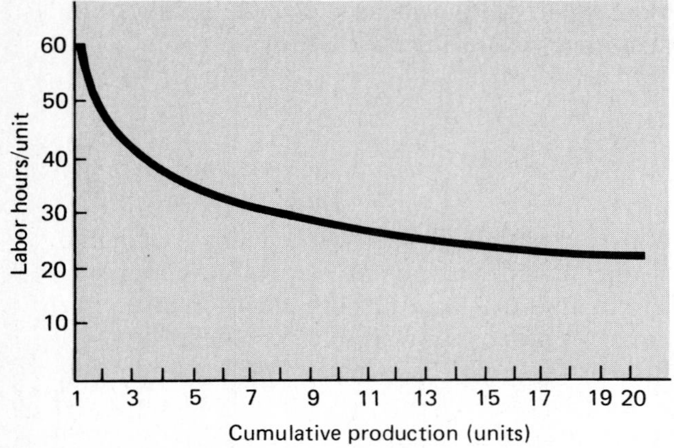

FIGURE 19.6
An 80 percent learning curve plotted on arithmetic coordinates: first unit requires 60 labor hours

ordinates in Figure 19.6. In it, the initial unit output requires 60 labor hours to manufacture. As output and experience continue, labor hours per unit diminish to about 23 for the twentieth unit. The general equation for this curve is:

$$Y_i = ki^b \qquad \textbf{(19.4)}$$

where

Y_i = labor hours required to produce the ith cumulative unit of output
k = labor hours required to produce the first unit of output (initial productivity)
b = index of learning

This exponential curve becomes a straight line when plotted on logarithmic coordinates (Figure 19.7).

Rate of Learning The rate of learning is not the same in all manufacturing applications. Learning occurs at a higher rate in some applications than others and is reflected by a more rapid descent of the curve. By convention the learning rate is specified as a percentage. A 90 percent curve, for example, means that each time cumulative output doubles, the newest unit of output requires 90 percent of the labor input of the reference unit; if unit 1 requires 100 labor hours, unit 2 will require 90 percent of 100, or 90 hours, unit 4 will require 90 percent of 90 hours, or 81 hours, and so on. Labor hours required for 70, 80, and 90 percent curves are shown here for various levels of cumulative output, assuming 100 labor hours are required for the first unit.

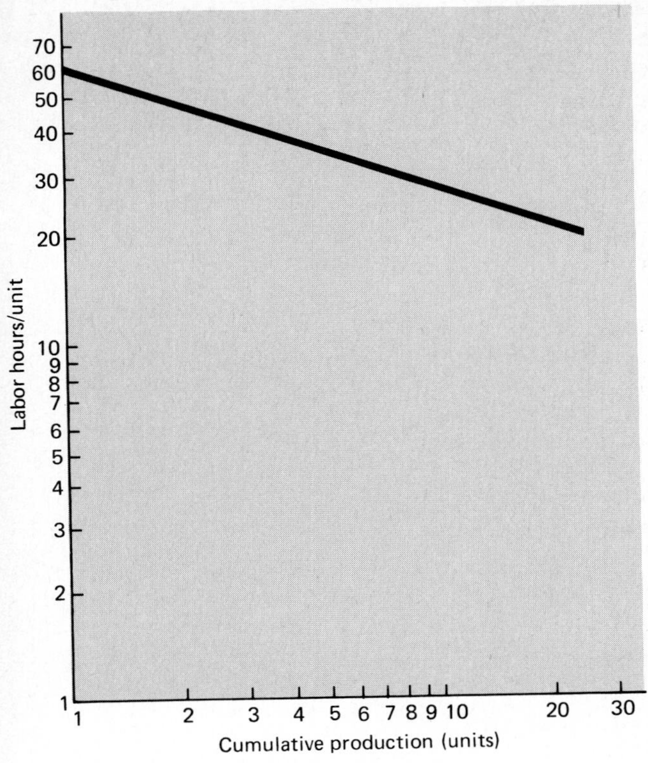

FIGURE 19.7
An 80 percent learning curve plotted on logarithmic coordinates: first unit requires 60 labor hours

Cumulative output i (units)	70% curve	Labor hours required for i^{th} cumulative unit 80% curve	90% curve
1	100.0	100.0	100.0
2	70.0	80.0	90.0
4	49.0	64.0	81.0
8	34.3	51.2	72.9
16	24.0	41.0	65.6

We have plotted three curves on arithmetic and logarithmic coordinates (Figure 19.8) for 16 cumulative units of output. Arithmetically, the rate of learning is reflected by b, the index of learning. The index b is shown in Figure 19.8 for each curve. The index of learning for the 90 percent learning curve is $-.1520$. Table 19.2 shows computed values of i^b for 80 and 90 percent curves. By using equation 19.4 you can extend these

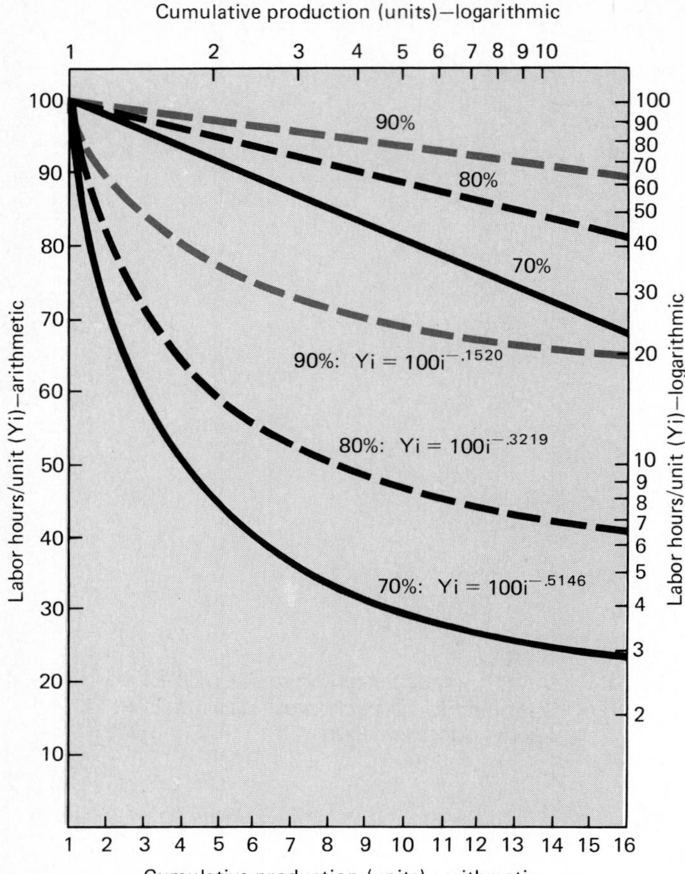

FIGURE 19.8
Arithmetic and logarithmic coordinates for 70, 80, and 90 percent learning curves: first unit requires 100 labor hours

calculations to cover any desired level of cumulative output beyond those given in the table.

EXAMPLE

Surefloat Boat Builders has been receiving customer orders for a new model yacht. Based on previous experience at introducing new models, Surefloat engineers estimate that an 80 percent improvement curve is applicable and that the first unit of the new model will require 500 hours of labor. Surefloat has received customer orders for delivery in the next five months as follows:

Month	Number of yachts ordered
1	2
2	6
3	10
4	10
5	15
	43

The manufacturing manager is concerned about the manpower requirements for meeting these commitments to customers. The manufacturing engineer was asked to provide some information that could be used for manpower planning.

TABLE 19.2
Computed values of i^b for 80% and 90% curves: 50 units

i (unit number)	80% curve ($b = -.3219$)	90% curve ($b = -.1520$)	i (unit number)	80% curve ($b = -.3219$)	90% curve ($b = -.1520$)
1	1.0000	1.0000	26	.3504	.6094
2	.7999	.9000	27	.3461	.6059
3	.7021	.8462	28	.3421	.6026
4	.6400	.8100	29	.3379	.5994
5	.5957	.7830	30	.3346	.5963
6	.5617	.7616	31	.3311	.5934
7	.5345	.7440	32	.3277	.5905
8	.5120	.7290	33	.3245	.5878
9	.4930	.7161	34	.3214	.5851
10	.4766	.7047	35	.3184	.5825
11	.4621	.6946	36	.3155	.5800
12	.4494	.6854	37	.3128	.5776
13	.4380	.6771	38	.3101	.5753
14	.4276	.6696	39	.3075	.5730
15	.4182	.6626	40	.3050	.5708
16	.4096	.6561	41	.3026	.5687
17	.4017	.6501	42	.3002	.5666
18	.3944	.6445	43	.2980	.5646
19	.3876	.6392	44	.2958	.5626
20	.3819	.6342	45	.2937	.5607
21	.3753	.6295	46	.2916	.5588
22	.3697	.6251	47	.2896	.5570
23	.3645	.6209	48	.2876	.5552
24	.3595	.6169	49	.2857	.5535
25	.3548	.6131	50	.2839	.5518

Equation 19.4 applied to the Surefloat situation becomes:

$$Y_i = (500)i^{-0.3219} \tag{19.5}$$

Using equation 19.5 (or tabled values) for the 80 percent curve, the engineer generated the data in Table 19.3. Surefloat management can use these data to decide how many yachts to produce each month so that the manpower requirements are smoothed across months. The data also enable determination of work force size. Notice the effects of learning in the data. Commitments to customers in month 2 are 200 percent greater than in month 1; yet the manpower to accomplish this increases by only 98 percent over the previous month. As the second column shows, labor hours are reduced rather dramatically initially and then taper off to relatively small increments as the effects of learning diminish with experience.

TABLE 19.3
Engineering data for use in manpower planning

Yacht (cumulative)	Labor hours* per yacht (rounded)	Month	Number of yachts promised	Labor hours needed for monthly commitments	Change in labor hours from previous month	Change in output from previous month	Monthly** manpower equivalents (number of people)
1	500	1	2	900			5.62
2	400						
3	351	2	6	1,773	+98.1%	+200.0%	11.08
4	320						
5	298						
6	281						
7	267						
8	256						
9	246	3	10	2,185	+23.2	+ 67.7	13.65
10	238						
11	231						
12	225						
13	219						
14	214						
15	209						
16	205						
17	201						
18	197						
19	194	4	10	1,816	– 16.8	0	11.35
20	191						
21	188						
22	185						

TABLE 19.3 (Cont.)
Engineering data for use in manpower planning

Yacht (cumulative)	Labor hours* per yacht (rounded)	Month	Number of yachts promised	Labor hours needed for monthly commitments	Change in labor hours from previous month	Change in output from previous month	Monthly** manpower equivalents (number of people)
23	182						
24	180						
25	177						
26	175						
27	173						
28	171						
29	169	5	15	2,373	+31.0	+ 50.0	14.83
30	167						
31	165						
32	164						
33	162						
34	161						
35	159						
36	158						
37	156						
38	155						
39	154						
40	153						
41	151						
42	150						
43	149						
			Total labor hours = 9,047			Total yachts = 43	

*Obtained from Table 19.2 and equation 19.4, labor hours for yacht one = Y_1 = (500)(1.000) = 500.
**A person is assumed to work 20 days per month, 8 hours per day. Thus, a "manpower equivalent" is 20 × 8 = 160 labor hours per month. For each month the manpower equivalent is found by dividing the monthly labor hours by 160. Hence, for month one, 900 ÷ 160 = 5.62.

EXAMPLE

Surefloat management has decided on a selling price of $12,000 per yacht. It expects to receive payment the month following delivery. Each yacht will be produced and delivered during the month in which it was promised previously. Work force size will equal the monthly manpower equivalents shown in Table 19.4. Standard wages are $1,000 per month per employee. Costs of direct materials, variable materials, overhead, and fixed administrative and marketing overhead are also shown in Table 19.4. All these costs will be incurred during the month of production.

TABLE 19.4
Cash flow for six months: Surefloat Boat Builders

	Month					
	1	2	3	4	5	6
Units produced and delivered	2	6	10	10	15	15
Cash inflow from sales	—0—	$24,000	$72,000	$120,000	$120,000	$180,000
Outflows						
Wages	$5,620	11,080	13,650	11,350	14,830	13,500
Direct materials ($6,000 per yacht)	12,000	36,000	60,000	60,000	90,000	90,000
Variable materials overhead (10% of direct materials)	1,200	3,600	6,000	6,000	9,000	9,000
Fixed administrative and marketing overhead	10,000	10,000	$10,000	$ 10,000	10,000	10,000
Monthly outflow	$28,820	60,680	89,650	87,350	123,830	122,500
Net monthly cash flow (inflow-outflow)	(28,820)*	(36,680)	(17,650)	32,650	(3,830)	57,500
Cumulative cash flow position (month-end)	(28,820)	(65,500)	(83,150)	(50,500)	(54,330)	3,170

*Parentheses denote negative cash flow.

Uses of Learning Curves Just as learning curve analysis can be used for manpower planning, it can also be helpful in cash flow planning.[7] Cash flow planning involves identifying the timing of cash outlays and inflows associated with a new product. The analysis indicates when we will need to borrow funds to finance our operations until revenues begin to make the project self-supporting.

Notice that monthly inflows are less than outlays for each of the first 3 months. Cumulative cash flows are negative through month 5, and Surefloat will have to borrow funds or divert them from other projects to finance operations on the new model yacht during these months. By using learning curve analysis, we can estimate manpower needs and the costs (outflows) necessary to complete a cash flow analysis.

Parameter Estimation Two parameters, k and b, must be estimated for learning curve analysis. If these parameters are seriously in error, results can be very misleading. Estimates of labor hours for the initial unit are based primarily on staff experience and familiarity with the history of the conversion process. Estimation accuracy will be closely related to the degree of conversion similarity between the new and previous products. Es-

[7]Use of the learning curve in decision making is discussed in Woody M. Liao, "Effects of Learning on Resource Allocation Decisions," *Decision Sciences* 10, no. 1 (January 1979), pp. 116–25.

timation of the appropriate learning rate is typically accomplished by regression analysis on data from experiences with similar past products.

Sources of Improvement While the learning curve depicts productivity improvement over time, improvement does not take place solely because workers are learning. The sources of productivity changes are numerous, but they include changes in work methods, product engineering modifications, facilities layout improvements, equipment redesign, employee training, and others. We intend the term "learning curve" to subsume the effects of all these sources of productivity progress in summary measure. Learning curve analysis is generally of greatest benefit in labor-intense conversion processes.

System Dynamics

In Chapter 18, when we described system dynamics, we mentioned that system dynamics models can provide information to many kinds of managers. One way these models are often used is for examining the effects of policy and structure changes in the organization. The analysis procedure involves three basic steps: creating a valid model of the system of interest as it currently exists, modifying the model to incorporate new policies or changes in structure, and recording and comparing simulated system performance before and after the changes. With this procedure, we can use such variability measures as service to customers, inventory levels, manpower levels, and output levels to evaluate the overall effects of change in the system.

A system dynamics simulation model is a mathematical representation of some system of interest. Without presenting the mathematics, we will discuss its general structure and form and show how it might be manipulated to provide useful managerial information. To use this model, the major components of the system must first be identified. Next, relationships among the components must be determined; in particular, flows of people, information, and materials within the system must be specified in detail. Usually these flows involve time delays, which must be represented in the model. Finally, the decision rules used for day-to-day operations within the components must be built into the model.

These model characteristics are shown in Figure 19.9 for a hypothetical production-distribution system. In the system is a factory, which sends the finished product to a nearby factory warehouse for storage. From inventory in the warehouse, finished goods are shipped to a few regional distributors, who order (purchase) from the factory warehouse when their existing inventory levels begin to deplete. Similarly, shipments enter local distributors' inventories when they are received from their regional distributors. Local distributors then supply retailers, who sell to the retail customers. Overall there are five sectors in this production-distribution system. In the factory is a production component, which creates the final product; a production decision component; and a purchase decision component. As the

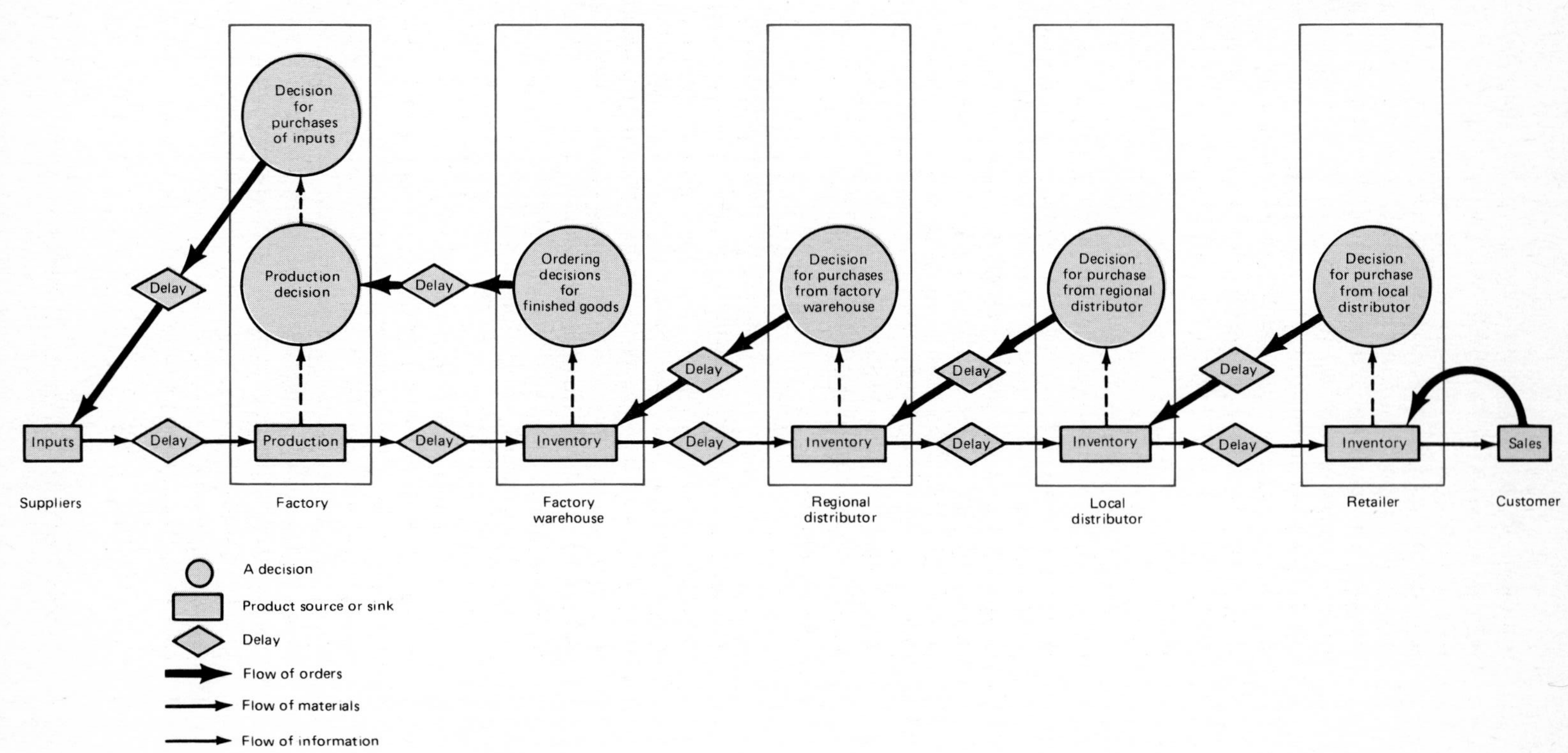

FIGURE 19.9
Production-distribution system

diagram shows, the production decision depends on information about current production rate and the quantity of new orders received from the factory warehouse. Only after the production decision has been made can managers decide to purchase factory inputs. Each of the other four sectors contains a pool of inventory, which is depleted when orders from downstream are filled and replenished when purchase orders from upstream are filled. In each sector the purchase decision is based on information about the current inventory level in that sector.

Two general characteristics of relationships among sectors should be noted. First, materials and finished goods flow downstream, and orders for goods flow upstream. Second, there are delays in receiving orders and in receiving replenishment supplies. The restricted information flows, the delays, and the use of inventory-based rules for purchasing decisions result in wide fluctuations throughout the system, particularly in those sectors farthest removed from the retail customers. Say that a sudden increase in retail sales causes retail inventories to go below desired levels. The retailer may respond by purchasing both larger amounts from the local distributor to restore inventory and some additional amount in anticipation of higher retail sales demand. After some delay, the local distributor receives the larger order from retailers, fills them from existing inventory, and then places larger orders to the regional distributor. In each sector inventory levels decline and backorders begin to accumulate; and these variations are amplified as they progress upstream. By the time the factory begins gearing up in response to the large increase in orders from the factory warehouse, retail customer sales may have dropped off. Retailers subsequently reduce orders to local distributors who, in turn, order less from regional distributors, and so on. Meanwhile, back at the factory, production rates and employment levels are beginning to fluctuate wildly as a result of all these changes in demand.

What can management do to improve the performance of this production-distribution system? Can production, inventories, and backorders be stabilized to provide better customer service and lower production costs? By building a simulation model of the existing system, managers can experimentally evaluate proposed changes. Perhaps some proposed changes require only minor modifications of the model, while others involve major remodeling efforts. If purchase order decision rules, for example, were tested for each sector within the existing model, the experimental simulation results would reveal the extent to which system performance is affected by these decision rules. The manager may find that they have relatively limited impact and that more extensive model modification is warranted. Say that the manager proposes establishing a new information flow in which current retail consumer demand becomes a direct input to production decisions at the factory. In this way demand information would bypass the three intermediate sectors. The existing model would be modified to incorporate this new information link, and subsequent simulation runs would indicate its potential effect on system behavior. A more extensive managerial proposal might consider restructuring the production-distribution system by consolidating two or more sectors into one. Perhaps by consolidating local and regional distributorships we could eliminate some existing delays in ordering and receiving. This type of system change could be evaluated by restructuring the model and then simulating system performance.

The system dynamics approach is useful because it helps the manager understand the structure and behavior of systems. However, it remains an experimental procedure, and the user has no assurance that the experimental results will materialize when changes suggested by the analysis are implemented. Furthermore, because of the modeling efforts and computer time required the analyses can be expensive. Still, system dynamics is one of the most formalistic approaches to anticipating the effects of policy and structural changes in organizations.

SUMMARY

The operations manager is part of a dynamic organization that requires changes in technology, structure, and behavior. Since the effects of change are so pervasive, the manager seeks to guide change in a rational manner toward the accomplishment of system goals. To help guide change in the organization, financial analysis, research and development, learning curve analysis, and system dynamics are all useful techniques.

With financial analysis the manager can evaluate the economic aspects of proposed changes. He or she can compare alternatives against one another or against a specified criterion before making a choice. The form of the analysis rests on basic concepts used in accounting, economics, and finance. After all the economic consequences of a proposal have been considered, the manager is in a better position to weigh them against noneconomic or nonquantifiable factors and make a more enlightened decision.

The research and development function is a major means by which organizations can plan for change. Proactive rather than reactive, R&D accepts the fact that change is an inherent part of organizational life. At the heart of R&D is the concept of product and process life cycles, a useful idea in phasing new products and processes into adoption so that transitions can be smooth and economical. This process is not cost-free, however; establishing R&D efforts is expensive in terms of the people, equipment, and facilities required. Furthermore, the very nature of the R&D process is risky; we can never be sure that a new product or process will materialize when it is needed.

Learning curves can be useful for manpower planning, cash flow analysis, and product pricing. Manpower planning and cash flow analysis help smooth the transition when new products or new models are introduced in the product line. The product pricing decision is vital to the organization's profitability.

System dynamics is a framework for evaluating changes in policy and structure on an experimental basis. It is applicable when one wishes to evaluate how changes in one or more parts of the system will affect both other parts and system performance overall. Modeling, of great potential value in system dynamics, helps the manager understand system interrelationships and behavior.

CASE

Cleanair Corporation

Cleanair Corporation designs and manufactures small contaminant filtration units. These units are used in various industrial facilities to reduce emissions contributing to air pollution. Cleanair's research and development department has developed and tested a new model, the Minigasp III, which it believes is now suitable for full-scale marketing. Minigasp I has been successfully marketed for eight years and Minigasp II for four, and Cleanair management believes that Minigasp III faces even brighter marketing prospects. Although similar in many ways to its predecessors, Minigasp III contains an innovative chemical processing system that should give Cleanair a competitive edge in the industry. Management must now decide whether or not to add Minigasp III to its product line.

The marketing manager says that a $3,000 per unit selling price would be very competitive and anticipates sales of one unit in each of months 1 and 2, two units in month 3, three units in month 4, and four units per month thereafter. Payment by the customer is expected during the month of purchase. The operations manager believes he can meet these market demands if the changeover of facilities is started immediately. An initial outlay of $30,000 will be necessary to renovate part of the plant and equipment. Costs of manufacture have been estimated as follows:

Direct materials	=	$700 per unit
Indirect materials	=	10 percent of direct materials cost
Direct labor	=	$7 per man hour
Indirect labor	=	20 percent of direct labor cost
Additional administrative and marketing costs	=	$3,000 per month

In addition, maintenance expenses will be $1,000 in month 1, $750 in month 2, and $500 per month thereafter. Production engineers estimate the initial unit of Minigasp III will require 200 hours of labor to manufacture. Thereafter, they believe an 80 percent learning curve is applicable.

The finance manager questions the advisability of adopting the new product because of the risks involved. If new government regulations were to be created, always a major factor in this industry, the marketability of Minigasp III could be prematurely damaged. Consequently, he suggests the project not be undertaken unless the funds from sales can fully recover the initial $30,000 outlay during the first year of production. As operations manager you are expected to respond to the finance manager.

REVIEW AND DISCUSSION QUESTIONS

1. What is mean by "rational approaches to change"?
2. Identify three examples of organizational changes for which the rational approach is helpful to the operations manager.
3. Discuss examples for which the rational approaches to change are of limited value.
4. Discuss difficulties of applying financial and economic analysis to behavioral changes in organizations.
5. What is the role of return on investment in financial and economic analysis of change alternatives?

6. Define the following:
   (a) opportunity costs
   (b) sunk costs
   (c) salvage value
   (d) depreciation
7. Define accounting life, machine life, and economic life of an asset.
8. How does an organization determine the appropriate discount rate for use in financial analysis?
9. Compare the major features of payback, net present value, and internal rate of return methods of evaluation.
10. The concept of product and process life cycles has implications for both rational approaches to change and organizational structure. Discuss these implications.
11. Under what circumstances is learning curve analysis most applicable?
12. What are the sources of productivity improvement that cause the learning phenomenon?
13. For what kinds of operating decisions can learning curve analysis provide data?
14. Discuss the role of system dynamics in analyzing organizational changes.

PROBLEMS

Solved Problems

1. What is the present value of $6,500 to be received 9 years from now if the prevailing interest rate is 8 percent? 10 percent?

Solution:

This is a cash flow pattern of the form. Given a future sum of money, find the equivalent present sum, or "given S to find P."

(1) for 8 percent:

$$PWF(s)_i^n \text{ or } PWF(s)_{.08}^9 = 0.5002 \text{ from Appendix B.}$$
$$P = \$6{,}500(0.5002) = \$3{,}251.30$$

(b) for 10 percent:

$$P = \$6{,}500(0.4241) = \$2{,}756.65$$

2. The current plans of Whataflop Corporation indicate a need to replace a worn out air compressor. One supplier, Airco, can provide a compressor costing $15,000 with a salvage value of $3,000 at the end of its three-year life. A second supplier, Compo, can provide a compressor for $10,000 initial cost with a salvage value of $2,000 at the end of its two-year life. Annual operating costs are estimated at $1,000 for both compressors. If money is worth 10 percent, which compressor do you recommend? Why?

Solution:

The Airco and Compo compressors have different life spans, therefore the computation of present worth costs is made over six years, the least common multiple.

$$\text{NPV (Airco)} = -\$15000 + (\$3{,}000 - \$15000)(.7513) + (\$3000)(.5645) = -\$22{,}322.10$$

$$\text{NPV (Compo)} = -\$10000 + (\$2000 - \$10000)(.8264) + (\$2000 - \$10000)(.6830) + (\$2000)(.5645) = -\$20{,}946.20$$

Based on this analysis, the Compo compressor provides the lowest costs and is alternative that should be chosen. Notice that the cash flows were not diagrammed in this solution. This probably made the solution difficult to follow, and increased the chance of logic errors. These steps were skipped to illustrate that point for you.

Reinforcing Fundamentals

3. What is the present value of $1,000 to be invested for 7 years at 8 percent interest? At 10 percent interest?
4. What is the present value of a 15-year series of $800 investments if the interest rate is 8 percent? 10 percent?
5. What is the present value of $12,000 to be received 13 years from now if the prevailing interest rate is 8 percent? 10 percent?
6. Show-Me is considering two alternative locations for a new movie theater. Show-Me is using a ten-year planning horizon with a 10 percent cost of capital. Location 1 involves a land purchase and construction costs totaling $300,000; this property's estimated resale value after ten years is $400,000. Annual revenues will be $82,000; annual expenses will be $47,000. Location 2 requires a ten-year lease agreement; in addition to an initial outlay of $45,000 the annual lease payment is $30,000 per year. Annual revenues at location 2 are expected to be $95,000; annual operating expenses will be $32,000. Which location is best?
7. A company is considering two alternative relayout designs. Alternative 1 requires an initial investment of $100,000, will result in $20,000 in annual cost savings for the next ten years, and is expected to have equipment salvage value of $20,000 at the end of ten years. Alternative 2 requires an $80,000 initial investment, will result in $16,000 annual cost savings, and will have no salvage value after ten years. The interest rate is 10 percent.
   (a) Which alternative is best using the payback criterion?
   (b) Which alternative is best using the net present value criterion?
8. The current plans of Russell's Auto Clinic indicate a need to replace a worn out welder. One supplier, Lincoln, can provide a welder costing $4500 with a salvage value of $3500 at the end of its four-year life. A second supplier, Weldit, can provide a welder for $3500 initial cost with a salvage value of $1000 at the end of its two-year life. Annual operating costs are estimated at $400 for both welders. If money is worth 10 percent, which welder do you recommend? Why?
9. Fastback Trucking Company is considering two alternative types of trucks. Truck *A*, a less expensive used model, has a useful economic life of two years, an initial cost of $3,000, estimated salvage value of $300 after two years, and annual maintenance costs of $800. Truck *B*, a newer and faster model, will have a useful economic life of four years, an initial cost of $8,000, estimated salvage value of $2,000 after four years, annual maintenace costs of $200, and will increase revenues from deliveries by $500 each year. Interest is 8%. Which alternative is most attractive?
10. An investment alternative requires an initial outlay of $71,500, is expected to have a five-year useful life, and will have a salvage value of $10,600 after five years. Annual incremental revenues will be $20,500 and annual increment operating expenses will be $7,200 during the useful life. What is the internal rate of return for this alternative?
11. A hospital is evaluating which of two machines to purchase to use in the analysis of blood samples. One unit is more expensive than the other, but because of its high degree of automation it has a lower labor cost. Both machines meet the hospital's needs and are essentially worthless at the end of their economic life. Money is worth 10 percent.

	Unit 1	Unit 2
Purchase cost	$15,000	$22,000
Economic life	3 years	3 years
Labor costs per year	$14,000	$ 9,000
Installation cost	$ 4,000	$ 5,000
Maintenance costs		
First year	$ 500	$ 1,000
Increase per year	100	$ 500
Book value		
End of first year	$15,000	$20,000
End of third year	$ 3,000	$ 3,000

(a) Using *present worth,* which unit should the hospital purchase?
(b) Explain to the pathologist (an MD) in charge of the lab how the *present worth* approach can provide useful data for capital budgeting purposes.

Challenging Exercises

12. Growthco's investment policy requires a 10 percent minimum internal rate of return for justifying any potential investment. Two alternatives, *A* and *B,* are under consideration. Which alternative should be adopted?

	Alternative A	Alternative B
Useful life	6 years	6 years
Initial outlay	$100,000	$130,000
Salvage value (at end of useful life)	$20,000	$22,000
Incremental annual revenue	$45,000	$50,000
Incremental annual expenses	$26,000	$30,000

13. As purchasing agent for Kansas City Industries, you have the following two equipment replacement alternatives.

	Alternative 1	Alternative 2
Machine life	2	3
Economic life	1	2
Initial investment	Negotiable	$20,000
Annual maintenance cost	0	$ 1,000
Salvage value end of machine life	$1,000	$ 2,000
Salvage value end of economic life	$4,000	$ 5,000
Value of money	10%	10%

Your problem is to find the upper bound (or maximum amount) of the initial investment you are willing to negotiate in alternative 1 (that is, any amount greater than the upper bound would make alternative 2 the most economical). Use present worth to determine the upper bound.

14. Insurance Associates, Inc. (IAI) needs a new photocopy machine to meet commitments to customers. The cost of capital to IAI is 10 percent. One of two alternatives must be selected. What is your recommendation?

	Alternative A	Alternative B
Useful life	3 years	6 years
Initial outlay	$45,000	$70,000
Salvage value (at end of useful life)	$4,000	$9,000
Annual maintenance and operating cost (years 1–3)	$8,000	$6,000
(years 4–6)	—	$10,000

15. In response to a consumer inquiry, a manufacturing company is estimating the costs of twenty-five units of a new product, which is similar to an existing one. Estimates indicate that 400 labor hours will be required to produce the first unit. Draw graphs of labor requirements for units 1 through 25 for 80 percent and 90 percent learning curves.
16. Reconsider problem 15 using the 80 percent improvement curve. Direct labor and variable overhead are estimated at $9 per labor hour. Direct materials will cost $600 for each unit produced. Initial tooling for the product costs $15,000. Monthly overhead will cost $6,000 per month during the life of the project. The available work force consists of ten operators, each available for 160 hours per month. If a profit of 10 percent on selling price is desired, what should be the selling price?
17. The vice president of operations for a telephone company has decided to replace a central dispatching office. In one of the design details, two alternatives are proposed. The more costly of the two alternatives will require an additional investment (over and above the other alternative) of $35,000 in construction costs. However, under this alternative it will be easier to bring in additional cables, since service expansion is required later. The estimated savings are $6,000 per year for the fifth to ninth year. What must the minimum savings be from the tenth to twentieth years in order to make the additional investment attractive, if the rate of interest is 10 percent and the estimated life of the structure is twenty years? No savings are expected for the first four years.

GLOSSARY

Accounting life Length of an asset's life determined for the purpose of developing a depreciation schedule.

Applied research Investigation directed to discovery of new scientific knowledge with specific commercial objectives toward products or processes.

Basic research Original investigation for the advancement of scientific knowledge.

Depreciation Accounting concept used to recover outlays for assets over their lives.

Development Technical activities encountered in translating research findings into products or processes.

Economic life Useful life of an asset.

Internal rate of return Interest rate at which the present value of inflows equals the present value of outflows.

Learning curve Pattern of input resources consumed in creating successive units of a product; generally initial units require higher amounts of inputs, and later units require progressively fewer inputs.

Life cycle Pattern of demand throughout the product's life; similar patterns and stages can be identified for the useful life of a process.

Machine life Length of time an asset (machine) is capable of functioning.

Net present value Technique of discounting all cash flows of an investment back to their present values and netting out the inflows against the outflows.

Opportunity costs Returns that are lost or forgone as a result of selecting one alternative over another.

Payback period Period of time required for investment net income to equal net outlays.

Present value of a future sum Future sum divided by the growth rate of funds over the relevant time period.

Research and development Organizational efforts directed toward product and process innovation; includes stages of basic research, applied research, development, and implementation.

Salvage value Income received from sale of an asset.

Sunk costs Past expenditures that are irrelevant to current decisions.

Time value of money Concept that recognizes that a sum of money has the potential for generating returns (revenues) over time.

SELECTED READINGS

Abernathy, W. J. "Production Process Structure and Technological Change." *Decision Sciences 7*, no. 4 (October 1976), pp. 607–19.

_____ and P. L. Townsend. "Technology, Productivity and Process Change." *Technological Forecasting and Social Change 7*, no. 4 (1975), pp. 379–96.

_____ and K. P. King. "The Limits of the Learning Curve." *Harvard Business Review* 52, no. 5 (September–October 1974), pp. 109–19.

Adam, Everett E. Jr. and Michael F. Pohlen. "A Scoring Methodology for Equipment Replacement Model Evaluation." *AIIE Transactions* 6, no. 4 (December 1974), pp. 338–44.

Conway, R. W. and A. Schultz. "The Manufacturing Progress Function." *The Journal of Industrial Engineering* 10 (1959), pp. 39–54.

de Kluyver, C. A. "Innovation and Industrial Product Life Cycles." *California Management Review* 20, no. 1 (Fall 1977), pp. 21–33.

Grant, E. L., W. G. Ireson, and R. S. Leavenworth. *Principles of Engineering Economy*, 6th ed. New York: Ronald Press, 1976.

Hakala, N. V. "Administration of Industrial Technology." *Business Horizons* 20, no. 5 (October 1977), pp. 4–10.

Hertz, David B. "Risk Analysis in Capital Investment." *Harvard Business Review* 42 (January–February 1964), pp. 95–106.

Hetzner, William A., Louis G. Tornatzky, and Katherine J. Klein. "Manufacturing Technology in the 1980's: A Survey of Federal Programs and Practices." *Management Science* 29, no. 8 (August 1983), pp. 951–961.

Liao, W. M. "Effects of Learning on Resource Allocation Decisions." *Decision Sciences* 10, no. 1 (January 1979), pp. 116–25.

Schmenner, Roger W. "Every Factory Has a Cycle." *Harvard Business Review* 61, no. 2 (March–April 1983), pp. 121–129.

Terbough, George. *Business Investment Management.* Washington, D.C.: Machinery and Allied Products Institute, 1967.

U.S. National Science Foundation (NSF 74-313). *An Analysis of Federal R&D Funding by Function: Fiscal Years 1969–1975.* Washington, D.C.: Surveys of Science Resources Series, 1974.

Yelle, L. E. "The Learning Curve: Historical Review and Comprehensive Survey." *Decision Sciences* 10, no. 2 (April 1979), pp. 302–28.

Supplement to Chapter 19

USEFUL TECHNICAL APPROACHES TO CHANGE

In this supplement we discuss concepts and models important to financial analysis relating to changes in technology and structure. Capital budgeting and engineering economic concepts in this supplement include depreciation and taxes in replacement, additional replacement models, and model selection. Derivation of compound interest factors may be found in Grant or a similar engineering economics or finance book.[1]

Depreciation and Taxes

Depreciation Depreciation is an accounting procedure for recovering outlays (expenditures) for assets over their lives. Companies invest in equipment and facilities with the expectation that future income benefits will be realized. The resulting income cannot be called profit until the expenses necessary to generate the income have been deducted. To accomplish this, the initial investment is subdivided across several years and charged off against income in each of those years. When considering investments in new facilities or equipment, management should determine depreciation. Different methods of depreciation can be selected; the choice affects the attractiveness of decision alternatives because of its effect on taxation.

Basically, depreciation methods fall into two categories, straight line and accelerated. Straight line depreciation is used to recover asset expenditures evenly over the asset's expected life. The annual amount of depreciation is determined by using equation S19.1.

$$\text{Annual amount of depreciation} = \frac{\text{Asset cost} - \text{salvage value}}{\text{Estimated asset life}} \tag{S19.1}$$

Suppose a machine is purchased for $20,000 and has a life expectancy of six years and an expected salvage value of $2,000 after year 6. Using equation S19.1,

$$\text{Annual amount of depreciation} = \frac{\$20{,}000 - 2{,}000}{6} = \$3{,}000 \text{ per year}$$

As we see in Table S19.1, the company reduces its taxable income each year by $3,000, the annual depreciation amount.

In contrast to the straight line approach are several accelerated methods of depreciation. These methods allow the firm to reduce taxable income by larger amounts in the earlier years of asset life but small amounts in the later years. Although several accelerated methods exist, we will present only one, the sum-of-years-digits. It should be noted that one does not have complete freedom in selecting an accelerated method. Choice in the United States is constrained by Internal Revenue Service regulations and depends upon the circumstances involved.

To use sum-of-years-digits, one first determines the total amount to be depreciated: amount to be depreciated (y) = asset cost − salvage value. Next, the number of years over which depreciation is to occur is deter-

[1] Eugene L. Grant, W. Grant Ireson, and Richard S. Leavenworth, *Principles of Engineering Economy*, 6th ed. (New York: The Ronald Press Company, 1976).

TABLE S19.1
Straight line depreciation schedule for machine costing \$20,000 initially with 6 year life and \$2,000 salvage value

Year	Book value Beginning value of asset	Depreciation	Book value Ending value of asset	
1	\$20,000	\$ 3,000	\$17,000	
2	17,000	3,000	14,000	
3	14,000	3,000	11,000	
4	11,000	3,000	8,000	
5	8,000	3,000	5,000	
6	5,000	3,000	2,000	
		\$18,000		(salvage value)

mined, and the sum of these years is calculated: for n years the sum is $1 + 2 + \ldots + n = x$. Then the amount of depreciation for each of the n years is determined as follows:

$$\text{First year depreciation} = \left(\frac{n}{x}\right) y$$

$$\text{Second year depreciation} = \left(\frac{n-1}{x}\right) y$$

Continue until the last (nth year), when

$$\text{Final year depreciation} = \left(\frac{1}{x}\right) y$$

Let us use the previous example to illustrate. The amount to be depreciated overall is:

$$\begin{aligned} y &= \text{Asset cost} - \text{salvage value, or} \\ y &= \$20{,}000 - \$2{,}000 \\ &= \$18{,}000 \end{aligned}$$

The expected life is six years, the sum of which is $x = 1 + 2 + 3 + 4 + 5 + 6$, or 21. Therefore the amount of depreciation for year 1 is:

$$\begin{aligned} \left(\frac{n}{x}\right) y &= \left(\frac{6}{21}\right) (\$18{,}000) \\ &= \$5{,}143 \end{aligned}$$

For the remaining years the depreciation schedule is shown on Table S19.2.

TABLE S19.2
Sum-of-years digits depreciation schedule

Year	Book Value Beginning value of asset	Depreciation rate	Depreciation	Book Value Ending value of asset
1	$20,000	(6/21) (18,000)	$5,143	$14,857
2	14,857	(5/21) (18,000)	4,286	10,571
3	10,571	(4/21) (18,000)	3,429	7,142
4	7,142	(3/21) (18,000)	2,571	4,571
5	4,571	(2/21) (18,000)	1,714	2,857
6	2,857	(1/21) (18,000)	857	2,000 (salvage value)
		21/21 (18,000) 100%	$18,000	

Observe the patterns of annual depreciation for the two methods over the six-year life of the equipment. Overall, the entire $18,000 is depreciated in both cases. Under straight line, it occurs evenly, $3,000 per year; under the accelerated method, the initial year is $5,143, and depreciation diminishes annually thereafter. This means that under accelerated methods there is less taxable income initially. The tax implications of these methods are discussed next.

Taxes Taxes have a direct effect on the financial benefits associated with investment decisions. In our discussion we consider only United States federal taxes on income and profit. However, a complete analysis should also consider state, local, and other relevant taxes.

In the United States, companies are taxed annually by the federal government in relation to their end of year profit picture. Medium and large companies are taxed at a rate of approximately 50 percent of profit. Recall that annual profit equals annual income minus annual costs of operation. Therefore, for a specified amount of annual income, the appropriate tax payment depends on the level of annual cost of operation. If costs are high, tax payments will be lower than if costs are low. With this in mind, you can see how different depreciation methods affect the benefits of investment proposals. To illustrate this let's calculate the tax implications of the two depreciation methods discussed earlier. Table S19.3 summarizes the calculations assuming a tax rate of 50 percent.

As columns 3 and 5 show, both methods result in an overall tax reduction of $9,000, because the cost of the equipment was charged off against income in determining profit in each year of the asset's life. The two methods differ in the way the $9,000 reduction is dispersed over the six years.

TABLE S19.3
Tax implications of two depreciation methods

	Straight line		Sum-of-years digits	
1 Year	2 Reduction in taxable income (amount of depreciation)	3 Reduction in taxes (50%)	4 Reduction in taxable income (amount of depreciation)	5 Reduction in taxes (50%)
1	$3,000	$1,500	$5,143	$2,572
2	3,000	1,500	4,286	2,143
3	3,000	1,500	3,429	1,714
4	3,000	1,500	2,571	1,286
5	3,000	1,500	1,714	857
6	3,000	1,500	857	428
		$9,000		$9,000

Taxes also enter into the analysis if an asset's selling price differs from its depreciated or book value. For example, if the book value of equipment is $2,000 at the time the equipment is sold for $1,000, a $1,000 loss can be declared, and taxes can be reduced accordingly.

EXAMPLE

Consider two investment alternatives for Consolidated Dryers, Inc. (COD). Alternatives *A* and *B* are two cut-off machines for manufacturing dryers. Machine *A* costs $10,000 and will require maintenance of $1,000 per year. Machine *B* costs $12,000 but requires maintenance of only $500 per year. COD uses straight line depreciation. The economic life of the asset is six years with no expected salvage value. Which machine should be purchased?

Using net present value, but short-cutting special analysis steps, we can solve the problem as shown in Table S19.4. Note that because of higher cash flow from more depreciation and lower maintenance costs, machine *B* is the more favorable investment even though *B* had higher initial costs.

There are many additional considerations such as the accelerated cost recovery (ACR) approach, introduced in the U.S. tax code in 1981, and the frequent use of the investment tax credit, to stimulate investment. ACR's allow for fast write-offs of investments; investment tax credits are allowances that directly reduce the income tax owed. These are mentioned simply to reinforce the need for competent tax advice. Even if you understood these tax concepts, you still must know the tax law at any point in time.

TABLE S19.4
Net present value of two alternatives for COD depreciation and tax effects added (50% tax rate)

Time (year)	Initial outlay	Annual maintenance	Annual depreciation	Tax savings		Net outflows		Present value
				Machine *A*				
0	−$10,000					−$10,000		−$10,000
1		−1,000	$1,667	$833	(−$1,000 + 833) =	−167		
2		−1,000	1,667	833		−167		
3		−1,000	1,667	833		−167	$167 × 4.355 →	
4		−1,000	1,667	833		−167		−727
5		−1,000	1,667	833		−167		
6		−1,000	1,667	833		−167	Total =	−$10,727
				Machine *B*				
0	−$12,000					−$12,000		−$12,000
1		−$500	$2,000	$1,000	(−$500 + 1,000) =	500		
2		− 500	2,000	1,000		500		
3		− 500	2,000	1,000		500	$500 × 4.355 →	
4		− 500	2,000	1,000		500		+2,178
5		− 500	2,000	1,000		500		
6		− 500	2,000	1,000		500		
							Total =	−$9,822

Additional Replacement Models

Risk Analysis *Description of the model.* Many decisions are based on discounted cash flow calculations. Management might be told, for example, that replacement alternative X had an expected internal rate of return of 9.2 percent and for replacement Y a 10.3 percent return can be expected. With risk analysis, the manager obtains the above information *plus* a distribution of other possible rates of return on each investment. You might tell the managers, for example, that X has 1 chance in 20 of being a total loss, 1 in 10 of earning from 4–5 percent, 2 in 10 of paying 10–12 percent, and 1 chance in 50 of attaining a 30 percent rate of return. From another schedule he learns what the most likely rate of return is from Y. These alternatives are graphically portrayed in Figure S19.1. Notice that the *shape* of the distribution gives the manager additional information about the variability of each proposal.

The model. The basic model is present value, present worth, discounted cash flow, or internal rate of return. However, instead of computing only the most likely rate of return, we compute several for each alternative. Data concerning the variables in the model are collected by obtaining estimates through such questions as:

1. Given that the expected annual cost of maintenance is $510, what is the probability that the cost will exceed $550?
2. Is there any chance that the cost will exceed $650?
3. How likely is it that the cost will drop below $475?

Answers to these kinds of questions give a distribution for each variable used in the discounted cash flow determination of return on investment.

FIGURE S19.1
Alternative investment distribution of returns

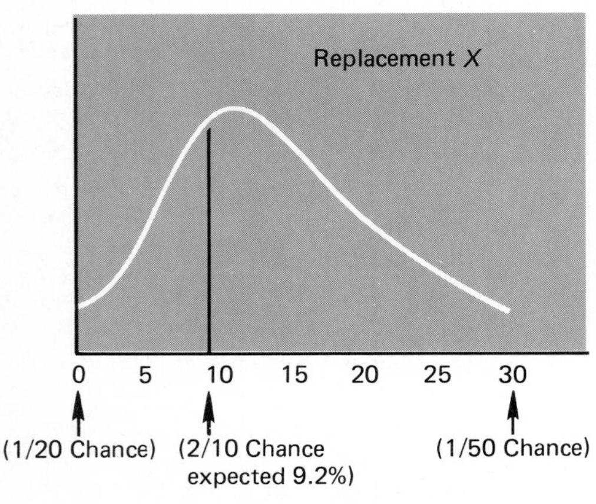

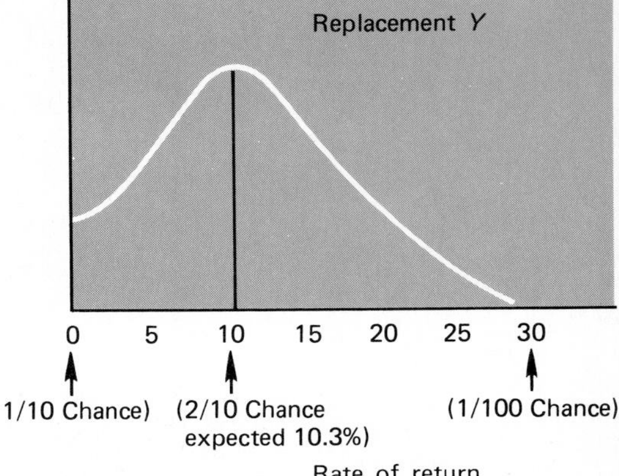

As you might suspect, estimation errors can enter into the analysis from many possible sources—salvage values, expenses, and revenues. If we attempted to reiterate the analysis for each source, we could easily end up with an overwhelming amount of computation. Fortunately, risk analysis is adaptable to computer simulation. Essentially the process involves programming the investment model and then inputing distributions of annual cash inflows, cash outflows, salvage value, useful life, and annual interest rate. In one simulation run, the Monte Carlo method is used to select at random a value from each of these distributions. The net present value for that run is calculated and recorded. Each of many such simulation runs, say 500 of them, would be performed, and the result would be 500 net present values. We then classify these observations into a frequency distribution that conveys a picture of just how much variation in net present value is to be expected. This information may be more useful to the operations manager than a single estimate.

The Machinery and Allied Products Institute (MAPI) Model[2] The MAPI formula may be characterized as an "adjusted" after-tax rate of return criterion. The entire focus of the calculation is to determine a rate of return for the next year on net investment, relative to the conditions that would prevail if the company went on without the proposed project. The steps involved in the MAPI analysis are:

1. Determine the net capital investment in the piece of equipment.
2. Determine the after-income-tax net operating advantage of the proposed addition. This is actually a calculation to see how much earnings have increased by using the new piece of equipment. This is usually reflected by increased revenue, decreased cost, or a combination of both.
3. Find the next-year capital consumption avoided by the project. This is the fall in salvage value from holding an existing asset one more year, plus the next-year allocation of possible capital additions or renewals.
4. Next-year capital consumption incurred is determined. This is the allowance for obsolescence and deterioration of the proposal taken from a MAPI chart. It is a function of the estimated terminal salvage value as a percent of cost and estimated service life.
5. Next-year income tax adjustment is found as the *net* increase in income tax resulting from the project.
6. Now you can calculate the after-tax return, called the "urgency rating." The actual mechanics of calculation vary slightly from this form:

$$\text{After-tax return} = \frac{\text{Net monetary advantage from project}}{\text{Net investment required by project}} \times 100$$

$$= \frac{(2) + (3) - (4) - (5)}{(1)} \times 100$$

[2]See George Terborgh, *Business Investment Management* (Washington, D.C.: Machinery and Allied Products Institute, 1967) and *A Practical Method of Investment Analysis: The MAPI System* (Washington, D.C.: Machinery and Allied Products Institute and Council for Technological Advancement, 1971).

To use the MAPI procedure, you need a MAPI summary form and charts (graphs). The details of the procedure are beyond our introductory treatment; if you're interested, the Machinery and Allied Products Institute can provide you with clear procedures to follow.

Model Selection

Further insight into the recommendation of combining payback with net present value is provided by a study on replacement model selection. This study developed a ranking methodology including the opinion and evaluations of users and actual computational and data requirements regarding each of several models on actual replacement problems.[3]

Criteria that users were asked to evaluate models against were:

1. Recognition of the time value of money. This refers to the allowance for variations in value that money will have in time periods other than the present. It involves the rate used to discount future amounts of money.
2. Recognition of the time pattern of money. The time pattern of money is the order (pattern) in which money is received or expended throughout the replacement life cycle, i.e. the flow of revenue and expenses to and from the equipment in each time period.
3. Treatment of risk and uncertainty. Risk refers to the ability to incorporate probabilities associated with possible outcomes. Uncertainty refers to a lack of any information concerning probabilities of possible outcomes.
4. Utilization of market values. This refers primarily to the value assigned to the equipment at the time of purchase or salvage. It involves the question of using market values for the receipts from the equipment to be replaced, as well as expenditures for the new equipment at the time of its purchase and its salvage at a later date.
5. Accuracy. Accuracy is the precision or exactness of the model as it relates to the actual equipment replacement problem. This does not refer to the computational accuracy of the model. It is the state of being free from error as an evaluation device.
6. Simplicity. Simplicity is the degree to which the model is easy to understand and apply. It is the equality or state of not being complex. Simplicity reflects clarity.

These evaluations were combined with actual replacement data, allowing the inclusion of two additional factors: computational difficulty and number of data points. All eight factors were combined in a scoring rule that provided the results shown in Table S19.5. The profit maximization model is the continuous function representation of present value. In Table S19.5, the higher the total score, the better the model *relative to the other models*. No model was "best" in an optimal sense. We can see that payback ranked highest (148), followed by risk analysis (111) and present value (101).

Even though payback was ranked low on some criteria, the high score on simplicity (123) offset those factors. Because of the low scores on some

---

[3]Everet E. Adam, Jr. and Michael F. Pohlen, "A Scoring Methodology for Equipment Replacement Model Evaluation," *AIIE Transactions* 6, no. 4 (December 1974), pp. 338–44.

TABLE S19.5
Weighting function results

Criteria	Payback	Present value	MAPI	Risk analysis	Profit maximization
			Models		
Time value	−18	20	−1	10	4
Time pattern	−1	17	2	3	10
Treatment of risk	−5	0	−9	38	−4
Market values	−8	4	9	1	10
Accuracy	57	80	55	56	74
Simplicity	123	−20	11	3	2
Total score	148	101	67	111	96

Source: Adam and Pohlen, "A Scoring Methodology for Equipment Replacement Model Evaluation," *AIIE Transactions* 6, no. 4 (December 1974), p. 342. Copyright American Institute of Industrial Engineers, Inc., 25 Technology Park/Atlanta, Norcross, Georgia 30092.

of the factors, the authors felt that the simplicity of payback alone was not enough to recommend the model by itself. We cannot, however, overlook the importance of simplicity to the user and the high ranking that payback received on that criterion. We concur, therefore, with the authors in their final recommendation to use payback in conjunction with either risk analysis or present value analysis.

REVIEW AND DISCUSSION QUESTIONS

1. Illustrate how depreciation affects the relative financial attractiveness of investment alternatives.
2. Contrast the effects of straight line and accelerated methods of asset depreciation.
3. Of what value is risk analysis in evaluating alternative investment proposals?
4. Describe the main features of the MAPI model.
5. Discuss the major considerations in selecting replacement models.

PROBLEMS

1. An asset has an initial cost of $150,000, an estimated life of eight years, and salvage value of $22,000. Develop schedules of depreciation for straight line and sum-of-years-digits methods of depreciation (similar to Tables S19.1 and S19.2).
2. For problem 1, develop a table of tax implications (similar to Table S19.3).
3. Using a 10 percent interest rate, calculate the net present value implications of the two depreciation methods for the data in problem 1.
4. Agribin, Inc., wants to build a new equipment facility but cannot invest in projects returning less than a 10 percent return. Alternative *A* requires a $300,000 investment,

will have an economic useful life of eight years, and will create net inflows (revenues minus expenses) from operations of $80,000 annually. Alternative *B* requires a $200,000 initial outlay, is expected to have zero salvage value after eight years of useful economic life, and will create net inflows of $65,000 per year. None of these estimates includes depreciation and tax considerations.

(a) Which alternative is better if straight line depreciation is used?
(b) Which is better if sum-of-years-digits is used?
(c) Compare after tax net present values for both alternatives.
(d) Which, if either, alternative should be selected?

20 Your Future in Operations Management

The United States is engaged in a difficult struggle to retain its industrial leadership in the global marketplace. This is a matter of great concern for the American people, and meeting the challenge is important to the future of the country. The standard of living, economic survival, and national defense are at stake. If industrial leadership declines, it will not be long before the rest of this society goes with it.

The United States has been slow to appreciate that foreign competitors exist for 70 percent of our industrial products. Lack of competitiveness has resulted in a flood of imports and loss of U.S. jobs. The top ten imports from Japan are industrial products such as radios, cars, and videotape machines. It is estimated that for every $1 billion in imports, 25,000 American manufacturing jobs are lost. Over 30 million manufacturing jobs have been lost since 1970, 3 million in *Fortune* 500 companies in the last five years. Fortunately there is a new American spirit emerging to face this challenge. The rush for the automated factory is creating a revolution in how the United States deals with manufacturing. This will have significant impact on the business organization as a whole.

Since the economic recovery began, there has been increased spending by the private sector for plant and equipment at the rate of 25 percent since late 1982. Sustaining this trend long enough to significantly modernize the industrial base will be the challenge for the future.

There are many exciting changes occurring in the field of manufacturing. While some critics lament the demise of U.S. manufacturing, total industrial production is actually over 30 percent higher today than what it was in 1970. It is a myth that the manufacturing base of the United States is shrinking. However, rapid modernization will be necessary to retain a competitive advantage in the global marketplace.

Richard A. Stimson
Director Industrial Productivity
Office of the Under Secretary of Defense
Washington, D.C.

Mr. Stimson's comments reflect a sense of concern and urgency over the future of U.S. industry. How will we respond to the global competitive challenge? Are we so tightly anchored to our past conventional practices that we cannot reorient our operations resources soon enough? In this, our final chapter, we look to the past, the present, and the future of production and operations management. Whether we agree with Edmund Burke that "You can never plan the future by the past" or with Patrick Henry that "I know of no way of judging the future but by the past," we must at least admit that the past, after all, is all we have. As a basis for prediction, it may be limited, but it is a beginning. Together we'll review the history of production and operations management in the hope it will help us see the future of the field. We'll review current practice and speculate on emerging trends and future events that might shape your future role as a production/operations manager.

THE PAST AS A BASIS FOR THE FUTURE

The Transition from Manufacturing to Operations Management

Manufacturing Management Manufacturing management was built upon the subdivision and specialization of labor, the recognition of differential skills in labor, and the scientific approach to studying work. With this approach, which spanned the late 1700s to about 1930, the focus was upon technology and logic at the manufacturing core.

Production Management Production management, the general term used to describe this discipline from the 1930s through the 1950s, emphasized the production of goods and services in industrialized societies. Production management, continuing the application of Frederic Taylor's scientific, logical techniques, developed such areas as time and motion study and scheduling. Statistical applications in quality control, fundamentals of mathematical programming (primarily linear programming), and further development of inventory theory highlight this period. The use of the shorthand logic of mathematics to formulate production problems emerged as a prominent methodology. Finding new ways to produce larger volumes of output efficiently to supply insatiable consumer needs became a necessity.

The Hawthorne studies typify the emergence of a human relations approach to management in the 1940s. During the decades of the 1940s and 1950s, our concept of employees changed from Taylor's mechanistic view to an understanding that people are complex individuals with psychological as well as material needs. In the late 1950s, the digital computer emerged, a significant event for the future of the field. Also during this time, the economy continued to shift employment from agriculture to services. As farm mechanization increased and our society grew in wealth, people began demanding more services.

Operations Management The digital computer accomplished several things for production managers. First, it relieved a tremendous clerical burden in production planning, costing, and control. Second, it gave production managers more information than ever before about a process that has always been data rich. Finally, in the later 1960s and throughout the 1970s, the computer began to be used as an analytical tool to assist in large-scale modeling and understanding of production processes.

Because many felt the word *production* had overly restrictive connotations, operations management became a term used to encompass both the manufacturing segment of the economy and the service sector. To the extent that the conversion process requires management, whether in manufacturing or a service industry, an operations manager is necessary.

The distinguishing feature of operations management is its continuation of the logical analysis developed in production settings and the application of these useful techniques to the service sector where, generally, management has not reaped its potential benefits. Operations management is not new in itself; it is a broadening of production management to include delivery of services.

CURRENT PRACTICE IN PRODUCTION/ OPERATIONS MANAGEMENT

Production/ Operations Management Activities

As you have seen throughout, Figure 20.1 is the general model of this book. Think about what practicing managers have indicated their major problems to be and the techniques they found most useful as you review this general model. The managerial process, the conversion process, activities of production/operations managers, and models and behavior should now fit together. It is our belief that this general model provides a framework for application that you may rely upon in your career as a production/ operations manager or as a general manager responsible for this function.

Production/ Operations Management: Systems View

During the 1960s, the systems approach emerged as a new framework for studying organizations. Whereas the approaches used during the preceding half-century emphasized detailed *analysis* of organizational components, the systems approach focuses on *synthesis*. The systems approach encour-

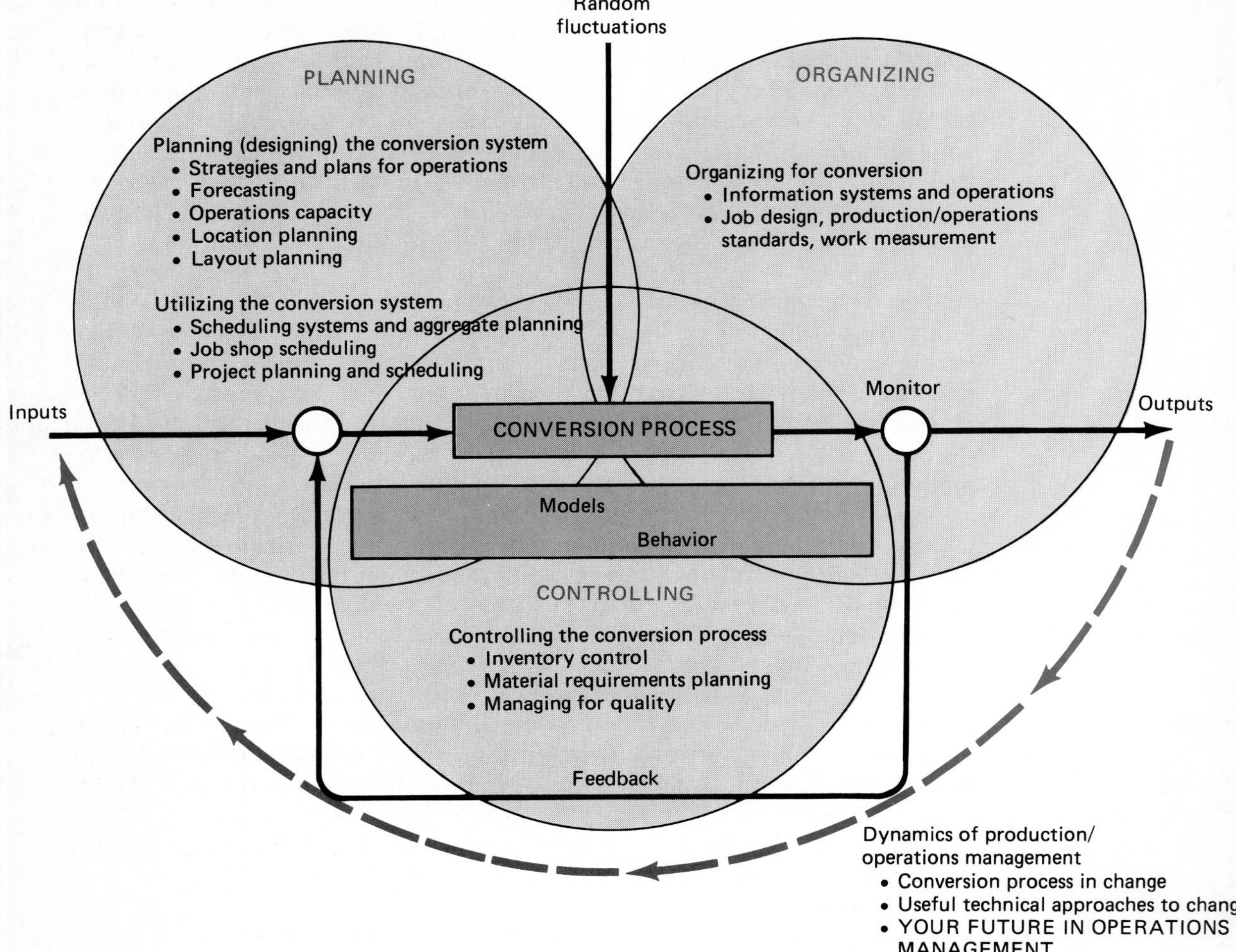

FIGURE 20.1
General model for managing operations management

ages managers to view the organization in its entirety rather than becoming preoccupied with a single subcomponent. If managers understand why organizations function as they do overall, they can keep the total organization's goals and objectives in view. The operations subsystem, remember, is but one component in a larger network of interrelated components. Together, all the subsystems, interrelating with one another, make up the larger system, the organization itself.

Although the systems approach remains largely at a conceptual/descriptive stage of development, its importance today is greater than ever. Increasingly, more companies are questioning their strategic missions and clarifying how to coordinate their marketing, finance, and operations functions more effectively. Then, they can bring more coherence and focus to the diverse problems they face with new technologies, international competition, and day-to-day operational issues throughout the organization.

Operations Strategies

In production/operations strategic planning, the broad overall planning, which precedes the more detailed operational planning, has never been more important. Increasingly, pressures and opportunities within a complex business environment force a strategic planning role upon the operations manager. Costs, both short-run and long-run, are often set by strategies developed within the operations function.

Process and product design strategies are critical to the health of the organization. Capacity strategies—decisions about if, how much, and when to bring new facilities onstream or to delete old ones—interact with product design, process layout, and job design strategies. Quality strategies are critical. Inventory and material, staffing, scheduling, aggregate planning—all of these operations management activities require sound strategies to guide day-to-day decision making. These operations strategies and functional strategies in marketing, finance, and personnel must all be linked through corporate strategy.[1] Strategic planning in production/operations is a critical linkage for successful organization performance.

Economic Trends and Service Sector Applications

Employment in the U.S. economy has shifted from a balance among the agriculture, manufacturing, and service sectors toward a manufacturing and service sector orientation. In 1920 in the United States, agriculture employed 30 percent, manufacturing 39 percent, and services 31 percent of the work force. By 1982, the figures had shifted dramatically; agriculture employed only 4 percent, manufacturing 26 percent, and services 70 percent of the work force.

The real challenge to service sector operations management is transferring existing tools and techniques from the manufacturing sector to the service sector. Unfortunately, existing technology may not be adequate for totally meeting the challenge. Nevertheless, insurance companies, banks, savings and loan institutions; schools and universities; local, state, and federal government; long-term care facilities, clinics, hospitals; food services, recreation, motels, and hotels; transportation; communication—these are all large institutionalized segments of our economy that are fruitfully applying existing operations management techniques.

The challenges are to identify the components of the conversion process; to plan, organize, and control the conversion process; and to deliver

---

[1]See Wickham Skinner, *Manufacturing in the Corporate Strategy* (New York: John Wiley and Sons, 1978), pp. 27–29.

services as outputs from the conversion process efficiently and effectively. These are substantial challenges, at both the strategic and operational levels, due to the distinctive characteristics of service organizations.[2] Convincing general management and administration that the rationality of the production core, and the tools and techniques so useful in analysis there, are often useful in delivery of services is a challenge in itself.

Management Problem Areas

In Chapter 1 we saw the diversity of operational problems encountered and the activities that organizations emphasize to improve their operations.[3] In addition, the surveys reported in Chapter 3 revealed some dominant concerns over problems in cost control, production control, labor/industrial relations, quality control, and production planning. Further, the techniques managers use most frequently appear to be network analysis (PERT, CPM), linear programming, time series analysis (exponential smoothing especially), regression and correlation, and computer simulation.

Notice, again, that most of these problems are planning and control oriented. To solve today's problems, one must understand the underlying concepts and available models. Further, it seems clear that the employee's behavior requires our attention in operations management, especially where the worker is more critical to the conversion process than are machines and materials. This book has attempted to respond to these expressed current needs of practicing managers and to provide concepts and orientation for those who are preparing for future careers in this area.

Production/Operations Management: Life Cycle View

At several places in this book we have talked about life cycles. We've mentioned the product life cycle, an important concept to product design and research and development efforts. The physical facility, equipment, and information systems also have life cycles. They must be designed, brought on stream in operations, used in the conversion process, and eventually revised or discarded. As an operations manager, you will benefit from an exposure to the field from a life cycle perspective.[4] Although the life cycle orientation differs from ours, the planning, organizing, and controlling subfunctions play vital roles in it too.

When one is studying a discipline like production/operations management, it's sometimes difficult to know which approach to take. Is the managerial process approach best? What about the systems view? The life-cycle approach? Don't get too worried about questions like these. In our own managerial process approach, we have made use of the systems orientation

---

[2]See R. S. Sullivan, "The Service Sector: Challenges and Imperatives for Research in Operations Management," *Journal of Operations Management* 2, no. 4 (August 1982), pp. 211–14.

[3]See *The Manufacturing Futures Project: Summary of Survey Responses* (Boston University School of Management, 1982).

[4]The life cycle approach is explained in detail in Richard B. Chase and Nicholas J. Aquilano, *Production and Operations Management*, 4th ed. (Homewood, Ill.: Richard D. Irwin, Inc., 1985).

(in discussions of the dynamics of P/O management; interfaces of planning, organizing, and controlling; and interactions of operations, other functions, and the environment) and the life-cycle approach too. Had we emphasized either of these other approaches, we would have found ourselves discussing the managerial, modeling, and behavioral dimensions we have tended to concentrate on in our own approach. *The fact is that within any contemporary framework, regardless of its primary orientation, the focus is on managing the conversion process, which converts economic inputs into outputs of goods and services.*

Computerization

Before 1960, a relatively small percentage of organizations in the United States, Canada, and the world were using the digital computer in manufacturing and operations. The digital computer was developed in 1955, and by the mid-1960s most major firms in the United States and Canada were using it in accounting activities and introducing it into manufacturing for data collection and dissemination purposes. The percentage of total firms using the computer for manufacturing and operations activities, however, remained rather low. By the 1980s this situation changed dramatically. Significant events increasing computer applications during this period included:

1. *Pricing umbrellas.* In the United States, computer companies were forced to separate the pricing of computer hardware (equipment) and software (programs for application). This appears to have encouraged competition for software applications in general and in production/operations in particular.
2. *Microcomputers.* The push for computers with large storage and faster processing capacities during the 1960s has been moderated by development of microcomputers in a price range that smaller companies can now afford.
3. *Time sharing.* Accounting firms, banks, consulting firms, and computer specialty firms are offering computer time to other users. Under time sharing, the user firm buys central processing unit time rather than the entire computer.
4. *Consumer acceptance.* Every year development of computerized systems in government, retailing, and finance continues, the more each of us as consumers accepts computers as a way of life. This same phenomenon is occurring within organizations in which production/operations managers are the consumers.
5. *Information systems and planning and control systems.* Information systems using the computer are being applied to a considerable extent in operations management. Typical are Material Requirements Planning (MRP) and other more broadscale manufacturing planning and control systems. These systems provide integrated planning, from the aggregate level on down through shop floor control, for both output and capacity management.

Systems Modeling and Analysis

Today's production/operations managers *cannot* operate solely within the walls of the office or factory; they do not have the luxury of treating conversion as a rational closed process. Adopting a *systems viewpoint,* operations managers must accept *suboptimization* in the conversion subsystem as the price of getting closer to optimization for the entire system.

Trends in operations analysis include *computer simulations* of the business firm, the conversion function, including its interactions with such business functions as distribution and finance, and individual processes within the conversion function. These simulations allow analysts and managers to test alternative proposed actions in a hypothetical environment that simulates the real operating process. Decision alternatives can be tested economically, without upsetting existing operations. To the extent that the simulation is logically consistent with and represents the real world situation, the simulation methodology can be a very useful tool for examining production/operations subsystems as they relate to larger systems.

Simulations have been conducted in production/operations on such functional problems as:

- facilities location
- plant layout
- aggregate scheduling
- job shop scheduling
- project scheduling
- forecasting
- inventory control
- physical distribution

The use of simulation and other analytical techniques has brought about the existence of the operations analyst, a specialist who is highly skilled in the technical problems in modeling and analysis of operations.

Government Regulation

In the 1970s, the government took an increasing role in regulating aspects of production/operations. Price controls, for example, were instituted in the early 1970s, although they were generally lifted, except for the oil industry, by 1976. Utilities, transportation and communications organizations, among other service groups, were continually regulated by the government. Table 20.1 lists various federal regulatory agencies. Despite periodic grumbling in Congress and partial deregulation of airlines (1978–79), trucking (1980), and energy (1979–81), we have learned from the past that such regulation swings with world political and economic conditions. As such it is an important aspect of the environment that warrants a watchful eye because of its potential impact on operations.

With continuing dependence on foreign oil by the United States, Canada, Europe, and Japan, most of the industrialized world is sensitive to potential energy shortages. Businesses and consumers pay considerable energy costs to obtain the material goods for our current consumption patterns.

Pressures continue on production/operations managers for fuel economy in plants and equipment used in the conversion process. Although most organizations have fuel conservation programs in place, with strikingly successful results in many cases, the point is that conversion processes and products have experienced radical changes.[5] Production/

[5]See, for example, James M. Shirley and Wayne C. Turner, "Industrial Energy Management—First Steps Are Easy," *Industrial Engineering* 10, no. 5 (May 1978), pp. 34–41.

TABLE 20.1
Regulatory agencies of the U.S. government

Year	Agency	Function
	Independent Agencies	
1887	Interstate Commerce Commission	Regulates rails, trucks
1913	Federal Reserve Board	Regulates banks, monetary policy
1914	Federal Trade Commission	Administers antitrust, packaging, advertising
1916	U.S. Tariff Commission	Investigates tariff and foreign trade
1924	U.S. Tax Court	Adjudicates federal tax cases
1926	National Mediation Board	Mediates labor disputes in air and rails
1930	Federal Power Commission	Regulates electricity and natural gas
1932	Federal Home Loan Bank Board	Provides credit reserve for home finance
1933	Federal Deposit Insurance Corporation	Insures deposits, supervises some banks
1934	Federal Communications Commission	Regulates radio, TV, telephone, telegraph
1934	Securities and Exchange Commission	Regulates securities industry
1935	National Labor Relations Board	Regulates unfair labor practices
1936	Federal Maritime Commission	Regulates foreign trade of steamships
1938	Civil Aeronautics Board	Regulates and promotes air travel
1946	Atomic Energy Commission	Regulates and promotes atomic energy
1952	Federal Coal Mine Safety Board	Hears appeals to Coal Mine Safety Act
1964	Equal Employment Opportunity Commission	Investigates discrimination charges
1970	Environmental Protection Agency	Monitors environmental matters
1974	Federal Energy Administration	Regulates energy production and use
	Executive Branch Agencies	
1824	Army Corps of Engineers	Builds and maintains rivers and harbors
1836	Patent Office	Administers patent and trademark laws
1862	Internal Revenue Service	Administers federal tax programs
1863	Comptroller of the Currency	Regulates national banks
1903	Antitrust division, Justice Department	Enforces antitrust laws
1915	U.S. Coast Guard	Regulates seaworthiness of ships
1916	Packers and Stockyards Administration	Regulates livestock and meat marketing
1922	Commodity Exchange Authority	Regulates commodity exchanges
1931	Food & Drug Administration	Regulates food and drug safety and labeling
1933	Bureau of Employment Security	Administers unemployment compensation
1933	Social Security Administration	Administers federal retirement programs
1933	Commodity Credit Corporation	Administers farm price support programs
1935	Rural Electrification Administration	Administers REA loan programs
1936	Maritime Administration	Promotes merchant marine
1951	Renegotiation Board	Renegotiates defense contracts
1953	Small Business Administration	Promotes small businesses
1958	Federal Aviation Administration	Regulates aircraft and air systems
1959	Oil Import Administration	Regulates petroleum imports
1963	Labor Management Services Administration	Regulates employee welfare and pensions
1964	Office of Economic Opportunity	Administers federal poverty/youth programs
1966	Federal Highway Administration	Administers road building and safety programs
1966	Federal Railroad Administration	Administers high-speed and safety programs
1966	National Transportation Safety Board	Investigates transportation accidents
1971	Occupational Safety & Health Administration	Issues and enforces industrial standards
1972	Consumer Product Safety Commission	Administers federal product safety laws

Source: William D. Brinckloe and Mary T. Coughlin, *Managing Organizations* (Encino, Calif.: Glencoe Press, 1977), p. 550.

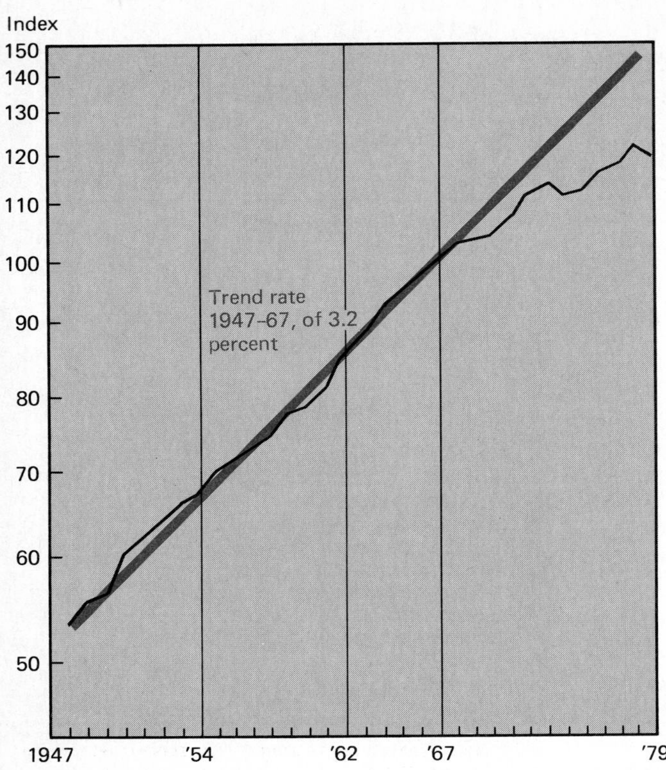

FIGURE 20.2
Output per hour in private business economy, 1947–79 actual levels and 1947–67 trend (1967 equal 100)

Source: Bureau of Labor Statistics.

operations managers have reacted to this external force by changing equipment and tooling and by retraining workers. We will discuss energy again, since we think the past energy shortages will periodically recur to challenge production/operations management in the future.

Inflation

Continuing inflation appears to be a fact of life in many economies throughout the world. If it is not controlled, inflation can assume runaway proportions, as has happened in Latin America, South America, and Great Britain. Inflation hurts production/operations managers through increased costs and disenchanted employees. In inflationary times, it's hard to determine how much of increased costs are attributable to the inflationary costs of labor, equipment, and materials and what costs are attributable to poor managerial and worker performance. Since operations managers are continually pressured to control costs, inflationary conditions can sometimes encourage managers to shelter poor performance under an inflation umbrella, an action that is not conducive to overall organization effectiveness.

Productivity

The Productivity Problem in the United States and Other Nations Since 1967 the United States' rate of productivity growth has slowed down substantially. Figure 20.2 illustrates this change, the 1947–1967 trend rate of 3.2

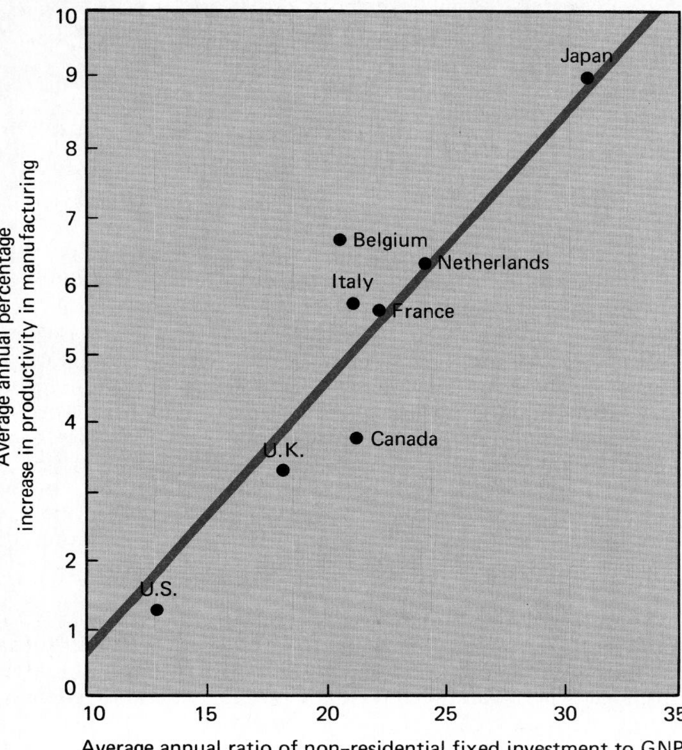

FIGURE 20.3
Investment and productivity in the U.S. and other nations, 1960–76

Source: *Productivity Perspectives,* American Productivity Center, Inc.

percent productivity annual growth contrasting sharply with the 1972–1978 growth rate of 1.2 percent. While this growth rate increased somewhat in the early 1980s, it still has not matched the growth of earlier years. The United States has not fared well in comparison to other nations either, as Figure 20.3 shows. United States' annual productivity growth of 1.2 percent contrasts sharply, for example, with Japan's 9 percent annual productivity growth into 1976. Although it was narrowed by 1982, it still remained a wide gap.

What are the sources of the productivity slowdown? The problem is complex and our explanations are partial at best. One expert suggests the sources to be one or more of the following: physical capital per worker is not increasing adequately; the quality of labor is not improving as in the past; and the efficiency with which capital and labor are combined has declined.[6] We should not throw our hands in the air and say the possibility of improvement is hopeless. In fact, much of what we have presented in this book is aimed at equipping you, as a production/operations manager,

[6]Stephen P. Zell, "Productivity in the U.S. Economy: Trends and Implications," *Economic Review* (Federal Reserve Bank of Kansas City, November 1979), pp. 13–26.

to directly influence the last two reasons for productivity decline. We believe much can be done within operations in the firm to improve our productivity record. Let's examine what others are doing also.

Business and Government Interest in Productivity Productivity, a general measure of efficiency, is receiving renewed interest by business and government. Examples of this trend are:

1. *Unions.* Unions are interested in sharing productivity improvements with management and owners. Within several unions, for example, productivity committees have been established to assist in improvement efforts.
2. *Business.* Individual firms have undertaken extensive productivity improvement programs. Collectively, through trade associations, efforts are being made to assess industry productivity and changes within any one industry over time. An unresolved problem is a clear identification of which productivity gains are attributable to capital, which to technology, and which to labor. Productivity institutes to investigate issues of interest to business are being formed on many college campuses and by business consortiums. One example of the latter is the American Productivity Center, which was formed in 1977 and is located in Houston, Texas. This productivity center is funded by scores of businesses with a general mission of productivity improvement in the private sector.
3. *Government.* There are numerous examples of action for productivity within government. The Civil Service Commission of the federal government has a productivity group. The U.S. Price Commission has evolved into a national Productivity Commission. The Board of Governors of the Federal Reserve Banking System has underway a productivity measurement and improvement program. At a more basic level, government has undertaken research programs, such as the productivity measurement program sponsored by the National Science Foundation, to better understand issues in the productivity area. There are similar state and municipal programs underway also.

Productivity Measurement As we discussed in Chapter 2, one problem in productivity improvement has been the measurement of outputs and inputs. How do you measure outputs of a barber? By the amount of time spent in productive effort? Persons served? Dollars of revenue generated? Further, what are the inputs consumed and how are they measured? Are inputs labor hours? Labor dollars? Should the barber chair be measured as original cost or depreciated cost? For meaningful comparison, inputs and outputs must be on equivalent scales, and the subcomponents of each must allow aggregation. This is often attempted by using dollars, or some other monetary measure.

Using dollars is a good approach for outputs that can be evaluated easily in terms of their market price, but what about government services? Because of the absence of a clearly identifiable market for the services provided, government services are particularly difficult to measure. Furthermore, the need for measurement is crucial in government because government has no direct responsibility to the owners of capital as is the case in the private sector. Since a before-and-after comparison is required to evaluate any improvement procedure, measurement is crucial to productivity improvement.[7] Although significant strides have been made since the 1970s, the problem of productivity measurement remains as a major concern today.

Consumerism

The United States government, consumer interest groups, and individual consumers are placing demands on private business as never before. The impact is significant on production/operations managers. Product and service liability cases proliferate in our court system. Consumers, no longer willing to "let the buyer beware," assume an adversary relationship with business should their purchase not meet expectations. Society, in general, seems to support this change.

Recalls are common for many products, including automobiles and tires. Many engineers, scientists, and attorneys have become product liability experts. Recently a physician, a urologist, informed us that standard liability insurance for his medical practice was so substantial that he estimated the cost to his patients at $4–$6 per office call. As this example vividly illustrates, consumerism remains an environmental variable that has direct and significant impacts on operations management.

SPECULATIONS IN PRODUCTION/OPERATIONS MANAGEMENT

As we discussed important trends in the preceding section, perhaps you noticed several factors external to the organization: government regulation, energy, and inflation. In our speculations, we'll consider these and other external forces that will mold the character of operations management in the future. Perhaps the greatest single lesson the operations manager can learn from all this is the necessity of being able and ready to adapt to future environmental intrusions. Systems must be designed not only for short-run economies of operation but for flexibility as well.

Energy

Almost any energy forecast suggests that potential energy shortages and dependence on foreign oil are likely to continue in the free world in the years ahead. Many oil companies have changed their identities from oil companies to energy companies, with the implicit idea of diversifying their operations. With limited U.S. and free world oil reserves, increasing attention is being given to coal, nuclear, and solar energy sources.

Although coal reserves are substantial in the United States, emission standards set by the federal government restrict low quality, high sulfur content coal. The implications of just this kind of environmental dilemma

[7]For details on measurement procedures and applications see Everett E. Adam, Jr., James C. Hershauer, and William A. Ruch, *Productivity and Quality: Measurement as a Basis for Improvement* (Englewood Cliffs, NJ: Prentice-Hall, 1981).

trouble consumers and policy makers alike. What kinds of tradeoffs are we willing to make between *environmental control* and the *benefits from energy*? The benefits from energy are visible everywhere; in transportation, heating, air conditioning, and consumer products, each of us consumes energy daily. How much are we willing to pay in personal effort (walking) or nonconsumption (staying home) for a cleaner environment? Although most of us are willing to sacrifice considerably for a clean environment, we would like our energy too.

How does all this affect the production/operations manager? An energy shortage will affect our ability to operate conversion processes, just as much as it affects consumers. Social issues that affect workers, products, and regulation affect variables critical to effective operations too.

Whether the trend in the next ten years is toward increased domestic oil production, foreign oil, shale oil, or such other energy sources as nuclear, solar, synthetic fuels, or coal, the plant and equipment design decisions, product decisions, and conversion process costs will all be affected in a dramatic way. As potential production/operations managers, you must keep aware of current energy developments and trends and their effects on the decisions you must make in operations.

International Business

World-wide economic competition is intensifying and, seemingly, the world is shrinking. Improvements in transportation, international banking, and communication have heightened the pace of international commerce and trade. Increasingly, products are produced in locations where the combination of labor, material, and transportation can be most economically supplied to the consumer. A typical American multinational company, for example, might export its technology in the form of equipment and technical expertise to an underdeveloped country, produce one product component in that country, and then ship the component to the United States for final assembly and ultimate consumption. Perhaps Japan, more than any other country, illustrates how international production can be accomplished in a reasonably short period of time. Since World War II, Japan has recovered enough to influence production in electronics, steel, automobiles, and shipbuilding, to name only a few industries, throughout the world.

Production/operations managers can learn from other countries. By comparing their production methods and costs with our own, managers can improve methods and reduce costs. Because of worldwide costs and prices, production executives are keenly aware of opportunities to make or purchase parts in other countries. International production is significant in operations today, and we believe this phenomenon will increase in the next decade.

Population

Although population is leveling in the United States and Canada, in many countries population explosions make it increasingly difficult to provide the essential food and shelter requirements for subsistence. Should this continue, production must be devoted toward agriculture and basic housing and clothing needs. Population trends have an impact on the allocation of factors of production, and these trends shape the production process, a matter of clear importance to production and operations managers.

Real Worth and the Productivity Crisis

Although the Gross National Product, the measure of output for the United States economy, increases annually, real growth was slowed in the 1970s before turning upward modestly. This situation presents a dilemma for managers. When output increases, new plants and equipment are necessary to keep up with demand. But when real growth slows down, companies tend to hold back on new facilities. What should managers do?

Should the economy in general or a particular industry spurt forward, there could be serious capacity problems unless new plants and equipment are ready. In 1975, for the first time in twenty-five years, utilization of capacity dipped below 70 percent in the United States. The 1980 recession again highlighted pockets of excess capacity. Should we continue to operate below capacity, the equipment that is unused will become obsolete before it is worn out. Furthermore, operating below capacity makes it more difficult to earn enough profits to replace obsolete plants and equipment. And since there is no capacity pressure, there's little incentive to invest in new facilities.

The point is clear. When real growth is slowed capacity remains unused and expenditures for plant and equipment are reduced. Under these conditions, the production/operations manager finds it increasingly difficult to introduce new technology into the conversion process. Productivity improvements will be more difficult than ever.

Business/Labor/Government Cooperative Efforts?

United States capitalism encourages a free-enterprise system in which markets are the control and stabilizing mechanism. Over decades, an adversary relationship has developed between business and labor, business and government, and in some instances labor and government. United States' practice contrasts sharply with other societies', in which organization structures and cooperation range from the Israeli Kibbutz (a small, self-contained social and work system within a supportive Israeli society) to Yugoslavia's commitment to the elimination of worker alienation, to Sweden's welfare state, to Japan's direct government support for selected industries.[8]

In which direction is the United States moving—toward or away from cooperative efforts? Our experience with the city of New York and Chrysler Corporation suggests that triparty relationships can be formed in the U.S. Rather than speculate, we merely raise the issue and ask you to think about just what cooperative changes, if any, will take place among business, labor, and government in the remainder of the 1980s and in the 1990s.

[8]For a discussion of these ideologies and their impact on organization structure and outcomes, see Robert H. Miles, *Macro Organizational Behavior* (Santa Monica, California: Goodyear Publishing Company, 1980), pp. 387–432.

Information Systems

Technological changes in computer hardware, software, and information systems will continue to affect the operations manager's role throughout the balance of the 1980s and the decade ahead. Manufacturing has adapted quickly to new computer and software developments that help managers make decisions in operations. Material requirements planning (MRP) is a prime example. In the mid-1970s MRP was new, results on usage and successes were mixed, and the impact of MRP systems in manufacturing was not known. Since then, MRP and more comprehensive operations planning and control systems have come into wide-spread favor. Further developments are on the horizon for decision support systems as well as the integration of robotics and computer-aided design in manufacturing.

We believe information systems that positively affect operations, such as office automation, will continue to be developed and will find increasing applications in service sectors. The checkless society, for example, *is a reality* for certain governmental agencies. A branch of the U.S. armed services has massive monthly payroll transfers through the wire services of the Federal Reserve Banking System into individual accounts in commercial banks throughout the nation. How does this affect banking operations? It means changes in job design, equipment, and personnel skills; and it generates substantial scheduling and control problems.

Service Sector Technology

In the labor-intense service sector, we believe that job specialization and mechanization will increase. Quasi-manufacturing processes, small assembly lines, and special-purpose equipment will probably be used as much as possible in an effort to reduce high labor costs. Consider the fast-food chains we see everywhere. Compared with traditional restaurants, these chains make use of much more food that has been prepared at a factory located away from where it is consumed, and they employ much more specialized labor. French fries, for example, are precut and frozen at a factory. Then they are transported to the store, where one or two people do nothing but deep fry them. We imagine that parallel examples of specialized labor and location will become increasingly prevalent in financial, health care, educational, and governmental services.

SUMMARY

Although the future of P/OM is not predictable in any precise sense, its general orientation is strongly influenced by its beginnings and its recent history. The basic notions of striving for system efficiency and effectiveness will continue, but with much more emphasis on finding specific priorities for enhancing each organization's specific competitive mission.

One discernible thrust of current and near-term efforts in operations management is in the service sector. Perhaps the greatest increase in application will be in governmental operations at the local and national levels. As economic and environmental issues continue to dominate the world, decisions that were traditionally politically based will be approached more systematically.

As for the future nature of conversion processes themselves, one can only point to the many unpredictable environmental elements that must be recognized and dealt with. We must expect and respond to changes in population, technology, and economic conditions. These requirements point to the need for designing conversion systems that are not only adaptive to changing needs but operated efficiently and effectively. These two sometimes-conflicting requirements will present a challenge of great proportions to the future production/operations manager.

REVIEW AND DISCUSSION QUESTIONS

1. It is helpful in determining the future of production/operations management to remember the past. Trace the transition from manufacturing to operations management.
2. Study Figure 20.1, production/operations management activities. Lay the figure aside and try to reproduce it. Which parts of the figure do you think are essential as a framework for practicing as an operations manager? Why?
3. Several discernible trends in production/operations management were presented in this chapter. Select one that you believe should be expanded and expand it. Likely, we overlooked one or more trends. Select a trend in production/operations that you believe should have been summarized and summarize it.
4. One speculation concerning production/operations management was that energy shortages will impact conversion processes in dramatic ways in the future. Provide some factual evidence not provided in this book that supports or refutes this speculation.
5. Large amounts of effort and resources have been devoted to studying productivity in the service sector in recent years. Why has this occurred?
6. One problem in productivity improvement has been the measurement of system inputs and outputs. Explain why this is a problem, and give examples of it.
7. Is it possible to have an efficient conversion system that is at the same time a flexible system? Discuss this question.
8. Explain what a contemporary production/operations manager could contribute to our productivity crisis. What could a recent college graduate contribute?

SELECTED READINGS

Adam, Everett E., James C. Hershauer, and William A. Ruch, *Productivity and Quality: Measurement as a Basis for Improvement*. Englewood Cliffs, NJ: Prentice-Hall, 1981.

Chase, Richard B. and Nicholas J. Aquilano. *Production and Operations Management: A Life Cycle Approach*. 4th ed. Homewood, Ill: Richard D. Irwin, Inc., 1985.

Gaither, N. "The Adoption of Operations Research Techniques by Manufacturing Organizations." *Decision Sciences* 6, no. 3 (October 1975), pp. 797–813.

Green, Thad B., Walter B. Newsom, and S. Roland Jones. "A Survey of the Application of Quantitative Techniques to Production/Operations Management in Large Corporations." *Academy of Management Journal* 20, no. 4 (December 1977), pp. 669–76.

Miles, Robert H. *Macro Organizational Behavior*. Santa Monica, California: Goodyear Publishing Company, 1980.

Skinner, Wickham. *Manufacturing in the Corporate Strategy*. New York: John Wiley and Sons, 1978.

Sullivan, R. S. "The Service Sector: Challenges and Imperatives for Research in Operations Management." *Journal of Operations Management* 2, no. 4 (August 1982), pp. 211–14.

Zell, Stephen P. "Productivity in the U.S. Economy: Trends and Implications." *Economic Review*, Federal Reserve Bank of Kansas City (November 1979), pp. 13–26.

Appendix

APPENDIX TABLE A
Areas of a Standard Normal Distribution*

An entry in the table is the proportion under the entire curve which is between $z = 0$ and a positive value of z. Areas for negative values of z are obtained by symmetry.

z	.00	.01	.02	.03	.04	.05	.06	.07	.08	.09
0.0	.0000	.0040	.0080	.0120	.0160	.0199	.0239	.0279	.0319	.0359
0.1	.0398	.0438	.0478	.0517	.0557	.0596	.0636	.0675	.0714	.0753
0.2	.0793	.0832	.0871	.0910	.0948	.0987	.1026	.1064	.1103	.1141
0.3	.1179	.1217	.1255	.1293	.1331	.1368	.1406	.1443	.1480	.1517
0.4	.1554	.1591	.1628	.1664	.1700	.1736	.1772	.1808	.1844	.1879
0.5	.1915	.1950	.1985	.2019	.2054	.2088	.2123	.2157	.2190	.2224
0.6	.2257	.2291	.2324	.2357	.2389	.2422	.2454	.2486	.2517	.2549
0.7	.2580	.2611	.2642	.2673	.2703	.2734	.2764	.2794	.2823	.2852
0.8	.2881	.2910	.2939	.2967	.2995	.3023	.3051	.3078	.3106	.3133
0.9	.3159	.3186	.3212	.3238	.3264	.3289	.3315	.3340	.3365	.3389
1.0	.3413	.3438	.3461	.3485	.3508	.3531	.3554	.3577	.3599	.3621
1.1	.3643	.3665	.3686	.3708	.3729	.3749	.3770	.3790	.3810	.3830
1.2	.3849	.3869	.3888	.3907	.3925	.3944	.3962	.3980	.3997	.4015
1.3	.4032	.4049	.4066	.4082	.4099	.4115	.4131	.4147	.4162	.4177
1.4	.4192	.4207	.4222	.4236	.4251	.4265	.4279	.4292	.4306	.4319
1.5	.4332	.4345	.4357	.4370	.4382	.4394	.4406	.4418	.4429	.4441
1.6	.4452	.4463	.4474	.4484	.4495	.4505	.4515	.4525	.4535	.4545
1.7	.4554	.4564	.4573	.4582	.4591	.4599	.4608	.4616	.4625	.4633
1.8	.4641	.4649	.4656	.4664	.4671	.4678	.4686	.4693	.4699	.4706
1.9	.4713	.4719	.4726	.4732	.4738	.4744	.4750	.4756	.4761	.4767
2.0	.4772	.4778	.4783	.4788	.4793	.4798	.4803	.4808	.4812	.4817
2.1	.4821	.4826	.4830	.4834	.4838	.4842	.4846	.4850	.4854	.4857
2.2	.4861	.4864	.4868	.4871	.4875	.4878	.4881	.4884	.4887	.4890
2.3	.4893	.4896	.4898	.4901	.4904	.4906	.4909	.4911	.4913	.4916
2.4	.4918	.4920	.4922	.4925	.4927	.4929	.4931	.4932	.4934	.4936
2.5	.4938	.4940	.4941	.4943	.4945	.4946	.4948	.4949	.4951	.4952
2.6	.4953	.4955	.4956	.4957	.4959	.4960	.4961	.4962	.4963	.4964
2.7	.4965	.4966	.4967	.4968	.4969	.4970	.4971	.4972	.4973	.4974
2.8	.4974	.4975	.4976	.4977	.4977	.4978	.4979	.4979	.4980	.4981
2.9	.4981	.4982	.4982	.4983	.4984	.4984	.4985	.4985	.4986	.4986
3.0	.4987	.4987	.4987	.4988	.4988	.4989	.4989	.4989	.4990	.4990

*Source: Paul G. Hoel, *Elementary Statistics,* 2nd edition (New York: John Wiley & Sons, Inc., 1966), p. 329.

APPENDIX TABLE B

8% Compound Interest Factors*

	Single payment		Uniform series				
n	Compound amount factor Given P to find S $(1+i)^n$	Present worth factor Given S to find P $\frac{1}{(1+i)^n}$	Sinking fund factor Given S to find R $\frac{i}{(1+i)^n-1}$	Capital recovery factor Given P to find R $\frac{i(1+i)^n}{(1+i)^n-1}$	Compound amount factor Given R to find S $\frac{(1+i)^n-1}{i}$	Present worth factor Given R to find P $\frac{(1+i)^n-1}{i(1+i)^n}$	n
1	1.0800	0.9259	1.000 00	1.080 00	1.000	0.926	**1**
2	1.1664	0.8573	0.480 77	0.560 77	2.080	1.783	**2**
3	1.2597	0.7938	0.308 03	0.388 03	3.246	2.577	**3**
4	1.3605	0.7350	0.221 92	0.301 92	4.506	3.312	**4**
5	1.4693	0.6806	0.170 46	0.250 46	5.867	3.993	**5**
6	1.5869	0.6302	0.136 32	0.216 32	7.336	4.623	**6**
7	1.7138	0.5835	0.112 07	0.192 07	8.923	5.206	**7**
8	1.8509	0.5403	0.094 01	0.174 01	10.637	5.747	**8**
9	1.9990	0.5002	0.080 08	0.160 08	12.488	6.247	**9**
10	2.1589	0.4632	0.069 03	0.149 03	14.487	6.710	**10**
11	2.3316	0.4289	0.060 08	0.140 08	16.645	7.139	**11**
12	2.5182	0.3971	0.052 70	0.132 70	18.977	7.536	**12**
13	2.7196	0.3677	0.046 52	0.126 52	21.495	7.904	**13**
14	2.9372	0.3405	0.041 30	0.121 30	24.215	8.244	**14**
15	3.1722	0.3152	0.036 83	0.116 83	27.152	8.559	**15**
16	3.4259	0.2919	0.032 98	0.112 98	30.324	8.851	**16**
17	3.7000	0.2703	0.029 63	0.109 63	33.750	9.122	**17**
18	3.9960	0.2502	0.026 70	0.106 70	37.450	9.372	**18**
19	4.3157	0.2317	0.024 13	0.104 13	41.446	9.604	**19**
20	4.6610	0.2145	0.021 85	0.101 85	45.762	9.818	**20**
21	5.0338	0.1987	0.019 83	0.099 83	50.423	10.017	**21**
22	5.4365	0.1839	0.018 03	0.098 03	55.457	10.201	**22**
23	5.8715	0.1703	0.016 42	0.096 42	60.893	10.371	**23**
24	6.3412	0.1577	0.014 98	0.094 98	66.765	10.529	**24**
25	6.8485	0.1460	0.013 68	0.093 68	73.106	10.675	**25**
26	7.3964	0.1352	0.012 51	0.092 51	79.954	10.810	**26**
27	7.9881	0.1252	0.011 45	0.091 45	87.351	10.935	**27**
28	8.6271	0.1159	0.010 49	0.090 49	95.339	11.051	**28**
29	9.3173	0.1073	0.009 62	0.089 62	103.966	11.158	**29**
30	10.0627	0.0994	0.008 83	0.088 83	113.283	11.258	**30**
31	10.8677	0.0920	0.008 11	0.088 11	123.346	11.350	**31**
32	11.7371	0.0852	0.007 45	0.087 45	134.214	11.435	**32**
33	12.6760	0.0789	0.006 85	0.086 85	145.951	11.514	**33**
34	13.6901	0.0730	0.006 30	0.086 30	158.627	11.587	**34**
35	14.7853	0.0676	0.005 80	0.085 80	172.317	11.655	**35**
40	21.7245	0.0460	0.003 86	0.083 86	259.057	11.925	**40**
45	31.9204	0.0313	0.002 59	0.082 59	386.506	12.108	**45**
50	46.9016	0.0213	0.001 74	0.081 74	573.770	12.233	**50**
55	68.9139	0.0145	0.001 18	0.081 18	848.923	12.319	**55**
60	101.2571	0.0099	0.000 80	0.080 80	1 253.213	12.377	**60**
65	148.7798	0.0067	0.000 54	0.080 54	1 847.248	12.416	**65**
70	218.6064	0.0046	0.000 37	0.080 37	2 720.080	12.443	**70**
75	321.2045	0.0031	0.000 25	0.080 25	4 002.557	12.461	**75**
80	471.9548	0.0021	0.000 17	0.080 17	5 886.935	12.474	**80**
85	693.4565	0.0014	0.000 12	0.080 12	8 655.706	12.482	**85**
90	1 018.9151	0.0010	0.000 08	0.080 08	12 723.939	12.488	**90**
95	1 497.1205	0.0007	0.000 05	0.080 05	18 701.507	12.492	**95**
100	2 199.7613	0.0005	0.000 04	0.080 04	27 484.516	12.494	**100**

*Source: Adapted from Eugene L. Grant, W. Grant Ireson, and Richard S. Leavenworth, *Principles of Engineering Economy,* 6th ed.

APPENDIX TABLE C
10% Compound Interest Factors*

	Single payment		Uniform series				
n	Compound amount factor Given P to find S $(1+i)^n$	Present worth factor Given S to find P $\frac{1}{(1+i)^n}$	Sinking fund factor Given S to find R $\frac{i}{(1+i)^n-1}$	Capital recovery factor Given P to find R $\frac{i(1+i)^n}{(1+i)^n-1}$	Compound amount factor Given R to find S $\frac{(1+i)^n-1}{i}$	Present worth factor Given R to find P $\frac{(1+i)^n-1}{i(1+i)^n}$	n
1	1.1000	0.9091	1.000 00	1.100 00	1.000	0.909	**1**
2	1.2100	0.8264	0.476 19	0.576 19	2.100	1.736	**2**
3	1.3310	0.7513	0.302 11	0.402 11	3.310	2.487	**3**
4	1.4641	0.6830	0.215 47	0.315 47	4.641	3.170	**4**
5	1.6105	0.6209	0.163 80	0.263 80	6.105	3.791	**5**
6	1.7716	0.5645	0.129 61	0.229 61	7.716	4.355	**6**
7	1.9487	0.5132	0.105 41	0.205 41	9.487	4.868	**7**
8	2.1436	0.4665	0.087 44	0.187 44	11.436	5.335	**8**
9	2.3579	0.4241	0.073 64	0.173 64	13.579	5.759	**9**
10	2.5937	0.3855	0.062 75	0.162 75	15.937	6.144	**10**
11	2.8531	0.3505	0.053 96	0.153 96	18.531	6.495	**11**
12	3.1384	0.3186	0.046 76	0.146 76	21.384	6.814	**12**
13	3.4523	0.2897	0.040 78	0.140 78	24.523	7.103	**13**
14	3.7975	0.2633	0.035 75	0.135 75	27.975	7.367	**14**
15	4.1772	0.2394	0.031 47	0.131 47	31.772	7.606	**15**
16	4.5950	0.2176	0.027 82	0.127 82	35.950	7.824	**16**
17	5.0545	0.1978	0.024 66	0.124 66	40.545	8.022	**17**
18	5.5599	0.1799	0.021 93	0.121 93	45.599	8.201	**18**
19	6.1159	0.1635	0.019 55	0.119 55	51.159	8.365	**19**
20	6.7275	0.1486	0.017 46	0.117 46	57.275	8.514	**20**
21	7.4002	0.1351	0.015 62	0.115 62	64.002	8.649	**21**
22	8.1403	0.1228	0.014 01	0.114 01	71.403	8.772	**22**
23	8.9543	0.1117	0.012 57	0.112 57	79.543	8.883	**23**
24	9.8497	0.1015	0.011 30	0.111 30	88.497	8.985	**24**
25	10.8347	0.0923	0.010 17	0.110 17	98.347	9.077	**25**
26	11.9182	0.0839	0.009 16	0.109 16	109.182	9.161	**26**
27	13.1100	0.0763	0.008 26	0.108 26	121.100	9.237	**27**
28	14.4210	0.0693	0.007 45	0.107 45	134.210	9.307	**28**
29	15.8631	0.0630	0.006 73	0.106 73	148.631	9.370	**29**
30	17.4494	0.0573	0.006 08	0.106 08	164.494	9.427	**30**
31	19.1943	0.0521	0.005 50	0.105 50	181.943	9.479	**31**
32	21.1138	0.0474	0.004 97	0.104 97	201.138	9.526	**32**
33	23.2252	0.0431	0.004 50	0.104 50	222.252	9.569	**33**
34	25.5477	0.0391	0.004 07	0.104 07	245.477	9.609	**34**
35	28.1024	0.0356	0.003 69	0.103 69	271.024	9.644	**35**
40	45.2593	0.0221	0.002 26	0.102 26	442.593	9.779	**40**
45	72.8905	0.0137	0.001 39	0.101 39	718.905	9.863	**45**
50	117.3909	0.0085	0.000 86	0.100 86	1 163.909	9.915	**50**
55	189.0591	0.0053	0.000 53	0.100 53	1 880.591	9.947	**55**
60	304.4816	0.0033	0.000 33	0.100 33	3 034.816	9.967	**60**
65	490.3707	0.0020	0.000 20	0.100 20	4 893.707	9.980	**65**
70	789.7470	0.0013	0.000 13	0.100 13	7 887.470	9.987	**70**
75	1 271.8952	0.0008	0.000 08	0.100 08	12 708.954	9.992	**75**
80	2 048.4002	0.0005	0.000 05	0.100 05	20 474.002	9.995	**80**
85	3 298.9690	0.0003	0.000 03	0.100 03	32 979.690	9.997	**85**
90	5 313.0226	0.0002	0.000 02	0.100 02	53 120.226	9.998	**90**
95	8 556.6760	0.0001	0.000 01	0.100 01	85 556.760	9.999	**95**
100	13 780.6123	0.0001	0.000 01	0.100 01	137 796.123	9.999	**100**

*Source: Adapted from Eugene L. Grant, W. Grant Ireson, and Richard S. Leavenworth, *Principles of Engineering Economy*, 6th ed.

APPENDIX TABLE D
Random Digits*

85387	51571	57714	00512	61319	69143	08881	01400	55061	82977
84176	03311	16955	59504	54499	32096	79485	98031	99485	16788
27258	51746	67223	98182	43166	54297	26830	29842	78016	73127
99398	46950	19399	65167	35082	30482	86323	41061	21717	48126
72752	89364	02150	85418	05420	84341	02395	27655	59457	55438
69090	93551	11649	54688	57061	77711	24201	16895	64936	62347
39620	54988	67846	71845	54000	26134	84526	16619	82573	01737
81725	49831	35595	29891	46812	57770	03326	31316	75412	80732
87968	85157	84752	93777	62772	78961	30750	76089	23340	64637
07730	01861	40610	73445	70321	26467	53533	20787	46971	29134
32825	82100	67406	44156	21531	67186	39945	04189	79798	41087
34453	05330	40224	04116	24597	93823	28171	47701	76201	68257
00830	34235	40671	66042	06341	54437	81649	70494	01883	18350
24580	05258	37329	59173	62660	72513	82232	49794	36913	05877
59578	08535	77107	19838	40651	01749	58893	99115	05212	92309
75387	24990	12748	71766	17471	15794	68622	59161	14476	75074
02465	34977	48319	53026	53691	80594	58805	76961	62665	82855
49689	08342	81912	92735	30042	47623	60061	69427	21163	68543
60958	20236	79424	04055	54955	73342	14040	72431	99469	41044
79956	98409	79548	39569	83974	43707	77080	08645	20949	56932
04316	01206	08715	77713	20572	13912	94324	14656	11979	53258
78684	28546	06881	66097	53530	42509	54130	30878	77166	98075
69235	18535	61904	99246	84050	15270	07751	90410	96675	62870
81201	04314	92708	44984	83121	33767	56607	46371	20389	08809
80336	59638	44368	33433	97794	10343	19235	82633	17186	63902
65076	87960	92013	60169	49176	50140	39081	04638	96114	63463
90879	70970	50789	59973	47771	94567	35590	23462	33993	99899
50555	84355	97066	82748	98298	14385	82493	40182	20523	69182
48658	41921	86514	46786	74097	62825	46457	24428	09245	86069
26373	19166	88223	32371	11570	62078	92317	13378	05734	71778
20878	80883	26027	29101	58382	17109	53511	95536	21759	10630
20069	60582	55749	88068	48589	01874	42930	40310	34613	97359
46819	38577	20520	94145	99405	47064	25248	27289	41289	54972
83644	04459	73253	58414	94180	09321	59747	07379	56255	45615
08636	31363	56033	49076	88908	51318	39104	56556	23112	63317
92058	38678	12507	90343	17213	24545	66053	76412	29545	89932
05038	18443	87138	05076	25660	23414	84837	87132	84405	15346
41838	68590	93646	82113	25498	33110	15356	81070	84900	42660
15564	81618	99186	73113	99344	13213	07235	90064	89150	86359
74600	40206	15237	37378	96862	78638	14376	46607	55909	46398
78275	77017	60310	13499	35268	47790	77475	44345	14615	25231
30145	71205	10355	18404	85354	22199	90822	35204	47891	69860
46944	00097	39161	50139	60458	44649	85537	90017	18157	13856
85883	21272	89266	94887	00291	70963	28169	95130	27223	35387
83606	98192	82194	26719	24499	28102	97769	98769	30757	81593
66888	81818	52490	54272	70549	69235	74684	96412	65186	87974
63673	73966	34036	44298	60652	05947	05833	27914	57021	58566
37944	16094	39797	63253	64103	32222	65925	64693	34048	75394
93240	66855	29336	28345	71398	45118	01454	72128	09715	29454
40189	76776	70842	32675	81647	75868	21288	12849	94990	21513

*Source: Reproduced with permission from the Rand Corporation, *A Million Random Digits with 100,000 Normal Deviates*. Copyright, 1955, The Free Press: Glencoe, IL, p. 259.

Index

A

B

C

D

J

K

L

M

N

O

R

S

T

U

V

W